Pearson Education

PEARSON EDUCATION
SECONDARY GROUP

1 Lake Street
Upper Saddle River, NJ 07458
201-236-5401...781-455-1309
Fax: 201-236-5553...781-433-8425
E-Mail: marty.smith@phschool.com

Martha G. Smith
President
Pearson Education
Secondary Group

To the Teacher:

As a former social studies teacher, I cannot imagine a more important time to be a social studies educator.

Since the terrorist attacks on New York City and Washington, D.C., on September 11, 2001, you have served at the front line of efforts to understand the causes and effects of those momentous events. In the social studies classroom, you have helped your students understand our nation's heritage of unity and determination in times of crisis. You have had the opportunity to instill in your students the core values of democracy, free enterprise, and the rule of law. Your students have probably explored concepts of freedom and justice, through primary sources from the Declaration of Independence to the "I Have a Dream" speech, and the rights and responsibilities of citizenship, through the Constitution of the United States. They may be learning and applying critical thinking skills as well—debating, for example, the benefits and challenges of living in an open and tolerant society.

As a social studies educator, you can help your students master the fundamentals of history, geography, civics, and economics, providing a context within which to analyze current events. With your guidance, this knowledge can inform and encourage young people's participation in the democratic process.

Today more than ever, you play a crucial role in the maturing of responsible citizens. You help create tomorrow's leaders—the future defenders of America's freedoms, as defined by one President during another time of great crisis:

> *"In the future days which we seek to make secure, we look forward to a world founded upon four essential human freedoms. The first is freedom of speech and expression—everywhere in the world. The second is freedom of every person to worship God in his own way—everywhere in the world. The third is freedom from want . . . everywhere in the world. The fourth is freedom from fear . . . anywhere in the world."*
>
> —President Franklin Delano Roosevelt
> State of the Union Address, January 6, 1941

Sincerely,

Martha G. Smith

TEACHER'S EDITION

PRENTICE HALL

WORLD EXPLORER

PEOPLE, PLACES, AND CULTURES

James B. Kracht

Prentice Hall

In Association with DK Publishing

Needham, Massachusetts
Upper Saddle River, New Jersey
Glenview, Illinois

Acknowledgments appear on pp. 706–708, which constitutes an extension of this copyright page.

Prentice Hall

ISBN 0-13-068366-3

2 3 4 5 6 7 8 9 10   02 03 04 05

CONTENTS

Teacher's Edition

Student Edition

Connect students to the world.

Program Components

- Student Edition
- Teacher's Edition

Classroom Resources

- Teaching Resources
  - Program Overview
  - Pacing Charts
  - Letters Home
  - Guided Reading and Review
  - Chapter Summary
  - Vocabulary
  - Reteaching
  - Enrichment
  - Critical Thinking
  - Activity Atlas
  - Cooperative Learning Activities
  - Rubrics
  - Section Quiz
  - Chapter Tests (Forms A and B)
  - Unit Tests (Forms A and B)
  - Social Studies and Geography Skills
  - Guide to the Essentials, English
  - Guide to the Essential, Teacher's Manual
  - Primary Sources and Literature Readings
  - Outline Maps
  - Using the Internet
  - The Middle Grades Experience
  - Glossary of Geographic Terms Poster
- DK Atlas
- Guided Reading and Review, Student Edition
- Guided Reading and Review, Teacher's Edition
- Color Transparencies
- Section Reading Support Transparency System
- How People Live Transparencies

Assessment

Prentice Hall Assessment System
- Chapter Tests with ExamView®
  Test Bank CD-ROM
- Alternative Assessment
- Diagnostic Tests for Middle Grades
  Social Studies Skills
- Test-Taking Strategies Posters
- Test-Taking Strategies with Transparencies
  for Middle Grades
- Review Book for World Studies
- Test Prep Book for Middle Grades World Studies

Examview® Test Bank CD-ROM

Technology

Student Edition on Audio CD
Resource Pro® CD-ROM
Passport to the World CD-ROM
Social Studies Skills Tutor CD-ROM
World Video Explorer
Companion Web Site

PH SuccessNet

Spanish Components

Student Edition
Teacher's Edition
Teaching Resources
Guide to the Essentials, Spanish
Guided Reading and Review, Student Edition
Guided Reading and Review, Teacher's Edition
Color Transparencies
Section Reading Support Transparency System
How People Live Transparencies
Chapter Tests with ExamView® Test Bank CD-ROM
Diagnostic Tests for Middle Grades Social Studies Skills
Review Book for World Studies
Test Prep Book for Middle Grades World Studies
Student Edition on Audio CD
Resource Pro® CD-ROM

Program Highlights:

- Makes content accessible to all learners
- Provides interdisciplinary connections
- Develops social studies skills
- Offers a variety of assessment options

But I'm Not a Reading Teacher!

Few people choose to be social studies teachers in order to focus on reading. Yet a significant number of today's students lack reading proficiency. Without it, they cannot access the wealth of social studies content they need to absorb from textbooks, primary sources, literature, and more. When students can't read well, they don't read and won't read.

Lack of reading skills is a nationwide problem. The National Assessment of Educational Progress (NAEP) Reading Report Card in 1998 revealed that only 33 percent of eighth-grade students and 40 percent of twelfth-grade students were proficient readers, the standard that all students should reach. NAEP findings also indicated that 60 percent of twelfth-graders will not be able to function effectively in college or in the workplace in the future.

How can a social studies teacher build students' reading skills and still cover all of the content required in the curriculum? Begin by looking for reading difficulties in the classroom. Watch for these student behaviors that signal reading problems.

Reading Proficiency in Secondary Students

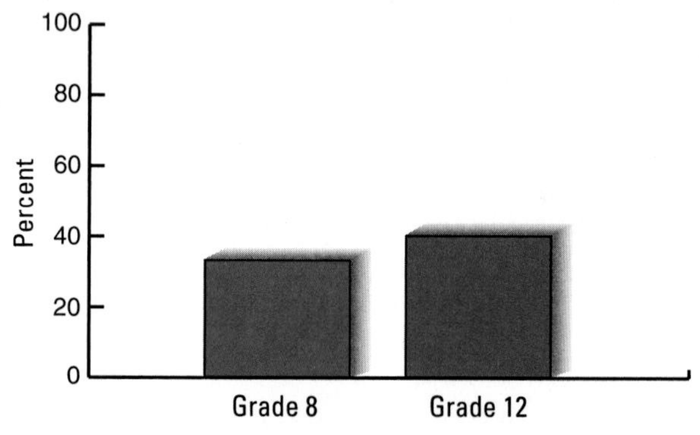

100
80
60
40
20
0
Percent
Grade 8
Grade 12

Source: NAEP Reading Report Card

Behaviors That Signal Reading Problems

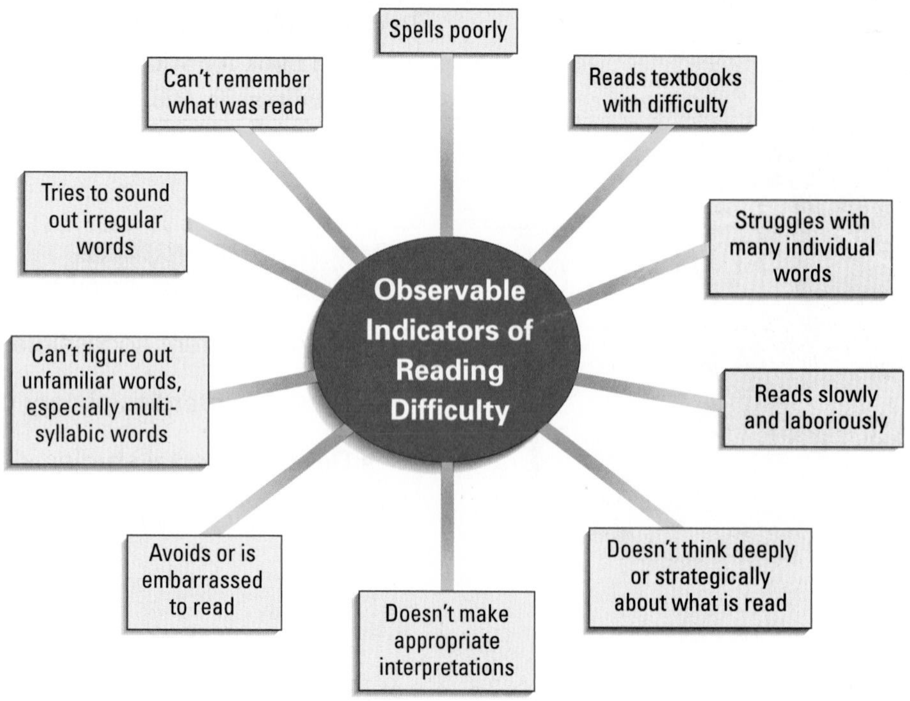

Observable Indicators of Reading Difficulty
Spells poorly
Reads textbooks with difficulty
Struggles with many individual words
Reads slowly and laboriously
Doesn't think deeply or strategically about what is read
Doesn't make appropriate interpretations
Avoids or is embarrassed to read
Can't figure out unfamiliar words, especially multi-syllabic words
Tries to sound out irregular words
Can't remember what was read

Best Practices in Reading

Instead of plunging in and plodding through a section, students need a plan of action, a strategy. The best practices for teaching reading in social studies focus on **comprehension strategies**—teaching students what to do *before reading, during reading,* and *after reading.*

Comprehension Strategies

Before Reading	During Reading	After Reading
• Activate prior knowledge • Build needed prior knowledge • Focus attention • Set purpose for reading • Make predictions	• Confirm predictions • Read and self-monitor • Take notes and ask questions	• Recall information • Respond to new learning • Extend and transfer new learning • Assess reading success

Here are some ways to implement these strategies with struggling readers:

Before Reading Both teacher and student preparations precede reading.

- Use an anecdote, photo, artifact, or audio to set the scene.
- Display a map or other visual aid to encourage students to identify what they already know and to make predictions to apply this knowledge to a new situation.
- Model for students how to look at pictures, captions, and headings in order to predict what they will be learning.

During Reading Student-directed, individual activities take place during reading. Providing guided practice will help students develop these habits.

- Show students how to take notes, using graphic organizers that match the type of information they are reading. For example, use a Venn diagram for comparing and contrasting, a flow chart for sequencing, and a concept web for finding main idea and supporting details.
- Teach students to ask themselves questions as they read.
- Demonstrate for students how to make connections between what they read and what they already know.

After Reading Both student-directed and teacher-directed activities can follow reading.

- Conduct a sample self-check for students—"What have I learned?"
- Teach students to ask themselves, "How does this relate to what I already know?"
- Demonstrate both formal and informal assessments that students will encounter.

Reading success happens when students can construct meaning from information.

Prentice Hall Reading Support in the Student Edition

The structure of each Prentice Hall program embeds the development of solid reading skills in the Student Edition. Each section of the text starts with suggestions to the student for before reading and during reading.

Notice that the *Reading Focus* questions align with the subheadings in the section.

BEFORE YOU READ

READING FOCUS

1. How does the movement of the Earth around the sun affect our environment?
2. What is the effect of latitude on climate?

KEY TERMS

environment
orbit
revolution
axis
rotation
latitude
low latitudes
high latitudes
middle latitudes

KEY PLACES

Equator
Tropic of Cancer
Tropic of Capricorn
Arctic Circle
Antarctic Circle

NOTE TAKING

Copy the concept web shown here. As you read the section, fill in the blank ovals with information about the Earth. Add as many ovals as you need.

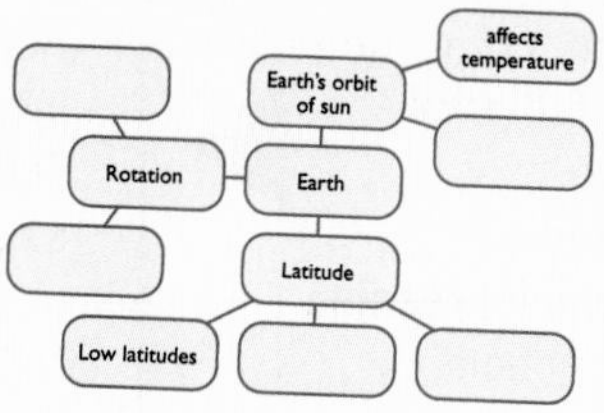

MAIN IDEA

The relationship between the Earth and the sun creates our days, seasons, and climate, and influences our environment.

AS YOU READ

Draw Inferences How do you think the cultural diversity of West Africa affects the lives of its people?

Notice how the *As You Read* annotations ask students to think critically about the text.

Setting the Scene

"The Sky Father opened his hand. Within every crease there lay innumerable grains of shining maize [corn]. In his thumb and forefinger he took some of the shining grains and placed them in the sky as brilliant stars to be a guide to humans when the bright sun was hidden."

This is part of an ancient myth of the Pueblos, who live in what today is the southwestern United States. They used the story to explain the appearance of the night sky.

The Surface of the Sun

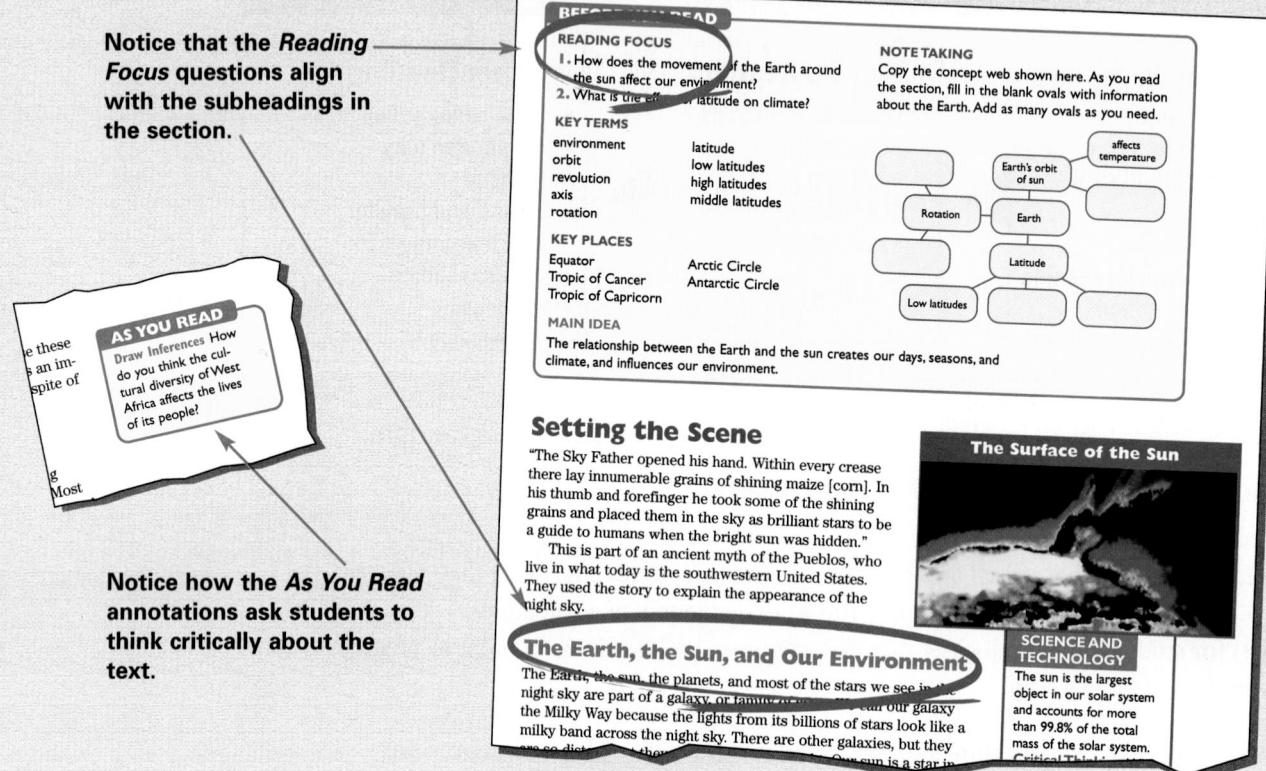

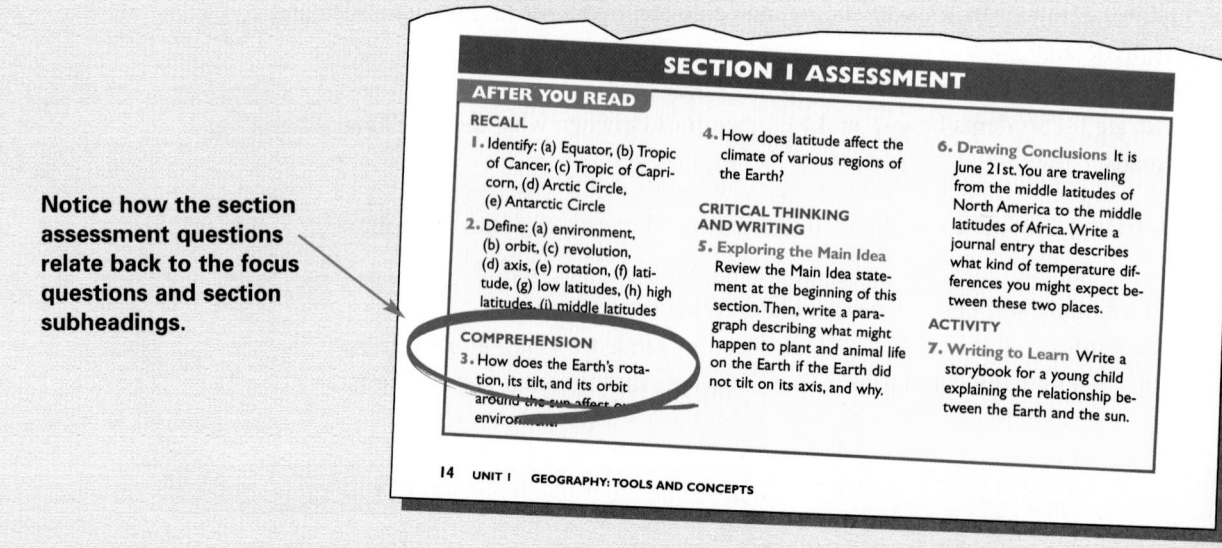

SCIENCE AND TECHNOLOGY

The sun is the largest object in our solar system and accounts for more than 99.8% of the total mass of the solar system.

The Earth, the Sun, and Our Environment

The Earth, the sun, the planets, and most of the stars we see in the night sky are part of a galaxy, or family of stars. We call our galaxy the Milky Way because the lights from its billions of stars look like a milky band across the night sky. There are other galaxies, but they are so distant that ... Our sun is a star in ...

At the end of each section, students will find opportunities to recall and apply information and construct meaning from it.

Notice how the section assessment questions relate back to the focus questions and section subheadings.

SECTION 1 ASSESSMENT

AFTER YOU READ

RECALL

1. Identify: (a) Equator, (b) Tropic of Cancer, (c) Tropic of Capricorn, (d) Arctic Circle, (e) Antarctic Circle
2. Define: (a) environment, (b) orbit, (c) revolution, (d) axis, (e) rotation, (f) latitude, (g) low latitudes, (h) high latitudes, (i) middle latitudes

COMPREHENSION

3. How does the Earth's rotation, its tilt, and its orbit around the sun affect our environment?
4. How does latitude affect the climate of various regions of the Earth?

CRITICAL THINKING AND WRITING

5. **Exploring the Main Idea** Review the Main Idea statement at the beginning of this section. Then, write a paragraph describing what might happen to plant and animal life on the Earth if the Earth did not tilt on its axis, and why.
6. **Drawing Conclusions** It is June 21st. You are traveling from the middle latitudes of North America to the middle latitudes of Africa. Write a journal entry that describes what kind of temperature differences you might expect between these two places.

ACTIVITY

7. **Writing to Learn** Write a storybook for a young child explaining the relationship between the Earth and the sun.

14 UNIT 1 GEOGRAPHY: TOOLS AND CONCEPTS

Prentice Hall Reading Support Beyond the Student Edition

Look for additional support for building reading skills in the Teacher's Edition, Teaching Resources box, and technology components.

Teacher's Edition

Ways to customize instruction for different student populations give you focused strategies to improve students' comprehension.

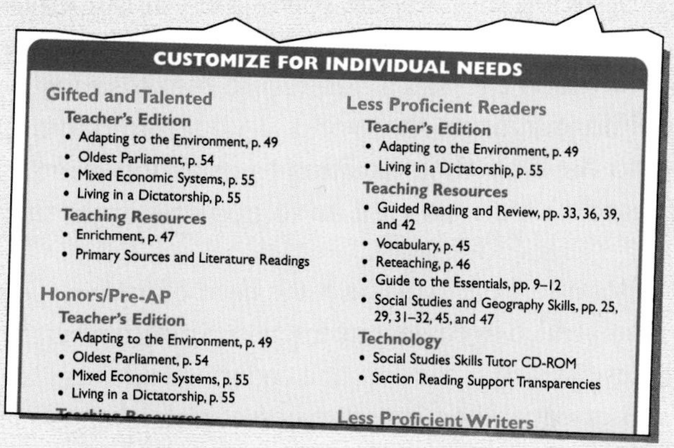
CUSTOMIZE FOR INDIVIDUAL NEEDS

Gifted and Talented
Teacher's Edition
- Adapting to the Environment, p. 49
- Oldest Parliament, p. 54
- Mixed Economic Systems, p. 55
- Living in a Dictatorship, p. 55

Teaching Resources
- Enrichment, p. 47
- Primary Sources and Literature Readings

Honors/Pre-AP
Teacher's Edition
- Adapting to the Environment, p. 49
- Oldest Parliament, p. 54
- Mixed Economic Systems, p. 55
- Living in a Dictatorship, p. 55

Less Proficient Readers
Teacher's Edition
- Adapting to the Environment, p. 49
- Living in a Dictatorship, p. 55

Teaching Resources
- Guided Reading and Review, pp. 33, 36, 39, and 42
- Vocabulary, p. 45
- Reteaching, p. 46
- Guide to the Essentials, pp. 9–12
- Social Studies and Geography Skills, pp. 25, 29, 31–32, 45, and 47

Technology
- Social Studies Skills Tutor CD-ROM
- Section Reading Support Transparencies

Less Proficient Writers

Section Reading Support Transparency System

Every section of the text has a companion reading support transparency that delivers the main points through a graphic organizer.

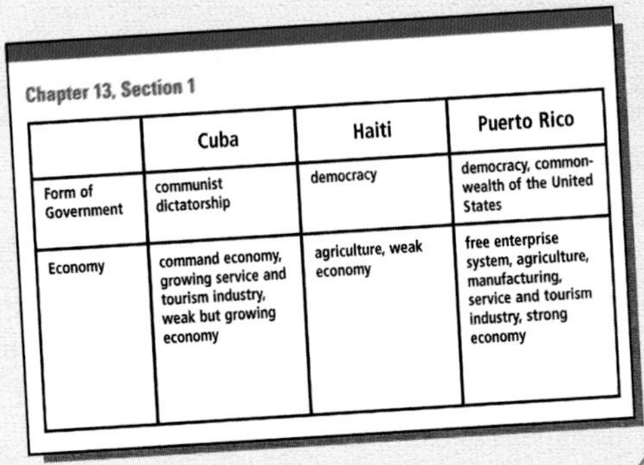
Chapter 13, Section 1

	Cuba	Haiti	Puerto Rico
Form of Government	communist dictatorship	democracy	democracy, commonwealth of the United States
Economy	command economy, growing service and tourism industry, weak but growing economy	agriculture, weak economy	free enterprise system, agriculture, manufacturing, service and tourism industry, strong economy

Guide to the Essentials

Look in the Teaching Resources box for the Guide to the Essentials in both English and Spanish. Students use this book to review and master new content through summaries written below grade level.

Text Summary

Graphic Summary

Questions

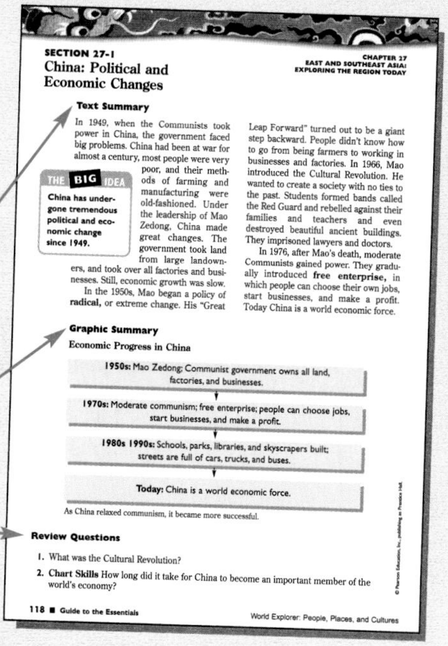
SECTION 27-1
China: Political and Economic Changes

CHAPTER 27
EAST AND SOUTHEAST ASIA: EXPLORING THE REGION TODAY

Text Summary

In 1949, when the Communists took power in China, the government faced big problems. China had been at war for almost a century, most people were very poor, and their methods of farming and manufacturing were old-fashioned. Under the leadership of Mao Zedong, China made great changes. The government took land from large landowners, and took over all factories and businesses. Still, economic growth was slow.

In the 1950s, Mao began a policy of **radical**, or extreme change. His "Great Leap Forward" turned out to be a giant step backward. People didn't know how to go from being farmers to working in businesses and factories. In 1966, Mao introduced the Cultural Revolution. He wanted to create a society with no ties to the past. Students formed bands called the Red Guard and rebelled against their families and teachers and even destroyed beautiful ancient buildings. They imprisoned lawyers and doctors.

In 1976, after Mao's death, moderate Communists gained power. They gradually introduced **free enterprise**, in which people can choose their own jobs, start businesses, and make a profit. Today China is a world economic force.

THE BIG IDEA
China has undergone tremendous political and economic change since 1949.

Graphic Summary
Economic Progress in China

1950s: Mao Zedong: Communist government owns all land, factories, and businesses.
1970s: Moderate communism; free enterprise; people can choose jobs, start businesses, and make a profit.
1980s 1990s: Schools, parks, libraries, and skyscrapers built; streets are full of cars, trucks, and buses.
Today: China is a world economic force.

As China relaxed communism, it became more successful.

Review Questions
1. What was the Cultural Revolution?
2. Chart Skills How long did it take for China to become an important member of the world's economy?

118 ■ Guide to the Essentials   World Explorer: People, Places, and Cultures

Student Edition on Audio CD

Auditory learners, less proficient readers, and English language learners can benefit from listening to the book on CD as they read the text.

Why Should I Teach Skills?

> **“Give a man a fish, and he eats for a day. Teach a man to fish and he eats for a lifetime.”**
>
> — Author Unknown

Following this advice, if we present our students with only content, we are, in essence, giving them a fish. If we are to prepare students for life, we need to teach the skills needed to make sense out of the increasing volume of information in the world. To help students become lifelong learners, we need to develop their abilities to question, read, analyze, interpret, and evaluate information, as well as to communicate their ideas to others.

Because these skills lie at the heart of understanding social studies, they need to be embedded in content instruction. Think of social studies content as having three levels: facts, concepts, and enduring understandings or “big ideas.” Skills development is essential for comprehension at each level, as in this example.

Topic: Colonization

	Example	Skill
Facts	Location of colonies	Map reading
Concepts	Migration	Cause and effect
Big Ideas	People make choices to meet needs	Problem solving

The Power of Skills for Life

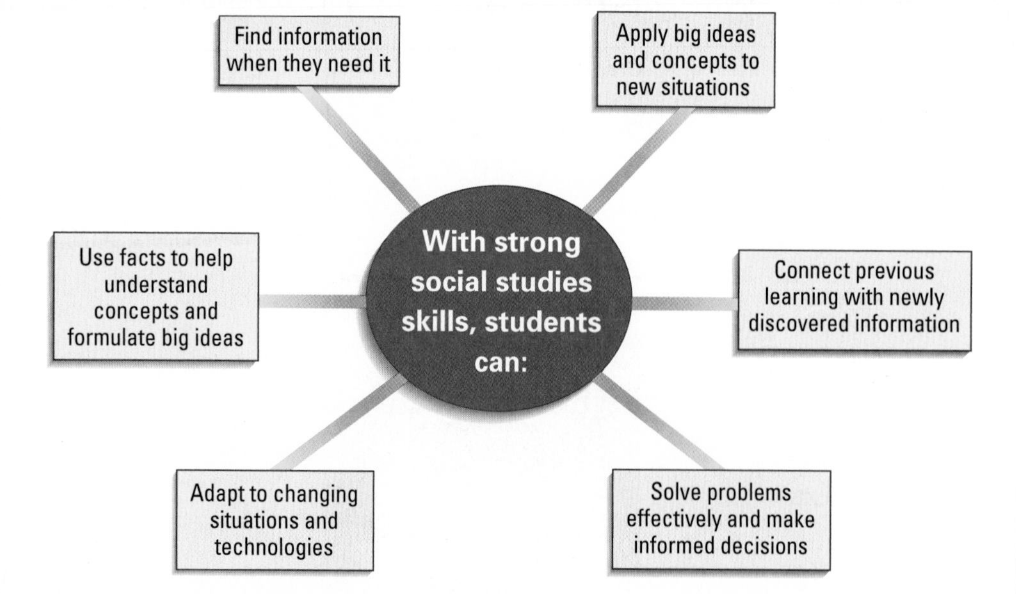

With strong social studies skills, students can:
Find information when they need it
Apply big ideas and concepts to new situations
Use facts to help understand concepts and formulate big ideas
Connect previous learning with newly discovered information
Adapt to changing situations and technologies
Solve problems effectively and make informed decisions

Best Practices in Skills Integration

These guidelines will help you to embed skills development within content instruction.

1. **Plan each chapter around an enduring understanding or big idea.** For example, if the chapter you are about to teach is Africa: Shaped by History, the big idea might be "Africa's cultures were greatly affected by European colonization."

2. **Develop each lesson around the facts, concepts, and skills students need to be able to connect the content to the big idea.**

Topic: African History		
	Example	**Skill**
Facts	African trade with Europeans	Note Taking
Concepts	Supply and demand	Cause and effect
Big Ideas	Africa's cultures were greatly affected by European colonization	Synthesizing information

3. **Teach skills that are new or that add another level of complexity to a previously mastered skill.** Follow the elements of good skill instruction:
    - Set a purpose for using the skill.
    - Present the steps to follow.
    - Model the process for using the skill.
    - Guide practice and provide feedback.
    - Apply to a prompt such as a picture, map, or reading passage.

4. **Reinforce skills whenever possible.** Ask critical thinking questions about maps, photos, graphs, charts, and primary sources.

5. **Assess both content and skills mastery regularly.** It is important to determine whether students are remembering important information, but equally important to determine whether they are internalizing skills as lifelong learners.

6. **Include skills in big projects.** Give students opportunities to combine their thinking and research abilities at least several times a year.

Elements of Skill Instruction

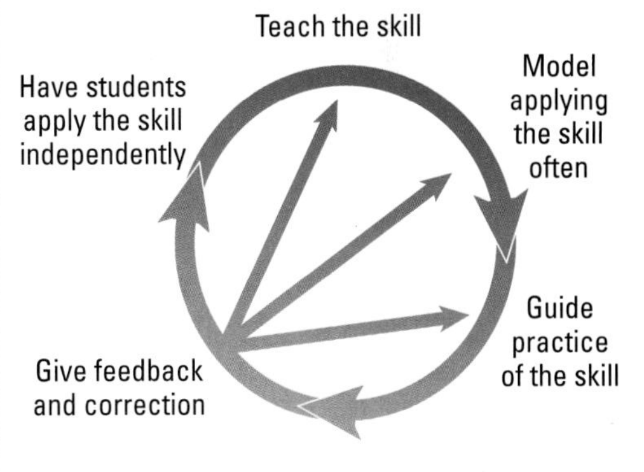
Teach the skill
Model applying the skill often
Guide practice of the skill
Give feedback and correction
Have students apply the skill independently

Prentice Hall Support for Skills

Skills mastery means developing habits of mind that enable us to turn information into meaning. To achieve mastery, students need both instruction and continuous reinforcement—many, many opportunities to practice and apply skills in new situations. Every Prentice Hall social studies program contains a wealth of resources to build skills for life.

Skills pages in the Student Edition provide three-step instruction strategy.

Learn **Practice** **Apply**

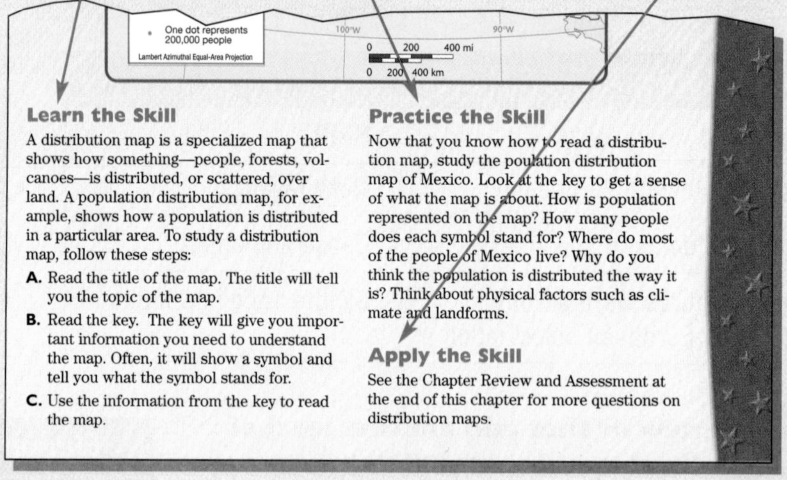

Learn the Skill

A distribution map is a specialized map that shows how something—people, forests, volcanoes—is distributed, or scattered, over land. A population distribution map, for example, shows how a population is distributed in a particular area. To study a distribution map, follow these steps:

A. Read the title of the map. The title will tell you the topic of the map.

B. Read the key. The key will give you important information you need to understand the map. Often, it will show a symbol and tell you what the symbol stands for.

C. Use the information from the key to read the map.

Practice the Skill

Now that you know how to read a distribution map, study the population distribution map of Mexico. Look at the key to get a sense of what the map is about. How is population represented on the map? How many people does each symbol stand for? Where do most of the people of Mexico live? Why do you think the population is distributed the way it is? Think about physical factors such as climate and landforms.

Apply the Skill

See the Chapter Review and Assessment at the end of this chapter for more questions on distribution maps.

Skills reinforcement appears in all caption questions.

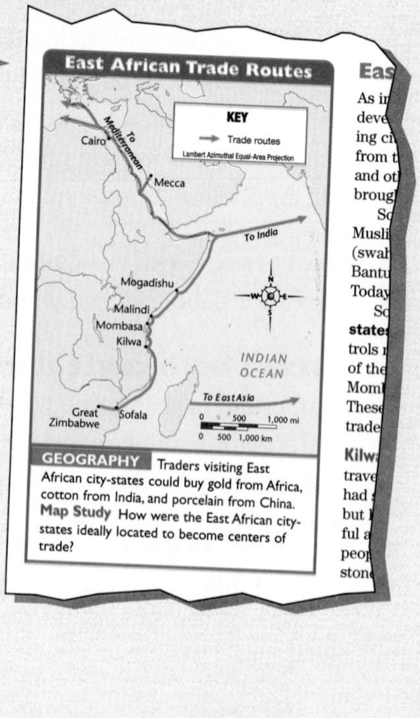

GEOGRAPHY Traders visiting East African city-states could buy gold from Africa, cotton from India, and porcelain from China. **Map Study** How were the East African city-states ideally located to become centers of trade?

Mini Lessons in the Teacher Edition reinforce key skills.

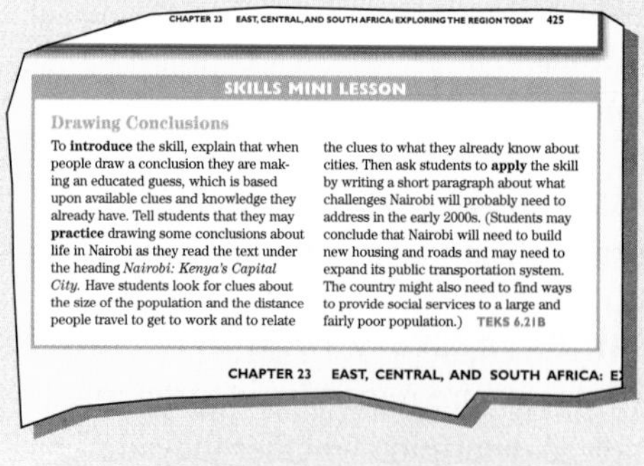

CHAPTER 23 EAST, CENTRAL, AND SOUTH AFRICA: EXPLORING THE REGION TODAY 425

SKILLS MINI LESSON

Drawing Conclusions

To **introduce** the skill, explain that when people draw a conclusion they are making an educated guess, which is based upon available clues and knowledge they already have. Tell students that they may **practice** drawing some conclusions about life in Nairobi as they read the text under the heading *Nairobi: Kenya's Capital City.* Have students look for clues about the size of the population and the distance people travel to get to work and to relate the clues to what they already know about cities. Then ask students to **apply** the skill by writing a short paragraph about what challenges Nairobi will probably need to address in the early 2000s. (Students may conclude that Nairobi will need to build new housing and roads and may need to expand its public transportation system. The country might also need to find ways to provide social services to a large and fairly poor population.) TEKS 6.21B

CHAPTER 23 EAST, CENTRAL, AND SOUTH AFRICA: E

Social Studies Skills Tutor CD-ROM provides two levels of interactive instruction and practice in 20 core social studies skills.

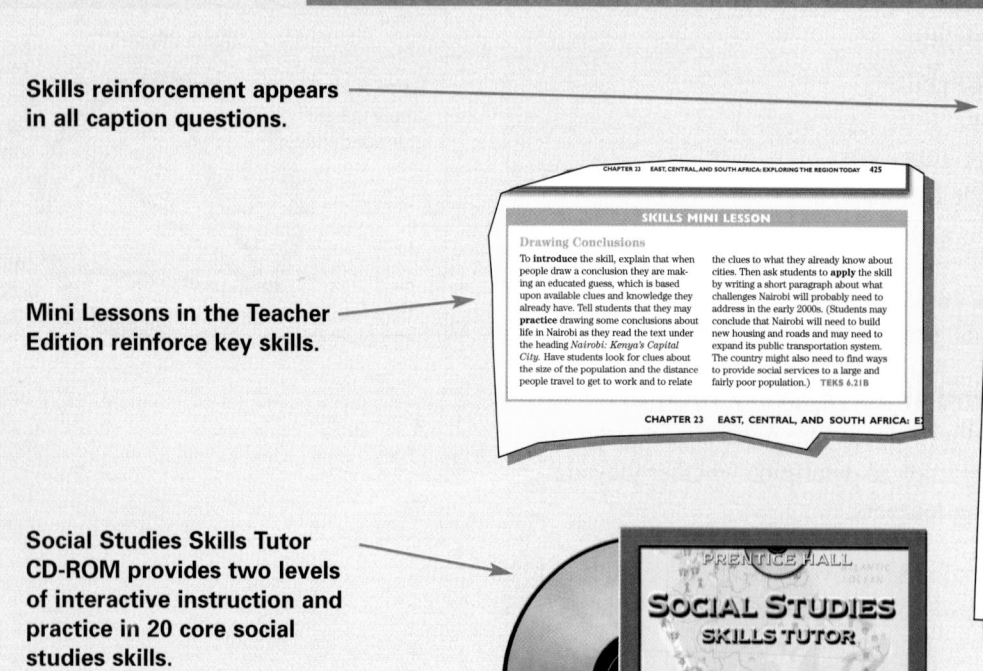

The Prentice Hall Vertical Alignment System

Mastery also requires that students learn skills at increasing levels of complexity as they progress through school. Prentice Hall takes the guesswork out of aligning skills instruction by developing 20 core social studies skills with increasing difficulty from grade to grade in every Prentice Hall program.

Here you see how three Prentice Hall programs build and elaborate the skill of analyzing graphic data.

Analyzing Graphic Data

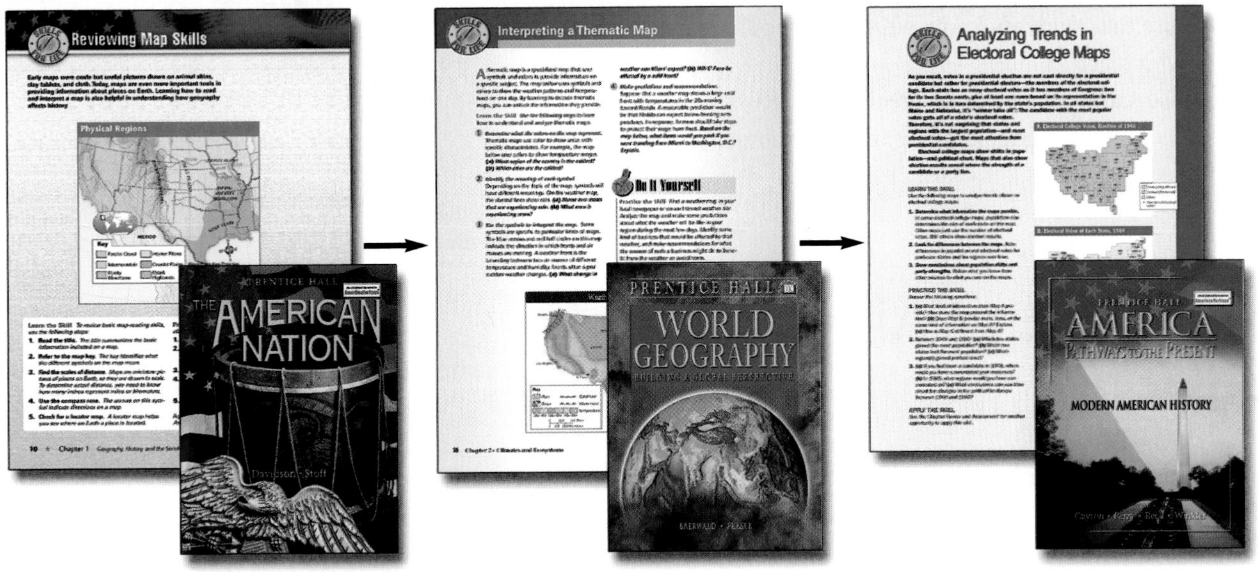

The 20 Core Social Studies Skills

1.	Using the Cartographer's Tools	11.	Comparing and Contrasting
2.	Using Special Purpose Maps	12.	Analyzing Primary Sources
3.	Analyzing Graphic Data	13.	Recognizing Bias and Propaganda
4.	Analyzing Images	14.	Identifying Frame of Reference and Point of View
5.	Identifying Main Ideas/Summarizing	15.	Decision-making
6.	Sequencing	16.	Problem-solving
7.	Identifying Cause and Effect/ Making Predictions	17.	Using Reliable Information
8.	Drawing Inferences and Conclusions	18.	Transferring Information from One Medium to Another
9.	Making Valid Generalizations	19.	Synthesizing Information
10.	Distinguishing Fact and Opinion	20.	Supporting a Position

Should I Teach to the Test?

The increasing importance of state standards and student accountability leads many teachers to wonder whether they must limit their classes to the content of high-stakes exams. While based on state standards and student needs, a truly effective social studies program requires **alignment of curriculum, instruction,** and **assessment.** When each of these elements dovetails with the others, *all* instruction prepares students for assessment based on curriculum objectives.

In an aligned system, both teacher and student know what is expected. There are no secrets or surprises. To ensure alignment:

- Teach the objectives in your standards to the specified level of understanding.
- Make sure that students know what they should learn before you teach.
- Test those same objectives as precisely as possible to the same depth of understanding that the standards require.

Tyler Triangle

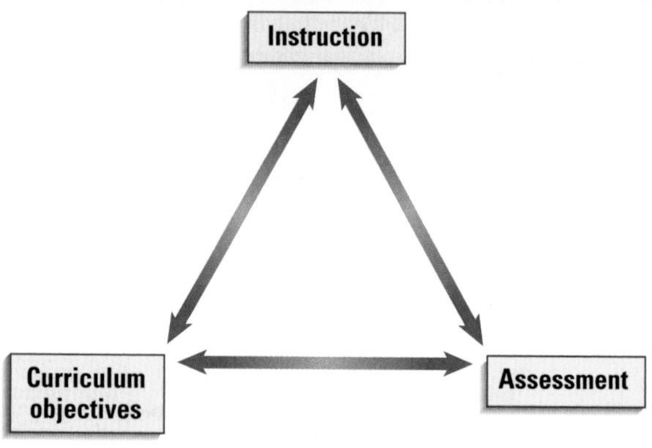

Constructing Aligned Assessments

The principle of aligning assessment questions to curriculum objectives and instruction needs to be applied for both standardized tests and teacher-created exams.

At the state level

To create assessments based on state standards, test writers dissect the objectives for the pieces of appropriate content and the thinking level required of the student. Test questions are written, reviewed, piloted, reviewed once again, and placed in testing banks.

At the classroom level

While state tests occur perhaps once a year, teachers must use an ongoing system of testing to measure student learning throughout the year. Teachers need to plan instruction and assessment simultaneously, with both of them based on the state curriculum objectives.

Best Practices in Assessment

Good assessment is part of an integrated cycle that is repeated throughout the school year. Following the principle of alignment, good assessment grows out of preparation that begins long before any test is administered and leads to improvements in teaching and learning long after the test. Here are some ways to integrate ongoing assessment into instruction:

<table>
<tr><th colspan="2">Assessment Techniques</th></tr>
<tr><td>Diagnose and Prescribe
Evaluate student abilities at the beginning of the year.</td><td>The best way to know if students are ready for the difficulty level you intend to use is to give a diagnostic test when school opens. Students will not know the content you are about to teach them, but they should bring with them a number of social studies skills that they will apply to new content. Evaluate student facility in these areas:
• Map and globe skills
• Critical thinking and reading
• Graph and chart skills
• Communications</td></tr>
<tr><td>Plan and Align
Plan instruction to align with assessment.</td><td>• Examine objectives carefully.
• Choose learning activities making sure that more than a knowledge level (or memorized level) is expected of students.
• Test students on all of the objectives, omitting none. Do not test information not contained in an objective.
• Test skill development at the same time you assess content.
• Integrate skill and content questions so that students must use what they know and combine it with new information that they gather.
• Test students' understanding of the objectives on many levels of thinking.</td></tr>
<tr><td>Review and Reteach
Weave ongoing review into aligned instruction and assessment.</td><td>One quick and easy way to check how much students remember from one unit to the next is to include some review questions on each of your tests.
• Find ways to connect new learning to previous learning as you put your lessons together. This previous learning could come from units previously studied during the same year or from content studied in other courses.
• Choose review questions that are aligned to your current lessons.</td></tr>
<tr><td>Practice and Assess
Apply assessment results to improve teaching and learning.</td><td>• Use individual student information for tutoring and devising individualized plans for improvement.
• Use whole-class data to determine if your teaching was aligned to the assessment. If many students missed an item, it was probably not aligned to your instruction and intent. Make changes when you teach this unit again.
• Use review data on both individuals and the whole class to make a list of those objectives with which students may have difficulty on an end-of-year test.</td></tr>
</table>

Prentice Hall Assessment System

The Prentice Hall Assessment System provides comprehensive support for both program content assessment and preparation for high-stakes standardized tests.

Program Assessment

Use the Chapter Tests to assess core content for every chapter.

Develop your own customized tests and practice worksheets with the ExamView Test Bank CD-ROM, selecting from hundreds of test questions and using the word-processing and editing capabilities. Create online tests and study guides and receive instant feedback on student progress.

Use a variety of assessment options to evaluate students' performance, such as activity-based assessment or portfolio assessment.

Give students clear expectations and a means of self-assessment through a variety of rubrics, which include criteria, indicators, and standards.

Writing Assignment Rubric

Name ____________ Date ______
Class ____________

	Distinguished	Proficient	Limited	Unsatisfactory
CONTENT:				
Introduction	Attitude is defined; thesis is clearly focused; subject is significant	Thesis is clear; provides direction for essay	Unclear; formulaic; not creative	Introduction is incomplete, ineffective, or missing
Idea Development	Interesting; sophisticated; insightful	Clear and thoughtful	Simplistic; uneven in quality; lacking in relevance	Absent or ineffective
Support or Evidence	Detailed; accurate; convincing	Sufficient and accurate	Uneven	Vague, missing, or inaccurate
Word Choice	Engaging and powerful choice of words	Appropriate to task	Uneven	Limited, monotonous, inappropriate
Conclusion	Extends; connects; comments on topics	Purposeful and perceptive	Summarizes previously stated information	Absent, incomplete, or unfocused
ORGANIZATION:				
Topic Sentences	Clearly related to thesis; comprehensive; incorporates effective transitions	Comprehensive and logical	Provides bland restatement of thesis; narrow or inaccurate	Absent
Paragraph Order	Contributes to an effective argument; reinforces the content	Demonstrates a clear plan	Ineffective or inconsistent	Random
Transitions	Effective and varied	Clear and functional	Mechanical	Absent
MECHANICS:				
Sentence Structure	Complete; varied; interesting	Complete and correct	Variety is present; some errors are evident	Repetitious; fragments and run-ons are frequent
Punctuation /Spelling	Error-free	Present but do not interfere with meaning	Careless or distracting	Block meaning
Voice	Distinctive; appropriate to task and audience	Clear and authentic	Mechanical, formulaic	Unclear

ALTERNATIVE ASSESSMENT

Standardized Test Preparation

Prentice Hall Assessment System gives you the tools to help your students succeed on standardized tests, from the beginning of the year to the culminating high-stakes exam.

Diagnose and Prescribe

Profile student skills with Diagnostic Tests A & B.

Address student needs with program resources correlated to diagnostic test questions.

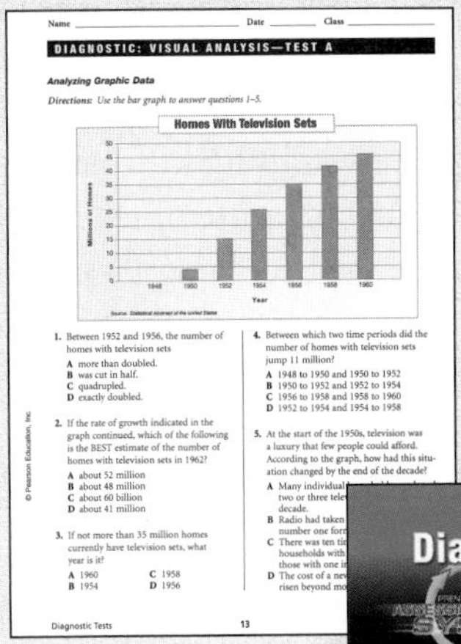

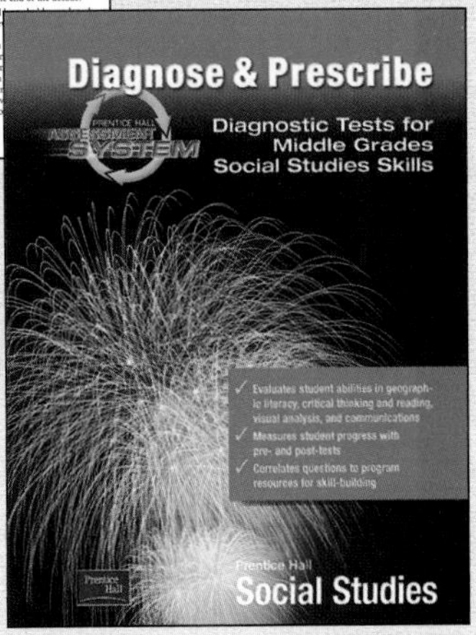

Review and Reteach

Provide cumulative content review with unit-level questions and study sheets.

Practice and Assess

Build assessment skills using Test-Taking Strategies with Transparencies.

Reinforce assessment skills with Test-Taking Posters.

Practice taking tests and improve scores on standardized tests with the Test Preparation Workbook.

How Am I Doing?

Paired with the demand for high student achievement has come the drive for greater teacher accountability. More and more states and districts are establishing standards for teaching and new systems of teacher evaluation.

In the past, professional appraisals focused on teacher behaviors. Nationwide, the focus of teacher evaluation is now shifting to what students are able to do. Student success emerges as the most critical measure of teaching—the teacher has not taught if students have not learned. The goal is becoming the learner-centered class, alive with critical thinking, problem-solving activities, collaborative learning, projects, and investigations. Evaluation criteria now measure how well teachers promote this kind of learning.

Prentice Hall social studies programs provide a variety of ways to support learner-centered instruction. Below you will find a guide to program resources to help you address criteria commonly found in teacher evaluations.

Common Criteria	Where to Look for Support
Active, successful student participation in the learning process	• Structured reading support • Activities at section and chapter levels • Group and individual activities
Learner-centered instruction	• Critical thinking questions in every caption • Strategies for different learner needs • Technology for students: Social Studies Skills Tutor CD-ROM, Companion Web site
Evaluation and feedback on student progress	• Section and chapter assessments in student edition • ExamView® Test Bank
Classroom management of students, time, and materials	• Pacing charts • Chapter interleaf • Resource Pro®
Professional communications	• Letters to families • Resource Pro® lesson plans for supervisors
Improvement of student performance	• Prentice Hall Assessment System
Professional development	• eTeach • Skylight • PHSuccessNet.com

Prentice Hall offers professional development opportunities that are not only standards-driven, and results-based, but also available in a variety of formats. From quality instructional materials to online support, Prentice Hall is committed to help you meet your immediate and long-term professional development goals.

Annotated Teacher's Edition

Management of student discipline, instructional strategies, time, and materials are made easy with point-of-use notes and planning tools. Throughout each chapter, inset notes support customized lesson plans right where you need them—so it's simple to meet the needs of all your students.

eTeach

This exclusive online teacher-to-teacher exchange lets you participate in an online seminar and discussion about the teaching of social studies. Each month, a new Master Teacher hosts a different topic.

eTeach
Meet This Month's Master Teacher
MARSHA K. RUSSELL, a lifelong Texan, earned a Bachelor of Music degree in Vocal Performance from Southwestern University, and a Master of Arts in English Literature at the University of Texas at Austin, where she has also done post-graduate work. During the first seven of her sixteen years as a public school teacher in Austin, she taught seventh and eighth grade English and American History, and during the past nine years she has been on the faculty of the Liberal Arts Academy, a magnet school for gifted students housed at A. S. Johnston High School. Here she has created programs in Humanities - World History examined through the lens of art, literature, music, architecture, city layouts, law codes, religious traditions, and other human products - and its

Resource Pro® CD-ROM

Unmatched classroom management tool!

- Planning lessons—Create customized lesson plans with a few clicks of a mouse.
- Meeting local standards—Import your own local or state objectives into lesson plans.
- Making planning easier—Transport hundreds of pages of resources in electronic format—no more carrying resource books back and forth from school to home.

Prentice Hall Professional Development and Training

Professional development starts with the resources you use every day. The combination of print, onsite, and online teacher resources offers a variety of ongoing, accessible support available anytime, anywhere.

Through our partnership with Skylight Professional Development, Prentice Hall now offers customized in-service programs based on individual educational goals, grade levels, and state standards and curriculum.

Prentice Hall is committed to being your partner in education.

PRENTICE HALL

WORLD EXPLORER

PEOPLE, PLACES, AND CULTURES

James B. Kracht

Prentice Hall

In Association with DK Publishing

Needham, Massachusetts
Upper Saddle River, New Jersey
Glenview, Illinois

Acknowledgments appear on pp. 706–708, which constitutes an extension of this copyright page.

Prentice Hall

ISBN 0-13-068365-5

2 3 4 5 6 7 8 9 10   02 03 04 05

Author

James B. Kracht serves as advisor and board member for numerous organizations and agencies including the International Center of the Bush Presidential Library Complex. He is a Fellow of the Grosvenor Center for Geographic Education and frequently serves as a consultant to international schools in Latin America. He is a recipient of the Extraordinary Service Award from Texas A&M University and the Distinguished Service Award from the Texas Council for the Social Studies.

In 1995, Dr. Kracht was named Director of the writing team for the Texas Essential Knowledge and Skills for Social Studies and in 1996 was selected as Director of the Social Studies Center for Educator Development. Dr. Kracht is currently Associate Dean for Undergraduate Programs and Teacher Education in the College of Education at Texas A&M University. He has been a faculty member in the Department of Geography and the Department of Teaching, Learning, and Culture at Texas A&M University since 1974. He is also a professional development specialist for the Texas Social Studies Center and co-director of a national demonstration project for interdisciplinary curriculum development at the middle grades.

IN ASSOCIATION WITH DK **Dorling Kindersley** is an international publishing company specialising in the creation of high quality reference content for books, CD-ROMs, online, and video. The hallmark of DK content is its unique combination of educational value and strong visual style. This combination allows DK to deliver appealing, accessible, and engaging educational content that delights children, parents, and teachers around the world.

iii

Teacher Reviewers

Betty Adair
Cameron Middle School
Nashville, Tennessee

Marietta Clark
Northview Middle School
Kodak, Tennessee

Nan Elmore
Beardon Middle School
Knoxville, Tennessee

Kristi Karis
West Ottawa Middle School
Holland, Michigan

Deborah J. Miller
Detroit Public Schools
Detroit, Michigan

Nancy Myers
Carter Middle School
Strawberry Plains, Tennessee

Rebecca Revis
Sylvan Hills Junior High School
Sherwood, Arkansas

Flossie Ware
Bellevue Junior High School
Memphis, Tennessee

iv

Program Reviewers

Reading Specialist

Bonnie Armbruster, Ph.D.
Professor of Education
University of Illinois at Urbana-Champaign
Champaign, Illinois

Curriculum and Assessment Specialist

Jan Moberley
Dallas, Texas

Special Program Consultant

Landon Risteen
Chicago, Illinois

Program Advisors

Pat Easterbrook
Social Studies Consultant
Cary, North Carolina

Michal Howden
Social Studies Consultant
Zionsville, Indiana

Kathy Lewis
Social Studies Consultant
Fort Worth, Texas

Rick Moulden
Social Studies Consultant
Federal Way, Washington

Sharon Pope
Social Studies Consultant
Houston, Texas

Joe Wieczorek
Social Studies Consultant
Baltimore, Maryland

v

TABLE OF CONTENTS

UNIT 1

Geography: Tools and Concepts

vi

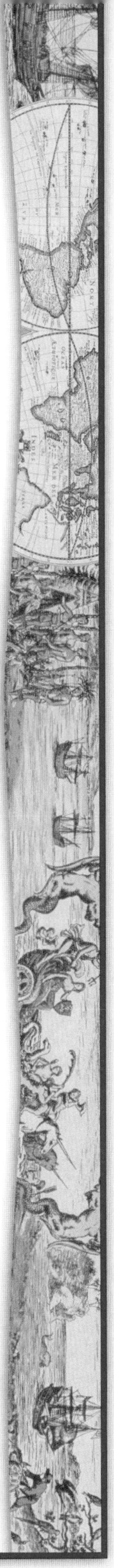

vii

UNIT 2

The United States and Canada

viii

ix

UNIT 3

Latin America 158

x

xi

UNIT 4

Europe and Russia ... 250

xii

xiii

UNIT 5

Africa

xiv

xv

UNIT 6

Asia

xvi

xvii

UNIT 7

The Pacific Realm

xviii

xix

Special Features

Adapted from the Dorling Kindersley Illustrated Children's Encyclopedia

Explore the world through the fascinating images and content of Dorling Kindersley.

Country and Regional Profiles

Examine countries and regions in-depth through special maps, charts, and data.

xx

Skills for Life

Master the essential social studies skills that you will use all your life.

Links to . . .

See how social studies links to other subjects you study in school.

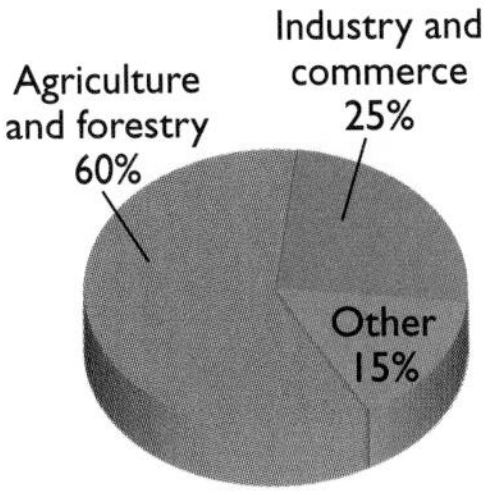

China Labor Force

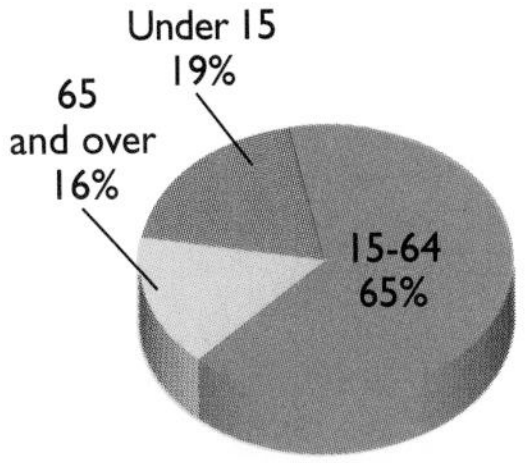

United Kingdom Age Structure (in years)

xxi

Connections

Investigate the connections among social studies topics.

Regional Database

Find data, including statistics, locator maps, and flags, for every country in a region.

Charts, Graphs, and Tables

SIZE OF CONTINENTS

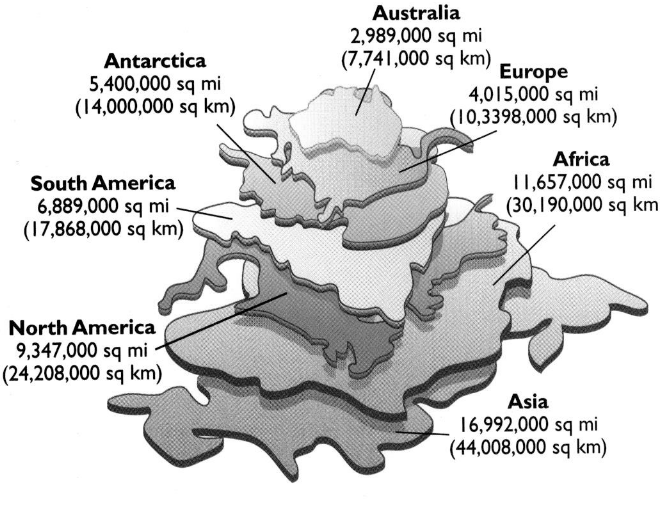

xxiii

Maps

Chapter Maps

How Latitude and Longitude Form the Global Grid

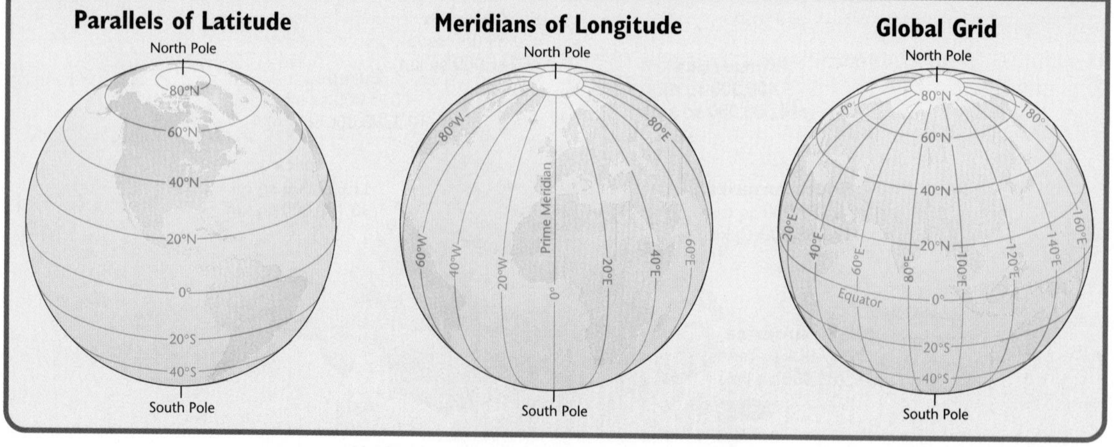

xxiv

World Precipitation

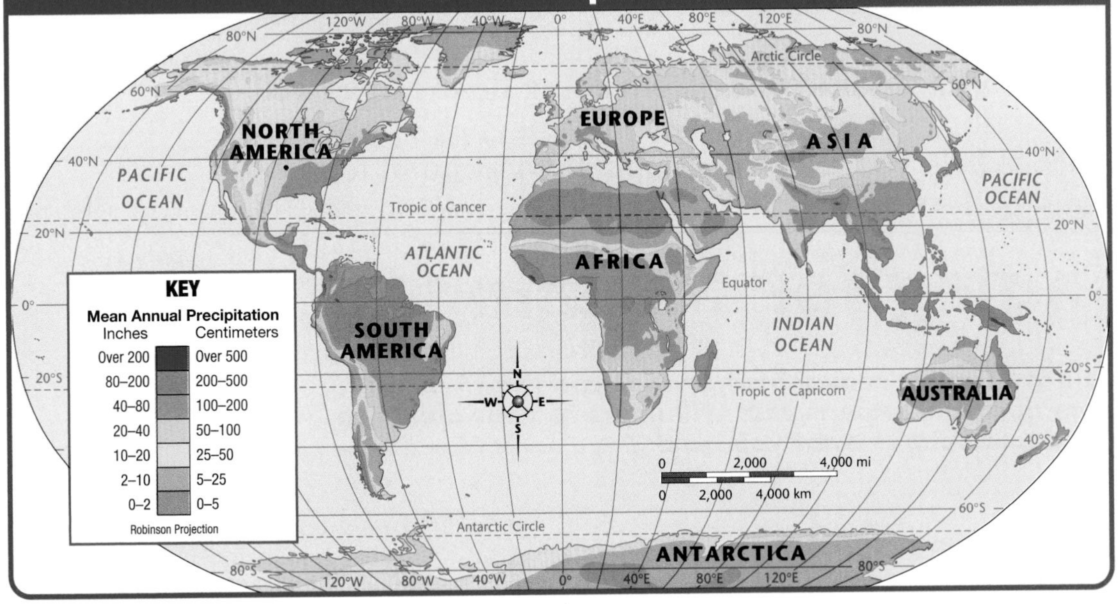
NORTH AMERICA
SOUTH AMERICA
EUROPE
ASIA
AFRICA
AUSTRALIA
ANTARCTICA
PACIFIC OCEAN
PACIFIC OCEAN
ATLANTIC OCEAN
INDIAN OCEAN
Arctic Circle
Tropic of Cancer
Equator
Tropic of Capricorn
Antarctic Circle
80°N
60°N
40°N
20°N
0°
20°S
40°S
60°S
80°S
120°W
80°W
40°W
40°E
80°E
120°E
N
S
E
W
0
2,000
4,000 mi
0
2,000
4,000 km
KEY
Mean Annual Precipitation
Inches
Centimeters
Over 200
Over 500
80–200
200–500
40–80
100–200
20–40
50–100
10–20
25–50
2–10
5–25
0–2
0–5
Robinson Projection

Atlas

xxv

Student Success Handbook

Success in social studies comes from doing three things well—reading, testing, and writing. The following pages present strategies to help you read for meaning, understand test questions, and write well.

Reading for Meaning

Do you have trouble remembering what you read? Here are some tips from experts that will improve your ability to recall and understand what you read:

BEFORE YOU READ

Preview the text to identify important information.
Like watching the coming attractions at a movie theater, previewing the text helps you know what to expect. Study the questions and strategies below to learn how to preview what you read.

Ask yourself these questions:	Use these strategies to find the answers:
• What is the text about?	Read the headings, subheadings, and captions. Study the photos, maps, tables, or graphs.
• What do I already know about the topic?	Read the questions at the end of the text to see if you can answer any of them.
• What is the purpose of the text?	Turn the headings into *who, what, when, where, why,* or *how* questions. This will help you decide if the text compares things, tells a chain of events, or explains causes and effects.

xxvi STUDENT SUCCESS HANDBOOK

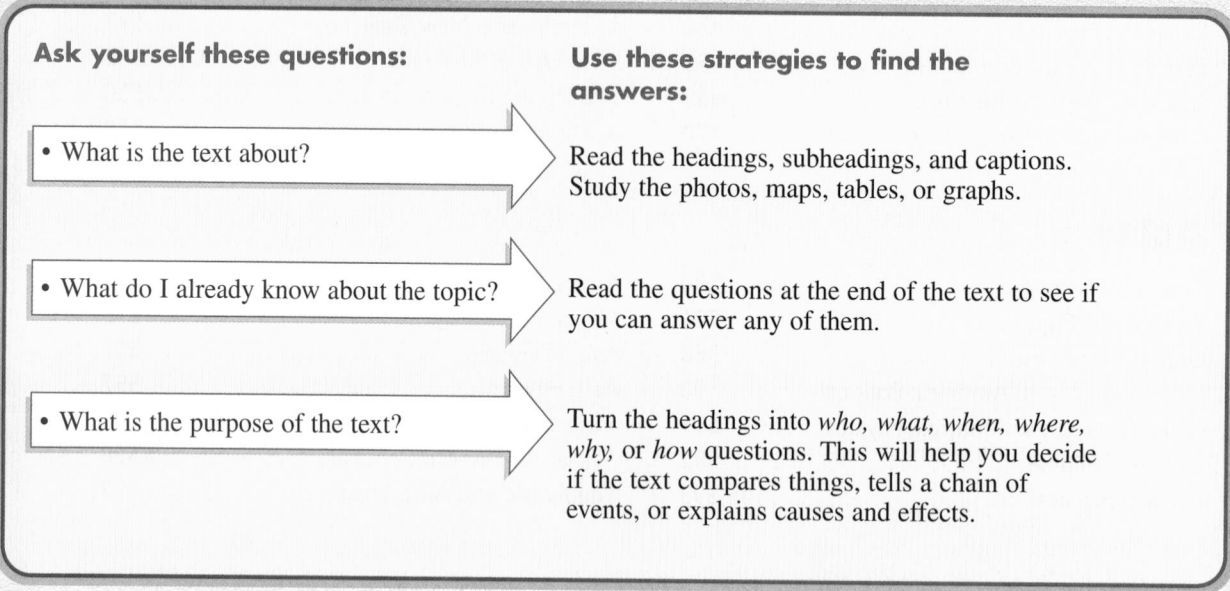

AS YOU READ

Organize information in a way that helps you see meaningful connections or relationships.

Taking notes as you read will improve your understanding. Use graphic organizers like the ones below to record the information you read. Study these descriptions and examples to learn how to create each type of organizer.

Sequencing

A **flowchart** helps you see how one event led to another. It can also display the steps in a process.

Use a flowchart if the text—

- tells about a chain of events.
- explains a method of doing something.

TIP▸ List the events or steps in order.

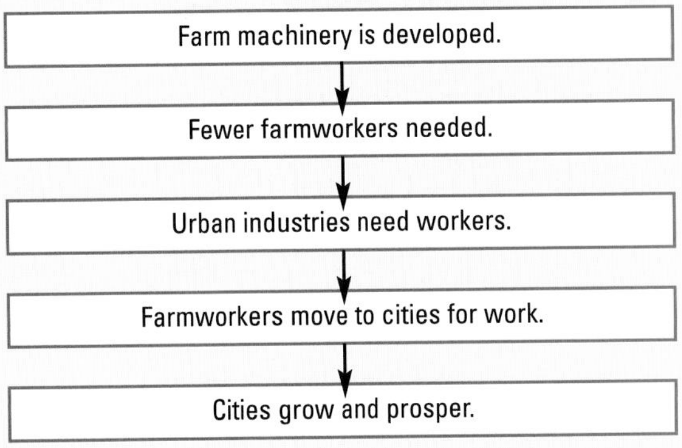

Comparing and Contrasting

A **Venn diagram** displays similarities and differences.

Use a Venn diagram if the text—

- compares and contrasts two individuals, groups, places, things, or events.

TIP▸ Label the outside section of each circle and list differences.
Label the shared section and list similarities.

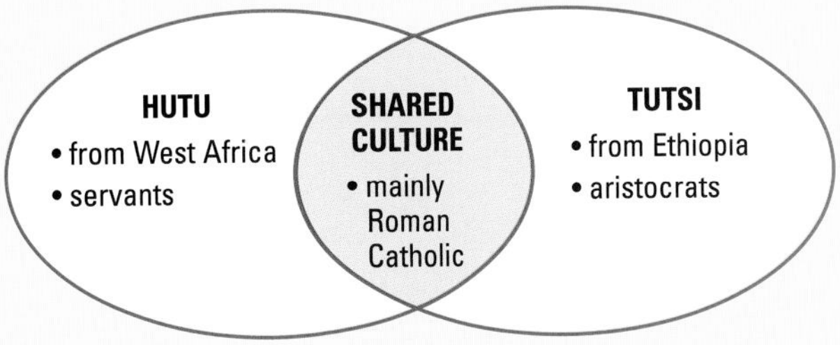

STUDENT SUCCESS HANDBOOK xxvii

AS YOU READ

(continued)

Categorizing Information

A **chart** organizes information in categories.

Use a chart if the text—

- lists similar facts about several places or things.
- presents characteristics of different groups.

TIP▸ Write an appropriate heading for each column in the chart to identify its category.

COUNTRY	FORM OF GOVERNMENT	ECONOMY
Cuba	communist dictatorship	command economy
Puerto Rico	democracy	free enterprise system

Identifying Main Ideas and Details

A **concept web** helps you understand relationships among ideas.

Use a concept web if the text—

- provides examples to support a main idea.
- links several ideas to a main topic.

TIP▸ Write the main idea in the largest circle. Write details in smaller circles and draw lines to show relationships.

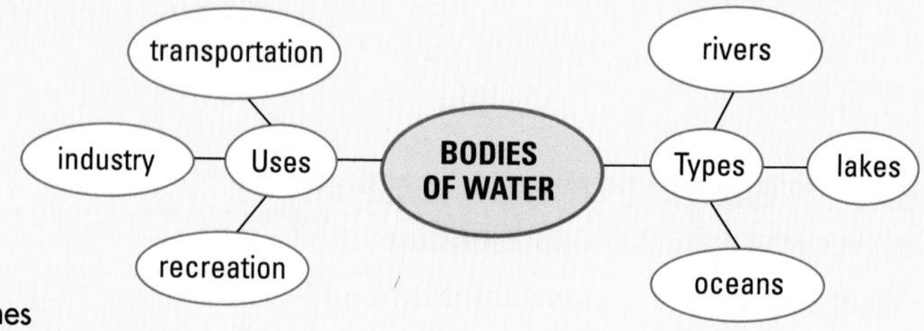

xxviii STUDENT SUCCESS HANDBOOK

Organizing Information

An **outline** provides an overview, or a kind of blueprint for reading.

Use an outline to organize ideas—
- according to their importance.
- according to the order in which they are presented.

TIP▶ Use Roman numerals for main ideas, capital letters for secondary ideas, and Arabic numerals for supporting details.

I. Differences Between the North and the South
- **A.** Views on slavery
  - **1.** Northern abolitionists
  - **2.** Southern slave owners
- **B.** Economies
  - **1.** Northern manufacturing
  - **2.** Southern agriculture

Identifying Cause and Effect

A **cause-and-effect** diagram shows the relationship between what happened (effect) and the reason why it happened (cause).

Use a cause-and-effect chart if the text—
- lists one or more causes for an event.
- lists one or more results of an event.

TIP▶ Label causes and effects. Draw arrows to indicate how ideas are related.

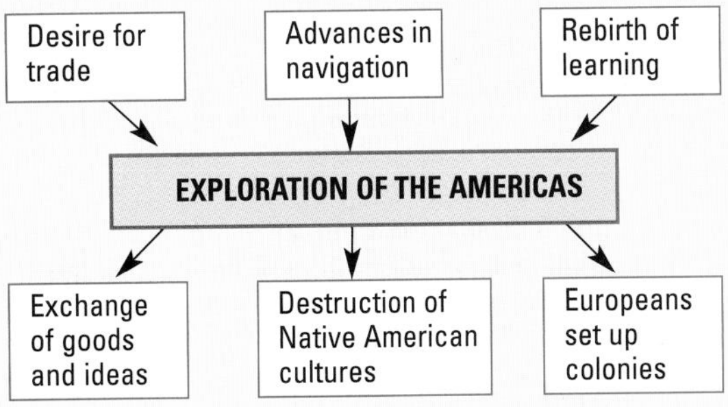

AFTER YOU READ

Test yourself to find out what you learned from reading the text.
Go back to the questions you asked yourself before you read the text. You should be able to give more complete answers to these questions:
- What is the text about?
- What is the purpose of the text?

You should also be able to make connections between the new information you learned from the text and what you already knew about the topic.

Study your graphic organizer. Use this information as the *answers.* Make up a meaningful *question* about each piece of information.

STUDENT SUCCESS HANDBOOK xxix

Taking Tests

Do you panic at the thought of taking a standardized test? Here are some tips that most test developers recommend to help you achieve good scores.

MULTIPLE-CHOICE QUESTIONS

Read each part of a multiple-choice question to make sure you understand what is being asked.

Many tests are made up of multiple-choice questions. Some multiple-choice items are **direct questions.** They are complete sentences followed by possible answers, called distractors.

Direct Question	What is a narrow strip of land that has water on both sides and joins two larger bodies of land called?
The **distractors** list the possible answers.	**A** a bay **B** an isthmus **C** a lake **D** an island
Try each distractor as an answer to your question. Rule out the ones that don't work.	You can rule out A and C because they are bodies of water, not land. You can rule out D because an island is completely surrounded by water.

Other multiple-choice questions are **incomplete sentences** that you are to finish. They are followed by possible answers.

The **stem** tells you what the question is looking for	A narrow strip of land that has water on both sides and joins two larger bodies of land is called
Distractors	**A** a bay **B** an isthmus **C** a lake **D** an island
Turn the stem into a direct question, using *who, what, when, where,* or *why.*	What is a narrow strip of land that has water on both sides and joins two larger bodies of land called?

XXX STUDENT SUCCESS HANDBOOK

WHAT'S BEING TESTED?

Identify the type of question you are being asked.

Social studies tests often ask questions that involve reading comprehension. Other questions may require you to gather or interpret information from a map, graph, or chart. The following strategies will help you answer different kinds of questions.

Reading Comprehension Questions

What to do:	How to do it:
1. Determine the content and organization of the selection.	Read the **title.** Skim the selection. Look for key words that indicate time, cause-and-effect, or comparison.
2. Analyze the questions. Do they ask you to *recall facts?*	Look for **key words** in the stem: According to the selection . . . The selection states that . . .
Do they ask you to *make judgments?*	The main idea of the selection is . . . The author would likely agree that . . .
3. Read the selection.	Read quickly. Keep the questions in mind.
4. Answer the questions.	Try out each distractor and choose the best answer. Refer back to the selection if necessary.

Example:

A Region of Diversity The Khmer empire was one of many kingdoms in Southeast Asia. Unlike the Khmer empire, however, the other kingdoms were small because Southeast Asia's mountains kept people protected and apart. People had little contact with those who lived outside their own valley.

Why were most kingdoms in Southeast Asia small?

A disease killed many people
B lack of food
C climate was too hot
D mountains kept people apart

TIP▸ The key word because tells why the kingdoms were small.

(The correct answer is D.)

STUDENT SUCCESS HANDBOOK xxxi

WHAT'S BEING TESTED?

(continued)

Map Questions

What to do:	How to do it:
1. Determine what kind of information is presented on the map.	Read the map **title.** It will indicate the purpose of the map. Study the **map key.** It will explain the symbols used on the map. Look at the **scale.** It will help you calculate distance between places on the map.
2. Read the question. Determine which component on the map will help you find the answer.	Look for **key words** in the stem. About <u>how far</u> . . . [use the scale] <u>What crops</u> were grown in . . . [use the map key]
3. Look at the map and answer the question in your own words.	Do not read the distractors yet.
4. Choose the best answer.	Decide which distractor agrees with the answer you determined from the map.

Example

In which of these countries are Thraco-Illyrian languages spoken?

A Romania
B Albania
C Hungary
D Lithuania

TIP▸ Read the labels and the key to understand the map.
(The correct answer is B.)

xxxii STUDENT SUCCESS HANDBOOK

Graph Questions

What to do:	How to do it:
1. Determine the purpose of the graph.	Read the graph **title.** It indicates what the graph represents.
2. Determine what information on the graph will help you find the answer.	Read the **labels** on the graph or on the key. They tell the units of measurement used by the graph.
3. Choose the best answer.	Decide which distractor agrees with the answer you determined from the graph.

Example

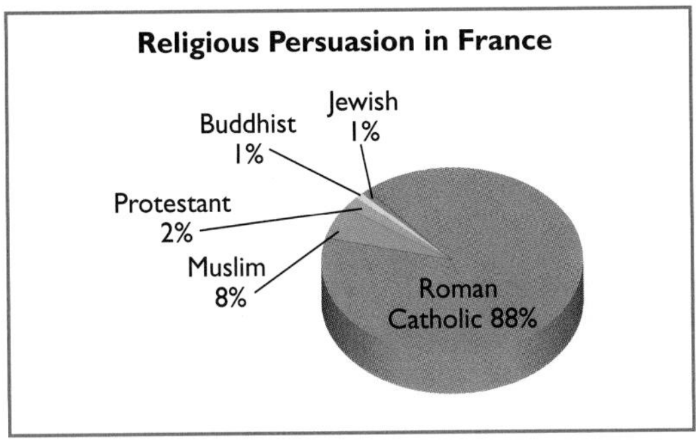

A **circle graph** shows the relationship of parts to the whole in terms of percentages.

After Roman Catholics, the next largest religious population in France is
A Buddhist **C** Jewish
B Protestant **D** Muslim

TIP▶ Compare the percentages listed in the labels.
(The correct answer is D.)

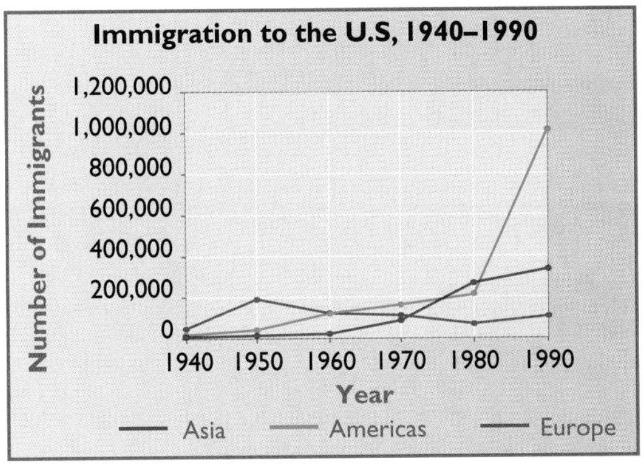

A **line graph** shows a pattern or change over time by the direction of the line.

Between 1980 and 1990, immigration to the U.S. from the Americas
A decreased a little **C** stayed about the same
B increased greatly **D** increased a little

TIP▶ Compare the vertical distance between the two correct points on the line graph.
(The correct answer is B.)

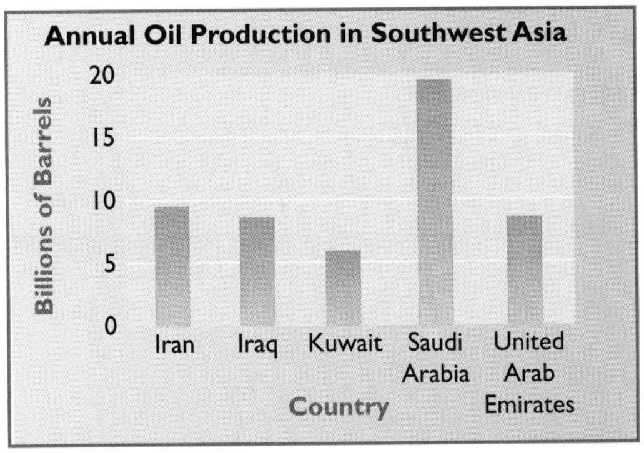

A **bar graph** compares differences in quantity by showing bars of different lengths.

Saudi Arabia produces about how many more billions of barrels of oil a year than Iran?
A 5 billion **C** 15 billion
B 10 billion **D** 20 billion

TIP▶ Compare the heights of the bars to find the difference.
(The correct answer is B.)

STUDENT SUCCESS HANDBOOK xxxiii

Writing for Social Studies

When you face a writing assignment, do you think, "How will I ever get through this?" Here are some tips to guide you through any writing project from start to finish.

THE WRITING PROCESS

Follow each step of the writing process to communicate effectively.

Step 1. Prewrite

- Establish the purpose.
- Define the topic.
- Determine the audience.
- Gather details.

Step 2. Draft

- Organize information logically in an outline or graphic organizer.
- Write an introduction, body, and conclusion.
- State main ideas clearly.
- Include relevant details to support your ideas.

Step 3. Revise

- Edit for clarity of ideas and elaboration.

Step 4. Proofread

- Correct any errors in spelling, grammar, and punctuation.

Step 5. Publish and Present

- Copy text neatly by hand, or use a typewriter or word processor.
- Illustrate as needed.
- Create a cover, if appropriate.

xxxiv STUDENT SUCCESS HANDBOOK

TYPES OF WRITING FOR SOCIAL STUDIES

Identify the purpose for your writing.

Each type of writing assignment has a specific purpose, and each purpose needs a different plan for development. The following descriptions and examples will help you identify the three purposes for social studies writing. The lists of steps will help you plan your writing.

Writing to Inform

Purpose: to present facts or ideas

Example

During the 1960s, research indicated the dangers of the insecticide DDT. It killed insects but also had long-term effects. When birds and fish ate poisoned insects, DDT built up in their fatty tissue. The poison also showed up in human beings who ate birds and fish contaminated by DDT.

TIP▶ Look for these **key terms** in the assignment: explain, describe, report, narrate

How to get started:

- Determine the topic you will write about.
- Write a topic sentence that tells the main idea.
- List all the ideas you can think of that are related to the topic.
- Arrange the ideas in logical order.

Writing to Persuade

Purpose: to influence someone

Example

Teaching computer skills in the classroom uses time that could be spent teaching students how to think for themselves or how to interact with others. Students who can reason well, express themselves clearly, and get along with other people will be better prepared for life than those who can use a computer.

TIP▶ Look for these **key terms** in the assignment: convince, argue, request

How to get started:

- Make sure you understand the problem or issue clearly.
- Determine your position.
- List evidence to support your arguments.
- Predict opposing views.
- List evidence you can use to overcome the opposing arguments.

Writing to Provide Historical Interpretations

Purpose: to present the perspective of someone in a different era

Example

The crossing took a week, but the steamship voyage was hard. We were cramped in steerage with hundreds of others. At last we saw the huge statue of the lady with the torch. In the reception center, my mother held my hand while the doctor examined me. Then, my father showed our papers to the official, and we collected our bags. I was scared as we headed off to find a home in our new country.

TIP▶ Look for these **key terms** in the assignment: go back in time, create, suppose that, if you were

How to get started:

- Study the events or issues of the time period you will write about.
- Consider how these events or issues might have affected different people at the time.
- Choose a person whose views you would like to present.
- Identify the thoughts and feelings this person might have experienced.

STUDENT SUCCESS HANDBOOK XXXV

RESEARCH FOR WRITING

Follow each step of the writing process to communicate effectively.

After you have identified the purpose for your writing, you may need to do research. The following steps will help you plan, gather, organize, and present information.

Step 1. Ask Questions

Ask yourself questions to help guide your research.	What do I already know about the topic? What do I want to find out about the topic?

Step 2. Acquire Information

Locate and use appropriate sources of information about the topic.	Library Internet search Interviews
Take notes.	Follow accepted format for listing sources.

Step 3. Analyze Information

Evaluate the information you find.	Is it relevant to the topic? Is it up-to-date? Is it accurate? Is the writer an authority on the topic? Is there any bias?

Step 4. Use Information

Answer your research questions with the information you have found. (You may find that you need to do more research.)	Do I have all the information I need?
Organize your information into the main points you want to make. Identify supporting details.	Arrange ideas in outline form or in a graphic organizer.

Step 5. Communicate What You've Learned

Review the purpose for your writing and choose an appropriate way to present the information.

Purpose	Presentation
inform	formal paper, documentary, multimedia
persuade	essay, letter to the editor, speech
interpret	journal, newspaper account, drama

Draft and revise your writing, and then evaluate it. Use a rubric for self-evaluation.

xxxvi STUDENT SUCCESS HANDBOOK

EVALUATING YOUR WRITING

Use the following rubric to help you evaluate your writing.

	Excellent	Good	Acceptable	Unacceptable
Purpose	Achieves purpose—to inform, persuade, or provide historical interpretation—very well	Informs, persuades, or provides historical interpretation reasonably well	Reader cannot easily tell if the purpose is to inform, persuade, or provide historical interpretation	Lacks purpose
Organization	Develops ideas in a very clear and logical way	Presents ideas in a reasonably well-organized way	Reader has difficulty following the organization	Lacks organization
Elaboration	Explains all ideas with facts and details	Explains most ideas with facts and details	Includes some supporting facts and details	Lacks supporting details
Use of Language	Uses excellent vocabulary and sentence structure with no errors in spelling, grammar, or punctuation	Uses good vocabulary and sentence structure with very few errors in spelling, grammar, or punctuation	Includes some errors in grammar, punctuation, and spelling	Includes many errors in grammar, punctuation, and spelling

STUDENT SUCCESS HANDBOOK xxxvii

UNIT 1

Introducing the Unit

This unit was developed around seven strands of essential knowledge and skills that relate to the study of the people, places, and cultures of the contemporary world. These strands areas include **History, Geography, Economics, Government, Citizenship, Culture,** and **Science, Technology, and Society.** These seven strands, and the related Guiding Questions on the next pages, are intended as an organizational focus for the unit. All of the chapter content, activities, questions, and assessments relate to the seven strands, which act as an umbrella under which all of the material falls.

Using the Pictures

Invite students to discuss the photographs. Use them as a prompt for a discussion of what students know about history, geography, economics, government, citizenship, culture, and science and technology.

- You may want to begin a K-W-L chart on the chalkboard for the tools and concepts of geography, with the headings What We **K**now About Geography, What We **W**ant to Know About Geography, and What We **L**earned About Geography.
- Have students fill in the first column with several things they agree they already know. Then, ask them to brainstorm what they would like to know about geography to add to the second column.
- Students can fill in the third column as they work through the text.

eTeach

Be sure to check out this month's discussion with a Master Teacher. Go to **phschool.com**.

UNIT 1

Geography: Tools and Concepts

GOVERNMENT

Learn about different forms of government . . .

SCIENCE, TECHNOLOGY, AND SOCIETY

See how people change their environment . . .

HISTORY

Discover who helped build America . . .

Resource Directory

Teaching Resources

Program Overview includes a guide to the Prentice Hall World Explorer program. You may wish to refer to the overview as you plan your instruction.

Pacing Charts for Unit 1 offer a variety of course configurations.

What do you want to learn?

ECONOMICS

Follow workers as they earn a living . . .

CULTURE

Examine differences among cultures . . .

CITIZENSHIP

Recognize our rights and duties . . .

GEOGRAPHY

Learn where people live, and why they live there . . .

A journal can be your personal record of discovery. As you learn about the tools and concepts of geography, you can include journal entries about what you read, write, think, and create. For your first entry, write about how geography affects you. How does it affect where you live, what you wear, what you eat, and when you sleep?

GEOGRAPHY: TOOLS AND CONCEPTS 1

Using the Explorer's Journal

Have students begin their Explorer's Journal as the paragraph on the student page suggests. If at all possible, encourage students to use a separate small notebook for their Explorer's Journal entries. They can add to this journal as they learn more about the tools and concepts of geography.

Project Possibilities

The projects in this book are designed to provide students with hands-on involvement in the content area. Write the following project ideas on the chalkboard and have students preview them and discuss which they might want to do. Students should work in pairs or small groups to complete the activities.

The Geography Game

Create a team game the whole class can play. Write clues about the unique physical features, climate, population, culture, and natural resources of a country. Challenge classmates to guess the country.

World News Today

Prepare a short speech about a country's economy and natural resources. Use a collection of newspaper articles.

Country Profile

Set up a classroom map and picture display based on your research of the geography, climate, and population of a country.

Resource Directory

Technology

Social Studies Skills Tutor CD-ROM provides two levels of interactive instruction and practice in 20 core social studies skills.

Resource Pro® CD-ROM allows you to create customized lesson plans and print all resources directly from the CD-ROM.

Introducing

Guiding Questions

The Guiding Questions that appear on the reduced student edition pages to the right should act as a guide for learning about the Earth and for encouraging students to relate what they learn to their own experience. The Guiding Questions that relate to the content of each chapter in the unit also appear on the Chapter Opener pages in this Teacher's edition.

- You may wish to add your own Guiding Questions to the list in order to tailor them to your particular course. Or, as a group activity, ask your class to develop its own Guiding Questions.

ACTIVITY

Using the Guiding Questions

Ask a volunteer to read aloud the Guiding Questions to the class.

- Have students write the seven headings on a separate piece of paper or in their Explorer's Journal. Have them think about what information they would like to learn about geography, and write a question that relates to each heading.
- Create a master list of questions grouped under the seven headings. As students read about geography tools and concepts, have them answer the questions on the list.
- At the end of the unit, if any questions remain unanswered, have students research and find the answers to those questions.

Guiding Questions

What questions do I need to ask to understand the tools and concepts of geography?

Asking questions is an important part of learning. Think about what information you would want to know if you were visiting a new place, and what questions you might ask to find the answers. The questions on these pages can help guide your study. You might want to try adding a few of your own!

GEOGRAPHY

Many physical processes have shaped our planet. Some of these processes are violent. Earthquakes and volcanoes can change the landscape in a matter of minutes. Other processes are slow, and almost unnoticeable. Wind slowly wears down rocks and rain carries soil into rivers. Gradually the Earth changes. Mountains, rivers, valleys, and even whole continents are created and changed.

1 What are some features of the Earth's geography?

HISTORY

People have been living on the Earth for a long time. Geography has played an important role in their history. People move from place to place, seeking better ways of life. Sometimes, they move because of environmental disasters. Other times, they are driven to a new place by war or uncaring governments. The study of geography includes the histories of people and places.

2 How can knowing a people's history help to better understand them?

CULTURE

Every group of people has a special way of doing things. They have a particular set of beliefs and values. All of these things are affected by geography. Culture can unite people, and it can separate them from other people. The physical landscape of an area gives every group a special set of challenges to meet in order to survive. As people learn to meet these challenges, they develop culture.

3 Are the world's many cultures more alike or more different?

2 UNIT I GEOGRAPHY: TOOLS AND CONCEPTS

GOVERNMENT

In order to live together, people need a government. It organizes the way people live and protects them. Yet there are many forms of government, and people must make important choices. Around the world, wherever you go, you will find many examples of the choices they have made.

4 Under what kinds of government do people live?

ECONOMICS

People around the world find many ways to make a living. Some raise crops, herd sheep, or mine for metals. Some labor in steel mills or automobile factories. Others work in medicine or law. Everyone, in fact, takes part in the economy. Learning about the economic choices people make will help you better understand and succeed in the world of work.

5 How do people use the world's resources?

CITIZENSHIP

No matter where they live, people have duties and responsibilities as citizens. These duties, however, depend on the kind of government they have. In some countries, such as the United States, people enjoy many rights, but they must also accept many responsibilities.

6 How do people fulfill their responsibilities as citizens?

SCIENCE, TECHNOLOGY, AND SOCIETY

Science and technology have changed both the face of the Earth and the societies that people have created. People have the ability to change their environment. They can build houses to protect themselves from the weather and climate. They can change the course of rivers and cut down forests.

7 What are the benefits and challenges created by science and technology?

Take It to the NET

For more information on geography, visit the World Explorer: People, Places, and Cultures companion Web site at **phschool.com.**

ACTIVITY

Identifying Cause-and-Effect Relationships

Physical Processes Explain to students that many physical processes have formed the Earth as we see it today. Among these processes are earthquakes, volcanoes, weathering, and erosion. These processes continue today. Ask students to work independently or in pairs to research one of these physical processes. Encourage them to create diagrams and other visual displays to help explain the process. When they are finished gathering information, have them deliver an oral presentation of their findings.

Verbal/Linguistic, Visual/Verbal

ACTIVITY

Comparing and Contrasting

Regional Characteristics Ask students to work in pairs and together list all the characteristics they can think of that describe the region in which they live. Tell them to consider these points:

- what the land looks like
- what the climate is like
- the people who live there
- the government and other institutions
- types of businesses

Then, tell them to select another country. As they read the unit, have them do research to learn about the country and to discover how it is similar to and different from their region of the world. Encourage them to use primary as well as secondary resources. Challenge them to create a means of sharing their discoveries with the class.

Verbal/Linguistic

ACTIVITY ATLAS

Lesson Objectives

1. Define the term *geography* and explain what geographers do.
2. Describe the features of physical, population density, climate, and vegetation maps.
3. Explain how physical, political, precipitation, and economic activity maps are used.

Lesson Plan

1 Engage

Warm-Up Activity

Tell students to imagine that they are creating a twin community to your own. To begin, have them describe your community's physical and human geography. If necessary, prompt students with questions such as *What is the land like? What is the weather like? How many people live in our community? How do people earn a living in our community?*

Activating Prior Knowledge

Ask students to name as many map types as they know. Post the common suggestions on the chalkboard and define them as a class. Talk about how the maps differ and what their possible uses might be.

ACTIVITY ATLAS

Geography: Tools and Concepts

Learning about geography tools and concepts requires you to be an explorer, and no explorer would start out without first checking some facts. Begin by exploring the maps and answering the questions on the following pages.

World: Physical

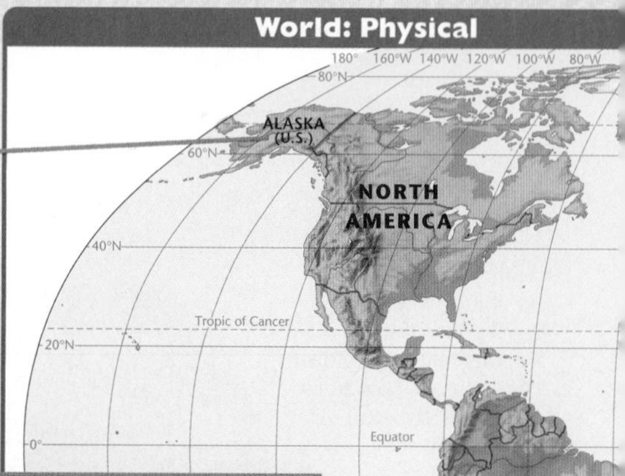

▲ Why do people in this place wear this type of clothing?

▶ Why do visitors to this area become short of breath easily?

Take It to the NET

Items marked with this logo are periodically updated on the Internet. To get current information about geography, go to **phschool.com.**

4 UNIT I GEOGRAPHY

Resource Directory

Teaching Resources

Activity Atlas in the Unit I Teaching Resources, pp. 57–63

▲ Why did ancient people in this area become expert sailors?

▲ Why do relatively few people live in this area?

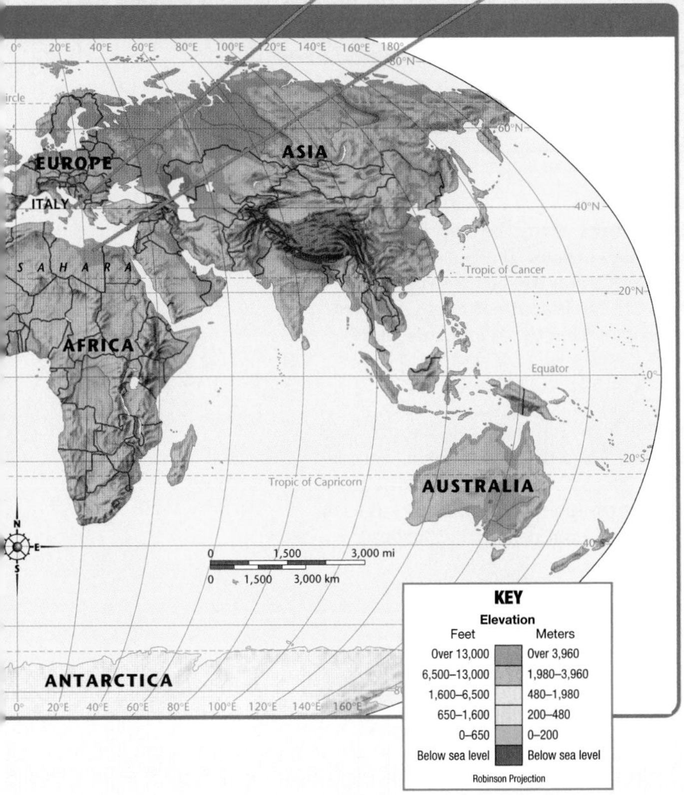

1. PLACE
Analyze the Meaning and Purpose of Geography Think about the word *geography*. The word part *geo* comes from a Greek word meaning "earth." *Graphy* means "science of," from an earlier word that meant "to write." How would you define *geography*?

People who are interested in geography are very curious about our world. Look at the pictures on these two pages. The question that accompanies each picture is the type of question that geographers ask. For each picture, write another question a geographer might ask.

❷ Explore

Generate, discuss, and record questions that must be answered in order to describe clearly your community's geographic twin. Then, have students carefully read the Activity Atlas materials. Ask them to list new questions that arise as they read. Discuss how maps might help answer each question.

❸ Teach

Begin a concept web about geography by writing the word *geography* on the chalkboard. Have a volunteer write a sentence in the center of the web defining the term. Students can then complete the web by adding a second row of elements describing the maps geographers use and a third row explaining the information each map provides.

❹ Assess/Reteach

Concept webs should define geography as the science of the Earth and should list physical, political, climate, cultural, population, and economic activity maps as well as the information each map provides.

Resource Directory

Teaching Resources

Outline Maps The World, pp. 2–3

Answers to...

PLACE

1. Geography is the science of the Earth. Possible questions: How do people adapt to their environment? What makes a place an attractive location to live? What major body of water influences life in a town? What challenges face people living at great elevations?

ACTIVITY ATLAS

Practice in the Themes of Geography

Place Have students use the material in the Activity Atlas to write one or two sentences describing a chosen place. Explain that each place can be described in terms of its physical and/or human geography. (Possible answer: Alaska is a sparsely populated, harsh land in the far north of North America.)

Location Ask students to name the continent on which Italy is located (Europe). Then, ask them what two continents are nearest to Italy (Asia and Africa).

Movement Tell students to imagine that their family wants to relocate from one continent to another. Ask students which continent their family would be on if they had to cross a large body of water to reach any other continent (Australia).

Regions Ask students to identify a mountain range that extends along the west coast of South America (Andes Mountains).

Human-Environment Interaction Ask students to locate areas on the world climate map that are arid. Then, have them locate those regions on the world economic activity map. Have students draw conclusions about how climate affects human activities.

ACTIVITY ATLAS

The World: Continents, Oceans, and Seas

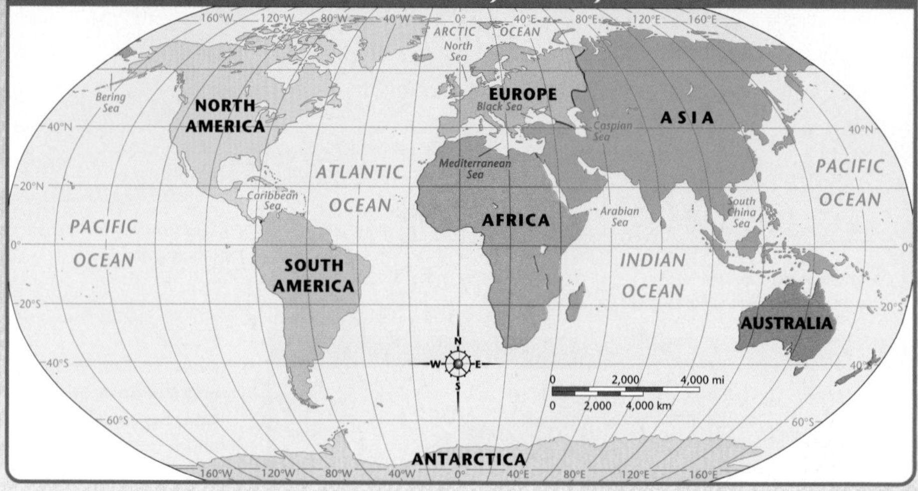

2. LOCATION

Locate the Continents and Oceans Study the map above to learn the locations of the continents and oceans. The United States is on the continent of North America. What ocean lies between North America and Africa? Which continent is south of North America? Which ocean lies north of Europe? What two continents share borders with Asia?

3. LOCATION

Compare the Continents This map shows the relative sizes and shapes of the continents because it is a flat map. Look closely. Is Africa smaller, larger, or about the same size as North America? How much larger is Asia than North America? Is Europe larger or smaller than South America? Which continent is the smallest?

Answers to...

LOCATION

2. Atlantic Ocean; South America; Arctic Ocean; Europe and Africa

LOCATION

3. Africa is larger; twice as large; South America is larger; smaller; Australia is the smallest

Resource Directory

Teaching Resources

Outline Maps The World, pp. 2–3

Technology

Color Transparencies 8 The World: Continents and Oceans Map

4. MOVEMENT

Explore Transportation Corridors Seventy-five percent of the world is covered by water, most of it in the oceans. Ships follow regular trade routes from country to country. This map shows some of the trade routes in the Pacific Ocean.

A. *Imagine that a manufacturer is shipping goods from Jakarta, Indonesia, to Vancouver, Canada. At what cities would the ship stop?*

B. *Which trip covers more distance: Wellington, New Zealand to Tokyo, Japan or Lima, Peru to Los Angeles?*

C. *Having a good ocean port allows a nation to send and receive goods from other countries. What other benefits do countries gain from being on a trade route?*

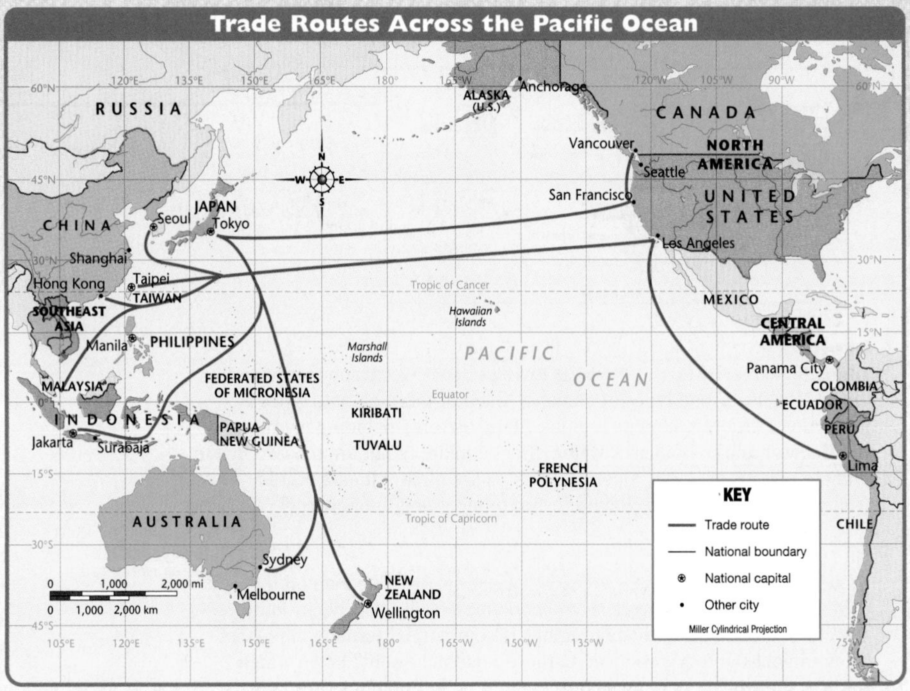

HISTORY

Impact of Physical Processes on the Environment

Alfred Lothar Wegener (1880–1930) studied astronomy and meteorology, so continents were not his field of expertise. Nonetheless, in looking at the shapes of the continent, he was struck by a ground shaking idea. The continents looked as though they could be fit together like the pieces of a puzzle. In 1912, he proposed that the Earth's surface was once comprised of a single large landmass that broke apart into the continents we see today. As evidence, he pointed to closely related fossil organisms and similar rock strata that occur on the continents. Geologists dismissed Wegener's ideas at the time. Forty years later, though, precise dating of rocks on the opposite sides of the Atlantic Ocean demonstrated that Wegener's ideas were not only plausible, but likely.

Resource Directory

Teaching Resources

Social Studies and Geography Skills,
Reading a Trade Map, p. 37

Answers to...

MOVEMENT

4. **A.** Tokyo and San Francisco
   B. Wellington to Tokyo
   C. Ocean ports place countries in close contact with other countries, allowing them to learn about new knowledge, information, and technologies developed elsewhere. These countries also benefit from the exchange of culture, which occurs naturally in seaports.

ACTIVITY ATLAS

ACTIVITY

Effects of the Physical Environment

Economic Activities Ask students to work in pairs and to choose a region of the world where a certain type of economic activity is predominant. Have them research the activity to learn more about what is produced. Ask: What geographic factors may have led people to develop that activity in that region? Have students report on their findings to the class.

Verbal/Linguistic

ACTIVITY ATLAS

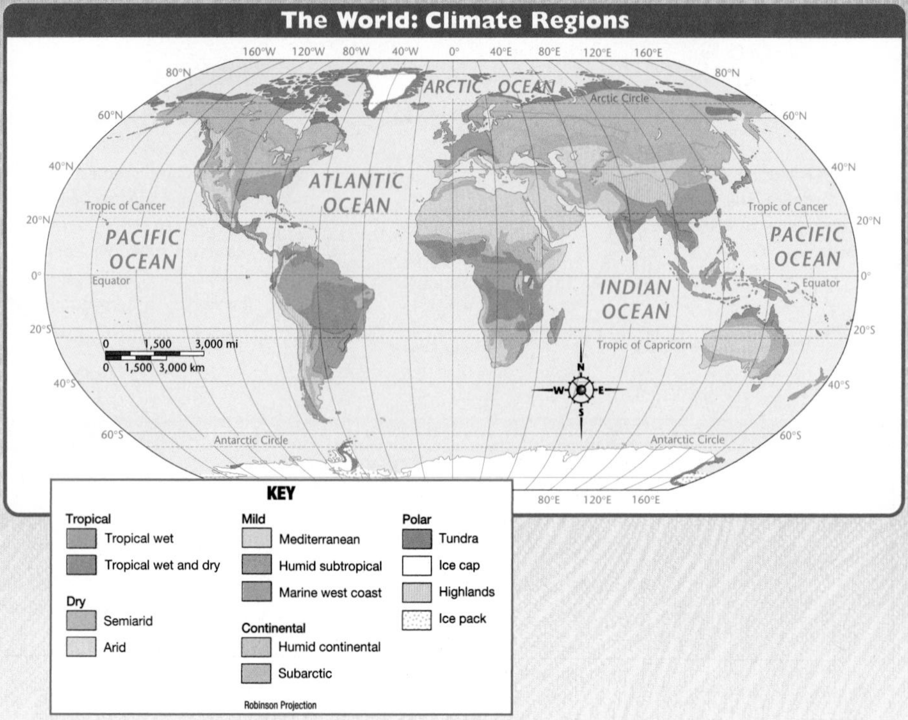

5. REGIONS

Identify Patterns in the Physical Environment Geographers divide the world into five broad types of climates. Each of these climate types is made up of different climate regions. Many factors, including nearness to the Equator and to bodies of water, affect climate. What are the two major climate regions of South America? What is the major climate region of Australia? What is the major climate region found along the Equator?

6. REGIONS

Examine the Effect of the Physical Environment The map on the next page shows the important types of economic activity that occur in different parts of the world. In what regions is commercial farming important? Where might the food produced in these regions be sent? From which parts of the world might these farming regions get manufactured goods?

Answers to...

REGIONS

5. tropical wet, tropical wet and dry; arid; arid

REGIONS

6. Much of eastern and central North America, most of Europe; and isolated regions around the edges of other continents. The food might be shipped to areas where manufacturing and trade are the principal activities. These regions would have concentrations of people and produce little food. The farming regions would get manufactured goods from the manufacturing and trade centers.

Resource Directory

Teaching Resources

Social Studies and Geography Skills,
Reading a Climate Map, p. 24

World Economic Activity

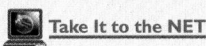

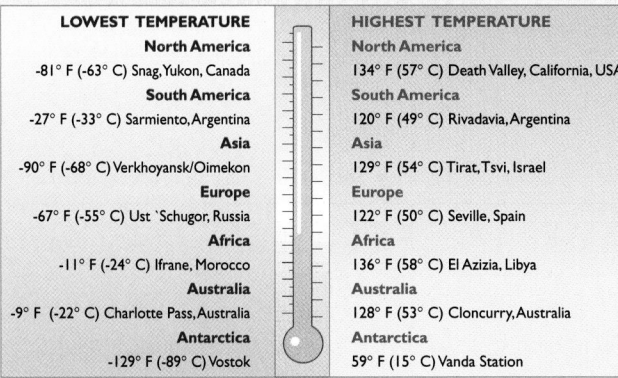

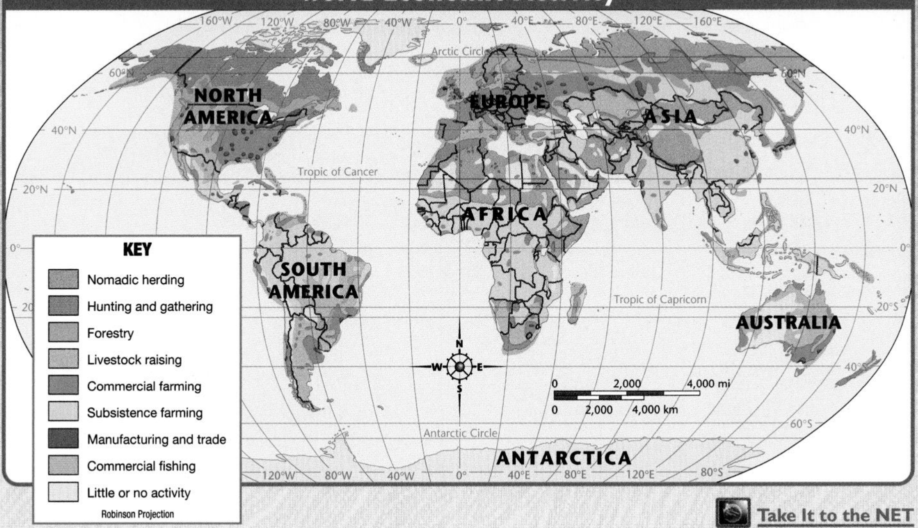

Take It to the NET

Going to Extremes

7. PLACE

Compare Geographic Factors The diagram below gives information about the highest and lowest recorded temperatures around the world. What place has the world's highest recorded temperature? What place has the world's lowest recorded temperature? What is the hottest temperature recorded in North America? How many degrees (in Fahrenheit) higher is the hottest place than the coldest place, according to the diagram?

LOWEST TEMPERATURE	HIGHEST TEMPERATURE
North America	**North America**
-81° F (-63° C) Snag, Yukon, Canada	134° F (57° C) Death Valley, California, USA
South America	**South America**
-27° F (-33° C) Sarmiento, Argentina	120° F (49° C) Rivadavia, Argentina
Asia	**Asia**
-90° F (-68° C) Verkhoyansk/Oimekon	129° F (54° C) Tirat, Tsvi, Israel
Europe	**Europe**
-67° F (-55° C) Ust `Schugor, Russia	122° F (50° C) Seville, Spain
Africa	**Africa**
-11° F (-24° C) Ifrane, Morocco	136° F (58° C) El Azizia, Libya
Australia	**Australia**
-9° F (-22° C) Charlotte Pass, Australia	128° F (53° C) Cloncurry, Australia
Antarctica	**Antarctica**
-129° F (-89° C) Vostok	59° F (15° C) Vanda Station

Take It to the NET

ACTIVITY

Discovery Learning

Global Geography Game To play the game, you will need a globe or a world map and a game piece that can be attached to either. Start the game by prompting students with a location clue. Clues may include data from the Atlas maps, photos, or text. Continue giving clues until the students identify the correct place and tell what kind of map would include the clue information. Place the game piece on the location. The student who identifies the location then gives clues for a second location to another student. Once that location is identified, move the game piece to the next location. Continue the game until all students have correctly identified one place.

Logical/Mathematical

Resource Directory

Teaching Resources

Social Studies and Geography Skills,
Reading an Economic Activity Map, p. 25

Answers to...

PLACE

7. El Azizia, Libya, which reached 136° F; Vostok in Antarctica, which reached –129° F; Death Valley, California, which reached a temperature of 134° F; 265°F

Chapter 1 Planning Guide

Resource Manager

	CORE INSTRUCTION	READING/SKILLS
Chapter-Level Resources	**Teaching Resources** Program Overview Pacing Charts **Technology** Resource Pro® CD-ROM Companion Web site, phschool.com • eTeach	**Technology** Social Studies Skills Tutor CD-ROM Student Edition on Audio CD, Ch. 1
1 Understanding the Earth 1. Explain how the movement of the Earth around the sun affects our environment. 2. Explain the effect of latitude on climate.	**Teaching Resources** **Unit 1** Classroom Manager, p. 2 Guided Reading and Review, p. 3	**Teaching Resources** Guide to the Essentials, p. 1 **Technology** Section Reading Support Transparencies
2 The Five Themes of Geography 1. Define the study of geography. 2. Identify the five themes of geography and use them to learn about the world.	**Teaching Resources** **Unit 1** Classroom Manager, p. 5 Guided Reading and Review, p. 6	**Teaching Resources** Guide to the Essentials, p. 2 Social Studies and Geography Skills, pp. 5, 8, and 9 **Technology** Section Reading Support Transparencies
3 Using the Tools of Geography 1. Understand the advantages and disadvantages of globes and maps in depicting the Earth's surface. 2. Appreciate how geographers have tried to create accurate maps. 3. Identify the main parts of a map.	**Teaching Resources** **Unit 1** Classroom Manager, p. 8 Guided Reading and Review, p. 9 Chapter Summary, p. 11 Vocabulary, p. 12 Reteaching, p. 13	**Teaching Resources** **Unit 1** Critical Thinking, p. 15 Guide to the Essentials, p. 3 Social Studies and Geography Skills, pp. 6–7, 10–16 **Technology** Section Reading Support Transparencies

ENRICHMENT / PRE-AP

Teaching Resources
Primary Sources and Literature Readings

Other Print Resources
DK Atlas

Technology
World Video Explorer: Journey Over the World and Five Themes of Geography
Companion Web site, phschool.com

Technology
Color Transparencies 2–3

Technology
Color Transparencies 4–6

Teaching Resources
Unit 1
Enrichment, p. 14
Cooperative Learning Activity, pp. 64–67

Technology
Color Transparencies 7

ASSESSMENT

Prentice Hall Assessment System

Core Assessment
Chapter Tests with ExamView® Test Bank, Ch. 1
ExamView® Test Bank CD-ROM, Ch. 1

Standardized Test Preparation
Diagnose and Prescribe
Diagnostic Tests for Middle Grades Social Studies Skills
Review and Reteach
Review Book for World Studies
Practice and Assess
Test-taking Strategies with Transparencies for Middle Grades Test Prep Book
Test-taking Strategies Posters

Teaching Resources
Unit 1
Section Quizzes, pp. 4, 7, and 10
Chapter Tests, pp. 82–87

Technology
Companion Web site, phschool.com
Ch. 1 Self-Test

World Video Explorer
Each region of the world is explored through regional flyovers and investigative field trips. Case study segments give students an in-depth view of the history, economy, government, and culture of a key place in each region. Case studies include Nigeria, Mexico, China, British Columbia, and the Czech Republic.

In Your Classroom

CUSTOMIZE FOR INDIVIDUAL NEEDS

Gifted and Talented

Teacher's Edition
- Describing the Universe, p. 13
- Map Perspectives, p. 21

Teaching Resources
- Enrichment, p. 14
- Primary Sources and Literature Readings

Honors/Pre-AP

Teacher's Edition
- Map Perspectives, p. 21

Teaching Resources
- Critical Thinking, p. 15
- Primary Sources and Literature Readings

ESL

Teacher's Edition
- Making Maps, p. 21

Teaching Resources
- Guided Reading and Review, pp. 3, 6, and 9
- Vocabulary, p. 12
- Reteaching, p. 13
- Guide to the Essentials, pp. 1–3
- Social Studies and Geography Skills, pp. 6–16

Technology
- Social Studies Skills Tutor CD-ROM
- Section Reading Support Transparencies

Less Proficient Readers

Teacher's Edition
- The Continents, p. 17

Teaching Resources
- Guided Reading and Review, pp. 3, 6, and 9
- Vocabulary, p. 12
- Reteaching, p. 13
- Guide to the Essentials, pp. 1–3
- Social Studies and Geography Skills, pp. 6–16

Technology
- Social Studies Skills Tutor CD-ROM
- Section Reading Support Transparencies

Less Proficient Writers

Teacher's Edition
- Describing the Universe, p. 13

Teaching Resources
- Guided Reading and Review, pp. 3, 6, and 9
- Vocabulary, p. 12
- Guide to the Essentials, pp. 1–3
- Social Studies and Geography Skills, pp. 6–16

Technology
- Social Studies Skills Tutor CD-ROM
- Section Reading Support Transparencies

DORLING KINDERSLEY

At the end of each unit, you will find information adapted from Dorling Kindersley's *Illustrated Children's Encyclopedia* that connects to the region being studied and to one of the seven content strands. In addition, your resources include Dorling Kindersley's *Atlas*, which contains valuable information about countries from around the world.

TEACHER'S EDITION INDEX

Activities describing the universe, p. 13; the continents, p. 17; making maps, p. 21

Connections desert regions, p. 17; atlas's task, p. 20; map perspectives, p. 21

Skills Mini Lessons Organizing Your Time, p. 16; Assessing Your Understanding, p. 21

CHAPTER 1 PACING SUGGESTIONS

For 90-minute Blocks

See suggestions in the Teaching Resources Pacing Charts for Chapter 5. Use Color Transparencies 2, 3, 4, and 5.

Running Out of Time?

See the Guide to the Essentials, pp. 1–4.

INTERDISCIPLINARY LINKS

Middle Grades Math: Tools for Success
Course 2, Lesson 1-4, **Mean, Median, and Mode**

Science Explorer
Earth's Changing Surface, Lesson 1-4, **Topographic Maps**

Prentice Hall Literature
Copper, The Loch Ness Monster

BIBLIOGRAPHY

For the Teacher

Eyewitness History of the World. Dorling Kindersley, 1995. CD-ROM

World Desk Reference. Dorling Kindersley, 2001.

For the Student

Easy

VanCleave, Jancie. *Janice VanCleave's Geography for Every Kid: Easy Activities That Make Learning Geography Fun.* Wiley, 1993.

Average

The Visual Dictionary of the Earth. Dorling Kindersley, 2001.

Guide to Savage Earth. Dorling Kindersley, 2001.

Challenging

Lasky, Kathryn. *The Librarian Who Measured the Earth.* Little Brown, 1994.

Literature Connection

Fisher Staples, Suzanne. *Shabanu: Daughter of the Wind.* Knopf, 1989.

Houston, James. *Drifting Snow: An Arctic Search.* McElderry, 1992.

Take It to the NET

The World Explorer companion Web site, found on **phschool.com**, offers activities for exploring geographical, historical, and cultural resources on the Internet. It also provides on-line links for key content and all Section and Chapter Assessment activities.

The **Teacher site** also provides teachers with regional data and ideas for student research and activities.

Students can use the **Student site** to find chapter-by-chapter Internet resource links and to access Self-Tests.

CHAPTER 1

Connecting to the Guiding Questions

In this chapter, students will read about the tools and concepts of geography. Content in this chapter corresponds to the following Guiding Question outlined at the beginning of the unit.

- What are some important features of the Earth's geography?

Using the Map Activities

Point out to students the differences in the two maps on pp. 6 and 10. Discuss the difficulties that might be involved in making an accurate representation of the earth, which is round, on a flat piece of paper.

- Students should recognize the major differences in the sizes and shapes of the continents, a result of the differences between the knowledge of the Earth in 1589 and today. Point out to students, for example, the words *Terra Incognita* at the top of North America. This phrase is Latin for "unknown land."
- Tell students that their maps should show important features in their neighborhoods, from hills and lakes to significant buildings and roads. Have students list the important features they want to include before they begin drawing them.

Heterogeneous Groups

The following activities are suitable for heterogeneous groups.

Making Connections

Describing the Universe, p. 13

Drawing Conclusions

The Continents, p. 17

eTeach

Be sure to check out this month's discussion with a Master Teacher. Go to **phschool.com**.

CHAPTER 1

Using Geography Skills

SECTION 1
Understanding the Earth

SECTION 2
The Five Themes of Geography

SECTION 3
Using the Tools of Geography

Historical Map

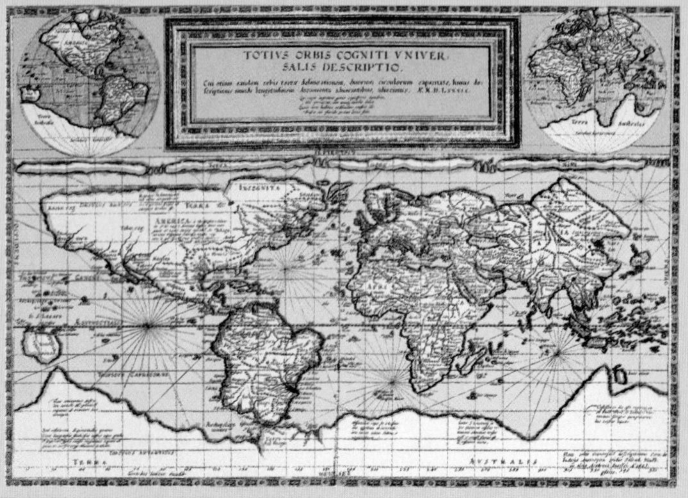

USING MAPS

A map is a drawing that shows the distribution and arrangement of features on the Earth. There are many different kinds of maps, and people have been creating and using them ever since they began to explore the world around them. The map above is from 1589. Looking at older maps can tell us a great deal about how earlier peoples thought the world looked.

Comparing Maps

Look at the map on this page and compare it with the map of the world in the Activity Atlas on page 6. What differences do you see? What are some reasons for these differences?

Making a Map

Maps can show anything from a specific place to the entire world. Create a map of your neighborhood, including any important features. Display your map in the classroom.

Resource Directory

Teaching Resources

Primary Sources and Literature Readings extend content with a selection related to the concepts in this chapter.

Other Print Resources

DK Atlas

Technology

Journey Over the World, from the World Video Explorer, introduces students to major landforms throughout the world.

Five Themes of Geography, from the World Video Explorer, enhances understanding of geography though an examination of the Pacific Islands.

Student Edition on Audio CD, Ch. 1

SECTION 1

Understanding the Earth

BEFORE YOU READ

READING FOCUS

1. How does the movement of the Earth around the sun affect our environment?
2. What is the effect of latitude on climate?

KEY TERMS

environment
orbit
revolution
axis
rotation
latitude
low latitudes
high latitudes
middle latitudes

KEY PLACES

Equator
Tropic of Cancer
Tropic of Capricorn
Arctic Circle
Antarctic Circle

NOTE TAKING

Copy the concept web shown here. As you read the section, fill in the blank ovals with information about the Earth. Add as many ovals as you need.

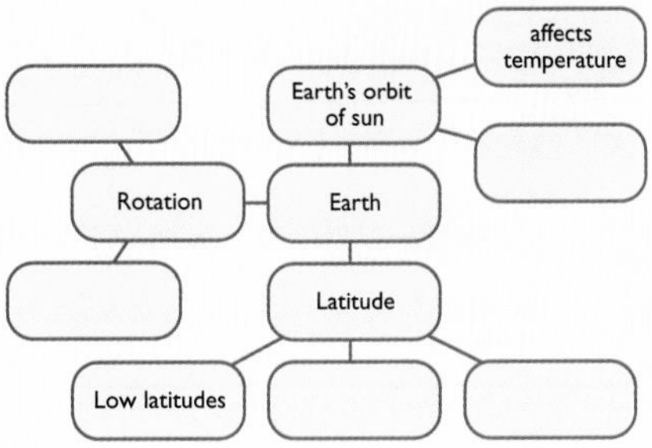

MAIN IDEA

The relationship between the Earth and the sun creates our days, seasons, and climate, and influences our environment.

Setting the Scene

"The Sky Father opened his hand. Within every crease there lay innumerable grains of shining maize [corn]. In his thumb and forefinger he took some of the shining grains and placed them in the sky as brilliant stars to be a guide to humans when the bright sun was hidden."

This is part of an ancient myth of the Pueblos, who live in what today is the southwestern United States. They used the story to explain the appearance of the night sky.

The Surface of the Sun

SCIENCE AND TECHNOLOGY

The sun is the largest object in our solar system and accounts for more than 99% of the total mass of the solar system. **Critical Thinking** What are some of the ways that the sun affects life on the Earth?

The Earth, the Sun, and Our Environment

The Earth, the sun, the planets, and most of the stars we see in the night sky are part of a galaxy, or family of stars. We call our galaxy the Milky Way because the lights from its billions of stars look like a milky band across the night sky. There are other galaxies, but they are so distant that they are only specks of light. Our sun is a star in the Milky Way. The sun provides light and the energy needed for life on the Earth. It affects our **environment,** or surroundings, in countless ways.

SECTION 1

Lesson Objectives

1. Explain how the movement of the Earth around the sun affects our environment.
2. Explain the effect of latitude on climate.

Lesson Plan

1 Engage

Warm-Up Activity

Ask students to orient themselves so that they can point to the east, where the sun rises, and to the west, where the sun sets. (You may wish to have a directional compass on hand to confirm students' observations.)

Activating Prior Knowledge

Write the words *Summer, Fall, Winter, Spring* on the chalkboard. Ask students to describe the type of clothing they wear, the activities they engage in, and foods they eat during each season. Then, ask students to explain what causes the change in seasons. Does the sun feel as warm in the winter or in the summer? What causes this change in warmth?

Resource Directory

Teaching Resources

Classroom Manager in the Unit 1 Teaching Resources, p. 2

Guided Reading and Review in the Unit 1 Teaching Resources, p. 3

Guide to the Essentials, p. 1

Technology

Section Reading Support Transparencies

Answers to...

CRITICAL THINKING

Students may say that the sun allows plants and trees to grow and provides us with a source of energy.

Lesson Plan continued

2 Explore

After students read the section, have them describe the Earth's position in the solar system. Encourage them to include answers to the following questions in their descriptions. Why does a model of the solar system include moving planets? How would a different slant to the axis of the Earth change the temperature of the surface of the Earth?

3 Teach

Have students make a model of the Earth with clay, a round balloon, or a ball. Have them indicate the locations of the poles, the Equator, and the Southern and Northern hemispheres. Then have students use their models to demonstrate the Earth's rotation and revolution. This activity should take about 20 minutes.

Questions for Discussion

GEOGRAPHY Why are seasons different in the Northern and Southern hemispheres?

Because of the tilt of the Earth's axis, the two hemispheres receive different amounts of direct sunlight during the year.

GEOGRAPHY The Earth revolves and the Earth rotates. What is the difference between the two?

The Earth revolves around the sun as it travels in its orbit. The Earth also rotates, or turns on its own axis.

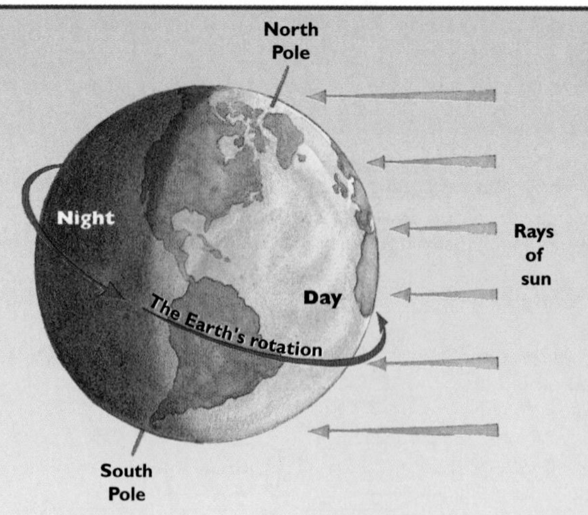

How Night Changes Into Day

GEOGRAPHY This diagram shows how places on the Earth move from night into day. Today, it takes almost 24 hours for the Earth to make one complete rotation. One-half of the Earth is always lighted by the sun, while the other half is in darkness. **Chart Study** As time passes, the Earth spins more and more slowly. What will eventually happen to the length of a day? Find North America on the globe. Which coast receives daylight first?

Understanding Days and Nights The sun may be about 93 million miles (150 million km) away, but it still provides the Earth with heat and light. The Earth travels around the sun in an oval-shaped path called an **orbit.** It takes 365 1/4 days, or just a little more than one year, for the Earth to complete one **revolution,** or journey, around the sun.

As the Earth revolves around the sun, it is also spinning in space. The Earth turns around its **axis**—an imaginary line running through it between the North and South poles. Each complete turn, which takes about 24 hours, is called a **rotation.** As the Earth rotates, it is daytime on the side facing the sun, and it is night on the side away from the sun.

Understanding Seasons At certain times of the year and in certain places, days are longer than nights, and at other times, nights are longer than days. This happens, in part, because the Earth's axis is at an angle. At some points in the Earth's orbit, the tilt causes a region to face toward the sun for more hours than it faces away from the sun. Days are longer. At other times, the region faces away from the sun for more hours than it faces toward the sun. Days are shorter.

The Earth's tilt and orbit also cause changes in temperatures. The warmth you feel depends on how directly the sunlight falls on the region in which you live. Some regions receive much fairly direct sunlight, while other regions receive no direct sunlight.

The amount of sunlight also partly determines how much food we produce and where people live. For example, fewer crops grow in regions that receive little direct sunlight, so fewer people live there. Regions that get more sunlight, like the United States, can grow more food to feed large populations.

Resource Directory

Technology

Color Transparency 3 Day and Night Diagram

Answers to...

CHART STUDY

Days will get longer. The east coast of North America receives daylight first.

The Effect of Latitude

Imaginary lines, called lines of **latitude,** are east-west circles around the globe. Some of these lines of latitude have special names. They divide the Earth into regions according to the amount of sunlight they receive.

Look at the diagram below. The **Equator** is a latitude line that circles the Earth exactly halfway between the North Pole and the South Pole. On about March 21 and September 23, the sun is directly over the Equator. At those times, days are almost exactly as long as nights. These days are the spring and fall equinoxes.

Two other lines of latitude are the **Tropic of Cancer** and the **Tropic of Capricorn.** On June 21 or 22, the sun shines directly above the Tropic of Cancer. This day is the summer solstice (SOHL stiss), in the Northern Hemisphere. On December 21 or 22, the sun shines directly above the Tropic of Capricorn. This day marks the winter solstice in the Northern Hemisphere. The seasons are reversed in the Southern Hemisphere. When would the summer solstice occur there?

The area between the Tropic of Cancer and the Tropic of Capricorn is called the **low latitudes,** or the tropics. Any location in the

LINKS TO Science

Midnight Sun The Earth's axis is at an angle, which makes the Earth seem to lean. When the North Pole leans toward the sun, the sun never sets. At the same time, the South Pole leans away from the sun, so at the South Pole, the sun never rises. This lasts for six months. When the South Pole leans toward the sun, this pole has six months of continuous sunlight.

Seasons of the Northern Hemisphere

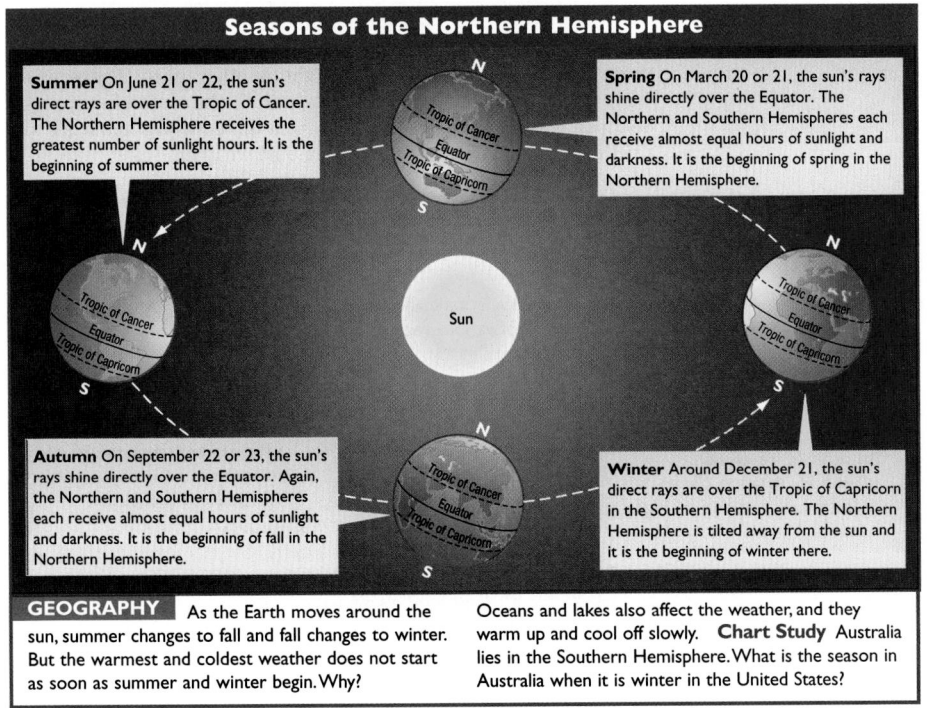

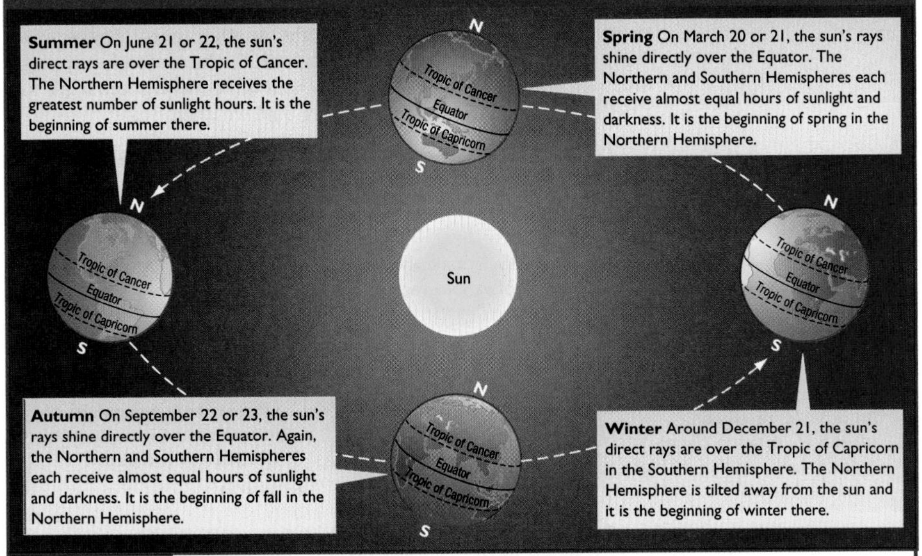

Summer On June 21 or 22, the sun's direct rays are over the Tropic of Cancer. The Northern Hemisphere receives the greatest number of sunlight hours. It is the beginning of summer there.
Spring On March 20 or 21, the sun's rays shine directly over the Equator. The Northern and Southern Hemispheres each receive almost equal hours of sunlight and darkness. It is the beginning of spring in the Northern Hemisphere.
Sun
N
S
Tropic of Cancer
Equator
Tropic of Capricorn
Autumn On September 22 or 23, the sun's rays shine directly over the Equator. Again, the Northern and Southern Hemispheres each receive almost equal hours of sunlight and darkness. It is the beginning of fall in the Northern Hemisphere.
Winter Around December 21, the sun's direct rays are over the Tropic of Capricorn in the Southern Hemisphere. The Northern Hemisphere is tilted away from the sun and it is the beginning of winter there.

GEOGRAPHY As the Earth moves around the sun, summer changes to fall and fall changes to winter. But the warmest and coldest weather does not start as soon as summer and winter begin. Why? Oceans and lakes also affect the weather, and they warm up and cool off slowly. **Chart Study** Australia lies in the Southern Hemisphere. What is the season in Australia when it is winter in the United States?

4 Assess/Reteach

See the answers to the Section 1 Review. You may also use students' models as an assessment.

Acceptable use of the model includes positioning the poles opposite one another, the Equator equidistant from the poles, and identifying the hemispheres correctly.

Commendable use of the model demonstrates the rotation and revolution of the Earth in relation to a point designated as the sun.

Outstanding use of the model includes correctly demonstrating the tilt of the Earth's axis in relation to the sun as well as rotation and revolution.

ACTIVITY

Making Connections

Describing The Universe Ask students why the Pueblo image of innumerable grains of corn in the Sky Father's palm is effective (page 11). Have them think of other metaphors that express the vastness of the universe, or the change from day into night. Students can also draw pictures or make a book of images.

Visual/Spatial, Verbal/Linguistic

Resource Directory

Technology

Color Transparency 2 The Earth's Revolutions and the Seasons Diagram

Answers to...

CHART STUDY

It is summer in Australia.

SECTION 1 ASSESSMENT

AFTER YOU READ

1. (a) a line of latitude that circles the Earth exactly halfway between the North Pole and the South Pole, (b) (23.5°N) the northern boundary of the tropics, (c) (23.5°S) the southern boundary of the tropics, (d) (66°N) line of latitude around the Earth near the North Pole, (e) (66°S) line of latitude around the Earth near the South Pole
2. (a) all of the surroundings and conditions that affect living things, (b) path followed by an object in space as it moves around another object, (c) one complete orbit of the Earth around the sun, (d) imaginary line around which a planet turns, (e) spinning motion of the Earth around its axis, (f) imaginary lines that circle the Earth parallel to the Equator, (g) the region between the Tropic of Cancer and the Tropic of Capricorn, (h) regions between the Arctic Circle and the North Pole and the Antarctic Circle and the South Pole, (i) regions between the Tropic of Cancer and the Arctic Circle and the Tropic of Capricorn and the Antarctic Circle
3. The Earth's rotation creates our days and nights; the side facing the sun has daylight. The orbit around the sun takes one year. During the year, the tilt of the Earth exposes certain portions of the Earth to more direct sunlight than other portions, creating seasons.
4. Latitude reflects the amount of sunlight that falls on portions of the Earth. The higher the latitude (greater distance from the Equator), the less direct sunlight is received, creating cooler climates.
5. Paragraphs should include that plant and animal life would change because there would no longer be seasonal cycles.
6. Entries should describe the temperature as being cooler because it would be winter in the Southern hemisphere.

GEOGRAPHY This field of icebergs creates a beautiful, if eerie landscape. Icebergs are large, floating masses of ice that have broken away from glaciers. **Critical Thinking** In what regions are you most likely to find icebergs?

low latitudes receives direct sunlight at some time during the year. In this region, it is almost always hot.

Two other latitude lines set off distinct regions. To the north of the Equator, at 66°N, is the **Arctic Circle.** To the south of the Equator, at 66°S, is the **Antarctic Circle.** The regions between these circles and the poles are the **high latitudes,** or the polar zones. The high latitudes receive no direct sunlight. It is very cool to bitterly cold there.

Two areas remain: the **middle latitudes** of the northern and southern hemispheres, or the temperate zones. At some times of the year, these areas receive fairly direct sunlight. At other times, they receive fairly indirect sunlight. So, the middle latitudes have seasons: spring, summer, winter, and fall. Each lasts about three months and has distinct patterns of daylight, temperature, and weather.

SECTION 1 ASSESSMENT

AFTER YOU READ

RECALL

1. Identify: (a) Equator, (b) Tropic of Cancer, (c) Tropic of Capricorn, (d) Arctic Circle, (e) Antarctic Circle
2. Define: (a) environment, (b) orbit, (c) revolution, (d) axis, (e) rotation, (f) latitude, (g) low latitudes, (h) high latitudes, (i) middle latitudes

COMPREHENSION

3. How do the Earth's rotation, its tilt, and its orbit around the sun affect our environment?
4. How does latitude affect the climate of various regions of the Earth?

CRITICAL THINKING AND WRITING

5. **Exploring the Main Idea** Review the Main Idea statement at the beginning of this section. Then, write a paragraph describing what might happen to plant and animal life on the Earth if the Earth did not tilt on its axis, and why.
6. **Drawing Conclusions** It is June 21st. You are traveling from the middle latitudes of North America to the middle latitudes of Africa. Write a journal entry that describes what kind of temperature differences you might expect between these two places.

ACTIVITY

7. **Writing to Learn** Write a storybook for a young child explaining the relationship between the Earth and the sun.

7. Encourage students to add appropriate illustrations to their storybooks.

Answers to...

CRITICAL THINKING

Icebergs would most likely be found in polar regions where it is very cold.

Resource Directory

Teaching Resources

Section Quiz in the Unit 1 Teaching Resources, p. 4

SECTION 2

The Five Themes of Geography

BEFORE YOU READ

READING FOCUS

1. What is geography?
2. How can the five themes of geography help you understand the world?

KEY TERMS

geography
parallel
degree
longitude
meridian
Prime Meridian

MAIN IDEA

Geographers study the Earth according to five themes: location, place, human-environment interaction, movement, and regions.

NOTE TAKING

Copy the outline shown here. As you read the section, fill in the blanks with information about the five themes of geography. Create more lettered and numbered entries as needed.

I. Geography
- A. Study of the Earth
  - 1.
  - 2.

II. Five Themes of Geography
- A. Location
  - 1. absolute location
  - 2.
- B. Place
- C. Human–Environment Interaction
- D. Movement
- E. Regions

Setting the Scene

Michael Collins, an astronaut who went to the moon, described Earth as he saw it from his spaceship in July 1969, about 200 miles above the Earth.

"The Indian Ocean flashes incredible colors of emerald jade and opal in the shallow water surrounding the Maldive Islands.... Now the sun glints in unusual fashion off the ocean near Formosa [Taiwan]. There are intersecting surface ripples just south of the island, patterns which are clearly visible and which, I think, must be useful to fishermen who need to know about these currents."

GEOGRAPHY Huge clouds drift over the Indian Ocean while the nearby land remains clearly visible. **Critical Thinking** What features of the land can you identify?

The Study of Geography

From his high perch, Michael Collins was looking at the world as a geographer does. **Geography** is the study of the Earth. Geographers analyze the Earth from many points of view. They discuss how far one place is from another. They study oceans, plant life, landforms, and people. Geographers study how the Earth and its people affect each other.

SECTION 2

Lesson Objectives

1. Define the study of geography.
2. Identify the five themes of geography and use them to learn about the world.

Lesson Plan

1 Engage

Warm-Up Activity

Have students do a quick-write about what they think the subject of geography covers. Let them share their thoughts in a discussion. Ask students to create a preliminary definition of *geography*. Suggest that they record their definitions and check them once or twice as they read the section. Encourage them to revise or rewrite their definitions as they learn more about geography.

Activating Prior Knowledge

Invite students to give directions from their homes to school. Tell students that these directions are examples of geography at work in their lives. Use these directions as a springboard for listing other occasions in which students use geography.

2 Explore

After students read the section, discuss the following aspects of geography: Why is the study of people and their activities part of geography? What is the difference between a natural and a human feature of a place? What are the two main questions that geographers ask? What are some reasons why people move from one place to another?

Answers to...

CRITICAL THINKING

Students should be able to identify mountains.

Resource Directory

Teaching Resources

Classroom Manager in the Unit 1 Teaching Resources, p. 5

Guided Reading and Review in the Unit 1 Teaching Resources, p. 6

Guide to the Essentials, p. 2

Technology

Section Reading Support Transparencies

CHAPTER 1 USING GEOGRAPHY SKILLS 15

Lesson Plan continued

❸ Teach

Ask students to list the five themes of geography and then use them to create a chart with the following headings: *Theme, Definition, Example.* Tell students that they can use examples from the text, but that original examples are preferred. With the class, create a definition of *geography* that includes the five themes.

Questions for Discussion

GEOGRAPHY What two things about the environment of a place does the theme of interaction stress?

The theme stresses how people affect their environment as well as the consequences of people's actions.

GEOGRAPHY What might you tell people who think that geography is only the study of places and not people?

Geography includes the study of people and cultures, where people live and why they live there as well as how people interact with the environment in which they live.

❹ Assess/Reteach

See answers to the Section Review. You may also use students' charts as an assessment.

Acceptable charts include accurate definitions and examples from the text.

Commendable charts include some original examples.

Outstanding charts have all original examples.

Answers to...

MAP STUDY

Australia

How Latitude and Longitude Form the Global Grid

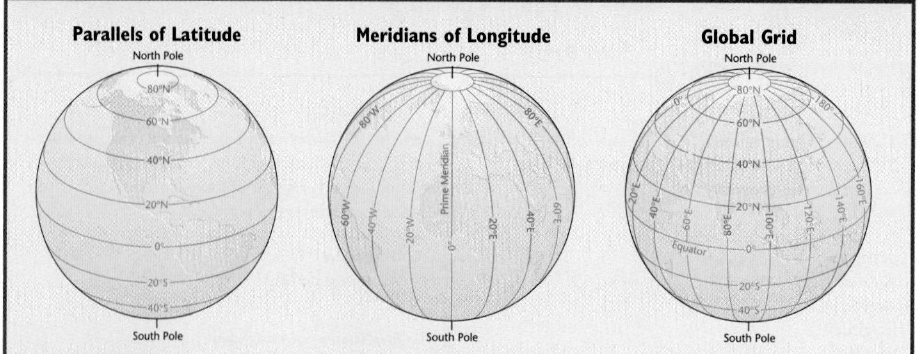

GEOGRAPHY
Latitude and longitude lines can help you find the absolute location, or geographic address, of a place. You can give the address as, for example, 20°S, 140°E. **Map Study** Find 20°S, 140°E on the Global Grid. What continent is found at this location?

The Themes of Geography: Five Ways to Look at the Earth

In their work, geographers are guided by two basic questions: (1) Where are things located? and (2) Why are they there? The answers can be organized according to five themes: location, place, human-environment interaction, movement, and regions.

Location Geographers begin a study of a place by describing its location. They identify the absolute location by using two kinds of imaginary lines around the Earth: latitude and longitude.

Lines of latitude are the imaginary east-west circles around the globe. They are also called **parallels,** because they are parallel to one another. These circles divide the globe into units called **degrees.** In the middle of the globe is the parallel called the Equator, which is 0° latitude. Geographers measure locations north and south of the Equator. The farthest latitude north of the Equator is 90° north, the location of the North Pole. The farthest latitude south of the Equator is 90° south, the location of the South Pole.

Geographers also must pinpoint a place from east to west. For this they use lines of **longitude.** These lines, also called **meridians**, circle the globe from north to south. All meridians begin and end at the North and South poles. The **Prime Meridian**, which runs through Greenwich, England, is 0° longitude. Geographers describe locations as east or west of the Prime Meridian. The maximum longitude is 180°, halfway around the world from the Prime Meridian.

SKILLS MINI LESSON

Organizing Your Time

You may **introduce** the skill by pointing out that making a timetable for each step of a larger task can help ensure that there is enough time to complete a project. Help students **practice** the skill by creating a model timetable for a cooperative assignment—listing the steps needed to complete the project; estimating the time needed to complete each step; adding extra time to each step for delays and problems and for the group to meet. Have students **apply** the skill by asking them to create their own timetable for a cooperative project.

The Hemispheres

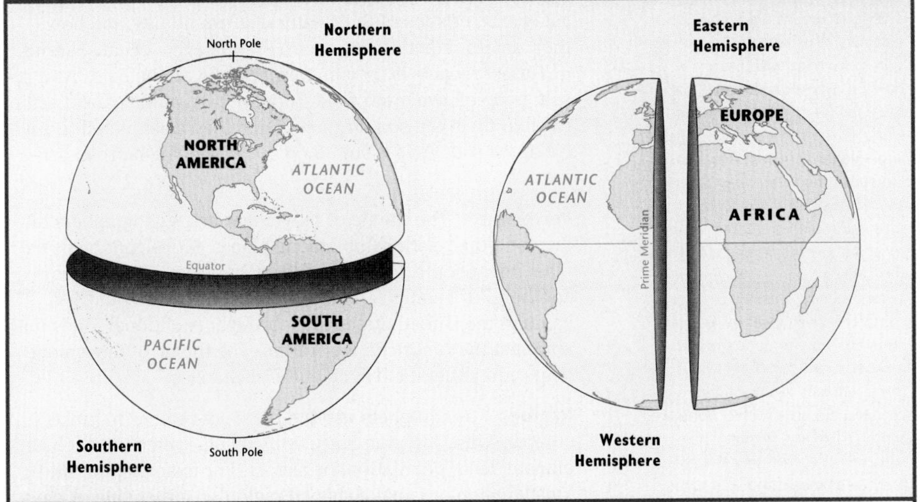

GEOGRAPHY The Equator and the Prime Meridian both divide the Earth in two. Each half is called a hemisphere. The Equator divides the Earth into Northern and Southern hemispheres. The Prime Meridian divides the Earth into Eastern and Western hemispheres. **Map Study** In which two hemispheres is your town or city located? Use the diagram above and a globe to help answer the question.

Geographers also discuss relative location. This explains where a place is by describing places near it. Suppose you live in Victoria, Texas. Victoria's relative location is about 120 miles southeast of Austin, the capital city.

Place Geographers also study place. This includes a location's physical and human features. To describe physical features, you might say the climate is hot or that the land is hilly. Human features include how many people live in a place and the work they do.

On maps, geographers use color or special symbols to show regions. A place can be part of several regions at the same time. For example, Houston, Texas, is in both a plains region and an oil-producing region.

LINKS TO
Math

Using Latitude Latitude can be used to measure distance north or south. One degree of latitude is equal to about 69 miles. For example, Wichita Falls, Texas, is located about 5 degrees north of San Antonio. Therefore, we can determine that Wichita Falls is about 345 miles north of San Antonio (5 x 69 = 345).

ACTIVITY
Drawing Conclusions

The Continents Point out to students that there are seven continents. (North and South America, Europe, Asia, Africa, Australia, and Antarctica). Ask students to refer to the illustration and list the names of the continents that lie mostly or completely in the Southern Hemisphere. Which lie in the Western Hemisphere? Have students evaluate their responses and then draw a conclusion identifying any additional information they may need to complete their lists.

Logical/Mathematical

GEOGRAPHY
Global Perspectives

Desert Regions Although all deserts have very little rainfall, some desert regions do receive enough rainfall to support plants, animals, and people. In the Kalahari Desert of Southern Africa, there are bushes, shrubs, trees, and an occasional meadow. Plant life is sufficient to support antelopes and other animals. The animals, in turn, are hunted by the !Kung San people.

Resource Directory

Teaching Resources
Social Studies and Geography Skills, Understanding Hemispheres, p. 5; Understanding Latitude and Longitude, p. 8; Using Latitude and Longitude, p. 9

Technology
Color Transparencies 4 Latitude and Longitude Grid map; **5** The Hemispheres diagram; **6** The Global Grid diagram

Answers to...
MAP STUDY

Students should be able to correctly identify the hemispheres in which their town or city is located.

SECTION 2 ASSESSMENT

AFTER YOU READ

1. (a) study of the Earth's surface and the processes that shape it, (b) imaginary lines that circle the Earth parallel to the Equator; latitude line (c) unit of measure used to determine absolute location, (d) series of imaginary lines that extend north and south from one pole to the other; meridian (e) imaginary line that extends north and south from one pole to the other; longitude (f) imaginary line that runs from the North Pole to the South Pole through Greenwich, England
2. People study geography to learn about the Earth and the people, plants, and animals that inhabit it.
3. The five themes are location, place, human-environment interaction, movement, and regions.
4. Paragraphs should explain how the study of geography gives insight to how the Earth and its people affect each other and why this information is important.
5. The symbol *S* for latitude indicates the city is south of the Equator. Therefore it is in the Southern hemisphere. The symbol *W* for longitude indicates it is west of the Prime Meridian. Therefore it is in the Western hemisphere.
6. Students' maps should show an understanding of latitude and longitude and correctly identify their locations.

GOVERNMENT

The government plays an important role in balancing the interaction of humans with the environment. For example, the Missouri River once supported some of the most abundant fish and wildlife in North America. However, the river often flooded and barges could not always navigate it. People wanted to tame the river. As a result, in the late 1800s the United States government began building a series of huge dams. The river channel was also straightened and deepened to make it easier for barges to travel the river. As a result of the changes, the river could no longer support fish and wildlife. In the late twentieth century, the government recognized this and took some steps to restore parts of the river.

Critical Thinking Why do you think the government wanted to control the river? Do you think governments should try to change the natural environment?

Human-Environment Interaction The theme of interaction stresses how people affect their environment, the physical characteristics of their natural surroundings, and how their environment affects them. For instance, because farms in Turkey receive little rain, farmers irrigate the land. As a result, people have more food. However, irrigation causes salt to build up in the soil. Farmers must then treat to soil to get rid of the salt. As a result, food could become more expensive.

Movement The theme of movement helps geographers understand the relationship among places. Movement helps explain how people, goods, and ideas get from one place to another. For example, when people from other countries came to the United States, they brought traditional foods that enriched the American way of life. The theme of movement helps you understand such cultural changes.

Regions Geographers use the theme of regions to make comparisons. A region has a unifying characteristic such as climate, land, population, or history. For example, the Nile Valley region is a snake shaped region on either side of the Nile River. The region runs through several countries. Life in the valley is much different from life in the regions alongside the valley. There, the landscape is mostly desert.

SECTION 2 ASSESSMENT

AFTER YOU READ

RECALL

1. Define (a) geography, (b) parallel, (c) degree, (d) longitude, (e) meridian, (f) Prime Meridian

COMPREHENSION

2. Why do people study geography?
3. What are the five themes of geography?

CRITICAL THINKING AND WRITING

4. **Exploring the Main Idea** Review the Main Idea statement at the beginning of this section. Then, write a paragraph explaining why it is important to study the geography of the earth.
5. **Drawing Conclusions** The city of Buenos Aires is at approximately 34° S latitude and 58° W longitude. From this information, how can you tell in which hemispheres this city is located?

ACTIVITY

Take It to the NET

6. **Measuring Latitude and Longitude** Measure the degrees of latitude and longitude that show your location on the Earth. Draw a map that includes lines of latitude and longitude, and indicate your location on the map. Visit the World Explorer: People, Places, and Cultures section of **phschool.com** for help in completing this activity.

Resource Directory

Teaching Resources

Section Quiz in the Unit 1 Teaching Resources, p. 7

Answers to...

CRITICAL THINKING

The land near the river flooded frequently, making it difficult to live or farm. They wanted to earn money by shipping goods on the river. Answers will vary for second question, but students should give reasons to support their answers.

SECTION 3

Using the Tools of Geography

BEFORE YOU READ

READING FOCUS

1. What are the advantages and disadvantages of globes and maps in showing the Earth's surface?
2. How did Mercator try to create an accurate map?
3. What are the parts of a map?

KEY TERMS

globe
scale
distortion
projection
compass rose
cardinal direction
key
grid

KEY PEOPLE

Gerhardus Mercator
Arthur Robinson

MAIN IDEA

Representing the Earth as a globe and as a flat map present different problems.

NOTE TAKING

Copy the concept web shown here. As you read the section, fill in the ovals with information about the tools of geography. Add as many ovals as you need.

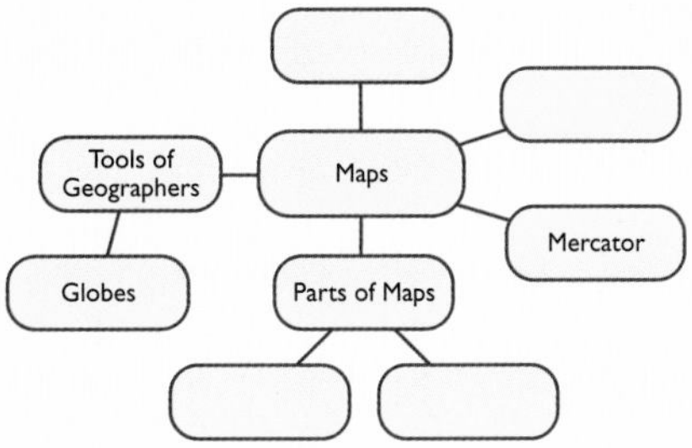

Setting the Scene

You might expect a map to be printed on a piece of paper. But hundreds of years ago, people made maps out of whatever was available. The Inuit (IN oo it) people carved detailed, accurate maps on pieces of wood. They needed maps that were portable, durable, and waterproof.

Globes and Maps

In those days, people knew very little about the land and water beyond their own homes. Their maps showed only the areas they traveled.

As people explored the Earth, they collected information about the shapes and sizes of islands, continents, and bodies of water. Mapmakers wanted to present this information accurately. The best way was to put it on a **globe,** a round model of the Earth itself. By using the same shape, mapmakers could show the continents and oceans of the Earth much as they really are. The only difference would be the **scale,** or size.

CULTURE The Marshall Islanders made wood maps of the southwest Pacific Ocean. Palm sticks show wave patterns and ocean currents and shells show islands. **Critical Thinking** Why do you think the people made their maps out of these materials? Why was it important to show ocean currents on their maps?

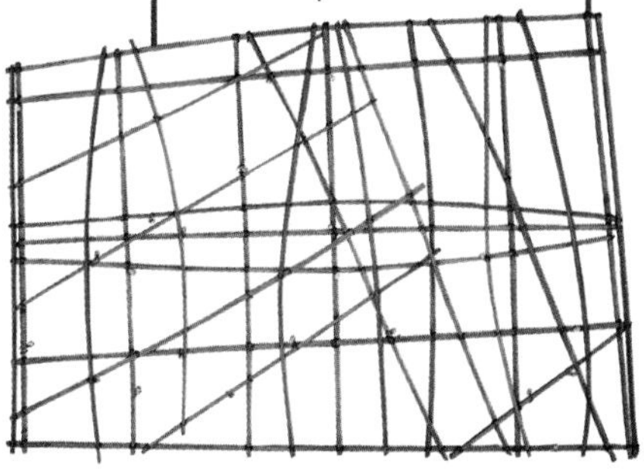

SECTION 3

Lesson Objectives

1. Understand the advantages and disadvantages of globes and maps in depicting the Earth's surface.
2. Appreciate how geographers have tried to create accurate maps.
3. Identify the main parts of a map.

Lesson Plan

1 Engage

Warm-Up Activity

Prepare the following demonstration for the class. Draw two same-size circles on an orange, one near the "equator" of the orange, another near one of the "poles." Ask students what they think will happen to the circles when the orange is peeled and the peel is laid flat. Peel the orange and flatten the peel. Point out that the circles no longer appear to be the same size.

Activating Prior Knowledge

Write *Maps* on the chalkboard. Then, ask students to name and describe the kinds of maps they use. List their suggestions. Prompt them by asking if they ever use the map in a shopping mall to find a particular store or a map of a library to find the fiction books. Emphasize that we all use maps in our daily lives without even thinking about it.

Resource Directory

Teaching Resources

Classroom Manager in the Unit 1 Teaching Resources, p. 8

Guided Reading and Review in the Unit 1 Teaching Resources, p. 9

Guide to the Essentials, p. 3

Technology

Section Reading Support Transparencies

Answers to...

CRITICAL THINKING

The Marshall Islanders used the materials available to them to make the maps. Understanding ocean currents would be important for sailing safely.

Lesson Plan continued

❷ Explore

Have students read the section. Then, review with them the illustrations showing the variety of map projections. Help students use clues in the illustrations to answer the questions in each caption. Record their answers.

❸ Teach

Ask students to work in small groups to develop a chart listing the advantages and disadvantages of each type of projection. Challenge students to find at least three disadvantages—involving distance, shape, or size—in each map.

Question for Discussion

GEOGRAPHY **Why are there so many different kinds of map projections?**

Geographers have developed many different kinds of projections to eliminate the distortions in flat maps. All have some distortion, however.

❹ Assess/Reteach

See the answers to the Section Review. You may choose to use students' charts of advantages and disadvantages as an assessment.

Acceptable charts include three advantages and disadvantages per map.

Commendable charts include additional disadvantages per map and present an example in each category: distance, shape, and size.

Outstanding charts explain why there is distortion in each map.

The World: A Mercator Projection

GEOGRAPHY Mercator maps make areas near the poles look bigger than they are. This is because on a globe, the lines of longitude meet at the poles, but on a flat Mercator map, they are parallel. Mercator maps are useful to navigators because the longitude and latitude lines appear straight. Navigators can use these lines and a compass to plot a ship's route. **Map Study** Here Greenland looks bigger than it really is. What other areas do you think might look larger than they should? Why?

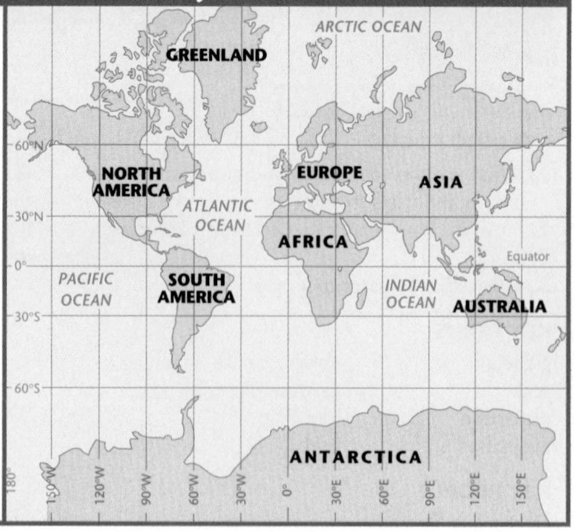

But there is a problem with globes. A globe cannot be detailed enough to be useful and at the same time be small enough to be convenient. People, therefore, also need flat maps.

Flat maps, however, present another problem. Because the Earth is round it is impossible to show the Earth on a flat surface without some **distortion,** or change in the accuracy of its shapes and distances. Something is going to look larger or smaller than it really is.

AS YOU READ

Monitor Your Reading What question would you ask Gerhardus Mercator about the map he made in 1569?

Making Maps

In 1569, a geographer named **Gerhardus Mercator** (juh RAHR duhs muhr KAYT uhr) created a flat map to help sailors navigate long journeys around the globe. To make his map flat, Mercator expanded the area between longitudes near the poles. Mercator's map was very useful to sailors. They made careful notes about the distortions they found on their journeys. More than 400 years later, those notes and the Mercator **projection,** or method of putting a map of the Earth onto a flat piece of paper, are used by nearly all deep-sea navigators.

When Mercator made his map, he made sure that the shape of the landmasses and ocean areas was similar to the shapes on a globe. But he had to stretch the spaces between the longitudes. This distorted the sizes of some of the land. Land near the Equator was about right, but land near the poles became much larger. For example, on Mercator's map, Greenland looks bigger than South America when it is only one eighth the size.

CULTURE

Atlas's Task

An ancient legend tells the story of a battle between the Titans and the Greek gods. The Titans were defeated and one of them, Atlas, was made to hold the whole world on his shoulders. Maps made hundreds of years ago showed a drawing of Atlas holding the world on his shoulders. That is why Mercator coined the term *atlas* to describe a collection of maps.

Answers to...

MAP STUDY

Antarctica, and possibly northern North America and northern Asia look larger. Areas near the poles look bigger than they are.

AS YOU READ

Students might ask how he came up with the idea of his projection and how he felt about the distortions on his map.

Resource Directory

Teaching Resources

Social Studies and Geography Skills, Understanding Grids, p. 6; Using a Map Grid, p. 7; Understanding Distortions in Map Projections, pp. 10–16

Technology

Color Transparency 7 Map Projections Diagram

The World: Interrupted and Robinson Projections

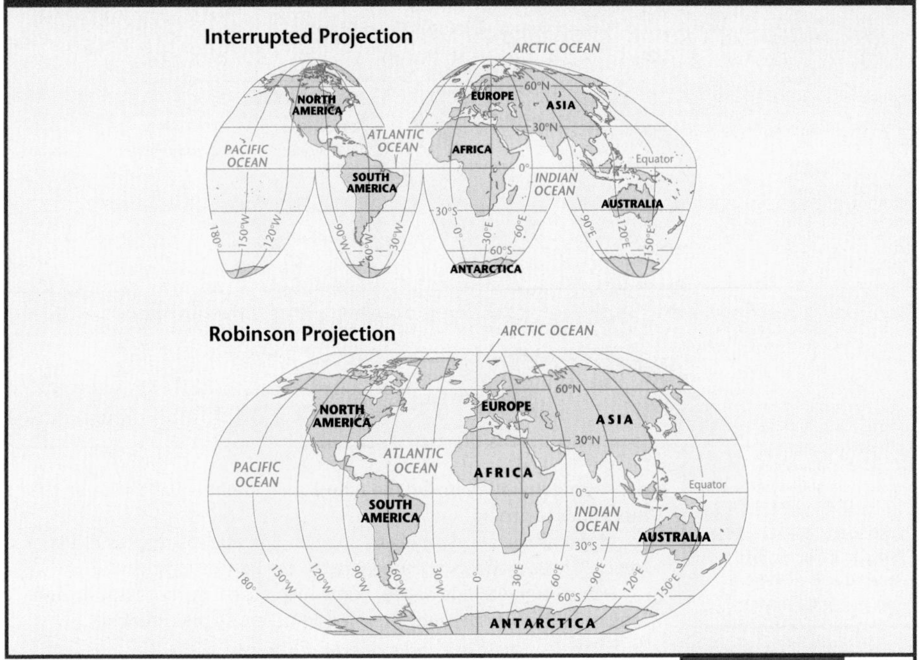

GEOGRAPHY There are many ways to show a globe on a flat map. The interrupted projection map, on the left, shows the real sizes and shapes of continents. While the Robinson projection does distort the globe a little, it shows the sizes and shapes of countries most accurately. **Critical Thinking** Do you think the Robinson projection would be as useful to a navigator as the Mercator projection? Why or why not?

Mapmakers have tried other techniques. The interrupted projection is like the ripped peel of an orange. By creating gaps in the picture of the world, mapmakers showed the size and shape of land accurately. The gaps make it impossible to figure distances correctly. You could not use this projection to chart a course across an ocean.

Today, many geographers believe **Arthur Robinson's** projection is the best world map available. This projection shows the size and shape of the land quite accurately. Sizes of the oceans and distances are also fairly accurate. However, even a Robinson projection has distortions, especially in areas around the edges of the map.

There are many other types of projections. Each has advantages and drawbacks. It all depends on how you want to use each one.

The Parts of a Map

Geographers use symbols and tools on maps. One of the most important is a **compass rose,** which is a model of a compass. It tells the **cardinal directions,** which are north, south, east, and west.

Maps also have an indicator for scale that tells what a certain distance on the map stands for on the surface of the Earth. Scales vary

ACTIVITY

Making Connections

Making Maps Have students draw a map of a room in their home or at school to scale. The scale might be 1 inch equals 1 foot, or 1 inch equals 2 feet, depending on the size of the room. Provide a compass so that students can correctly place a compass rose on their map. Encourage students to create a legend or key with symbols for various objects in the room. This activity can be extended by having students draw a map of the school building to scale as a class project.

Visual/Spatial, Logical/Mathematical

CULTURE

Map Perspectives

The way a culture draws its maps can tell us how people in that culture see their world. For example, the Aborigines of Australia believed that the world was created by the dreams of ancestral beings. Aboriginal maps have abstract designs of circles and wavy lines and represent how the world looked to the ancestral beings. In the 1600s in China, maps showed China at the center and the direction south was at the top of the map. This allowed the Chinese emperor to look out over the world he claimed to rule. Today, we in the United States place our country at the center of world maps—other countries often place themselves at the center.

SKILLS MINI LESSON

Assessing Your Understanding

To **introduce** the skill, point out to students that only they can judge whether or not they understand what they have read. Suggest that they **practice** the skill by asking themselves the following questions after they have read the section. Point out that if they are unsure of any answer, this is the best time to reread the text and reexamine the illustrations.

- Which map shows the correct shapes of landforms but not the true distances or sizes?
- Which map shows the real sizes and shapes of landforms but not the correct distances between places?
- Which map shows the correct sizes, but alters the shapes of landforms?

Answers to...

CRITICAL THINKING

The Robinson projection would not be as useful for navigation as the Mercator projection because the lines of longitude are not straight.

SECTION 3 ASSESSMENT

AFTER YOU READ

1. (a) Gerhardus Mercator created the Mercator Projection in 1569 (b) Arthur Robinson created the most accurate flat map available
2. (a) a round model of the Earth that shows the continents and oceans in their true shapes (b) the size of an area on a map as compared with an area's actual size (c) a misrepresentation of the true shape (d) a representation of the Earth's rounded surface on a flat piece of paper (e) a map feature that usually shows the four cardinal directions (f) one of the four compass points: north, south, east, and west (g) the section of a map that explains the symbols for the map features (h) a map feature used to make identifying a location on the map easier
3. Globes accurately depict to scale the shape of the Earth's features and the distances from point to point. Maps are convenient to use but always include distortions.
4. Distances cannot be determined correctly.
5. The scale shows distance; the compass rose shows the cardinal directions; a key tells what the symbols used on the map stand for.
6. Lists will vary but should include the challenge of dealing with map distortion and allowing navigators to figure distances correctly.
7. The road map provides information on how to get to the park, while the park map shows how to reach features inside the park.
8. Make sure students' maps accurately reflect the area. Encourage them to add a scale, compass rose, and key to their maps.

A Road Map

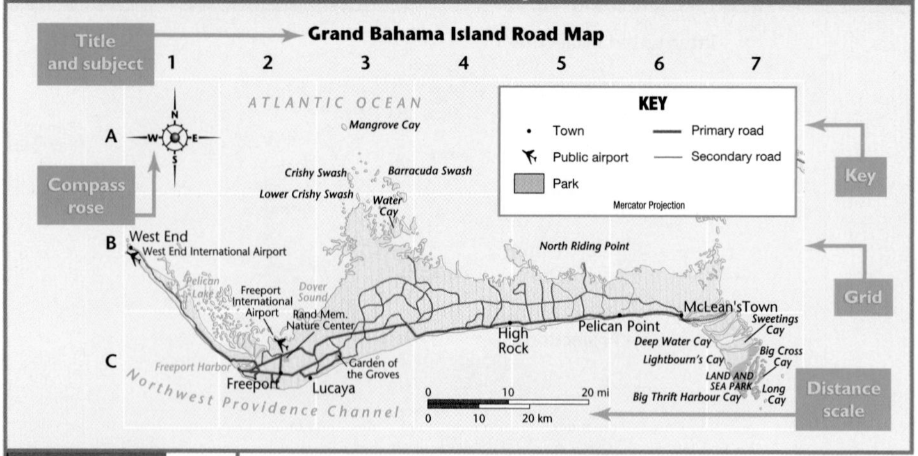

GEOGRAPHY The road map above has a grid of numbers and letters to help locate places. **Map Study** What airport is located at B-1? Where can you find Freeport?

depending on the map. On the map 1 inch might equal 1 mile or 100 miles on the ground.

Mapmakers use symbols to indicate landmarks, such as roads or towns. These symbols are explained in the **key,** or legend.

Maps often include a **grid.** Some maps use a grid of latitude and longitude lines. Other maps use a grid of letters and numbers.

SECTION 3 ASSESSMENT

AFTER YOU READ

RECALL

1. Identify the people: (a) Gerhardus Mercator, (b) Arthur Robinson
2. Define: (a) globe, (b) scale, (c) distortion, (d) projection, (e) compass rose, (f) cardinal direction, (g) key, (h) grid

COMPREHENSION

3. Compare the use of maps and globes for showing the Earth.
4. What is the main problem with the interrupted projection?
5. Why are the different parts of a map important?

CRITICAL THINKING AND WRITING

6. **Exploring the Main Idea** Review the Main Idea statement at the beginning of this section. Then list some of the obstacles faced by mapmakers.
7. **Making Comparisons** You are planning a hiking trip to a nearby state park. You have two maps: a road map and a map of the park. What advantages does each map have?

ACTIVITY

8. **Writing to Learn** Think of a place you like to visit. How would you tell a friend to get there? Make some notes about directions and landmarks you could include in a map. Then, make a map that shows how to get there.

Resource Directory

Teaching Resources

Section Quiz in the Unit 1 Teaching Resources, p. 10

Chapter Summary in the Unit 1 Teaching Resources, p. 11

Vocabulary in the Unit 1 Teaching Resources, p. 12

Reteaching in the Unit 1 Teaching Resources, p. 13

Enrichment in the Unit 1 Teaching Resources, p. 14

Critical Thinking in the Unit 1 Teaching Resources, p. 15

Answers to...

CRITICAL THINKING

West End International Airport; C-2

Studying Distribution Maps

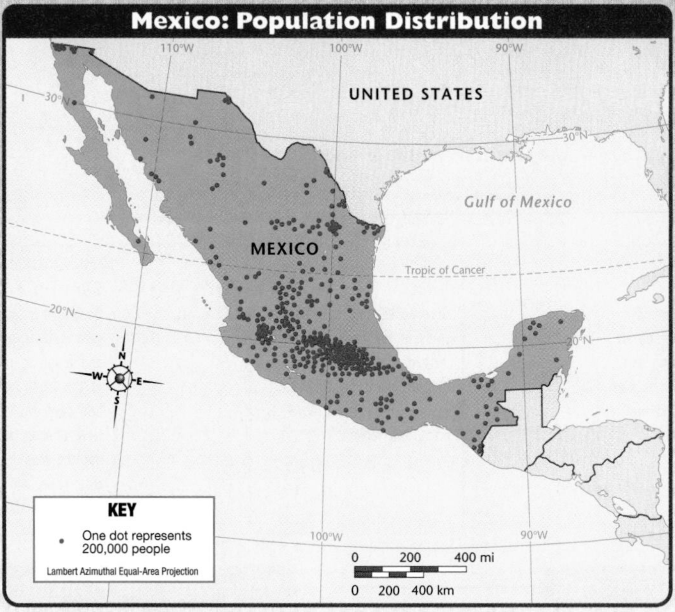

Learn the Skill

A distribution map is a specialized map that shows how something—people, forests, volcanoes—is distributed, or scattered, over land. A population distribution map, for example, shows how a population is distributed in a particular area. To study a distribution map, follow these steps:

A. Read the title of the map. The title will tell you the topic of the map.

B. Read the key. The key will give you important information you need to understand the map. Often, it will show a symbol and tell you what the symbol stands for.

C. Use the information from the key to read the map.

Practice the Skill

Now that you know how to read a distribution map, study the population distribution map of Mexico. Look at the key to get a sense of what the map is about. How is population represented on the map? How many people does each symbol stand for? Where do most of the people of Mexico live? Why do you think the population is distributed the way it is? Think about physical factors such as climate and landforms.

Apply the Skill

See the Chapter Review and Assessment at the end of this chapter for more questions on distribution maps.

Resource Directory

Teaching Resources

Social Studies and Geography Skills, Reading a Population Distribution Map, p. 31

Technology

Social Studies Skills Tutor CD-ROM

Answers to...

PRACTICE THE SKILL

Population is represented by dots, with each dot representing 200,000 people. Most people live in central Mexico, around Mexico City.

Lesson Objectives

1. Identify the features of distribution maps.
2. Read and use a population distribution map.

Lesson Plan

1 Engage

Have students determine the root word of "distribution" and talk about what the word means. If students need help, refer them to a dictionary or thesaurus.

2 Explore

Explain to students that they will be studying a population distribution map of Mexico. Review the steps with students. Make sure students understand the key—one dot on the map represents 200,000. From the distribution of the dots, students should be able to understand the distribution of the population.

3 Teach

Have students work with partners to study the map and answer the questions in the text. For additional reinforcement, have students come up with two to three more questions that can be answered by studying the map.

4 Assess/Reteach

Students should be able to answer the questions by studying the distribution map.

To further assess students' understanding of distribution maps, have them complete the "Applying Your Skills" part of the Chapter Review and Assessment at the end of the chapter.

CHAPTER 1

Review and Assessment

Reviewing Key Terms

1. a **2.** c **3.** g **4.** f **5.** d **6.** e **7.** b **8.** h

Reviewing the Main Ideas

1. The Earth rotates completely every twenty-four hours. The side of the Earth that faces the sun has daylight; the opposite side has night. The Earth is also tilted on its axis. As the Earth revolves around the sun, certain parts of the planet receive more direct sunlight than others. Areas that get the most direct light are warmer. As the Earth orbits the sun, the areas getting the most direct sunlight change, creating the seasons.
2. The theme of location describes where a place is. The theme of place describes the human and physical features of the location.
3. The human-environment interaction theme deals with how people adapt to and modify their environment. It also focuses on the results of human modification of the environment.
4. Students should identify certain characteristics that describe their region and compare it to another region that has different characteristics.
5. No map is perfect because it attempts to depict the rounded surface of the Earth on a flat piece of paper. Consequently, mapmakers create different maps to make them as useful as possible for specific purposes.
6. A globe is a three-dimensional model of the entire Earth. A map is a flat representation, and can represent everything from the entire Earth to a single town.
7. Distortion matters because it affects the size and shape of continents and oceans on a map, as well as distances between things.
8. *Grid* refers to breaking down of the parts of a map into equal sections. Lines of latitude and longitude or numbers and letters are used on the grid to help make locating a place on the map easier.

CHAPTER 1

Review and Assessment

Chapter Summary

The following ideas are important to remember about Chapter 1:

GEOGRAPHY: TOOLS AND CONCEPTS

Section 1
The Earth revolves around the sun while rotating on its axis. It is tilted on this axis. The combination of these elements creates our days and nights and our seasons.

Section 2
Geographers organize their study of the Earth by organizing it into five themes: location, place, human-environment interaction, movement, and regions.

Section 3
Geographers have created various tools, including globes and maps, to make the study of the Earth both accurate and easy. These include a variety of map projections. They use the map key, compass rose, scale, and grid to give information about a map.

Reviewing Key Terms

Match the following geography terms with their definitions.

Column I	Column II
1. globe	**a.** model of the Earth
2. latitude	**b.** imaginary line that circles the globe halfway between the North and South poles
3. scale	**c.** imaginary lines that circle the Earth from east to west
4. geography	**d.** imaginary lines circling the globe from north to south
5. longitude	**e.** a line of longitude that runs through Greenwich, England
6. Prime Meridian	**f.** the study of the Earth
7. Equator	**g.** the size of an area on a map as compared to the area's actual size
8. cardinal direction	**h.** north, south, east, or west

Reviewing the Main Ideas

1. How does the physical relationship between the Earth and the sun create our days, seasons, and climate? (Section 1)
2. What is the difference between the geographic themes of place and location? (Section 2)
3. What is the human-environment interaction theme of geography? (Section 2)
4. Use the theme of regions to compare your region to another. (Section 2)
5. Why have geographers created so many different types of maps? (Section 3)
6. What is the difference between a globe and a map? (Section 3)
7. Why does "distortion" matter? (Section 3)
8. How do you use the term *grid* in geography? (Section 3)

Map Activity

The Globe

For each place listed below, write the letter from the globe that shows its location on your own paper.

1. Prime Meridian
2. Equator
3. North Pole
4. South Pole
5. Europe
6. Africa
7. South America
8. North America

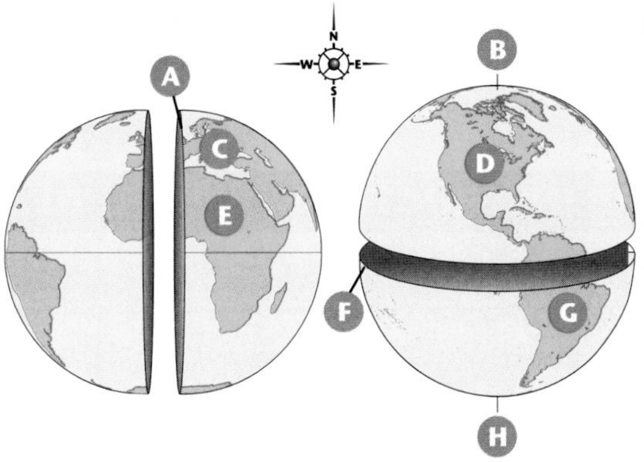

Take It to the NET

Enrichment For more map activities using geography skills, visit the Social Studies section of **phschool.com.**

Writing Activity

Writing a Paragraph

1. Write a paragraph describing ways that you have seen people use maps. You may include such things as road maps, maps for seats in a sports arena or areas in a museum, or even hand-drawn maps to a friend's house.

Writing a Report

2. Write a brief report explaining why spring arrives earlier in some parts of the United States than in other parts. You may include illustrations showing the tilt of the Earth in relation to the sun, or maps showing the different regions of the United States and when spring arrives in those regions.

Critical Thinking

1. Making Inferences If the sun is directly over the Tropic of Capricorn, how many months will it be before spring arrives in the United States?

2. Generalizing All maps of the Earth that are drawn on a flat piece of paper include distortions. Are there also distortions on maps of small areas, such as your town? Explain your answer.

Applying Your Skills

Turn to the Skills for Life activity on p. 23 to help you complete the following activity.

Find a distribution map in the library or on the Internet. Write a series of questions that test an understanding of how to read and use the map. Trade your map and questions with a partner and answer each other's questions.

Take It to the NET

Activity Create a map of your city or town and include a legend or key. Visit the World Explorer: People, Places, and Cultures section of **pschool.com** for help in completing this activity.

Chapter 1 Self-Test As a final review activity, take the Chapter 1 Self-Test and get instant feedback on your answers. To take the test, visit the Social Studies section of **phschool.com.**

Map Activity

1. A **2.** F **3.** B **4.** H **5.** C **6.** E **7.** G **8.** D

Writing Activity

1. Students' paragraphs should identify the type of map used and why.

2. Students' paragraphs should describe the movement of the Earth in relationship to the sun in explaining why spring arrives earlier in some places than in others.

Critical Thinking

1. Three months

2. Yes, there are distortions on all maps regardless of how small an area shown. However, the smaller the area shown, the less significant those distortions become.

Applying Your Skills

You may want to provide students with a distribution map for them to use for the activity. Review the topic of the map and the map key with them before they begin.

Resource Directory

Teaching Resources

Cooperative Learning Activity in the Unit 1 Teaching Resources, pp. 64–67

Chapter Tests Forms A and B in the Unit 1 Teaching Resources, pp. 82–87

Guide to the Essentials, Ch. 1 Test, p. 4

Other Print Resources

Chapter Tests with ExamView® Test Bank, Ch. 1

Technology

ExamView® Test Bank CD-ROM, Ch. 1

Resource Pro® CD-ROM

Chapter 2 Planning Guide

Resource Manager

	CORE INSTRUCTION	READING/SKILLS
Chapter-Level Resources	**Teaching Resources** Program Overview Pacing Charts **Technology** Resource Pro® CD-ROM Companion Web site, phschool.com • eTeach	**Technology** Social Studies Skills Tutor CD-ROM Student Edition on Audio CD, Ch. 2
1 Physical Features and Processes 1. Identify the physical processes that occur within the Earth. 2. Identify the physical processes that occur on the Earth's surface. 3. Describe the characteristics of air and water and explain their importance.	**Teaching Resources** **Unit 1** Classroom Manager, p. 17 Guided Reading and Review, p. 18	**Teaching Resources** Guide to the Essentials, p. 5 Social Studies and Geography Skills, p. 19 **Technology** Section Reading Support Transparencies
2 Geographic Factors and Natural Resources 1. Define and identify natural resources. 2. Explain the scarcity of energy as a natural resource.	**Teaching Resources** **Unit 1** Classroom Manager, p. 20 Guided Reading and Review, p. 21	**Teaching Resources** Guide to the Essentials, p. 6 **Technology** Section Reading Support Transparencies
3 Climate and Vegetation 1. Identify the difference between weather and climate. 2. Explain the role of wind and water in creating the Earth's climate. 3. Identify the Earth's five major climate regions and types of vegetation characteristic of each region.	**Teaching Resources** **Unit 1** Classroom Manager, p. 23 Guided Reading and Review, p. 24 Chapter Summary, p. 26 Vocabulary, p. 27 Reteaching, p. 28	**Teaching Resources** **Unit 1** Critical Thinking, p. 30 Guide to the Essentials p. 7 Social Studies and Geography Skills, pp. 23–24 **Technology** Section Reading Support Transparencies

ENRICHMENT / PRE-AP

Teaching Resources
Primary Sources and Literature Readings

Other Print Resources
DK Atlas

Technology
World Video Explorer: Forces That Shape the Earth and Weather and Climate
Companion Web site, phschool.com

Technology
Color Transparencies 154–156

Technology
Color Transparencies 154–156

Teaching Resources
Unit 1
Enrichment, p. 29
Cooperative Learning Activity, pp. 68–71

Technology
Color Transparencies 12–14; 16–18

ASSESSMENT

Prentice Hall Assessment System

Core Assessment
Chapter Tests with ExamView® Test Bank, Ch. 2
ExamView® Test Bank CD-ROM, Ch. 2

Standardized Test Preparation
Diagnose and Prescribe
Diagnostic Tests for Middle Grades Social Studies Skills
Review and Reteach
Review Book for World Studies
Practice and Assess
Test-taking Strategies with Transparencies for Middle Grades Test Prep Book
Test-taking Strategies Posters

Teaching Resources
Unit 1
Section Quizzes, pp. 19, 22, and 25
Chapter Tests, pp. 88–93

Technology
Companion Web site, phschool.com
Ch. 2 Self-Test

World Video Explorer
Each region of the world is explored through regional flyovers and investigative field trips. Case study segments give students an in-depth view of the history, economy, government, and culture of a key place in each region. Case studies include Nigeria, Mexico, China, British Columbia, and the Czech Republic.

In Your Classroom

CUSTOMIZE FOR INDIVIDUAL NEEDS

Gifted and Talented

Teacher's Edition

- Making a Circle Graph, p. 29
- Drawing Conclusions, p. 29
- Influences From the Past, p. 29

Teaching Resources

- Enrichment, p. 29
- Primary Sources and Literature Readings

Honors/Pre-AP

Teacher's Edition

- Making a Circle Graph, p. 29
- Drawing Conclusions, p. 29

Teaching Resources

- Critical Thinking, p. 30
- Primary Sources and Literature Readings

ESL

Teacher's Edition

- Drawing Conclusions, p. 29

Teaching Resources

- Guided Reading and Review, pp. 18, 21, and 24
- Vocabulary, p. 27
- Reteaching, p. 28
- Guide to the Essentials, pp. 5–7
- Social Studies and Geography Skills, pp. 23–24, 60

Technology

- Social Studies Skills Tutor CD-ROM
- Section Reading Support Transparencies

Less Proficient Readers

Teacher's Edition

- Making a Circle Graph, p. 29
- Drawing Conclusions, p. 29

Teaching Resources

- Guided Reading and Review, pp. 18, 21, and 24
- Vocabulary, p. 27
- Reteaching, p. 28
- Guide to the Essentials, pp. 5–7
- Social Studies and Geography Skills, pp. 23–24, 60

Technology

- Social Studies Skills Tutor CD-ROM
- Section Reading Support Transparencies

Less Proficient Writers

Teacher's Edition

- Making a Circle Graph, p. 29
- Drawing Conclusions, p. 29
- Influences From the Past, p. 29

Teaching Resources

- Guided Reading and Review, pp. 18, 21, and 24
- Vocabulary, p. 27
- Guide to the Essentials, pp. 5–7
- Social Studies and Geography Skills, pp. 23–24, 60

Technology

- Social Studies Skills Tutor CD-ROM
- Section Reading Support Transparencies

DORLING KINDERSLEY

At the end of each unit, you will find information adapted from Dorling Kindersley's *Illustrated Children's Encyclopedia* that connects to the region being studied and to one of the seven content strands. In addition, your resources include Dorling Kindersley's *Atlas*, which contains valuable information about countries from around the world.

TEACHER'S EDITION INDEX

CHAPTER 2 PACING SUGGESTIONS

For 90-minute Blocks

See suggestions in the Teaching Resources Pacing Charts for Chapter 2. Use Color Transparencies 12–14, 16–18, and 154–156

Running Out of Time?

See the Guide to the Essentials, pp. 5–7.

INTERDISCIPLINARY LINKS

Middle Grades Math: Tools for Success

Course 2, Lesson 1-5, **Reading and Understanding Graphs;** Lesson 10-7, **Graphing on the Coordinate Plane**

Science Explorer

Earth's Changing Surface, Chapter 1, **Mapping Earth's Surface**

Inside Earth, Lesson 1-3, **Drifting Continents**

Weather and Climate, Lesson 1-4, **What Causes Climate?**

Prentice Hall Literature

Bronze, A Boy and a Man

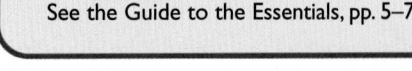

BIBLIOGRAPHY

For the Teacher

Farndon, John. *Dictionary of the Earth.* Dorling Kindersley, 1995.

Smith, Miranda. *Living Earth.* Dorling Kindersley, 1996.

For the Student

Easy

Eyewitness Visual Dictionary of the Earth. Dorling Kindersley, 2001.

Average

McVey, Vicki. *The Sierra Club Book of Weather-Wisdom.* Sierra Club/Little, Brown, 1991.

Van Rose, Susanna. *The Earth Atlas.* Dorling Kindersley, 1994.

Challenging

Macquitty, Miranda. *Desert.* Knopf, 1994.

Literature Connection

George, Jean Craighead. *Everglades.* HarperCollins, 1995.

Jacobs, Francine. *A Passion for Danger: Nansen's Arctic Adventures.* Putnam, 1994.

Thaxter, Celia; Loretta Krupinski, adaptor and illustrator. *Celia's Island Journal.* Little, Brown, 1992.

Take It to the NET

The World Explorer companion Web site, found on **phschool.com**, offers activities for exploring geographical, historical, and cultural resources on the Internet. It also provides on-line links for key content and all Section and Chapter Assessment activities.

The **Teacher site** also provides teachers with regional data and ideas for student research and activities.

Students can use the **Student site** to find chapter-by-chapter Internet resource links and to access Self-Tests.

CHAPTER 2

Connecting to the
Guiding Questions

In this chapter, students will read about the Earth's physical geography. Content in this chapter corresponds to the following Guiding Questions outlined at the beginning of the unit:

- What are some important features of the Earth's geography?
- How do people use the world's resources?

Using the Map Activities

Explain to students that the map shows the distribution of natural resources around the world. Review with students the resources in the map key. Ask students if the world's natural resources are evenly spread among all the continents.

- You may want to have students complete the activity in pairs or small groups. Encourage students to find out which countries are the leading producers of each of the resources listed. Students can create a classroom display with images of the products made from these resources.
- Students may say that most natural resources must be changed before they can be sold for profit. Not all countries have well developed industries to perform such tasks.

Heterogeneous Groups

The following activities are suitable for heterogeneous groups.

Making Connections

Making a Circle Graph, p. 29

Critical Thinking

Drawing Conclusion, p. 29

eTeach

Be sure to check out this month's discussion with a Master Teacher. Go to **phschool.com**.

CHAPTER 2

Earth's Physical Geography

SECTION 1
Physical Features and Processes

SECTION 2
Geographic Factors and Natural Resources

SECTION 3
Climate and Vegetation

The World: Natural Resources

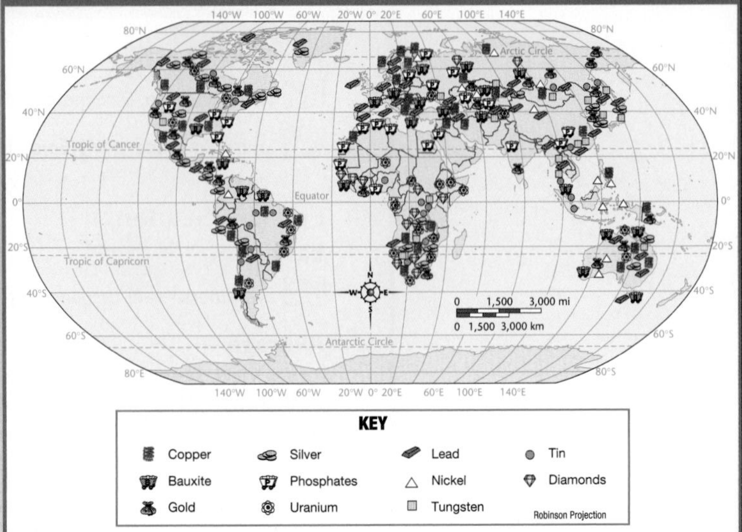

Using Maps

Study the natural resources map. Then, complete the following activities.

Learning About Resources

Visit the library or the Internet to learn about the uses of the natural resources listed in the map key. Organize the information you find in a brief report, making sure to explain why these resources are important.

Drawing Conclusions

Many countries have a wealth of natural resources. Yet not all of these countries have prospered from these resources. Work with a partner to make a list of reasons as to why this might be so.

Resource Directory

Teaching Resources

Primary Sources and Literature Readings extend content with a selection related to the concepts in this chapter.

Other Print Resources

DK Atlas

Technology

Forces That Shape the Earth, from the World Video Explorer, enhances students' understanding of plate tectonics, earthquakes, and volcanoes.

Weather and Climate, from the World Video Explorer, enhances students' understanding of the forces that create weather and climate

Student Edition on Audio CD, Ch. 2

SECTION 1

Physical Features and Processes

BEFORE YOU READ

READING FOCUS QUESTIONS

1. What physical processes occur within the Earth?
2. What physical processes occur on the Earth's surface?
3. Describe air and water—two of the most important natural resources needed for life on Earth.

KEY TERMS

landform	plate tectonics
mountain	plate
hill	weathering
plateau	erosion
plain	atmosphere

KEY PLACES

Pangaea

MAIN IDEA

Physical processes both within the Earth and on its surface are constantly changing and renewing its physical features: its land, air, and water.

NOTE TAKING

Copy the outline shown here. As you read the section, fill in the outline with information about Earth. Add headings and details to make the outline more complete.

- **I. Physical features and processes inside Earth**
  - A. Earth's structure
    - 1. 75 percent water
    - 2.
  - B. Pangaea
- **II. Physical features and processes on Earth's surface**
  - A. Weathering
  - B.
- **III. Natural resources**
  - A. Air
  - B.

Setting the Scene

Earthquakes and volcanic eruptions are two forces that shape and reshape the Earth. They provide clues about the Earth's structure and are one reason why the Earth's surface constantly changes.

Physical Processes Inside the Earth

To understand events like volcanic eruptions and earthquakes, geographers study the Earth's structure. Pictures of the Earth show a great deal of water and some land. The water covers about 75 percent of the Earth's surface in lakes, rivers, seas, and oceans. Only 25 percent of the Earth's surface is land.

In part, continents are unique because of their **landforms,** or shapes and types of land. **Mountains** are landforms that rise usually more than 2,000 feet (610 m) above sea level. They are wide at the bottom and rise steeply to a narrow peak or ridge. **Hills** are lower and less steep than mountains. A **plateau** is a large, elevated piece of flat land. **Plains** are large areas of flat or gently rolling land. Many are along coasts, while others are in the interior.

CULTURE Hawaii Island has the largest active volcano in the world. Molten lava formed the islands one at a time. Eventually, plants and animals arrived. About 2,000 years ago, the first humans settled on the islands. **Critical Thinking** What kinds of challenges might the first settlers have faced? How might these people have changed the land they found?

Resource Directory

Teaching Resources

Classroom Manager in the Unit 1 Teaching Resources, p. 17

Guided Reading and Review in the Unit 1 Teaching Resources, p. 18

Guide to the Essentials, p. 5

Technology

Section Reading Support Transparencies

SECTION 1

Lesson Objectives

1. Identify the physical processes that occur within the Earth.
2. Identify the physical processes that occur on the Earth's surface.
3. Describe the characteristics of air and water and explain their importance.

Lesson Plan

1 Engage

Warm-Up Activity

Have students cut pictures of landscapes from magazines and then sort the photographs by landforms, such as mountains, hills, seashores, plains, and plateaus. Then, have them make a poster collage. As they complete the chapter, they can return to their posters and label the landforms represented.

Activating Prior Knowledge

Ask students to list some of their favorite outdoor activities, such as bicycling. Then, invite students to describe how the activity is affected as land changes from flat to hilly.

2 Explore

After students read the section, have them discuss the following questions. What do geographers who study volcanoes and earthquakes learn about the Earth? Why is it important to study what's happening under the ocean? How are the massive plates of the Earth's surface able to move?

Answers to...

CRITICAL THINKING

The first settlers would have faced unsettled wilderness. They would have changed the land by clearing land for homes, fields, and pastures.

Lesson Plan continued

3 Teach

Have students trace the continents to make a puzzle map. Have them experiment with moving the continents in the directions indicated on this page. This activity should take about 30 minutes.

Questions for Discussion

GEOGRAPHY Look at the physical map of the world on pp. 4–5 and carefully examine the continents. Do you notice anything about the shapes of the continents that might help prove the theory of plate tectonics?

The continents have interlocking shapes which might prove that they were once all part of a larger landmass.

GEOGRAPHY Examine the map of plate boundaries on p. 29. What relationships do you see among plate boundaries, earthquake zones, and volcanoes?

Most earthquake zones and volcanoes are found along plate boundaries. There are many weak spots in the Earth's crust along plate boundaries, which allow the crust to move. This causes earthquakes and volcanoes.

4 Assess/Reteach

See the answers to the Section 1 Assessment. You may also assess student's use of their puzzle maps.

Acceptable use includes accurate placement of the continents as they are now.

Commendable use includes an ability to reconstruct the plate movement.

Outstanding use includes an ability to reconstruct, using the reference map, the current movements of the plates.

Answers to...

MAP STUDY

Accept any reasonable answer that suggests using fossils or rock formations as clues.

The Movement of the Continents

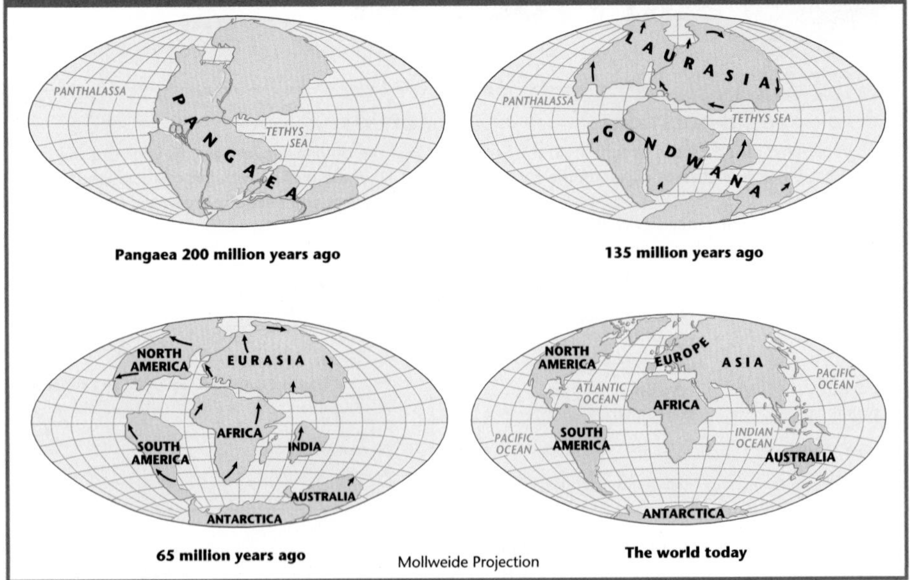

GEOGRAPHY These diagrams, based on the theory of plate tectonics, show how Pangaea broke apart and formed the continents we know today. **Map Study** If you were a scientist trying to prove the theory of plate tectonics, what clues would you look for?

Pangaea: The Supercontinent Geographers theorize that at one time the Earth had only one huge landmass, called **Pangaea** (pan JEE uh). They think that Pangaea split into pieces and began to pull apart, with the pieces forming our continents.

Geographers explain the movement of continents with a theory called **plate tectonics.** According to this theory, the outer skin of the Earth, called the crust, is broken into huge pieces called **plates.** The continents and oceans are the top of the crust. Below the plates is a layer of rock called magma, which is hot enough to be fairly soft. The plates float on the magma. Over time, the plates move about, taking the continents with them. This movement is very slow. A plate that moves quickly might shift just 2 inches (5 cm) a year.

Volcanoes, Earthquakes, and Shifting Plates The vast plates move in different directions. Some ocean plates move apart, and magma leaks through cracks in the crust. Over time, the cooling rock builds up to form lines of underwater mountains called ridges. In other places, the plates push against one another, forcing one plate under the other. Tremendous pressure and heat build up. Molten rock moves upward, sometimes exploding onto the surface and producing a volcano.

28 UNIT I GEOGRAPHY: TOOLS AND CONCEPTS

SKILLS MINI LESSON

Predicting

You may **introduce** the skill by indicating to students that previewing a reading selection is a bit like using a menu in a restaurant or watching the "Coming Attractions" at a theatre. Previewing provides clues about the content to come. Have students **practice** and **apply** the skill by asking them to make a list of the headings and subheadings in the section. Then, ask them to predict what information they will find in reading the text. Ask them how changing the order of the items on their list might affect their prediction. After completing the section, return to the list and have the students evaluate their earlier predictions.

Plate Boundaries

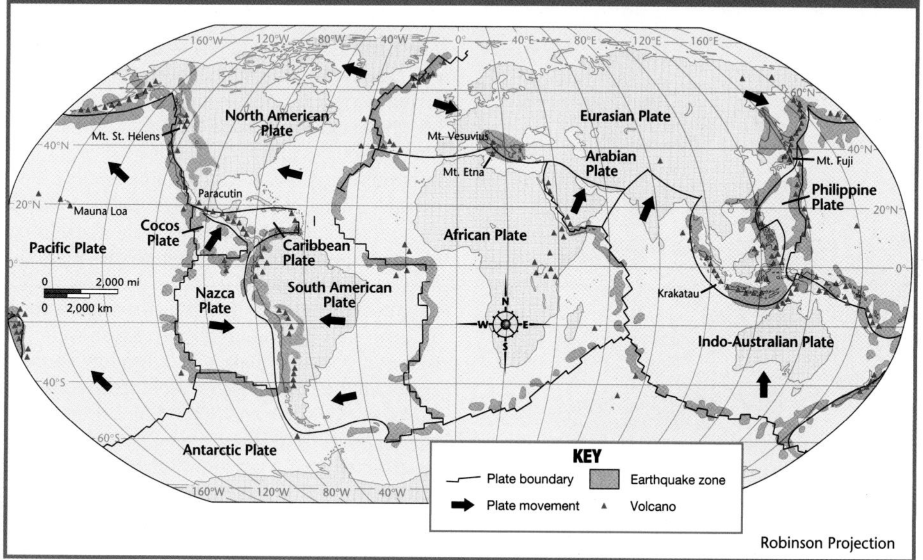

Along plate boundaries, there are many weak places in the Earth's crust. When plates push against one another, the crust cracks and splinters from the pressure. The cracks are called faults. When the crust moves along faults, it releases great amounts of energy in the form of earthquakes. These movements can cause dramatic changes.

GEOGRAPHY The Earth's plates move very slowly—a fast moving plate moves even slower than your hair grows. When plates move away from each other, they create oceans and valleys. When they push into one other, they create mountains and volcanoes. **Movement** Based on the direction the plates are moving, name the areas where you think oceans are getting bigger.

Physical Processes on the Earth's Surface

Forces like volcanoes slowly build up the Earth; other forces slowly break it down. Often, the forces that break the Earth down are not as dramatic as volcanoes, but the results can last just as long.

Weathering is a process that breaks rocks down into tiny pieces. Three things cause weathering: wind, rain, and ice. Slowly but surely, they wear away the Earth's landforms. Hills and low, rounded mountains show what weathering can do. The Appalachian Mountains in the eastern United States once were as high as the Rocky Mountains of the western United States. Wind and rain have weathered them into much lower peaks. Weathering helps create soil, too. Tiny pieces of rock combine with decayed animal and plant material to form soil.

Once this breaking down has taken place, small pieces of rock may be carried to new places by a process called **erosion.** Weathering and erosion slowly create new landforms.

HISTORY

Influences from the Past

Colonists settling in the green hills of Guatemala in 1543 chose a site in a valley surrounded by volcanic peaks for the capital of the region. Not surprisingly, Antigua, Guatemala, was troubled by the shaking and shifting of the earth. It withstood serious earthquakes in 1581, 1590, 1651, 1751, and 1773, as well as other minor tremors. The architectural history of Antigua shows the development of building styles intended to withstand earthquakes. Buildings have thick stone walls; high windows; strong, shallow arches; and short towers incorporated into walls for added strength. Despite the architectural innovations, Antigua was virtually destroyed by the earthquake of 1773.

ACTIVITY

Making Connections

Making a Circle Graph Point out to students that while 97 percent of the Earth's water is salt water, the remaining 3 percent is made up of ice (2 percent) and fresh water (1 percent). Have students construct a circle graph reflecting these relationships. Ask students to indicate what part of the Earth's water supply is available for drinking, bathing, and irrigating crops. (1 percent).

Logical/Mathematical, Visual/Spatial

ACTIVITY

Critical Thinking

Drawing Conclusions *Suitable as a whole class activity.* Scientists have discovered the bones of a dinosaur called a *Mesosaurus* in locations such as eastern South America and West Africa. Ask students how this information might help scientists conclude that the continents once formed one large landmass.

Logical/Mathematical

Resource Directory

Teaching Resources

Social Studies and Geography Skills, Four Types of Landforms, p. 19

Technology

Color Transparencies 154 Major Types of Plate Movement Diagram; **155** Plate Collisions Diagram; **156** Types of Volcanoes Diagram

Answers to...

MOVEMENT

Students may say in the Pacific, between the Pacific and Nazca plates, and in the Atlantic, between the North American and Eurasian plates.

SECTION I ASSESSMENT

AFTER YOU READ

1. single landmass that scientists theorize existed millions of years ago
2. (a) an area of the Earth's surface with a definite shape, (b) a landform with steep sides that rises more than 2,000 feet above sea level, (c) a landform that rises above the surrounding land and has a rounded top, (d) a large, mostly flat area that rises above the surrounding land, (e) a large area of flat or gently rolling land, (f) theory that the Earth's crust is made up of huge, slowly moving plates, (g) a huge section of the Earth's crust, (h) the breaking down of rocks by wind, rain, or ice, (i) process by which water, wind, or ice wears away landforms and carries the material to another place, (j) air; the gases that surround the Earth
3. Inside the Earth, the rock is molten, allowing the crust to float about. Volcanoes, earthquakes, and movement of the continents are the effects.
4. On the Earth's surface, weathering and erosion occur. These processes wear down mountain ranges and create new landforms.
5. The air provides oxygen for people and animals and carbon dioxide for plants. It holds in the heat of the sun and distributes it around the world in its winds. About 97 percent of the Earth's water is in the oceans. Only a small portion is fresh water, and most of that is frozen into ice at the poles. Water continually passes through the water cycle, replenishing water supplies.
6. Answers will vary. Students will probably observe wind, rain, weathering, and erosion. They should comment on how landforms have been affected.
7. They can construct buildings to withstand earthquakes. They can avoid building in high-risk areas.

The Water Cycle

SCIENCE AND TECHNOLOGY Ocean water is too salty to drink or to irrigate crops. However, the oceans are a source of fresh water. How does this happen? When water evaporates from the ocean's surface, salt is left behind. The water vapor rises and forms clouds. The rain that falls to the Earth is fresh. **Chart Study** Once rain has fallen, how does water return to the ocean?

Air and Water: Natural Resources Needed for Life

The Earth is surrounded by a thick layer of special gases called the **atmosphere.** It provides life-giving oxygen for people and animals and life-giving carbon dioxide for plants. The atmosphere also acts like a blanket. It holds in the right amount of heat from the sun, making life possible. Without this blanket, solar heat would rise out back into space, making the Earth too cold to support life. Winds help to distribute this heat around the globe.

About 97 percent of the Earth's water is found in its oceans. This water is salty. Fresh water, or water without salt, makes up only a tiny percentage of all the Earth's water. Most fresh water is frozen at the North and South Poles. Fresh water comes from lakes, rivers, and rain. Also, fresh water, called groundwater, is stored in the soil and in rock layers below the surface of the Earth. This diagram shows the movement of all the water on the Earth's surface, in the ground, and in the air. The Earth does have enough water for people. However, some places have too much water and other places have too little.

SECTION I ASSESSMENT

AFTER YOU READ

RECALL

1. Identify: (a) Pangaea
2. Define: (a) landform, (b) mountain, (c) hill, (d) plateau, (e) plain, (f) plate tectonics, (g) plate, (h) weathering, (i) erosion, (j) atmosphere

COMPREHENSION

3. What are some physical processes that occur inside of the Earth, and what has been their effect?
4. What are some physical processes that occur on the Earth's surface, and what has been their effect?
5. What should people know about air and water and how they affect life on the Earth?

CRITICAL THINKING AND WRITING

6. **Exploring the Main Idea** Review the Main Idea statement at the beginning of this section. Write a paragraph responding to the following questions. (a) What physical processes can you see in your neighborhood? (b) How are they changing the features of the land?
7. **Recognizing Cause and Effect** List reasons why it is helpful for people to understand the causes of earthquakes and volcanoes.

ACTIVITY

8. **Writing to Learn** Suppose you were able to see the region you live in 10,000 years from now. Describe how the landforms might look. Explain what might have caused those changes.

8. Answers will vary. Students' descriptions should show an understanding of the causes of the changes in landforms.

Answers to...

CHART STUDY

It returns through runoff from rivers, streams, and through groundwater.

Resource Directory

Teaching Resources

Section Quiz in the Unit 1 Teaching Resources, p. 19

SECTION 2

Geographic Factors and Natural Resources

BEFORE YOU READ

READING FOCUS QUESTIONS

1. What are natural resources?
2. Why is energy a scarce natural resource?

KEY TERMS

natural resource
raw material
recyclable resource
renewable resource
nonrenewable resource
fossil fuel

MAIN IDEA

The Earth has many natural resources; some can be recycled, some can be renewed, while others are nonrenewable.

NOTE TAKING

Copy the concept web shown here. As you read the section, fill in the ovals with information about geographic factors and natural resources. Add as many ovals as you need.

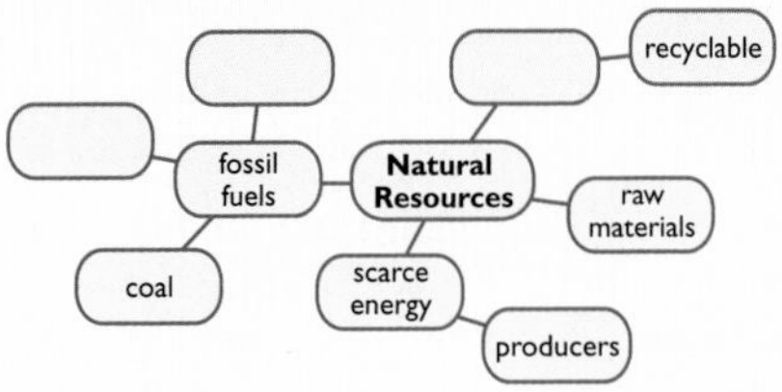

Setting the Scene

What can we do with the garbage we create? People are searching for answers. In 1995, architect Kate Warner built a house in Martha's Vineyard, Massachusetts. She used materials most people call trash. The builders mixed concrete with ash left over from furnaces that burn trash. Then they used the mixture to make the foundation of the house. Warner wanted glass tiles in the bathroom. So she had glassmakers create them out of old car windshields. "By making use of waste materials, the manufacturers of these new building materials are creating exciting new markets and completing a loop," Warner said. In this loop, materials are used over and over again.

ECONOMICS Factories make new steel for bicycles and buildings by combining iron and other natural resources with recycled "scrap" steel. **Critical Thinking** What might happen if people did not recycle scrap steel?

Natural Resources

Like many people, Kate Warner wants to use the Earth's natural resources wisely. She believes this is the only way for humans to survive. A **natural resource** is anything from the Earth that people use in meeting their needs for food, clothing, and shelter. Examples of these resources include soil, water, minerals, and vegetation.

Resource Directory

Teaching Resources

Classroom Manager in the Unit 1 Teaching Resources, p. 20

Guided Reading and Review in the Unit 1 Teaching Resources, p. 21

Guide to the Essentials, p. 6

Technology

Section Reading Support Transparencies

SECTION 2

Lesson Objectives

1. Define and identify natural resources.
2. Explain the scarcity of energy as a natural resource.

Lesson Plan

1 Engage

Warm-Up Activity

Ask students to identify an object in the classroom that is in its natural form. Then, have the students name the raw materials used to make several classroom objects. Ask them to describe how they think trees are changed for human use.

Activating Prior Knowledge

Ask students what they know about recycling. Does their family recycle trash? Their school? What kinds of materials? Then ask them to think about the materials they do not recycle. Have them identify types of items. List their responses on the chalkboard.

2 Explore

Direct students to read the section. Encourage them to look for answers to questions such as these: How are some natural resources changed before they are used? What happens if a renewable resource is not replaced? Why is it a good idea to use recycled materials? Why have people started looking for new energy resources?

Answers to...

CRITICAL THINKING

Our supplies of steel would become scarce and steel products would become more costly. Eventually, we would run out of steel. Government, manufacturers, and the public all have a responsibility for recycling.

Lesson Plan continued

3 Teach

Have students identify the basic materials they see around them in the classroom and create a chart with the following column headings:

- Item
- Wood, Metal, or Plastic?
- Renewable or Nonrenewable?
- Recyclable?
- Energy Resources Used to Produce?

Ask students to complete the chart. Use completed charts as a basis for discussion about how resources are used in your society. This activity should take about 30 minutes.

Question for Discussion

GEOGRAPHY **Why are fossil fuels considered to be a nonrenewable resource?**

Fossil fuels are created from the remains of prehistoric plants and animals. There is a limited amount of these remains, so they are a nonrenewable resource.

4 Assess/Reteach

See the answers to the Section 2 Assessment. You may also use students' completed charts as an assessment.

Acceptable charts include indications of the raw materials used and whether they are renewable or nonrenewable, as well as one energy source used in the production of each item.

Commendable charts include reference to the energy expended in transferring goods as well as in manufacturing them.

Outstanding charts indicate a grasp of the complexities of energy use for modern products, from the extraction of raw materials to consumption.

World Petroleum Production and Consumption

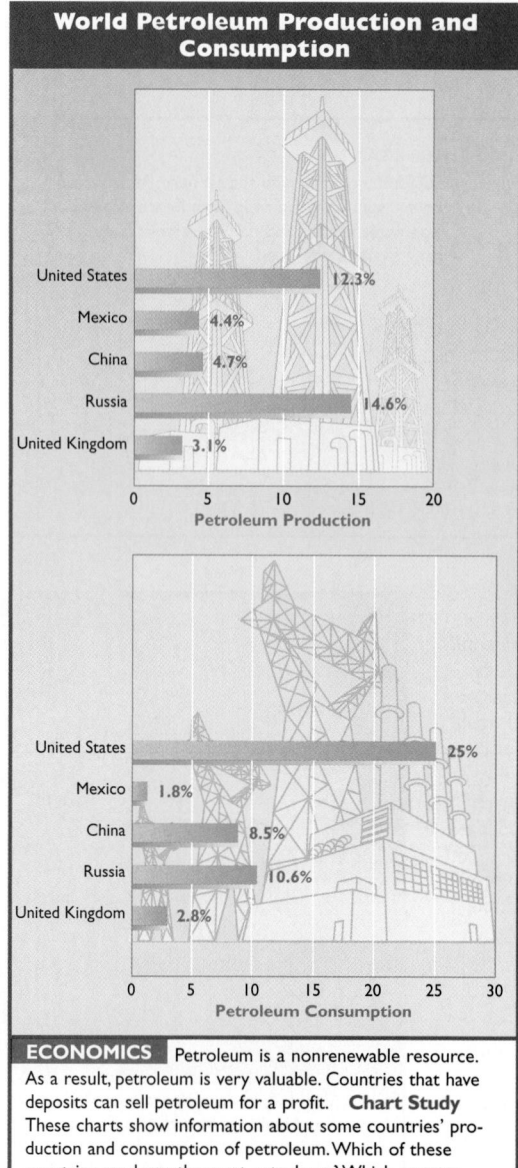

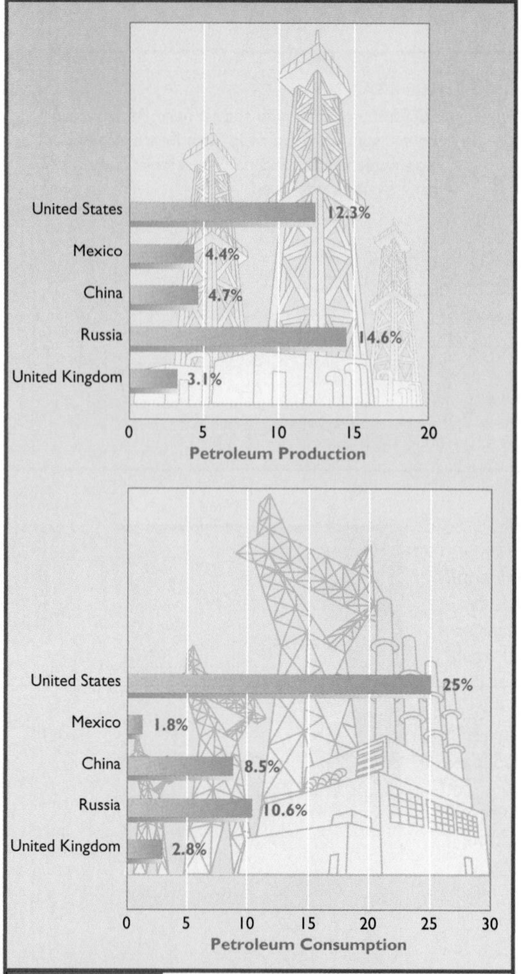

ECONOMICS Petroleum is a nonrenewable resource. As a result, petroleum is very valuable. Countries that have deposits can sell petroleum for a profit. **Chart Study** These charts show information about some countries' production and consumption of petroleum. Which of these countries produces the most petroleum? Which country consumes the most?

People use some resources just the way they come from nature. Water is one example. But most resources must be changed in some way to make them useful. These resources are called raw materials. Trees, for example, are a **raw material**. They must be processed to make them into useful materials such as paper and lumber.

Three Kinds of Resources Geographers divide the Earth's natural resources into three groups. The first group is **recyclable resources**. Water, nitrogen, and carbon are examples of recyclable resources. These resources recycle through our environment naturally. The water cycle, for instance, naturally recycles our fresh water supply.

A second group of resources is called **renewable resources**. Examples include trees and other living things on the Earth. These resources are different from recyclable resources because they can be replaced. For instance, a timber company may harvest all the trees in an area. If the company plants new trees to replace them, however, they are renewing the resource.

The third group of resources is called **nonrenewable resources**. When they are used up, they cannot be replaced. Most nonliving things, such as minerals, coal, natural gas, and petroleum, are nonrenewable resources.

Ancient Energy: Fossil Fuel Often people take some things for granted. Lights turn on when a switch is flicked. The house is warm in winter or cool in summer. The car runs. All of these things require **fossil fuels,** which include coal, natural gas, and petroleum. Fossil fuels were created over millions of years from the remains of prehistoric plants and animals. These fuels are no longer being created. As a result, fossil fuels are nonrenewable resources.

SKILLS MINI LESSON

Interpreting Graphs

To **introduce** the skill, tell students that information can sometimes be compared more easily if it is presented in a graph. For example, a bar graph allows readers to compare numerical quantities by comparing the lengths of bars on the graph. Help students **practice** the skill by directing their attention to the graphs on this page. Ask what the title tells them about the graphs. What information is shown along the horizontal axis of each? Along the vertical axes? What is the greatest number a bar could represent on one graph? How does the petroleum consumption of Mexico compare with that of the United Kingdom? Have students **apply** the skill by writing three questions that can be answered with information in the graphs.

Answers to...

CHART STUDY

Russia produces the most petroleum and the United States consumes the most petroleum.

A Scarce Natural Resource: Energy

Everyone in the world needs energy. Much of these energy needs are filled by fossil fuels like petroleum, natural gas, and coal. But these energy resources are not evenly spread around the world. Certain areas are rich in some energy resources, while others have very few.

Countries like Saudi Arabia and Mexico have huge amounts of oil. Others, like the United States and China, have coal and natural gas. Countries with many rivers, such as the countries of northwestern Europe, can use water energy to create electricity. Others, such as Japan, have very few energy sources.

Growing Needs and the Search for New Supplies In 1973, members of the Organization of Petroleum Exporting Countries (OPEC) raised their oil prices. In addition, some members decided to produce less oil. In the United States, this caused a shortage of gasoline, which is made from oil. When there is a shortage of something, it is more expensive. In this case, the price of gas more than doubled. Companies that used oil to make electricity asked people to use as little electricity as possible.

Just because a country uses large amounts of energy does not mean that country has its own large energy resources. The biggest users of energy are industrial countries like the United States and the nations of Western Europe. Japan, which has few petroleum resources of its own, uses over twice as much energy as all of Africa. If a country does not have enough energy resources of its own, it must buy them from other countries. The oil shortages of the 1970s made people see they needed more sources of energy, including petroleum.

AS YOU READ

Use Prior Knowledge What things can you and your family do to use less fossils fuels in your everyday life?

SECTION 2 ASSESSMENT

AFTER YOU READ

RECALL

1. Define: (a) natural resource, (b) raw material, (c) recyclable resource, (d) renewable resource, (e) nonrenewable resource, (f) fossil fuel

COMPREHENSION

2. What are the different types of natural resources?
3. What factors have made energy scarce?

CRITICAL THINKING AND WRITING

4. **Exploring the Main Idea** Review the Main Idea statement at the beginning of this section. Make a list of reasons why people must be careful about how they use nonrenewable resources.
5. **Drawing Inferences** What do you think might happen to the United States if it could no longer buy petroleum from other countries?

ACTIVITY

6. **Finding Solutions** Work with a partner and choose a specific natural resource, such as wood, petroleum, or steel. Then brainstorm a list of ways to protect our supply of that resource. You might consider ways to limit use, to recycle, or to replace it when used. List your five best ideas and share them with your class.

SECTION 2 ASSESSMENT

AFTER YOU READ

1. (a) any useful material found on the Earth, (b) a material in its natural state, before being processed into a useful product, (c) a material that cycles through natural processes in the environment, (d) a material that the environment continues to supply or replace as it is used, (e) a material that cannot be replaced once it is used up, (f) any of several nonrenewable resources, such as coal, oil, or natural gas, that were created long ago from the remains of plants and animals
2. There are raw materials as well as resources that can be used directly. There are also recyclable, renewable, and nonrenewable natural resources.
3. Energy is scarce because it is produced from nonrenewable resources. It is not evenly distributed in different parts of the world, and some countries use more of it than others do. Producers have created scarcity by limiting production in order to raise prices.
4. As they are used up, they become more scarce and therefore more expensive. Once gone, the resources are gone forever.
5. Students may say that the United States might try to develop alternative sources of energy, such as solar, wind, or hydroelectric energy.
6. Answers will vary. Students should try to provide at least five specific ideas and clear explanations of how they would protect the resource.

Resource Directory

Teaching Resources

Section Quiz in the Unit 1 Teaching Resources, p. 22

Answers to...

AS YOU READ

Students may suggest things like carpooling to save gas, limiting the use of electricity at home, or keeping the thermostat lower in the winter.

SECTION 3

Lesson Objectives

1. Identify the difference between weather and climate.
2. Explain the role of wind and water in creating the Earth's climate.
3. Identify the Earth's five major climate regions and types of vegetation characteristic of each region.

Lesson Plan

1 Engage

Warm-Up Activity

Ask students what they think would be different about their lives if they lived in a different climate region. Would the school building or their homes be constructed differently? Would they wear different clothes? Eat different foods? Play different games or sports?

Activating Prior Knowledge

Have students name and describe some of the plant life they see in their neighborhood. How much rain and sunlight the plants seem to need? How do they respond to unusual weather? Do they show signs of seasonal change?

2 Explore

Once students have read the section, ask them to discuss the following questions. Why does the sun rise earlier during the summer months than during the winter months? What makes some months colder than others? What is the deciding factor between rain and snow?

Answers to...

CRITICAL THINKING

Students may say that people can be more aware of weather conditions that may cause tornadoes or go to a safe place, such as the basement, during a tornado. Tornadoes and severe weather can cause severe damage to property.

SECTION 3

Climate and Vegetation

BEFORE YOU READ

READING FOCUS QUESTIONS

1. What is the difference between weather and climate?
2. What role do wind and water play in creating our climate?
3. What are the five major climate regions and what kinds of vegetation grow in each region?

KEY TERMS

weather
temperature
precipitation
climate
vegetation

MAIN IDEA

The climate of an area affects the vegetation that will grow there, as well as the ways in which people and animals live.

NOTE TAKING

Copy the cause-and-effect chart shown here. As you read the section, fill in the chart with causes and effects of climate and vegetation. Add more topics to the chart with information from the section.

Causes
1. Earth rotates.
2. Hot air rises.

Wind and Climate

Effects
1. Wind spreads heat over the Earth.

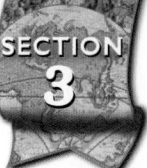

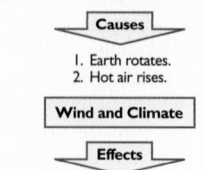

GEOGRAPHY Tornadoes can easily flatten buildings. Tornado winds are the most powerful and violent winds on the Earth. **Critical Thinking** How can people protect themselves from the dangers of tornadoes? What is the economic effect of tornadoes and other severe weather?

Setting the Scene

In late May 1996, a tornado's furious winds tore down the movie screen of a drive-in theater in St. Catherine's, Ontario, Canada. Ironically, the week's feature movie was *Twister*, a film about tornadoes.

The Difference between Weather and Climate

Weather is the day-to-day changes in the air. It is measured primarily by temperature and precipitation. **Temperature** is how hot or cold the air feels. **Precipitation** is water that falls to the ground as rain, sleet, hail, or snow.

Climate is the average weather of a place over many years. Weather, on the other hand, is what people see from day to day. The Earth has many climate regions. Climate varies among different latitudes and is also greatly affected by wind, water, and landforms.

Resource Directory

Teaching Resources

Classroom Manager in the Unit I Teaching Resources, p. 23

Guided Reading and Review in the Unit I Teaching Resources, p. 24

Guide to the Essentials, p. 7

Technology

Section Reading Support Transparencies

The World: Precipitation

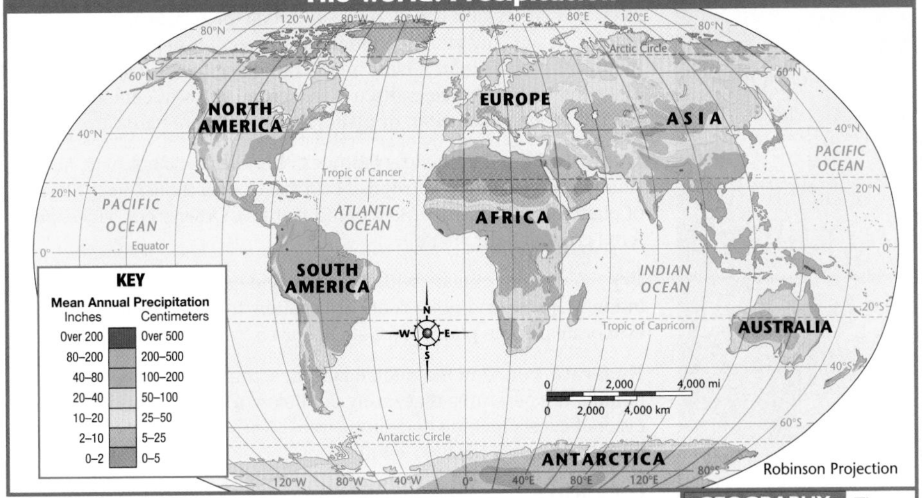

GEOGRAPHY The mean annual precipitation is the amount of rain or snow that falls in a region in an average year. **Map Study** Which areas get the most precipitation? Which get the least?

The Impact of Wind and Water

Without wind and water, the Earth would overheat. Together, wind and water moderate the effect of the sun's heat. Heat causes air to rise, especially near the Equator and over warm ocean water. Cold air sinks towards the surface away from the Equator. Wind blows from places where air is sinking towards places where air is rising. The Earth's rotation bends this flow to create circular wind patterns. So, depending on where you are in a circling weather system, the wind may be blowing north, south, east, or west.

The Earth's rotation also creates ocean currents, which are like rivers in the oceans. Some currents carry warm water from near the Equator toward the north and the south. Other currents carry cold water from the poles toward the Equator. Oceans also moderate the climate of nearby land just by their presence. Water takes longer to heat and cool than land. As a result, when the land has warmed during the summer, the nearby ocean remains cooler. Air blowing over the ocean becomes cool and then cools the land. In the winter, the opposite occurs.

Raging Storms Wind and water can make climates milder, but they also create storms. Hurricanes are storms that form over the ocean in the tropics. Hurricanes rotate in a counter-clockwise direction around an "eye." They have winds of at least 74 miles (124 km) per hour and usually involve heavy rainfall. Tornadoes are just as dangerous, but they affect smaller areas. Their wind can range from 40 miles (67 km) per hour to over 300 miles (501 km) per hour and wreck anything in their path.

LINKS TO Science

Smog Normally, air is cooler at higher altitudes. During a temperature inversion, however, a layer of warm air sits on top of the cooler air. The warm air traps pollution near the ground. This mixture of dangerous smoke and fog is called *smog.* The brown air seen in cities such as Los Angeles and Denver is smog caused by car exhaust.

Resource Directory

Teaching Resources

Social Studies and Geography Skills, Reading a Natural Vegetation Map, p. 23; Reading a Climate Map, p. 24

Technology

Color Transparencies 12 Temperature Regions and Ocean Currents Map; **13** Forest Vegetation Regions Map; **14** Grassland Vegetation Regions Map; **16** The World: Annual Precipitation Map; **17** Tropical Climate Regions Map; **18** Desert and Desert Scrub Vegetation Regions Map

3 Teach

Have students keep a weather record on daily weather conditions such as temperature, precipitation, and wind direction. Have them record observations each day for one week. Use these weather records as the basis for a discussion about weather and climate in your region. This activity should take 10 minutes each day, and 15 minutes for discussion at the end of the week.

Questions for Discussion

GEOGRAPHY Compare the map of climate regions in the Activity Atlas on p. 8 with the map of world precipitation on this page. What relationship exists between the amount of precipitation that regions in Africa receive and their climates?

Areas that receive more precipitation are located in tropical climate regions. Areas that receive very little precipitation are in dry regions.

GEOGRAPHY Choose a climate region. Why do certain kinds of plants *not* grow there?

Students' responses will vary, but should be supported with information from the section. For example, in polar climates, trees do not grow. The climate is too cold for such vegetation.

4 Assess/Reteach

See the answers to the Section 3 Assessment. You may also use students' weather records as an assessment.

Acceptable records include information on temperature and precipitation.

Commendable records include more detailed information, including a description based on personal observation each day.

Outstanding records indicate a recognition of weather patterns.

Answers to...

MAP STUDY

areas near the Equator; polar regions, north Africa, central Australia, central Asia

SECTION 3 ASSESSMENT

AFTER YOU READ

1. (a) condition of the air over a short period of time, (b) degree of hotness or coldness, (c) all forms of water, including rain, sleet, hail, and snow, that fall to the ground from the air, (d) weather patterns of an area typical over a long period of time, (e) plants
2. Weather is the condition of the surrounding air over a short period of time, whereas climate is the condition of the air over a long period of time. Examples of weather: tornadoes and thunderstorms. Examples of climate: tropical and continental.
3. Wind and water moderate the temperature of the Earth by carrying warm air and water from near the Equator to cooler areas near the poles and cool air and water from the polar regions to warmer regions near the Equator.
4. Tropical: rain forest, shrubs, leafy vegetation; Dry: sparse vegetation often with small leaves; Moderate: varied vegetation including deciduous forests, shrubs, bushes, and grasses; Continental: grasslands and both deciduous and coniferous forests; Polar: low shrubs, mosses, lichens
5. Charts should correctly identify your local climate region, explain how wind, water, and latitude create that climate, and give specific description of the vegetation.
6. Students should recognize that climate influences how people live, earn a living, and the traditions, culture, and civilization that they have.
7. Students can also refer to the map of climate regions in the Activity Atlas on p. 8 to help them with the activity.

Desert Vegetation

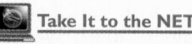

GEOGRAPHY Cacti have waxy skins that hold moisture in. Prickly spines protect a cactus from being eaten by animals. **Critical Thinking** Why do you think cacti have developed these distinct features?

Climate and Vegetation

Every climate region has its own special characteristics, such as amount of rain and sunlight, temperature, and nutrients, or elements, that plants use as food. Plants adapt, or adjust, to the characteristics of a climate. Geographers discuss five broad types of climates. Each has its unique **vegetation,** or plants that grow there naturally.

Tropical Found in the low latitudes, this climate is hot, wet, and sunny. The vegetation is tropical rain forest with thousands of kinds of plants. Trees grow to 130 feet (40 meters). Other trees, vines, and ferns grow in their shade.

Dry A dry, hot climate with little rain and sandy, gravelly soil. Vegetation is sparse and plant roots are shallow to absorb water before it evaporates. Some plants have small leaves, which lose little moisture.

Moderate Found in the middle latitudes, this climate has moderate rainfall, temperatures that rarely fall below freezing, and varied vegetation. Forests include deciduous trees (trees that lose their leaves in fall), shrubs, low bushes, wildflowers, and a variety of grasses.

Continental Summer temperatures are moderate to hot; winters are cold. Vegetation includes grasslands and forests. Large deciduous forests occur where temperatures are moderate, while colder regions have coniferous trees (trees with needles and cones).

Polar This climate is found in the high latitudes and is cold all year. Vegetation includes low shrubs, mosses, and lichens (plants that grow on rocks). There are no trees and few flowering plants.

SECTION 3 ASSESSMENT

AFTER YOU READ

RECALL

1. Define: (a) weather, (b) temperature, (c) precipitation, (d) climate, (e) vegetation

COMPREHENSION

2. Compare weather and climate and give an example of each.
3. How do wind and water influence climate?
4. Name the five major climate regions of the world and describe the vegetation in each.

CRITICAL THINKING AND WRITING

5. **Exploring the Main Idea** Review the Main Idea statement at the beginning of this section. Then make a chart. In the first column, identify the climate region. In the second column, tell what factors help create that climate. In the third column, describe the vegetation that grows there.
6. **Predicting** How can understanding the differences in climate regions help you better understand differences among civilizations and cultures? Write a paragraph to explain.

ACTIVITY

Take It to the NET

7. **Making a Climate Map** Create a map showing the Earth's climate zones. Use a different color to indicate each zone. Visit the World Explorer: People, Places and Cultures section at **phschool.com** for help in completing this activity.

Resource Directory

Teaching Resources

Section Quiz in the Unit I Teaching Resources, p. 25

Chapter Summary in the Unit I Teaching Resources, p. 26

Vocabulary in the Unit I Teaching Resources, p. 27

Reteaching in the Unit I Teaching Resources, p. 28

Enrichment in the Unit I Teaching Resources, p. 29

Critical Thinking in the Unit I Teaching Resources, p. 30

Understanding Charts

The World's Highest Active Volcanoes		
Peak	Country	Elevation (in feet)
San Pedro	Chile	20,161
Arácar	Argentina	19,954
Guallatiri	Chile	19,918
Tupungatito	Chile/ Argentina	19,685
Sabancaya	Peru	19,577

Learn the Skill

Charts are helpful because they organize information in a way that makes it easy to read and understand. To understand and use charts, follow these steps:

A. Read the title to identify the topic of the chart. This chart's title tells you that it contains information about the highest active volcanoes in the world.

B. Read the chart. Use the column heads to understand the information in each row of the chart. The column heads in this chart provide information about the volcano peak, the country in which it is located, and its elevation measure in feet. Using this information, you can tell that the San Pedro Peak in Chile is 20,161 feet and that the Sabancaya Peak in Peru is 19,577 feet.

C. Interpret the chart. By comparing the information in the chart, you can tell that three of the world's highest active volcanoes are located in Chile. You can also determine that the Arácar Peak in Argentina is 36 feet higher than the Guallatiri Peak in Chile.

Practice the Skill

Study the chart about temperature and precipitation in Charleston, South Carolina. How much precipitation does Charleston get in January? In April? During which month does Charleston get the most precipitation? During which month is the average temperature 67 degrees? Which month is the hottest? Which month is the coldest?

Temperature and Precipitation in Charleston		
Month	Temperature (Fahrenheit)	Precipitation (inches)
January	48	3.5
February	51	3.5
March	58	4.5
April	65	3.0
May	73	4.0
June	78	6.5
July	82	7.0
August	81	7.0
September	76	5.0
October	67	3.0
November	58	2.5
December	51	3.0

Apply the Skill

See the Chapter Review and Assessment at the end of this chapter for more questions about charts.

Lesson Objectives

1. Describe how information is organized in a chart.
2. Read and interpret information in a chart.

Lesson Plan

1 Engage

Give students an opportunity to share examples of times when they have used other charts to help them organize or present information. Some students may find it easier to sketch the chart on the chalkboard as an option to describing it. Remind students that charts are common in textbooks and encyclopedias.

2 Explore

Direct students to read the steps under "Learn the Skill." Answer any questions they may have. When finished, have each student write a question that can be answered from the volcanoes chart. Then, ask students to exchange questions.

3 Teach

Direct students' attention to the chart "Temperature and Precipitation in Charleston." Explain that Charleston is a city in South Carolina, and have them find it on a map. Read the questions aloud as students use the chart to find the answers.

4 Assess/Reteach

To assess students' understanding, have students find charts in textbooks or encyclopedias and ask each other questions that can be answered by reading the charts.

To further assess students' understanding of charts, have them complete the "Applying Your Skills" part of the Chapter Review and Assessment at the end of this chapter.

Resource Directory

Teaching Resources

Social Studies and Geography Skills, Reading a Table, p. 60

Technology

Social Studies Skills Tutor CD-ROM

Answers to...

PRACTICE THE SKILL

3.5 inches; 3.0 inches; July and August; October; July; January

CHAPTER 2

Review and Assessment

Creating a Chapter Summary

Students' summaries will vary.

Physical Features The physical features of the Earth are a result of physical processes which occur within the Earth and on the Earth's surface. Air and water are two of the most important natural resources needed for life.

Natural Resources There are three types of natural resources: recyclable, renewable, and nonrenewable. Energy is a scarce natural resource.

Climate and Vegetation The Earth has many different climate regions. The movement of wind and water affects these regions. There are five major climate regions, and each has its own unique vegetation.

Reviewing Key Terms

Students' definitions should show an understanding of each key term.

Reviewing the Main Ideas

1. Plates continually move, creating volcanoes and earthquakes and shifting the continents. Weathering breaks down rocks and erosion carries rocks and soil to new places. Together they create new landforms. Water continuously passes through the water cycle, renewing itself and our water supplies.
2. As the Earth's plates move apart, magma oozes out and forms new land. As plates meet, they can grind against each other, causing earthquakes or volcanoes. The slow pressure of plates pressing together can push up mountains.
3. Geographers divide the Earth's natural resources into three groups: recyclable resources, such as water; renewable resources, such as trees; and nonrenewable resources, such as minerals.
4. Renewable resources, such as trees, chickens, and corn, can be replaced when they are used. Nonrenewable resources, such as petroleum and coal cannot be replaced.
5. Weather is the day-to-day changes in the air. Climate is the average weather of a place over many years.
6. tropical climate, rainforests; dry climate, sparse vegetation, often with small leaves; moderate climate, varied vegetation including deciduous trees, shrubs, bushes, and grasses; continental climate, grasslands and deciduous and coniferous forests; polar climate, low shrubs, mosses, and lichens

CHAPTER 2

Review and Assessment

Creating a Chapter Summary

On a separate piece of paper, copy this web. Then, add more ovals and fill them in with information summarizing what you have learned about each topic.

Earth's Physical Geography
- Physical Features
- Natural Resources
- Climate and Vegetation

Reviewing Key Terms

Write a definition for each of the following words.

1. landform
2. plate tectonics
3. atmosphere
4. erosion
5. natural resource
6. fossil fuel
7. climate
8. vegetation

Reviewing the Main Ideas

1. How do the Earth's physical processes change and renew the physical features of our planet? (Section 1)
2. How do plate tectonics shape the Earth? (Section 1)
3. What are the three groups that geographers divide the Earth's natural resources into? Give examples of each. (Section 2)
4. What is the difference between renewable and nonrenewable resources? Give an example of each. (Section 2)
5. Explain the difference between climate and weather. (Section 3)
6. What are the Earth's major climate regions? Give an example of the kinds of vegetation that grow in each of the climate regions. (Section 3)

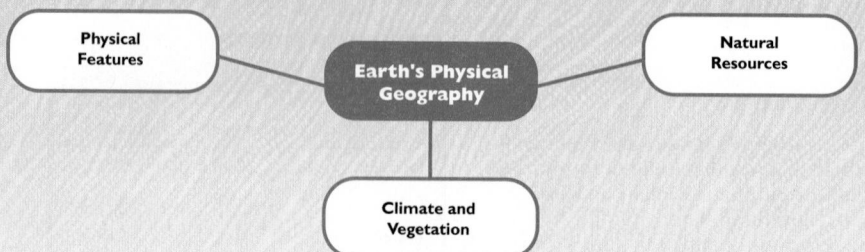

Map Activity

Geography

For each place listed below, write the letter on the map that shows its location. Use the Atlas at the back of the book to complete the exercise.

1. Australia
2. North Pole
3. Equator
4. Atlantic Ocean
5. Tropic of Capricorn

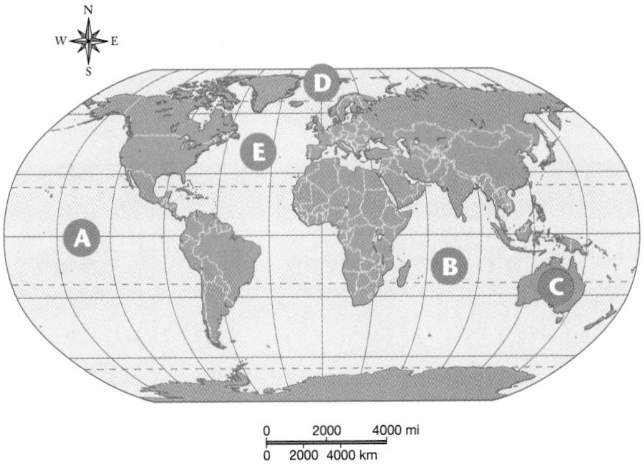

Take It to the NET

Enrichment For more map activities using geography skills, visit the social studies section of **phschool.com.**

Writing Activity

1. **Writing a News Report** Choose a well-known natural disaster such as Hurricane Mitch or the eruption of Mount St. Helens. Find out where it happened, why it happened, and what the immediate and long-term effects were. Then, write a news report that describes the natural disaster in geographic terms.
2. **Predicting Events** Write a paragraph about the possibility of predicting earthquakes, volcanoes, and other natural events. Do you think scientists can make these predictions? Why or why not?

Critical Thinking

1. **Identifying Central Issues** How does water affect a region's landforms and climate?
2. **Recognizing Cause and Effect** Why is the Earth continually changing its form?

Applying Your Skills

Turn to the Skills for Life activity on p.37 to help you complete the following activity.

Scan a recent newspaper or magazine for a chart. Write four or five statements based on the information in the chart.

Take It to the NET

Activity What are the physical features of the region in which you live? Click on each link to learn about the different biones and ecosystems of the world. Visit the World Explorer: People, Places, and Cultures section of **phschool.com** for help in completing this activity.

Chapter 2 Self-Test As a final review activity, take the Chapter 2 Self-Test and get instant feedback on your answers. To take the test, visit the Social Studies section of **phschool.com.**

Map Activity

1. C **2.** D **3.** A **4.** E **5.** B

Writing Activity

1. Students' news reports will vary but should answer where, what, and when, and give a simple description of the cause and effects of the disaster.
2. Students' paragraphs will vary, but they should express an opinion about whether scientists will learn to predict earthquakes and volcanoes based on what they have learned about these phenomena in the text.

Critical Thinking

1. Answers will vary. Students should refer to patterns of precipitation and the effects of weathering and erosion on local landforms and the moderating effects of large bodies of water on climate.
2. Answers will vary. Students may refer to forces from within the Earth that change its form, such as the movement of tectonic plates, earthquakes, and volcanoes. They may also cite the effects of weathering and erosion and mention the more dramatic changes that can be caused by storms.

Applying Your Skills

You may want to have students work in pairs to complete the activity. If possible, provide students with a chart for them to use.

Resource Directory

Teaching Resources

Cooperative Learning Activity in the Unit 1 Teaching Resources, pp. 68–71

Chapter Tests Forms A and B in the Unit 1 Teaching Resources, pp. 88–93

Guide to the Essentials, Ch. 2 Test, p. 8

Other Print Resources

Chapter Tests with ExamView® Test Bank, Ch. 2

Technology

ExamView® Test Bank CD-ROM, Ch. 2

Resource Pro® CD-ROM

Chapter 3 Planning Guide

Resource Manager

	CORE INSTRUCTION	READING/SKILLS
Chapter-Level Resources	**Teaching Resources** Program Overview Pacing Charts **Technology** Resource Pro® CD-ROM Companion Web site, phschool.com • eTeach	**Technology** Social Studies Skills Tutor CD-ROM Student Edition on Audio CD, Ch. 3
1 Population Patterns in Places and Regions 1. Understand population distribution. 2. Explain population density. 3. Describe the growth of Earth's population.	**Teaching Resources** **Unit 1** Classroom Manager, p. 32 Guided Reading and Review, p. 33	**Teaching Resources** Guide to the Essentials, p. 9 Social Studies and Geography Skills, pp. 29 and 31 **Technology** Section Reading Support Transparencies
2 The Influences of Human Migration 1. Identify reasons why people migrate. 2. Understand the effect of migration on cities	**Teaching Resources** **Unit 1** Classroom Manager, p. 35 Guided Reading and Review, p. 36	**Teaching Resources** Guide to the Essentials, p. 10 **Technology** Section Reading Support Transparencies
3 Culture and Cultural Institutions 1. Define the meaning of culture. 2. Identify the institutions that make up a culture's social structure. 3. Explain the effect of language on culture. 4. Describe the relationship between religion and culture.	**Teaching Resources** **Unit 1** Classroom Manager, p. 38 Guided Reading and Review, p. 39	**Teaching Resources** **Unit 1** Guide to the Essentials, p. 11 Social Studies and Geography Skills, pp. 47 **Technology** Section Reading Support Transparencies
4 Economic and Political Systems 1. Identify the four kinds of industry and the products they produce. 2. Describe basic economic systems. 3. Identify forms of government.	**Teaching Resources** **Unit 1** Classroom Manager, p. 41 Guided Reading and Review, p. 42 Chapter Summary, p. 44 Vocabulary, p. 45 Reteaching, p. 46	**Teaching Resources** **Unit 1** Guide to the Essentials, p. 12 Social Studies and Geography Skills, pp. 25 and 45 **Technology** Section Reading Support Transparencies

ENRICHMENT / PRE-AP

Teaching Resources
Primary Sources and Literature Readings

Other Print Resources
DK Atlas

Technology
World Video Explorer: Where People Live
How People Live Transparencies, Unit 1
Companion Web site, phschool.com

Technology
Color Transparencies 15, 24, 25, 27

Teaching Resources
Unit 1
Enrichment, p. 29
Cooperative Learning Activity, pp. 68–71

Technology
Color Transparencies 12–14; 16–18

ASSESSMENT

Prentice Hall Assessment System

Core Assessment
Chapter Tests with ExamView® Test Bank, Ch. 3
ExamView® Test Bank CD-ROM, Ch. 3

Standardized Test Preparation
Diagnose and Prescribe
Diagnostic Tests for Middle Grades Social Studies Skills
Review and Reteach
Review Book for World Studies
Practice and Assess
Test-taking Strategies with Transparencies for Middle Grades
Test Prep Book
Test-taking Strategies Posters

Teaching Resources
Unit 1
Section Quizzes, pp. 34, 37, 40, and 43
Chapter Tests, pp. 94–99

Technology
Companion Web site, phschool.com
Ch. 3 Self-Test

World Video Explorer
Each region of the world is explored through regional flyovers and investigative field trips. Case study segments give students an in-depth view of the history, economy, government, and culture of a key place in each region. Case studies include Nigeria, Mexico, China, British Columbia, and the Czech Republic.

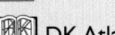

In Your Classroom

CUSTOMIZE FOR INDIVIDUAL NEEDS

Gifted and Talented

Teacher's Edition
- Adapting to the Environment, p. 49
- Oldest Parliament, p. 54
- Mixed Economic Systems, p. 55
- Living in a Dictatorship, p. 55

Teaching Resources
- Enrichment, p. 47
- Primary Sources and Literature Readings

Honors/Pre-AP

Teacher's Edition
- Adapting to the Environment, p. 49
- Oldest Parliament, p. 54
- Mixed Economic Systems, p. 55
- Living in a Dictatorship, p. 55

Teaching Resources
- Critical Thinking, p. 48
- Primary Sources and Literature Readings

ESL

Teacher's Edition
- Living in a Dictatorship, p. 55

Teaching Resources
- Guided Reading and Review, pp. 33, 36, 39, and 42
- Vocabulary, p. 45
- Reteaching, p. 46
- Guide to the Essentials, pp. 9–12
- Social Studies and Geography Skills, pp. 25, 29, 31–32, 45, and 47

Technology
- Social Studies Skills Tutor CD-ROM
- Section Reading Support Transparencies

Less Proficient Readers

Teacher's Edition
- Adapting to the Environment, p. 49
- Living in a Dictatorship, p. 55

Teaching Resources
- Guided Reading and Review, pp. 33, 36, 39, and 42
- Vocabulary, p. 45
- Reteaching, p. 46
- Guide to the Essentials, pp. 9–12
- Social Studies and Geography Skills, pp. 25, 29, 31–32, 45, and 47

Technology
- Social Studies Skills Tutor CD-ROM
- Section Reading Support Transparencies

Less Proficient Writers

Teacher's Edition
- Adapting to the Environment, p. 49
- Oldest Parliament, p. 54
- Mixed Economic Systems, p. 55

Teaching Resources
- Guided Reading and Review, pp. 33, 36, 39, and 42
- Vocabulary, p. 45
- Guide to the Essentials, pp. 9–12
- Social Studies and Geography Skills, pp. 25, 29, 31–32, 45, and 47

Technology
- Social Studies Skills Tutor CD-ROM
- Section Reading Support Transparencies

DORLING KINDERSLEY

At the end of each unit, you will find information adapted from Dorling Kindersley's *Illustrated Children's Encyclopedia* that connects to the region being studied and to one of the seven content strands. In addition, your resources include Dorling Kindersley's *Atlas*, which contains valuable information about countries from around the world.

TEACHER'S EDITION INDEX

CHAPTER 3 PACING SUGGESTIONS

For 90-minute Blocks

See suggestions in the Teaching Resources Pacing Charts for Chapter 3. Use Color Transparencies 15, 24, 25, and 27.

Running Out of Time?

See the Guide to the Essentials, pp. 9–12.

INTERDISCIPLINARY LINKS

Middle Grades Math: Tools for Success

Course 1, Lesson 10-6, **Graphing Functions**

Course 2, Lesson 10-7, **Interpreting Graphs**

Science Explorer

Earth's Changing Surface, Lesson 1-1, **Exploring Earth's Surface**

Prentice Hall Literature

Copper, The Stone, Moving Mountains, Tenochtitlan

BIBLIOGRAPHY

For the Teacher

Bowker, John. *World Religions.* Dorling Kindersley, 2001.

Fry, Plantagenet Somerset. *The Dorling Kindersley History of the World.* Dorling Kindersley, 1994.

Sandler, Martin W. *Immigrants.* HarperCollins, 1995.

Winckler, Suzanne, and Mary M. Rodgers. *Population Growth.* Lerner, 1991.

For the Student

Easy

Lewin, Ted. *Sacred River.* Clarion, 1995.

Average

Copsey, Susan Elizabeth, and Anabel Kindersley. *Children Just Like Me.* Dorling Kindersley, 1995.

Morris, Ann. *Dancing to America.* Dutton, 1994.

Challenging

Mozeson, I. E., and Lois Stavsky. *Jerusalem Mosaic: Young Voices from the Holy City.* Four Winds/Simon & Schuster, 1994.

Literature Connection

Strete, Craig Kee. *The World in Grandfather's Hands.* Clarion, 1995.

Whelan, Gloria. *Goodbye, Vietnam.* Knopf, 1992.

Take It to the NET

The World Explorer companion Web site, found on **phschool.com**, offers activities for exploring geographical, historical, and cultural resources on the Internet. It also provides on-line links for key content and all Section and Chapter Assessment activities.

The **Teacher site** also provides teachers with regional data and ideas for student research and activities.

Students can use the **Student site** to find chapter-by-chapter Internet resource links and to access Self-Tests.

CHAPTER 3

Connecting to the Guiding Questions

In this chapter, students will read about the Earth's human and cultural geography. Content in this chapter corresponds to the following Guiding Questions outlined at the beginning of the unit.

- How can knowing a people's history help to better understand them?
- Are the world's many cultures more alike or more different?
- Under what kind of government do people live?
- How do people use the world's resources?
- How do people fulfill their responsibilities as citizens?

Using the Map Activities

Point out to students that different regions of the world are in different time zones, which means that the time of day is different depending on where in the world you live. Have students think about what it means to have 24 different time zones, and how this affects people around the world as they travel and communicate with one another.

- Students should write questions that can be answered from the World Time Zones map and use the map to answer accurately the questions.
- Students should give specific descriptions of, and reasonable explanations for their own method of dividing the world into different time zones.

Heterogeneous Groups

The following activities are suitable for heterogeneous groups.

Journal Writing

Living in a Dictatorship, p. 55

eTeach

Be sure to check out this month's discussion with a Master Teacher. Go to **phschool.com**.

CHAPTER 3

Earth's Human and Cultural Geography

World Time Zones

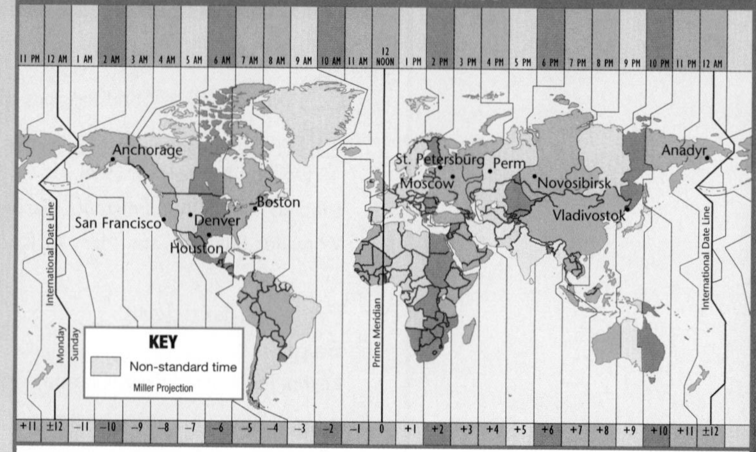

Using Maps

When it is 6 a.m. in Houston, it is 3 p.m. in Moscow. That is because the world has been divided into 24 Standard time zones—one for each hour of the day. Without world time zones, every place would have to determine its own time. There would be so many different local times that it would cause confusion. Use the World Time Zones map to complete these activities.

Interpreting Maps

Study the map and try to figure out how to read it. Then, write three questions that can be answered by studying the map. Exchange questions with a classmate and try to find the answers using the map.

Problem Solving

Think about what the world would be like without 24 Standard time zones. Write a brief report on whether these 24 zones are a good idea or whether they should be changed. If you think they should be changed, present a new system that you think should replace the old one.

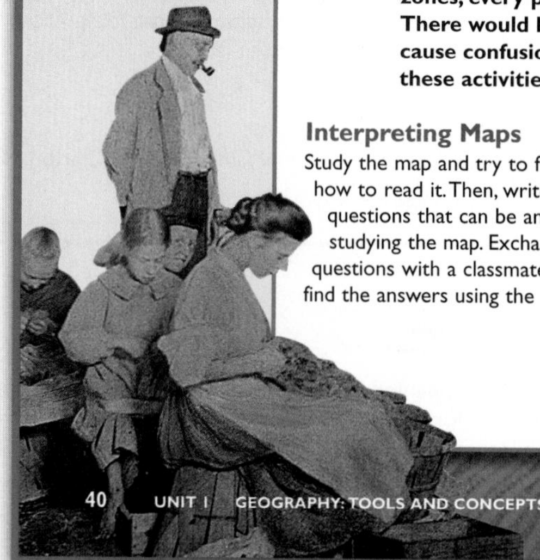

Resource Directory

Teaching Resources

Primary Sources and Literature Readings extend content with a selection related to the concepts in this chapter.

Other Print Resources

DK Atlas

Technology

Where People Live, from the World Video Explorer, enhances students' understanding of the geographic factors that influence population distribution.

How People Live Transparencies, Unit 1

Student Edition on Audio CD, Ch. 3

SECTION 1

Population Patterns in Places and Regions

BEFORE YOU READ

READING FOCUS QUESTIONS

1. What accounts for the distribution of the Earth's population?
2. What is population density?
3. What are the causes of population growth?

KEY TERMS

population
population distribution
demographer
population density
birthrate
death rate
life expectancy
Green Revolution

MAIN IDEA

The Earth's population is growing rapidly, due to modern technology and scientific developments, and is concentrated in areas where it is easiest to live.

NOTE TAKING

Copy the cause-and-effect chart shown here. As you read the section, fill in the chart with information about population patterns. Add more topics and cause-and-effect sequences to the chart.

Causes
1. Rivers and lakes
2. Flat, fertile soil
3.
4.

Populaton Distribution

Effects
1.
2.

Setting the Scene

Imagine that you go to school in Tokyo, the capital of Japan. Every day you ride a train to school. People jam the train. Most people must stand. Often, special station guards push people inside so the doors can close behind them.

This is not an exaggeration. Japan is smaller than California, but it is home to 125 million people and extremely crowded.

CULTURE At rush hour in Tokyo, white-gloved guards jam two more passengers onto an already full train. **Critical Thinking** Compare the crowded conditions in Japan with crowding you've experienced. How do very crowded situations make you feel?

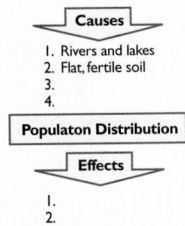

What Is Population Distribution?

The world's **population,** or total number of people, is spread unevenly over the Earth's surface. **Population distribution** describes how the population is spread out across the world.

Demographers, scientists who study population, know that many factors affect where people live. Most major civilizations began along bodies of water. Rivers and lakes form transportation corridors for trade and travel and are a source of water for drinking and farming. Most people chose places with flat, fertile soil, adequate rainfall, a suitable climate, and ample natural resources. Many of these factors still influence where people live. Consider the population distribution of the different continents.

Resource Directory

Teaching Resources

Classroom Manager in the Unit 1 Teaching Resources, p. 32

Guided Reading and Review in the Unit 1 Teaching Resources, p. 33

Guide to the Essentials, p. 9

Technology

Section Reading Support Transparencies

SECTION 1

Lesson Objectives

1. Understand population distribution.
2. Explain population density.
3. Describe the growth of Earth's population.

Lesson Plan

1 Engage

Warm-Up Activity

Briefly tell students the story of Robinson Crusoe, who was shipwrecked on an island. Then, ask students to imagine that they are shipwrecked on such an island. Have them make a geography "survival chart" telling what kind of climate, vegetation, and landforms would help them live comfortably on the island.

Activating Prior Knowledge

Create a chart on the chalkboard. Write the headings *Country* and *City* above each column. Write *Advantages* and *Disadvantages* as row heads. Have students fill in the chart as a class activity. Then, ask students whether they would prefer to live in the country or in a city. Tell them to use details from the chart to support their answers.

Answers to...

CRITICAL THINKING

Students may never have experienced crowding like that depicted in the picture. They should provide details from personal experiences in a comparison. Students may have different feelings about crowds.

Lesson Plan continued

2 Explore

Have students read the section, looking for answers to the following questions: What are some important characteristics about the places where people live? In what ways do fertile soil, natural resources, and fresh water affect population in an area? Why was population growth slower in past centuries?

3 Teach

Have students name several factors that affect population growth and describe how each factor works to increase or decrease population growth. Ask them which factor they think is the most serious and to give reasons for their opinions.

Questions for Discussion

GEOGRAPHY **What geographic factors contribute to the high percentage of the Earth's population living in Asia, Europe, and North America?**

Favorable landforms, fertile soil, fresh water, and rich natural resources contribute to the population distribution.

GEOGRAPHY **How has new technology allowed farmers in the United States to increase the world's food supply?**

Scientists have developed new ways to protect crops from insects, new fertilizers to enrich the soil, and new varieties of food crops.

4 Assess/Reteach

See the answers to the Section 1 Assessment. The students' charts can also be valuable assessment tools.

Acceptable charts include two supporting facts for each column.

Commendable charts include several supporting entries and some indication of the benefits associated with some climates and landforms.

Outstanding charts include several supporting entries and some indication of the benefits associated with some climates and landforms, as well as the disadvantages associated with others.

More than 81 percent of Earth's population lives in Asia, Europe, and North America. These continents total about 53 percent of the world's land. However, these continents have large areas of fertile soil, favorable landforms, ample fresh water, rich natural resources, and good climates.

Other continents have smaller populations partly because it is harder to live there. For example, about 309 million people live in South America. Many live along the Atlantic coast. Other regions have mountains, dry plains, and rain forests. Fewer people live there.

What Is Population Density?

The average number of people who live in a square mile (or square kilometer) is called **population density.** In a country with a high density, people are crowded together. Japan has one of the highest population densities in the world. In Tokyo, more than 25,000 people live in one square mile (9,664 people per sq km).

In contrast, Canada has a lower population density. It has about eight persons per square mile (about three persons per sq km). Many factors affect Canada's population. For instance, its cool climate has a short growing season, which limits farming.

Studying Population Density Demographers measure population density by dividing the number of people living in a place by the number of square miles (or sq km) of that place. Remember that population density is an *average.* People are not evenly distributed over the land. New York City, for example, has a very dense population. However, New York state has many fewer people per square mile. Even in the city, some areas are more densely populated than others.

GEOGRAPHY For hundreds of years the world's population rose very slowly. Recently, however, the rate of growth has skyrocketed. **Critical Thinking** How does the graph show the change in the growth of the world's population?

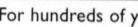

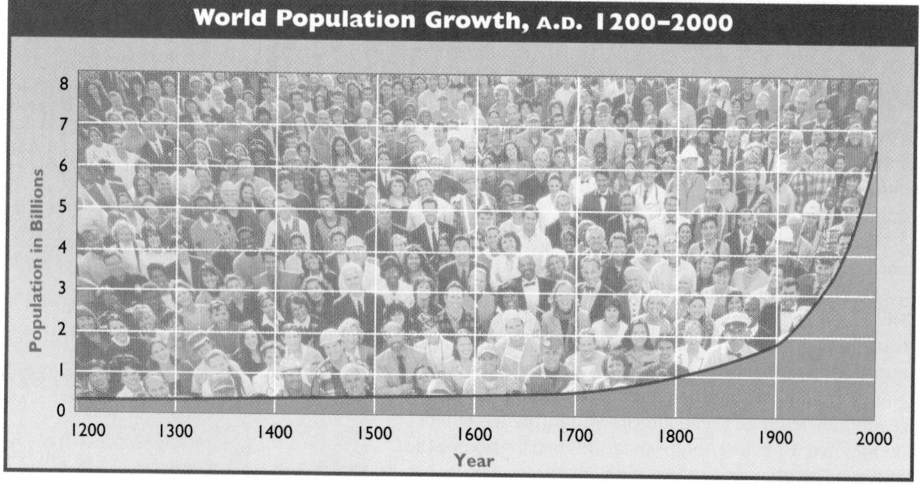

Answers to...

CRITICAL THINKING

A line rises or curves upwards to correspond with the vertical axis showing population in billions.

Resource Directory

Teaching Resources

Social Studies and Geography Skills, Reading a Population Density Map, p. 29

Technology

Color Transparencies 15 Population Density Map; **24** The World: Life Expectancy Map; **25** The World: Infant Mortality Map; **27** The World: Growth in Urban Population Map

Population Growth

Today, the Earth's population is growing steadily. Population growth depends on the birthrate and the death rate. The **birthrate** is the number of live births each year per 1,000 people. The **death rate** is the number of deaths each year per 1,000 people. By comparing these numbers, demographers can figure out population growth.

For centuries, the world population grew slowly. Without modern technology, food was often scarce. Also, many people died of disease. Although the birthrate was high, so was the death rate. **Life expectancy,** the average number of years that people live, was short.

Reasons for Population Growth Today Population growth occurs because the birth rate is higher than the death rate. In the United States, for example, the average life expectancy for women is about 80 years and for men about 73 years.

Two scientific developments have made this possible. First, new farming methods have greatly increased the world's food supply. Scientists have developed new varieties of food crops and new ways to protect crops from insects. New fertilizers can enrich the soil, and scientists have also discovered ways to raise crops with less water. These changes in agriculture are called the **Green Revolution.**

Scientists have also made advancements in medicine and health. Doctors can now treat people who once died of illnesses and injuries. As a result, people live longer lives.

SCIENCE, TECHNOLOGY, AND SOCIETY

Changing the Earth's Physical Environment

We use coal and petroleum to make energy. Burning these fossil fuels creates gases that build up in the atmosphere. These gases trap heat from the sun, which makes the Earth warmer. As a result the Earth's polar ice is melting. This is causing the oceans to rise. Some scientists say ocean levels may rise 1 1/2 feet by 2100. Cities like San Francisco, Sydney, and Rio de Janeiro, which lie along ocean coastlines, would flood.

Critical Thinking What can we do to stop the ice caps from melting? Who do you think is responsible for solving the problem?

SECTION 1 ASSESSMENT

AFTER YOU READ

RECALL

1. Define: (a) population, (b) population distribution, (c) demographer, (d) population density, (e) birthrate, (f) death rate, (g) life expectancy, (h) Green Revolution

COMPREHENSION

2. Why is the Earth's population unevenly distributed around the world?
3. Explain population density and give examples.
4. Why is the Earth's population growing faster now than in the past?

CRITICAL THINKING AND WRITING

5. **Exploring the Main Idea** Review the Main Idea statement at the beginning of this section. Write a paragraph explaining how population distribution adds to the challenge of dealing with our rapid population growth.
6. **Making Comparisons** A large percentage of the world's population lives on a small portion of the Earth's land. How do the population distributions in Japan and Canada reflect this fact?

ACTIVITY

7. **Writing to Learn** You are a demographer studying the population of your community. Make a list of questions to ask and possible sources for answers.

Resource Directory

Teaching Resources

Section Quiz in the Unit 1 Teaching Resources, p. 34

Answers to...

CRITICAL THINKING

Limiting the use of fossil fuels will help stop ice caps from melting. Some students may say countries that pollute the most are responsible, and others may say that every country is responsible for solving the problem.

SECTION 1 ASSESSMENT

AFTER YOU READ

1. (a) the number of people living in an area, (b) how a population is spread over an area, (c) scientist who studies human populations, (d) average number of people living in an area, (e) the number of live births each year per 1,000 people, (f) the number of deaths each year per 1,000 people, (g) the number of years that a person may be expected, on average, to live, (h) changes in agriculture that have greatly increased the world's food supply
2. People choose to live where climate, soil fertility, rainfall, and fresh water are most suited to living. Because these areas are unevenly spread across Earth, so is the population.
3. Population density is the number of people living in an area. For example, Canada has a low population density whereas Japan has one of the highest population densities in the world.
4. People are healthier, birthrates are higher, death rates are lower, and there is a more abundant food supply.
5. Students should recognize that because uneven distribution of population concentrates population in certain areas, those areas are subject to greater pressure from rapid population growth. These areas will continue to grow faster than other areas, which will put additional strain on these regions to provide public services, jobs, housing, and other necessities.
6. The population of Japan is densely concentrated in its major cities, which comprise only a small part of Japan's total land area. Canada's population is concentrated along its southern border in several large cities. The vast northern area of Canada has a small population.
7. Make sure students' questions address factors that affect population, such as what kind of climate exists, the presence of natural resources, the presence of water for farming, drinking, and so forth.

SECTION 2

Lesson Objectives

1. Identify reasons why people migrate to new places.
2. Understand the effect of migration on cities.

Lesson Plan

1 Engage

Warm-Up Activity

Ask students how many of them have lived in another city, state, or country. Then, ask whether they remember what it was like when their families moved. What things did they find familiar? What things were new or different? Did they feel at home in the new place at first? Ask them to describe how they made friends at school and with neighbors.

Activating Prior Knowledge

Ask students if they know children who have moved into their neighborhoods from other cities, towns, or countries. How do they think those children felt? What challenges did they face? Then, have students tell what they can do to make newcomers feel welcome. List their ideas on the chalkboard.

SECTION 2

The Influences of Human Migration

BEFORE YOU READ

READING FOCUS QUESTIONS

1. Why do people migrate?
2. What effect is migration having on cities?

KEY TERMS

migration
immigrant
"push-pull" theory
urbanization
rural area
urban area

KEY PLACES

Cuba
Jakarta
São Paulo

MAIN IDEA

The world's population is on the move.

NOTE TAKING

Copy the chart shown here. As you read the section, fill in the chart with information about migration. Add more bulleted points to the chart.

Reasons People Migrate	Effects of Urbanization
• Poverty	• Overcrowded cities
• Unable to find work	• Lack of adequate housing
•	•
•	•

Fleeing Cuba

HISTORY These men are preparing to leave Cuba on a makeshift raft, hoping to arrive in Florida. They are fleeing the regime of the dictator Fidel Castro. **Critical Thinking** What conflicts do you know about that have resulted in migration? What effect might migration have on the countries that take in refugees?

Setting the Scene

Roberto Goizueta (goy zoo AY tuh) was the former head of Coca-Cola, one of the largest companies in the world. Yet, when he came to the United States from **Cuba** in 1960, he had nothing. This is how he described his escape from the largest island nation in the Caribbean Sea:

"When my family and I came to this country [the United States], we had to leave everything behind…our photographs hung on the wall, our wedding gifts sat on the shelves."

Like millions of others who came to the United States, Roberto Goizueta helped the nation become a land of prosperity.

Migration: The Movement of People

Humans have always been on the move. When they move from one place to another, it is called **migration. Immigrants** are people who leave one country and move to another. For centuries, hundreds of thousands of people have migrated to the United States. Since the late 1970s, more than 700,000 people migrated here from Vietnam, 800,000 from Central America, 900,000 from Caribbean islands.

Answers to...

CRITICAL THINKING

Possible answer: The conflicts in Bosnia or the Middle East. Refugees must be fed and provided with medical care. Their children must be educated. They must be provided with social services. Refugees also enrich the culture and provide additional workers.

Resource Directory

Teaching Resources

Classroom Manager in the Unit 1 Teaching Resources, p. 35

Guided Reading and Review in the Unit 1 Teaching Resources, p. 36

Guide to the Essentials, p. 10

Technology

Section Reading Support Transparencies

Demographers use the **"push-pull" theory** to explain immigration. It says that people migrate because certain things "push" them to leave. Often, the reasons are economic. People may be poor, unable to find work or buy land. Sometimes people are pushed to move by war or other conflict, or by the actions of a government.

For instance, in 1959 there was a revolution in Cuba led by Fidel Castro. He established a Communist government where the people have little say in that government. Some Cubans who opposed the Communists fled to America to find safety, freedom, and better opportunities.

What about the "pull" part of the theory? The hope for better living conditions "pulls" people to a country. Cubans settled in Florida because it was near their former home. It had a large Spanish-speaking population and a climate and vegetation similar to Cuba's. In addition, the United States has a limited government, which means that the government's power over citizens is limited. People enjoy freedom and have a right to vote for their leaders. All these factors "pulled" many Cubans to America.

Other Kinds of Immigration Sometimes, people are forced to migrate. Australia was colonized by English immigrants. Some were convicts who served their sentences in Australia and stayed when their sentences were done. War also forces people to migrate. In the mid-1990s, war broke out among three ethnic groups in the former Yugoslavia, in Eastern Europe. Many refugees fled to escape the warfare. Also, victorious soldiers of one group often forced entire communities of other groups to leave. Millions of immigrants flooded into other countries in Eastern and Western Europe.

Cuba and Florida: Climate Regions

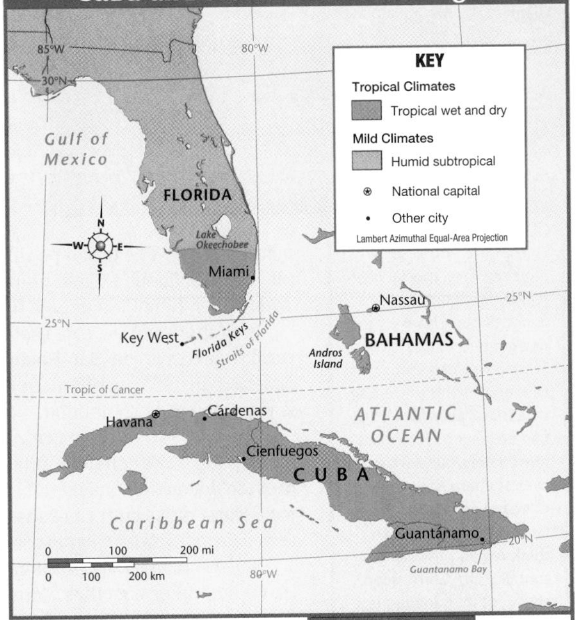

GEOGRAPHY Since 1959, about one million Cubans have fled their communist-ruled country to find a new life in the United States. Many have settled in Florida. **Map Study** Use the map scale to determine about how far Cuba lies from the mainland of Florida. How are the climates of southern Florida and Cuba similar?

The World Becomes More Urban

One of the biggest challenges to today's nations is people migrating to cities from farms and small villages. In recent years, the population of major cities has grown tremendously. The movement of people to cities and the growth of cities is called **urbanization.**

2 Explore

The United States is often called "a nation of immigrants." As students read the section, ask what evidence they can find to support this statement. What peoples have come to the United States in recent decades? What were some of the reasons for their migration?

3 Teach

Have students create a two-column chart, *The "Push-Pull" of Migration*. Have students fill in each column of their chart with facts from the section. When they have completed their charts, have them rank the items in each column by numbering them from most to least important. This activity should take about 20 minutes.

Question for Discussion

GOVERNMENT **What kind of government does Cuba have?**

Cuba has an unlimited government. It has a Communist government where people have little say in government policies.

4 Assess/Reteach

See the answers to the Section 2 Assessment. You may also use students' completed charts as an assessment.

Acceptable charts list three correct entries in each column.

Commendable charts list three entries in each column and a ranking that places survival "pushes" at the top of the list.

Outstanding charts include an indication of the cause-and-effect relationships between push and pull factors.

SKILLS MINI LESSON

Drawing Conclusions

To **introduce** the skill, indicate to students that they can use what they know in concert with what they learn to draw conclusions about events in the world around them. Help students **practice** the skill by asking them to name the main reasons for which people migrate to another country. List their responses on the chalkboard. Then, help students use these facts to make a generalized statement, a conclusion, that explains migration. Encourage students to **apply** the skill by listing reasons for migration from rural areas to cities and by using the reasons to draw a conclusion about rural-urban migration. Remind students that their conclusions must be supported by relevant facts.

Answers to...

MAP STUDY

Cuba lies about 150 miles (240 km) from Florida's mainland. Southern Florida and Cuba both have a tropical wet and dry climate.

SECTION 2 ASSESSMENT

AFTER YOU READ

1. (a) largest island country in the Caribbean Sea, (b) capital and largest city of the Republic of Indonesia, (c) largest city in Brazil
2. (a) movement of people from one country or region to another to live there, (b) person who moves to a new country in order to settle there, (c) theory of migration that says people migrate because certain things "push" them to leave, and certain things in a new place "pull" them there, (d) growth of city populations caused by movement of people to cities, (e) area with low population density, (f) area with a high population density
3. poverty, lack of land, war or conflict, actions of their government
4. better living conditions, available land, good climate and vegetation, freedom
5. Migration is causing cities to grow rapidly, causing problems such as overcrowding and straining the cities' abilities to provide adequate services.
6. Students should recognize that migration will affect both urban and rural areas. Cities will suffer from overcrowding and related problems. Rural areas will suffer from a lack of population. There may not be enough workers for agriculture.
7. Answers will vary, but students will probably recognize some pattern of growth or decline in population.
8. Answers will vary, but students may consider drawbacks to include how they will feel about leaving friends and relatives behind, and the difficulties of moving to an unfamiliar place. Benefits might include the possibility of finding better working and living conditions.

ECONOMICS

Across the world, growing cities face special challenges. Sometimes, there is not enough housing for newcomers to the cities. Sometimes, newcomers cannot afford the housing that is available. Until they find better housing, many newcomers build whatever shelters they can.

Critical Thinking What kinds of factors do you think would push people to a city like Cairo, seen above, despite inadequate housing?

What pushes people from rural areas and pulls them to cities?

Growing Cities, Growing Challenges

Cities in Indonesia are an example of urbanization. In the past, most Indonesians were farmers, fishers, and hunters. They lived in **rural areas,** or villages in the countryside. Recently more and more Indonesians have moved to **urban areas,** or cities and nearby towns. The urban population is increasing rapidly. For example, in 1978, about 4.5 million people lived in the capital of **Jakarta.** Today over 10 million people live there.

In South America, too, vast numbers of people are moving from rural to urban areas. **São Paulo, Brazil** is now the largest city in South America. In 1995, its population was nearly 16 million, and by 2015, it is expected to be 21 million.

The problem of urbanization is complex. Cities suffer because too many people are coming too fast. Cities are overcrowded and cannot provide adequate housing, jobs, schools, hospitals, and other services. Rural areas suffer because of lack of people. Fewer people mean fewer farmers. Less food is produced, and everybody suffers.

With so many daily problems, why do immigrants flock to São Paulo and other big cities? Most are seeking a better life for their families. They are looking for jobs, decent houses, and good schools. Above all, most want more opportunities for their children.

SECTION 2 ASSESSMENT

AFTER YOU READ

RECALL

1. Identify: (a) Cuba, (b) Jakarta, (c) São Paulo
2. Define: (a) migration, (b) immigrant, (c) "push-pull" theory, (d) urbanization, (e) rural area, (f) urban area

COMPREHENSION

3. What "pushes" people from one country to another?
4. What "pulls" people to one country from another?
5. How is migration changing the world's cities?

CRITICAL THINKING AND WRITING

6. **Exploring the Main Idea** Review the Main Idea statement at the beginning of this section. Write a paragraph predicting what effect increasing urbanization might have on the world.
7. **Making Inferences** Think about how population movement affects the community you live in, then make a list of examples that show the ways your community is affected.

ACTIVITY

8. **Writing to Learn** When people migrate from rural to urban areas, they may face hardships and challenges. Imagine that you are considering whether or not to move from a rural area to a city. Make a two-column chart listing the benefits of moving to the city in one column, and the drawbacks in the other. Use the list to help you decide whether or not to move.

46 UNIT 1 GEOGRAPHY: TOOLS AND CONCEPTS

Answers to...

CRITICAL THINKING

Possible answers: Lack of jobs in rural areas and more opportunities in the city might push people to a city like Cairo.

Resource Directory

Teaching Resources

Section Quiz in the Unit 1 Teaching Resources, p. 37

SECTION 3

Culture and Cultural Institutions

BEFORE YOU READ

READING FOCUS QUESTIONS

1. How is culture a total way of life?
2. What institutions are basic to all societies?
3. How is language part of culture?
4. What is the relationship among philosophy, religion, and culture?

KEY TERMS

culture	institution
cultural trait	social structure
culture region	nuclear family
technology	extended family
cultural landscape	ethics

MAIN IDEA

Culture affects everything a group of people does, what they believe, how they behave, and how they organize their society.

NOTE TAKING

Copy the outline shown here. As you read the section, fill in the outline with information about culture. Add headings and details to make the outline more complete.

I. Culture: A Total Way of Life
- A. Elements of culture
  - 1. Cultural traits
  - 2.
- B. How land affects culture

II. Institutions Basic to all Societies
- A. Family

III. Language as Culture

IV. Religion and Culture

Setting the Scene

"All right, students," your teacher says, "time to clean the room. Kaitlyn—I'd like you to sweep the floor today. Guy and Keisha, please dust the shelves and windowsills. Eric and Bobby, you do the lunch dishes."

Would you be surprised if this happened in your classroom? There are many differences between Japanese and American schools. In Japan, students are expected to help keep their classrooms clean. Japanese students generally spend more time studying than American students do. They go to school five and one-half days a week.

Of course, Japanese schools are also very much like American schools. In both places, students study math, science, literature, and history. They enjoy sports, music, art, and drama.

CULTURE These students in Japan are listening closely as their classmate speaks. **Critical Thinking** How is your classroom like a classroom in Japan? How is it different?

Culture: A Total Way of Life

If you met students from Japan, you might have many questions. What do you eat for lunch? What kinds of music do you like? What makes you laugh?

SECTION 3

Lesson Objectives

1. Define the meaning of culture.
2. Identify the institutions that make up a culture's social structure.
3. Explain the effect of language on culture.
4. Describe the relationship between religion and culture.

Lesson Plan

1 Engage

Warm-Up Activity

Write the following four headings on the chalkboard: *sports*, *foods*, *clothing*, and *entertainment*. Ask students to list, under each heading, things that are important parts of American life. Ask for specific items. Summarize by saying that these different parts of our way of life are only part of American culture.

Activating Prior Knowledge

Tell students that they have a particular way of doing some things, such as greeting their friends, celebrating holidays, speaking, and gesturing. Many of these ways of doing things are personal mannerisms. Others they share with the people around them. Invite students to give examples of each.

Resource Directory

Teaching Resources

Classroom Manager in the Unit 1 Teaching Resources, p. 38

Guided Reading and Review in the Unit 1 Teaching Resources, p. 39

Guide to the Essentials, p. 11

Technology

Section Reading Support Transparencies

Answers to...

CRITICAL THINKING

Answers will vary, but students should note specific details about the classroom that are different from and similar to their own.

Lesson Plan continued

❷ Explore

Point out to students that geographers study how people affect their environment as well as how the environment affects people. Discuss how tools, fire, agriculture, and writing each contributed to the development of culture.

❸ Teach

Have students work in small groups to create a cause-and-effect graphic showing how the environment affects people living in their community.

Cause ⟶	Effect
Climate ⟶	
Landforms ⟶	
Vegetation ⟶	
Natural resources ⟶	

Direct students to list results or effects of each cause in a connecting box. Use the completed graphics to discuss how the local environment has shaped life in your community.

Invite students to tell what they know about each of the following terms: *nuclear family, extended family,* and *social class.* Have them work in pairs to create their own definitions for the words. Suggest that as students read the section, they edit and revise their definitions and include examples of each term.

Question for Discussion

CULTURE How has slavery and the experience of African Americans affected music in the United States?

Two American music forms, jazz and blues, are expressions of how African Americans feel about the history of slavery and their experiences as African Americans in the United States.

CULTURE How people live is part of their culture. Different cultures sometimes interact with their environment in similar ways. In mountainous Japan, farmers build terraces on the hillsides to increase the amount of land available for farming. Terrace farming is also used in other cultures, including those in South America and South Asia. **Critical Thinking** How else do you think different cultures interact with their environments in similar ways?

Answers to these questions will tell you something about the culture of Japan. **Culture** is the way of life of a group of people who share similar beliefs and customs. The language Japanese students speak, how they dress, what they study, and what they do after school are part of their culture.

Elements of Culture Culture includes the work people do, their behaviors, their beliefs, their ways of doing things, and their creative expressions. A particular group's distinct skills, customs, and ways of doing things are called **cultural traits.** Over time, cultural traits may change, but cultures change very slowly.

The people of Japan have a unique culture. So do the people of the United States. Each of these groups of people live in a **culture region,** an area in which people share the same cultural traits. These traits are influenced by the issues in the society in which people live. American music is an example. Slavery and the experiences of African Americans led them to develop blues and jazz. This music expressed their feelings about their experiences.

Although every culture region has its own culture traits, some aspects of culture are shared. For example, Shakespeare wrote plays that are part of the English culture. However, he wrote about universal themes—ideas that are of interest to all people. His work has been translated into other languages for people of many cultures to read and appreciate.

People and Their Land Geographers study culture in relation to the environment. They want to know how landforms, climate, vegetation, and resources affect culture.

Geographers are also interested in the effect people have on their environment. Often the effect is linked to a culture's **technology,** or tools and the skills people need to use them. Technology helps people use natural resources and change the environment, and includes computers and the Internet as well as other tools and the skills needed to make them.

A group's **cultural landscape** includes any changes to its environment. It also includes technology used to make the changes. For example, Bali, in Indonesia, has many mountains. Therefore, people carved terraces in them to make flat farmland. Central India, on the other hand, has much level land. Farmers there would probably not develop technology to create terraces.

Culture and Political Boundaries Culture changes slowly but political boundaries sometimes change rapidly. War and changes in political leadership can divide culture regions, but the culture often survives. For example, Austria and Germany are part of the same culture region. Austria has been long separated from Germany. And following World War II, Germany itself was divided into two countries, a separation that lasted more than 40 years. Through all this, the culture of Austria, East Germany, and West Germany remained closely linked.

Answers to...

CRITICAL THINKING

Students may mention use of irrigation methods in desert landscapes and farming methods, such as hothouses, in cold climates.

Resource Directory

Teaching Resources

Social Studies and Geography Skills, Recognizing Cause and Effect, p. 47

Institutions Basic to All Societies

Every culture has basic institutions that help people organize their lives together. An **institution** is an important practice, relationship, or organization in a society or culture. Among these are government, economic, educational, religious, and family institutions. These are all part of a culture's **social structure.** This is a way of organizing people into smaller groups. Each smaller group has certain tasks. Some groups gather food, others protect the community, while others raise children. Social structure helps people work together to meet the basic needs of individuals, families, and communities.

The family is the basic social unit of any culture. Families teach customs and traditions of the culture. They teach children how to grow up, behave, treat others, and learn.

Kinds of Families In some cultures, the basic family unit is the **nuclear family.** It is made up of a mother, a father, and their children.

Another type of family is the **extended family.** It includes parents and their children. It may also include grandparents, aunts, uncles, cousins, and other relatives. These family members may live in the same house or close by.

LINKS TO
Language Arts

Cultural Borrowing The Phoenicians were ancient traders along the Mediterranean Sea. Their alphabet had 22 letters, and they wrote from right to left. The Greeks saw this writing system and based their own alphabet on it—with one difference. The Greeks, like us, wrote from left to right. We owe our alphabet, in part, to these two ancient cultures.

Language and Culture

All cultures have language. In fact, every culture is based on language. It lets people communicate everything they need to share in their culture. Without language, people could not pass on what they know or believe to their children.

A culture's language reflects the things that its people think are important. For example, English has the word *snow* for the white stuff that falls in some places in winter. But the Inuits of North America have over 13 words for snow. Why? Where the Inuits live, snow covers the ground for a good part of the year. Snow is a more important part of their environment than it is to people of other cultures. The Inuits, therefore, have created words to meet their needs.

In some countries, people speak different languages. For example, the official language of Egypt is Arabic. It is spoken by most Egyptians. But some Egyptians speak Italian, Greek, or Armenian. Canada has two official languages, French and English, and Native Americans there speak a number of other languages. People who speak these languages are culturally different in some ways from other people in their country. They may celebrate different festivals, wear different clothes, or have different customs for such things as dating or education.

CULTURE The end of Ramadan, a month-long period of spiritual reflection, means a joyous celebration for these Egyptian Muslims. **Critical Thinking** What important religious or cultural events do you and your family observe?

4 Assess/Reteach

See the answers to the Section 3 Assessment. You may also use students' completed graphics as an assessment.

Acceptable graphics contain at least two effects per cause.

Commendable graphics show a greater number of effects.

Outstanding graphics include a greater variety of effects.

HISTORY

Adapting to the Environment

Early civilizations grew as people learned to control their environment. In the Indus Valley, in what is now Pakistan and western India, people learned to irrigate with river water and to control floods about 4,500 years ago. This led to the growth of the cities of Harappa and Mohenjo-Daro, which were highly civilized, with public buildings, an organized system of producing and storing grains and other foods, and homes with interior baths and drains to carry sewage away from the houses.

SKILLS MINI LESSON

Organizing Information

To **introduce** the skill, point out to students that as they do research, they will often need to take notes. Identify for students these steps in taking notes and organizing information.

- Use key words and phrases to record the main idea and to record details.
- Double-check your notes.

Have students **practice** the skill by taking notes on this section of the text. Suggest that students **apply** the skill by researching the languages, religions, and customs of people who live in their area or of cultures represented in their school.

Answers to...

CRITICAL THINKING

Answers will vary. Students may mention Christmas, Easter, Thanksgiving, Passover, Chanukah, and so forth.

SECTION 3 ASSESSMENT

AFTER YOU READ

1. (a) language, religious beliefs, values, customs, and other ways of life shared by a group of people, (b) behavioral characteristic of a people, such as a language, skill, or custom, (c) area in which most of the people share the same cultural traits, (d) tools and the skills that people need to use them, (e) landscape that has been changed by humans and that reflects their culture, (f) an important practice, relationship, or organization, (g) the ways in which people within a culture are organized into small groups, (h) family unit that includes a mother, a father, and their children, (i) family unit that may include parents, children, grandparents, aunts, uncles, cousins, and other relatives, often living with or near one another, (j) the standards of moral behavior that distinguishes right from wrong for a particular person, religion, or group
2. Culture is all around each of us and our behavior has been modified by it. Therefore, everything we do is in some way affected by culture.
3. Answers will vary, but students should recognize that many institutions will exist in almost every culture.
4. People use language to communicate and it reflects what people think is important. Language also isolates people from other people who do not speak the same language and unites those who do.
5. Students should understand that religion helps define values that people believe are important.
6. Answers will vary, but students should demonstrate an understanding of cultural traits and the uniqueness of their own culture.
7. Have students form groups to work on their charts. Then, have them present their charts to the rest of the class.

Religions of the World

	Christianity	Buddhism	Islam	Hinduism	Judaism	Confucianism
Deity	God	Various gods	God (Allah)	Brahman	God (Yahweh)	None
Founder	Jesus Christ	The Buddha	Muhammad	No single founder	Abraham	Confucius
Holy Book	Bible	Tripitika	Quran	Numerous sacred writings	Hebrew Bible, Torah	Writings of Confucius
Clergy	Ministers, priests	Monks and ministers	Imam	Guru, Holy Man, Brahman	Rabbis	None
Members	1.9 billion	300 million	1 billion	793 million	14 million	5 million

Religion and Culture

Religion is basic to every culture. Religion helps answer questions about the meaning and purpose of life. It helps define the values that people believe are important. Religion can also guide people in **ethics,** or standards of accepted behavior.

Religious beliefs vary, but most believers expect people to treat one another well and to behave properly. The chart above lists major religions of the world. Every religion celebrates important people and events in its history. Muslims celebrate Ramadan. Christians celebrate Christmas. Buddhists celebrate the birth and death of Buddha. These celebrations remind believers of the sacrifices others have made and of the joy of their faith.

SECTION 3 ASSESSMENT

AFTER YOU READ

RECALL

1. Define: (a) culture, (b) cultural trait, (c) culture region, (d) technology, (e) cultural landscape, (f) institution, (g) social structure, (h) nuclear family, (i) extended family, (j) ethics

COMPREHENSION

2. How does culture affect all aspects of a person's life?
3. What institutions would you find in every society?
4. How does language influence culture?
5. Explain the relationship between religion and culture.

CRITICAL THINKING AND WRITING

6. **Exploring the Main Idea** Review the Main Idea statement at the beginning of this section. Then, list cultural traits that are characteristic of your culture.

ACTIVITY

Take It to the NET

7. **Identifying Regional Characteristics** Create a chart showing the characteristics of the region in which you live. Model your chart on the information and data included on the web site. Visit the World Explorer: People, Places, and Cultures section of **phschool.com** for help in completing this activity.

Resource Directory

Teaching Resources

Section Quiz in the Unit I Teaching Resources, p. 40

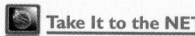

SECTION 4

Economic and Political Systems

BEFORE YOU READ

READING FOCUS QUESTIONS

1. What are the categories of industry and what do they produce?
2. What are the basic economic systems in use around the world?
3. What are the important types of government?

KEY TERMS

economy
producer
goods
services
consumer
primary industry
secondary industry
tertiary industry
quaternary industry
traditional economy
market economy
capitalism
free enterprise
command economy
government
direct democracy
monarchy
constitution
representative democracy
dictatorship

NOTE TAKING

Copy the concept web shown here. As you read the section, fill in the circles with information about economic and political systems. Add more circles to make the web more complete.

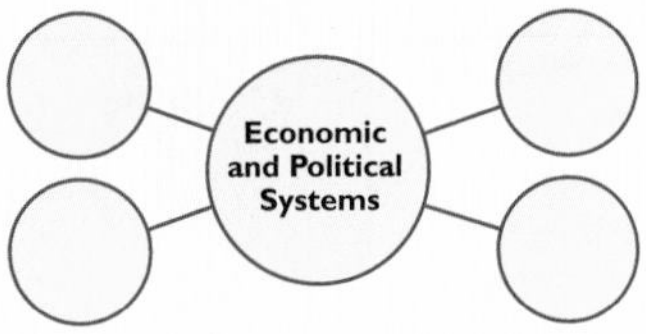

MAIN IDEA

Societies make various choices in how to organize their economies and governments in order to provide for the needs of their people.

Setting the Scene

Muhammad Yunnus was a professor of economics in the country of Bangladesh (bahng gluh DESH), a poor nation in South Asia. Yunnus wanted to help poor Bangladeshis improve their lives.

In the early 1970s, Yunnus met Sufiya Khatun. She made bamboo stools but earned only two cents a day because she could only make a few stools. If she had more money for supplies, she could have made more, but Sufiya had no way to borrow money. Forty-two other people in her village also needed money to build their businesses. They needed an average of just $26 each, but banks wouldn't bother making loans for just $26.

In 1976, Yunnus opened a bank to loan small amounts of money only to poor people. Yunnus's bank has loaned money to 2 million customers.

ECONOMICS Most of Muhammad Yunnus's customers are women seeking to open small businesses. This woman used her loan to start a weaving shop. **Critical Thinking** List some ways that the loans improved the lives of the people. How do you think these loans improved the economy of Bangladesh?

SECTION 4

Lesson Objectives

1. Identify the four kinds of industry and the products they produce.
2. Describe the basic economic systems in use in the world.
3. Identify the important forms of government.

Lesson Plan

1 Engage

Warm-Up Activity

Discuss with students their answers to the following questions: What do they do when they want a glass of milk? How does milk get from the cow to their glass? Who owns the cows? Who owns the trucks that move the milk from one place to another? Elicit from students that some people choose to run farms that produce milk that they then sell directly to consumers.

Activating Prior Knowledge

Guide a discussion of elections. Ask students why people vote. What kinds of decisions do they make? Who is permitted to vote? Have students give examples of elections they know about. Then, ask students whether or not they think the same kind of voting occurs in other nations.

Resource Directory

Teaching Resources

Classroom Manager in the Unit 1 Teaching Resources, p. 41

Guided Reading and Review in the Unit 1 Teaching Resources, p. 42

Guide to the Essentials, p. 12

Technology

Section Reading Support Transparencies

Answers to...

CRITICAL THINKING

Possible answer: the loans enable the people to begin or expand their businesses, increase their incomes, and improve their lives and the lives of their families. The loans also improve the economy of Bangladesh because even though each business produces a very small income, it is multiplied by millions of people. Altogether, it amounts to a significant increase in economic activity and prosperity.

Lesson Plan continued

2 Explore

Have students read the section. Then, ask them to make a chart that identifies the roles of producers, consumers, and the government in market and command economies. Next, have students make an organizational chart comparing the hierarchies of power in a monarchy, representative democracy, and a dictatorship.

3 Teach

Organize students into six groups and assign each group one of the economic or political systems discussed in this section. Direct each group to prepare for a "press conference" about their topic. Class members can act as newspaper, magazine, or television reporters, asking group members about the principles, benefits, and disadvantages of their form of government or economic system. This activity should take about an hour.

Questions for Discussion

ECONOMICS How does the economic system of the Tuareg people in northern Africa differ from the economic system of the United States?

The Tuareg are a nomadic people who operate within a traditional economy. In this economy, the customs, traditions, and habits of the group dictate what is produced, bought, and sold. The United States has a market economy. Most businesses are privately owned and companies sell their products for profit.

Answers to...

MAP STUDY

North America and Europe are the most developed countries because they both have large areas of commercial farming and industry.

AS YOU READ

Answers will vary.

The World: Economic Activity

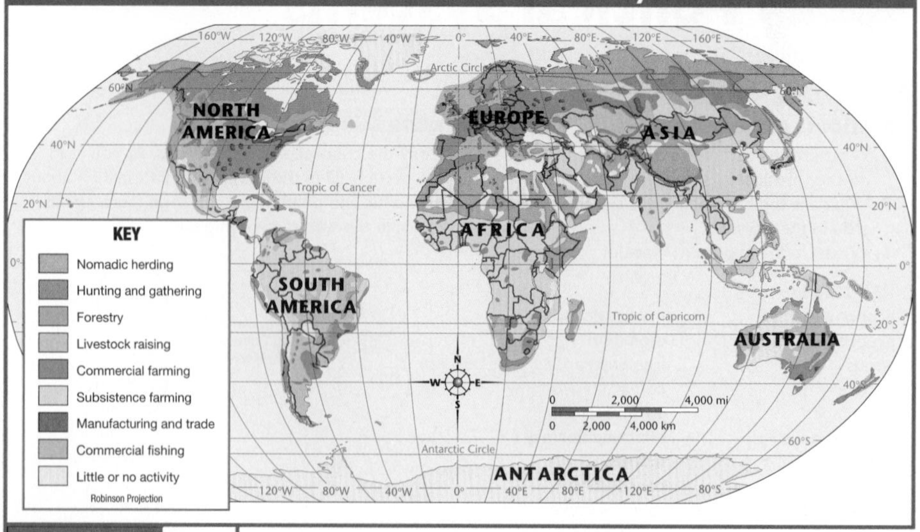

ECONOMICS This map uses a color-coded key to show the most common economic activities that take place across the world. Use the key to make comparisons among the continents. **Map Study** After you read the paragraphs on developed and developing countries on page 54, look at the map and identify the continents where you think the most developed countries might be located. Explain your answer.

AS YOU READ

Use Prior Knowledge Think about each member of your family and what he or she does. Is each a consumer, a producer, or both? Explain why.

Categories of Industry

Banks like the one Yunnus started help people become productive members of their nation's economy. An **economy** is a system for producing, distributing, and consuming goods and services. Owners and workers are **producers.** They make products, such as bamboo baskets or automobiles. Those products are called **goods.** Some products are really **services** that producers perform for other people. They may style hair, edit books, or heal diseases. **Consumers** are people who buy the goods and use the services.

There are four categories of economic activities or industries. **Primary industry** is the part of the economy that produces raw materials. Examples include agriculture, fishing, mining, and forestry. **Secondary industry** refers to manufacturing businesses. They take materials from primary industries and other secondary industries and make them into goods. **Tertiary industry** refers to service companies. Examples include banking, transportation, health care, and police protection. **Quaternary industry** refers to information technologies. Quaternary industries provide Internet services, computer software, and cable and telephone service.

Economic Systems

Cultures choose the way they organize their economies. There are three basic systems: traditional, market, and command economies. In a **traditional economy,** the customs, traditions, and habits of the group

Resource Directory

Teaching Resources

Social Studies and Geography Skills, Reading an Economic Activity Map, p. 25

influence the producing, buying, and selling of goods. The Tuareg of the Sahara in northern Africa are an example. These people are nomadic herders who travel about the region in search of food and water for their animals. They produce most of the things they need and trade with others for what they need and cannot produce.

In a **market economy,** most businesses are privately owned. When a company sells its products, it earns a profit, or money. Owners decide how much to pay workers and how to use profits. Consumers are important in a market economy. A company may produce goods, but consumers may not buy them or be willing to pay what the company wants for the products. Prices will then have to be lowered. A market economy is also called **capitalism** or **free enterprise.** It is the type of economic system we have in the United States.

In a **command economy,** economic decisions are made by the central government. The government decides what products are made, how much is produced, and what the goods cost. Consumers and businesses have little control of the goods. There are two major types of command economies—socialism and communism.

In a socialist system, the government owns most basic industries. The government decides how much to pay workers and how much to charge for goods. It uses profits to pay for services such as health and education. Other industries and services follow the capitalist model. They are

Capitalism Replaces Communism

ECONOMICS This photograph was taken in Berlin shortly after communist East Germany united with capitalist West Germany. These East German children had never seen so many different school supplies before. **Critical Thinking** Why would these children not be used to seeing so many different school supplies for sale?

SKILLS MINI LESSON

Recognizing Bias

Remind students that not everything they read is fact—often personal opinion or bias is represented as fact. **Introduce** the skill by indicating to students that as they read about cultures, economies, and governments, they will need to be able to recognize bias. To help students **practice** the skill, encourage them to bring in articles from newspapers and periodicals discussing governmental and economic policies. Work with students as they scan the articles looking for opinions and loaded words and phrases (such as *backward economic policies*). Have students describe the tone of the article as positive, negative, supportive, or insulting. Suggest that students **apply** this skill on their own as they read publications or watch political campaign announcements.

ECONOMICS How are primary and secondary industries related to one another?

Secondary industries use the raw materials produced by primary industries to make goods and products.

GOVERNMENT What is a direct democracy, and what society was one of the first to use this type of democracy?

A direct democracy is a system of government in which every member of a group participates in the running of the group's affairs. Greece had a direct democracy in about 500 B.C.

4 Assess/Reteach

See the answers to the Section 4 Assessment. You may use the presentations for an assessment.

Acceptable presentations reiterate the material in the text.

Commendable ones show an effective presentation of ideas and accurate responses to questions.

Outstanding presentations show imagination and ingenuity in addition to effectiveness.

Answers to...

CRITICAL THINKING

In communist East Germany, government factories provided goods to the citizens. There were no privately owned factories to create competing brands.

GOVERNMENT

Oldest Parliament

Althing, the parliament of Iceland, was founded in the year 930 and functioned almost continuously until it was abolished in 1800 during Denmark's absolutist rule of the country. During the 1800s, an independence movement flourished among Icelanders and Althing was reestablished. In 1944, Althing moved to establish Iceland as a republic, cutting all formal ties with Denmark.

CITIZENSHIP

The Chinese National Day Parade

Chinese citizens mark the 22nd anniversary of Communist rule in their country at Beijing's Gate of Heavenly Peace Square. **Critical Thinking** How does your community mark important events in America's history?

privately owned and consumers decide which products to buy. A few countries follow socialism or have socialist programs. These countries include Spain, Portugal, and Italy.

In a communist system, the central government owns all property, such as farms and factories. It controls all aspects of citizens' lives, including the price of goods and services, how much is produced, and how much workers are paid. Today, only a few of the world's nations practice communism. They include Cuba, China, and North Korea.

Developed and Developing Countries Cultures can also be described by how many industries they have. About one quarter of the people of the world live in developed nations. These are countries such as the United States, Canada, Japan, and most Western European countries. They have many industries and machinery and technology are in wide use. Most citizens can get a good education and health care. Large commercial farms use modern technology. They need fewer workers but produce large amounts of food.

The majority of the world's population lives in developing countries. These nations have few industries and most are poor. People often suffer from disease, food shortages, unsafe water, poor education and health services, and changing governments.

Types of Government

Government is the system that sets up and enforces a society's laws and institutions. Some governments are controlled by a few people. Others are controlled by many.

Resource Directory

Teaching Resources

Social Studies and Geography Skills, Recognizing Bias, p. 45

Answers to...

CRITICAL THINKING

Answers will vary. Students may say parades, fairs, carnivals, festivals, and so forth.

Direct Democracy The earliest governments were probably simple. People lived in small groups and practiced some form of **direct democracy.** That means that everyone participated in running the affairs of the group, though chiefs or elders made most decisions. Individuals had a responsibility to the group. Decisions were based on the culture's customs and beliefs.

The first complex society to try direct democracy was Greece in about 500 B.C. It was not completely democratic. Only men could vote, but every man had both the right and the responsibility to vote for laws and government policies.

Monarchy Until about 100 years ago, one of the most common forms of government was a **monarchy.** In this system, a king or queen rules the government. The ruler inherits the throne by birth. At one time, many monarchies were forms of unlimited government. That is, the ruler had almost complete authority. Citizens had little say in the affairs of their country.

Monarchies still exist today. Sweden, Denmark, Great Britain, Spain, and Swaziland are examples. However, these monarchies do not have unlimited power. People believe they have the right to participate in running their countries. As a result, the power of the rulers and of government is limited. These countries have **constitutions,** or sets of laws that define and often limit the government's power.

CULTURE In Great Britain's constitutional monarchy, the monarch has little authority. The real power is wielded by Parliament, an elected body like our Congress. **Critical Thinking** If the monarchy has little authority in Great Britain, why do you think it still exists?

Representative Democracy In a **representative democracy,** the people indirectly hold the power to govern and rule. They elect representatives who create laws. If the people do not like what a representative does, they can refuse to re-elect that person. They can also work to change laws they do not like because the citizens have a responsibility to participate in government. They should keep informed about issues affecting the country, and know about the leaders who serve them, and accept responsibility for voting. The United States and Canada are examples of representative democracy.

ACTIVITY

Journal Writing

Living in a Dictatorship Challenge students to write about what it would be like to live in a dictatorship in which they had no power over the government. What would they fear? How would their daily lives be affected? If students have knowledge of life under a particular dictatorship they can write about it in their Explorer's Journal, if they are keeping one.

Verbal/Linguistic

ECONOMICS

Mixed Economic Systems

Sweden is an example of a mixed economy. The government owns mining, public transportation, energy, and telecommunications industries. In addition, the government provides medical care and monetary aid to ensure a high living standard for all.

Resource Directory

Teaching Resources

Vocabulary in the Unit 1 Teaching Resources, p. 45

Critical Thinking in the Unit 1 Teaching Resources, p. 48

Answers to...

CRITICAL THINKING

Answers will vary. Students may say that the monarchy still exists because it is a cultural tradition.

HISTORY

Josef Stalin was one of the world's cruelest dictators. He ruled the former Soviet Union from the 1920s until 1953. He controlled every aspect of Soviet life and jailed or executed anybody who opposed him.

Critical Thinking How do you think dictators gain control of their countries' governments?

Representative democracy developed from direct democracy. However, it took many centuries for modern representative democracy to develop. Gradually citizens began demanding more personal freedoms. They demanded protection from actions of their own government, and wanted a voice in the decisions made by government. The democracy established in the United States provided these rights and freedoms.

Dictatorship A **dictatorship** is a form of government in which one person, the dictator, holds almost total power to govern. It is another type of unlimited government. Dictators decide what happens in their countries. They make the laws and decide if there will be elections. Citizens have few rights. When dictators take over, they often make promises that sound good, like ending crime or providing better social services. Sometimes they keep their promises, but more often, they do not. Either way, people lose the right to make their own decisions.

SECTION 4 ASSESSMENT

AFTER YOU READ

RECALL

1. Define: (a) economy, (b) producer, (c) goods, (d) services, (e) consumer, (f) primary industry, (g) secondary industry, (h) tertiary industry, (i) quaternary industry, (j) traditional economy, (k) market economy, (l) capitalism, (m) free enterprise, (n) command economy, (o) government, (p) direct democracy, (q) monarchy, (r) constitution, (s) representative democracy, (t) dictatorship

COMPREHENSION

2. Describe the basic types of economic activities and give examples of each.
3. What types of economic systems do nations use?
4. What are the differences in the types of government?

CRITICAL THINKING AND WRITING

5. **Exploring the Main Idea** Review the Main Idea statement at the beginning of this section. Which economic and government systems do you think are best? List reasons for your choices.
6. **Drawing Conclusions** The newspaper reports that a new leader has been elected president of a foreign country. The next day, the newspaper reports that the president has declared that the country's representatives will not meet. He has also stated that no elections will be held until further notice. What kind of a government does this country now have? How do you know?

ACTIVITY

7. **Writing to Learn** Imagine that you have begun a project to increase voting in your community. A statewide election is approaching. Write a letter to a newspaper. Describe two reasons why people should vote in the election.

SECTION 4 ASSESSMENT

AFTER YOU READ

1. (a) system for producing, distributing, consuming, and owning goods, services, and wealth, (b) person or business that makes products, (c) products made to be sold, (d) work done for other people, (e) person who buys goods and services, (f) businesses that produce raw materials, (g) businesses that manufacture products, (h) service companies, (i) businesses that use information technology, (j) economy governed by customs, traditions, and habits of the group, (k) economy in which businesses are privately owned and consumers affect the price of goods, (l) similar to market economy, (m) similar to market economy, (n) an economic system where a central agency controls business, (o) system that establishes and enforces the laws and institutions of a society, (p) system of government in which the people participate directly in decision making, (q) system of government headed by a king or queen who inherits the throne, (r) set of laws that defines and limits a government's power, (s) system of government in which the people elect representatives to run the affairs of the country, (t) system of government in which one person holds almost total power
2. Primary industries are companies that produce raw materials. Secondary industries are companies that use raw materials to produce goods. Tertiary industries are service companies. Quaternary industries are companies that use or produce information technologies.
3. They use either a traditional economy, market economy, or command economy.
4. A direct democracy allows every member of a society a voice in all decisions. A representative democracy provides representatives who speak for the people. A monarchy is a government by a king or queen who historically had almost total power. Today, the power of monarchs is limited by a constitution. A dictatorship is rule by one person. Citizens have little say in their government.
5. Most students will choose a market system and a representative democracy.
6. The country has a dictatorship.
7. Answers will vary.

Answers to...

CRITICAL THINKING

Answers will vary. Students may say dictators gain control through force, such as a military coup.

Resource Directory

Teaching Resources

Section Quiz in the Unit I Teaching Resources, p. 43

Chapter Summary in the Unit I Teaching Resources, p. 44

Reteaching in the Unit I Teaching Resources, p. 46

Enrichment in the Unit I Teaching Resources, p. 47

Using Special Purpose Maps

Learn the Skill

Language is a part of culture. People who study languages have divided all of the world's different languages into several groups. English is a part of the Indo-European language family. Languages in the same group may have several things in common, including the same or a similar alphabet. Japanese and Korean alphabets, for example, are completely different from the English alphabet. Spanish and English, on the other hand, have a similar alphabet as well as many similar words.

Language groups can be shown on a special purpose map. This map shows major language groups throughout the world. To read a special purpose map, do the following:

A. Locate the title. This tells you what the map is about. What is the subject of this map?

B. Study the key. This map is color-coded. A different color is used on the map for each of the world's language groups. Count the number of language groups. How many are there? What group includes English and Spanish? What color is it?

C. Check the map itself. Notice that is it a world map. Find North America and South America on the left side of the map. Find Europe, Asia, Africa, Australia, and Antarctica. Are all areas of the world shown on this map?

Practice the Skill

Use the map to answer these questions: What language group can be found in Northern Africa? What are the two main language groups of South America? Where are the Ural-Altaic language groups spoken? What language group can be found in Southern India? Which language group covers the greatest area on the map? Which language group is spoken more in Europe—Ural-Altaic or Indo-European? On how many continents does the Indo-European language group exist?

Apply the Skill

See the Chapter Review and Assessment at the end of this chapter for more questions on special purpose maps.

Major Language Groups

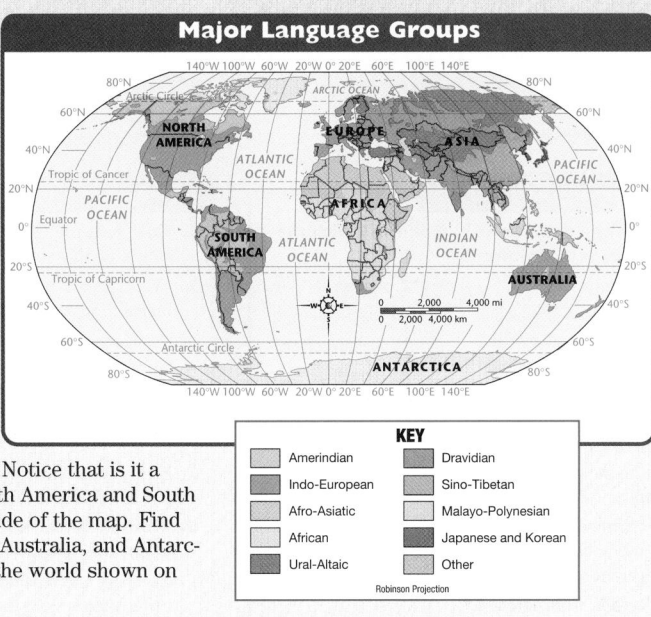

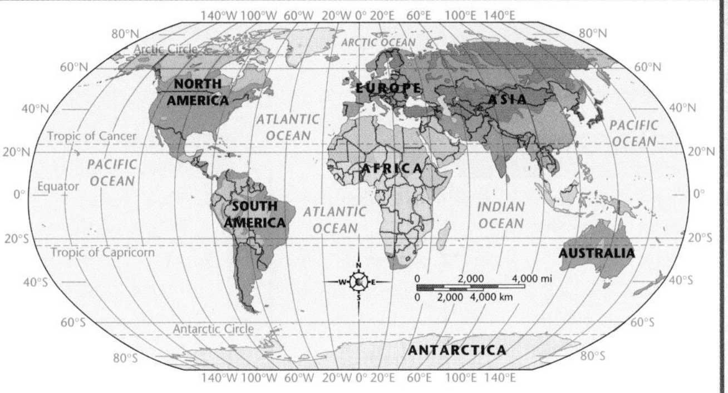

KEY

Amerindian	Dravidian
Indo-European	Sino-Tibetan
Afro-Asiatic	Malayo-Polynesian
African	Japanese and Korean
Ural-Altaic	Other

Robinson Projection

Lesson Objectives

1. Identify the various parts of a special purpose map.
2. Read a special purpose map.

Lesson Plan

1 Engage

To introduce the skill, read the opening text under "Learn the Skill" aloud. Make sure students understand that the key gives language groups, not languages. If students are not familiar with the language group names, explain that this map activity will provide them with a good introduction to a new area of study. Relate the activity to Chapter 1 by asking students to identify the map as a world map.

2 Explore

Direct students to read the steps under "Learn the Skill" and to find the areas referred to. Then, have students answer the questions. Make sure students know how to use the key to determine which language groups are spoken throughout the world.

3 Teach

Have students answer the questions using the map. For additional reinforcement, challenge students to write their own questions and have a partner answer them.

4 Assess/Reteach

Students should be able to answer questions regarding the special purpose map.

To further assess students' understanding of special purpose maps, have them complete the "Applying Your Skills" part of the Chapter Review and Assessment at the end of this chapter.

Resource Directory

Teaching Resources

Social Studies and Geography Skills, Reading a Population Distribution Map, p. 31; Reading a Natural Resources Map, p. 32

Technology

Social Studies Skills Tutor CD-ROM

Answers to...

PRACTICE THE SKILL

Afro-Asiatic; Amerindian and Indo-European; Asia and Europe; Dravidian; Indo-European; Indo-European; six

CHAPTER 3

Review and Assessment

Creating a Chapter Summary

Student summaries will vary.

Sample summary:

Population Answers will vary. Sample summary: The Earth's population is distributed unevenly. Some countries have high population densities, while others have low densities. The population on our planet is growing rapidly.

Culture Answers will vary. Sample summary: Culture is the way of life of a group of people who share similar beliefs and customs. Culture includes the work people do, their behaviors, their beliefs, their ways of doing things, and their artistic, creative, and literary expressions. Cultures choose how to organize their economies and government. These choices provide citizens with greater or lesser freedom.

Economic and Political Institutions An economy is a way of producing, distributing, and consuming goods and services. Government is the system that sets up and enforces society's laws and institutions.

Reviewing Key Terms

1. b **2.** c **3.** d **4.** e **5.** a

Reviewing the Main Ideas

1. People tend to settle in regions where the climate, landforms, vegetation, water supply and other geographic features provide a comfortable environment.
2. The factors are a decrease in death rate, increase in birthrate, and the Green Revolution.
3. "Push" factors include wars, lack of jobs, changes in governments, the search for a better life, and lack of land. "Pull" factors include the promise of better living conditions, similar climate and vegetation, the expectation of owning land, and more freedom.
4. People are moving from rural to urban areas to find jobs, homes, and opportunities to improve their lives.
5. Culture is a group's shared way of life. It determines the work people do, their behaviors, their beliefs, their ways of doing things, and their artistic, creative, and literary expressions.
6. Possible answers: government, economic, educational, religious, and family institutions
7. In a traditional economic system, economic activities are governed by culture and traditions. People often follow in their parents' footsteps in choosing occupations. In a market economy, businesses are privately owned, and consumers have a strong influence on prices of goods through their buying preferences. In a command economy, a central agency controls businesses. It sets prices and amounts produced.
8. direct democracy, monarchy, representative democracy, dictatorship

CHAPTER 3

Review and Assessment

Creating a Chapter Summary

On a sheet of paper, draw a chart like this one. Include the information that has already been completed. Then, complete the remaining boxes with details summarizing what you have learned.

Population	Migration	Culture	Economic and Political Institutions
	People migrate for many reasons. Sometimes, certain things, such as war, "push" them to leave. Other times they leave because hope for better conditions "pulls" them to another place. One effect of migration is rapid urbanization.		

Reviewing Key Terms

Match the definitions in Column I with the key terms in Column II.

Column I

1. growth of city populations caused by the movement of people to cities
2. products that are made to be sold
3. the average number of people living in an area
4. economic system in which businesses are privately owned
5. area in which most of the people share the same cultural traits

Column II

a. culture region
b. urbanization
c. goods
d. population density
e. market economy

Reviewing the Main Ideas

1. How does the Earth's physical geography affect where people settle? (Section 1)
2. What factors are causing a rapid increase in human population? (Section 1)
3. What are some conditions that push people to leave their country and pull them to migrate to another country? (Section 2)
4. Why are people in many parts of the world moving from rural to urban areas? (Section 2)
5. How does culture affect what a group does and believes? (Section 3)
6. What are three institutions that are basic to all cultures? (Section 3)
7. Compare the traditional, market, and command economic systems. (Section 4)
8. What systems have societies developed for organizing their governments? (Section 4)

Map Activity

Continents

For each place listed below, write the letter from the map that shows its location.

1. Asia
2. Antarctica
3. Africa
4. South America
5. North America
6. Europe
7. Australia

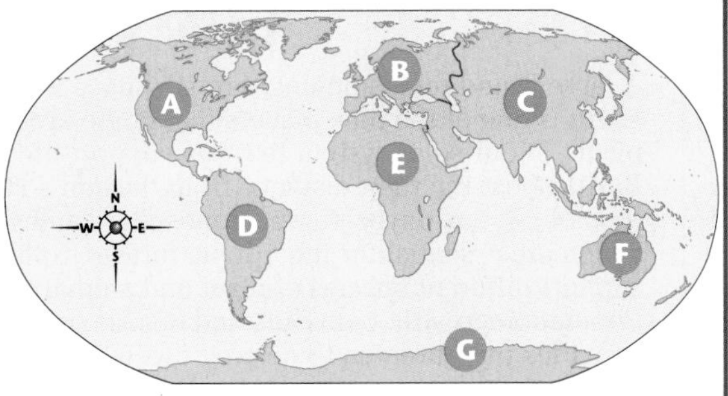

Take It to the NET

Enrichment For more map activities using geography skills, visit the social studies section of **phschool.com.**

Writing Activity

1. **Writing a Report** Visit your school or local library and gather information to learn how the population of your state has changed in the past fifty years. Write a brief report explaining why people migrated to or from your state.
2. **Writing a Public Service Message** Imagine that your town is having a "culture fair." The fair will introduce people to cultures from other countries. It will also introduce people to different cultures within the United States. Write a public service message for the fair for the local radio station. A public service message includes the time, place, and purpose of the event. It should also tell people how and why they should get involved with the fair.

Critical Thinking

1. **Recognizing Cause and Effect** How have Africa's landforms and climate affected its population distribution?
2. **Drawing Conclusions** Explain the meaning of this statement: "Today, many countries of the world are becoming more urban." What does this statement tell you about the movement of people?

Applying Your Skills

Turn to the Skills for Life activity on p. 57 to help you complete the following activity.

Use your school or local library or the Internet to find information on a cultural topic such as distribution of ethnic groups, religions, or types of music in the United States. Using this information, draw a special purpose map of the United States that shows this information. Then, write a series of questions to test an understanding of the map. Trade your map and questions with a partner and answer each other's questions.

Take It to the NET

Activity Patterns of human migration have shaped cultures and regions around the world. What impact has migration had on the region in which you live? Visit the World Explorer: People, Places, and Cultures section of **phschool.com** for help in completing this activity.

Chapter 3 Self-Test As a final review activity, take the Chapter 3 Self-Test and get instant feedback on your answers. To take the test, visit the Social Studies section of **phschool.com.**

Map Activity

1. C **2.** G **3.** E **4.** D **5.** A **6.** B **7.** F

Writing Activity

1. Answers will vary, depending on the state. Sample answer: The state of Washington's population has grown rapidly over the last 50 years. State population was just under 3 million people in 1960, rising to almost 5.5 million people in the mid-1990s. Over the last five years, population has grown almost 10 percent. Many factors have contributed to the growth. Washington has a mild climate that is dominated by the Pacific Ocean and protected by the Rocky Mountains. Seattle is a major port city. Many computer/technology companies thrive. Year-round outdoor recreation, state parks, and beaches make the state a very pleasant place to live.
2. Students' messages should include good reasons why people should attend and also participate in the culture fair.

Critical Thinking

1. Africa has two huge deserts, one in the north and one in the south, large areas of lands that receive little rainfall, and rain forest along the Equator. Thus most people live along the coasts.
2. People are moving from rural areas to the cities.

Applying Your Skills

1. Students' maps will vary, but should include the elements discussed in the "Skills for Life" activity, including a map title and map key.

Resource Directory

Teaching Resources

Cooperative Learning Activity in the Unit 1 Teaching Resources, pp. 72–75

Chapter Tests Forms A and B in the Unit 1 Teaching Resources, pp. 94–99

Guide to the Essentials, Ch. 3 Test, p. 13

Unit Test Forms A and B in the Unit 1 Teaching Resources, pp. 100–105

Other Print Resources

Chapter Tests with ExamView® Test Bank, Ch. 3

Technology

ExamView® Test Bank CD-ROM, Ch. 3

Resource Pro® CD-ROM

UNIT I

Introduction

The introduction on the student page on the right provides key facts and general information about the Earth.

- Students should read the introduction first to gain a basic knowledge of the subject before reading on.
- Have students read all of the subentries, which provide further information on the earth, particularly focusing on the formation. Have students also read the annotations that accompany and explain the photos and illustrations.
- When students have finished reading all of the information, discuss the connections between the information on these pages and what they have learned about how geography affects life on our planet.

ACTIVITY

Creating a Model of the Earth

Have students work with partners to create three-dimensional models of the Earth. Partners should first gather information on the major landforms and physical features of the Earth, such as oceans, continents, and islands. Supply each group with a Styrofoam ball that can be used to represent the planet. Students can cut away a portion of the ball to show the mantle and the outer and inner core. Have them use clay, papier mache, and found objects to depict landforms and features of the Earth's surface. Groups should share their models with the rest of the class and use them to create a classroom display.

Visual/Spatial

Adapted from the Dorling Kindersley Illustrated Children's Encyclopedia

The Earth

A large round rock spinning through space is our home in the universe. The Earth is one of the nine planets that circle around the sun, and it is the only planet in our solar system that can support life. Unlike the other planets, the Earth is just the right distance from the sun so that it is not too hot and not too cold. It has oxygen in the atmosphere and water in the oceans, both of which are essential for life. Alpine forests, rolling prairies, and vast deserts all support different species of plant and animal life in a fragile balance of nature. Population growth, pollution, and misuse of natural resources are human activities that threaten to destroy this balance.

? How do geographic features influence population centers around the globe? What can people do to preserve the balance of nature that is critical to the future of the planet?

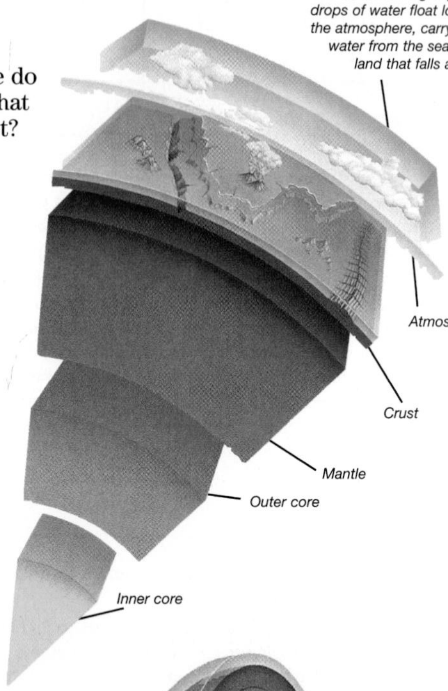

Clouds containing tiny drops of water float low in the atmosphere, carrying water from the seas and land that falls as rain.
Atmosphere
Crust
Mantle
Outer core
Inner core

OCEANS
The oceans are large water-filled hollows in the Earth's crust. Their average depth is 2.2 miles (3.5 km).

CRUST
The top layer of rock at the Earth's surface is called the crust. It can be 44 miles (70 km) deep below the continents but only 4 miles (6 km) deep below the ocean floor. The temperature at the bottom of the crust is about 1,900°F (1,050°C).

MANTLE
Under the Earth's crust is the mantle. It is a layer of rock about 1,800 miles (2,900 km) thick. At the base of the mantle, the temperature can be as high as 6,700°F (3,700°C). The high pressure pushing against the mantle keeps it from turning into a liquid.

OUTER CORE
The center of the Earth has an outer core. It is about 1,240 miles (2,000 km) thick and is made of liquid iron. Its temperature is about 4,000°F (2,200°C).

INNER CORE
The center of the Earth is a ball of solid iron and nickel. It is about 1,712 miles (2,740 km) across. Its temperature is about 8,100°F (4,500°C).

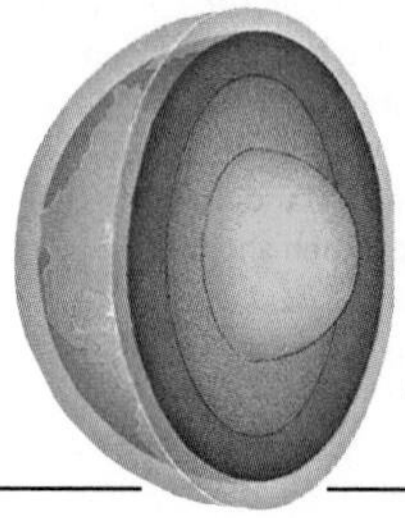

The Earth is made of layers of air, water, iron, nickel, and rock around a core of iron and nickel.

60 UNIT I GEOGRAPHY

GEOGRAPHY

The Geography of the Earth

The geography of the different regions of the Earth influences everything from where people live to their political systems. Landforms that developed over millions of years determine the location and availability of natural resources, and the way in which human populations are distributed over the Earth's surface. Understand-ing the Earth and its geography will help students appreciate the need for conservation and care of our atmosphere, land, and oceans, and the resources they provide.

GEOGRAPHY

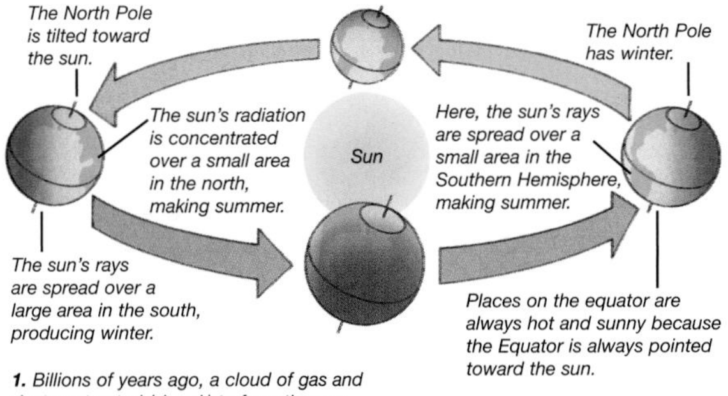

The North Pole is tilted toward the sun.
The sun's radiation is concentrated over a small area in the north, making summer.
Sun
The North Pole has winter.
Here, the sun's rays are spread over a small area in the Southern Hemisphere, making summer.
The sun's rays are spread over a large area in the south, producing winter.
Places on the equator are always hot and sunny because the Equator is always pointed toward the sun.

Seasons

North and south of the Equator, seasons change as the Earth moves around the sun. The Earth is tilted at an angle of 23.5° compared to its orbit. This angle makes the poles point toward or away from the sun at different times of the year.

Formation of the Earth

Scientists have calculated that the Earth is billions of years old. Some moon rocks and meteorites (pieces of rock that fall to the Earth from space) are the same age, which suggests that the whole solar system formed at the same time. The sun, the Earth, and the other planets were formed from a huge cloud of gas and dust in space.

1. Billions of years ago, a cloud of gas and dust contracted (shrank) to form the sun. The rest of the cloud then contracted even more. It broke up into large clumps made up of particles of ice and rock. After a short time, the particles stuck to each other and began to form the planets.

2. When the Earth was forming, rock particles crashing into each other made the planet very hot. The surface was liquid and gave off a red-hot glow. It took the Earth about 100 million years to form into a ball of rock.

3. Radioactivity in the rock particles produced heat. The whole planet melted. Liquid iron sank to the center of the Earth to form the core. Lighter rocks floated above the iron. The surface cooled to form the crust. Volcanoes erupted and poured out gases. These gases formed the atmosphere. Steam from the volcanoes turned to a liquid and filled the world's oceans with water.

4. About 3.5 billion years ago, tiny living things began to grow. About 2.5 billion years ago, some of these organisms produced oxygen. The oxygen began to build up in the atmosphere. Parts of the crust broke up and slowly moved to create the world's landforms as they are today.

Theories of the Earth

People once believed that the Earth was flat. About 2,500 years ago, the Greeks found out that the Earth is round. In 260 B.C., a Greek scientist named Aristarchus suggested that the Earth moves around the sun. It was not until 1543 that Polish astronomer Nicolaus Copernicus (1473–1543) proved that Aristarchus was right.

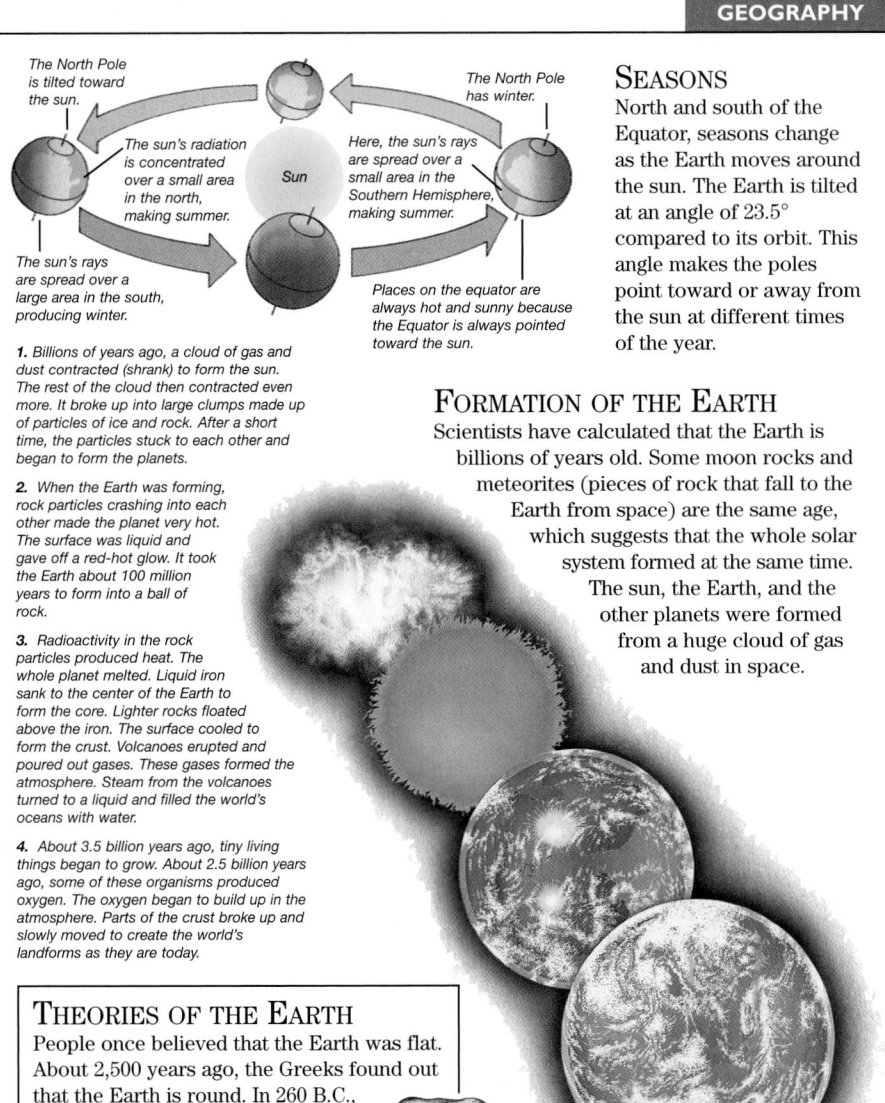

ACTIVITY

Creating a Continental Profile

Have students form small groups. Assign one of the Earth's continents to each group and have them work together to create a continental profile. Students can find out the highest and lowest elevations, largest city, main resources, busiest port, largest and smallest nation, deepest lake, longest river, and similar information for their continent. Groups should present their findings to the class in a chart, annotated map, or other graphic organizer. Groups can use the data collected to make global comparisons.

Verbal/Linguistic

GEOGRAPHY

Prince Henry the Navigator

Prince Henry the Navigator of Portugal was known for his passion for exploration and search for knowledge about the Earth. Although he never participated in any of the seafaring expeditions that he sponsored, he was a key figure in the Age of Exploration and the quest for a westerly route to the East. In 1418, Henry founded the Institute at Sagres, located at Cape Saint Vincent, once known as the western edge of the Earth. There, scientists, cartographers, and geographers from all over the world studied in the library, used the observatory, designed vessels for the ship-building facility, taught navigation, and collected and compiled the geographical information brought home by explorers.

THE EARTH 61

UNIT 2

Introducing the Unit

This unit was developed around seven strands of essential knowledge and skills that relate to the study of people, places, and cultures of the contemporary world. These strands include **History, Geography, Economics, Government, Citizenship, Culture,** and **Science, Technology, and Society.** These seven strands, and the related Guiding Questions on the next pages, are intended as an organizational focus for the unit. All of the chapter content, activities, questions, and assessments relate to the seven strands, which act as an umbrella under which all of the material falls. In this unit, students will learn to identify the locations and geographic characteristics of the United States and Canada, learn about different economic and governmental systems in the United States and Canada, compare different cultural institutions, and learn how technology affects societies in the United States and Canada.

Using the Pictures

Invite students to discuss the photographs and captions on these pages. Use them as a prompt for a discussion of what students know about history, geography, economics, government, citizenship, culture, and science and technology.

- You may want to begin a K-W-L chart on the chalkboard for the United States and Canada, with the headings What We **K**now, What We **W**ant to Know, and What We **L**earned.
- Have students fill in the first column with several things they agree they already know. Then, ask them to brainstorm what they would like to know about the United States and Canada to add to the second column.
- Students can fill in the third column as they work through the text.

eTeach

Be sure to check out this month's discussion with a Master Teacher. Go to **phschool.com**.

UNIT 2

Welcome to The United States and Canada

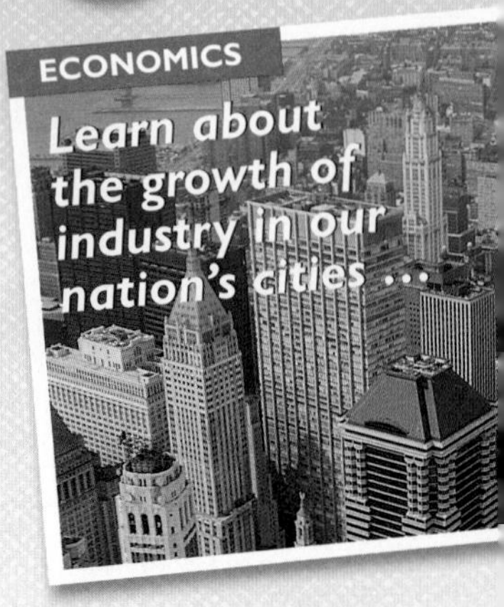

ECONOMICS *Learn about the growth of industry in our nation's cities ...*

SCIENCE, TECHNOLOGY, AND SOCIETY *Learn how technology helped people settle the West ...*

CULTURE *Study the creative arts of Canada's native people ...*

Resource Directory

Teaching Resources

Program Overview includes a guide to the Prentice Hall World Explorer program. You may wish to refer to the overview as you plan your instruction.

Pacing Charts for Unit 2 offer a variety of course configurations.

What do you want to learn?

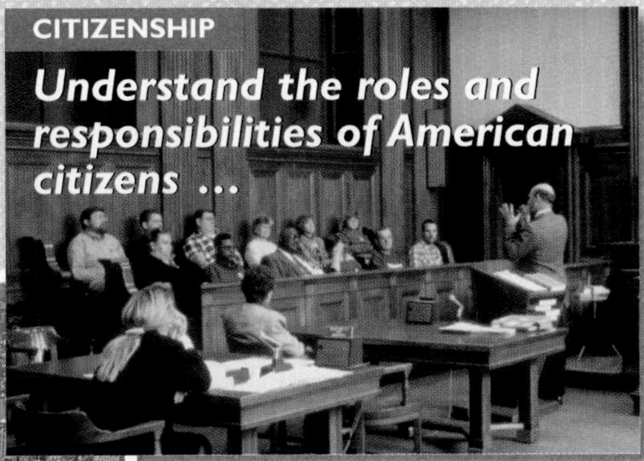

CITIZENSHIP
Understand the roles and responsibilities of American citizens ...

Witness Quebec's vote on independence ...

GEOGRAPHY
Climb one of the region's tallest mountains ...

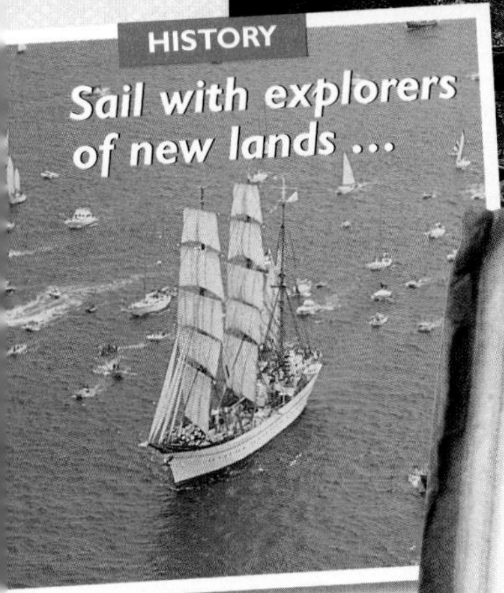

Sail with explorers of new lands ...

A journal can be your personal record of discovery. As you learn about the United States and Canada, you can include journal entries about what you read, write, think, and create. For your first entry, write your thoughts on where in the United States and Canada you would like to go and what you would want to see there.

Resource Directory

Technology

Social Studies Skills Tutor CD-ROM provides two levels of interactive instruction and practice in 20 core social studies skills.

Resource Pro® CD-ROM allows you to create customized lesson plans and print all resources directly from the CD-ROM.

Using the Explorer's Journal

Have students begin their Explorer's Journal as the paragraph on the student book page suggests. If at all possible, encourage students to use a separate small notebook for their Explorer's Journal entries. They can add to this journal as they learn more about the United States and Canada.

Project Possibilities

The projects in this book are designed to provide students with hands-on involvement in the content area. Write the following project ideas on the chalkboard and have students preview them and discuss which they might want to do. Students should work in pairs or small groups to complete the activities.

Writing a Children's Book

Write a short book for young students about a topic in the United States and Canada. In your story, include information about one or more of the cultures in one of these two countries.

Make a Timeline of Local History

Make an illustrated timeline of the history of your community. In your timeline, include information about contributions to your community made by individuals or groups.

Set Up a Weather Station

Keep a log of local weather conditions. Compare your weather to other parts of the U.S. and Canada. Write a paragraph describing how the weather patterns affect the way people live in this region.

Introducing

Guiding Questions

The Guiding Questions that appear on the reduced student edition pages to the right should act as a guide for learning about the United States and Canada and for encouraging students to relate what they learn to their own experience. The Guiding Questions that relate to the content of each chapter in the unit also appear on the Chapter Opener pages in this Teacher's Edition.

- You may wish to add your own Guiding Questions to the list in order to tailor them to your particular course. Or, as a group activity, ask your class to develop its own Guiding Questions.

ACTIVITY

Using the Guiding Questions

Ask a volunteer to read aloud the Guiding Questions to the class. These questions will guide students as they learn about the United States and Canada.

- Have students write the seven headings on a separate piece of paper or in their Explorer's Journal. Have them think about what information they would like to learn about the United States and Canada, and write a question that relates to each heading.
- Create a master list of questions grouped under the seven headings. As you read about the United States and Canada, try to answer the questions on the list.
- At the end of the unit, if any questions remain unanswered, have students research and find the answers to those questions.

Guiding Questions

What questions do I need to ask to understand the United States and Canada?

Asking questions is a good way to learn. Think about what information you would want to know if you were visiting a new place, and what questions you might ask to find the answers. The questions on these pages can help guide your study of the United States and Canada. You might want to try adding a few of your own!

GEOGRAPHY

The United States and Canada offer a rich variety of physical features that have affected the history and settlement patterns of these two nations. Vast regions of desert and tundra, rich farming plains, and natural harbors and waterways have greatly affected where and how people live. As people have learned to adapt to and modify the physical environment, they have used these geographic factors to build prosperous nations.

1 How has physical geography affected the settlement patterns and the economies of the United States and Canada?

HISTORY

The early history of the United States and Canada is full of challenges, victories, and conflicts. Europeans arriving in the Americas struggled with native peoples for control of the land, and later, England and France fought for control of territories. The American colonies fought for, and won, their independence from Britain, and went on to build a powerful nation. In both Canada and the United States, citizens have worked to maintain their freedom and unity as a people.

2 How have historical events affected the cultures of the United States and Canada?

CULTURE

When European settlers arrived in what is now the United States and Canada, they brought elements of their own cultures with them, and also adopted the ways of the native people. As the nations grew and welcomed immigrants from around the world, these citizens contributed to what would become new, uniquely diverse cultures.

3 How has cultural diversity benefited and challenged these two nations?

GOVERNMENT

The governments of the United States and Canada have evolved from colonial rule to democratic forms of government in which the people have a strong voice. In its early history, not all citizens of the United States had a voice in government. Today, however, people in both countries are working to ensure equal representation of all citizens.

4 How have the United States and Canada developed the strong, democratic forms of government they have today?

ECONOMICS

The United States and Canada are rich in fertile lands that have made both countries important agricultural producers. Natural resources such as minerals and lumber have contributed to the economies of both nations. With the development of industry, the two nations have grown into world economic powers.

5 How did the United States and Canada become two of the wealthiest nations in the world?

CITIZENSHIP

In both the United States and Canada, citizens are encouraged to participate in the political process through voting, running for public office, and speaking out about important issues. In both countries, individual citizens are free to voice their opinions, and to work to guarantee individual rights and equal justice for all people within the nation.

6 How have ordinary citizens in the United States and Canada worked to achieve justice and equality for all?

SCIENCE, TECHNOLOGY, AND SOCIETY

Since the 1800s, technology has been used to improve farming, manufacturing, and health care in the United States and Canada. Today, the economies of both nations rely heavily on technology in industry, and are using new methods to help improve and protect the environment. In addition, both countries are world leaders in scientific research.

7 How has modern technology both benefited and created challenges for the United States and Canada?

Take It to the NET

For more information on the United States and Canada, visit the World Explorer: People, Places, and Cultures companion Web site at **phschool.com.**

ACTIVITY

Using Primary and Secondary Sources

History Ask students to think about their own daily routines and how those routines are affected by the history of their country or their community. Discuss what life might have been like in their community, or in other parts of the country, in the past, and how it might have been different from life today. Have students work in pairs to create an outline that shows the activities they do on a typical day. Then, have each pair choose a time period, such as a time previous to the arrival of Europeans, a period from the first settlements, colonial times, the 1800s, or the early 1900s. Have students research that time period to try to find information on the daily activities of the people who lived then. Encourage students to use primary resources in their research, including letters, interviews, biographies, and Internet sources.

Verbal/Linguistic

ACTIVITY ATLAS

Lesson Objectives

1. Describe the size and relative location of Canada and the United States.
2. Relate land use in Canada and the United States to each country's physical features.
3. Analyze major climate regions in Canada and the United States.
4. Compare significant physical features of the United States and Canada.

Lesson Plan

1 Engage

Warm-Up Activity

Invite students to describe some physical features near their homes. Urge students to list the features or write a short descriptive paragraph about them.

Activating Prior Knowledge

Ask students why it might be important, as U.S. residents, to learn both about other parts of the United States as well as the neighboring country of Canada.

ACTIVITY ATLAS

The United States and Canada

To learn about Canada and the United States, start by checking some facts. Begin by exploring the maps of the United States and Canada and answering the questions on the following pages.

Relative Location

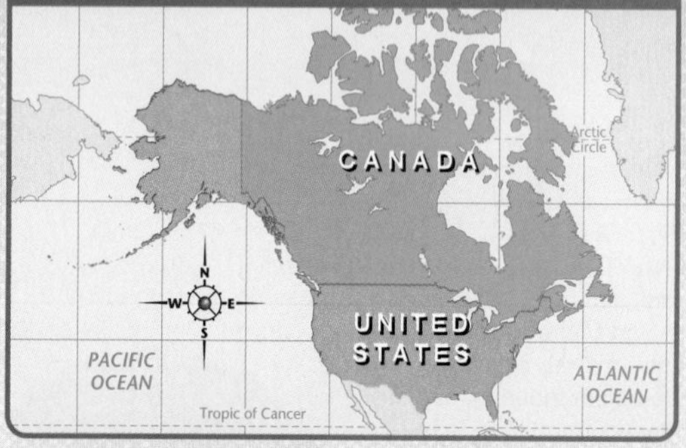

1. LOCATION

Locate the United States and Canada Look at the map at the left. In this unit, you will read about the United States, which is colored orange on the map, and Canada, which is green. Which country extends farther north? If you were on the east coast of the United States, which direction would you travel to get to the Pacific Ocean?

Relative Size

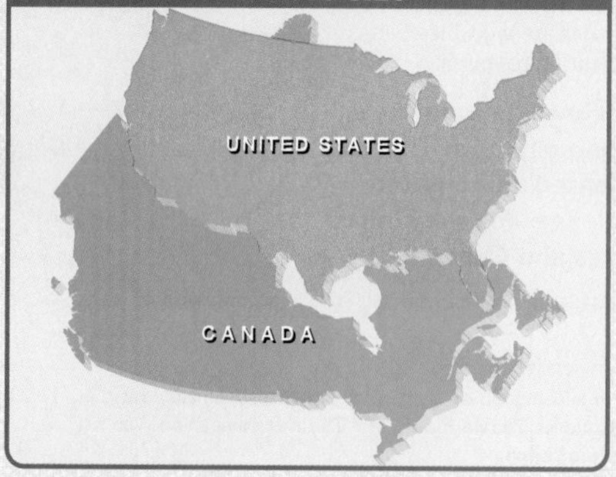

2. REGIONS

Compare the United States and Canada Look at the map to the left. Compare it to the map above. Notice that not all of the United States is shown on the second map. Which country do you think is bigger, the United States mainland or Canada?

Take It to the NET

Items marked with this logo are periodically updated on the Internet. To get current information about the geography of the United States and Canada, go to **phschool.com.**

Answers to...

LOCATION

1. Canada extends farther north than does the United States. To get to the Pacific Ocean from the east coast, travel west.

REGIONS

2. Canada is larger than the United States.

Resource Directory

Teaching Resources

Activity Atlas in the Unit 2 Teaching Resources, pp. 95–103

United States and Canada: Political

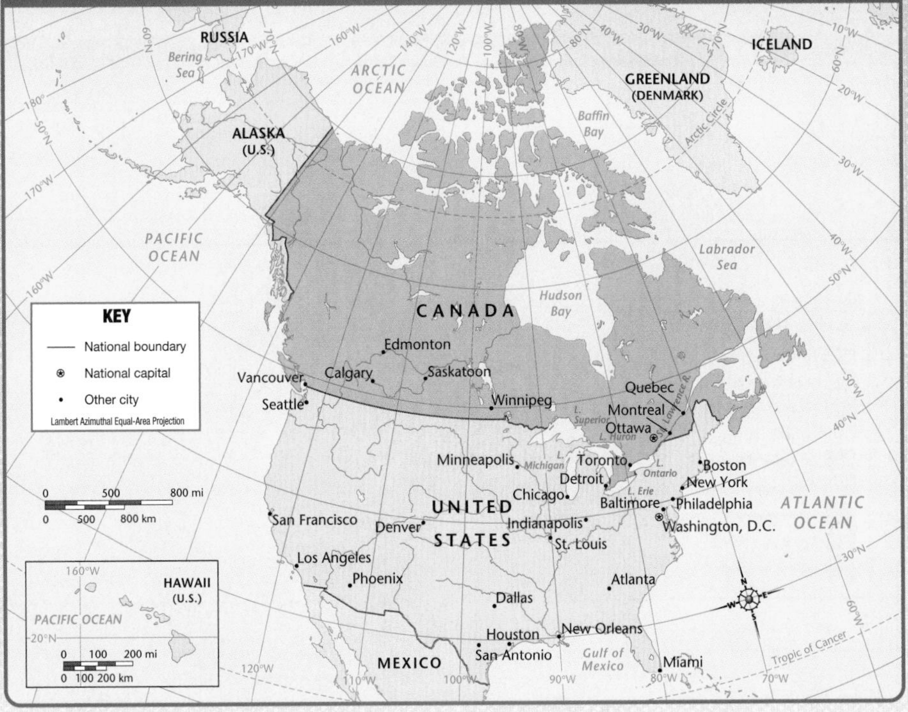

3. LOCATION

Identify Places in the United States and Canada The United States and Canada together take up most of the continent of North America. Look at the map. What other country is on the same continent? What country borders Canada? What countries border the United States? Name the cities that are the national capitals of the United States and Canada. What two states in the United States do not share a border with any other state? Which of the Canadian cities on the map is the farthest south? North?

4. PLACE

Locate Bodies of Water in the United States and Canada Rivers, lakes, and oceans are vital to a nation's development. Look at the map. What three oceans border the United States and Canada? Find the Great Lakes on the map. How many are there? Which one lies entirely within the United States? What river connects the Great Lakes to the Atlantic Ocean? The largest bay in the world is located in Canada. What is its name? Would you enter the bay from the Pacific Ocean or from the Atlantic Ocean?

2 Explore

Direct students to read the Activity Atlas. Urge them to take notes as they read.

3 Teach

On the chalkboard, model a Venn diagram by labeling one circle *Canada* and the other *United States.* Create an overlap labeled *Shared Features.* Have students use data from the Activity Atlas to complete the diagram.

4 Assess/Reteach

Diagrams should note that both Canada and the United States are on the same continent, and that they share many climatic and physical features. Diagrams should identify Canada as having colder climates and less farming and manufacturing. They should note that the United States has warmer climates and more farming and manufacturing.

Resource Directory

Teaching Resources

Outline Maps United States and Canada, pp. 12–13

Technology

Color Transparencies 28 The United States and Canada: Physical-Political Map

Answers to...

LOCATION

3. Mexico is also part of North America. The United States borders Canada. Canada and Mexico border the United States. Ottawa is Canada's capital; Washington, D.C., is the U.S. capital. Alaska and Hawaii do not share a border with any other state. Toronto; Edmonton

PLACE

4. The Arctic, Pacific, and Atlantic Oceans surround the United States and Canada. There are five Great Lakes. Lake Michigan is entirely within the United States. The St. Lawrence River connects the Great Lakes to the Atlantic. Hudson Bay; the Atlantic Ocean

ACTIVITY ATLAS

Practice in the Themes of Geography

Instruct students to use the maps in the Activity Atlas to complete the following questions and activities concerning the five themes of geography.

Place Have students create two postcards—one describing a place in Canada, the other describing a place in the United States. Encourage students to illustrate their postcards and provide some geographical clues. Encourage students to "send" their postcards to a classmate and have the classmate identify the location.

Regions Ask students to identify a mountain range shared by Canada and the United States (the Rocky Mountains).

Movement Ask students how climate might challenge the movement of people and goods in Canada's Northwest Territories. (Extreme cold, icy conditions, and storms may cause difficulties.)

Interaction Have students identify areas on the land use map where there is little or no activity. Then have them locate those regions on the climate map. Have students draw conclusions about climatic conditions and land use.

Location Have students identify cities in the United States and Canada located on or near the two nations' shared border (Canada: Vancouver, Winnipeg, Quebec, Montreal, Ottawa, Toronto; United States: Seattle, Detroit).

Answers to...

HUMAN-ENVIRONMENT INTERACTION

5. nine; hunting and gathering; commercial farming; students may say that the climate is too cold to support other uses of the land.

REGIONS

6. Bodies of water, such as lakes, rivers, and oceans, are close to most manufacturing areas because it makes the transportation of raw materials and goods easier.

ACTIVITY ATLAS

Take It to the NET

United States and Canada: Land Use

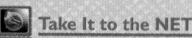

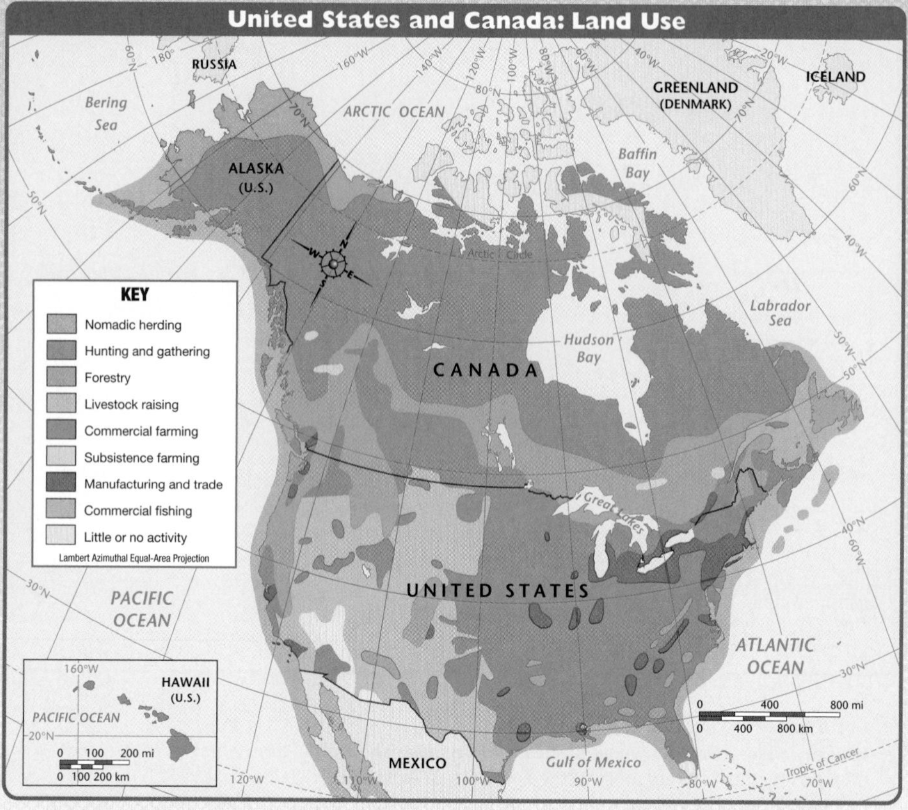

5. HUMAN-ENVIRONMENT INTERACTION

Compare Land Use in the United States and Canada How many different types of land use are identified on this map? Which is the most common use of the land in Canada? In the United States? Why do you think hunting and gathering is the most common use of land in northern Canada?

6. REGIONS

Compare Land Use to Physical Features Look at the physical map on the next page. Compare it to the land use map above. What physical feature is close to most manufacturing areas? Why do you think manufacturing areas are located near these features?

7. LOCATION

Identify Relative Location A friend is traveling around North America. She sends you postcards with clues to her whereabouts. Use her clues and the map below to identify her relative location in the United States and Canada.

A. *Whew! I've been hiking through the Rocky Mountains! Right now I'm heading south. I just crossed the Colorado River. What country am I in?*

B. *Today, I crossed the northern border of the United States, and I'm flying to Vancouver Island in Canada. In which direction am I traveling?*

C. *Now I'm on a ship. We're heading from the Gulf of St. Lawrence to the Great Lakes. What river will we travel on?*

United States and Canada: Physical

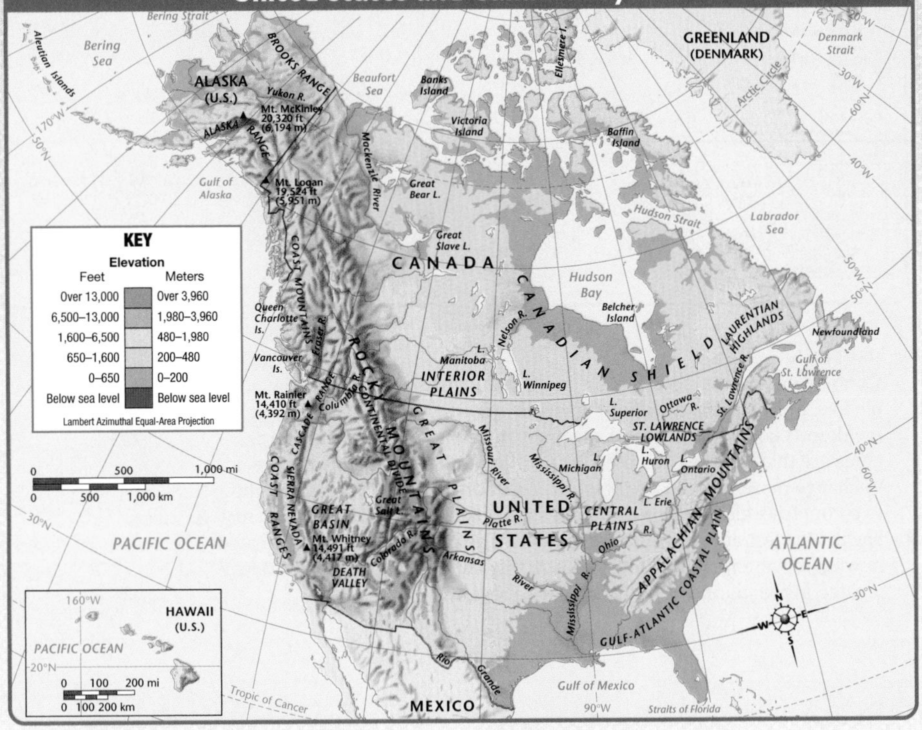

GEOGRAPHY

Acid Rain

Activities in the United States have contributed to environmental damage in Canada. As emissions generated by U.S. automobiles and industries rise into the atmosphere, winds blow them toward Canada's eastern lands. These pollutants combine with moisture in the atmosphere and fall as acid rain. This rain has polluted some of Canada's rivers, streams, and lakes. It also threatens wildlife and damages buildings.

Resource Directory

Teaching Resources

Outline Maps United States and Canada, pp. 12–13

Technology

Color Transparencies 28 The United States and Canada: Physical-Political Map

Answers to...

LOCATION

7. **A.** the United States
   B. west
   C. St. Lawrence River

ACTIVITY ATLAS

ACTIVITY

Interdisciplinary Connections

Science Have students use an atlas or an almanac to locate average monthly temperatures and precipitation figures for four major cities in different regions of the United States and Canada. Have students collect data for the months of January, April, July, and October. Then have students find the same data for your community. Students may display the data in a chart. Have students use their charts to identify which cities experience climatic conditions most similar to and most different from your community.

Verbal/Linguistic

ACTIVITY ATLAS

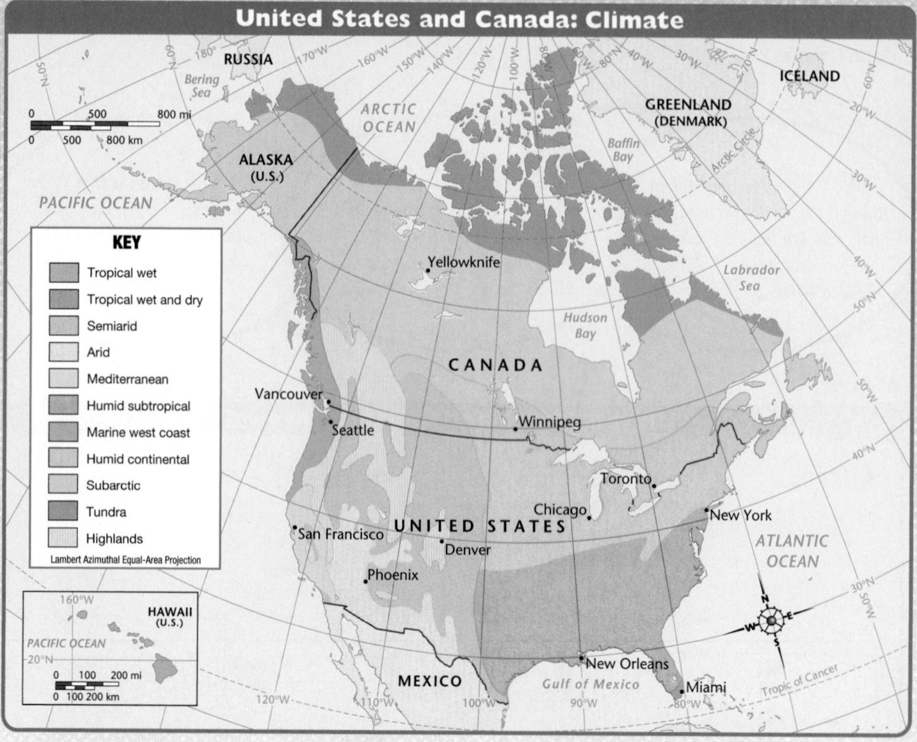

8. REGIONS

Compare Climates You already know that climate affects the way people live. For example, you don't find snowplows on the beach or skis in the desert! Look at this map. How many different types of climate regions are there in the United States and Canada? Do the climates seem to change more from east to west or from north to south? Which of the two countries has a region of humid subtropical climate? Which country has the biggest area of subarctic climate? The city of Winnipeg is located in what climate region? Which cities in the United States and Canada are located in the marine west coast climate region?

Answers to...

REGIONS

8. There are 11 different climate regions. There is a more extreme change from north to south. The United States has a humid subtropical region. Canada has the biggest area of subarctic climate. Winnipeg is located in the humid continental climate region. Vancouver and Seattle are located in the marine west coast climate region.

Resource Directory

Teaching Resources

Social Studies and Geography Skills, Reading a Climate Map, p. 24

The Tallest, Longest, Largest, and Deepest...

THE TALLEST MOUNTAINS OF THE UNITED STATES AND CANADA

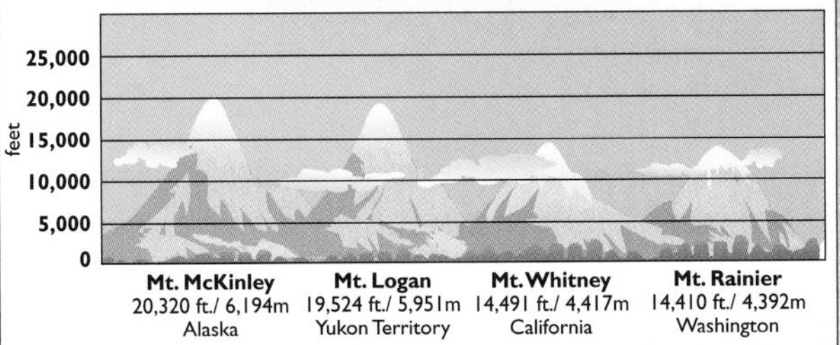

THE LONGEST RIVERS OF THE UNITED STATES AND CANADA

River	Mouth	Length
Mackenzie	Beaufort Sea	2,635 mi/4,241 km
Mississippi	Gulf of Mexico	2,348 mi/3,779 km
Missouri	Mississippi River	2,315 mi/3,726 km
Yukon	Bering Sea	1,979 mi/3,185 km
St. Lawrence	Gulf of St. Lawrence	1,900 mi/3,058 km
Rio Grande	Gulf of Mexico	1,885 mi/3,034 km
Arkansas	Mississippi River	1,459 mi/2,348 km

THE LARGEST LAKES OF THE UNITED STATES AND CANADA

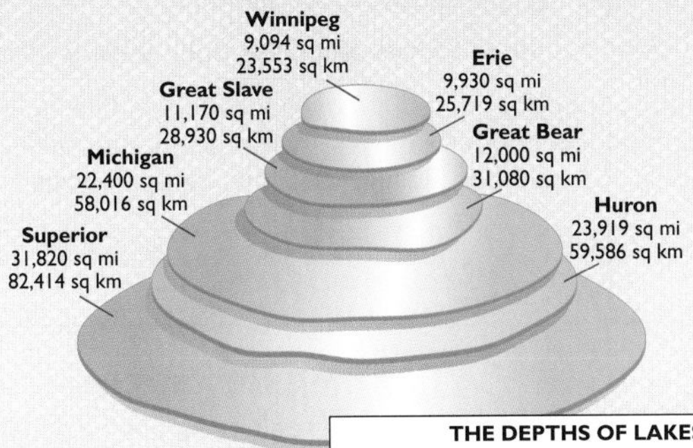

THE DEPTHS OF LAKES IN THE UNITED STATES AND CANADA

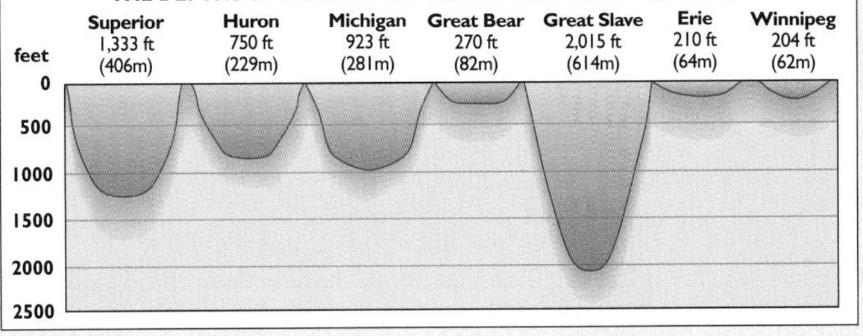

9. PLACE

Compare Physical Features The United States and Canada have many different types of landforms. Study the charts, graphs, and diagrams on this page. Locate each of the landforms on the maps in this Activity Atlas. How much deeper is Great Slave Lake than Lake Superior? Which river is almost twice as long as the Arkansas River? How much bigger is Lake Huron than Lake Winnipeg? Which rivers have their mouths, or end, in other rivers? Where would you go to climb the highest mountain in the United States and Canada?

ACTIVITY

Discovery Learning

Scouting Locations Have students choose one of the following roles: travel agent, filmmaking locations scout, or real estate agent. In pairs, students should first brainstorm the features each agent would be seeking. Then, one student can pose as a "client," presenting a list of required features to the "agent" student. For example, the client might ask the agent for a place that has a humid continental climate and is located near one of the Great Lakes. The agent must then locate a place in Canada or the United States possessing the requested features. Have pairs switch roles.

Logical/Mathematical

Resource Directory

Teaching Resources

Social Studies and Geography Skills, Reading a Bar Graph, p. 51; Reading a Diagram, p. 54

Answers to...

PLACE

9. Great Slave Lake is about 682 ft (208 m) deeper than Lake Superior. The Mackenzie River is almost twice as long as the Arkansas River. Lake Huron is about 14,825 sq mi (36,033 sq km) larger than Lake Winnipeg. The Missouri and Arkansas Rivers both end in the Mississippi. The highest mountain is Mt. McKinley in the United States (Alaska).

Chapter 4 Planning Guide

Resource Manager

	CORE INSTRUCTION	READING/SKILLS
Chapter-Level Resources	**Teaching Resources** Program Overview Pacing Charts **Technology** Resource Pro® CD-ROM Companion Web site, phschool.com • eTeach	**Technology** Social Studies Skills Tutor CD-ROM Student Edition on Audio CD, Ch. 4
1 Physical Features 1. Describe the relative locations of the United States and Canada. 2. Identify the main landforms of the United States and Canada. 3. Identify the major bodies of water in the United States and Canada.	**Teaching Resources** **Unit 2** Classroom Manager, p. 2 Guided Reading and Review, p. 3	**Teaching Resources** Guide to the Essentials, p. 14 Social Studies and Geography Skills, p. 19 **Technology** Section Reading Support Transparencies
2 Humans and the Physical Environment 1. Identify and describe the climate zones of the United States and Canada. 2. Identify and describe the four types of vegetation zones in the United States and Canada.	**Teaching Resources** **Unit 2** Classroom Manager, p. 5 Guided Reading and Review, p. 6	**Teaching Resources** Guide to the Essentials, p. 15 **Technology** Section Reading Support Transparencies
3 Geographic Factors and Natural Resources 1. Identify the natural resources of the United States and Canada. 2. Explain how natural resources affect the American and Canadian economies.	**Teaching Resources** **Unit 2** Classroom Manager, p. 8 Guided Reading and Review, p. 9 Chapter Summary, p. 11 Vocabulary, p. 12 Reteaching, p. 13	**Teaching Resources** **Unit 2** Critical Thinking, p. 15 Guide to the Essentials, p. 16 **Technology** Section Reading Support Transparencies

ENRICHMENT / PRE-AP

Teaching Resources
Primary Sources and Literature Readings

Other Print Resources
DK Atlas

Technology
World Video Explorer: Journey Over the United States and Canada
Companion Web site, phschool.com

Technology
Color Transparencies 28

Teaching Resources
Unit 2
Enrichment, p. 14
Cooperative Learning Activity, pp. 104–107

ASSESSMENT

Prentice Hall Assessment System

Core Assessment
Chapter Tests with ExamView® Test Bank, Ch. 4
ExamView® Test Bank CD-ROM, Ch. 4

Standardized Test Preparation
Diagnose and Prescribe
Diagnostic Tests for Middle Grades Social Studies Skills
Review and Reteach
Review Book for World Studies
Practice and Assess
Test-taking Strategies with Transparencies for Middle Grades Test Prep Book
Test-taking Strategies Posters

Teaching Resources
Unit 2
Section Quizzes, pp. 4, 7, and 10
Chapter Tests, pp. 132–137

Technology
Companion Web site, phschool.com
Ch. 4 Self-Test

World Video Explorer
Each region of the world is explored through regional flyovers and investigative field trips. Case study segments give students an in-depth view of the history, economy, government, and culture of a key place in each region. Case studies include Nigeria, Mexico, China, British Columbia, and the Czech Republic.

In Your Classroom

CUSTOMIZE FOR INDIVIDUAL NEEDS

Gifted and Talented

Teacher's Edition
- Great Lakes Journey, p. 75

Teaching Resources
- Enrichment, p. 14
- Primary Sources and Literature Readings

Honors/Pre-AP

Teacher's Edition
- Great Lakes Journey, p. 75

Teaching Resources
- Critical Thinking, p. 15
- Primary Sources and Literature Readings

ESL

Teaching Resources
- Guided Reading and Review, pp. 3, 6, and 9
- Vocabulary, p. 12
- Reteaching, p. 13
- Guide to the Essentials, pp. 14–16
- Social Studies and Geography Skills, p. 19

Technology
- Social Studies Skills Tutor CD-ROM
- Section Reading Support Transparencies

Less Proficient Readers

Teacher's Edition
- Art, p. 75

Teaching Resources
- Guided Reading and Review, pp. 3, 6, and 9
- Vocabulary, p. 12
- Reteaching, p. 13
- Guide to the Essentials, pp. 14–16
- Social Studies and Geography Skills, p. 19

Technology
- Social Studies Skills Tutor CD-ROM
- Section Reading Support Transparencies

Less Proficient Writers

Teacher's Edition
- Art, p. 75

Teaching Resources
- Guided Reading and Review, pp. 3, 6, and 9
- Vocabulary, p. 12
- Guide to the Essentials, pp. 14–16
- Social Studies and Geography Skills, p. 19

Technology
- Social Studies Skills Tutor CD-ROM
- Section Reading Support Transparencies

DORLING KINDERSLEY

At the end of each unit, you will find information adapted from Dorling Kindersley's *Illustrated Children's Encyclopedia* that connects to the region being studied and to one of the seven content strands. In addition, your resources include Dorling Kindersley's *Atlas*, which contains valuable information about countries from around the world.

TEACHER'S EDITION INDEX

CHAPTER 4 PACING SUGGESTIONS

For 90-minute Blocks

See suggestions in the Teaching Resources Pacing Charts for Chapter 4. Use Color Transparencies 28.

Running Out of Time?

See the Guide to the Essentials, pp. 14–16.

INTERDISCIPLINARY LINKS

Middle Grades Math: Tools for Success

Course 1, Lesson 1-1, **Organizing and Displaying Data**

Course 2, Lesson 9-8, **Estimating Population Size**

Science Explorer

Weather and Climate, Lesson 1-2, **Air Quality;** Lesson 4-1, **What Causes Climate;** Lesson 4-2, **Climate Regions**

Prentice Hall Literature

Bronze, How the Snake Got Poison

Copper, Thunder Butte

BIBLIOGRAPHY

For the Teacher

DK *DK Essential World Atlas.* Dorling Kindersley, 2001.

Fisher, Ron. *Heartland of a Continent: America's Plains and Prairies.* National Geographic, 1991.

Malcolm, Andrew H. *The Land and People of Canada.* HarperCollins, 1991.

For the Student

Easy

Burns, Diane L. *Rocky Mountain Seasons: From Valley to Mountaintop.* Macmillan, 1993.

Gibbons, Gail. *The Great St. Lawrence Seaway.* Morrow, 1992.

Average

DK *Eyewitness North American Indian.* Dorling Kindersley, 2001.

Fraser, Mary Ann. *In Search of the Grand Canyon.* Holt, 1995.

Challenging

DK Schullery, Paul. *America's National Parks.* Dorling Kindersley, 2001.

Literature Connection

Hobbs, Will. *Far North.* Morrow, 1996.

Siebert, Diane. *Sierra.* HarperCollins, 1991.

Take It to the NET

The World Explorer companion Web site, found on **phschool.com**, offers activities for exploring geographical, historical, and cultural resources on the Internet. It also provides on-line links for key content and all Section and Chapter Assessment activities.

The **Teacher site** also provides teachers with regional data and ideas for student research and activities.

Students can use the **Student site** to find chapter-by-chapter Internet resource links and to access Self-Tests.

CHAPTER 4

Connecting to the Guiding Questions

In this chapter, students will read about the physical geography of the United States and Canada. Content in this chapter corresponds to the following Guiding Questions outlined at the beginning of the unit.

- How has the physical geography affected the settlement patterns and economies of the United States and Canada?

Using the Map Activities

Have students study the map and map key. Point out the great variety of natural resources shown, and have students note the way that certain resources, such as petroleum, cluster in the same geographic regions.

- Resources not found in Canada: phosphates and bauxite; Resources found along the Gulf of Mexico: petroleum, phosphates; Resources found just north of the Great Lakes: uranium, iron, silver, gold, hydroelectric power
- Students might suggest that in order to conserve resources, governments might limit the amount of nonrenewable resources that can be used for industry, and might find ways to replenish renewable resources.

Heterogeneous Groups

The following activities are suitable for heterogeneous groups.

Interdisciplinary Connections

Art, p. 75

Cooperative Learning

Great Lakes Journey, p. 75

eTeach

Be sure to check out this month's discussion with a Master Teacher. Go to **phschool.com**.

CHAPTER 4

THE UNITED STATES AND CANADA: Physical Geography

SECTION 1
Physical Features

SECTION 2
Humans and the Physical Environment

SECTION 3
Geographic Factors and Natural Resources

United States and Canada: Natural Resources

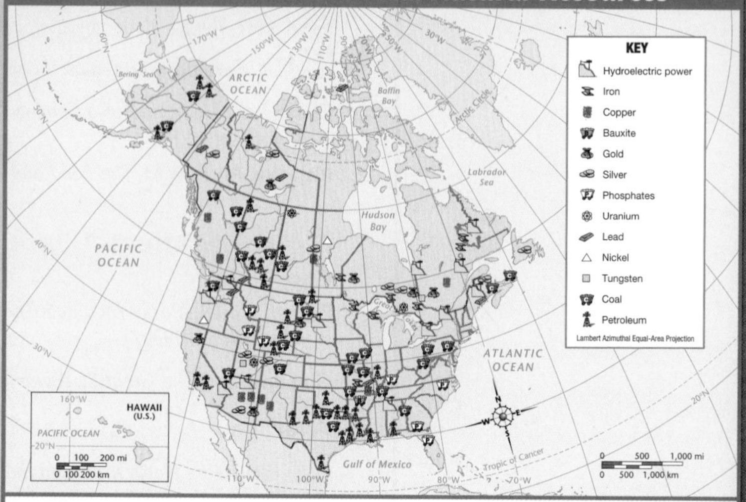

USING MAPS

The United States and Canada are rich in natural resources. Both countries have used their resources to build a variety of industries. Study the map and the map key. Then, complete the following activities.

Locating Natural Resources

Make lists to answer the following questions: Which resources are not found in Canada? Which resources are found along the Gulf of Mexico? Which resources are found just north of the Great Lakes? If you are unfamiliar with some of the resources, look them up in a dictionary.

Conserving Resources

Some resources, such as gold or petroleum, are not renewable and could someday be used up. What do you think governments should do to conserve their resources? What would you suggest to conserve some of the resources shown on the map?

72 UNIT 2 THE UNITED STATES AND CANADA

Resource Directory

Teaching Resources

Primary Sources and Literature Readings extend content with a selection related to the concepts in this chapter.

Other Print Resources

DK Atlas

Technology

Journey Over the United States and Canada, from the World Video Explorer, introduces students to the major landforms of the United States and Canada.

Geography: Three Native American Cultures, from the World Video Explorer, enhances students' understanding of how Native Americans adapted to different environments.

Student Edition on Audio CD, Ch. 4

SECTION 1

Physical Features

BEFORE YOU READ

READING FOCUS

1. Where in the world are the United States and Canada located?
2. What are the main landforms of the United States and Canada?
3. What are the major bodies of water in the United States and Canada?

KEY TERMS

Continental Divide
glacier
transportation corridors
tributary

KEY PLACES

Rocky Mountains
Appalachian Mountains
Death Valley
Great Lakes
St. Lawrence River
Mississippi River

NOTE TAKING

Copy the chart below. As you read the section, fill in the chart with information about the physical features of the United States and Canada.

	United States	Canada
Land Forms		
Bodies of Water		

MAIN IDEA

The United States and Canada have a wide variety of unique physical features, including mountains, farmlands, great lakes, and mighty rivers.

Setting The Scene

Alaska's Mount McKinley is the highest mountain in North America and attracts thousands of visitors every year. In 1992, Ruth Kocour joined a team of climbers to scale the 20,320-foot (6,194-m) peak. After the team had set up camp at 9,500 feet (2,896 m), the first storm arrived. The team quickly built walls of packed snow to shield their tents from the wind. They dug a snow cave to house their kitchen and waited for the storm to blow itself out. Kocour recalls, "Someone on another team went outside for a few minutes, came back, and had a hot drink. His teeth cracked."

Maybe camping in the cold mountains is not for you. Perhaps you would prefer the sunny beaches of the South or the giant forests of the Northwest. Maybe you would like to see the Arizona desert or the vast plains of central Canada. The landscape of the United States and Canada varies greatly.

Climbing Mount McKinley

GEOGRAPHY

Dressed for warmth and carrying heavy backpacks, hikers stride across Mount McKinley's Kahiltna Glacier. **Critical Thinking** Why might hiking on this mountain be dangerous?

Resource Directory

Teaching Resources

Classroom Manager in the Unit 2 Teaching Resources, p. 2

Guided Reading and Review in the Unit 2 Teaching Resources, p. 3

Guide to the Essentials, p. 14

Technology

Section Reading Support Transparencies

SECTION 1

Lesson Objectives

1. Describe the relative locations of the United States and Canada.
2. Identify the main landforms of the United States and Canada.
3. Identify the major bodies of water in the United States and Canada.

Lesson Plan

1 Engage

Warm-Up Activity

Ask students to consider the physical geography of your community. What features are most noticeable? Invite students to list some of these features on the chalkboard. Discuss whether these features are unique to your community or whether students would expect to find them in other places in the United States or Canada.

Activating Prior Knowledge

If possible, take the class to the top of a hill or a tall building. Alternatively, show students photographs taken from such a location. Compare how land, people, and buildings look from this viewpoint and from students' usual viewpoint.

2 Explore

Prompt students to look for answers to the following questions as they read. What physical features do both Canada and the United States share? What role do the Great Lakes play in transportation between Canada and the United States? What geographic features link Canada and the United States?

Answers to...

CRITICAL THINKING

Hikers face extreme weather conditions that present numerous physical challenges.

Lesson Plan continued

3 Teach

Have students write a short paragraph in which they compare and contrast the major physical features of Canada and the United States. This activity should take about 20 minutes.

Questions for Discussion

GEOGRAPHY Why do you think few people settled in the Canadian Shield region?

The region is made up of ancient rock covered by a thin layer of soil. This would not be a good place to settle because it would be difficult to grow crops.

CULTURE Why do you think Native Americans call the Mississippi River the "Father of Waters"?

It is the largest river in the United States and a number of other major rivers flow into it.

4 Assess/Reteach

See the answers to the Section 1 Assessment. You may also assess students' paragraphs.

Acceptable paragraphs correctly list major physical features.

Commendable paragraphs note both similarities and differences.

Outstanding paragraphs recognize that without political boundaries, the United States and Canada could in many ways be described as one place.

Answers to...

AS YOU READ

The Rocky Mountains, the Appalachian Mountains (Laurentian Highlands in Canada), Great and Central Plains (the Interior Plains in Canada)

Where in the World Are We?

The United States and Canada are located in North America. To the east is the Atlantic Ocean, to the west, the Pacific. To the north, Canada borders the Arctic Ocean, while to the south, the United States borders Mexico and the Gulf of Mexico. The United States also includes Alaska and Hawaii.

Canada is larger than the United States and is the second-largest country in the world. The United States is the fourth largest country. But the United States has almost 10 times as many people as Canada.

Landforms of the United States and Canada

From outer space, the United States and Canada appear as one landmass, with mountain ranges and vast plains running from north to south. Locate the following land forms on the physical map in the Activity Atlas on page 69.

Extending about 3,000 miles (4,830 km) along the western section of the continent, the **Rocky Mountains** are the largest mountain system in North America. Along the spine of the Rockies runs the **Continental Divide,** the boundary that separates the flow of rivers to the oceans. On the east side of the Rockies, rivers flow to the Atlantic Ocean, the Arctic Ocean, and the Gulf of Mexico. On the west side, they flow to the Pacific Ocean.

The second largest mountain system, the **Appalachian Mountains,** lies in the east. The Appalachians stretch about 1,600 miles (2,570 km), becoming the Laurentian Highlands in Canada.

AS YOU READ
Summarize What are the major landforms of the United States and Canada?

Between the Rockies and the Appalachians lies a huge plains area. In Canada, these lowlands are called the Interior Plains. In the United States, they are called the Great Plains and the Central Plains. Much of this region has rich soil. In the wetter eastern area, farmers grow crops like corn and soybeans, while in the drier western area, farmers grow wheat, and ranchers raise livestock.

Special Features of the United States The United States has several unique features. A plains area runs along its eastern and southern coasts. In the Northeast, this plain is narrow; it broadens as it spreads south and west. Flat, fertile land and access to the sea attracted many settlers to this area, and large cities developed.

West of the Rockies lies a region of plateaus and basins. The largest of these basins, the Great Basin, is the site of the Great Salt Lake in the west and **Death Valley,** the hottest place in North America, in the southwest. Farther west lie two more mountain ranges, the Sierra Nevada in California and the Cascades in Washington and Oregon.

Far to the north, snow and ice cover Alaska's many mountains. **Glaciers,** huge, slow-moving sheets of ice, fill many of the valleys between these mountains. Most of Alaska's people live along the warmer southern coast.

SKILLS MINI LESSON

Previewing

To **introduce** the skill, tell students that previewing what they are about to read can help them develop some expectations about it. List the following previewing techniques on the chalkboard: *(1) Note the headings and subheadings. (2) Study the pictures and captions. (3) Relate the subject matter to your own life.* Have students **practice** the skill by allowing them a few minutes to use the techniques to preview Section 1. Encourage students to jot down notes as they preview. Students may then **apply** the skill by developing a one- or two-sentence preview of the section.

Special Features of Canada Canada, too, has a number of unique features. East of Alaska lies the Yukon (YOO kahn) Territory of Canada. Mount Logan, Canada's highest peak, is here. It is part of the Coast Mountains, which stretch south along the Pacific almost to the United States border.

East of the Interior Plains lies the Canadian Shield, a region of ancient rock covered by a thin layer of soil that covers about half of Canada, where few people live. Southeast of the shield are the St. Lawrence Lowlands, home to more than half of the country's population. While these fertile lowlands produce about one third of the country's crops, the region is also Canada's manufacturing center.

Major Bodies of Water

Both the United States and Canada have important lakes and rivers. Many American and Canadian cities developed near these bodies of water. As you read, find these water bodies on the physical map in the Activity Atlas on page 69.

Lakes Superior, Michigan, Huron, Erie, and Ontario make up the **Great Lakes,** the world's largest group of freshwater lakes. Only Lake Michigan lies entirely in the United States. The other four lakes are part of the border between the United States and Canada.

Melting ice from ancient glaciers formed the Great Lakes. Today, the Great Lakes are important waterways in both the United States and Canada. Shipping on the Great Lakes helped industry to develop in the two countries.

A Ship on the St. Lawrence Seaway

GEOGRAPHY This picture shows a ship passing through the Welland Canal on the St. Lawrence Seaway. The canal, which connects Lakes Erie and Ontario, is 27.6 miles (44.4 km) long. **Critical Thinking** Why do you think that people sometimes call the St. Lawrence Seaway "Canada's highway to the sea"? Where does it start and end?

ACTIVITY

Interdisciplinary Connections

Art Invite students to create a photo exhibit about some of the magnificent physical features of the United States and Canada. Students may include postcards, personal photographs, and magazine ads in the exhibit. Tell students to write captions that identify and locate the places shown in the photos. Students may add to the exhibit throughout their study of the chapter.

Visual/Spatial

ECONOMICS

Transcontinental Border

The long transcontinental border that divides the United States and Canada has become more expensive to police. The terrorism of September 11, 2001 led to increased surveillance. Long border delays also take an economic toll on businesses and tourism.

ACTIVITY

Cooperative Learning

Great Lakes Journey Organize students into groups. Assign each group one of the five Great Lakes to study. Tell students that they will produce a narrative for a guided tour of their group's lake. Encourage groups to focus their research on topics such as wildlife, industry, human settlement, and environmental issues.

Verbal/Linguistic

Resource Directory

Teaching Resources

Social Studies and Geography Skills, Four Types of Landforms, p. 19

Technology

Color Transparencies 28 The United States and Canada: Physical-Political Map

Answers to...

CRITICAL THINKING

The canal allows ships from Canada's interior to reach the Atlantic Ocean. It starts at the Great Lakes and ends at the Atlantic Ocean.

CHAPTER 4 THE UNITED STATES AND CANADA: PHYSICAL GEOGRAPHY 75

SECTION 1 ASSESSMENT

AFTER YOU READ

1. (a) largest mountain system in North America, (b) second-largest mountain system in North America, known as Laurentian Highlands in Canada, (c) hottest place in North America, (d) world's largest group of freshwater lakes, (e) major Canadian river that links the Great Lakes to the Atlantic Ocean, (f) largest river in the United States
2. (a) boundary formed by the Rocky Mountains separating rivers flowing toward opposite sides of the continent, (b) huge, slow-moving sheet of ice, (c) routes used for transportation of people and goods, (d) stream that flows into a larger river
3. The United States and Canada are both located in North America. The United States borders Canada to the north and Mexico to the south. Canada borders the Arctic Ocean. To the west of both countries is the Pacific Ocean, and to the east is the Atlantic Ocean.
4. Possible answers: About one third of Canada's crops are grown in the St. Lawrence Lowlands because the soil is fertile there. In the United States, people grow crops in the fertile soil of the Great Plains and the Central Plains.
5. They are important shipping waterways and have helped industry develop in both the United States and Canada.
6. Possible answers: The Great Basin, the Great Lakes, the Canadian Shield, the Appalachian Mountains, the Great Plains
7. Students should recognize that people need access to water for farming and transportation.
8. Students can begin by listing the major physical features of both countries and then choosing features from their lists. Make sure students support their choices with reasons.

GEOGRAPHY As the Mississippi River flows into the Gulf of Mexico, it dumps silt, forming a huge triangular plain called a delta. This satellite image shows the shape of the delta. The waters of the Mississippi are shown as light blue, and the land is shown in shades of black. **Critical Thinking** Do you think a delta would be a good place to raise crops? Why?

Mighty Rivers Canada has two major rivers. The Mackenzie River, the country's longest, forms in the Rockies and flows north into the Arctic Ocean. The **St. Lawrence River** connects the Great Lakes to the Atlantic Ocean. People have modified their environment by building a system of locks and canals that enable large ships to navigate the river. As a result, the St. Lawrence is one of North America's most important **transportation corridors.**

In Canada, the St. Lawrence is called the "Mother of Canada." In the United States, America's largest river has an equally grand title. Native Americans call the **Mississippi River** the "Father of Waters." It begins in Minnesota and flows through the Central Plains to the Gulf of Mexico. Two other major rivers, the Ohio and the Missouri, are tributaries of the Mississippi. A **tributary** (TRIB yoo ter ee) is a stream that flows into a larger river.

SECTION 1 ASSESSMENT

AFTER YOU READ

RECALL

1. Identify: (a) Rocky Mountains, (b) Appalachian Mountains, (c) Death Valley, (d) Great Lakes, (e) St. Lawrence River, (f) Mississippi River
2. Define: (a) Continental Divide, (b) glacier, (c) transportation corridors, (d) tributary

COMPREHENSION

3. Describe the locations of the United States and Canada in relation to other countries and major bodies of water.
4. Describe two ways in which the physical features have affected life in the United States and Canada.
5. How do people of the United States and Canada use the major bodies of water in these two countries?

CRITICAL THINKING AND WRITING

6. **Exploring the Main Idea** Review the Main Idea statement at the beginning of this section. Then list five unique physical features found in the United States and Canada.
7. **Making Inferences** Hundreds of years ago, many people coming to the United States and Canada settled along coastal plains and rivers. Why do you think these areas attracted settlers?

ACTIVITY

8. **Writing a Paragraph** Suppose that you are planning a vacation. If you had your choice, what physical features of the United States and Canada would you like to see? Write a paragraph describing the places you would like to visit and why.

Answers to...

CRITICAL THINKING

Yes, because the silt would provide fertile soil for crops.

Resource Directory

Teaching Resources

Section Quiz in the Unit 2 Teaching Resources, p. 4

SECTION 2

Humans and the Physical Environment

BEFORE YOU READ

READING FOCUS

1. What types of climate zones can be found in the United States and Canada?
2. What are the four types of natural vegetation zones that can be found in the United States and Canada?

KEY TERMS

rain shadow
tropics
tundra
permafrost
prairie

MAIN IDEA

The wide range of climate and vegetation zones found in the United States and Canada is caused by a variety of factors.

NOTE TAKING

Copy the concept web shown below. As you read the section, fill in the web with information about the climate of each type of vegetation zone and where each zone is located.

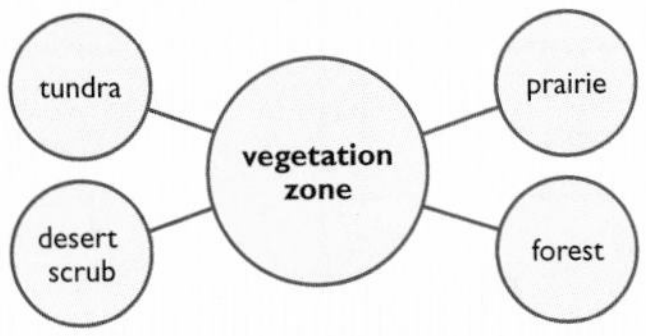

Setting the Scene

On a hot and sunny February morning, a reporter left his home in Miami Beach, Florida, and headed for the airport. Wearing lightweight trousers and a short-sleeved shirt, he boarded a plane to snowy Toronto. Was he forgetting something? Surely he knew that the temperature would be below freezing in Toronto.

He did, indeed, know all about the bitter cold that would greet him when he got off the plane. But he was going to do research for an article on Toronto's tunnels and underground malls. He wanted to find out whether people could really visit hotels, restaurants, and shops without having to go outside.

Coping with the Climate

GEOGRAPHY Whatever the weather might be outside, it is always pleasant in climate-controlled Eaton Center, a shopping mall in Toronto, Ontario. **Critical Thinking** What are some of the ways that you modify your environment to cope with the climate in your region?

Climate Zones

Climate zones in the United States and Canada range from the polar climate of northern Canada to the desert climate of the southwestern United States. Factors such as the size of a region, latitude, mountains, and oceans affect the kinds of climates found in a region.

Canada's Climates—Braving the Cold Generally, the farther a location is from the Equator, the colder its climate. Since Canada lies well to the north of the Equator, much of it is very cold!

SECTION 2

Lesson Objectives

1. Identify and describe the climate zones of the United States and Canada.
2. Identify and describe the four types of vegetation zones in the United States and Canada.

Lesson Plan

1 Engage

Warm-Up Activity

Mention to students that some places have earned nicknames based on a typical aspect of their climate. For example, Florida is known as the "Sunshine State" because it is warm and sunny for much of the year. Challenge students to invent a climate-related nickname for your community or state.

Activating Prior Knowledge

Encourage students who have lived in or visited other places in the United States or Canada to compare those climates to your local climate. Have students discuss possible reasons for the similarities or differences in climate.

2 Explore

Direct students to look for answers to the following questions as they read the section: What factors influence the climate in Canada and the United States? Why do lands in rain shadows receive little rainfall? What different types of vegetation zones can be found in the United States and Canada?

Answers to...

CRITICAL THINKING

Answers will vary. Students might mention the kinds of clothing they wear to cope with heat or cold, the use of heat and air conditioning, and the types of houses they live in.

Resource Directory

Teaching Resources

Classroom Manager in the Unit 2 Teaching Resources, p. 5

Guided Reading and Review in the Unit 2 Teaching Resources, p. 6

Guide to the Essentials, p. 15

Technology

Section Reading Support Transparencies

Lesson Plan continued

3 Teach

Have students write weather reports about two places in the United States and Canada. Reports should be based on information about the region and should include data about vegetation. Students may also consult the climate regions map in the Activity Atlas. Students may deliver their reports orally. This activity should take about 25 minutes.

Questions for Discussion

GEOGRAPHY Examine the world climate regions map on p. 70 and the vegetation map on this page. In what area of the United States would you expect to find the least amount of people living? Why?

The southwest would have the least amount of people because it has a very dry climate and has little or no vegetation.

GEOGRAPHY How do mountains in the western United States help contribute to the semiarid and desert climates in Nevada, Utah, and Arizona?

Winds coming from the Pacific Ocean rise when they reach the mountains, cooling and releasing their moisture. The areas on the other side of the mountains, therefore, receive little rainfall.

4 Assess/Reteach

See the answers to the Section 2 Assessment. You may also assess students' weather reports.

Acceptable reports present accurate climate and vegetation information.

Commendable reports recognize the impact of climate on vegetation.

Outstanding reports highlight key data about climate and vegetation.

Answers to...

MAP STUDY

Alaska's vegetation patterns are most similar to those in Canada.

United States and Canada: Vegetation

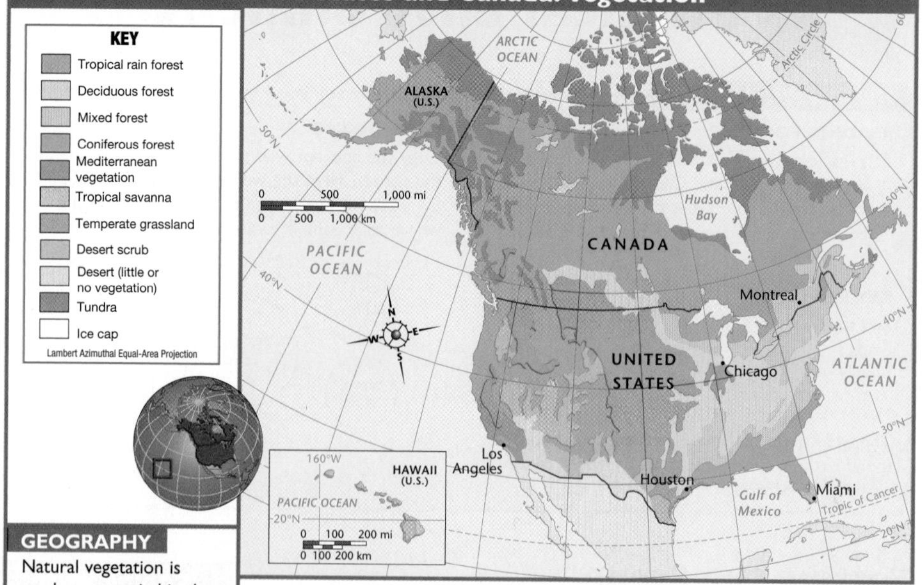

GEOGRAPHY Natural vegetation is much more varied in the United States than it is in Canada. **Map Study** In terms of natural vegetation, what part of the United States has the most in common with Canada?

The ocean affects Canada's climates, too. Areas that are near an ocean may have milder climates than areas inland. The waters of the Pacific Ocean help make the climate of the northwestern coast of Canada mild all year, while inland areas often have climate extremes.

Finally, mountains influence climate, especially rainfall. Winds blowing from the Pacific Ocean rise as they meet the mountains in the west, cooling and dropping their moisture. The air is dry when it reaches the other side of the mountains. This area of **rain shadow** is on the dry, sheltered side of a mountain that receives little rainfall.

Climates of the United States Latitude also influences climate in the United States. On the climate map in the Activity Atlas on page 70, you will see that Alaska lies far from the Equator and is cold for a good part of the year. The southern tip of Florida and Hawaii lie near or within the **tropics,** the area between the 23°N and 23°S lines of latitude. Here, it is almost always warm.

As in Canada, wet winds from the Pacific Ocean drop their moisture before they cross the western mountains, leaving the eastern sections of California and the states of Nevada, Utah, and Arizona semiarid or desert.

East of the Great Plains, the country has continental climates. In the north, summers are warm and winters are cold and snowy. In the south, summers tend to be long and hot, while winters are mild.

SKILLS MINI LESSON

Using the Writing Process

To **introduce** students to the skill, write the following headings on the chalkboard: *Prewrite, Draft, Revise, Proofread, Publish.* Help students become familiar with the process by discussing each step in the writing process before they **practice** and **apply** the step to writing a report about tornadoes, a weather phenomenon associated with a particular region of the United States and Canada. In the *prewriting* stage, they would conduct research and record data in an outline. Next, the research notes would be used to *draft* sentences and paragraphs that focus on a main idea. To *revise* the draft, they would edit out nonessential ideas and rework awkward sentences. Writers should always *proofread* their work by checking for spelling and grammatical errors. Finally, a writer would *publish* the report, which involves making the report available for others to read.

Natural Vegetation Zones

Climate determines the different vegetation zones. There are four major kinds of natural vegetation or plant life.

Northern Tundras The **tundra** is a cold, dry region in the far north that is covered with snow for more than half the year. The Arctic tundra contains **permafrost,** or permanently frozen soil. During the short, cool summer, the surface of the permafrost thaws. Mosses, grasses, and bright wildflowers grow there.

Prairies **Prairies,** also known as grasslands, are regions of flat or rolling land covered with grasses. The world's largest prairie covers much of the American central states and stretches into the provinces of Alberta, Saskatchewan (suh SKACH uh wun), and Manitoba in Canada.

Desert Scrub With little rainfall, desert and semiarid regions have few plants. The Great Basin is a large, very dry region between the Rocky Mountains and the Sierras in the United States.

Forests Forests cover nearly one third of the United States and almost one half of Canada. The mild climate of the northern Pacific Coast, for example, encourages great forests of trees.

Cattle Raising in the West

GEOGRAPHY Many people in the plains and other lowland areas of western North America make a living by raising cattle. These cowhands in Texas are rounding up cattle and bringing them into a fenced area.
Critical Thinking Why do you think that areas of flat or rolling land are better for raising cattle than mountainous areas?

SECTION 2 ASSESSMENT

AFTER YOU READ

RECALL

1. Define: (a) rain shadow, (b) tropics, (c) tundra, (d) permafrost, (e) prairie

COMPREHENSION

2. How do the climate zones of the United States differ from those of Canada?
3. List the four types of natural vegetation zones found in the United States and Canada.

CRITICAL THINKING AND WRITING

4. **Exploring the Main Idea** Review the Main Idea statement at the beginning of this section. Then create a chart showing the types of climate zones mentioned in this section and the causes for each type of climate zone.
5. **Comparing and Contrasting** Write a paragraph that compares and contrasts the climate and vegetation of the tundra with that of the area around the Great Lakes. Use the climate map in the Activity Atlas to help you.

ACTIVITY

6. **Creating a Travel Brochure** Create a short travel brochure, inviting tourists to visit one of the climate zones described in this section. Use words and illustrations to describe the area and why tourists would find it appealing.

Resource Directory

Teaching Resources

Section Quiz in the Unit 2 Teaching Resources, p. 7

Answers to...

CRITICAL THINKING

Possible answer: It would be harder to feed and round up cattle in the mountains.

SECTION 2 ASSESSMENT

AFTER YOU READ

1. (a) area on the dry, sheltered side of a mountain that receives little rainfall (b) area between the 23 1/2°N and 23 1/2°S lines of latitude where it is usually hot (c) cold, dry climate region in the far north (d) permanently frozen soil (e) region of flat or rolling land covered with grasses
2. Much of Canada's climate is very cold. The climate zones in the Unites States are more varied.
3. tundra: far north areas of Canada and Alaska; grassland: Great Plains of the American central states stretching into the Canadian provinces of Alberta, Saskatchewan, and Manitoba; desert shrub: area known as the Great Basin between the Rocky Mountains and the Sierras in the United States; forest: northern Pacific coast, area from the Great Lakes across southeastern Canada and New England and down to the southeastern United States.
4. Charts should include polar climate, caused by being in the far north, having vegetation such as tundra grasses, mosses, and wildflowers; tropical climates, caused by being near the Equator, having tropical savannas and tropical rain forests; semiarid or desert climate, caused by lack of moisture when the mountains interfere with flow of cloud-carrying rain, having grassland, desert scrub, or little or no vegetation; continental climates of hot summers and cold winters, caused by being so far inland, having vegetation such as deciduous, coniferous, and mixed forests.
5. Students should note that the Great Lakes area has extreme seasonal climate differences while the tundra is cold year-round. The tundra will not support much vegetation while the Great Lakes area has both coniferous and deciduous forests.
6. Students brochures should demonstrate an understanding of the climate zone and the type of vegetation associated with it.

CHAPTER 4 THE UNITED STATES AND CANADA: PHYSICAL GEOGRAPHY 79

SECTION 3

Lesson Objectives

1. Identify the natural resources of the United States and Canada.
2. Explain how natural resources affect the American and Canadian economies.

Lesson Plan

1 Engage

Warm-Up Activity

Invite a volunteer to empty his or her backpack. Identify the natural resources that were used to make the displayed items.

Activating Prior Knowledge

Have students write down four or five activities that they do in a typical day, such as taking a shower, eating lunch, riding the bus to school, and so on. Help them identify the natural resources that play a part in these activities.

2 Explore

As students read the section, urge them to answer the following questions: What are some of the most important resources in the United States? How are mineral resources in the United States used by people and industry? Why are so few Canadians farmers? Where are most of Canada's minerals found?

SECTION 3

Geographic Factors and Natural Resources

BEFORE YOU READ

READING FOCUS

1. What are the important natural resources of the United States, and how do they contribute to the economy?
2. What are the important natural resources of Canada, and how do they contribute to the economy?

KEY TERMS

alluvial
hydroelectricity

KEY PLACES

Grand Coulee Dam
St. Lawrence Lowlands

NOTE TAKING

Copy the chart shown here. As you read the section, fill in locations of where you can find each type of natural resource in the United States and Canada.

Type of Resource	United States	Canada
soil/farmland		
water/hydroelectric power		
oil		
forests		

MAIN IDEA

The rich natural resources of the United States and Canada have helped to build two of the leading economies in the world.

Preserving the Forest

GEOGRAPHY These redwood trees are part of Muir Woods National Monument, a national park just northwest of San Francisco, California. **Critical Thinking** Is it important to preserve our natural resources? Why?

Setting the Scene

Surrounded by redwood forests, Carlotta, California, has little more than a gas station and a general store. Yet on one day in September 1996, police arrested more than 1,000 people here. It was the scene of a showdown. A logging company wanted to cut down some of the oldest redwood trees in the world. Protesters wanted to preserve the forest and the animals that live there. Both sides believed in the importance of natural resources. But they disagreed about how to use them.

Natural Resources of the United States

Native Americans, pioneers, and explorers knew North America was a land of abundant fertile soil, water, forests, and minerals.

Soil The Midwest and the South have rich, dark soils called **alluvial** (uh LOO vee ul) soils, the fertile topsoil left by rivers after a flood. Areas that have good soil are suitable for farming.

Water Water is a vital resource for drinking, growing crops, industries, and transportation. Some rivers, such as the Mississippi, Ohio, and Missouri Rivers, also serve as important shipping routes.

Resource Directory

Teaching Resources

Classroom Manager in the Unit 2 Teaching Resources, p. 8

Guided Reading and Review in the Unit 2 Teaching Resources, p. 9

Guide to the Essentials, p. 16

Technology

Section Reading Support Transparencies

Answers to...

CRITICAL THINKING

Students should recognize the importance of preserving natural resources for recreation, industry, and energy.

The World's First Oil Well

HISTORY The modern oil industry began almost 150 years ago on a farm near Titusville, Pennsylvania. On August 27, 1859, a retired railroad conductor named Edwin L. Drake (on the left in this picture) struck oil almost 70 feet (21 m) underground. At first, the oil fetched $20 a barrel. After Drake showed neighbors how to drill their own wells, however, oil prices plunged to 10 cents a barrel. **Critical Thinking** Why do you think oil prices fell after Drake shared his knowledge with neighbors?

Water is used for other purposes, too. Dams along many rivers generate **hydroelectricity** (hy dro ee lek TRIS ih tee), or power generated by moving water. The **Grand Coulee** (KOO lee) **Dam** on the Columbia River in the state of Washington produces more hydroelectricity than any other U.S. dam.

Abundant Energy and Mineral Resources The United States is the second-largest producer of coal, petroleum, and natural gas in the world. Abundant energy resources have fueled industrial expansion and have helped to provide Americans with one of the world's highest standards of living.

The United States also has valuable deposits of copper, gold, granite, iron ore, and lead and these minerals are very important to many industries.

A Wealth of Trees America's forests are an important resource. In the Pacific Northwest, the South, the Appalachians, and areas around the Great Lakes, forests produce lumber, wood pulp for paper, and fine hardwoods for furniture.

Natural Resources of Canada

Canada's first European settlers earned their living as fur trappers, loggers, fishers, and farmers. Today, less than 5 percent of Canada's workers earn their living in these ways.

SCIENCE AND TECHNOLOGY

The Grand Coulee Dam is 5,223 feet (1,592 meters) long and 550 feet (168 meters) high. At its base, it is 500 feet (152 meters) thick.

Hydroelectric power generated by the Grand Coulee and other dams on the Columbia River has encouraged the industrial development of the Pacific Northwest. Aluminum plants were built along the river. Aircraft factories were built in the state of Washington.

The dam was completed in 1942 and created the Franklin D. Roosevelt Lake, which is 151 miles (243 kilometers) long. Water from the lake is pumped into an irrigation system that provides water for more than 1 million acres (400,000 hectares) of land, turning the arid region into productive farmland.

In addition, the lake provides recreation such as boating, swimming, fishing, and other water-related activities.

Critical Thinking If you lived in the region affected by the Grand Coulee Dam, how might you benefit personally?

3 Teach

Have students create two concept webs that show the natural resources of Canada and the United States. Each web should have the country name in the center. Secondary circles can contain major resources, and tertiary circles can identify the resources' uses. This activity should take about 25 minutes.

Questions for Discussion

ECONOMICS **What do you think is the most important natural resource in the United States and Canada? Why?**

Students' responses will vary. Make sure they support their choices with details from the text or from their own experiences.

GEOGRAPHY **The middle portion of the United States is an agricultural center. Why is this? Consider the factors of climate and natural resources in your answer.**

This area occupies the humid continental and humid subtropical climate regions. They have moderate temperatures and precipitation which makes for good crop-growing weather. Also, this region contains very fertile soil, which is also good for crops.

4 Assess/Reteach

See the answers to the Section 3 Assessment. You may also assess students' webs.

Acceptable webs should contain at least three natural resources for each country.

Commendable webs should contain at least three natural resources for each country and should list some uses.

Outstanding webs should contain at least three natural resources for each country and should name at least one use for each resource listed.

SKILLS MINI LESSON

Assessing Your Understanding

You might **introduce** the skill by asking a volunteer to explain why a Section Review is included at the end of each section. Discuss how these questions enable teachers—and students—to assess understanding. Point out that difficulties in answering a particular question indicate a part of the text students should review. Students may work in pairs to **practice** and **apply** the skill by completing the Section 3 Review.

Answers to...

CRITICAL THINKING

If more people were drilling for oil, there would be more oil available. This would cause a drop in oil prices.

CRITICAL THINKING

Students may suggest that they would benefit by having access to jobs, ample electrical power, and places for recreation.

SECTION 3 ASSESSMENT

AFTER YOU READ

1. (a) dam on the Columbia River in Washington that produces more hydroelectricity than any other dam in the country (b) major agricultural region in Canada
2. (a) deposited by a river or stream, relating to soil (b) power generated by moving water
3. Water is necessary to human life and to most businesses. Water is used for irrigation, drinking, cooling industrial machines, transportation, and hydroelectric power.
4. Canada has farmland that produces grains, milk, fruits, and vegetables; minerals for energy and industry; and forests for wood products.
5. Students' paragraphs should demonstrate an understanding of the major natural resources and how they are used.
6. Possible answer: Canada and the Unites States both have prairie lands, tall mountains, major lakes and rivers, and some overlapping climate zones.
7. The plan should accurately identify a resource in the community and give persuasive reasons for protecting the resource.

ECONOMICS Powerful tugboats tow huge booms of logs harvested from Canada's forests.
Critical Thinking
What wood products do you use in your daily life? How important are these products to you?

Farmland About 12 percent of Canada's land is suitable for farming. Most is located in the Prairie Provinces, and produces most of Canada's wheat and beef. The **St. Lawrence Lowlands** are another major agricultural region and produce grains, milk, vegetables, and fruit.

Minerals and Energy Resources About 85 percent of the nation's iron ore comes from mines near the Quebec-Newfoundland border. The region also has large deposits of gold, silver, zinc, copper, and uranium. The Prairie Provinces, particularly Alberta, have large oil and natural gas deposits.

Canada harnesses the rivers of Quebec Province to make hydroelectricity. These rivers generate enough hydroelectric power so that some can be exported to the northeastern United States.

Forests With almost half its land covered in forests, Canada is a leading producer of timber products. These products include lumber, paper, plywood, and wood pulp. The major timber-producing provinces include British Columbia, Quebec, and Ontario.

SECTION 3 ASSESSMENT

AFTER YOU READ

RECALL

1. Identify: (a) Grand Coulee Dam, (b) St. Lawrence Lowlands
2. Define: (a) alluvial, (b) hydroelectricity

COMPREHENSION

3. Why is water an important resource in the United States and how is it used?
4. Describe the major natural resources in Canada.

CRITICAL THINKING AND WRITING

5. **Exploring the Main Idea** Review the Main Idea statement at the beginning of this section. Then write a paragraph describing the natural resources of the United States and Canada, and explain how they benefit the economies of the two nations.
6. **Comparing and Contrasting** Based on what you know about the physical geography of the two countries, why do you think their resources are similar?

ACTIVITY

Take It to the NET

7. **Protecting Natural Resources** Think of a natural resource in your community that needs to be protected, such as a forest or wetland. As a class, develop a plan to protect this resource. Visit the World Explorer: People, Places, and Cultures section of **phschool.com** for help in completing this activity.

Resource Directory

Teaching Resources

Section Quiz in the Unit 2 Teaching Resources, p. 10

Chapter Summary in the Unit 2 Teaching Resources, p. 11

Vocabulary in the Unit 2 Teaching Resources, p. 12

Reteaching in the Unit 2 Teaching Resources, p. 13

Enrichment in the Unit 2 Teaching Resources, p. 14

Critical Thinking in the Unit 2 Teaching Resources, p. 15

Answers to...

CRITICAL THINKING

Students may mention school supplies, furniture, building materials, and sports equipment, all of which they will consider to be important.

Using Graphic Organizers

What You Need
- paper
- pencil

Learn the Skill

Knowing how to organize can help you keep track of the information you read. One good way to organize information is to use a graphic organizer. Graphic organizers can help you visually sort and understand information that you read. One helpful kind of graphic organizer is the concept map or web. With this type of graphic organizer, the subject or main topic is written in an oval in the center of the map. Features and details about this topic are written in ovals around the center. Read the following passage and then follow the steps below to help you organize the information into a concept map.

Bodies of Water

Water is one of the most important resources on the Earth. There are many different types of bodies of water found around the world, and they are used for a variety of purposes.

Types Some of the largest bodies of water include oceans, which contain salt water. Seas are also large bodies of salt water, but they are smaller than oceans. Lakes are smaller bodies of water, usually containing fresh water and surrounded by land. Rivers are large streams that usually flow into lakes and other large bodies of water.

Uses Water is used for many different things. People require water for nourishment, and they also enjoy rivers, lakes, and oceans for recreation. In addition, many industries rely on water to create electricity and help run factories. Finally, water is an important means of transportation of both people and goods.

A. Gather the materials you need.

B. Draw an oval in the middle of a sheet of paper. Write the topic for the map inside the oval. The topic for this map is "Bodies of Water."

C. Think about the different features of the topic. Look for headings and subheadings in the text to help you determine the features to include in the map. For example, two features for the topic "Bodies of Water" include the different types of bodies of water and the uses of bodies of water. Note how the features have been added to the map.

D. Add details from the text to each feature. Look at the map to see how details from the text about each of the features have been added.

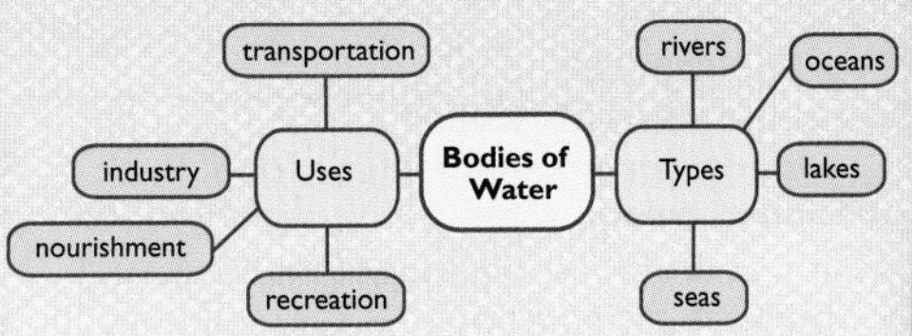

Practice the Skill

Read the text about the natural resources of the United States on pp. 80–81. Follow the steps you learned to create a concept map to organize this information.

Apply the Skill

See the Chapter Review and Assessment at the end of this chapter for more questions on using graphic organizers.

Lesson Objectives

1. Understand what graphic organizers are and how they are used to organize information.
2. Learn how to create a concept map to organize information from text.

Lesson Plan

1 Engage

Ask students if they are familiar with concept maps. Some of the students may be more familiar with the term "concept webs." Have students give definitions for concept maps. Make sure they understand that the web can be constructed in various configurations.

2 Explore

Direct students to read the steps under "Learn the Skill" and to refer to the concept map titled "Bodies of Water" to understand how the map organizes information from the passage.

3 Teach

Have students make their own concept maps following the instructions under "Practice the Skill." Remind them that their concept map must have three parts—subject, features, and details.

For additional reinforcement, invite students to draw concept maps for subjects that they know well. For example, they might make a map for a hobby or an extracurricular activity.

4 Assess/Reteach

Students' concept maps should be clearly written and easy to follow. They should include a subject, features, and several details for each feature.

To further assess students' understanding of concept maps, have them complete the "Applying Your Skills" part of the Chapter Review and Assessment at the end of this chapter.

Resource Directory

Technology

Social Studies Skills Tutor CD-ROM

Answers to...

PRACTICE THE SKILL

Make sure students create their concept maps around the heading and subheadings of the text.

SECTION 4

Review and Assessment

Creating a Chapter Summary

Student summaries will vary.

Sample summary:

Physical Features (Canada) Canada has many mountains and rivers. The Canadian Shield is a region of ancient rock, covered by a thin layer of soil. Southeast of the Shield are the St. Lawrence Lowlands, a very fertile area.

Physical Environment (U.S. and Canada) There are a wide range of climate and vegetation zones found in the United States and Canada. Factors such as the size of a region, latitude, mountains, and oceans affect the kinds of climate found in a region. The four major kinds of natural vegetation found here are tundra, grassland, desert scrub, and forest.

Natural Resources (U.S. and Canada) Both countries have abundant mineral and energy resources. The U.S. has coal, petroleum, and natural gas, as well as deposits of copper, gold, iron ore, and lead. Canada also has large oil and natural gas deposits, as well as deposits of gold, silver, zinc, copper, and uranium. Both countries also have vast resources of water and trees.

Reviewing Key Terms

1. C **2.** A **3.** D **4.** A **5.** B

Reviewing the Main Ideas

1. Possible responses: Great Basin and Rocky Mountains; Great Lakes and Mississippi River
2. Possible responses: Canadian Shield, St. Lawrence Lowlands; St. Lawrence River, Mackenzie River
3. the size of the region, the latitude, mountains, and oceans
4. tundra, prairies or grassland, desert scrub, and forest
5. Possible responses: Water is important as a source of drinking, irrigation, recreation, and hydroelectric power; petroleum is an important source of power for heating and for industrial use.
6. Possible responses: Farmland is important to produce grains, milk, vegetables, and fruits; forests produce timber products such as lumber, paper, plywood, and wood pulp.

CHAPTER 4

Review and Assessment

Creating a Chapter Summary

On a separate piece of paper draw a chart like this one, and include the information that summarizes the physical features of the United States. Then, fill in the remaining boxes with summaries of the information you learned in this chapter.

	United States	Canada
Physical Features		
Physical Enviroment	The United States has a wide variety of physical features ranging from the glaciers of northern Alaska, to Death Valley in the Great Basin. There are mountain ranges, vast plains, and important rivers and lakes.	
Natural Resources		

Reviewing Key Terms

Choose the correct word(s) for each of the definitions below.

1. an area that receives little rainfall on the dry, sheltered side of a mountain
   A tributary **C** rain shadow
   B tundra **D** river
2. a large mass of ice that flows slowly over land
   A glacier **C** tundra
   B prairie **D** mountain
3. a cold dry region that is covered with snow for more than half the year
   A summit **C** prairie
   B alluvial **D** tundra
4. a stream that flows into a larger river
   A tributary **C** alluvial
   B glacier **D** lake
5. relating to fertile soil deposited by a river or stream
   A tundra **C** tributary
   B alluvial **D** prarie

Reviewing the Main Ideas

1. Describe two major landforms and bodies of water in the United States. (Section 1)
2. Describe two major landforms and bodies of water in Canada. (Section 1)
3. What factors influence the types of climate and vegetation found in the United States and Canada? (Section 2)
4. What are the four major types of natural vegetation found in the United States and Canada? (Section 2)
5. List two natural resources for the United States and describe their importance to the nation's economy. (Section 3)
6. List two natural resources for Canada and describe their importance to the nation's economy. (Section 3)

Map Activity

United States and Canada

For each place listed below, write the letter from the map that shows its location. Use the maps in the Activity Atlas to help you.

1. Canadian Shield
2. Great Basin
3. Great Plains
4. Rocky Mountains
5. Appalachian Mountains
6. Pacific Ocean
7. Atlantic Ocean
8. Great Lakes

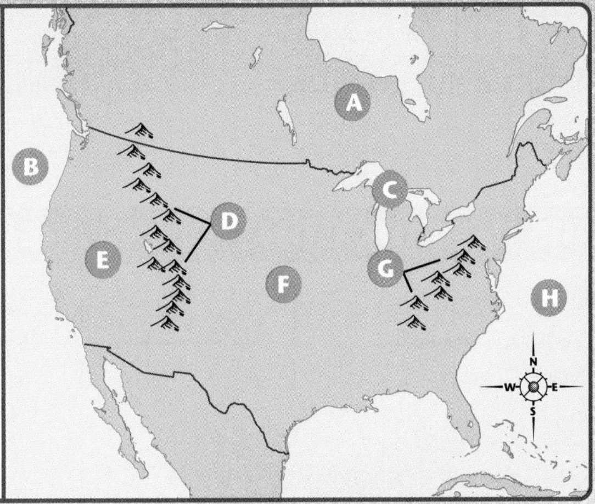

Take It to the NET

Enrichment For more map activities using geography skills, visit the social studies section of **phschool.com.**

Writing Activity

1. **Writing a Poem** Write a poem describing some aspect of the geography of the region where you live. Choose from landforms, bodies of water, climate, vegetation, or other natural resources.
2. **Writing a Travel Postcard** Imagine that you are vacationing in one of the regions described in this chapter. Write a postcard to a friend at home describing some of the physical features and vegetation that you've seen, and what the weather is like.
3. **Creating a Chart** What are the similarities and differences between the natural resources of the United States and Canada? Create a chart that shows these similarities and differences.

Applying Your Skills

Turn to the Skills for Life activity on p. 83 to help you complete the following activity.

Visit the library or the Internet to learn more about the Rocky Mountains. Create a concept web to organize the information you learned about these mountains.

Critical Thinking

1. **Drawing Conclusions** If you were going to build a new city in the United States or Canada, where would you locate it? What geographic features would influence your decision?
2. **Recognizing Cause and Effect** How does climate affect the growth of vegetation in the United States and Canada? Give two examples.

Take It to the NET

Activity Create a shaded relief map showing the major physical features of Canada. Visit the World Explorer: People, Places, and Cultures section of **phschool.com** for help in completing this activity.

Chapter 4 Self-Test As a final review activity, take the Chapter 4 Self-Test and get instant feedback on your answers. To take the test, visit the Social Studies section of **phschool.com.**

Map Activity

1. A **2.** E **3.** F **4.** D
5. G **6.** B **7.** H **8.** C

Writing Activity

1. Poems should use vivid language to create a mental picture of the local geography.
2. Postcards should include descriptions of landforms. Descriptions of climate and vegetation should be consistent with the region described.
3. Charts should accurately identify the resources that are similar and those that are different.

Critical Thinking

1. Answers should accurately identify a U.S. or Canadian location and explain the climate, physical features, and natural resources that make it appealing.
2. In Canada's far north, extreme cold freezes the soil and severely limits vegetation, while in the mild climate on the Pacific Coast of both countries, abundant rainfall helps forests grow.

Applying Your Skills

Have students share their concept webs with the class and explain how they decided which information that they read would be included in their organizers.

Resource Directory

Teaching Resources

Cooperative Learning Activity in the Unit 2 Teaching Resources, pp. 104–107

Chapter Tests Forms A and B in the Unit 2 Teaching Resources, pp. 132–137

Guide to the Essentials Ch. 4 Test, p. 17

Other Print Resources

Chapter Tests with ExamView® Test Bank, Ch. 4

Technology

ExamView® Test Bank CD-ROM, Ch. 4

Resource Pro® CD-ROM

Chapter 5 Planning Guide

Resource Manager

	CORE INSTRUCTION	READING/SKILLS
Chapter-Level Resources	**Teaching Resources** Program Overview Pacing Charts **Technology** Resource Pro® CD-ROM Companion Web site, phschool.com • eTeach	**Technology** Social Studies Skills Tutor CD-ROM Student Edition on Audio CD, Ch. 5
1 Exploration in the Americas **1.** Identify the first Americans. **2.** Describe the effect of European settlement on the Native Americans. **3.** Explain how the United States gained independence from Great Britain.	**Teaching Resources** **Unit 2** Classroom Manager, p. 17 Guided Reading and Review, p. 18	**Teaching Resources** Guide to the Essentials, p. 18 **Technology** Section Reading Support Transparencies
2 Growth and Conflict in the United States **1.** Explain how the United States increased in size under President Thomas Jefferson. **2.** Identify some effects of westward movement in the United States. **3.** Explain causes and effects of the U.S. Civil War.	**Teaching Resources** **Unit 2** Classroom Manager, p. 20 Guided Reading and Review, p. 21	**Teaching Resources** Guide to the Essentials, p. 19 **Technology** Section Reading Support Transparencies
3 The Emergence of a World Power **1.** Explain the effects of the Industrial Revolution on the United States. **2.** Trace the U.S. path to world power. **3.** Identify some ways in which American society has worked toward equality among citizens.	**Teaching Resources** **Unit 2** Classroom Manager, p. 23 Guided Reading and Review, p. 24	**Teaching Resources** Guide to the Essentials, p. 20 **Technology** Section Reading Support Transparencies
4 Settlement, Trade, and Independence in Canada **1.** Explain the reasons for French and British rivalry in Canada. **2.** Trace Canada's path to independence. **3.** Explain how Canada became a world power.	**Teaching Resources** **Unit 2** Classroom Manager, p. 26 Guided Reading and Review, p. 27 Chapter Summary, p. 29 Vocabulary, p. 30 Reteaching, p. 31	**Teaching Resources** **Unit 2** Critical Thinking, p. 33 Guide to the Essentials, p. 21 **Technology** Section Reading Support Transparencies

ENRICHMENT / PRE-AP

Teaching Resources
Primary Sources and Literature Readings

Other Print Resources
DK Atlas

Technology
World Video Explorer: Daily Life: Life During the Civil War
Passport to the World CD-ROM
Companion Web site, phschool.com

Teaching Resources
Outline Maps, pp. 14 and 15

Teaching Resources
Outline Maps, p. 3

Technology
Color Transparencies 40, 49

Teaching Resources
Unit 2
Enrichment, p. 32
Cooperative Learning Activity, pp. 108–111
Outline Maps, pp. 12 and 16

Technology
Color Transparencies 32

ASSESSMENT

Prentice Hall Assessment System

Core Assessment
Chapter Tests with ExamView® Test Bank, Ch. 5
ExamView® Test Bank CD-ROM, Ch. 5

Standardized Test Preparation
Diagnose and Prescribe
Diagnostic Tests for Middle Grades Social Studies Skills
Review and Reteach
Review Book for World Studies
Practice and Assess
Test-taking Strategies with Transparencies for Middle Grades Test Prep Book
Test-taking Strategies Posters

Teaching Resources
Unit 2
Section Quizzes, pp. 19, 22, 25, and 28
Chapter Tests, pp. 138–143

Technology
Companion Web site, phschool.com
Ch. 5 Self-Test

World Video Explorer
Each region of the world is explored through regional flyovers and investigative field trips. Case study segments give students an in-depth view of the history, economy, government, and culture of a key place in each region. Case studies include Nigeria, Mexico, China, British Columbia, and the Czech Republic.

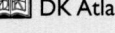

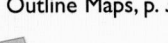

In Your Classroom

CUSTOMIZE FOR INDIVIDUAL NEEDS

Gifted and Talented

Teacher's Edition

- Expressing Problems Clearly, p. 96

Teaching Resources

- Enrichment, p. 32
- Primary Sources and Literature Readings

Honors/Pre-AP

Teacher's Edition

- Math, p. 92

Teaching Resources

- Critical Thinking, p. 33
- Primary Sources and Literature Readings

ESL

Teaching Resources

- Guided Reading and Review, pp. 18, 21, 24, and 27
- Vocabulary, p. 30
- Reteaching, p. 31
- Guide to the Essentials, pp. 1–3

Technology

- Social Studies Skills Tutor CD-ROM
- Section Reading Support Transparencies

Less Proficient Readers

Teaching Resources

- Guided Reading and Review, pp. 18, 21, 24, and 27
- Vocabulary, p. 30
- Reteaching, p. 31
- Guide to the Essentials, pp. 18–21
- Social Studies and Geography Skills, pp. 6–16

Technology

- Social Studies Skills Tutor CD-ROM
- Section Reading Support Transparencies

Less Proficient Writers

Teaching Resources

- Guided Reading and Review, pp. 18, 21, 24, and 27
- Vocabulary, p. 30
- Guide to the Essentials, pp. 18–21

Technology

- Social Studies Skills Tutor CD-ROM
- Section Reading Support Transparencies

DORLING KINDERSLEY

At the end of each unit, you will find information adapted from Dorling Kindersley's *Illustrated Children's Encyclopedia* that connects to the region being studied and to one of the seven content strands. In addition, your resources include Dorling Kindersley's *Atlas*, which contains valuable information about countries from around the world.

TEACHER'S EDITION INDEX

Activities math, p. 92; expressing problems clearly, p. 96

Connections Harriot Tubman, p. 92; influenza, p. 96

Skills Mini Lessons Recognizing Cause and Effect, p. 88; Using a Time Line, p. 96

CHAPTER 5 PACING SUGGESTIONS

For 90-minute Blocks

See suggestions in the Teaching Resources Pacing Charts for Chapter 5. Use Color Transparencies 32, 40, and 79.

Running Out of Time?

See the Guide to the Essentials, pp. 18–21.

INTERDISCIPLINARY LINKS

Middle Grades Math: Tools for Success

Course 1, Lesson 6-6, **Draw a Diagram**
Course 1, Lesson 7-1, **Exploring Ratios**
Course 2, Lesson 6-1, **Exploring Ratios**

Science Explorer

Environmental Science, Lesson 4-1, **Conserving Land and Soil**
Earth's Changing Surface, Lesson 3-4, **Glaciers**

Prentice Hall Literature

Copper, A Backwoods Boy
Bronze, Real Story of a Cowboy's Life

BIBLIOGRAPHY

For the Teacher

Morley, Jacqueline, and David Antram. *Exploring North America.* Bedrick, 1996.

Wakin, Edward, with Daniel Wakin. *Photos That Made U. S. History. Vol I: From the Civil War Era to the Atomic Age. Vol II: From the Cold War to the Space Age.* Walker, 1993.

For the Student

Easy

Lincoln, Abraham. *The Gettysburg Address.* Houghton, 1995.

Average

DK *Eyewitness Civil War.* Dorling Kindersley, 2001.

Challenging

DK McPherson, James, and Alan Brinkley, editors. *Days of Destiny: Crossroads in American History.* Dorling Kindersley, 2001.

DK Schmidt, Tom, and Jeremy Schmidt. *The Saga of Lewis & Clark.* Dorling Kindersley, 2001.

Literature Connection

Cutler, Jane. *My Wartime Summers.* Farrar, 1994.

London, Jack. *The Call of the Wild.* Holt, 1991.

Take It to the NET

The World Explorer companion Web site, found on **phschool.com**, offers activities for exploring geographical, historical, and cultural resources on the Internet. It also provides on-line links for key content and all Section and Chapter Assessment activities.

The **Teacher site** also provides teachers with regional data and ideas for student research and activities.

Students can use the **Student site** to find chapter-by-chapter Internet resource links and to access Self-Tests.

CHAPTER 5

Connecting to the Guiding Questions

In this chapter, students will read about the history of the U.S. and Canada. Content in this chapter corresponds to the following Guiding Questions outlined at the beginning of the unit.

- How have historical events affected the cultures of the United States and Canada?
- How have the United States and Canada developed the strong, democratic forms of government they have today?
- How did the United States and Canada become two of the wealthiest nations in the world?

Using the Primary Sources Activities

Point out to students that the excerpt is in John Glenn's own words, reflecting his own experience as an astronaut.

- Students may say that to continue to be a world power, the U.S. needed to have a space program. Building a strong space program was necessary for the national security of the country.
- Information gathered as the result of Glenn's flight was used on future flights. Reasons for exploration might include gathering information for scientific and educational purposes.

Heterogeneous Groups

The following activities are suitable for heterogeneous groups.

Interdisciplinary Connections

Math, p. 92

Critical Thinking

Expressing Problems Clearly, p. 96

eTeach

Be sure to check out this month's discussion with a Master Teacher. Go to **phschool.com**.

CHAPTER 5

THE UNITED STATES AND CANADA: Shaped by History

An Astronaut's Answers: An Interview with John Glenn

On February 20, 1962, American John Glenn orbited the Earth three times in the spacecraft Friendship 7. He was the first American to travel around the Earth in space. He recently answered the question about why space exploration is necessary by saying in an interview:

"The crucial hands-on experience of my flight in the Mercury program helped make the Gemini flights possible. The Gemini flights then helped make the Apollo missions to the moon a reality. Apollo gave us valuable information for the Shuttle missions, and the Shuttle/Mir program prepares us for the International Space Station. This is the nature of progress. Each of the missions has built on the knowledge gained from the previous flights.

We are a curious, questing people and our research in this new laboratory of space represents an opportunity to benefit people right here on Earth and to increase our understanding of the universe. The potential scientific, medical, and economic benefits from space are beyond our wildest dreams. That's why astronauts went to the moon, and that's why we continue to pursue our dreams of space exploration."

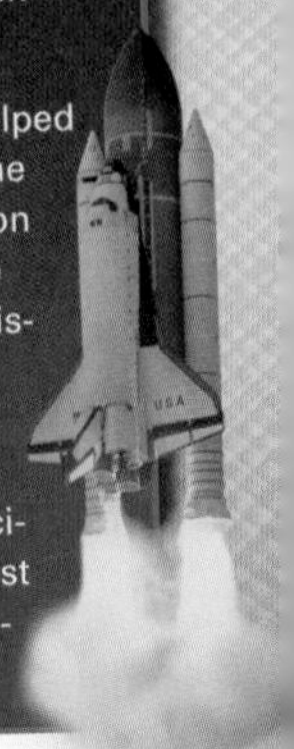

USING PRIMARY SOURCES

When reading a text, especially for the purposes of gathering information, it is important to distinguish between primary and secondary sources. A primary source is an original document, such as a speech, novel, poem, diary, eyewitness account, or interview. A secondary source is a commentary on a primary source, such as a book review.

Using Interviews

Working with a partner, make a list of the ways that John Glenn says his flight strengthened the position of the United States as a world power. Then, summarize your ideas and share them with the rest of the class. Be sure to give details from Glenn's interview to support your conclusions.

Writing an Essay

Write an essay about the future of space exploration in the United States. Answer these questions in your essay:

1. How do you think John Glenn's flight prepared the way for future space exploration in the United States?
2. Predict possible reasons for space exploration in the future.

Resource Directory

Teaching Resources

Primary Sources and Literature Readings extend content with a selection related to the concepts in this chapter.

Other Print Resources

DK Atlas

Technology

Daily Life: Life During the Civil War, from the World Video Explorer, enhances students' understanding of daily life for Americans living during the Civil War.

Student Edition on Audio CD, Ch. 5

Passport to the World CD-ROM This interactive CD-ROM allows students to explore each region of the world. Students view regional videos, take a photo tour, and explore a historical timeline. Students record their travels in an Explorer's Journal and receive passport stamps when they pass regional quizzes.

SECTION 1

Exploration in the Americas

BEFORE YOU READ

READING FOCUS

1. Who were the first Americans?
2. What effect did the arrival of Europeans have on Native Americans?
3. How did the United States win its independence from Great Britain?

KEY TERMS

indentured servant
plantation
boycott
Revolutionary War
Declaration of Independence
Constitution

KEY PEOPLE AND PLACES

Christopher Columbus
Jamestown
William Penn
Pennsylvania Colony
Thomas Jefferson
George Washington

NOTE TAKING

Copy the flow chart below. As you read the section, fill in the events that occurred in the Americas up to the time the British colonies gained independence.

30,000 years ago Hunters and gatherers reach North America
↓
1400s Christopher Columbus reaches lands in the Caribbean
↓
1500s
↓
1600s
↓
1700ss

MAIN IDEA

European settlers and colonizers spread out across the Americas, took control of Native American lands, and eventually gained their independence.

Setting the Scene

Perhaps as early as 30,000 years ago, small family groups of hunters and food gatherers reached North America from Asia. This human migration took place during the last ice age. Some scientist think that, at that time, so much water froze into thick ice sheets that the sea level dropped, exposing a land bridge between Siberia and Alaska. Hunters followed herds of bison and mammoths across this land bridge. Other migrating people may have paddled boats and fished along the coasts.

Early Tools

HISTORY This bone tool was found near the area where scientists think a land bridge once connected Asia and North America. **Critical Thinking** Why do you think the first Americans used bone as a material for making tools?

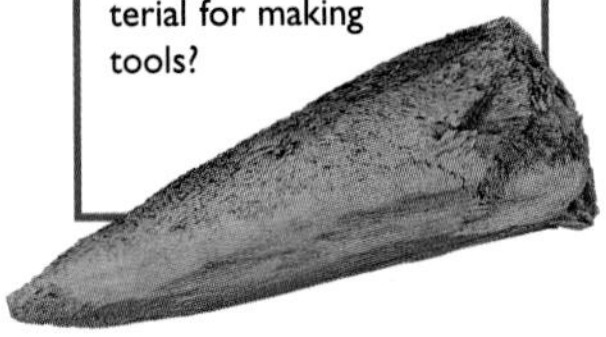

Who Were the First Americans?

In the novel *The Crown of Columbus*, Louise Erdrich, an American writer, describes the variety of Native American cultures before the Europeans arrived:

> "[They] had hundreds of societies, millions of people, whose experience had told them that the world was a pretty diverse place. Walk for a day in any direction and what do you find: A tribe with a whole new set of gods, a language as distinct from your own as Tibetan is from Dutch—very little, in fact, that's even slightly familiar."

The Europeans Arrive

Native Americans' ways of life began to change forever after 1492 when **Christopher Columbus** explored islands in the Caribbean Sea.

Resource Directory

Teaching Resources

Classroom Manager in the Unit 2 Teaching Resources, p. 17

Guided Reading and Review in the Unit 2 Teaching Resources, p. 18

Guide to the Essentials, p. 18

Technology

Section Reading Support Transparencies

SECTION 1

Lesson Objectives

1. Identify the first Americans.
2. Describe the effect of European settlement on Native Americans.
3. Explain how the United States gained independence from Great Britain.

Lesson Plan

1 Engage

Warm-Up Activity

Ask the class to answer the following questions as well as they can:

- Who were the first Americans?
- What were the 13 colonies?
- How did the United States gain its independence?

Students should verify or revise their answers as they read the section.

Activating Prior Knowledge

Encourage students to think about times they have arrived in new places such as a new school or a new community. Discuss the ambivalent feelings such experiences sometimes produce.

2 Explore

As students read the section prompt them to answer these questions: Why did English and French settlers come to the Americas? Why did American colonists want to become independent? What are the Declaration of Independence and the Constitution?

Answers to...

CRITICAL THINKING

Animal bones were readily available, and were a strong material for making tools.

Lesson Plan continued

3 Teach

Have students create a sequence chart showing the events discussed in the section. Suggest boxes linked by arrows as a chart format. Students may note cause-and-effect relationships among events if these can be supported by the text. This activity should take about 20 minutes.

Questions for Discussion

HISTORY How did the native peoples of America aid the economy of Spain?

Native people provided the labor for Spanish settlers who had enslaved them to work in mines or on farms.

GOVERNMENT What are some of the main characteristic of the government formed by the Constitution?

It is a central government of three branches in which the government's power is limited and citizens have rights that the government cannot take away.

4 Assess/Reteach

See the answers to the Section 1 Assessment. You may also assess students' charts.

Acceptable charts include at least six accurate events in correct sequence.

Commendable charts note some cause-and-effect relationships with supporting text references.

Outstanding charts show an understanding of the enormous changes that occurred when Europeans arrived.

Answers to...

MAP STUDY

Spain; Britain

North America in the Early 1700s

GEOGRAPHY Three different European countries—Spain, England, and France—controlled much of North America in the early 1700s.

Map Study Which European country held the largest territory? Which country had the territory farthest north?

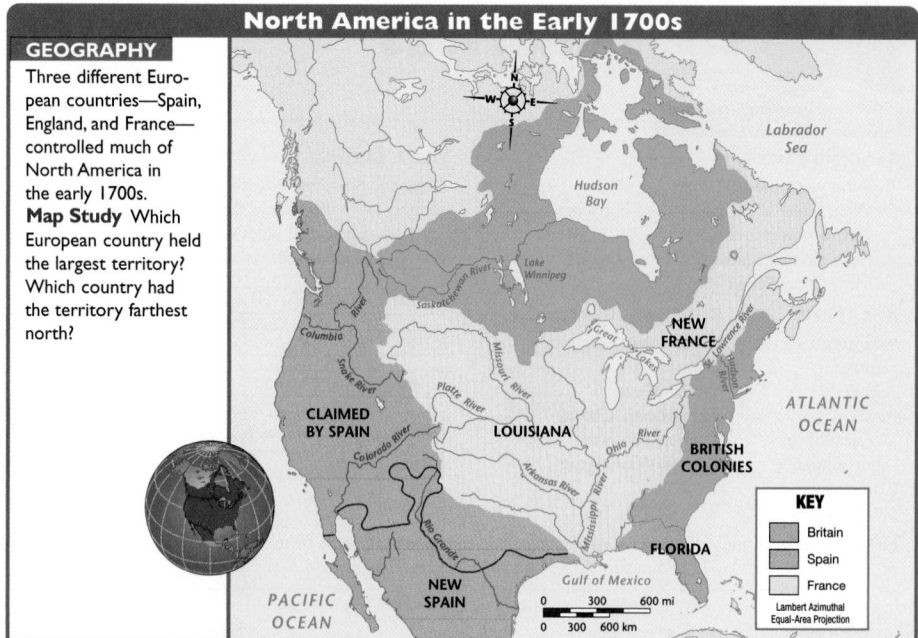

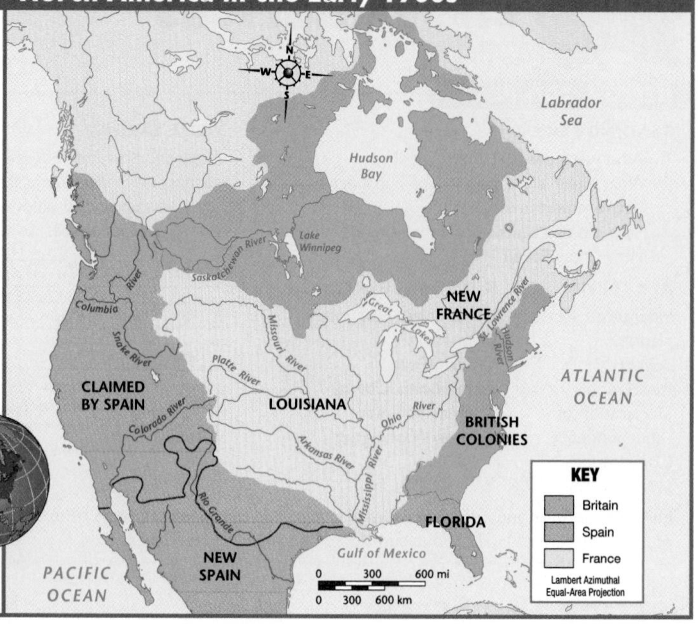

Spanish and French Claims to the Americas During the 1500s, Spanish settlers spread out across the Americas. They often enslaved native peoples, forcing them to work in mines or on farms under harsh conditions.

Spain gained great wealth from her American colonies, and soon other countries wanted colonies in the Americas. France, for example, sent explorers to claim land along the St. Lawrence and Mississippi rivers.

The English Colonists Grow Powerful English settlers established 13 colonies along the Atlantic Coast where they came to start new lives, be free from debt, own land, and practice their religion freely.

The first permanent English settlement was **Jamestown,** Virginia, founded in 1607 and, by 1619, it had the beginnings of self-government. In the same year, the first Africans arrived here as **indentured servants,** people who had to work for a period of years to gain freedom. Later, about 1640, Africans were brought as slaves. Many were forced to work on the **plantations,** large farms in the South.

In 1620, the Pilgrims arrived in Massachusetts from England. They wanted to worship God in their own way and to govern themselves. They named their settlement Plymouth. About 60 years later, **William Penn** founded the **Pennsylvania Colony.**

SKILLS MINI LESSON

Recognizing Cause and Effect

To **introduce** the skill, surround a marble with an outer circle of marbles. Have a volunteer use the middle finger and thumb to shoot the center marble at the outer circle. Point out the cause—the moving marble—and the effect—the disruption of the outer circle of marbles. Explain that a causal event must do more than occur before an effect—it must *cause* the effect. Have students **practice** using the skill with the text under the heading *Spanish and French Claims to America.* Write *Europeans Arrive* on the chalkboard and work with students to list some ways that the arrival of Europeans caused Native American life to change. To **apply** the skill, have students complete a two-column cause-and-effect chart for the remaining text in the section.

Problems developed between France and Britain, and in 1754, they went to war over land in North America. Americans call this war the French and Indian War. With the colonists' help, the British were victorious.

The Break With Britain

To help pay the cost of war with France, Great Britain imposed many kinds of taxes on the colonies, and goods bought from Britain were also taxed. Since no one represented the colonists in the British Parliament, the colonists demanded, "no taxation without representation." They also **boycotted,** or refused to buy, British goods.

Patriots such as Samuel Adams, Thomas Paine, and Patrick Henry encouraged colonists to rebel against British rule, and the **Revolutionary War** began in 1775. **Thomas Jefferson** wrote the official **Declaration of Independence,** and in July 1776, representatives from each colony voted for independence. **George Washington** led the American forces to victory in 1781. The Treaty of Paris, signed in 1783, made American independence official for the 13 new states.

To form a strong central government, state representatives met in Philadelphia in 1787 and wrote the **Constitution.** The Constitution, approved in 1789, established a government of three branches in which the government's powers are limited and citizens have rights that the government cannot take away.

CITIZENSHIP

Patriotism and the Sons of Liberty

To fight British rule, American patriots organized themselves in 1765 when the Stamp Act, a tax, was passed. A wealthy Boston merchant, Andrew Oliver, was appointed as the Distributor of Stamps for the British. Angry colonists hung an effigy of Oliver from a tree, and they stormed his house. Oliver barely escaped and quickly resigned his tax-collecting job. Encouraged by their success, the protesting colonists formed the Sons of Liberty who, in turn, formed the Committees of Correspondence to keep in touch with one another and oppose importing British goods. These Sons of Liberty risked their lives to help win American independence.

Critical Thinking Why do you think the Sons of Liberty are considered patriotic?

SECTION I ASSESSMENT

AFTER YOU READ

RECALL

1. Identify: (a) Christopher Columbus, (b) Jamestown, (c) William Penn, (d) Pennsylvania Colony, (e) Thomas Jefferson, (f) George Washington
2. Define: (a) indentured servant, (b) plantation, (c) boycott, (d) Revolutionary War, (e) Declaration of Independence, (f) Constitution

COMPREHENSION

3. Where do many scholars think the first Americans came from?
4. Identify and explain causes for a major conflict between Native Americans and the European colonists.
5. What did American colonists do to resist British rule in the American colonies?

CRITICAL THINKING AND WRITING

6. **Exploring the Main Idea** Review the Main Idea statement at the beginning of this section. Write a paragraph describing how the Spanish and the French treated the Native Americans.
7. **Recognizing Cause and Effect** Why did the colonists object to the taxes placed on them by the British?

ACTIVITY

Take It to the NET

8. **Plymouth** Learn about the lives and history of the Pilgrims of Plymouth, Massachusetts. Write and perform a skit depicting the daily lives of Pilgrims or one significant event such as the first Thanksgiving. Visit the World Explorer: People, Places, and Cultures section of **phschool.com** for help in completing this activity.

Resource Directory

Teaching Resources

Section Quiz in the Unit 2 Teaching Resources, p. 19

SECTION I ASSESSMENT

AFTER YOU READ

1. (a) sea captain who explored the Caribbean islands (b) first permanent English settlement in America (c) founder of Pennsylvania Colony (d) colony founded by William Penn (e) writer of the Declaration of Independence (f) leader of American revolutionary forces
2. (a) person who works for a period of years to gain freedom (b) large farm in the American South (c) to refuse to buy (d) war in which American colonists fought for independence from Great Britain (e) formal declaration of the 13 colonies announcing the separation of the colonies from Great Britain (f) formal document which states the fundamental principles of the government of the United States
3. Asia
4. Europeans took control of the Native Americans' lands.
5. They boycotted British goods; they refused to pay the stamp taxes; they declared independence
6. Students' paragraphs should reflect that the Spanish enslaved Native Americans; the French traded with them, and lived among them to learn their ways.
7. Colonists objected because they had no representation in the British Parliament, and they wanted "no taxation without representation."
8. Have students form groups and share their skits. Then, have each group choose a skit and present it to the rest of the class.

Answers to...

CRITICAL THINKING

They resisted British rule and supported American independence, even though they endangered their lives to do so.

SECTION 2

Lesson Objectives

1. Explain how the United States increased in size under President Thomas Jefferson.
2. Identify some effects of westward movement in the United States.
3. Explain the causes and effects of the U.S. Civil War.

Lesson Plan

1 Engage

Warm-Up Activity

Ask students to think of how toddlers who have recently learned to walk sometimes charge forward uncertainly and bump into things or fall down. Relate this moment in human development to the young United States during the 1800s.

Activating Prior Knowledge

Have students imagine their neighborhood before human settlement by mentally removing buildings and roads and adding forests or prairies. Invite them to describe what they see in their imaginations.

SECTION 2

Growth and Conflict in the United States

BEFORE YOU READ

READING FOCUS

1. How was President Jefferson responsible for doubling the size of the United States?
2. How did the United States begin to grow and prosper?
3. What were the causes and effects of the United States Civil War?

KEY TERMS

Louisiana Purchase
immigrant
Industrial Revolution
abolitionist
Confederacy
Civil War
Reconstruction
segregate

KEY PEOPLE

Meriwether Lewis
William Clark
Andrew Jackson
Abraham Lincoln

NOTE TAKING

Copy the chart shown below. As you read the section, fill in information about the ways in which the United States grew, and the conflicts the United States faced.

Growth	Conflicts
Louisiana Purchase	War with Mexico

MAIN IDEA

After growing to include land from the Atlantic to the Pacific Oceans, the United States was torn apart by the Civil War in the 1860s.

The Lewis and Clark Expedition

HISTORY It took Meriwether Lewis (left) and William Clark (right) three years to complete their exploration of the lands west of the Mississippi River. **Critical Thinking** Why do you think the information gathered by Lewis and Clark was so valuable to America?

Setting the Scene

In 1803, President Thomas Jefferson sent **Meriwether Lewis** and **William Clark** to explore land west of the Mississippi River. As they journeyed all the way to the Pacific Coast, Lewis and Clark found plants and animals completely new to them. With this new information, Lewis and Clark created accurate, highly valuable maps of the region. They also met Native American groups along the way. During these meetings, the two men tried to learn about the region and set up trading alliances. Few of those Native Americans had any idea how this visit would change their way of life.

A Growing Nation

In 1803, President Jefferson bought all the land between the Mississippi River and the eastern slopes of the Rocky Mountains from France for only $15 million. This sale of land, called the **Louisiana Purchase,** doubled the size of the United States. Since little was known about this land, Lewis and Clark were sent to explore it.

Resource Directory

Teaching Resources

Classroom Manager in the Unit 2 Teaching Resources, p. 20

Guided Reading and Review in the Unit 2 Teaching Resources, p. 21

Guide to the Essentials, p. 19

Technology

Section Reading Support Transparencies

Answers to...

CRITICAL THINKING

It provided Americans with maps of the area and information about the land. Once Americans had this information, they began to move west and, in many areas, displace the Native Americans.

The Nation Prospers

As the country grew, so did the meaning of democracy. In the 13 original states, only white males who owned property could vote. New states passed laws giving the vote to all white men 21 years old or older, whether they owned property or not. Soon, all states gave every adult white male the right to vote. Women and African Americans, however, could not vote.

In 1828, voters elected **Andrew Jackson** as president. He supported the interests of poor farmers, laborers, and settlers who wanted Native American lands in the Southeast.

More Room to Grow The United States also continued to gain land. In 1836, American settlers in the Mexican territory of Texas rebelled against Mexican authority. With a force of more than 4,000 men, Antonio López de Santa Anna, Mexico's new leader, marched towards San Antonio to personally put down the rebellion. Although Santa Anna would defeat the Texans at the Alamo and Goliad, he would lose decisively to Sam Houston, the leader of the Texas volunteers, and his men at the Battle of San Jacinto on April 21, 1836. The territory was named the Lone Star Republic of Texas. In 1845, Texas became part of the United States. Only a year later, the United States went to war with Mexico and gained much of what is now the Southwest region. In the 1840s, American wagon trains began to cross the continent heading for the West as Americans started to settle this new land.

The Industrial Revolution At the same time, thousands of people were pouring into cities in the Northeast. Many were **immigrants,** or people who moved from one country to another. This movement was spurred by the **Industrial Revolution,** or the change from making goods by hand to making them by machine.

The first industry to change was clothmaking, or textiles. New spinning machines and power looms enabled people to make cloth more quickly than they could by hand. Other inventions, such as the steam engine, made travel easier and faster. Steamboats and steam locomotives moved people and goods rapidly. By 1860, railroads linked most major Northeastern and Southeastern cities.

HISTORY In the 1820s, a Cherokee leader named Sequoyah developed a system of writing that enabled his people to read and write in their own language. **Critical Thinking** What do you think were some of the benefits of this system of writing?

The Civil War and Reconstruction

In the late 1700s, a new machine called the cotton gin was invented. It quickly removed seeds from cotton, which made the crop more profitable. Cotton wore out the soil, though, and plantation owners wanted to expand into new western lands. Growing cotton still required many laborers for planting and harvesting. Since plantation owners relied on slaves, that meant that slavery would spread into the new territories. Some people did not want this and a debate began. Should the states or the federal government decide about slavery in the new territories?

AS YOU READ
Monitor Your Reading How did the cotton gin and new land affect slavery in the United States?

2 Explore

Urge students to answer the following questions as they read the section: What allowed the United States to double its size? What happened to Native Americans as settlers moved westward? Why did many people from other countries move to the United States? Why did the North and South go to war?

3 Teach

Have students make timelines reflecting the dates and explaining events highlighted in the section. This activity should take about 20 minutes.

Questions for Discussion

HISTORY How did the Louisiana Purchase eventually affect the United States' policy towards Native Americans?

Settlement of this land purchased from France meant that Native Americans would have to give up their land.

HISTORY What actions of the abolitionists greatly disturbed Southern slave owners?

They helped slaves escape to freedom.

Resource Directory

Teaching Resources

Outline Maps, The United States: Physical, p. 14; The United States: Political, p. 15

Answers to...

CRITICAL THINKING

The system of writing allowed for better communication among the Cherokee people.

AS YOU READ

The cotton gin made the cotton crop more profitable, and new land meant that slavery would continue.

Lesson Plan continued

4 Assess/Reteach

See the answers to the Section 2 Assessment. You may also assess students' timelines.

Acceptable timelines include at least four dates and events and some explanatory information.

Commendable timelines include at least six dates and events and explanatory information about most events.

Outstanding timelines include at least six dates and events and explanatory information about all listed events.

HISTORY

Harriet Tubman (c. 1820–1913)

Harriet Tubman spent the first 29 years of her life as a slave. In 1849 she escaped to the North but returned to guide other slaves to freedom. Tubman soon became one of the most tireless "conductors" on the Underground Railroad. The secret flights were very dangerous for all involved, and Tubman did not tolerate any risky behavior. She kept people in line by making sure they knew she carried a gun. Such no-nonsense behavior led abolitionist John Brown to admiringly dub her "General Tubman."

ACTIVITY

Interdisciplinary Connections

Math Tell students that the Louisiana Purchase consisted of 828,000 square miles (2,144,520 sq km) of land. Using the purchase price of $15 million, have students calculate the price per square mile and per square kilometer ($18.11/square mile; $7.00/square kilometer). Explain that this works out to less than 3 cents per acre—a real bargain by today's standards.

Logical/Mathematical

Growth of the United States From 1783

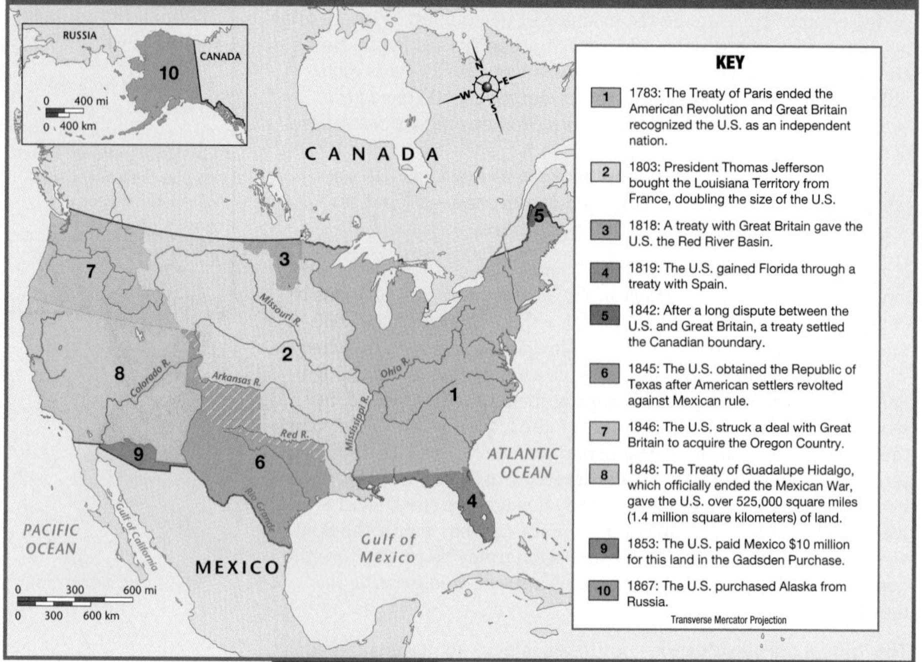
RUSSIA
CANADA
10
0 400 mi
0 400 km
CANADA
KEY
1 1783: The Treaty of Paris ended the American Revolution and Great Britain recognized the U.S. as an independent nation.
2 1803: President Thomas Jefferson bought the Louisiana Territory from France, doubling the size of the U.S.
3 1818: A treaty with Great Britain gave the U.S. the Red River Basin.
4 1819: The U.S. gained Florida through a treaty with Spain.
5 1842: After a long dispute between the U.S. and Great Britain, a treaty settled the Canadian boundary.
6 1845: The U.S. obtained the Republic of Texas after American settlers revolted against Mexican rule.
7 1846: The U.S. struck a deal with Great Britain to acquire the Oregon Country.
8 1848: The Treaty of Guadalupe Hidalgo, which officially ended the Mexican War, gave the U.S. over 525,000 square miles (1.4 million square kilometers) of land.
9 1853: The U.S. paid Mexico $10 million for this land in the Gadsden Purchase.
10 1867: The U.S. purchased Alaska from Russia.
Transverse Mercator Projection
Missouri R.
Arkansas R.
Colorado R.
Red R.
Mississippi R.
Ohio R.
Rio Grande
Gulf of California
ATLANTIC OCEAN
PACIFIC OCEAN
Gulf of Mexico
MEXICO
0 300 600 mi
0 300 600 km

GEOGRAPHY The region known as the United States grew to its present size over a period of about 100 years. As you can see, the United States made agreements with many countries in order to gain land.
Map Study What parts of the United States were once claimed by Great Britain? How did the United States acquire the Louisiana Territory? How did the United States acquire Alaska?

Causes of Conflict Until 1850, there were equal numbers of slave and free states in the United States. Then, California was admitted to the union as a free state. When the Southern states objected because California's admission upset the balance, Congress passed the Fugitive Slave Act. It said people anywhere in the country must return runaway slaves to their owners. Before this law, a slave who could make the journey safely into a free state was considered free. The Fugitive Slave Act only increased the argument over slavery.

Thousands of Northerners became **abolitionists** (ab uh LISH un ists), people who wanted to end slavery. Many helped slaves escape to Canada where slavery was illegal. Most Southerners, however, felt that abolitionists were robbing them of their property.

When **Abraham Lincoln,** a Northerner, was elected president in 1860, many Southerners feared they would have little say in govern-

Answers to...

MAP STUDY

Most eastern lands from the Atlantic Ocean to the Mississippi River were once claimed by Britain. In addition, Britain also claimed the Red River Basin in the north-central part of the country and Oregon Country in the Pacific Northwest. The United States gained the Louisiana Territory by buying it from France and bought Alaska from Russia.

ment. Some Southern states seceded, or withdrew, from the United States. They founded the Confederate States of America, or the **Confederacy.**

Conflict Erupts Into War In 1861, the **Civil War** between the North and the South erupted and lasted four years. The North, known as the Union, had more industry, wealth, and soldiers; the Confederacy had experienced military officers and cotton. Southerners hoped that the foreign countries that bought cotton would help supply the Confederacy with the materials necessary to fight the war.

In 1863, Lincoln issued the Emancipation Proclamation which freed slaves in areas loyal to the Confederacy. After this, thousands of African Americans joined the fight against the South.

The Civil War ended with a Union victory in 1865. Lincoln wanted the Southern states to return willingly to the Union. This was the first step for the **Reconstruction,** or rebuilding, of the nation.

Reconstructing the Union Less than a week after the end of the war, Lincoln was assassinated and Congress took control of Reconstruction. The Union Army governed the South until new state officials were elected. But as soon as the Union Army withdrew, Southern lawmakers voted to **segregate,** or separate, blacks from whites. The conflict between North and South ended with preserving the United States, but segregation affected all aspects of life for nearly a hundred years. The long struggle to guarantee equality to all Americans still lay ahead.

Fighting for Their Cause

CITIZENSHIP The picture shows African American soldiers outside their barracks at Fort Lincoln, Washington, D.C., in early 1865. Twenty-one African Americans received the Congressional Medal of Honor, the country's highest award for bravery. **Critical Thinking** Why do you think African Americans were willing to fight for the Union?

SECTION 2 ASSESSMENT

AFTER YOU READ

RECALL

1. Identify: (a) Meriwether Lewis, (b) William Clark, (c) Andrew Jackson, (d) Abraham Lincoln
2. Define: (a) Louisiana Purchase, (b) immigrant, (c) Industrial Revolution, (d) abolitionist, (e) Civil War, (f) Reconstruction, (g) segregate, (h) Confederacy

COMPREHENSION

3. What land did the United States gain as a result of the Louisiana Purchase?
4. What region did the United States gain through war with Mexico in 1846?
5. Why did the Southern states withdraw from the Union?

CRITICAL THINKING AND WRITING

6. **Exploring the Main Idea** Review the Main Idea statement at the beginning of this section. Then, write three paragraphs explaining how the westward expansion of the United States affected Native Americans, slaves, and citizens of the Southern states.
7. **Identifying Cause and Effect** How did the issue of slavery become a cause of the Civil War?

ACTIVITY

8. **Making a Chart** The Native Americans had a different attitude about the land than the white settlers had. Find out more about the Native Americans who were forced to leave the southeastern states and move to Oklahoma. Make a chart that compares and contrasts how these attitudes toward the land separated the Native American culture and the white settlers' culture.

SECTION 2 ASSESSMENT

AFTER YOU READ

1. (a and b) explorers who traveled and mapped land west of the Mississippi (c) president who removed Native Americans from their land (d) president during the Civil War who issued the Emancipation Proclamation
2. (a) U.S. purchase of land between the Mississippi and the Rockies (b) person who moves from one country to another (c) change from making goods by hand to making them with machines (d) person who wanted to end slavery (e) war between Northern and Southern states (f) rebuilding the nation (g) to separate (h) Southern states that separated from the United States after the election of Lincoln in 1860
3. The United States gained all the land between the Mississippi River and the eastern slopes of the Rocky Mountains.
4. The United States gained the Southwest region through the war with Mexico in 1846.
5. Southern slave owners feared President Lincoln would abolish slavery.
6. Students' paragraphs should mention that Native Americans were pushed from their land, slavery expanded as more land became available for plantations, Southerners worried about the increased opposition to slavery as more states were added to the Union.
7. Northerners and Southerners disagreed about slavery.
8. Students' charts should demonstrate an understanding of the different attitudes of white settlers and Native Americans toward land ownership and use.

Resource Directory

Teaching Resources

Section Quiz in the Unit 2 Teaching Resources, p. 22

Answers to...

CRITICAL THINKING

The Union was against slavery.

SECTION 3

Lesson Objectives

1. Explain the effects of the Industrial Revolution on the United States.
2. Trace the U.S. path to world power.
3. Identify some ways in which American society has worked toward equality among citizens.

Lesson Plan

1 Engage

Warm-Up Activity

Summarize the 1964 Civil Rights Act and read the 19th Constitutional Amendment aloud to students. (The text of the documents can be found in an encyclopedia or other reference.) Tell students that laws granting civil rights and the right to vote to women are just two of the many changes that have occurred in the United States since the Civil War. Today, we may take these rights for granted, however, they represent important milestones in American history.

Activating Prior Knowledge

Ask volunteers to share their experiences and knowledge of city life. How are neighborhoods in a city different? Urge those students with limited urban experiences to recall films, books, or visits to cities.

Answers to...

CRITICAL THINKING

He probably wanted people to work for changes in housing laws and in labor laws that would give workers a fair wage so they could live decently; he probably wanted people to give charity to help the poor.

SECTION 3

The Emergence of a World Power

BEFORE YOU READ

READING FOCUS

1. What events were taking place in the United States from 1865 to 1914?
2. What events led to United States involvement in World War I and World War II?
3. How did the United States change after World War II?

KEY TERMS

labor force
settlement house
Homestead Act
Holocaust
communism
Cold War
civil rights movement

KEY PEOPLE

Jacob Riis
Jane Addams
Franklin D. Roosevelt
Harry S. Truman
Martin Luther King, Jr.

NOTE TAKING

Copy the web diagram shown here. As you read the section, fill in the empty ovals with forces that made the United States a world power.

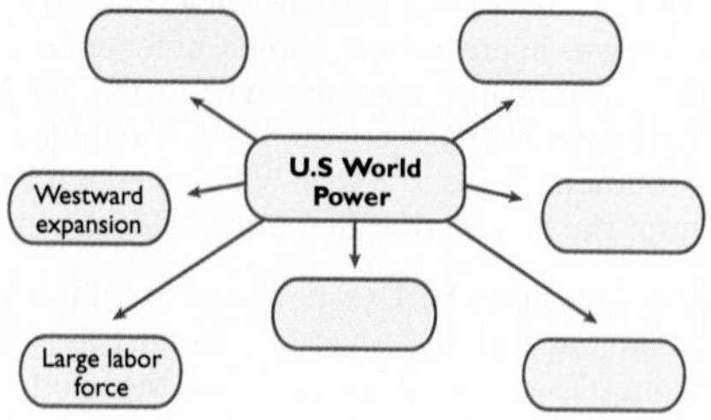

MAIN IDEA

As the United States expanded and its economy grew, it began to play a more important role in world affairs.

Crowded City Life

ECONOMICS Jacob Riis argued that tenements like these in New York City, which crowded as many as 10 people to a room, bred misery, disease, and crime. **Critical Thinking** What do you think Jacob Riis wanted "the other half" of the people to do about tenements and poverty?

Setting the Scene

Jacob Riis was an angry man. In his book *How the Other Half Lives*, he took his readers on tours of tenement life in the late 1800s. He wanted other people to be angry, too—angry enough to change things.

"Come over here. Step carefully over this baby—it is a baby, in spite of its rags and dirt—under these iron bridges called fire escapes, but loaded down...with broken household goods, with wash-tubs and barrels, over which no man could climb from a fire....That baby's parents live in the rear tenement here....There are plenty of houses with half a hundred such in."

Riis himself had experienced these conditions first hand. Like many immigrants before him, Riis had suffered in the years following his arrival in the United States. Though he overcame the obstacles to become a journalist, Riis never forgot his past and worked hard for reform.

Resource Directory

Teaching Resources

Classroom Manager in the Unit 2 Teaching Resources, p. 23

Guided Reading and Review in the Unit 2 Teaching Resources, p. 24

Guide to the Essentials, p. 20

Technology

Section Reading Support Transparencies

Life in the West

SCIENCE, TECHNOLOGY, AND SOCIETY

New technology helped settlers turn vast areas of the West into productive farmland. Above, a huge combine harvester cuts wheat on a farm in Washington State. **Critical Thinking** Why was the development of new farming technology important to the settling of the Plains region?

The United States From 1865 to 1914

The Industrial Revolution made life easier for the rich and the middle class, but life did not improve for many of the poor. City slums were crowded with poor immigrants, many of whom could not speak English. These newcomers were a huge **labor force,** or supply of workers. But employers paid them very little, and even small children had to work so that families could make ends meet.

Reformers like Jacob Riis began to protest such poverty. In Chicago, **Jane Addams** set up a **settlement house,** or community center, for poor immigrants. Mary Harris Jones traveled across the country to help miners organize for better wages. Because of her work to end child labor, people called her "Mother Jones."

To escape poverty, many people moved to the open plains and prairies of the Midwest. When the United States government passed the **Homestead Act** in 1862, it gave 160 acres (65 hectares) of land to any adult willing to farm it and live on it for five years. Railroads helped connect the East and West coasts, which speeded up settlement. But life on the plains was not easy because trees and water were often in short supply, and settlers faced swarms of insects, wild prairie fires, and temperatures that were very hot in summer and cold in winter. Still, most homesteaders held on for the five years.

The United States Expands Beyond Its Shores The United States also expanded beyond its immediate borders. In 1867, Secretary of State William Seward arranged for the United States to buy the territory of Alaska from Russia. In 1898, the United States took control of Hawaii, another territory. In the same year, the United States fought and won the Spanish-American War, gaining control of the Spanish lands of Cuba, Puerto Rico, Guam, and the Philippines. Because America had a strong economy and military strength, it was able to gain overseas territory.

Resource Directory

Teaching Resources

Outline Maps, The World: Political, p. 3

Technology

Color Transparencies 40 The United States: Political Map; **79** *Troops Rising* Fine Art

2 Explore

As students read, invite them to answer the following questions: How was life different for rich, middle-class, and poor people during the late 1800s? What did the Homestead Act do? What were some causes of the U.S. involvement in World Wars I and II? Why were the United States and the Soviet Union at odds during the Cold War?

3 Teach

Have students create a glossary of important terms linked to the period of American history covered in the section. Students may use the section's key terms as a starting point and should add other terms that they feel are important in creating a picture of the time period. Urge students to use their own words when writing definitions. This activity should take about 30 minutes.

Questions for Discussion

HISTORY What caused Jacob Riis, Jane Addams, and Mary Harris Jones to call for civil reform and worker's rights in the late 19th century?

The Industrial Revolution had brought prosperity to the rich and middle class, but created new hardships for the poor. Poor living conditions for the new labor force, many of them immigrants, lack of worker's rights, and child labor moved these individuals to action.

GOVERNMENT What kind of government did Germany have during WWII?

Germany was a dictatorship led by Adolph Hitler.

Answers to...

CRITICAL THINKING

New farming technology made it possible to profitably cultivate the land and probably encouraged many more people to risk moving to the West.

Lesson Plan continued

4 Assess/Reteach

See the answers to the Section 3 Assessment. You may also assess students' glossaries.

Acceptable glossaries include all key terms with correct definitions.

Commendable glossaries include all key terms with correct definitions and at least two other terms with correct definitions.

Outstanding glossaries include all key terms with correct definitions and include other terms and definitions that indicate insight into the events that have shaped recent history.

HISTORY

Influenza

As World War I was ending, many countries around the world were fighting a different war. The influenza epidemic of 1918 swept through India, Russia, China, Europe, and the United States. Worldwide, about 20 million people died. In fact, the influenza outbreak of 1918 ranks alongside the Black Death as one of the most destructive epidemics in history. Hardest hit were the very old and very young and those living in cities where overcrowding and malnutrition allowed deadly secondary bacterial infections to set in.

ACTIVITY

Critical Thinking

Expressing Problems Clearly
Suitable as an individual or a whole class activity. Ask students to scan several current national and local newspapers. Challenge them to identify some major problems facing the United States today as a result of the events of September 11, 2001 and its aftermath. Then, have students express these problems in either question or statement form.

Logical/Mathematical

GOVERNMENT
During World War I, the United States government paid for the war effort by selling bonds. These were certificates that included a promise to pay back the face amount plus interest. Posters like this urged Americans to buy bonds to win the war.
Critical Thinking Why do you think many people felt it was their duty as citizens of a democratic society to participate in buying bonds?

The World at War

As a player in world affairs, the United States was drawn into international conflicts. In 1914, World War I broke out in Europe. The United States joined the Allied Powers of Great Britain and France three years later. They fought against the Central Powers, which included Germany, Austria-Hungary, and Turkey. With American help, the Allies won the war in 1918.

In the United States, the economy boomed during the 1920s. Women enjoyed new freedoms and the hard-won right to vote. More and more people bought cars, refrigerators, radios, and other modern marvels.

In 1929, however, the world faced an economic disaster called the Great Depression. In America, factories closed, people lost their jobs, and farmers lost their farms. Many banks closed, and people lost their life savings. In 1933, President **Franklin D. Roosevelt** took office. He created a plan called the New Deal. This was a series of government programs to help people get jobs and to restore the economy. Some of these programs, like Social Security, are still in place today.

The Great Depression was very hard on Germany and its people lost hope. In 1933, they responded by turning to Adolf Hitler who became dictator of Germany. Hitler convinced Germans they were a superior ethnic group and should take over Europe. In 1939, Hitler's armies invaded Poland, starting World War II. The allied powers of Great Britain, France, and Russia fought against the Axis Powers of Germany, Italy, and Japan.

Hitler forced countless Jews, Gypsies, Slavs, and others into brutal prison camps murdering millions of people, including some six million Jews. This horrible mass murder is called the **Holocaust** (HAHL uh kawst).

Up to this point, however, the United States did not get involved in the war. But in 1941, Japan attacked a United States naval base at Pearl Harbor, Hawaii. The Japanese were allied with the Germans, so the United States declared war on both nations and sent armed forces to fight in Europe and in the Pacific. President Roosevelt, who led the nation in war, died in April 1945, and Vice President **Harry S. Truman** became president.

In May 1945, the Allies defeated the Germans. During the summer, President Truman decided to drop two atomic bombs on Japan, which convinced Japan to give up. Finally, World War II was over.

Answers to...

CRITICAL THINKING

People probably felt that it was their duty to contribute money to help win the war and preserve their nation.

SKILLS MINI LESSON

Using a Timeline

To **introduce** the skill, ask students to locate the earliest and latest time periods covered in this section. Explain that one way to trace the sequence of events over an extended time period is with a timeline. Students may **practice** the skill by creating a timeline for the events in this section. Students may **apply** the skill as they answer a partner's questions about the dates and events shown on the timeline.

Postwar Responsibilities

After World War II, the United States took on new international responsibilities. The Soviet Union had been created in 1922. It adopted a form of government called **communism** where the state owns all property, such as farms and factories. After World War II, the communist Soviet Union took control of many Eastern European countries and imposed communism on them. The leader of the Soviet Union, Joseph Stalin, was a dictator who had complete control over the government and over the lives of the people. Unlike the United States, where officials are elected by the people and have to answer to them, Stalin answered to no one.

The United States feared that the Soviets were trying to spread communism throughout the world. As a result, the United States and the Soviet Union entered the **Cold War.** This was a period of great tension which lasted more than 40 years, although the two countries never faced each other in an actual war. Two wars grew out of this tension—the Korean War and the Vietnam War.

The economy of the United States boomed after World War II. But not all citizens shared in the benefits. In many areas, segregation was a way of life. People like **Martin Luther King, Jr.,** led the **civil rights movement** to end segregation and win rights for African Americans. This success inspired others who felt they were treated unequally.

ECONOMICS

Citizens from all over the nation took part in the 1963 March on Washington to support a civil rights bill. Martin Luther King, Jr., summed up their common hopes in his "I Have a Dream" speech. **Critical Thinking** In the civil rights movement, many people broke the law by fighting for equality. Do you think their actions were justified? Why?

SECTION 3 ASSESSMENT

AFTER YOU READ

RECALL

1. Identify: (a) Jacob Riis, (b) Jane Addams, (c) Franklin D. Roosevelt, (d) Harry S. Truman, (e) Martin Luther King, Jr.
2. Define: (a) labor force, (b) settlement house, (c) Homestead Act, (d) Holocaust, (e) communism, (f) Cold War, (g) civil rights movement

COMPREHENSION

3. How did the Industrial Revolution affect economic conditions in the United States?
4. What effect did the Great Depression have on the United States and Germany?
5. What were some of the challenges faced by the United States after World War II?

CRITICAL THINKING AND WRITING

6. **Exploring the Main Idea** Review the Main Idea statement at the beginning of this section. Then, write a paragraph describing how the United States carried out its responsibilities as a world power.
7. **Recognizing Cause and Effect** How did the Homestead Act help settle the Plains?

ACTIVITY

8. **Using Primary Sources** People who stay home during a war also find ways to help their country. Interview family and friends who remember the period of time during World War II. Ask questions about such things as rationing, volunteer work, and the employment of women during the war. Then, write a report about what life was like at home during the war.

Resource Directory

Teaching Resources

Section Quiz in the Unit 2 Teaching Resources, p. 25

Answers to...

CRITICAL THINKING

Yes, because these very laws promoted inequality.

SECTION 3 ASSESSMENT

AFTER YOU READ

1. (a) author whose writing showed how poor Americans lived (b) founder of settlement house in Chicago (c) president during Great Depression and World War II, creator of the New Deal (d) president at end of World War II, ordered the use of atomic bombs against Japan (e) leader of civil rights movement
2. (a) supply of workers (b) community center for poor immigrants (c) government program that offered free land to settlers (d) the mass murder of Jews, Gypsies, Slavs and others by Germany during WWII (e) system of government in which the state owns all industry and people share work and rewards equally (f) period of great tension between the United States and the Soviet Union (g) movement to end segregation and gain rights for African Americans
3. The wealthy and the middle class prospered. Poor immigrants made up the bulk of the labor force and lived in crowded city slums.
4. In America, factories and other businesses closed. People lost their jobs, their farms, and their life's savings. In Germany, people responded to the Great Depression by turning to Adolph Hitler for hope. Hitler invaded Poland and World War II began.
5. The United States had new international responsibilities such as opposing the spread of communism. The Civil Rights movement fought to end segregation and win rights for African Americans and other minorities.
6. Students' paragraphs should mention fighting the Cold War and fighting to protect civil rights.
7. Many settlers were attracted by the fact that the act gave them 160 acres of land for free.
8. Students' reports should contain particular points to illustrate what life was like at home during the war.

SECTION 4

Lesson Objectives

1. Explain the reasons for French and British rivalry in Canada.
2. Trace Canada's path to independence.
3. Explain how Canada became a world power.

Lesson Plan

1 Engage

Warm-Up Activity

Write the following headings on the chalkboard: *People, Languages, History, Land, and Laws.* Challenge students to categorize their knowledge of Canada according to the listed headings. As students study the section, invite them to add to the list. Students may also suggest revisions or corrections to the list.

Activating Prior Knowledge

Tell students that fads have been around a long time. Fads can make a company rich. Ask the class to list some of this year's most popular fashion items or fads among students their age. Discuss how fads like these can drive sales and what companies might do to ensure the popularity and sales of their products.

SECTION 4

Settlement, Trade, and Independence in Canada

BEFORE YOU READ

READING FOCUS

1. Why were France and Britain rivals in Canada?
2. How did Canada become an independent nation?
3. How did Canada become a world power?

KEY TERMS

dominion
bilingual

KEY PEOPLE AND PLACES

Ontario
Quebec
Louis Papineau
William Mackenzie

NOTE TAKING

Copy the flowchart shown below. As you read the section, fill in the important events that led to Canada becoming a strong and independent industrial power.

1713 Treaty gives Great Britain the Hudson Bay and Acadia
↓
1754
↓
1867
↓
World War I & II
↓
1982

MAIN IDEA

Canada won independence from Great Britain, grew industrially, and established close relations with the United States, but the tensions between the French and British cultures in Canada remain.

The Fur Trade in Canada

ECONOMICS The trade in beaver furs is an example of a primary economic activity which supplied the raw materials for beaver hats, like the one shown here. These hats were the height of fashion in Europe during the 1700s and 1800s, making the trade in beaver furs highly profitable.

Critical Thinking What do you think happened to the demand for beaver hats when fashions changed in Europe?

Setting the Scene

The Haida are one of Canada's First Nations, living on the Queen Charlotte Islands off the coast of British Columbia. Haida mythology is very rich and complex. As in many Native American folktales, animals play an important role in Haida mythology. The Haida believe, for example, that the Raven created the Earth when he became tired of flying over a world covered with water. The Beaver is another important figure in Haida mythology. Imagine how the Haida felt when European trappers killed almost all of the beavers to make fur hats.

The French and the British in Canada

The profitable fur trade in Canada brought two European powers—France and Great Britain—into conflict. In 1713, they signed a peace treaty, giving Great Britain the Hudson Bay region and southeastern Canada, called Acadia. But this peace was uneasy. Against their will, French Catholics in Acadia came under the rule of British Protestants. The French controlled

Resource Directory

Teaching Resources

Classroom Manager in the Unit 2 Teaching Resources, p. 26

Guided Reading and Review in the Unit 2 Teaching Resources, p. 27

Guide to the Essentials, p. 21

Technology

Section Reading Support Transparencies

Answers to...

CRITICAL THINKING

The demand for beaver fur eventually decreased, making the trade less profitable.

the lowlands south of Hudson Bay and around the St. Lawrence River, and both countries wanted to control the Ohio River Valley, farther to the south. The French wanted beavers for furs; the British wanted land for settlement.

The contest for this region was so intense that in 1754, it erupted into the Seven Years' War, called the French and Indian War in the United States. The British won the decisive Battle of Quebec in 1759 and gained complete control over Canada. Some French settlers returned to France and those who stayed resisted English culture. The Quebec Act gave the French people there the right to speak their own language, practice their own religion, and follow their own customs.

During the American Revolution, Americans who did not want independence were called British Loyalists. After the war, many Loyalists moved to Canada. But most did not want to live in a French culture. Great Britain divided the land into two colonies, Upper and Lower Canada. Most Loyalists moved into Upper Canada, now called **Ontario**. French Canadians remained in Lower Canada, now **Quebec.**

The Battle of Quebec, 1759

HISTORY The Battle of Quebec was a turning point in the French and Indian War. This painting illustrates how British troops found a path through the cliffs that protected Quebec. **Critical Thinking** Do you think that Quebec would have fallen to the British if troops had not found a path in? Why or why not?

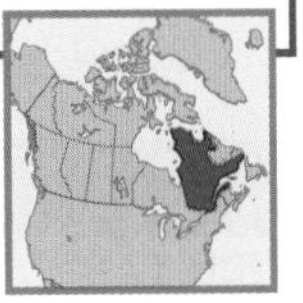

Canada Seeks Self-Rule

Both French Canadians and British Canadians hated British rule, but the two groups did not join in rebellion. In 1837, a French Canadian named **Louis Papineau** (pah pee NOH) organized a revolt in Lower Canada. His goal was to establish the region as a separate country. In Upper Canada, **William Mackenzie** led the people against British rule. The British easily defeated the rebels in both cases.

British leaders, afraid more trouble was coming, agreed to give Canadians more control of their government by uniting Upper and Lower Canada to form the Province of Canada. Because the British feared the Canadians might make a successful rebellion, not all the provinces were included in the union.

But Canadians felt that all provinces should be represented for their government to be effective. In 1864, leaders from every province met and worked out a plan to form a union. On July 1, 1867, the British Parliament accepted the plan and passed the British North American Act. This made Canada "one Dominion under the name of Canada." A **dominion** is a self-governing area but still subject to Great Britain. But now a central government would run the country. Canada had won its "peaceful revolution."

Canada Takes Its Place in the World When Britain entered World War I, Canadians were still British subjects. Canada, therefore, entered the war, too. Canada contributed so much in resources and soldiers to the Allied victory that the young country became a world power. Great Britain recognized Canada's new strength and granted it more independence. During the Great Depression, Canada focused on solving problems at home, but when World War II began in 1939, Canada took part. Once again, Canadian efforts helped win the war.

Resource Directory

Teaching Resources

Outline Maps, The United States and Canada: Political, p. 12; Canada: Political, p. 16

Technology

Color Transparencies 32 Canada: Political Map

Answers to...

CRITICAL THINKING

No, because the cliffs acted as a natural barrier to intruders.

2 Explore

Encourage students to answer these questions as they read the section: Why was the Seven Years' War fought? What was the relationship between French Canadians and British Canadians during the 1700s and 1800s? What is Canada's current relationship to Great Britain?

3 Teach

Tell students to create a children's story about the history of Canada. Using data from the section text and their own art, students should develop a narrative format while staying true to the facts. This activity should take about 35 minutes.

Questions for Discussion

HISTORY How has British and French colonization affected the Canadian culture?

Canada has two distinct cultures within its borders: the British-influenced culture of greater Canada and the French Canadian culture of Quebec. Both French and English are official languages of Canada.

GOVERNMENT What kinds of government did Canada have after Great Britain passed the British North American Act in 1867?

A dominion—a self-governing area still subject to the rule of Great Britain. A Canadian central government ran the country.

4 Assess/Reteach

See the answers to the Section 4 Assessment. You may also assess students' stories.

Acceptable stories should contain accurate information linked to each main section heading.

Commendable stories should use illustrations to capture important moments in Canadian history.

Outstanding stories should incorporate facts from the section into a coherent and engaging illustrated narrative.

SECTION 4 ASSESSMENT

AFTER YOU READ

1. (a) province that was once known as Upper Canada (b) province that was once known as Lower Canada (c) French Canadian organizer of 1837 revolt in Lower Canada (d) leader of revolt against British rule in Upper Canada
2. (a) self-governing area (b) having or using two languages
3. The French wanted to trap beavers there and sell their fur. The British wanted to settle the land.
4. Canadian leaders from every province worked out a plan to form a union, and in 1867 the British Parliament accepted the plan and made Canada an independent dominion.
5. Canadians built factories during the war to produce goods not available from Europe. After the war, Europeans bought these Canadian factory-made goods. Immigrants added to industry's labor pool.
6. Students' editorials should include references to: the French and British conflict over control of land in Canada and in the Ohio valley; the French and Indian War; the separation into Upper and Lower Canada; and the ongoing cultural clash between English-speaking Canadians and the French-speaking Canadians who want the province of Quebec to be independent from Canada.
7. Students' cartoons should demonstrate an understanding of the conflict between French-speaking and English-speaking Canadians.

Canada: Postwar to the Present

During the war, Canadians built factories. They made war supplies and goods like clothes and shoes. Because of the war, people could not get such products from Europe. After the war, Canadian goods found a ready market in Europe.

Also during the postwar years, immigrants poured into Canada. They came from Asia, Europe, Africa, and the Caribbean. The newcomers filled jobs in new factories and other businesses. Soon, Canada became the world's fourth-largest industrial nation.

Canada and the United States—Trading Partners and Friends

As Canada grew in industrial power, Canada and the United States became cooperative neighbors. They worked together to clean up industrial pollution in Lake Erie. They signed an agreement to control air pollution. Trade between Canada and the United States also became increasingly important to both countries.

Old Conflicts Arise

Industrialization brought not only new friends but old conflicts. British Canadians built new factories in Quebec, alarming French Canadians. By 1976, some French Canadians were tired of being part of Canada. Quebec, they argued, should be independent. Instead, new laws made Canada a **bilingual** country. That is, Canada had two official languages—English and French. In addition Canadians could now change their constitution without Great Britain's permission. Canada was completely independent.

SECTION 4 ASSESSMENT

AFTER YOU READ

RECALL

1. Identify: (a) Ontario, (b) Quebec, (c) Louis Papineau, (d) William Mackenzie
2. Define: (a) dominion, (b) bilingual

COMPREHENSION

3. Explain why the Ohio River Valley was important to both the French and the English.
4. Describe Canada's "peaceful revolution."
5. How did Canada become an industrial power after World War II?

CRITICAL THINKING AND WRITING

6. **Exploring the Main Idea** Review the Main Idea statement at the beginning of this section. Then, write an editorial supporting either the French or English point of view regarding the problems in Canada.

ACTIVITY

7. **Drawing a Political Cartoon** French Canadians have argued that Quebec should be separate and independent from Canada. Draw a political cartoon that might have appeared in a French Canadian newspaper favoring independence for Quebec.

Resource Directory

Teaching Resources

Section Quiz in the Unit 2 Teaching Resources, p. 28

Chapter Summary in the Unit 2 Teaching Resources, p. 29

Vocabulary in the Unit 2 Teaching Resources, p. 30

Reteaching in the Unit 2 Teaching Resources, p. 31

Enrichment in the Unit 2 Teaching Resources, p. 32

Critical Thinking in the Unit 2 Teaching Resources, p. 33

Sequencing Events on a Timeline

What You Need

You can make your own timeline. You will need:

- a sheet of paper
- a ruler
- a pencil or pen

Learn the Skill

A timeline is an easy way to make sense of dates and events of the past. It is a simple diagram that shows how dates and events relate to one another. To sequence events on a timeline, follow these steps to create a timeline of your life:

A. Gather the materials you need.

B. Use the ruler to draw a straight line across the sheet of paper. Draw a big dot on the left end of the line.

C. Mark the years. Next to the first dot, write the year you were born. Measure 1/2 inch down from the first dot, mark the spot with another dot, and write the next year under the dot. Continue until you reach the current year. Then write "Present" under the last dot.

D. Add the events. Above the first dot, write "Born in (write the name of the town where you were born.)" Now write several other important events in your life next to other dates on the timeline. Connect each label to the right place on the timeline by drawing a line.

E. Give your timeline a title.

Practice the Skill

Read the following paragraph about Canada's road to self-rule. Sequence the events in the paragraph on a timeline.

> France and Great Britain signed a peace treaty in 1713, giving Great Britain the Hudson Bay region and the southeastern corner of Canada. However, 41 years later both countries would enter the French and Indain War over the issue of land. In 1763, the Treaty of Paris gave Great Britain control over all of Canada. Twenty years later, British loyalists from the United States began to move to upper Canada after the end of the American Revolution. At this time, French Canadians lived in Quebec in lower Canada. Soon, the French and British would align to defend themselves in Canada against the United States during the War of 1812.
> In 1837, citizens across Canada organized revolts against Great Britain, but were defeated. Thirty years later, the British North America Act made Canada a self-governing area.

Apply the Skill

See the Chapter Review and Assessment at the end of this chapter for more questions on timelines.

Lesson Objectives

1. Understand what a timeline is and how it is used.
2. Make an autobiographical timeline.
3. Make a historical timeline of events during the 1700s and 1800s.

Lesson Plan

1 Engage

To introduce the skill, read aloud the opening text under "Learn the Skill." Draw two lines, one horizontal and one vertical. Point out that some timelines run horizontally across the page but that timelines can also run vertically. Explain that the scale on timelines varies. A time line scale might include each year, or it might show intervals of 10, 50, or 100 years.

2 Explore

Direct students to read the steps under "Learn the Skill." Have them construct a simple time line of their own lives by following the steps. Help students as needed. Encourage students to think of an event for each year in their lives.

3 Teach

Help students read and interpret the paragraph. Make sure they understand that the events are presented chronologically. Remind them that each dot in their timeline will represent one event in Canada's road to self-rule.

4 Assess/Reteach

Students' historical timelines should be well organized and easy to follow. An event should be listed with each date given.

To further assess students' understanding of timelines, have them complete the "Applying your Skills" part of the Chapter Review and Assessment at the end of this chapter.

Resource Directory

Teaching Resources

Social Studies and Geography Skills, Reading a Timeline, p. 59

Technology

Social Studies Skills Tutor CD-ROM

Answers to...

PRACTICE THE SKILL

Make sure students use the dates effectively to construct their timelines.

CHAPTER 5

Review and Assessment

Creating a Chapter Summary

Student timelines will vary.

Sample summaries:

Section 2 1803: Louisiana Purchase, and Lewis and Clarke sent to explore the new land; 1836: Lone Star Republic formed; 1845: Texas joins the U.S.; 1840s: Americans begin to settle to West; mid-1800s: Industrial Revolution (steamboats, railroads, cotton gin); 1860: Abraham Lincoln; 1861: Civil War begins; 1863: Emancipation Proclamation; 1865: Union victory, then Reconstruction begins

Section 3 1800s: immigrants arrive to U.S. and face poor living conditions; 1862: Homestead Act; 1867: purchase of Alaska; 1898: U.S. takes control of Hawaii; 1914: WWI begins; 1918: Allies win war; 1929: Great Depression; 1939: WWII begins; 1941: Japan attacks Pearl Harbor; 1945: Allies defeat Germany and U.S. drops two bombs on Japan, ending the war; post-WWII: Cold War with the Soviet Union lasts 40 years

Section 4 1713: Great Britain and Canada sign peace treaty after fighting over land; 1754: French and Indian war begins between Great Britain and France; 1759: Great Britain wins Battle of Quebec; 1763: Great Britain gains control over Canada; 1837: French Canadian Louis Papineau organizes revolt in Lower Canada and William Mackenzie leads a revolt in Upper Canada; 1867: Canada become a dominion; post-1976: French and English become official languages of Canada; Canada becomes independent from Great Britain

Reviewing Key Terms

1. American Revolution
2. abolitionist
3. Reconstruction
4. boycott
5. Cold War

CHAPTER 5

Review and Assessment

Creating a Chapter Summary

On a separate sheet of paper, draw a diagram like this one, and include the information that summarizes Section 1. Then, create three other timelines to summarize the events you read about in Sections 2, 3, and 4.

Exploration in the Americas

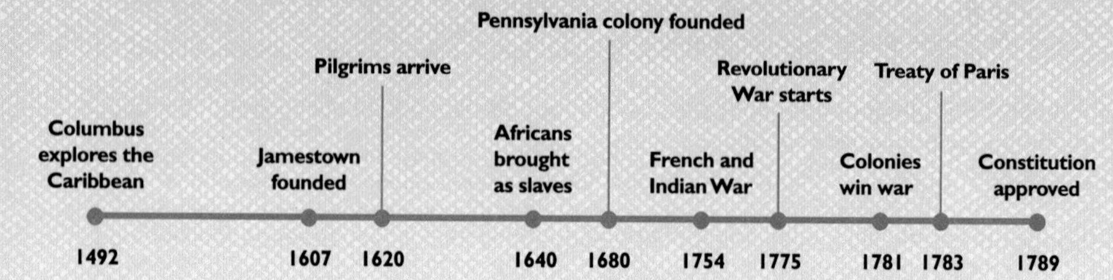

Reviewing Key Terms

Complete each sentence with a word or words from the list below.

Reconstruction	boycott
abolitionist	American Revolution
Cold War	

1. The American colonies won their independence from Great Britain in the ________.
2. An ________ is a person who believed slavery was wrong and wanted to end the practice.
3. The plan to rebuild the United States after the Civil War was known as ________.
4. A ________ is a refusal to buy goods from a company or country.
5. The ________ was a period of great tension between the United States and the Soviet Union.

Reviewing the Main Ideas

1. How did the first people get to North America? (Section 1)
2. How did Europeans change Native American ways of life? (Section 1)
3. Why did early colonists want to break away from Great Britain? (Section 2)
4. How did the United States expand its territory? (Section 2)
5. Name one cause of the Civil War. (Section 2)
6. Besides African Americans, which groups campaigned for civil rights after the 1950s? (Section 3)
7. Why did Canada become more independent from Britain after World War I? (Section 4)
8. After World War II, Canada's influence on the rest of the world increased. Why? (Section 4)

Reviewing the Main Ideas

1. They migrated from Asia along a land bridge between Siberia and Alaska.
2. Europeans sometimes enslaved Native Americans or tried to convert them to European religions.
3. They did not have representation in Parliament, but Great Britain still made them pay high taxes.
4. The United States made the Louisiana Purchase, gained Texas as a state, and gained territory in the Southwest from Mexico.
5. Slavery and the rights of states to determine whether they should be free or slave states were two of the major factors that caused the Civil War.
6. Mexican American farmworkers, women, and disabled people
7. Great Britain saw that Canada, which had helped the Allied nations win the war, had become a world power and granted it more independence.
8. Canada's factories were able to produce goods that were in high demand. Canada eventually became the world's fourth-largest industrial nation.

Map Activity

Canada

For each place listed below, write the letter from the map that shows its location.

1. Ontario
2. Quebec
3. Lake Erie
4. St. Lawrence Seaway

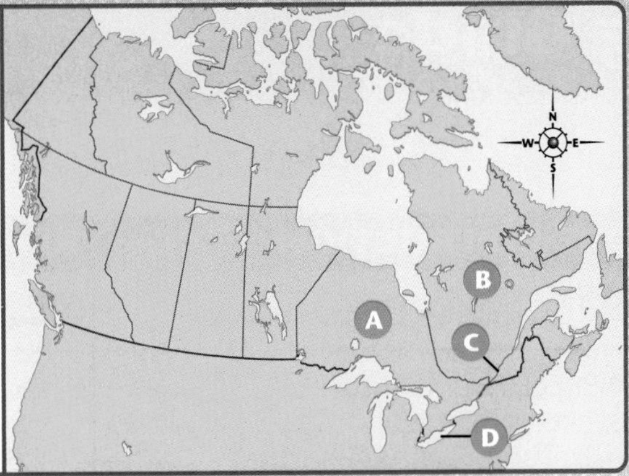

Take It to the NET

Enrichment For more map activities using geography skills, visit the social studies section of **phschool.com.**

Writing Activity

1. **Writing a Summary** Think about ways in which the United States and Canada are similar. How are they different? Write a summary comparing the two countries.
2. **Using Primary Sources** Some of the events described in this chapter were written about first-hand. Choose one event from the chapter to research. Visit your school or local library and use primary sources such as autobiographies, journals, or letters written by someone who participated in the event. You might also use additional information about the event, such as current books or articles describing the events, or information from the Internet. When you are done collecting information, write a brief report using direct quotations from your primary source to make your report more lively.

Critical Thinking

1. **Identifying Central Issues** Explain why Southern colonists thought that they needed slaves.
2. **Making Comparisons** Compare the ways in which the United States and Canada gained their independence from Great Britain.
3. **Drawing Conclusions** Why do you think many French Canadians want to be independent from English-speaking Canadians?

Applying Your Skills

Turn to the Skills for Life activity on p. 101 to help you complete the following activity.

Interview a family member and gather information about important events in their life, and the years in which these events occurred. Use this information to create a timeline of that person's life.

Take It to the NET

Activity Create a timeline of significant events of one of the historic periods you read about. Visit the World Explorer: People, Places, and Cultures section of **phschool.com** for help in completing this activity.

Chapter 5 Self-Test As a final review activity, take the Chapter 5 Self-Test and get instant feedback on your answers. To take the test, visit the Social Studies section of **phschool.com** for help in completing this activity.

Resource Directory

Teaching Resources

Cooperative Learning Activity in the Unit 2 Teaching Resources, pp. 108–111

Chapter Tests Forms A and B in the Unit 2 Teaching Resources, pp. 138–143

Guide to the Essentials Ch. 5 Test, p. 22

Other Print Resources

Chapter Tests with ExamView® Test Bank, Ch. 5

Technology

ExamView® Test Bank CD-ROM, Ch. 5

Resource Pro® CD-ROM

Map Activity

1. A **2.** B **3.** D **4.** C

Writing Activity

1. Summaries should note that the two nations have similar geographies, settlement histories, and government and economic structures. Students should note important differences such as how independence was won, how civil differences have been resolved, and the presence of two official languages in Canada.
2. Students' reports may cover a range from recounting Civil War battles, to the daily life of a slave, to the Trail of Tears or other event involving Native Americans. The reports should demonstrate a clear understanding of the events about which students are writing. The reports should include some direct quotes from autobiographies, letters, or diaries, or some other primary source material.

Critical Thinking

1. Cotton growing required many workers.
2. Canada acquired independence through negotiation with Great Britain. The United States fought a war with Great Britain to win independence.
3. French Canadians probably feel that they are in a minority among the English-speaking Canadians; their culture and language is so different that they feel they should be a separate country; they have a long-standing history of conflict with English-speaking Canadians.

Applying Your Skills

1. Students' timelines should be organized according to the details outlined in the "Skills for Life" activity, and should include important events for each date listed.

Chapter 6 Planning Guide

Resource Manager

	CORE INSTRUCTION	READING/SKILLS
Chapter-Level Resources	**Teaching Resources** Program Overview Pacing Charts **Technology** Resource Pro® CD-ROM Companion Web site, phschool.com • eTeach	**Technology** Social Studies Skills Tutor CD-ROM Student Edition on Audio CD, Ch. 6
1 Cultural Diversity in the United States and Canada 1. Identify sources of cultural diversity in the United States and Canada. 2. Explain how cultural diversity has affected people's lives in the United States and Canada. 3. Explain the factors that led to religious diversity in the United States and Canada.	**Teaching Resources** **Unit 2** Classroom Manager, p. 35 Guided Reading and Review, p. 36	**Teaching Resources** Guide to the Essentials, p. 23 **Technology** Section Reading Support Transparencies
2 Creative Expression and Artistic Traditions 1. Explain how the literature and music of the United States and Canada reflect diverse cultures. 2. Explain how the art and architecture of the United States and Canada reflect these nations' history and landscape.	**Teaching Resources** **Unit 2** Classroom Manager, p. 38 Guided Reading and Review, p. 39	**Teaching Resources** Guide to the Essentials, p. 24 **Technology** Section Reading Support Transparencies
3 Conflict and Cooperation Among Cultures 1. Explain how the governments of Canada and the United States have tried to resolve conflicts with indigenous peoples. 2. Identify examples of conflicts that different groups in Canada and the United States have faced, as well as ways that those conflicts have been resolved.	**Teaching Resources** **Unit 2** Classroom Manager, p. 41 Guided Reading and Review, p. 42 Chapter Summary, p. 44 Vocabulary, p. 45 Reteaching, p. 46	**Teaching Resources** Critical Thinking, p. 48 Guide to the Essentials, p. 25 **Technology** Section Reading Support Transparencies

ENRICHMENT / PRE-AP

Teaching Resources
Primary Sources and Literature Readings

Other Print Resources
DK Atlas

Technology
World Video Explorer: Cultures of the United States and Canada
How People Live Transparencies, Unit 2
Companion Web site, phschool.com

Technology
Color Transparencies 40

Technology
Color Transparencies 50–51, 149

Teaching Resources
Unit 2
Enrichment, p. 47
Cooperative Learning Activity, pp. 112–115
Outline Maps, p. 16

Technology
Color Transparencies 32

ASSESSMENT

Prentice Hall Assessment System

Core Assessment
Chapter Tests with ExamView® Test Bank, Ch. 6
ExamView® Test Bank CD-ROM, Ch. 6

Standardized Test Preparation
Diagnose and Prescribe
Diagnostic Tests for Middle Grades Social Studies Skills
Review and Reteach
Review Book for World Studies
Practice and Assess
Test-taking Strategies with Transparencies for Middle Grades Test Prep Book
Test-taking Strategies Posters

Teaching Resources
Unit 2
Section Quizzes, pp. 37, 40, and 43
Chapter Tests, pp. 144–149

Technology
Companion Web site, phschool.com
Ch. 6 Self-Test

World Video Explorer
Each region of the world is explored through regional flyovers and investigative field trips. Case study segments give students an in-depth view of the history, economy, government, and culture of a key place in each region. Case studies include Nigeria, Mexico, China, British Columbia, and the Czech Republic.

In Your Classroom

CUSTOMIZE FOR INDIVIDUAL NEEDS

Gifted and Talented

Teacher's Edition
- Math, p. 107

Teaching Resources
- Enrichment, p. 47
- Primary Sources and Literature Readings

Honors/Pre-AP

Teacher's Edition
- Mobile Words, p. 107
- Language Issues, p. 115

Teaching Resources
- Critical Thinking, p. 48
- Primary Sources and Literature Readings

ESL

Teacher's Edition
- Language Issues, p. 115

Teaching Resources
- Guided Reading and Review, pp. 36, 39, and 42
- Vocabulary, p. 45
- Reteaching, p. 46
- Guide to the Essentials, pp. 23–25

Technology
- Color Transparencies 32, 40, 50–51, 149
- Social Studies Skills Tutor CD-ROM
- Section Reading Support Transparencies

Less Proficient Readers

Teacher's Edition
- Music, p. 111
- Language Issues, p. 115

Teaching Resources
- Guided Reading and Review, pp. 36, 39, and 42
- Vocabulary, p. 45
- Reteaching, p. 46
- Guide to the Essentials, pp. 23–25

Technology
- Social Studies Skills Tutor CD-ROM
- Section Reading Support Transparencies

Less Proficient Writers

Teacher's Edition
- Music, p. 111

Teaching Resources
- Guided Reading and Review, pp. 36, 39, and 42
- Vocabulary, p. 45
- Guide to the Essentials, pp. 23–25

Technology
- Social Studies Skills Tutor CD-ROM
- Section Reading Support Transparencies

DORLING KINDERSLEY

At the end of each unit, you will find information adapted from Dorling Kindersley's *Illustrated Children's Encyclopedia* that connects to the region being studied and to one of the seven content strands. In addition, your resources include Dorling Kindersley's *Atlas*, which contains valuable information about countries from around the world.

TEACHER'S EDITION INDEX

CHAPTER 6 PACING SUGGESTIONS

For 90-minute Blocks

See suggestions in the Teaching Resources Pacing Charts for Chapter 6. Use Color Transparencies 32, 40, 50–51, and 149.

Running Out of Time?

See the Guide to the Essentials, pp. 23–25.

INTERDISCIPLINARY LINKS

Middle Grades Math: Tools for Success

Course 1, Lesson 1-3, **Mean, Median and Mode**

Course 2, Lesson 1-7, **Random Samples and Surveys**

Science Explorer

Environmental Science, Lesson 4-3, **Hazardous Wastes;** Lesson 6-3, **Nuclear Energy**

Motion, Forces, and Energy, Introduction, **Nature of Science**

Prentice Hall Literature

Copper, Jackie Robinson—Justice at Last, The All American Slurp

BIBLIOGRAPHY

For the Teacher

Art: A World History. Dorling Kindersley, 2001.

Cultures of America series (10 titles). Cavendish, 1994.

Reimers, David. *A Land of Immigrants.* Chelsea, 1995.

For the Student

Easy

Herold, Maggie Rugg. *A Very Important Day.* Morrow, 1995.

Average

Eyewitness Dance. Dorling Kindersley, 2001.

Challenging

Myers, Walter Dean. *One More River to Cross: An African American Photograph Album.* Harcourt, 1995.

Wyman, Bill. *Bill Wyman's Blues Odyssey.* Dorling Kindersley, 2001.

Literature Connection

Cox, Clinton. *Mark Twain: America's Humorist, Dreamer, Prophet—A Biography.* Scholastic, 1995.

Ehrlich, Amy, ed. *When I Was Your Age: Original Stories About Growing Up.* Candlewick, 1996.

Take It to the NET

The World Explorer companion Web site, found on **phschool.com**, offers activities for exploring geographical, historical, and cultural resources on the Internet. It also provides on-line links for key content and all Section and Chapter Assessment activities.

The **Teacher site** also provides teachers with regional data and ideas for student research and activities.

Students can use the **Student site** to find chapter-by-chapter Internet resource links and to access Self-Tests.

CHAPTER 6

Connecting to the Guiding Questions

In this chapter, students will read about the cultures of the United States and Canada. Content in this chapter corresponds to the following Guiding Questions outlined at the beginning of the unit.

- How have historical events affected the cultures of the United States and Canada?
- How has cultural diversity benefited and challenged these two nations?

Using the Architecture Activities

Explain to students that there are many different ways of looking at and using architecture—you can admire buildings for their architectural style, for their history, and for their functionality.

- Encourage students to share the particular feature of the building that they most admire, and explain why they admire it.
- Students should gather information on a particular building in their community, and, if possible, use first-hand information in their report.

Heterogeneous Groups

The following activities are suitable for heterogeneous groups.

Cooperative Learning
Mobile Words, p. 107

Interdisciplinary Connections
Music, p. 111

Journal Writing
Language Issues, p. 115

eTeach
Be sure to check out this month's discussion with a Master Teacher. Go to **phschool.com**.

CHAPTER 6

THE UNITED STATES AND CANADA: Rich in Culture

Toronto and the CN Tower

Understanding Architecture

The photograph above shows the skyline in Toronto, Ontario. The distinct building topped with a needle-like structure is the CN Tower, a communications and observation tower in downtown Toronto.

Studying Landmark Buildings

If you were asked to paint a picture of a landmark building in your community, which one would you choose? Why? Choose a landmark building and take a photograph of it. Then, paint a picture that shows the unique features of that particular building, such as the materials it is made from, the shape or size of the building, or the style of architecture.

Using Primary and Secondary Sources

Visit your local library or historical society and find information about the landmark building you chose to paint, including the style of architecture it represents, and the time period in which it was built. If possible, interview people in your community who might have first-hand information about the building and its history. Present your findings to the rest of the class in a brief oral report.

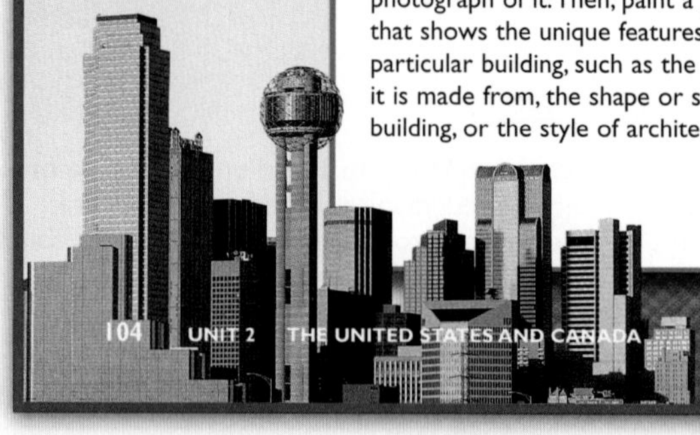

Resource Directory

Teaching Resources

Primary Sources and Literature Readings extend content with a selection related to the concepts in this chapter.

Other Print Resources

DK Atlas

Technology

Cultures of the United States and Canada, from the World Video Explorer, introduces students to the cultures of the United States and Canada.

How People Live Transparencies, Unit 2

Student Edition on Audio CD, Ch. 6

SECTION 1

Cultural Diversity in the United States and Canada

BEFORE YOU READ

READING FOCUS

1. What led to cultural diversity in North America?
2. How did various ethnic groups affect the culture of the United States and Canada?
3. What led to religious diversity in the United States and Canada?

KEY TERMS

cultural diversity
cultural exchange
ethnic group
religious diversity

NOTE TAKING

Copy the web diagram below. As you read the section, fill in the ovals with the items, including religion, which various cultures have exchanged or brought to North America.

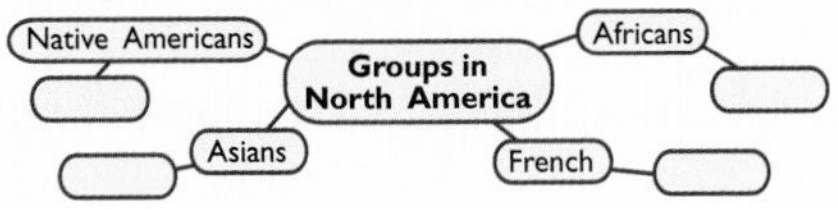

MAIN IDEA

People from all over the world have immigrated to North America, making the United States and Canada culturally and religiously diverse countries.

Setting the Scene

This view of **cultural diversity,** or a wide variety of cultures, comes from Tito, a teenager from Mexico.

"My parents say, 'you have to learn the American culture.' I listen to them, but then I think about an ideal society where there's a little bit of every culture and it goes together just right. Different ideas would come together and make everything a whole lot better."

Diverse Cultures in North America

North America has always been culturally diverse. When the first Europeans arrived, they found many different Native American groups. These groups spoke different languages and had different ways of life. The cultures of the first Americans reflected their different environments. Native American people living near the ocean ate a great deal of fish and told stories about the sea. People living in the forest hunted and trapped forest animals. These groups traded with one another and when groups trade, they also share ideas and ways of doing things. This process is called **cultural exchange.**

When Europeans began to explore and colonize North America, they changed Native American life in a number of ways.

Chinese New Year

CULTURE Chinese American Boy Scouts in San Francisco proudly show off a dragon, which symbolizes Chinese New Year. **Critical Thinking** What elements of cultural exchange can you identify from this photo?

SECTION 1

Lesson Objectives

1. Identify sources of cultural diversity in the United States and Canada.
2. Explain how cultural diversity has affected people's lives in the United States and Canada.
3. Explain the factors that led to religious diversity in the United States and Canada.

Lesson Plan

1 Engage

Warm-Up Activity

As a class, discuss a main business street in your community. Have students list evidence of cultural diversity. For example, students might note restaurants serving ethnic foods, signs printed in languages other than English, shops selling goods and services linked to other cultures, or people wearing the clothing of their cultures.

Activating Prior Knowledge

Ask students how they can learn about cultural influences in their area or throughout the United States. Direct students toward sources such as the phone book, books and films available in your school or local library, or a calendar of local cultural events.

Resource Directory

Teaching Resources

Classroom Manager in the Unit 2 Teaching Resources, p. 35

Guided Reading and Review in the Unit 2 Teaching Resources, p. 36

Guide to the Essentials, p. 23

Technology

Section Reading Support Transparencies

Answers to...

CRITICAL THINKING

Answers will vary. Students should recognize that the celebration is Chinese, but the boys in the photo are American and probably celebrate elements of both American and Chinese culture.

Lesson Plan continued

2 Explore

As students read, urge them to locate answers to the following questions: How did early Native Americans learn about each other's cultures? Why do some immigrants prefer not to fully adopt American customs? What are some of the cultures that have influenced the United States?

3 Teach

Have students use information from the section to create a concept web with *U.S. and Canadian Culture* at the center. Concepts in the outside circle should be influences on the diversity of culture in the United States and Canada. Students may also include their own ideas as long as they are based on fact and related to the topics of the section. This activity should take about 15 minutes.

Questions for Discussion

GEOGRAPHY Why were Native American cultures in different environments in North America different from one another?

Environmental features such as climate, landforms, and available food influenced the customs, skills, and cultures that Native Americans developed.

CULTURE What is the significance of the Islamic holy month of Ramadan?

It celebrates when God first revealed himself to Muhammad.

4 Assess/Reteach

See the answers to the Section 1 Assessment. You may also assess students' concept webs.

Acceptable webs accurately identify at least three key influences.

Commendable webs accurately identify more than three influences.

Outstanding webs accurately identify more than three influences and include original ideas related to section topics.

For example, early Spanish explorers brought horses with them. Native Americans had never before seen horses, but these animals soon became an important part of their culture. Native Americans also learned to use the rifle brought by later European settlers.

Native Americans contributed many things to European culture as well. They taught the French how to trap and survive in the forest. They taught English families how to grow local foods such as corn and pumpkins.

AS YOU READ
Summarize What kinds of things did the Europeans learn from Native Americans?

Cultural exchange also took place between enslaved Africans and their owners. The Africans learned English and used European tools. African music and foods often entered the daily lives of slave owners.

Immigration and Cultural Exchange

Over the centuries, more and more Europeans and people from other areas flocked to North America. The immigrants made up different **ethnic groups**—people who share a language, history, and culture. When these groups settled in Canada and the United States, hoping for a better life, they made important contributions. For example, when Russian settlers came to the Great Plains, they brought a kind of hardy wheat that grew well in the cold climate of their home country. Farmers soon learned that this tough wheat grew well in the Great Plains climate. These immigrants helped the Great Plains become the leading wheat-growing area in the United States today.

For the first two hundred years, mainly European immigrants came to North America. By the mid-1800s Asian immigrants began arriving. Waves of Asian immigrants from China, Japan, and later from

Canada: Ethnic Groups

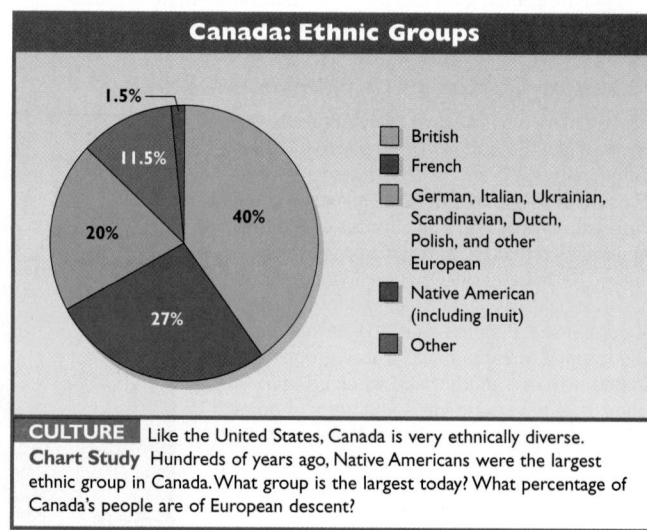

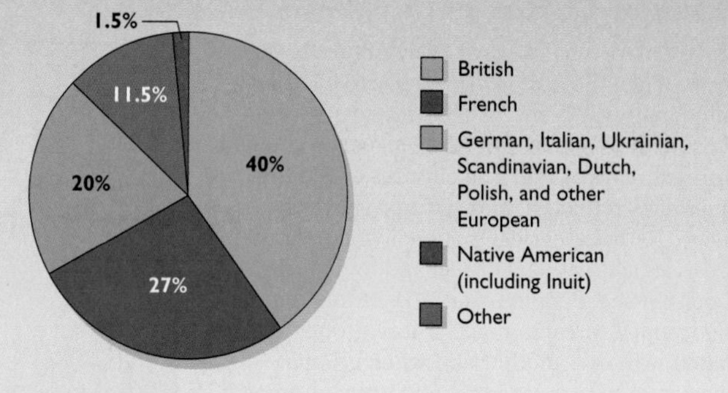

CULTURE Like the United States, Canada is very ethnically diverse.
Chart Study Hundreds of years ago, Native Americans were the largest ethnic group in Canada. What group is the largest today? What percentage of Canada's people are of European descent?

Answers to...

AS YOU READ

From Native Americans, the Europeans learned how to trap forest animals, survive in the woods, and cultivate corn and pumpkins.

CHART STUDY

People of British extraction make up the largest group. Eighty-seven percent of Canadians are of European descent.

Resource Directory

Technology

Color Transparencies 40 The United States: Political Map

Thailand, Vietnam, Cambodia, and other nations have settled in the United States and Canada. In recent years there has also been an increase in immigrants coming from South Asian countries, such as India and Pakistan. All these immigrants have brought with them their special foods, holidays such as the Chinese New Year, martial arts such as the Japanese *judo* and Korean *tae kwan do*, and acupuncture, an ancient Chinese method of treating disease. In return, these immigrants have absorbed many things from U.S. and Canadian culture.

When immigrants move from one country to another, they must make difficult decisions. For instance, what parts of their original culture should they keep and what should they change? They must learn the language, laws, and manners of the people in the new country without losing the traditions of their former cultures.

Almost all immigrants cling to things that remind them of their former homes. Think about your family or your friends' families. Does someone play a musical instrument special to their heritage? Do they use special phrases from the language they learned from their parents or grandparents? These customs give people a sense of identity. They also help to enrich life in North America.

LINKS TO Math

Using Your Fingers and Toes Native Americans created the first number systems north of the Mexican border. The San Gabrielino in California used "all my hand finished" to mean 10. "All my hand finished and one foot" was 15. The Chukchee used their fingers to count. Their word for "five" is *hand*, for "ten" *both hands*, and for "twenty" *man*—meaning both hands and both feet.

Religious Diversity in North America

Just as there has always been cultural diversity in North America, there has always been **religious diversity** as well. When European explorers and colonists first arrived in the Americas, they found Native Americans practicing a wide variety of religions. Different tribes held different philosophical beliefs, but common to most tribes was the belief in a powerful and mysterious spirit force. This powerful spirit lived in nature and could be contacted by certain people or through certain ceremonies. Many Native Americans in the United States and Canada continue to hold their ancient beliefs and practice some of the ceremonies.

The earliest European settlers of North America were Christian. Many, such as the pilgrims of Plymouth Colony, came to escape religious persecution in England. As more colonies were established, a

Major Religious Holidays

Christian	Jewish	Islamic
Christmas–Commemorates the birth of Jesus Christ **Easter**–Commemorates the resurrection of Jesus Christ	**Rosh Hashanah**–The Jewish New Year **Yom Kippur**–Day of Atonement	**Ramadan**–The Islamic holy month commemorating when God first revealed Himself to the prophet Muhammad

CULTURE This chart highlights some of the major religious holidays celebrated in North America. **Chart Study** Who is the focus of both Christian holidays? Which holidays are celebrated in your community?

ACTIVITY

Interdisciplinary Connections

Math Direct students to survey a group of local people—the school band or orchestra, a school sports team, or a neighborhood—to determine how different ethnic or cultural groups are represented in the group. Remind students to respect respondents' desire for privacy. Ask students to calculate the results of their survey in percentage form and display them as a bar or circle graph.

ACTIVITY

Cooperative Learning

Mobile Words Tell students that many words now part of the English language originated in other languages. Cultural exchange has incorporated them into English. Have pairs of students use dictionaries to report on the origins of the following words: *barbecue, cafeteria, chauffeur, chef, confetti, coyote, delicatessen, foyer, frankfurter, graffiti, kindergarten, memoir, mesa, omelet, opera, pretzel, spaghetti, thug,* and *umbrella.*

Verbal/Linguistic

SKILLS MINI LESSON

Locating Information

To **introduce** the skill, ask students to list their favorite music, sport, and food. Explain that students can do research to discover the cultural origins of these things. Ask students to **practice** the skill by listing some possible information sources. In addition to the standard library resources, suggest that students consult community or cultural organizations and adult family members as sources of information. Ask students to **apply** the skill by checking the resources on their list to determine the cultural origins of their favorite music, sport, and food. Volunteers may share their findings with the class; invite them also to discuss how they located the information they needed.

Answers to...

CHART STUDY

Jesus Christ is the focus of both Christian holidays shown on the chart. Encourage students to discuss the holidays celebrated by different cultures within their community.

SECTION I ASSESSMENT

AFTER YOU READ

1. (a) presence of a wide variety of cultures (b) process of sharing ideas and ways of doing things among different cultures (c) group of people who share a language, history, and culture (d) presence of a wide variety of religions
2. Native Americans taught the French how to trap and to survive in the forest. They taught English settlers how to grow foods native to the region. Europeans brought horses and rifles, both of which were absorbed into the culture of many Native Americans.
3. The U.S. Constitution gives people the right to practice whatever religion they choose.
4. Answers will vary. Students may mention things such as different foods, holidays, languages, tools, clothing, music, and lifestyles.
5. Answers will vary. Students may suggest that colonists would not have been able to survive, or that they would have abandoned their colonies.
6. You might encourage students to consult print sources (including local histories, collections of photographs, and newspapers); local and state government Web sites; and knowledgeable individuals, such as notable religious leaders, business people, and librarians.

Freedom of Religion

CULTURE This image shows the Puritans arriving in North America in the 1600s. They left Great Britain in search of religious freedom. **Critical Thinking** Do you think that the freedom to practice religion is important to people? Why?

spirit of toleration for different religions spread. When the United States Constitution was written, it guaranteed that no one would have to pay taxes to support religion. It also guaranteed that people could practice any religion they chose.

Religious tolerance attracted many immigrants to the United States and Canada. Jews fled religious persecution in Europe in the 1800s and 1900s to settle here. In the later 1900s, many people who practice the religion of Islam immigrated here. Today, people of Christian, Jewish, Islamic, and other religions practice their faith freely in the United States and Canada.

SECTION I ASSESSMENT

AFTER YOU READ

RECALL

1. Define: (a) cultural diversity, (b) cultural exchange, (c) ethnic group, (d) religious diversity

COMPREHENSION

2. Describe the cultural exchange that occurred between Native Americans and Europeans.
3. How is freedom of religion protected in the United States?

CRITICAL THINKING AND WRITING

4. **Exploring the Main Idea** Review the Main Idea statement at the beginning of this section. Then, list as many ways as you can think of that immigrants from various ethnic groups have contributed to culture in the United States and Canada.
5. **Drawing Conclusions** Write a paragraph describing how development in North America might have been different if Native Americans had not shared their cultural knowledge.

ACTIVITY

Take It to the NET

6. **Creating a Cultural Scrapbook** Create a cultural scrapbook with stories and illustrations showing the cultural diversity of your state or community. Model your scrapbook on the one shown on the web site. Visit the World Explorer: People, Places, and Cultures section of **phschool.com** for help in completing this activity.

Resource Directory

Teaching Resources

Section Quiz in the Unit 2 Teaching Resources, p. 37

Answers to...

CRITICAL THINKING

Students may respond that many people who have come to the United States from other countries have suffered religious oppression, and therefore they value the freedom to practice their own religion in the United States.

108 UNIT 2 THE UNITED STATES AND CANADA

SECTION 2

Creative Expression and Artistic Traditions

BEFORE YOU READ

READING FOCUS

1. How do the literature and music of the United States and Canada reflect diverse cultures?
2. How do the art and architecture of the United States and Canada reflect the history and landscape of the nations?

KEY TERMS

Quebecois literature
improvisation
Group of Seven

KEY PEOPLE

Langston Hughes
Andrew Wyeth

NOTE TAKING

Copy the chart shown here. As you read the section, fill in the chart with information in each category.

	Literature	Music	Art	Architecture
United States				
Canada				

MAIN IDEA

The literature, music, art, and architecture of the United States and Canada reflect the history, landscape, and cultural diversity of the two countries.

Setting the Scene

As immigrants settled into life in the United States and Canada, they began to create their own unique cultures. Their art, literature, and music reflected their experiences in the new land. This excerpt is from a short story by American author Willa Cather, about a Czech immigrant who built a life on the American plains.

"When Rosicky went out to his wagon, it was beginning to snow—the first snow of the season, and he was glad to see it. He rattled out of town and along the highway through a wonderfully rich stretch of country, the finest farms in the county. He admired this High Prairie, as it was called, and always liked to drive through it. His own place lay in a rougher territory, where there was some clay in the soil and it was not so productive. When he bought his land, he hadn't the money to buy on High Prairie; so he told his boys, when they grumbled, that if their land hadn't some clay in it, they wouldn't own it at all. All the same, he enjoyed looking at these fine farms, as he enjoyed looking at a prize bull."

Literature and Music

Like Willa Cather, other American authors often wrote about the lives of common people. In John Steinbeck's novel, *The Grapes of Wrath*, a poor farm family escapes dust storms in the Southern Great Plains in the 1930s. African American poet **Langston**

The American Experience

CULTURE The work of U.S. and Canadian authors and artists, such as Willa Cather (pictured below), draws on the unique character of the North American landscape and the history and experience of its inhabitants.
Critical Thinking Was the physical geography of the land important in the work of American authors? Why?

109

SECTION 2

Lesson Objectives

1. Explain how the literature and music of the United States and Canada reflect diverse cultures.
2. Explain how the art and architecture of the United States and Canada reflect these nations' history and landscape.

Lesson Plan

1 Engage

Warm-Up Activity

Ask students to name some types of music they enjoy. Then, ask them if they can identify what culture or musical tradition influenced that music. Encourage discussion of how musical traditions influence one another. Explain to students that most music today is influenced by different cultures and musical traditions.

Activating Prior Knowledge

Tell students that much of the art and literature of the United States and Canada has been influenced by the landscapes of those countries. Have students list different types of landscapes, landforms, and climates in the United States and Canada. Ask them if they recall any artwork or any stories that feature some of these geographic characteristics.

Resource Directory

Teaching Resources

Classroom Manager in the Unit 2 Teaching Resources, p. 38

Guided Reading and Review in the Unit 2 Teaching Resources, p. 39

Guide to the Essentials, p. 24

Technology

Section Reading Support Transparencies

Answers to...

CRITICAL THINKING

Students may suggest that because America's physical geography had such an impact on how people lived and worked it became an important part of the American literary tradition.

Lesson Plan continued

2 Explore

As students read, challenge them to answer the following questions: How do art, literature, and music reflect a culture? How do conflicts and issues in society affect creative expression? What is the relationship between a group's ethnic identity and its art?

3 Teach

Have students use information from this section to sketch a mural depicting the artistic traditions of the United States and Canada. Students should depict visually some of the specific literature, music, art, and architecture mentioned in the section. For example, they might sketch a picture of a whale, a farm in a dust storm, a street in Harlem, or a young girl representing Anne. Murals might also include sketches of musical instruments, bands playing, Inuit or other artists at work, the Empire State Building or other skyscrapers or structures. This activity should take about 30 minutes.

Question for Discussion

CULTURE How does American society influence American music?

The cultural diversity of America influences the music. Different cultural groups contribute to create a unique American musical tradition.

4 Assess/Reteach

See the answers to the Section 2 Assessment. You may also assess students' murals.

Acceptable murals accurately depict at least three key items from the section.

Commendable murals accurately depict more than three key items.

Outstanding murals accurately depict more than three key items and show originality, thoughtfulness, and care in design and layout.

Hughes describes life in Harlem, New York City, in the early 1900s. Although Hughes was writing from his experience as an African American, his work was appreciated by people from a variety of backgrounds, and his poetry created a link among different cultures. Hughes' work helped many white people understand the African American experience.

Unique Voices in Literature

The novels and stories of many American authors reflect the wide range of American culture. Herman Melville wrote New England whaling stories, including the classic novel *Moby Dick.* Mark Twain wrote about life on the Mississippi River, as well as "tall tales" that expressed a uniquely American humor. In the second half of the 1800s, Walt Whitman wrote poetry full of vivid images and energetic language. His work expressed the growing self-confidence of American writers.

Canadian writers achieved fame for their work as well. Mark Twain highly praised Lucy Maud Montgomery's coming-of-age stories that began with the book, *Anne of Green Gables.* The heroine, Anne, was "the dearest and most moving and delightful child since Alice in Wonderland," Twain said. Today, Canadian writers such as Margaret Atwood and Alice Munro receive high praise for their work.

Canadian literature is often written in both French and English. French Canadian literature is called **Quebecois** (keh beh KWAH) **literature,** after the province of Quebec whose citizens speak French as their primary language. *Quebecois* literature is an example of how issues and conflicts in society influence creative expression. Until the 1830s, no French-Canadian poets or novelists had any of their work published in Canada. In the 1960s Quebec poets worked to create a French-Canadian identity. Paul Chamberland, in his book called *Terre Quebec*, which means "the land of Quebec," encourages readers to take pride in their French roots.

CULTURE In the picture below, Louis Armstrong poses with his band, the Hot Five. With his brilliant trumpet playing and his inventive musical mind, Louis Armstrong was one of the most influential figures in jazz history.
Critical Thinking What does this picture tell you about the musical style of jazz? How does jazz relate to the American spirit?

Musical Traditions

Have you ever listened to music at a Caribbean carnival, heard Cajun Zydeco music from Louisiana, or bluegrass music from the Southeast? These are just a few of the different musical styles in American culture.

One of the most important American musical styles is jazz. An important element in jazz is **improvisation,** in which musicians do not follow music written down, but spontaneously create their own. This has allowed jazz to grow to include a variety of cultural influences.

Answers to...

CRITICAL THINKING

The musicians are African American, suggesting the cultural influence on jazz. The body language of the musicians conveys a sense of movement, dynamism, and informality. There is also no written sheet music, suggesting that they are improvising.

Resource Directory

Technology

Color Transparencies 50 Toronto and the CN Tower Student Art; **51** Here's the Pitch Student Art

Jazz began with black American music and African rhythms. It later included elements of folk and classical music from Africa, Europe, Asia, and other places. Jazz is a uniquely American blend of sounds from many cultures. It has become popular throughout the world as a style of music that goes beyond the boundaries of society.

One of the most important jazz musicians of all time was Louis "Satchmo" Armstrong. In the 1920s and 1930s Armstrong became known as the world's greatest jazz trumpet and cornet player. He was also a singer whose rough, gravelly voice was recognized around the world. Armstrong introduced the "swing" style of jazz and popularized a kind of jazz singing without words called *scat.* Through his immense popularity as an entertainer, Armstrong brought American jazz to the whole world.

CULTURE An Inuit artist uses a drill to put the finishing touches on a soapstone carving. Creating such traditional artwork is one way the Inuit retain their identity. **Critical Thinking** What figures are shown in this sculpture? How do you think sculpture like this reflects the Inuit identity?

Art and Architecture

As in literature, the art and architecture of the United States and Canada have been influenced by history and by the landscape.

Art Painter **Andrew Wyeth** is one of America's most popular artists. His works focus on rural scenes that are reminders of a way of life long gone—old buildings, abandoned boats, deserted beaches. Other American landscape artists include Fitz Hugh Lane, who painted the seacoasts of New England, and Georgia O'Keeffe, known for her landscape paintings of the desert Southwest.

Native Americans have a long artistic tradition. From ancient times gifted artists have created beautiful pottery, baskets, woven cloth and rugs, beadwork, and metal jewelry. Many Native American artists continue this tradition today. Native groups such as the Haida of Canada's northwest coast produce fine woodcarvings. These artists express the close relationship that exists between their lives and their art.

In Canada, several painters formed the **"Group of Seven"** in the 1920s and 1930s. These artists developed bold new techniques for their paintings of Canada's landscapes. The group inspired other Canadian artists to experiment. Some ethnic artists followed other paths. Inuit printmakers and sculptors give new life to the images and ideas of their ancestors.

ACTIVITY

Interdisciplinary Connections

Music Arrange for students to listen to a variety of American musical genres, including rock, jazz, blues, gospel, country and western, and folk, as well as those listed in the text. Invite interested students to find out about the historical development of one of the genres they enjoy.

Musical/Rhythmic

CULTURE

The American Musical

The American musical developed in the early 1900s as a sort of democratic hybrid of the European traditions of operetta and ballet and the American traditions of vaudeville, burlesque, and minstrel shows. By the mid-1900s, the American musical was flourishing. Musicals such as *Show Boat*, *Oklahoma!*, *The Music Man*, *Guys and Dolls*, *Of Thee I Sing*, *Girl Crazy*, and *West Side Story* featured uniquely American themes and brought American composers such as George Gershwin, Cole Porter, and Leonard Bernstein international acclaim. Today, the American musical is firmly anchored as one of the most important contributions of the United States to modern world theater.

Resource Directory

Technology

Color Transparencies 149 *The Letter*
Fine Art

Answers to...

CRITICAL THINKING

Students may recognize the figures in the carving as animals and/or human figures. The Inuit people identify strongly with art as a part of their culture and way of life.

SECTION 2 ASSESSMENT

AFTER YOU READ

1. (a) African American poet who wrote about life in Harlem, (b) popular painter from the United States
2. (a) French Canadian literature (b) the spontaneous creation of music or some other form of performing art (c) group of Canadian artists
3. African American cultures, and rhythms and sounds from Africa, Europe, and Asia have contributed to jazz. American writers such as Willa Cather have been influenced by the immigrant experience in America.
4. Canadian artists and architects have been influenced by the different landscapes of their country. Many Canadian architects have adapted buildings to fit those landscapes.
5. Students' charts should demonstrate an understanding of the material in the section.
6. Answers will vary. Students should show that they understand that jazz reflects the cultural diversity that is uniquely American. Jazz appeals to people from other countries for a variety of reasons, ranging from its multicultural roots to its engaging rhythms to the excitement of improvisation.
7. Students' paragraphs should demonstrate an understanding of the poetry and how it relates to American life.

"Fallingwater"

CULTURE The "Fallingwater" house is located in Mill Run, Pennsylvania, and was designed by the American architect, Frank Lloyd Wright. Built for Edgar J. Kaufmann and his family in 1935 as a weekend retreat, "Fallingwater" is one of the most influential works of twentieth-century architecture. **Chart Study** What about this house is special? What does it say about architecture and nature?

Architecture The very diverse landscapes of the United States and Canada have influenced architecture in both countries. In the United States, architect Frank Lloyd Wright became famous for designing homes in the prairie style that blended with the landscape of the Midwest. The cool white and pastel stucco homes of the Southwest reflect the hot climate of the region. The Canadian architect Arthur Erickson designed buildings in Vancouver, British Columbia that are in harmony with the landscape.

In the 1900s, architects began to design new kinds of commercial buildings. A famous "race for the sky" took place in New York City. In the summer of 1929, an automobile tycoon, Walter Chrysler, battled Wall Street's Manhattan Trust Company for the title of the world's tallest building. Work on the buildings proceeded at break-neck speed, and just as it appeared that the bank would take the title in the spring of 1930, a crew atop the Chrysler Building put up a thin spire on the building to claim the title of world's tallest building at 1,046 feet. However, the title would be short-lived. Only four months later, the Empire State Building was completed.

In this new era, skyscrapers reflected the new wealth and power of the United States and Canada.

SECTION 2 ASSESSMENT

AFTER YOU READ

RECALL

1. Identify: (a) Langston Hughes, (b) Andrew Wyeth
2. Define: (a) *Quebecois* literature, (b) improvisation, (c) Group of Seven

COMPREHENSION

3. How have the different cultures of the United States influenced American music and literature?
4. How has the physical geography of Canada influenced Canadian art and architecture?

CRITICAL THINKING AND WRITING

5. **Exploring the Main Idea** Review the Main Idea statement at the beginning of this section and the chart you completed as you read. Then, write a paragraph that explains how art, literature, and music reflect the history, the physical landscape, and the cultural diversity of the United States and Canada.
6. **Drawing Conclusions** Write a paragraph explaining why you think that jazz is both uniquely American, and also appealing to people from all over the world.

ACTIVITY

7. **Reading Poetry** Read a poem by Langston Hughes or Walt Whitman. Write a paragraph explaining in what ways the poem reflects American life.

Resource Directory

Teaching Resources

Section Quiz in the Unit 2 Teaching Resources, p. 40

Answers to...

CRITICAL THINKING

Students may note the arresting shapes and their unique arrangement in the structure. The building is set into the landscape in a way that suggests a connection between architecture and nature.

SECTION 3

Conflict and Cooperation Among Cultures

BEFORE YOU READ

READING FOCUS

1. How were conflicts settled between the indigenous peoples and the governments of Canada and the United States?
2. What conflicts have ethnic groups faced in Canada and the United States?

KEY TERMS
reservation
indigenous
quota

KEY PEOPLE AND PLACES
Chippewa
Nunavut

NOTE TAKING

Copy the chart shown below. As you read the section, fill in information about conflicts and their solutions that culture groups faced in the United States and Canada.

	Conflicts	Solutions
United States		
Canada		

MAIN IDEA

Conflicts among groups within Canada and the United States have, at times, been resolved peacefully, though some continue.

Setting the Scene

During World War II, the Canadian army took over the land of the **Chippewa** tribe for a military base. The Chippewa were sent to a **reservation,** or area that the government set aside for them. The government said it would return the land after the war. Although the war ended in 1945, the land was not returned until 1994. Chippewa chief Thomas M. Bressette felt that his people deserved better treatment from the government:

"While our people were giving their lives [in the war] in Europe, the Government here in Canada was taking their land away from them and putting us on postage-stamp [size] reserves. We're asking for a share in the resources. We don't want to appear as beggars dependent on the government handouts, but we are now being denied the resources that we so willingly gave up to support this nation."

Remembering Canada's History

CULTURE The community of Chemainus, British Columbia, is famous for its collection of 33 larger-than-life historical murals. This mural honors the role that the indigenous peoples have played in Canada's history.
Critical Thinking How do you think this mural might promote cooperation between Canada's indigenous people and other Canadians?

Government and Native Peoples: Conflict and Cooperation

From the time the first European explorers arrived in North America, there was both conflict and cooperation between the Europeans and the native peoples. Early European settlers in North America took

Resource Directory

Teaching Resources

Classroom Manager in the Unit 2 Teaching Resources, p. 41

Guided Reading and Review in the Unit 2 Teaching Resources, p. 42

Guide to the Essentials, p. 25

Technology

Section Reading Support Transparencies

SECTION 3

Lesson Objectives

1. Explain how the governments of Canada and the United States have tried to resolve conflicts with indigenous peoples.
2. Identify examples of conflicts that different groups in Canada and the United States have faced, as well as ways that those conflicts have been resolved.

Lesson Plan

1 Engage

Warm-Up Activity

Ask students to think about the people in their community. Have them describe some ways in which their neighbors' cultural traditions or ways of life are similar to or different from their own. Then, discuss any conflicts that might arise because of these differences. Have students brainstorm some rules for maintaining good relationships between neighbors.

Activating Prior Knowledge

Ask students to think about disagreements that they have had with their siblings or friends. What was the cause of each disagreement? Ask volunteers to report how some disagreements were settled. Did a third party intervene to help settle the disagreement? Do students think the settlement was fair? Why or why not? Tell students that finding satisfactory solutions to conflicts between groups of people can be hard to achieve, despite people's best efforts.

Answers to...

CRITICAL THINKING

The mural honors the role that indigenous peoples have played in Canadian history. The mural may help these groups to feel that they are recognized and respected by the government.

Lesson Plan continued

❷ Explore

Challenge students to answer the following questions as they read: What are some conflicts encountered by the indigenous peoples of Canada and the United States? What steps have been taken to solve the conflicts between French Canadians and English-speaking Canadians? What are the some of the conflicts that have arisen between U.S. citizens and new immigrants?

❸ Teach

Have students develop a layout for a Web site about immigration to the United States and Canada. The layout should include text and graphics. Data should include information about the diverse origins of the immigrants, and the problems some of them faced after arriving. Encourage students to devise four "frequently asked questions" about immigrants and to include answers to those questions. This activity should take about 35 minutes.

Question for Discussion

CULTURE **How have Canada's national government and Quebec's provincial government acted to protect French culture?**

The governments have enacted laws requiring bilingual signs and establishing two official languages.

❹ Assess/Reteach

See the answers to the Section 3 Assessment. You may also assess students' Web site layouts.

Acceptable layouts include accurate information about immigrants and their origins and include appropriate graphics.

Commendable layouts include accurate information about immigrants and their origins, appropriate graphics, and provide and answer some frequently asked questions.

Outstanding layouts use text and graphics to link various groups of immigrants and the problems they faced, and they also provide and answer some frequently asked questions.

Native Americans and Europeans, 1753

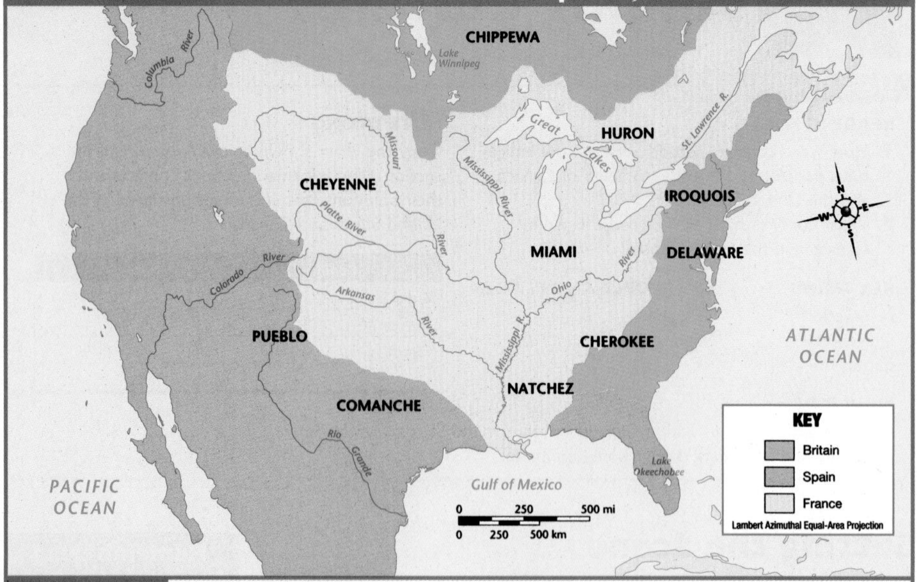

GEOGRAPHY By 1753, European countries had claimed land in North America. However, most of North America was still populated by Native Americans. This map shows some of the largest Native American groups who lived in European-claimed areas.
Map Study What European country claimed the land where the Cheyenne lived?

over the land of **indigenous** peoples, the people who were natives of North America. Many indigenous people were sent to reservations, while others were denied equal rights and facilities.

AS YOU READ
Monitor Your Reading How is the history of Canada's indigenous peoples similar to that of Native Americans in the United States?

Indigenous People in Canada

Despite being forced off of their land, indigenous people in Canada worked hard to hold onto their cultural identity and to regain their rights. Today, new laws in Canada allow indigenous peoples to use their own languages in their schools, and native people are working to have their own languages on street signs in their communities.

For centuries, the Inuit, nomadic hunters, lived in the Arctic. They had great survival skills and were fine craftsmen and artists. As times changed however, many Inuit lost their traditional artistic skills and feared that they would slowly lose their identity as Inuit people as well. In the early 1990s, the Inuit people convinced the Canadian government to grant them a vast section of land, once part of the Northwest Territory. On April 1, 1999, they moved to this new homeland, and called it ***Nunavut*** (NOO nah voot), or "Our Land."

Answers to...

MAP STUDY

France claimed the land where the Cheyenne lived.

AS YOU READ

Both groups were forced off their land and were denied civil rights by their respective governments.

Resource Directory

Teaching Resources

Outline Maps, Canada, p. 16

Technology

Color Transparencies 32 Canada: Political Map

114 UNIT 2 THE UNITED STATES AND CANADA

Native Americans and the United States Government

In the 1700s, as more and more settlers came to the United States, Native American peoples were squeezed into smaller and smaller areas of land. By the late 1800s, many groups were forcibly moved to and confined on reservation land under the control of the government. Without land, these Native Americans could no longer support themselves in their traditional ways, such as by hunting. Little by little, they were forced to become dependent upon government assistance.

During the mid 1900s, Native Americans worked along with other groups in the United States to gain civil rights. By the late 1900s, conflicts between Native Americans and the United States government were being settled peacefully by the courts. Native leaders won back important rights including fishing, forest, and mineral rights on tribal lands.

GOVERNMENT

The Bureau of Indian Affairs

In 1824, the Bureau of Indian Affairs was established by the U. S. government. It began as part of the War Department and later became part of the Department of Interior. Its job was to control the property and the lives of Native Americans living on reservations. The Bureau could lease the mineral, water, and other rights to reservation lands to non-Indians. At that time, the Native American people had almost no say in their own affairs. It was not until the 1900s that Congress passed laws allowing tribes to make their own decisions about their schools, courts, law enforcement, and other community activities.

Critical Thinking How do you think Native Americans felt about the Bureau of Indian Affairs? What do you think caused the most recent changes in government policy concerning Native Americans?

Citizens and Immigrants in Conflict

For centuries people from all over the world have flocked to the rich lands of North America. As waves of immigrants arrived, conflicts sometimes between among the newcomers and those already established.

The Quebec Question

From the beginning, Canada's leaders made immigration easy. At first they preferred European settlers and laws set limits on immigrants who were Jews, Asians, or Africans. But that has changed. Today, people of all ethnic groups may move to Canada as long as they can financially support themselves.

French Canadians are the focus of one of the greatest conflicts. These are mainly descendants of people who stayed after the British won control of Canada from France. The French Canadians of Quebec are very concerned about preserving their heritage. The Canadian government attempts to cooperate with the needs of French Canadians. For example, both English and French are official languages. In Quebec special laws promote French culture and language, but many French Canadians want more. They want Quebec to become a separate country, while the Canadian government wants Canada to remain one country. This conflict between French Canadians and English-speaking Canadians still remains unresolved.

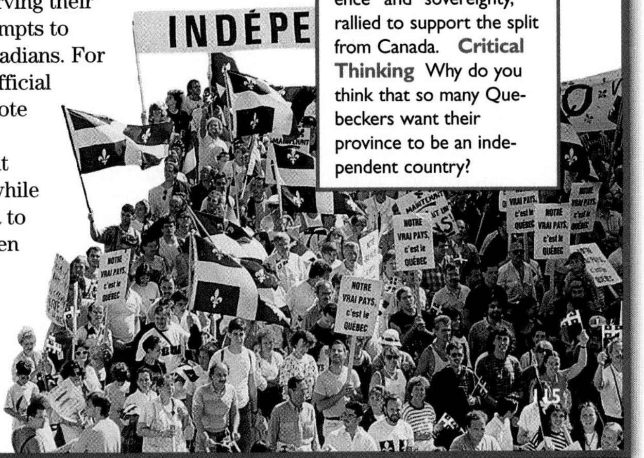

Disagreement on Separation

GEOGRAPHY Just before the 1995 referendum, Quebeckers, carrying signs calling for "independence" and "sovereignty," rallied to support the split from Canada. **Critical Thinking** Why do you think that so many Quebeckers want their province to be an independent country?

CULTURE

Adapting to the Physical Environment

Inuits in Greenland Greenland, a huge island to the northeast of Canada that is administered by Denmark, is also home to the Inuit people. The Inuits of Greenland live in an Arctic climate in ways similar to the Canadian Inuits. One difference, however, has been in housing. Traditional Canadian Inuits spent their summers in tents made from caribou hide. Greenland Inuits built more permanent homes of sod and stones or logs.

ACTIVITY

Journal Writing

Language Issues Some indigenous peoples want signs in their community to be written in their own languages. Ask students to carefully consider the pros and cons of such an undertaking (pros: preservation of the languages, reinforcement of cultural identity; cons: possible isolation from the rest of Canada, confusion among visitors to the community). Have students decide upon a position on the issue and explain their stance in their journals.

Verbal/Linguistic

SKILLS MINI LESSON

Drawing Conclusions

You may **introduce** the skill by encouraging the students to describe their understanding of the relationship between French-speaking and English-speaking Canadians. Suggest that they reread the section material about the people of Quebec before answering. To help students **practice** the skill, ask them to think about a time when they wanted to do something very different from their family or friends. Discuss the conflicting emotions the experience created and how these might relate to the Canadian situation. Have students **apply** their skill by writing a one- to two-sentence discussion based on the text just discussed. (Possible conclusion: The emotional atmosphere between English-speaking and French-speaking Canadians is tense, with both sides wanting to preserve their cultures. As members of a national "family," however, Canadians probably are distressed that there is such strife.)

Answers to...

CRITICAL THINKING

Students may recognize that Native Americans saw the actions of the Bureau as a departure from the government's earlier policy and were angered by it. The number of Native Americans was growing, and the government was under pressure to reform its policy.

CRITICAL THINKING

Students may speculate that these people feel that the cultural gulf between themselves and other Canadians is wide enough to justify Quebec's secession.

SECTION 3 ASSESSMENT

AFTER YOU READ

1. (a) indigenous people of Canada (b) homeland of the Inuit people
2. (a) an area set aside for native peoples (b) native to a certain area (c) a certain number allowed
3. They have granted the Inuit people a large tract of land as their homeland.
4. They were unable to support themselves in traditional ways, such as hunting.
5. Many French Canadians want Quebec to become a separate country, whereas the Canadian government wants the province to remain a part of Canada.
6. Students' paragraphs should demonstrate an understanding of the conflicts encountered by native peoples and the different steps each country took to resolve these conflicts.
7. Answers will vary. Students' paragraphs should reflect an understanding of the issues described in the section.

Panning for Gold

CULTURE Along with prospectors from all over the United States and its territories, the California Gold Rush of the mid-nineteenth century brought many immigrants to the state searching for work and a new life on the frontier. In the picture above, Chinese immigrants pan for gold in a California creek. **Critical Thinking** Besides work-related accidents, what other risks might immigrants have encountered when working in a new land?

Citizens and Immigrants in the United States

Poverty, political problems, and famine caused thousands of Europeans to come to the United States during the 1800s. At first the newcomers were welcome. The land was big, and there was plenty of work to do. But conflicts soon arose between new immigrants and U.S. citizens. During the 1850s, thousands of Chinese came to the United States to work in the California gold mines and to build the railroads. As their numbers grew, many other groups felt the Chinese were taking too many jobs. In 1882 the United States passed the Chinese Exclusion Act, which stopped Chinese workers from coming to the United States. Americans began to worry about the large number of immigrants from certain European countries, too. After World War I, the United States established **quotas,** certain numbers allowed, for various ethnic groups.

During the 1900s, many Spanish-speaking people immigrated to the United States from Mexico and Central and South America. Conflicts have arisen over whether public school classes should be taught in Spanish as well as English. Some people have tried to pass a law making English the official language of the United States.

Today, conflicts between cultural groups within the United States continue to exist. However, most Americans attempt to find peaceful solutions to these problems, and ways to cooperate with one another.

SECTION 3 ASSESSMENT

AFTER YOU READ

RECALL

1. Identify: (a) Chippewa, (b) *Nunavut*
2. Define: (a) reservation, (b) indigenous, (c) quota

COMPREHENSION

3. How has the Canadian government cooperated with the Inuit people to help them preserve their culture?
4. As Native Americans became confined on reservations in the United States, why did they become more dependent on government assistance?
5. Describe the main conflict between French Canadians and the Canadian government.

CRITICAL THINKING AND WRITING

6. **Exploring the Main Idea** Review the Main Idea statement at the beginning of this section. Then, write a paragraph comparing how the governments of the United States and Canada each handled conflicts with native peoples in those two countries.

ACTIVITY

7. **Making Predictions** Write a paragraph explaining why you think returning homelands to indigenous peoples will create more conflict or will ease conflict. List at least two reasons for your opinion.

Resource Directory

Teaching Resources

Section Quiz in the Unit 2 Teaching Resources, p. 43

Chapter Summary in the Unit 2 Teaching Resources, p. 44

Vocabulary in the Unit 2 Teaching Resources, p. 45

Reteaching in the Unit 2 Teaching Resources, p. 46

Enrichment in the Unit 2 Teaching Resources, p. 47

Critical Thinking in the Unit 2 Teaching Resources, p. 48

Answers to...

CRITICAL THINKING

Students may mention risks relating to a lack of understanding of the English language or those stemming from some Americans' resentment of immigrants.

Identifying Primary and Secondary Sources

What You Need

To figure out the differences between primary and secondary sources, you will need:

- Several sources including magazines, newspapers, nonfiction books, a textbook, an encyclopedia, and a copy of the Constitution of the United States, which can be found in an encyclopedia.
- Paper
- A pen or pencil

Learn the Skill

You must use sources in order to do research. The best sources of information are often primary sources. Primary sources are written by people who experienced a particular event or time period firsthand. They are writing from their own experience. Examples of primary sources are:

letters, journals, autobiographies, government documents, such as declarations or laws, speeches, interviews, and home videos.

Secondary sources are written by people who did not experience a particular event or time period firsthand. These people are reporting what they have heard or read about an event. Examples of secondary sources are:

nonfiction books, textbooks, most magazine and newspaper articles

You can learn to identify primary and secondary sources by doing the following:

A. Gather the materials you need.

B. Make a two-column chart. Label the first column "Primary Sources." Label the second column "Secondary Sources."

C. Decide whether each source is a primary source or a secondary source. If you need help, reread the definitions above.

D. Write the names of your sources into the correct column of your chart.

E. When finished, compare your chart with a partner.

Practice the Skill

Below are two articles about the Gourd Dance. A Gourd Dance is a traditional Native American dance performed by the Kiowa people. One article is written by N. Scott Momaday, a Kiowa author and poet. The other article is written by a sixth grade student. Which article is a primary source? Which article is a secondary source? How do you know?

> It's in Oklahoma in July. It's apt to be very humid and very hot and we wear blankets. But once the movement starts and the drum starts gathering momentum, reaching a certain pitch, you get deep into the motion of the dance, and that feeling is indescribable. It's wonderful…I know why those warriors danced before they went out on raiding expeditions. It is a great way to gather yourself up, and you feel very much alive.
>
> —*N. Scott Momaday*
>
> Source: Bolton, Jonathan, and Claire Wilson. *Scholars, Writers, and Professionals (American Indian Lives)*, New York: Facts on File, 1994. p. 113

> The Gourd Dance is a dance of the Kiowa Indians. The men of this Native American tribe dance it while wearing blankets. They are accompanied by the drum. The dancers wear blankets, even in hot, humid weather. The dance prepares them for raiding expeditions.
>
> —*Jonathan Smith, Sixth Grader*

Apply the Skill

See the Chapter Review and Assessment at the end of this chapter for more questions on interpreting primary sources.

Lesson Objectives

1. Recognize the differences between primary and secondary sources.
2. Determine which kinds of sources provide the best information.

Lesson Plan

1 Engage

To introduce the skill, read aloud the opening text under "Learn the Skill." Ask students to give definitions in their own words for primary and secondary sources. Then, name various sources and have students determine whether they are primary or secondary sources.

2 Explore

Direct students to read the steps under "Learn the Skill." Have them collect various sources from the classroom or library, including textbooks and encyclopedia articles. Make sure students understand that a copy of a primary source, found in an encyclopedia is still a primary source.

3 Teach

Have students read the two articles and determine which is a primary source. If necessary, have students reread the definitions under "Learn the Skill."

Then, have students turn to various pages in their text. Ask them to determine whether the page contains a primary or a secondary source.

4 Assess/Reteach

Check to make sure students have listed sources on their charts correctly.

To further assess students' understanding, have them complete the "Applying Your Skills" part of the Chapter Review and Assessment at the end of this chapter.

Resource Directory

Technology

Social Studies Skills Tutor CD-ROM

Answers to...

PRACTICE THE SKILL

N. Scott Momaday's article is the primary source because it relates a firsthand experience; Jonathan Smith's article is a secondary source because it is a written report of an event he did not experience firsthand.

CHAPTER 6

Review and Assessment

Creating a Chapter Summary

Student summaries will vary.

Sample summaries:

Section 2 People of the United States and Canada combined many different cultural traditions to form unique cultures of their own. Literature, music, art, and architecture reflected the histories of these nations, and were influenced by the impact of physical geography on people's lives.

Section 3 As settlers in North America moved steadily westward, conflicts arose over land ownership between the settlers and the native peoples. Later, as more and more immigrants came to the United States and Canada, conflicts arose between citizens and new immigrants. Many of these conflicts were resolved, but some continue today.

Reviewing Key Terms

1. b **2.** a **3.** d **4.** c **5.** h **6.** i **7.** e **8.** g **9.** f

Reviewing the Main Ideas

1. Native Americans taught the French to trap and to live in the forest. They taught the English how to grow local foods.
2. Different immigrant groups have contributed different things to American culture, including different types of foods, music, language, crops and farming methods, and religious practices and beliefs.
3. Artists paint pictures of landscapes and of reminders of the past; authors may write stories set in the past, and they often make the physical geography of a specific region an important part of the story.
4. American music has been influenced by African American culture, rhythms from Africa, and sounds from Europe and Asia.
5. Native American tribes were given control over their lands and their affairs. Sometimes tribes went through the courts to achieve their rights.
6. Citizens may believe that new immigrants are taking too many jobs; they may resent immigrants wanting to use their own language in the public schools.

CHAPTER 6

Review and Assessment

Creating a Chapter Summary

On a separate sheet of paper, draw a diagram like this one, and include the information that summarizes Sections 1. Then fill in the second and third box with a summary of Sections 2 and 3.

THE UNITED STATES AND CANADA: RICH IN CULTURE

Section 1
Europeans arriving in North America encountered different cultural and religious beliefs among Native Americans. Different ethnic groups immigrating to North America made the United States and Canada culturally diverse.

Section 2

Section 3

Reviewing Key Terms

Match the definitions in Column I with the key terms in Column II.

Column I	Column II
1. the exchange of customs, ideas, or things between two cultures	a. cultural diversity
2. a wide variety of cultures	b. cultural exchange
3. an area set aside for native peoples	c. ethnic group
4. people who share a language, history, and culture	d. reserve
5. a certain number allowed	e. indigenous
6. the act of spontaneously creating something	f. religious diversity
7. native to a certain area	g. *Quebecois* literature
8. work by French Canadian authors	h. quota
9. a wide variety of religions	i. improvisation

Reviewing the Main Ideas

1. What contributions have Native Americans made to American culture? (Section 1)
2. What are some important contributions that immigrants have made to American culture? (Section 1)
3. How are history and landscape reflected in the art and literature of Canada and the United States? (Section 2)
4. How has cultural diversity helped shape American music? (Section 2)
5. How have conflicts between Native American groups and the U. S. Government begun to be resolved? (Section 3)
6. Why has there been conflict between U.S. citizens and new immigrants in the past and in more recent times? (Section 3)

118 UNIT 2 THE UNITED STATES AND CANADA

Map Activity

Native American Groups

For each Native American group listed below, write the letter from the map that shows its location.

1. Miami
2. Chippewa
3. Cherokee
4. Iroquois
5. Pueblo
6. Cheyenne
7. Comanche
8. Huron

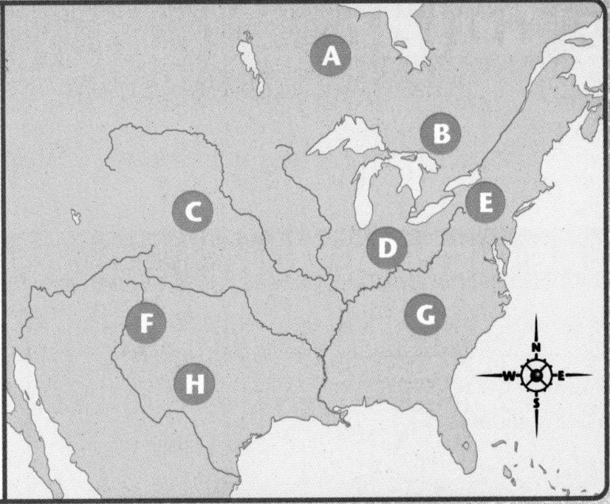

Take It to the NET

Enrichment For more map activities using geography skills, visit the social studies section of **phschool.com.**

Writing Activity

1. **Writing a Poem** Much of the literature of America has been influenced by the history, landscape, and cultural diversity of the country. Write a short poem that shows one or more of these influences. The poem might be about your own family history, or that of your neighbors or classmates. It might be about the history of the place where you live, or about an historical event. Or it might be about the landscape where you live, or of places you have visited.
2. **Writing a Journal** Imagine that your family has just immigrated to the United States from another country. (You choose the country!) Write three journal entries describing your experiences and feelings on your first day of school in America, during your first trip to the grocery store, and watching an American television program or movie.

Critical Thinking

1. **Drawing Conclusions** What are some advantages of having many different cultures influence your own culture? What are some disadvantages?
2. **Making Predictions** Think about the Inuit people moving to *Nunavut*, their new homeland. What do you think might happen to their culture in this new place? How will their lives be changed?

Applying Your Skills

For each of the following, decide whether it is a primary or secondary source. Make sure to explain your answers.

1. an encyclopedia entry about architecture in the United States
2. a journal entry
3. a research report about the Inuit
4. an interview with Willa Cather in a literary journal

Take It to the NET

Activity Canada's history and cultural identity have been shaped by a variety of cultural groups. Compare and contrast different cultural groups on the "Canadian Museum of Civilization" Web site. Visit the World Explorer: People, Places, and Cultures section of **phschool.com** for help in completing this activity.

Chapter 6 Self-Test As a final review activity, take the Chapter 6 Self-Test and get instant feedback on your answers. To take the test, visit the Social Studies section of **phschool.com.**

Map Activity

1. D **2.** A **3.** G **4.** E **5.** F **6.** C **7.** H **8.** B

Writing Activity

1. The poem should clearly reflect a specific ethnic background, make reference to the history of a specific place, or describe a specific landscape.
2. Students should produce three distinct journal entries, each giving specific sensory details and describing their feelings about each situation.

Critical Thinking

1. Students may suggest that some advantages are adding variety to their culture, with new music, new foods, new ways of doing things; some disadvantages might be that the old culture changes too much and traditions are lost.
2. Students may predict that their native culture will be strengthened because there will be fewer outside influences or control over matters that may not be fully understood by people outside of the Inuit culture.

Applying Your Skills

1. secondary—writer did not experience architectural creations and eras firsthand
2. primary—contains writer's firsthand impressions
3. secondary—contains information about Inuit by a non-Inuit
4. primary—Cather's responses are firsthand

Resource Directory

Teaching Resources

Cooperative Learning Activity in the Unit 2 Teaching Resources, pp. 112–115

Chapter Tests Forms A and B in the Unit 2 Teaching Resources, pp. 144–149

Guide to the Essentials, Ch. 6 Test, p. 26

Other Print Resources

Chapter Tests with ExamView® Test Bank, Ch. 6

Technology

ExamView® Test Bank CD-ROM, Ch. 6

Resource Pro® CD-ROM

Chapter 7 Planning Guide

Resource Manager

	CORE INSTRUCTION	READING/SKILLS
Chapter-Level Resources	**Teaching Resources** Program Overview Pacing Charts **Technology** Resource Pro® CD-ROM Companion Web site, phschool.com • eTeach	**Technology** Social Studies Skills Tutor CD-ROM Student Edition on Audio CD, Ch. 7
1 The Northeast: An Urban Center 1. Identify the ways in which the people of the Northeast contribute to the economy of the United States. 2. Explain why the Northeast is home to people of many different cultures.	**Teaching Resources** **Unit 2** Classroom Manager, p. 50 Guided Reading and Review, p. 51	**Teaching Resources** Guide to the Essentials, p. 27 Social Studies and Geography Skills, p. 29 **Technology** Section Reading Support Transparencies
2 The South: Growth in Population and Industry 1. Describe why the South's land and water are important to the region's economy. 2. Explain how the growth of industry has changed the South.	**Teaching Resources** **Unit 2** Classroom Manager, p. 53 Guided Reading and Review, p. 54	**Teaching Resources** Guide to the Essentials, p. 28 **Technology** Section Reading Support Transparencies
3 The Midwest: Technology Brings Change 1. Explain how technology is changing agriculture in the Midwest. 2. Discuss how changes in agriculture affect the growth of cities there.	**Teaching Resources** **Unit 2** Classroom Manager, p. 56 Guided Reading and Review, p. 57	**Teaching Resources** Guide to the Essentials, p. 29 **Technology** Section Reading Support Transparencies
4 The West: Land of Precious Resources 1. Identify the natural resources of the West. 2. Describe how people work to balance conservation with the use of natural resources.	**Teaching Resources** **Unit 2** Classroom Manager, p. 59 Guided Reading and Review, p. 60 Chapter Summary, p. 62 Vocabulary, p. 63 Reteaching, p. 64	**Teaching Resources** **Unit 2** Critical Thinking, p. 66 Guide to the Essentials, p. 30 **Technology** Section Reading Support Transparencies

ENRICHMENT / PRE-AP

Teaching Resources
Primary Sources and Literature Readings

Other Print Resources
DK Atlas

Technology
World Video Explorer: Spotlight On: Immigration and Case Study: Land Preservation
Companion Web site, phschool.com

Teaching Resources
Outline Maps, pp. 14–15

Technology
Color Transparencies 34–36, 41–42
Passport to the World CD-ROM

Teaching Resources
Outline Maps, pp. 14–15

Technology
Color Transparencies 34–35, 37, 41–42
Passport to the World CD-ROM

Teaching Resources
Outline Maps, pp. 14–15

Technology
Color Transparencies 34–35, 38, 41–42
Passport to the World CD-ROM

Teaching Resources
Unit 2
Enrichment, p. 65
Cooperative Learning Activity, pp. 116–118

Technology
Color Transparencies 34–35, 39, 41–42
Passport to the World CD-ROM

ASSESSMENT

Prentice Hall Assessment System

Core Assessment
Chapter Tests with ExamView® Test Bank, Ch. 7
ExamView® Test Bank CD-ROM, Ch. 7

Standardized Test Preparation
Diagnose and Prescribe
Diagnostic Tests for Middle Grades Social Studies Skills
Review and Reteach
Review Book for World Studies
Practice and Assess
Test-taking Strategies with Transparencies for Middle Grades Test Prep Book
Test-taking Strategies Posters

Teaching Resources
Unit 2
Section Quizzes, pp. 52, 55, 58, and 61
Chapter Tests, pp. 150–155

Technology
Companion Web site, phschool.com
Ch. 7 Self-Test

World Video Explorer
Each region of the world is explored through regional flyovers and investigative field trips. Case study segments give students an in-depth view of the history, economy, government, and culture of a key place in each region. Case studies include Nigeria, Mexico, China, British Columbia, and the Czech Republic.

In Your Classroom

CUSTOMIZE FOR INDIVIDUAL NEEDS

Gifted and Talented

Teacher's Edition
- Identifying Central Issues, p. 127
- Environmental Responsibility, p. 135

Teaching Resources
- Enrichment, p. 65
- Primary Sources and Literature Readings

Honors/Pre-AP

Teacher's Edition
- Cotton, p. 127
- Depleting Natural Resources, p. 135

Teaching Resources
- Critical Thinking, p. 66
- Primary Sources and Literature Readings

ESL

Teacher's Edition
- Beantown, p. 123
- Art, p. 131

Teaching Resources
- Guided Reading and Review, pp. 51, 54, 57, and 60
- Vocabulary, p. 63
- Reteaching, p. 64
- Guide to the Essentials, pp. 27–30
- Social Studies and Geography Skills, p. 29

Technology
- Social Studies Skills Tutor CD-ROM
- Section Reading Support Transparencies

Less Proficient Readers

Teacher's Edition
- Weekend Getaway, p. 123
- Language Arts, p. 131

Teaching Resources
- Guided Reading and Review, pp. 51, 54, 57, and 60
- Vocabulary, p. 63
- Reteaching, p. 64
- Guide to the Essentials, pp. 27–30
- Social Studies and Geography Skills, p. 29

Technology
- Social Studies Skills Tutor CD-ROM
- Section Reading Support Transparencies

Less Proficient Writers

Teacher's Edition
- Art, p. 131
- Depleting Natural Resources, p. 135

Teaching Resources
- Guided Reading and Review, pp. 51, 54, 57, and 60
- Vocabulary, p. 63
- Guide to the Essentials, pp. 27–30
- Social Studies and Geography Skills, p. 29

Technology
- Social Studies Skills Tutor CD-ROM
- Section Reading Support Transparencies

DORLING KINDERSLEY

At the end of each unit, you will find information adapted from Dorling Kindersley's *Illustrated Children's Encyclopedia* that connects to the region being studied and to one of the seven content strands. In addition, your resources include Dorling Kindersley's *Atlas*, which contains valuable information about countries from around the world.

TEACHER'S EDITION INDEX

CHAPTER 7 PACING SUGGESTIONS

For 90-minute Blocks

See suggestions in the Teaching Resources Pacing Charts for Chapter 5. Use Color Transparencies 34–39, 41–42.

Running Out of Time?

See the Guide to the Essentials, pp. 27–30.

INTERDISCIPLINARY LINKS

Middle Grades Math: Tools for Success

Course 1, Chapter 3, **Math Toolbox, Spreadsheets and Bank Statements**

Course 2, Lesson 1-8, **Using Data to Persuade**

Science Explorer

Environmental Science, Lesson 5-3, **Finding Pollution Solutions;** Lesson 2-4, **Earth's Biomes**

Weather and Climate, Lesson 4-2, **Climate Regions**

Prentice Hall Literature

Bronze, Melting Pot

BIBLIOGRAPHY

For the Teacher

Cohn, Amy L., ed. *From Sea to Shining Sea.* Scholastic, 1993.

Mead, Robin, Polly Mead, and Gary A. Lewis. *The Fifty States.* Smithmark, 1992.

World Desk Reference. Dorling Kindersley, 2001.

For the Student

Easy

Eyewitness Technology. Dorling Kindersley, 2001.

Jaspersohn, William. *Timber!* Little, Brown, 1996.

Average

Bial, Raymond. *Portrait of a Farm Family.* Houghton Mifflin, 1995.

Krull, Kathleen. *The Other Side: How Kids Live in a California Latino Neighborhood.* Lodestar, 1994.

Challenging

Hilton, Suzanne. *A Capital Capital City, 1790–1814.* Atheneum, 1992.

Literature Connection

George, Jean Craighead. *There's an Owl in the Shower.* HarperCollins, 1995.

Holt, David, and Bill Mooney. *Spiders in the Hairdo: Modern Urban Legends.* August House, 1999.

Take It to the NET

The World Explorer companion Web site, found on **phschool.com**, offers activities for exploring geographical, historical, and cultural resources on the Internet. It also provides on-line links for key content and all Section and Chapter Assessment activities.

The **Teacher site** also provides teachers with regional data and ideas for student research and activities.

Students can use the **Student site** to find chapter-by-chapter Internet resource links and to access Self-Tests.

CHAPTER 7

Connecting to the Guiding Questions

In this chapter, students will read about regions in the United States. Content in this chapter corresponds to the following Guiding Questions outlined at the beginning of the unit.

- How has physical geography affected the settlement patterns and the economies of the United States?
- How has cultural diversity benefited and challenged these two nations?
- How did the United States and Canada become two of the wealthiest nations in the world?
- How has modern technology both benefited and created challenges for the United States and Canada?

Using the Song Activities

Point out to students that the song was originally written as a poem, and then set to music later.

- Students should recognize different physical regions of the country as described in the song's lyrics. Students also should recognize the writer's respect and awe for the physical greatness of the country.
- Poems should clearly depict a physical landscape with vivid language.

Heterogeneous Groups

The following activities are suitable for heterogeneous groups.

Cooperative Learning
Weekend Getaway, p. 123

Interdisciplinary Connection
Art, p. 131

Journal Writing
Environmental Responsibility, p. 135

eTeach

Be sure to check out this month's discussion with a Master Teacher. Go to **phschool.com**.

CHAPTER 7

THE UNITED STATES: Exploring the Region Today

America the Beautiful

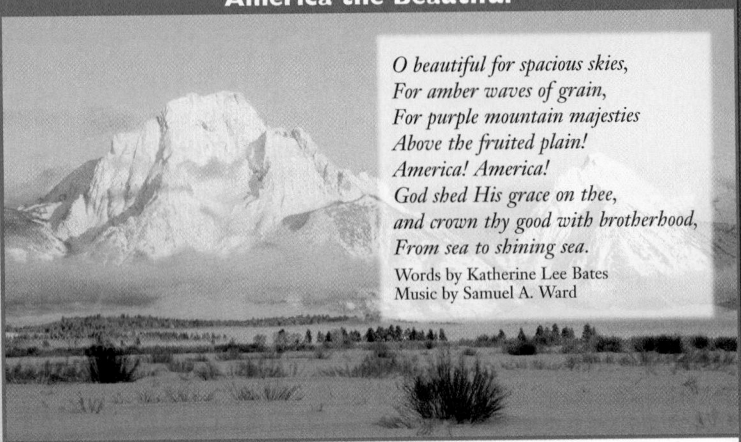

O beautiful for spacious skies,
For amber waves of grain,
For purple mountain majesties
Above the fruited plain!
America! America!
God shed His grace on thee,
and crown thy good with brotherhood,
From sea to shining sea.
Words by Katherine Lee Bates
Music by Samuel A. Ward

Understanding Song

Katherine Lee Bates wrote the words to "America the Beautiful" in 1893. Bates was a Massachusetts poet and a teacher. She attended Wellesley College, where she also taught. Later, Samuel A. Ward set her poem to music. The song has become a popular American hymn. First read the words, then listen to a recording of the song. Think about how Ward's music adds to Bates's poem.

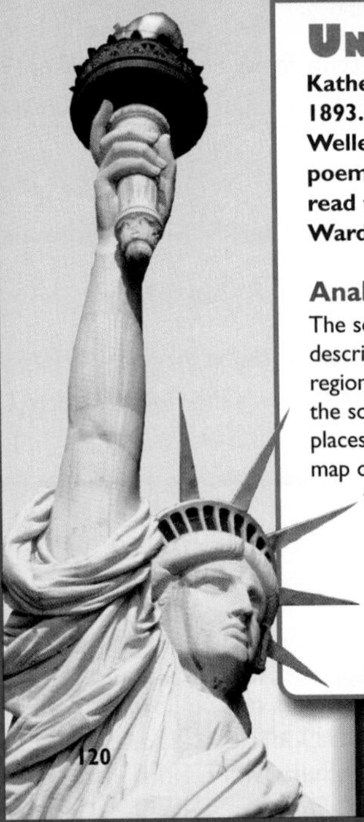

Analyzing Song Lyrics

The song, "America the Beautiful" describes several different geographic regions in America. Read the lyrics to the song and then make a list of the places that the song describes. Study a map of the United States and try to figure out where you might find the places described. What kinds of words and images does the song's writer use to describe each place? How do you think the writer felt about America, based on the lyrics of the song?

Writing Song Lyrics

Writing song lyrics is a lot like writing poetry. Think about a place or a landscape that you know and love. Make a list of words that you think best describe that place. Be as specific as possible, and think about the images that your words will convey to someone. Share your lyrics with a partner, and discuss for which kind of music your lyrics would be best suited.

120 UNIT 2 THE UNITED STATES AND CANADA

Resource Directory

Teaching Resources

Primary Sources and Literature Readings extend content with a selection related to the concepts in this chapter.

Other Print Resources

DK Atlas

Technology

Spotlight On: Immigration, from the World Video Explorer, enhances understanding of the effects of immigration in the United States.

Case Study: Land Preservation, from the World Video Explorer, enhances understanding of issues surrounding land preservation in the United States.

Student Edition on Audio CD, Ch. 7

SECTION 1

The Northeast

An Urban Center

BEFORE YOU READ

READING FOCUS

1. How does the population of the Northeast affect the economy of the United States?
2. Why is the Northeast a region of many cultures?

KEY TERMS
commute
megalopolis

KEY PLACES
Philadelphia
Boston
New York City

NOTE TAKING
Copy the chart below. As you read the section, fill in the chart with details about cities in the Northeast.

Philadelphia	Boston	New York

MAIN IDEA
The coastal region of the Northeast is densely populated, and its culturally diverse cities are important economic centers.

Setting the Scene

For at least a century, life in New York City has been described in one way: crowded. One hundred years ago, horse-drawn carriages caused traffic jams. Now, 5 million riders squeeze into New York's subway cars every day. Others travel the 1,745 miles (2,807 km) of bus lines, catch one of the city's 12,000 taxis, or ride the ferry boat. And many people drive their own cars through the city's busy streets.

New York is not unique. Washington, D.C., Philadelphia, and Boston are also crowded. In these big cities, millions of people **commute**, or travel to work, each day. Many drive to the city from the suburbs, but many who live in the city travel from one area to another in order to work.

City Streets

GEOGRAPHY

During rush hour, New York City's streets fill with cars. If you are in a hurry, try walking or grabbing a subway train instead of driving.
Critical Thinking What does this traffic tell you about where and how people live in this region?

A Region of Cities

Did you ever hear of Bowash? That is what some people call the chain of cities from Boston to New York to Washington, D.C. This coastal region of the Northeast is a **megalopolis** (meg uh LAHP uh lis), a type of region where cities and suburbs have grown so close together they form one big urban area. Look at the map on page 123 to see how large this area is.

SECTION 1

Lesson Objectives

1. Identify the ways in which the people of the Northeast contribute to the economy of the United States.
2. Explain why the Northeast is home to people of many different cultures.

Lesson Plan

1 Engage

Warm-Up Activity

Write *New York City*, *Philadelphia*, and *Boston* on the chalkboard. Ask students what they think these cities have in common. Then, ask students to brainstorm some characteristics or impressions they have of each of the listed cities. Record students' responses on the chalkboard. Revise or add to the list during a class discussion of the section.

Activating Prior Knowledge

Suggest that students move all of their desks to the center of the classroom. Have them suppose that each desk represents a household or a business in a city with a high population density. Guide students in identifying the advantages and disadvantages of high population density.

2 Explore

As students read the section, ask them to find answers to the following questions: How would you describe the population density of the Northeast? How do Philadelphia, Boston, and New York City each contribute to the nation as a whole? Why have the cities of the Northeast been called *gateways*?

Answers to...

CRITICAL THINKING
Traffic indicates an urban area where many people live and commute.

Resource Directory

Teaching Resources

Classroom Manager in the Unit 2 Teaching Resources, p. 50

Guided Reading and Review in the Unit 2 Teaching Resources, p. 51

Guide to the Essentials, p. 27

Technology

How People Live Transparencies, Unit 2

Section Reading Support Transparencies

Lesson Plan continued

3 Teach

Have students create a "Major Cities of the Northeast" chart. Each chart should have three columns: *City Name, Economy,* and *Other Interesting Facts.* The three rows of the chart should correspond to the three cities discussed in the section. This activity should take about 30 minutes.

Questions for Discussion

GEOGRAPHY If you were looking for work in the Northeast, what kinds of jobs might you find?

Possibilities include manufacturing, finance, commerce, communications, government, transportation, farming, and working in the timber industry.

GEOGRAPHY Locate Philadelphia on the map on page 602. Why is its location good for an industrial center?

It is located near the mouth of the Delaware River, providing an important transportation route. It also is located near important land transportation routes.

4 Assess/Reteach

See the answers to the Section 1 Assessment. You may also assess students' charts.

Acceptable charts contain one fact in each cell.

Commendable charts contain a minimum of one fact per cell, with many cells containing several facts.

Outstanding charts contain several facts in most cells and clearly convey each city's unique features.

Answers to...

CHART STUDY

The highest population density is in New York City and Boston and the areas surrounding those two cities. The least densely populated areas are in northwestern Maine. Most Northeasterners live in the urban areas along the coast.

REGIONAL PROFILE

The Northeast

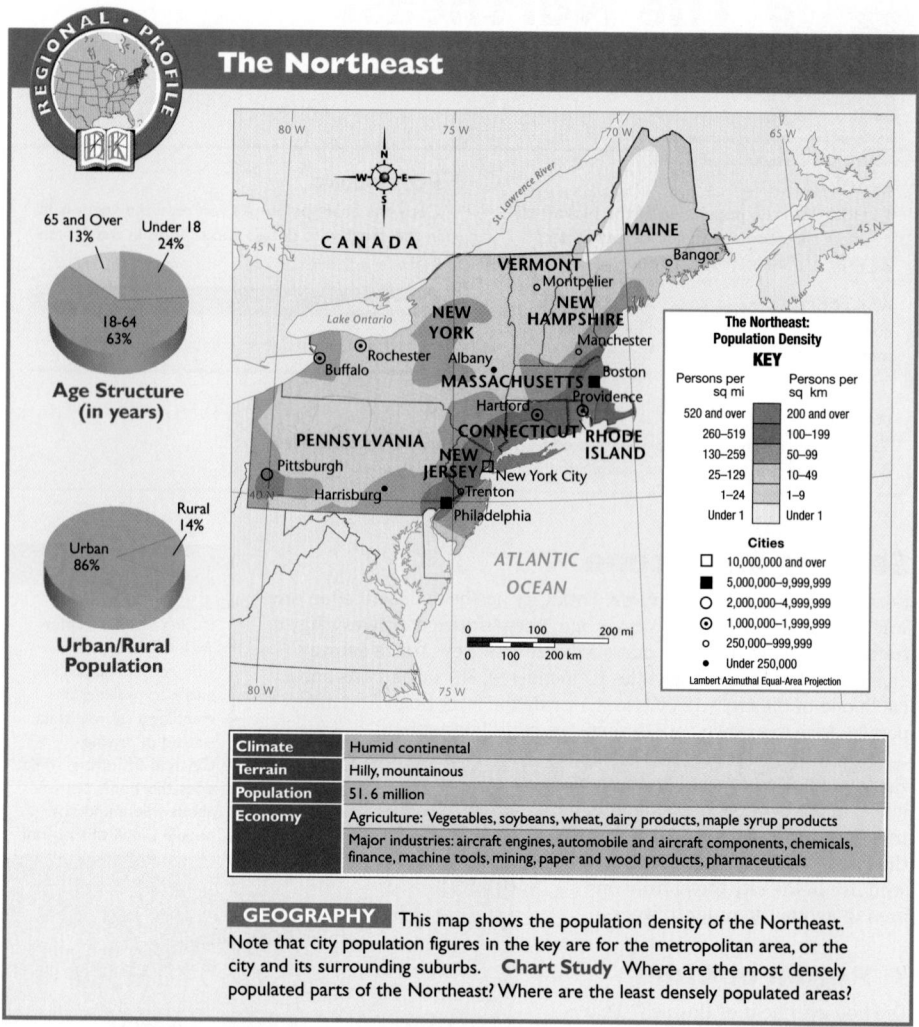

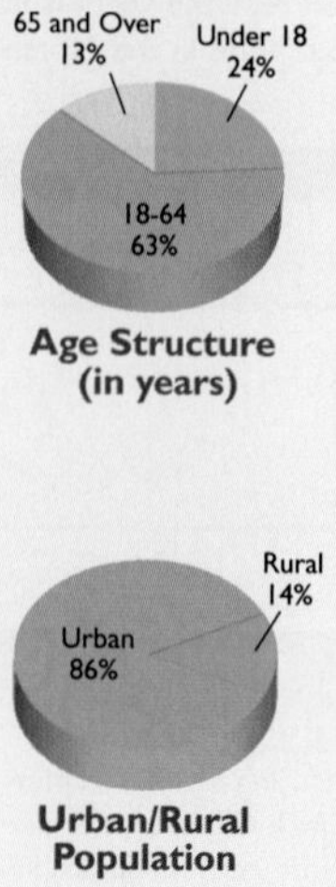

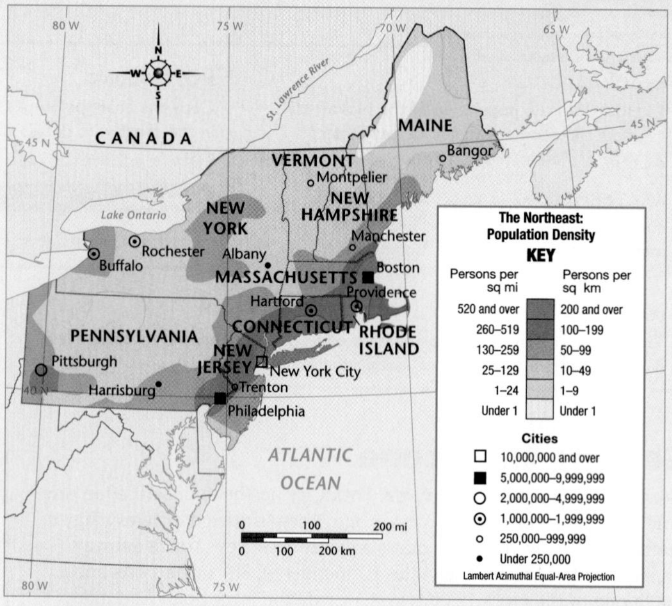

Climate	Humid continental	
Terrain	Hilly, mountainous	
Population	51.6 million	
Economy	Agriculture: Vegetables, soybeans, wheat, dairy products, maple syrup products	
	Major industries: aircraft engines, automobile and aircraft components, chemicals, finance, machine tools, mining, paper and wood products, pharmaceuticals	

GEOGRAPHY This map shows the population density of the Northeast. Note that city population figures in the key are for the metropolitan area, or the city and its surrounding suburbs. **Chart Study** Where are the most densely populated parts of the Northeast? Where are the least densely populated areas?

The Northeast is the most densely populated region of the United States. A region's population density is the average number of people per square mile (or square kilometer). The population is denser in parts of New Jersey than in crowded countries like India or Japan!

The Northeast's economy is based on cities, many founded in colonial times, along rivers or near the ocean as transportation and trade centers. Today, manufacturing, finance, communications, and government employ millions of urban Northeasterners.

122 UNIT 2 UNITED STATES AND CANADA

Resource Directory

Teaching Resources

Outline Maps, The United States, pp. 14–15

Social Studies and Geography Skills, Reading a Population Density Map, p. 29

Technology

Color Transparencies 35 The United States and Canada: Population Distribution Map; **36** The United States: Northeast: Physical-Political Map

Passport to the World CD-ROM This interactive CD-ROM allows students to explore each region of the world. Students view regional videos, take a photo tour, and explore a historical timeline. Students record their travels in an Explorer's Journal and receive passport stamps when they pass regional quizzes.

An Urban Megalopolis

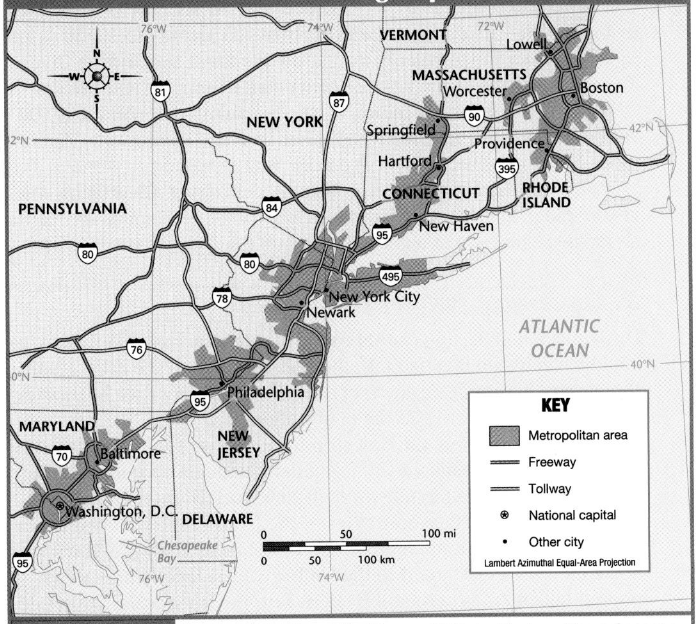

GEOGRAPHY You can drive from Washington, D.C., to Boston, Massachusetts, almost entirely within urban areas. **Map Study** Compare this map with the one in the Regional Profile. What similarities are there between the two maps?

Philadelphia and Boston **Philadelphia** and Boston were important in our nation's early history. In Philadelphia, America's founders adopted the Declaration of Independence and the Constitution. Some early struggles against the British took place in Boston.

Today, Philadelphia is an industrial powerhouse located near the mouth of the Delaware River. Important land and water transportation routes pass through here as ships, trucks, and trains bring in raw materials from all over the world. Thousands of factories process food, refine petroleum, and manufacture chemicals. Hundreds of products are then shipped out for sale.

The **Boston** area is home to more than 20 colleges and universities. Cambridge (KAYM brij), a Boston suburb, is the home of Harvard, the oldest university in the United States. The city is also famous for its science and technology centers. Boston's universities and scientific companies often work together to design new products and to carry out medical research.

AS YOU READ

Find Main Ideas In what ways are Philadelphia and Boston important to the United States?

CULTURE

Beantown

Sometimes elements of culture, such as special foods, can be linked in surprising ways to places and to time periods. Some of Boston's most influential early white settlers were the Puritans, who in 1629 had left England because they were being persecuted for their religious beliefs. Since Puritans did not believe in cooking on the Sabbath, on Saturday nights the Puritan women of Boston often prepared baked beans, which they served for Sunday dinner. Thus was born the classic American dish Boston baked beans and Boston's nickname, "Beantown."

ACTIVITY

Cooperative Learning

Weekend Getaway Organize students into groups of four to design a television commercial urging people to visit New York City for a weekend. Students should supplement information in the text with independent research. Encourage groups to integrate music, narrative, and visuals in their commercials.

Visual/Spatial

SKILLS MINI LESSON

Using a Map Key

To **introduce** the skill, remind students that map keys can be used to convey almost any kind of information about a place. For example, on the Regional Profile map on the opposite page, each color indicates the number of persons per square mile or square kilometer living in a particular area. In other words, the colors show the population densities of several areas in the northeastern United States. Allow students to **practice** the skill by asking them to identify all the areas with a population density of 260 to 519 persons per square mile. Then ask them which city has the greater population—Hartford, Connecticut, or Trenton, New Jersey (Hartford). Ask students to **apply** the skill by supposing that they are traveling from Boston, Massachusetts, to Montpelier, Vermont. Have them describe the changes in the population density during such a trip.

Answers to...

MAP STUDY

The megalopolis coincides with areas of high population density.

AS YOU READ

Students should note that these cities are centers of industry, education, and technology.

SCIENCE, TECHNOLOGY, AND SOCIETY

September 11, 2001

The key east coast cities of New York and Washington, D.C. suffered heavily in the terrorist attacks of September 11, 2001. The hijacking of commercial passenger planes to destroy the twin towers of the World Trade Center in New York and part of the Pentagon in Washington, D.C. was a new and terrifying misuse of the science and technology that produced the planes. The destruction of the buildings that took so many innocent lives also created challenges for architecture of the future.

SECTION 1 ASSESSMENT

AFTER YOU READ

1. (a) large industrial city in the Northeast (b) large city in the Northeast famous for its colleges and universities (c) large city in the Northeast that is the nation's "money capital"
2. (a) to travel to work (b) region in which cities and suburbs have grown so close together that they form one big urban area
3. Answers will vary, but students should refer to the fact that people who live in cities work in businesses and industries instead of on farms.
4. Various ethnic neighborhoods and ethnic restaurants are plentiful in the Northeast.
5. Philadelphia has many factories; it is an important land and water corridor. Boston is home to many universities that work with scientific companies to create new products and carry out research. New York is the money capital, a center of fashion, publishing, advertising, television, radio, and the arts.
6. Diagrams should show similarities between the two cities such as their importance in the nation's early history, and differences such as Philadelphia being a more industrial city and Boston being a city with many colleges and high-tech companies.

LINKS TO Language Arts

Good-bye City Life In 1845, Henry David Thoreau moved to Walden Pond in Massachusetts. His life there was an experiment in living alone and with only the essentials. He cut down trees and built a one-room house. He planted a vegetable garden and gathered wild fruit. There he wrote *Walden,* a classic of American literature.

New York City One word describes New York City—huge. More than 7 million people live there. Most states do not have populations that large. The city covers an area of about 320 square miles (830 sq km) on islands and the mainland around the mouth of the Hudson River. The various parts of the city are connected by tunnels and bridges.

New York City is our nation's "money capital" and about 500,000 New Yorkers work for banks and other financial institutions. The famous New York Stock Exchange is on Wall Street.

New York is also a center of fashion, publishing, advertising, television, radio, and the arts. New York's Broadway is famous for its theaters where more than eight million people see plays every year.

A Gateway for Immigrants

On January 1, 1892, 15-year-old Annie Moore who had sailed from Ireland by steamship stepped into the registry room of the Ellis Island Immigrant Station. Here she received a $10 gold piece for being the first immigrant to arrive at the new station.

From 1892 to 1943, the first stop for millions of immigrants to the United States was Ellis Island. From here, immigrants could see the Statue of Liberty, half a mile away in New York Harbor.

New York and other port cities of the Northeast have been important gateways for immigrants. In the 1800s, many Irish, Germans, and Scandinavians immigrated to the United States. Later, immigrants poured in from Southern and Eastern Europe. During the 1900s, people also came from the Caribbean, Asia, and Africa.

After entering the port cities, many immigrants stayed in those cities and built new lives. Today, New York is rich in ethnic diversity.

SECTION 1 ASSESSMENT

AFTER YOU READ

RECALL

1. Identify: (a) Philadelphia, (b) Boston, (c) New York City
2. Define: (a) commute, (b) megalopolis

COMPREHENSION

3. How does the population density of the Northeast affect the ways people live and work?
4. How have immigrants affected the culture of the Northeast?

CRITICAL THINKING AND WRITING

5. **Exploring the Main Idea** Review the Main Idea statement at the beginning of this section. Then, make a list of reasons why the cities of Philadelphia, Boston, and New York are so important to the economy of the United States.
6. **Making Comparisons** Think about the histories of, and major industries in, Philadelphia and Boston. Construct a Venn diagram to show how the two cities are similar and different.

ACTIVITY

7. **Writing a Journal Entry** Imagine you are a young immigrant arriving at Ellis Island. Write a journal expressing your feelings about coming to a new land.

7. Journal entries should convey the writers' emotions about the reality of immigration.

Resource Directory

Teaching Resources

Section Quiz in the Unit 2 Teaching Resources, p. 52

SECTION 2

The South

Growth in Population and Industry

BEFORE YOU READ

READING FOCUS

1. How are the South's land and water important to its economy?
2. How has the growth of industry changed the South?

KEY TERMS

petrochemical
industrialization
Sun Belt

KEY PLACES

Atlanta
Washington, D.C.

NOTE TAKING

Copy the table below. As you read the section, fill in the table with information about the South's agriculture, natural resources, and industry, and the locations of each.

Agriculture	Natural Resources	Industries

MAIN IDEA

While the South produces a wide variety of agricultural products and natural resources, in the past fifty years, it has become industrialized as well.

Setting the Scene

From July 19 to August 4, 1996, the city of **Atlanta,** Georgia, was the center of the world. More than two million people from 172 countries visited the city during that time to see a very special event. It was the 1996 Summer Olympic Games.

Atlanta today is a center of trade, transportation, and communication. It is located in one of the fastest-growing regions of the United States—the South.

The Varied Land of the South

The South's geography makes many different types of jobs possible. The South is warmer than regions farther north, it receives plenty of rain, and the plains along the Atlantic Ocean and the Gulf of Mexico have rich soil. Together, these features make much of the South a great place for growing crops and raising animals.

Farming in the South Farming has always been important to the South's economy and farmers once depended on cotton as their only source of income. Today, cotton still brings a lot of money to the South, especially to Alabama, Mississippi, and Texas, but "King Cotton" no longer rules this region. Most southern farmers produce a wide variety of crops and farm animals.

Atlanta Hosts the Olympics

ECONOMICS

Famous boxer Muhammad Ali lights the Olympic torch at the 1996 Summer Olympic Games in Atlanta, Georgia. **Critical Thinking** In what ways do you think hosting the Olympics benefited the city of Atlanta?

Resource Directory

Teaching Resources

Classroom Manager in the Unit 2 Teaching Resources, p. 53

Guided Reading and Review in the Unit 2 Teaching Resources, p. 54

Guide to the Essentials, p. 28

Technology

Section Reading Support Transparencies

SECTION 2

Lesson Objectives

1. Describe why the South's land and water are important to the region's economy.
2. Explain how the growth of industry has changed the South.

Lesson Plan

1 Engage

Warm-Up Activity

Write the following on the chalkboard: *cotton, oranges, peaches, petroleum, coal, fish, timber, furniture, cloth, aerospace, tourism,* and *shipping.* Ask students which of the above they associate with the South and have them explain the reasons for their associations. Explain that all of the items are part of the South's diverse economy.

Activating Prior Knowledge

Ask students to think about a time in their lives when they experienced a big change—perhaps a move to a new community or school. Discuss with students the difficulties involved in adapting to new situations.

2 Explore

As students read the section, ask them to find answers to the following questions: Why has farming always been a part of the South's economy? What are some of the South's most important natural resources? Why does transportation play a large role in the South's economy? Why is the South nicknamed the Sun Belt?

Answers to...

CRITICAL THINKING

Many new jobs were generated, and visitors' spending money in restaurants, hotels, and shops boosted the economy.

Lesson Plan continued

3 Teach

Have students develop a quiz containing five questions and answers about the main ideas of the section. Then have students exchange quizzes and answer the questions. This activity should take about 30 minutes.

Questions for Discussion

GEOGRAPHY **Early in the 1900s, the South was a mostly rural region. Today, more southerners live in urban areas than live in rural areas. What change in the South's economy might have contributed to this population change?**

Industrialization contributed to a change in population distribution.

ECONOMICS **What made the South a good location for a growing textile industry?**

Cotton had always been important to the southern economy, and it provided the raw material for the textile industry.

4 Assess/Reteach

See the answers to the Section 2 Assessment. You may also use students' completed quizzes as an assessment.

Acceptable quizzes include five questions with correct answers.

Commendable quizzes include five questions and answers that cover several main ideas.

Outstanding quizzes include five questions and answers that show a thorough understanding of the main ideas of the section.

Answers to...

MAP AND CHART STUDY

Southerners could use the rivers to ship goods and to produce hydroelectric power.

REGIONAL PROFILE

The South

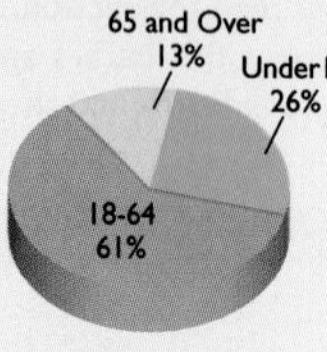

Age Structure (in years)

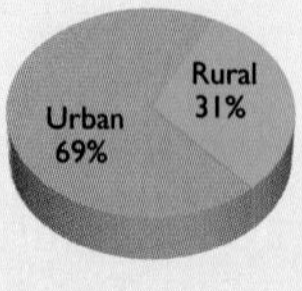

Urban/Rural Population

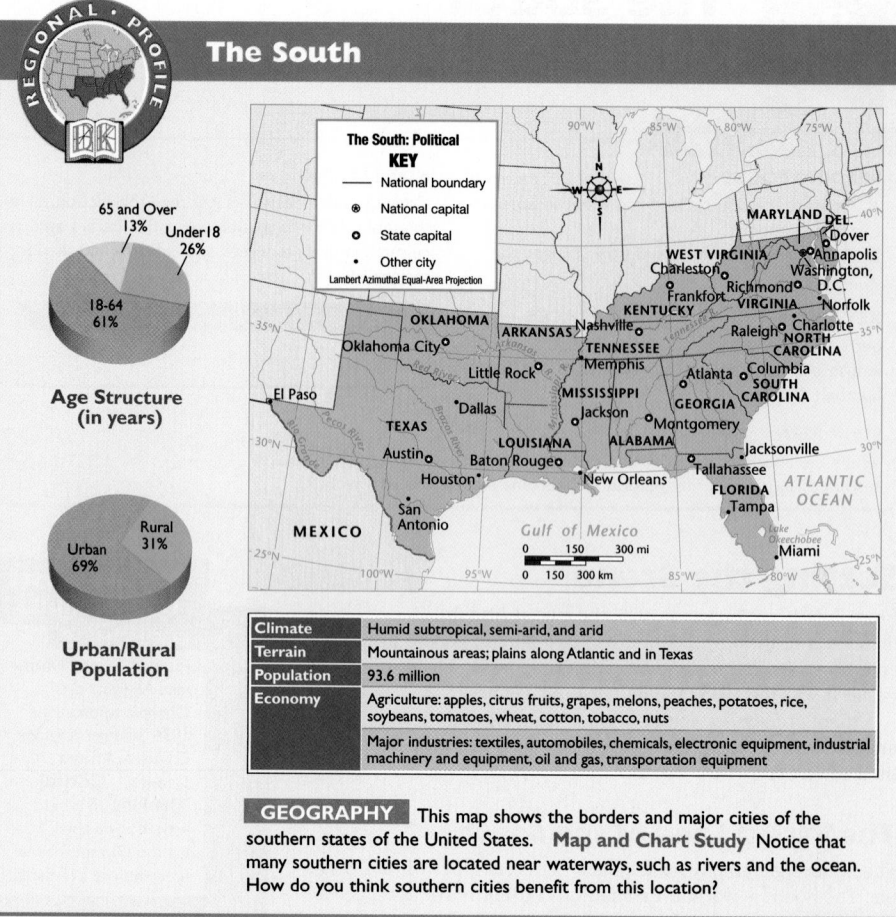

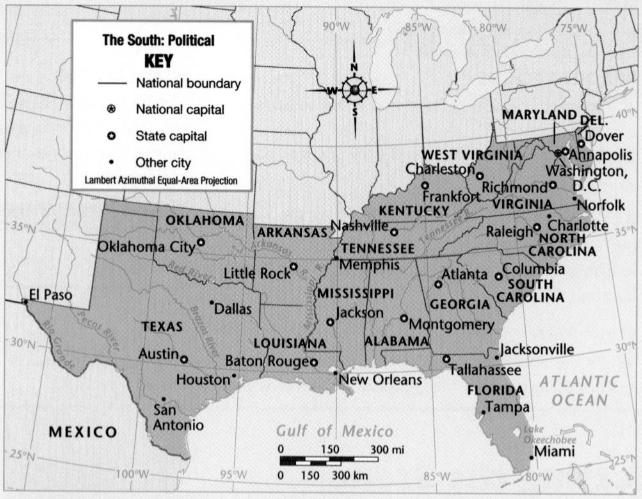

Climate	Humid subtropical, semi-arid, and arid
Terrain	Mountainous areas; plains along Atlantic and in Texas
Population	93.6 million
Economy	Agriculture: apples, citrus fruits, grapes, melons, peaches, potatoes, rice, soybeans, tomatoes, wheat, cotton, tobacco, nuts
	Major industries: textiles, automobiles, chemicals, electronic equipment, industrial machinery and equipment, oil and gas, transportation equipment

GEOGRAPHY This map shows the borders and major cities of the southern states of the United States. **Map and Chart Study** Notice that many southern cities are located near waterways, such as rivers and the ocean. How do you think southern cities benefit from this location?

Some of these crops need special growing conditions. Citrus fruits require year-round warmth and sunshine. Florida has plenty of both and more oranges, tangerines, grapefruits, and limes are grown here than in any other state. Rice needs the warm moist growing conditions found in Arkansas, Louisiana, and Mississippi, so it is grown along the coast of the Gulf of Mexico and also in the Mississippi River valley.

Some areas of the South have become famous for their agricultural products. Georgia is known as the Peach State and is famous for its peanuts and pecans. Texas raises more cattle than any other state. Arkansas raises the most chickens and turkeys. These items are just a sample of what is produced.

126 UNIT 2 UNITED STATES AND CANADA

Resource Directory

Teaching Resources

Outline Maps The United States, pp. 14–15

Technology

Color Transparencies 34 The United States and Canada: Economic Activity; **35** The United States and Canada: Population Distribution; **37** The United States: South: Physical-Political; **41** The United States: Percent Change in States Population; **42** The United States: Agricultural Regions

Passport to the World CD-ROM This interactive CD-ROM allows students to explore each region of the world. Students view regional videos, take a photo tour, and explore a historical timeline. Students record their travels in an Explorer's Journal and receive passport stamps when they pass regional quizzes.

Drilling and Mining in the South In some parts of the South, what is under the soil is as important as what grows in it. In Louisiana, Oklahoma, and Texas, companies drill for oil and natural gas to be used as fuel. These resources are also made into **petrochemicals,** such as plastics and paint. In Alabama, Kentucky, West Virginia, and Tennessee, miners dig for coal. Southern states are also leading producers of salt, sulfur, lead, zinc, and bauxite—a mineral used to make aluminum.

Southern Fish and Forests People in the South can also make a living in fishing and forestry. The Chesapeake Bay area near Maryland and Virginia is famous for its shellfish. However, the South's fishing industry is strongest in Louisiana and Texas. The timber industry is found in nearly every southern state. Softwood trees are used for building or for paper, and hardwood trees for furniture.

Southern Cities and Industries

Over the past 50 years, the South has gone through many changes. Though the South's rural areas are important, most people in the South today live in cities. They work in factories, high-technology firms, tourism, or in one of the other industries in this region's growing economy. This change from an agriculture-based economy to an industry-based economy is called **industrialization.**

Textiles and Technology One of the most important industries in the South is the textile industry, which makes cloth.

Textile mills were first built in this region to use the South's cotton and many still make cotton cloth today. Many others now make cloth from synthetic, or human-made, materials. The textile industry is strongest in Georgia, the Carolinas, and Virginia.

CITIZENSHIP

Stephen F. Austin, Patriot and Pioneer

Stephen F. Austin is remembered as a true Texas patriot. In 1821, when Texas was still part of Mexico, Moses Austin, Stephen's father, received permission from Mexico's government to colonize Texas. He died before he could but Stephen Austin followed in his father's footsteps and started the colony, San Felipe de Austin, near the Brazos River in 1822. He worked for the independence of Texas from Mexico, but the Mexicans accused him of trying to help Texas join the United States. He was sent to prison, but was never tried. He returned to Texas, and with his help, Texas became a Republic in 1836. Austin served as the Secretary of State and worked to help the United States annex Texas. He died in 1836, however, before Texas became a state. The city of Austin is named after him, and a statue in his honor is in the United States Capitol building in Washington, D.C.

Critical Thinking How did the work of Stephen F. Austin help Texas achieve statehood?

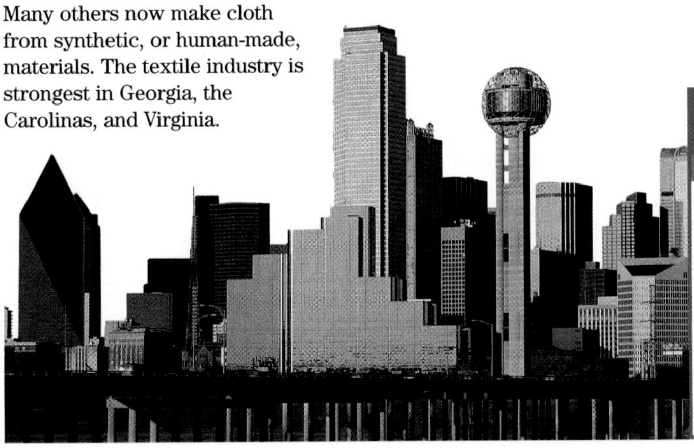

An Economic Center

ECONOMICS One of the largest cities in the United States, Dallas, Texas, is a center of banking, industry, and trade. **Critical Thinking** How has a move from an agriculture-based economy, to a more industrialized economy, changed the South?

ECONOMICS

Cotton

Cotton is one of the most important crops in the world. China leads the world in cotton production, but the United States, India, Pakistan, and Uzbekistan are also major producers. More than 75 percent of the world's population wears clothes made from cotton fibers. But other parts of the cotton plant are also valuable. Cottonseed is used to make products such as cosmetics, linoleum, and margarine. Even the short, fuzzy fibers (called linters) on cottonseeds are used in the manufacture of cotton balls, mattresses, varnish, cellophane, and explosives.

ACTIVITY

Critical Thinking

Identifying Central Issues *Suitable as an individual or a whole class activity.* Have students read the paragraph under the heading *Southern Cities and Industries.* Review strategies for identifying the central issue, or main idea, in a piece of writing, and then read students the following statements. Ask them which one best identifies the paragraph's central issue. Have students explain their responses.

1. During the past 50 years, the South's economy has shifted from being mostly agricultural and based in rural areas to being much more industrial and urban.
2. More southerners live in cities than in rural areas.
3. Some people in the South work in the tourism industry.

Verbal/Linguistic

SKILLS MINI LESSON

Using Regional Maps

You might **introduce** this skill by directing students to study the regional map of the South on the opposite page. Point out that the map zeros in on the South and shows more detail for that region than would a map of the entire United States. Allow students to **practice** the skill by using the map of the South to answer the following questions: *What region does the map show?* (the South) *About how wide is the region from east to west?* (1,600 miles) *How far does it extend from north to south?* (about 1,000 miles) Students may **apply** the skill by using the regional map to describe the relative locations (using the distance scale and compass rose) of the following cities mentioned in the section: Atlanta, Georgia; Houston, Texas; Raleigh, North Carolina; Austin, Texas; Miami, Florida; New Orleans, Louisiana; and Washington, D.C.

Answers to...

CRITICAL THINKING

Austin worked as Secretary of State and worked to help the United States annex Texas.

CRITICAL THINKING

Students may mention the growth of cities and the movement of more people from rural areas into urban areas.

SECTION 2 ASSESSMENT

AFTER YOU READ

1. (a) Georgia city that is a center of trade, transportation, and communication (b) the nation's capital, located in the District of Columbia between the states of Maryland and Virginia
2. (a) substance such as plastic, paint, or asphalt that is made from petroleum (b) change from an agriculture-based economy to an industry-based economy (c) area from the southern Atlantic Coast to the coast of California that is known for its warm weather
3. The South is warmer than regions of the United States farther north. Most of the region also receives plenty of rain. These factors make the South an excellent agricultural area. The area is also rich in natural resources including minerals, timber, and fish.
4. The cities have become industrialized, and people move there for job opportunities.
5. Students' lists should include examples of agricultural activities, fishing and forestry, and industry.
6. People move to the South because the diverse economy offers a wide variety of jobs. Retired people have also settled in the area because it offers a mild climate year-round.
7. Students' advertisements will vary but will probably highlight job opportunities and climate.

New industries are growing all across the South. One is the high-technology industry where workers try to improve computers and figure out better ways to use them. Some centers of high technology are Raleigh, North Carolina, and Austin, Texas. In Cape Canaveral, Florida, Houston, Texas, and Huntsville, Alabama, people work for the National Aeronautics and Space Administration (NASA) running the nation's space exploration program.

Transportation and Tourism Some of the South's largest cities play big roles in the transportation industry. Miami, Florida, is a center for goods and people going to and from Central and South America. New Orleans, Louisiana, is a gateway between the Gulf of Mexico and the Mississippi River system.

Thousands of people come to work in the South's new industries, but thousands more choose to move there because of the climate. The South is part of the **Sun Belt,** a broad area of the United States stretching from the southern Atlantic Coast to the coast of California. It is known for its warm weather. Some arrivals are older adults who want to retire to places without cold winters. Others come to take advantage of both the weather and the work that the Sun Belt offers. Still others come to the South as tourists.

Our Nation's Capital The city of Washington is not in any state. Instead, it is in the District of Columbia, which lies between the states of Maryland and Virginia. This area of land was chosen as the site for the nation's capital in 1790. Located on the shore of the Potomac River, **Washington, D.C.** is home to the nation's leaders and to hundreds of foreign diplomats.

SECTION 2 ASSESSMENT

AFTER YOU READ

RECALL

1. Identify: (a) Atlanta, (b) Washington, D.C.
2. Define: (a) petrochemical, (b) industrialization, (c) Sun Belt

COMPREHENSION

3. How do the geography and climate of the South help make it an important agricultural region?
4. Why have many people in the South moved from rural areas to urban areas?

CRITICAL THINKING AND WRITING

5. **Exploring the Main Idea** Review the Main Idea statement at the beginning of this section. Then, make a list of some of the most important economic activities of the South.
6. **Recognizing Cause and Effect** In this section you have learned that the population of the South is growing. Write a paragraph explaining how the South's geography and economy were affected by this growth.

ACTIVITY

7. **Writing an Advertisement** Imagine you work in an advertising firm in Atlanta, Georgia, in Houston, Texas, or in Miami, Florida. Create an advertisement to persuade people to move to your city or state. The advertisement can be designed for a newspaper or a magazine, or for radio, television, or the Internet.

Resource Directory

Teaching Resources

Section Quiz in the Unit 2 Teaching Resources, p. 55

SECTION 3

The Midwest

Technology Brings Change

BEFORE YOU READ

READING FOCUS

1. How is technology changing agriculture in the Midwest?
2. How is the change in agriculture affecting the growth of cities?

KEY TERMS
mixed-crop farm
recession
corporate farm
capital

KEY PLACES
Chicago
Detroit
St. Louis

NOTE TAKING

Copy the cause-and-effect chart below. As you read the section, fill in the chart with the causes and effects of technological changes in agriculture.

Causes
1.
2.
Changes in agriculture bring growth to cities
Effects
1.
2.

MAIN IDEA

Along with the growth of large corporate farms, many people have moved from family farms to the growing cities in the Midwest.

Setting the Scene

Camille LeFevre grew up in Black River Falls, Wisconsin. Her family included generation after generation of farmers, and she spent her childhood on her parents' sheep farm.

Camille remembers her childhood with deep affection. Yet, like thousands of farm children who grew up in the 1980s and 1990s, she did not follow in her parents' footsteps. Farming in the Midwest changed, and Camille chose a different path for herself.

Technology Brings Changes to the Midwest

The Midwest is often called "the heartland" because it is the agricultural center of our nation. The soil is rich, and the climate is suitable for producing corn, soybeans, and livestock. Technology helped make farms productive. Inventions like the steel plow, the windmill, and barbed wire helped settlers carve out farms on the plains. Today, technological innovations continue to shape the world of agriculture and the way people farm the land.

ECONOMICS On most farms, sheep-shearing takes place once a year. The wool from this breed of sheep—the Suffolk—is used to make industrial and upholstery fabrics. **Critical Thinking** Raising sheep for wool is an example of a primary industry. Industries that turn wool into thread and fabrics are secondary industries. What do you think happens to the fabrics made from the wool of these sheep?

129

Resource Directory

Teaching Resources

Classroom Manager in the Unit 2 Teaching Resources, p. 56

Guided Reading and Review in the Unit 2 Teaching Resources, p. 57

Guide to the Essentials, p. 29

Technology

Section Reading Support Transparencies

SECTION 3

Lesson Objectives

1. Explain how technology is changing agriculture in the Midwest.
2. Discuss how changes in agriculture affect the growth of cities there.

Lesson Plan

1 Engage

Warm-Up Activity

Invite students to share their perceptions of the Midwest: where it is, why it is so named, and what defining characteristics the region has. Explain that these perceptions may change as they read about some important changes taking place in the Midwest.

Activating Prior Knowledge

Ask students to describe the physical geography of the Midwest. Then, ask them to describe some of the economic activities they would expect to find there based on the region's physical geography.

2 Explore

As students read the section, ask them to find answers to the following questions: What has been happening to family farms in the Midwest? How did a recession help change the nature of farming in the Midwest? What are corporate farms? Do most people in the Midwest live on farms or in cities? What are some of the unique features of the large cities in the Midwest?

Answers to...

CRITICAL THINKING

Students may respond that the fabric made from the wool of the sheep may be used to upholster furniture, or to make clothing or blankets.

Lesson Plan continued

3 Teach

Have students create Venn diagrams that compare and contrast family farms and corporate farms. Have students consider such things as ownership, size, business methods, and history. This activity should take about 20 minutes.

Questions for Discussion

ECONOMICS Ideally, how do mixed-crop farms help individual farmers stay secure financially?

A farmer is protected from financial disaster in the event of the failure of one or two crops.

SOCIAL STUDIES SKILLS

Compare the two line graphs on page 131. Has the decrease in the number of farms occurred at a similar rate to the increase in the average size of farms? How can you tell?

Yes, the rates are similar. Both graphs show similar rates from 1960 to 1975 and then from 1975 to 1995.

4 Assess/Reteach

See the answers to the Section 3 Assessment. You may also assess students' completed Venn diagrams.

Acceptable diagrams show one similarity and one difference between family farms and corporate farms.

Commendable diagrams show two similarities and two differences between family farms and corporate farms.

Outstanding diagrams show at least two similarities and two differences between family farms and corporate farms and indicate that some land now part of corporate farms was once family owned.

Answers to...

MAP AND CHART STUDY

Minnesota, Wisconsin, Illinois, Indiana, Michigan, and Ohio border the Great Lakes. Most people must work in the industry and services sector, because farms tend to be in rural areas, and only 28 percent of the population live in rural areas.

REGIONAL · PROFILE

The Midwest

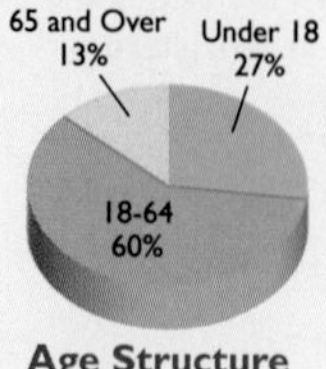

Age Structure (in years)

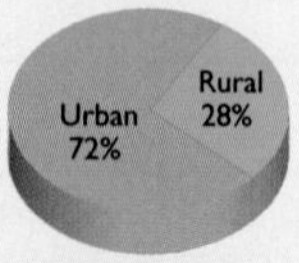

Urban/Rural Population

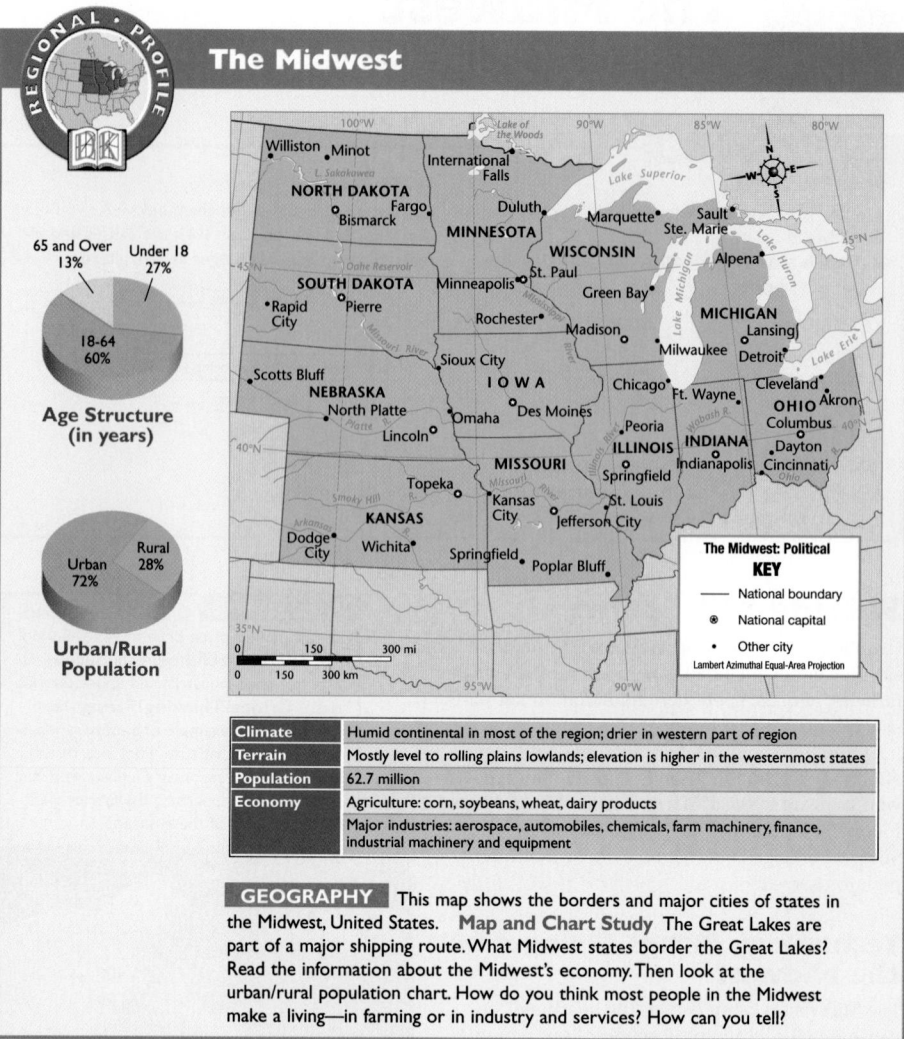

Climate	Humid continental in most of the region; drier in western part of region
Terrain	Mostly level to rolling plains lowlands; elevation is higher in the westernmost states
Population	62.7 million
Economy	Agriculture: corn, soybeans, wheat, dairy products
	Major industries: aerospace, automobiles, chemicals, farm machinery, finance, industrial machinery and equipment

GEOGRAPHY This map shows the borders and major cities of states in the Midwest, United States. **Map and Chart Study** The Great Lakes are part of a major shipping route. What Midwest states border the Great Lakes? Read the information about the Midwest's economy. Then look at the urban/rural population chart. How do you think most people in the Midwest make a living—in farming or in industry and services? How can you tell?

Family Farms Dwindle Until the 1980s, small family farms operated in this region, and many were **mixed-crop farms.** That is, they grew several different crops, so, if one crop failed, the farm had others.

In the 1960s and 1970s, family farms prospered. The world population was rising, and demand for American farm products was high. Farmers felt that they could increase their business if they enlarged their farms. To build bigger farms, many farmers bought more land and equipment, borrowing money from local banks.

Resource Directory

Teaching Resources

Outline Maps The United States, pp. 14–15

Technology

Color Transparencies 34 The United States and Canada: Economic Activity; **35** The United States and Canada: Population Distribution; **38** The United States: Midwest: Physical-Political; **41** The United States: Percent Change in States Population; **42** The United States: Agricultural Regions

Passport to the World CD-ROM This interactive CD-ROM allows students to explore each region of the world. Students view regional videos, take a photo tour, and explore a historical timeline. Students record their travels in an Explorer's Journal and receive passport stamps when they pass regional quizzes.

In the early 1980s, there was a country-wide **recession** (rih SESH un), or a downturn in business activity. The demand for farm products dropped at the same time interest rates on loans increased. As a result, many farmers were not able to make enough money to pay their loans. Some families sold or left their farms. In fact, over one million American farmers have left their land since 1980.

Corporate Farms Expand

Some of the farms that were sold were bought by agricultural companies that combined small farms to form large ones called **corporate farms.** Large agricultural companies had more **capital,** or money used to expand a business. They could afford to buy the expensive land and equipment that modern farming requires. These large farms could be run more efficiently.

Corporate farmers rely on machines and computers to do much of the work. Kansas offers a good example of corporate farming—having fewer workers and larger farms. In Kansas, 90 percent of the land is farmland or ranchland, but less than 10 percent of the people are farmers or ranchers.

Not every farm in the Midwest is a corporate farm. But most small farms do not earn enough money to support a family so family farmers usually have another job as well. Young adults often leave the farm and move to the cities where there are more opportunities.

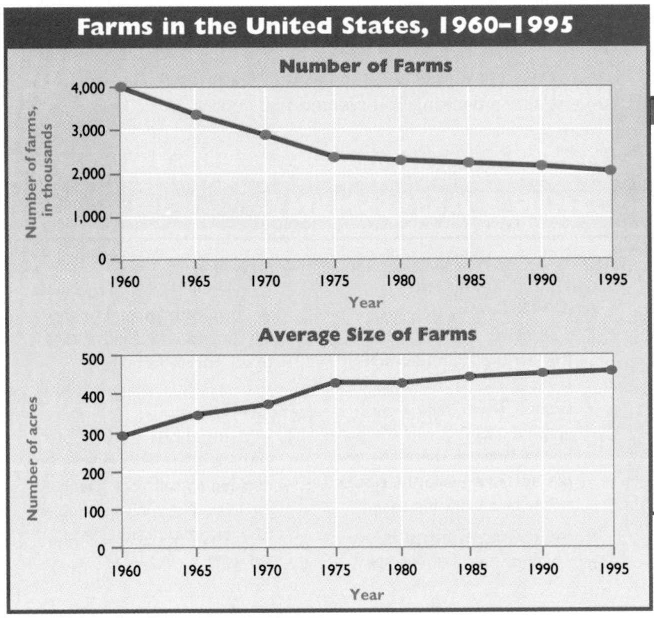

ECONOMICS As this graph shows, the number of farms has decreased, while the size of farms has grown. These changes came about because many owners of small family farms could not make enough money to cover their expenses. As a result, they sold their farms and left the land. **Chart Study** When was there the greatest change in the number of farms and farm size in the United States—between 1960 and 1975 or between 1980 and 1995?

SKILLS MINI LESSON

Reading Tables and Analyzing Statistics

Allow the students a few moments to study the table shown in the Regional Profile on the opposite page, and then **introduce** the skill by telling them that this table shows statistics, or numerical data, and other important data about the Midwest. Point out that the numerical data are presented in the form of circle graphs. Together, these data provide information about the Midwest's geography, economy, and people. Work with students to **practice** reading the table, identifying how the data are related. For example, the information about climate and terrain can help students understand why the Midwest is suitable for farming. Have students **apply** the skill by asking them to use the table to write one statement each about the geography, economy, and people of the Midwest.

ACTIVITY

Interdisciplinary Connections

Art Read aloud the following excerpts from Carl Sandburg's poem "Chicago."

Hog Butcher for the World,
Tool Maker, Stacker of Wheat,
Player with Railroads and the
  Nation's Freight Handler;
Stormy, husky, brawling,
City of the Big Shoulders:

. . .

Fierce as a dog with tongue
  lapping for action, cunning
  as a savage pitted against the
  wilderness,
Bareheaded,
Shoveling,
Wrecking,
Planning,
Building, breaking, rebuilding

Compare Sandburg's words with the text's description of industrial Chicago and invite students to convey the imagery of the poem and the facts from the text in a mural. Groups or the whole class may cooperate to make the mural.

Visual/Spatial

ACTIVITY

Interdisciplinary Connections

Language Arts Have students consider the skills a person working on a family farm and a person working on a corporate farm would need. Which skills would be important for workers on both kinds of farms? Then, ask students to write two help-wanted advertisements—one for a corporate farmworker and one for a family farmworker. Advertisements should describe the skills, education, and background desired by each employer.

Verbal/Linguistic

Answers to...

CHART STUDY

The greatest change occurred between 1960 and 1975.

SECTION 3 ASSESSMENT

AFTER YOU READ

1. (a) large city in Illinois located on Lake Michigan, once a meat-packing and manufacturing center (b) large city in Michigan, called "the Motor City" because it is the headquarters of the American automobile industry (c) large city in Missouri located on the Mississippi River that is today a banking and commercial center
2. (a) farm that grows several different kinds of crops (b) downturn in business activity (c) large farm owned and operated by an agricultural company (d) money used to expand a business
3. Farmers had borrowed money to expand their farms. During the recession of the early 1980s, demand for farm products dropped, and interest rates on loans increased. Many families could not afford to pay back their loans.
4. The city was surrounded by farms, and farmers sent their products to Chicago to be processed and shipped east. Railroads made it even more important as a transportation hub. Steel and manufacturing industries were built.
5. Farmers had borrowed heavily in the 1960s and 1970s. When recession came they could not repay their debts and were forced to sell. Agricultural corporations had the capital and technology to make large farms profitable.
6. Possible answer: Advantages: greater efficiency, higher profits; Disadvantages: fewer jobs, fewer family farms
7. Letters will vary, but should include reasons supported by information from the text.

Answers to...

CRITICAL THINKING

Students should recognize that the city's skyscrapers are a physical indication of Chicago's importance to the nation's economy.

ECONOMICS This view from the shores of Lake Michigan shows the many skyscrapers in Chicago's downtown area. The Sears Tower, to the left, is the tallest building in the United States **Critical Thinking** What do the skyscrapers of Chicago tell you about the economic importance of that city?

The Midwest Grows Cities

Most people in the Midwest today live in towns and cities. Yet many of these cities got their start as places to process and ship farm products.

Chicago: At the Center of Things **Chicago,** Illinois, is a good example. Located on Lake Michigan, it was surrounded by prairies and farms in the mid-1800s. Farmers sent their corn, wheat, cattle, and hogs to Chicago. Mills and meat-packing plants turned these products into foods and shipped them east on the Great Lakes. When railroads were built, Chicago really boomed. By the late 1800s, it had become a steel-making and manufacturing center. Farm equipment was one of the most important manufactured products made in Chicago.

Today, Chicago is the biggest city in the heartland. It is known for its ethnic diversity and lively culture. It is the hub of major transportation routes—highways, railroads, airlines, and shipping routes. Chicago is also the home of the first skyscraper to be built in the Midwest.

Other Cities The Midwest has other large cities. Two of them—**Detroit** and **St. Louis**—have played an important role in the country's history. Detroit, Michigan, is called "the Motor City." Here, you will find the headquarters of the American automobile industry.

Covered wagons, not cars, used to roll through St. Louis, Missouri. Located on the Mississippi River, this city was the starting point for pioneers heading west. Today, a huge stainless steel arch beside the river marks St. Louis as the "Gateway to the West." St. Louis is also a banking and commercial center.

SECTION 3 ASSESSMENT

AFTER YOU READ

RECALL

1. Identify: (a) Chicago, (b) Detroit, (c) St. Louis
2. Define: (a) mixed-crop farm, (b) recession, (c) corporate farm, (d) capital

COMPREHENSION

3. Why did family farmers face hard times in the 1980s?
4. What caused Chicago to boom during the 1800s?

CRITICAL THINKING AND WRITING

5. **Exploring the Main Idea** Review the Main Idea statement at the beginning of this section. Then, write a paragraph explaining why the number of farms in the Midwest has declined while the size of family farms has increased.
6. **Identifying Central Issues** Think of how farming has changed with the development of corporate farms. List the advantages and disadvantages of corporate farming.

ACTIVITY

7. **Writing a Letter** Suppose you are a farmer and you have decided to sell your farm and move to a city. Write a letter to a friend explaining your decision.

Resource Directory

Teaching Resources

Section Quiz in the Unit 2 Teaching Resources, p. 58

SECTION 4

The West

Land of Precious Resources

BEFORE YOU READ

READING FOCUS

1. What are the resources of the West?
2. How are people working to balance conservation with the need to use natural resources?

KEY TERMS

forty-niner
mass transit

KEY PLACES

Sierra Nevada
Pacific Northwest
Portland
San Jose

NOTE TAKING

Copy the chart below. As you read the section, fill in the table with information about the resources of the West, where they are found, and what concerns there are over conserving each resource.

Resource	Where Found	Concerns

MAIN IDEA

The West has many natural resources, but as the population grows, protecting the environment and using resources wisely is becoming a challenge.

Setting the Scene

An American president stood before Congress and made the following statement:

"The conservation of our natural resources and their proper use constitute the fundamental problem which underlies almost every other problem of our national life. . . . But there must be . . . a realization . . . that to waste, to destroy our natural resources, to skin and exhaust the land instead of using it so as to increase its usefulness, will result in undermining . . . the very prosperity which we ought by right to hand down to [our children]."

President Theodore Roosevelt made this statement nearly one hundred years ago. He understood that the vast resources of the West would not last without proper care.

A Wealth of Resouces

An incredible wealth of natural resources has drawn people to the West for well over 400 years. The Spanish were well established on the West Coast even before the Pilgrims settled in New England in the 1620s. Then, after Lewis and Clark's exploration of the Louisiana Territory in the early 1800s, more people began to move westward.

Preserving the Physical Environment

GEOGRAPHY

Congress declared Yosemite a national park in 1890. Yosemite Falls, which drops some 2,425 feet (740 m), is higher than any big-city skyscraper. **Critical Thinking** Why do you think so many people visit national parks like Yosemite?

SECTION 4

Lesson Objectives

1. Identify the natural resources of the West.
2. Describe how people work to balance conservation with the use of natural resources.

Lesson Plan

1 Engage

Warm-Up Activity

Challenge students to brainstorm a list of the "most important" natural resources. Encourage them to list basic resources, such as water, soil, and clean air. Record their responses on the chalkboard. When you have developed a substantial list, circle the resources that are found in the West.

Activating Prior Knowledge

Invite volunteers to describe some of the recycling or conservation efforts that they and their families make. Ask them what difference they think it would make if everyone in the country made similar efforts to conserve natural resources.

2 Explore

As students read the section, ask them to find answers to the following questions: What precious natural resources are found in the West? Which natural resources first drew settlers to the West? What were the effects of the Gold Rush? How have people affected the environment of the West?

Answers to...

CRITICAL THINKING

Students may mention that people want to experience the wilderness and see its natural beauty and wildlife.

Resource Directory

Teaching Resources

Classroom Manager in the Unit 2 Teaching Resources, p. 59

Guided Reading and Review in the Unit 2 Teaching Resources, p. 60

Guide to the Essentials, p. 30

Technology

Section Reading Support Transparencies

Lesson Plan continued

3 Teach

Ask students to use the section text and graphics to create a "Natural Resources of the West" chart. Each chart should list a natural resource of the West in the first column and the ways each resource is used in the second column. Students may add a third column for listing conservation issues. This activity should take about 30 minutes.

Question for Discussion

GEOGRAPHY **In the 1800s, many people moved to the West to live in the region's wide open spaces. Look at the urban/rural population chart. Do you think that most people move to the West for the same reason today? Why or why not?**

Because the West is overwhelmingly urban, people probably are not moving to the region in order to live in the wide open spaces.

4 Assess/Reteach

See the answers to the Section 4 Assessment. You may also use students' completed charts as an assessment tool.

Acceptable charts list two natural resources and describe how they are used.

Commendable charts list three natural resources, describe how they are used, and include at least one conservation issue.

Outstanding charts list more than three natural resources, describe how they are used, and include several conservation issues.

Answers to...

MAP AND CHART STUDY

New Mexico, Colorado, Wyoming, Montana, Alaska, and California have petroleum deposits. Hawaii's resources are mostly agricultural. Alaska, California, and New Mexico experienced gold rushes.

REGIONAL PROFILE

The West

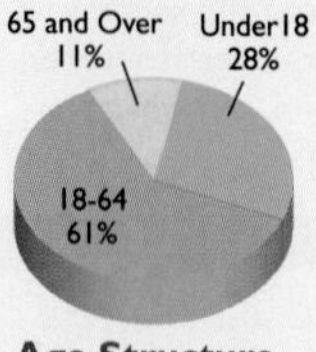

Age Structure (in years)

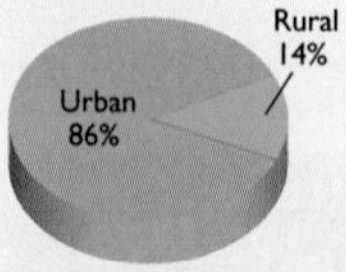

Urban/Rural Population

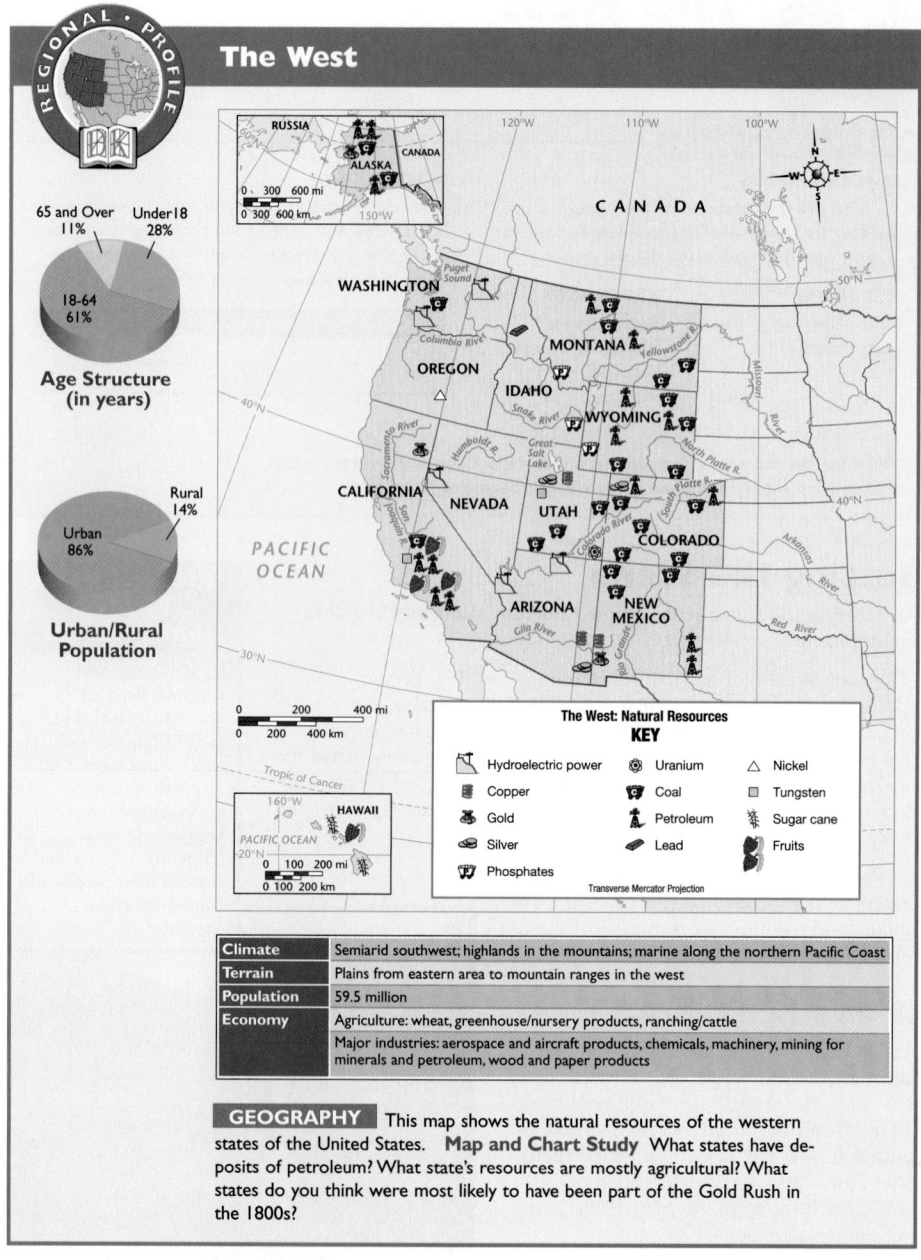

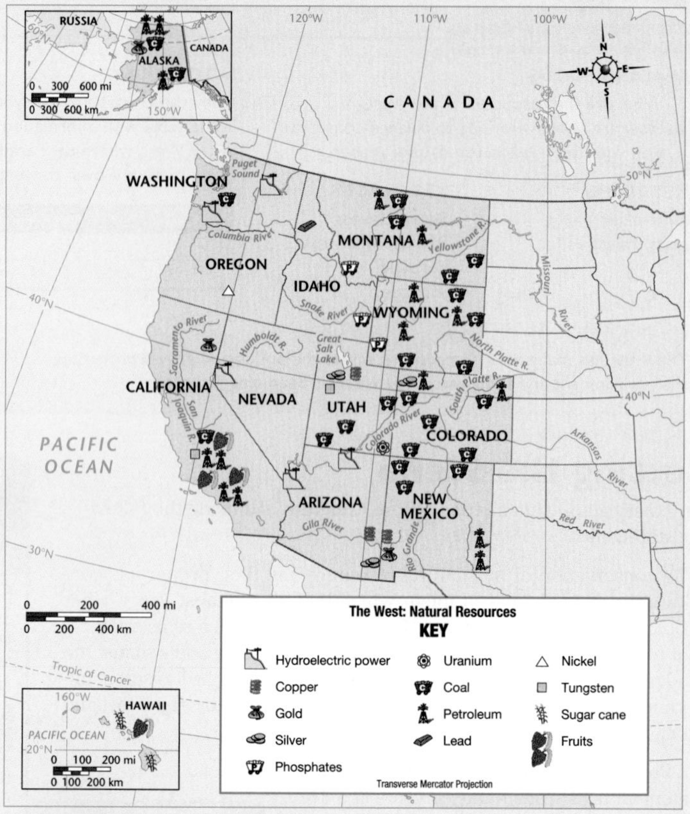

Climate	Semiarid southwest; highlands in the mountains; marine along the northern Pacific Coast
Terrain	Plains from eastern area to mountain ranges in the west
Population	59.5 million
Economy	Agriculture: wheat, greenhouse/nursery products, ranching/cattle
	Major industries: aerospace and aircraft products, chemicals, machinery, mining for minerals and petroleum, wood and paper products

GEOGRAPHY This map shows the natural resources of the western states of the United States. **Map and Chart Study** What states have deposits of petroleum? What state's resources are mostly agricultural? What states do you think were most likely to have been part of the Gold Rush in the 1800s?

Resource Directory

Teaching Resources

Outline Maps The United States, pp. 14–15

Technology

Color Transparencies 34 The United States and Canada: Economic Activity; **35** The United States and Canada: Population Distribution; **39** The United States: West: Physical-Political; **41** The United States: Percent Change in States Population; **42** The United States: Agricultural Regions

Passport to the World CD-ROM This interactive CD-ROM allows students to explore each region of the world. Students view regional videos, take a photo tour, and explore a historical timeline. Students record their travels in an Explorer's Journal and receive passport stamps when they pass regional quizzes.

Resources and Population With the California Gold Rush in 1849, the population of the region exploded. The sleepy port of San Francisco boomed into a prosperous city as hopeful miners arrived there, bought supplies, and headed off to the **Sierra Nevada** expecting to strike it rich.

Further discoveries of valuable minerals drew more and more people westward. New settlers needed timber to build homes and after the Civil War, logging camps, sawmills, and paper mills sprang up in the **Pacific Northwest.**

At first, the resources of the West seemed unlimited. The use of these resources did create wealth and many jobs. However, it also created new challenges.

Managing Resources in the Sierras For many years, people searching for gold treated the Sierra Nevada carelessly. The **forty-niners,** the first miners of the Gold Rush, washed small bits of gold from the streams, but to get at larger deposits, big mining companies used water cannons to blast away entire hillsides. They left behind huge, ugly piles of rock.

After the Gold Rush, California's population soared. To meet the demand for new houses, loggers cleared many forests and engineers built dams to send water through pipes to coastal cities. Next to the dams, they built hydroelectric (hy droh ee LEK trik) plants. Cities like San Francisco got water and power this way, but the dams flooded whole valleys of the Sierras.

To save parts of the West as natural wilderness, Congress created several national parks and forests. Yet these, too, have developed problems. Yosemite (yoh SEM ut ee) National Park now gets so many visitors that it has traffic jams and air pollution in the summer, and must limit the number of campers in the park. Dam-building has

A Black Bear in its Natural Habitat

GEOGRAPHY

Many westerners are working to preserve the land areas where black bears and other wild animals live. Parts of the West have been made into national parks, forests, and wilderness areas. In addition, logging companies are working to preserve the environment by planting new trees to replace the ones that have been cut down.

Critical Thinking
Does conservation of natural resources in a certain region affect the wildlife that lives in that region? In other regions?

135

HISTORY

Depleting Natural Resources

As a result of the discovery of gold and other precious metals, a number of makeshift towns came into existence. These boomtowns had few amenities; they developed simply to cater to the needs of miners. Local shops erected large false fronts that gave a small building the appearance of grandeur. But the miners themselves made do with very little. They ate an unvaried diet of meat and biscuits or flapjacks, as fresh vegetables and fruits were difficult to get. Miners had little money for furniture or fine housing; they built improvised shacks out of rocks, packing cases, and empty bottles, and used newspaper for insulation. As soon as the mines were mined out, the miners moved on, and these frontier boomtowns became ghost towns.

ACTIVITY

Journal Writing

Environmental Responsibility Remind students how vital natural resources are to our environment and how many of these resources are being threatened. Point out that each succeeding generation has fewer natural resources to draw on. Ask students to think about the responsibility of the current adult generation to protect natural resources for them. Then, have them further explore this topic by writing a journal entry in response to the question: *What responsibility do I have for protecting our natural resources for future generations?*

Verbal/Linguistic

SKILLS MINI LESSON

Distinguishing Facts From Opinions

You may **introduce** this skill by stating: *This chapter is about the regions of the United States* and *This is the best chapter in the textbook.* Challenge students to identify the differences between the two statements. Guide them in identifying the first statement as a fact, which can be proved true, and the second statement as an opinion, which is an individual belief. Allow students to **practice** using the skill by having volunteers make oral statements about the West and having their classmates call out whether each statement is a fact or an opinion. Discuss ways to identify each statement. To **apply** the skill, ask students to write five facts and five opinions about the West. Students should then challenge a classmate to identify each statement as a fact or an opinion.

Answers to...

CRITICAL THINKING

Students should recognize that conserving natural resources helps to protect the habitats that wild animals need in order to survive.

SECTION 4 ASSESSMENT

AFTER YOU READ

1. (a) western mountain range, site of the California Gold Rush (b) northern region of the West that provided settlers with timber for building (c) port city in Oregon near the junction of the Willamette and Columbia rivers (d) city in California that is part of "Silicon Valley"
2. (a) one of the first miners of the California Gold Rush (b) transit system that replaces individual cars with energy-saving buses or trains
3. People mined for gold, used timber to build houses, and used water to produce electricity and to pipe into cities.
4. Large areas of wilderness have been declared national parks; dam building has stopped; laws protect wildlife habitats and limit logging; governments are cleaning up rivers, and cities have built mass transit systems.
5. Lists should include the need that people in cities have for water and timber; pollution of air and water caused by automobile and industry; large numbers of people visiting the wilderness.
6. Paragraphs will vary, but may include the idea that rapid urban growth has caused deforestation and air and water pollution.
7. Responses will vary, but should include specific strategies for achieving conservation of a regional natural resource.

CITIZENSHIP

To Be a Leader

Cesar Chavez and his family made a living as migrant farmworkers. Pay was low, and working conditions were hard. Chavez wanted to build a better future for migrant farmworkers. He helped to set up a farmworkers' union that organized national boycotts of farm products. As a result, farm owners agreed to improve pay and working conditions. Chavez had achieved his goal—fair treatment of migrant farmworkers.

stopped. Laws protect the habitats of certain animals. In addition, logging companies are limited in the amount of timber they can cut down.

Using and Preserving Resources

Most westerners today are not miners, farmers, or loggers. Rather, they work and live in cities. Their challenge is to figure out how to use natural resources wisely.

Portland, Oregon **Portland** was founded in 1845 near the junction of the Willamette and Columbia rivers. Portland became a trade center for lumber, furs, grain, salmon, and wool. In the 1930s, new dams produced cheap electricity and Portland attracted many manufacturing industries. Over time, the factories polluted the Willamette River. Federal, state, and local governments—and industries—have worked to clean up this valuable resource.

San Jose, California Urban sprawl is a problem in **San Jose.** The area around San Jose was known as "Valley of the Heart's Delight" for its beautiful orchards and farms. Now it is called "Silicon Valley," because it is the heart of the computer industry.

San Jose's most valuable resource is its people and they come from all parts of the world. The greater population density has created crowded freeways and air pollution. To counter these problems, San Jose has built a light-rail mass transit system. **Mass transit** replaces individual cars with energy-saving buses or trains.

SECTION 4 ASSESSMENT

AFTER YOU READ

RECALL

1. Identify: (a) Sierra Nevada, (b) Pacific Northwest, (c) Portland, (d) San Jose
2. Define: (a) forty-niner, (b) mass transit

COMPREHENSION

3. How have people used the resources of the West?
4. How are these resources being protected today?

CRITICAL THINKING AND WRITING

5. **Exploring the Main Idea** Review the Main Idea statement at the beginning of this section. Then, list some of the challenges people of the West face in preserving and protecting their natural resources.
6. **Recognizing Cause and Effect** Write a paragraph explaining how rapid urban growth has affected the natural resources of the West.

ACTIVITY

Take It to the NET

7. **Developing a Conservation Plan** California's forests are one of its most valuable natural resources. Think about the importance of conservation as you read about California's forests. Develop a conservation plan for one of the natural resources in your region. Visit the World Explorer: People, Places, and Cultures section of **phschool.com** for help in completing this activity.

Resource Directory

Teaching Resources

Section Quiz in the Unit 2 Teaching Resources, p. 61

Chapter Summary in the Unit 2 Teaching Resources, p. 62

Vocabulary in the Unit 2 Teaching Resources, p. 63

Reteaching in the Unit 2 Teaching Resources, p. 64

Enrichment in the Unit 2 Teaching Resources, p. 65

Critical Thinking in the Unit 2 Teaching Resources, p. 66

Understanding Special Purpose Maps

United States: Railroad Routes of the Late 1800s

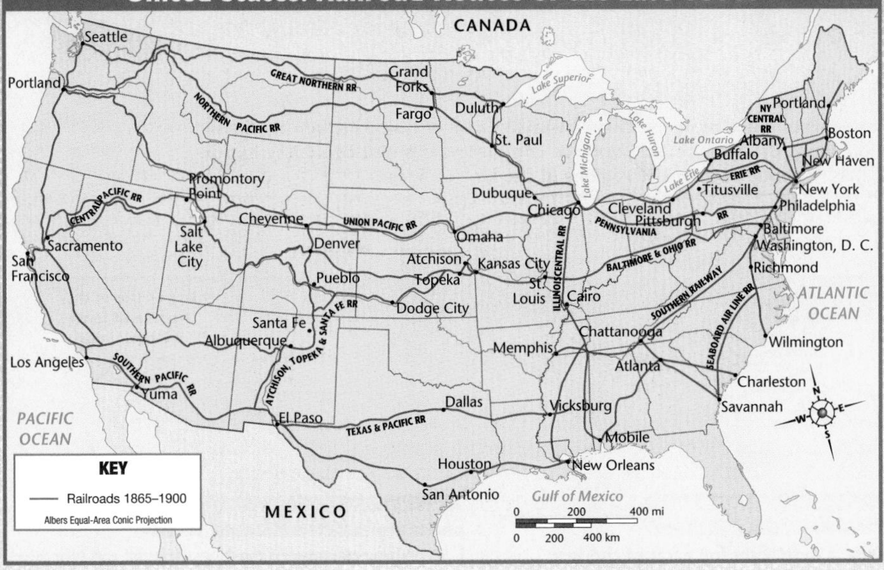

Learn the Skill

As you explore the world, you will encounter many different kinds of special purpose maps. You have already encountered some special purpose maps in previous chapters. To help you learn more about how to understand and use special purpose maps, follow these steps:

A. Read the title of the map. The title will tell you the purpose and content of the map. The title of the map above tells you that it is about railroad routes in the United States from the late 1800s.

B. Read the information in the map key. Even though a special purpose map shows only one kind of information, it may present many pieces of data. The map key above shows railroad lines from 1865 to 1900 in red.

C. Study the map to identify its main ideas and try to draw conclusions based on the information.

Practice the Skill

Use the map to answer these questions:

- How many states did the Pennsylvania Railroad run through?
- How many states did not have railroad routes running through them?
- If you were traveling from Baltimore to St. Louis, which railway line would you take?

Apply the Skill

See the Chapter Review and Assessment at the end of this chapter for more questions on understanding special purpose maps.

Lesson Objectives

Use a special purpose map to find information and answer questions.

Lesson Plan

1 Engage

To introduce the skill, ask students to brainstorm for a list of the kinds of information found in maps. If possible, show the class a road map, as well as a few special purpose maps. Then, lead students in a discussion of how maps convey information graphically as well as with words.

2 Explore

Read aloud with students the text under "Learn the Skill." Remind students that reading a map's title and key helps tell them quickly what the map is about and whether it will be useful to their specific needs.

3 Teach

Encourage students to answer the three practice questions. Point out that they will need to look not only at the red lines showing railroad routes, but also the gray lines showing state borders. Point out that the map shows the names of cities but not of states.

4 Assess/Reteach

Students should be able to answer the questions by studying the map.

To further assess students' understanding of special purpose maps, have them complete the "Applying Your Skills" part of the Chapter Review and Assessment at the end of the chapter.

Resource Directory

Technology

Social Studies Skills Tutor CD-ROM

Answers to...

PRACTICE THE SKILL

The Pennsylvania Railroad ran through three states; five states did not have railroads running through them; and to travel from Baltimore to St. Louis, you would take the Baltimore and Ohio Railroad.

CHAPTER 7

Review and Assessment

Creating a Chapter Summary

Student summaries will vary.

Sample summaries:

South rich farmland and plenty of water resources; important agricultural area; in recent decades, has become more industrialized; more of its people now live in urban areas

Midwest 1980s recession sees many family farms sold to large corporate farms formed out of many smaller family farms; new technology makes the farms more efficient and profitable; many people move to cities to make a living

West rich in natural resources; 1800s sees resources damaged or depleted by careless use and growing cities; 1900s sees conservation efforts begun; today, people attempt to balance use of natural resources with conservation.

Reviewing Key Terms

Students' sentences will vary, but should demonstrate an understanding of each term.

Reviewing the Main Ideas

1. Students may mention New York City, Philadelphia, and Boston.
2. From 1892 to 1943, millions of immigrants entered the United States via Ellis Island off New York City. Other northeastern port cities were also gateways for immigrants.
3. The farming, mining, fishing, forestry, manufacturing, technology, and tourism industries are all employers of people in the South.
4. People, such as retirees, relocate to the South, and many people vacation in the South because of the mild climate. Increased population and tourism benefit the economy.
5. Since the 1980s, there has been a decrease in the number of family farms and an increase in the number of corporate farms.
6. Corporate farms are large farms owned by agricultural companies. Machines and computers do much of the work. Family farms are smaller farms owned by families.
7. minerals such as gold, copper, silver, and lead; forests; soil; and water
8. Answers will vary, but should refer to the dramatic changes in population and in the number and size of cities.

CHAPTER 7

Review and Assessment

Creating a Chapter Summary

On a separate piece of paper, draw a web like this one, and include the information about the Northeast. Continue completing the web by adding important details about each of the regions in the United States.

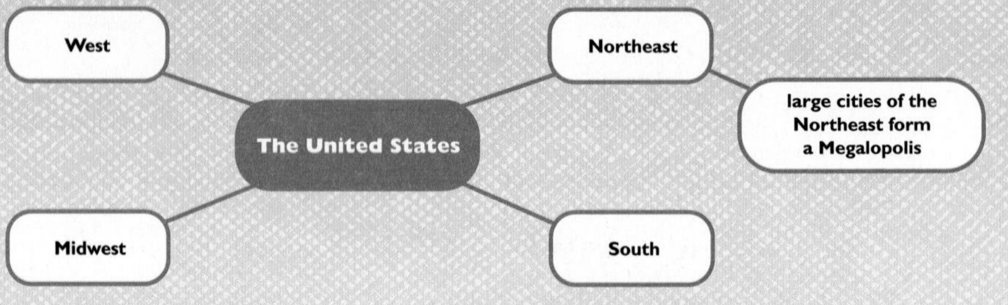

Reviewing Key Terms

Write a definition for each of the key terms. Then, use each term in a sentence.

1. commute (p. 121)
2. megalopolis (p. 121)
3. industrialization (p. 127)
4. mixed-crop farm (p. 130)
5. recession (p. 131)
6. capital (p. 131)
7. forty-niner (p. 135)
8. mass transit (p. 136)

Reviewing the Main Ideas

1. What are some of the large cities of the Northeast? (Section 1)
2. How does the Northeast serve as a gateway to the country? (Section 1)
3. How do people in the South make a living? (Section 2)
4. How does warm weather affect the economy of the South? (Section 2)
5. What major changes have occurred in the Midwest since the 1980s? (Section 3)
6. Describe the differences between family farms and corporate farms. (Section 3)
7. What are the main natural resources of the West? (Section 4)
8. How has life in the West changed since the days of the California Gold Rush? (Section 4)

Map Activity

United States

For each place listed below, write the letter from the map that shows its location.

1. Boston	**5.** Chicago
2. New York City	**6.** Dallas
3. Washington, D.C.	**7.** Portland
4. Atlanta	**8.** San Jose

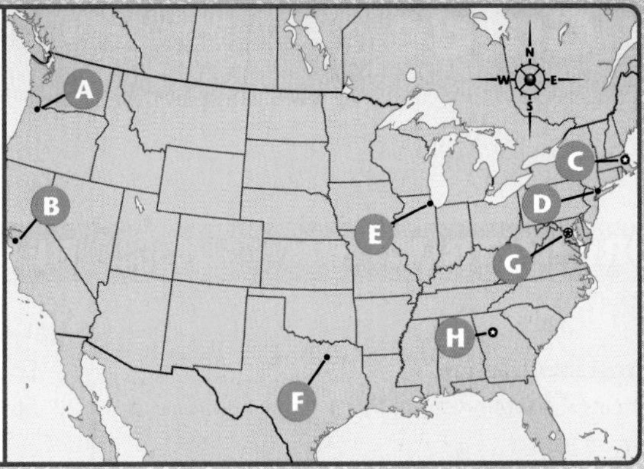

Take It to the NET

Enrichment For more map activities using geography skills, visit the social studies section of **phschool.com.**

Writing Activity

1. **Writing a Travel Guide** If you had friends who were visiting the United States for the first time, what information would you want to share with them? Which cities would you tell them to visit? Write a brief travel guide for your friends that takes them to all four regions. Suggest activities for each region. Provide background information to help your friends understand the history and culture of each region.
2. **Using Primary Sources** Miners and other people in the gold rush towns left letters and journals that give us a picture of life during the gold rush. Use your local or school library, or the Internet, to find some of these primary sources. Then, using the information you find, write a brief report on some aspect of the gold rush.

Applying Your Skills

Turn to the Skills for Life activity on p. 137 to help you complete the following actvity.

Look at the map on p. 134. Write a series of questions that can be answered by studying the map. Exchange your questions with a classmate and answer each other's questions.

Critical Thinking

1. **Making Comparisons** Identify at least one major trend that two or more regions of the United States have in common.
2. **Compare and Contrast** Create a chart that shows the similarities and differences between the Northeast and the South.
3. **Drawing Conclusions** If the use of resources continues in the West as it has, what are some likely results?

Take It to the NET

Activity Read an overview of the United States economy. How do the location, population, and resources of a region impact its economy? How do these factors impact the economy in your region? Visit the World Explorer: People, Places, and Cultures section of **phschool.com** for help in completing this activity.

Chapter 7 Self-Test As a final review activity, take the Chapter 7 Self-Test and get instant feedback on your answers. To take the test, visit the Social Studies section of **phschool.com.**

Map Activity

1. C **2.** D **3.** G **4.** H **5.** E **6.** F **7.** A **8.** B

Writing Activity

1. Travel guides will vary, but should be accurate and refer to all four regions of the United States and include activities and background information.
2. Students' reports should give a clear and accurate description of the gold rush era and should show clear evidence of use of primary sources through direct quotations.

Critical Thinking

1. Answers may include population growth, industrialization, and the growth of cities.
2. The South is becoming more industrialized like the North. Its cities are growing large and are home to important economic activities that affect the nation. The South produces many agricultural products, and it has important industries such as fishing and forestry that depend on local natural resources.
3. Answers will vary. Possibilities include the exhaustion of resources and widespread pollution.

Applying Your Skills

Sample questions: In which state can lead be found? (Idaho) What is Nevada's only siginificant natural resource? (hydroelectric power)

Resource Directory

Teaching Resources

Cooperative Learning Activity in the Unit 2 Teaching Resources, pp. 116–118

Chapter Tests Forms A and B in the Unit 2 Teaching Resources, pp. 150–155

Guide to the Essentials, Ch. 7 Test, p. 31

Other Print Resources

Chapter Tests with ExamView® Test Bank, Ch. 7

Technology

ExamView® Test Bank CD-ROM, Ch. 7

Resource Pro® CD-ROM

Chapter 8 Planning Guide

Resource Manager

	CORE INSTRUCTION	READING/SKILLS
Chapter-Level Resources	**Teaching Resources** Program Overview Pacing Charts **Technology** Resource Pro® CD-ROM Companion Web site, phschool.com • eTeach	**Technology** Social Studies Skills Tutor CD-ROM Student Edition on Audio CD, Ch. 8
1 Quebec: A Quiet Revolution 1. Understand the origins of French culture in Quebec. 2. Explain why French Canadians are concerned about preserving their culture. 3. Describe how French Canadian in Quebec have worked to preserve their culture.	**Teaching Resources** **Unit 2** Classroom Manager, p. 68 Guided Reading and Review, p. 69	**Teaching Resources** Guide to the Essentials, p. 32 **Technology** Section Reading Support Transparencies
2 Ontario: A Thriving Economy 1. Explain why Ontario is the industrial heartland of Canada. 2. Describe the resources that help make Ontario wealthy.	**Teaching Resources** **Unit 2** Classroom Manager, p. 71 Guided Reading and Review, p. 72	**Teaching Resources** Guide to the Essentials, p. 33 **Technology** Section Reading Support Transparencies
3 The Plains and British Columbia: Cultural and Economic Changes 1. Explain how the lives of indigenous people of Canada were changed by immigrants from other countries. 2. Describe how geography links British Columbia to the Pacific Rim.	**Teaching Resources** **Unit 2** Classroom Manager, p. 74 Guided Reading and Review, p. 75 Chapter Summary, p. 77 Vocabulary, p. 78 Reteaching, p. 79	**Teaching Resources** **Unit 2** Critical Thinking, p. 81 Guide to the Essentials, p. 34 Social Studies and Geography Skills, pp. 53, and 100 **Technology** Section Reading Support Transparencies

ENRICHMENT / PRE-AP

Teaching Resources
Primary Sources and Literature Readings

Other Print Resources
DK Atlas

Technology
World Video Explorer: Making a Living: Canada, A Trip to French Canada
Companion Web site, phschool.com

Technology
Color Transparencies 28, 32
Passport to the World CD-ROM

Technology
Color Transparencies 50
Passport to the World CD-ROM

Teaching Resources
Unit 2
Enrichment, p. 80
Cooperative Learning Activity, pp. 120–123

Technology
Color Transparencies 31
Passport to the World CD-ROM
World Video Explorer: British Columbia Case Study

ASSESSMENT

Prentice Hall Assessment System

Core Assessment
Chapter Tests with ExamView® Test Bank, Ch. 8
ExamView® Test Bank CD-ROM, Ch. 8

Standardized Test Preparation
Diagnose and Prescribe
Diagnostic Tests for Middle Grades Social Studies Skills
Review and Reteach
Review Book for World Studies
Practice and Assess
Test-taking Strategies with Transparencies for Middle Grades Test Prep Book
Test-taking Strategies Posters

Teaching Resources
Unit 2
Section Quizzes, pp. 70, 73, and 76
Chapter Tests, pp. 156–161

Technology
Companion Web site, phschool.com
Ch. 8 Self-Test

World Video Explorer
Each region of the world is explored through regional flyovers and investigative field trips. Case study segments give students an in-depth view of the history, economy, government, and culture of a key place in each region. Case studies include Nigeria, Mexico, China, British Columbia, and the Czech Republic.

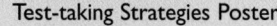

In Your Classroom

CUSTOMIZE FOR INDIVIDUAL NEEDS

Gifted and Talented

Teacher's Edition
- Drawing Conclusions, p. 143
- Proposal for a Movie, p. 147

Teaching Resources
- Enrichment, p. 80
- Primary Sources and Literature Readings

Honors/Pre-AP

Teacher's Edition
- Drawing Conclusions, p. 143

Teaching Resources
- Critical Thinking, p. 81
- Primary Sources and Literature Readings

ESL

Teacher's Edition
- Gold Rush Editorial, p. 151

Teaching Resources
- Guided Reading and Review, pp. 69, 72, and 75
- Vocabulary, p. 78
- Reteaching, p. 79
- Guide to the Essentials, pp. 32–34
- Social Studies and Geography Skills, pp. 53, 100

Technology
- Social Studies Skills Tutor CD-ROM
- Section Reading Support Transparencies

Less Proficient Readers

Teacher's Edition
- Gold Rush Editorial, p. 151

Teaching Resources
- Guided Reading and Review, pp. 69, 72, and 75
- Vocabulary, p. 78
- Reteaching, p. 79
- Guide to the Essentials, pp. 32–34
- Social Studies and Geography Skills, pp. 53, 100

Technology
- Social Studies Skills Tutor CD-ROM
- Section Reading Support Transparencies

Less Proficient Writers

Teacher's Edition
- Gold Rush Editorial, p. 151

Teaching Resources
- Guided Reading and Review, pp. 69, 72, and 75
- Vocabulary, p. 78
- Guide to the Essentials, pp. 32–34
- Social Studies and Geography Skills, pp. 53, 100

Technology
- Social Studies Skills Tutor CD-ROM
- Section Reading Support Transparencies

DORLING KINDERSLEY

At the end of each unit, you will find information adapted from Dorling Kindersley's *Illustrated Children's Encyclopedia* that connects to the region being studied and to one of the seven content strands. In addition, your resources include Dorling Kindersley's *Atlas*, which contains valuable information about countries from around the world.

TEACHER'S EDITION INDEX

CHAPTER 8 PACING SUGGESTIONS

For 90-minute Blocks

See suggestions in the Teaching Resources Pacing Charts for Chapter 6. Use Color Transparencies 28, 31, 32, and 50.

Running Out of Time?

See the Guide to the Essentials, pp. 32–34.

INTERDISCIPLINARY LINKS

Middle Grades Math: Tools for Success

Course 1, Lesson 3-8, **Metric Units of Length**

Course 2, Lesson 9-3, **Theoretical Probability, Math Toolbox, Odds**

Science Explorer

Weather and Climate, Lesson 3-1, **Air Masses and Fronts;** Lesson 3-2, **Storms;** Lesson 3-4, **Predicting the Weather**

Prentice Hall Literature

Bronze, I am a Native of North America, The Cremation of Sam Magee

Copper, The King of Mazy May

BIBLIOGRAPHY

For the Teacher

Collins, Carolyn Strom, and Christina Wyss Eriksson. *The Anne of Green Gables Treasury.* Viking, 1991.

Hello, Canada series (13 books). Lerner, 1995-1996.

World Desk Reference. Dorling Kindersley, 2001.

For the Student

Easy

Bannatyne-Cugnet, Jo. *A Prairie Year.* Tundra, 1994.

Average

Bowers, Vivien. *British Columbia.* Lerner, 1995.

Hamilton, Janice. *Quebec.* Lerner, 1996.

Challenging

Kendall, Russ. *Eskimo Boy: Life in an Inupiaq Eskimo Village.* Scholastic, 1992.

Literature Connection

Burnford, Sheila. *The Incredible Journey.* Little Brown, 1965.

Lingard, Joan. *Between Two Worlds.* Lodestar, 1991.

Murphy, Claire Rudolf. *The Prince and the Salmon People.* Rizzoli, 1993.

Take It to the NET

The World Explorer companion Web site, found on **phschool.com**, offers activities for exploring geographical, historical, and cultural resources on the Internet. It also provides on-line links for key content and all Section and Chapter Assessment activities.

The **Teacher site** also provides teachers with regional data and ideas for student research and activities.

Students can use the **Student site** to find chapter-by-chapter Internet resource links and to access Self-Tests.

CHAPTER 8

Connecting to the Guiding Questions

In this chapter, students will read about regions in Canada today. Content in this chapter corresponds to the following Guiding Questions outlined in the beginning of the unit.

- How have historical events affected the cultures of the United States and Canada?
- How has cultural diversity benefited and challenged these two nations?
- How have ordinary citizens in the United States and Canada worked to achieve justice and equality for all?
- How has modern technology both benefited and created challenges for the United States and Canada?

Using the Picture Activities

Have students study the photograph and think about the long journey that the grain must take from farms, to the towns and cities where it will be sold.

- Student reports should include information on why they chose a particular job, and should include details about the duties and responsibilities of a person holding that job.

Heterogeneous Groups

The following activities are suitable for heterogeneous groups.

Critical Thinking

Drawing Conclusions, p. 143

Creating a Visual Record

Proposal for a Movie, p. 147

Journal Writing

Gold Rush Editorial, p. 151

eTeach

Be sure to check out this month's discussion with a Master Teacher. Go to **phschool.com**.

CHAPTER 8

CANADA: Exploring the Region Today

Using Photographs

This train is taking on a load of wheat from the nearby grain elevator. The train takes the wheat west to the Pacific Coast or east to the Great Lakes. The wheat then is loaded on ships for export. Canada is the world's second leading grain exporter and the United States is the first.

Understanding Economics

Study the photo. Make a list of all of the steps you think might be involved in growing wheat and transporting it to mills to be made into flour. Start with a farmer planting a seed. End with a loaf of bread on the table. Which steps may be represented in this photograph?

Jobs in Agriculture

Think about the many different kinds of jobs that the agricultural industry provides. Which job would you want? Would you enjoy being a farmer? Or would you rather work on a train or ship that hauls grain? Visit your school or local library or the Internet and research different jobs in agriculture. Then, find someone with such a job and interview them about the work they do. Write a report using the information you gather and share it with the rest of the class.

Resource Directory

Teaching Resources

Primary Sources and Literature Readings extend content with a selection related to the concepts in this chapter.

Other Print Resources

DK Atlas

Technology

Making a Living: Canada, from the World Video Explorer, enhances students' understanding of the different ways of making a living in Canada.

A Trip To: French Canada, from the World Video Explorer, enhances students' understanding of French culture in the province of Quebec.

Student Edition on Audio CD, Ch. 8

SECTION 1

Quebec

A Quiet Revolution

BEFORE YOU READ

READING FOCUS

1. Why is the French culture so strong in Quebec?
2. What are some of the concerns of Quebec's citizens?
3. What have French Canadians in Quebec done to preserve their culture?

KEY TERMS

Francophone
separatist
Quiet Revolution
referendum

KEY PEOPLE AND PLACES

Jacques Cartier
Quebec City
Montreal

NOTE TAKING

Copy the web diagram below. As you read the section, fill in the diagram with information about how the people of Quebec are preserving French culture.

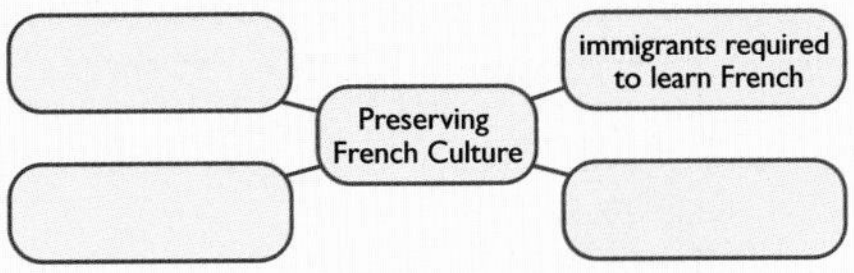

MAIN IDEA

Many of Quebec's citizens work hard to preserve their French culture, and some want Quebec to become independent from the rest of Canada.

Setting the Scene

In 1977, a new law in the province of Quebec said that all street signs must be in French only. That pleased the majority of Quebeckers who speak French, but it upset other Quebeckers. In 1993, a change in the law allowed English on signs as well. But French is the only language used in Quebec government, commerce, and education.

Canadian law states that the country has two official languages—English and French. French-speaking people live in every province. In Quebec, however, the first language of 83 percent of the people is French. English is the first language of 12 percent and the remaining 5 percent speak 35 different languages! Still, until the 1960s, government and business in Quebec were conducted in English, just as they were in the rest of Canada. It took a long political battle to change things in Quebec.

One Country, Two Languages

CULTURE

In Quebec, traffic signs say "STOP" in Canada's two official languages, French and English. **Critical Thinking** Why do you think it is important to the people of Quebec to have signs appear in two languages?

The French Influence in Quebec

Canada's history explains why Quebec is so French. In the 1530s, **Jacques Cartier** (ZHAHK kahr TYAY), a French explorer, sailed up the St. Lawrence River near today's **Quebec City.**

Resource Directory

Teaching Resources

Classroom Manager in the Unit 2 Teaching Resources, p. 68

Guided Reading and Review in the Unit 2 Teaching Resources, p. 69

Guide to the Essentials, p. 32

Technology

Section Reading Support Transparencies

SECTION 1

Lesson Objectives

1. Understand the origins of French culture in Quebec.
2. Explain why French Canadians are concerned about preserving their culture.
3. Describe how French Canadians in Quebec have worked to preserve their culture.

Lesson Plan

1 Engage

Warm-Up Activity

Ask students to suppose that their class speaks a different language from the rest of the school. Discuss with students how they would get along with the rest of the school. How might the class and the rest of the school communicate? What kinds of compromises might be needed? How could the rest of the school and the class learn about and benefit from each other's differences?

Activating Prior Knowledge

Ask the class to suppose that two class members want to be class president. There is a vote and each person gets half of the votes. What happens next? How can the class decide on the winner? Challenge students to identify the most democratic of these proposed solutions: the teacher decides; elections are held until there is a winner; the election is determined by coin toss. Encourage students to see that for some problems it is difficult to find a solution that will please everyone.

Answers to...

CRITICAL THINKING

Having signs appear in both English and French recognizes the importance of both of these cultures in Quebec.

Lesson Plan continued

2 Explore

As students read the section, ask them to find answers to the following questions: Why is there such a strong French influence in Quebec? Why has Quebec's unique situation led to a struggle among the people of Quebec?

3 Teach

To ensure that students understand the basic historical reasons for Quebec's French heritage, have students write a paragraph that answers the question: Why do many Quebeckers want Quebec to be a distinct society within Canada? This activity should take about 20 minutes.

Questions for Discussion

CITIZENSHIP **How were the citizens of Canada given the opportunity to participate in the issues concerning the province of Quebec?**

Referendums were held in 1990 and 1992 to ensure that Canadian citizens had a voice in whether to change the Canadian constitution to recognize the province of Quebec as a "distinct society" within Canada. The referendums failed.

SOCIAL STUDIES SKILLS **Look at the Provincial Profile on this page. How do the place names in Quebec reflect the cultural history of the province?**

The place names are either of French, British, or native origin, and reflect the historical dominion that these groups held over the region at different times.

Answers to...

MAP AND CHART STUDY

Quebec shares a border with the United States. Quebec's French heritage is evident in the number of French names on the map. Seventy-four percent of Quebeckers are of French extraction. Quebec's population has grown by over 700,000 people since 1985.

PROVINCIAL PROFILE

Quebec

Population Growth

Year	Population
1985	6,690,000
1990	7,021,000
1995	7,334,000
2000	7,372,448

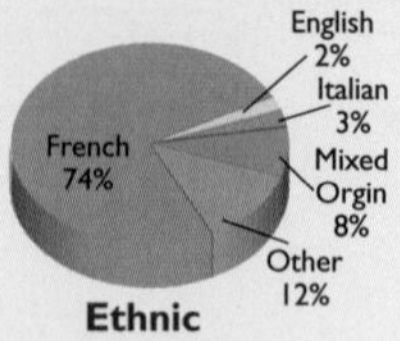

Ethnic Groups

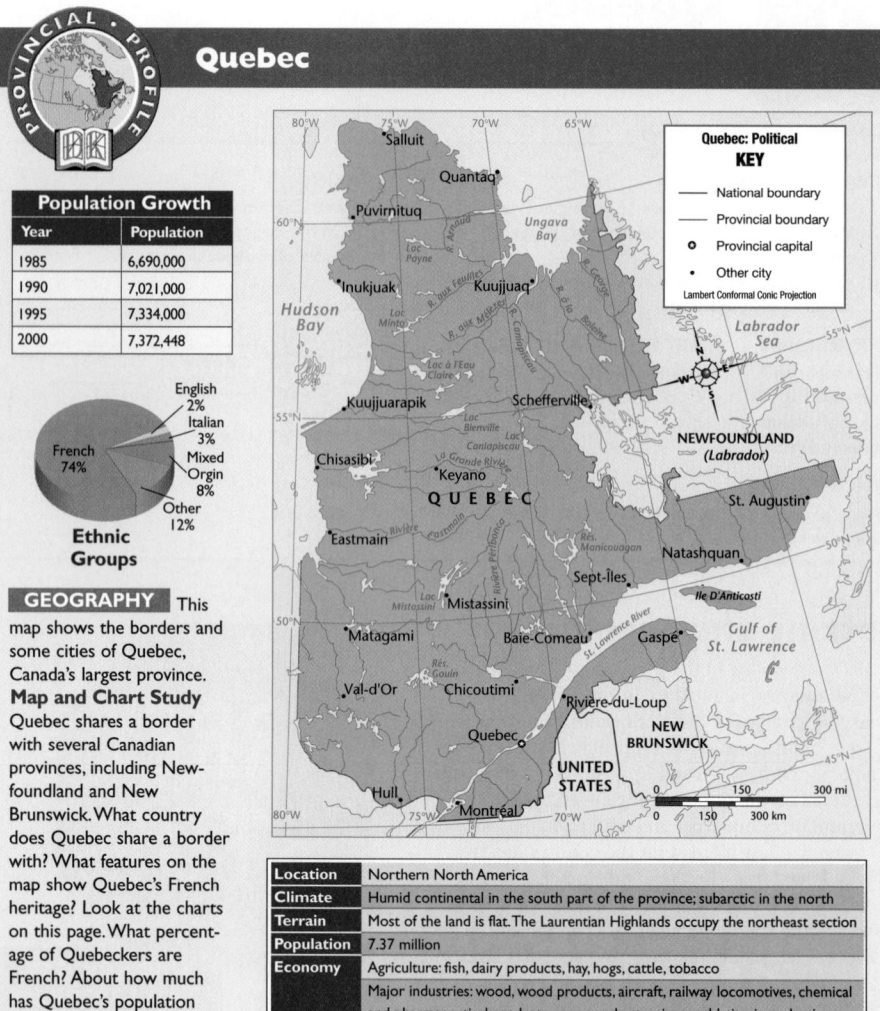

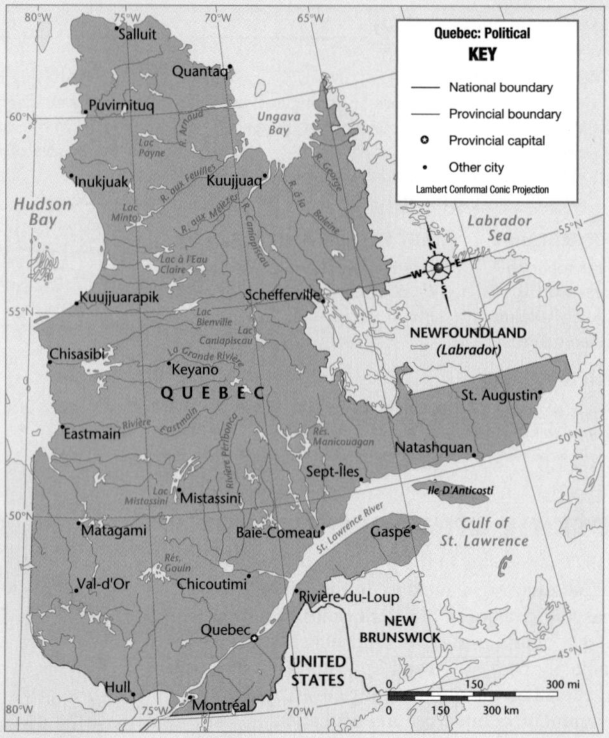

GEOGRAPHY This map shows the borders and some cities of Quebec, Canada's largest province. **Map and Chart Study** Quebec shares a border with several Canadian provinces, including Newfoundland and New Brunswick. What country does Quebec share a border with? What features on the map show Quebec's French heritage? Look at the charts on this page. What percentage of Quebeckers are French? About how much has Quebec's population grown since 1985?

Location	Northern North America
Climate	Humid continental in the south part of the province; subarctic in the north
Terrain	Most of the land is flat. The Laurentian Highlands occupy the northeast section
Population	7.37 million
Economy	Agriculture: fish, dairy products, hay, hogs, cattle, tobacco
	Major industries: wood, wood products, aircraft, railway locomotives, chemical and pharmaceutical products, copper, asbestos, iron, gold, titanium, aluminum

Cartier and his men became friends with the Stadacona (stad uh KOH nuh), the native people of the area. Some places in Quebec and elsewhere in Canada have Stadacona names. Cartier and later explorers gave other places French names. **Montreal,** for instance, is French for "Mount Royal."

Cartier claimed the region we now know as Quebec for France. But England also claimed the region. The two countries eventually

Resource Directory

Technology

Color Transparencies 28 The United States and Canada: Physical-Political Map; **32** Canada: Political Map

Passport to the World CD-ROM This interactive CD-ROM allows students to explore each region of the world. Students view regional videos, take a photo tour, and explore a historical timeline. Students record their travels in an Explorer's Journal and receive passport stamps when they pass regional quizzes.

fought over it. France lost, and in 1763 the territory went to the British. However, tens of thousands of French colonists lived in the region. Today, their descendants make up the majority of Quebec's population. They are **Francophones** (FRANG koh fohnz), or people who speak French as their first language.

Quebec: A Distinct Society within Canada

In the 1960s, some Francophones began to demand independence from the rest of Canada. They opposed using English as the only official language, and worried that their language and culture might die. They also believed that they were contributing much to Canada but getting little back. For the most part, Francophones held only low-paying jobs. They faced prejudice because they were French speakers.

Francophones who wanted independence were called **separatists.** They wanted Quebec to separate, or break away, from Canada. Separatists formed a political party, which won control of the Quebec provincial legislature in 1976. This peaceful change in Quebec's government is called the **Quiet Revolution.**

French became the official language, to be used in education, government, and commerce. Immigrants were required to learn French. Still, Quebec remained a province of Canada.

In 1980, the provincial government held a **referendum.** In a referendum, voters cast ballots for or against an issue. This referendum asked voters whether Quebec should become a separate nation. A majority voted no.

The Canadian government feared separatists could force the nation to separate, so they tried to meet their demands. Quebeckers wanted their province to be a "distinct society" within Canada with its own special way of life. If this was guaranteed, they would stay part of Canada. There was only one way to do this—change Canada's constitution. In 1990 and 1992, the government held referendums

CITIZENSHIP

Quebeckers, carrying signs calling for "independence" and "sovereignty," rallied to support the split from Canada. By the narrowest of margins, Quebeckers voted to remain part of Canada.
Critical Thinking Why do you think that so many Quebeckers want their province to be an independent country?

4 Assess/Reteach

See the answers to the Section 1 Assessment. You may also use students' paragraphs as an assessment tool.

Acceptable paragraphs cite language and cultural differences.

Commendable paragraphs cite historical, language, and cultural differences.

Outstanding paragraphs cite historical, language, and cultural differences and discuss some Quebeckers' desire to have Quebec become a separate nation.

ACTIVITY

Critical Thinking

Drawing Conclusions Remind students that Montreal is French for "Mount Royal," and that the name was given to the city when the French settled the area. Explain that place names often reveal much about the history and culture of a place. Point out several other French place names on the Provincial Profile map such as Rivière-du-Loup and Val-d'Or. Have students note the region of the province in which they see the most French names. Then point out some communities such as Inukjuak and Quantaq, which have indigenous language names. Have students note the locations of these places, and ask them to draw some conclusions about settlement patterns in Quebec.

SKILLS MINI LESSON

Recognizing Bias

To **introduce** the skill, write the following statement on the chalkboard: *The Fête des Neiges is Canada's most exciting festival; all other Canadian festivals are dull and boring by comparison.* Explain that the statement is biased because it presents a slanted opinion. It uses loaded words such as *dull* and *boring* to describe other festivals, yet it does not present any facts to support the statement. Re-write the statement as follows: *The Fête des Neiges, which celebrates winter, is one of many Canadian festivals.* Explain that this statement contains facts and does not use loaded words to try to sway readers. Help students **practice** and **apply** the skill by asking them to write a biased statement about their school. Have students exchange papers with partners and write down why their partners' statements are biased and rewrite them in a way that does not display bias.

Answers to...

CRITICAL THINKING

Many French-speaking Quebeckers are concerned about preserving their French heritage.

SECTION I ASSESSMENT

AFTER YOU READ

1. (a) French explorer who explored Canada (b) capital of Quebec (c) major city in Quebec
2. (a) person who speaks French as his or her first language (b) Francophone Quebecker who wants Quebec to separate from Canada (c) peaceful change in Quebec's government (d) election in which voters cast ballots for or against an issue
3. In the 1530s, French explorer Jacques Cartier landed near what is today Quebec City, and later claimed the region for France. Many French colonists moved to the region. Today their descendents make up a majority of Quebec's population.
4. The Canadian government has held referendums to change the Canadian constitution.
5. Many festivals take place. French cooking and architecture are found throughout Quebec.
6. Lists will vary, but should refer to the dominance of French culture in Quebec in contrast to the rest of Canada and the concern that French Canadians have about preserving their culture.
7. Answers will vary but should reflect an understanding of the issues that the people of Quebec face and should give specific reasons for opinions.
8. Lists and reports will vary but should reflect a general understanding of the region.

Winter Carnival

CULTURE During Quebec's Winter Carnival, artists compete to make the best sculptures of ice or packed snow. **Critical Thinking** Why do you think Quebeckers are so concerned with preserving and celebrating their culture?

about the issue. Quebeckers voted to change the constitution but Canadians in other provinces voted not to. The referendums failed.

In 1995, Quebec held another referendum. Again, Quebeckers voted to remain part of Canada. But the margin was very slim. Canada's Prime Minister promised to try to change the constitution again. But Quebec's separatist leader warned, "The battle for a country is not over. And it will not be until we have one." The close vote on election day guaranteed that the issue will continue to be discussed.

Preserving Quebec's Culture

One of the ways in which Quebeckers celebrate their culture is through festivals. The Fête des Neiges (FET day NEZH), or winter festival, lasts 17 days. It even includes canoe races along the St. Lawrence River.

Another festival honors Jean Baptiste (ZHAHN bah TEEST), the patron saint, or special guardian, of French Canadians. The festival is held June 24. All over the province, people celebrate with bonfires, firecrackers, and street dances.

French style and cooking are alive in Quebec—with Quebec variations. Sugar pie, for example, uses maple sugar from the province's forests. Quebec has French architecture—with Quebec variations. All in all, Quebeckers have a lively culture to preserve and protect.

SECTION I ASSESSMENT

AFTER YOU READ

RECALL

1. Identify: (a) Jacques Cartier, (b) Quebec City, (c) Montreal
2. Define: (a) Francophone, (b) separatist, (c) Quiet Revolution, (d) referendum

COMPREHENSION

3. Explain the early history of French influence in Quebec.
4. What has the Canadian government done to try to meet the demands of the separatists?
5. Describe some of the ways Quebeckers celebrate their French culture today.

CRITICAL THINKING AND WRITING

6. **Exploring the Main Idea** Review the Main Idea statement at the beginning of this section. Then, make a list of reasons why many people in Quebec want to separate from Canada.
7. **Supporting a Point of View** Quebeckers are split almost evenly on the issue of independence from Canada. Write a paragraph giving your opinion on whether Quebec should become independent or not. Give reasons for your point of view.

ACTIVITY

8. **Asking Good Questions** Make a list of questions that ask about some of the features of Quebec culture that you would like to know more about. Visit the library and try to find the answers to your questions. Write a brief report on the information you find.

Resource Directory

Teaching Resources

Section Quiz in the Unit 2 Teaching Resources, p. 70

Answers to...

CRITICAL THINKING

Answers will vary. Some students may say pride in family and cultural origins are cause for celebration.

SECTION 2

Ontario

A Thriving Economy

BEFORE YOU READ

READING FOCUS

1. Why is Ontario considered the industrial heartland of Canada?
2. What resources contribute to Ontario's wealth?

KEY TERMS

United Empire Loyalists
Golden Horseshoe

KEY PLACES

Ottawa
Toronto

MAIN IDEA

Ontario's industrial and agricultural production and its abundance of natural resources make it the wealthiest Canadian province.

NOTE TAKING

Copy the chart below. As you read the section, fill in the chart with details about Ontario's major industries.

ONTARIO'S INDUSTRIES			
Service Industries	Manufacturing	Agriculture	Mining
Banking			
Tourism			

Setting the Scene

"Which is better—to be ruled by one tyrant three thousand miles away or by three thousand tyrants one mile away?" These words of Rev. Mather Byles reflected the attitude of thousands of people in the United States who remained loyal to Great Britain during the American Revolution.

In 1784, the American Revolution had ended with a British defeat, and thousands of colonists loyal to Great Britain had lost their wealth and their homes. Even their lives were threatened. Canada welcomed these **United Empire Loyalists,** as they were called. By 1785, about 6,000 of these Loyalists settled west of the Ottawa River in what is now Ontario. They brought their English heritage into a land that had been dominated by French culture. Their loyalty to Great Britain contributed to the establishment of the province of Ontario and helped shape modern-day Canada.

British Influence in Ontario

CITIZENSHIP

This Latin motto on the Ontario coat of arms means "Loyal She Began, Loyal She Remains." It reflects the influence of the United Empire Loyalists in Ontario. **Critical Thinking** Why do you think the British government helped the United Empire Loyalists settle in Canada?

The Industrial Heartland of Canada

Ontario is not only the wealthiest province in Canada, it also has the largest population. About one-third of Canada's population lives there and nearly half of them have some English ancestry. Ontario is a center of manufacturing, service industries, and agriculture with almost half of Canada's industrial workers employed in the province.

SECTION 2

Lesson Objectives

1. Explain why Ontario is the industrial heartland of Canada.
2. Describe the resources that help make Ontario wealthy.

Lesson Plan

1 Engage

Warm-Up Activity

Call students' attention to the title of the section. Tell them that Ontario is the wealthiest of all Canada's provinces. Then have them turn to the Provincial Profile on page 146. Have students point out the waterways and clusters of cities shown on the map. Tell them that Ontario's economy depends on agriculture, mining, manufacturing, and service industries such as banking and health care. Ask them to look at the map and think about where these different types of activities might take place and what role the waterways might play in the economy.

Activating Prior Knowledge

Tell students that some of Ontario's early settlers were British loyalists who left the United States after the American Revolution. Ask students to name some groups of immigrants who came to the United States to begin a new life in unsettled territories. Encourage them to think about how these people built communities, and later cities, and made the region prosperous.

Resource Directory

Teaching Resources

Classroom Manager in the Unit 2 Teaching Resources, p. 71

Guided Reading and Review the Unit 2 Teaching Resources, p. 72

Guide to the Essentials, p. 33

Technology

Section Reading Support Transparencies

Answers to...

CRITICAL THINKING

Possible responses: They wanted to increase the population of Canada; they wanted people loyal to Britain to immigrate to Canada; they wanted people who would develop the land.

Lesson Plan continued

❷ Explore

As students read the section, ask them to find answers to the following questions: Where do the majority of Ontario's people live? How are the cities of Ottawa and Toronto alike? How are they different? What is the economic importance of the Golden Horseshoe? What does the land of the Canadian Shield provide to Ontario's economy?

❸ Teach

Have students trace a copy of the Provincial Profile map of Ontario on page 146. Then, have them illustrate the map with pictures of goods, services, or agricultural products in various parts of the province. For example, they might use an illustration of an automobile near Toronto, or cattle or poultry in the agricultural areas, or a ship near Thunder Bay. This activity should take about 25 minutes.

Question for Discussion

HISTORY **How did the American Revolution help shape the province of Ontario and modern-day Canada?**

When the American Revolution ended in 1784, colonists who remained loyal to Great Britain settled west of the Ottawa River in what is now Ontario. They brought their English heritage into what had been a land dominated by French culture, thus changing the influence on Canadian culture from French (except in Quebec) to English.

PROVINCIAL · PROFILE

Ontario

GEOGRAPHY This map shows the borders and major cities of Ontario. **Map Study** Where are most of Ontario's major cities located?

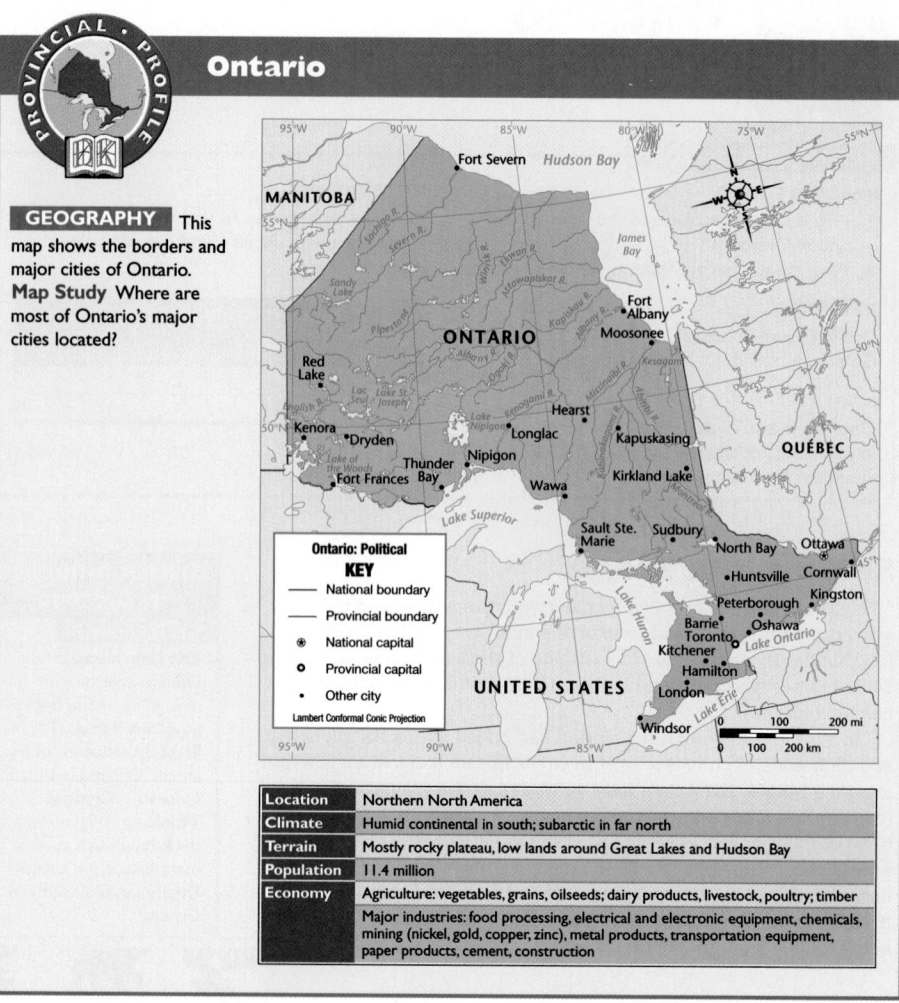

Location	Northern North America
Climate	Humid continental in south; subarctic in far north
Terrain	Mostly rocky plateau, low lands around Great Lakes and Hudson Bay
Population	11.4 million
Economy	Agriculture: vegetables, grains, oilseeds; dairy products, livestock, poultry; timber
	Major industries: food processing, electrical and electronic equipment, chemicals, mining (nickel, gold, copper, zinc), metal products, transportation equipment, paper products, cement, construction

Cities of Ontario Ontario's great cities lie in the warmer southern portion of the province, where about 90 percent of the population lives. Although there are rich agricultural lands in this region, most of the people live in cities and make up Ontario's large skilled labor force. Service industries such as banking, education, health care, legal services, and data processing employ nearly three-fourths of Ontario's workers.

Resource Directory

Technology

Color Transparencies 50 Toronto and the CN Tower Student Art

Passport to the World CD-ROM This interactive CD-ROM allows students to explore each region of the world. Students view regional videos, take a photo tour, and explore a historical timeline. Students record their travels in an Explorer's Journal and receive passport stamps when they pass regional quizzes.

Answers to...

MAP AND CHART STUDY

Most of Ontario's cities are in the southern portion, especially the southeast.

Ottawa is the national capital of Canada. It lies on the south bank of the Ottawa River, which forms the border between the provinces of Ontario and Quebec. Canada's three Parliament buildings sit on Parliament Hill overlooking the Ottawa River. Ottawa's most important employer is the Canadian government, which employs more than 100,000 of the Ottawa area's residents. Many people work in the technology, tourism, and manufacturing industries as well.

Toronto is Ontario's capital, as well as Canada's largest city. It is the commercial, cultural, and financial center of Canada. Headquarters for Canada's largest banks and insurance companies are located in Toronto and the offices for many of these businesses are found in Toronto's skyscrapers. Three of the world's 50 tallest buildings are located in downtown Toronto.

Toronto: Canada's Largest City

ECONOMICS The tall tower to the right in this photo is the CN (Canadian National) tower, the tallest free-standing structure in the world. **Critical Thinking** How do you think the tower is used?

The Golden Horseshoe The sprawling metropolitan area that includes Toronto is the center of Ontario's richest manufacturing region. The area, known as the **Golden Horseshoe,** follows the curve of the western shore of Lake Ontario. Most of Ontario's automobile plants are located here in the cities that cluster around the lakeshores. Manufacturing automobiles is Ontario's major industry but other important industries include electrical equipment, meat-packing, chemicals, textiles, industrial machinery, and furniture.

A Wealth of Resources

Ontario is rich in natural resources such as timber, minerals, and fertile soils. It is also close to large population centers in North America. This is a great advantage for Ontario's economy because big cities provide markets for goods and services.

4 Assess/Reteach

See the answers to the Section 2 Assessment. You may also use students' illustrated maps as a means of assessment.

Acceptable maps accurately depict the shape of the province of Ontario and will have two or more illustrations of goods.

Commendable maps accurately depict the shape of Ontario and include detailed illustrations of three or more products in the appropriate places on the map.

Outstanding maps accurately depict the shape of Ontario and include well-done, detailed illustrations of most of the major economic products of Ontario located in the appropriate places on the map.

ACTIVITY

Creating a Visual Record

Proposal for a Movie Have students develop a proposal for a film to be set in Ontario. Students may choose to make a contemporary documentary or a historical film. As part of the proposal, students should "scout" locations by consulting appropriate references. They should also outline the events or plot of the film on a storyboard—a series of sketches that show the sequence of major scenes in the film.

Verbal/Linguistic, Visual/Spatial

SKILLS MINI LESSON

Organizing Your Time

You may **introduce** this skill to students by having them brainstorm a list of the benefits of organizing their time (completing assignments on time, better grades, more leisure time, and so on). Have students **practice** the skill by asking them to develop a timetable for a report about an aspect of Ontario that interests them. Draw a two-week calendar on the board, and guide students in how to allocate time for research, prewriting, writing, revising, and publishing. Students may **apply** the skill by keeping a log of their activities as they work on their reports. At the completion of the assignment, have students compare their log with their timetable to locate discrepancies between planned time and actual time spent. Encourage students to use these data to realistically plan future assignments.

Answers to...

CRITICAL THINKING

Answers will vary. Students may say the tower is used as an observation tower, a tourist attraction, for communication purposes, and so forth.

SECTION 2 ASSESSMENT

AFTER YOU READ

1. (a) national capital of Canada, (b) capital of Ontario
2. (a) immigrants loyal to Great Britain who came to Ontario from the United States during the American Revolution (b) the region around the western shore of Lake Ontario, which is Ontario's richest manufacturing region
3. Automobiles are the most important manufactured product.
4. Being close to large cities provides a market for Ontario's goods and services.
5. It allows Ontario's goods to be sent to markets easily; it allows goods such as raw materials to be shipped from one point to another for manufacturing; it allows Ontario to import goods as needed and to have tourists visit.
6. Paragraphs should indicate that the southern part of Ontario is warmer; it is more fertile; manufacturing and service industries are clustered in the cities.
7. Student reports should have detailed examples of how the region's natural resources help shape the economy of that region.

Shipping in the Saint Lawrence Seaway

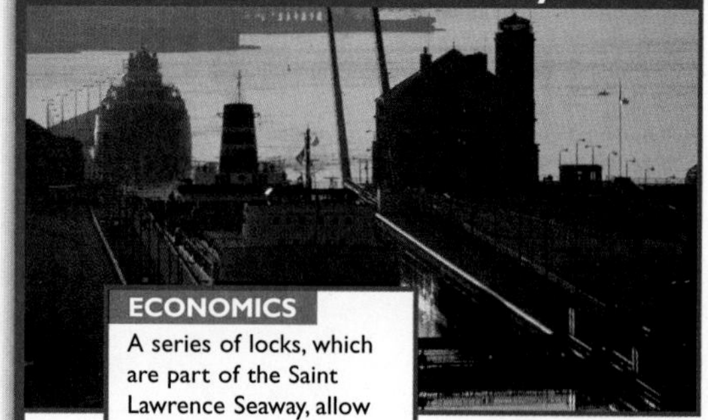

ECONOMICS

A series of locks, which are part of the Saint Lawrence Seaway, allow ships to travel through the Great Lakes to the Atlantic Ocean. In the picture above, a cargo ship travels through locks connecting Lake Superior to Lake Huron.

Critical Thinking How does the Saint Lawrence Seaway affect Canada's economic relationship with the United States and Europe?

Major transportation corridors such as the St. Lawrence Seaway, and Great Lakes, allow shipment of goods to ports in the United States and overseas, giving Ontario another great advantage. Thunder Bay on Lake Superior is a major port where ships pick up loads of grain from western provinces, or bring in goods from other areas.

Agriculture Ontario is Canada's leading producer of fruits and vegetables, as well as eggs and poultry products. Tobacco is an important cash crop, but most farms produce beef and dairy cattle in the rich pasturelands between Lake Ontario and Lake Huron. About 55 percent of the income from agriculture comes from livestock and livestock products. Milk is the most important product, followed by beef and pork.

Mining The rocky ground of the Canadian Shield in the central and northern regions of Ontario contains a variety of minerals. Nickel is the most important metal produced. Ontario mines provide a large percentage of the world's nickel. Copper is the second most important metal. Others include zinc, gold, uranium, iron ore, and silver.

Other riches mined from the earth include natural gas, petroleum, sand, and gravel. Limestone, marble, and granite mined in Ontario are used in buildings around the world.

SECTION 2 ASSESSMENT

AFTER YOU READ

RECALL

1. Identify: (a) Ottawa, (b) Toronto
2. Define: (a) United Empire Loyalists, (b) Golden Horseshoe

COMPREHENSION

3. What is Ontario's most important manufacturing industry?
4. How does being close to large population centers benefit Ontario's economy?

CRITICAL THINKING AND WRITING

5. **Exploring the Main Idea** Review the Main Idea statement at the beginning of this section. Then, list three ways that Ontario's access to transportation helps contribute to its thriving economy.
6. **Drawing Conclusions** Write a paragraph explaining why most of Ontario's population is located in the southern portion of the province, and why most of those people live in cities.

ACTIVITY

Take It to the NET

7. **Understanding Natural Resources and the Economy** Lanark County in Ontario, Canada enjoys a thriving economy. Write a short report describing how a region's natural resources can help shape the economy. Use what you learn on the Web site as a basis for your report. Visit the World Explorer: People, Places, and Cultures section of **phschool.com** for help in completing this activity.

Resource Directory

Teaching Resources

Section Quiz in the Unit 2 Teaching Resources, p. 73

Answers to...

MAP AND CHART STUDY

Students may say that the transportation corridor boosts the economies of both the United States and Canada because it allows for the swift movement of raw materials and goods.

SECTION 3

The Plains and British Columbia

Cultural and Economic Changes

BEFORE YOU READ

READING FOCUS

1. How were the lives of the native peoples of the Canadian Plains disrupted by immigrants?
2. How does geography tie British Columbia to the Pacific Rim?

KEY TERMS
indigenous
immunity
totem poles
boomtown

KEY PLACES
Vancouver
Saskatchewan
Fraser River
Pacific Rim

NOTE TAKING
Copy the chart below. As you read the section, fill in the chart with details about the history and economic activities of the Canadian Plains and British Columbia.

	Canadian Plains	British Columbia
customs of native peoples		
effects of European immigrants		
modern economic activities		

MAIN IDEA
European immigrants settled on Canada's plains and in British Columbia, bringing cultural change to the lives of the region's native peoples, and new economic activities to these regions.

Setting the Scene

One August day in 1821, after a long, difficult journey, about 195 Swiss immigrants reached their new land. It was summertime, but it was chilly on the Hudson Bay in northern Canada. The settlers had come to this land to become Canadian farmers. They had heard that these vast plains had good land and an excellent climate. However, they soon discovered that no shelter, food, or supplies were waiting for them and they survived only with the help of the native people. The settlers stayed on, enduring harsh winters and summers during which they fought drought, floods, and swarms of grasshoppers.

Over 180 years later and hundreds of miles west in the city of **Vancouver,** people are speaking Dutch, Japanese, Spanish, German, and English. On the city's streets, signs are written in English, Chinese, and other languages, restaurants serve the food of many different countries, and people practice the customs of many different cultures.

In both of these regions—the Canadian Plains and British Columbia—native people once practiced a unique culture. Today, these regions have undergone dramatic changes in both their cultures and in their economies.

Settling the Plains

HISTORY This photograph, taken in 1928, shows a group of young men on board the ship *Montcalm*. They are on their way from Great Britain to Canada to start a new life in the Prairie Provinces. **Critical Thinking** Why do you think these young men were so eager to settle in Canada?

149

SECTION 3

Lesson Objectives

1. Explain how the lives of indigenous people of Canada were changed by immigrants from other countries.
2. Describe how geography links British Columbia to the Pacific Rim.

Lesson Plan

1 Engage

Warm-Up Activity

Draw students' attention to the section's title. Ask them to speculate about what kind of changes took place on the Canadian Plains and British Columbia during the 1800s and 1900s. Remind them about what happened on the Great Plains of the United States.

Activating Prior Knowledge

Glowing advertisements offering rich fertile lands ready for the plow brought immigrants to the Canadian Plains. They were not prepared, however, for the hardships, such as drought, heat, cold, and insects. Ask students to discuss something they heard that led them to believe that some experience was going to be wonderful. Ask them if they were ever disappointed when the real experience turned out to be less than what they had hoped for. What did they do? Did they try to maintain a good attitude?

Resource Directory

Teaching Resources

Classroom Manager in the Unit 2 Teaching Resources, p. 74

Guided Reading and Review the Unit 2 Teaching Resources, p. 75

Guide to the Essentials, p. 34

Technology

Section Reading Support Transparencies

Answers to...

CRITICAL THINKING

Possible responses: They thought that life would be better in a new land; they wanted an adventure; they thought they would prosper in Canada.

Lesson Plan continued

❷ Explore

As students read the section, ask them to find the answers to the following questions: How did the ways of life of indigenous people of the Plains and British Columbia differ? How did the coming of European immigrants affect the lives of indigenous peoples in the Plains and British Columbia? What events caused the dramatic changes in the population of these regions? What is life like on the Plains and in British Columbia today?

❸ Teach

Have students create a timeline of the history of the Canadian Plains and British Columbia. The timeline should begin when traders first arrived in British Columbia and continue to today, identifying the dates of significant events and briefly describing each one. The activity should take about 30 minutes.

Questions for Discussion

GEOGRAPHY What geographic factors contribute to the economic and cultural relationship between British Columbia and the Pacific Rim?

Mountain ranges separate British Columbians from their fellow Canadians to the east, and two-thirds of British Columbians live along the coast of the Pacific Ocean, which provides easy access for Asian trade.

SOCIAL STUDIES SKILLS Look at the Provincial Profile on p. 151. Why do you think the largest group in Ethnic Groups graph is one of mixed origin?

Answers will vary. Students may say that the various European and Asian immigrants mixed with each other and with the indigenous population of British Columbia.

Answers to...

CRITICAL THINKING

Possible answer: Immigrants want to retain their heritage.

Religious Diversity in Saskatchewan

CULTURE

The onion-shaped domes of St. Julien's Greek Orthodox Church pierce the blue sky of Alvena. This small town is located in central Saskatchewan. Other Christian churches include Roman Catholic, Ukrainian Orthodox, and various Protestant denominations. **Critical Thinking** Why do you think that immigrant groups maintain the traditions and ways of life of the countries they came from?

The Canadian Plains

Throughout the 1800s, European settlers trickled into the Canadian Plains, bringing changes to the cultures of the **indigenous** peoples. These are people descended from the people who first lived in the region. Settlers brought trade goods, such as pots, needles, and guns but they also brought European diseases such as measles. Europeans had **immunity,** or natural resistance to the diseases. But the indigenous peoples did not and as many as 75 percent of them died.

By the late 1870s, the ways of life of many native peoples living in the Plains region had ended. They had depended upon the buffalo for their way of life. They suffered greatly when most of the buffalo herds were killed off by European settlers. New immigrants from northern and eastern Europe moved to the Plains region, bringing a variety of languages and cultures with them. By the turn of the century, the Canadian Plains were a checkerboard of different ethnic settlements.

LINKS TO Science

Sanctuary Visitors to Saskatchewan's Grasslands National Park see some of North America's last untouched prairies. Ancient grasses called wheat grass, snowberry, and silver sage blow in the wind. The park is also home to 12 endangered and threatened species. They include certain kinds of hawks, burrowing owls, and short-horned lizards.

Maintaining Traditions

About one quarter of Canada's farmland is in the province of **Saskatchewan.** Most European immigrants became wheat farmers. Two thirds of Saskatchewan's farmland is still devoted to wheat. For this reason, the province is sometimes called "Canada's Breadbasket."

Today, immigrants still come to the Canadian prairies. Each year, prairie cities celebrate Ukrainian, Icelandic, and German festivals that include traditional dancing, art, and music. In some small towns, people still maintain the European languages and customs of their ancestors.

British Columbia

The first people who lived in what is now British Columbia belonged to several ethnic groups. Each group spoke its own language and had its own customs and complex society. Along the coast, people caught fish, whales, and shellfish. They also carved giant **totem poles,** which were symbols for a group, a clan, or a family. Other groups hunted game in dense inland forests.

In the late 1500s, Spanish, British, and Russian traders began to arrive in the area. Trade did not change the native peoples' lives a great deal, but in 1858, gold was discovered along the **Fraser River.** Within

SKILLS MINI LESSON

Interpreting Graphs

In order to **introduce** the skill to students, display several line graphs from textbooks, magazines, or other publications. Identify and explain how to use the vertical and horizontal scales, and mention that line graphs are very useful for quickly showing how any variable has changed over time. Have students study the Provincial Profile on the next page, and point out that the population information in the table could be communicated in a line graph. Work with the class to **practice** the skill by asking them how they would set up a line graph using the values in the Provincial Profile table. Allow students to sketch a preliminary line graph to work out appropriate increments for the vertical scale. Students may **apply** the skill by using the data from the table to make an accurately scaled line graph that shows how British Columbia's population has changed from 1985 to 2000.

PROVINCIAL PROFILE: British Columbia

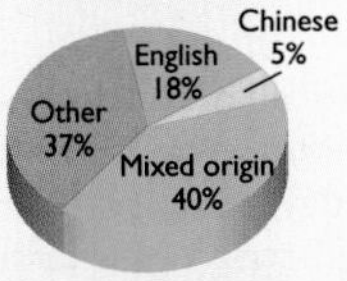

Ethnic Groups

Population Growth	
Year	**Population**
1985	2,990,000
1990	3,300,000
1995	3,766,000
2000	4,063,760

GEOGRAPHY This map shows the borders and major cities of British Columbia. **Map and Chart Study** Look at the charts and the economic information on this page. Is any one ethnic group much larger than the others? About how much has the population grown since 1985? How does British Columbia's growing population make a living?

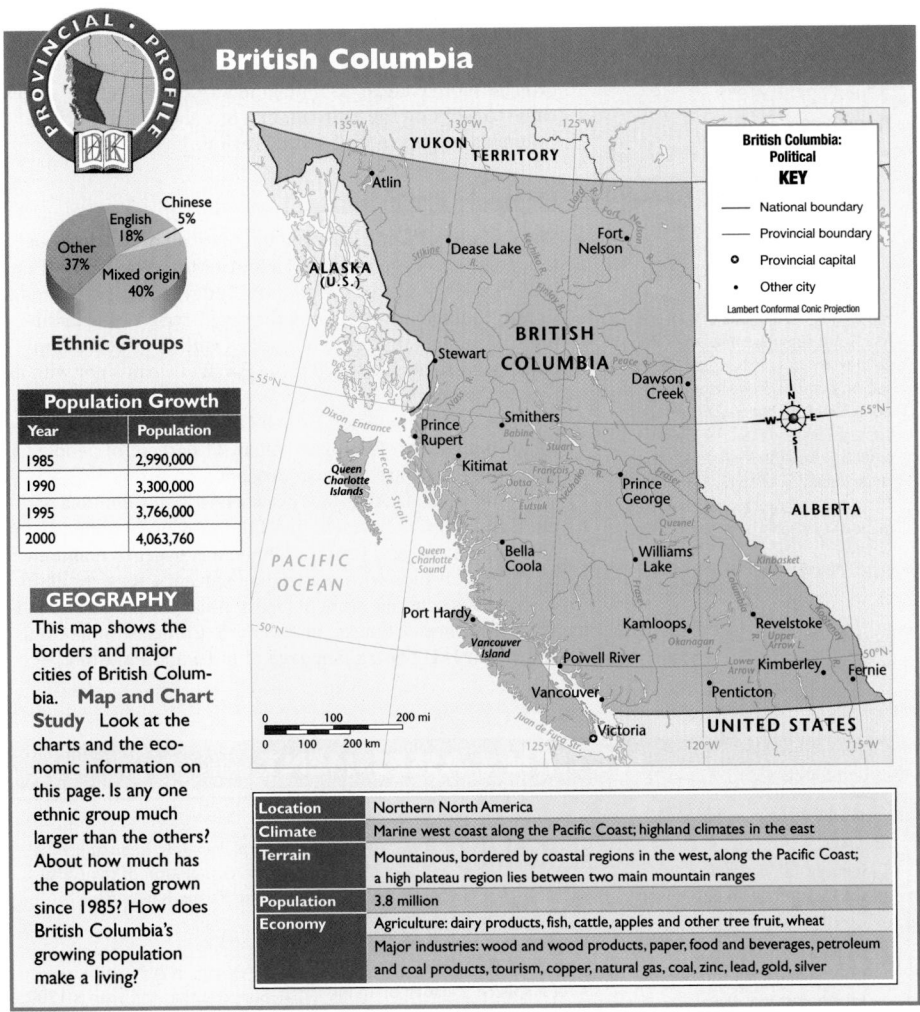

Location	Northern North America
Climate	Marine west coast along the Pacific Coast; highland climates in the east
Terrain	Mountainous, bordered by coastal regions in the west, along the Pacific Coast; a high plateau region lies between two main mountain ranges
Population	3.8 million
Economy	Agriculture: dairy products, fish, cattle, apples and other tree fruit, wheat
	Major industries: wood and wood products, paper, food and beverages, petroleum and coal products, tourism, copper, natural gas, coal, zinc, lead, gold, silver

weeks, tens of thousands of people had arrived in the town of Victoria on Vancouver Island. When gold was discovered in the Cariboo Mountains, more miners came, and **boomtowns** sprang up. A boomtown is a settlement that quickly springs up to serve the needs of miners.

Native people soon became the smallest minority of the population and were pushed onto small land areas, called reserves. Many of their customs, religions, and languages were banned.

AS YOU READ

Draw Inferences How did the discovery of gold affect life in British Columbia?

4 Assess/Reteach

See the answers to the Section 3 Assessment. You may also assess students' completed time lines.

Acceptable time lines include descriptions of three chronological events.

Commendable time lines include descriptions of more than three chronological events.

Outstanding time lines include descriptions of most events mentioned in the section in chronological order.

ACTIVITY

Journal Writing

Gold Rush Editorial Discuss with students the consequences of the arrival of miners in Victoria. In what different ways might the established citizens react? Would they be excited, wary, angry, welcoming? How would the population increase affect the community's businesses? What actions might the local government take? Have students consider these questions, and then ask them to write a journal entry in the form of a newspaper editorial that expresses the point of view of one of the townspeople.

Verbal/Linguistic

Resource Directory

Teaching Resources

Social Studies and Geography Skills, Reading a Circle Graph, p. 53

Technology

Color Transparencies 31 Canada: Physical-Political Map

World Video Explorer See the British Columbia case study for an overview of British Columbia's history, economy, government, and culture. Discussion questions are included.

Passport to the World CD-ROM This interactive CD-ROM allows students to explore each region of the world. Students view regional videos, take a photo tour, and explore a historical timeline. Students record their travels in an Explorer's Journal and receive passport stamps when they pass regional quizzes.

Answers to...

MAP AND CHART STUDY

No single ethnic group forms a significant majority, but the English population is about 3.5 times that of the Chinese population. The population has grown by about 1,100,000 since 1985. People hold agricultural jobs and work in industries that rely upon natural resources such as forests and minerals.

AS YOU READ

It brought more miners to the area, and boomtowns sprang up. Native people soon became the minority and were pushed onto reserves.

CHAPTER 8 CANADA: EXPLORING THE REGION TODAY 151

SECTION 3 ASSESSMENT

AFTER YOU READ

1. (a) a major city in British Columbia (b) a province in the Canadian Plains (c) major river in British Columbia (d) nations that border the Pacific Ocean
2. (a) originally living in an area (b) natural resistance to a disease (c) a carved pole symbolic of a group, a clan, or a family (d) fast-growing settlement near a mine
3. They brought European diseases that killed many Native Americans; they pushed the Native Americans off the land; they brought their own culture from various European countries.
4. The fact that British Columbia is on the Pacific Coast means that it is closer to Asia than any other province. British Columbia actively trades with Pacific Rim countries. In addition, a significant number of British Columbians are of Asian ancestry, and their customs, languages, and traditions are evident in British Columbia.
5. Student outlines should include references to the grievances that native people had against the government.
6. Paragraphs should discuss how the railway linked the eastern and western parts of Canada and opened up the West for settlement.
7. Posters will vary, but should reflect information presented in the text.

GOVERNMENT

The Northwest Mounted Police

As more and more settlers came to the prairies, the Canadian government needed to maintain law and order. In 1882 the Northwest Mounted Police set up headquarters in Saskatchewan at Pile O'Bones Creek (present-day Regina). Today, mostly for the benefit of tourists, a few Royal Canadian Mounted Police, as they are now called, can be spotted on horseback wearing the traditional uniform, but most Mounties are not highly visible. As Canada's federal police force, their duties include subduing terrorists, smugglers, and drug traffickers—tasks that demand they keep a low profile.

In 1881, Canadians began to build a railroad to link Vancouver to the eastern part of Canada. The railroad project brought more change, as immigrants from all over the world came to work on the railroad. In a few short years, British Columbia became a well-settled region.

British Columbia Today

The Canadian Pacific Railroad did unite all of Canada, but the mountains have remained a barrier between British Columbia and the rest of the country. Today, about two thirds of British Columbians live along the coast, west of the mountains. Many feel that their future lies with the **Pacific Rim** countries—those that border the Pacific Ocean—not with the rest of Canada.

Another link between British Columbia and the Pacific Rim is a diversity of cultures. About 11 percent of people living in the region are of Asian descent.

Trade is yet another link between British Columbia and the Pacific Rim. Forty percent of the province's trade is with Asian countries, and British Columbia is eager to maintain good relationships with her trading partners. As a result, in many of the region's schools, students learn Asian languages, including Japanese, Cantonese Chinese, or Mandarin Chinese. Some even learn Punjabi (pun JAH bee), a language of India and Pakistan.

SECTION 3 ASSESSMENT

AFTER YOU READ

RECALL

1. Identify: (a) Vancouver, (b) Saskatchewan, (c) Fraser River, (d) Pacific Rim
2. Define: (a) indigenous, (b) immunity, (c) totem pole, (d) boomtown

COMPREHENSION

3. How did European immigrants change the culture of the Canadian Plains?
4. What ties exist between the people of British Columbia and the Pacific Rim?

CRITICAL THINKING AND WRITING

5. **Exploring the Main Idea** Review the Main Idea statement at the beginning of this section. Then, make an outline of a speech a leader of an indigenous tribe might give to Canadian government officials, explaining how government policies have affected his tribe's way of life.
6. **Identifying Central Issues** In the late 1800s, the Canadian Pacific Railroad connected the eastern provinces to British Columbia. Write a paragraph explaining the importance of the completion of the Canadian Pacific Railroad.

ACTIVITY

7. **Writing an Advertisement** Suppose that the year is 1900. You want to encourage people to come and start farms in Saskatchewan. The government will give 160 acres of land to anyone willing to try. Make a poster advertising free land. You may show weather, soil, scenery, or settler communities. Describe conditions so many will want to come.

Resource Directory

Teaching Resources

Section Quiz in the Unit 2 Teaching Resources, p. 76

Chapter Summary in the Unit 2 Teaching Resources, p. 77

Vocabulary in the Unit 2 Teaching Resources, p. 78

Reteaching in the Unit 2 Teaching Resources, p. 79

Enrichment in the Unit 2 Teaching Resources, p. 80

Critical Thinking in the Unit 2 Teaching Resources, p. 81

Summarizing Information

What You Need

You can summarize information. You will need:
► book or textbook lesson
► paper or notebook
► pencil or pen

Learn the Skill

You probably read many things in one day. It's not possible to remember everything you read. Summarizing information will help you pick out the main points of what you read, and can even help you study for tests. More importantly, it will help you make sense of the ideas you read or hear about. To learn the skill of summarizing, think about your activities yesterday. Your goal will be to describe the main points of your day from when you woke up to when you went to sleep.

A. Work from start to finish. When you summarize, it's best to start at the beginning and work through to the end. When summarizing your day, start with when you woke up.

B. List the main points. Remember that a summary describes the main points, not the small details.

C. Add a few details to the list. Although you do not want to list too many details, it helps to list a few that may help jog your memory. For example, you might write, "ate breakfast" as a main point. You can add the details of what you ate if the meal was special in some way. As you make your list, add details after some of the main points.

D. Turn your list into a summary. Summaries are usually in paragraph form. Once you have made your list, you can add transitions to make it into a paragraph. Transitions are words that connect one idea to the next by showing how the ideas are related to each other. For example, if your

list reads: 1) woke up, 2) got dressed, 3) ate breakfast, you might write, "First I woke up. Then, after I got dressed, I ate breakfast."

Summary

> After I woke up yesterday morning, I got dressed and put on my new sweater. Then I ate blueberry pancakes for breakfast. My first class at school was math, and we did fractions. Then I went to gym class. After an assembly, I ate lunch. We had a field trip to the town hall in the afternoon. After school, I went to my Grandpa's house for dinner. Then I did homework and went to bed.

Practice the Skill

Summarizing a day is good for journal writing, but not much help in your schoolwork. However, the steps you just took will help you in school when you apply them to what you read or hear.

Practice by writing a summary of this chapter. Follow the four steps you took when summarizing your day. The headings in the chapter will help you pick the main points to list. Topic sentences in paragraphs will also help you find main points and interesting details. Remember to turn your list into a written summary, different from the diagram summary in the chapter review.

Apply the Skill

See the Chapter Review and Assessment at the end of this chapter for more questions about summarizing information.

CHAPTER 8 SKILLS FOR LIFE 153

Resource Directory

 Teaching Resources

Social Studies and Geography Skills, Summarizing and Taking Notes, p. 100

 Technology

Social Studies Skills Tutor CD-ROM

Answers to...

PRACTICE THE SKILL

Make sure students understand to use only the main points of the chapter in their summaries, and not the small details.

Lesson Objectives

1. Define summarizing and understand why it is useful.
2. Write a summary following step-by-step instructions.

Lesson Plan

❶ Engage

To introduce the skill, read the opening paragraph under "Learn the Skill." Make sure students understand that a summary is a retelling of the most important ideas in a book or textbook lesson.

❷ Explore

Direct students to read the steps under "Learn the Skill," and then follow the steps to make a list of yesterday's activities. Make sure they understand that they will first make a list of activities in the order in which they occurred. When they are finished with their lists, they will use transitions to turn the information into a short paragraph.

❸ Teach

Have students write a summary of the chapter as described in "Practice the Skill." Page through the chapter with students, pointing out the various headings and subheadings. Point out that the main ideas of the chapter are often found in the headings. Students should follow the same directions as in "Learn the Skill."

❹ Assess/Reteach

Students should apply the skill by completing a summary of the chapter. Their summaries should give several main ideas for each province in Canada.

To further assess students' understanding of concept maps, have them complete the "Applying Your Skills" part of the Chapter Review and Assessment at the end of this chapter.

CHAPTER 8

Review and Assessment

Creating a Chapter Summary

Student summaries will vary.

Sample summaries:

Section 2 Ontario was settled by British loyalists from the United States, who brought with them many of the customs of the British culture. Today Ontario is the wealthiest Canadian province, with an economy based on service industries, manufactured and agricultural goods, and raw materials such as metals and petroleum.

Section 3 Indigenous people who lived on the Canadian Plains and in British Columbia had their own distinct cultures. Settlers new to the region eventually pushed the Native people off of their lands, and established farms and communities that reflected their own cultural heritage. Today, British Columbia is a vital center for trade with the Pacific Rim countries.

Reviewing Key Terms

1. c **2.** g **3.** d **4.** a **5.** f **6.** b **7.** e

Reviewing the Main Ideas

1. French Canadians
2. for Quebec to be designated a distinct society within Canada
3. There are many service industries that require skilled labor, such as banking, health care, education, and data processing.
4. The southern part of Ontario is warmer and has fertile soils.
5. wheat
6. indigenous peoples, the British, the Spanish, Russians, Chinese, Americans, and many others

CHAPTER 8

Review and Assessment

Creating a Chapter Summary

On a separate piece of paper, draw a diagram like this one, and include the information that summarizes Section 1. Then, fill in the remaining two boxes with summaries of Sections 2 and 3.

CANADA: EXPLORING THE REGION TODAY

Section 1	Section 2	Section 3
Quebec is a distinct society within Canada. Many people living in Quebec speak French and are of French descent. They are working to preserve their French cultural heritage, and many want Quebec to separate from Canada and become independent.		

Reviewing Key Terms

Match the key terms in Column I with the definitions in Column II.

Column I	Column II
1. Francophone	**a.** a ballot or vote in which voters decide for or against a certain issue
2. separatist	**b.** a natural resistance to disease
3. Quiet Revolution	**c.** a person who speaks French as his or her first language
4. referendum	**d.** a peaceful change in the government of Quebec, making French the official language
5. Golden Horseshoe	**e.** a tall, carved wooden pole containing symbols
6. immunity	**f.** the sprawling metropolitan area that includes Toronto
7. totem pole	**g.** someone who wants Quebec to break away

Reviewing the Main Ideas

1. What is the largest cultural group in Quebec? (Section 1)
2. What is the main political aim of many French Canadians? (Section 1)
3. Why does Ontario need a large skilled labor force? (Section 2)
4. Why does most agricultural activity take place in the southern part of Ontario? (Section 2)
5. What is Saskatchewan's main contribution to Canada's economy? (Section 3)
6. Identify different groups of people who have shaped British Columbia's culture. (Section 3)

Resource Directory

Teaching Resources

Cooperative Learning Activity in the Unit 2 Teaching Resources, pp. 120–123

Chapter Tests Forms A and B in the Unit 2 Teaching Resources, pp. 156–161

Guide to the Essentials, Ch. 8 Test, p. 35

Unit Tests Forms A and B in the Unit 2 Teaching Resources, pp. 162–167

Map Activity

Canada

For each place listed below, write the letter from the map that shows its location.

1. Quebec
2. Montreal
3. Ontario
4. Ottawa
5. Toronto
6. British Columbia
7. Vancouver

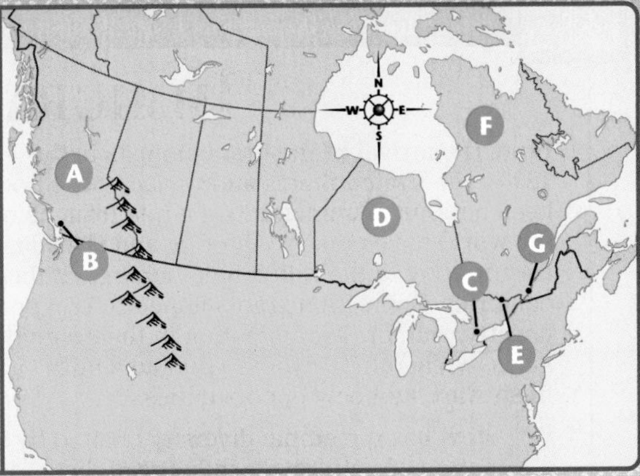

Take It to the NET

Enrichment For more map activities using geography skills, visit the social studies section of **phschool.com.**

Writing Activity

1. **Recognizing Bias** The slogans "Masters in Our Own House" and "United From Sea to Sea" are from the dispute over Quebec. Determine which side of the issue each slogan supports.
2. **Drawing Conclusions** Many immigrants came to Ontario in the late 1700s. What advantages and disadvantages do you think this move had for them?
3. **Recognizing Cause and Effect** Identify several different events in western Canada that led to the decline of the native peoples' cultures.

Critical Thinking

1. **Writing a Paragraph** Make a list of the distinguishing characteristics of Quebec, Saskatchewan, and British Columbia. Then pick one province. Write a letter to a friend, trying to convince your friend to move to the province.
2. **Writing a Report** The native peoples of British Columbia had close ties to their natural environment. Visit the library and gather information on one of the tribes of native peoples living in British Columbia. Write a report detailing the ways that they used their natural resources for food, shelter, and cultural traditions.

Applying Your Skills

Turn to the Skills for Life Activity on p. 153 to help you complete the following activity.

Find a newspaper or magazine article on a topic that interests you. Read the article and then follow the steps for writing a summary in order to summarize the information you have read.

Take It to the NET

Activity Read about the industries that fuel Canada's economy. How would your life be different without the products and industries you read about? Visit the World Explorer: People, Places, and Cultures section of **phschool.com** for help in completing this activity.

Chapter 8 Self-Test As a final review activity, take the Chapter 8 Self-Test and get instant feedback on your answers. To take the test, visit the Social Studies section of **phschool.com.**

Resource Directory

Other Print Resources

Chapter Tests with ExamView® Test Bank, Ch. 8

Technology

ExamView® Test Bank CD-ROM, Ch. 8

Resource Pro® CD-ROM

Map Activity

1. F **2.** G **3.** D **4.** E **5.** C **6.** A **7.** B

Writing Activity

1. "Masters in Our Own House" is a slogan of the separatists. "United From Sea to Sea" is a slogan of those who want Canada to remain united.
2. Advantages: being in a country where people were loyal to the British crown; getting free land; being free from persecution. Disadvantages: having to leave homes and families; having to start all over in a strange country.
3. Answers will vary. Possibilities include the immigration of thousands of Europeans, exposure to European diseases, the killing of buffalo herds, the forced movement of indigenous peoples onto reserves, and the building of the Canadian Pacific Railway.

Critical Thinking

1. Lists and letters will vary, but should be accurate. Possible distinguishing characteristics include the following: Quebec: French culture and language; British Columbia: diverse population and ties to the Pacific Rim.
2. Reports should detail the relationship between the chosen tribe and its natural environment. Invite students to present their reports to the class.

Applying Your Skills

1. Students' summaries should include the main points of the article they have chosen, as well as a few details. Summaries should be in paragraph form.

UNIT 2

Introduction

The introduction on the student page on the right provides key facts and general information about immigration in the United States and Canada.

- Students should read the introduction first to gain a basic knowledge of the subject before reading on.
- Have students read all of the subentries, which provide further information on immigration, particularly focusing on what it means to be a citizen. Have students also read the annotations that accompany and explain the photos and illustrations.
- When students have finished reading all of the information, discuss the connections between the information on these pages and what they have learned about the United States and Canada. Students might want to review information in Chapters 5 and 6.

ACTIVITY

Creating a Travel Brochure

Have students work in small groups to create travel brochures highlighting several cities across Canada, including Vancouver, Calgary, Toronto, and Quebec City. Brochures should include information about the different ethnic groups that make up the population in each city, including native peoples and immigrants from other countries. Suggest that students think of graphic devices to represent the heritage and background of people who are citizens of Canada.

Visual/Spatial

Adapted from the Dorling Kindersley Illustrated Children's Encyclopedia

IMMIGRATION

From the arrival of the first colonists in the 1600s, the United States and Canada have both been nations of immigrants. People from all over the world have come to the U.S. and Canada, contributing to the rich ethnic heritage of these countries. Some immigrants hoped to escape poverty, war, or discrimination in their native lands, while others came to find adventure, a fresh start, and new opportunities.

FLEEING FAMINE AND POVERTY
More than seven million people entered the U.S. from 1820 to 1870, mostly from Northern and Western Europe. About a third were Irish, seeking escape from a famine brought on by potato crop failures in the 1840s. Another third were from Germany, where political unrest forced thousands to flee. While most new immigrants settled on the East Coast, many Germans traveled to the rich farmlands in the middle of the country.

? How has the ethnic diversity created by a nation of immigrants influenced the cultures of the United States and Canada?

THE FIRST IMMIGRANTS

Most of the early colonists who settled in what became the United States came from England in the 17th and 18th centuries. Some of these early immigrants could not afford the travel costs and came as indentured servants. These people agreed to work for a fixed number of years to pay for their passage. Others were African slaves who were brought to the colonies against their will.

Reenacting a Pilgrim harvest in Plymouth Rock, MA

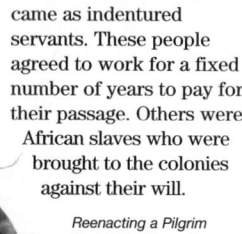

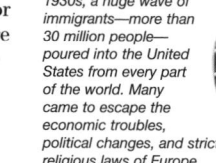

THE GREAT WAVE
From the early 1900s to the Great Depression of the 1930s, a huge wave of immigrants—more than 30 million people—poured into the United States from every part of the world. Many came to escape the economic troubles, political changes, and strict religious laws of Europe.

RELIGIOUS FREEDOM

Many people came to America seeking the freedom to practice their chosen religion, a right that would be later guaranteed by the First Amendment to the Constitution. In colonial times, religious groups such as the Quakers and the Puritans fled from harsh treatment in England. More that two and a half million Jews from Eastern Europe emigrated to the United States between 1880 and 1920 to escape cultural and religious persecution.

156 UNIT 2 UNITED STATES AND CANADA

CITIZENSHIP

Immigration Laws

Throughout American history, there have been attempts to limit the number of immigrants coming into the country. In the late 1800s and early 1900s, many native-born Americans were worried by the rising number of immigrants. They were threatened by the different languages and religions, and felt that they were competing with new immigrants for jobs. Urged by these "nativists," Congress began to place restrictions on immigration. In 1882, Congress passed the Chinese Exclusion Act, which banned Chinese workers from coming to the United States. In the early 1920s, Congress passed other immigration laws limiting the number of immigrants from eastern and southern Europe. It wasn't until 1965 that Congress eased these restrictions when it passed the Immigration and Nationality Act.

Chinese Immigration

In the mid-1800s, many Chinese people crossed the Pacific Ocean. They came to California in search of gold. Instead, they found violent anti-Chinese protests, unfair taxes, and laws to prevent their families from joining them. Labor shortages led companies to hire Chinese workers to help build transcontinental railroads in both the U.S. and in Canada.

VANCOUVER
Vancouver is located in southwestern British Columbia. It is Canada's leading Pacific port and reflects the great cultural diversity of the province. Many of its citizens are descended from the Chinese immigrants who helped to build the Canadian west.

An immigrant family arrives in New York in 1910.

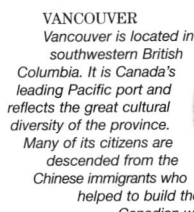

PRESERVING HERITAGE
Many immigrants choose to settle in communities made up of people from their native lands. Most American cities contain ethnic neighborhoods, where residents continue to speak their native language as well as English. These neighborhoods have ethnic shops, places of worship, and businesses. They are also the site of many traditional festivals.

Immigration Limits

By 1910, most immigrants were coming from Southern and Eastern Europe. Some native-born Americans felt threatened by their large numbers. Consequently, Congress passed the first quota laws limiting the number of people allowed into the country.

ACTIVITY

Understanding the Bill of Rights

Have students work with partners to compare the U.S. Bill of Rights, which was adopted in 1791, to the Canadian Bill of Rights, which was adopted in 1985. Have students use the library or Internet to find each country's bill of rights. Then, have students make a chart or diagram to record their observations and share their conclusions with the rest of the class.

Verbal/Linguistic

CITIZENSHIP

Pierre Trudeau

Pierre Elliot Trudeau, a native of Montreal, was elected Prime Minister of Canada in 1968. He came to power at a time when Canada was asserting its independence from Great Britain. At the same time, citizens in Quebec were launching a strong and sometimes violent separatist movement.

Trudeau's father was Quebecois and his mother was Scottish, and this dual ethnicity reinforced Trudeau's commitment to a united Canada. He believed that a strong federal government and constitutional reforms would enable citizens of any cultural background to coexist in harmony.

UNIT 3

Introducing the Unit

This unit was developed around seven strands of essential knowledge and skills that relate to the study of people, places, and cultures of the contemporary world. These strands include **History, Geography, Economics, Government, Citizenship, Culture,** and **Science, Technology, and Society.** These seven strands, and the related Guiding Questions on the next pages, are intended as an organizational focus for the unit. All of the chapter content, activities, questions, and assessments relate to the seven strands, which act as an umbrella under which all of the material falls.

Using the Pictures

Use the photographs on the reduced student pages as a prompt for a discussion of what students know about the history, geography, economics, government, citizenship, culture, and science and technology of Latin America.

- You may want to begin a **K-W-L** chart on the chalkboard for Latin America, with the headings What We **K**now About Latin America, What We **W**ant to Know About Latin America, and What We **L**earned About Latin America.
- Have students fill in the first column with several things they agree they already know. Then, ask them to brainstorm what they would like to know about Latin America to add to the second column.
- Students can fill in the third column as they work through the text.

eTeach

Be sure to check out this month's discussion with a Master Teacher. Go to **phschool.com**.

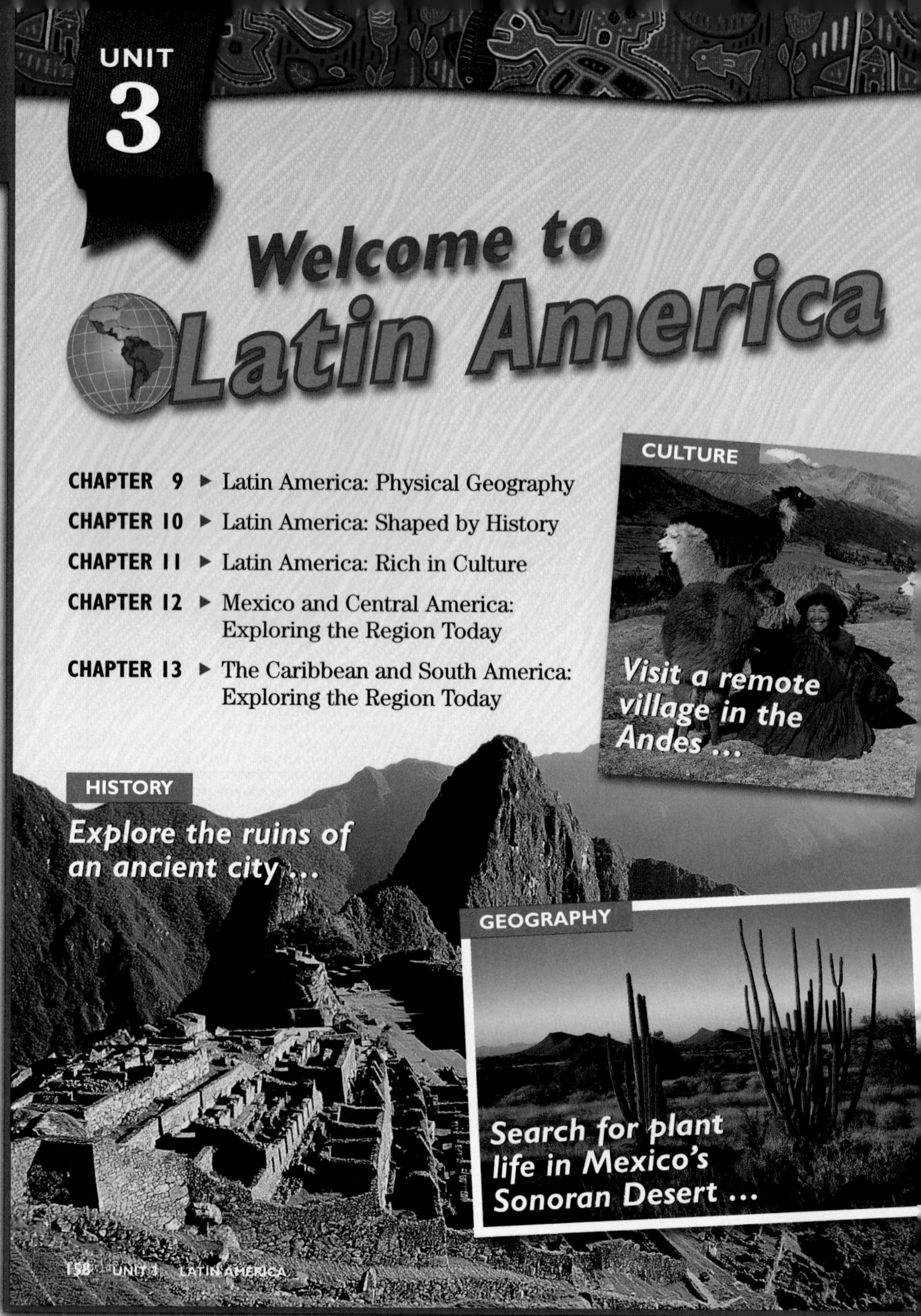

UNIT 3

Welcome to Latin America

CULTURE

Visit a remote village in the Andes ...

HISTORY

Explore the ruins of an ancient city ...

GEOGRAPHY

Search for plant life in Mexico's Sonoran Desert ...

Resource Directory

Teaching Resources

Program Overview includes a guide to the Prentice Hall World Explorer program. You may wish to refer to the overview as you plan your instruction.

Pacing Charts for Unit 2 offer a variety of course configurations.

What do you want to learn?

ECONOMICS

Visit an open-air market in Lima ...

SCIENCE, TECHNOLOGY, AND SOCIETY

Build a television on an assembly line ...

GOVERNMENT

See the "Pink House," the home of Argentina's government in Buenos Aires ...

CITIZENSHIP

Celebrate the return of a democratic president ...

A journal can be your personal record of discovery. As you learn about Latin America, you can create journal entries about what you read, write, think, and create. For your first entry, think about the geography of Latin America. How have Latin America's physical features influenced life in this region of the world? How is life in rural areas different from life in urban areas?

UNIT 3 WELCOME TO LATIN AMERICA 159

Using the Explorer's Journal

Have students begin their Explorer's Journal as the paragraph on the student book page suggests. If at all possible, encourage students to use a separate small notebook for their Explorer's Journal entries. They can add to this journal as they learn more about Latin America.

Project Possibilities

The projects in this book are designed to provide students with hands-on involvement in the content area. Write the following project ideas on the chalkboard and have students preview them and discuss which they might want to do. You may assign projects as cooperative activities, whole-class projects, or individual projects.

A Latin American Concert

Research Latin American music. Choose one or more Latin American countries to focus on. Find examples of popular songs and song lyrics, and share them with the class.

Latin American Physical Geography

Create a topographical model of a Latin American region. Research and write a report on how physical geography affects the way people live in this region.

Latin America in the News

Collect articles on Latin American culture from current magazines and newspapers, and create a bulletin board display that shows how people live in that region. Categories might include food, arts and entertainment, and sports.

Explorer's Dictionary

Create an illustrated dictionary of important terms translated from Latin American languages.

Resource Directory

 Technology

Social Studies Skills Tutor CD-ROM provides two levels of interactive instruction and practice in 20 core social studies skills.

Resource Pro® CD-ROM allows you to create customized lesson plans and print all resources directly from the CD-ROM.

Introducing

Guiding Questions

The seven Guiding Questions that appear on the reduced student edition pages to the right should act as a guide for learning about Latin America, and for encouraging students to relate what they learn to their own experience. The Guiding Questions that relate to the content of each chapter in the unit also appear on the Chapter Opener pages in this Teacher's Edition.

- You may wish to add your own Guiding Questions to the list in order to tailor them to your particular course. Or, as a group activity, ask your class to develop its own Guiding Questions.

ACTIVITY

Using the Guiding Questions

Ask a volunteer to read aloud the Guiding Questions to the class.

- Have students write the seven headings on a separate piece of paper or in their Explorer's Journal. Have them think about what information they would like to learn about Latin America, and write a question that relates to each heading.
- Have students share their questions with the rest of the class, and discuss any similarities.
- Create a master list of questions grouped under the seven headings. As you read about Latin America, try to answer the questions on the list.
- At the end of the unit, if any questions remain unanswered, have students research and find the answers to those questions.

Guiding Questions

What questions do I need to ask to understand Latin America?

Asking questions is a good way to learn. Think about what information you would want to know if you were visiting a new place, and what questions you might ask to find out. The questions on these pages can help guide your study of Latin America. You might want to try adding a few of your own!

GEOGRAPHY

Latin America is a region of variety, contrast, and extremes. Its rugged mountains, dense tropical rain forests, and rushing rivers are valuable natural resources but can make travel and communication difficult. Volcanoes along the Pacific Coast produce fertile soil, yet limited types of crops are produced. While vast arid regions remain sparsely populated, wet tropical areas produce sugar, bananas, and cotton. Today, Latin Americans are working together to develop their natural resources.

1 How has geography influenced the social and economic development of Latin America?

HISTORY

When explorers from Europe arrived in Latin America in the 1500s, Native American civilizations had already flourished there for hundreds of years. Groups such as the Mayas, Aztecs, and Incas had built great cities and established rich cultures. Rather than live peaceably with the indigenous people, the Europeans claimed their land and treasures as their own. Many Native Americans perished, while others were enslaved. The history of Latin America tells of conquests, political struggles, and a blending of cultures from around the world.

2 How has Latin America's history influenced modern day Latin American societies?

CULTURE

The different regions in which Latin Americans live together define Latin American culture. Many people in Latin America are mestizos of Spanish and Native American descent. Others maintain indigenous cultures or cultural traditions that come from Africa, Europe, or Asia. Their customs and religions are as diverse and varied as those found in other parts of the world, including the United States.

3 How are Latin American cultures alike? How are they different?

GOVERNMENT

Political rivalries and military government control have played a major role in Latin America's history. Often the Latin American people are caught in the middle and must struggle for their civil and human rights. Today, however, countries in Latin America are slowly moving toward democratic governments similar to that in the United States, with two or more political parties and peaceful transfers of power.

4 How have the governments of Latin America changed over time, and how are they organized today?

ECONOMICS

Traditionally, agriculture has been the basis for Latin America's economy. But not all Latin American countries have fertile farmland. Instead of farming, some countries have relied on one or two products to support their economies, which made them weak when these products were not in demand. Now, however, many Latin American countries are developing new resources to diversify and improve their sources of income and to boost their economies.

5 What economic activities support the people of Latin America?

CITIZENSHIP

Since first breaking ties with European rulers to gain independence, citizens of Latin America have worked to have a voice in their governments. Yet, difficult economic conditions, illiteracy, and ruthless political leaders have hindered their efforts. As Latin American countries move toward democracy and free elections, the people of Latin American are finding more opportunities to voice their opinions.

6 What opportunities do citizens of Latin America have to participate in the political process?

SCIENCE, TECHNOLOGY, AND SOCIETY

Ancient scientists developed the astrolabe, a tool used by Spanish explorers to help guide their ships. Had these sailors not reached the shores of Latin America, the history of that region would have been written differently. The development of science and technology in Latin America has been slow but is growing steadily. Latin American countries are becoming more industrialized as they build their economies for the global marketplace.

7 How have technology and science helped shape Latin America today?

Take It to the NET

For more information on Latin America, visit the World Explorer: People, Places, and Cultures companion Web site at **phschool.com.**

ACTIVITY

Using Primary and Secondary Sources

Daily Life Ask students to think about their own daily routines and how those routines are affected by the part of the world in which they live. Discuss what life might be like in some Latin American countries, and how it may be different from life in the United States.

- Have students work in pairs to create an outline that shows what activities they do on a typical day.
- Have each pair choose a country from Latin America and research that country to try to find information on the daily activities of the people who live there.
- Encourage students to use primary sources in their research, including letters, interviews, biographies, and Internet sources.

Verbal/Linguistic

ACTIVITY ATLAS

Lesson Objectives

1. Describe the relative location and size of Latin America.
2. Analyze how Portuguese and Spanish became the major languages of Latin America.
3. Name the major physical features of Latin America.
4. Explain the effects of hydroelectric dams on the environment.

Lesson Plan

1 Engage

Warm-Up Activity

Ask students to define the word *neighbor*. Ask them to list the qualities of a good neighbor.

Activating Prior Knowledge

Ask students why they think the United States wishes to have good relations with the countries of Latin America.

ACTIVITY ATLAS

Latin America

Being an explorer and a geographer means first checking some facts. Begin by exploring the maps of Latin America on the following pages.

Relative Location

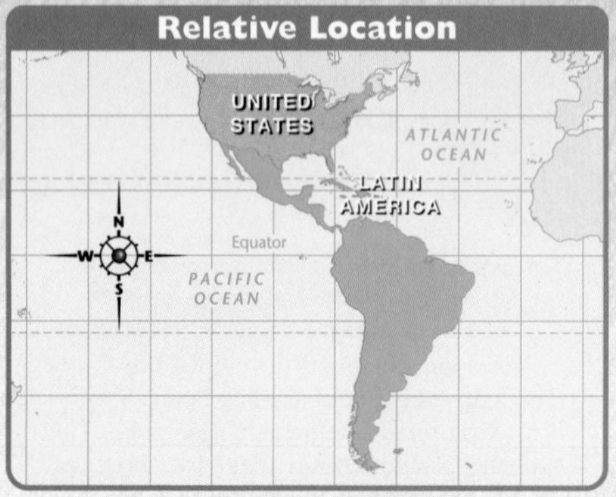

1. LOCATION

Locate Latin America and the United States Notice where the United States and Latin America are located relative to the Equator. On the other side of the Equator, seasons come at the opposite time of year. When it's summer here, it's winter there. In what season does your birthday fall? In what season would it fall if you lived below the Equator in Latin America?

Relative Size

2. REGIONS

Estimate Latin America's Size How long is Latin America's west coast? To get an idea, roughly measure the length of the west coast of the United States. Then, measure the length of the west coast of Latin America. Begin at the edge of the Pacific Ocean where Mexico borders California. Finish at the southern tip of South America. About how many times longer is Latin America's Pacific coast than that of the United States?

Take It to the NET

Items marked with this logo are periodically updated on the Internet. To get current information about the geography of Latin America, go to **phschool.com.**

Resource Directory

Teaching Resources

Activity Atlas in the Unit 3 Teaching Resources, pp. 95–102

Answers to...

LOCATION

1. Students should note that their birthdays would be in the opposite season of those in a Latin American country below the Equator.

REGIONS

2. The Pacific Coast of Latin America is almost four times as long as the Pacific Coast of the continental United States.

Latin America: Political

3. LOCATION

Compare the Size of Countries The map above shows the countries that make up Latin America. Which two countries are the biggest in land area?

4. MOVEMENT

Analyze the Migration of People by Their Languages Long ago, settlers from other countries took control of Latin America. Where were they from? Clues: Portuguese is the official language of Brazil, and Spanish is spoken in most other Latin American countries.

2 Explore

Direct students to read the six pages of the Activity Atlas. Then, ask students to work in pairs to study the maps and illustrations in the Activity Atlas and to think of one or two questions about the countries of Latin America. Have students write the questions and hold onto them. They can see if they can answer all the questions at the end of their study of Latin America.

3 Teach

Ask students to create a concept map of Latin America. Write Latin America on the chalkboard, draw a circle around it, and ask volunteers to add secondary circles with additional information.

4 Assess/Reteach

Concept maps should locate Latin America relative to the United States and to the Equator. They should identify Latin America as an enormous area, with rain forests, deserts, high mountains, and many rivers, some of which are harnessed for hydroelectric power. Maps should note that most people speak either Spanish or Portuguese.

Resource Directory

Teaching Resources

Outline Maps Latin America, pp. 6–7

Technology

Color Transparencies 55 Latin America: Physical-Political Map

Answers to...

LOCATION

3. Brazil and Argentina

MOVEMENT

4. People from Portugal and Spain took control of most of Latin America.

ACTIVITY ATLAS

Practice in the Themes of Geography

Place Ask students to use the Latin America physical map to find the Amazon Basin. What is the elevation of this place? (0–650 ft.)

Regions Ask students what continent is along the north border of Latin America. (North America)

Movement Ask students which of the following cities they could reach by boat: Manaus, Brazil; Buenos Aires, Argentina; La Paz, Bolivia; Santiago, Chile. (Manaus, Buenos Aires) Which map did they use? (Latin America political map)

Interactions Ask students where in Latin America they think most people live—along the coasts or in the interior? (along the coasts)

ACTIVITY ATLAS

Latin America: Physical

5. PLACE

Explore the Physical Features of Latin America Volcanoes created many of Latin America's dramatic features. Long ago, they formed the Andes Mountains and others became a chain of islands called the Lesser Antilles. Central America has volcanic mountains, too. Some are still active! Trace the Andes Mountains, the Lesser Antilles, and the mountains in Central America with your finger. Which of these areas has the highest altitude? Which is largest?

Resource Directory

Teaching Resources

Outline Maps Latin America, pp. 6–7

Technology

Color Transparencies 55 Latin America: Physical-Political Map

Answers to...

PLACE

5. The Andes Mountains have the highest altitudes and are the largest.

6. REGIONS

Locate Latin America's Physical Features Your favorite aunt has once again taken off on an adventure. This time, she is traveling around Latin America by ship. Occasionally, she takes time to write you a postcard. Each contains a clue about her location. Use the map below and the map on the opposite page to answer her questions.

A. *Our ship is on the south side of the island of Hispaniola. A dense rain forest covers the island's mountain slopes. Which way will we sail to reach the Panama Canal?*

B. *We are sailing south past one of the Earth's driest deserts. It is in a long, skinny South American country that extends north and south along the continent's west coast. Where are we?*

C. *From the Falkland Islands, we traveled north and sailed past desert scrub for days. Finally, we saw tropical rain forest along the coast. What two major cities will we come to next?*

Take It to the NET

Latin America: Natural Vegetation

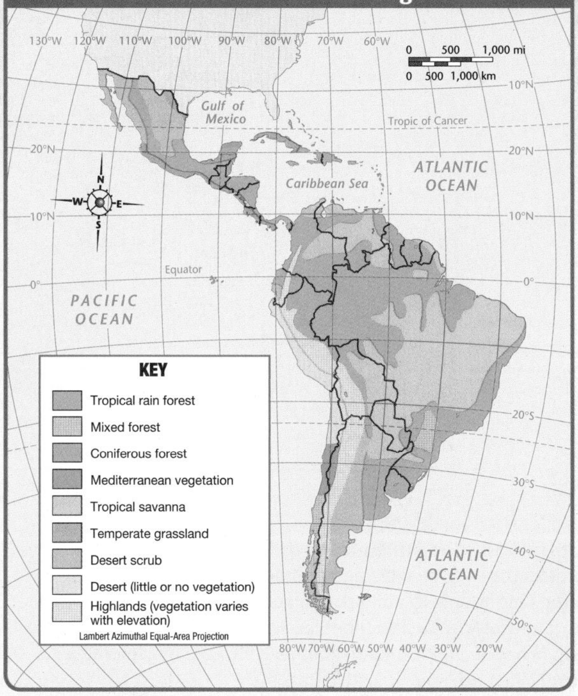

GEOGRAPHY

Elevation

Elevation is an important factor in everyday life in Latin America because elevation helps govern climate. Assuming that air is not moving, air is 3.5°F (1.9°C) cooler for every 1,000 feet (305 meters) one climbs. Thus, while the city of Guayaquil on the coast of Ecuador may be very hot and sticky, at the same time in the city of Quito it is almost cold. That is because Quito is located high in the Andes Mountains.

Resource Directory

Teaching Resources

Social Studies and Geography Skills, Reading a Natural Vegetation Map, p. 23

Answers to...

REGIONS

6. A. They will sail southwest.

B. Your aunt is passing Chile.

C. Buenos Aires and Montevideo

ACTIVITY

Interdisciplinary Connections

Mathematics Ask students to use an atlas or an almanac to find the heights of the six highest mountains in South America (Aconcagua, Argentina, 22,831 ft. [6,959 m]; Ojos del Salado, Argentina-Chile, 22,572 ft. [6,880 m]; Bonete, Argentina, 22,546 ft. [6,872 m]; Tupungato, Argentina-Chile, 22,310 ft. [6,800 m]; Pissis, Argentina, 22,242 ft. [6,779 m]; Mercedario, Argentina, 22,211 ft. [6,769 m]). Ask students to create a bar graph comparing the heights of these mountains to the height of Mt. McKinley, the highest peak in the United States at 20,320 ft. (6,194 m).

Logical/Mathematical

Answers to...

HUMAN-ENVIRONMENT INTERACTION

7. Some advantages of dams include power, recreation, and jobs. Disadvantages include loss of habitat for plants and animals, loss of homes, and changes in ecosystems.

ACTIVITY ATLAS

Latin America: Major Hydroelectric Plants

7. HUMAN-ENVIRONMENT INTERACTION

Examine Ways People Have Modified Latin America's Physical Environment Hydroelectricity is electric power that is made by harnessing the power of water. One way is to build a dam across a river. The dam creates a large lake, lake water runs into the river, and turns a wheel, which creates electricity. What do you think are some advantages of building a dam across a river? What are some disadvantages?

Latin America's Longest and Highest ...

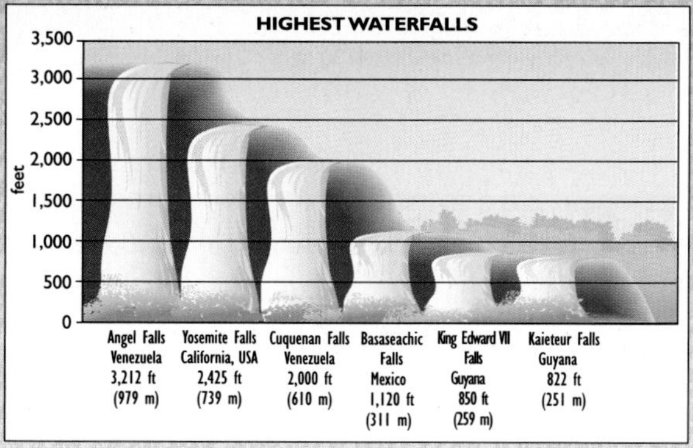

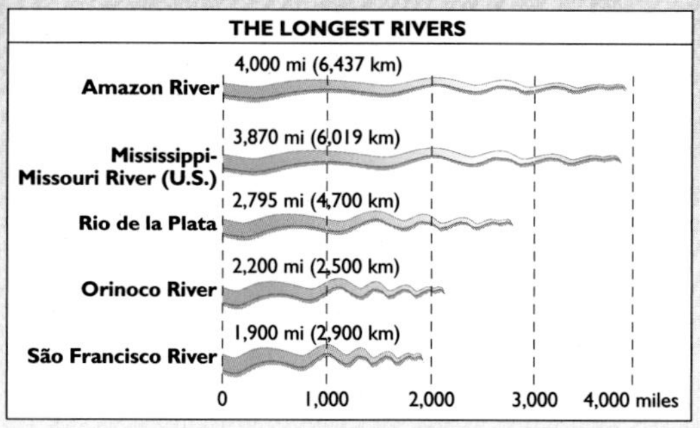

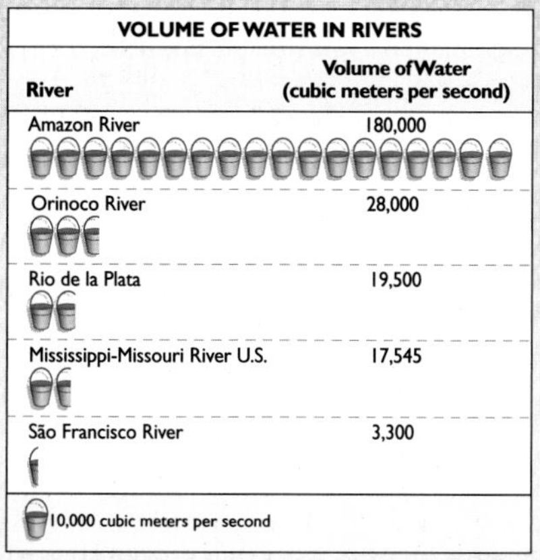

Take It to the NET

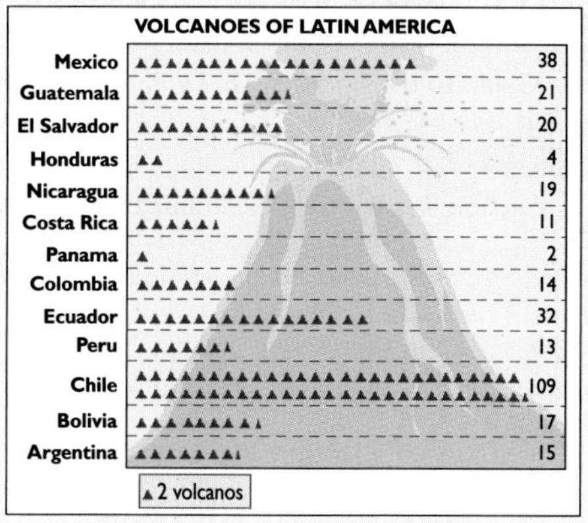

8. PLACE

Compare Physical Features Latin America's Angel Falls waterfall is the highest in the world. The Amazon River is the second longest river in the world and carries more water than any other...by far! Latin America is also one of the most active volcanic regions in the world. Study these charts and diagrams. What country would you visit to see the world's highest waterfall? How much higher is this waterfall than the second highest in Latin America? Which is the second longest river in Latin America? How many times more water does the Amazon carry than does the Mississippi? Which Latin American country has the most volcanoes? How many?

ACTIVITY

Discovery Learning

What Country Am I? Ask students to write three or four "Who Am I?" questions about countries in Latin America. For example, *My capital is Lima. What country am I?* (Peru) Put a large map of Latin America on display and have students work in pairs. One member of a pair reads a question to an opposing pair. The designated "runner" in that pair goes to the map and points out the correct country. Continue until each pair has asked one question and answered one question.

Visual/Spatial

Resource Directory

Teaching Resources

Social Studies and Geography Skills, Reading a Bar Graph, p. 51; Reading a Diagram, p. 54

Answers to...

PLACE

8. Angel Falls is in Venezuela. It is 1,212 ft (369 m) higher than Cuquenan Falls. The Rio de la Plata is the second longest river. The Amazon carries more than ten times as much water as the Mississippi-Missouri. Chile has the most volcanoes: 109.

Chapter 9 Planning Guide

Resource Manager

	CORE INSTRUCTION	READING/SKILLS
Chapter-Level Resources	**Teaching Resources** Program Overview Pacing Charts **Technology** Resource Pro® CD-ROM Companion Web site, phschool.com • eTeach	**Technology** Social Studies Skills Tutor CD-ROM Student Edition on Audio CD, Ch. 9
1 Physical Features 1. Identify Latin America's main geographic regions. 2. Describe how the physical features of Latin America affect people's lives.	**Teaching Resources** **Unit 3** Classroom Manager, p. 2 Guided Reading and Review, p. 3	**Teaching Resources** Guide to the Essentials, p. 36 **Technology** Section Reading Support Transparencies
2 Humans and the Physical Environment 1. Describe the climate and vegetation of Latin America. 2. Explain ways in which climate and vegetation affect how and where the people of Latin America live.	**Teaching Resources** **Unit 3** Classroom Manager, p. 5 Guided Reading and Review, p. 6	**Teaching Resources** Guide to the Essentials, p. 37 **Technology** Section Reading Support Transparencies
3 Geographic Factors and Natural Resources 1. Describe Latin America's important natural resources. 2. Explain why it is important for Latin American countries to have more than one source of income.	**Teaching Resources** **Unit 3** Classroom Manager, p. 8 Guided Reading and Review, p. 9 Chapter Summary, p. 11 Vocabulary, p. 12 Reteaching, p. 13	**Teaching Resources** **Unit 3** Critical Thinking, p. 15 Guide to the Essentials, p. 38 **Technology** Section Reading Support Transparencies

ENRICHMENT / PRE-AP

Teaching Resources
Primary Sources and Literature Readings

Other Print Resources
DK Atlas

Technology
World Video Explorer: Opener: Journey Over Latin America and Geography: The Gauchos of Argentina
Companion Web site, phschool.com

Teaching Resources
Outline Maps, pp. 6–7

Technology
Color Transparencies 55

Teaching Resources
Unit 3
Enrichment, p. 14
Cooperative Learning Activity, pp. 103–105

ASSESSMENT

Prentice Hall Assessment System

Core Assessment
Chapter Tests with ExamView® Test Bank, Ch. 9
ExamView® Test Bank CD-ROM, Ch. 9

Standardized Test Preparation
Diagnose and Prescribe
Diagnostic Tests for Middle Grades Social Studies Skills
Review and Reteach
Review Book for World Studies
Practice and Assess
Test-taking Strategies with Transparencies for Middle Grades Test Prep Book
Test-taking Strategies Posters

Teaching Resources
Unit 3
Section Quizzes, pp. 4, 7, and 10
Chapter Tests, pp. 130–135

Technology
Companion Web site, phschool.com
Ch. 9 Self-Test

World Video Explorer
Each region of the world is explored through regional flyovers and investigative field trips. Case study segments give students an in-depth view of the history, economy, government, and culture of a key place in each region. Case studies include Nigeria, Mexico, China, British Columbia, and the Czech Republic.

In Your Classroom

CUSTOMIZE FOR INDIVIDUAL NEEDS

Gifted and Talented

Teacher's Edition
- Making a Puzzle Map, p. 171

Teaching Resources
- Enrichment, p. 14
- Primary Sources and Literature Readings

Honors/Pre-AP

Teacher's Edition
- Asia's Mighty Himalaya Mountains, p. 171

Teaching Resources
- Critical Thinking, p. 15
- Primary Sources and Literature Readings

ESL

Teacher's Edition
- Making a Puzzle Map, p. 171

Teaching Resources
- Guided Reading and Review, pp. 3, 6, and 9
- Vocabulary, p. 12
- Reteaching, p. 13
- Guide to the Essentials, pp. 36–38

Technology
- Social Studies Skills Tutor CD-ROM
- Section Reading Support Transparencies

Less Proficient Readers

Teacher's Edition
- Making a Puzzle Map, p. 171

Teaching Resources
- Guided Reading and Review, pp. 3, 6, and 9
- Vocabulary, p. 12
- Reteaching, p. 13
- Guide to the Essentials, pp. 36–38

Technology
- Social Studies Skills Tutor CD-ROM
- Section Reading Support Transparencies

Less Proficient Writers

Teacher's Edition
- Asia's Mighty Himalaya Mountains, p. 171

Teaching Resources
- Guided Reading and Review, pp. 3, 6, and 9
- Vocabulary, p. 12
- Guide to the Essentials, pp. 36–38

Technology
- Social Studies Skills Tutor CD-ROM
- Section Reading Support Transparencies

DORLING KINDERSLEY

At the end of each unit, you will find information adapted from Dorling Kindersley's *Illustrated Children's Encyclopedia* that connects to the region being studied and to one of the seven content strands. In addition, your resources include Dorling Kindersley's *Atlas*, which contains valuable information about countries from around the world.

TEACHER'S EDITION INDEX

CHAPTER 9 PACING SUGGESTIONS

For 90-minute Blocks

See suggestions in the Teaching Resources Pacing Charts for Chapter 9. Use Color Transparencies 55.

Running Out of Time?

See the Guide to the Essentials, pp. 36–38.

INTERDISCIPLINARY LINKS

Middle Grades Math: Tools for Success

Course 1, Lesson 10-7, **Graphing on the Coordinate Plane**

Course 2, Lesson 3-4, **Subtracting Integers**

Science Explorer

From Bacteria to Plants, Lesson 1-1, **What is Life?**

Cells and Heredity, Lesson 1-1, **Discovering Cells**

BIBLIOGRAPHY

For the Teacher

DK Essential World Atlas. Dorling Kindersley, 2001.

National Geographic Picture Atlas of Our World. National Geographic, 1993.

South America. National Geographic 51441, 1991. Video

For the Student

Easy

Eye Wonder Rain Forest. Dorling Kindersley, 2001.

Average

Blue, Rose, and Corinne Naden. *Andes Mountains.* Raintree, 1995.

Eyewitness Jungle. Dorling Kindersley, 2001.

Challenging

Bernhard, Brendan. *Pizarro, Orellana, and the Exploration of the Amazon.* Chelsea, 1991.

Literature Connection

Brill, Marlene Targ. *Journey for Peace: The Story of Rigoberta Menchu.* Dutton, 1996.

Cherry, Lynne. *The Great Kapok Tree: A Tale of the Amazon Rain Forest.* Harcourt, 1990.

Take It to the NET

The World Explorer companion Web site, found on **phschool.com**, offers activities for exploring geographical, historical, and cultural resources on the Internet. It also provides on-line links for key content and all Section and Chapter Assessment activities.

The **Teacher site** also provides teachers with regional data and ideas for student research and activities.

Students can use the **Student site** to find chapter-by-chapter Internet resource links and to access Self-Tests.

CHAPTER 9

Connecting to the
Guiding Questions

In this chapter, students will read about the physical geography of Latin America. Content in this chapter corresponds to the following Guiding Questions outlined in the beginning of the unit.

- How has geography influenced the social and economic development of Latin America?
- How have technology and science shaped Latin America?

Using the Picture Activities

Lead a class discussion of the picture, focusing on significant details such as the snow on the mountain peaks and the lack of snow at the lower elevations.

- Encourage students to list as many adjectives as they can to describe the landscape shown in the picture and the landscape of their own region, including words that describe the colors, topography, weather, and natural vegetation found in both places.
- Students should recognize that the climate is usually different at higher elevations—the temperatures are often colder and weather may be more severe. Encourage students to share their own experiences with mountain climbing, where they may have needed to wear different, more protective clothing at the higher elevations.

Heterogeneous Groups

The following activity is suitable for heterogeneous groups.

Geography

Making a Puzzle Map, p. 171

eTeach

Be sure to check out this month's discussion with a Master Teacher. Go to **phschool.com**.

CHAPTER 9

LATIN AMERICA: Physical Geography

Looking at the Land

Using Pictures

These rugged mountains are the Andes (AN deez). They stretch along the entire length of South America.

Comparing Geographic Regions

Think about where you live. Do you live in an area with mountains, or at a lower elevation? What do you think it would be like to live in or near the Andes? Brainstorm a list of adjectives that describe the landscape in this picture, then brainstorm another list that describes the landscape where you live. Write the two lists side by side so that you can compare them. How are the two different? How are they similar?

Understanding Climate

Have you ever been mountain climbing? How did the temperature change as you climbed higher? Based on your experience, do you think the climate is the same at the top of the Andes as at the bottom? Where would it be colder? Where would it be warmer? Would these changes affect the vegetation? The wild life? Where people live? How they live?

Resource Directory

Teaching Resources

Primary Sources and Literature Readings extend content with a selection related to the concepts in this chapter.

Other Print Resources

DK Atlas

Technology

Opener: Journey Over Latin America, from the World Video Explorer, introduces students to the varied landforms of the region.

Geography: The Gauchos of Argentina, from the World Video Explorer, enhances students' understanding of how the physical geography of the Pampas of Argentina contributes to the region's economy and way of life.

Student Edition on Audio CD, Ch. 9

SECTION 1

Physical Features

BEFORE YOU READ

READING FOCUS

1. What are some major landforms and regions in Latin America?
2. What are some major rivers in Latin America, and how do they affect the lives of the people living in the region?

KEY TERMS

plateau
isthmus
coral
tributary

KEY PLACES

Mexico
Central America
Caribbean
South America

NOTE TAKING

Copy the chart below. As you read the section, fill in the chart with information about Latin America's geographic features, including its landforms and bodies of water.

Physical Features	Important Landforms	Important Bodies of Water	Other Water Resources
The Caribbean			
Mexico and Central America			
South America			

MAIN IDEA

Latin America's geographic features make it a region of variety and contrast.

Setting the Scene

Latin America is located in the Western Hemisphere south of the United States. Latin America includes all the nations from Mexico to the tip of the continent of South America. It also includes the islands that dot the Caribbean (ka ruh BEE un) Sea. Geographic features divide Latin America into three smaller regions. They are (1) Mexico and Central America, (2) the Caribbean, and (3) South America.

The Amazon River's Many Uses

GEOGRAPHY The people who live near the Amazon River in Brazil rely on it for transportation, fish, and water. Families also wash their laundry right at the river bank. **Critical Thinking** What are some of the ways that your life is affected by the physical features of the region where you live? Make a list.

Resource Directory

Teaching Resources

Classroom Manager in the Unit 3 Teaching Resources, p. 2

Guided Reading and Review in the Unit 3 Teaching Resources, p. 3

Guide to the Essentials, p. 36

Technology

Section Reading Support Transparencies

SECTION 1

Lesson Objectives

1. Identify Latin America's main geographic regions.
2. Describe how the physical features of Latin America affect people's lives.

Lesson Plan

1 Engage

Warm-Up Activity

Ask students to describe the physical features of the area in which they live. Prompt students by asking whether the land is flat or hilly. Are there lakes or wooded areas? Are there open areas of land, such as parks, or do buildings and roads take up nearly all the space? List features on the chalkboard. Then, discuss with students how these features affect their lives and the lives of other people living in the area.

Activating Prior Knowledge

Point out that every place in the world has unique features. In addition, explain that people adjust to the physical features around them in various ways. For example, people living near a river may build a bridge across it; people living near a lake may use boats to travel from one place to another. Ask for other examples of how people interact with their surroundings.

Answers to...

CRITICAL THINKING

Student responses might include mention of how life is affected by physical features such as rivers, lakes, or oceans, or proximity to desert, mountains, or farmland.

Lesson Plan continued

2 Explore

Direct students to read the section. Have them locate on a world map and then briefly describe the three regions that make up Latin America: the Caribbean, Mexico and Central America, and South America. Ask how mountains and rivers in Latin America affect travel in the area.

3 Teach

Have students draw three boxes. Label the boxes *The Caribbean*, *Mexico and Central America*, and *South America*. Tell students to list one or more physical features of the area in each box. Then, ask them to describe ways in which the feature or features affect people's lives. Use students' work as the basis for a discussion of Latin America's regions and features. This activity should take about 20 minutes.

Questions for Discussion

GEOGRAPHY **What landforms influence where most of Mexico's people live?**

Although Mexico has many mountainous areas, most Mexicans live on the Central Plateau between the two major mountain ranges because it takes up half of the area of Mexico and is mostly level land, making farming and ranching easier.

GEOGRAPHY **Why have farmers moved to the Andes region, despite the difficulty they pose to transportation to and from the region?**

The soil in the Andes is very good for farming.

Answers to...

CRITICAL THINKING

North America and South America; the Caribbean and the Pacific Ocean

AS YOU READ

Students may say that like the United States, Latin America probably has mountains, plains, deserts, rivers, and so forth.

The Regions of Latin America

GEOGRAPHY Mexico and Central America are also called Middle America because they are located between two continents. **Critical Thinking** Which two continents does Middle America lie between? What bodies of water make up the coastline of Middle America?

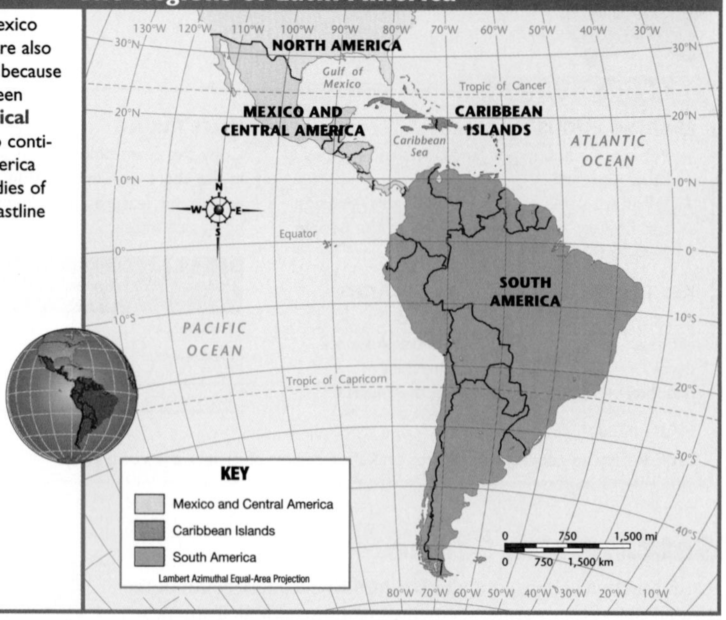

About 500 years ago, Europeans sailed to Latin America and brought their own languages and ways of life with them. Since most came from Spain and Portugal, almost all Latin Americans today speak Spanish or Portuguese. These languages have their roots in the ancient language of Latin and as a result, the region is known as Latin America.

AS YOU READ

Monitor Your Reading How do you think the physical features of Latin America might be like those of the United States?

Latin America's Major Landforms and Regions

Imagine mountains that pierce the clouds and grassy plains that never seem to end. Picture wet rain forests, sunbaked deserts, and broad rivers. This is Latin America, a region of variety and contrast.

Mexico and Central America **Mexico** and **Central America** stretch 2,500 miles (4,023 km) from the U.S. border to South America. It is a distance that is almost equal to the width of the mainland United States. Mountains dominate this region and are a part of a huge system of mountain ranges that extends from Canada through the United States all the way to the tip of South America.

Between the mountains in Mexico lies Mexico's Central Plateau. A **plateau** (pla TOH) is a large raised area of mostly level land. Mexico's

Resource Directory

Teaching Resources

Outline Maps, Latin America, pp. 6–7

Technology

Color Transparencies 55 Latin America: Physical-Political Map

Central Plateau makes up more than half of the country's area and most of Mexico's people live here. However, the surrounding mountains make it hard for people to travel to and from the Central Plateau.

Central America, located south of Mexico, is an isthmus. An **isthmus** is a narrow strip of land that has water on both sides and joins two larger bodies of land. Find Central America on the map in the Activity Atlas on page 163. What two large bodies of land does the isthmus of Central America connect? As in Mexico, narrow plains run along Central America's coasts. Between these coastal plains are rugged, steep mountains. More than a dozen of these mountains are active volcanoes. Volcanic ash has made the soil good for farming.

The Caribbean Imagine islands made of skeletons, or others that are the tips of underwater mountains. The **Caribbean** is made up of these two types of islands. The smaller islands were formed from the skeletons of tiny sea animals. Over hundreds of years, the skeletons formed a rocklike substance called **coral.**

The larger islands of the Caribbean are the tops of huge underwater mountains. Most people on the islands make a living farming.

South America **South America** contains many types of landforms, which you can see on the map in the Activity Atlas on page 164. Perhaps the most impressive landform is the Andes Mountains which run some 4,500 miles (7,250 km) along the western coast of South America. In some places, the Andes rise to heights of more than 20,000 feet (6,100 m).

The Andes are steep and difficult to cross. But their rich soil has drawn farmers to the region. East of the Andes are rolling highlands. These highlands spread across parts of Brazil, Venezuela (ven uh ZWAY luh), Guyana (gy AN uh), and other South American countries. Farther south are the Pampas (PAHM puz), a large plains area that stretches through Argentina (ar jun TEE nuh) and Uruguay (YOOR uh gway).

Herding Cattle on the Pampas
GEOGRAPHY
Grasslands known as the Pampas can also be found in Brazil. These grasslands are perfect for raising cattle. **Critical Thinking** How are these grasslands similar to the Great Plains in the United States?

171

Answers to...

CRITICAL THINKING

The Great Plains area is also suitable for raising livestock.

4 Assess/Reteach

See answers to the Section 1 Assessment. You may also use the students' completed boxes of physical features for assessment purposes.

Acceptable responses include three factually correct entries in each box.

Commendable responses include statements of cause and effect, relating geography and people's lives.

Outstanding responses show an understanding of how the effect of one cause can be the cause of other effects.

GEOGRAPHY

Asia's Mighty Himalaya Mountains

Only the Himalaya Mountains, a mountain system in Asia, stand taller than the Andes. The Himalaya Mountains make up the tallest range in the world. They extend along the India-Tibet border and through Pakistan, Nepal, China, and Bhutan. Have students find the Himalaya Mountains on a relief map. The tallest peak of this range is the well known—and often climbed—Mount Everest. At 29,028 feet (8,848 m) above sea level, Everest stands more than a mile higher than the tallest peak in the Andes.

ACTIVITY

Geography

Making a Puzzle Map Students can work in groups of four to create a puzzle map of one or more regions of Latin America. Remind students to include and label important places and physical features mentioned in the text.

One student can be responsible for researching the information, another for drawing the map on construction paper. You may wish to refer students to the physical map of Latin America in the Activity Atlas. Students may trace this map. A third student can mount the map onto cardboard, and the fourth can cut the map into jigsaw pieces. Have groups exchange puzzles and try to reassemble one another's puzzles.

Bodily/Kinesthetic

SECTION I ASSESSMENT

AFTER YOU READ

1. (a) country south of the United States (b) isthmus joining Mexico and South America (c) region that includes small islands made of coral and larger islands that are the tops of huge underwater mountains (d) continent that contains many types of landforms, including the Andes
2. (a) a large, raised area of mostly level land (b) narrow strip of land that has water on both sides and joins two larger bodies of land (c) rock-like substance formed of skeletons of tiny sea animals (d) river or stream that flows into a larger river
3. Student descriptions should mention that the Caribbean region is made up of islands; Mexico and Central America is a region of mountains and plateaus; South America is a region of mountains, plains, and forests.
4. Rivers help people transport goods. The fish that swim in the river waters provide food. Rushing water provides power for electricity.
5. Answers will vary. Responses should reflect the variety and contrast of the three Latin American regions. Within South America there are mountains, plains, and forests. Between regions there are contrasts in the land ranging from mountains, to islands, to plains, to plateaus.
6. Answers will vary. Possible differences: the Caribbean is the only region made up of islands; South America is a broad landmass, while Mexico and Central America are more narrow.
7. Answers will vary. Students should support their answers with reasons.

The plains areas, the eastern highlands, and the Andes frame the Amazon River Basin. The Amazon River Basin contains the largest tropical rain forest in the world. This dense forest covers more than a third of the continent.

The Rivers of Latin America

Latin America's rivers and lakes are some of the longest and largest bodies of water in the world. Rivers serve as transportation corridors in places where it is hard to build roads. The fish that swim the waters of Latin America provide food, and rushing water from large rivers provides power for electricity.

Amazon: The Ocean River Latin America's Amazon (AM uh zahn) River is the second-longest river in the world, flowing 4,000 miles (6,437 km) from Peru across Brazil into the Atlantic Ocean. Only the Nile River in Africa is longer.

The Amazon River also carries more water than any other river in the world. In fact, it contains about 20 percent of all the fresh river water on the Earth. The Amazon River gathers power from the more than 1,000 **tributaries** (TRIB yoo tehr eez) that spill into it. Tributaries are the rivers and streams that flow into a larger river. With its tributaries, the Amazon drains an area of more than two million square miles

Other Rivers and Lakes Latin America has many other bodies of water besides the Amazon. The Paraná (pah rah NAH), Paraguay, and Uruguay rivers form the Río de la Plata system. The Río de la Plata separates Argentina and Uruguay. Lake Titicaca is the highest lake in the world on which ships can travel. It lies high in the Andes Mountains on the border between Peru and Bolivia.

SECTION I ASSESSMENT

AFTER YOU READ

RECALL

1. Identify: (a) Mexico, (b) Central America, (c) Caribbean, (d) South America
2. Define: (a) plateau, (b) isthmus, (c) coral, (d) tributary

COMPREHENSION

3. Describe the major landforms of the three regions that make up Latin America.
4. Describe how Latin America's rivers affect the lives of people in the region.

CRITICAL THINKING AND WRITING

5. **Exploring the Main Idea** Review the Main Idea statement at the beginning of this section. Then, list two ways the physical features of Latin America show that it is a region of variety and contrast.
6. **Making Comparisons** Describe two ways in which the three regions of Latin America are different.

ACTIVITY

7. **Expressing a Point of View** Suppose that your family was planning to move to Latin America. If you had your choice, in which of the three regions of Latin America would you live? Explain why.

172 UNIT 3 LATIN AMERICA

Resource Directory

Teaching Resources

Section Quiz in the Unit 3 Teaching Resources, p. 4

SECTION 2 Humans and the Physical Environment

BEFORE YOU READ

READING FOCUS

1. What is the climate of Latin America like?
2. What is the natural vegetation of Latin America like, and how is it affected by climate?

KEY TERMS

elevation

KEY PLACES

Andes
Atacama Desert
Patagonia
Amazonian rain forest

NOTE TAKING

Copy the concept web below. As you read the section, fill in and add more circles with information about Latin America's climate and vegetation.

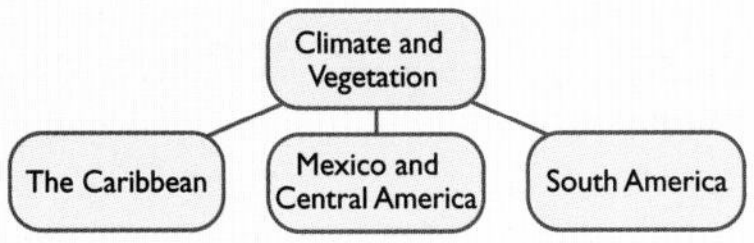

MAIN IDEA

Latin America's physical environment, such as its climate and vegetation, varies greatly even within each country and affects how the people there live.

Setting the Scene

What's the climate like where you live? Is it hot? Cold? Rainy? Dry? If you lived in Latin America, the climate might be any of these. Climate in Latin America can vary greatly even within the same country.

In parts of the **Andes,** below-zero temperatures would set your teeth chattering. Travel down to the Amazon Basin, and you may be sweating in 90°F (32°C) heat. If you prefer dry weather, visit the **Atacama** (ah tah KAH mah) **Desert** in Chile or the Sonoran Desert in Mexico. These are two of the driest places on the Earth.

Climate: Hot, Cold, and Mild

The climate of the Caribbean is usually sunny and warm. From June to November, however, the region is often hit with fierce hurricanes. Winds from hurricanes can blow at over 180 miles per hour (300 km/hr) causing waves nearly 20 feet (6 m) high to smash into the coast. The storms tear roofs off houses, shatter windows, and yank huge trees from the ground.

Hurricanes are a part of life for people living in the Caribbean. But climate affects the people of Latin America in other ways,

GEOGRAPHY Mexico's Sonoran Desert shows that even a hot, dry desert can be full of plant life. **Critical Thinking** What kinds of plants might you find growing in a desert? Why?

Resource Directory

Teaching Resources

Classroom Manager in the Unit 3 Teaching Resources, p. 5

Guided Reading and Review in the Unit 3 Teaching Resources, p. 6

Guide to the Essentials, p. 37

Technology

Section Reading Support Transparencies

SECTION 2

Lesson Objectives

1. Describe the climate and vegetation of Latin America.
2. Explain ways in which climate and vegetation affect how and where the people of Latin America live.

Lesson Plan

1 Engage

Warm-Up Activity

Ask students how climate affects their daily life. For example, how do seasonal weather changes affect the clothing they wear, the activities they do, and the amount of time they spend outdoors? Ask how their lives might be different if they lived in a colder or warmer climate.

Activating Prior Knowledge

Point out that climate affects vegetation as well as people. For example, plants need water and suitable temperatures and soil to grow. Ask students for examples of places that are too dry or too cold for most plant life to survive.

2 Explore

Direct students to read the section. Have them describe how Latin American climate and vegetation vary. Have students compare the climates in Latin America with the climate in their own city or town. Is there as much climate variation in their region? Why or why not?

Answers to...

CRITICAL THINKING

Students' responses should reflect an understanding that the kinds of plants found in the desert would need to be adaptable to the environment and survive with little water and with a hot, sunny climate.

Lesson Plan continued

3 Teach

Using the climate regions map, discuss Latin America's climate regions. Have students describe the different climates. Next use the vegetation map to discuss Latin America's vegetation. Help students recognize links between climate and vegetation. Then, have students write a description that tells how climate and vegetation affect Latin Americans' lives and livelihood. Total discussion time should be about 20 minutes.

Question for Discussion

GEOGRAPHY **How do farms in Patagonia differ from farms in the north of Argentina?**

Farmers in Patagonia raise sheep because the climate is cold and arid; farmers in the north are able to raise more crops because the climate is subtropical, which produces hot, wet summers and cool winters.

4 Assess/Reteach

See answers to the Section 2 Assessment. You may also use students' classroom discussion to gauge their understanding.

Acceptable responses include two factually correct descriptions of climate and vegetation, their relationship, and their effects on people's lives and livelihood.

Commendable responses include three factually correct descriptions of climate and vegetation, their relationship, and their effects on people's lives and livelihood.

Outstanding responses compare and contrast climate, vegetation, and livelihood in at least three areas of Latin America.

Answers to...

CHART STUDY

14,000 feet; potatoes, wheat, barley, apples

AS YOU READ

Students should understand that as they climb higher, they will see less vegetation along the way.

Vertical Climate Zones

GEOGRAPHY If you climb high enough on a mountain, you will reach a place where the temperature never warms up. This chart shows how the temperature near the equator can vary with elevation. **Chart Study** Based on this chart, above what elevation will snow not melt? What grows beneath the tree line?

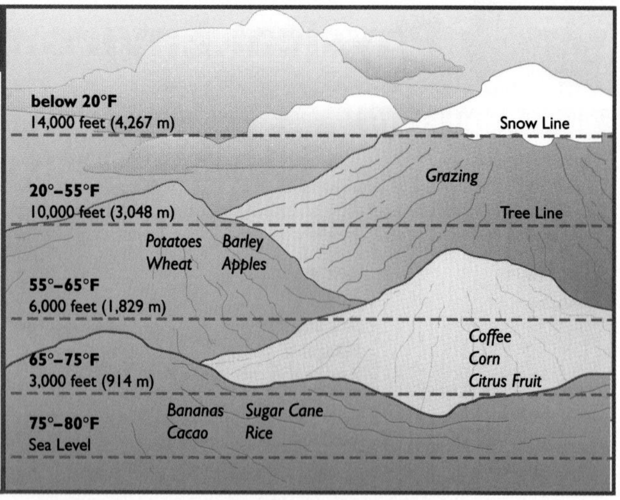

too. For example, people who live in the mountains need warm clothing and shelter to protect them against cool temperatures. The higher up the mountains you go, the cooler it gets.

Climate Regions of Latin America Many parts of Latin America have a tropical wet climate. A tropical wet climate means hot, humid, rainy weather all year round. Rain forests thrive in this type of climate.

Other parts of Latin America have a tropical wet and dry climate. These areas are equally hot, but the rainy season does not last all year long. Parts of Mexico and Brazil and most of the Caribbean have a tropical wet and dry climate.

Much of Argentina, Uruguay, and Paraguay has a humid subtropical climate, similar to that of parts of the southern United States. People living in this climate usually have hot, wet summers and cool winters. Farmers in these areas can raise such crops as wheat and apples, which need a cold season to grow well. Farther south, the climate turns arid. Farmers raise sheep on the plains of this colder, drier area, called **Patagonia** (pat uh GOH nee uh).

AS YOU READ
Summarize Suppose that you were climbing a mountain. How would the vegetation you see change as you climb higher?

What Factors Affect Climate? **Elevation,** the height of land above sea level, is a key factor in the climate of mountainous Latin America. The higher the elevation, the colder the temperature. Suppose it is a warm 80°F (27°C) at sea level. Continue up to 6,000 feet (1,829 m), and the temperature may now be only about 60°F (16°C). Above 10,000 feet (3,048 m), the temperature may remain below freezing—too cold for people to live permanently.

SKILLS MINI LESSON

Organizing Information

To **introduce** the skill, suggest that students organize information by summarizing what they read. Point out that headings, pictures, maps, and charts can help them focus on important ideas and facts. To **practice** the skill, have students work in pairs to develop written summaries of Section 2. Indicate to students that (1) the summaries should incorporate the headings—rewritten using the students' own words—to present the most important ideas of each part of the text, and that (2) students should support these ideas with facts, details, and examples. Encourage students to **apply** the skill of organizing information as they read the next section.

Other factors also affect Latin America's climate. Regions close to the Equator are generally warmer than those farther away.

Wind patterns affect the climate too. Winds move colder, drier air from the North and South Poles toward the Equator. They also move warmer, moister air from the Equator toward the Poles. In the Caribbean, sea breezes blowing toward shore help keep tempertures moderate. More rain falls on the sides of islands facing the wind than on sides facing away.

Tree Dwellers

GEOGRAPHY Tree sloths live in the rain forest trees of South America. They rarely descend from the trees. **Critical Thinking** Look carefully at the photograph. How do you think the sloth is well adapted to living in the trees?

Natural Vegetation and Climate

Imagine a forest so dense and lush that almost no sunlight reaches the ground. Broad, green leaves, tangled vines, and thousands of species of trees and plants surround you. The air is hot and heavy with moisture. Welcome to the **Amazonian rain forest.**

Now, suppose you have traveled to the coast of northern Chile. You're in the Atacama Desert. There is very little moisture to this barren land, and there is little sign of life. The Andes shield this dry region from rain. Because winds move from east to west in this region, rain falls only on the eastern slope of the Andes at this latitude. This leaves the western side dry.

Elevation also affects vegetation. To grow at higher elevations, plants must be able to withstand cooler temperatures, chill winds, and irregular rainfall.

SECTION 2 ASSESSMENT

AFTER YOU READ

RECALL

1. Identify: (a) Andes, (b) Atacama Desert, (c) Patagonia, (d) Amazonian rain forest
2. Define: (a) elevation

COMPREHENSION

3. How does climate affect life in Latin America?
4. How does climate affect the natural vegetation of Latin America?

CRITICAL THINKING AND WRITING

5. **Exploring the Main Idea** Review the Main Idea statement at the beginning of this section. Then, list three examples that support the statement: "The physical environment of Latin America varies greatly."
6. **Drawing Conclusions** In what ways would the life of a family living on a Caribbean island be different from a family living high in the Andes?

ACTIVITY

7. **Expressing an Opinion** Latin America has been called a land of extremes. Do you agree or disagree? Write a paragraph or more telling why. Support your opinion with examples.

Resource Directory

Teaching Resources

Section Quiz in the Unit 3 Teaching Resources, p. 7

SECTION 2 ASSESSMENT

AFTER YOU READ

1. (a) mountain system extending along the western coast of South America (b) desert in Chile (c) plains region in southern South America (d) hot, humid area with dense vegetation
2. (a) the height of land above sea level.
3. Accept reasonable responses. Possibilities may include the following: People living in cool mountain areas need warm clothes and shelter; climate and vegetation help determine whether an area is suitable for farming or ranching. Climate helps determine what types of crops can be raised.
4. Answers may vary. Sample answers: Tropical wet climates have tropical rain forest vegetation. Arid climates tend to have desert or desert scrub vegetation.
5. Answers will vary. Possibilities may include: Climates can be extreme from being very cool and dry, such as in the Andes or mountains of Mexico and Central America, to very warm and wet in the Amazonian rain forest; climates can vary within one region; the climate in the Caribbean is tropical but can be either wet or dry; the vegetation varies as well from the desert plants in the Atacama Desert to the tropical plants of the Amazonian rain forest.
6. Answers will vary. Responses should focus on how location, climate, and vegetation would affect the way families in two different locations live.
7. Answers will vary, but most students will agree. Students may contrast the barren desert with the lush rain forest, or the warm and steamy coastal lowlands with the cold and dry mountains. Be sure students use specific examples.

Answers to...

CRITICAL THINKING

Students may say the long claws on the sloth's paws help it to live in trees.

SECTION 3

Lesson Objectives

1. Describe Latin America's important natural resources.
2. Explain why it is important for Latin American countries to have more than one source of income.

Lesson Plan

1 Engage

Warm-Up Activity

Ask students what keeps their homes warm in the winter or heats water for home use. Elicit or explain that homes and water are heated using oil, natural gas, wood, or electricity. Point out that substances such as oil, gas, wood, and coal are natural resources. Ask why natural resources are valuable to a nation. Guide students in understanding that a nation can both use the resources and sell them.

Activating Prior Knowledge

Water and coal are natural resources. People drink water; we use it to cook, bathe, raise crops, and travel. Coal can be burned as fuel. Tell students that oil is a particularly valuable resource. Elicit or explain the information that oil products include gasoline and fuel for heating. Ask students to name the sources of the oil used by the United States. (countries in the Middle East and Latin America)

Answers to...

CRITICAL THINKING

Dependence on one crop or industry may make economies vulnerable to disasters such as drought and hurricanes. Exported goods may be vulnerable to falling prices.

SECTION 3

Geographic Factors and Natural Resources

BEFORE YOU READ

READING FOCUS

1. What are Latin America's important natural resources?
2. Why is it important for Latin American nations not to rely too much on one resource?

KEY TERMS

hydroelectricity
diversify

KEY PLACES

Jamaica
Venezuela
Brazil
Colombia

NOTE TAKING

Copy the chart below. As you read the section, fill in the chart with information about factors that cause incomes from natural resources to decrease.

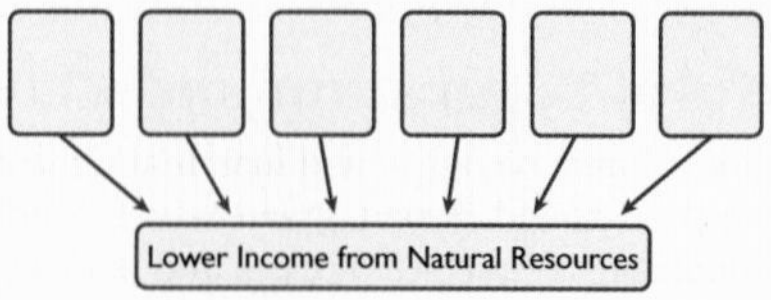

MAIN IDEA

The distribution and use of natural resources in Latin America influence the economies of countries there.

An Agricultural Economy

ECONOMICS Many Latin American economies are based on agriculture. Half of Colombia's exports are coffee. **Critical Thinking** What problems do you think the economy of a country like Colombia might face?

Setting the Scene

Bolivia has always depended on mineral resources for wealth. At first, silver helped to bring money into Bolivia's treasury. Soon, however, another metal became even more important than silver. That metal was tin.

For many years, Bolivia enjoyed the good times that wealth from tin brought. Then, in the 1920s and 1930s, a world-wide economic crisis hit. Industries stopped buying tin, as well as other natural resources, and Bolivia suffered as its main resource failed to bring money into the economy. This economic crisis hit all of Latin America hard. It brought home a problem many Latin American nations have: They rely too much on one resource.

Latin America's Natural Resources

Fish, petroleum, water, silver, and forests are all natural resources of Latin America and are as varied as its physical features and climate.

Mexico and Central America: Riches of Land and Sea Mexico is a treasure chest of minerals. The country has deposits of silver, gold,copper, coal, iron ore, and just about any other mineral you can name. Mexico also has huge amounts of oil and natural gas.

Resource Directory

Teaching Resources

Classroom Manager in the Unit 3 Teaching Resources, p. 8

Guided Reading and Review in the Unit 3 Teaching Resources, p. 9

Guide to the Essentials, p. 38

Technology

Section Reading Support Transparencies

In addition, trees cover nearly a quarter of Mexico's land. Wood from these trees is turned into lumber and paper products.

Central America's climate and rich soil are good for farming. The people grow coffee, cotton, sugar cane, and bananas. They also plant cacao trees. Cacao seeds are made into chocolate and cocoa.

Not all of Central America's resources are on land. People catch fish and shellfish in the region's waters. Central Americans use the energy of flowing water to produce power. This type of power is called **hydroelectricity** (hy droh ee lek TRIS ih tee) and is produced by huge dams that harness and control the energy.

Harnessing Water Power

ECONOMICS The hydroelectric power plant at Itaipú Dam is the largest in the world. It harnesses the energy of the Paraná River to provide electric power to Paraguay and Brazil. **Critical Thinking** What detail in this picture is a clue that the dam is used to produce electricity?

The Caribbean: Farming Resources Caribbean countries also have rich soil and a good climate for farming. Farmers grow sugar cane, coffee, bananas, cacao, citrus fruits, and other crops. The Caribbean has other resources as well. **Jamaica** is one of the world's main producers of bauxite—a mineral used to make aluminum. Cuba and the Dominican Republic have nickel deposits, while Trinidad is rich in oil.

South America: A Wealth of Resources Like Mexico, South America is rich in minerals. Businesses drill for oil in many South American countries, but much of the oil is found in **Venezuela.**

South America's plants and fish are natural resources, too. Forests cover about half the continent and trees from these forests provide everything from wood for building to coconuts for eating. People harvest many rain forest plants to make medicines. Tuna, anchovies, and other fish are plentiful.

Like other parts of Latin America, South America has rich soil so farmers can grow many different crops there. Coffee is a key crop in **Brazil** and **Colombia.** Many South American economies rely on the production of sugar cane, cotton, and rice.

Natural Resources and Economy

Not every country shares in the wealth of Latin America's resources. Some Latin American countries have many resources, while others have few. Some countries do not have the money they need to develop all of their resources.

Economic Factors and Weather Depending on one resource or crop can lead to problems. Many people in Latin America make their living by farming. Some Latin American countries depend on one or two crops, such as coffee, bananas, or sugar. When the price of a crop goes down, exports of that crop bring less money into the country. As a result, workers' wages may drop, and some workers may lose their jobs.

2 Explore

Direct students to read the section. Have them list Latin America's natural resources on the chalkboard. Ask students which of the resources are most important and why. Stress that a nation's people may consume and export a resource. For example, people in Latin American raise cattle for their own consumption as well as for export.

3 Teach

Have students draw three circles, one for each region of Latin America. Tell them to label the circles *The Caribbean*, *Mexico and Central America*, and *South America.* Direct students to write, in each circle, the region's major natural resources. Use students' diagrams as the basis for a discussion of Latin America's resources. This activity should take about 20 minutes.

Question for Discussion

SCIENCE, TECHNOLOGY, AND SOCIETY

In what ways do the resources of the Caribbean influence the economies of the region?

The region has very rich soil and a good climate for farming, so agriculture is an important part of the economy.

4 Assess/Reteach

See answers to the Section 3 Assessment. For assessment purposes, you may also check students' circles showing Latin America's major natural resources. You may also evaluate students' grasp of concepts by their responses during the classroom discussion.

SKILLS MINI LESSON

Reading Actively

You may **introduce** the skill by informing students that they can be active readers by asking themselves questions as they read. Looking for answers to the questions will help them focus on important points. Help students **practice** the skill by suggesting questions that they might ask themselves as they read: *What are the natural resources of the Caribbean? Why are these resources important? What role do people play in developing these resources?* Help students **apply** this skill by directing them to choose two pages of text and then write questions they might ask themselves while reading the information.

Answers to...

CRITICAL THINKING

Students may say the numerous electrical cables are clues to the dam's use.

SECTION 3 ASSESSMENT

AFTER YOU READ

1. (a) island country in the Caribbean (b) country in northern South America (c) largest country in South America (d) country in northwestern South America
2. (a) electricity generated by moving water (b) to add variety
3. Important natural resources include oil and natural gas; fertile soil; fish; forests; and minerals such as copper, gold, bauxite, nickel, and iron.
4. Answers may vary but should reflect students' understanding of the danger of depending on only one resource. Sample answer: If that one resource is damaged or decreases in value, the country's economy would be severely hurt.
5. Possible response: Resources provide a source of income for the nations and their people. Nations must use the resources they have to generate income and strengthen their economies. Their incomes and strong economies allow both the nations and the people living there to purchase items they may need or want.
6. Answers may vary. Students may respond that workers would be unemployed and their families might not have enough money to live on. The coffee industry workers could no longer buy goods. Coffee shippers would have no coffee to ship, and the country would not have coffee to sell to other nations.
7. Answers will vary. Make sure students use specific examples to back up their position.

Answers to...

CRITICAL THINKING

Problems such as lower workers' wages and unemployment occur when the prices of the crops that the country depends on fall and exports bring less money into the country.

Cash Crop Farming

ECONOMICS Many Latin American economies are based on agriculture. For example, one third of Honduras's exports are bananas. **Critical Thinking** What problems do you think one-crop economies face?

Weather and disease also cause people and businesses to lose money. Hurricanes, droughts, and plant disease can damage crops, and weather can also hurt the fishing industry.

Depending on Oil Oil is one of Latin America's most valuable resources. But it is risky to depend on oil because oil prices increase and decrease, sometimes suddenly. Mexico, like Venezuela, is a major oil producer. In the mid-1980s, oil companies produced more oil than the world needed. As a result of this decrease in demand, prices dropped and Mexico earned much less income than it had expected. The same thing happened to Trinidad.

There are other problems as well. In the 1960s, oil was discovered in Ecuador. Soon, oil became the country's main export. But in 1987, earthquakes destroyed Ecuador's major oil pipeline and the country's income was slashed.

Avoiding the Problems of a One-Resource Country Latin American nations know the risks of depending on one resource or crop and they are trying to diversify their economies. To **diversify** is to add variety. When Latin American nations try to diversify their economies, it means that they are looking for other ways to make money. Many are building factories to make products that can be sold to bring more money into the economy. Factories also provide jobs for people.

Venezuela has been trying to set up more factories and farms rather than relying only on oil production. Brazil has been building up its various industries, exporting machinery, steel, and chemicals, and encouraging cotton farming. El Salvador used to depend too heavily on its coffee crop. Now, cotton, sugar, corn, and other crops play an important role in the nation's economy.

SECTION 3 ASSESSMENT

AFTER YOU READ

RECALL

1. Identify: (a) Jamaica, (b) Venezuela, (c) Brazil, (d) Colombia
2. Define: (a) hydroelectricity (b) diversify

COMPREHENSION

3. Describe the important natural resources of Latin America.
4. Why is it important for Latin American nations to diversify their economies?

CRITICAL THINKING AND WRITING

5. **Exploring the Main Idea** Review the Main Idea statement at the beginning of this section. Then, write a paragraph explaining how the economies of the nations of Latin America are tied to its resources.
6. **Recognizing Cause and Effect** Suppose a disease destroyed Colombia's coffee crop. How would this loss affect coffee-plantation workers and their families?

ACTIVITY

Take It to the NET

7. **Writing a Position Paper** Write a paper discussing your views about the conservation of the rainforests. Visit the World Explorer: People, Places, and Cultures section of **phschool.com** for help in completing this activity.

Resource Directory

Teaching Resources

Section Quiz in the Unit 3 Teaching Resources, p. 10

Chapter Summary in the Unit 3 Teaching Resources, p. 11

Vocabulary in the Unit 3 Teaching Resources, p. 12

Reteaching in the Unit 3 Teaching Resources, p. 13

Enrichment in the Unit 3 Teaching Resources, p. 14

Critical Thinking in the Unit 3 Teaching Resources, p. 15

Using Reliable Information

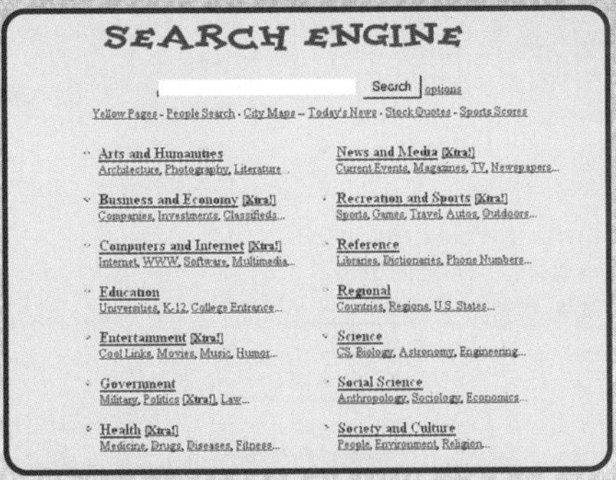

Learn the Skill

You know that you can find a great deal of information on the Internet, which provides contact with other computers around the world. People use the Internet to search for information on nearly every topic. However, you need to make sure that the information you find is reliable and accurate.

You can follow these steps to help you decide if the information you find is reliable.

A. Is the information true?

- Make sure any facts you find are supported. Remember that a fact can proven true, but opinions cannot. Be on the lookout for opinions presented as facts.
- Look for spelling or grammatical mistakes. These mistakes may show that the information was not checked or reviewed.

B. Who is responsible for the information?

- Check to see what person or organization put the information on the Internet. Is this person or organization qualified to provide information about this topic? How do you know? Is there a way to contact the author or organization by email or phone?

C. Is the information fair?

- Check to see if the information provides a balanced view on the topic.
- Identify the purpose of the information. Are you being persuaded to believe or do something? Is the information provided by a business that wants to sell you a product or service? If so, the information might not be as reliable as it seems.

D. Is the information up to date?

- Check to see when the Web page was first created. Also, make sure you can tell when the page was last updated. If there are no dates on the page, then the information might not be reliable.

E. How in-depth is the information?

- Decide if the Web page goes into enough detail on the topic. Also, check to see if there are links to other resources and Web sites. Are these links working?

You may not be able to find answers to all these questions for every Web page you visit. However, it's important for you to keep these questions in mind when you use the Internet.

Practice the Skill

Use the Internet to find out information about Latin America. First, write a question that you can answer, such as "What kinds of animals live in the Andes Mountains?" Then, use a search engine to find Web pages related to your topic. Choose three Web sites from your search and follow the steps you learned to decide if the information on each page is reliable. Record your observations.

Apply the Skill

See the Chapter Review and Assessment at the end of this chapter for more questions on using reliable information.

Resource Directory

Teaching Resources

Social Studies and Geography Skills, Distinguishing Fact and Opinion, p. 41

Technology

Social Studies Skills Tutor CD-ROM

Answers to...

PRACTICE THE SKILL

Students' observations should employ the five questions to determine whether each of the three Web sites is reliable.

Lesson Objectives

1. Use the Internet to conduct research on a topic.
2. Evaluate the quality of an Internet source.

Lesson Plan

1 Engage

To introduce the skill, read the opening text under "Learn the Skill" aloud. Make sure students understand the terms that relate to computers. You might want to write technical terms, such as *database, Internet, URL, browser, search engine,* and *hyperlink*, on the chalkboard and help students define them. Students can copy the definitions for later use.

2 Explore

Direct students to read the steps under "Learn the Skill." Make sure they understand that there are several ways to check on the reliability of information. Using a computer, show students examples of reliable and unreliable Web pages. Educational sites from schools or reputable businesses are the best examples of reliable Web pages.

3 Teach

Allow students time on a computer to explore. Then, have students use key words to find answers to questions about Latin America. They can share their results with the class.

For additional reinforcement, provide questions to students and have them search for the answers on the Internet.

4 Assess/Reteach

Students should be able to distinguish between reliable and unreliable information during Internet research.

To further assess students' recognition of reliable information on the Internet, have them complete the "Applying Your Skills" part of the Chapter Review and Assessment at the end of this chapter.

CHAPTER 9

Review and Assessment

Creating a Chapter Summary

Student summaries will vary.

Sample summaries:

Physical Environment Latin America's physical environment, such as its climate and vegetation varies greatly even within each country. The physical environment affects how people in Latin America live.

Natural Resources Latin America has a rich variety of natural resources. The distribution and use of natural resources influence the economies of Latin American countries.

Reviewing Key Terms

1. isthmus
2. elevation
3. plateau
4. hydroelectricity
5. coral

Reviewing the Main Ideas

1. The Caribbean, Mexico and Central America, and South America. Sample answers: The Caribbean is mostly islands; Mexico and Central America are mostly mountains and plateaus; South America is mostly mountains, plains, and forests.
2. Accept reasonable answers. For example, students may mention that mountains make travel difficult or that many islanders in the Caribbean rely on fishing for a living.
3. Climates are colder at higher elevations.
4. Accept reasonable answers. Possibilities include: the warm, rainy weather near the equator helps create the lush vegetation of the rain forest. The dry, hot climate is responsible for the dry and barren deserts of Chile. People within the rain forests can hunt or gather their food. Few people live in the desert regions of Latin America.
5. Accept reasonable answers. Answers might include: Minerals, oil, and trees are found in Mexico and Central America; rich soil and bauxite are found in the Caribbean; minerals, oil, fish, and rich soil are found in South America.
6. If the one source of income is reduced or lost, the country's economy would be severely hurt. Examples will vary.

CHAPTER 9

Review and Assessment

Creating a Chapter Summary

On a separate piece of paper, draw a web like this one, and include the information that summarizes part of the information in Section 1. Then, add more ovals to summarize the remaining information you learned in this chapter.

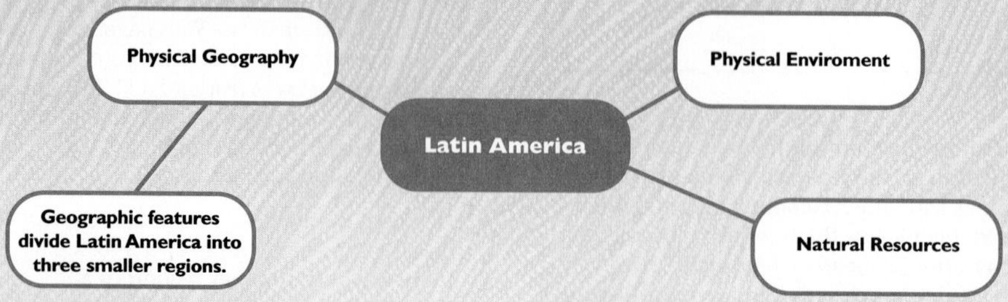

Reviewing Key Terms

Complete each sentence with a word from the list below.

hydroelectricity
elevation
coral
plateau
isthmus

1. An ________ is a narrow strip of land that has water on both sides and joins two larger bodies of land.
2. ________ refers to the height of land above sea level.
3. A large, raised area of mostly level land is called a ________.
4. ________ generates power using moving water.
5. ________, a rock-like substance, is formed by the skeletons of tiny sea animals.

Reviewing the Main Ideas

1. List the three main regions of Latin America. Then choose two and describe their physical features. (Section 1)
2. In what ways do the physical features of Latin America affect the people and their way of life? (Section 1)
3. How does elevation affect climate? (Section 2)
4. Give an example of how climate in one region of Latin America affects the vegetation that grows there. How does this affect the way in which people live? (Section 2)
5. List two natural resources found in each of the three regions of Latin America. (Section 3)
6. What problems arise when a country depends too heavily on a single source of income? Support your answer with one or two examples. (Section 3)

180 UNIT 3 LATIN AMERICA

Map Activity

For each place listed below, write the letter from the map that shows its location.

1. Colombia
2. Brazil
3. Jamaica
4. Mexico
5. Venezuela

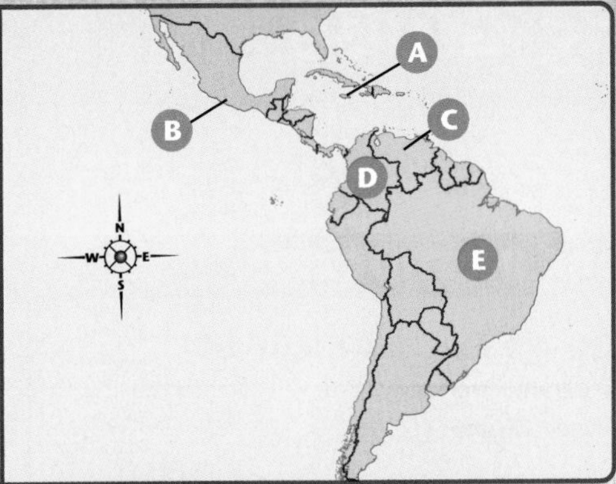

Take It to the NET

Enrichment For more map activities using geography skills, visit the social studies section of **phschool.com.**

Writing Activity

1. Writing a Letter Imagine that you are a visitor to Latin America. You are touring the whole region: Mexico, Central America, the Caribbean, and South America. Write a letter home describing your trip. Write about such items as these: the weather, interesting facts you've learned about Latin America's physical features, places that you liked or didn't like, and the economy in at least one of the regions.

2. Writing a Report Choose a country in Latin America for further study. Visit the library or the Internet and gather information on the physical geography and climate of that country. Write a short report explaining how the geography and climate affect the economy and way of life in that country.

Critical Thinking

1. Supporting a Point of View Write a paragraph using examples to support this point of view: "The weather in Latin America is a great friend to the people, but also an enemy."

2. Drawing Conclusions "How a country uses its natural resources affects the well-being of its people." Do you agree or disagree with this statement? Explain your answer.

3. Making Comparisons Compare the physical geography of the Caribbean to that of South America. Which region do you think has a more beneficial geography? Explain.

Applying Your Skills

Turn to the Skills for Life activity on p. 179 to help you complete the following activity.

Use the Internet to search for information about the Amazon River. Find one web page that is a good example of reliable information and one that is a bad example. Support your choices using the information you learned on p. 179.

Take It to the NET

Activity Draw or trace a map of Latin America. Label each country, and list three distinctive geographicals for each one. Visit the World Explorer: People, Places, and Cultures section of **phschool.com** for help in completing this activity.

Chapter 9 Self-Test As a final review activity, take the Chapter 9 Self-Test and get instant feedback on your answers. To take the test, visit the Social Studies section of **phschool.com.**

Resource Directory

Teaching Resources

Cooperative Learning Activity in the Unit 3 Teaching Resources, pp. 103–105

Chapter Tests Forms A and B in the Unit 3 Teaching Resources, pp. 130–135

Guide to the Essentials, Ch. 9 Test, p. 39

Other Print Resources

Chapter Tests with ExamView® Test Bank, Ch. 9

Technology

ExamView® Test Bank CD-ROM, Ch. 9

Resource Pro® CD-ROM

Map Activity

1. D **2.** E **3.** A **4.** B **5.** C

Writing Activity

1. Students should write about various places visited during their imaginary tour of Latin America. Letters should contain specific descriptive details about the region. Students should support their opinions with reasons.
2. Reports should contain specific examples of the ways in which physical geography and climate affect the economy and way of life in the chosen country.

Critical Thinking

1. Accept reasonable answers. Students may mention that ample sun and rain help farmers grow crops, but hurricanes and the effects of El Niño cause great destruction.
2. Most students will agree. Students' answers should reflect sound reasoning. For example, Venezuela is setting up factories and farms to produce and export crops and other products besides oil. This provides people with different job and livelihood options and other ways to make money. In turn, this means more jobs and more income for the nation.
3. Answers will vary. Students should mention at least one comparison of physical features, climate, vegetation, and/or natural resources. Explanations of why one is more beneficial than the other should be supported with details such as better climate, better soil, and more variety of resources.

Applying Your Skills

Make sure students support their choices with the skills they learned to distinguish reliable information from unreliable information.

Chapter 10 Planning Guide

Resource Manager

	CORE INSTRUCTION	READING/SKILLS
Chapter-Level Resources	**Teaching Resources** Program Overview Pacing Charts **Technology** Resource Pro® CD-ROM Companion Web site, phschool.com • eTeach	**Technology** Social Studies Skills Tutor CD-ROM Student Edition on Audio CD, Ch. 10
1 Early Civilizations 1. Describe the chief characteristics and accomplishments of the Mayan civilization. 2. Describe the chief characteristics and accomplishments of the Aztec civilization. 3. Describe the chief characteristics and accomplishments of the Incan civilization.	**Teaching Resources** **Unit 3** Classroom Manager, p. 17 Guided Reading and Review, p. 18	**Teaching Resources** Guide to the Essentials, p. 40 **Technology** Section Reading Support Transparencies
2 European Exploration: Short and Long Term Effects 1. Summarize the reasons that Europeans sailed to the Americas. 2. Analyze the short- and long-term effects of European rule in the region. 3. Consider long-term effects of European rule over Native Americans.	**Teaching Resources** **Unit 3** Classroom Manager, p. 20 Guided Reading and Review, p. 21	**Teaching Resources** Guide to the Essentials, p. 41 **Technology** Section Reading Support Transparencies
3 Independence and the Spread of Democracy 1. Describe how Latin American nations won independence from their European rulers. 2. Analyze the ways the American and French Revolutions influenced events in Latin America. 3. Describe challenges Latin America faced as a result of independence.	**Teaching Resources** **Unit 3** Classroom Manager, p. 23 Guided Reading and Review, p. 24 Chapter Summary, p. 26 Vocabulary, p. 27 Reteaching, p. 28	**Teaching Resources** **Unit 3** Critical Thinking, p. 30 Guide to the Essentials, p. 42 **Technology** Section Reading Support Transparencies

ENRICHMENT / PRE-AP

Teaching Resources
Primary Sources and Literature Readings

Other Print Resources
DK Atlas

Technology
World Video Explorer: A Trip to the Ruins
Companion Web site, phschool.com

Technology
Color Transparencies 52, 53

Technology
Color Transparencies 52, 53

Teaching Resources
Unit 3
Enrichment, p. 29
Cooperative Learning Activity, pp. 107–110

Technology
Color Transparencies 61, 65

ASSESSMENT

Prentice Hall Assessment System

Core Assessment
Chapter Tests with ExamView® Test Bank, Ch. 10
ExamView® Test Bank CD-ROM, Ch. 10

Standardized Test Preparation
Diagnose and Prescribe
Diagnostic Tests for Middle Grades Social Studies Skills
Review and Reteach
Review Book for World Studies
Practice and Assess
Test-taking Strategies with Transparencies for Middle Grades Test Prep Book
Test-taking Strategies Posters

Teaching Resources
Unit 3
Section Quizzes, pp. 19, 22, and 25
Chapter Tests, pp. 136–141

Technology
Companion Web site, phschool.com
Ch. 10 Self-Test

World Video Explorer
Each region of the world is explored through regional flyovers and investigative field trips. Case study segments give students an in-depth view of the history, economy, government, and culture of a key place in each region. Case studies include Nigeria, Mexico, China, British Columbia, and the Czech Republic.

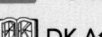

In Your Classroom

CUSTOMIZE FOR INDIVIDUAL NEEDS

Gifted and Talented
Teacher's Edition
- Talking With Liberators, p. 191

Teaching Resources
- Enrichment, p. 29
- Primary Sources and Literature Readings

Honors/Pre-AP
Teacher's Edition
- Talking With Liberators, p. 191

Teaching Resources
- Critical Thinking, p. 30
- Primary Sources and Literature Readings

ESL
Teacher's Edition
- A Soldier's Diary, p. 191

Teaching Resources
- Guided Reading and Review, pp. 18, 21, and 24
- Vocabulary, p. 27
- Reteaching, p. 28
- Guide to the Essentials, pp. 40–42

Technology
- Social Studies Skills Tutor CD-ROM
- Section Reading Support Transparencies

Less Proficient Readers
Teacher's Edition
- A Soldier's Diary, p. 191

Teaching Resources
- Guided Reading and Review, pp. 18, 21, and 24
- Vocabulary, p. 27
- Reteaching, p. 28
- Guide to the Essentials, pp. 40–42

Technology
- Social Studies Skills Tutor CD-ROM
- Section Reading Support Transparencies

Less Proficient Writers
Teacher's Edition
- A Soldier's Diary, p. 191

Teaching Resources
- Guided Reading and Review, pp. 18, 21, and 24
- Vocabulary, p. 27
- Guide to the Essentials, pp. 40–42

Technology
- Social Studies Skills Tutor CD-ROM
- Section Reading Support Transparencies

TEACHER'S EDITION INDEX

Activities talking with liberators, p. 191; a soldier's diary, p. 191

Connections hieroglyphics, p. 184

Skills Mini Lessons Recognizing Bias, p. 187

CHAPTER 10 PACING SUGGESTIONS

 For 90-minute Blocks
See suggestions in the Teaching Resources Pacing Charts for Chapter 10. Use Color Transparencies 52, 53, 55, and 61.

 Running Out of Time?
See the Guide to the Essentials, pp. 40–42.

INTERDISCIPLINARY LINKS

Middle Grades Math: Tools for Success
Course 1, Lesson 1-3, **Mean, Median, and Mode**
Course 1, Lesson 11-4, **Theoretical Probability**

Science Explorer
Cells and Heredity, Lesson 4-1, **Human Inheritance**
From Bacteria to Plants, Lesson 1-3, **Classifying Organisms**

Prentice Hall Literature
Bronze, Mi Amigo Mark
Copper, The Circuit
Copper, The King of Mazy May

DORLING KINDERSLEY

At the end of each unit, you will find information adapted from Dorling Kindersley's *Illustrated Children's Encyclopedia* that connects to the region being studied and to one of the seven content strands. In addition, your resources include Dorling Kindersley's *Atlas*, which contains valuable information about countries from around the world.

BIBLIOGRAPHY

For the Teacher

Arnold, Caroline. *City of the Gods: Mexico's Ancient City of Teotihuacán.* Clarion, 1994.

Eyewitness Aztec, Inca, and Maya. Dorling Kindersley, 2001.

Fritz, Jean, et al. *The World in 1492.* Holt, 1992.

For the Student

Easy

Defrates, Joanna. *What Do We Know About the Aztecs?* Bedrick, 1995.

Average

Garcia, Guy. *Spirit of the Maya: A Boy Explores His People's Mysterious Past.* Walker, 1995.

Challenging

Mason, Antony. *Ancient Civilizations of the Americas.* Dorling Kindersley, 2001.

Meyer, Carolyn, and Charles Gallenkamp. *The Mystery of the Ancient Maya.* McElderry, 1995.

Literature Connection

Dorris, Michael. *Morning Girl.* Hyperion, 1992.

Lourie, Peter. *Lost Treasure of the Inca.* Boyds Mills, 1999.

Take It to the NET

The World Explorer companion Web site, found on **phschool.com**, offers activities for exploring geographical, historical, and cultural resources on the Internet. It also provides on-line links for key content and all Section and Chapter Assessment activities.

The **Teacher site** also provides teachers with regional data and ideas for student research and activities.

Students can use the **Student site** to find chapter-by-chapter Internet resource links and to access Self-Tests.

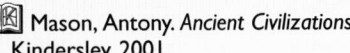

CHAPTER 10

Connecting to the Guiding Questions

In this chapter, students will read about the history of Latin America. Content in this chapter corresponds to the following Guiding Questions outlined at the beginning of the unit.

- How has geography influenced the social and economic development of Latin America?
- How has Latin America's history influenced modern day Latin American societies?
- How have the governments of Latin America changed over time, and how are they organized today?
- What opportunities do citizens of Latin America have to participate in the political process?

Using the Map Activities

Have students study the map and compare and contrast the sizes, locations, and dates of the three civilizations.

- Ask students to combine their accomplishments for each civilization into three master lists. Then, ask them to find similar accomplishments and unique ones for these civilizations.
- Students should consider accessible shoreline as well as natural barriers, such as mountains, rivers, and deserts.

Heterogeneous Groups

The following activities are suitable for heterogeneous groups.

Cooperative Learning

Talking With Liberators, p. 191

Journal Writing

A Soldier's Diary, p. 191

eTeach

Be sure to check out this month's discussion with a Master Teacher. Go to **phschool.com**.

CHAPTER 10

LATIN AMERICA: Shaped by History

SECTION 1
Early Civilizations

SECTION 2
European Exploration
SHORT AND LONG TERM EFFECTS

SECTION 3
Independence and the Spread of Democracy

Mayan, Aztec, and Incan Civilizations

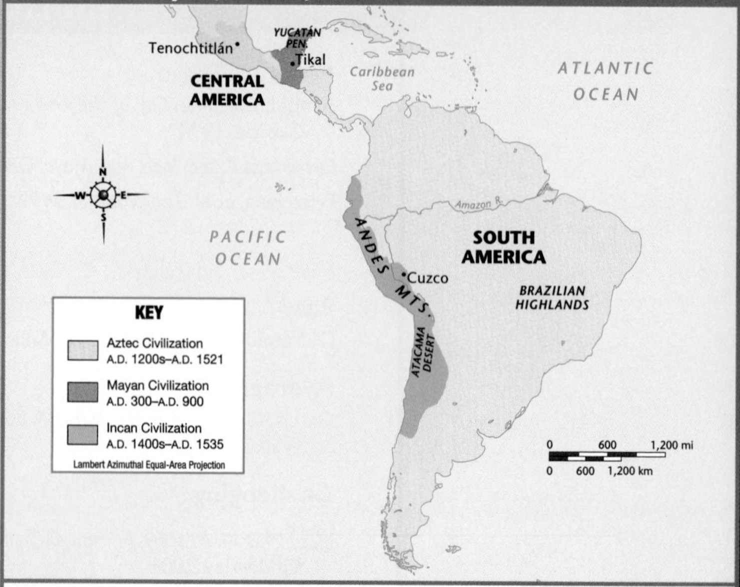

USING A MAP

This map shows the location of three civilizations in Latin America that existed before Europeans arrived in the region.

Understanding Ancient Civilizations

Each of these civilizations was highly advanced. Visit your local library or the Internet to find out some of the major accomplishments of each of these civilizations. Make a list of your findings.

Evaluating the Geography

Look at the map and describe the location of each of the three civilizations. Which civilization do you think was the most difficult to defend from invaders? Explain your answer.

Resource Directory

Teaching Resources

Primary Sources and Literature Readings extend content with a selection related to the concepts in this chapter.

Other Print Resources

DK Atlas

Technology

A Trip to: Ruins of the Maya, from the World Video Explorer, enhances students' understanding of ancient Mayan culture and its contributions to Latin America culture today.

Student Edition on Audio CD, Ch. 10

SECTION 1

Early Civilizations

BEFORE YOU READ

READING FOCUS

1. What were the chief cultural characteristics and accomplishments of the Mayan civilization?
2. What were the chief cultural characteristics and accomplishments of the Aztec civilization?
3. What were the chief cultural characteristics and accomplishments of the Incan civilization?

KEY TERMS

maize
hieroglyphics
aqueduct

KEY PLACES

Copán
Valley of Mexico
Tenochtitlán
Cuzco

NOTE TAKING

Copy the Venn diagram below. As you read the section, complete the diagram to show how the ancient Mayan, Aztec, and Incan civilizations were alike and how they were different.

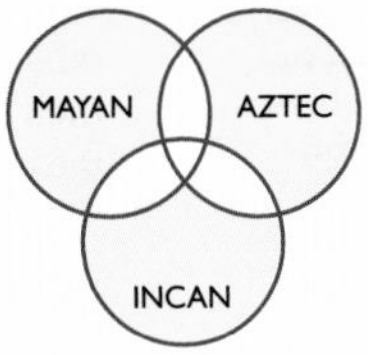

MAIN IDEA

The Mayas, Aztecs, and Incas had developed unique civilizations in Latin America before Europeans arrived.

Setting the Scene

Fans cheered as the players brought the ball down the court. Suddenly, the ball flew into the air and sailed through the hoop. Fans and players shouted and screamed. Although this may sound like a championship basketball game, it is actually a moment of a game played over 1,000 years ago. Pok-a-tok was a game played by ancient Mayas.

Ancient Mayan Games

CULTURE This pok-a-tok court is in Copán, Honduras. **Critical Thinking** In what ways do you think sporting events or games played by the ancient Mayas were similar to those played today?

Mayan Civilization and Culture

Mayan civilization thrived in Central America and southern Mexico from about A.D. 300 to A.D. 900. By studying ruins, scientists have learned much about Mayan civilization.

The Mayas built great cities that were also religious centers. Two of these cities were **Copán** (ko PAHN) in present-day Honduras and Tikal (tee KAHL) in Guatemala. Large pyramid-shaped temples, where Mayas worshipped, stood in the center of the cities. Mayan farmers worked in the fields surrounding the cities.

SECTION 1

Lesson Objectives

1. Describe the chief characteristics and accomplishments of the Mayan civilization.
2. Describe the chief characteristics and accomplishments of the Aztec civilization.
3. Describe the chief characteristics and accomplishments of the Incan civilization.

Lesson Plan

1 Engage

Warm-Up Activity

Write the word *civilization* on the board. Ask students to suggest all the things that they think of when they hear this word. Write their responses on the chalkboard. Invite discussion.

Activating Prior Knowledge

Tell students that, generally, a civilization is a culture that has built cities and has developed a writing system, the arts, the sciences, and a system of education. The culture also generally has a government, public buildings, and commerce. Ask students to name some features of American civilization.

2 Explore

Have students read the section and use the illustrations to investigate the Mayan, Aztec, and Incan civilizations. Students should find supporting details for the following topics: Major Achievements and Reasons for Decline.

Resource Directory

Teaching Resources

Classroom Manager in the Unit 3 Teaching Resources, p. 17

Guided Reading and Review in the Unit 3 Teaching Resources, p. 18

Guide to the Essentials, p. 40

Technology

Section Reading Support Transparencies

Answers to...

CRITICAL THINKING

They played some games on a court; an audience often watched the games; they used a ball.

Lesson Plan continued

3 Teach

Have students create three concept maps titled *Mayas*, *Aztecs*, and *Incas*. The maps should include facts for subtopics such as Cities, Achievements, Decline, and Religion. Discuss how the achievements of the three civilizations have influenced students' lives.

Questions for Discussion

GEOGRAPHY **How did the Incas modify their physical environment?**

They built stone terraces into the sides of mountains. They built aqueducts to irrigate their land.

CULTURE **What are some similarities of the Mayan, Aztec, and Incan cultures?**

They all built cities; they had religion and priests, a government, language, arts, and science.

4 Assess/Reteach

See the answers to the Section 1 Assessment. You may also assess students' completed concept maps.

Acceptable maps include one fact for each subtopic.

Commendable maps include at least two facts for each subtopic.

Outstanding maps include more than two facts for each subtopic.

CULTURE

Hieroglyphics

The Egyptians and the Mayas both used hieroglyphics, or picture writing. Most Egyptian symbols stood for a word. The Mayan symbols, however, were unusual because each stood for a syllable in a word.

LINKS TO **Math**

The Concept of Zero The Mayas created a numbering system that included the idea of zero. Zero is important in math because it is a symbol that shows that there is none of something. For example, to write the number 308, you need a symbol to show that there are no tens. Mathematicians consider the idea of zero to be one of the world's greatest inventions.

Aztec Calendar

SCIENCE AND TECHNOLOGY

The Aztecs observed the stars and planets carefully and like the ancient Greeks, named them after their gods. The Aztecs used their knowledge of astronomy to make calendars like the one below. **Critical Thinking** Who do you think designed and used the calendar? Why?

Science, Technology, and Religion The most important Mayan crop was **maize,** or corn, which was the main food in the Mayan diet. Farmers also grew beans, squash, peppers, avocados, and papayas. Mayan priests studied the stars and planets and designed an accurate calendar, which they used to decide when to hold religious ceremonies. They also developed a system of writing using signs and symbols called **hieroglyphics** (hy ur oh GLIF iks) along with a number system similar to the present-day decimal system.

The Great Mystery of the Mayas About A.D. 900, the Mayas suddenly left their cities, but no one knows why. Crop failures, war, disease, drought, or famine may have killed many, or perhaps people rebelled against the control of the priests and nobles. The Mayas left their cities, but stayed in the region and millions of them still live in the countries of Mexico, Belize, Guatemala, Honduras, and El Salvador.

Aztec Civilization and Culture

Another ancient civilization is that of the Aztecs. They arrived in the **Valley of Mexico** in the 1100s. The Valley of Mexico is in Central Mexico.

The Aztecs found a permanent home in 1325 when they settled on an island in Lake Texcoco. They changed the swampy lake into a magnificent city, which they called **Tenochtitlán** (tay nawch tee TLAHN). Tenochtitlán stood on the site of present-day Mexico City.

The Aztecs Expand Their Empire In the 1400s, Aztec warriors conquered other people in the region. They forced the people they conquered to pay tribute, or taxes. Tribute was paid in food, cotton, gold, or slaves. The Aztecs grew rich from the tribute.

An emperor ruled over all Aztec lands and their society had several classes. Nobles and priests helped the emperor, warriors fought battles, and traders carried goods throughout the empire and beyond. Craftworkers created jewelry, garments, pottery, sculptures, and other goods. Most people, however, were farmers.

Aztec Science and Technology Tenochtitlán was a center of trade and learning. Aztec doctors made more than 1,000 medicines from plants. Aztec astronomers predicted eclipses and the movements of planets. Aztec priests kept records using hieroglyphics similar to those used by the Mayas.

Incan Civilizations and Culture

In about 1200, the Incas settled in **Cuzco** (KOOS koh), a village in the Andes that is now a city in the country of Peru. Most Incas were farmers who grew maize and other crops. Through wars and conquest, the Incas won control of the entire Cuzco Valley, one of many valleys that extend from the Andes to the Pacific Ocean.

Answers to...

CRITICAL THINKING

Priests may have designed and used the calendar so that they could tell people when to plant, harvest, and celebrate special days.

Resource Directory

Teaching Resources

Outline Maps, Latin America: Physical, p. 6; Latin America: Political, p. 7

Technology

Color Transparencies 52 Middle America: Political Map; **53** South America: Political Map

At one time, the Incan Empire stretched some 2,500 miles (4,023 km) from what is now Ecuador south along the Pacific coast through Peru, Bolivia, Chile, and Argentina. The 12 million people ruled by the Incas lived mostly in small villages and their descendants still live in present-day Peru, Ecuador, Bolivia, Chile, and Colombia. They speak Quechua (KECH wah), the Incan language.

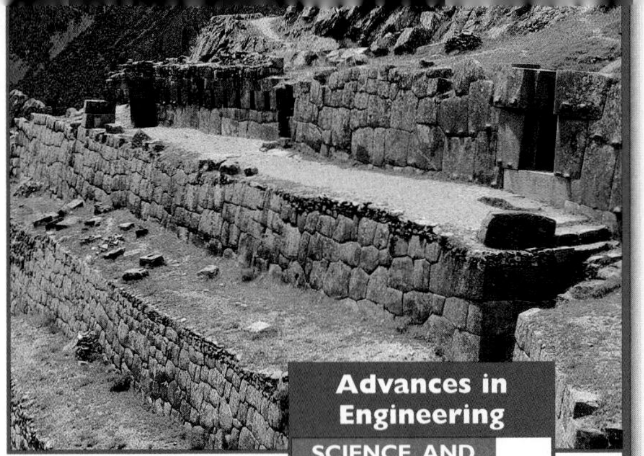

Advances in Engineering

SCIENCE AND TECHNOLOGY

The Incas shaped their stones so well that they did not need cement to hold a wall together. **Critical Thinking** How well do you think the structures of the Incas held up over time? How does this affect what we know about the Incas today?

Incan Accomplishments The Incan capital, Cuzco, was the center of government, trade, learning, and religion. The emperor and the nobles who helped him run the empire lived in the city near the central plaza. Most of the farmers and workers lived outside Cuzco in mud huts.

The Incas were excellent farmers, builders, and managers. They built more than 19,000 miles (30,577 km) of roads. The roads went over some of the most mountainous land in the world. This road system helped the Incas to govern their vast empire. They increased their farmland by building stone terraces into the sides of steep slopes and **aqueducts,** pipes or channels designed to carry water from a distant source. Aqueducts allowed the Incas to irrigate land to grow crops.

SECTION I ASSESSMENT

AFTER YOU READ

RECALL

1. Identify : (a) Copán, (b) Valley of Mexico, (c) Tenochtitlán, (d) Cuzco
2. Define: (a) maize, (b) hieroglyphics, (c) aqueduct

COMPREHENSION

3. What were the main accomplishments of the Mayan civilization?
4. What were the main accomplishments of the Aztec civilization?
5. What were the main accomplishments of the Incan civilization?

CRITICAL THINKING AND WRITING

6. **Exploring the Main Idea** Review the Main Idea statement at the beginning of this section. Then, describe some of the ways that the ancient civilizations of the Mayas, Aztecs, and Incas influenced Latin America's present-day cultures.
7. **Distinguishing Fact from Opinion** Tell if the following statements are facts or opinions. Explain why.

   (a) Mayan calendars were very accurate. (b) Aztec civilization was more important than Mayan civilization.

ACTIVITY

Take It to the NET

8. **Exploring Early Latin American Civilizations** Imagine you are an archeologist and examine some of the artifacts you see on the Web site. Interpret the object's use or purpose, and how it represents the culture. Visit the World Explorer: People, Places, and Cultures section of **phschool.com** for help in completing this activity.

SECTION I ASSESSMENT

AFTER YOU READ

1. (a) Mayan city in present-day Honduras (b) area inhabited by Aztecs in the 1100s (c) central city of Aztec empire at the site of present-day Mexico City (d) Incan capital
2. (a) corn (b) a kind of writing, using signs and symbols (c) a pipe or channel designed to carry water from a distant source
3. Mayan accomplishments: great cities, accurate calendar, system of writing, number system
4. Aztec accomplishments: great cities, calendars, system of writing, medicine, arts and crafts
5. Incan accomplishments: great cities, roads, aqueducts, terraced land for increased farmland, organized government, strong buildings
6. Present-day cultures eat some of the same kinds of foods and speak some of the same languages as those of the ancient Latin American civilizations.
7. (a) fact (b) opinion. Explanations will vary.
8. Students may not accurately identify all the artifacts, but encourage them to think about what it could be used for.

Resource Directory

Teaching Resources

Section Quiz in the Unit 3 Teaching Resources, p. 19

Answers to...

CRITICAL THINKING

Incan structures were well built, so they lasted for 600 years. We are able to learn about their culture by studying their architecture and buildings.

SECTION 2

Lesson Objectives

1. Summarize the reasons that Europeans sailed to the Americas.
2. Analyze the short- and long-term effects of European rule in the region.
3. Consider long-term effects of European rule over Native Americans.

Lesson Plan

1 Engage

Warm-Up Activity

Ask students to list reasons why countries today explore outer space and the ocean floor. List their responses on the board. Ask students to evaluate the reasons and choose the one that they think is the most important.

Activating Prior Knowledge

Ask students how they decide what is right and wrong. They may provide a variety of responses, including: principles of their religion, learning from their parents, knowing the rules, and looking at a situation and realizing "It isn't the way I would like to be treated."

2 Explore

Ask students to skim the section and note the main headings. Have them find answers to the following questions: Why did Europeans come to America? How did Spanish explorers treat the Native Americans living in the Americas? How did Spain and Portugal organize their empires in the Americas?

SECTION 2

European Exploration

Short and Long Term Effects

BEFORE YOU READ

READING FOCUS

1. Why did Europeans sail to the Americas?
2. What were some of the short-term effects of European exploration in Latin America?
3. What were some of the long-term effects of European rule over Native Americans in the region?

KEY TERMS

Treaty of Tordesillas
treaty
Line of Demarcation
conquistador
mestizo
hacienda

KEY PEOPLE

Hernán Cortés
Christopher Columbus
Moctezuma
Francisco Pizarro

NOTE TAKING

Copy the chart below. As you read the section, fill in the chart with information about the causes and effects of Spain's colonization of Latin America.

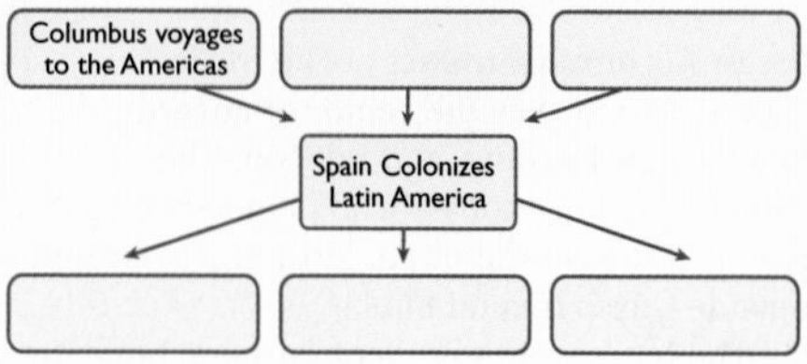

MAIN IDEA

As European explorers expanded their wealth and claimed land in Latin America for their countries, their exploration and conquests damaged many Native American civilizations.

Early Navigation

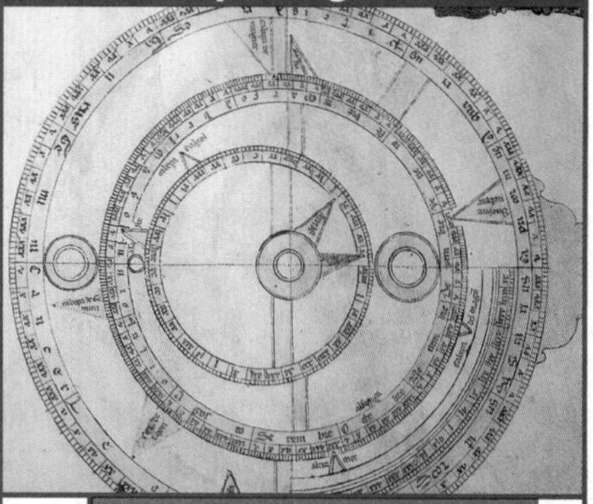

SCIENCE AND TECHNOLOGY

Sailors in the 1400s guided their ships using only the stars, a compass, and an astrolabe. Above is a drawing of an astrolabe. **Critical Thinking** Why did sailors use the stars? How could they do that?

Setting the Scene

Hernán Cortés was the Spanish soldier who conquered the Aztecs. He landed in Mexico in 1519 and soon met Malinche (mah LIHN chay), the daughter of a Mayan leader. Malinche quickly learned Spanish and became Cortés's main translator. She also kept an eye on Aztec spies. Without Malinche, Cortés could not have conquered the Aztecs.

Europeans Arrive in the Americas

In the 1400s, Spain and Portugal searched for new trade routes to Asia. They knew that in Asia they would find expensive goods such as spices and silks that could be traded for a profit.

Explorer **Christopher Columbus** thought he could reach Asia by sailing west across the Atlantic Ocean. Columbus knew the world was round, but he believed the distance around the world was shorter than it was.

Columbus asked Spain to sponsor a voyage, and he set sail in early August 1492. On October 12, he spotted

Answers to...

CRITICAL THINKING

Sailors used the stars to navigate because the stars were identifiable and could be located at night, no matter where a ship was, and used to determine a ship's position.

Resource Directory

Teaching Resources

Classroom Manager in the Unit 3 Teaching Resources, p. 20

Guided Reading and Review in the Unit 3 Teaching Resources, p. 21

Guide to the Essentials, p. 41

Technology

Section Reading Support Transparencies

land. Columbus thought he had reached the East Indies in Asia, so he described the people there as Indians. In fact, the land he saw was an island in the Caribbean Sea.

Spain and Portugal soon became fierce rivals. Each country tried to stop the other from claiming land in the Americas. In 1494, Spain and Portugal signed the **Treaty of Tordesillas** (tor day SEE yas). A **treaty** is an agreement in writing made between two or more countries. The treaty set an imaginary line from the North Pole to the South Pole at about 50° longitude, called the **Line of Demarcation.** It gave Spain the right to settle and trade west of the line. Portugal could do the same east of the line. The only part of South America that is east of the line is roughly the eastern half of present-day Brazil. Because of the Treaty of Tordesillas, the language and background of Brazil are Portuguese.

Spanish explorers heard stories of wealthy kingdoms in the Americas where they hoped to find gold and other treasures. Spanish rulers did not pay for the trips of the explorers. Instead, they gave the **conquistadors** (kon KEES ta dors), or conquerors, the right to hunt for treasure. In exchange, conquistadors agreed to give Spain one fifth of any treasures they found.

A Court Welcome

HISTORY This historical painting shows Moctezuma welcoming Cortés to his court. **Critical Thinking** Based on this painting, what conclusions can you draw about Aztec wealth?

Cortés Conquers the Aztecs

In 1519, Hernán Cortés sailed to the coast of Mexico in search of treasure. He brought a small army of 500 men and 16 horses with him. The Aztec ruler **Moctezuma** (mahk tuh ZOOM uh) heard that a strange ship was offshore and sent spies to find out about it. The spies, who had never seen horses before, described the Spanish as "supernatural creatures riding on hornless deer, armed in iron, fearless as gods." Moctezuma thought Cortés might be a god.

When Cortés and his soldiers arrived in Tenochtitlán, Moctezuma welcomed them. But the peace did not last. Spanish soldiers killed some Aztecs and a bloody battle began. Moctezuma was killed, and with the help of native groups who were enemies of the Aztecs, Cortés surrounded and attacked Tenochtitlán. In 1521, the Aztecs surrendered after nearly 240,000 Aztecs and 30,000 of Cortés's allies had died. The Aztec Empire lay in ruins.

Pizarro Conquers the Incas **Francisco Pizarro** (fran SIS koh pih ZAR oh), like Cortés, was a Spanish conquistador. He heard stories about the rich Incan kingdom in South America, so in 1531, Pizarro set sail with a small force of 180 Spanish soldiers. Pizarro captured and killed the Incan emperor and other leaders. By 1535, Pizarro had conquered most of the Incan empire, including the capital, Cuzco.

Within 15 years, the conquistadors defeated the two most powerful empires in the Americas. They had guns, cannons, and horses that Native Americans had never seen. The Europeans also carried diseases, such as smallpox, that wiped out entire villages.

3 Teach

Have students write an essay that answers the question: How did European rule affect both the Europeans and the Native Americans in the Americas? Encourage students to include specific examples from this section in their essays.

Questions for Discussion

HISTORY **Who was Hernan Cortés and why was he important?**

Cortés was a Spanish explorer who conquered the Aztec empire.

SCIENCE, TECHNOLOGY, AND SOCIETY

What kinds of technology did the conquistadors bring to the Americas and what were the effects of these technologies?

They brought guns, cannons, and horses to help them conquer the Native Americans. These weapons made defeating the Native Americans much easier.

4 Assess/Reteach

See answers to the Section 2 Assessment. You may also use students' completed essays as an assessment.

Acceptable essays include the facts that Europeans gained land and wealth and that the Native Americans lost their empires.

Commendable essays include details about the conquistadors and how they conquered the Native Americans.

Outstanding essays provide information about the Portuguese and Spanish empires and the effects of the cultural interaction between the Native Americans and the Europeans.

SKILLS MINI LESSON

Recognizing Bias

As a way to **introduce** the skill, tell students that bias, or prejudice, involves judging what a person is like based on assumptions or a stereotype, rather than on that person's individual qualities. Help students **practice** this skill by discussing how European actions, such as demanding taxes or labor from Native Americans, shows that the Europeans prejudged the Native Americans. Ask students what kinds of biases or opinions the Spanish might have had concerning the Native Americans that would have led to this treatment.

Answers to...

CRITICAL THINKING

The Aztecs had enormous wealth.

SECTION 2 ASSESSMENT

AFTER YOU READ

1. (a) Spanish soldier who conquered the Aztecs (b) explorer who reached the Americas in 1492 (c) Aztec ruler (d) Spanish conquistador who conquered the Incas
2. (a) treaty between Spain and Portugal that gave Spain the right to settle and trade west of the Line of Demarcation. Portugal could do the same east of the Line. (b) an agreement in writing between two or more countries (c) imaginary line from the North Pole to the South Pole at about 50 degrees longitude (d) conqueror (e) person of Spanish and Native American descent (f) plantation owned by Spaniards or the Catholic church
3. Europeans originally hoped to find new trade routes to Asia.
4. European explorers and conquistadors achieved wealth, fame and glory.
5. Native Americans were forced to work on farms for the settlers. They also died from diseases brought by Europeans, and their great civilizations were destroyed.
6. The Spanish had advantages such as guns, cannons, and horses that Native Americans could not defend themselves against. The Spanish allied themselves with other Native American groups that were the enemies of the groups they tried to conquer. The Europeans introduced diseases that Native Americans had no immunity to.
7. Europeans believed that Native Americans were inferior and that the settlers were entitled to take their wealth, land, and labor.
8. Remind students that the Europeans recognized much of what they encountered, whereas much about the Europeans was new and puzzling to the Native Americans.

A Family in the Americas

CULTURE This painting shows a Native American man, his Mestizan wife, and their child. **Critical Thinking** What do you think the family in this painting is doing?

Colonization

By the 1540s, Spain claimed land throughout much of the Americas. Spain's lands stretched from what today is Kansas all the way south to the tip of South America. Brazil was claimed by Portugal.

Spain Organizes Its Empire Spain divided its territory into provinces and set up a strong government. The two most important provinces were New Spain and Peru. The capital of New Spain was Mexico City and Lima became the capital city of Peru.

The most powerful citizens lived in the center of Lima. They either came from Spain or had Spanish parents. **Mestizos,** people of mixed Spanish and Native American descent, lived on the outskirts of the city. Native Americans, the least powerful class, continued to live in the countryside. The Spanish forced them to work on haciendas. A **hacienda** (hah see EN duh) was a plantation owned by Spaniards or the Catholic Church.

The Effect of European Rule Spain gave its settlers rights to demand taxes or labor from Native Americans. Many Native Americans died from overwork, malnutrition, and European diseases. In 1519, New Spain had a Native American population of 25 million. Only 3 million survived the first 50 years of Spanish rule.

SECTION 2 ASSESSMENT

AFTER YOU READ

RECALL

1. Identify : (a) Hernán Cortés, (b) Christopher Columbus, (c) Moctezuma, (d) Francisco Pizarro
2. Define: (a) Treaty of Tordesillas, (b) treaty, (c) Line of Demarcation, (d) conquistador, (e) mestizo, (f) hacienda

COMPREHENSION

3. What did European explorers originally hope to achieve by sailing west across the Atlantic Ocean?
4. What were the short-term effects of European exploration of Latin America?
5. How did Spanish colonization affect Native Americans?

CRITICAL THINKING AND WRITING

6. **Exploring the Main Idea** Review the Main Idea statement at the beginning of this section. Then, write a paragraph listing some of the factors that led to the decline of Native American cultures in the Americas.
7. **Recognizing Bias** Native Americans were not asked about the Treaty of Tordesillas, though it directly affected their lives. What do you think this says about European attitudes toward Native Americans?

ACTIVITY

8. **Writing to Learn** Write two paragraphs: one by a Native American who has just seen a European for the first time and another by a European who has just seen a Native American for the first time.

Answers to...

CRITICAL THINKING

Students' responses will vary, but should be supported with details from the painting.

Resource Directory

Teaching Resources

Section Quiz in the Unit 3 Teaching Resources, p. 22

SECTION 3

Independence and the Spread of Democracy

BEFORE YOU READ

READING FOCUS

1. How did Latin American nations win independence from their European rulers?
2. How did the American and French revolutions influence events in Latin America?
3. What are some of the challenges Latin America faced as a result of gaining independence?

KEY TERMS

revolution
criollo
caudillo
invest
economy

KEY PEOPLE

Toussaint L'Ouverture
Miguel Hidalgo
Agustín de Iturbide
Simón Bolívar
José de San Martín

NOTE TAKING

Copy the chart below. As you read the section, fill in the chart with information about how and when Latin American countries gained independence.

Late 1770s: British colonies in North America revolt for freedom from British rule
Late 1780s: French citizens revolt against royal rulers
Criollos in Latin America become interested in revolutions

→ Haiti | Mexico | Western South America | Brazil

MAIN IDEA

Inspired by revolutions in other countries, Latin American countries fought for and gained their independence from European rule.

Setting the Scene

The first colony in Latin America to start a revolution was Saint-Domingue (san duh MANG) in the Caribbean. Tired of French colonial rule and mistreatment by white masters, and led by a former slave, **Toussaint L'Ouverture** (too SAN loo vur TOOR), the slaves there fought for 10 years and finally gained independence in 1804. They called their new country Haiti.

The flame of liberty sparked in Haiti soon spread across Latin America. By 1825, most of the region was independent. Latin Americans would no longer be ruled by Europe.

Haitian Independence

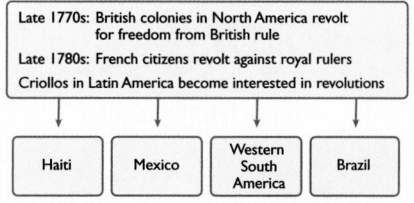

HISTORY Toussaint L'Ouverture was captured by the French, but his followers won Haiti's independence. **Critical Thinking** What qualities do you think make a hero? Why?

Independence in Mexico

Haiti's leaders drew encouragement from two famous revolutions. One type of **revolution** is a political movement in which the people overthrow a government and set up another. During the 1770s and early 1780s, the 13 British colonies in North America fought a war to free themselves from Britain's rule. In 1789, the common people of France staged a violent uprising against their royal rulers. These actions inspired not only the people of Haiti, but also people across Latin America.

SECTION 3

Lesson Objectives

1. Describe how Latin American nations won independence from their European rulers.
2. Analyze the ways the American and French Revolutions influenced events in Latin America.
3. Describe challenges Latin America faced as a result of independence.

Lesson Plan

1 Engage

Warm-Up Activity

Write *Fourth of July* on the board. Ask students what they think of when they see these words. Then, ask students what the Fourth of July commemorates. Ask them why they think Americans continue to celebrate this day.

Activating Prior Knowledge

Ask students to name people whom they consider heroes. Why are they heroic?

Resource Directory

Teaching Resources

Classroom Manager in the Unit 3 Teaching Resources, p. 23

Guided Reading and Review in the Unit 3 Teaching Resources, p. 24

Guide to the Essentials, p. 42

Technology

Section Reading Support Transparencies

Answers to...

CRITICAL THINKING

Answers will vary. Students may say that bravery, enthusiasm, hard work, and perseverence are qualities that make a hero.

Lesson Plan continued

2 Explore

Have students read the section. Ask students to focus on the significance of the following people to the independence movement in Latin America: Toussaint L'Ouverture, Miguel Hidalgo, Simón Bolívar, and José de San Martín.

3 Teach

Ask partners to create an illustrated poster titled *Independence in Latin America* using the information in this section. Encourage them to include information about the people who worked for independence, the locations of battles, the countries that gained their independence as a result of the movement, and the years they became independent. Display and discuss completed posters.

Questions for Discussion

SOCIAL STUDIES SKILLS **What were the different points of view of Father Hidalgo held by the Mexican people and the Spanish government?**

To the Mexican people, he was a hero. To the Spanish government, he was a traitor.

ECONOMICS **How did a rise in the price of oil affect the Latin American economy?**

Latin American countries borrowed money, causing a huge foreign debt, which they are still paying off.

AS YOU READ

Draw Conclusions What do you think the attitude of Mexican criollos was toward the revolution?

Criollos (kree OH yohz) paid particular attention to these events. A **criollo** had Spanish parents, but had been born in Latin America. Criollos often were the wealthiest and best-educated people in the Spanish colonies but few criollos had any political power because only people born in Spain could hold government office.

The "Cry of Dolores" Mexico began its struggle for self-government in 1810. **Miguel Hidalgo** (mee GEHL ee DAHL goh) led the way. He was a criollo priest in the town of Dolores. With other criollos in Dolores, he planned to begin a revolution.

In September 1810, the Spanish government discovered Hidalgo's plot. But before the authorities could arrest him, Hidalgo took action. He wildly rang the church bells. A huge crowd gathered. "Recover from the hated Spaniards the land stolen from your forefathers," he shouted.

Hidalgo's call for revolution became known as the "Cry of Dolores." It attracted some 80,000 fighters in a matter of weeks, mostly mestizos and Native Americans. They wanted revenge against the Spanish government. The rebels won some victories, but their luck changed and by the beginning of 1811, they were in full retreat. Hidalgo tried to flee the country but was captured. He was tried, convicted of treason, and executed in July 1811.

The Cry of Dolores

CULTURE Father Hidalgo made the "Cry of Dolores" on September 16. Mexico celebrates every year on that day. **Critical Thinking** Why do you think that the painter of this mural included so many people in the background behind Father Hidalgo? What can you tell about these people?

Independence Finally Comes Small rebel groups kept fighting. Then **Agustín de Iturbide** (ee toor BEE day) joined the rebels. He was a high-ranking officer in the Spanish army. Many people who had opposed the rebellion felt they could trust Iturbide to protect their interests. They decided to support the rebellion and in 1821, Iturbide defeated the Spanish and declared Mexico independent.

South American Independence

Simón Bolívar (see MOHN boh LEE vahr) almost certainly was the greatest Latin American revolutionary leader.

Bolívar joined the fight for Venezuelan independence in 1804. Six years later he became its leader. By 1822, Bolívar's troops had freed a large area from Spanish rule (the future countries of Colombia, Venezuela, Ecuador, and Panama). This newly liberated region formed Gran Colombia. Bolívar became its president.

José de San Martín (san mahr TEEN), an Argentine, had lived in Spain and served in the Spanish army. When Argentina began its fight for freedom, he quickly offered to help. In 1817, he led his soldiers

Answers to...

AS YOU READ

Answers will vary. Students may say that criollos probably supported the Mexican Revolution because they had little political power and could not hold government offices.

CRITICAL THINKING

The painter may have wanted to show how many people supported Hidalgo. These people came from all levels of society.

Resource Directory

Technology

Color Transparencies 61 Mexico: Political Map

through the high passes in the Andes into Chile. This bold action took the Spanish completely by surprise and in a matter of months, Spain was defeated. San Martín declared Chile's independence. Then he turned his attention to Peru.

Again, San Martín took an unexpected action. This time, he attacked from the sea. In July 1821, San Martín pushed inland and seized Lima, the capital of Peru.

A year later, San Martín met with Bolívar to discuss the fight for independence. Afterward, San Martín suddenly gave up his command and left Bolívar to continue the fight alone. Eventually, Bolívar drove the remaining Spanish forces out of South America altogether. By 1825, only Cuba and Puerto Rico were still ruled by Spain.

Brazil Takes a Different Route to Freedom In the early 1800s, French armies invaded Spain and Portugal. Portugal's royal family fled to Brazil for safety. The king returned to Portugal in 1821, and left his son, Dom Pedro, to rule the colony. Dom Pedro declared Brazil independent in 1822. Three years later, Portugal quietly admitted that Brazil was independent.

Challenges of Independence

After winning independence from Europe in the mid-1800s, Latin American leaders faced hard challenges and had to decide how to govern their nations. Bolívar set the standard for Latin American leaders, most of whom were **caudillos** (kow DEE yohs), military officers who ruled very strictly with unlimited powers. Unlike Bolívar, though, most caudillos just wanted to stay in power and get rich. Following years of fighting and now under strict control, Latin American nations were very poor.

Agriculture and the Economy

ECONOMICS

Many large-scale farming operations in Latin America are still foreign-owned. **Critical Thinking** How would having many foreign-owned farming operations affect a country's economy?

Resource Directory

Technology

Color Transparencies 55 Latin America: Physical-Political Map

4 Assess/Reteach

See answers to the Section 3 Assessment. You might also use students' completed posters as an assessment.

Acceptable posters include basic information about three of the major figures involved.

Commendable posters include basic information about the people involved and illustrate the locations of battles.

Outstanding posters present the basic information as well as information about the influences of the American and French Revolutions on the Latin American revolutions.

ACTIVITY

Cooperative Learning

Talking With Liberators Organize students into groups of six or seven. Have each group prepare a talk show featuring the heroes of the Latin American independence movement as guests. Individual group members should work on the following tasks: preparing questions to ask the heroes, creating props, writing the script, assigning roles for heroes and talk-show host, rehearsing the show. Let groups present their shows to the class.

Verbal/Linguistic

ACTIVITY

Journal Writing

A Soldier's Diary Ask students to imagine that they are soldiers in San Martín's army. Have students write a journal entry describing their experiences about fighting for independence. Invite volunteers to share their journal entries with the class.

Verbal/Linguistic

Answers to...

CRITICAL THINKING

Profit from the farms would go to the foreign country rather than to Latin Americans.

SECTION 3 ASSESSMENT

AFTER YOU READ

1. (a) ex-slave who led Haiti to independence (b) led struggle for Mexican independence (c) declared Mexico's independence from Spain in 1821 (d) led fight for independence for Colombia, Venezuela, Ecuador, Panama (e) led fight for independence for Chile and Peru
2. (a) political movement in which people overthrow the government and set up another (b) person of Spanish parents born in Latin America (c) military officer who ruled very strictly (d) to spend money to earn money (e) the ways goods and services are produced and made available to people
3. Most fought battles with Spanish government soldiers and were led by Latin American revolutionary leaders. Brazil was peacefully granted independence by the royal family of Portugal. Haiti's slaves fought against French colonial rule for ten years.
4. Revolutions in North America and France in the late 1700s inspired people across Latin America.
5. They built factories, grew more crops, developed resources, and limited foreign investment. They also began cooperating with each other.
6. Caudillos, or military leaders were very strict and often more interested in personal gain than in helping the newly independent countries. Also, the countries were poor after years of fighting.
7. The economies would have remained poor, because the rulers would have taken most of the money.
8. Display examples of poems in different formats so students can see their poetic options.

Answers to...

CRITICAL THINKING

Students may say factory workers need manual dexterity, patience, and an ability to work carefully and pay attention.

Building Televisions on an Assembly Line

ECONOMICS In the last 50 years, Latin American countries have begun to produce many more products in factories like this one in Brazil. **Critical Thinking** What skills do you think these factory workers need?

Economic Issues

In the 1900s, many foreign companies invested in Latin America. **Investing** means spending money to earn more money. As a result, foreign companies became powerful in Latin American economies. A country's **economy** is made up of the ways that goods and services are produced and made available to people. Money from the sale of goods and services affects a country's economy. Foreign companies made huge profits but did little to help Latin American countries build their economies.

To improve their economies, Latin American countries built their own factories to make goods and began to grow different kinds of crops to develop their resources. By the 1970s Latin American economies improved. But in the 1980s, the price of oil to run factories rose. In addition, prices for Latin American goods dropped. Latin American countries spent more money but were making less. To make up the difference, they borrowed money from wealthy countries, causing huge foreign debt.

Today, Latin American countries continue to expand their economies. Foreign companies still invest in Latin America, but most Latin American countries limit how investments can be made. They want to prevent foreign countries from having too much control over their economies. Latin American countries are also cooperating with one another and trading for a variety of different products.

SECTION 3 ASSESSMENT

AFTER YOU READ

RECALL

1. Identify: (a) Toussaint L'Ouverture, (b) Miguel Hidalgo, (c) Agustín de Iturbide, (d) Simón Bolíver, (e) José de San Martín
2. Define: (a) revolution, (b) criollo, (c) caudillo, (d) invest, (e) economy

COMPREHENSION

3. Describe how Latin American countries won their independence.
4. What world events influenced the independence movement in Latin America?
5. What steps did Latin American countries take to improve their economies after winning independence?

CRITICAL THINKING AND WRITING

6. **Exploring the Main Idea** Review the Main Idea statement at the beginning of this section. Then, list some of the political and economic challenges faced by the new, independent countries of Latin America.
7. **Making Predictions** Write a paragraph explaining what you think might have happened to Latin American economies if the countries had not gained independence and had stayed under colonial rule.

ACTIVITY

8. **Writing to Learn** Imagine you are a poet and have been asked to write a patriotic poem for a newly independent country in Latin America. Write a poem about the country's independence. Be sure to include the country's name and details about its struggle for independence.

Resource Directory

Teaching Resources

Section Quiz in the Unit 3 Teaching Resources, p. 25

Chapter Summary in the Unit 3 Teaching Resources, p. 26

Vocabulary in the Unit 3 Teaching Resources, p. 27

Reteaching in the Unit 3 Teaching Resources, p. 28

Enrichment in the Unit 3 Teaching Resources, p. 29

Critical Thinking in the Unit 3 Teaching Resources, p. 30

Making Decisions

IDENTIFY THE SITUATION

GATHER INFORMATION

CONSIDER THE OPTIONS
Option 1
Option 2
Option 3

PREDICT THE CONSEQUENCES
1.
2.
3.

MAKE A DECISION

Learn the Skill

Making good decisions requires thought and effort. To make good decisions, follow these steps:

A. Identify the Situation. Make sure you have a clear picture of the issues involved. It is sometimes helpful to write out the situation, explaining reasons why it needs to be considered and what needs to be changed.

B. Gather Information. To clarify the issues further, it is helpful to collect specific information about the situation being considered. A situation develops over the course of time. Often this history—the history of the situation—can offer facts that will aid you in making your decision.

C. Consider the Options. Before jumping to conclusions and acting too quickly, take some time to write down several options, or different possible courses of action. When Christopher Columbus wanted to find a better trade route to the East, he probably considered several different routes. Brainstorming as many ideas as possible and writing them down will give you more information to work with.

D. Predict the Consequences. Think about each option and the possible consequences of each action. Write down the risks as well as the outcome not only for yourself, but for everyone involved. Some decisions affect not only you but your family, school, and community. Others, such as which candidate to vote for or which political issue to support, may affect your entire state or country. It's better to know these possible outcomes before your decision is made.

E. Make a Decision. Choose one of the options. Using what you have learned, decide what action to take that is best for everyone involved. The best decision is not always the easiest solution or the one that brings the quickest results. Choose the one that will best solve the problem in the long run.

Practice the Skill

Miguel Hidalgo began a revolution that led to Mexican independence. No doubt this priest struggled with his decision to rally the people to war. He may have pondered his decision over a period of months or even years. Think about the decision he made and examine it in light of the five decision-making steps. What was the situation? What were the options? Consider the consequences of each option. Tell why you think Hidalgo made the decision he did. Do you think he made the right decision? Tell why or why not.

Apply the Skill

See the Chapter Review and Assessment at the end of this chapter for more questions on making decisions.

Lesson Objectives

1. Identify the steps needed to make good decisions.
2. Analyze the decision-making process.

Lesson Plan

1 Engage

Discuss with students the ways they make decisions every day. For instance, when they get up, they decide what to wear and what to eat for breakfast. Discuss the possible consequences of deciding to wear shorts on a cold day, or of skipping breakfast. Point out that some decisions have more far-reaching consequences than other decisions.

2 Explore

Have students read the steps under "Learn the Skill." Make sure students understand the meaning of *options* and *consequences.* Have them point to the boxes on the flow chart and explain in their own words what they are to do at each stage.

3 Teach

If students cannot remember the story of Miguel Hidalgo, have them reread page 190. Have them work through the flow chart, predicting Hidalgo's thoughts and ideas during each of the four stages.

For additional reinforcement, have students choose a decision they must make, such as which sport to play, then follow the four steps to make a decision.

4 Assess/Reteach

Students should be able to list the four steps, explain what to do for each, and use them to make a decision.

To further assess students' understanding of making decisions, have them complete the "Applying Your Skills" part of the Chapter Review and Assessment at the end of this chapter.

Resource Directory

Technology

Social Studies Skills Tutor CD-ROM

Answers to...

PRACTICE THE SKILL

Answers will vary with some questions. Situation: In 1810, the Spanish government discovered Hidalgo's plot to overthrow it; Options: to abort the plot or to continue on as planned; Consequences: if he had stopped the plot, the Spanish probably would have remained in power much longer than they did.

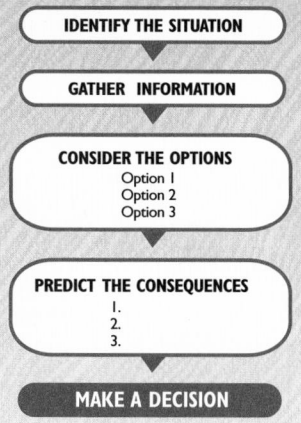

CHAPTER 10

Review and Assessment

Creating a Chapter Summary

Student summaries will vary.

Sample summaries:

Section 2 European explorers came to Latin America looking for gold and other treasures and to claim land. Native American cultures were destroyed as a result of European exploration and conquest.

Section 3 Some Latin American countries started revolutions in order to gain independence from Europe, while others gained independence in different ways. With independence came new political and economic challenges.

Reviewing Key Terms

1. e **2.** b **3.** c **4.** a **5.** f **6.** d

Reviewing the Main Ideas

1. Mayan accomplishments: great cities, calendar, system of writing, number system; Aztec accomplishments: great cities, calendars, system of writing, medicine, arts and crafts; Incan accomplishments: great cities, roads, aqueducts, terraced land, organized government, strong buildings.
2. Many people in Mexico today eat foods similar to those eaten by the Aztecs, such as corn; Mayan and Incan languages are still spoken.
3. They built canals and aqueducts to carry water to their crops. They also made terraces to increase farmland.
4. The Mayas and Aztecs both had calendars, written language based on hieroglyphics, great cities, religions, and priests that studied the stars and planets. They were also farmers.
5. The Line of Demarcation divided the land in such a way that Spain received most of Latin America and Portugal received Brazil.
6. They supported the fight for independence. Miguel Hidalgo, a criollo priest, began the fight for independence by assembling an army.
7. They have built more factories, diversified their crops, and limited investment by foreign countries. They are also working with each other to develop trade.

CHAPTER 10

Review and Assessment

Creating a Chapter Summary

On a separate piece of paper, draw a diagram like this one, and include the information that summarizes the first section of the chapter. Then, fill in the second and third boxes with summaries of Sections 2 and 3.

LATIN AMERICA: SHAPED BY HISTORY

Section 1	Section 2	Section 3
Three advanced civilizations—those of the Mayas, Aztecs, and Incas—existed in Latin America before the arrival of Europeans. Each had its own important cultural practices and institutions.		

Reviewing Key Terms

Match the definitions in Column I with the key terms in Column II.

Column I

1. a pipe or channel designed to carry water from a distant source
2. conqueror
3. a kind of writing, using signs and symbols
4. a political movement in which people overthrow the government and set up another
5. people of mixed Spanish and Native American descent
6. the ways in which goods and services are produced and made available

Column II

a. revolution
b. conquistador
c. hieroglyphics
d. economy
e. aqueduct
f. mestizo

Reviewing the Main Ideas

1. Name one major accomplishment of each of the Mayan, Aztec, and Incan civilizations. (Section 1)
2. Give two examples of how the Mayan, Aztec, or Incan civilizations affect culture in Latin America today. (Section 1)
3. How were the Incas able to change their environment in order to grow more food? (Section 1)
4. List two ways in which the Mayan and Aztec civilizations were alike. (Section 1)
5. Why did Spain gain control over most of Latin America while Portugal gained control over only Brazil? (Section 2)
6. What role did the criollos play in the fight for Latin American independence? (Section 3)
7. How have many Latin American countries been trying to improve their economies in recent years? (Section 3)

Map Activity

For each civilization or place listed below, write the letter from the map that shows its location.

1. Andes
2. Incan civilization
3. Mayan civilization
4. Aztec civilization

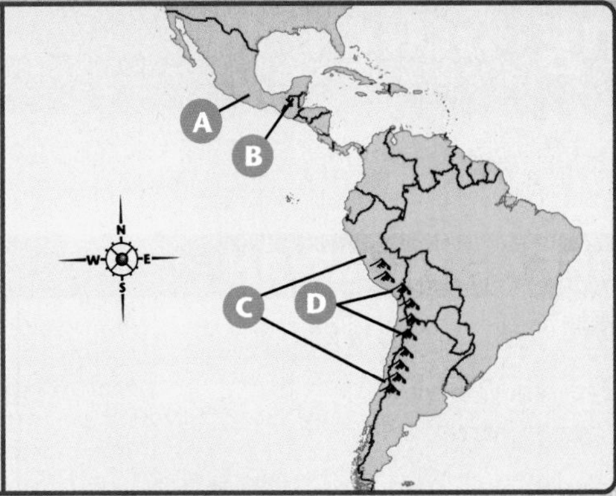

Take It to the NET

Enrichment For more map activities using geography skills, visit the social studies section of **phschool.com.**

Writing Activity

1. **Writing a Song** The Mayas, Aztecs, and Incas had spoken histories. Information is passed from generation to generation in stories and songs. Imagine that you lived at the time of the Spanish conquest. Write a song that tells about the conquest from a Mayan, Aztec, or Incan point of view.
2. **Writing a Journal** You are supporter of Miguel Hidalgo who has just heard the "Cry of Dolores." Write a journal entry telling how you feel about Hidalgo's efforts toward making Mexico an independent nation, free of Spanish rule.

Critical Thinking

1. **Recognizing Cause and Effect** What were two causes of the fall of the Aztec and Incan civilizations? What were two long-term effects of European rule on the Native American people of the region?
2. **Recognizing Point of View** Hidalgo shouted to the people, "Recover from the hated Spaniards the land stolen from your forefathers!" Why would criollos, who had Spanish parents but who had been born in Latin America, be sympathetic to his cry for freedom from Spain?

Applying Your Skills

Turn to the Skills for Life page to answer the following questions.

1. During which step of the decision-making process would you ponder the consequences of your actions?
   - **a.** Identify the Situation
   - **b.** Gather Information
   - **c.** Consider the Options
   - **d.** Predict the Consequences
   - **e.** Make a Decision
2. Define an issue that you must make a decision about in your life, such as what sports to play after school, how to spend your summer, or what topic to choose for a research report. Outline and use the steps in the decision-making process to make a decision about this issue.

Take It to the NET

Activity Read about the conquistadors and early civilizations in Latin America. How have the conquistadors influenced life in present-day Latin America? Visit the World Explorer: People, Places, and Cultures section of **phschool.com** for help in completing this activity.

Chapter 10 Self-Test As a final review activity, take the Chapter 10 Self-Test and get instant feedback on your answers. To take the test, visit the Social Studies section of **phschool.com.**

Map Activity

1. D **2.** C **3.** B **4.** A

Writing Activity

1. Students songs should include the names of the conquistadors and the time of the conquest. Songs should contain specific descriptive details about the conquest. Encourage volunteers to perform their songs for the class.
2. Entries should include feelings about being independent from Spain and details that support feelings.

Critical Thinking

1. Possible causes: killing the leader and taking over the capital. Possible effects: The Native Americans were forced to work for the Spanish settlers; they died from European diseases.
2. Although criollos had Spanish parents, they could not hold government positions and they had no political power. They wanted to have the right to govern themselves. Freedom from Spain would give them those opportunities.

Applying Your Skills

1. d
2. Students' outlines should include the elements discussed in the decision-making process in the "Skills for Life" activity.

Resource Directory

Teaching Resources

Cooperative Learning Activity in the Unit 3 Teaching Resources, pp. 107–110

Chapter Tests Forms A and B in the Unit 3 Teaching Resources, pp. 136–141

Guide to the Essentials, Ch. 10 Test, p. 43

Other Print Resources

Chapter Tests with ExamView® Test Bank, Ch. 10

Technology

ExamView® Test Bank CD-ROM, Ch. 10

Resource Pro® CD-ROM

Chapter 11 Planning Guide

Resource Manager

	CORE INSTRUCTION	READING/SKILLS
Chapter-Level Resources	**Teaching Resources** Program Overview Pacing Charts **Technology** Resource Pro® CD-ROM Companion Web site, phschool.com • eTeach	**Technology** Social Studies Skills Tutor CD-ROM Student Edition on Audio CD, Ch. 11
1 The Cultures of Mexico **1.** Identify the main cultural groups in Mexico. **2.** Describe population trends in Mexico. **3.** Explain the economic causes of emigration from Mexico to the U.S.	**Teaching Resources** **Unit 3** Classroom Manager, p. 32 Guided Reading and Review, p. 33	**Teaching Resources** Guide to the Essentials, p. 44 Social Studies and Geography Skills, p. 31 **Technology** Section Reading Support Transparencies
2 The Cultures of Central America **1.** Describe the cultural heritage of the people of Central America. **2.** Explain the important role of religion in Central American life. **3.** Identify the causes of the population shift to the cities of Central America and to the U.S.	**Teaching Resources** **Unit 3** Classroom Manager, p. 35 Guided Reading and Review, p. 36	**Teaching Resources** Guide to the Essentials, p. 45 **Technology** Section Reading Support Transparencies
3 The Cultures of the Caribbean **1.** Describe how European, African, and Native American cultures blended to create unique Caribbean cultures. **2.** Explain how various cultures influence present-day ethnic groups, languages, and religions found in the Caribbean. **3.** Identify the key cultural influences that affect the lifestyles, music, foods, and entertainment in the Caribbean.	**Teaching Resources** **Unit 3** Classroom Manager, p. 38 Guided Reading and Review, p. 39	**Teaching Resources** Guide to the Essentials, p. 46 **Technology** Section Reading Support Transparencies
4 The Cultures of South America **1.** Explain how geography has created diversity in South America. **2.** Describe the role of farming in South American life. **3.** Explain how rapid population growth is affecting cities in South America.	**Teaching Resources** **Unit 3** Classroom Manager, p. 41 Guided Reading and Review, p. 42 Chapter Summary, p. 44 Vocabulary, p. 45 Reteaching, p. 46	**Teaching Resources** **Unit 3** Critical Thinking, p. 48 Guide to the Essentials, p. 47 **Technology** Section Reading Support Transparencies

ENRICHMENT / PRE-AP

Teaching Resources
Primary Sources and Literature Readings

Other Print Resources
DK Atlas

Technology
World Video Explorer: Cultures of Latin America
Companion Web site, phschool.com

Teaching Resources
Outline Maps, p. 8

Technology
Color Transparencies 60
World Video Explorer, Mexico Case Study

Teaching Resources
Unit 3
Enrichment, p. 47
Cooperative Learning Activity, pp. 111–113

ASSESSMENT

Prentice Hall Assessment System

Core Assessment
Chapter Tests with ExamView® Test Bank, Ch. 11
ExamView® Test Bank CD-ROM, Ch. 11

Standardized Test Preparation

Diagnose and Prescribe
Diagnostic Tests for Middle Grades Social Studies Skills

Review and Reteach
Review Book for World Studies

Practice and Assess
Test-taking Strategies with Transparencies for Middle Grades Test Prep Book
Test-taking Strategies Posters

Teaching Resources
Unit 3
Section Quizzes, pp. 34, 37, 40, and 43
Chapter Tests, pp. 142–147

Technology
Companion Web site, phschool.com
Ch. 11 Self-Test

World Video Explorer

Each region of the world is explored through regional flyovers and investigative field trips. Case study segments give students an in-depth view of the history, economy, government, and culture of a key place in each region. Case studies include Nigeria, Mexico, China, British Columbia, and the Czech Republic.

In Your Classroom

CUSTOMIZE FOR INDIVIDUAL NEEDS

Gifted and Talented

Teacher's Edition
- Travel Diary, p. 208

Teaching Resources
- Enrichment, p. 47
- Primary Sources and Literature Readings

Honors/Pre-AP

Teacher's Edition
- Travel Diary, p. 208

Teaching Resources
- Critical Thinking, p. 48
- Primary Sources and Literature Readings

ESL

Teacher's Edition
- Travel Diary, p. 208

Teaching Resources
- Guided Reading and Review, pp. 33, 36, 39, and 42
- Vocabulary, p. 45
- Reteaching, p. 46
- Guide to the Essentials, pp. 44–47
- Social Studies and Geography Skills, p. 31

Technology
- Social Studies Skills Tutor CD-ROM
- Section Reading Support Transparencies

Less Proficient Readers

Teacher's Edition
- Travel Diary, p. 208

Teaching Resources
- Guided Reading and Review, pp. 33, 36, 39, and 42
- Vocabulary, p. 45
- Reteaching, p. 46
- Guide to the Essentials, pp. 44–47
- Social Studies and Geography Skills, p. 31

Technology
- Social Studies Skills Tutor CD-ROM
- Section Reading Support Transparencies

Less Proficient Writers

Teacher's Edition
- Travel Diary, p. 208

Teaching Resources
- Guided Reading and Review, pp. 33, 36, 39, and 42
- Vocabulary, p. 45
- Guide to the Essentials, pp. 44–47
- Social Studies and Geography Skills, p. 31

Technology
- Social Studies Skills Tutor CD-ROM
- Section Reading Support Transparencies

DORLING KINDERSLEY

At the end of each unit, you will find information adapted from Dorling Kindersley's *Illustrated Children's Encyclopedia* that connects to the region being studied and to one of the seven content strands. In addition, your resources include Dorling Kindersley's *Atlas*, which contains valuable information about countries from around the world.

TEACHER'S EDITION INDEX

CHAPTER 11 PACING SUGGESTIONS

For 90-minute Blocks

See suggestions in the Teaching Resources Pacing Charts for Chapter 11. Use Color Transparencies 60.

Running Out of Time?

See the Guide to the Essentials, pp. 44–47.

INTERDISCIPLINARY LINKS

Middle Grades Math: Tools for Success

Course 1, Lesson 1-3, **Mean, Median, and Mode;** Lesson 11-4, **Theoretical Probability**

Science Explorer

Cells and Heredity, Lesson 4-1, **Human Inheritance**

From Bacteria to Plants, Lesson 1-3, **Classifying Organisms**

Prentice Hall Literature

Bronze, Mi Amigo Mark

Copper, The Circuit

BIBLIOGRAPHY

For the Teacher

Moss, Joyce. *People of the World: The Culture, Geographical Setting, and Historical Background of 42 Latin American Peoples.* Gale Research, 1989.

Machado, Ana Maria. *Exploration into Latin America.* New Discovery, 1995.

World Desk Reference. Dorling Kindersley, 2001.

For the Student

Easy

Dorros, Arthur. *Tonight Is Carnaval.* Dutton, 1992.

Average

Lehtinen, Ritva, and Kari E. Nurmi. *The Grandchildren of the Incas.* Carolrhoda, 1991.

Challenging

Peterson, Marge. *Argentina: A Wild West Heritage.* Dillon, 1990.

Literature Connection

Joseph, Lynn. *Coconut Kind of Day: Island Poems.* Lothrop, 1990.

O'Dell, Scott. *The Black Pearl.* Houghton Mifflin, 1967.

Wisniewski, David. *Rain Player.* Clarion, 1991.

Take It to the NET

The World Explorer companion Web site, found on **phschool.com**, offers activities for exploring geographical, historical, and cultural resources on the Internet. It also provides on-line links for key content and all Section and Chapter Assessment activities.

The **Teacher site** also provides teachers with regional data and ideas for student research and activities.

Students can use the **Student site** to find chapter-by-chapter Internet resource links and to access Self-Tests.

CHAPTER 11

Connecting to the Guiding Questions

In this chapter, students will read about the cultures of Latin America. Content in this chapter corresponds to the following Guiding Questions outlines at the beginning of the unit.

- How has geography influenced the social and economic development of Latin America?
- How are Latin American cultures alike? How are they different?
- What economic activities support the people of Latin America?
- How have technology and science helped shape Latin America today?

Using the Literature Activities

Choose a student volunteer to read aloud the poem by Octavio Paz. Point out to students the relationship among the three elements in the poem, and the repetition of these elements.

- Some students may prefer to make a sculpture, collage, mobile, or other artwork to represent the poem.
- The poet is writing about how the three elements of wind, water, and stone, all act in different ways to influence and change each other until they become almost interchangeable. Students' poems should reflect an understanding of other close relationships in nature.

Heterogeneous Groups

The following activity is suitable for heterogeneous groups.

Journal Writing

Travel Diary, p. 208

eTeach

Be sure to check out this month's discussion with a Master Teacher. Go to **phschool.com**.

CHAPTER 11

LATIN AMERICA: Rich in Culture

"Wind and Water and Stone" by Octavio Paz

The water hollowed the stone,
the wind dispersed the water,
the stone stopped the wind.
Water and wind and stone.

The wind sculpted the stone,
the stone is a cup of water,
the water runs off and is wind,
Stone and wind and water.

The wind sings in its turnings,
the water murmurs as it goes,
the motionless stone is quiet.
Wind and water and stone.

One is the other, and is neither;
among their empty names
they pass and disappear,
water and stone and wind.

Understanding Literature

Analyzing Poetry

A poet often attempts to give meaning to something through the words he or she uses. The poet, Octavio Paz, shows the relationship between wind, water, and stone in this poem. Reread the poem and then choose one of the poem's four stanzas and draw or paint a picture that you think captures the images used in this poem. You might recreate the scene as the poet describes it, or use symbolism or abstract art to illustrate the stanza.

Creating a Poem

Read the poem by Octavio Paz again. What do you think the poet is saying about the relationship between wind, water, and stone? How do these three elements relate to each other? Think of other elements in nature that have a close relationship, such as the ocean's tides and the beach, clouds and rain, or sun and light. Write a poem that illustrates such a relationship, using images from nature.

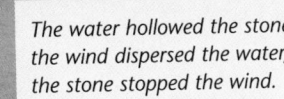

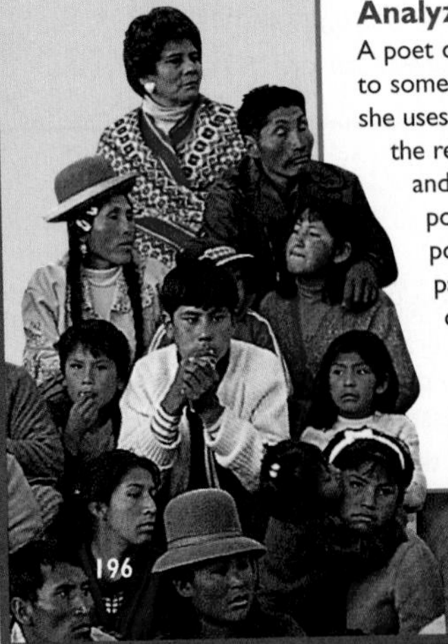

Resource Directory

Teaching Resources

Primary Sources and Literature Readings extend content with a selection related to the concepts in this chapter.

Other Print Resources

DK Atlas

Technology

Cultures of Latin America, from the World Video Explorer, provides students with a visual overview of the region's many cultures.

Student Edition on Audio CD, Ch. 11

SECTION 1

The Cultures of Mexico

BEFORE YOU READ

READING FOCUS

1. What are three of the cultures that influence Mexico?
2. What population trends affect Mexico today?
3. What economic factors have caused emigration from Mexico to the United States?

KEY TERMS

campesinos
rural
urban
maquiladora
emigrate

KEY PLACES

Mexico City

MAIN IDEA

Mexico's diverse peoples are affected by shifting population patterns and economic circumstances.

NOTE TAKING

Copy the concept web below. As you read the section, fill in the web with information about the culture of Mexico. Add more ovals as you need them.

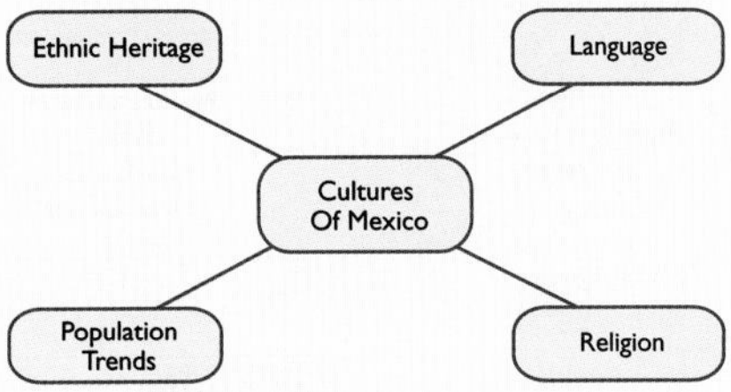

Setting the Scene

Modern Mexico is greatly influenced by its past. For centuries it was the home of advanced, ancient Native American civilizations. When the Spanish colonized the region in the 1500s, they brought their language, religion, architecture, and music with them. The combination of these two cultures gave rise to another culture, the mestizo. Mexico blends these cultures.

Mexico's Cultural Influences

Mestizos have both Spanish and indigenous ancestors. About 20 percent of the people of Mexico are indigenous people, but Spanish is the first language for most Mexicans. Some Mexicans also speak Native American languages.

Religion is important to the people of Mexico. In the 1500s and 1600s, Spanish Catholic missionaries converted many Native Americans to Christianity and the Roman Catholic Church has been important to this region ever since. Native Americans, however, have blended many elements of their religions with Christianity.

A Rural Marketplace

ECONOMICS This market is in Oaxaca (wah HAH kah), Mexico. People in rural Mexico buy many of their groceries and housewares from markets like these. **Critical Thinking** What details in this photograph show similarities between rural markets and urban supermarkets? What details show differences?

Resource Directory

Teaching Resources

Classroom Manager in the Unit 3 Teaching Resources, p. 32

Guided Reading and Review in the Unit 3 Teaching Resources, p. 33

Guide to the Essentials, p. 44

Technology

Section Reading Support Transparencies

SECTION 1

Lesson Objectives

1. Identify the main cultural groups in Mexico.
2. Describe population trends in present-day Mexico.
3. Explain the economic causes of emigration from Mexico to the U.S.

Lesson Plan

1 Engage

Warm-Up Activity

Ask students to name three things that come to mind when they think of Mexico. Extract key words or terms to make a list of geographical features, clothing, food items, and so on. Add to the list as students progress through the chapter.

Activating Prior Knowledge

Ask volunteers to share what they know about where their great-great-grandparents, great-grandparents, grandparents, or parents were born and what they know about their cultural backgrounds.

2 Explore

Have students read the section. Then, have them describe the predominant cultures in Mexico. Prompt them with questions such as, *What groups of people live in Mexico? Who are the mestizos and what is their cultural background? What is the main language and religion of Mexico?*

Answers to...

CRITICAL THINKING

Similarities: food is sold in both places, and the produce stalls in the rural market are similar to the produce section of a grocery store. Differences: rural markets are often open-air markets with different products sold by different vendors.

Lesson Plan continued

3 Teach

Work with students to begin creating Mexican heritage poster-collages of images depicting cultural influences. Have them add images to their posters as they read through the section. The following questions may provide prompts to get poster-collages started: *How could you include an image for language in your poster? What images might you show to depict Spanish or Native American influences?*

Questions for Discussion

CULTURE **What aspects of Native American culture are found in Mexico today?**

One finds aspects such as religion, language, music, and architecture.

HISTORY **What cultural aspects demonstrate Spain's historical influence on Mexico?**

Spanish is the first language for most Mexicans, and the major religion is Christianity.

4 Assess/Reteach

See answers to the Section 1 Assessment. You may also use students' completed poster-collages as an assessment.

Acceptable poster-collages include images of basic cultural factors such as language, religion, clothing, and food.

Commendable poster-collages include images of basic cultural factors as well as other specific Spanish, Native American, and mestizo influences.

Outstanding poster-collages include images as listed above as well as depicting living styles found in rural and urban areas and political and economic cultural influences.

Answers to...

MAP STUDY

Most people live in or around Mexico City. More job opportunities exist in the city and the potential for making a better living is likely to be available in urban areas rather than rural areas.

Mexico

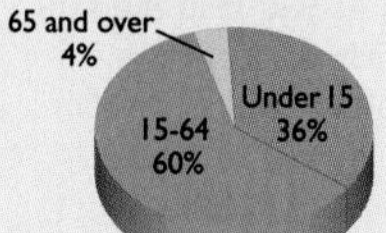

Age Structure (in years)

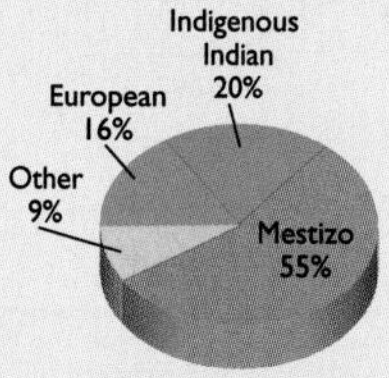

Ethnic Makeup

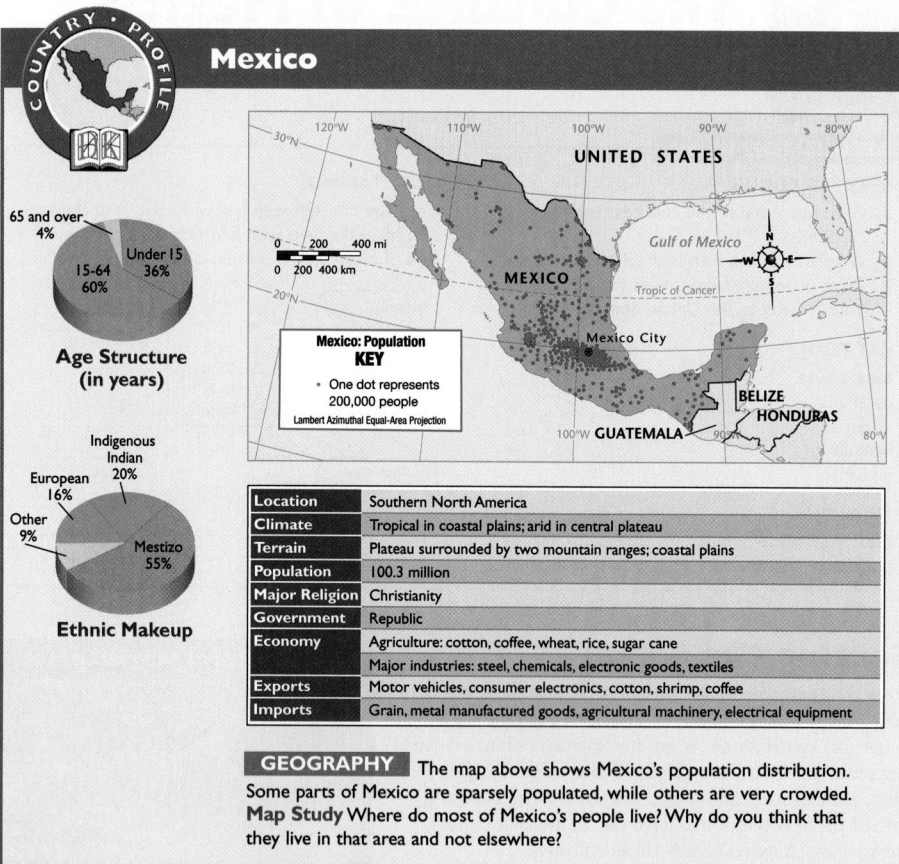

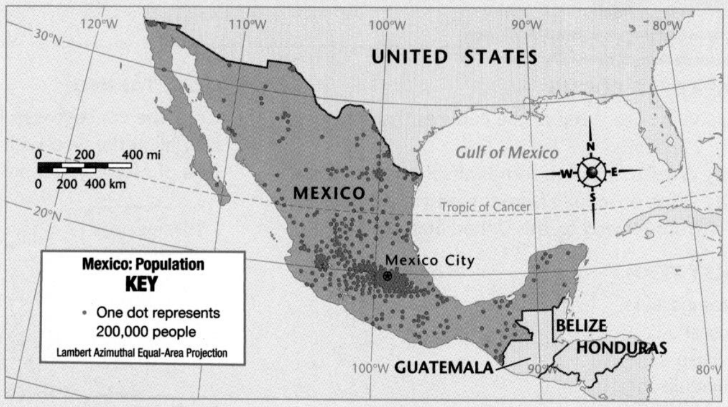

Location	Southern North America
Climate	Tropical in coastal plains; arid in central plateau
Terrain	Plateau surrounded by two mountain ranges; coastal plains
Population	100.3 million
Major Religion	Christianity
Government	Republic
Economy	Agriculture: cotton, coffee, wheat, rice, sugar cane
	Major industries: steel, chemicals, electronic goods, textiles
Exports	Motor vehicles, consumer electronics, cotton, shrimp, coffee
Imports	Grain, metal manufactured goods, agricultural machinery, electrical equipment

GEOGRAPHY The map above shows Mexico's population distribution. Some parts of Mexico are sparsely populated, while others are very crowded. **Map Study** Where do most of Mexico's people live? Why do you think that they live in that area and not elsewhere?

Changing Population Patterns

Most farm families in Mexico are poor. The poor farmers, who are known as **campesinos** (kahm peh SEE nohs), plow the land and harvest their crops by hand because they cannot afford expensive equipment.

Although some people of Mexico live in **rural,** or countryside, areas, about 74 percent live in cities and large towns. Mexico's population has risen dramatically over the last 20 years, growing at a rate of more than two percent each year—a rate that will cause the poulation to double in 20 to 30 years. Rapid population growth makes it hard for young people in rural areas to find jobs and many leave home to look for work in **urban,** or city, areas.

Many people have moved from rural areas to **Mexico City,** Mexico's largest city. If you count the people in all the outlying areas,

Resource Directory

Teaching Resources

Social Studies and Geography Skills, Reading a Population Distribution Map, p. 31

Outline Maps Mexico, p. 8

Technology

Color Transparencies 60 Mexico: Physical-Political Map

World Video Explorer See the Mexico case study for an overview of Mexico's history, economy, government, and culture. Discussion questions are included.

Mexico City has more than 23 million people. There are many contrasts between the lives of city dwellers in Mexico City. Wealthy people in Mexico City have a lifestyle similar to that of wealthy people in the United States. For the poor, however, life in the city can be very hard.

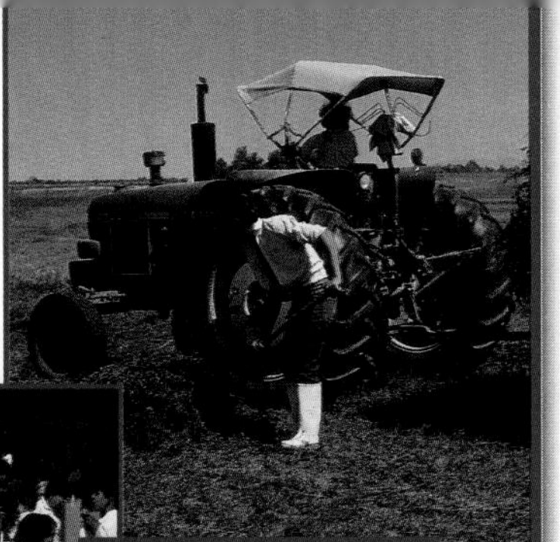

Economics and Emigration

Some people in Mexico move to towns along the border with the United States. There they can work in factories owned by American companies, but located in Mexico because wages are lower than in the United States. These border factories are called **maquiladoras** (ma kee la DOR as).

As people flood into Mexican cities and border towns, jobs become scarcer and some people have decided to emigrate. **Emigrate** means to move permanently from one country to another. Thousands of people have emigrated from Mexico to the United States. Some of these emigrants enter the United States illegally, a problem that the U.S. and Mexican governments are attempting to solve.

Fermin Carrillo (fair MEEN kah REE yoh) is one worker who did just that. Because there were no more jobs and his parents needed food and medical care, he left his hometown in Mexico and moved to Oregon. He found work in a fish processing plant and sends most of the money he earns home to his parents.

Rural and Urban Living

ECONOMICS

Above, a farmer in rural Mexico makes his living by raising alfalfa. To the left, people hurry to destinations in Mexico City. **Critical Thinking** How do you think the challenges of living in urban areas in Mexico might be different from the challenges of living in rural areas?

SECTION I ASSESSMENT

AFTER YOU READ

RECALL

1. Identify: (a) Mexico City
2. Define: (a) campesinos, (b) rural, (c) urban, (d) maquiladora, (d) emigrate

COMPREHENSION

3. What cultures influence Mexico today?
4. Why is the population in Mexico shifting from rural to urban areas?
5. Describe economic factors that have influenced emigration from Mexico to the United States.

CRITICAL THINKING AND WRITING

6. **Exploring the Main Idea** Review the Main Idea statement at the beginning of this section. Then write a paragraph telling how and why the population patterns in Mexico are changing.
7. **Supporting a Point of View** Write a journal entry from the point of view of a person moving from a rural to urban setting. Write about how the person's life has changed as a result of his or her move.

ACTIVITY

Take It to the NET

8. **Mexican Culture and Cooking** Food and cooking are important aspects of Mexican culture. Cook some of the recipes you find on the Web site and sample some traditional Mexican food. Visit the World Explorer: People, Places, and Cultures section of **phschool.com** for help in completing this activity.

SECTION I ASSESSMENT

AFTER YOU READ

1. (a) the capital of Mexico
2. (a) poor farmers who have only a small amount of land (b) having to do with countryside (c) having to do with cities (d) Mexican factory near the U.S. border (e) to move from one country to another
3. Spanish, Native American, and mestizo
4. The population in Mexico is shifting from rural to urban as people look for ways other than farming to make a living.
5. American companies open factories in Mexico near the border because wages are low. There are not enough jobs for all the Mexicans who move to these towns, so many of them choose to immigrate to the United States.
6. Paragraphs should mention that with increased population in rural areas, there are fewer jobs available. People are moving to cities to find work to support themselves and their families.
7. Journal entries should cite specific reasons for moving, challenges faced, goals, and feelings.
8. Ask students how Mexican food is similar to and different from food they usually eat.

Resource Directory

Teaching Resources

Section Quiz in the Unit 3 Teaching Resources, p. 34

Answers to...

CRITICAL THINKING

Students might mention the challenges of dealing with physical geography and climate in rural areas, as well as scarcity of jobs. Challenges in urban areas might include higher cost of living, higher crime rate, and greater competition for jobs.

SECTION 2

Lesson Objectives

1. Describe the cultural heritage of the people of Central America.
2. Explain the important role of religion in Central American life.
3. Identify the causes of the population shift to the cities of Central America and to the United States.

Lesson Plan

1 Engage

Warm-Up Activity

Ask students what comes to mind when they hear the words *urban* and *rural*. Ideas can encompass geography, ways of life, clothing, foods, and standards of living. Make a list of their ideas.

Activating Prior Knowledge

Ask students what their hopes and dreams are for the future. Ask if they plan to continue their education, or what kinds of careers they would like to have.

2 Explore

As students read the section, have them identify the major characteristics of Central American culture. The following questions may provide prompts: *What groups of people live in these countries? What is the main language in most countries? Which religion is common in all the countries?*

Answers to...

CRITICAL THINKING

Modern farming equipment might make it easier for farmers to farm more land in less time, or to grow a greater variety of crops. This might strengthen the economy, but it might also harm the environment.

SECTION 2

The Cultures of Central America

BEFORE YOU READ

1. What is the cultural heritage of the people of Central America?
2. How does religion affect the lives of Central Americans?
3. Why have many Central Americans moved to cities or to the United States?

KEY TERMS
diversity
injustice

KEY PLACES
Honduras

MAIN IDEA
There is great diversity and rich heritage among the cultures of Central America.

NOTE TAKING
Copy the Venn diagram below. As you read the section, fill in the diagram with information about rural and urban life in Central America.

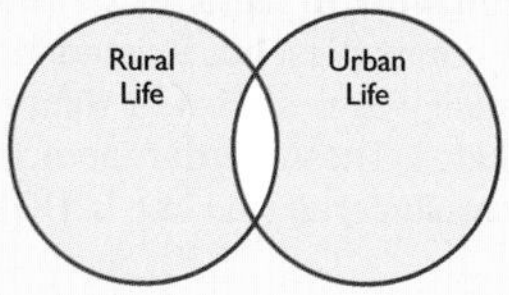

Farming Methods

SCIENCE, TECHNOLOGY, AND SOCIETY

In El Salvador, many farmers do not have modern farming equipment. They use traditional wooden plows and oxen. **Critical Thinking** How might modern farming equipment change farming methods in El Salvador? How would this affect the economy?

Setting the Scene

Elvia Alvarado (el VEE ah ahl vah RAH doh) walks the back roads of rural **Honduras** to help poor campesinos make a living. Honduran campesinos, like rural people in all of Central America, have little land of their own. It is hard for them to make enough money to support their families.

Alvarado is a mother and grandmother and she works for an organization of campesinos. She helps people get loans to buy seeds and farm machinery and to get more land. She also works with community groups.

Alvarado's work is not easy. "The communities we work in are hard to get to," she says. "Sometimes I don't eat all day, and in the summertime the streams dry up and there's often no water to drink." Sometimes Alvarado does not get paid. "But I couldn't be happy if my belly was full while my neighbors didn't have a plate of beans and tortillas to put on the table," she says. "My struggle is for a better life for all Hondurans."

Resource Directory

Teaching Resources

Classroom Manager in the Unit 3 Teaching Resources, p. 35

Guided Reading and Review in the Unit 3 Teaching Resources, p. 36

Guide to the Essentials, p. 45

Technology

Section Reading Support Transparencies

Cultural Heritage

Honduras, where Alvarado lives and works, is one of seven nations in Central America. Together these countries form a crooked, skinny isthmus. The isthmus links Mexico and South America.

One Region, Many Faces There is much **diversity,** or variety, among the people of Central America. Hondurans, like Alvarado, are mostly mestizo with both Spanish and indigenous ancestors. About half of Guatemala's people are mestizo while the other half are indigenous. Many Costa Ricans are direct descendants of Spaniards, and more than half the people of Belize are of African or mixed African and European descent.

Spanish is the main language in six of the seven countries. However, these countries have many other languages. Guatemala is home to more than 20 languages. Spanish is the language of government and business, but the indigenous people in Guatemala speak their own languages, as do indigenous people in Panama, El Salvador, and Nicaragua. People in Belize speak English.

CITIZENSHIP

Oscar Arnulfo Romero, Archbishop of El Salvador

Oscar Arnulfo Romero y Galdamez was born in Ciudad Barrios, El Salvador in 1917. He became a priest in 1942 and was appointed archbishop in 1977. At first, Romero avoided political affairs. Later, he thought that the church should help its people obtain social justice. Romero spoke out against injustice, human rights abuses, and violence committed against the poor by the military regime. In 1980, while celebrating mass, Romero was assassinated.

Religion and Citizenship

Religion is important to the people of Central America. Just as in Mexico, Spanish Catholic missionaries who came to Central America in the 1500s and 1600s converted many Native Americans to Christianity. Today, most Central Americans are Catholic but some Native American religions also blend elements of their traditional religions with Christianity.

The Roman Catholic Church fights injustice in Central America. **Injustice** is the unfair treatment of people and often happens in countries with undemocratic governments. Examples of injustice include people having their property taken away from them and people being imprisoned without first having a fair trial. Catholic clergy members work for the fair treatment of the people, and many citizens take their own steps to end poverty and injustice.

Art and Heritage

CULTURE The people of El Salvador are mostly mestizo, and this mixed heritage often is reflected in their art. **Critical Thinking** Why would people choose to reflect their mixed heritage in the art they create?

SKILLS MINI LESSON

Recognizing Cause and Effect

To **introduce** the skill, drop a book on the floor. Indicate that the noise is an effect caused by the book hitting the floor. Explain that many conditions are the results, or *effects,* of other actions. The things that create the effects are *causes.* Help students **practice** the skill by reading the following pair of sentences. Ask which is the cause and which is the effect.

- *Thousands of young people in the countryside are unable to find jobs.* (cause)
- *Thousands move to cities to find work.* (effect)

Encourage students to **apply** the skill by writing a pair of sentences about the migrant worker in the photo on p. 202. Have students describe a cause in one sentence and an effect in the other.

3 Teach

Help students create an "Urbanization and Emigration" chart.

Urbanization and Emigration	
Conditions/ Problems in Central America	Results/ Solutions

Work with the class to put one or two items in each column. Then, suggest that students complete the chart with facts from the section. Indicate to students that case histories can help support their entries. Use the completed chart as the basis for discussion about the future of Central America.

Questions for Discussion

CITIZENSHIP How is Elvia Alvarado's work an example of good citizenship?

She tries to build better lives for all Hondurans rather than just thinking about herself.

ECONOMICS There is too much labor (workers) and too little capital (money) in Honduras. How does this affect the movement of people in the region?

Many people move to the cities, to other Central American countries, or to the United States to escape poverty.

4 Assess/Reteach

See answers to the Section 2 Assessment. You may also use students' completed charts as an assessment.

Acceptable charts include three factually correct entries in each column.

Commendable charts mention case histories along with factual entries.

Outstanding charts indicate some of the political and economic injustices that have long existed in the region.

Answers to...

CRITICAL THINKING

Their heritage is important to them. They want to celebrate it and share it with others.

SECTION 2 ASSESSMENT

AFTER YOU READ

1. (a) one of seven countries in Central America; located south of Guatemala and east of El Salvador
2. (a) variety (b) unfair treatment of people
3. (a) Spanish, Roman Catholic (b) Sample answer: The Spanish brought the Spanish language and Catholic religion when they explored the area and conquered the indigenous people.
4. Most Central Americans are Roman Catholic, and the Catholic church fights injustices done by the government.
5. Most Central Americans immigrate because they cannot find work in their home countries and because rising prices there have made life more and more expensive.
6. Paragraphs should include the fact that in Central America there are not only people of European (Spanish) and Native American descent, but also people of African and a mix of African and European descent. In addition, although Spanish is the main language, in some countries Native American languages are still spoken.
7. Journal entries should cite the country from which the person emigrated and specific causes for immigrating to the United States. They should also include specific effects that have resulted from the move. Details might include the fact that there were no jobs in the town where the person came from and he or she needed make more money than could be made in the country of origin.
8. Maps should show all seven countries of Central America and major cities. Each country should be labeled with the cultures found there. Maps might also include the languages spoken.

Harvesting Crops

ECONOMICS

Many immigrants from Central America come to the United States to find jobs on farms, harvesting crops. The worker in the photograph is harvesting broccoli in Texas' Rio Grande Valley. **Critical Thinking** Why must people who make a living harvesting crops move around so often?

A Search for Economic Opportunity

Much like the population of Mexico, Central America's population is growing rapidly. The population has increased dramatically in both the rural and urban areas. As the population expands in rural areas, many campesinos have decided that making a living from the land is just too difficult. They have left the land and gone to the cities in the hopes of finding better economic opportunities. This move has resulted in the rapid growth in the populations of large cities, where populations have increased the most.

In the cities, the wealthy people live in big houses on wide streets. They send their children to good schools and can afford to pay for medical care. For the poor, however, city life is difficult since there is a housing shortage. Rising prices have made living even more expensive. It is not easy to find work, or to feed a family.

Most people in Central America move somewhere else within their own country if they cannot find work. Some have left their countries to find work in places such as the United States. They have become immigrants, people who have moved into one country from another. Some of these immigrants want to remain in the countries to which they have moved. Others want to return home after earning some money to help their families.

Although some Central Americans have left the region in search of a better life, many more have followed Elvia Alvarado's example. They have stayed and begun to build a better life for themselves at home.

SECTION 2 ASSESSMENT

AFTER YOU READ

RECALL

1. Identify: (a) Honduras
2. Define: (a) diversity, (b) injustice

COMPREHENSION

3. (a) What are the main language and religion of the people of Central America? (b) How do the languages and religions of the region reflect Central America's history?
4. What role does religion play in the lives of Central Americans?
5. What is one reason that Central Americans are immigrating to the United States?

CRITICAL THINKING AND WRITING

6. **Exploring the Main Idea** Review the Main Idea statement at the beginning of this section. Then write a paragraph describing the diversity of cultures found in Central America.
7. **Identifying Cause and Effect** Imagine that you are an immigrant from Central America who has come to the United States. Write a journal entry telling about the reasons that led to your immigration and about the effects your immigration has had on you and your family.

ACTIVITY

8. **Making a Cultural Map** Make a map showing the countries of Central America and labeling each with the cultures found in that country. Include labels for major cities.

202 UNIT 3 LATIN AMERICA

Answers to...

CRITICAL THINKING

Because different crops are harvested at different times of the year, workers must follow the harvest from region to region.

Resource Directory

Teaching Resources

Section Quiz in the Unit 3 Teaching Resources, p. 37

SECTION 3

The Cultures of the Caribbean

BEFORE YOU READ

READING FOCUS

1. How did European, African, and Native American cultures come together to create unique Caribbean cultures?
2. Which cultures influence the ethnic groups, religions, and languages found in the Caribbean today?
3. What are the key cultural elements that make up the present-day cultures of the Caribbean?

KEY TERMS

ethnic group
Carnival

KEY PLACES

Jamaica
Cuba
Trinidad and Tobago

MAIN IDEA

Caribbean lifestyles, music, foods, art, and entertainment are influenced by a rich blend of cultures.

NOTE TAKING

Copy the outline below. As you read the section, fill in the outline with information about the cultures of the Caribbean islands.

- **I. Cultural Links with the Past**
  - A. Native American, indigenous people
  - B.
  - C.
  - D.
- **II. Ethnic Variety and Cultural Traits**
  - A. Race
  - B. Language
  - C. Religion
- **III. Cultural Blend of Past and Present**
  - A. Sports/Entertainment
  - B. Food
  - C. Caribbean Music
  - D. Carnival

Setting the Scene

Dorothy Samuels is a ten-year-old from **Jamaica,** a tropical island in the Caribbean Sea. She lives in a village near the ocean and goes to a village school. She hopes one day to go to college in Kingston, Jamaica's capital city. Jamaican laws require that women have as much opportunity for education as men have.

Dorothy's family are farmers. They plant vegetables, fruits, and cocoa beans. Every Saturday, Dorothy's mother and grandmother take their fruits and vegetables to the market to sell. All the traders at the market are women.

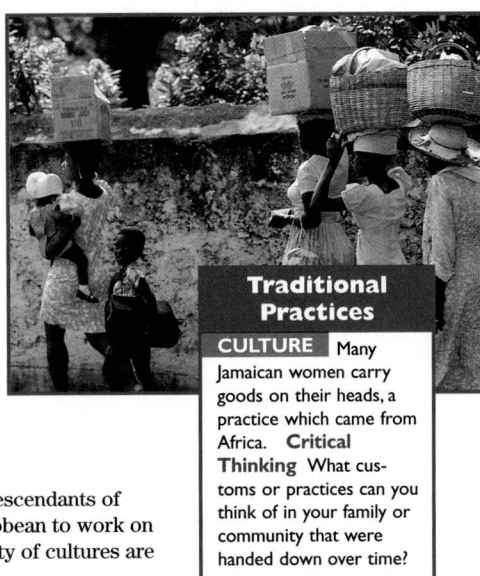

Traditional Practices

CULTURE Many Jamaican women carry goods on their heads, a practice which came from Africa. **Critical Thinking** What customs or practices can you think of in your family or community that were handed down over time?

The People and Cultures of the Caribbean

Many Jamaicans, like most Caribbean people, are descendants of African slaves. The slaves were brought to the Caribbean to work on sugar plantations built by Europeans. Today, a variety of cultures are found in this region.

SECTION 3

Lesson Objectives

1. Describe how European, African, and Native American cultures blended to create unique Caribbean cultures.
2. Explain how various cultures influence present-day ethnic groups, languages, and religions found in the Caribbean.
3. Identify the key cultural influences that affect the lifestyles, music, foods, and entertainment in the Caribbean.

Lesson Plan

1 Engage

Warm-Up Activity

Ask students how they would feel if they had to travel by boat to a neighboring city rather than by car or bus. Encourage students to imagine living on an island. Prompt their imaginations with questions about how they might make a living. How would they visit friends on another island?

Activating Prior Knowledge

If any students have experienced island living, allow them to describe their views of island life. If no students have had the experience, encourage the class to discuss what island life might be like.

Resource Directory

Teaching Resources

Classroom Manager in the Unit 3 Teaching Resources, p. 38

Guided Reading and Review in the Unit 3 Teaching Resources, p. 39

Guide to the Essentials, p. 46

Technology

Section Reading Support Transparencies

Answers to...

CRITICAL THINKING

Students may suggest food, music, clothing styles, celebrations, and holidays.

Lesson Plan continued

2 Explore

Have students read the section. Then, ask them to describe the unique blend of cultures on the Caribbean islands, addressing the following characteristics: many islands; first inhabitants were Native Americans called the Ciboney; most natives died from overwork and disease once Spain established rule over the islands; Caribbean culture today is a blend of Native American, African, European, Asian, and Middle Eastern cultures.

3 Teach

Provide the following topic sentence for a paragraph: *Caribbean culture is known for its liveliness.* Direct students to write a paragraph that supports the sentence using details from the section to identify the rich traditions in food, music, art, and entertainment from the Caribbean region. This activity should take from 20 to 30 minutes.

Question for Discussion

CULTURE **What is one way that religion has influenced culture in the Caribbean?**

The tradition of Carnival is related to the Catholic period of Lent. Even people who are not Catholic celebrate Carnival.

4 Assess/Reteach

See answers to the Section 3 Assessment. You may also use students' completed paragraphs as an assessment.

Acceptable paragraphs include at least four factually correct supporting details, one for each cultural element.

Commendable paragraphs include some specific examples from countries mentioned in the text.

Outstanding paragraphs mention the origins of some of these cultural traditions.

AS YOU READ

Use Prior Knowledge What ethnic groups do you think live in the Caribbean today?

The First People of the Caribbean

The island chain that makes up the Caribbean stretches some 2,000 miles (3,219 km) through the Caribbean Sea. Jamaica, like other Caribbean islands, has fertile soil and adequate rainfall that is especially good for sugar and cotton production. Small valleys produce fruits and vegetables.

Native Americans called the Ciboney (SEE boh nay) lived on the islands for thousands of years. In about 300 B.C., a South American group called Arawaks (AR ah wahks) joined them. In about A.D. 1000, another South American group called the Caribs (KA ribs) joined the population and gave the region its name. They lived there for more than 400 years before the first Europeans came to the area.

When Christopher Columbus landed on the Caribbean islands, he thought he had reached the Indies in Asia, so he called the native peoples there Indians. Columbus and other explorers, who sailed from Spain to the Caribbean islands, enslaved the Native Americans, and as a result, most of the Caribs, Arawaks, and other groups died of overwork and of diseases the Spanish brought with them. Today, just a few hundred Caribs still live on the island of Dominica.

Dutch, French, and English colonists followed the Spanish. They claimed territory in the 1600s and brought enslaved Africans to work on their plantations. The descendants of the Africans, Europeans, and of immigrants who came to the Caribbean from China, India, and the Middle East add to the rich blend of present-day Caribbean cultures.

Ethnic Variety and Cultural Traits The Caribbean population has grown to about 37 million. Nearly one-third of these people live on the region's largest island, **Cuba.**

Because so many people came to the Caribbean as colonists, slaves, or immigrants, the area has great ethnic variety. An **ethnic group** is a group of people who share race, language, religion, or cultural traditions. The ethnic groups of the Caribbean are Native American, African, European, Asian, and Middle Eastern.

The people of the Caribbean islands speak one of several European languages or their language may be a mixture of European and African languages. Most West Indians are Christians, but there are also small groups of Hindus, Muslims, and Jews. Some people practice traditional African religions.

A Caribbean Family

CULTURE

Family life is very important to people in the Caribbean. This family, from Montserrat, British West Indies, is made up of parents and their children. Many people in the Caribbean live in family groups that also include grandparents, uncles, aunts, and cousins.

Critical Thinking What members make up your family? How does your family compare to a Caribbean family?

A Cultural Blend of Past and Present

Caribbean culture is known for its liveliness. People play music, dance, and tell stories. People also play many sports. Baseball, soccer, and track and field are popular.

Answers to...

AS YOU READ

Students may mention Native Americans, Africans, Europeans, Asians, and Middle Easterners.

CRITICAL THINKING

Students' responses will vary. Encourage students to think about the people who live in their homes as well as relatives who live elsewhere.

SKILLS MINI LESSON

Using the Writing Process

You may **introduce** the skill by reviewing the basic steps of the writing process: prewriting, writing, editing, and presenting. Have students **practice** by following the steps to write a paragraph about Caribbean culture. Help students **apply** the skill by following the writing process as they develop writing assignments throughout this book.

Food Caribbean food is a mixture from all the cultures of the islands. Caribbean people enjoy abundant seafood. Bammy—a bread made from the cassava plant—is still made the way the Arawaks made it. People also cook spicy curries from India, sausages from England, and Chinese dishes.

Music Caribbean music is famous around the world. Calypso, which originated in Trinidad and Tobago, is a form of song that often is played on steel drums. These instruments are made from recycled oil drums. A steel drum can be "tuned" so that different parts of it play different tones. Reggae is another popular form of music from the Caribbean, which originated in Jamaica.

Carnival Many islanders observe the Roman Catholic tradition of Lent, which is the period of 40 days before Easter Sunday. People consider Lent to be a very solemn time, so just before Lent they throw a huge party called **Carnival.**

Different countries celebrate Carnival in different ways. The biggest Carnival takes place in **Trinidad and Tobago.** People spend all year making costumes and floats. At 5 a.m. the Monday before Lent, people go into the streets in their costumes. Calypso bands play and thousands of fans follow the bands through the streets, dancing and celebrating. At the stroke of midnight Tuesday, the party stops. Lent has begun.

Tradition and Celebration

CULTURE Many people in Caribbean countries dress in lavish, colorful costumes to celebrate Carnival. **Critical Thinking** What similar celebrations take place in the United States?

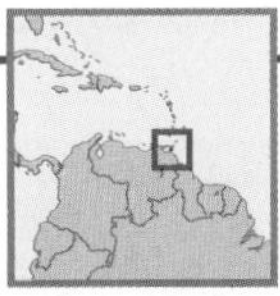

SECTION 3 ASSESSMENT

AFTER YOU READ

RECALL

1. Identify: (a) Jamaica, (b) Cuba, (c) Trinidad and Tobago
2. Define: (a) ethnic group, (b) Carnival

COMPREHENSION

3. How did the Caribbean's unique cultures come together?
4. Which cultures have influenced the ethnic makeup, language, and religion of the Caribbean?
5. What are some of the customs that contribute to present-day Caribbean culture?

CRITICAL THINKING AND WRITING

6. **Exploring the Main Idea** Review the Main Idea statement at the beginning of this section. Then list at least four different cultures that influence the traditions, food, art, entertainment, and music found in the Caribbean.
7. **Making Comparisons** What common elements in their histories have shaped the cultures of the various Caribbean islands?

ACTIVITY

8. **Comparing Cultures** Select one aspect of Caribbean culture (food, music, religion, and so on) and take notes on what you have learned about it in this section. Then, write ways in which it is similar to and different from your own culture.

Resource Directory

Teaching Resources

Section Quiz in the Unit 3 Teaching Resources, p. 40

Answers to...

CRITICAL THINKING

Mardi Gras, annual parades celebrating different countries of origin

SECTION 3 ASSESSMENT

AFTER YOU READ

1. (a) large tropical island in the Caribbean (b) the largest island in the Caribbean (c) Caribbean islands where the largest Carnival celebration takes place
2. (a) group of people who share a race, language, religion, or cultural traditions (b) celebration just before Lent
3. The Native Americans were enslaved or died during the European colonization of the area. Europeans brought enslaved Africans to work on the plantations. The people of the Caribbean are the descendants of these groups.
4. The ethnic groups of the Caribbean are Native American, African, European, Asian, and Middle Eastern. The people speak European languages or a language that blends European and African influences. Most people practice Christianity, but there are also Hindus, Muslims, Jews, and people who practice African religions.
5. Present-day Caribbean culture includes foods from all the cultures of the islands, music such as Calypso and reggae, and entertainment such as storytelling, sports, and Carnival.
6. Lists might include: traditions—African; food—Native American, Indian (from India), English, Chinese; entertainment—European (Carnival), American (United States, baseball); music—Caribbean.
7. Answers may include the following: The Spanish enslaved the native populations of the islands. Enslaved Africans were brought from Africa to work in the islands.
8. Let volunteers read their comparisons to the class.

SECTION 4

Lesson Objectives

1. Explain how geography has created diversity in South America.
2. Describe the role of farming in South American life.
3. Explain how rapid population growth is affecting cities in South America.

Lesson Plan

1 Engage

Warm-Up Activity

Ask students to recall the major ethnic groups that live in Mexico, Central America, and the Caribbean. Then, have students predict what they think the present-day cultures of South America might be like, and why.

Activating Prior Knowledge

Ask students to think about the music they listen to and the clothes they wear. Explain that these are elements of their culture. Ask them where they think their culture comes from. Students may mention that their culture is a result of their families or the part of the country they are from.

2 Explore

After students read the section, ask them to identify the major cultural groups of South America. Elicit the following information: Many Native Americans live high in the Andes. People have lived in South America since prehistoric times. Most South Americans are descended from Native Americans, Africans, Europeans, or a blend of these.

Answers to...

CRITICAL THINKING

walking, riding animals, riding in carts pulled by animals, four-wheel drive vehicles

SECTION 4

The Cultures of South America

BEFORE YOU READ

READING FOCUS

1. How has geography created diversity in South America?
2. How does farming shape the lives of South Americans?
3. How has rapid population growth affected the cities of South America?

KEY TERMS

subsistence farmer
import

KEY PLACES

Andes Mountains

MAIN IDEA

Within South America's four cultural regions, there is great diversity in lifestyles.

NOTE TAKING

Copy the chart below. As you read the section, fill in the chart with information about the different cultural regions of South America.

Cultural Regions of South America			
Colombia Venezuela Guyana Suriname French Guiana	Peru Ecuador Bolivia	Chile Argentina Uruguay Paraguay	Brazil

Building Boats

CULTURE The Native Americans who live on Lake Titicaca use totora reeds to make boats. **Critical Thinking** What forms of transportation might the Native Americans use to travel through the Andes?

Setting the Scene

Between Peru and Bolivia is a deep lake called Lake Titicaca. It lies high in the **Andes Mountains.** This area is bitterly cold with few trees. Native Americans here make their living from totora reeds, a kind of thick, hollow grass that grows on the lakeshore. They use these reeds to make houses, boats, mats, hats, ropes, sails, toys, roofs, and floors. They eat the reeds, feed them to livestock, and brew them into tea. Totora reeds can even be made into medicine. Long ago, some Native American groups built floating islands with totora reeds. They used the islands to hide from the Incas. Today, some Native Americans live on floating islands.

Resource Directory

Teaching Resources

Classroom Manager in the Unit 3 Teaching Resources, p. 41

Guided Reading and Review in the Unit 3 Teaching Resources, p. 42

Guide to the Essentials, p. 47

Technology

Section Reading Support Transparencies

The People of South America

Most South Americans today are descended from Native Americans, Africans, or Europeans. In this way, they are like the people of Mexico and Central America. South America's history is also like that of its neighbors to the north. It was colonized mainly by Spain, so most South Americans speak Spanish and are Catholic. Each nation has its own unique culture, however.

Regions Within South America There are four cultural regions in South America. The first region includes Colombia, Venezuela, Guyana, Suriname, and French Guiana, which are in the northern part of South America. They each border the Caribbean Sea. The cultures of these countries are like those of the Caribbean islands.

To the south and west, the culture is very different. Peru, Ecuador, and Bolivia are Andean countries. Many Native Americans live high in the Andes. In Bolivia, there are more indigenous people than mestizos. The Quechua and Aymara (eye MUH rah) people each speak their own languages.

The third cultural region consists of Chile, Argentina, and Uruguay. The long, thin country of Chile has mountains, beaches, deserts, forests, and polar regions. Most people in Chile are mestizos. The big cities of Argentina and Uruguay, however, are very diverse, and many different ethnic groups live there. Another culture exists on Argentina's Pampas, or plains. On the Pampas, gauchos (GOW chohz), or cowhands, herd cattle.

Brazil is South America's largest country and fourth region. Brazil was a colony of Portugal so its people speak Portuguese. However, Brazil is culturally diverse. Many Native Americans live in Brazil and so do people of African and mixed descent.

Raising Llamas in Peru

CULTURE Some of the indigenous people of the Andes raise llamas, a relative of the camel. **Critical Thinking** How do you think the people of the Andes use llamas?

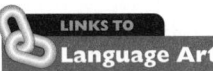

Rural and Urban Life

South America is made up of very large cities, along with numerous villages throughout the countryside. However, there are vast areas with hardly any people at all.

Farming in South America Outside of Chile, Argentina, and Uruguay, most rural people with small plots of land are **subsistence farmers.** That means they grow only enough food for their families to eat. Farmers plant corn, beans, potatoes, and rice.

LINKS TO Language Arts

Gabriela Mistral
Chilean poet Gabriela Mistral was awarded the Nobel Prize for Literature in 1945. But Mistral considered herself to be more a teacher than a writer. Mistral taught school in rural Chile in the early 1900s, but she was frustrated by the low quality of the textbooks that were available. In response, Mistral began to write poetry and prose for children.

3 Teach

Begin a four-column chart on the chalkboard for each of the four regions discussed. Place two categories along the side of the chart: *Geographic Characteristics* and *Cultural Characteristics*. Work with students to fill in the first cell on the chart. Let students complete their own charts by using the information from the section. Use the charts to discuss the features of each region.

Questions for Discussion

GEOGRAPHY **What are some ways that Native Americans have adapted to living in the Andes?**

They use tortora reeds for everything from rope to roofs to food. They raise llamas.

ECONOMICS **What is one positive and one negative effect of the continued growth of cities in South America?**

There will be more jobs for people, but probably not enough to support everyone who comes to the cities looking for work. This could result in more slums and poor neighborhoods.

4 Assess/Reteach

See answers to the Section 4 Assessment. You may also use students' completed charts as an assessment.

Acceptable charts include at least one characteristic for each country and category.

Commendable charts include two or three facts for each.

Outstanding charts include some cause-and-effect relationships linking culture and unique features.

SKILLS MINI LESSON

Assessing Your Understanding

To **introduce** the skill, point out that building knowledge of a subject is much like building a house. What students learn today forms the foundation for what they learn next week or next year. One way to ensure that their foundation is strong is to check their learning as they go. Help students **practice** assessing their understanding by asking them to read the section "Regions Within South America." Tell students to read one paragraph and then stop and restate the ideas from the paragraph in their own words. After reading another paragraph, students might list the important points. If students have trouble restating or summarizing a paragraph, they should reread it and try again.

Answers to...

CRITICAL THINKING

for food, milk, wool and to carry loads

ACTIVITY

Journal Writing

Travel Diary Ask students to write a travel diary or journal entry about one of the regions mentioned in the section. Explain that they should describe physical and human characteristics. Students might include illustrations from travel magazines to illustrate their entries.

SECTION 4 ASSESSMENT

AFTER YOU READ

1. huge mountain range that runs almost the whole length of the west coast of South America
2. (a) farmer who grows enough food for his or her own family (b) to buy goods from another country
3. People in the Andes raise llamas. People in the Pampas herd cattle.
4. Many families living in rural areas have small farms and grow only enough food for themselves. Large farms grow crops to export to other countries. Because so much land is used for these export, or cash crops, South America has to import food for its people to eat.
5. Rapid population growth makes it difficult for South American countries to maintain their large cities. City governments try to provide electricity and running water to everyone, but it is hard to keep up. Many people end up in poor neighborhoods.
6. In rural areas, most people are farmers. In urban areas, people work in offices.
7. One cause is the huge migration of people from the farm areas into the cities to find work. One effect is that newcomers often have difficulty finding places to live; another is that slums have developed. A third effect is that it is difficult for city governments to keep up with the demand for services.
8. Small groups can each choose a region. Groups can combine their completed brochures into one comprehensive guidebook.

SCIENCE, TECHNOLOGY, AND SOCIETY

Brasília: Brazilian Innovation

Brasília is a planned city. Some people think the layout of the city looks like a bow and arrow. Others think it looks like a jet plane. Government offices and shopping areas are located in the center of the city, where the two "wings" meet. The Plaza of the Three Powers is the center of government. The Presidential Palace is located at the tip of the city, on Lake Paranoa. The wings contain superblocks, or residential neighborhoods. Each includes 10 to 16 apartment buildings, a school, and shops.

Very large farms grow crops such as coffee, sugar, and cocoa, to export to other countries. Export farming uses so much land for cash crops that South America has to import food to eat. To **import** means to buy from another country.

The population of South America is booming. Latin America is the fastest-growing region in the world. Like Mexicans and Central Americans, South Americans cannot find enough jobs in rural areas. Every day, thousands of rural South Americans move to the cities looking for work.

Urban Issues The cities of South America illustrate the region's mix of cultures. Many major cities—Lima, Peru, and Buenos Aires, Argentina, for example—were built by Spanish colonists more than 400 years ago. Some of the buildings follow Native American designs. In contrast, modern office blocks and apartment buildings of concrete, steel, and glass tower above the downtown areas. Brasília, the Brazilian capital, was constructed in the 1950s. It was a completely planned city, designed to draw people to the country's interior.

By contrast, slums in many South American cities were unplanned. They are called favelas (FUH vez luz) in Brazil and barrios (BAR ee ohs) in Venezuela. As more and more people migrate into the cities they have ended up in these poor neighborhoods. City governments try to provide electricity and running water to everyone. But people move into cities so quickly that it is hard for city governments to keep up.

SECTION 4 ASSESSMENT

AFTER YOU READ

RECALL

1. Identify: Andes Mountains
2. Define: (a) subsistence farmer, (b) import

COMPREHENSION

3. Name two ways in which the geography of South America has shaped how people live.
4. How does farming contribute to the lives of the people and to the economies of South America?
5. What pressures does rapid population growth place on the cities of South America?

CRITICAL THINKING AND WRITING

6. **Exploring the Main Idea** Review the Main Idea statement at the beginning of this section. Then list the ways in which life differs in rural and urban areas of South America.
7. **Recognizing Cause and Effect** Write a paragraph explaining two causes and two effects of rapid population growth in the cities of South America.

ACTIVITY

8. **Creating a Travel Brochure** Design a travel brochure for a region in South America. Tell what countries a traveler might visit and what the people are like there. Include other facts that someone visiting might like to know. Illustrate your brochure with a drawing or a map.

Resource Directory

Teaching Resources

Section Quiz in the Unit 3 Teaching Resources, p. 43

Chapter Summary in the Unit 3 Teaching Resources, p. 44

Vocabulary in the Unit 3 Teaching Resources, p. 45

Reteaching in the Unit 3 Teaching Resources, p. 46

Enrichment in the Unit 3 Teaching Resources, p. 47

Critical Thinking in the Unit 3 Teaching Resources, p. 48

Analyzing Images

Learn the Skill

Have you stopped to think about how the images around you communicate meaning? Understanding how images communicate meaning can help you analyze their messages. Follow these steps to help you analyze this image:

A. Identify the subject of the image. From looking at the painting, you can see that it depicts some kind of a celebration that is taking place in front of a church.

B. Look at the elements of design. Elements of design include line and color. Line refers to the overall shapes and patterns of elements in the image. Color is one of the most important elements in images. You can see that the painting above has very strong patterns of circles and lines. Also, by putting the church in the center of the painting, the artist draws the viewer's attention to it. In addition, the use of bright colors creates a very festive atmosphere.

C. Think about the purpose of the image. Why was the image created? Some images, such as advertisements, are created to persuade you to buy something or think a certain way. Other images, such as those in a magazine article, are meant to inform you about a topic. This painting was probably meant to entertain the viewer and capture the excitement of a celebration.

D. Respond to the image. Think about the feelings that the subject matter and design elements create in you. How does the image make you feel? Happy? Sad? Scared? In the painting above, the people dancing, the fireworks, and the bright colors work together to create a sense of joy and excitement in the viewer.

Practice the Skill

Turn to p. 190 in Chapter 10 of your book. Look at the mural of Father Hidalgo. Answer the following questions to help you analyze the image:

- What is the subject matter of this mural?
- What elements of design are in the mural? Pay careful attention to and describe the artist's use of line and color.
- Why do you think the artist created it?
- How does the mural make you feel? Why?

Apply the Skill

See the Chapter Review and Assessment at the end of this chapter for more questions on analyzing images.

Lesson Objectives

1. Recognize images.
2. Analyze and respond to images.

Lesson Plan

1 Engage

Ask students to describe images they saw on their way to school today—signs, billboards, even graffiti and t-shirts. What was the purpose of the images? Did they succeed in their purpose? Why or why not?

2 Explore

Direct students to read the steps under "Learn the Skill" as they look at the picture. For part D, ask students to tell their responses. Any response is acceptable, but encourage students to explain their reactions.

3 Teach

Ask students to be art critics as they analyze the mural of Father Hidalgo. Have them write a paragraph describing the mural and explaining why it is successful or unsuccessful.

4 Assess/Reteach

Students' paragraphs should offer their opinions along with reasons to support their views.

To further assess students' understanding of images, have them complete the "Applying Your Skills" part of the Chapter Review and Assessment at the end of this chapter.

Resource Directory

Teaching Resources

Social Studies and Geography Skills, Analyzing Art, p. 57

Technology

Social Studies Skills Tutor CD-ROM

Answers to...

PRACTICE THE SKILL

Possible responses: Hidalgo's instigating the crowd against Spanish government; Hidalgo large in foreground, mass of people in middle- and background, strong vertical lines contrast Hidalgo's horizontal arms, Hidalgo's solid black contrasts other colors; to commemorate Hidalgo's heroism and a crucial historical event; admiring, interested

CHAPTER 11

Review and Assessment

Creating a Chapter Summary

Student summaries will vary.

Sample summaries:

Section 2 The cultures of Central America are diverse and vary from region to region. Due to economic hardship, an increasing number of people are leaving rural areas for urban areas in the hopes of finding jobs.

Section 3 A rich blend of cultures unique to the Caribbean influences lifestyle, music, food, art, and entertainment.

Section 4 South America's cultural background is much like that of Mexico, Central America, and the Caribbean. Within its four cultural regions there is a great diversity of lifestyles, from traditional Native Americans to modern urban dwellers.

Reviewing Key Terms

1. correct
2. Maquiladoras are factories on the U.S.-Mexico border.
3. correct
4. correct
5. To import means to buy goods from another country.

Reviewing the Main Ideas

1. Spanish, Native American, and mestizo
2. Possible answer: The population from rural areas is shifting to urban areas as people look for ways other than farming to make a living. Urban areas are becoming more crowded.
3. Roman Catholic; Spanish
4. Central Americans are moving to the United States to find jobs.
5. European, African, Native American
6. Present-day Caribbean culture is enriched by foods from the many cultures of the islands, music such as calypso and reggae, and the tradition of Carnival.
7. Native American, African, European
8. The rapid population growth has caused more people to move into the cities. The cities have become more crowded and people need more services. It is hard for city governments to provide all the necessary services, such as running water and electricity.

CHAPTER 11

Review and Assessment

Creating a Chapter Summary

On a separate piece of paper, draw a chart like this one, and include the information that summarizes the first section of the chapter. Then, fill in the remaining boxes with information that summarizes what you learned about the cultures of Latin America.

Mexico	• The cultures of Mexico include Spanish, Native American, and mestizo influences. • Due to Mexico's increasing population, more people are searching for new places to live and make a living.
Central America	
Caribbean	
South America	

Reviewing Key Terms

Decide whether the definition for each term below is correct. If it is incorrect, rewrite the definition to correct it.

1. Campesinos are poor farmers who plant and harvest their crops by hand.
2. Maquiladoras are people who move permanently from Mexico to the United States.
3. Injustice is the unfair treatment of people.
4. A subsistence farmer grows only enough food to feed his or her family.
5. To import means to sell goods to another country.

Reviewing the Main Ideas

1. Name the predominant cultures of Mexico. (Section 1)
2. Name one way Mexico's population pattern is changing. (Section 1)
3. What are the main religion and language of Central America? (Section 2)
4. To which country are some Central Americans going to find jobs? (Section 2)
5. What blend of three cultures makes up a unique culture found in the Caribbean today? (Section 3)
6. Name some of the key elements of present-day Caribbean culture. (Section 3)
7. What are the three main cultural groups found in South America today? (Section 4)
8. Name one way the cities of South America have been affected by rapid population growth. (Section 4)

Map Activity

For each place listed below, write the letter from the map that shows its location.

1. Andes
2. Argentina
3. Brazil
4. Honduras
5. Jamaica
6. Mexico City

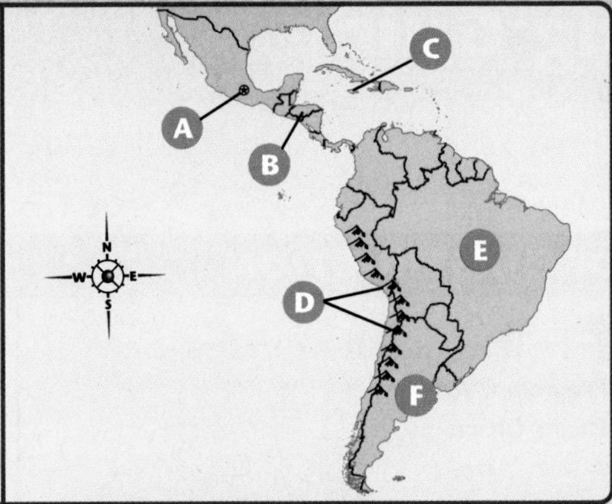

Take It to the NET

Enrichment For more map activities using geography skills, visit the social studies section of **phschool.com.**

Writing Activity

1. **Writing a Magazine Article** In this chapter, you've taken a guided tour of the cultures of Latin America. Write an article for a travel magazine describing the "high points" of your tour. As you write, consider how historical events and geography influenced the region's culture.
2. **Writing a Dialogue** You are a young adult from a campesino family in Mexico who is planning to leave the farm to live in Mexico City. Write a dialogue between you and one of your parents as you explain why you think you need to go to the city.

Critical Thinking

1. **Making Comparisons** Consider these regions of Latin America: Mexico, Central America, the Caribbean, South America. What do the cultures of these regions have in common? How are they different?
2. **Recognizing Cause and Effect** What is the main reason that many Latin Americans move from rural to urban areas?
3. **Drawing Conclusions** In what ways are maquiladoras important to the economy of Mexico?

Applying Your Skills

Turn to the Skills for Life activity on p. 209 to help you complete the following activity.

With a partner, look through magazines and newspapers to find three or four images. Try to choose a variety of images—an advertisement, a photograph, and a drawing. Follow the steps you learned to analyze the images you chose.

Take It to the NET

Activity Examine the paintings found on the Web site. Choose one and write a short description describing what is happening in the painting and what it tells you about the Mayan community. Visit the World Explorer: People, Places, and Cultures section of **phschool.com** for help in completing this activity.

Chapter 11 Self-Test As a final review activity, take the Chapter 11 Self-Test and get instant feedback on your answers. To take the test, visit the Social Studies section of **phschool.com.**

Map Activity

1. D **2.** F **3.** E **4.** B **5.** C **6.** A

Writing Activity

1. Students should write about the various places mentioned in the chapter. Magazine articles should include specific descriptive details about the region, where it is located, the cultures that exist today, and the roots of those cultures.
2. Dialogues should include reasons stated in the chapter, such as a need for jobs and a need to make more money to support the family.

Critical Thinking

1. Possibilities include the fact that Native Americans, Africans, and Europeans, especially Spaniards, influenced the cultures and histories of Latin American regions. Geographically, these regions are quite diverse, and their living conditions may vary accordingly.
2. Thousands of Latin Americans move because they cannot find work in rural areas.
3. The maquiladoras provide work for many Mexicans who cannot find work in the areas where they were raised.

Applying Your Skills

1. Stress that partners' analyses and opinions need not agree, as long as students can justify their views.

Resource Directory

Teaching Resources

Cooperative Learning Activity in the Unit 3 Teaching Resources, pp. 111–113

Chapter Tests Forms A and B in the Unit 3 Teaching Resources, pp. 142–147

Guide to the Essentials, Ch. 11 Test, p. 48

Other Print Resources

Chapter Tests with ExamView® Test Bank, Ch. 11

Technology

ExamView® Test Bank CD-ROM, Ch. 11

Resource Pro® CD-ROM

Chapter 12 Planning Guide

Resource Manager

	CORE INSTRUCTION	READING/SKILLS
Chapter-Level Resources	**Teaching Resources** Program Overview Pacing Charts **Technology** Resource Pro® CD-ROM Companion Web site, phschool.com • eTeach	**Technology** Social Studies Skills Tutor CD-ROM Student Edition on Audio CD, Ch. 12
1 Mexico: Urban Migration 1. Explain reasons for the migration of rural Mexicans to urban centers. 2. Describe challenges faced by poor people who move to cities. 3. Summarize the environmental problems of growing cities in Mexico.	**Teaching Resources** **Unit 3** Classroom Manager, p. 50 Guided Reading and Review, p. 51	**Teaching Resources** Guide to the Essentials, p. 49 Social Studies and Geography Skills, p. 1 **Technology** Section Reading Support Transparencies
2 Guatemala and Nicaragua: Economic and Political Change 1. Identify the main issues facing the indigenous people of Guatemala. 2. Describe recent changes in Guatemala. 3. Understand the events that have led to Nicaragua's unstable economy.	**Teaching Resources** **Unit 3** Classroom Manager, p. 53 Guided Reading and Review, p. 54	**Teaching Resources** Guide to the Essentials, p. 50 Social Studies and Geography Skills, p. 17 **Technology** Section Reading Support Transparencies
3 Panama: A Transportation Corridor 1. Summarize the challenges faced during the building of the Panama Canal. 2. Describe how Panama gained control of the canal.	**Teaching Resources** **Unit 3** Classroom Manager, p. 56 Guided Reading and Review, p. 57 Chapter Summary, p. 59 Vocabulary, p. 60 Reteaching, p. 61	**Teaching Resources** **Unit 3** Critical Thinking, p. 63 Guide to the Essentials, p. 51 Social Studies and Geography Skills, p. 1 **Technology** Section Reading Support Transparencies

ENRICHMENT / PRE-AP

Teaching Resources
Primary Sources and Literature Readings

Other Print Resources
DK Atlas

Technology
World Video Explorer: Case Study: Cleaning Up the Air in Mexico City
How People Live Transparencies, Unit 3
Companion Web site, phschool.com

Teaching Resources
Outline Maps, p. 8

Technology
Passport to the World CD-ROM
World Video Explorer, Mexico Case Study

Teaching Resources
Outline Maps, pp. 6–7

Technology
Color Transparencies 55

Teaching Resources
Unit 3
Enrichment, p. 62
Cooperative Learning Activity, pp. 115–117

ASSESSMENT

Prentice Hall Assessment System

Core Assessment
Chapter Tests with ExamView® Test Bank, Ch. 12
ExamView® Test Bank CD-ROM, Ch. 12

Standardized Test Preparation
Diagnose and Prescribe
Diagnostic Tests for Middle Grades Social Studies Skills
Review and Reteach
Review Book for World Studies
Practice and Assess
Test-taking Strategies with Transparencies for Middle Grades Test Prep Book
Test-taking Strategies Posters

Teaching Resources
Unit 3
Section Quizzes, pp. 52, 55, and 58
Chapter Tests, pp. 148–153

Technology
Companion Web site, phschool.com
Ch. 12 Self-Test

World Video Explorer
Each region of the world is explored through regional flyovers and investigative field trips. Case study segments give students an in-depth view of the history, economy, government, and culture of a key place in each region. Case studies include Nigeria, Mexico, China, British Columbia, and the Czech Republic.

In Your Classroom

CUSTOMIZE FOR INDIVIDUAL NEEDS

Gifted and Talented

Teacher's Edition
- Timeline, p. 215
- Canals Change the World, p. 223

Teaching Resources
- Enrichment, p. 62
- Primary Sources and Literature Readings

Honors/Pre-AP

Teacher's Edition
- A Guatemalan Hero, p. 219
- Math, p. 223

Teaching Resources
- Critical Thinking, p. 63
- Primary Sources and Literature Readings

ESL

Teacher's Edition
- Timeline, p. 215

Teaching Resources
- Guided Reading and Review, pp. 51, 54, and 57
- Vocabulary, p. 60
- Reteaching, p. 61
- Guide to the Essentials, pp. 49–51
- Social Studies and Geography Skills, pp. 1 and 17

Technology
- Social Studies Skills Tutor CD-ROM
- Section Reading Support Transparencies

Less Proficient Readers

Teacher's Edition
- Timeline, p. 215
- Math, p. 223

Teaching Resources
- Guided Reading and Review, pp. 51, 54, and 57
- Vocabulary, p. 60
- Reteaching, p. 61
- Guide to the Essentials, pp. 49–51
- Social Studies and Geography Skills, pp. 1 and 17

Technology
- Social Studies Skills Tutor CD-ROM
- Section Reading Support Transparencies

Less Proficient Writers

Teacher's Edition
- Earthquakes in Urban Centers, p. 215
- Math, p. 223

Teaching Resources
- Guided Reading and Review, pp. 51, 54, and 57
- Vocabulary, p. 60
- Guide to the Essentials, pp. 49–51
- Social Studies and Geography Skills, pp. 1 and 17

Technology
- Social Studies Skills Tutor CD-ROM
- Section Reading Support Transparencies

DORLING KINDERSLEY

At the end of each unit, you will find information adapted from Dorling Kindersley's *Illustrated Children's Encyclopedia* that connects to the region being studied and to one of the seven content strands. In addition, your resources include Dorling Kindersley's *Atlas*, which contains valuable information about countries from around the world.

TEACHER'S EDITION INDEX

CHAPTER 12 PACING SUGGESTIONS

For 90-minute Blocks

See suggestions in the Teaching Resources Pacing Charts for Chapter 12. Use Color Transparencies 55.

Running Out of Time?

See the Guide to the Essentials, pp. 49–51.

INTERDISCIPLINARY LINKS

Middle Grades Math: Tools for Success
Course 1, Lesson 9-8, **Proportions and Changing Dimensions**

Science Explorer
Cells and Heredity, Lesson 5-1, **Darwin's Voyage**

Prentice Hall Literature
Bronze, Tenochtitlán, Barrio Boy
Copper, Señor Coyote and the Tricked Trickster

BIBLIOGRAPHY

For the Teacher

Ancona, George. *The Piñata Maker: El Piñatero.* Harcourt, 1994.

Nye, Naomi Shihab, ed. *The Tree Is Older Than You Are: A Bilingual Gathering of Poems and Stories from Mexico with Paintings by Mexican Artists.* Simon & Schuster, 1995.

Silverthorne, Elizabeth. *Fiesta!: Mexico's Great Celebrations.* Millbrook, 1992.

For the Student

Easy

Herrera, Juan Felipe. *Calling the Doves/El canto de las palomas.* Children's Book Press, 1995.

Average

Delf, Brian, and Richard Platt. *Great Events That Changed the World.* Dorley Kindersley, 2001.

Challenging

Dolan, Edward F. *Panama and the United States: Their Canal, Their Stormy Years.* Watts, 1990.

Literature Connection

Casteñada, Omar S. *Among the Volcanoes.* Lodestar, 1992.

Strasser, Todd. *The Diving Bell.* Scholastic, 1992.

Take It to the NET

The World Explorer companion Web site, found on **phschool.com**, offers activities for exploring geographical, historical, and cultural resources on the Internet. It also provides on-line links for key content and all Section and Chapter Assessment activities.

The **Teacher site** also provides teachers with regional data and ideas for student research and activities.

Students can use the **Student site** to find chapter-by-chapter Internet resource links and to access Self-Tests.

CHAPTER 12

Connecting to the Guiding Questions

In this chapter, students will read about countries in Latin America. Content in this chapter corresponds to the following Guiding Questions outlines at the beginning of the unit.

- How has geography influenced the social and economic development of Latin America?
- How has Latin America's history influenced modern day Latin American societies?
- How are Latin American cultures alike? How are they different?
- How have the governments of Latin America changed over time, and how are they organized today?
- What economic activities support the people of Latin America?
- What opportunities do citizens of Latin America have to participate in the political process?
- How have technology and science helped shape Latin America today?

Using the Biography Activities

Explain to students that Diego Rivera was a Mexican artist best known for his large wall mural paintings.

- Point out to students that this excerpt reveals Diego Rivera to be a man of great artistic skill.
- After they read, ask students to write the answers to their questions.

Heterogeneous Groups

The following activity is suitable for heterogeneous groups.

Making Predictions

Timeline, p. 215

eTeach

Be sure to check out this month's discussion with a Master Teacher. Go to **phschool.com**.

CHAPTER 12

MEXICO AND CENTRAL AMERICA: Exploring the Region Today

Artistic Mexico

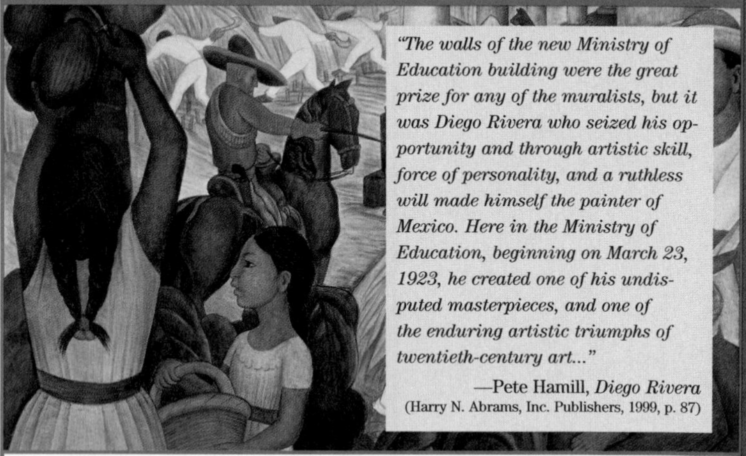

"The walls of the new Ministry of Education building were the great prize for any of the muralists, but it was Diego Rivera who seized his opportunity and through artistic skill, force of personality, and a ruthless will made himself the painter of Mexico. Here in the Ministry of Education, beginning on March 23, 1923, he created one of his undisputed masterpieces, and one of the enduring artistic triumphs of twentieth-century art..."

—Pete Hamill, *Diego Rivera* (Harry N. Abrams, Inc. Publishers, 1999, p. 87)

Jose Diego Maria Rivera, "Sugar Cane," 1931. Fresco. 57 1/8 x 94 1/8 in. (145.1 x 239.1 cm). Philadelphia Museum of Art. Gift of Mr. and Mrs. Herbert Cameron Morris, 1943-46-2. (C)Banco de Mexico Diego Rivera Museum Trust.

Using Biography

If you visit any public buildings in Mexico, chances are you will see the work of Mexican artist Diego Rivera, best known for painting large wall murals. He chose as his themes his country's revolution and the social problems of the early 1900s.

Understanding Biographies

Read the excerpt from the biography of Diego Rivera. A biography is a book written about the life of a real person. What does this excerpt tell you about Diego Rivera?

Using Biographies

Choose a well-known person who is of interest to you, and find a biography written about that person. Make a list of questions that you would like to answer by reading the biography, such as, "Where did this person live?" "How was this person affected by where he or she lived?" "How did the influence of family and friends affect this person's life?" Read the biography and try to answer as many of the questions on your list as possible.

Resource Directory

Teaching Resources

Primary Sources and Literature Readings extend content with a selection related to the concepts in this chapter.

Other Print Resources

DK Atlas

Technology

Case Study: Cleaning Up the Air in Mexico City, from the World Video Explorer, enhances students' understanding of one of the major consequences of urbanization and what Mexico City is doing to meet this challenge.

How People Live Transparencies, Unit 3

Student Edition on Audio CD, Ch. 12

SECTION 1

Mexico

Urban Migration

BEFORE YOU READ

READING FOCUS

1. Why have many Mexicans been moving from rural to urban areas?
2. What challenges do Mexicans from the country face when they build new lives in the city?
3. What environmental problems result when urban areas like Mexico City experience rapid population growth?

KEY TERMS

migrant farmworker
squatter

KEY PLACES

Mexico City

NOTE TAKING

Copy the table below. As you read the section, fill in the table with information about rural and urban life in Mexico.

Life in Rural Mexico: Benefits	Life in Rural Mexico: Drawbacks	Life in Urban Mexico: Benefits	Life in Urban Mexico: Drawbacks

MAIN IDEA

In recent times, many Mexicans have begun migrating to urban areas where they must meet the challenge of finding housing and jobs, and of living with pollution.

Setting the Scene

Ramiro Avila (rah MEE roh ah VEE lah) is one of seven children. He grew up in the state of Guanajuato (gwah nuh HWAH toh), in central Mexico. In his small village, Ramiro knew everyone and everyone knew him.

Ramiro's family were campesinos who owned no land. Even as a young child, Ramiro had to work to help support the family and he and his father had jobs as **migrant farmworkers.** Migrant farmworkers do not own land, but work on large farms owned by rich landowners and travel from one area to another, picking crops that are in season. Ramiro and his father made less than a dollar a day. There is not enough farm work for all the migrant workers, so many move to the cities because they cannot find work in the countryside.

Life in Mexico City

CULTURE This photo shows people walking on a crowded street in Mexico City. **Critical Thinking** How do you think the challenges of living in a city might be different from the challenges of living in a rural area?

Urban Migration to Mexico City

Ramiro's village is located in the southern part of the Mexican Plateau. This area has Mexico's best farmland, and is home to more than half of the country's people. Not surprisingly, it is the location of Mexico's largest city—**Mexico City.**

Resource Directory

Teaching Resources

Classroom Manager in the Unit 3 Teaching Resources, p. 50

Guided Reading and Review in the Unit 3 Teaching Resources, p. 51

Guide to the Essentials, p. 49

Technology

Section Reading Support Transparencies

SECTION 1

Lesson Objectives

1. Explain reasons for the migration of rural Mexicans to urban centers.
2. Describe challenges faced by poor people who move to cities.
3. Summarize the environmental problems of growing cities in Mexico.

Lesson Plan

1 Engage

Warm-Up Activity

Ask students whether they have ever worked and been paid for their work. Write responses on the board. Ask them to name some of the things they bought with their earnings. Help students distinguish between working by cleaning the garage, baby-sitting, or helping an uncle at a restaurant and working to support a family.

Activating Prior Knowledge

Ask students who have moved to tell how they felt about changing schools and moving to a new neighborhood.

2 Explore

Have students read the section. Then, discuss with them life in rural Mexico, identifying characteristics of that life that lead people to move to cities. Point out that new problems arose when Ramiro's family moved. Ask students to list things Ramiro might like about living in the country and things he might like about living in the city.

Answers to...

CRITICAL THINKING

Cities are more crowded and noisier than rural areas. It is more expensive to live in a city.

Lesson Plan continued

3 Teach

Have students create a cause-effect tree based on information in the section. Direct students to list causes such as the following: family cannot earn enough in the country; family could not afford house in the city; Mexico's population rising dramatically; Mexico's cities growing quickly. For each cause, ask students to write at least one effect. Use their completed charts as a springboard for a discussion of possible solutions to the problems of Mexico's cities. This activity should take about 20 minutes.

Questions for Discussion

GEOGRAPHY **How does Mexico City's geography contribute to the problem of pollution?**

The mountains around the city help trap the pollution, preventing winds from blowing it away.

SOCIAL STUDIES SKILLS

Compare and contrast Ramiro's life in the country and in the city.

He worked hard and earned low wages in both places. He knew everyone in his village, but he knows only a few people in the city.

4 Assess/Reteach

See answers to the Section 1 Assessment. You may also use students' completed charts as an assessment.

Acceptable charts include one factually correct effect for each cause.

Commendable charts include two additional effects for last two causes.

Outstanding charts show that an effect can, in turn, become a cause for another effect.

Answers to...

MAP STUDY

Yes. Possible answer: The lava from volcanoes makes fertile soil.

Mexico: Volcanoes and Earthquake Faults

GEOGRAPHY The Earth's crust is made up of many large plates. Usually, earthquakes occur and volcanoes erupt along faults, places where two plates collide or pull apart. Many parts of Mexico have had earthquakes and volcanic eruptions. Volcanic ash makes much of Mexico's soil rich and fertile. Notice the volcanic eruption and earthquake patterns.

Map Study Compare this map with the one in the Country Profile of Mexico in Chapter 11 on page 198. Do many Mexicans live near volcanoes? What is one reason why someone might want to live near a volcano?

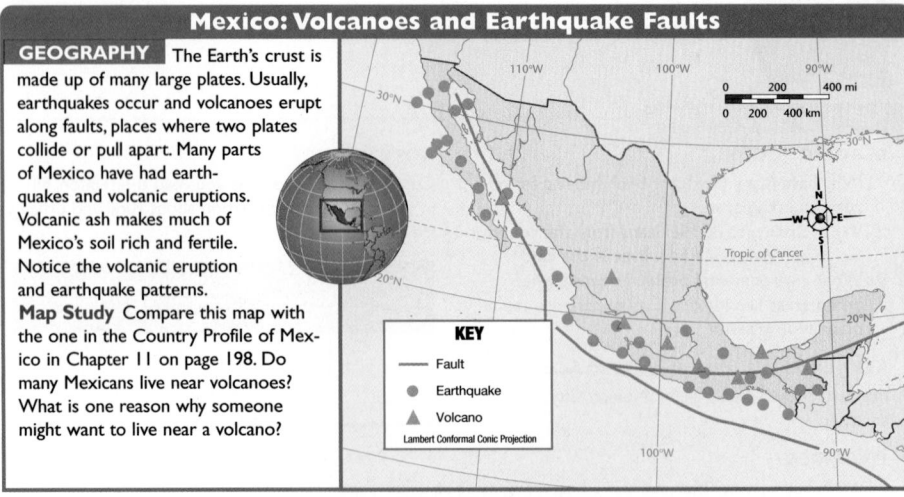

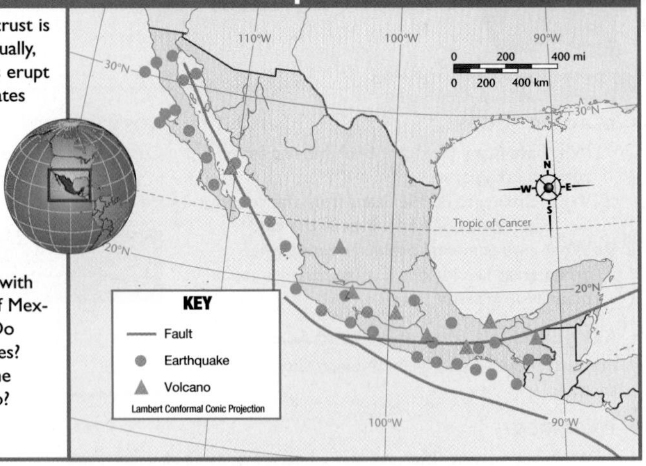

When Ramiro was 13, his parents decided to move the family to Mexico City where they hoped to find better work. The city was far away and their lives would be completely different, but moving offered them a chance to make a decent living.

Life in the City

Like thousands of other campesino families coming to the city, Ramiro's family did not have much money. When they arrived in Mexico City, they could not afford a house. They went to live in Colonia Zapata, which is one of many neighborhoods where poor people become **squatters.** That means they settle on someone else's land without permission. Many small houses of squatters cling to the sides of a steep hill in the Colonia. The older houses near the bottom of the hill are built of concrete. However, most people cannot afford to make sturdy houses when they first arrive. Therefore, many of the newer houses higher up the hill are constructed of scrap metal.

Ramiro's family made a rough, one-room house of rock. Ramiro felt that his new house was ugly. He and his family hoped that soon they would be able to buy land from the government. Then they could build a real house with a garden and a patio.

In Mexico City small neighborhoods of very wealthy people are tucked away from the rest of the city. But most of the residents are not wealthy. The poor live in all areas of the city, but many of the poorest, like Ramiro and his family, live on the outskirts. Some must travel hours each day to get to and from their jobs.

Resource Directory

Teaching Resources

Outline Maps Mexico, p. 8

Technology

Passport to the World CD-ROM This interactive CD-ROM allows students to explore each region of the world. Students view regional videos, take a photo tour, and explore a historical timeline. Students record their travels in an Explorer's Journal, and receive passport stamps when they pass regional quizzes.

Urban Migration and the Growth of Mexico City

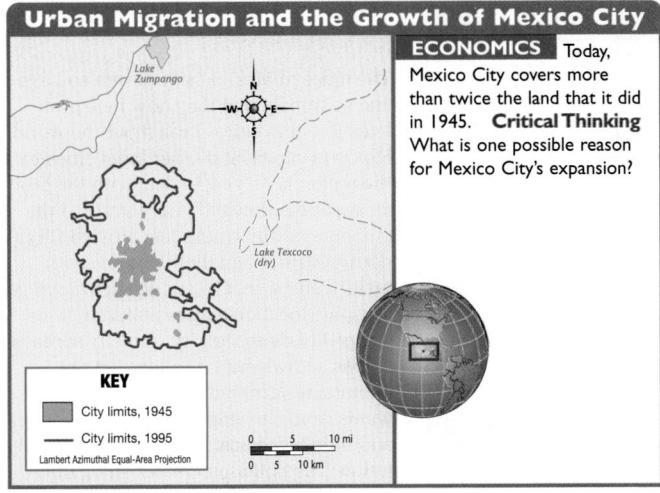

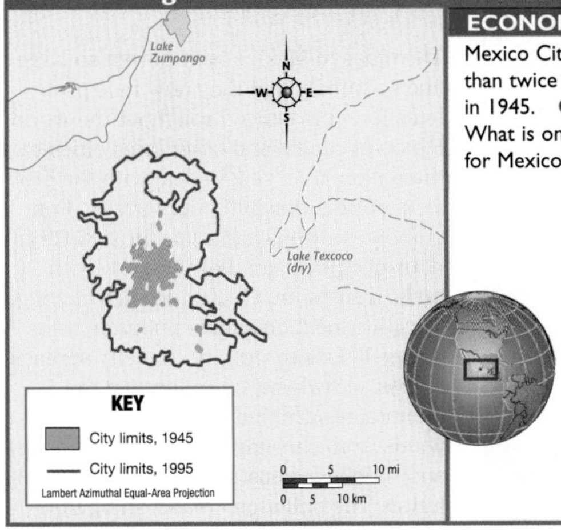

ECONOMICS Today, Mexico City covers more than twice the land that it did in 1945. **Critical Thinking** What is one possible reason for Mexico City's expansion?

Mexico City is huge. Its population sprawls over a large area. It is a megacity, an urban center where many of Mexico's people live. Unlike most big cities, Mexico City does not have many skyscrapers and major streets. Two- and three-story buildings still form its downtown, and only a few streets are wide enough for the city's traffic. The subway, or underground railroad system, carries thousands of people each day.

AS YOU READ

Monitor Your Reading What problems might occur as more people move into a city?

Shortages and the Economy Large cities offer many ways to make a living. Factories and offices employ millions of people. Ramiro works as a cook in a tiny restaurant from 7 A.M. to 2 P.M. For these seven hours of work he earns about $3. His mother and some of his brothers and sisters work, too. Ramiro's sister, Carmela, works as a street vendor. She sells juice at a stand in the bus station near their neighborhood. Every morning, she gets up at 5:30 to make juice from oranges and carrots. People on their way to work buy her juice for their long trip into the city.

Ramiro also goes to a school in Mexico City that holds night classes. After work, he attends classes until 9:30 at night.

Ramiro's father could not get a job in Mexico City. He decided to go to Texas in the United States. He found work as a migrant farmworker. He sends money home every month. It became Ramiro's job to look after his younger brothers and sisters while his father is gone. Ramiro's life is very different from how it had been in his village where life changed little over the years.

SCIENCE, TECHNOLOGY, AND SOCIETY

Earthquakes in Urban Centers

Although the volcanoes that ring Mexico City are dormant, the land is still seismically active. Major earthquakes have occurred in Mexico City as recently as 1985. Other cities that lie on earthquake faults include San Francisco, Tokyo, and Katmandu.

ACTIVITY

Making Predictions

Timeline Have students use an almanac or the Internet to find out when major earthquakes and volcanic eruptions have occurred in Mexico. Ask students to show these events on a timeline. Then, ask questions such as *Are these events becoming more or less frequent? Do you predict that there will be another occurrence soon? Why?*

Visual/Spatial

Resource Directory

Technology

Social Studies Skills Tutor CD-ROM

World Video Explorer See the Mexico case study for an overview of Mexico's history, economy, government, and culture. Discussion questions are included.

Answers to...

CRITICAL THINKING

The city's expansion may have resulted from people moving there to find work.

AS YOU READ

Possible answers include overcrowding, housing shortages, and poverty.

SECTION I ASSESSMENT

AFTER YOU READ

1. (a) capital city of Mexico where millions of people have migrated to live
2. (a) worker who travels with the seasons and the crops to work on large farms (b) person who settles on someone else's land without permission
3. Mexicans from rural areas migrate to Mexico City to find jobs.
4. Possible answers: People have to find or create housing when they move to the city. Some children work part of the day. It may take hours to get to and from jobs.
5. More people have caused more pollution in the city as factories produce more smoke and automobiles create more exhaust fumes. It is also more crowded.
6. Possible benefits: There is the possibility of more work and opportunities for schooling; drawbacks: housing is often poor and people have to live with more pollution that could affect their health.
7. The city will become more crowded and more polluted. There will not be enough jobs for all the new people.
8. Let volunteers read their journal entries to the class.

Pollution and the Environment

GEOGRAPHY Even on a sunny day, buildings a few blocks away appear dim and blurry in Mexico City because of heavy smog. **Critical Thinking** Why do you think Mexico City has so much smog? How can people living in Mexico City work to protect the environment from pollution?

Urban Growth and the Environment

The cities in Mexico have grown so large and so rapidly that they now face problems found in cities throughout the world. Mexico's capital and other large cities in the region are trying to deal with the problems of pollution and heavy traffic. Four million cars and trucks jam Mexico City's narrow streets and they compete with taxis, trolleys, and buses. Mexico City's geographic location causes pollution to be trapped close to the city. The city spreads across a bowl-shaped valley, and the mountains surrounding the valley stop winds from carrying away factory smoke, automobile exhaust fumes, and other pollution. The pollution creates smog that hangs over the city like a dark cloud.

Mexico City is not the only city that is growing. All of Mexico's major cities are becoming more crowded. City life is not easy for most Mexicans, but hard work and hope keep people going.

SECTION I ASSESSMENT

AFTER YOU READ

RECALL

1. Identify: (a) Mexico City
2. Define: (a) migrant farmworker, (b) squatter

COMPREHENSION

3. Why have many people from rural areas in Mexico been migrating to urban areas?
4. What are some of the problems that people from rural areas face when they move to Mexico City?
5. How has urban migration affected Mexico City's physical environment?

CRITICAL THINKING

6. **Exploring the Main Idea** Review the Main Idea statement at the beginning of this section. Then list two benefits and two drawbacks for people who leave Mexico's rural areas for its cities.
7. **Making Predictions** Write a paragraph about the future of Mexico City. Tell what you think will happen to the environment and to the city's residents as more and more people move there.

ACTIVITY

8. **Writing a Journal** Write an entry in your Explorer's Journal comparing and contrasting Ramiro's life with your own. How are your lives different? What similarities do you notice?

Resource Directory

Teaching Resources

Section Quiz in the Unit 3 Teaching Resources, p. 52

Answers to...

CRITICAL THINKING

Cars, trucks, and factories cause smog. People can reduce smog by riding in buses rather than cars. Government can force factories to use cleaner manufacturing processes.

SECTION 2

Guatemala and Nicaragua

Economic and Political Change

SECTION 2

BEFORE YOU READ

READING FOCUS

1. What are the main issues that the indigenous people of Guatemala face?
2. What kinds of changes have been taking place in Guatemala recently?
3. What political events have led to Nicaragua's unstable economy?

KEY TERMS

ladino
political movement
strike
Creole
dictator
guerrilla

KEY PLACES

Guatemala
Nicaragua

MAIN IDEA

While the Maya people of Guatemala have struggled for hundreds of years to earn a voice in their government, in Nicaragua, the people struggle to keep the government and economy stable.

NOTE TAKING

Copy the outline below. As you read the section, complete the outline with information about Guatemala and Nicaragua.

I. **Guatemala: Struggle for Land**
   A. History
      1.
      2.
      3.
      4.
   B. Mayas Struggle for Rights
      1.
      2.
      3.
      4.
II. **Nicaragua: Changes in Government**
   A. History
      1.
      2.
      3.
   B. Many Changes in Government
      1.
      2.

Setting the Scene

Many Latin American countries are working hard to keep their democratic republics alive. Struggles for land, conflicts among people, and changes in government are often part of everyday life. Two countries in Central America—**Guatemala** and **Nicaragua**—share similar histories. Both countries were conquered and colonized by the Spanish in the early 1500s. Yet their challenges are different.

The Struggle for Land in Guatemala

Guatemala has the largest population among Central American countries. The Native Americans are the majority of the population. They form 23 ethnic groups, each with its own language and customs. The largest group is the Quiche Maya.

In Guatemala, most Mayas live in the mountains because at one time it was the only land available to Native Americans. Most land in Guatemala belongs to a few rich landowners called **ladinos** (luh DEE nohs), mestizos who are descended from Native Americans and Spaniards.

Rural Challenges

ECONOMICS Most Mayas who live in the highlands of Guatemala have only small plots of land to farm. **Critical Thinking** What challenges face Mayas who have only small farms?

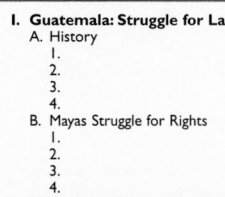

Lesson Objectives

1. Identify the main issues facing the indigenous people of Guatemala.
2. Describe recent changes in Guatemala.
3. Understand the events that have led to Nicaragua's unstable economy.

Lesson Plan

1 Engage

Warm-Up Activity

Ask students to imagine that one day soldiers come to all the houses in their neighborhood and order the people to leave. Prompt the discussion by asking, *How would you feel? What would you do?* Have students try to imagine what life is like in a country where such actions really happen.

Activating Prior Knowledge

Ask students if they have ever felt that they had an important opinion about something, but no one was interested in listening. Then, ask them how people can try to voice their opinions or help change the way things are.

Resource Directory

Teaching Resources

Classroom Manager in the Unit 3 Teaching Resources, p. 53

Guided Reading and Review in the Unit 3 Teaching Resources, p. 54

Guide to the Essentials, p. 50

Technology

Section Reading Support Transparencies

Answers to...

CRITICAL THINKING

hunger and poverty, little or no access to education and medical care

Lesson Plan continued

❷ Explore

Direct students to read the section. Ask them to explain who the indigenous people of Guatemala are and what happened to them. Review how various people and groups became involved in fighting for rights for campesinos and other indigenous people in Guatemala. Then, ask them to discuss the political changes in Nicaragua. Ask what are the differences between the struggles in Guatemala and in Nicaragua.

❸ Teach

Have students create two posters, one showing who the indigenous people of Guatemala are and how they are trying to reshape their lives after civil war, and the other showing how governments in Nicaragua have changed. Remind students to use facts from the section to support their work. Use completed posters to discuss the future of Guatemala and Nicaragua. This activity should take about 40 minutes.

Questions for Discussion

CULTURE In what ways is the current government in Guatemala cooperating with the Mayas?

It appointed 21 Mayan priests to advise officials. It promised to rebuild Mayan communities damaged by civil war.

GOVERNMENT Compare the previous government of Nicaragua with its government today.

Nicaragua used to be ruled by dictators. Today, it is a democracy with elected officials.

COUNTRY • PROFILE Guatemala

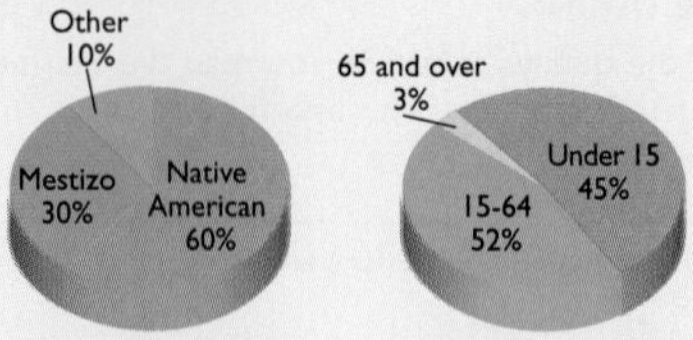

Ethnic Makeup **Age Structure (In years)**

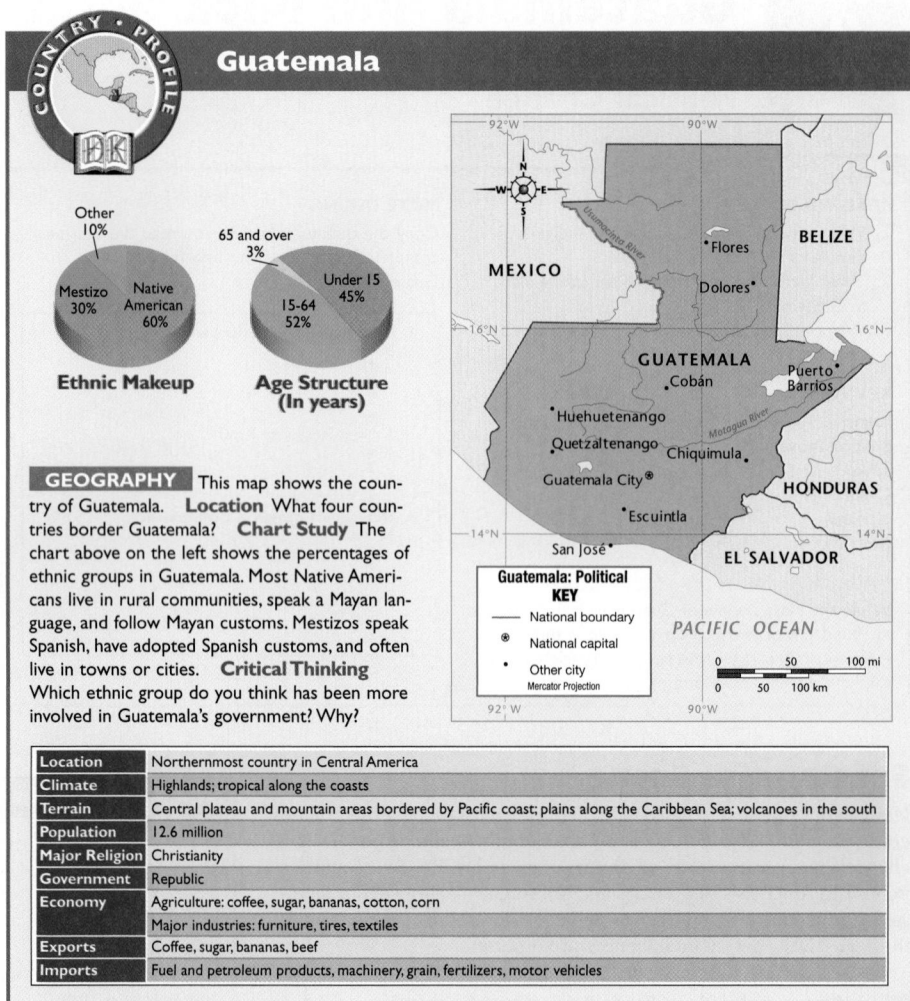

GEOGRAPHY This map shows the country of Guatemala. **Location** What four countries border Guatemala? **Chart Study** The chart above on the left shows the percentages of ethnic groups in Guatemala. Most Native Americans live in rural communities, speak a Mayan language, and follow Mayan customs. Mestizos speak Spanish, have adopted Spanish customs, and often live in towns or cities. **Critical Thinking** Which ethnic group do you think has been more involved in Guatemala's government? Why?

Location	Northernmost country in Central America
Climate	Highlands; tropical along the coasts
Terrain	Central plateau and mountain areas bordered by Pacific coast; plains along the Caribbean Sea; volcanoes in the south
Population	12.6 million
Major Religion	Christianity
Government	Republic
Economy	Agriculture: coffee, sugar, bananas, cotton, corn
	Major industries: furniture, tires, textiles
Exports	Coffee, sugar, bananas, beef
Imports	Fuel and petroleum products, machinery, grain, fertilizers, motor vehicles

Though Native American families work hard to make their land produce crops, they have many challenges to overcome since the soil is not very good, and soil erosion is a serious problem. Also, most Native Americans in Guatemala cannot read or write. Many have not filed papers with the government showing that they own land. As a result, they have no way to prove that their land belongs to them.

Resource Directory

Teaching Resources

Social Studies and Geography Skills,
Reading a Political Map, p. 17

Answers to...

CRITICAL THINKING

Mestizos have been more involved because they are rich landowners who probably do not want things to change.

The Struggle for Change

When a civil war started in Guatemala in 1961, it caught many Mayas in the middle. In hundreds of villages, soldiers came to challenge the Mayas. Sometimes the soldiers were sent by landowners to claim the Mayas' land. Other times, they wanted to exert control over the Mayas by taking away their land and possessions. Most Mayan survivors lost all of their belongings and were forced out of their villages.

Some Mayas started **political movements,** large groups of people who work together to defend their rights or to change the leaders in power. They teach people the history of their land and how to read. They also help organize meetings, protests, and **strikes,** or work stoppages. Above all, they are determined to defend Native American land rights.

All of these efforts have brought about change in Guatemala. For the first time, Mayas have a voice in their own government. For example, Guatemala appointed 21 Mayan priests to advise officials about Mayan culture and the government has promised to rebuild indigenous communities damaged by civil war. Now, the people of Guatemala must make sure that justice is carried out.

Nicaragua: Political and Economic Divisions

Nicaragua is the largest country in Central America, yet it is the least populated. The majority of Nicaraguans are mestizos. Spanish is spoken throughout most of Nicaragua and most of the people are Roman Catholics.

Just as Guatemalans have struggled with injustice and civil war, so have their neighbors to the south in Nicaragua. Many of Nicaragua's struggles are a result of political revolts and changes in government.

Nicaragua shares a similar history with its neighbors in Middle America. Spanish colonists established two cities, Leon and Granada, where a history of political and economic conflicts emerged between conservatives, who favored traditional political ideals, and liberals, who favored non-traditional ideals. British colonists established a logging industry on Nicaragua's eastern coast on the Caribbean Sea.

Spanish is spoken by nearly everyone in the fertile Pacific lowlands and central highlands, where most of the country's population lives. English is spoken on the Caribbean side, which is sparsely populated by people of indigenous, African, and Creole descent. A **Creole** is a person born in the Caribbean of European, usually French, and African descent. Miskito, an indigenous language, is also spoken on the Caribbean side.

LINKS TO Language Arts

The Mosquito Coast (1986) *The Mosquito Coast* is a film about an American inventor, Allie Fox (played by Harrison Ford), who moves his family to a rain forest in Central America to create a simpler life alongside nature, while bringing progress to the indigenous population. While mosquitoes are part of the film's jungle setting, the word *mosquito* in the film's title actually refers to the region on the east coast of Nicaragua and Honduras. This region is named for the Miskito, the native people who inhabit the area.

4 Assess/Reteach

See answers to the Section 2 Assessment. You may also use students' completed posters as an assessment.

Acceptable posters reflect at least four facts about Guatemala and Nicaragua.

Commendable posters include opinions supported by facts from the section.

Outstanding posters demonstrate a sophisticated grasp of Guatemala's indigenous people and of how they have organized politically and socially and Nicaragua's political turmoil.

HISTORY

A Guatemalan Hero

Justo Rufino Barrios (1835–1885) served as president of Guatemala from 1873 to 1885. Barrios strengthened local government. Under his administration, education improved, roads were built, and employment figures rose. Barrios hoped that someday the countries of Central America would unite to form a strong political force.

Resource Directory

Teaching Resources

Outline Maps Latin America, pp. 6–7

Technology

Color Transparencies 55 Latin America: Physical-Political Map

SECTION 2 ASSESSMENT

AFTER YOU READ

1. (a) Central American country with the largest population located just south of Mexico (b) largest Central American country with the smallest population located between Honduras and Costa Rica
2. (a) rich landowner; mestizo descended from Native Americans and Spaniards (b) large group of people who work together to defend their rights (c) work stoppage (d) a person born in the Caribbean of European, usually French, and African descent (e) a ruler who has complete power (f) a person who takes part in undeclared warfare as a member of an independent group
3. The soil where they farm is poor and does not yield much; they have not been able to prove ownership of land; they have played a very minor role in their government.
4. The Mayas are taking a more active political role to gain more of a voice in their government and to defend their rights.
5. Changes in government in Nicaragua have weakened that nation's economy, making it one of the poorest in Latin America. Dictators took money from the country, and their governments built up huge foreign debt.
6. political movements; organizing meetings, protests, and strikes; teaching people about the history of their land, how to read, how to defend their rights
7. Answers will vary, but should be supported with facts.
8. Students' journal entries should reflect actions appropriate to a Maya or Nicaraguan person facing hardship, and to a president who must consider all the people.

Answers to...

CRITICAL THINKING

Answers will vary. Students may say that even though women provided support for the armies, the civil war greatly affected family life.

Cooking for Contra Rebels

CULTURE In the picture above, a Nicaraguan woman prepares food for Contra rebels. **Critical Thinking** How do you think women and children were affected by Nicaragua's civil war?

Independence and Political Changes From the mid 1800s and into the late 1990s, civil war and political differences tore Nicaragua apart, mostly as a result of dictators. A **dictator** is a ruler who has complete power.

Although it is now a republic with a democratic form of government and elected officials, Nicaragua's leaders have placed government controls on the people and have taken land from citizens. Some also took money from the country to build their personal wealth. At the same time, their governments borrowed money from other countries and built up a huge debt.

Economic and Social Changes From the 1970s to the late 1980s, violent political warfare between two political groups—the Sandinistas and Contras—plunged Nicaragua into deep economic and social trouble. Both groups sometimes used guerrilla tactics to get what they wanted. A **guerrilla** is a person who takes part in undeclared warfare as a member of an independent group. In 1999, both the Sandinistas and Contras were disbanded, yet the differences between them still remain.

Today, Nicaragua is one of the poorest nations in Latin America although the government is working to pull the country out of its economic crisis. Nicaragua's main hope is its wealth of unused natural resources. With proper management of these resources, Nicaragua could experience economic growth in the 21st century.

SECTION 2 ASSESSMENT

AFTER YOU READ

RECALL

1. Identify: (a) Guatemala (b) Nicaragua
2. Define: (a) ladino, (b) political movement, (c) strike, (d) Creole, (e) dictator, (f) guerrilla

COMPREHENSION

3. What are some of the current economic and political difficulties that the indigenous people of Guatemala face?
4. How has the Mayan role in the Guatemalan government changed over time?
5. How have the changes in government affected the economy of Nicaragua?

CRITICAL THINKING AND WRITING

6. **Exploring the Main Idea** Review the Main Idea statement at the beginning of this section. Then list three steps the Mayas of Guatemala have taken to gain in voice in their government.
7. **Making a Prediction** What do you think the future holds for the economy of Nicaragua?

ACTIVITY

8. **Writing a Journal** Write a journal entry explaining what you would have done if you were a Mayan villager of Guatemala or a campesino whose land was taken away by the government in Nicaragua during a civil war. Then, explain what you would do if you were the president of either Guatemala or Nicaragua.

Resource Directory

Teaching Resources

Section Quiz in the Unit 3 Teaching Resources, p. 55

220 UNIT 3 LATIN AMERICA

SECTION 3

Panama

A Transportation Corridor

BEFORE YOU READ

READING FOCUS

1. What geographic and political challenges did the builders of the Panama Canal face?
2. How did Panama eventually gain control of the Canal?

KEY TERMS
lock
transportation corridor

KEY PLACES
Panama
Panama Canal
Canal Zone

NOTE TAKING
Copy the flow chart below. As you read the section, fill in the chart with information about the Panama Canal. Add more boxes as needed.

1500s - Sailors dream of transportation corridor through Central America
↓
[ ]
↓
[ ]
↓
[ ]

MAIN IDEA
The Panama Canal is an important transportation corridor providing a shortcut across the Western Hemisphere between the Atlantic and the Pacific Ocean.

Setting the Scene

Cruising through the Pacific Ocean, ships filled with cargo or passengers approach the country of **Panama** heading for the **Panama Canal.** When they reach the canal, they will get in line and perhaps wait for up to 20 hours. Ships pass through this 40-mile (64.4-km) canal 24 hours a day, 365 days a year. A trip through the canal takes at least eight hours and costs thousands of dollars.

It is a worthwhile shortcut, the only way in the Western Hemisphere to get from the Pacific to the Atlantic Ocean by ship without going around the tip of South America. The Panama Canal eliminates about 7,800 miles (12,553 km) in travel distance.

Ships enter the Panama Canal at sea level. But parts of the canal go through mountains. The ships need to be raised and lowered several times in locks as they travel through the canal. A **lock** is a section of waterway in which a ship is raised and lowered by adjusting the water level. Each ship passes through a set of gates into a lock chamber. The water in the chamber starts at sea level. Then, more water comes pouring into the chamber. When the water rises high enough, the ship passes through a second set of gates and enters a small lake. It proceeds to the next lock. Ships pass through two more sets of locks and zigzag through a passage cut through the mountains. After sailing through a huge lake, they exit at the city of Colón (kuh LOHN) into a bay in the Atlantic Ocean.

Panama's Tropical Rain Forest

GEOGRAPHY

Panama's Barro Colorado rain forest is near the Panama Canal. **Critical Thinking** This photograph shows a trail through the rain forest. Where is the trail? Based on this photograph, what difficulties might Panama Canal workers have faced?

SECTION 3

Lesson Objectives

1. Summarize the challenges faced during the building of the Panama Canal.
2. Describe how Panama gained control of the canal.

Lesson Plan

1 Engage

Warm-Up Activity

Use a cardboard box or a three-dimensional drawing on the board to show the size of a cubic yard. Ask students to estimate how many such boxes could fit in their classroom or in their school. Have students judge how many of the boxes could fit in a football field. Then, tell students that to build the Panama Canal, workers scooped out and removed 211 million cubic yards of earth and rock. Explain that the Panama Canal is considered one of the great engineering feats of all time. In this section, students will read why this is so.

Activating Prior Knowledge

Ask students if they have ever agreed to a deal or given away something and then wondered if they made the best decision. What did they do—if anything—to solve the problem?

Resource Directory

Teaching Resources

Classroom Manager in the Unit 3 Teaching Resources, p. 56

Guided Reading and Review in the Unit 3 Teaching Resources, p. 57

Guide to the Essentials, p. 51

Technology

Section Reading Support Transparencies

Answers to...

CRITICAL THINKING

The trail is in the middle of the photo. The rain forest is dense and hot and rainy. There are dangerous animals and insects.

Lesson Plan continued

② Explore

Have students read the section. Ask them to describe what traveling through the canal might be like. Have students consider how the United States gained the right to build the canal and what its construction was like. Finally, discuss how its ownership changed. Have students list some reasons why the United States transferred ownership.

③ Teach

Organize students into three groups of journalists assigned to cover the Panama Canal. Students in the first group will write brief news reports about traveling through the canal. Students in the second group will write a news report about the U.S. role in the canal. Students in the third group will write about the decision to return the canal to Panama. Then, have students form new groups of three in which each student has prepared a different report. Have them read their reports to one another.

Questions for Discussion

GEOGRAPHY Do you think the Panama Canal could have been built in 1800? Explain. How would construction have been different if the canal had been built in 2000?

The canal probably could not have been built in 1800 because the necessary machines and technology had not been invented yet. In 2000, construction would have been easier and cheaper because of improved technology.

SCIENCE, TECHNOLOGY, AND SOCIETY

How has the Panama Canal affected people all over the world?

It has made travel easier. All countries can ship goods more quickly and cheaply.

COUNTRY • PROFILE

Panama

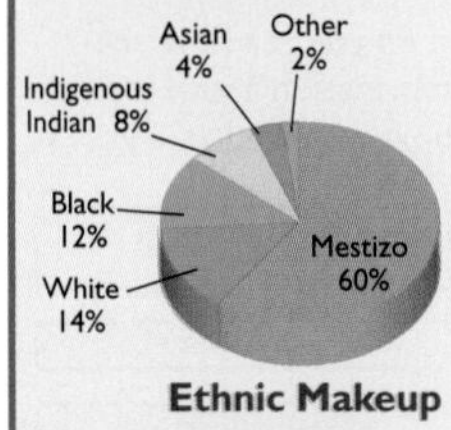

Ethnic Makeup

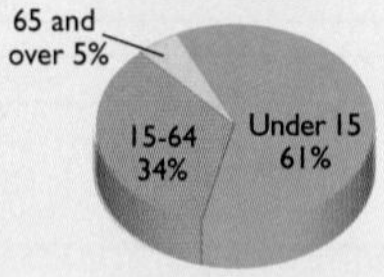

Age Structure (in years)

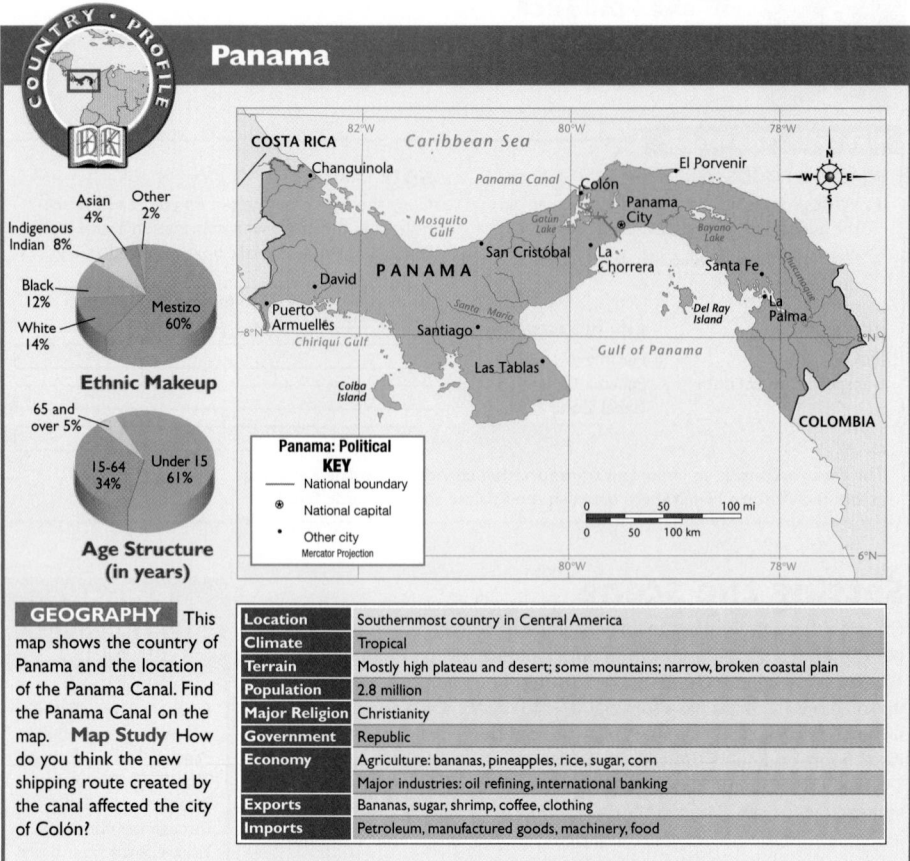

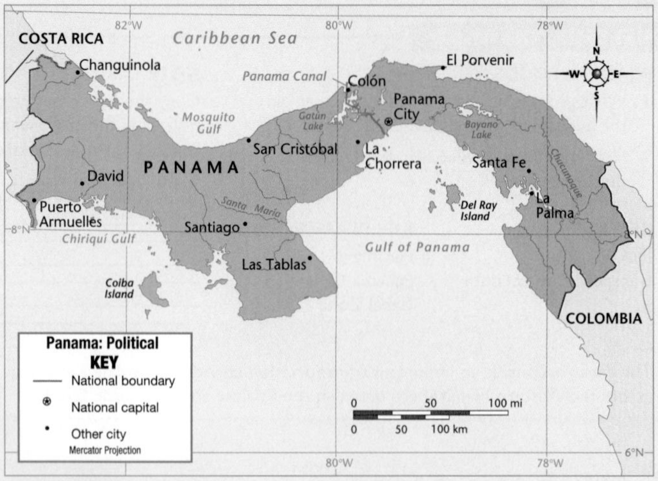

GEOGRAPHY This map shows the country of Panama and the location of the Panama Canal. Find the Panama Canal on the map. **Map Study** How do you think the new shipping route created by the canal affected the city of Colón?

Location	Southernmost country in Central America
Climate	Tropical
Terrain	Mostly high plateau and desert; some mountains; narrow, broken coastal plain
Population	2.8 million
Major Religion	Christianity
Government	Republic
Economy	Agriculture: bananas, pineapples, rice, sugar, corn
	Major industries: oil refining, international banking
Exports	Bananas, sugar, shrimp, coffee, clothing
Imports	Petroleum, manufactured goods, machinery, food

Building the Panama Canal: Geographic and Political Challenges

Since the 1500s, sailors dreamed of a transportation corridor through Central America to shorten the trip from the Atlantic to the Pacific. A **transportation corridor** is a passageway through which people can travel by foot, vehicle, rail, ship, or airplane. A canal would cut the cost of shipping goods.

In 1881, when Panama was part of Colombia, Colombia gave a French company the rights to build a canal. Digging through Panama posed several problems. The builders struggled with mudslides. A mountain range blocked the way. In addition, tropical diseases such as malaria and yellow fever killed 25,000 workers. After a few years, the French company went bankrupt and work on the canal stopped.

Answers to...

MAP STUDY

Colón probably had an economic boom because it is located at one end of the canal.

SKILLS MINI LESSON

Expressing Problems Clearly

To **introduce** the skill, tell students that expressing a problem clearly can help them find possible solutions to the problem. Help students **practice** the skill by having small groups choose the point of view of either the United States or Panama. Work with them to express clearly what the problems were. Have them list positive and negative effects of relinquishing control of the canal. You may want to have groups debate the issue.

Shipping Routes and the Panama Canal

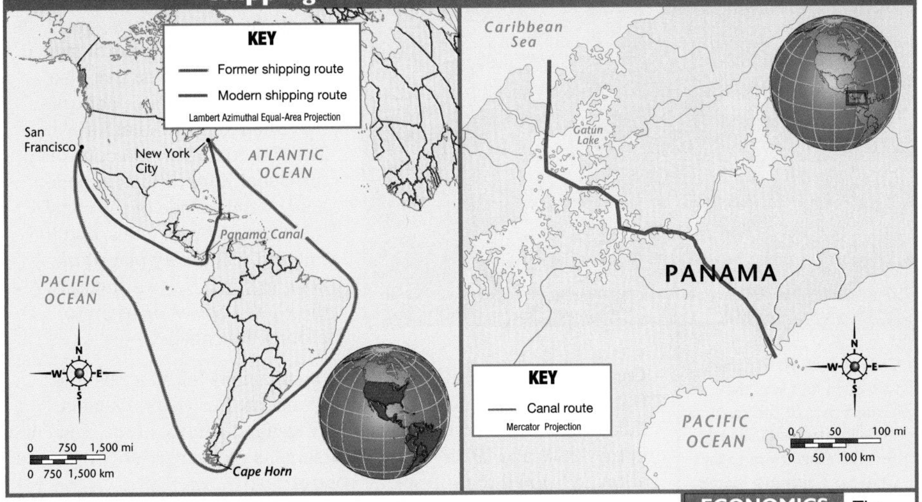

ECONOMICS The map on the left shows shipping routes from New York to San Francisco before and after construction of the Panama Canal. The map on the right is a close up of the Panama Canal route. Before the Panama Canal was built, ships had to travel more than 13,000 miles (20,900 km) around South America. After the Canal was built, ships only had to travel 5,200 miles (8,370 km).
Map Study What kind of savings would occur by shortening the trip 7,800 miles?

The United States Takes a Role In 1902, the United States government tried to get the rights to continue building the canal. Colombia refused and Panamanians who had hoped that the Canal would bring business to Panama were disappointed. Many Panamanians wanted freedom from Colombia's rule and they saw the canal as a chance to win independence.

In November 1903, the United States helped Panama revolt against Colombia. Two weeks after Panama declared independence, the United States received the rights to build the Canal.

Scientific Developments Make the Canal a Reality Builders continued to face problems building the Canal. Whenever the diggers carved a hole in the soft earth, more dirt slid into its place. A dam needed to be built to form a lake. Locks needed to be designed and built. But, the biggest problems were malaria and yellow fever.

In the early 1900s, doctors discovered that mosquitoes carried malaria and yellow fever. The mosquitoes bred in swamps and in drinking water. In 1904, the Panama Canal Company hired a doctor and a large crew to deal with the mosquito problem. Workers burned sulfur in every house to kill mosquitoes and they covered drinking water sources with wire mesh and filled swamps with dirt.

Without modern medicine and the scientific innovations of the early 1900s, as well as good planning, the Panama Canal could not have been built. Still, it took eight years and 45,000 workers, mostly Caribbean islanders, to make the waterway. The Panama Canal remains one of the greatest engineering feats of modern times.

4 Assess/Reteach

See answers to the Section 3 Assessment. You may also use students' news reports as an assessment.

Acceptable reports include facts from the text.

Commendable reports may include appropriate opinions, supported by facts.

Outstanding reports draw reasonable conclusions about the topic.

GEOGRAPHY

Canals Change the World

Other canals have significantly changed countries and world travel. For example, the Erie Canal, completed in 1825, changed American history. The canal linked Chicago, Detroit, and Buffalo to the Atlantic Ocean. The resulting industry made the Midwest a magnet for settlement by immigrants. In the Middle East, the Suez Canal—connecting the Mediterranean Sea to the Red Sea and the Indian Ocean—opened in 1869. The canal greatly shortens the distance between Europe and Asia.

ACTIVITY

Interdisciplinary Connections

Math Have students use their knowledge of math to answer the following question: If it takes 8 hours for a ship to pass through the canal, how many miles per hour does a ship average? (40 miles ÷ 8 hours = 5 miles per hour)

Logical/Mathematical

Resource Directory

Teaching Resources

Social Studies and Geography Skills, Using the Map Key, p. 1

Answers to...

MAP STUDY

People would save time and money.

SECTION 3 ASSESSMENT

AFTER YOU READ

1. (a) Southernmost country in Central America (b) constructed transportation corridor in Panama that links the Atlantic and Pacific oceans (c) land on either side of the canal, ports, port cities, and railroad
2. (a) a section of waterway in which a ship is raised and lowered by adjusting the water level (b) a passageway through which foot, vehicle, rail, shipping, or airplane traffic can travel
3. Workers had to cut through the mountains. They struggled with mudslides as they dug. They had to build a dam, a lake, and locks. They had to control yellow fever and malaria.
4. The original treaty gave the United States the right to build the canal and to control it forever. The new treaties gave Panama more control over the canal. In 1999, Panama was given ownership of the canal.
5. It cuts the distance between the Atlantic and Pacific Oceans by thousands of miles. It cuts the costs of shipping goods by thousands of dollars. It saves time, money, and distance. It has helped the economy develop in the Canal Zone.
6. It seems right to Panamanians to have control over their own country. It helps Panama's economy since the owner of the canal charges fees for passing through it.
7. Students can work together on a large display timeline.

Answers to...

CRITICAL THINKING

Workers and supplies were moved by rail.

Building the Canal

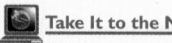

GEOGRAPHY Cutting through Panama's soft earth hills was the hardest part of the canal to build. Earth still slides into the canal there today. **Critical Thinking** Based on the picture, how do you think workers and supplies were moved to and from the canal?

Control of the Canal

When the United States gained the rights to build the canal, it signed a treaty with Panama that also gave the United States control over the Panama Canal forever. The United States also controlled the **Canal Zone,** which included land on either side of the canal, the ports, the port cities, and the railroad. The treaty placed the Zone under U.S. laws and gave the United States the right to protect the canal.

Conflict and Resolution Many Panamanians felt this gave the United States too much power over Panama. For years, Panama talked with the United States about regaining control of the canal and in the 1960s and 1970s, many Panamanians grew angry about the situation and rioted to protest U.S. control.

In 1978, U.S. President Jimmy Carter signed two new treaties with Panama. These treaties gave Panama more control over the canal. In 1999, Panama finally gained full control of the Panama Canal.

SECTION 3 ASSESSMENT

AFTER YOU READ

RECALL

1. Identify: (a) Panama, (b) Panama Canal, (c) Canal Zone
2. Define: (a) lock, (b) transportation corridor

COMPREHENSION

3. What were some of the political and geographical difficulties that the builders of the canal faced?
4. What countries controlled the Panama Canal at one time or another? How did Panama eventually gain control of the canal?

CRITICAL THINKING AND WRITING

5. **Exploring the Main Idea** Review the Main Idea statement at the beginning of this section. Then list at least three reasons why the Panama Canal is an important transportation corridor.
6. **Recognizing Point of View** Write a paragraph explaining why it has been important both politically and economically to Panamanians to have control of the Panama Canal.

ACTIVITY

Take It to the NET

7. **Creating a Timeline** The Panama Canal is an engineering marvel. Create a timeline of significant events pertaining to the construction of the Panama Canal. Visit the World Explorer: People, Places, and Cultures section of **phschool.com** for help in completing this activity.

Resource Directory

Teaching Resources

Section Quiz in the Unit 3 Teaching Resources, p. 58

Chapter Summary in the Unit 3 Teaching Resources, p. 59

Vocabulary in the Unit 3 Teaching Resources, p. 60

Reteaching in the Unit 3 Teaching Resources, p. 61

Enrichment in the Unit 3 Teaching Resources, p. 62

Critical Thinking in the Unit 3 Teaching Resources, p. 63

Using Standard English

Learn the Skill

Even in places where the same language is spoken, variations occur in different regions. In the United States, English phrases and accents are different in the South than in the North or West. Different ethnic and cultural groups also develop their own ways of speaking.

Most national and state standardized tests require you to know what is called "standard English." Questions on these tests usually require you to read a passage and answer multiple-choice questions. (See the sample test on this page.)

Standard English is what you learn when you study grammar, spelling, capitalization, and punctuation rules. Use these strategies to help you answer questions about English when taking tests:

A. Recognize grammar errors. Remember the rules you've learned. Don't confuse common spoken language for Standard English, for example, "ain't" instead of "am not." Check to see if the subject and verb agree, for example, "land and resources affect an economy," instead of "land and resources affects an economy."

B. Recognize spelling errors. Check the spelling of the words in the passage you are being tested on. Pay special attention to homophones (to, too, two), double vowels ("squeak," not "squeek"), suffixes ("*-ness*," not "*-nes*"), and words containing *-ie* or *-ei*.

C. Check for capitalization errors. Make sure that the first word in a sentence is capitalized, that proper nouns are capitalized, and that no words are capitalized unnecessarily. All the words in a compound proper noun should be capitalized, for example, "National Preparatory School."

D. Recognize punctuation errors. Check end punctuation, make sure that all necessary commas and no unnecessary commas are there, notice if both pairs of quotation marks are present, and look for a question mark where needed.

Practice the Skill

Read the sample test and try to find the errors in Standard English.

(1) Have you ever visited the Panama Canal.

A Spelling error B Punctuation error
C Grammar error D No error

(2) It crosses through Panama in central America.

A Capitalization error B Punctuation error
C Grammar error D No error

(3) The Canal Zone use to be controlled by the United States.

A Spelling error B Punctuation error
C Grammar error D No error

(4) In 1999, Panama finally gained complete control of it.

A Spelling error B Capitalization error
C Grammar error D No error

Apply the Skill

See the Chapter Review and Assessment at the end of this chapter for more questions on Standard English.

Lesson Objectives

1. Explain the importance of using Standard English.
2. Identify and correct errors in Standard English.

Lesson Plan

1 Engage

Read the opening text under "Learn the Skill" aloud. Make sure students understand the meaning of the terms. A *dialect* is a form of speech that is characteristic of a certain geographic region, such as the southern region of the United States. An *idiom* is an expression that has a special meaning different from the usual meaning of the words. Ask students to provide more examples of dialects and idioms.

2 Explore

Direct students to read the steps under "Learn the Skill." Discuss each example and have students provide more examples.

3 Teach

Have students read and answer the questions. Make sure students understand how to answer multiple-choice questions of this nature.

For additional reinforcement, provide more simple sentences that contain errors on the chalkboard.

4 Assess/Reteach

Students should know how to take standardized multiple-choice tests in which they must determine whether a sentence contains an error, and identify the kind of error.

To further assess students' understanding of Standard English, have them complete the "Applying Your Skills" part of the Chapter Review and Assessment at the end of this chapter.

Resource Directory

Teaching Resources

Social Studies and Geography Skills,
Revising: Editing Your Work, p. 83

Technology

Social Studies Skills Tutor CD-ROM

Answers to...

PRACTICE THE SKILL

1. B
2. A
3. C
4. D

CHAPTER 12

Review and Assessment

Creating a Chapter Summary

Student summaries will vary.

Sample summaries:

Section 2 The Mayas of Guatemala are working hard to keep their rights and to play a role in their government. Nicaragua's people struggle for political and economic stability.

Section 3 The Panama Canal is one of the most important transportation corridors in the world. Several countries, including the United States, have controlled the canal.

Reviewing Key Terms

1. d **2.** a **3.** h **4.** b **5.** g **6.** f **7.** c **8.** e

Reviewing the Main Ideas

1. Many Mexicans move from rural to urban areas to find of work, so they can better support their families.
2. People lack decent housing, and Mexico City now has more traffic congestion and air pollution from increased traffic and factory production.
3. Indigenous Guatemalans are struggling to hold on to their land and to gain equal rights.
4. They are organizing political movements and educating their people in order to have more of a voice in their government.
5. Most of Nicaragua's political leaders have weakened the economy by taking the country's money for themselves and by having the government borrow money from other countries, building up a huge foreign debt.
6. Guerrilla fighting between the Sandinistas and the Contras caused economic and social trouble. Land was taken away by the government.
7. It went through the rain forest. There were mudslides and disease.
8. It is part of their country. Panama charges fees to all ships using the canal.

CHAPTER 12

Review and Assessment

Creating a Chapter Summary

On a separate piece of paper, draw a diagram like this one, and include the information that summarizes the first section of the chapter. Then fill in the second and third boxes with summaries of Sections 2 and 3.

MEXICO AND CENTRAL AMERICA: EXPLORING THE REGION TODAY

Section 1	Section 2	Section 3
In recent times, many Mexicans have begun moving to urban areas like Mexico City. This migration from rural to urban areas brings many new challenges for people.		

Reviewing Key Terms

Match the definitions in Column I with the Key Terms in Column II.

Column I

1. ruler who has complete power
2. work stoppage
3. large group of people who work together to defend their rights
4. passageway through which foot, vehicle, rail, shipping, or airplane traffic can travel
5. a section of waterway in which a ship is raised and lowered by adjusting the water level
6. rich landowner of Guatemala or Nicaragua, or a Native American who follows European ways
7. landless farm worker who travels with the seasons and the crops
8. person who settles on someone else's land without permission

Column II

a. strike
b. transportation corridor
c. migrant farmworker
d. dictator
e. squatter
f. ladino
g. lock
h. political movement

Reviewing the Main Ideas

1. Describe Mexico's urban migration. Why are so many people making this move? (Section 1)
2. What housing and environmental problems has Mexico City experienced as a result of its rapid population growth? (Section 1)
3. What are the main challenges that indigenous Guatemalans face? (Section 2)
4. Name two steps Mayas in Guatemala are taking to ensure their rights. (Section 2)
5. How have political changes affected Nicaragua's economy? (Section 2)
6. Name one way civil war has played a role in Nicaragua's history. (Section 2)
7. Why was the Panama Canal so difficult to build? (Section 3)
8. Why is control of the Panama Canal important to Panama? (Section 3)

Map Activity

For each place listed below, write the letter from the map that shows its location.

1. Guatemala
2. Colón, Panama
3. Panama
4. Mexico City
5. Nicaragua
6. Panama City

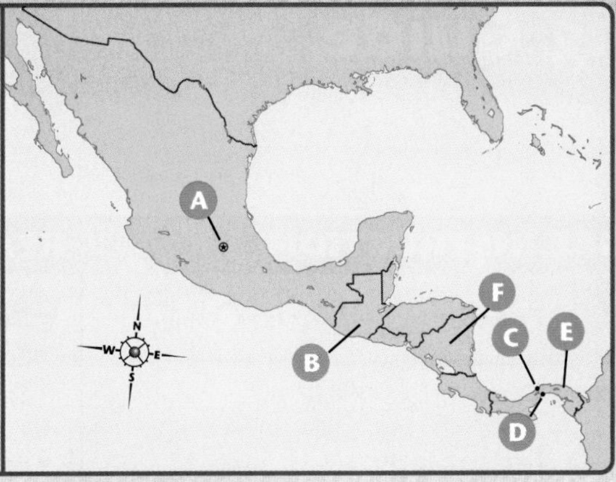

Take It to the NET

Enrichment For more map activities using geography skills, visit the social studies section of **phschool.com.**

Writing Activity

1. **Writing News Stories** Imagine you are a writer for a radio program. Write two brief news stories on urban migration in Mexico and the history of the Panama Canal.
2. **Writing a Dialogue** Imagine that you are a Maya from Guatemala. Write a dialogue between you and a person from Nicaragua. Discuss the political changes in your countries.

Critical Thinking

1. **Making Comparisons** What do people who move from rural Mexico to the city have to gain? What do they have to lose?
2. **Drawing Conclusions** Over the years, the United States has exercised economic and political influence in Central America. How does the history of the Panama Canal demonstrate U.S. influence in the region?

Applying Your Skills

Choose the letter answer below that correctly identifies the type of error in each sentence shown.

1. nicaragua is a country in Central America.
   - **A** Spelling error
   - **B** Punctuation error
   - **C** Capitalization error
   - **D** No error
2. Mayas in Guatemala now have a voice in their own goverment.
   - **A** Capitalization error
   - **B** Spelling error
   - **C** Grammar error
   - **D** No error
3. If you're planning too take a trip to South America, bring me along to!
   - **A** Capitalization error
   - **B** Spelling error
   - **C** Grammar error
   - **D** No error

Take It to the NET

Activity Create a graph illustrating the population growth in Mexico City over the past 50 years. What are some negative effects of such a rapid increase in population? What are some possible solutions? Visit the World Explorer: People, Places, and Cultures section of **phschool.com** for help in completing this activity.

Chapter 12 Self-Test As a final review activity, take the Chapter 12 Self-Test and get instant feedback on your answers. To take the test, visit the Social Studies section of **phschool.com.**

Map Activity

1. B **2.** C **3.** E **4.** A **5.** F **6.** D

Writing Activity

1. Students' news stories should contain the main ideas from sections 1 and 3.
2. Dialogues should include details about political changes and challenges in Guatemala and Nicaragua.

Critical Thinking

1. They gain more opportunities for education, work, and different kinds of jobs. They can often make more money. They might lose a feeling of closeness and familiarity with the community. Sometimes families are broken up in order for everyone to work.
2. The United States had nearly unlimited power in Central America; the United States helped Panama become independent, then took part of the country under its own control. The United States seems to be relinquishing its influence in the area, as evidenced by letting go of control of the canal.

Applying Your Skills

1. C **2.** B **3.** B

Resource Directory

Teaching Resources

Cooperative Learning Activity in the Unit 3 Teaching Resources, pp. 115–117

Chapter Tests Forms A and B in the Unit 3 Teaching Resources, pp. 148–153

Guide to the Essentials, Ch. 12 Test, p. 52

Other Print Resources

Chapter Tests ExamView® Test Bank, Ch. 12

Technology

ExamView® Test Bank CD-ROM, Ch. 12

Resource Pro® CD-ROM

Chapter 13 Planning Guide

Resource Manager

	CORE INSTRUCTION	READING/SKILLS
Chapter-Level Resources	**Teaching Resources** Program Overview Pacing Charts **Technology** Resource Pro® CD-ROM Companion Web site, phschool.com • eTeach	**Technology** Social Studies Skills Tutor CD-ROM Student Edition on Audio CD, Ch. 13
1 The Caribbean: Economic and Political Challenges 1. Identify the major industries of the Caribbean. 2. Describe some of the political changes facing the countries of the Caribbean.	**Teaching Resources** **Unit 3** Classroom Manager, p. 65 Guided Reading and Review, p. 66	**Teaching Resources** Guide to the Essentials, p. 53 Social Studies and Geography Skills, p. 3 **Technology** Section Reading Support Transparencies
2 Brazil and Peru: Natural Resources and Industry 1. Explain why Brazil's rain forests are a global concern. 2. Explain the importance of rain forests to Brazil's economy.	**Teaching Resources** **Unit 3** Classroom Manager, p. 68 Guided Reading and Review, p. 69	**Teaching Resources** Guide to the Essentials, p. 54 Social Studies and Geography Skills, p. 23 **Technology** Section Reading Support Transparencies
3 Chile and Venezuela: Growing Economies 1. Identify how Chile's government has worked to protect the environment. 2. Describe why agriculture is important to Chile's economy. 3. Explain how Venezuela's oil boom affected its people and economy.	**Teaching Resources** **Unit 3** Classroom Manager, p. 71 Guided Reading and Review, p. 72	**Teaching Resources** Guide to the Essentials, p. 55 **Technology** Section Reading Support Transparencies
4 Argentina: A Cultural Center 1. Compare Argentina's ethnic makeup to that of other South American countries. 2. Identify the two main cultural groups in Argentina. 3. Compare the culture of Argentina's gauchos to that of American cowboys.	**Teaching Resources** **Unit 3** Classroom Manager, p. 74 Guided Reading and Review, p. 75 Chapter Summary, p. 77 Vocabulary, p. 78 Reteaching, p. 79	**Teaching Resources** **Unit 3** Critical Thinking, p. 81 Guide to the Essentials, p. 56 Social Studies and Geography Skills, p. 17 **Technology** Section Reading Support Transparencies

ENRICHMENT/PRE-AP

Teaching Resources
Primary Sources and Literature Readings

Other Print Resources
DK Atlas

Technology
World Video Explorer: Spotlight On: Music of the Caribbean and Daily Life: Life on the Amazon River
Companion Web site, phschool.com

Technology
Color Transparencies 63
How People Live Transparencies, Unit 3

Technology
Color Transparencies 13, 57–58
Passport to the World CD-ROM

Technology
Color Transparencies 46
How People Live Transparencies, Unit 3

Teaching Resources
Unit 3
Enrichment, p. 80
Cooperative Learning Activity, pp. 119–121
Outline Maps, pp. 10–11

ASSESSMENT

Prentice Hall Assessment System

Core Assessment
Chapter Tests with ExamView® Test Bank, Ch. 13
ExamView® Test Bank CD-ROM, Ch. 13

Standardized Test Preparation
Diagnose and Prescribe
Diagnostic Tests for Middle Grades Social Studies Skills
Review and Reteach
Review Book for World Studies
Practice and Assess
Test-taking Strategies with Transparencies for Middle Grades Test Prep Book
Test-taking Strategies Posters

Teaching Resources
Unit 3
Section Quizzes, pp. 67, 70, 73, and 76
Chapter Tests, pp. 154–159

Technology
Companion Web site, phschool.com
Ch. 13 Self-Test

World Video Explorer
Each region of the world is explored through regional flyovers and investigative field trips. Case study segments give students an in-depth view of the history, economy, government, and culture of a key place in each region. Case studies include Nigeria, Mexico, China, British Columbia, and the Czech Republic.

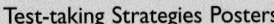

In Your Classroom

CUSTOMIZE FOR INDIVIDUAL NEEDS

Gifted and Talented

Teacher's Edition
- Create a Play, p. 231
- Identifying Central Issues, p. 235
- Cowboy Songs, p. 243

Teaching Resources
- Enrichment, p. 80
- Primary Sources and Literature Readings

Honors/Pre-AP

Teacher's Edition
- Oil Cartel, p. 239
- Juan Peron, p. 243

Teaching Resources
- Critical Thinking, p. 81
- Primary Sources and Literature Readings

ESL

Teacher's Edition
- Baseball, p. 231
- Capoeira, p. 235
- Pen Pal, p. 239

Teaching Resources
- Guided Reading and Review, pp. 66, 69, 72, and 75
- Vocabulary, p. 78
- Reteaching, p. 79
- Guide to the Essentials, pp. 53–56
- Social Studies and Geography Skills, pp. 3, 17, and 23

Technology
- Social Studies Skills Tutor CD-ROM
- Section Reading Support Transparencies

Less Proficient Readers

Teacher's Edition
- Create a Play, p. 231
- Cowboy Songs, p. 243

Teaching Resources
- Guided Reading and Review, pp. 66, 69, 72, and 75
- Vocabulary, p. 78
- Reteaching, p. 79
- Guide to the Essentials, pp. 53–56
- Social Studies and Geography Skills, pp. 3, 17, and 23

Technology
- Social Studies Skills Tutor CD-ROM
- Section Reading Support Transparencies

Less Proficient Writers

Teacher's Edition
- Create a Play, p. 231
- Identifying Central Issues, p. 235

Teaching Resources
- Guided Reading and Review, pp. 66, 69, 72, and 75
- Vocabulary, p. 78
- Guide to the Essentials, pp. 53–56
- Social Studies and Geography Skills, pp. 3, 17, and 23

Technology
- Social Studies Skills Tutor CD-ROM
- Section Reading Support Transparencies

DORLING KINDERSLEY

At the end of each unit, you will find information adapted from Dorling Kindersley's *Illustrated Children's Encyclopedia* that connects to the region being studied and to one of the seven content strands. In addition, your resources include Dorling Kindersley's *Atlas*, which contains valuable information about countries from around the world.

TEACHER'S EDITION INDEX

Activities create a play, p. 231; identifying central issues, p. 235; pen pal, p. 239; cowboy songs, p. 243

Connections baseball, p. 231; capoeira, p. 235; oil cartel, p. 239; juan peron, p. 243

Skills Mini Lessons Identifying Central Issues, p. 231; Interpreting Graphs: Circle Graphs, p. 239

CHAPTER 13 PACING SUGGESTIONS

For 90-minute Blocks

See suggestions in the Teaching Resources Pacing Charts for Chapter 13. Use Color Transparencies 13, 46, 57–58, and 63.

Running Out of Time?

See the Guide to the Essentials, pp. 53–56.

INTERDISCIPLINARY LINKS

Middle Grades Math: Tools for Success

Course 1, Lesson 8-8, **Congruent and Similar Figures**

Course 2, Lesson 11-2, **Graphing Linear Equations**

Course 3, Lesson 2-11, **Scientific Notation**

Science Explorer

Chemical Building Blocks, Lesson 3-1, **Organizing the Elements**

Electricity and Magnetism, Lesson 1-1, **Nature of Magnetism**

Environmental Science, Lesson 6-1, **Fossil Fuels**

Chemical Interactions, Lesson 1-2, **Describing Chemical Reactions**

Prentice Hall Literature

Bronze, I am a Native of North America, Amigo Brothers

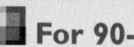

BIBLIOGRAPHY

For the Teacher

Ada, Alma Flor. *Where the Flame Trees Bloom.* Atheneum, 1994.

Aliotta, Jerome J. *The Puerto Ricans.* Chelsea House, 1995.

Beani, Laura, Francesco Dessi, and Massimo Pandolfi. *The Pampas, Andes, and Galapagos.* Steck-Vaughn, 1992.

DK *Wild South America.* Dorling Kindersley, 2001.

Sheehan, Sean. *Jamaica.* Cavendish, 1993.

For the Student

Easy

DK *Rain Forest* (*Eye Wonder* series). Dorling Kindersley, 2001.

Peru—In Pictures. Lerner, 1994.

Average

Schwartz, David. *Yanomami: People of the Amazon.* Lothrop, 1995.

Challenging

Temple, Frances. *Tonight, By Sea.* Orchard, 1995.

Literature Connection

Kendall, Sarita. *Ransom for a River Dolphin.* Lerner, 1993.

Taylor, Theodore. *The Cay.* Doubleday, 1969.

Take It to the NET

The World Explorer companion Web site, found on **phschool.com**, offers activities for exploring geographical, historical, and cultural resources on the Internet. It also provides on-line links for key content and all Section and Chapter Assessment activities.

The **Teacher site** also provides teachers with regional data and ideas for student research and activities.

Students can use the **Student site** to find chapter-by-chapter Internet resource links and to access Self-Tests.

CHAPTER 13

Connecting to the Guiding Questions

In this chapter, students will read about specific countries in Latin America. Content in this chapter corresponds to the following Guiding Questions outlined at the beginning of the unit.

- How are Latin American cultures alike? How are they different?
- How have the governments of Latin America changed over time, and how are they organized today?
- What economic activities support the people of Latin America?
- What opportunities do citizens of Latin America have to participate in the political process?

Using the Graph Activities

Explain to students that petroleum is what we usually call "oil." Review the parts of a bar graph—title, horizontal and vertical axes—and how to read the height of a bar that isn't exactly at a number to the left.

- Make sure that students ask questions that can be answered from the graph.
- You may want to divide the class into small groups and assign each group a particular product. Encourage students to include pictures and photographs of the products.

Heterogeneous Groups

The following activities are suitable for heterogeneous groups.

Cooperative Learning
Create a Play, p. 231

Journal Writing
Pen Pal, p. 239

eTeach

Be sure to check out this month's discussion with a Master Teacher. Go to **phschool.com**.

CHAPTER 13

THE CARIBBEAN AND SOUTH AMERICA: Exploring the Region Today

U.S Petroleum Imports From Venezuela, 1990–2000

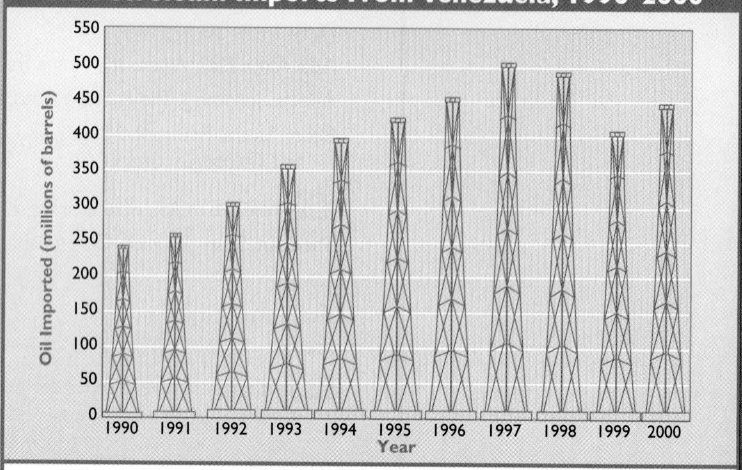

Understanding Graphs

Petroleum is one of the most valuable resources in the world. It comes from deep within the Earth in the form of crude oil, which is refined to use as fuel and to create thousands of other products. Venezuela has one of the largest reserves of petroleum in South America. The United States, which uses more petroleum than it can produce, imports petroleum from Venezuela.

Using the Graph

Study the graph, and then write a series of questions about the information in the graph. For example, about how many more millions of barrels were imported in 1998 than in 1992? Between what two years did petroleum imports increase the most? When you are finished, trade your questions with a partner and use the graph to answer them.

Researching Petroleum Products

Use your local library or the Internet to learn more about the uses of petroleum and the different kinds of products that are made from it. Write a brief report on your findings. Then, work with your classmates to create a bulletin board display showing the different kinds of products that are made from petroleum.

228 UNIT 3 LATIN AMERICA

Resource Directory

Teaching Resources

Primary Sources and Literature Readings extend content with a selection related to the concepts in this chapter.

Other Print Resources

DK Atlas

Technology

Spotlight on: Music of the Caribbean, from the World Video Explorer, enhances students' understanding of how the blending of Indian, European, and African influences has resulted in a unique Caribbean culture.

Daily Life: Life on the Amazon River, from the World Video Explorer, enhances understanding of the ways that people have adapted to the Amazon.

Student Edition on Audio CD, Ch. 13

SECTION 1

The Caribbean

Economic and Political Challenges

BEFORE YOU READ

READING FOCUS

1. What are the major industries in the Caribbean?
2. What are some of the political challenges facing countries in the Caribbean?

KEY TERMS

one-crop economy

KEY PEOPLE

Jean-Bertrand Aristide
René Préval

MAIN IDEA

The island nations of the Caribbean, some of which are independent and some of which remain dependent on other countries, have struggled with poverty and political unrest.

NOTE TAKING

Copy the diagram below. As you read the section, complete the diagram with information from the text.

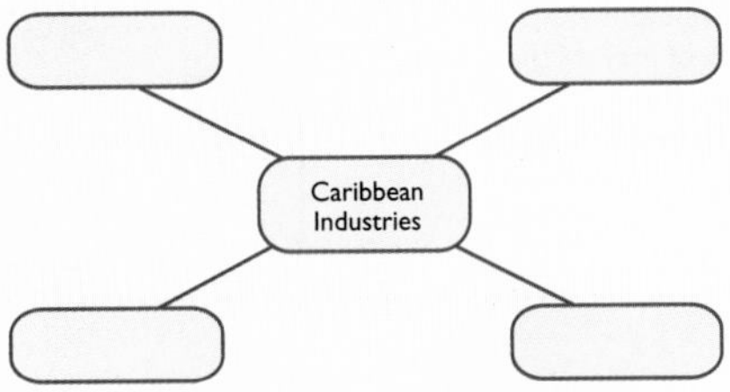

Setting the Scene

When farmer Pierre Joseph stands at the top of his land on the island of Haiti, he can see the calm waters of the Caribbean. When he looks down, he sees the dry, cracked earth of his one acre of land.

About two thirds of the people in Haiti make their living by farming. However, much of the land has been overused. Most trees have been cut down to make way for farmland and rain often washes the topsoil into the sea. "The land just doesn't yield enough," says Joseph. He points to the few rows of corn and beans that he can grow on his one acre.

Economic Challenges

Agriculture The Caribbean islands have very fertile soil and are located in a tropical region with moderate temperatures and adequate rainfall. This makes the land suitable for farming. Agriculture, therefore, is the chief economic activity on the Caribbean islands, and over half of the working population works in this industry. Sugar cane is the leading crop grown on the islands. It is grown on large plantations and exported to other countries. Other crops grown on large plantations include bananas, coffee, and cotton.

Sugar Cane Plantation

ECONOMICS

A Caribbean farm worker harvests sugar cane on a plantation in Saint Kitts. Sugar cane plantations in the Caribbean, like this one, were first established by Spanish and Portuguese settlers. **Critical Thinking** Judging from the photo, do you think harvesting sugar cane is an easy or difficult task? Why?

SECTION 1

Lesson Objectives

1. Identify the major industries of the Caribbean.
2. Describe some of the political changes facing the countries of the Caribbean.

Lesson Plan

1 Engage

Warm-Up Activity

Have students imagine what it must be like to live in a country ruled by dictators. Then suddenly they are able to have elections and vote for a leader. The new government promises better economic conditions, improved education, and more political freedom. Finally, have students consider how they might feel if that new government was not able to fulfill its promises to the people.

Activating Prior Knowledge

Ask students what they know about the Caribbean islands from their own experience or from books, movies, or television. Explain that as they read the lesson, their perceptions of what life in the Caribbean is like might change.

2 Explore

Have students read the section. Indicate that as they read they will find answers to questions such as these: Why are many Haitians poor? How have changes in government affected the economy in Haiti? How is life in Puerto Rico influenced by both the Caribbean and American cultures?

Answers to...

CRITICAL THINKING

It looks difficult. The sugarcane is tall and thick, and there is a lot of it. You have to chop it down and carry it away.

Resource Directory

Teaching Resources

Classroom Manager in the Unit 3 Teaching Resources, p. 65

Guided Reading and Review in the Unit 3 Teaching Resources, p. 66

Guide to the Essentials, p. 53

Technology

Section Reading Support Transparencies

Lesson Plan continued

3 Teach

Organize students into two groups of reporters. Assign one group one to cover Haiti and one to cover Puerto Rico. Each group should cover the following topics on the country assigned to them: (1) government, (2) economy, (3) standard of living, (4) future. Students should use the information in the text to collaborate on a short report on their topic.

Questions for Discussion

HISTORY **Why was Toussaint L'Ouverture important to Haiti?**

He was an ex-slave who took control of the government. He wanted Haitians to live as equals.

SOCIAL STUDIES SKILLS **What is the main idea of the section "Haiti's Journey to Democracy"?**

Haiti's journey to democracy has taken 200 years and has been very difficult.

4 Assess/Reteach

See answers to the Section 1 Assessment. You may also use students' completed charts as assessment.

Acceptable charts include at least four factually correct entries in each column.

Commendable charts show changes in the government, economy, and relations with the United States.

Outstanding charts explore the causes for changes in the economy and government.

Answers to...

MAP STUDY

Cuba, Havana; Dominican Republic, Santo Domingo; Haiti, Port-au-Prince; Jamaica, Kingston

---

The Caribbean Islands

GEOGRAPHY There are approximately 100 permanently inhabited Caribbean islands. The distances between islands vary greatly. But none is more than 124 miles (200 km) from its closest neighbor.
Map Study What are the four largest countries in the Caribbean? What are the capitals of each of these four countries?

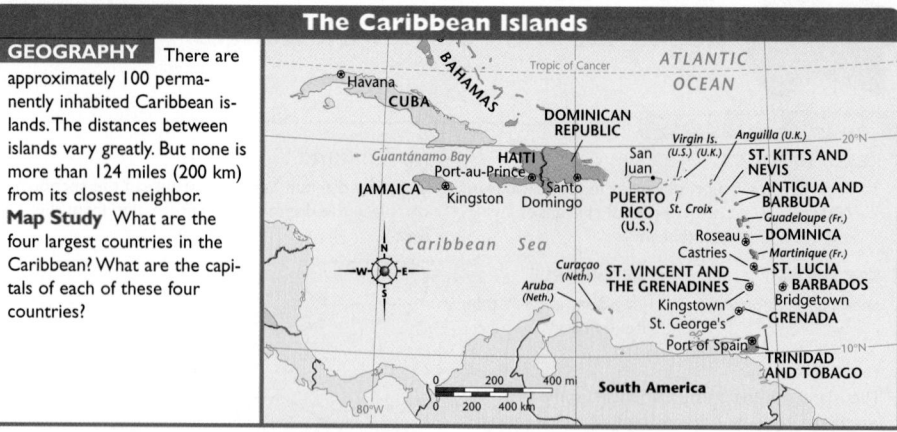

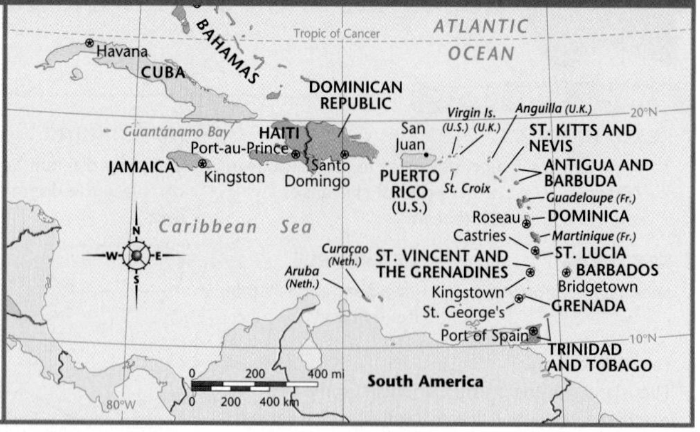

Many people who live in rural areas on the islands work as small farmers, like Pierre Joseph. They raise yams, corn, sweet potatoes and tropical fruits such as guavas and mangoes. Most of these farmers are poor, working one or two acres of land with simple farming tools. In addition to these farms, ranches are found throughout the Caribbean, where cattle, pigs and other livestock are raised.

For years, many Caribbean countries have relied on one type of crop for a majority of their income. Sugar cane, for example, is one of Cuba's largest crops, accounting for three-quarters of the country's agricultural exports.

Many Caribbean nations have begun to vary the crops that they raise. They have learned that it can be very risky to rely on a **one-crop economy,** in which only one crop provides a majority of a country's income. A single crop can be destroyed by disease or ruined by natural disasters, such as a hurricane, which could seriously hurt a country's economy.

Tourism Tourism is another important economic activity for these islands. Each year, millions of tourists travel to the islands to take advantage of the beautiful beaches and tropical weather. Shops, hotels, and restaurants employ about one third of the population. Because many Caribbean nations are so dependent on tourism, their economies can be badly hurt by natural disasters, such as hurricanes, or social problems. Jamaica, for example, has faced many social problems, including poverty and unemployment. In the 1960s and 1970s, Jamaicans became so upset that they began to riot and violent crimes began to increase, which adversely affected the tourism industry.

Resource Directory

Teaching Resources

Social Studies and Geography Skills, Using the Map Scale, p. 3

Technology

Color Transparencies 63 Central America and the Caribbean: Political Map

How People Live Transparencies, Unit 3

230 UNIT 3 LATIN AMERICA

Manufacturing and Mining Many goods are also produced on the islands. Clothing and medicine are just some of the products that are produced. A few islands are rich in natural resources. Trinidad, for example, has supplies of oil and natural gas. Jamaica is rich in bauxite, a mineral that is used to make aluminum. It is mined and exported to the United States and Canada.

Political Challenges

Today, the Caribbean islands fall into two major political groups—those countries that are independent and those that are still dependent on other countries. Some countries, such as Cuba, Haiti, and the Dominican Republic, have been independent from colonial powers for many years. Others have gained their independence more recently. However, there are still many countries in the Caribbean, including Puerto Rico, that are dependent on other countries' governments in one form or another. These countries usually manage their own affairs, but receive economic and military aid from their ruling powers.

Haiti's Journey to Democracy Haiti became the first independent Caribbean nation in 1804. In the 1790s, slaves working on plantations began to revolt against their French masters. One former slave, Toussaint L'Ouverture, took control of the government and offered Haitians a new way of life based on the idea that all people could live as equals. Unfortunately, he was captured by the French army and imprisoned in France. In the years that followed, Toussaint L'Ouverture's goal of freedom and equality was never fully realized. Most of Haiti's presidents became dictators when they got into power. A dictator is a person who rules with complete power and authority.

More recently, there have been attempts to bring democracy to Haiti. In 1990, **Jean-Bertrand Aristide** was elected president. Aristide was a Catholic priest who had long defended the rights of the poor. He was the first president to be democratically elected in many years. Aristide, however, only served as president for seven months. Haiti's military once again took control and forced him to leave the country. The country's economy remained weak and most people continued to live in poverty.

In 1994, Aristide came back to Haiti, restoring democratic government. In 1995, **René Préval** was elected as the new president of Haiti. Préval has been facing problems with the country's parliament. Because of constant quarreling, the government has not been able to help the economy and many people still remain in poverty.

Democracy in Haiti

GOVERNMENT

After his exile, Haitian President Jean-Bertrand Aristide returned to Haiti amid cheers of support. **Critical Thinking** Why was Aristide's return to Haiti so important to Haitians?

CULTURE

Daily Life

Baseball Many Caribbean people share America's passion for baseball. In Puerto Rico, *beisbol* has produced such stars as Roberto Clemente and Ruben Sierra. Puerto Rico has a league of six teams that play all over the island. Cubans also enjoy baseball. In America Latina stadium in Havana, crowds cheer their teams energetically, and even dance in the aisles to the sound of bongo drums to celebrate an exceptionally good play.

ACTIVITY

Cooperative Learning

Create a Play Organize students into small groups and have each find information about Toussaint L'Ouverture in one reference source. Students can then share information and choose events in his life they would like to dramatize. Each group can produce a scene, working cooperatively to cast roles, improvise dialogue, and stage the action. Conclude by having each group present its scene to the rest of the class.

Bodily/Kinesthetic

SKILLS MINI LESSON

Identifying Central Issues

To introduce the skill, indicate to students that the information on p. 232 has been organized around a central issue, which is a question or problem that Puerto Ricans face. Help students practice the skill by asking them to identify this issue. Record their responses on the chalkboard. If students need help; suggest that they review the headings and subheadings of the section for clues. Have students apply the skill by finding evidence in the text that supports their answer.

Answers to...

CRITICAL THINKING

Haitians suffered for many years under dictatorships and military rule. Aristide's return to Haiti signaled the restoration of a democratic government.

SECTION 1 ASSESSMENT

AFTER YOU READ

1. (a) former president of democratic Haiti (b) current elected president of Haiti
2. (a) an economy in which one crop provides most of the country's income
3. agriculture, tourism, manufacturing, mining
4. In the 1790s, slaves revolted against their French masters. Ex-slave Toussaint L'Ouverture took control of the government. Haiti became independent in 1804.
5. Puerto Rico has its own constitution but is still bound by American laws. It receives financial aid and investment from the U.S.
6. Students can read their completed paragraphs to the class.
7. After students have written their paragraphs, divide the class into two groups for a debate.
8. Since 1961, Americans have not been able to visit Cuba. Students will have to imagine that a travel ban has been lifted.

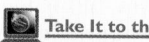

Celebrating Spanish Heritage

CULTURE These women are celebrating Puerto Rico's Spanish heritage. Puerto Ricans celebrate many holidays with traditional music and dancing. **Critical Thinking** What similar celebrations take place in the United States?

Puerto Rico's Ties to the U.S. Puerto Rico is an island of old cities as well as beautiful countryside. Farming is still very important to the economy. However, about 70 percent of Puerto Ricans live in cities and many of them work in factories. The standard of living is high in Puerto Rico and its economy is the strongest of all the Caribbean islands.

After defeating Spain in the Spanish-American War in 1898, the United States took control of Puerto Rico, which had been a Spanish colony. In 1951, Puerto Ricans voted to adopt their own constitution. A constitution is a statement of a country's basic laws and values. This gave the country its own group of lawmakers, but it was still connected to the United States. Puerto Rico is a commonwealth of the United States. A commonwealth is a place that has its own government but also has strong ties to another country. Puerto Ricans are U.S. citizens, but they cannot vote in U.S. presidential elections. They do not pay U.S. taxes and they have only a non-voting representative in the U.S. Congress.

SECTION 1 ASSESSMENT

AFTER YOU READ

RECALL

1. Identify: (a) Jean-Bertrand Aristide, (b) René Préval
2. Define: (a) one-crop economy

COMPREHENSION

3. What are some of the main industries of the Caribbean islands?
4. How did Haiti win its independence?
5. What is the political relationship between the United States and Puerto Rico?

CRITICAL THINKING

6. **Exploring the Main Idea** Review the Main Idea statement at the beginning of this section. Then, write a short paragraph discussing some economic and political challenges faced by the countries of the Caribbean.
7. **Drawing Conclusions** Some people in Puerto Rico want the country to separate from the United States. Others feel that it should become a state so that they can enjoy all the privileges of U.S. citizens. Write a paragraph in support of either Puerto Rico's becoming a state or separating completely from the United States.

ACTIVITY

Take It to the NET

8. **Writing a Travel Journal** Cuba is one of our nearest neighbors, but life in Cuba is very different from life in the United States. Use the information on the web site to write a travel journal of a trip to Cuba, and include information about daily life in Cuba. Visit the World Explorer: People, Places, and Cultures section of **phschool.com** for help in completing this activity.

Resource Directory

Teaching Resources

Section Quiz in the Unit 3 Teaching Resources, p. 67

Answers to...

CRITICAL THINKING

America celebrates its heritage on July 4. America also celebrates the heritage of immigrants on St. Patrick's Day, Cinco de Mayo, and many other festivals.

232 UNIT 3 LATIN AMERICA

SECTION 2

Brazil

Natural Resources and Industry

BEFORE YOU READ

READING FOCUS

1. Why are Brazil's rain forests a global concern?
2. How do the rain forests in Brazil affect its economy?

KEY TERMS

campesinos
canopy
photosynthesis

KEY PEOPLE AND PLACES

Rio de Janeiro
Brasília

MAIN IDEA

Brazil looks for ways to develop new industries, aware that what happens to its rain forests is important not only to Brazil, but also to the rest of the world.

NOTE TAKING

Copy the outline below. As you read the section, fill in the outline with information about the natural resources of Brazil.

Brazil's Natural Resource: Rain Forests

I. Importance of rain forests to Brazil
   A.
   B.
II. Importance of Brazil's rain forests to the world
   A.
   B.

Setting the Scene

Land is a valuable natural resource in Brazil. It provides places for people to settle and live, and places to grow crops. It contains valuable resources that can be used, made into other goods, or traded to other countries. It provides places for factories and cities to develop. How land is used and what happens to the resources the land produces greatly affect the economy of Brazil.

Brazilian Rain Forests: A Global Concern

Brazil, the largest country in South America, is nearly as large as the United States. It is also one of the richest countries in the world in land and resources. Until recently, its immense rain forests remained undisturbed. Only the few Native American groups that had lived in them for centuries ever explored them.

Brazil's rain forests take up about one half of the country. The rain forests are important to Brazil's economy. People cut timber, mine for gold, and farm there. In the past, the government of Brazil gave land to landless peasants and poor farmers, known as **campesinos** (kahm peh SEE nohs). The government moved the campesinos to the Amazonian rain forests where the farmers burned down trees to clear the land for their farms. After a few years, however, the soil in the rain forest became unfit for farming.

People around the world expressed concern about the clearing of the rain forest. Many scientists think that when people come to the rain forest, they upset the delicate balance of nature. Other people worry that the traditional way of life of native people who live in the rain forest may be altered or damaged.

Farming in a Rain Forest

ECONOMICS

This pepper farmer has cleared land on an island in the Amazon River, in northern Brazil.

Critical Thinking How does pepper farming contribute to Brazil's economy?

SECTION 2

Lesson Objectives

1. Explain why Brazil's rain forests are a global concern.
2. Explain the importance of rain forests to Brazil's economy.

Lesson Plan

1 Engage

Warm-Up Activity

Have students imagine that they share a pet dog with a friend. Have them discuss with a partner how they might divide fairly the time, chores, costs, and fun associated with pet care. Encourage volunteers to share with the class how they compromised to make a plan. What problems did they have in reaching an agreement? What solutions did they find?

Activating Prior Knowledge

On the chalkboard, create a KWL chart to record what students already know about the rain forests of Brazil and their importance to the enviroment. Suggest that students copy the chart and add infomation to it as they read the section.

What We Know About Brazil	What We Want to Learn About Brazil	What We Learned About Brazil

Resource Directory

Teaching Resources

Classroom Manager in the Unit 3 Teaching Resources, p. 68

Guided Reading and Review in the Unit 3 Teaching Resources, p. 69

Guide to the Essentials, p. 54

Technology

Section Reading Support Transparencies

Answers to...

CRITICAL THINKING

Pepper is a crop that can be sold/exported.

Lesson Plan continued

2 Explore

As students read the section, they should look for answers to the following questions: Which groups in Brazil use the rain forests for their livelihood? Why are Brazil's rain forests important to the world? What solutions have been found to the conflict over the use of the rain forest?

3 Teach

Have students work in groups of four to list the rain forest problems and solutions described in this section. Then, have them discuss whether they feel the solutions are fair. Ask each group to share with the class how they judged the fairness of the solutions.

Questions for Discussion

ECONOMICS What is the most important natural resource in Brazil? Why is it important?

Land is the most important natural resource in Brazil because it provides a place for people to live, work, and grow crops.

GEOGRAPHY Is oxygen/air a renewable or nonrenewable resource? How do you know?

It is renewable because plants and trees use carbon dioxide to produce oxygen.

Answers to...

MAP STUDY

Chile and Ecuador

COUNTRY PROFILE

Brazil

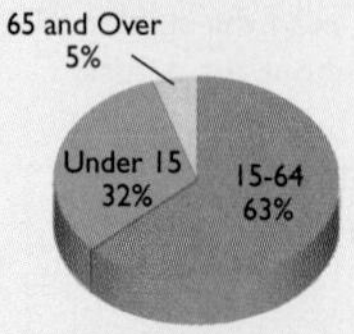

Age Structure (in years)

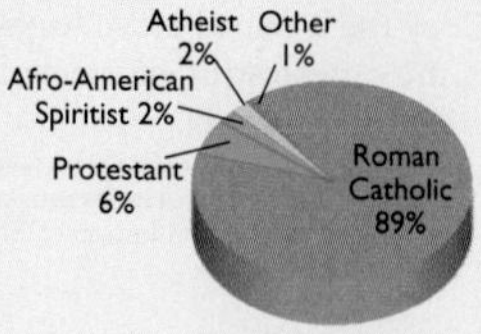

Religious Persuasion

GEOGRAPHY This map shows the vegetation regions of Brazil. Brazil contains over 1 million square miles (2,589,900 sq km) of rain forest. Northern Brazil contains part of the largest rain forest in the world, the Amazonian rain forest. Alaska could fit inside Brazil's Amazonian rain forest twice. Texas could fit inside it five times. **Map Study** Which are the only South American countries that do not border Brazil?

Location	Eastern half of South America
Climate	Tropical wet along the Amazon and southeast coast. Tropical wet and dry in the southeast interior
Terrain	Long Atlantic coastline, Amazon rain forest covering one half of the country, hilly upland plateaus and low mountains
Population	174.4 million
Major Religion	Christianity
Government	Republic
Economy	Agriculture: coffee (world's largest grower), soybeans, sugar, wheat, rice
	Major industries: steel, automobiles, appliances, chemicals, machinery, textiles, mining
Exports	Coffee, iron ore, soybeans, motor vehicle parts
Imports	Petroleum, coal, food, chemical products

A Valuable Natural Resource

Deep in the rain forest in Brazil, the light barely penetrates. At the top of the trees, the leaves form a dense, roof-like mass called a **canopy.** More species of plants and animals than any other place on Earth can be found living in and under the rain forest canopy. Scientists also estimate that rain forests produce about one third of the world's oxygen. In a process called **photosynthesis** (foht oh SIN thuh sis), green plants produce their own food using water and carbon dioxide, and oxygen is given off. The rain forests also hold about one fifth of the world's fresh water.

Resource Directory

Teaching Resources

Social Studies and Geography Skills, Reading a Natural Vegetation Map, p. 23

Technology

Color Transparencies 13 Forest Vegetation Regions Map

Passport to the World CD-ROM This interactive CD-ROM allows students to explore each region of the world. Students view regional videos, take a photo tour, and explore a historical timeline. Students record their travels in an Explorer's Journal, and receive passport stamps when they pass regional quizzes.

Using Technology to Protect the Rain Forest

Brazil's government is trying to use the resources of the rain forest without upsetting the natural balance. The government has begun using satellite technology to keep an eye on the rain forest. There are many threats for the government to watch out for. When part of the forest is destroyed, the animals and plants that live there may not survive. When plant life is destroyed, less oxygen is produced.

There is also a problem with smuggling in the rain forest. Each year, Brazil loses about 12 million animals to smugglers. Many of these animals are endangered. It is illegal to capture and kill these animals, but the smugglers often get away with it.

In the late 1980s, the discovery of gold attracted many miners to the rain forest. Gold mining caused pollution in streams in the rain forest, and made people in several villages sick. The government of Brazil passed strict laws about mining in the rain forest. As they work to protect the rain forests, Brazilian leaders must also look for ways to use the rain forest's resources to ensure Brazil's economic progress.

Brazil's African Heritage

CULTURE In Salvador, Brazil, people cook food similar to the food eaten in West Africa. Food in both places is seasoned with coconut milk, pepper, and palm oil, and cooked in earthenware pots. The women of Salvador wear lacy dresses and turbans, like many of the women of West Africa. **Critical Thinking** Why do you think these women dress in a West African fashion even though they live in Brazil?

Economic Challenges and Developing Industry

The Native Americans living in the rain forests were some of the first people to live in Brazil. Today, most Brazilians are a mix of Native American, African, and European heritages. Many parts of African culture still flourish in Brazil. Most of the people of African descent are ancestors of the millions of Africans brought to Brazil as slaves and forced to work the coffee plantations. Brazil used their labor to become the world's largest coffee grower. When the slaves were freed in the late 1800s, they became paid but cheap labor.

Coffee prices dropped in the first few years of the 1900s. Brazilians realized that they could not depend on one or two crops to survive. In the 1930s, the government discouraged coffee production and tried to diversify the economy by building more factories. Today, Brazil produces many goods, including iron and steel, cars, and electrical equipment. Since 1960, about 30 million people have left farms and plantations to get jobs in the large cities near the coast, such as **Rio de Janeiro** (REE oh day zhuh NER oh), far from the rain forests.

Resource Directory

Technology

Color Transparencies 57 The Amazon Rain Forest, Late 1980s Map; **58** The Amazon Rain Forest, 1940 Map

4 Assess/Reteach

See the Answers to the Section 2 Assessment. You may also use the student discussion for assessment.

Acceptable responses include several problems, solutions, and evaluations.

Commendable responses include more and show an understanding of why solutions are fair or unfair.

Outstanding responses include original, practical, and equitable solutions.

CULTURE

Daily Life

Capoeira *Capoeira*, a Brazilian combination of dance and martial arts, developed in the northeastern part of the country. The dance form was created by enslaved Africans. Forbidden to fight each other, the slaves developed a form of fighting to music that looked like dancing. Music was played on drums and on a *berimbau* made from a bow and a gourd. Today, young men, boys, and some girls study *capoeira*, just as American young people study karate, judo, and other martial arts.

ACTIVITY

Geography

Identifying Central Issues *Suitable for an individual or whole-class activity.* Encourage students to discuss what they think are the most important issues surrounding Brazil's rain forests. Then, have students prepare and deliver a one-minute news bulletin presenting the issues they feel are most important to the protection of the rain forests. Ask the class to evaluate the news bulletins, choosing three they feel accurately identify the central issues.

Verbal/Linguistic

Answers to...

CRITICAL THINKING

They want to honor and keep alive their African heritage.

CHAPTER 13 THE CARIBBEAN AND SOUTH AMERICA: EXPLORING THE REGION TODAY 235

SECTION 2 ASSESSMENT

AFTER YOU READ

1. (a) coastal city in Brazil (b) the capital of Brazil
2. (a) landless peasants and poor farmers (b) dense mass of leaves on the tallest trees in the rain forest (c) process by which green plants and trees produce their own food
3. The trees and plants of the rain forest convert carbon dioxide into oxygen that plants, animals, and humans need to breathe. The rain forests produce one-third of the Earth's oxygen and hold one-fifth of the Earth's fresh water.
4. Timber and gold are natural resources from the rain forest that provide income for the country. Native American groups depend on the rain forest for their livelihood. Farmers clear land for farming.
5. Answers will vary. Possible answer: The government is using satellites to keep an eye on what takes place in the rain forest, such as timber practices, smuggling, and monitoring pollution. It provides land to poor farmers, which they use to make a living, and also increases crop production.
6. Answers will vary. Students should include details and valid arguments to support arguments.
7. Students may prefer to work in groups or as a whole class to create a display.

GEOGRAPHY São Paolo is the largest city in Brazil. It contains more than 20,000 factories, which provide jobs for about 600,000 workers. **Critical Thinking** In what ways does São Paolo look similar to large cities in the United States? In what ways does it look different?

Brazilian cities are home to the rich and the very poor. Rio de Janeiro is a good example of these contrasts. Expensive hotels and shops for tourists are located in the south part of the city. Old palaces and government buildings are found in the downtown area, and north of the city are clusters of small houses where factory workers live. Beyond the factory workers' homes is an even poorer area. It is crowded with homes that have no electricity or running water. About a quarter of Rio's 12 million people live in these neighborhoods known as *favelas* (fuh VEH lus).

The New Capital: A Move for the Economy

In the 1950s, the Brazilian government moved the capital to a new city, **Brasília,** away from the coast and closer to the rain forest. The government thought that moving the capital there would attract some people from the coastal areas and help develop industry using resources from the rain forest. Brazilian leaders continue to face challenges as they try to help the economy without destroying the rain forest.

SECTION 2 ASSESSMENT

AFTER YOU READ

RECALL

1. Identify: (a) Rio de Janeiro, (b) Brasília
2. Define: (a) campesinos, (b) canopy, (c) photosynthesis

COMPREHENSION

3. Why is the Brazilian rain forest an important environmental concern for the world?
4. In what ways does the Brazilian economy depend upon the rain forests?

CRITICAL THINKING AND WRITING

5. **Exploring the Main Idea** Review the Main Idea statement at the beginning of this section. Then, list one way the Brazilian government is working to protect its rain forests, and one way it is trying to use resources from the rain forest to improve its economy.
6. **Supporting a Point of View** Some people want Brazil to stop using rain forests completely. Is this reasonable? What do you think it would do to Brazil's economy?

ACTIVITY

7. **Creating a Rain Forest Display** Work with a partner to find images that show the vegetation and animal life found in Brazil's rain forests. Write captions for the images you select and then create a classroom display.

Answers to...

CRITICAL THINKING

It has office buildings, homes, streets, and trees like other large cities. But most cities have offices and homes in separate areas.

Resource Directory

Teaching Resources

Section Quiz in the Unit 3 Teaching Resources, p. 70

SECTION 3

Chile and Venezuela

Growing Economies

BEFORE YOU READ

READING FOCUS

1. How does Chile's government work to protect the environment?
2. Why is agriculture important to Chile's economy?
3. How did Venezuela's oil boom affect its people and its economy?

KEY TERMS

boom
privatization

KEY PEOPLE AND PLACES

Santiago
Caracas

NOTE TAKING

Copy the chart below. As you read the section, fill in the chart with information about the economies of Chile and Venezuela.

	Chile	Venezuela
Economy Before 1980s		
Economy After Mid-1980s		

MAIN IDEA

As Chile and Venezuela develop and expand new industries and resources, their governments must meet the challenges of keeping their economies strong while protecting the environment.

Setting the Scene

Both Chile and Venezuela have experienced the prosperity and problems associated with growing economies. Before the 1980s, Chile's economy depended mostly on its copper exports and the primary industry of mining. In the early 1980s, world copper prices began to drop and Chile could no longer depend on copper to survive. One way to improve Chile's economy was to focus on agriculture.

Agriculture and the Economy

By the late 1980s, agriculture was especially important for Chile. It had become a billion dollar industry, providing jobs for about 900,000 Chileans. Like Chile, Venezuela experienced an economic **boom,** or period of increased prosperity. Venezuela's boom was in the sale of oil products. During the 1970s the price of oil went up. Then, like copper prices in Chile, the oil prices started to fall. Now, Venezuela must find other ways to make money. As demand for products has risen and fallen, so too have standards of living.

Chile's Varied Landscape

GEOGRAPHY

The Atacama Desert in Chile is barren and empty, but other areas of Chile are fertile and green. **Critical Thinking** What factors do you think make it possible for one country to have such different climates?

Resource Directory

Teaching Resources

Classroom Manager in the Unit 3 Teaching Resources, p. 71

Guided Reading and Review in the Unit 3 Teaching Resources, p. 72

Guide to the Essentials, p. 55

Technology

Section Reading Support Transparencies

SECTION 3

Lesson Objectives

1. Identify how Chile's government has worked to protect the environment.
2. Describe why agriculture is important to Chile's economy.
3. Explain how Venezuela's oil boom affected its people and economy.

Lesson Plan

1 Engage

Warm-Up Activity

Ask students what they already know about Chile and Venezuela. Have volunteers contribute to a K-W-L chart with these columns: *What We **K**now About Chile and Venezuela*, and *What We **W**ant to Find Out.* After reading the section, students can fill in a third column, *What We **L**earned About Chile and Venezuela.*

Activating Prior Knowledge

Ask students to speculate on where the peaches they eat in summer come from. Then, ask them to speculate on where peaches might come from when it is winter in the United States.

Answers to...

CRITICAL THINKING

Physical features such as mountains, ocean coast, and plains make it possible for such varied climates.

Lesson Plan continued

2 Explore

Have students read the section. Tell them to think about the following questions as they read: What are the important products of Chile? Why did the government encourage the growth of industry in the early 1980s? What problems did Venezuela face when oil prices dropped in the 1980s?

3 Teach

Direct student pairs to make a product map of Chile. Maps should show the country's main regions, important geographical features, and the products grown, manufactured, or mined in each region. This activity should take about 15 minutes.

Questions for Discussion

GEOGRAPHY **How do you think the discovery of oil in Venezuela affected world prices for oil?**

Because there was more oil on the market, prices probably decreased.

ECONOMICS **How do you think Venezuela's oil resources affect its relations with other countries?**

Venezuela has a product that many other countries need, so it may have more power when dealing with other nations.

4 Assess/Reteach

See the Answers to the Section 3 Assessment. You may also use students' product maps as assessment.

Acceptable maps show the main regions mentioned in the text and at least one product for each region.

Commendable maps include industrial and mining products as well as agricultural.

Outstanding maps show the major geographical features of each region as well as most of the products mentioned in the text.

Net Fishing Off Chile's Coast

ECONOMICS In northern Chile, the soil is not very good for farming. Many people here fish for a living. Chile's fishing industry is one of the largest in the world. **Critical Thinking** What difference do you see between people who fish for a living and those who fish for fun?

Chile's Physical Environment

Look at the physical map of Latin America in the Activity Atlas on page 164. Find the Andes Mountains. They extend down the whole length of the continent like a giant spine. Chile stretches 2,650 miles (4,265 km) down the Pacific Coast, and it reaches all the way to the tip of South America. It is the longest, narrowest country in the world.

Chile contains an amazing variety of lands and climates. In the north is the Atacama Desert. The long central valley near the coast has rolling hills, high grasses, and dense forests. This is the region where most of the people live.

Chile's Cultural Ties

Chile's early Spanish settlers married Native Americans already living there. Today, these mestizos make up about 75 percent of the population. Only 3 percent of Chileans are Native Americans.

The lifestyles of Chileans vary from region to region. In the far south, people raise sheep. Farther north in the central valley, farmers grow many vegetables and fruits. Few people live in the Atacama Desert of the far north. But the desert is rich in copper and dotted with copper mines. Chile exports more copper than any country in the world.

A visit to the city of **Santiago** is unforgettable. Old Spanish buildings stand near gleaming skyscrapers. The city is in the valley of the central plain, so the altitude is low enough to produce mild weather. The sea makes the air humid. Palm trees grow in the public parks with a backdrop of the snowcapped Andes in the east.

Protecting the Environment

The beautiful sights of Santiago, Chile's capital, are sometimes blocked by a thick layer of smog. How did pollution get to be so bad in Santiago? One cause is the city's location. It is surrounded by the Andes on three sides. The mountains trap the exhaust fumes from vehicles and smoke from factories in the valley.

Another cause is that in the early 1980s, the government relaxed the laws that protected the environment from pollution. Government leaders thought that if the laws were too strict, some private industries would not survive. Encouraging private industry was good for Chile's economy. The standard of living rose, but so did pollution levels. More people moved to the cities to get jobs in the new industries. More than 80 percent of Chile's people now live in cities.

During the 1990s, Chile's government took action to reduce the problems of pollution in the city. On days when the wind does not blow, industries are shut down, and only a limited number of cars may enter the city. The government may also require new cars to have special exhaust systems that do not produce much pollution.

AS YOU READ

Use Prior Knowledge What cities in the United States have problems with pollution? Which of these cities, like Santiago, are surrounded by mountains?

Answers to...

CRITICAL THINKING

People who fish for a living work hard. People who fish for fun can relax and enjoy themselves.

AS YOU READ

Students may mention an array of cities. Some, such as Los Angeles, Denver, Phoenix, and Boise, Idaho, are located in the mountainous areas.

Resource Directory

Technology

Color Transparencies 46 Sources of Pollution Diagram

How People Live Transparencies, Unit 3

Venezuela

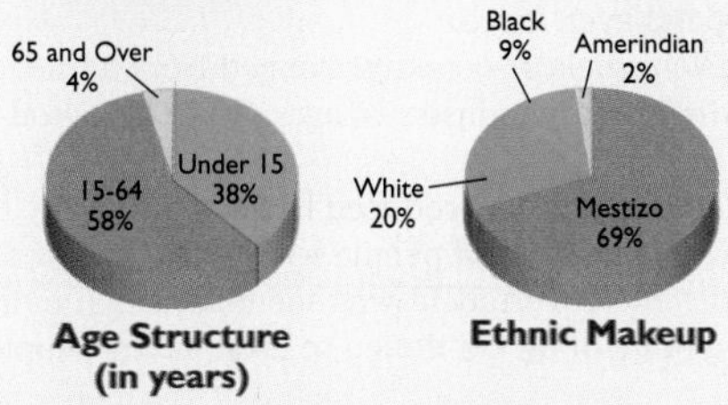

GEOGRAPHY This map shows the natural resources of Venezuela. Venezuela is famous for its deposits of petroleum. However, Venezuela also has many other resources, including soil that is good for farming and raising livestock. **Map Study** What part of Venezuela has the most natural resources? What area do you think has the most cities?

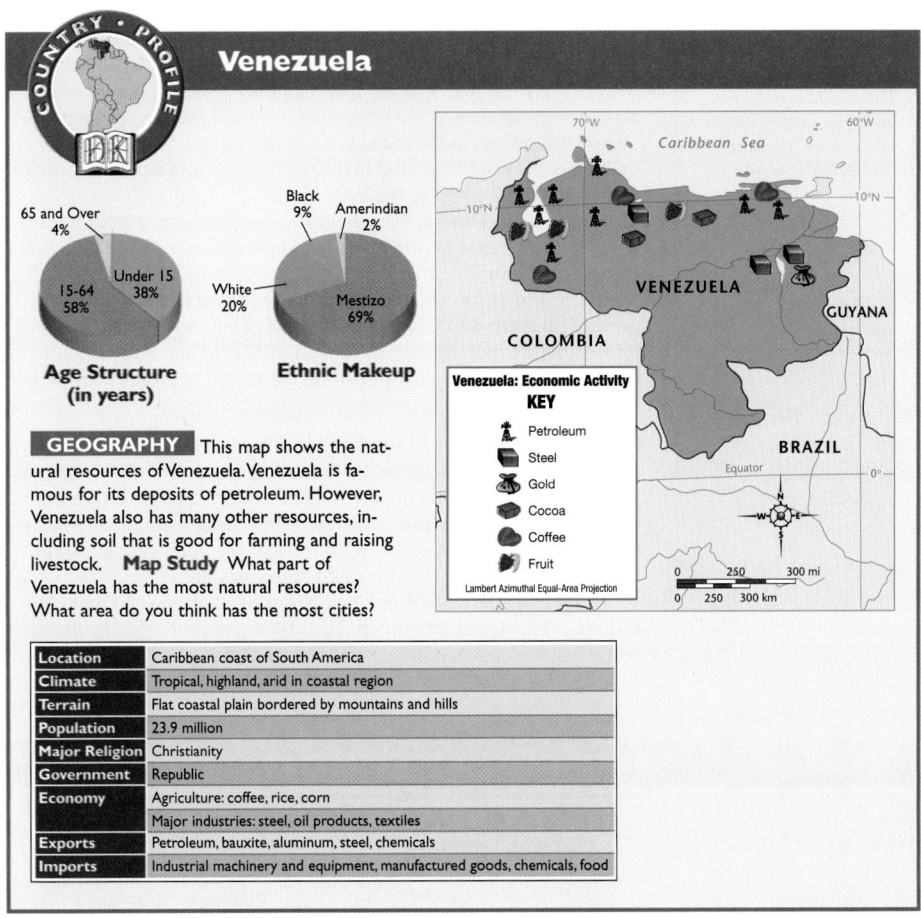

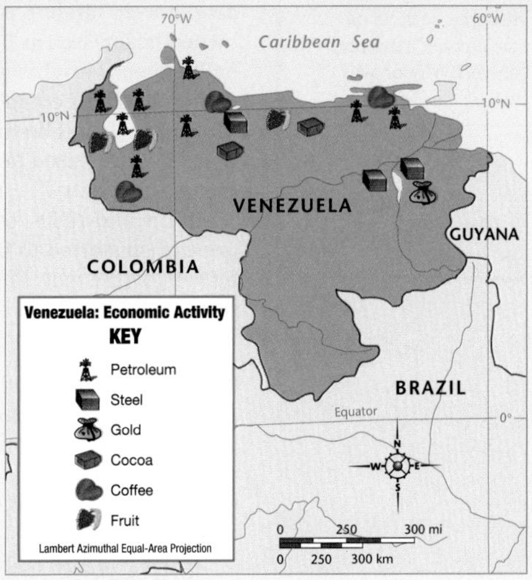

Location	Caribbean coast of South America
Climate	Tropical, highland, arid in coastal region
Terrain	Flat coastal plain bordered by mountains and hills
Population	23.9 million
Major Religion	Christianity
Government	Republic
Economy	Agriculture: coffee, rice, corn
	Major industries: steel, oil products, textiles
Exports	Petroleum, bauxite, aluminum, steel, chemicals
Imports	Industrial machinery and equipment, manufactured goods, chemicals, food

A Land Made Wealthy by Oil

Venezuela, located in the north of South America, has vast supplies of oil. The map above shows where this oil is located. Venezuela's oil has earned billions of dollars on the world market. Because of this, people have migrated from the countryside to work for the oil companies.

Venezuela's oil was discovered about 75 years ago. Since then, Venezuela has pumped about 67 billion barrels of oil. Except for the Persian Gulf region, Venezuela has the biggest oil reserves in the world.

ECONOMY

Oil Cartel

Venezuela was a founding member of the Organization of Petroleum Exporting Countries (OPEC), formed in 1960 so that oil-producing countries could control the price of oil throughout the world. Other members of OPEC are Iran, Iraq, Kuwait, Saudi Arabia, Qatar, Libya, and the United Arab Emirates in the Middle East; Algeria and Nigeria in Africa; and Indonesia in Asia. In late 1973, OPEC raised the price of oil by 200 percent, which greatly affected life in the industrial countries of the world. The costs of heating homes, running factories, and fueling motor vehicles skyrocketed.

ACTIVITY

Journal Writing

Pen Pal Ask students to choose Brazil, Chile, or Venezuela and consider what it would be like to have a pen pal there. Have students make a list of the things they would like to know about the country they chose. Then, direct them to write a letter to their pen pal, introducing themselves, telling about their lives, and asking questions.

Verbal/Linguistic

SKILLS MINI LESSON

Interpreting Graphs: Circle Graphs

To **introduce** the skill, tell students that important facts can be shown in a graph. Help students **practice** the skill by asking them to find the following information: the most common ethnic group (mestizo); the most common age group (15–64). Ask them to predict, then find, the sum of the percents shown in the Age Structure graph. Have students explain why the sum is 100 percent. Have students **apply** the skill by forming questions using the circle graphs. Students can share and answer one another's questions.

Answers to...

MAP STUDY

north; north

SECTION 3 ASSESSMENT

AFTER YOU READ

1. (a) capital city of Chile (b) largest city in Venezuela and the country's capital
2. (a) a period of increased prosperity during which more of a product is produced and sold (b) a government selling its industries to individuals and private companies
3. The government shuts down industries on days when the wind does not blow, and limits the number of cars that may enter the city. The government may also require cars to have special exhaust systems.
4. Chile began developing its agricultural industry because copper prices fell.
5. The oil boom allowed Venezuela to earn millions of dollars on the world market. The government had more money to spend, hired more people, and the economy prospered. Recently, Venezuela has worked to develop other industries to keep its economy stable.
6. Answers will vary. Possible answer: Chile has increased its agricultural production. It has taken steps to reduce pollution. Venezuela's economy is relying less on oil production. Venezuela privatized industry to help boost the production of other goods.
7. Answers will vary. Suggestions might include working within a budget and keeping debt at a minimum. They might also include being careful when developing new industries to ensure that they do not harm the environment.
8. Students can present their advertisements to the class. Ask the audience which ads were most persuasive and why.

Answers to...

AS YOU READ

Students will probably explain that even the most plentiful natural resources are finite.

AS YOU READ

Monitor Your Reading
Do you think that one resource, such as oil, can support a country forever? Why or why not?

During the 1970s, the price of oil went up and an oil boom began. The standard of living of many Venezuelans began to rise. That is when the government started spending huge sums of money. Many people were hired to run government agencies and government-owned businesses in **Caracas,** Venezuela's capital. The government built expensive subways and high-quality roads and began to borrow money so that it could spend even more.

During the oil boom, Venezuela's economy changed from a traditional culture based on the primary industry of agriculture to a modern urban country.

In the mid-1980s, too much oil was produced in the world. The price of oil started to fall, but millions of people were still employed by the government. Finally, the government was spending much more than it could earn. As the price of oil continued to drop, many people lost their jobs.

Government Industries Go Public The government's solution was a new policy of privatization. **Privatization** (pry vuh tih ZAY shun) occurs when the government sells its industries to individuals or private companies. In the late 1980s and the 1990s, the government decided to privatize some businesses. It hoped that the corporations would make big profits. The profits would help workers.

Venezuela also started new industries in an attempt to make its economy less dependent on oil. The country is producing goods such as steel, gold, cocoa, coffee, and tropical fruits.

SECTION 3 ASSESSMENT

AFTER YOU READ

RECALL

1. Identify: (a) Santiago, (b) Caracas
2. Define: (a) boom, (b) privatization

COMPREHENSION

3. What steps has the government taken to prevent pollution in Chile's cities?
4. Why did Chile begin developing its agricultural industry?
5. How has Venezuela's oil boom affected the economy in the past and more recently?

CRITICAL THINKING AND WRITING

6. **Exploring the Main Idea** Review the Main Idea statement at the beginning of this section. Then, list ways that Chile and Venezuela have worked to keep their economies strong, and their people and environment in good health.
7. **Drawing Conclusions** Write a paragraph about what you think Venezuela should do to avoid economic problems in the future, without harming the environment.

ACTIVITY

8. **Writing an Advertisement** With a partner, create a commercial to advertise a new product that would help the economies of either Chile or Venezuela. Make a poster to use as a prop for your commercial. Write a script that takes no longer than 60 seconds to present and that explains why it is important to have new products to help the economy.

Resource Directory

Teaching Resources

Section Quiz in the Unit 3 Teaching Resources, p. 73

SECTION 4

Argentina
A Cultural Center

BEFORE YOU READ

READING FOCUS

1. How is Argentina's ethnic makeup different from other countries in South America?
2. What are two of Argentina's distinct cultural groups?
3. How is the gaucho of Argentina's Pampas region like the American cowboy of the Great Plains in the United States?

KEY TERMS
cosmopolitan
gauchos
porteños
bolas
estancias

KEY PEOPLE AND PLACES
Buenos Aires
Pampas

MAIN IDEA

Argentina's cultural heritage is an unusual blend of European influences found in the capital city of Buenes Aires with a uniquely Argentinian culture from the plains.

NOTE TAKING

Copy the diagram below. As you read the section, fill in the diagram with information about the cultures of Argentina.

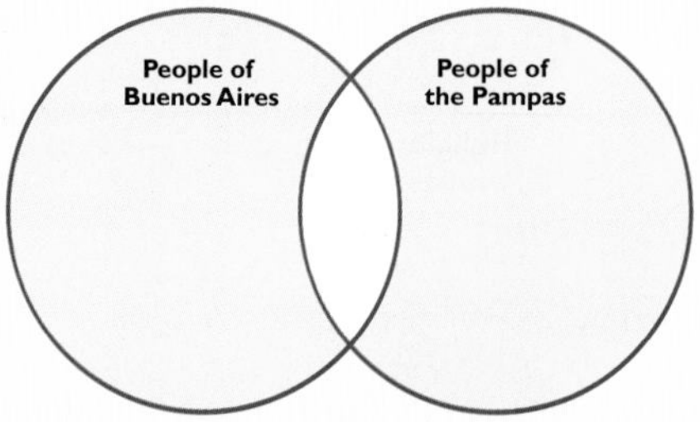

Setting the Scene

Walking through the colorful streets of **Buenos Aires,** the capital of Argentina, a traveler is likely to hear the country's official language, Spanish, being spoken with an Italian accent. Buenos Aires is a **cosmopolitan** city, or a city whose population is composed of people from many parts of the world.

Not far from Buenos Aires lies an area called the **Pampas** [PAHM puhs], a vast, flat grassland similar to the Great Plains in the United States. It was here, in the mid-18th century, that nomadic cowboys called **gauchos** (GOW chohz), became legends portrayed in ballads and stories.

Geographical and Cultural Diversity

Argentina spreads across almost the entire southern half of South America and it is the eighth largest country in the world. Argentina's geographical diversity begins in the north with

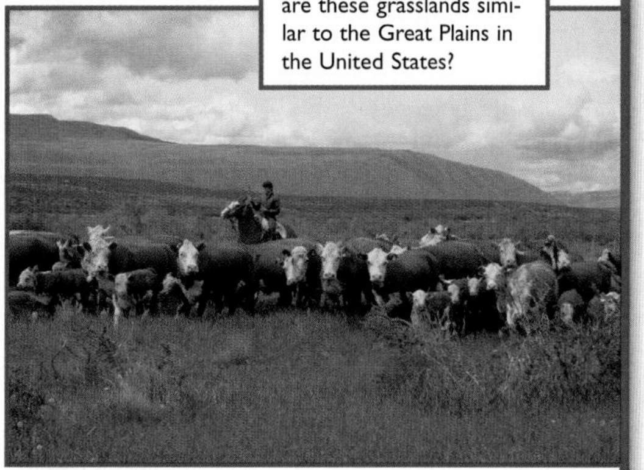

The Pampas

GEOGRAPHY The grasslands known as the Pampas in Argentina are perfect for raising cattle. **Critical Thinking** How are these grasslands similar to the Great Plains in the United States?

SECTION 4

Lesson Objectives

1. Compare Argentina's ethnic makeup to that of other South American countries.
2. Identify the two main cultural groups in Argentina.
3. Compare the culture of Argentina's gauchos to that of American cowboys.

Lesson Plan

1 Engage

Warm-Up Activity

Have students discuss why they think people want to emigrate from the countries where they were born to other countries. Ask students to share their ideas. Then, extract key words or terms to make a list of geographical reasons, economic reasons, political reasons, and cultural reasons.

Activating Prior Knowledge

Ask students what they know about Argentina and the gauchos of the Pampas. Have volunteers share their ideas.

2 Explore

As students read the section, have them identify major characteristics of Argentina's culture. The following questions may provide prompts: *What groups of people live there? What is the main language? How is the Spanish spoken there different from the Spanish in other Latin American countries?*

Answers to...

CRITICAL THINKING

Both are flat, open, and mostly treeless, and are ideal for grazing animals such as cattle.

Resource Directory

Teaching Resources

Classroom Manager in the Unit 3 Teaching Resources, p. 74

Guided Reading and Review in the Unit 3 Teaching Resources, p. 75

Guide to the Essentials, p. 56

Technology

Section Reading Support Transparencies

CHAPTER 13 THE CARIBBEAN AND SOUTH AMERICA: EXPLORING THE REGION TODAY 241

Lesson Plan continued

3 Teach

Work with students to create a chart to include details about the regions in Argentina and why they would be good places to settle. Help the class to put one or two items in each column. Then, have students complete the chart with facts from the section. Discuss reasons for the major settlements in Argentina.

Questions for Discussion

GOVERNMENT What was the difference between Argentina's centralists and federalists?

The centralists wanted more central government control. The federalists favored local control.

GEOGRAPHY How has human migration affected the character of Buenos Aires?

The many immigrants from Spain, Italy, and France wanted to make Buenos Aires more like a European city. The city reflects those influences.

4 Assess/Reteach

See answers to the Section 4 Assessment. You may also use students' completed charts as an assessment.

Acceptable charts include the four regions discussed and one or two descriptions of the climate or geography that make it habitable or uninhabitable.

Commendable charts mention some historical notes about the regions.

Outstanding charts include comparative adjectives and cultural information about the regions.

Answers to...

MAP STUDY

Yes. It is located on a bay and at the mouth of a river.

COUNTRY PROFILE

Argentina

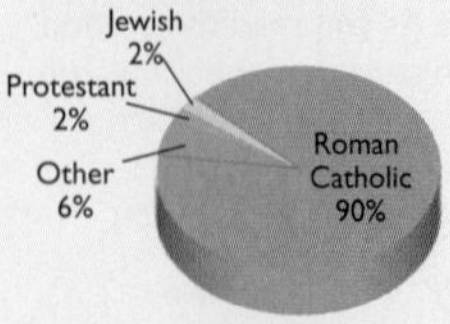

Religious Persuasion

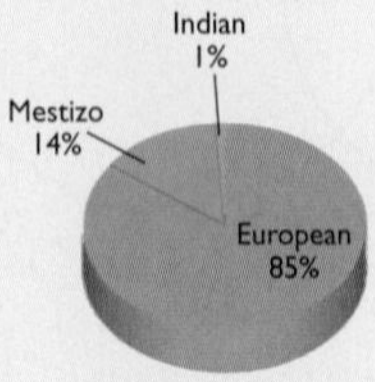

Ethnic Makeup

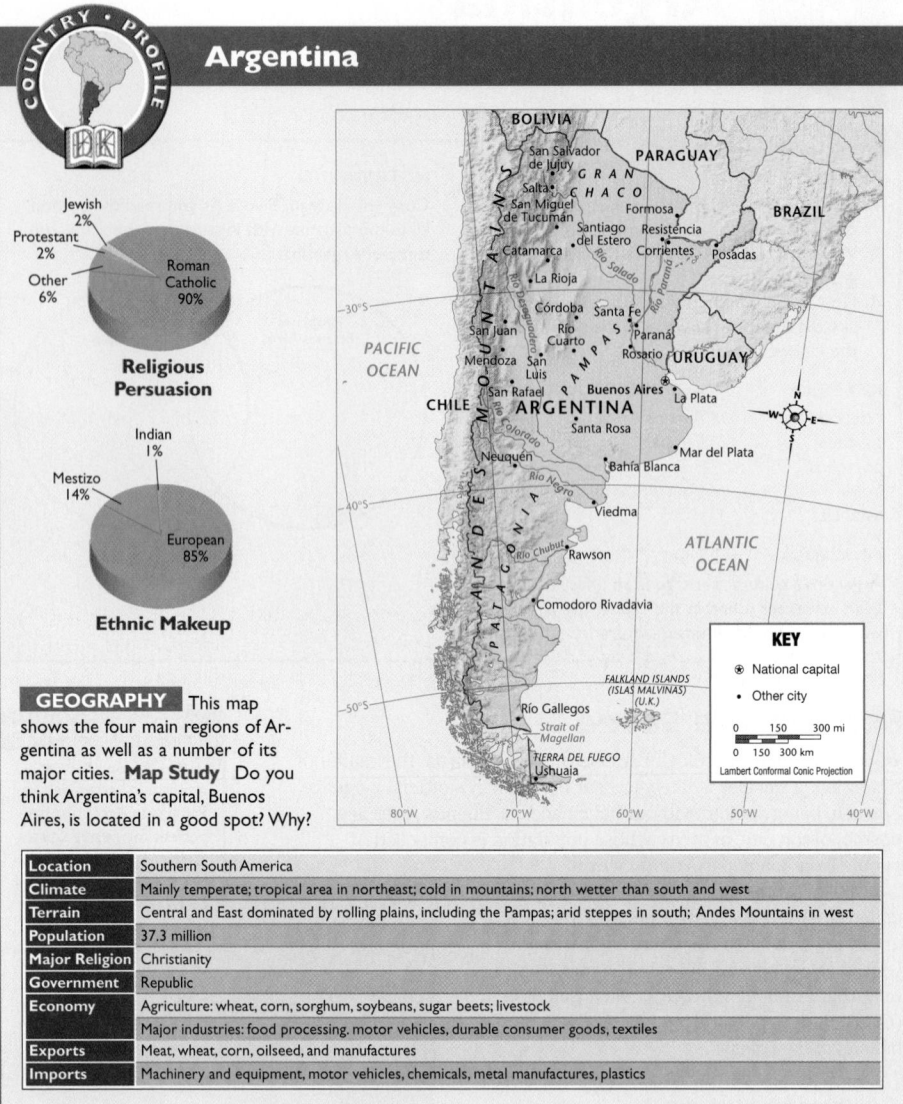

GEOGRAPHY This map shows the four main regions of Argentina as well as a number of its major cities. **Map Study** Do you think Argentina's capital, Buenos Aires, is located in a good spot? Why?

Location	Southern South America
Climate	Mainly temperate; tropical area in northeast; cold in mountains; north wetter than south and west
Terrain	Central and East dominated by rolling plains, including the Pampas; arid steppes in south; Andes Mountains in west
Population	37.3 million
Major Religion	Christianity
Government	Republic
Economy	Agriculture: wheat, corn, sorghum, soybeans, sugar beets; livestock
	Major industries: food processing, motor vehicles, durable consumer goods, textiles
Exports	Meat, wheat, corn, oilseed, and manufactures
Imports	Machinery and equipment, motor vehicles, chemicals, metal manufactures, plastics

a heavily forested, low, wet, hot region called the Gran Chaco. The central plains, or Pampas, lie south of the Gran Chaco and encompass a stretch of land from the East Coast, where Buenos Aires is located, to increasingly dry land toward the west. The Pampas is mostly flat, fertile land with a temperate climate where nearly 98 percent

Resource Directory

Teaching Resources

Social Studies and Geography Skills,
Reading a Political Map, p. 17

of the population lives. To the south of the Pampas is an arid region called Patagonia. This windswept plateau also contains some grassy valleys. The Andes Mountains in the west make up Argentina's fourth geographic region.

Political and Economic History

Argentina became a Spanish colony in the 16th century. Under Spanish control, Argentina was forbidden to trade with foreign countries. This trade policy angered the colonists. In the early 1800s, Argentina finally gained its independence from Spain. By the 1900s European immigrants came to farm and invest in businesses in Argentina.

Following its independence, a long struggle took place between the *centralists*, those who wanted more central government control, and the *federalists*, who favored local control. In recent times, the government has become more stable, and industry and agriculture have developed. Today, Argentina has a free market economy and people there enjoy one of the highest standards of living in Latin America.

GOVERNMENT

Working Together

From 1976 to 1983, Argentina had a military government. The government took thousands of people prisoner. Many were never seen again. The mothers and grandmothers of the "disappeared" marched in protest every day for six years in Buenos Aires. They wanted their marches to remind the government to keep investigating the disappearance of their relatives.

Two Distinct Cultures

Argentina's ethnic makeup is part Spanish but also a blend of European from other countries like Italy, England, France, and Germany, with nearly one half of the population of Italian descent. Also, unlike its neighbor Brazil and countries of the Caribbean, African slaves were not imported. Two distinct social groups of people settled in this vast land that we now call Argentina. One group crossed the Andes from Peru and established themselves in the fertile interior and central Pampas. Most of them were mestizos, or people of Spanish and Native American heritage. Others were of mixed European and African ancestry. The people of the interior learned to raise cattle and adopted rural lifestyles.

The people who settled in and around Buenos Aires were Europeans who came to the port city for trade. The **porteños** as they are sometimes called, wanted to make Buenos Aires a city much like those in Europe. These people of European heritage far outnumbered the small groups of mestizos who settled on the plains.

An Argentine Cultural Center

More than one third of Argentina's population lives in the capital city of Buenos Aires. Buenos Aires is located along the Rio de la Plata estuary and its location on the Atlantic coast in the sea lanes between the South Atlantic and South Pacific oceans places it in an important transportation corridor for trade.

GOVERNMENT

Juan Peron

During the 1940s, Juan Peron devoted his efforts to winning over the middle class and labor classes of Argentina. Peron and his wife, Evita, became popular for developing programs for mass housing, schools, hospitals and labor law reforms. Peron's work in foreign relations helped restore Argentina's international prestige. After Evita died in 1952, Peron's power began to fade. He finally was elected president in 1973 with his new wife Isabel as his running mate. Among the problems that faced the new president were a weak economy and political terrorism. Peron died in 1974. His wife replaced him but was removed from office by a military coup in 1976.

ACTIVITY

Culture

Cowboy Songs Have students research cowboy songs from the American Great Plains, such as "Home on the Range." Then, have partners write a song or ballad that might have been sung by a gaucho in the Pampas or a student living in Buenos Aires. Be sure students include details from the section.

Musical/Rhythmic

Resource Directory

Teaching Resources

Outline Maps South America, pp. 10–11

Vocabulary in the Unit 3 Teaching Resources, p. 78

Enrichment in the Unit 3 Teaching Resources, p. 80

Critical Thinking in the Unit 3 Teaching Resources, p. 81

CHAPTER 13 THE CARIBBEAN AND SOUTH AMERICA: EXPLORING THE REGION TODAY 243

SECTION 4 ASSESSMENT

AFTER YOU READ

1. (a) the capital city of Argentina (b) vast, flat grassland region similar to the U.S. Great Plains
2. (a) being composed of people from many parts of the world (b) nomadic horsemen and cowboys of the Pampas in Argentina (c) Europeans who settled and traded in the port city of Buenos Aires (d) a set of leather cords and three iron balls or stones thrown at the legs of animals to catch them (e) huge, privately owned estates in Argentina
3. Argentina's ethnic makeup is part Spanish but also a blend of other Europeans from Italy, England, France, and Germany. African slaves were not brought to Argentina, so few people are of African ancestry.
4. Two cultural groups are the people of the interior and central Pampas, mostly mestizos, or people of Spanish and Native American heritage. The others are people of European heritage who settled in Buenos Aires.
5. Both rode horses on the plains, herded horses and cattle, and became folk legends in their countries and internationally. They used similar tools such as lassos and knives.
6. The mestizos and the porteños who settled in Argentina came from different places and cultural backgrounds. The mestizos crossed the Andes from Peru and established themselves in the fertile interior and central Pampas. They raised cattle and adopted rural lifestyles. The porteños settled in and around Buenos Aires and were a mixture of Europeans who came to the port city for trade. They wanted to make Buenos Aires a city like those in Europe.
7. Buenos Aires's geographic location and cultural activities make it a desirable place to live.
8. Students can work in small groups, with each member responsible for a different aspect of gaucho life.

The Gauchos of Argentina

CULTURE This gaucho displays his horse on a ranch on the Pampas.
Critical Thinking Today, many Argentinian cowboys still wear the costume of the early gauchos. Why do you think they still dress like gauchos?

Like a European city, Buenos Aires is composed of small neighborhoods, each with its own special characteristics. It also houses tall, cosmopolitan skyscrapers that tower over homes built in the 19th century. Spanish colonial design with Italian and French influences enriches the city's fine buildings. The city offers a great variety of cultural activities such as opera, ballet, concerts, plays, literary events, and film festivals.

The Culture of the Pampas

Beyond Buenos Aires, where the Pampas stretches into the rich, fertile grassland of the interior, is the birthplace of the gaucho. The nomadic gauchos established a unique culture found only in Argentina. They wandered the Pampas and hunted herds of wild horses and cattle using lassos, knives, and **bolas** (BOH lahs), a set of leather cords and three iron balls or stones that they threw at the legs of animals to capture them.

The gauchos were part of a profitable, although illegal, trade in hides and tallow in the frontier regions near Buenos Aires. Known for their expert horsemanship, the gauchos played a major role in Argentina's history. They helped bring civilization to the Pampas, and fought in the struggle for independence and stability.

By the late 1800s, most of the Pampas had been fenced in as part of the huge **estancias** (eh STAHN see yahs), or estates owned by private owners. The gauchos became hired farmhands rather than the free-spirited cowboys they had once been.

SECTION 4 ASSESSMENT

AFTER YOU READ

RECALL

1. Identify: (a) Buenos Aires, (b) Pampas
2. Define: (a) cosmopolitan, (b) gauchos, (c) porteños, (d) bolas, (e) estancias

COMPREHENSION

3. What is unique about the ethnic makeup of the people in Argentina?
4. Describe Argentina's two distinct cultural groups.
5. What are some similarities between the gauchos of the Pampas and the cowboys of the Great Plains?

CRITICAL THINKING AND WRITING

6. **Exploring the Main Idea** Review the Main Idea statement at the beginning of this section. Then, write a paragraph describing how two distinct cultures came to exist in Argentina.
7. **Drawing Conclusions** Why do you think nearly 98 percent of the population lives in a small geographic area of Argentina called the Pampas?

ACTIVITY

8. **Learning About Gauchos** Find out more about gauchos by doing research on the Internet or in your school library. Write a short report about your findings and include any images that you find while doing your research.

Answers to...

CRITICAL THINKING

The clothing is appropriate for the work they do. They want to hold on to old customs and traditions.

Resource Directory

Teaching Resources

Section Quiz in the Unit 3 Teaching Resources, p. 76

Chapter Summary in the Unit 3 Teaching Resources, p. 77

Reteaching in the Unit 3 Teaching Resources, p. 79

Making Generalizations

Quality of Life

	Gross national product per capita (in U.S. dollars)	Life expectancy in years	People per doctor	Literacy rate	Infant mortality (per 1,000 live births)	Cars per 1,000 people
United States	$29,080	77	400	99%	7 deaths	489
Venezuela	$3,480	72	625	92%	21 deaths	68
Haiti	$380	54	10,000	46%	58 deaths	4
Brazil	$4,790	67	714	84%	34 deaths	128
Chile	$4,820	75	909	95%	11 deaths	71

Learn the Skill

A generalization is a broad statement that is based on data, or facts. It is a statement that links information or ideas together. To make a generalization based on data from a chart, follow these steps:

A. Study the information on the chart. Determine what information the chart provides by reading the title and the labels for each column and row. Also check out the data to determine ranges in numbers of percentages. Which numbers are highest? Which numbers are lowest? Are the numbers decimals? Are numbers provided in the millions?

B. Look for relationships in the information. On the chart on this page, for example, you can look for a relationship between life expectancy and the number of people per doctor. Look for other relationships that the chart reveals.

C. Make a general statement based on the facts. This statement might be a conclusion based on relationships that you've noted. You can make a general statement, or generalization, regarding a relationship between life expectancy and the number of people per doctor in the chart: As the number of people per doctor increases, life expectancy usually decreases.

Practice the Skill

Use the chart titled "Quality of Life" to practice making generalizations. To help you get started, answer these questions. Then, come up with your own generalizations by looking for relationships among data.

1. What are some characteristics of societies with high gross national products per capita?
2. What would you say are the characteristics of societies with low gross national products per capita?
3. What two suggestions would you make to improve the quality of life in societies that are less industrialized?
4. What relationship do you see between the number of people per doctor and infant mortality? What general statement about this relationship can you make?

Apply the Skill

See the Chapter Review and Assessment at the end of this chapter for more questions on making generalizations.

Lesson Objectives

1. Understand how to make generalizations.
2. Make generalizations using data from a chart.

Lesson Plan

1 Engage

To introduce the skill, read aloud the opening text under "Learn the Skill." Point out that students probably make generalizations every day. For example, if their bus is late and it's raining out, they might make the generalization that buses run late on rainy days. Have partners make a list of common generalizations they've made in the past.

2 Explore

Direct students to read the steps under "Learn the Skill." Encourage them to compare and contrast each category in order to find possible relationships.

3 Teach

Have students make generalizations using data from the chart. Answers to the questions: (1) Highly industrialized societies have a higher life expectancy, less people per doctor, and higher literacy rates. (2) Less-industrialized societies have the fastest-growing population, lower life expectancy, more people per doctor, and lower literacy rates. (3) Students might mention improving education or health care. (4) In general, infant mortality goes down as there are fewer people per doctor.

4 Assess/Reteach

Students should be able to make generalizations by looking for relationships in data in charts.

To further assess students' understanding of making generalizations, have them complete the "Applying Your Skills" part of the Chapter Review and Assessment at the end of the chapter.

Resource Directory

Technology

Social Studies Skills Tutor CD-ROM

Answers to...

PRACTICE THE SKILL

Possible responses:

1. higher life expectancy, literacy rate, and number of cars; lower infant mortality rate
2. lower life expectancy, literacy rate, and number of cars; higher infant mortality rate
3. increase the number of doctors and the amount of education
4. cause-and-effect relationship; the greater the number of doctors, the fewer infants die

CHAPTER 13

Review and Assessment

Creating a Chapter Summary

Student summaries will vary.

Sample summaries:

Section 2 As Brazil expands its economy, it looks for ways to use its natural resources to develop new industries. The government and people must find ways to use the land and other natural resources without harming the environment.

Section 3 As Chile and Venezuela develop their economies and expand industrial production, their governments must meet the challenges of keeping their economies strong, standards of living high, people in good health, and pollution levels low.

Section 4 Argentina has a unique cultural heritage. A blend of European cultures is evident in the capital city Buenos Aires, while in the plains region, a unique culture exists.

Reviewing Key Terms

1. f **2.** a **3.** c **4.** d **5.** b **6.** e

Reviewing the Main Ideas

1. Agriculture is the leading industry of most Caribbean nations because the islands have very fertile soil and are located in a tropical region with moderate temperatures and adequate rainfall.
2. With political unrest, instability of leadership, and continual changes in government, the economy has remained weak and dependent primarily on agriculture.
3. Puerto Rico is a commonwealth of the United States. It has its own constitution and lawmakers, but is bound by the laws of the United States.
4. The rain forests produce one-third of the world's oxygen and hold one-fifth of the world's fresh water. Oxygen produced there through photosynthesis is important to the large variety of rare plants and animals living in the rain forests.
5. The growth of agriculture saved the Chilean economy after the price of its chief export, copper, fell in the 1980s. Agriculture has allowed Chile not to depend on just one product to sustain its economy.
6. Venezuela earned millions of dollars on the world market; the government had more money to spend, it hired more people, and the economy prospered. However, relying on oil made the country dependent on one product and sensitive to changes in the income from that resource.
7. Argentina's ethnic makeup is part Spanish but also a blend of European cultures. Unlike in neighboring countries, there was no importation of African slaves to Argentina.
8. Mestizos, or people of Spanish and Native American heritage, and porteños, who settled in Buenos Aires to take advantage of the port city's trade and commerce.

CHAPTER 13

Review and Assessment

Creating a Chapter Summary

On a separate piece of paper, draw a diagram like this one, and include the information that summarizes the first section of the chapter. Then, fill in the remaining boxes with summaries of Sections 2, 3, and 4.

THE CARIBBEAN AND SOUTH AMERICA

Section 1	Section 2	Section 3	Section 4
The nations of the Caribbean face many economic and political challenges. Often, they have been influenced by the United States.			

Reviewing Key Terms

Match the definitions in Column I with the key terms in Column II.

Column I

a. people who own only small tracts of land in Latin America
b. nomadic cowboys of Argentina
c. the process of a government selling its industries to individuals and private companies
d. one crop provides a majority of a country's income
e. estates owned by private owners
f. a period of increased prosperity

Column II

1. boom
2. campesinos
3. privatization
4. one-crop economy
5. gauchos
6. estancias

Reviewing the Main Ideas

1. Why is agriculture the leading industry of most Caribbean nations? (Section 1)
2. How have Haiti's political problems influenced its economic problems? (Section 1)
3. What political ties exist between Puerto Rico and the United States? (Section 1)
4. Why are Brazil's rain forests a global concern? (Section 2)
5. How has producing more crops and increasing agriculture helped Chile's economy? (Section 3)
6. How did its oil boom affect Venezuela's people and its economy? (Section 3)
7. What makes Argentina's culture so unique? (Section 4)
8. What are two of Argentina's distinct cultural groups? (Section 4)

Map Activity

The Caribbean and South America

For each place listed below, write the letter from the map that shows its location.

1. Cuba
2. Haiti
3. Puerto Rico
4. Brazil
5. Chile
6. Brasília
7. Venezuela
8. Argentina

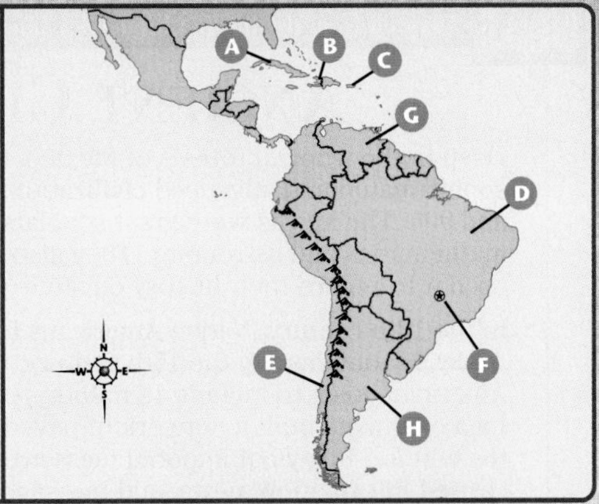

Take It to the NET

Enrichment For more map activities on the Caribbean and South America, visit the World Explorer section of **phschool.com.**

Writing Activity

1. **Using Primary Sources** Visit your school or local library or use the Internet to find newspaper and magazine articles and other primary sources with information about the current status of the Brazilian rain forests. Write a persuasive argument describing why it is important to protect the rain forests. Create a poster to illustrate your argument.
2. **Writing a Journal** You are a citizen of Puerto Rico. Tomorrow an election will be held to decide if Puerto Rico should remain a commonwealth, become the 51st state in the United States, or declare independence from the United States. Write how you feel about this decision in your journal. Include your feelings about how you will vote and why.

Applying Your Skills

Use the chart titled "Quality of Life" on p. 245. Look for a relationship by answering the questions, then write a generalization for each one based on data from the chart. Be sure to write in complete sentences.

1. Does the gross national product seem to have a bearing on the amount of cars owned?
2. Are the countries with the highest literacy rates the countries that are most industrialized or least industrialized?

Critical Thinking

1. **Making Comparisons** Compare the environmental concerns faced by the governments of Brazil and Chile. How are they similar? How are they different?
2. **Making Generalizations** What generalization can you make about the culture and people of Argentina?

Take It to the NET

Activity Search your home and make a list of items you find that are made from resources found in the rainforest. How can resources from the rainforest be used in sustainable ways? Visit the World Explorer: People, Places, and Cultures section of **phschool.com** for help in completing this activity.

Chapter 13 Self-Test As a final review activity, take the Chapter 13 Self-Test and get instant feedback on your answers. To take the test, visit the Social Studies section of **phschool.com.**

Map Activity

1. A **2.** B **3.** C **4.** D **5.** E **6.** F **7.** G **8.** H

Writing Activity

1. Student arguments and posters should reflect current conditions of the rain forests and scientific concerns.
2. Student responses should be logical and include arguments for and against the three choices.

Critical Thinking

1. Brazil currently faces serious environmental concerns over the future of the rain forest. Concerns include whether or not to develop the rain forest's natural resources and risk upsetting the delicate balance of nature. Past development, such as increased farming, damaged the soil and environment of the rain forests. Increased mining in the region could lead to problems similar to those Chile faced from extensive copper mining. In the 1980s, Chile encouraged private industry, which was good for its economy, but relaxed the laws that protected the environment from pollution. Both countries need to develop industry while protecting the environment.
2. The culture of Argentina is diverse and unique compared to many other Latin American countries.

Applying Your Skills

1. Yes. The higher the country's GNP, the more people own cars.
2. The most industrialized countries have the highest literacy rates.

Resource Directory

Teaching Resources

Cooperative Learning Activity in the Unit 3 Teaching Resources, pp. 119–121

Chapter Tests Forms A and B in the Unit 3 Teaching Resources, pp. 154–159

Unit Test Forms A and B in the Unit 3 Teaching Resources, pp. 160–165

Guide to the Essentials, Ch. 13 Test, p. 57

Other Print Resources

Chapter Test with ExamView® Test Bank, Ch. 13

Technology

ExamView® Test Bank CD-ROM, Ch. 13

Resource Pro® CD-ROM

UNIT 3

Introduction

The introduction on the student page on the right provides key facts and general information about the history of ancient civilizations in Latin America.

- Students should read the introduction first to gain a basic knowledge of the subject before reading on.
- Have students read all of the subentries, which provide further information on ancient civilizations, particularly focusing on how they have influenced future civilizations. Have students read the annotations that accompany and explain the photos and illustrations.
- When students have finished reading all of the information, discuss the connections between the information on these pages and what they have learned about Latin America. Students might want to review information about early civilizations in Chapter 10.

ACTIVITY

Creating a System of Writing

Have students work in pairs to create a writing system. Students can design their own symbols to stand for sounds and numbers, and pictures to show concrete information. Have students first create a key showing the symbols used and what they represent, and then have them use their writing system to record a current event, such as news of a bad storm, a sporting event, or a political election. When pairs have finished recording an event using their writing system, have them display it for the rest of the class, and allow others to try to "read" the message they have written using the symbol key.

Visual/Spatial

Adapted from the Dorling Kindersley Illustrated Children's Encyclopedia

Ancient Civilizations

Deep in the tropical forests of Mexico, the Mayan people created a sophisticated and advanced civilization. It reached its height between A.D. 250 and 900. The Mayas were great scholars who developed systems of mathematics and astronomy. They also created their own writing system and used it to record their history on stone plaques.

In the 12th century, Native Americans founded the Incan civilization in the Andes Mountains. By the 15th century, the empire stretched down the South American coast to include 12 million people. The Incas had a powerful army. Inca engineers built a network of paved roads that linked far-reaching parts of the empire. Relays of imperial messengers carried information, news, and messages to and from the capital city of Cuzco.

In the 13th century, a wandering tribe of Native Americans founded the Aztec civilization in the Valley of Mexico. Borrowing ideas from the Toltec and Olmec peoples with established civilizations in the area, the Aztec empire grew to 12 million people over a two hundred-year span.

? How have ancient civilizations influenced contemporary society in Latin America?

GLYPHS
Mayan writing was made up of a series of signs that archaeologists call glyphs. Many of the glyphs were simplified pictures of the objects they stood for. The Maya used glyphs to record their calendar and to write inscriptions about their history.

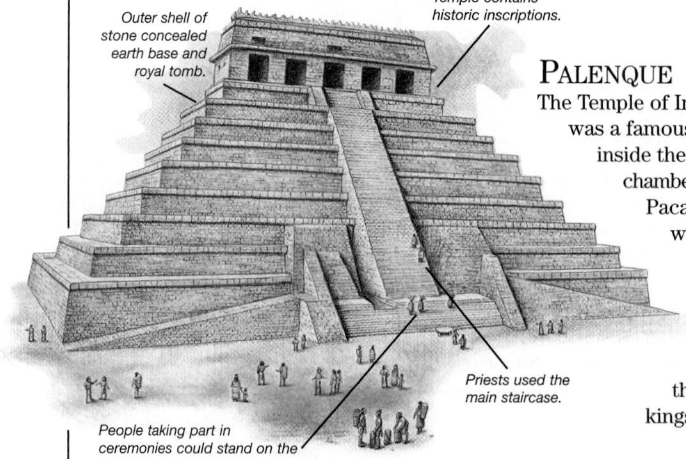

Outer shell of stone concealed earth base and royal tomb.
Temple contains historic inscriptions.
Priests used the main staircase.
People taking part in ceremonies could stand on the main stepped levels.

Palenque

The Temple of Inscriptions at Palenque was a famous Mayan pyramid. Deep inside the base was a secret chamber. It contained the tomb of Pacal. Pacal was a local king who died in about A.D. 684. A temple was built on top of the pyramid. Inside were stone tablets carved with glyphs that recorded the history of the local kings up to Pacal's reign.

HISTORY

Ancient Civilizations

Majestic ruins in the jungles of Mexico and on the hillsides of South America, shards and stone tools sifted from centuries of soil, and records and information recorded in stone carvings and knotted strands are the only traces left of the Inca and Aztec civilizations. These archeological remains provide the crucial links to the rich world of these long-lost peoples. Within a short amount of time, their culture had been all but erased by the Spanish conquistadors and the missionaries and colonists who followed them.

TENOCHTITLÁN

The Aztec capital was Tenochtitlán. It has been called a "floating city" because it was built on one natural island and a series of artificial islands in Lake Texcoco. Raised roads, or causeways, and canals linked the islands to the mainland. Today, Mexico City stands on the site of the ancient city.

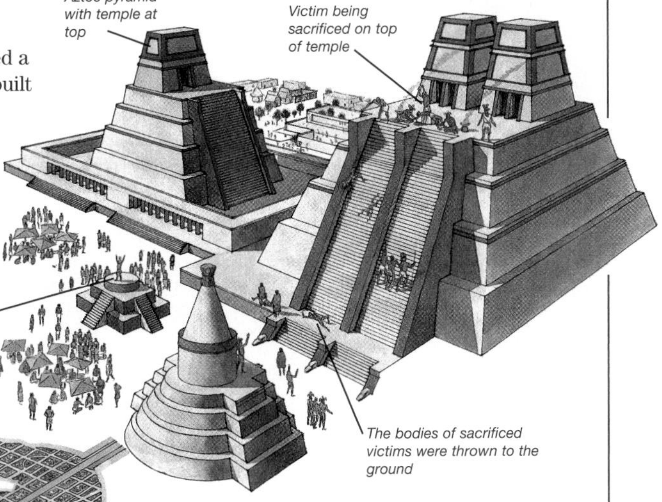

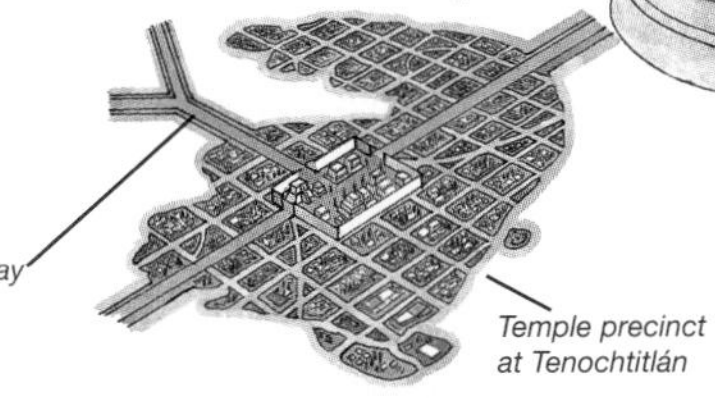

TRIBUTES
The Aztecs became very rich by collecting tributes (payments) from conquered tribes. Porters brought cloth, corn, pottery, and luxury goods to Tenochtitlán from the conquered cities. Goods were exchanged in four huge markets. Officials used picture writing to make lists of all the tributes that were paid. The Aztecs declared war on any tribe that refused to pay tribute.

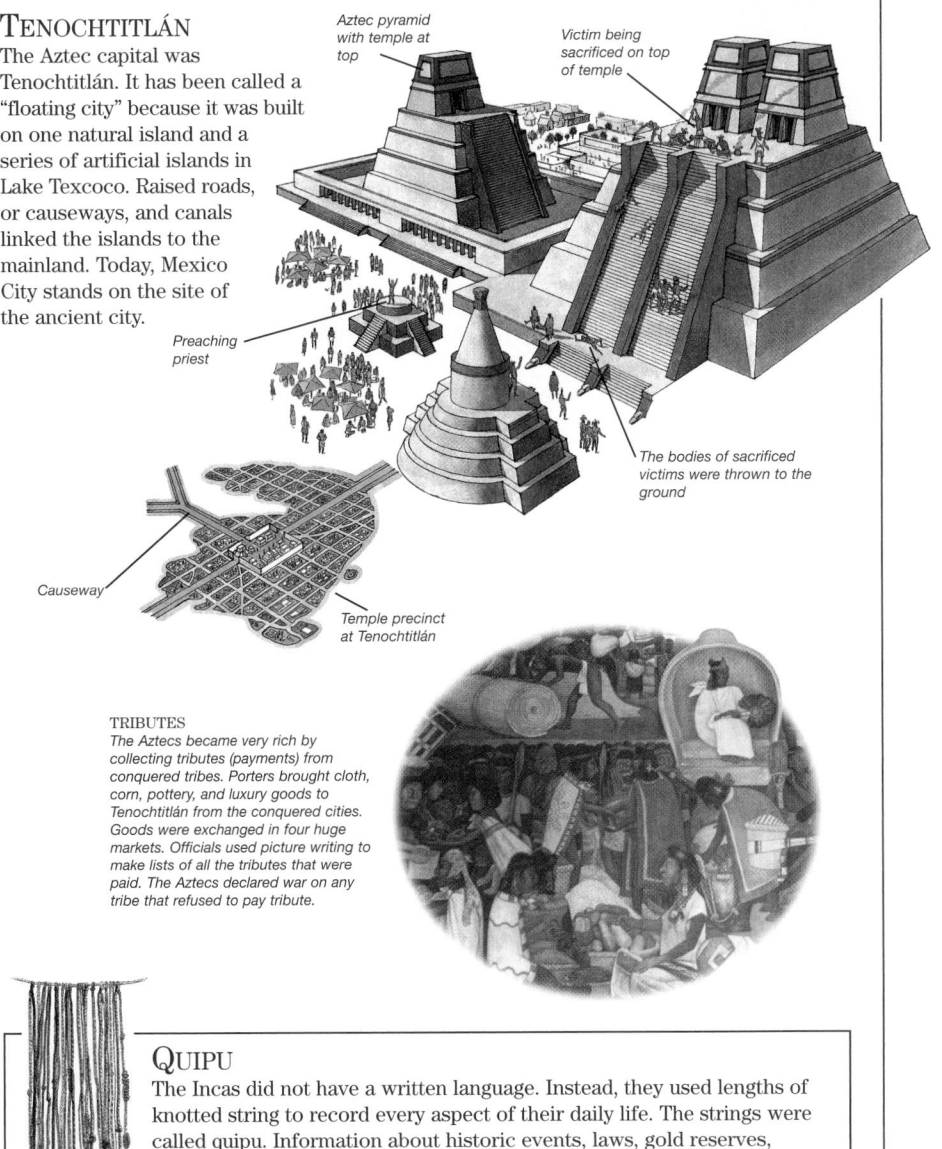

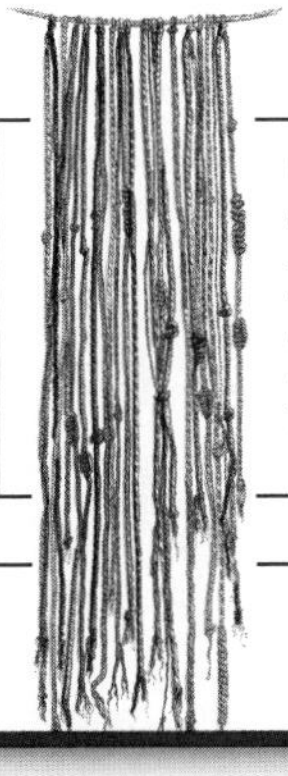

QUIPU

The Incas did not have a written language. Instead, they used lengths of knotted string to record every aspect of their daily life. The strings were called quipu. Information about historic events, laws, gold reserves, population statistics, and other news was accurately stored using these knotted strands.

ACTIVITY

Exploring Artifacts

Have students use library and Internet resources to learn more about the archeological ruins of ancient cultures. Have them gather information on the architecture and artifacts found on the sites where one of these three great civilizations existed. Students can use the information they find to write journal entries about daily life for people with different responsibilities in the empire, such as merchant, scribe, messenger, priest, soldier, builder, or farmer.

Verbal/Linguistic

HISTORY

Hernán Cortés

When the Spanish conquistador Hernán Cortés and his armada arrived in Tenochtitlán, the great Aztec ruler, Montezuma, thought that their arrival had been foretold in a series of omens. These portents were interpreted as a signal of the return of Quetzalcoatl, the creator. For this reason, when Cortés arrived on horseback—a two-headed creature on six legs, as some described it—he was welcomed into the kingdom. For the Aztecs, it was the beginning of the end of their powerful empire.

UNIT 4

Introducing the Unit

This unit was developed around seven strands of essential knowledge and skills that relate to the study of people, places, and cultures of the contemporary world. These strands include **History, Geography, Economics, Government, Citizenship, Culture,** and **Science, Technology, and Society.** These seven strands, and the related Guiding Questions on the next pages, are intended as an organizational focus for the unit. All of the chapter content, activities, questions, and assessments relate to the seven strands, which act as an umbrella under which all of the material falls.

Using the Pictures

Use the photographs on the reduced student pages as a prompt for a discussion of what students know about geography, history, economics, government, citizenship, culture, and science and technology of Europe and Russia.

- You may want to begin a **K-W-L** chart on the chalkboard for Europe and Russia, with the headings What We **K**now About Europe and Russia, What We **W**ant to Know About Europe and Russia, and What We **L**earned About Europe and Russia.
- Have students fill in the first column with several things they agree they already know. Then, ask them to brainstorm what they would like to know about Europe and Russia to add to the second column.
- Students can fill in the third column as they work throughout the text.

eTeach

Be sure to check out this month's discussion with a Master Teacher. Go to phschool.com.

UNIT 4

Welcome to Europe and Russia

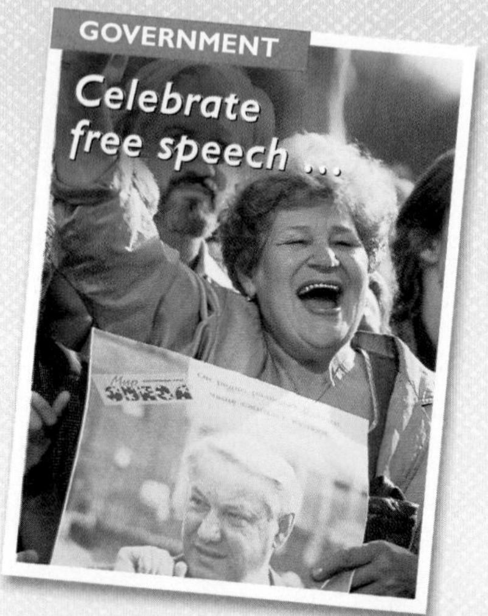

GOVERNMENT

Celebrate free speech ...

ECONOMICS

Shop with the new European currency ...

GEOGRAPHY

Explore important physical features ...

250 UNIT4 EUROPE AND RUSSIA

Resource Directory

Teaching Resources

Program Overview includes a guide to the Prentice Hall World Explorer program. You may wish to refer to the overview as you plan your instruction.

Pacing Charts for Unit 4 offer a variety of course configurations.

What do you want to learn?

CULTURE

Listen to the music of Italy ...

CITIZENSHIP

Climb over the Berlin Wall ...

HISTORY

Explore the ancient ruins of the Colosseum ...

SCIENCE, TECHNOLOGY, AND SOCIETY

Travel through France on a high-speed train ...

A journal can be your personal record of discovery. As you learn about Europe and Russia, you can create journal entries about what you read, write, think, and create. For your first entry, choose a region of Europe or Russia that you would like to visit. How might the history of this region be similar to the history of the region where you live? How might it be different?

UNIT 4 WELCOME TO EUROPE AND RUSSIA 251

Resource Directory

Technology

Social Studies Skills Tutor CD-ROM provides two levels of interactive instruction and practice in 20 core social studies skills.

Resource Pro® CD-ROM allows you to create customized lesson plans and print all resources directly from the CD-ROM.

Using the Explorer's Journal

Have students begin their Explorer's Journal as the paragraph on the student book page suggests. If at all possible, encourage students to use a separate small notebook for their Explorer's Journal entries. They can add to this journal as they learn more about Europe and Russia.

Project Possibilities

The projects in this book are designed to provide students with hands-on involvement in the content area. Write the following project ideas on the chalkboard and have students preview them and discuss which they might want to do. You may assign projects as cooperative activities, whole-class projects, or individual projects.

Changing Climates

Choose a European country near the Arctic or one near the Mediterranean. Find out about ways of life that have to do with the climate, and then write a survival guide for someone moving to that region from the other end of the continent.

Tourism and Eastern Europe

Choose a country in Eastern Europe. Read about its geography and culture. Decide which features might interest tourists from other countries. Create a travel brochure for the country you have chosen. Create your own pictures or cut them out of magazines, and write captions and descriptive text to sell your ideas.

Folklore and Culture Corner

Create a library of myths and folktales from Europe and Russia. As you read about a country, find an example of traditional literature that reflects the culture. Build a Folklore and Culture Corner in your classroom, and include books of folktales, as well as objects, drawings, and photographs that show cultural traits and customs.

Introducing

Guiding Questions

The seven Guiding Questions that appear on the reduced student edition pages to the right should act as a guide for learning about Europe and Russia, and for encouraging students to relate what they learn to their own experience. The Guiding Questions that relate to the content of each chapter in the unit appear on the Chapter Opener pages in the student edition.

- You may wish to add your own Guiding Questions to the list in order to tailor them to your particular course. Or, as a group activity, ask your class to develop its own Guiding Questions.

ACTIVITY

Using the Guiding Questions

Ask a volunteer to read aloud the Guiding Questions to the class.

- Have students write the seven headings on a separate piece of paper or in their Explorer's Journal. Have them think about what information they would like to learn about Europe and Russia, and write a question that relates to each heading.
- Have students share their questions with the rest of the class, and discuss any similarities.
- Create a master list of questions grouped under the seven headings. As you read about Europe and Russia, try to answer the questions on the list.
- At the end of the unit, if any questions remain unanswered, have students research and find the answers to those questions.

Guiding Questions

What questions do I need to ask to understand Europe and Russia?

Asking questions is a good way to learn. Think about what information you would want to know if you were visiting a new place, and what questions you might ask to find out. The questions on these pages can help guide your study of Europe and Russia. You might want to try adding a few of your own!

GEOGRAPHY

The continent of Europe is surrounded on three sides by water. Rivers wind through the land, leading to coastal harbors and inland seas. The steep slopes of ancient mountains separate regions of land and people. In the north, winters are long and cold, and in the south, summers are hot and dry. In the east, the Ural Mountains separate Europe from the vast, isolated region known as Siberia.

1 How has the geography of Europe and Russia influenced economic, political, and cultural differences in the region?

HISTORY

Events of the past have shaped the modern European world. These events include ethnic conflicts, colonization of distant lands, shifting political borders, and changing economic systems. To understand how Europeans are living today, it is important to understand how history has shaped the course of their lives.

2 How have the turbulent and triumphant events of the past influenced present-day Europe?

CULTURE

Some countries in Europe share a common language and religion, while others attempt to blend many different cultures successfully. Some regions have changed governments over centuries of war and peace. Different beliefs and customs have spread across the European continent for hundreds of years, but each nation manages to retain a cultural identity that is uniquely its own.

3 What are some cultural traits that European nations share, and what are some traits that make each nation unique?

GOVERNMENT

For many years, Western Europe was separated from Eastern Europe and Russia by an invisible but strong boundary called the Iron Curtain. In Eastern Europe, behind the Iron Curtain, dictatorships maintained strict control over all aspects of the people's lives. In Western Europe, governments were democratic and the people were free to choose their leaders and make and enforce their own laws. Both of these regions have seen great political change in recent times, and look forward to more change in the future.

4 How are people's lives changing with the freedom of the newly formed democracies of Eastern Europe?

ECONOMICS

The countries that share the continent of Europe also share limited natural resources. Economic stability and the ability to compete in worldwide markets depend on open transportation corridors and fair trade agreements. With these factors in mind, many countries of Europe have come together to form the European Union.

5 What are the economic advantages of participating in the European Union?

CITIZENSHIP

In democratic countries, citizens are allowed to be involved in government and are encouraged to participate in the political process. In countries where civil and human rights are violated, the freedom of all the people might depend on a group of citizens or even an individual leader speaking out for change, and inspiring reforms.

6 Why is it important for people in democratic societies to exercise their responsibilities as citizens?

SCIENCE, TECHNOLOGY, AND SOCIETY

People have moved from the cities to the countryside across the continent of Europe over the last century. Rapid technological advances in industry and telecommunications have made the world a smaller place. However, these advances have threatened traditional ways of life, especially in Europe's countryside.

7 How can people take advantage of new technologies and still maintain links to more traditional ways of life?

Take It to the NET

For more information on Europe and Russia, visit the World Explorer: People, Places, and Cultures companion Web site at **phschool.com.**

ACTIVITY

Using Primary and Secondary Sources

Daily Life Ask students to think about their own daily routines and how those routines are affected by the part of the world in which they live. Discuss what life might be like in some European countries, and in Russia, and how it may be different from life in the United States.

- Have students work in pairs to create an outline that shows what activities they do on a typical day.
- Have each pair choose a country from Europe (including Russia), and research that country to try to find information on the daily activities of the people who live there.
- Encourage students to use primary and secondary sources in their research, including letters, interviews, biographies, and Internet sources.

Verbal/Linguistic

ACTIVITY ATLAS

Lesson Objectives

1. Describe the relative size and location of Europe and Russia.
2. Explain how climate affects the ways of life and population densities in Europe and Russia.
3. Trace the changing political boundaries of Eastern Europe and the former Soviet Union.
4. Compare physical features of Russia and Europe.

Lesson Plan

1 Engage

Warm-Up Activity

Invite students to describe a patchwork quilt. Together, identify the materials used in such a quilt and discuss what holds the quilt together. Help students list the quilt's strengths and weaknesses in various uses.

Activating Prior Knowledge

Ask students how the different peoples and nations of Europe and Russia have related to one another through history. Note some of the students' ideas on the chalkboard.

ACTIVITY ATLAS

Europe and Russia

Learning about Europe and Russia means being an explorer and a geographer. No explorer would start out without first checking some facts. Begin by exploring the maps of Europe and Russia on the following pages.

Relative Location

1. LOCATION

Locate Europe and Russia A geographer must know where a place is. Use the map at left to describe Europe and Russia's location relative to the United States. Which area is closer to the Equator, Europe and Russia or the United States? Which is closer to the Arctic Circle? Many people think the climates of Europe and the United States are similar. Look at the map. Then list three reasons why this might be so.

Relative Size

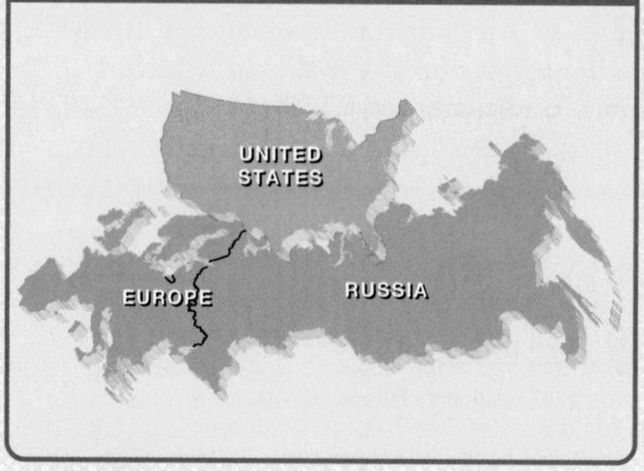

2. PLACE

Compare the Size of Europe, Russia, and the United States Are Europe and Russia together larger or smaller than the United States? How does the size of Russia alone compare to that of the continental United States?

Take It to the NET

Items marked with this logo are periodically updated on the Internet. To get current information about the geography of Europe and Russia, go to **phschool.com.**

Resource Directory

Teaching Resources

Activity Atlas in the Unit 3 Teaching Resources, pp. 97–106

Answers to...

LOCATION

1. The United States is closer to the Equator; Russia is closer to the Arctic Circle; possible reasons: many parts of the two regions are in the same latitudes, they both have Atlantic Ocean coastlines; both have humid and dry areas

PLACE

2. larger; Russia is larger

Europe and Russia: Climate Regions

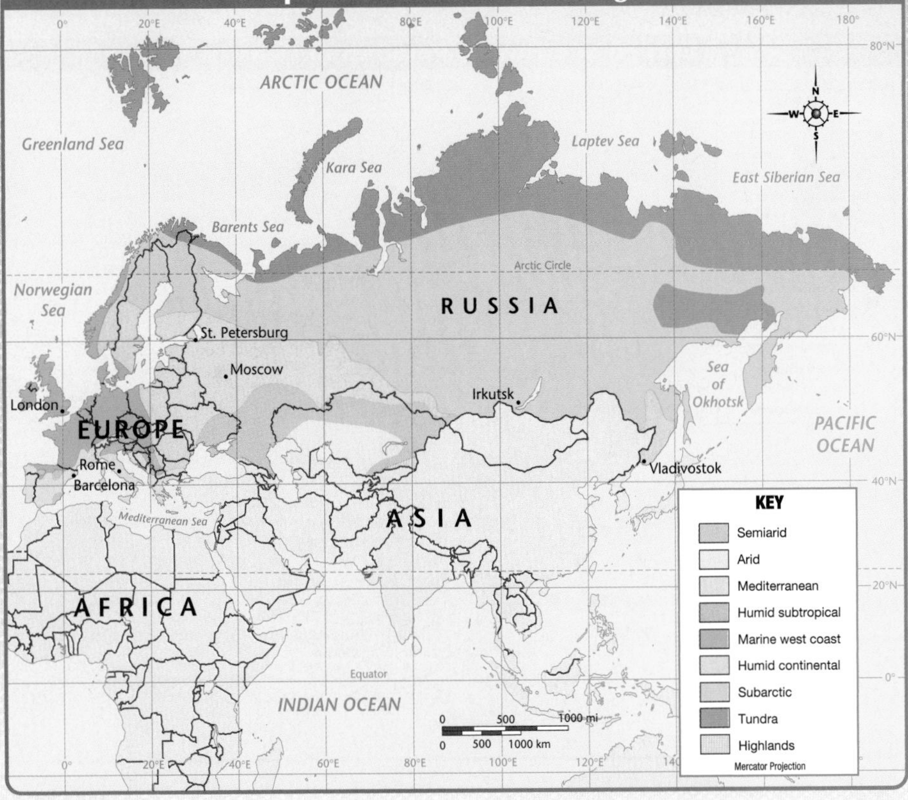

3. REGIONS

Compare Climates in Europe and Russia Find Russia on the map. What are its three major climate regions? How does Russia's latitude, or distance from the Equator, affect its climate? Compare Russia's climate regions with those in Europe. Does Europe have a greater or lesser variety of climate regions than Russia? Find Moscow and Rome on the map. Which city do you think has a warmer climate? Why?

4. HUMAN-ENVIRONMENT INTERACTION

Predict the Effect of Climate on How People Live In warm countries such as Spain, many people live in houses with thick walls, which remain cool in the hot sun. In colder countries like Sweden, houses often have steep roofs to keep the snow from piling up on them. In what other ways do you think people have adapted to their climates?

2 Explore

Have students carefully read the material in the Activity Atlas. As they read each activity, ask students to indicate which major maps best answer each group of questions. Urge students to generate their own questions linked to each geography theme. Post these on a classroom bulletin board and let all students respond.

3 Teach

Have students create a five-column chart about Europe and Russia. Column labels should correspond to the five geography themes. Information about Europe and Russia should appear in two rows. Students can then compare the two regions, addressing each geography theme in turn.

4 Assess/Reteach

Charts should correctly locate Europe and Russia relative to the United States, the Equator, and the North Pole. They should note Europe's diverse nations and describe both regions' changing political boundaries. Charts should note the range of climates in Europe and Russia and the link between population density and human movement.

Resource Directory

Teaching Resources

Outline Maps Western Europe, pp. 17–18; Eastern Europe, pp. 22–23; Russia, p. 27

Answers to...

REGIONS

3. tundra, subarctic, humid continental; distance from Equator causes colder climates; greater variety; Rome, because it is closer to the Equator and to large bodies of water

HUMAN-ENVIRONMENT INTERACTION

4. Possible answers include different clothing, different kinds of transportation, different types of foods that are grown, and different types of recreation.

ACTIVITY ATLAS

ACTIVITY

Interdisciplinary Connections

Language Arts Tell students to think carefully about what they now know about Europe and Russia. Then have them describe or draw some possible illustrations that could accompany the Activity Atlas. With each illustration, students should write a short caption telling what the illustration shows.

Visual/Spatial

ACTIVITY ATLAS

Take It to the NET

Europe and Russia: Population Density

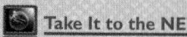

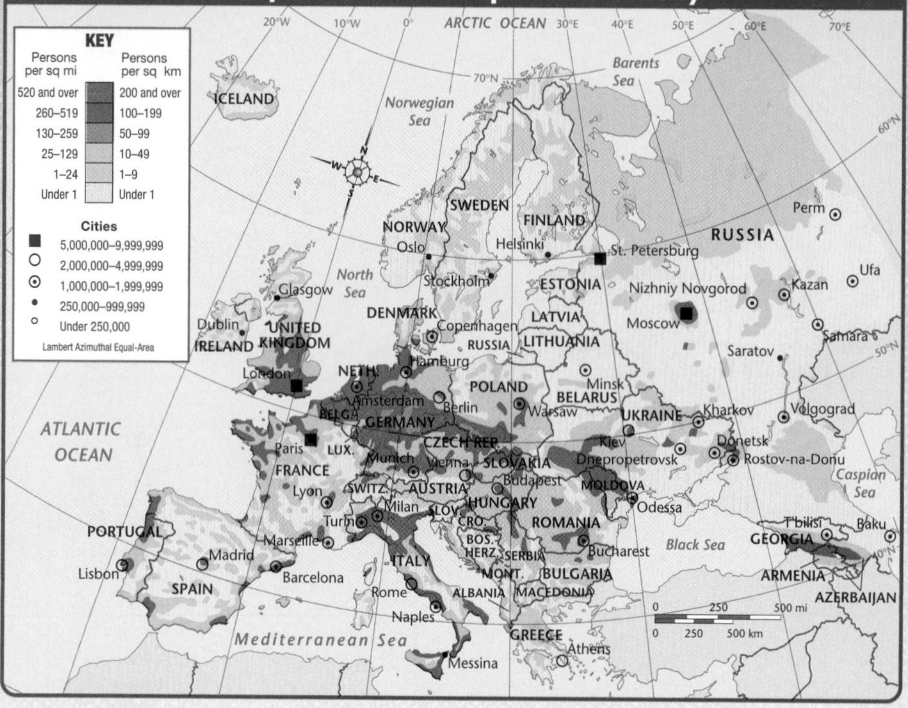

5. PLACE

Compare Population Densities Population density is the number of people living within a certain area. Compare the parts of Europe that have many people to the parts that have only a few people. Do the same for European Russia. How would you describe the population density of the two regions? What geographic features might explain the low population density of countries like Finland and Switzerland?

6. MOVEMENT

Analyze Population and Transportation Notice the population density in the northernmost part of Europe and European Russia. Now look at the same region on the railroad map on the next page. How many railroads do you see in this region compared to regions in central and southern Europe and European Russia? Do regions with more people tend to have more or fewer rail routes? In what other ways might population and transportation affect each other?

Answers to...

PLACE

5. Europe's population is relatively dense throughout, while Russia's varies from relatively dense to very sparse; cold temperatures and mountainous terrain.

MOVEMENT

6. fewer; more; possible answers: People will be more likely to locate in places accessible by transportation and that offer transporation to and from jobs.

Resource Directory

Teaching Resources

Social Studies and Geography Skills, Reading a Population Density Map, p. 29

7. MOVEMENT

Organize a Journey by Railway You've always wanted to visit Europe and Russia. Now you have the chance. Your family will be exploring Europe and Russia next summer by train. Together, you've set the following goals. Use the map below to plan which routes to take.

A. *Your flight from the United States will land in Paris. From there, you want to travel to Warsaw. What's the shortest route? List the cities you'll pass through.*

B. *From Warsaw, you will go to Moscow. What other Russian city can you visit on the way?*

C. *After Moscow, you are going to Rome. You want to see as many major cities as you can on the way. What's your route?*

D. *From Rome, you must head straight back to Paris. Can you find the shortest route?*

BONUS

Your trip is planned for March. What clothing should you pack for each part of your journey? Use the climate map on page 255 and information from the Map and Globe Handbook.

Europe: Major Railroad Lines

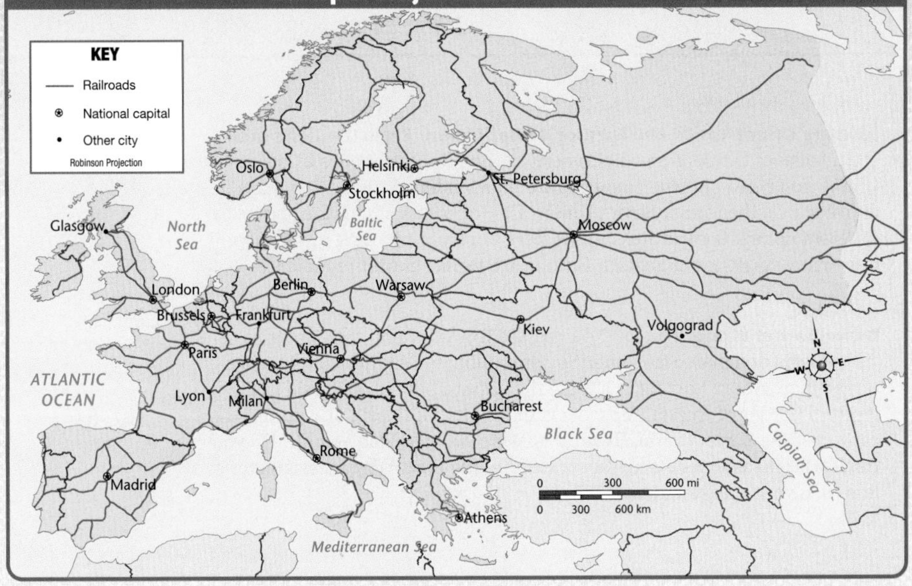

Practice in the Themes of Geography

Place Ask students to use the transportation map on this page to identify places that can be described as transportation centers. (any of the following: Paris, London, Madrid, Vienna, Warsaw, Moscow)

Regions Ask students to compare communication within Russia to that throughout Europe. (Students should note that Russia is a one-nation region united by language and government but divided by size, while Europe is a multinational region divided by language, government, and culture but linked by proximity.)

Movement Ask students what transportation challenges might face Russians trying to fully develop their nation's natural resources (limited rail service to certain parts of the country, huge distances).

Location Ask students to use the Climate Regions map to identify European nations that are located at least partly within the Arctic Circle (Finland, Sweden, and Norway).

Answers to...

MOVEMENT

7. A. Paris to Brussels to Berlin to Warsaw

B. Kiev

C. Kiev, Warsaw, Vienna, and Milan

D. Milan to Lyon to Paris

BONUS

Winter clothes will be needed for most of the journey, with perhaps lighter clothes for Italy.

ACTIVITY

Discovery Learning

Geography Quilt Using plain muslin fabric and fabric pens (permanent markers), have students create a geography quilt of Europe and Russia. Divide the nations of the two regions among student pairs. Have students use a wall map to trace each nation's shape on fabric. Pairs can then choose the data about each country that will best depict its geographic features on the quilt. Encourage students to draw these features on the fabric and then help the class assemble the quilt with thread or fabric glue.

Visual/Spatial

ACTIVITY ATLAS

Former Republics of the Soviet Union

8. REGIONS

Identify Countries of the Former Soviet Union From the 1920s until 1991, some of the countries in Eastern Europe were republics of the Soviet Union. Today, all of these countries are independent nations. The map above shows the former Soviet Union. The former republics are shown by different colors. Look at Russia's western border. According to the map, how many countries in Eastern Europe are former Soviet republics?

9. REGIONS

Describe the Size of Russia You can see from the map that, in terms of size, Russia dominated the other Soviet republics. Use the scale of miles on the map. About how far is it from the eastern border of Russia to the western border of Russia? Moscow is the capital of Russia. It was also the capital of the Soviet Union. How far is Moscow from Vladivostok? Do you think your measurements are accurate? Are the actual distances greater or less than your measurements? Why?

Resource Directory

Technology

Color Transparencies 74–76 Europe Today with Eastern Europe Updated (Base map with overlays)

Answers to...

REGIONS

8. six (Estonia, Latvia, Lithuania, Ukraine, Belarus, and Moldova)

REGIONS

9. Russia is approximately 4,750 miles (7,644 km) across. Moscow is about 4,500 miles (7,242 km) from Vladivostok. Not accurate; greater than; this map is flat so it is distorted.

The Biggest Lakes and Rivers

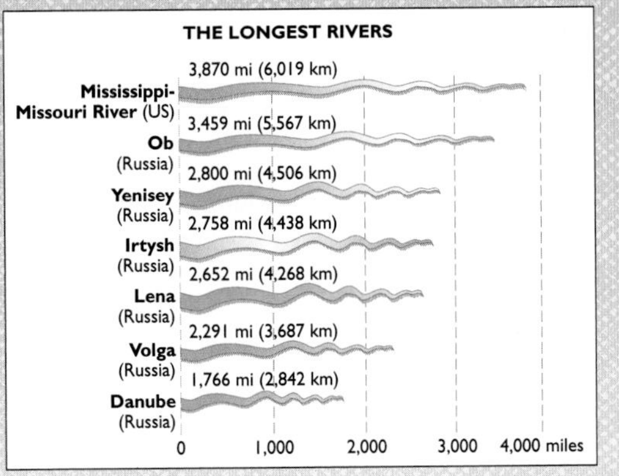

10. PLACE

Compare Physical Features Study these charts and diagrams. Using the maps in this Activity Atlas to locate the places listed in Russia and Europe. What lake has the largest volume of water? Some geographers say that the Caspian Sea is a lake. Others say it is a sea because its waters are salty. How does it compare to other lakes in size? What countries border it? What is the longest river in Russia and Europe?

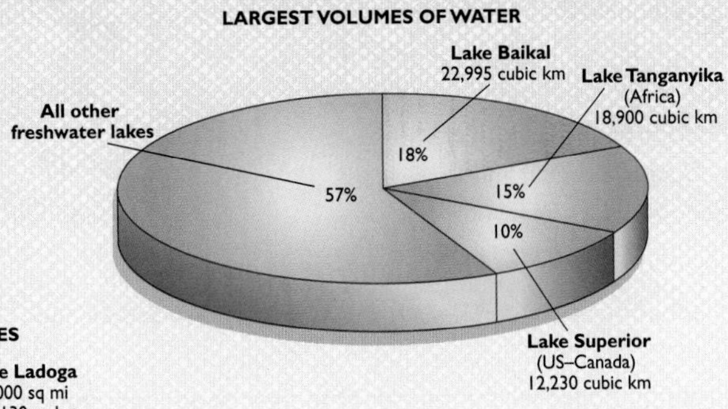

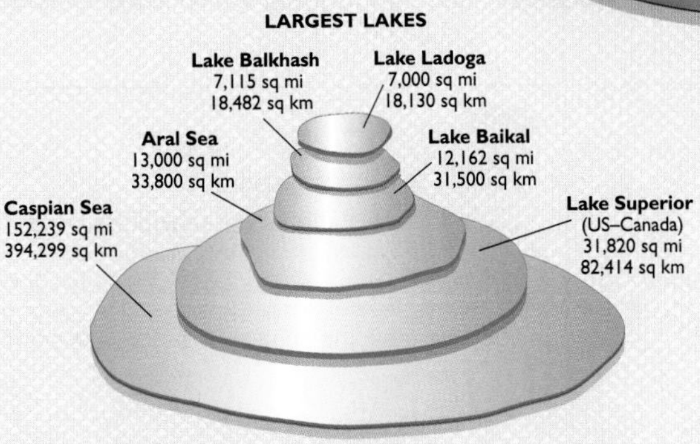

HISTORY

Russia's Geographic Challenges

In 1991, the Soviet Union was disolved. Russia and the former republics of the Soviet Union became separate nations once again. A move toward democracy replaced the region's crumbling communist governments. However, Russia's geographic challenges have remained the same. As the largest nation in the world—about 6,000 miles (9,650 km)—from east to west, it is difficult to communicate across, travel through, or govern.

Resource Directory

Teaching Resources

Social Studies and Geography Skills, Reading a Bar Graph, p. 51; Reading a Circle Graph, p. 53

Answers to...

PLACE

10. Lake Baikal; the Caspian Sea is five times larger than Lake Superior, the next largest lake; the Caspian Sea is bordered by Russia, Kazakstan, Turkmenistan, Iran, Azerbaijan; the longest river is the Ob River in Russia.

Chapter 14 Planning Guide

Resource Manager

	CORE INSTRUCTION	READING/SKILLS
Chapter-Level Resources	**Teaching Resources** Program Overview Pacing Charts **Technology** Resource Pro® CD-ROM Companion Web site, phschool.com • eTeach	**Technology** Social Studies Skills Tutor CD-ROM Student Edition on Audio CD, Ch. 14
1 Physical Features 1. Identify the main physical features of Europe and Russia. 2. Explain how the rivers of Europe and Russia create transportation corridors throughout the continent. 3. Explain how the physical processes of the ocean affect the continent of Europe.	**Teaching Resources** **Unit 4** Classroom Manager, p. 2 Guided Reading and Review, p.3	**Teaching Resources** Guide to the Essentials, p. 58 **Technology** Section Reading Support Transparencies
2 Humans and the Physical Environment 1. Describe how people adapt to the climate conditions in different parts of Europe and Russia. 2. Explain how people have modified the physical environment of Europe and Russia.	**Teaching Resources** **Unit 4** Classroom Manager, p. 5 Guided Reading and Review, p. 6	**Teaching Resources** Guide to the Essentials, p. 59 Social Studies and Geography Skills, p. 23 **Technology** Section Reading Support Transparencies
3 Geographic Factors and Natural Resources 1. Explain where fossil fuels come from and how they benefit Europe and Russia. 2. Explain how water resources are used in Europe and Russia. 3. Describe the geographic features that contribute to the fertile soil of Europe and Ukraine.	**Teaching Resources** **Unit 4** Classroom Manager, p. 8 Guided Reading and Review, p. 9 Chapter Summary, p. 11 Vocabulary, p. 12 Reteaching, p. 13	**Teaching Resources** Critical Thinking, p. 15 Guide to the Essentials, p. 60 **Technology** Section Reading Support Transparencies

NRICHMENT / PRE-AP

Teaching Resources
Primary Sources and Literature Readings

Other Print Resources
DK Atlas

Technology
World Video Explorer: Journey Over Europe and Russia and The Influence of Geography
Companion Web site, phschool.com

Teaching Resources
Outline Maps, pp. 18, 20–27

Technology
Color Transparencies 13

Teaching Resources
Unit 4
Enrichment, p. 14
Cooperative Learning Activity, pp. 107–109

ASSESSMENT

Prentice Hall Assessment System

Core Assessment
Chapter Tests with ExamView® Test Bank, Ch. 14
ExamView® Test Bank CD-ROM, Ch. 14

Standardized Test Preparation
Diagnose and Prescribe
Diagnostic Tests for Middle Grades Social Studies Skills
Review and Reteach
Review Book for World Studies
Practice and Assess
Test-taking Strategies with Transparencies for Middle Grades Test Prep Book
Test-taking Strategies Posters

Teaching Resources
Unit 4
Section Quizzes, pp. 4, 7, and 10
Chapter Tests, pp. 138–143
Guide to the Essentials, Ch. 14 Test, p. 61

Technology
Companion Web site, phschool.com
Ch. 14 Self-Test

World Video Explorer
Each region of the world is explored through regional flyovers and investigative field trips. Case study segments give students an in-depth view of the history, economy, government, and culture of a key place in each region. Case studies include Nigeria, Mexico, China, British Columbia, and the Czech Republic.

In Your Classroom

CUSTOMIZE FOR INDIVIDUAL NEEDS

Gifted and Talented

Teacher's Edition
- Language Arts, p. 267

Teaching Resources
- Enrichment, p. 14
- Primary Sources and Literature Readings

Honors/Pre-AP

Teacher's Edition
- Language Arts, p. 267

Teaching Resources
- Critical Thinking, p. 15
- Primary Sources and Literature Readings

ESL

Teaching Resources
- Guided Reading and Review, pp. 3, 6, and 9
- Vocabulary, p. 12
- Reteaching, p. 13
- Guide to the Essentials, pp. 58–60
- Social Studies and Geography Skills, p. 23

Technology
- Social Studies Skills Tutor CD-ROM
- Section Reading Support Transparencies

Less Proficient Readers

Teaching Resources
- Guided Reading and Review, pp. 3, 6, and 9
- Vocabulary, p. 12
- Reteaching, p. 13
- Guide to the Essentials, pp. 58–60
- Social Studies and Geography Skills, p. 23

Technology
- Social Studies Skills Tutor CD-ROM
- Section Reading Support Transparencies

Less Proficient Writers

Teaching Resources
- Guided Reading and Review, pp. 3, 6, and 9
- Vocabulary, p. 12
- Guide to the Essentials, pp. 58–60
- Social Studies and Geography Skills, p. 23

Technology
- Social Studies Skills Tutor CD-ROM
- Section Reading Support Transparencies

DORLING KINDERSLEY

At the end of each unit, you will find information adapted from Dorling Kindersley's *Illustrated Children's Encyclopedia* that connects to the region being studied and to one of the seven content strands. In addition, your resources include Dorling Kindersley's *Atlas*, which contains valuable information about countries from around the world.

TEACHER'S EDITION INDEX

CHAPTER 14 PACING SUGGESTIONS

For 90-minute Blocks

See suggestions in the Teaching Resources Pacing Charts for Chapter 14. Use Color Transparencies 13.

Running Out of Time?

See the Guide to the Essentials, pp. 58–60.

INTERDISCIPLINARY LINKS

Middle Grades Math: Tools for Success
Course 1, Lesson 10-7, **Graphing on a Coordinate Plane**

Science Explorer
Weather and Climate, Lesson 4-1, **What Causes Climate?**

Prentice Hall Literature
Bronze, A Boy and a Man

BIBLIOGRAPHY

For the Teacher

DK Essential World Atlas. Dorling Kindersley, 2001.

Europe. National Geographic, 1991. Videocassette.

Visual Geography Series (25 European countries). Lerner, 1990–1997.

For the Student

Easy

Mason, Antony. *Around the World in Eighty Pages.* Copper Beech, 1995.

Average

Rogers, Daniel. *The Thames.* Raintree, 1993.

Smalley, Mark. *The Rhine.* Raintree, 1993.

Challenging

Buettner, Dan. *Sovietrek: A Journey by Bicycle Across Russia.* Lerner, 1994.

Ultimate Pocket Book of the World Atlas & Fact File. Dorling Kindersley, 2001.

Literature Connection

Hautzig, Esther. *Endless Steppe: Growing Up in Siberia.* Crowell/HarperCollins, 1968.

Dexter, Catherine. *Safe Return.* Candlewick, 1996.

Take It to the NET

The World Explorer companion Web site, found on **phschool.com**, offers activities for exploring geographical, historical, and cultural resources on the Internet. It also provides on-line links for key content and all Section and Chapter Assessment activities.

The **Teacher site** also provides teachers with regional data and ideas for student research and activities.

Students can use the **Student site** to find chapter-by-chapter Internet resource links and to access Self-Tests.

CHAPTER 14

Connecting to the Guiding Questions

In this chapter, students will read about the physical geography of Europe and Russia. Content in this chapter corresponds to the following Guiding Questions outlines at the beginning of the unit.

- How has the geography of Europe and Russia influenced economic, political, and cultural differences in the region?
- How can people take advantage of new technologies and still maintain links to more traditional ways of life?

Using the Map Activities

As a class, study the map and trace the route of the Trans-Siberian Railroad. Review the map and key with students before they begin the activities.

- Students should list Siberian mineral resources and where they can be found. Conclusions about where to build the new rail line should reflect an understanding of the connection between mineral resources and the need to transport them from the cities and towns where they are found.
- Proposals should include persuasive arguments about the need for better access to Siberia's natural resources.

Heterogeneous Groups

The following activities are suitable for heterogeneous groups.

Critical Thinking

Recognizing Cause and Effect, p. 263

Interdisciplinary Connections

Language Arts, p. 267

eTeach

Be sure to check out this month's discussion with a Master Teacher. Go to **phschool.com**.

CHAPTER 14

EUROPE AND RUSSIA: Physical Geography

SECTION 1
Physical Features

SECTION 2
Humans and the Physical Environment

SECTION 3
Geographic Factors and Natural Resources

Trans-Siberian Railroad

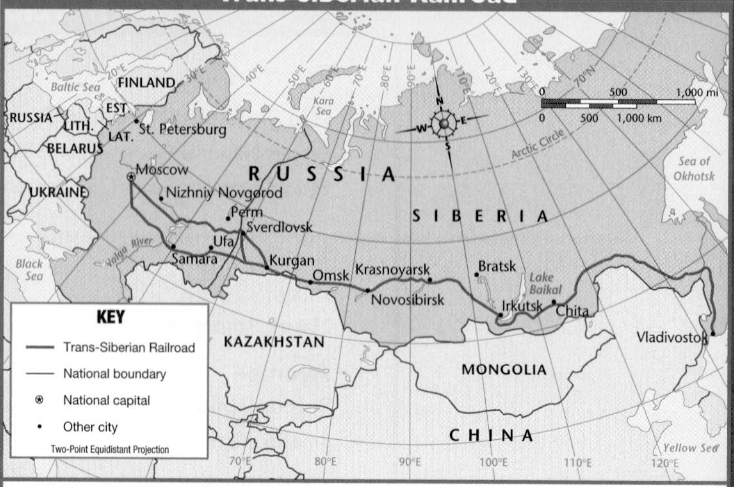

USING MAPS

This map shows the route of the Trans-Siberian Railroad, completed in 1916. The route is thousands of miles long, but it covers only a part of Siberia, which has many natural resources but few transportation routes. An addition to the rail line would make it easier to transport some of the region's many natural resources to other parts of Russia.

Planning a New Railroad Line

Look up Russia and Siberia in an encyclopedia. Make a list of Siberian mineral resources and where each can be found. Using this list, and other maps of Siberia, decide where you think a new rail line should run. Write down a list of cities and towns the route might pass through, and then draw a map showing both the old route and the new route.

Writing a Proposal

Write a proposal to persuade the Russian government to build a new rail line in Siberia. Start with a brief history of the Trans-Siberian Railroad. Then, tell where the new rail line will run, what purpose it will serve, and how the project will be paid for.

260 UNIT 4 EUROPE AND RUSSIA

Resource Directory

Teaching Resources

Primary Sources and Literature Readings extend content with a selection related to the concepts in this chapter.

Other Print Resources

DK Atlas

Technology

Journey Over Europe and Russia, from the World Video Explorer, introduces students to the major landforms of Europe and Russia.

The Influence of Geography, from the World Video Explorer, enhances understanding of the geographic factors that have influenced population distribution and land use in Europe and Russia.

Student Edition on Audio CD, Ch. 14

SECTION 1

Physical Features

BEFORE YOU READ

READING FOCUS

1. What are the main physical features of Europe and Russia?
2. How do the rivers of Europe and Russia create transportation corridors throughout the continent?
3. How do the physical processes of the ocean affect the continent of Europe?

KEY TERMS

plateau
tributary
navigable
peninsula

KEY PLACES

Eurasia
Europe
Russia
Ural Mountains
Siberia

MAIN IDEA

The physical features of the regions that make up Europe and Russia determine land use, population density, and transportation corridors.

NOTE TAKING

Copy the chart below. As you read the section fill in the chart with information about the physical features of Europe and Russia.

Region	Location	Features
Northwestern Highlands		
Plains and Uplands		

Setting the Scene

Eurasia is the world's largest landmass. It is made up of the continents of **Europe** and Asia and much of it lies in the northern latitudes. There the climate is colder and the growing season is shorter than in countries farther south.

Look at the map of Europe and Russia in the Activity Atlas on page 256. The continent of Europe is made up of 48 different countries and each country is about the size of an average state in the U.S. Included on the European continent is part of **Russia,** the largest country in the world. Beyond the **Ural** (YOOR uhl) **Mountains** that mark the boundary between Europe and Asia, the Russian region of **Siberia** (sy BIHR ee uh) extends for thousands of miles.

The Physical Features of Europe and Russia

Europe has four major land regions: The Northwestern Highlands, the North European Plain, the Central Uplands, and the Alpine Mountain System.

Far to the North

CULTURE This small church is located in the Scottish Highlands, which are in the Northwestern Highlands region. **Critical Thinking** What role might this small church play in its rural community?

Resource Directory

Teaching Resources

Classroom Manager in the Unit 4 Teaching Resources, p. 2

Guided Reading and Review in the Unit 4 Teaching Resources, p. 3

Guide to the Essentials, p. 58

Technology

Section Reading Support Transparencies

SECTION 1

Lesson Objectives

1. Identify the main physical features of Europe and Russia.
2. Explain how the rivers of Europe and Russia create transportation corridors throughout the continent.
3. Explain how the physical processes of the ocean affect the continent of Europe.

Lesson Plan

1 Engage

Warm-Up Activity

List these physical features on the chalkboard: *hot desert, tall mountain, marshy plain, jagged coastline,* and *rocky plateau.* For each feature, have students name a contrasting feature—cold tundra, coastal lowlands, and so on. Explain that the lands of Europe and Russia contain many of the features in both lists. Ask students to make a generalization about the physical features of Europe and Russia. (Europe and Russia have varied physical features.)

Activating Prior Knowledge

Ask students to compare the region where they live to Europe and Russia. Have them identify two physical features from their region that are also found in Europe and Russia and two that are not.

Answers to...

CRITICAL THINKING

This might be the main gathering place for social events, festivals, community meetings, and for passing along news and information, as well as a place of worship.

Lesson Plan continued

2 Explore

As they read the section, have students consider challenges the physical geography of Europe and Russia may present to the region's inhabitants. Invite volunteers to contribute their thoughts to a chalkboard list. Then, explore the reasons for each challenge, asking students to explain their thinking.

3 Teach

Have students record key information about the geographic patterns and processes of Europe and Russia in a four-column chart labeled *Region, Location, Features, Notes.* Students can compare the information they recorded and discuss their ideas about what they learned.

Questions for Discussion

GEOGRAPHY **How have the people in the Central Uplands adapted to their environment?**

The soil is not good for farming, so they raise goats and sheep instead.

GEOGRAPHY **What caused the bays, inlets, and harbors of Europe and Russia?**

Ocean waves have battered the coastline for millions of years, creating these bays, inlets, and harbors.

Europe: Land Regions

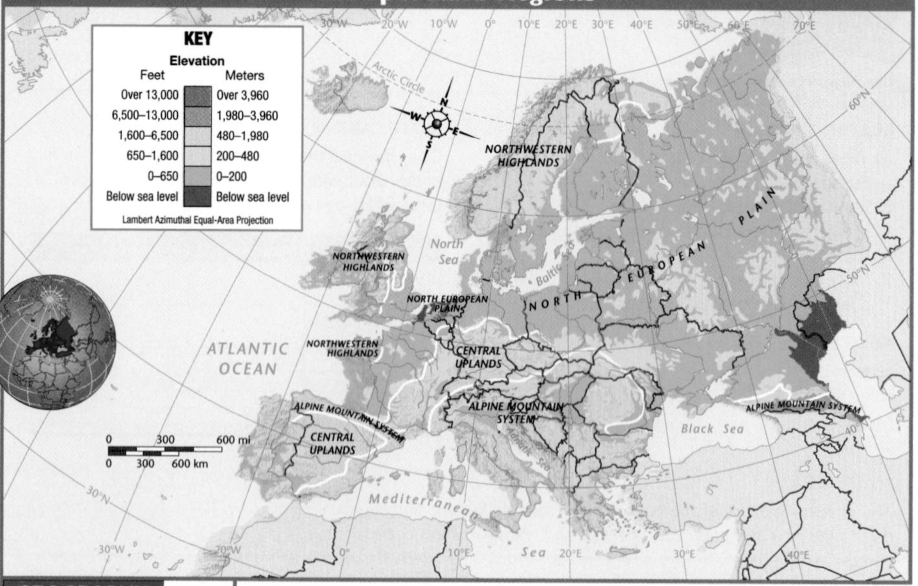

GEOGRAPHY
This map shows the four major land regions of Europe. **Map Study** Which of the four land regions covers the greatest area? Where in Europe can you find land that is below sea level?

The Northwestern Highlands

The ancient mountains of the Northwestern Highlands are found in the northern parts of France, Great Britain, and Scandinavia. These have been eroded by centuries of wind and weather. Few people live here, where the climate is severe, the soil is thin, and the farming is poor.

Plains and Uplands

The North European Plain extends from Southern England and France to the foot of the Ural Mountains in Russia. This is a region of rich soil, productive farmland, and a high population density, which is the average number of people living in an area.

The Central Uplands stretch across the center of southern Europe. This region is made up of mountains and **plateaus** (pla TOHZ), which are large raised areas of level land. The soil in this region is too rocky for farming, but the land is rich in minerals and is good for grazing goats and sheep.

Alpine Mountain System

The Alpine Mountain System is a series of high mountain ranges that cross Europe from Spain to the Balkans and extend to Georgia east

SKILLS MINI LESSON

Previewing

To **introduce** the skill, tell students that previewing helps readers know what to expect in their reading. Outline the strategy on the chalkboard: *1) Scan section titles and subheads; 2) Look at illustrations; 3) Read opening and closing paragraphs; 4) Develop predictions.* Have students **practice** the skill by previewing Section 1. Invite volunteers to record their findings for each step listed on the chalkboard outline. Then challenge students to **apply** their previewing skills to Sections 2 and 3.

Answers to...

MAP STUDY

North European Plain; on the western coast of the Black Sea and the northern coast of Belgium and the Netherlands

of the Black Sea. The Alps in Switzerland (SWIT sur lund) are a spectacular part of this region, and their majestic, snow-capped peaks are a favorite vacation spot for hikers and skiers. This region is home to families who work small farms in the valleys and meadows high in the mountains.

Siberia

Beyond the Ural Mountains lies a vast, low, marshy expanse called the West Siberian Plain. It covers more than a million square miles (2.58 million sq. km). It is known for its long, cold winters, harsh living conditions, and small, scattered population. At the eastern edge of the plain, the Central Siberian Plateau slopes upward. The land continues to rise, forming the East Siberian Uplands. This is a desolate region of rugged mountains, stark plateaus, and more than twenty active volcanoes.

ECONOMICS

These farm workers in Siberia are havesting strawberries. The best farming country in Siberia lies in the region's southwestern section. Here, in addition to strawberries, farm workers harvest wheat, oats, and rye. **Critical Thinking** Based on this photograph, what do you think a job harvesting strawberries would be like?

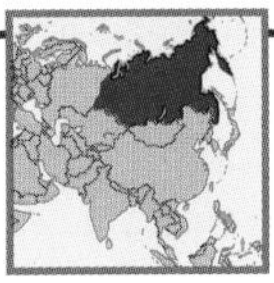

River Resources and Transportation Corridors

The highlands of Europe and Russia are the source for many important rivers. High in the Swiss Alps, melting glaciers form two streams that combine to become the Rhine (RYN) River. The Rhine winds for 865 miles (1,391 km) through forests and plains and past castles, factories, and cities before it flows into the North Sea. The Rhine and its canals and **tributaries** (TRIB yoo tehr eez), which are the smaller rivers and streams that connect to the main channel, form a network of transportation corridors that reach every part of Western Europe.

The Volga (VAHL guh) River is the longest river on the continent of Europe. It flows for 2,291 miles (3,687 km) through western Russia and empties into the Caspian Sea. Its tributaries and canals link the Volga to the Arctic Ocean and the Baltic Sea. However, the river is frozen for three months of the year, so during the winter, the Volga and many other rivers of Russia are not **navigable** (NAV ih guh bul), which means ships cannot travel on them.

The Danube (DAN yoob) River begins in the mountains of Germany and flows through eight countries before it empties into the Black Sea. It is the second longest river in Europe, and it is navigable year round. These factors make it an important transportation corridor for trade and travel. Ships from the Mediterranean Sea can travel up the Danube to ports in Romania. From there, the cargo can be transferred to smaller boats that can continue up the river.

Resource Directory

Teaching Resources

Outline Maps Western Europe, p. 18; Central Europe, p. 20; Mediterranean Europe, p. 21; Eastern Europe, pp. 22–23; Poland, p. 24; Northern Eurasia, pp. 25–26; Russia, p. 27

4 Assess/Reteach

See the answers to the Section 1 Assessment. If you wish, assess students' charts and notes.

Acceptable efforts include information about features of the four geographic regions of Europe and Russia.

Commendable efforts include details about specific locations and geographic patterns.

Outstanding efforts show an understanding of how the geographic patterns and processes affect the people and their way of life in each region.

ACTIVITY

Critical Thinking

Recognizing Cause and Effect
Suitable as an individual activity. Ask students why good harbors are important to a region's economy. Have students photocopy or draw pictures showing the cause-and-effect relationship between harbors and local economies and write captions.

Visual/Spatial

GEOGRAPHY

Barges on the Rhine

The Zoëtmulder family makes its living bringing goods to and from the Rhine Delta in the Netherlands and points upriver. The Zoëtmulders transport cargo such as sand, aluminum, coal, and farm crops on their 125-foot barge. A newer, larger barge will enable the Zoëtmulders to travel farther upriver to Basel, Switzerland— a journey of about 600 miles. The trip upriver will take about seven days. Currents will shorten the return trip to only five days.

Answers to...

CRITICAL THINKING

Harvesting strawberries would be hard work because the workers spend long hours bent over while picking the berries near the ground.

CHAPTER 14 EUROPE AND RUSSIA: PHYSICAL GEOGRAPHY 263

SECTION I ASSESSMENT

AFTER YOU READ

1. (a) the continents of Europe and Asia (b) a small continent with 48 countries (c) the largest country in the world (d) mountain range that marks the boundary between Europe and Asia (e) the Asian part of Russia
2. (a) a large, raised area of level land (b) river or stream that connects to a larger river (c) clear enough for ships to travel (d) a body of land nearly surrounded by water
3. The North European Plain covers a large area from southern England to the Ural Mountains, and it has rich soil and productive farms.
4. The Danube is navigable year round. Ships from the Mediterranean can travel up the Danube to ports in Romania.
5. Warm water from the Gulf Stream joins the North Atlantic Current.
6. Responses will vary. Students should discuss the change from fertile soil, long growing season, and large, level tracts of land for growing crops in the North European Plain compared with the short growing season and poorer soil in the small mountain valleys.
7. Responses will vary. Students should explore their feelings about population density and how it affects daily life and culture, to assess which location they would prefer to call home.
8. Encourage students to read their descriptions to the class.

Ocean Patterns and Processes

The continent of Europe forms a **peninsula** (puh NIN suh luh), a body of land nearly surrounded by water. It juts into the Atlantic Ocean and is bordered by the Mediterranean Sea, the North Sea, and the Norwegian Sea. The entire continent is affected by all of this water. The warm ocean current called the Gulf Stream begins in the Gulf of Mexico and flows northeast to join the North Atlantic Current that flows into the Arctic Ocean. The warm water keeps the northern coastlines of Great Britain and Norway from freezing in the winter, even if the land is covered in ice and snow.

Moist, warm air blows inland from the coast, sweeping across the North European Plain. West of the mountains, rainfall is heavy. When the moist air rises over the mountains, it cools and falls as snow along the ridges of the Alpine Mountain System. Not much moisture makes it over to the east side of the mountains, so this area is hotter and dryer.

The waves that have battered the coastline for millions of years, have formed bays, inlets, coves, and harbors. Look at the maps in the Activity Atlas on pages 255–256 to see how these natural features affect the climate and influence where people live.

SECTION I ASSESSMENT

AFTER YOU READ

RECALL

1. Identify: (a) Eurasia, (b) Europe, (c) Russia, (d) Ural Mountains, (e) Siberia
2. Define: (a) plateau, (b) tributary, (c) navigable, (d) peninsula

COMPREHENSION

3. Why does the North European Plain have the highest population density of all the major land regions?
4. What makes the Danube River a major transportation corridor?
5. What keeps the harbors of Northern England and Norway from freezing in the winter?

CRITICAL THINKING AND WRITING

6. **Exploring the Main Idea** Review the Main Idea statement at the beginning of this section. Write a paragraph to describe how your life would change if you moved from a farm in the North European Plain to a farm in the Alpine Mountain System.
7. **Comparing and Contrasting** Write a paragraph comparing life at a port city on the Rhine to life in a remote village in the Scottish highlands. In which place would you rather live? Give reasons for your answer.

ACTIVITY

Take It to the NET

8. **Creating a Map of Siberia** The physical geography of Siberia is varied and beautiful. Imagine that you are walking along the routes described on the Web site. Write a detailed account of your experience, including geographical features, climate, and vegetation. Visit the World Explorer: People, Places, and Cultures section of **phschool.com** for help in completing this activity.

Resource Directory

Teaching Resources

Section Quiz in the Unit 4 Teaching Resources, p. 4

SECTION 2

Humans and the Physical Environment

BEFORE YOU READ

READING FOCUS

1. How do people adapt to climate conditions in different parts of Europe and Russia?
2. How have people learned to modify and use the physical environment and natural vegetation of Europe and Russia?

KEY TERMS

deciduous
coniferous
taiga
prairies
steppe
tundra
permafrost

KEY PLACES

Barcelona
Irkutsk
Norway
Iceland

NOTE TAKING

Copy the concept web below. As you read the section fill in the concept web with information about the natural vegetation of Europe and Russia.

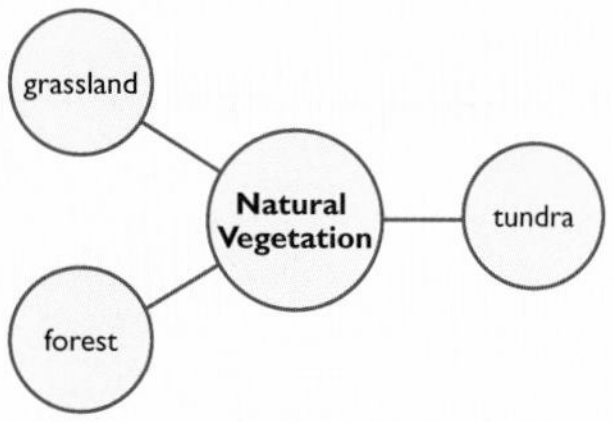

MAIN IDEA

People find ways to adapt to the climate and to modify the natural vegetation where they live.

Setting the Scene

It is February in **Barcelona** (bar suh LOH nuh), Spain. Twelve-year-old Isabella wakes up to a warm, sunny Saturday morning. It is 65°F (18°C)—the perfect day for a bike ride.

At that same moment, it is late afternoon in **Irkutsk** (ihr KOOTSK), a city in Southern Siberia. It is a clear, cold, sunny day. The temperature is –15°F (–26°C). Alexy is skiing home after a visit with his grandmother.

In Barcelona, which is located on the Mediterranean Sea, the winters are mild and rainy, while the summers are hot and dry. In Siberia, snow covers the ground for six months of the year. Winters are severe, with temperatures falling to –50°F (–46°C). Summers are cool and short. The temperature on a pleasant summer day in Irkutsk is the same as the temperature on a chilly winter day in Barcelona.

Skiing in Siberia

GEOGRAPHY In areas such as Siberia, where winters are long and snow covers the ground for six months of the year, cross-country skiing is an efficient way to get from place to place. **Critical Thinking** What other forms of transportation have people developed in response to their climate or physical environment?

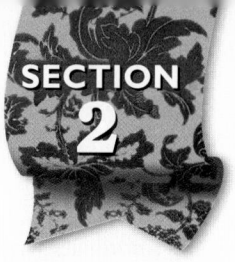

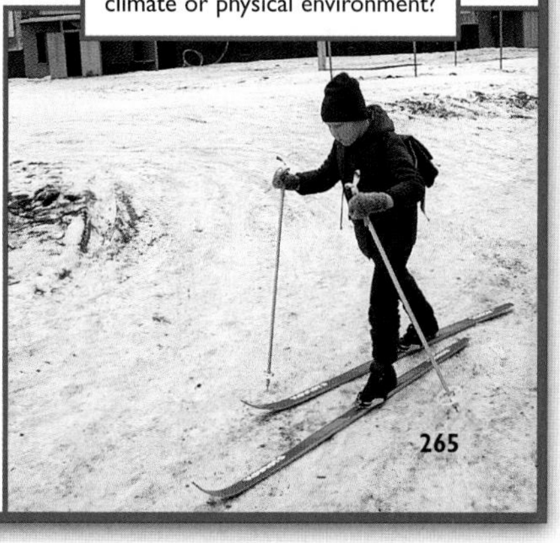

Humans Adapt to the Physical Environment

In Section 1, you read about how the ocean affects climate. Much of northwestern Europe, including the coast of **Nor-**

265

Resource Directory

Teaching Resources

Classroom Manager in the Unit 4 Teaching Resources, p. 5

Guided Reading and Review in the Unit 4 Teaching Resources, p. 6

Guide to the Essentials, p. 59

Technology

Section Reading Support Transparencies

SECTION 2

Lesson Objectives

1. Describe how people adapt to the climate conditions in different parts of Europe and Russia.
2. Explain how people have modified the physical environment of Europe and Russia.

Lesson Plan

1 Engage

Warm-Up Activity

Show students photographs of natural and human-made settings in Europe and Russia. Ask students to list both human-made and natural elements from the images. Urge students to respond to questions such as *What people, animals, buildings, and landforms are present? What does the landscape look like? What are the people doing?*

Activating Prior Knowledge

Ask students how the climate where they live affects clothing, architecture, industry, and recreation. Discuss activities that can and cannot be enjoyed during the year.

2 Explore

Direct students to read the text. Have them look for answers to these questions: How are climate and vegetation regions related? Why do wind and water currents change climate so dramatically? Where in Europe and Russia might cities be located?

Answers to...

CRITICAL THINKING

Answers may include sleds and snowshoes for northern climates; boats and barges for river and canal travel; bicycles, scooters, subways, and buses for busy urban centers.

Lesson Plan continued

3 Teach

Have students write a paragraph identifying the factors that influence climate and vegetation and explaining the cause-and-effect relationship between the factors. Students may use specific examples from the text if these support the cause-and-effect relationship.

Questions for Discussion

GEOGRAPHY How have Europeans modified their physical environment?

They have modified the environment by creating farmland and building cities.

GEOGRAPHY How have people in Iceland, Norway, and northern Russia adapted to their physical environment?

They found ways to raise food and build shelters that are adapted to the environment.

4 Assess/Reteach

See the answers to the Section 2 Assessment. Students' paragraphs may also provide a key to assessment.

Acceptable paragraphs correctly identify causes and effects.

Commendable paragraphs use examples from the text.

Outstanding paragraphs show an understanding of the complex relationship between location relative to large bodies of water, elevation, climate, and vegetation.

CULTURE

Summer Homes

Each summer, millions of Russians travel to their *dacha*, or "summer home." A dacha may be on a lakeshore, in a small wood, or set in a field. Many have gardens to take advantage of the milder climate.

Europe: Natural Vegetation

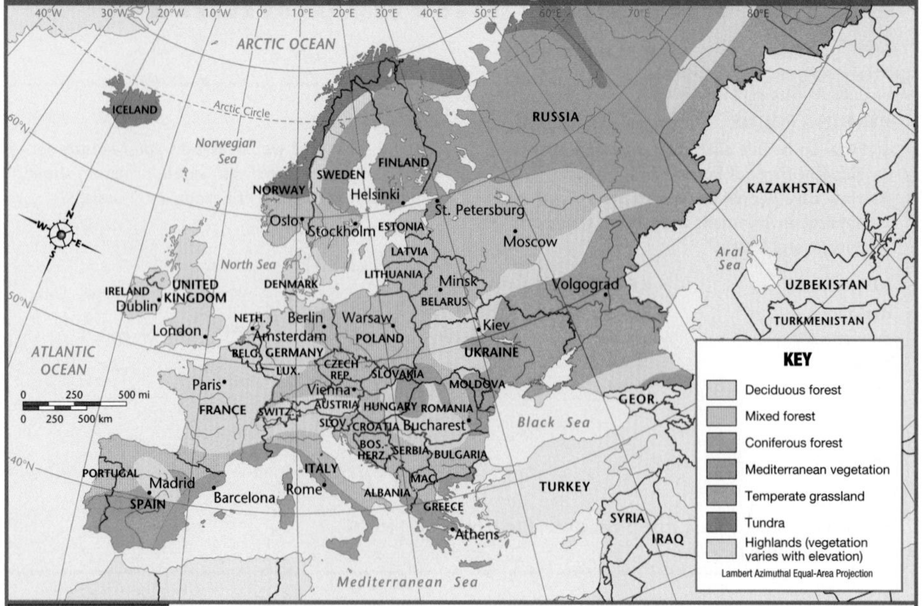

GEOGRAPHY Much of Europe and Russia was once covered with forests. **Map Study** What happens to the natural vegetation in this region as you move northward?

way and the southern tip of **Iceland,** has a marine west coast climate and is rainy year round.

The countries that ring the Mediterranean have a climate similar to that of Barcelona. Much of this region is in the rain shadow of the mountains of the Alpine Mountain System. A rain shadow is an area on the dry, sheltered side of a mountain that receives little rainfall.

Most of Eastern Europe is in the humid continental region. As you travel inland, you move out of the range of the warm, moist air blowing in from the Atlantic. People living here are prepared for longer, colder winters and very hot summers.

Few people live in the climate regions of the subarctic and tundra areas of Europe and Asia because during the long, dark winters, temperatures stay well below zero. In the summer, temperatures do not get much above freezing.

Modifying the Physical Environment

Temperature, rainfall, altitude, and latitude are factors that determine the natural vegetation, or plant life, of an area. Compare the vegetation map to the climate and landform maps you have seen.

Answers to...

MAP STUDY

The vegetation gets less diverse as you move northward, due to the poorer soil and colder climate. In the tundra, only moss and small grasses grow during the short season.

Resource Directory

Teaching Resources

Social Studies and Geography Skills, Reading a Natural Vegetation Map, p. 23

Technology

Color Transparencies 13 Forest Vegetation Regions Map

266 UNIT 4 EUROPE AND RUSSIA

Forests and Grasslands

Deciduous (duh SID joo us) forests, made up of trees that lose their leaves, once covered most of Europe. Over many years, people cleared the trees to create farmland and build cities. In Northern Europe and in Russia, there are large **coniferous** (koh NIF ur us) forests, which have trees with cones that carry and protect the seeds. In Russia, the **taiga** (TY guh), as this forested region is called, covers more than 4 million square miles (6.4 million sq km). The soil is not so good for farming, and the growing season is short.

The central and southern parts of the North European Plain were once covered with grasslands called **prairies.** People created farmland in this region. In Russia, the grasslands are called **steppes.** The fertile, black soil is good for farming.

Tundra

The **tundra** is a treeless plain where only grasses and mosses grow. Here, the ground is **permafrost,** or permanently frozen soil, and there is only a very short growing season. In Iceland, Norway, and northern Russia, the people have had to find ways to raise food and construct shelters without the natural resources that forests provide.

The Frozen Tundra

GEOGRAPHY The tundra stretches from northern Europe into northern Russia. The shapes visible on the ground here are caused by upheavals in permafrost. **Critical Thinking** What are some ways that people living here might raise food and construct shelters in the absence of natural resources?

SECTION 2 ASSESSMENT

AFTER YOU READ

RECALL

1. Identify: (a) Barcelona, (b) Irkutsk, (c) Norway, (d) Iceland
2. Define: (a) deciduous, (b) coniferous, (c) taiga, (d) prairie, (e) steppe, (f) tundra, (g) permafrost

COMPREHENSION

3. What are the advantages of living in the rain shadow of the Alps?
4. What makes the taiga an important resource for people living in Siberia?

CRITICAL THINKING AND WRITING

5. **Exploring the Main Idea** Review the Main Idea statement at the beginning of this section. Then, imagine that you are either Isabella or Alexy and write a letter describing your day. Explain how you stayed comfortable and what you saw when you were out.
6. **Drawing Conclusions** Considering the difficulties posed by the physical environment of the tundra, why do you think people choose to live there?

ACTIVITY

7. **Design a House** Design a house for life in the French countryside and for the tundra of Norway. Use materials found in each region. How will this house protect you from the climate? Include illustrations that detail your design ideas and construction methods.

Resource Directory

Teaching Resources

Section Quiz in the Unit 4 Teaching Resources, p. 7

Answers to...

CRITICAL THINKING

Accept all reasonable responses. Make sure students support their answers with details.

ACTIVITY

Interdisciplinary Connections

Language Arts Tell students that the forest is a common setting for fairy tales, such as "Hansel and Gretel" and "Little Red Riding Hood." Prompt students to write their own fairy tales set in the Black Forest of Germany. Urge them to use descriptive language to capture the forest setting.

Verbal/Linguistic

SECTION 2 ASSESSMENT

AFTER YOU READ

1. (a) a city in Spain with a Mediterranean climate (b) a city in Southern Siberia with a subarctic climate (c) a Scandinavian country on the North Sea (d) an island nation near the Arctic Circle
2. (a) trees that lose their leaves (b) cone-bearing trees (c) huge forested area in Russia (d) grassland (e) Russian grassland (f) treeless plain where the ground is permafrost (g) permanently frozen soil
3. The soil is good and the climate is dryer than on the western side of the mountains.
4. The timber from the taiga can be used for fuel, for construction, and for trade.
5. Responses will vary. Students should describe activities and clothing that are appropriate for the climate and geographical area they are writing about.
6. Not many people choose to live in the tundra. Those who do must like cold weather and may appreciate the wide open spaces and absence of city noise and pollution.
7. Students may want to choose one of each design and actually construct a scale model.

SECTION 3

Lesson Objectives

1. Explain where fossil fuels come from and how they benefit Europe and Russia.
2. Explain how water resources are used in Europe and Russia.
3. Describe the geographic features that contribute to the fertile soil of Europe and Ukraine.

Lesson Plan

1 Engage

Warm-Up Activity

Show students a variety of (pre-Euro) coins and currency issued by European countries and Russia. Point out that many of the coins' features relate to the nation's natural resources, vegetation, or wildlife. Challenge students to identify a feature and hypothesize about the coin's place of origin.

Activating Prior Knowledge

Have students define the term *natural resource.* Talk about sources such as almanacs, newspapers, and the Internet in which students can learn about the natural resources of a particular country.

Answers to...

CRITICAL THINKING

Yes. You have to build the oil rig and bring everything you need from far away. You may have to pay people high salaries to do this dangerous work far from home.

SECTION 3

Geographic Factors and Natural Resources

BEFORE YOU READ

READING FOCUS

1. Where do fossil fuels come from and how do they benefit Europe and Russia?
2. How are water resources used in Europe and Russia?
3. What geographic features contribute to the fertile soil of Europe and Ukraine?

KEY TERMS

fossil fuels
nonrenewable resources
turbine
hydroelectric power
loess

KEY PLACES

North Sea
Ruhr Valley
Silesia
Ukraine

MAIN IDEA

Europe and Russia are rich in both renewable and nonrenewable natural resources.

NOTE TAKING

Copy the Venn diagram below. As you read the section fill in the diagram with information about the natural resources of Europe and Russia.

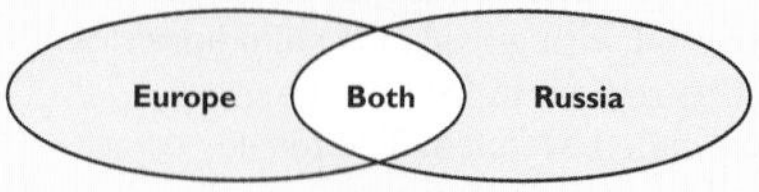

Off-Shore Oil Rigs

ECONOMICS Great Britain, Norway, and other nations around the North Sea depend on the oil and natural gas drilled from underwater petroleum deposits. **Critical Thinking** Do you think it is expensive to drill for oil in the North Sea? Why?

Setting the Scene

Europe is a wealthy region and a world leader in economic development. Part of this wealth and success comes from Europe's rich supply of natural resources, such as fertile soil, water, and fuels. Russia has a wide variety of resources, but its harsh climate, frozen rivers, and huge transportation distances have made it difficult to turn these resources into wealth.

Physical Processes that Produce Fossil Fuels

Fossil fuels in the form of oil, natural gas, and coal provide energy for industries. They are called fossil fuels because they are formed over millions of years from the remains of ancient animals and plants. Fossil fuels are **nonrenewable resources;** once they are used up, they are gone.

Millions of years ago, marine plants and animals called plankton died and settled on the ocean floor. Over the years, the plankton was

Resource Directory

Teaching Resources

Classroom Manager in the Unit 4 Teaching Resources, p. 8

Guided Reading and Review in the Unit 4 Teaching Resources, p. 9

Guide to the Essentials, p. 60

Technology

Section Reading Support Transparencies

Europe and Russia: Natural Resources

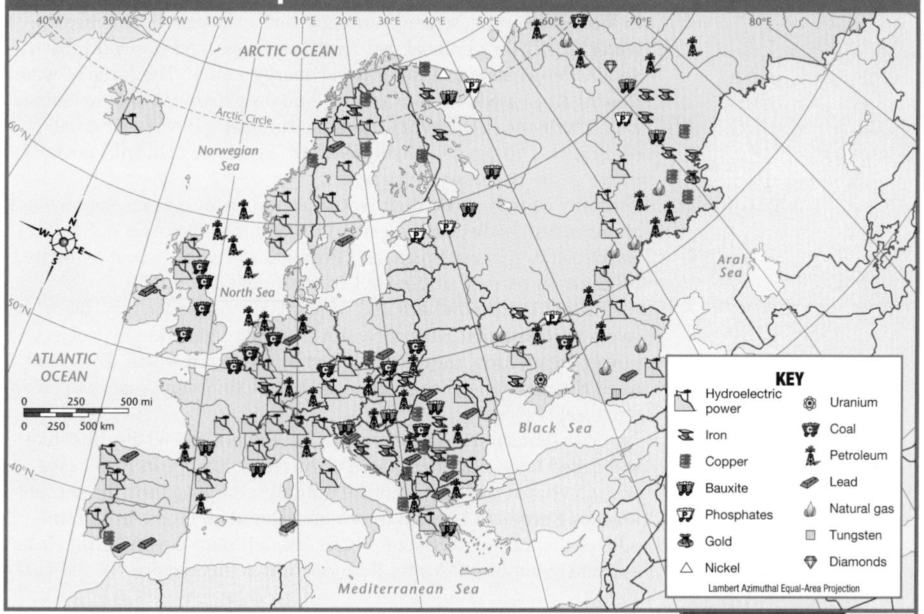

GEOGRAPHY Europe and Russia are rich in natural resources that are important for the development and strength of the economy of the region. **Map Study** How does the distribution of natural resources match the major population centers of Europe?

covered with mud and sand. The weight of this material gradually changed the plankton into oil trapped inside of porous rock. Oil drilling equipment cuts through the rock and removes the oil, which is called crude oil. Crude oil is then cleaned to make refined oil products that are used to run cars and heat homes.

There are oil and gas deposits under the ocean floor in the **North Sea** and Siberia. However, these resources in remote parts of Russia are thousands of miles from the country's industrial centers. They must be transported by pipeline.

Coal is made from ancient plant and animal materials that decay to form peat. Over millions of years, the pressure of materials heaped on top of peat deposits gradually changed the peat into brown coal. Increased pressure changed the brown coal into what is called soft coal that is used in industries worldwide.

Coal is mined in Great Britain; the **Ruhr Valley** of Germany; the industrial center called **Silesia** (sy LEE shuh), where Poland, the Czech (chek) Republic, and Germany come together; **Ukraine** (yoo KRAYN); and Russia, which has one-third of the world's coal reserves.

Russia also has great reserves of iron ore, which is used to make steel. Most of these mineral deposits are west of the Ural Mountains, which is where Russia's industrial centers are located.

AS YOU READ

Monitor Your Reading What kinds of natural resources have you used so far today?

SKILLS MINI LESSON

Using Distribution Maps

To **introduce** the skill, direct students' attention to the Europe and Russia: Natural Resources map. Explain that the map shows which resources can be found in which regions of Europe and Russia. Help students **practice** the skill by asking them to describe the information contained in the map key. Have them explain how they can use the key to read the map. Then have students **apply** the skill by identifing the following using the map: copper-mining regions, regions with hydroelectric power, diamond-producing regions.

2 Explore

After they read the section text, ask students to answer these questions: Why has Russia not fully developed its natural resources? What important resources have helped Europe's industries to grow?

3 Teach

Direct students to create a book cover about Europe and Russia. Covers should show data about the natural resources of Europe on one side and of Russia on the other. Students may add summarizing statements across the bottom.

Questions for Discussion

GEOGRAPHY Why are most large cities in Europe located near water?

People need water for drinking, washing, and cooking, for irrigating crops, for transporting goods, and as an energy resource.

GEOGRAPHY How is coal produced?

Ancient plants and animals decay to form peat. Over millions of years, the pressure on the peat changes it into brown coal. More pressure turns brown coal into the coal we use.

4 Assess/Reteach

See the answers to the Section 3 Assessment. You may also assess students' book covers.

Acceptable covers contain factual information about Europe and Russia.

Commendable covers creatively present visual images and text.

Outstanding covers describe differences and similarities of the regions.

Answers to...

MAP STUDY

Most areas that are rich in resources have the higher population densities.

AS YOU READ

Answers will vary.

ECONOMICS

Pipelines

The countries of Europe have natural gas reserves in the North Sea and buy natural gas from other nations, including Russia, which supplies 15 percent of Europe's natural gas. Most of it comes by pipeline from Siberia.

SECTION 3 ASSESSMENT

AFTER YOU READ

1. (a) the sea east of Great Britain, south of Scandinavia, and northwest of of Europe (b) German river valley with large coal deposits (c) the place where Poland, the Czech Republic, and Germany come together; region with large coal deposits (d) a large country in Eastern Europe with rich resources, including fertile soil
2. (a) fuels—coal, oil, and natural gas—that come from remains of ancient plants and animals (b) resources that are gone once they are used up (c) machines that spin to generate electricity (d) electricity generated by water (e) rich, dustlike soil
3. Russia has a hard time tapping into reserves and transporting oil and coal because of the harsh climate and long distances.
4. Most of the rivers of Russia are frozen; Europe's main rivers are located where dams can easily be built for hydroelectric power.
5. The winds carry loess and deposit it over the North European Plain.
6. Responses will vary. Students should consider population of Europe, size of the countries, natural barriers, and renewable and nonrenewable resources.
7. Responses will vary. Students should describe how Russia's resources can be developed and transported for distribution and for trade.
8. Students can write a "private" journal entry or a letter home to friends and/or family.

Geographic Processes

In Western Europe, water is an important resource. People use the water supply for personal use, irrigating crops, and transporting goods. People also use water as an energy source. The force of water flowing from a waterfall or from a dam on a river can spin machines called **turbines** (TUR bynz). Spinning turbines generate, or create, electricity. This is called **hydroelectric** (hy dro ee LEK trik) **power**; *hydro* is the Greek word for water.

Many countries use their water resources for power. Norway gets almost all of its electric power from water, and factories in Sweden, Switzerland, Austria, Spain, and Portugal all run on power generated by dams on rivers that flow out of the mountains.

Except in the southern and western part of the country, the frozen rivers in Russia and Siberia cannot be used to generate hydroelectric power. In addition, they are polluted by industrial waste. These polluted rivers will need to be restored before they can be developed as a natural resource.

Over thousands of years, winds have deposited fertile, dust-like soil called **loess** (LOH ess) across the North European Plain. This soil, combined with the plentiful rainfall and a long growing season, enables European farmers to produce abundant crops. In Ukraine, a black soil called *chernozem* (CHEHR nuh zem) is very fertile. It is extremely important for food production in this region.

SECTION 3 ASSESSMENT

AFTER YOU READ

RECALL

1. Identify: (a) North Sea, (b) Ruhr Valley, (c) Silesia, (d) Ukraine
2. Define: (a) fossil fuels, (b) nonrenewable resources, (c) turbine, (d) hydroelectric power, (e) loess

COMPREHENSION

3. Why are fossil fuels more beneficial to the economy of Europe than to the economy of Russia?
4. What prevents hydroelectric power from being developed in Russia compared to Europe?
5. How do the warm, moist winds blowing off the Atlantic Ocean contribute to the fertile soil of Europe?

CRITICAL THINKING AND WRITING

6. **Exploring the Main Idea** Review the Main Idea statement at the beginning of this section. Then, write a paragraph identifying the most important natural resource for Europe and for Russia. Give reasons for your ideas.
7. **Making Predictions** What will Russia's major natural resource be in twenty years? Write a paragraph describing the development of the resource and tell how it will affect the country's economy.

ACTIVITY

8. **Writing a Journal** Imagine that you are on an oil rig in the North Sea. Write a journal entry describing your important, dangerous work on the high seas.

Resource Directory

Teaching Resources

Section Quiz in the Unit 4 Teaching Resources, p. 10

Chapter Summary in the Unit 4 Teaching Resources, p. 11

Vocabulary in the Unit 4 Teaching Resources, p. 12

Reteaching in the Unit 4 Teaching Resources, p. 13

Enrichment in the Unit 4 Teaching Resources, p. 14

Critical Thinking in the Unit 4 Teaching Resources, p. 15

SKILLS FOR LIFE

Interpreting Graphs

Average Temperature in Irkutsk, Russia

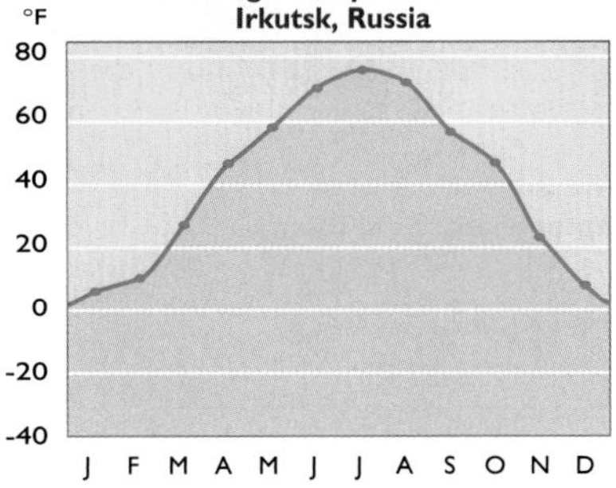

Oil Production, 2000

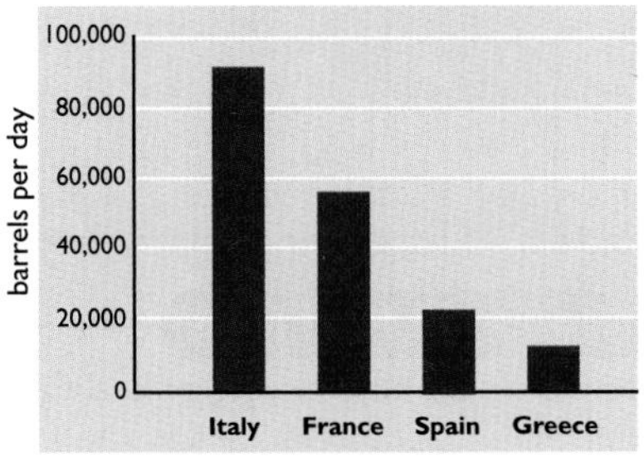

Electricity Generation in Russia

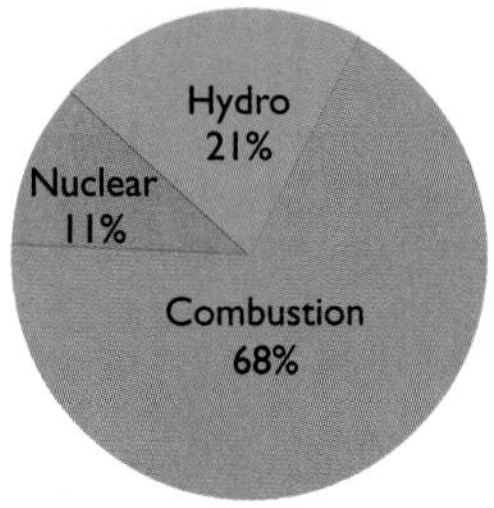

Learn the Skill

Graphs are helpful because they organize information in a simple, easy-to-read way. One of the most common types of graph is the line graph. A line graph shows how data values change over time.

Bar graphs use bars to show amounts. The length of the bar tells you the number value it represents.

Circle graphs use slices of the circle (like a pie) to show proportion, or the parts of a whole. The value of the entire circle is 100 percent.

To read a graph:

A. Read the title to find out what information the graph shows.

B. Figure out what kind of graph it is. Study the three graphs on this page. Which one is a line graph? Which is a circle graph? Which is a bar graph?

C. Read the information on the graph. Read the line graph to tell which month has the hottest weather in Irkutsk, Russia. Read the bar graph to tell which country produces the most oil. Read the circle graph to tell which method is used to generate the most electricity in Russia.

Practice the Skill

Compare the three graphs on this page. How does each type of graph show the value of the data? Do you think a circle graph could be used to show yearly temperature changes? Could a line graph show oil production in different countries?

Apply the Skill

See the Chapter Review and Assessment at the end of this chapter for more questions on comparing graphs.

SKILLS FOR LIFE

Lesson Objectives

1. Compare line graphs, bar graphs, and circle graphs
2. Understand how to read line graphs, bar graphs, and circle graphs

Lesson Plan

1 Engage

Ask students to find examples of these three kinds of graphs in newspapers and magazines and tell what kind of graphs they are. Collect and display as many samples as possible.

2 Explore

Direct students to read the steps under "Learn the Skill." Stress the importance of reading the title so students know what the graph is showing. Have them practice reading the three graphs on the page by asking them questions that they can answer by studying the graphs.

3 Teach

Make sure students understand the purpose of each graph and why certain graphs are better suited for some information than others. For example, students should understand that a circle graph cannot show yearly temperature changes and that a line graph cannot show oil production in different countries.

For additional reinforcement, have students write questions that can be answered by studying the graphs. They can exchange questions with a partner to answer.

4 Assess/Reteach

Students should be able to read and interpret the graphs.

To further assess students' understanding of graphs, have them complete the "Applying Your Skills" part of the Chapter Review and Assessment at the end of the chapter.

Resource Directory

Teaching Resources

Social Studies and Geography Skills, Reading a Bar Graph, p. 51; Reading a Line Graph, p. 52; Reading a Circle Graph, p. 53

Technology

Social Studies Skills Tutor CD-ROM

Answers to...

PRACTICE THE SKILL

with a line, with four bars, with a circle; a circle graph could not show temperature changes; a line graph could not show oil production in different countries

CHAPTER 14

Review and Assessment

Creating a Chapter Summary

Student summaries will vary.

Sample summaries:

Section 2 People in Europe and Russia have had to adapt to a variety of climates and living conditions. These range from areas with fertile soil in river valleys with a mild year-round climate, to the tundra, where the climate is harsh, the ground is frozen, and the growing season is very short.

Section 3 Europe and Russia are rich in natural resources. These resources include fossil fuels, timber, hydroelectric power, and cropland.

Reviewing Key Terms

1. d **2.** e **3.** f **4.** g **5.** a **6.** b **7.** c

Reviewing the Main Ideas

1. Northwestern Highlands, North European Plain, Central Uplands, Alpine Mountain System
2. Siberia
3. Ural Mountains
4. Volga
5. mild and rain year-round
6. deciduous forest
7. Great Britain, the Ruhr Valley, Silesia
8. They are thousands of miles from the industrial centers and there are no transportation corridors.

CHAPTER 14

Review and Assessment

Creating a Chapter Summary

On a separate piece of paper, draw a diagram like this one, and include the information that summarizes the first section of the chapter. Then, fill in the remaining boxes with summaries of Sections 2 and 3.

EUROPE AND RUSSIA: PHYSICAL GEOGRAPHY

Section 1	Section 2	Section 3
Europe and Russia have four major land regions. The population density in each of these regions depends on the climate, the quality of the soil, and the access to navigable rivers.		

Reviewing Key Terms

Match the definitions in Column I with the key terms in Column II.

Column I

1. Russian grassland
2. electricity generated by water
3. rich, dust-like soil
4. rivers or streams that connect to a larger river
5. able to be used by ships
6. treeless plain where the ground is permafrost
7. fuels—coal, oil, and natural gas—that come from remains of ancient plants and animals

Column II

a. navigable
b. tundra
c. fossil fuels
d. steppe
e. hydroelectric power
f. loess
g. tributaries

Reviewing the Main Ideas

1. Identify the four major land regions of Europe. (Section 1)
2. Identify the part of Russia that is in Asia. (Section 1)
3. Name the mountain range that separates Europe and Asia. (Section 1)
4. What is the longest river on the continent of Europe? (Section 1)
5. What is a marine west coast climate? (Section 2)
6. What kind of vegetation covered most of Europe long ago? (Section 2)
7. What parts of Europe have large reserves of coal? (Section 3)
8. Why is it difficult for Russia to take advantage of its natural resources? (Section 3)

Resource Directory

Teaching Resources

Cooperative Learning Activity in the Unit 4 Teaching Resources, pp. 107–109

Chapter Tests Forms A and B in the Unit 4 Teaching Resources, pp. 138–143

Guide to the Essentials, Ch. 14 Test, p. 61

Map Activity

Europe and Russia

For each place listed below, write the letter from the map that shows its location.

1. Europe
2. Ural Mountains
3. Alps
4. Siberia
5. Volga River
6. North Sea

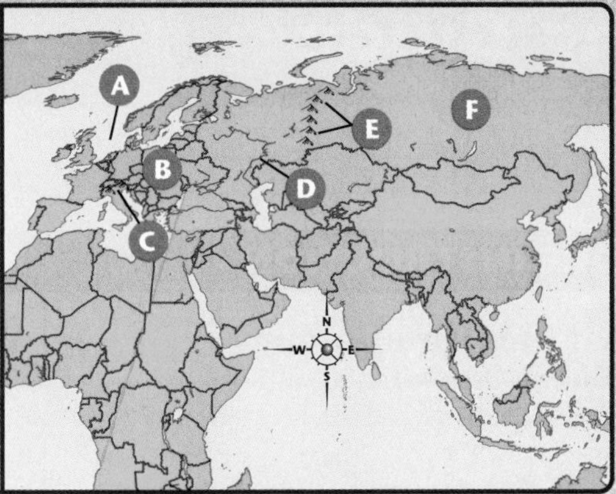

Take It to the NET

Enrichment For more map activities using geography skills, visit the social studies section of **phschool.com.**

Writing Activity

1. Using Primary Sources Find out more about one of the land regions of Europe or the expanse of Siberia. Visit your school or local library and use primary sources such as newspaper and magazine articles to find out more information about the towns in the region, details of daily life, how people make a living, and so on. Use the information to create a profile of a typical family in the region.

2. Write Catalogue You work for a coat manufacturer. You have just received a shipment of two new coats. One is perfect for the drizzle of London. The other is designed to keep off the Siberian chill. Write a paragraph describing the features of the two coats for your company catalogue, including details from the climate in these places.

Critical Thinking

1. Identifying Main Ideas How does the Gulf Stream affect the climate of the North European Plain? How does it affect the coastline of Norway?

2. Recognizing Cause and Effect Russia has had to build an extensive rail system and pipelines to transport resources out of Siberia. What are the reasons for needing to build these transportation corridors?

Applying Your Skills

Turn to the Skills for Life Activity on page 271 to answer the following questions.

1. Which graph would you NOT use to show population increases in Great Britain during the past 10 years?

A line graph **B** circle graph
C bar graph **D** none of the above

2. Which kind of graph would best show the percent of days with rain in Southern France?

A line graph **B** circle graph
C bar graph **D** both a and c

Take It to the NET

Activity Read about Europe's diverse physical geography. How are some of the geographic features of Europe similar to and different from the region where you live? Visit the World Explorer: People, Places, and Cultures section of **phschool.com** for help in completing this activity.

Chapter 14 Self-Test As a final review activity, take the Chapter 14 Self-Test and get instant feedback on your answers. To take the test, visit the Social Studies section of **phschool.com.**

Map Activity

1. B **2.** E **3.** C **4.** F **5.** D **6.** A

Writing Activity

1. Profiles may include information about the climate, geographic features, natural resources that tie into lifestyle and livelihood.

2. Encourage students to use vivid language to describe the special features of the coats and to describe how they suit the needs of the people living in these two climates.

Critical Thinking

1. The Gulf Stream mixes with the North Atlantic current. Warm, moist air blowing over the continent of Europe keep the temperatures mild and the rainfall plentiful for crops. The warm water of the North and Norwegian seas keeps the harbors of Norway from freezing in the winter.

2. The harsh climate in Siberia causes the rivers to freeze over so that they cannot be used to transport resources. The area of Russia that is rich in resources is thousands of miles from the main population centers on the west side of the Urals, where the climate is milder and the soil is rich.

Applying Your Skills

1. b
2. b

Resource Directory

Other Print Resources

Chapter Tests with ExamView® Test Bank, Ch. 14

Technology

ExamView® Test Bank CD-ROM, Ch. 14

Resource Pro® CD-ROM

Chapter 15 Planning Guide

Resource Manager

	CORE INSTRUCTION	READING/SKILLS
Chapter-Level Resources	**Teaching Resources** Program Overview Pacing Charts **Technology** Resource Pro® CD-ROM Companion Web site, phschool.com • eTeach	**Technology** Social Studies Skills Tutor CD-ROM Student Edition on Audio CD, Ch. 15
1 From Ancient Greece to Feudal Europe **1.** List key accomplishments of ancient Greeks and Romans. **2.** Describe the importance of Christianity and feudalism to life in the Middle Ages.	**Teaching Resources** **Unit 4** Classroom Manager, p. 17 Guided Reading and Review, p. 18	**Teaching Resources** Guide to the Essentials, p. 62 **Technology** Section Reading Support Transparencies
2 Renaissance and Revolution **1.** Explain why Europeans began exploring other parts of the world during the Renaissance. **2.** Trace how the Age of Revolution changed science and government.	**Teaching Resources** **Unit 4** Classroom Manager, p. 20 Guided Reading and Review, p. 21	**Teaching Resources** Guide to the Essentials, p. 63 **Technology** Section Reading Support Transparencies
3 Industrial Revolution and Nationalism **1.** Describe the connection between the Industrial Revolution and the Age of Imperialism. **2.** Explain the influence of the Industrial Revolution on nationalism.	**Teaching Resources** **Unit 4** Classroom Manager, p. 23 Guided Reading and Review, p. 24	**Teaching Resources** Guide to the Essentials, p. 64 **Technology** Section Reading Support Transparencies
4 The Russian Monarchy and Soviet Communism **1.** Identify the events leading to the fall of the Russian czars. **2.** Explain why communism failed in the Soviet Union.	**Teaching Resources** **Unit 4** Classroom Manager, p. 26 Guided Reading and Review, p. 27 Chapter Summary, p. 29 Vocabulary, p. 30 Reteaching, p. 31	**Teaching Resources** **Unit 4** Critical Thinking, p. 33 Guide to the Essentials, p. 65 Social Studies and Geography Skills, pp. 86–87 **Technology** Section Reading Support Transparencies

ENRICHMENT / PRE-AP

Teaching Resources
Primary Sources and Literature Readings

Other Print Resources
DK Atlas

Technology
World Video Explorer: Spotlight on: The Renaissance in Italy
Companion Web site, phschool.com

Teaching Resources
Outline Maps, p. 17

Technology
Color Transparencies 133, 89

Technology
Color Transparencies 68, 87

Technology
Color Transparencies 71

Teaching Resources
Unit 4
Enrichment, p. 32
Cooperative Learning Activity, pp. 111–114

Technology
Color Transparencies 73

ASSESSMENT

Prentice Hall Assessment System

Core Assessment
Chapter Tests with ExamView® Test Bank, Ch. 15
ExamView® Test Bank CD-ROM, Ch. 15

Standardized Test Preparation
Diagnose and Prescribe
Diagnostic Tests for Middle Grades Social Studies Skills
Review and Reteach
Review Book for World Studies
Practice and Assess
Test-taking Strategies with Transparencies for Middle Grades Test Prep Book
Test-taking Strategies Posters

Teaching Resources
Unit 4
Section Quizzes, pp. 19, 22, 25, and 28
Chapter Tests, pp. 144–149

Technology
Companion Web site, phschool.com
Ch. 15 Self-Test

World Video Explorer
Each region of the world is explored through regional flyovers and investigative field trips. Case study segments give students an in-depth view of the history, economy, government, and culture of a key place in each region. Case studies include Nigeria, Mexico, China, British Columbia, and the Czech Republic.

In Your Classroom

CUSTOMIZE FOR INDIVIDUAL NEEDS

Gifted and Talented

Teacher's Edition
- Math, p. 276

Teaching Resources
- Enrichment, p. 32
- Primary Sources and Literature Readings

Honors/Pre-AP

Teacher's Edition
- Math, p. 276

Teaching Resources
- Critical Thinking, p. 33
- Primary Sources and Literature Readings

ESL

Teacher's Edition
- Language Arts, p. 285

Teaching Resources
- Guided Reading and Review, pp. 18, 21, 24, and 27
- Vocabulary, p. 30
- Reteaching, p. 31
- Guide to the Essentials, pp. 62–65
- Social Studies and Geography Skills, pp. 86–87

Technology
- Social Studies Skills Tutor CD-ROM
- Section Reading Support Transparencies

Less Proficient Readers

Teacher's Edition
- Language Arts, p. 285

Teaching Resources
- Guided Reading and Review, pp. 18, 21, 24, and 27
- Vocabulary, p. 30
- Reteaching, p. 31
- Guide to the Essentials, pp. 62–65
- Social Studies and Geography Skills, pp. 86–87

Technology
- Social Studies Skills Tutor CD-ROM
- Section Reading Support Transparencies

Less Proficient Writers

Teacher's Edition
- Language Arts, p. 285

Teaching Resources
- Guided Reading and Review, pp. 18, 21, 24, and 27
- Vocabulary, p. 30
- Guide to the Essentials, pp. 62–65
- Social Studies and Geography Skills, pp. 86–87

Technology
- Social Studies Skills Tutor CD-ROM
- Section Reading Support Transparencies

DORLING KINDERSLEY

At the end of each unit, you will find information adapted from Dorling Kindersley's *Illustrated Children's Encyclopedia* that connects to the region being studied and to one of the seven content strands. In addition, your resources include Dorling Kindersley's *Atlas*, which contains valuable information about countries from around the world.

TEACHER'S EDITION INDEX

Activities math, p. 276; language arts, p. 285

Connections original Renaissance man, p. 280

CHAPTER 15 PACING SUGGESTIONS

For 90-minute Blocks

See suggestions in the Teaching Resources Pacing Charts for Chapter 15. Use Color Transparencies 68, 71, 73, 87, 89, 133.

Running Out of Time?

See the Guide to the Essentials, pp. 62–65.

INTERDISCIPLINARY LINKS

Middle Grades Math: Tools for Success

Course 1, Lesson 1-3, **Mean, Median, and Mode**

Course 2, Lesson 1-4, **Mean, Median, and Mode**

Science Explorer

Human Biology and Health, Lesson 1-2, **Keeping the Body in Balance**

Cells and Heredity, Lesson 5-1, **Darwin's Voyage**

Prentice Hall Literature

Bronze, **Suzy and Leah**

BIBLIOGRAPHY

For the Teacher

Fry, Plantagenet Somerset. *The Dorling Kindersley History of the World.* Dorling Kindersley, 1994.

Nardo, Don. *Life in Ancient Greece.* Lucent, 1995.

Symynkywicz, Jeffrey B. *1989: The Year the World Changed.* Dillon, 1995.

For the Student

Easy

Grant, R. G. *1848: Year of Revolution.* Thomson, 1995.

Langley, Andrew. *The Industrial Revolution.* Viking, 1994.

Average

DK *Renaissance* (*Eyewitness* series). Dorling Kindersley, 2001.

Marx, Trish. *Echoes of World War II.* Lerner, 1994.

Challenging

Kossman, Nina. *Behind the Border.* Beech Tree, 1996.

Literature Connection

Dickens, Charles. *Oliver Twist.* Random House, 2001.

Matas, Carol. *Sworn Enemies.* Bantam Doubleday Dell, 1993.

Take It to the NET

The World Explorer companion Web site, found on **phschool.com**, offers activities for exploring geographical, historical, and cultural resources on the Internet. It also provides on-line links for key content and all Section and Chapter Assessment activities.

The **Teacher site** also provides teachers with regional data and ideas for student research and activities.

Students can use the **Student site** to find chapter-by-chapter Internet resource links and to access Self-Tests.

CHAPTER 15

Connecting to the Guiding Questions

In this chapter, students will read about the history of Europe and Russia. Content in this chapter corresponds to the following Guiding Questions outlined at the beginning of the unit.

- How have the turbulent and triumphant events of the past and present influenced present-day Europe?
- How are people's lives changing with the freedom of the newly formed democracies of Eastern Europe?
- What are the economic advantages of participating in the European Union?
- How can people take advantage of new technologies and still maintain links to more traditional ways of life?

Using the Timeline Activities

As a class, study the timeline and discuss the inventions shown. Have students use an encyclopedia or dictionary if necessary to understand all of the inventions.

- Have students find or prepare and label an illustration of the invention they choose, and display it as they read their reports.
- Suggest that "modern" means an invention created after 1900.

Heterogeneous Groups

The following activities are suitable for heterogeneous groups.

Interdisciplinary Connections

Math, p. 276
Language Arts, p. 285

eTeach

Be sure to check out this month's discussion with a Master Teacher. Go to **phschool.com**.

CHAPTER 15

EUROPE AND RUSSIA: Shaped by History

Inventions in Industry

Michael Faraday's first electric generator

- 1733 John Kay, flying shuttle *England*
- 1764 James Hargreaves, spinning jenny *England*
- 1765 James Watt, improved steam engine *Scotland*
- 1779 Samuel Crompton, spinning mule *England*
- 1800 Alessandro Volta, electric battery *Italy*
- 1803 Richard Trevithick, first successful steam locamotive *Wales*
- 1831 Michael Faraday, electric generator *England*
- 1859 John-Joseph-Etienne Lenoir, first successful internal combustion engine *France*

1725 | 1750 | 1775 | 1800 | 1825 | 1850 | 1875

James Watt's steam engine changed heat into energy, which could be used to power machinery.

USING TIMELINES

This timeline shows European inventions in industry from the 1700s and 1800s.

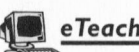

Exploring Early Inventions

Many of the inventions shown on the timeline helped pave the way for more advanced technology. Choose one of the inventions from the timeline. Visit the library or the Internet and gather information on that invention, including information about how and why the invention came about, and how it might have helped lead to the Industrial Revolution. Prepare a brief oral report on your findings and share it with the rest of the class.

Making a Timeline of Modern Inventions

People continue to invent technologies that change the world. Make a list of eight modern-day inventions that you would like to know more about. Use the library or the Internet to gather information about these inventions, including the year they were invented, who invented them, and what their purpose is. Create a timeline showing the information you gather.

Resource Directory

Teaching Resources

Primary Sources and Literature Readings extend content with a selection related to the concepts in this chapter.

Other Print Resources

DK Atlas

Technology

Spotlight on: The Renaissance in Italy, from the World Video Explorer, enhances students' understanding of the art and artists of the Italian Renaissance.

Student Edition on Audio CD, Ch. 15

SECTION 1

From Ancient Greece to Feudal Europe

BEFORE YOU READ

1. What were the main accomplishments of the ancient Greeks and Romans?
2. What impact did Christianity and feudalism have on life during the Middle Ages?

KEY TERMS
policy
empire
Pax Romana
feudalism
Middle Ages
serf

KEY PEOPLE AND PLACES
Greece
Athens
Alexander the Great
Rome
Jesus
Palestine

MAIN IDEA
Many achievements of the empires of the ancient world have had a lasting impact throughout history, and continue to this day.

NOTE TAKING
Copy the outline below. As you read the section, fill in the outline with information about ancient times and the Middle Ages.

I. Ancient Greeks and Romans
A. Greeks
1.
2.
3.
4.
B. Romans
1.
2.
3.
4.
II. Middle Ages
A. Feudalism
1.
2.
3.
4.

Setting the Scene

Athletes compete in the Olympics. Buildings are designed in a classical style. Judges make rulings based on written law. Citizens pay taxes to the state. All of these activities can be traced to ancient times.

Achievements of the Ancient Greeks and Romans

The ancient Greeks were Europe's first great philosophers, historians, poets, and writers. They borrowed ideas from older civilizations of Mesopotamia and Egypt and used them to develop new ways of thinking. Their observations led to scientific ways of gathering knowledge. Their method of rule led to democracy.

Origins of Democracy In ancient times, **Greece** was divided into over 100 city-states. Each city-state acted as an independent nation. The most famous was **Athens.** In Athens, free men were allowed to vote on their leaders, laws, and **policies.** Policies are the methods and plans a government uses to do work. Women, slaves, and non-Greeks could not vote. Even so, the idea that people should have a voice in how they are ruled had a strong impact on history.

Aristotle

HISTORY The Greeks and Romans made sculptures of their political and cultural figures. This is a sculpture of Aristotle, Alexander the Great's teacher. Aristotle is known for his observations about the natural world and creating rules for drama that are still used for plays, TV, and movies today.
Critical Thinking Why do you think the Greeks and Romans made sculptures of their political and cultural figures?

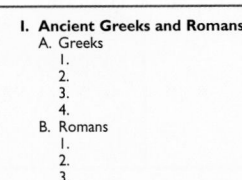

SECTION 1

Lesson Objectives

1. List key accomplishments of ancient Greeks and Romans.
2. Describe the importance of Christianity and feudalism to life in the Middle Ages.

Lesson Plan

1 Engage

Warm-Up Activity

Write the following phrases on the chalkboard: *Olympic games, alphabet, classical architecture, elected government.* Tell students that these and other aspects of our culture can be traced to ancient Greek and Roman cultures.

Activating Prior Knowledge

Help students define *accomplishment.* Ask students to name civic holidays that Americans celebrate. How do they highlight American accomplishments?

2 Explore

As students read the section, challenge them to answer these questions: How did Greek and Roman citizens participate in democracy? How did serfs live in the Middle Ages? What did people of the Middle Ages do to honor Christianity?

3 Teach

Have students write three questions and answers for an ancient and medieval history game. Each question should cover either ancient Rome, ancient Greece, or Europe of the Middle Ages.

Resource Directory

Teaching Resources

Classroom Manager in the Unit 4 Teaching Resources, p. 17

Guided Reading and Review in the Unit 4 Teaching Resources, p. 18

Guide to the Essentials, p. 62

Technology

Section Reading Support Transparencies

Answers to...

CRITICAL THINKING
To honor them and their achievements.

CHAPTER 15 EUROPE AND RUSSIA: SHAPED BY HISTORY 275

Lesson Plan continued

Questions for Discussion

HISTORY How do ancient Greek political ideas affect life in democracies today?

The Greeks believed that people should have a voice in how they are ruled. They voted to elect their leaders, as do people in modern democracies.

GEOGRAPHY Look at the map of the Roman Empire. What geographical feature enabled the Romans to control these areas?

The Roman Empire surrounded the Mediterranean Sea. The Romans could sail across and around the sea, conquering and controlling the areas around it.

4 Assess/Reteach

See the answers to the Section 1 Assessment. You may also assess students' game questions and answers.

Acceptable questions and answers are pertinent and factual.

Commendable questions and answers include conclusions drawn from and supported by the text.

Outstanding questions and answers require respondents to use critical-thinking skills.

ACTIVITY

Interdisciplinary Connections

Math Rome's emperor Hadrian had a wall built across northern England in order to defend his distant empire. The wall runs for about 75 miles (120 km). It was constructed of two stone walls separated by layers of rubble and earth and topped by a stone walk. Ask students how long it would have taken a patrolling Roman soldier to walk the entire length of the wall if the soldier's normal walking speed was 3 mph. (25 hours, or just over one day)

Logical/Mathematical

The Roman Empire

GEOGRAPHY This map shows the regions conquered by the Romans. These regions became part of the Roman Empire, which lasted for hundreds of years. **Map Study** Using what you know about the resources, climate, and natural barriers of Europe, describe the geography of the Roman Empire.

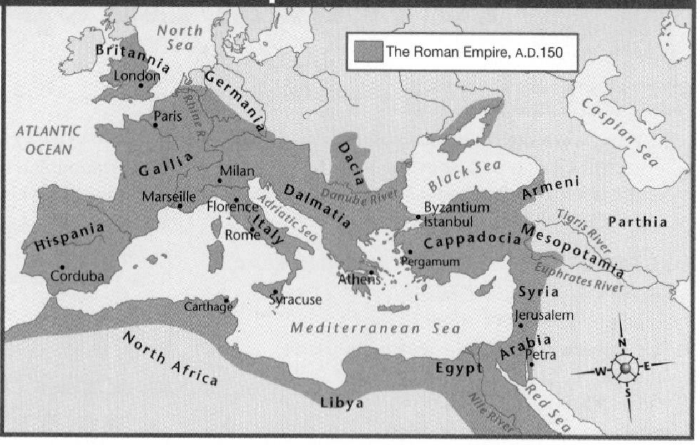

LINKS TO Science

The Volcano and the City of Pompeii The city of Pompeii stood at the foot of a volcano called Mt. Vesuvius. In A.D. 79, the volcano erupted. Smoke, ash, and cinders rained on the city. In two days, the eruption covered the city with about 20 feet (6.6 m) of ash. It sealed the city like a volcanic "time capsule." Archaeologists have uncovered Pompeii's buildings, almost perfectly intact. They have even found loaves of bread in ovens!

Spread of Greek Culture Greek language, ideas, and culture were spread throughout the Mediterranean by **Alexander the Great,** a king of Macedonia. Between 334 B.C. and 323 B.C., Alexander conquered an **empire** that spread eastward to the Indus River. An empire is a collection of lands ruled by a single government. When the Romans took over Alexander's lands they borrowed many Greek ideas.

The Roman Empire The Romans began to build their empire after Alexander died. Augustus, the first emperor of **Rome,** came to power in 27 B.C. His rule began 200 years of Roman peace, or **Pax Romana** (pahks ro MAH nah). During this time, Rome was the most powerful state in Europe. Magnificent cities were built, new technologies were developed, and the economy prospered.

Judges in the Roman Empire followed written laws to make decisions. These written laws protected all citizens in the empire, not only the rich and powerful. Modern ideas about law and citizenship used by democratic governments are based on Roman law.

The Pax Romana was followed by hundreds of years of war. More and more soldiers were needed to defend the empire's boundaries. The taxes raised to maintain the army hurt the economy. The emperor could no longer govern such a huge area, and the empire was divided into two parts. The western half of the empire began to crumble.

The Fall of Rome The Christian religion was based on the teachings of **Jesus,** who lived in the eastern Mediterranean region of **Palestine.** When the Roman emperor Constantine became a follower of Christianity, the religion quickly spread throughout the empire. Later, the empire collapsed. Government, law and order, and trade broke down, but Christianity survived. Without the empire, people were living in difficult, dangerous times. Christianity gave them hope.

Answers to...

MAP STUDY

The Roman Empire includes the parts of Europe that have fertile soil, mild climate, clear transportation corridors, and high population density.

Resource Directory

Teaching Resources

Outline Maps, Western Europe: Political, p. 17

Technology

Color Transparencies 133 Southwest Asia and North Africa: Physical-Political Map; **89** *The Discus Thrower* Fine Art; *Nike of Samothrace* Fine Art; Trojan Horse Student Art

Europe in the Middle Ages

Along with Christianity, **feudalism** (FYOOD ul iz um) was an important part of society in the **Middle Ages,** the time period that falls between ancient and modern times. Feudalism was a way to organize society when there was no central government. Peasants made up about 90% of the population. They worked as **serfs,** farming the land on manors owned by lords. The lords collected taxes for the king. The serfs were not slaves, but they had to follow the lord's rules. In return, they were given work and protection.

Over the centuries, life in Europe changed. Trade increased. Many serfs bought their freedom from the lords and moved into towns, where they could practice trades and take advantage of opportunities. Towns grew into cities. By the 1400s, a new way of life had begun to develop in Europe.

Notre Dame

CULTURE Picture a building like a hollow mountain of stones. Graceful arches sweep to the sky. This building is a cathedral, a great church. Many cathedrals were built in Europe during the Middle Ages. It took 150 years to build the cathedral of Notre Dame. Workers devoted their lives to the work, believing it was God's wish. This strong religious faith was a key part of life in Europe during the Middle Ages. **Critical Thinking** How do you think this long-term building project based on faith in God affected the society?

SECTION I ASSESSMENT

AFTER YOU READ

RECALL

1. Identify: (a) Greece, (b) Athens, (c) Alexander the Great, (d) Rome, (e) Jesus, (f) Palestine
2. Define: (a) policy, (b) empire, (c) Pax Romana (d) feudalism, (e) Middle Ages, (f) serf

COMPREHENSION

3. How did the ancient leaders of Greece and Rome unite their empires?
4. What were the positive effects of feudalism on Europe in the Middle Ages?

CRITICAL THINKING AND WRITING

5. **Exploring the Main Idea** Review the Main Idea statement at the beginning of this section. Write a paragraph describing how you have been influenced by the culture and ideas of the ancient world.
6. **Compare and Contrast** Describe some ways in which Europe under the Pax Romana was different from Europe in the Middle Ages.

ACTIVITY

7. **Writing a Journal** You are a Roman governor in Britain, far from your home and family in Rome. Write a journal entry describing the things you miss about Rome. Be as specific as you can.

Resource Directory

Teaching Resources

Section Quiz in the Unit 4 Teaching Resources, p. 19

SECTION I ASSESSMENT

AFTER YOU READ

1. (a) area on the north side of the Mediterranean Sea, composed of more than 100 city-states (b) most important Greek city-state (c) King of Macedonia who built an empire (d) most powerful empire in Europe (e) person whose teachings led to Christianity (f) region on the eastern Mediterranean where Jesus lived
2. (a) method and plans a government uses to do work (b) collection of lands ruled by a single government (c) period of peaceful rule (d) system in which there is no central government (e) period of time that falls between ancient and modern times (f) worker who is not a slave but obeys rules of a lord in exchange for work and protection
3. Alexander the Great brought Greek culture and ideas that united the people he conquered. The Romans increased trade and travel throughout their empire.
4. People were given work, protection, and a place to live. Feudalism also provided order to society.
5. Students can discuss how their lives are influenced by democracy, cultural elements like theater, well-planned cities, and laws.
6. During the Pax Romana, there was a strong central government and stable society. Europe in the Middle Ages lacked central government.
7. Entries should note accurate elements from Roman culture.

Answers to...

CRITICAL THINKING

Groups of workers with a common goal would strengthen the sense of community; work would be assured for a long time, which would make the economy stable.

SECTION 2

Lesson Objectives

1. Explain why Europeans began exploring other parts of the world during the Renaissance.
2. Trace how the Age of Revolution changed science and government.

Lesson Plan

1 Engage

Warm-Up Activity

Tell students that the European societies discussed in this section had no radios, televisions, or telephones. People knew little about other lands and cultures. Ask students what they think it would be like to live in such a time. How might people view newly discovered ideas, cultures, and places?

Activating Prior Knowledge

Discuss exotic places that students dream of visiting. Pair students to study maps and the travel sections of newspapers for possible locations. Have partners describe the geographic and cultural features of places they named.

2 Explore

Encourage students to find answers to the following questions as they read: How did Greek and Roman ideas influence Renaissance thinking? Why was the middle class important during the Renaissance? What changes occurred during the revolutions in England, France, and colonial America? How did the Scientific Revolution affect the relationship between science and religion?

Answers to...

CRITICAL THINKING

Few people traveled. Exotic goods came from the East, and Marco Polo's travels increased the desire for trade with the East.

SECTION 2

Renaissance and Revolution

BEFORE YOU READ

READING FOCUS

1. Why did Europeans begin to look outward to other continents?
2. How did the Age of Revolution change science and government?

KEY TERMS

monarch
middle class
Renaissance
humanism
revolution
Parliament
Scientific Revolution

KEY PEOPLE

Marco Polo
Louis XIV

NOTE TAKING

Copy the Cause and Effect chart below and as you read the section, fill in the chart.

Causes	Causes
1. 2. 3.	1. 2. 3.
Event: Age of Exploration	**Event: French Revolution**
Effects	**Effects**
1. 2. 3.	1. 2. 3.

MAIN IDEA

As explorers' knowledge of the world changed, so too did cultural expression, people's ideas, and the powers of competing nations.

Fine Art

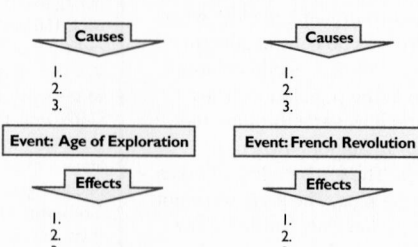

CULTURE Painters were still creating works to celebrate Marco Polo's adventures more than 100 years after his journey. **Critical Thinking** Why were Europeans excited by the idea of Marco Polo's travels?

Setting the Scene

At the end of the thirteenth century, **Marco Polo** traveled from Venice to the east and brought back marvelous tales of the voyage. He visited the Spice Islands, sources of cinnamon, nutmeg, and cloves—spices that Europeans loved. He earned great riches, only to be robbed on his way home to Italy. For centuries after, explorers searched the globe for routes that would lead to more riches.

The Age of Discovery

Two hundred years later, Christopher Columbus was inspired by Marco Polo's travels to set sail on a voyage of his own. Columbus believed that sailing west would lead to a new route to China, Japan, the Spice Islands, and India. Instead, Columbus came ashore in the New World and claimed it for Spain.

While Columbus was sailing across the Atlantic, the Portuguese were making their way down the western coast of Africa. They set up a very profitable trade in gold, ivory, and slaves. When they finally traveled around the Cape of Good Hope and reached the Indian Ocean, they were able to open trade corridors to the Spice Islands. To people

Resource Directory

Teaching Resources

Classroom Manager in the Unit 4 Teaching Resources, p. 20

Guided Reading and Review in the Unit 4 Teaching Resources, p. 21

Guide to the Essentials, p. 63

Technology

Section Reading Support Transparencies

in Europe, spices were more precious than any other resource.

Other European nations were quick to send explorers to faraway lands, seeking new trade routes and sources for exotic items. The rulers of Spain, France, England, and the Netherlands all wanted a share in the riches that the Portuguese enjoyed. As a result, wonderful goods poured into Europe. In additions to spices, there were precious minerals, gold and silver, and fur and tobacco.

The Renaissance The Age of Exploration made the European monarchs very rich. **Monarchs** were the king and queen in control of a nation. The traders and merchants got rich, too, and formed the new **middle class,** a group between the very poor and the very rich. The middle class paid taxes to the monarchs and soon, the monarchs did not need the support of the feudal lords. Feudalism began to disappear.

Members of the middle class used their money to support artists and scholars. They now had time to enjoy art and learning. This rebirth of interest in learning and art is called the **Renaissance** (REN uh sahns). It began in Italy in the 1300s and spread over the rest of the continent. It reached its peak in the 1500s.

Renaissance scholars and artists rediscovered the ideas of ancient Greece and Rome, and what they learned changed the culture. They began writing fresh, powerful poetry. They built glorious buildings and filled them with breathtaking paintings and sculpture. People focused on improving this world rather than hoping for a better life after death. This new approach to knowledge was called **humanism.**

Leonardo da Vinci

CULTURE Leonardo da Vinci (above), one of the best-known artists of the Renaissance, is famous for his paintings and drawings. But he also excelled as a scientist, an engineer, and an inventor.

The Age of Revolution

Revolution in Government Over time, the monarchs of Europe unified their countries and made them stronger. The kings were absolute monarchs who exercised complete power. **Louis XIV**, a powerful king of France from 1643 to 1715, said, "I am the state." His wishes were the law, and no one dared to disagree with him. He believed that his power to rule came from God. The French monarchs taxed citizens heavily to pay for their luxurious lifestyle.

By the end of the Age of Revolution, Europe was a continent of powerful nations. They were bustling with trade and bursting with new scientific ideas. Europe was about to begin a new kind of revolution. This time it would be an economic one—the rise of industry.

Europeans began to question their governments and think about

AS YOU READ

Use Prior Knowledge
How might humanism have influenced the Scientific Revolution?

3 Teach

Have students create a two-column chart headed *Key Ideas/Events of the Renaissance and Age of Revolution* and *Effects on Europe.* Students can complete the chart with chapter data. They may highlight the effects they find most significant, adding explanatory sentences with supporting facts.

Questions for Discussion

ECONOMICS **Why were the Portuguese interested in traveling along the coast of Africa and to the Spice Islands?**

These places had items the Portuguese lacked but wanted, such as gold, ivory, spices, and slaves.

CULTURE **Define *humanism* and tell how it affected art and architecture.**

Humanism focused on improving life in this world. Humanists built big, beautiful buildings and filled them with great paintings and sculptures.

4 Assess/Reteach

See the answers to the Section 2 Assessment. You may also assess students' charts.

Acceptable charts include four accurate entries in each column.

Commendable charts note key events/effects with explanations and supporting data.

Outstanding charts show an understanding of the sweeping changes Europe experienced during this period.

Resource Directory

Technology

Color Transparencies 68 Western Europe: Physical-Political Map; **87** *Eritrean Sibyl from the Sistine Chapel* Fine Art

Answers to...

AS YOU READ

Humanism focuses on improving the world, a similar goal of science.

BIOGRAPHY

Original Renaissance Man

Born in 1452 in Tuscany, Italy, Leonardo da Vinci was a true Renaissance man. He was a brilliant artist, architect, inventor, musician, and scientist. Leonardo's understanding of how things worked helped him imagine and design all manner of inventions. It also helped him see and capture the science of the human body in his artwork.

SECTION 2 ASSESSMENT

AFTER YOU READ

1. (a) Italian who journeyed to the Spice Islands at the end of the 13th century (b) King of France who believed his power was given to him by God
2. (a) king or queen in control (b) group between the poor and the rich (c) period of rebirth of art and learning (d) approach to knowledge based on Greek and Roman thinkers (e) far-reaching change (f) elected legislature (g) change from belief-based to fact-based scientific theories using observation and proof
3. Europeans' desire for wealth led to voyages of exploration. They sought new sources of raw materials, labor, and trade goods.
4. Traders and merchants formed the new middle class in Europe during the Age of Revolution.
5. Government became more representative, with a loss of power among monarchs. Science began to base theories on facts rather than religious beliefs.
6. Letters might include description of goods coming into port, money being made, the circulation of new ideas, new buildings being built, and artwork being created.
7. The French worker might describe the high taxes that he is forced to pay the king, the luxurious lifestyle the king enjoys, and the unlimited power of the king. He might ask the American questions about life after the Revolution.
8. Descriptions should use vivid language to evoke the reader's interest in the place.

GOVERNMENT

The Seeds of Change

The idea of a limited government spread from Great Britain to the thirteen colonies in North America. A colony is a territory ruled by another nation, usually one that is far away. In 1776, the colonies rebelled against the British king, and in 1789, the French Revolution overthrew King Louis XVI.

change—even the far-reaching change in government called **revolution.** In the 1600s, when England's king refused to share his power with **Parliament** (PAHR luh munt), the elected legislature, he was overthrown. For a time, there was no monarch in England. The monarchy was later restored, but not before the people realized the kind of limited government they wanted. The modern age of science and democracy had begun.

The Scientific Revolution At the time of the revolutions in America and in France, there was also a revolution going on in the world of science. For centuries European scientists had studied nature to explain how the world fit with their religious beliefs. During the Age of Revolution, that approach changed. Scientists started to base theories on facts by watching carefully to see what really happened in the world. This change is called the **Scientific Revolution.** The Scientific Revolution required new procedures, called the scientific method, in which ideas are tested with experiments and observation.

The scientific method led to dramatic advances. For example, in the Middle Ages, Europeans believed that the Earth was at the center of the universe. Renaissance scientists challenged this belief, but they could not prove their ideas. Then, during the Scientific Revolution, scientists used a new form of mathematics called calculus (KAL kyoo lus) to study the movement of the moon and planets.

SECTION 2 ASSESSMENT

AFTER YOU READ

RECALL

1. Identify: (a) Marco Polo, (b) Louis XIV
2. Recall: (a) monarch, (b) middle class, (c) Renaissance, (d) humanism, (e) revolution, (f) Parliament, (g) Scientific Revolution

COMPREHENSION

3. What factors led to Europe's voyages of exploration?
4. What groups formed the new middle class in Europe during the Age of Revolution?
5. How did government and science in Europe change during the Age of Revolution?

CRITICAL THINKING AND WRITING

6. **Exploring the Main Idea** Review the Main Idea statement at the beginning of this section. Imagine you are a merchant at a European port. Write a letter to a friend describing the changes in your life as trade ships arrive from all over the world.
7. **Making Valid Generalizations** The French Revolution took place thirteen years after the American Revolution. With a partner, write a dialogue between an American traveling in Europe in 1780 and a French worker who is thinking about the benefits of limited power in a ruler.

ACTIVITY

8. **Writing a Descriptive Paragraph** Marco Polo's writings about his travels excited readers and made them want to explore the world just as he had. Think about a place that you have visited. What makes it special? Write about that place in a descriptive way that would make a reader want to go there too.

Resource Directory

Teaching Resources

Section Quiz in the Unit 4 Teaching Resources, p. 22

SECTION 3

Industrial Revolution and Nationalism

BEFORE YOU READ

READING FOCUS

1. How are the Industrial Revolution and the Age of Imperialism connected?
2. How did the Industrial Revolution influence nationalism?

KEY TERMS

Industrial Revolution
textiles
imperialism
nationalism
alliance

NOTE TAKING

Copy the flow chart below. As you read the section, fill in a flow chart with information about the Industrial Revolution, imperialism, and nationalism.

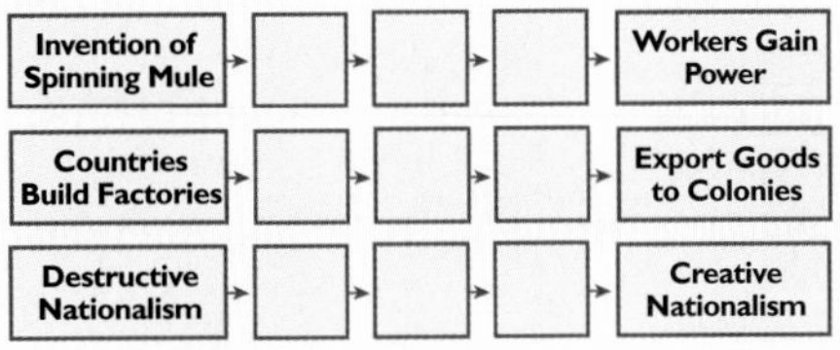

MAIN IDEA

The 1800s represent a century of change for the nations of Europe, change that left its mark on history and continues to influence contemporary life worldwide.

Setting the Scene

Until the late 1700s, everything that people needed was handmade. Goods were either produced at home or bought from small local shops. Then, inventors began to create machines that could make goods quickly and cheaply. Huge factories housed the machines. People left their homes to work in the factories and keep the machines running. This change in the way goods were made was called the **Industrial Revolution.** It was also a revolution in the ways people lived and worked.

Factories in England

GEOGRAPHY This picture from the 1800s shows factory smokestacks along the Don River in Sheffield, an industrial city in northern England. **Critical Thinking** Why are factory towns often located on or near rivers?

Technological Innovation Shapes the World

The Industrial Revolution began in Great Britain. The first machines were invented to speed up the spinning of thread and the weaving of **textiles,** or cloth products. Spinning mules were huge machines that could spin fiber such as cotton or linen into thread. A person using a spinning wheel would have to spin full time for nearly four years to produce the amount of thread that the spinning mule could produce in a single day.

Resource Directory

Teaching Resources

Classroom Manager in the Unit 4 Teaching Resources, p. 23

Guided Reading and Review in the Unit 4 Teaching Resources, p. 24

Guide to the Essentials, p. 64

Technology

Section Reading Support Transparencies

SECTION 3

Lesson Objectives

1. Describe the connection between the Industrial Revolution and the Age of Imperialism.
2. Explain the influence of the Industrial Revolution on nationalism.

Lesson Plan

1 Engage

Warm-Up Activity

Direct students to preview the European Imperialism map in this section. Ask students where they think most of the world's power was located. (Europe) What do they think was the reason for European expansion? (the need for resources)

Activating Prior Knowledge

Have students list their household chores, the amount of sleep they usually get, and time they have for fun. Discuss responsibility students have at home, at school, and in the community. How do students think this might compare to the responsibility of their great-grandparents as children?

2 Explore

List the following questions on the chalkboard for students to answer as they read the section: Why did workers gain power during the Industrial Revolution? How did the Industrial Revolution lead to imperialism? How did alliances among nations contribute to both peace and war? How was Europe different after World Wars I and II?

Answers to...

CRITICAL THINKING

Rivers provide the means for bringing raw materials needed for industry into the city, and the means for shipping goods out of the city.

Lesson Plan continued

3 Teach

Have students create storyboards for a television documentary about the Industrial Revolution and nationalism in Europe. Tell students to make a cell for each major topic, using text and illustrations to describe the scenes. Students may add narrative text explaining cause-and-effect relationships among the topics, but must include supporting facts.

Questions for Discussion

ECONOMICS How did factors of production—raw materials, labor, capital, and entrepreneurs—make the Industrial Revolution possible?

There were many people willing to work, people willing to spend money to build factories, and raw materials that factories could use to produce goods.

GOVERNMENT Why did nations become more democratic during the 1800s?

Workers formed unions, which gave working people more power. Because making and selling goods was important to the economy, workers were given a stronger voice in government.

4 Assess/Reteach

See the answers to the Section 3 Assessment. You may also assess students' storyboards.

Acceptable storyboards show accurate data from the section.

Commendable storyboards depict major topics linked to section subheads.

Outstanding storyboards highlight and explain cause-and-effect relationships.

European Imperialism, 1900

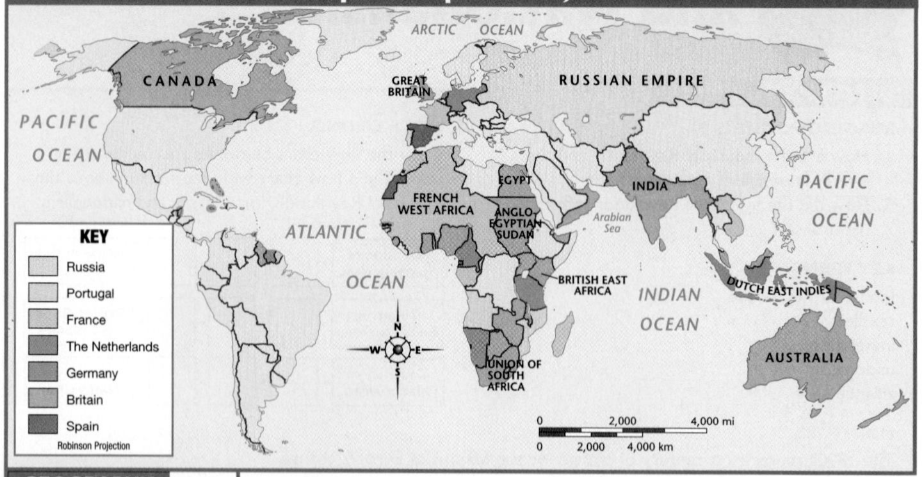

GEOGRAPHY This map shows the colonies held by the various countries of Europe in 1900.
Map Study Which three countries had the most colonies? Why do you think the Americas were mostly free of colonies? What geographic features prevented Russia from colonizing far-away lands?

The new factories made their owners very wealthy, and the revolution spread to other countries. By 1900, factories produced almost all goods made in the United States and most of Western Europe.

The Industrial Revolution changed life across Europe. For centuries, farmers had worked the land. Now they moved to cramped, dirty quarters in rapidly growing cities to find factory work.

The changes that people made in their lives were difficult. For many years, factory owners took advantage of workers. Factory conditions were not safe, and wages were low. Conditions gradually improved as workers formed unions that spoke up for their rights and laws were passed to protect them.

Governments had to respond to workers' complaints. Making and selling goods became a big part of each country's economy, and the work force was an important resource. Nations became more democratic as working people were given a stronger voice in passing laws and setting policies.

AS YOU READ
Find Main Ideas How did the Industrial Revolution promote democracy?

At the same time, European governments were becoming more aggressive abroad. During the 1800s, many nations took over other countries and turned them into colonies. This is called **imperialism.** Factories needed raw materials, such as cotton, wood, and metals, which colonies could provide. With plenty of raw materials, the factories were able to produce more goods than people could buy. Colonies also became a source for new customers.

The late 1800s are called the Age of Imperialism, but European nations had a long tradition of colonizing other parts of the world. They began colonizing the Americas in the 1500s. By 1900, most of the colonies in America had gained their independence. Belgium,

Answers to...

MAP STUDY

Britain, France, and Russia. By 1900, most of the colonies in the Americas were independent. Because of its climate and location, Russia did not pursue exploration by sea.

AS YOU READ

As factory workers formed unions and called for better conditions, governments had to respond. The working people were given a strong voice in passing laws and setting policy.

Resource Directory

Technology

Color Transparencies 71 Western Europe: Political Map

France, Italy, Spain, Portugal, and Great Britain concentrated their efforts on managing colonies in Africa, Southeast Asia, and the South Pacific. In time, struggles between these colonial powers would bring disaster to Europe.

Nationalism and Historic Events

At the start of the 1900s, the people of Europe were filled with **nationalism,** or pride in their country. Nationalism can be either destructive or creative, depending on how people express it.

Destructive Nationalism Destructive nationalism can make anger and hatred erupt between nations as they compete with each other for the world's resources, wealth, and power. In the early 1900s, this sense of competition made the nations of Europe team up. They made **alliances** (uh LY un sez), or agreements, to help each other in case of attack. Soon, Europe was divided into two alliances, with Germany, Austria-Hungary, and Italy on one side and Great Britain, France, and Russia on the other. When fighting broke out between these alliances, World War I began, and millions of people were killed.

In 1939, World War II broke out between the Axis powers and the Allies. The Axis powers included Germany, Italy, and Japan; the Allies were Great Britain and the Soviet Union, joined by the United States. More than fifty nations were involved in this war, the most destructive ever fought. When it ended in 1945, the Allies had won.

Creative Nationalism This period of war was followed by an era of creative nationalism. The United States and the Soviet Union took over as the world's leading nations while the Europeans rebuilt and repaired their societies. They began working together to establish a new type of European nationalism.

A Tunnel Connecting Britain to France

GEOGRAPHY In 1987, French and English workers began digging a tunnel underneath the English Channel separating Great Britain and France. In 1994, the men in this picture broke through to link the two nations. Today, trains use this tunnel known as "the Chunnel." **Critical Thinking** Do you think nationalism could have kept Great Britain and France from building the Chunnel before 1987?

SECTION 3 ASSESSMENT

AFTER YOU READ

RECALL

1. Define: (a) Industrial Revolution, (b) textiles, (c) imperialism, (d) nationalism, (e) alliance

COMPREHENSION

2. How did European nations' colonies help to boost the economy and increase wealth?
3. What happened in Europe as countries competed for wealth and power?

CRITICAL THINKING AND WRITING

4. **Exploring the Main Idea** Review the Main Idea statement at the beginning of this section. Write a paragraph describing the most important change that took place in Europe during the 1800s.
5. **Identifying Cause and Effect** Write an editorial that speaks out against the destructive nationalism that led Europe into the first world war.

ACTIVITY

6. **Writing a First-Person Account** During the Industrial Revolution, many people your age worked in factories 12 hours a day, 6 days a week. Imagine that you work in a spinning factory. Write a first-person account describing your very long, hard day.

SECTION 3 ASSESSMENT

AFTER YOU READ

1. (a) change in the way goods are made (b) cloth products (c) taking over countries and turning them into colonies (d) pride in one's country (e) agreement between nations
2. Colonies provided needed resources for the factories and new customers for the goods produced.
3. Nations began to form alliances, and eventually war broke out between the two most powerful groups.
4. Students should discuss how the economic change brought about by the Industrial Revolution gave nations the wealth and power needed to colonize faraway lands.
5. Editorials should encourage the nations of Europe to work together to produce goods, exchange resources, and build strong societies that work for a common goal instead of competing for power.
6. Accounts should include details about the working conditions in Europe's factories during the Industrial Revolution.

Resource Directory

Teaching Resources

Section Quiz in the Unit 4 Teaching Resources, p. 25

Answers to...

CRITICAL THINKING

Students may note that building the Chunnel required modern technology, or that Great Britain and France have not always had a friendly relationship.

SECTION 4

Lesson Objectives

1. Identify the events leading to the fall of the Russian czars.
2. Explain why Communism failed in the Soviet Union.

Lesson Plan

1 Engage

Warm-Up Activity

Tell students to imagine that a new leader of the school band has taken over the band, claiming that, with total control, he or she can ensure the band's success. Individuals will not have a vote in band policies, and they will have to pay for the leader's uniform or other supplies. As a result of the new leadership, the band might become more skilled and grow larger. Ask students whether they would support such a leader. Do they feel the band's expansion and improvement is worth the trade-off?

Activating Prior Knowledge

Invite volunteers to identify some U.S. laws. Encourage students to share their ideas about which laws they would change, and new laws they would pass. Have them give reasons for their ideas.

2 Explore

Prompt students to answer these questions as they read the section: How did the czars expand the empire and bring western culture to Russian society? What role did poverty play in Russian history? Why did the Communists close the U.S.S.R. off from Western culture?

Answers to...

CRITICAL THINKING

Life under Mongol rule was worse because Mongol rulers demanded high taxes and service in the army.

SECTION 4

The Russian Monarchy and Soviet Communism

BEFORE YOU READ

READING FOCUS

1. What events led to the overthrow of the Russian czars?
2. Why did Communism fail in the Soviet Union?

KEY TERMS

westernization
czar
Duma
Communism
dictator
Cold War

KEY PEOPLE

Golden Horde
Ivan the Terrible
Catherine the Great
Vladimir Lenin
Mikhail Gorbachev

NOTE TAKING

Copy the concept web below. As you read the section, fill in the concept web with information about the history of Russia under the czars and under Communism.

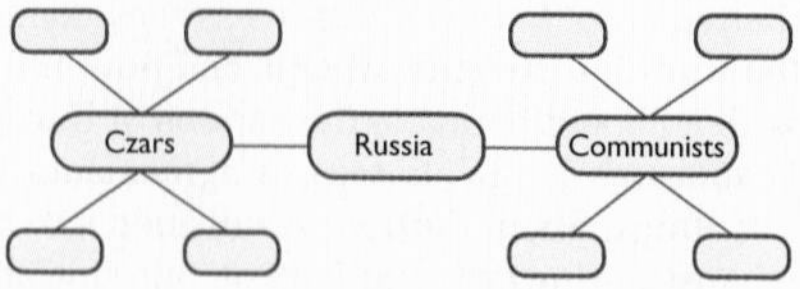

MAIN IDEA

Russia has changed from a small, occupied state into an empire stretching across Asia, into a communist dictatorship and now into an independent nation.

A Mongol Archer

HISTORY Mongol warriors like this archer plundered and burned Kiev and other Russian towns. They killed so many Russians that a historian claimed "no eye remained to weep for the dead."
Critical Thinking Do you think life for the Russian people was better under Mongol rule, or Czarist rule? Why?

Setting the Scene

While Western Europe was exploring the world and establishing colonies, Russia was building a vast empire. The history of Russia is a story with three themes: expansion, the harsh treatment of the common people, and slow westernization. **Westernization** is the process of becoming more like Western Europe and North America.

The Rise and Fall of the Russian Czars

Muscovy (MUHS kuh vee), or Moscow, was once a collection of lands ruled by weak princes who did not get along. Kiev (KEE ev), the most important city in the region, was ruled by the grand prince. In 1238, Mongol conquerors called the **Golden Horde** swept into the region from Asia and quickly defeated the weak princes. By 1240, the Mongols had conquered Kiev. The whole territory became part of the Mongol empire that lasted for 250 years.

Resource Directory

Teaching Resources

Classroom Manager in the Unit 4 Teaching Resources, p. 26

Guided Reading and Review in the Unit 4 Teaching Resources, p. 27

Guide to the Essentials, p. 65

Technology

Section Reading Support Transparencies

The Mongols kept the people cut off from the culture of Western Europe. They demanded service in the army and high taxes, which were collected by princes they appointed. Little by little, the princes gained land and power until they were able to overthrow the Mongolian rule.

The Rise of the Czars As Muscovy spread its control throughout Russia, its grand prince became known as a **czar** (ZAR), or emperor. The first czar, Ivan IV, was crowned in 1547. He conquered western Siberia and the Mongol lands to the southeast. He was known as **Ivan the Terrible** because of his cruelty.

After Ivan IV's death, Russians suffered through 30 years of war until 1613, when the Romanov (ROH muh nawf) family came to power. The Romanovs continued to expand Russian territory. Over time, seaports on the Baltic (BAWL tik) and Black seas were added to the empire, along with territories in Poland, Turkey, China, and Sweden.

In 1689, Peter the Great came to power, and in 1762, **Catherine the Great** took the throne. Both of them opened their court to the teachers, thinkers, and scientists of Western Europe and encouraged their people to adopt western customs.

However, the serfs of Russia wanted freedom, and the czars would not give it to them. The Russian people became divided between the very rich and the very poor, and the poor were starving. Finally, in 1905, violence erupted. Serfs and workers demonstrated, demanding reforms. Hundreds were killed and Czar Nicholas II was forced to establish the **Duma** (DOO mah), a congress whose members were elected by the people. Establishing the Duma was not enough, however, to save the monarchy.

Catherine the Great

GOVERNMENT

Catherine the Great was a German princess who came to Russia as a young bride of 16. Her husband became czar, but he was a weak ruler. With the support of the people, the military, and the church, Catherine seized control of the throne. **Critical Thinking** What qualities might Catherine the Great have had that appealed to the people?

The Rise and Fall of Soviet Communism

Russian involvement in World War I caused severe food and fuel shortages at home. The people listened to leaders speaking out to overthrow the government. In November 1917, **Vladimir Lenin** and his supporters took over the government and set up a new communist regime. **Communism** (KAHM yoo nizum) is a form of unlimited government in which the state owns the farms and factories and decides what will be grown and produced. Lenin turned the Russian Empire into the Union of Soviet Socialist Republics (U.S.S.R.) called the Soviet Union.

3 Teach

Have students create a sequence chart showing Russia's path from Muscovy to an empire. Each event in the chart should appear in its own box and be briefly described. On arrows connecting the boxes, students may explain cause-and-effect relationships among the events.

Questions for Discussion

GOVERNMENT Is communism a form of limited or unlimited government? Explain.

It is a form of unlimited government because the state owns the farms and factories and decides what will be grown and produced.

HISTORY What was the result of the serfs' uprising?

Czar Nicholas was forced to establish the Duma, a congress elected by the people.

4 Assess/Reteach

See the answers to the Section 4 Assessment. You may also assess students' sequence charts.

Acceptable charts show events in correct sequence, and they are accurately described.

Commendable charts include cause-and-effect relationships among events.

Outstanding charts recognize the key impact of serfs' living conditions on the final collapse of Russia's czars.

Resource Directory

Technology

Color Transparencies 73 Northern Eurasia: Political Map

Answers to...

CRITICAL THINKING

She was a strong leader who would have made Russia a powerful nation.

ACTIVITY

Interdisciplinary Connections

Language Arts Tell students that the Russian word *czar* derives from the Roman term *caesar*, or ruler. The German word *kaiser* shares the same history. Ask students to name what some other countries call or have called their leaders. Have them list the terms and investigate the word origins of each.

Verbal/Linguistic

SECTION 4 ASSESSMENT

AFTER YOU READ

1. (a) Mongol conquerors (b) first czar of Russia (c) Russian ruler who encouraged westernization (d) first Communist leader of Russia and founder of the Soviet Union (e) Russian leader who granted reforms
2. (a) a process of becoming more like Western Europe (b) emperor or empress (c) a congress whose members are chosen by the people (d) the government owns the farms and factories (e) leader who rules with unlimited power (f) period of tension without warfare
3. The serfs were suffering from terrible poverty for many years, and their demands for freedom led to revolution.
4. Under Lenin and Stalin's rule, the work of the people went to support state projects instead of meeting people's needs.
5. Students should recall details about the hardship in the lives of the serfs and the geography and natural resources of Russia.
6. Paragraphs should identify the disadvantages of communism, for example, a low standard of living and a lack of personal freedom.
7. Students can look back at page 274 for an example of a timeline.

Vladimir Lenin

SCIENCE AND TECHNOLOGY

In this picture, Lenin is seen giving a fiery speech to the workers of Moscow. **Critical Thinking** How might today's technology have affected the way Lenin called people to action? How would today's technology have made it difficult to cut the Soviet people off from the west?

Iron Curtain The Communists jailed or killed anyone who was an enemy of the revolution. When Lenin died in 1924, Josef Stalin took his place as **dictator** (DIK tayt ur). A dictator is a leader with unlimited power. All of the Soviet Union lived in terror of Stalin's harsh policies.

When World War II ended, the Communists established governments across Eastern Europe. The imaginary barrier called the Iron Curtain was created, again cutting the people off from the west.

The Cold War In the decades following World War II, Communism was seen by the United States as a corrupt system of government. Both countries developed enough weapons to destroy the planet while they engaged in a **Cold War,** a period of tension without actual warfare. At the same time, the people were losing faith in unlimited control by the communist system. Their labor supported state projects instead of their families.

Government Reform In 1985, **Mikhail Gorbachev** (mee khah EEL GOR buh chawf) came into power. He granted the people more personal freedom and fewer economic controls. By 1991, the Soviet Union had broken apart into independent nations struggling for democracy. After years of harsh rule, the Eastern European and Russian people now control their own fate.

SECTION 4 ASSESSMENT

AFTER YOU READ

RECALL

1. Identify: (a) Golden Horde, (b) Ivan the Terrible, (c) Catherine the Great, (d) Vladimir Lenin, (e) Mikhail Gorbachev
2. Define: (a) westernization, (b) czar, (c) Duma, (d) Communism, (e) dictator, (f) Cold War

COMPREHENSION

3. How did the living conditions of serfs lead to opposition to the czars?
4. What happened in the Soviet Union under the leadership of Lenin and Stalin?

CRITICAL THINKING AND WRITING

5. **Exploring the Main Idea** Review the Main Idea statement at the beginning of this section. Imagine you are a serf. Write a journal entry explaining how frustrated you are by your way of life but how strongly you are connected to Russia's land and people.
6. **Comparing and Contrasting** Some people in Russia want to go back to the old communist way of life. Write a paragraph comparing life before and after communism, and arguing against a return to communism.

ACTIVITY

Take It to the NET

7. **Creating a Timeline of the Russian Revolution** The Russian Revolution began an era of communist dictatorship in Russia that lasted until the end of the twentieth century. Create a timeline showing significant events leading up to and following the Russian Revolution of 1917. Visit the World Explorer: People, Places, and Cultures section of **phschool.com** for help in completing this activity.

Answers to...

CRITICAL THINKING

Lenin would have used media such as radio and TV to get his point across. At the same time, access to technology and the media would have prevented the Soviet people from being cut off from Western society, influence, and thought.

Resource Directory

Teaching Resources

Section Quiz in the Unit 4 Teaching Resources, p. 28

Chapter Summary in the Unit 4 Teaching Resources, p. 29

Vocabulary in the Unit 4 Teaching Resources, p. 30

Reteaching in the Unit 4 Teaching Resources, p. 31

Enrichment in the Unit 4 Teaching Resources, p. 32

Critical Thinking in the Unit 4 Teaching Resources, p. 33

Supporting a Position

Learn the Skill

Ivan IV was one of Russia's cruelest and most violent czars.

When you write a paper, give a speech, or debate a point, it's very important to support your position or argument. By providing support for your ideas, your position becomes more persuasive, or believable. For example, in the statement above, the writer says that Ivan IV was a cruel and violent leader. However, the statement would be much more persuasive if the writer supported her idea with details and examples. Follow these steps to learn how to support a position or argument:

A. Use facts and statistics to reinforce your position. Remember that your position or argument is an opinion that needs to be supported by facts.

B. Use explanations and definitions to make your ideas more clear. Don't assume that your readers will understand all the terms and words that you use. Your argument will be clearer if you take the time to explain and define your ideas.

C. Use examples to strengthen your argument. Examples can help illustrate your ideas and make your argument more convincing to readers.

D. Use quotations to offer support for your position. By using the words of other writers and experts, you can make your own argument more persuasive.

Practice the Skill

Read this passage about Ivan IV. Then, answer the questions that follow.

The Reign of Terror

Ivan IV was one of Russia's cruelest and most violent czars. As legend states, a terrible thunderstorm shook Moscow on the day that he was born. A Russian priest warned Ivan's father that a wicked son would succeed him.

As a child, Ivan began to distrust everyone around him. He believed that the Russian nobles and ministers around him wanted him dead so that they could control the country. When he became czar in 1547, his suspicions only grew. Ivan ordered many arrests and executions to protect himself. He also passed a new code of laws that only he could change. Once, in a fit of rage, he even killed his own son. Ivan died in 1584, ending his reign of terror.

A. What is the writer's position or argument?

B. Identify the ways in which the writer supports her position.

C. Do you think the writer's position is well-supported and convincing? Why?

D. What other ways could the writer support her position to make it more convincing?

Apply the Skill

See the Chapter Review and Assessment at the end of this chapter for more questions on supporting a position.

Lesson Objectives

1. Learn how to support a position or argument.
2. Identify examples of support.

Lesson Plan

1 Engage

To introduce the skill, read aloud the opening text under "Learn the Skill." Give examples of facts (It is raining today) and opinions (I hate rain) and ask students to identify them.

2 Explore

Direct students to read the steps under "Learn the Skill." Point out that they need not use every kind of support to bolster an argument. Some positions lend themselves to different types of backup.

3 Teach

Have students complete "Practice the Skill" independently. Then, compare their answers.

For additional reinforcement, have students indicate places in the paragraphs where explanations, definitions, examples, and/or annotations would be effective and helpful.

4 Assess/Reteach

Student should be able to identify examples used to support a position or argument.

To further assess students' understanding of supporting a position, have them complete the "Applying Your Skills" part of the Chapter Review and Assessment at the end of the chapter.

Resource Directory

Teaching Resources

Social Studies and Geography Skills, Determining Tone, Purpose, and Audience, p. 86; Writing to Persuade, p. 87

Technology

Social Studies Skills Tutor CD-ROM

Answers to...

PRACTICE THE SKILL

A. Ivan IV was Russia's cruelest and most violent czar.

B. The writer's position is supported by historical facts that are examples of cruelty.

C. Answers will vary, but students should see that the writer's position is supported.

D. Answers will vary.

CHAPTER 15

Review and Assessment

Creating a Chapter Summary

Student summaries will vary.

Sample summaries:

Section 2 Exploration opened up new trade that made the European monarchies wealthy. Rediscovery of the thinkers of the ancient world introduced new ideas and an understanding of the natural world.

Section 3 The Industrial Revolution and Imperialism increased competition between nations for natural resources, economic opportunities, and increased wealth and power.

Section 4 Centuries of unlimited rule and harsh conditions led the serfs of Russia to overthrow their leaders. Communism cut the people of the Soviet Union off from Western culture until demands for freedom led to changes that ended Communist rule.

Reviewing Key Terms

1. dictator
2. Renaissance
3. Industrial Revolution
4. czar
5. Communism

Reviewing the Main Ideas

1. The Greeks and Romans influence us with their ideas about democracy, written laws, rights of citizens, scientific method, and architecture.
2. The feudal system gave serfs a place to work and live with protection during uncertain times. Christianity gave them hope for a better life after death.
3. The absolute monarchs were strong-willed and ruthless if opposed.
4. Life under an absolute monarchy and the fact that the citizens were heavily taxed to pay for the luxurious lifestyle of the French monarchs led to the French Revolution.

CHAPTER 15

Review and Assessment

Creating a Chapter Summary

On a separate piece of paper, draw a chart like this one, and include the information that summarizes the first section of the chapter. Then, fill in the chart with summaries of Sections 2, 3, and 4.

Section 1	• The ancient Greek and Roman empires spread cultural ideas and practices throughout Europe. • The influence of these ancient empires is still felt today.
Section 2	
Section 3	
Section 4	

Reviewing Key Terms

Complete each sentence with a term from the list below.

czar communism dictator
Industrial Revolution Renaissance

1. A ________ is a leader who rules with unlimited power.
2. The ________ was a period of artistic and intellectual rebirth.
3. During the ________, there were many changes in the ways that goods and products were made.
4. A ruling emperor or empress in Russia was called a ________.
5. ________ is a system of government in which the state decides what is best for its citizens.

Reviewing the Main Ideas

1. Identify how the accomplishments of the Greeks and Romans influence our lives today. (Section 1)
2. Identify how Christianity and feudalism affected the lives of people in the Middle Ages. (Section 1)
3. Describe life under the rule of Europe's absolute monarchs. (Section 2)
4. What factors led to the French Revolution? (Section 2)
5. How did the Industrial Revolution change life for people in Europe? (Section 3)
6. How did nationalism in Europe lead to world war? (Section 3)
7. Describe the ways in which the rule of the Russian czars was different from the rule of the Soviet dictators. (Section 4)
8. What factors led to the fall of Soviet communism? (Section 4)

5. The Industrial Revolution provided jobs and made some Europeans in the new middle class wealthy, but it also resulted in poor living and working conditions for many workers, especially in cities.
6. Countries formed alliances, leading to two powerful groups. When fighting broke out, it involved all the European nations.
7. The czars were ruthless, but they had connections to Western culture and ideas. Soviet dictators suppressed many freedoms and isolated people from the rest of the world.
8. Soviet communism failed because people became frustrated with a system that did not allow personal freedom and that forced them to work for the benefit of state-owned projects rather than for themselves and their families.

Map Activity

Europe and Russia

For each place listed below, write the letter from the map that shows its location. Use the maps in the Activity Atlas to help you.

1. Athens
2. Rome
3. Italy
4. France
5. Great Britain
6. Russia
7. Greece
8. Spain

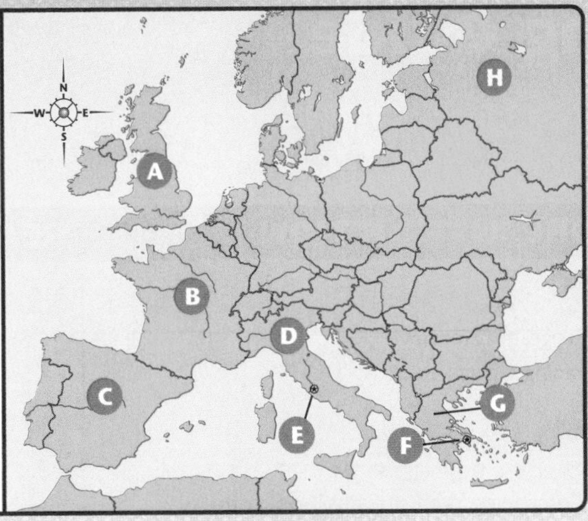

Take It to the NET

Enrichment For more map activities using geography skills, visit the social studies section of **phschool.com.**

Writing Activity

1. **Using Primary Sources** Find out more about what is going on in the former Soviet Union today. Visit your school or local library and use primary sources such as newspaper and magazine articles to find out more information about the people, current leaders, the economy, and the culture. Use the information to write a brief report on life in Russia today.
2. **Writing an Interview** Choose a historical figure from this chapter. Think of questions that you would like to ask that person. Find out more about the person so that you can get a better idea of how he or she might have answered you. Then write the "interview" as if you were asking that person the questions and he or she was answering them.

Critical Thinking

1. **Identifying Main Ideas** Describe some of the advantages of feudalism.
2. **Drawing Conclusions** How did the growth of towns lead to strong monarchies and increased nationalism?
3. **Recognizing Cause and Effect** Why did the Communist dictators consider exposure to western ideas and culture such a danger?

Applying Your Skills

Turn to the Skills for Life activity on p. 287 to help you complete the following activity.

Write a one-page report supporting the argument that the Renaissance was one of the most creative periods in European history. You may want to find more information about the Renaissance in the library or on the Internet to help you support this position.

Take It to the NET

Activity The Industrial Revolution was a time of great change that shaped the way we live and work today. How would your life be different if the Industrial Revolution had never happened? Visit the World Explorer: People, Places and Cultures section of **phschool.com** for help in completing this activity.

Chapter 15 Self-Test As a final review activity, take the Chapter 15 Self-Test and get instant feedback on your answers. To take the test, visit the Social Studies section of **phschool.com.**

Map Activity

1. F **2.** E **3.** D **4.** B **5.** A **6.** H **7.** G **8.** C

Writing Activity

1. Students should include contrasts with life in the Soviet Union of the past.
2. Encourage students to try to capture the personality of the interview subject in the answers that he or she gives.

Critical Thinking

1. If you were a serf, you were given work and protection if you followed the lord's rules. If you had a fair lord, you were treated well. If you were a lord, you had a work force to take care of your land and to add to your wealth as a landowner.
2. Towns helped create a central government ruled by the king. The increased power of this central government gave the people a sense of identity.
3. The dictators did not agree with western values; however, since life in Russia did not improve, they may also have been worried that seeing the freedom of the West and the standard of living would lead to more unrest.

Applying Your Skills

1. Students should include opinions, supported by facts, explanations, and examples.

Resource Directory

Teaching Resources

Cooperative Learning Activity in the Unit 4 Teaching Resources, pp. 111–114

Chapter Tests Forms A and B in the Unit 4 Teaching Resources, pp. 144–149

Guide to the Essentials, Ch. 15 Test, p. 66

Other Print Resources

Chapter Tests with ExamView® Test Bank, Ch. 15

Technology

ExamView® Test Bank CD-ROM, Ch. 15

Resource Pro® CD-ROM

Chapter 16 Planning Guide

Resource Manager

	CORE INSTRUCTION	READING/SKILLS
Chapter-Level Resources	**Teaching Resources** Program Overview Pacing Charts **Technology** Resource Pro® CD-ROM Companion Web site, phschool.com • eTeach	**Technology** Social Studies Skills Tutor CD-ROM Student Edition on Audio CD, Ch. 16
1 The Cultures of Western Europe 1. Explain how industry influenced Western European cities. 2. Describe the positive effects of immigrants in Western Europe. 3. Explain how the development of the European Union has changed Western Europe.	**Teaching Resources** **Unit 4** Classroom Manager, p. 35 Guided Reading and Review, p. 36	**Teaching Resources** Guide to the Essentials, p. 67 Social Studies and Geography Skills, p. 53 **Technology** Section Reading Support Transparencies
2 The Cultures of Eastern Europe 1. Identify the major ethnic groups of Eastern Europe. 2. Explain the reasons for ethnic conflict in Eastern Europe.	**Teaching Resources** **Unit 4** Classroom Manager, p. 38 Guided Reading and Review, p. 39	**Teaching Resources** Guide to the Essentials, p. 68 **Technology** Section Reading Support Transparencies
3 The Cultures of Russia 1. Describe the role that ethnic groups have played in the history of Russia. 2. Explain how Russia is recovering its heritage.	**Teaching Resources** **Unit 4** Classroom Manager, p. 41 Guided Reading and Review, p. 42 Chapter Summary, p. 44 Vocabulary, p. 45 Reteaching, p. 46	**Teaching Resources** **Unit 4** Critical Thinking, p. 48 Guide to the Essentials, p. 69 **Technology** Section Reading Support Transparencies

NRICHMENT / PRE-AP

Teaching Resources
Primary Sources and Literature Readings

Other Print Resources
DK Atlas

Technology
World Video Explorer: Cultures of Europe and Russia, A Trip to: Three Capitals
Companion Web site, phschool.com

Teaching Resources
Outline Maps, p. 17–18

Technology
Color Transparencies 68
Passport to the World CD-ROM

Teaching Resources
Outline Maps, p. 22–23

Technology
Color Transparencies 72

Teaching Resources
Unit 4
Enrichment, p. 47
Cooperative Learning Activity, pp. 118–120
Outline Maps, p. 27

ASSESSMENT

Prentice Hall Assessment System

Core Assessment
Chapter Tests with ExamView® Test Bank, Ch. 16
ExamView® Test Bank CD-ROM, Ch. 16

Standardized Test Preparation
Diagnose and Prescribe
Diagnostic Tests for Middle Grades Social Studies Skills
Review and Reteach
Review Book for World Studies
Practice and Assess
Test-taking Strategies with Transparencies for Middle Grades Test Prep Book
Test-taking Strategies Posters

Teaching Resources
Unit 4
Section Quizzes, pp. 37, 40, and 43
Chapter Tests, pp. 150–155

Technology
Companion Web site, phschool.com
Ch. 16 Self-Test

World Video Explorer
Each region of the world is explored through regional flyovers and investigative field trips. Case study segments give students an in-depth view of the history, economy, government, and culture of a key place in each region. Case studies include Nigeria, Mexico, China, British Columbia, and the Czech Republic.

In Your Classroom

CUSTOMIZE FOR INDIVIDUAL NEEDS

Gifted and Talented

Teacher's Edition
- Train Travel, p. 293

Teaching Resources
- Enrichment, p. 47
- Primary Sources and Literature Readings

Honors/Pre-AP

Teacher's Edition
- Train Travel, p. 293

Teaching Resources
- Critical Thinking, p. 48
- Primary Sources and Literature Readings

ESL

Teacher's Edition
- Train Travel, p. 293

Teaching Resources
- Guided Reading and Review, pp. 36, 39, and 42
- Vocabulary, p. 45
- Reteaching, p. 46
- Guide to the Essentials, pp. 68–70
- Social Studies and Geography Skills, p. 53

Technology
- Social Studies Skills Tutor CD-ROM
- Section Reading Support Transparencies

Less Proficient Readers

Teacher's Edition
- Train Travel, p. 293

Teaching Resources
- Guided Reading and Review, pp. 36, 39, and 42
- Vocabulary, p. 45
- Reteaching, p. 46
- Guide to the Essentials, pp. 68–70
- Social Studies and Geography Skills, p. 53

Technology
- Social Studies Skills Tutor CD-ROM
- Section Reading Support Transparencies

Less Proficient Writers

Teacher's Edition
- Train Travel, p. 293

Teaching Resources
- Guided Reading and Review, pp. 36, 39, and 42
- Vocabulary, p. 45
- Guide to the Essentials, pp. 68–70
- Social Studies and Geography Skills, p. 53

Technology
- Social Studies Skills Tutor CD-ROM
- Section Reading Support Transparencies

DORLING KINDERSLEY

At the end of each unit, you will find information adapted from Dorling Kindersley's *Illustrated Children's Encyclopedia* that connects to the region being studied and to one of the seven content strands. In addition, your resources include Dorling Kindersley's *Atlas*, which contains valuable information about countries from around the world.

TEACHER'S EDITION INDEX

CHAPTER 16 PACING SUGGESTIONS

For 90-minute Blocks

See suggestions in the Teaching Resources Pacing Charts for Chapter 16. Use Color Transparencies 68, 72.

Running Out of Time?

See the Guide to the Essentials, pp. 68–70.

INTERDISCIPLINARY LINKS

Middle Grades Math: Tools for Success

Course 1, Lesson 1-2, **Make a Table**

Course 2, Lesson 7-8, **Circle Graphs**

Science Explorer

Cells and Heredity, Lesson 4-2, **Human Genetic Disorders**

Prentice Hall Literature

Copper, The Ant and the Dove, Arachne

BIBLIOGRAPHY

For the Teacher

Collins, Michael, and Matthew Price. *The Story of Christianity: A Celebration of 2,000 Years of Faith.* Dorling Kindersley, 2001.

Circling the Globe: A Young People's Guide to Countries and Cultures of the World. Kingfisher, 1995.

The Russian Way of Life. AIMS Media, 1995. Videocassette.

For the Student

Easy

Dance (*Eyewitness* series). Dorling Kindersley, 2001.

Kendall, Ross. *Russian Girl: Life in an Old Russian Town.* Scholastic, 1994.

Average

Richardson, Wendy. *Cities: Through the Eyes of Artists.* Children's Press, 1991.

Challenging

Glancey, Jonathon. *The Story of Architecture.* Dorling Kindersley, 2001.

Literature Connection

Hicyilmaz, Gaye. *The Frozen Waterfall.* Farrar, 1994.

Pushkin, Alexander. *The Tale of Tsar Saltan.* Dial, 1996.

Take It to the NET

The World Explorer companion Web site, found on **phschool.com**, offers activities for exploring geographical, historical, and cultural resources on the Internet. It also provides on-line links for key content and all Section and Chapter Assessment activities.

The **Teacher site** also provides teachers with regional data and ideas for student research and activities.

Students can use the **Student site** to find chapter-by-chapter Internet resource links and to access Self-Tests.

CHAPTER 16

Connecting to the Guiding Questions

In this chapter, students will read about the cultures of Europe and Russia. Content in this chapter corresponds to the following Guiding Questions outlined in the beginning of the unit.

- How has the geography of Europe and Russia influenced economic, political, and cultural differences in the region?
- What are some cultural traits that European nations share, and what are some traits that make each nation unique?
- How are people's lives changing with the freedom of the newly formed democracies of Eastern Europe?
- What are the economic advantages of participating in the European Union?
- Why is it important for people in democratic societies to exercise their responsibilities as citizens?

Using the Literature Activities

As a class, read the excerpt and discuss the description of the village.

- Most students will probably say that the feudal system wasn't fair. They may note differences in daily or common tasks, as well.
- Paragraphs should use descriptive language to paint a picture of life in a city or town today.

Heterogeneous Groups

The following activity is suitable for heterogeneous groups.

Journal Writing

Train Travel, p. 293

eTeach

Be sure to check out this month's discussion with a Master Teacher. Go to **phschool.com**.

CHAPTER 16

EUROPE AND RUSSIA: Rich in Culture

Pearl in the Egg

Sir Geoffrey was lord of the manor, which included his great stone house and all the land surrounding it. He owned this tiny village. He even owned most of the people in it. A few, like the baker, the miller, and the soapmaker, were freemen and free women. They worked for themselves and paid the lord taxes....

But the serfs were not free. They could never leave the manor, or marry without the lord's permission. They could not fish in the streams or hunt in the forest....The serfs also paid taxes. Each year they gave Sir Geoffrey a portion of their crops. He took a share of their eggs; if a flock of sheep or geese increased, he took a share; and if a cow had a calf, he took that also. On certain days of the week each family had to send a man—and an ox if they had one—to help plow the lord's fields, harvest his crops, and do their work. Each woman had to weave one garment a year for the lord and his family.

—from *Pearl in the Egg* by Dorothy Van Woerkom

Using Literature

This description of life in the Middle Ages is from a novel based on the life of a girl who lived in the 1200s. Because it is set during a certain historical period, it reveals a great deal about life in that particular place and time.

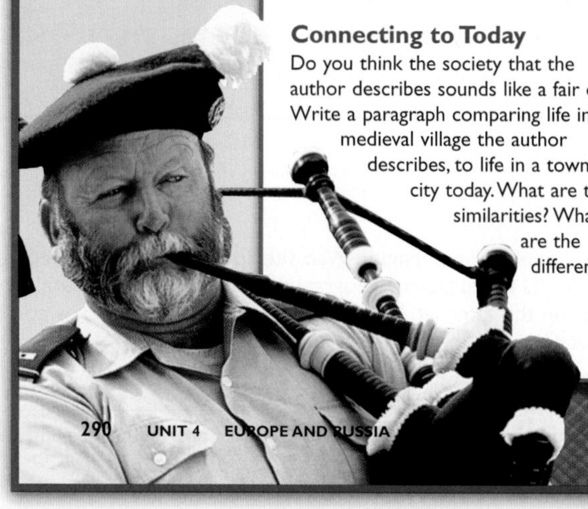

Connecting to Today

Do you think the society that the author describes sounds like a fair one? Write a paragraph comparing life in the medieval village the author describes, to life in a town or city today. What are the similarities? What are the differences?

Writing a Descriptive Paragraph

If the author were writing about your community, how might she describe it? Reread her description of the village in the novel. Then, make a list of important points to include in a description of the place where you live. Use your notes to write a paragraph describing it to someone who might live 500 years from now.

Resource Directory

Teaching Resources

Primary Sources and Literature Readings extend content with a selection related to the concepts in this chapter.

Other Print Resources

DK Atlas

Technology

Cultures of Europe and Russia, from the World Video Explorer, enhances understanding of the many facets of European and Russian culture.

A Trip to: Three Capitals, from the World Video Explorer, enhances understanding of the history and culture of London, Paris, and Moscow.

How People Live Transparencies, Unit 4

Student Edition on Audio CD, Ch. 16

SECTION 1

The Cultures of Western Europe

BEFORE YOU READ

READING FOCUS

1. How has industry shaped the cities of Western Europe?
2. How do immigrants enrich Europe's cultural centers?
3. How has the development of the European Union influenced Western Europe?

KEY TERMS
urbanization
multicultural
tariff

KEY PLACES
Paris
London
Madrid
Berlin
Stockholm

NOTE TAKING

Copy the flow chart below. As you read the section, fill in the chart with information about Western Europe.

Farm machinery is developed. → □ → □ → □ →

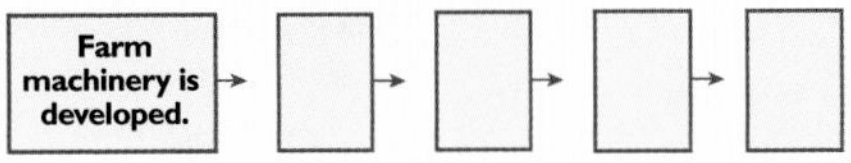

MAIN IDEA

Western Europe has prospered because of the change from an agricultural to an industrial economy, from a closed to a multicultural society, and from several competing nations to a single union.

Setting the Scene

The capital cities of Western Europe have distinctive characters. **Paris,** France attracts scholars, writers, and artists. **London,** England is known for its grand historic buildings, theaters, and parks. **Madrid** (muh DRID), Spain is friendly and relaxing. **Berlin,** Germany is full of activity. **Stockholm,** Sweden combines Viking history with modern design.

Most Western European cities are a mix of the old and the new. Buildings from the Middle Ages stand beside modern apartments and office complexes. Cars and buses travel over cobblestone streets built by the Romans. People travel to these cities to enjoy the cultural attractions, past and present.

Growth in Industry

The prosperity, or wealth, of Western Europe is based on industry. Factories in Western Europe make consumer goods that are in great demand around the world, as well as steel, cars, machines, and many other important products.

British Theater

CULTURE "The Mousetrap," a play by mystery writer Agatha Christie, has been playing continuously in London since its opening in November 1952. **Critical Thinking** What cultural activities and events help to define the city or town where you live?

Lesson Objectives

1. Explain how industry influenced Western European cities.
2. Describe the positive effects of immigrants in Western Europe.
3. Explain how the development of the European Union has changed Western Europe.

Lesson Plan

① Engage

Warm-Up Activity

Have students use the political map of Europe in the Atlas at the back of this book to locate several cities in Western Europe, such as Barcelona, Paris, Berlin, and Rome. Point out that even though these cities are separated by only several hundred miles, each is in a different country and is home to a different language and culture. Explain that, by contrast, students could travel nearly three thousand miles (from New York to Los Angeles) and still be in the United States, where most people share the same language and culture.

Activating Prior Knowledge

Have the class list cultural events and historical details that are unique to their community (fairs, pageants, monuments, entertainment attractions).

Resource Directory

 Teaching Resources

Classroom Manager in the Unit 4 Teaching Resources, p. 35

Guided Reading and Review in the Unit 4 Teaching Resources, p. 36

Guide to the Essentials, p. 67

 Technology

Section Reading Support Transparencies

Answers to...

CRITICAL THINKING

Possible answers might include theater, art museums, sporting events, religious celebrations and practices, and educational opportunities.

Lesson Plan continued

2 Explore

Have students read the section and explore the following questions: What are some differences among European cities? Why did Europeans move from farms to cities? Why did people begin to immigrate to Western Europe? How do immigrants affect their new countries?

3 Teach

Have students work in pairs to develop a quiz containing five questions and answers covering the main ideas of this section. Then, have student pairs challenge the class to answer their questions. This activity should take about 30 minutes.

Questions for Discussion

HISTORY **Why do you think it was important to the Allies to rebuild Germany as a democracy?**

Students may suggest that rebuilding Germany as a democracy might lessen the chances of another dictator leading Germany into war.

ECONOMICS **How did the European Union increase trade both between EU nations and with the rest of the world?**

Between 1958 and 1970, the EU ended tariffs. There was six times more trade between EU nations and three times more trade with the rest of the world.

Answers to...

CHART STUDY

The Netherlands and Norway have the most service workers. Spain and Austria have the most industrial workers. Cities would have more service and industrial workers because these occupations require a dense concentration of people.

CRITICAL THINKING

The combination of both old and the new elements is typical of Western Europe.

The Labor Force in Selected Western European Countries

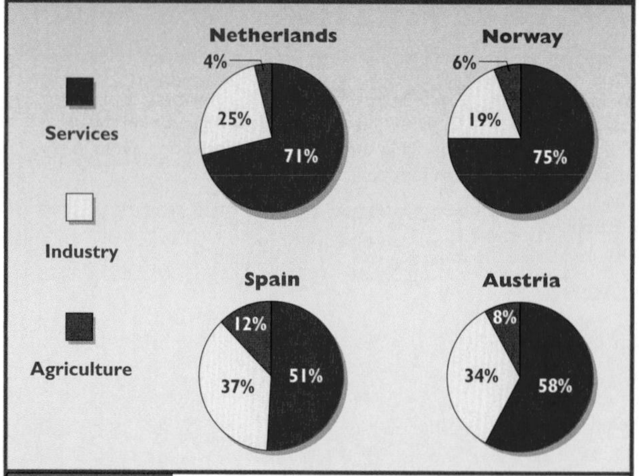

ECONOMICS Today, most people in the Netherlands, Norway, Spain, and Austria make their living in services, performing tasks for other people. Workers in industry make products. Workers in agriculture grow crops and raise livestock. **Chart Study** Of the countries shown here, which two have the largest proportion of service workers? Which two have the largest proportion of industrial workers? Would you expect to find service and industrial workers in cities or in rural areas? Why?

Technological Innovation Two hundred years ago, most Europeans worked in agriculture. As machinery was developed and farming techniques were improved, fewer workers were needed on the land.

The need for farmworkers decreased just as the Industrial Revolution began. Farmworkers moved to the cities to fill factory jobs. This growth of cities, or **urbanization** (ur bun ih ZAY shun), increased after World War II. Money from the United States to help Western Europe recover from the destruction of the war helped make the region's industrial centers stronger than ever.

Today, most Western Europeans work in factories or in service industries such as banking, education, and health care. And most Western European workers earn good wages and have comfortable lives. For example, a visitor to Germany would see a fast-paced society that is run without a lot of waste or extra effort by hardworking people. City streets, buses, parks, and playgrounds are clean. Hotels are efficient. German cars are well designed and long-lasting. Travel from place to place is swift, either on the excellent highway system or on high-speed trains.

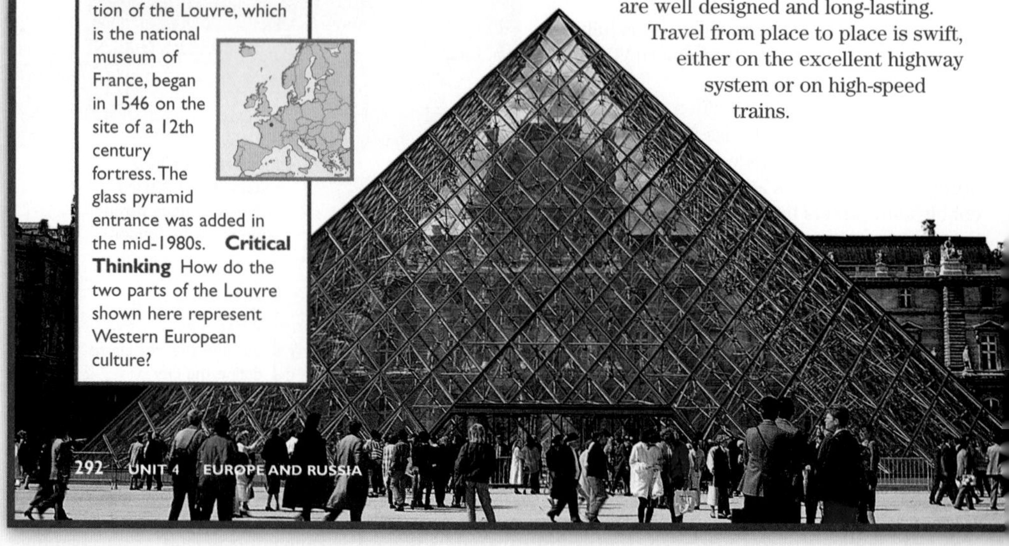

The Louvre

CULTURE Construction of the Louvre, which is the national museum of France, began in 1546 on the site of a 12th century fortress. The glass pyramid entrance was added in the mid-1980s. **Critical Thinking** How do the two parts of the Louvre shown here represent Western European culture?

Resource Directory

Teaching Resources

Outline Maps Western Europe, pp. 17–18

Social Studies and Geography Skills, Reading a Circle Graph, p. 53

Technology

Color Transparencies 68 Western Europe: Physical-Political Map

Passport to the World CD-ROM This interactive CD-ROM allows students to explore each region of the world. Students view regional videos, take a photo tour, and explore a historical timeline. Students record their travels in an Explorer's Journal, and receive passport stamps when they pass regional quizzes.

However, life is not all hard work. Many people are given up to six weeks of vacation each year. The mountains and rivers are popular spots for all forms of outdoor recreation. Cities offer many cultural festivals and celebrations, as well as museums, plays, and concerts that are enjoyed by citizens and tourists alike.

British Schoolchildren

CULTURE The children in this picture are on a school outing in London. **Critical Thinking** How do you think the culture these children experience is different from that of their parents? Their grandparents?

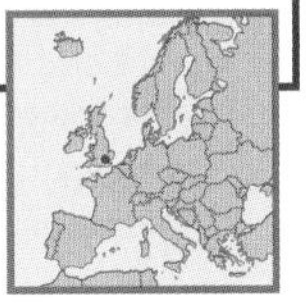

Immigration and Culture

Life in Western Europe was not always so good. In the 1800s and early 1900s, millions of people left Europe to find a better life in the United States, Canada, and South America. However, since World War II, the direction of human movement has changed. As industry developed in the postwar years, more workers were needed. Western Europeans did not leave their homeland, and people began moving in from other parts of the world, including Eastern Europe, North Africa, Asia, and the Middle East. Today, these immigrants make up about 6 percent of the workforce in Western Europe.

When immigrants leave their homelands, they bring their languages, religious beliefs, values, and customs. But most immigrants make changes in their way of life. They may change the way they dress, or discover new ways of cooking. Most of them learn the language of their new country.

Immigration has changed the cultures of Western Europe. In countries such as Britain and France, people from many different backgrounds live and work together. They learn about each other's way of life, and in the process, they begin to blend their backgrounds. As a result, many Western European countries are multicultural. **Multicultural** (mul ti KUHL chur ul) means a country's way of life is influenced by many different cultures.

The Influence of the European Union

If you look at a map of Europe, you can see that most of the countries are small and close together. High-speed trains can take travelers from one country to another in a matter of hours. Ideas, goods, and raw materials can travel very quickly as well. The open exchange of ideas and items has helped make Western Europe prosperous and strong.

4 Assess/Reteach

See the answers to the Section 1 Assessment. You may also use students' completed quizzes as an assessment.

Acceptable quizzes include five questions with correct answers.

Commendable quizzes include questions and answers that cover several main ideas.

Outstanding quizzes show a thorough understanding of the main ideas of the section.

ACTIVITY

Journal Writing

Train Travel Tell students they are on a train traveling across Europe from west to east. Then have them write a journal entry describing their journey, telling what countries they pass through, and at what cities the train stops. Encourage students to include other details, such as the language spoken in each country. If students are keeping an Explorer's Journal as described in the opening pages of their book, you may wish to do this writing activity as part of that journal.

Verbal/Linguistic

SKILLS MINI LESSON

Interpreting Graphs

You may **introduce** the skill by explaining that a circle graph is a way of showing the percentage distribution of information about any subject or subjects. Circle graphs can also be compared with other circle graphs containing the same information in order to show the relative distribution of the subject or subjects in different places or at different times. For example, the circle graph on the preceeding page compares the percentages of labor force distribution among four selected countries. Ask questions such as, *Which country has the smallest percentage of its labor force working in agriculture?* To **apply** the skill, students should write three true-or-false questions that can be answered using the information in the graphs.

Answers to...

CRITICAL THINKING

Students may explain that continual immigration to Britain in recent decades has made British culture increasingly rich and diverse.

SECTION I ASSESSMENT

AFTER YOU READ

1. (a) capital of France (b) capital of Great Britain (c) capital of Spain (d) capital of Germany (e) capital of Sweden
2. (a) growth of cities caused by farmworkers' moving to cities (b) influenced by many different cultures (c) fee that government charges for goods entering the country
3. Machinery was developed to improve farming techniques and increase crop production, and it reduced the need for farmworkers. People moved to the cities to fill the need for more workers in the factories.
4. A multicultural society has the benefit of exposure to a variety of ideas, beliefs, traditions, customs, and points of view.
5. The EU has strengthened the economy, preserved peace, and allowed for the free exchange of people, ideas, goods, and services across the boundaries of Europe.
6. Paragraphs will vary. Students should describe the specific ways that Western Europe has changed and prospered.
7. Answers will vary. Accept all reasonable responses.

Europe's New Money—The Euro

ECONOMICS

To make it easier for member nations to trade among themselves, the European Union adopted a single currency called the European Currency Unit, or ECU. Later, the ECU was renamed the Euro. In 1999, consumers began using the Euro, but only through checks, credit cards, or bank transfers. Actual bank notes and coins appeared in 2002, replacing the national currencies of participating EU members. **Critical Thinking** How might the Euro make travel and trade among the European countries easier?

It was not always so easy for people, goods, and ideas to move throughout Western Europe. Until World War II, many countries kept their borders closed. Changes began in 1950, when France and Germany agreed to work together to rebuild after World War II. Other nations soon joined them to create an organization called the European Union (EU). In 2002, the EU had 15 member nations and plans for adding more. The EU works to expand trade in Europe. One way to do this is to end **tariffs,** or fees that a government charges for goods entering the country. Between 1958 and 1970, when these tariffs were ended, there was six times more trade between EU member nations and three times more trade with the rest of the world. The EU hopes to maintain an alliance that continues to enable people, money, goods, and services to move freely among member countries.

SECTION I ASSESSMENT

AFTER YOU READ

RECALL

1. Identify: (a) Paris, (b) London, (c) Madrid, (d) Berlin, (e) Stockholm
2. Define: (a) urbanization, (b) multicultural, (c) tariff

COMPREHENSION

3. What caused the shift in Western Europe from an agricultural to an industrial economy?
4. What are the strengths of a multicultural society?
5. What has the European Union accomplished over the past 50 years?

CRITICAL THINKING AND WRITING

6. **Exploring the Main Idea** Review the Main Idea statement at the beginning of this section. Write a paragraph describing how change has benefited Western Europe and helped it to prosper.

ACTIVITY

Take It to the NET

7. **Exploring Baroque Architecture** Architecture can teach you about the history and culture of past societies. View the images on the web site. What does the Baroque architecture tell you about the time period, the people, and the culture? Visit the World Explorer: People, Places and Cultures section of **phschool.com** for help in completing this activity.

Answers to...

CRITICAL THINKING

Answers will vary. One possibility is that people traveling to several countries can carry just one kind of currency with them, instead of several. Also, trade will be easier since companies importing or exporting goods will not have to worry about the exchange rates of various currencies.

Resource Directory

Teaching Resources

Section Quiz in the Unit 4 Teaching Resources, p. 37

SECTION 2

The Cultures of Eastern Europe

BEFORE YOU READ

READING FOCUS

1. How have Slavic cultures shaped life in Eastern Europe?
2. What are the causes of ethnic conflict in Eastern Europe?

KEY TERMS

migration
ethnic group
NATO

KEY PLACES

Czech Republic
Slovakia

MAIN IDEA

The people of Eastern Europe share many cultural traits, but it is their cultural differences that give them a national identity.

NOTE TAKING

Copy the concept web below. As you read the section, complete the web with information about the cultural traits of Eastern Europeans. Add additional ovals as needed.

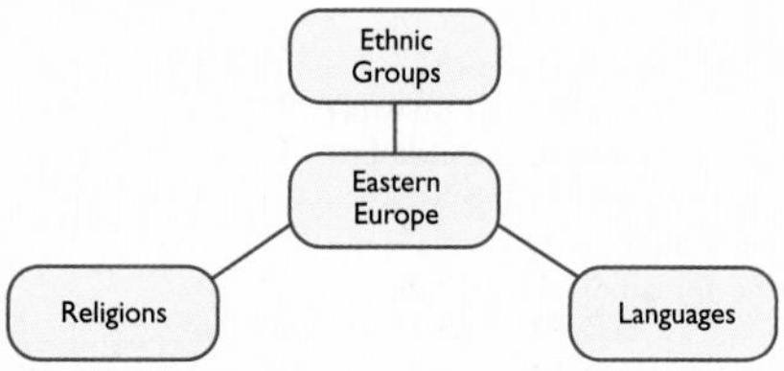

Setting the Scene

Look at a map of Europe in 1900 and you may notice something odd. Poland is missing. From 1795 to 1918, this nation disappeared from the maps of Europe.

A geographer could quickly solve this mystery of the missing country. Poland lies on the North European Plain. There are few mountains or other natural barriers to keep invaders out. In 1795, Russia, Prussia, and Austria moved into Poland and divided it among themselves. Poland did not become independent again until the end of World War I.

Movement throughout much of Eastern Europe is easy. For thousands of years, groups have entered or crossed this region. This movement from place to place, called **migration** (my GRAY shun), is still happening today.

There are many reasons for migration in Eastern Europe. Long ago, people moved to find places with a good supply of natural resources. Sometimes people moved to escape enemies. In more recent times, people have fled places where their religious or political beliefs put them in danger. And they have often moved to find a better life.

Europe in 1871

GEOGRAPHY From 1795 to 1918, the nation of Poland disappeared from maps such as the one shown here. **Critical Thinking** How did the geography of Eastern Europe affect the takeover of Poland?

SECTION 2

Lesson Objectives

1. Identify the major ethnic groups of Eastern Europe.
2. Explain the reasons for ethnic conflict in Eastern Europe.

Lesson Plan

1 Engage

Warm-Up Activity

Ask students to imagine that residents of each state in the United States spoke a language different from residents of other states. Have students discuss how this might change travel between states. How might residents of different states feel about one another?

Activating Prior Knowledge

Have students name holidays celebrated by their families. Discuss whether everyone in the class celebrates the same holidays. Then discuss whether all families celebrate the same holidays in the same way.

Resource Directory

Teaching Resources

Classroom Manager in the Unit 4 Teaching Resources, p. 38

Guided Reading and Review in the Unit 4 Teaching Resources, p. 39

Guide to the Essentials, p. 68

Technology

Section Reading Support Transparencies

Answers to...

CRITICAL THINKING

Poland lies on the North European Plain. There are few mountains or other natural barriers to keep invaders out.

Lesson Plan continued

2 Explore

Have students read the section and explore the following questions: What are some major differences among the Slavs? What are some other ethnic groups in Eastern Europe? Why did some Eastern European countries break into smaller countries? What happened when these countries broke up?

3 Teach

Have students develop a chart with the following headings: *Nation*, *Language*, and *Religion*. Have students fill in each column with facts about ethnic groups mentioned in the section. Then have students write a paragraph explaining how differences can lead to conflict among ethnic groups. This activity should take about 30 minutes.

Questions for Discussion

CULTURE **How do you think ethnic conflicts affect the ways in which people think of people from other cultures, and how can people's attitudes make it harder to solve these conflicts?**

Answers will vary, but may include the idea that when ethnic groups fight, each group may consider the other to be cruel. People may be unwilling to make peace with a group they hold responsible for killing or hurting family members.

CULTURE **What cultural aspects link the Slavs in Eastern Europe? What aspects separate them?**

Slavs now speak different languages and live in different nations. But because they came from the same ethnic group, they still share many customs and do similar kinds of work, including farming.

Answers to...

MAP STUDY

Invite students to share their observations about cultural connections, migration, and apparent isolation that are suggested by the map.

Eastern Europe: Language Groups

CULTURE Most people in Eastern Europe speak Indo-European languages. These include Slavic languages, like Czech, Polish, and Russian, and Baltic languages, which come from northern European countries like Latvia and Lithuania. Romance languages come from France, Italy, Portugal, Romania, and Spain. The Finno-Ugric languages of Estonia, Hungary, and Romania do not belong to the Indo-European family. **Map Study** How do these languages show the spread of cultural traits?

Ethnic Groups in Eastern Europe

Among the groups that long ago migrated to Eastern Europe were the Slavs (slahvz). These people first lived in the mountains of modern Slovakia (sloh VAH kee uh) and Ukraine. By the 700s, they had spread south to Greece, west to the Alps, and north to the coast of the Baltic Sea.

Slavic Cultures Today, the Slavs are one of the major ethnic groups in Eastern Europe. People of the same **ethnic group** share things, such as a culture, a language, and a religion, that set them apart from their neighbors. Two thousand years ago, there was a single Slavic language. But as the Slavs separated, different Slavic languages were born. Today, some 10 Slavic languages are spoken in Eastern Europe. These include Czech, Polish, and Russian.

Though the Slavs now have different languages and live in different nations, they still have many of the same customs. Large numbers of Eastern Europeans still work as farmers, and live in rural areas where customs change more slowly than in cities.

Resource Directory

Teaching Resources

Outline Maps, Eastern Europe, pp. 22–23

Technology

Color Transparencies 72 Eastern Europe: Political Map

World Video Explorer See the Czech Republic's case study for an overview of the Czech Republic's history, economy, government, and culture. Discussion questions are included.

Other Ethnic Groups Such countries as Poland, Croatia (kroh AY shuh), Slovenia (sloh VEE nee uh), and the **Czech Republic** are almost entirely Slavic. But many other ethnic groups live in Eastern Europe. About 95 percent of the people of Hungary belong to an ethnic group called the Magyars (MAG yarz). In the country of Romania, most people belong to yet another ethnic group, the Romanians. Similarly, the Bulgars of Bulgaria and the Albanians of Albania are separate ethnic groups. And people belonging to the German ethnic group live in several of the countries of Eastern Europe.

Religion in Eastern Europe

CULTURE There are major religious differences among Slavs. Some follow the Eastern Orthodox faith, some are Protestant, and some are Roman Catholic. The women in this photograph are Muslims. **Critical Thinking** How can religious differences in a region lead to cultural conflicts?

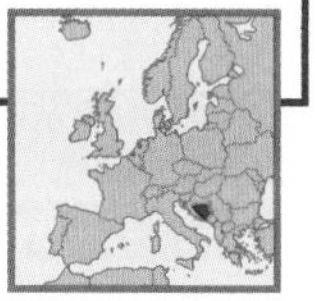

Ethnic Conflict

In some Eastern European countries, people of different ethnic groups live together in harmony. But in other places, there have been ethnic conflicts.

Czechs and Slovaks: A Peaceful Division For most of the 1900s, Czechoslovakia (CHECK uh sloh VAH kee uh) was a single country. The two main ethnic groups were the Czechs and the Slovaks.

Czechoslovakia was a parliamentary democracy from 1918 to 1935, but after World War II, the Soviet Union controlled Czechoslovakia. Almost overnight, the Communist Party took over the country. Many people were not happy with the communist government. From the 1960s to the 1980s, students and writers formed groups promoting a return to democracy. Vaclav Havel, a playwright, was a major voice of protest. He spoke out against the government for more than 20 years and was repeatedly put in jail. The government urged him to move out of the country, but he always refused.

Mass protests forced the communist government to consider changes. In 1989, the Communist Party gave up its power and worked in cooperation with the democratic groups. This generally nonviolent change is called the Velvet Revolution. Havel later was elected president of Czechoslovakia.

The Czechs and the Slovaks disagreed about how to carry out the goals of the newly democratic country. In 1993, they agreed to separate, and the countries of the Czech Republic and **Slovakia** were born. Perhaps because most Czechs and Slovaks already lived in separate parts of the country, the split was peaceful.

4 Assess/Reteach

See the answers to the Section 2 Assessment. You may also use students' completed charts as an assessment.

Acceptable charts comprise most of the facts included in the section; paragraphs may show some understanding of the conflicts.

Commendable charts include all of the facts given in the section; paragraphs indicate that students have a good understanding of the conflicts.

Outstanding charts include a full description of all the facts given in the section; paragraphs give a clear, concise explanation of the ethnic conflicts.

HISTORY

Not on the Maps

Poland was missing from maps of Europe published during World War II. In 1939, Germany and Russia secretly agreed to divide Poland. To that end, Germany invaded Poland from the west, and Russia from the east. The Poles were defeated in just a few weeks. Germany and Russia then divided the country between them, erasing Poland from the map. With the defeat of Germany at the end of the war in 1945, a new Poland was formed from the lands that Germany had seized. Russia, however, kept most of the Polish lands it had taken in 1939.

SKILLS MINI LESSON

Distinguishing Fact From Opinion

As you **introduce** the skill, explain that to have an accurate picture of world events, students need to be able to distinguish fact from opinion. Point out that a statement of fact can be supported by evidence. An opinion cannot be verified. Have students **practice** the skill by asking them to determine whether each of the following statements are fact or opinion and to explain how they can tell. (1) Traditions change more slowly in rural areas. (fact; it is an observable phenomenon) (2) Changing traditions is a good idea. (opinion; it cannot be proved) Suggest that students **apply** the skill by collecting newspaper and periodical articles about the region and highlighting the opinions.

Answers to...

CRITICAL THINKING

Religious differences can imply a fundamental disagreement about life that may be difficult for people to overlook as they try to set common goals.

SECTION 2 ASSESSMENT

AFTER YOU READ

1. (a) country formed when Czechoslovakia divided (b) country formed when Czechoslovakia divided
2. (a) movement from place to place (b) people who share things such as language, culture, and religion (c) North Atlantic Treaty Organization—an alliance among the United States and other western nations
3. The Slavic language and culture spread throughout the region hundreds of years ago to make the Slavs one of the major ethnic groups in Eastern Europe, and one of the most influential.
4. Factors include religious differences, language differences, and different ethnic identities.
5. Students may mention details such as the Serbs' Slavic language and the Albanians' Thraco-Illyrian language.
6. Students should recognize the comparative isolation of rural communities, the small number of immigrants there, and the limited amount of migration there.
7. Students may explain that the term is appropriate because of the ethnic, cultural, and national tensions among so many different groups of people in the region.

Answers to...

CRITICAL THINKING

Some students may say that the constant threat of armed conflict would be frightening to live with, whereas others may say that having UN troops on patrol would be reassuring.

A Fragile Peace

HISTORY In the war-torn country of Bosnia-Herzegovina, United Nations troops struggle to keep a fragile peace among the warring parties. **Critical Thinking** How would it feel to live in a city with armed troops patrolling the streets?

Yugoslavia: Violent Division Most of the people of Yugoslavia were part of the same ethnic group—the Slavs. However, various groups within the country had distinct religions and cultures. These differences led to the breakup of Yugoslavia in 1991. The new countries of Bosnia-Herzegovina (BAHZ nee uh herts uh goh VEE nuh), Croatia, Slovenia, Serbia and Montenegro, and Macedonia were formed. War broke out, and thousands of people, mainly Bosnians, were killed. In 1995, **NATO** forces helped bring peace to the region. NATO (North Atlantic Treaty Organization) is an alliance among the United States, Canada, and other western nations. NATO was formed in 1949 with the goal of protecting the interests of the member nations and promoting international cooperation.

By 1999, conflict had again broken out, this time between the Serbs and ethnic Albanians who live in Kosovo, a province of Serbia. As a result, NATO forces were again sent to the region. Though a cease-fire was reached, tensions increased again in 2001 in Macedonia, and the future of the region is uncertain.

SECTION 2 ASSESSMENT

AFTER YOU READ

RECALL

1. Identify: (a) Czech Republic, (b) Slovakia
2. Define: (a) migration, (b) ethnic group, (c) NATO

COMPREHENSION

3. What influence have Slavic cultures had in Eastern Europe?
4. What factors have contributed to ethnic conflict in Eastern Europe?

CRITICAL THINKING AND WRITING

5. **Exploring the Main Idea** Review the Main Idea statement at the beginning of this section. Write a paragraph describing the cultural differences between the Serbs and Albanians.
6. **Recognizing Cause and Effect** Why do you think cultural traits change more slowly in rural areas than in urban areas?

ACTIVITY

7. **Writing a Journal** Write a paragraph in your Explorer's Journal about why you think Eastern Europe has been called "the powder keg of Europe."

Resource Directory

Teaching Resources

Section Quiz in the Unit 4 Teaching Resources, p. 40

SECTION 3

The Cultures of Russia

BEFORE YOU READ

READING FOCUS

1. How have ethnic groups in and around Russia affected Russian history?
2. How are the people of Russia reconnecting with their cultural traditions?

KEY TERMS

heritage
repress
propaganda

KEY PEOPLE AND PLACES

Leo Tolstoy
Peter Tchaikovsky
St. Petersburg

MAIN IDEA

Although the Soviet government of the 20th century tried to control the Russian people's religious beliefs and creative expression, many of their cultural traditions have survived.

NOTE TAKING

Copy the table below. As you read the section, fill in the table with information about cultural expression in Soviet Russia and in present-day Russia.

Cultural Expression in Soviet Union	Cultural Expression in Federation of Russia
forbid practice of religious beliefs	renewed practice of religious beliefs

Setting the Scene

For many years, Russians passing the Church of Saints Cosmas and Damian in Moscow never heard a choir or religious services. The communist government of the Soviet Union owned the church and used it as a printing shop. In the Soviet Union, people were restricted from practicing religion.

In 1991, the Soviet Union collapsed. Two years later, Russians who had never given up their faith took back their church. Now Saints Cosmas and Damian is filled with people singing songs of worship. In recent years, hundreds of other churches in Moscow and across all of Russia have reopened their doors. It is one way the Russian people are reclaiming their culture.

Reclaiming Cultural Traditions

CULTURE Under communism, worship in Soviet churches was restricted. Now, the doors of churches all over the former Soviet Union are open again for worshippers. **Critical Thinking** How would you feel if your government did not allow you to freely practice your religion? What could you do about it?

Russia's Ethnic Mix

The Russian Orthodox religion, a branch of Christianity, has been a powerful bond among Russians for hundreds of years. It is part of the Russian **heritage** (HEHR ut ij), the customs and practices that are passed from one generation to the next. Another part of the Russian heritage is ethnic identity.

SECTION 3

Lesson Objectives

1. Describe the role that ethnic groups have played in the history of Russia.
2. Explain how Russia is recovering its heritage.

Lesson Plan

1 Engage

Warm-Up Activity

Ask student volunteers to discuss their visits to art museums and to describe some of the art that they liked. Ask the class to discuss whether they think that artists should or should not be allowed to create whatever they wish without government involvement.

Activating Prior Knowledge

Ask students to name the holidays celebrated by different ethnic groups in their families and communities. Then have them describe the different ways in which ethnic groups might celebrate the same holiday.

2 Explore

Have students read the section and explore the following questions: What role has religion played in Russian history? How have Russia's many ethnic groups reacted to the breakup of the Soviet Union? Why is St. Petersburg considered an elegant city? How has education changed in Russia since the breakup of the Soviet Union?

Answers to...

CRITICAL THINKING

Students may respond that that they would feel dissatisfied with or resentful towards the government, or that they would try to find ways to practice their religion in private.

Resource Directory

Teaching Resources

Classroom Manager in the Unit 4 Teaching Resources, p. 41

Guided Reading and Review in the Unit 4 Teaching Resources, p. 42

Guide to the Essentials, p. 69

Technology

Section Reading Support Transparencies

Lesson Plan continued

3 Teach

Have students develop a chart with two column headings: *In the Soviet Union* and *In the New Russia.* The rows should have the following headings: *Religion, Art, Ethnic Groups,* and *Education.* Have students fill in each box with examples from the section. This activity should take about 20 minutes.

Question for Discussion

CULTURE How has Russia's ethnic mix created challenges for the new Russian government?

Ethnic groups seeking more freedom have challenged the government. The government has tried to give them more autonomy, but when some groups have demanded complete independence, the government has repressed them.

4 Assess/Reteach

See the answers to the Section 3 Assessment. You may also use students' completed charts as an assessment.

Acceptable charts include most of the facts included in the section.

Commendable charts include all of the facts given in the section.

Outstanding charts include a full description of all the facts given in the section and demonstrate a clear understanding of the differences between the Soviet Union and the new Russia.

Siberia's Ethnic Groups

CULTURE Many ethnic groups live in Siberia, Russia's largest region. This father and child are Nentsy, an ethnic group that lives in northwest Siberia. **Critical Thinking** Would the isolation of Siberia from the rest of Russia affect the cultural traits of its different ethnic groups? In what ways?

More than 80 percent of the Russian people belong to the ethnic group of Russian Slavs. These people generally speak the Russian language and live in western parts of the country.

Other Ethnic Groups Besides the Slavs, more than 75 different ethnic groups live in Russia. The Finns and Turks live in regions of the Ural and Caucasus (KAW kuh sus) mountains. Armenians and Mongolians live along Russia's southern edges. The Yakuts (yah KOOTS) live in small areas of Siberia. These groups speak languages other than Russian and they also follow different religions. Muslims make up Russia's second-largest religious group, after Russian Orthodox believers. Many followers of Buddhism (BOOD izum) live near Russia's border with China.

United or Divided? When the Soviet Union came apart, some non-Russian ethnic groups broke away from Russia and formed their own countries. Since that time, other ethnic groups have tried to break ties with Russia.

The new Russian government has tried to keep the country unified by giving ethnic groups the right to rule themselves. At times, however, groups have called for complete independence from Russia. In response, the Russian government has sent the army to **repress,** or put down, the independence movements.

Russian Culture Past and Present and Education

Russia has produced many great artists, thinkers, and writers. Russia's artistic heritage includes outstanding architecture, fine religious paintings, great plays, and intricate art objects. Novelist **Leo Tolstoy** (TOHL stoy) wrote powerful stories of life in Russia in the 1800s. **Peter Tchaikovsky** (chy KAWF skee) composed moving classical music. Russian painters, such as Vasily Kandinsky (kan DIN skee), were leaders in the modern art movement in the early 1900s. In a way, creating works of art is a tradition among Russians.

SKILLS MINI LESSON

Drawing Conclusions

You may wish to **introduce** the skill by explaining that drawing conclusions means looking at several facts or pieces of information, putting them together, and then arriving at a conclusion based on the facts. Point out that students can draw some conclusions about why some ethnic groups wished to form their own countries. Have students **practice** the skill by listing some facts about an ethnic group (for example, its language, culture, and religion). Then have students look at a map of Russia in the Activity Atlas. Point out some geographic features of Russia, as well as its enormous size. To **apply** the skill, have students discuss how these facts might affect a group's desire for its own country. Record students' conclusions on the chalkboard.

Answers to...

CRITICAL THINKING

Students should understand that groups that are relatively isolated from outside influence preserve their cultural traits with little change over the centuries.

Under communism, the creation of great new works of art nearly came to a halt. The Soviet government believed that the purpose of art was to glorify communism. The government banned any art it did not like and jailed countless artists. The only art that the government did like was **propaganda**—the spread of ideas designed to support some cause, such as communism. With the collapse of communism, the Russian people eagerly returned to creating new works of art.

Elegant St. Petersburg An important center of Russian culture is the city of **St. Petersburg.** Visitors to the city can clearly see the Russian mixture of European and Slavic cultures. Peter the Great founded it in 1703. His goal was to create a Russian city as beautiful as any Western European city.

Elegant is the best word for St. Petersburg. The Neva (NYEH vuh) River winds gracefully through the city. Along the river's banks are palaces and public buildings hundreds of years old. St. Petersburg's grandest sight, the Winter Palace, is on the Neva. This 1,000-room palace was the winter home of Russia's czars. Part of the palace is the Hermitage (HUR mih tij) Museum. This museum houses one of the world's finest art collections.

Education in Russia One of the few strengths of the old Soviet Union was its free public education. Under this system, the number of Russians who could read and write rose from about 40 percent to nearly 100 percent.

The new Russia has continued free public schooling for children between ages 6 and 17. Schools are updating their old courses of study, which told only the communist point of view. New courses, such as business management, are preparing students for the new, non-communist Russia. Some private schools run by the Orthodox Church offer similar courses, as well as religious instruction.

A Monument to Heroic Workers

CULTURE Socialist realism was the only style of art permitted in the Soviet Union. Socialist realist paintings and sculptures showed idealized views of heroic workers and farmers, often struggling against great odds. The only purpose of socialist realist art was to further the aims of the Soviet government. This sculpture in Moscow is a monument to Soviet workers. The two workers are holding aloft a hammer and sickle, the symbols of the Soviet Union.

Critical Thinking What aspects of socialist realist art does this sculpture illustrate?

Resource Directory

Teaching Resources

Outline Map, Russia, p. 27

HISTORY

St. Petersburg

The name of the city now called St. Petersburg has changed several times during the city's history. Peter the Great, who founded the city, was heavily influenced by Western European culture, and he used the German word *burg,* meaning "city," as part of his city's name, St. Petersburg. However, in 1914, when Russia and Germany went to war, the city's name was changed from the German to the Russian word *Petrograd,* meaning "Peter's city." When the Communists came to power, the city's name was again changed, this time to *Leningrad,* after one of the founders of Russian communism, V. I. Lenin. Finally, when the Sovier Union collapsed, the city's name was changed back to its original, St. Petersburg.

HISTORY

Teacher and Novelist

Count Leo Tolstoy (1828–1910) was born into wealth and privilege on a country estate, where he spent a good part of his life. Tolstoy, always concerned with the conditions of the peasants in Russia, opened a successful school on his estate for peasant children. Tolstoy, who worked as the teacher, believed that each student should be taught according to his or her individual needs, an idea far ahead of its time. Tolstoy's writings reflect his desire for social reform. His novel *War and Peace* is a story about the experiences of several families during Napoleon's 1812 invasion of Russia. *Anna Karenina* is one of the world's great love stories.

Answers to...

CRITICAL THINKING

Student should recognize that the statue shows workers proudly and triumphantly supporting the symbol of the Soviet government indicating that the workers themselves are the very foundation of the government.

SECTION 3 ASSESSMENT

AFTER YOU READ

1. (a) novelist who wrote about Russia in the 1800s (b) classical composer (c) an elegant Russian city founded by Peter the Great
2. (a) customs and practices that are passed from one generation to the next (b) to put down (c) spread of ideas designed to support some cause
3. (a) the Slavs; (b) The government has given ethnic groups the right to rule themselves, but it has repressed independence movements.
4. Russia has a long history of great artists and writers. But under the Soviet government the only form of artistic expression allowed was in the form of propaganda. Once communism ended, the Russian people eagerly returned to their artistic traditions.
5. Students should point out that language represents a strong connection to one's heritage and preserves cultural patterns passed down from generation to generation.
6. Responses will vary. Students should develop persuasive arguments in favor of independence in their speeches.
7. Letters might include mention of elegant old palaces and public buildings, the Winter Palace, and the Hermitage Museum.

Russian Treasures

CULTURE Visitors to St. Petersburg's Hermitage Museum can view priceless art objects in the Emblem Hall.
Critical Thinking Why do you think it is important to Russians to preserve the homes of the czars even though Russia is no longer ruled by a czar?

These changes show that Russia is trying to recover the riches of its past even as it prepares for a new future. Religion and art, two important parts of Russia's cultural heritage, can now be freely expressed. And Russia's young people, unlike their parents, can grow up making more decisions for themselves.

SECTION 3 ASSESSMENT

AFTER YOU READ

RECALL

1. Identify: (a) Leo Tolstoy, (b) Peter Tchaikovsky, (c) St. Petersburg
2. Define: (a) heritage, (b) repress, (c) propaganda

COMPREHENSION

3. (a) What is Russia's major ethnic group? (b) How has the government treated Russia's smaller ethnic groups?
4. What role has art played in connecting the Russian people with their cultural heritage?

CRITICAL THINKING AND WRITING

5. **Exploring the Main Idea** Review the Main Idea statement at the beginning of this section. Write a paragraph describing the role that language may have played in preserving the cultural traditions and traits of ethnic peoples across Russia.
6. **Identifying Point of View** Some of Russia's ethnic groups have demanded their independence. Write a speech in favor of independence for a group you belong to.

ACTIVITY

7. **Writing a Letter** Imagine that you are on a visit to St. Petersburg. Write a letter to your family, describing the works of art and other expressions of the Russian culture that you are experiencing.

Answers to...

CRITICAL THINKING

Students' responses should indicate that the homes of the czars are time capsules of Russia's past history and culture. Preserving these structures helps Russian citizens have an understanding of their heritage.

Resource Directory

Teaching Resources

Section Quiz in the Unit 4 Teaching Resources, p. 43

Chapter Summary in the Unit 4 Teaching Resources, p. 44

Vocabulary in the Unit 4 Teaching Resources, p. 45

Reteaching in the Unit 4 Teaching Resources, p. 46

Enrichment in the Unit 4 Teaching Resources, p. 47

Critical Thinking in the Unit 4 Teaching Resources, p. 48

Synthesizing Information

The diamond at the top of the egg covers a portrait of the czarina.

The windows of the coach are made of a clear type of rock crystal quartz.

The colors of the egg match the colors of the gown Czarina Alexandra wore when she and Czar Nicholas II were crowned in 1896.

The egg holds a model of the coach used for the czar and czarina's crowning. The coach has working doors and folding steps.

This handcrafted egg was given by Czar Nicholas II to his wife, Czarina Alexandra. It was made by the jewelry company Fabergé. The egg is 5 inches (12.6 cm) tall. The miniture coach, encrusted with diamonds, rubies, and rock crystal, is about 3 3/4 inches (9.3 cm) long. Fabergé made 56 Imperial eggs for the czars. Master goldsmiths, jewelers, enamelers, and miniature painters worked on each egg. The eggs never failed to hold a surprise. Inside, something either moved or played a song. Some eggs even contained other objects like this one.

Learn the Skill

When you combine details from different sources to make decisions or draw conclusions, you are synthesizing information. You've already had practice with this skill by looking at images and reading captions in your text and then answering questions about the information. Synthesizing helps you to better understand the information you see, hear, and read. To learn how to synthesize information, follow these steps:

A. Identify the common topic of the different sources of information.

B. Identify the main idea and details of each source of information. The purpose of this skill is to get information on a particular topic from different sources. Before you can compare these sources, you need to focus on each one separately.

C. Identify the similarities and differences between or among the sources. Paying attention to these similarities and differences will help you better understand the topic.

D. Draw conclusions based on the information.

Practice the Skill

Study the two pieces of information above about Fabergé eggs. Then, answer the questions below to help you practice the skill.

- What is the topic of these two sources of information?
- What information about the egg does the photograph contain? The text?
- Based on the information, how special do you think a Fabergé egg was? Do you think a single egg was expensive to produce? Why?

Apply the Skill

See the Chapter Review and Assessment at the end of this chapter for more questions on synthesizing information.

Resource Directory

 Technology
Social Studies Skills Tutor CD-ROM

Answers to...

PRACTICE THE SKILL

Students should be able to determine these answers: an egg made by Fabergé; photograph and captions—overall view of the object, various visual details and facts about the egg's construction and design; text—various facts about the egg's history, form, and construction; extremely special and expensive to produce due to time-consuming work of expert craftspeople.

Lesson Objectives

1. Learn strategies for synthesizing information.
2. Use two sources to synthesize information about a historical topic.

Lesson Plan

1 Engage

To introduce the skill, ask students what they might learn about a familiar topic (for example, the American flag) from a color photograph. From a written explanation of the flag's design? Ask them whether or not it would further their understanding to combine details from these two sources.

2 Explore

Read aloud with students the text under "Learn the Skill." Point out that several sources of information can appear on a single page of a book. Remind students that each source must be approached and understood separately before one attempts to synthesize information.

3 Teach

Invite students to answer the questions under "Practice the Skill." Point out that they will need to study each source closely to glean key details as well as overall impression of the subject.

4 Assess/Reteach

Students should be able to answer the questions. To further assess students' understanding of how to synthesize information, have them complete the "Applying Your Skills" part of the Chapter Review and Assessment at the end of the chapter.

CHAPTER 16

Review and Assessment

Creating a Chapter Summary

Student summaries will vary.

Sample summaries:

Eastern Europe The Slavic people of Eastern Europe share many of the same cultural traits. Regions within each country have distinct cultural identities that have either helped or hindered the process of independence.

Russia Russians are renewing their cultural ties to the past as they move further away from the restrictive policies of the old communist government.

Reviewing Key Terms

1. ethnic group
2. tariff
3. Migration
4. propaganda
5. heritage

Reviewing the Main Ideas

1. They have many cultural attractions such as museums, concerts, restaurants, and plays; they are a mix of old and new; and each city is different from any other.
2. People, goods, and ideas can travel easily from one country to another,. This situation has led to prosperity.
3. Slavs, a major ethnic group in Eastern Europe, live in many countries of Eastern Europe; there are 10 Slavic languages spoken in Eastern Europe, but Slavs still share many of the same customs.
4. Czechoslovakia divided peacefully, but the breakup of Yugoslavia was violent.
5. Many have formed their own separate countries; others who wished to form their own countries but were repressed by the Russians have reacted violently.
6. religious and artistic traditions

CHAPTER 16

Review and Assessment

Creating a Chapter Summary

On a separate piece of paper, draw a web like this one, and include the information about the cultures of Western Europe. Then, add more ovals and summarize the information you learned about the culture of Eastern Europe and Russia.

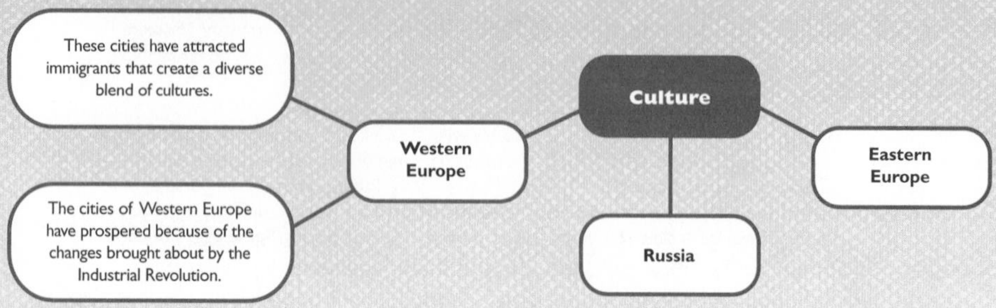
These cities have attracted immigrants that create a diverse blend of cultures.
The cities of Western Europe have prospered because of the changes brought about by the Industrial Revolution.
Western Europe
Culture
Eastern Europe
Russia

Reviewing Key Terms

Complete each sentence with a term from the list below.

propaganda, ethnic group, heritage, tariff, migration

1. An ________ is made up of people who share language, culture, and religion.
2. The fee a government charges for goods entering a country is called a ________.
3. ________ is the movement of people from place to place.
4. The spread of ideas designed to support a cause is called ________.
5. A person's ________ is made up of customs passed down from older generations.

Reviewing the Main Ideas

1. What features make the cities in Western Europe great centers for culture? (Section 1)
2. How do open borders and free trade affect the way Western Europeans live? (Section 1)
3. Who are the Slavs and why are they an important part of the population of Eastern Europe? (Section 2)
4. How was the breakup of Czechoslovakia different from the breakup of Yugoslavia? (Section 2)
5. How have non-Russian ethnic groups reacted to recent events in Russia? (Section 3)
6. What traditions are Russians reviving following the collapse of the Soviet Union? (Section 3)

Resource Directory

Teaching Resources

Cooperative Learning Activity in the Unit 4 Teaching Resources, pp. 118–120

Chapter Tests Forms A and B in the Unit 4 Teaching Resources, pp. 150–155

Guide to the Essentials, Ch. 16 Test, p. 70

Map Activity

Europe and Russia

For each place listed below, write the letter from the map that shows its location.

1. France
2. Poland
3. Russia
4. Germany
5. Slovakia
6. St. Petersburg

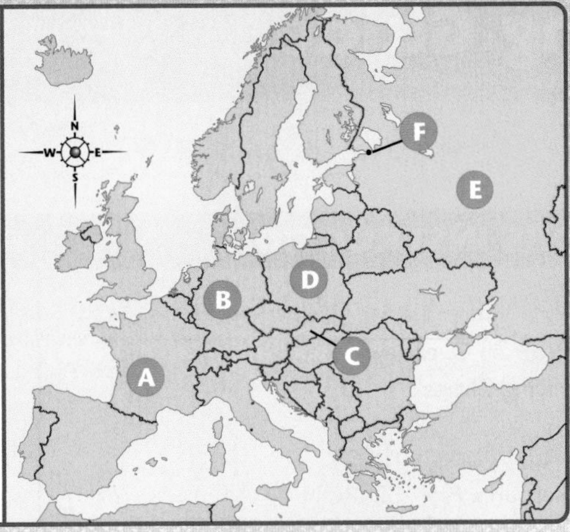

Take It to the NET

Enrichment For more map activities using geography skills, visit the social studies section of **phschool.com.**

Writing Activity

1. **Using Primary Sources** Visit your school or local library and use primary sources such as newspaper and magazine articles to gather information on the lives of non-Russian ethnic groups since the collapse of the Soviet Union. Use the information to describe a day in the life of a non-Russian person.
2. **Create a Travel Guide** Choose six cultural centers from Western Europe, Eastern Europe, and Russia. Create a travel guide that describes a cultural tour that visits each of these six places. Describe the highlights of the trip for each place. Provide as much interesting background information as possible, in order to convince travelers to take the tour.

Critical Thinking

1. **Drawing Conclusions** Why do Western Europeans generally have a higher standard of living than Eastern Europeans?
2. **Identifying Central Issues** How has life changed for the Russian people since the collapse of the Soviet Union?

Applying Your Skills

Turn to the Skills for Life Activity on p. 303 to help you complete the following activity.

Choose a current movie in theaters that you have not yet seen. Look through a newspaper for an ad for the movie. Locate a few reviews for the film in a newspaper or on the Internet. Use these sources to write a paragraph that analyzes and synthesizes the information you found.

Take It to the NET

Activity Examine the paintings found at the Web site. What can you learn about Russia and Russian culture from looking at these paintings? Visit the World Explorer: People, Places and Cultures section of **phschool.com** for help in completing this activity.

Chapter 16 Self-Test As a final review activity, take the Chapter 16 Self-Test and get instant feedback on your answers. To take the test, visit the Social Studies section of **phschool.com.**

Map Activity

1. A **2.** D **3.** E **4.** B **5.** C **6.** F

Writing Activity

1. Students should demonstrate an understanding of the daily lives of a non-Russian ethnic group and should describe details about that specific culture.
2. Students should demonstrate an understanding of the main ideas of the chapter, identify the important cities and cultural highlights, and give accurate and complete background information.

Critical Thinking

1. There is more industry in Western Europe, and trade goods can move quickly and easily among the countries.
2. People have more freedom; they are able to practice their religions and to create art freely; they are reconnecting with their cultural heritage.

Applying Your Skills

Students' paragraphs should combine details from multiple sources in order to draw conclusions about the film.

Resource Directory

Other Print Resources

Chapter Tests with ExamView® Test Bank, Ch. 16

Technology

ExamView® Test Bank CD-ROM, Ch. 16

Resource Pro® CD-ROM

Chapter 17 Planning Guide

Resource Manager

	CORE INSTRUCTION	READING/SKILLS
Chapter-Level Resources	**Teaching Resources** Program Overview Pacing Charts **Technology** Resource Pro® CD-ROM Companion Web site, phschool.com • eTeach	**Technology** Social Studies Skills Tutor CD-ROM Student Edition on Audio CD, Ch. 17
1 Great Britain and Ireland: Historic Roots of Modern Conflict **1.** Identify the historical events that led to the development of democracy in Great Britain. **2.** Describe the key issues and events that have contributed to the conflict in Northern Ireland.	**Teaching Resources** **Unit 4** Classroom Manager, p. 50 Guided Reading and Review, p. 51	**Teaching Resources** Guide to the Essentials, p. 71 Social Studies and Geography Skills, p. 39 **Technology** Section Reading Support Transparencies
2 Belgium and the Netherlands: Changing Economies **1.** Identify the main products and industries of Belgium and the Netherlands. **2.** Describe how the European Union might affect the relationship between Belgium and the Netherlands.	**Teaching Resources** **Unit 4** Classroom Manager, p. 53 Guided Reading and Review, p. 54	**Teaching Resources** Guide to the Essentials, p. 72 **Technology** Section Reading Support Transparencies
3 Germany: Political and Economic Reunion **1.** Explain the historical causes for the division and reunification of Germany. **2.** Describe how the traditional ways of former East Germany and West Germany are changing under the pressure of modern times.	**Teaching Resources** **Unit 4** Classroom Manager, p. 56 Guided Reading and Review, p. 57	**Teaching Resources** Guide to the Essentials, p. 73 **Technology** Section Reading Support Transparencies
4 France and Italy: Cultural Influence on the World **1.** Explain how the past informs contemporary French culture. **2.** Identify some of the traditions and traits of French culture. **3.** Explain the importance of religion in Italy. **4.** Describe some of the cultural characteristics that define Italy.	**Teaching Resources** **Unit 4** Classroom Manager, p. 59 Guided Reading and Review, p. 60 Chapter Summary, p. 62 Vocabulary, p. 63 Reteaching, p. 64	**Teaching Resources** **Unit 4** Critical Thinking, p. 66 Guide to the Essentials, p. 74 **Technology** Section Reading Support Transparencies

ENRICHMENT / PRE-AP

Teaching Resources
Primary Sources and Literature Readings

Other Print Resources
DK Atlas

Technology
World Video Explorer: Case Study: Germany Reunites
Companion Web site, phschool.com

Technology
Color Transparencies 71, 78
How People Live Transparencies, Unit 4

Teaching Resources
Outline Maps, p. 18

Technology
Color Transparencies 74–76

Technology
Color Transparencies 71, 88
Passport to the World CD-ROM

Teaching Resources
Unit 4
Enrichment, p. 65
Cooperative Learning Activity, pp. 122–125

Technology
Color Transparencies 71, 84–85
Passport to the World CD-ROM

ASSESSMENT

Prentice Hall Assessment System

Core Assessment
Chapter Tests with ExamView® Test Bank, Ch. 17
ExamView® Test Bank CD-ROM, Ch. 17

Standardized Test Preparation
Diagnose and Prescribe
Diagnostic Tests for Middle Grades Social Studies Skills
Review and Reteach
Review Book for World Studies
Practice and Assess
Test-taking Strategies with Transparencies for Middle Grades Test Prep Book
Test-taking Strategies Posters

Teaching Resources
Unit 4
Section Quizzes, pp. 52, 55, 58, and 61
Chapter Tests, pp. 156–161

Technology
Companion Web site, phschool.com
Ch. 17 Self-Test

World Video Explorer
Each region of the world is explored through regional flyovers and investigative field trips. Case study segments give students an in-depth view of the history, economy, government, and culture of a key place in each region. Case studies include Nigeria, Mexico, China, British Columbia, and the Czech Republic.

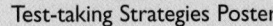

In Your Classroom

CUSTOMIZE FOR INDIVIDUAL NEEDS

Gifted and Talented

Teacher's Edition
- Investing in Industries, p. 313
- The Wall, p. 317

Teaching Resources
- Enrichment, p. 65
- Primary Sources and Literature Readings

Honors/Pre-AP

Teacher's Edition
- Investing in Industries, p. 313
- The Wall, p. 317

Teaching Resources
- Critical Thinking, p. 66
- Primary Sources and Literature Readings

ESL

Teacher's Edition
- Music, p. 309
- Art, p. 321
- Go North Young Man, p. 321

Teaching Resources
- Guided Reading and Review, pp. 51, 54, 57, and 62
- Vocabulary, p. 63
- Reteaching, p. 64
- Guide to the Essentials, pp. 71–74
- Social Studies and Geography Skills, p. 39

Technology
- Social Studies Skills Tutor CD-ROM
- Section Reading Support Transparencies

Less Proficient Readers

Teacher's Edition
- Music, p. 309
- Art, p. 321
- Go North Young Man, p. 321

Teaching Resources
- Guided Reading and Review, pp. 51, 54, 57, and 62
- Vocabulary, p. 63
- Reteaching, p. 64
- Guide to the Essentials, pp. 71–74
- Social Studies and Geography Skills, p. 39

Technology
- Social Studies Skills Tutor CD-ROM
- Section Reading Support Transparencies

Less Proficient Writers

Teacher's Edition
- Music, p. 309
- Art, p. 321
- Go North Young Man, p. 321

Teaching Resources
- Guided Reading and Review, pp. 51, 54, 57, and 62
- Vocabulary, p. 63
- Guide to the Essentials, pp. 71–74
- Social Studies and Geography Skills, p. 39

Technology
- Social Studies Skills Tutor CD-ROM
- Section Reading Support Transparencies

DORLING KINDERSLEY

At the end of each unit, you will find information adapted from Dorling Kindersley's *Illustrated Children's Encyclopedia* that connects to the region being studied and to one of the seven content strands. In addition, your resources include Dorling Kindersley's *Atlas*, which contains valuable information about countries from around the world.

TEACHER'S EDITION INDEX

CHAPTER 17 PACING SUGGESTIONS

For 90-minute Blocks

See suggestions in the Teaching Resources Pacing Charts for Chapter 17. Use Color Transparencies 71, 74–76, 78, 84–85, 88.

Running Out of Time?

See the Guide to the Essentials, pp. 71–74.

INTERDISCIPLINARY LINKS

Middle Grades Math: Tools for Success

Course 1, Lesson 9-1, **Estimating Area**

Course 2, Lesson 9-8, **Estimating Population Size**

Science Explorer

Waters, Lesson 3-3, **Freshwater Pollution**; Lesson 5-4, **Resources from the Ocean**

Prentice Hall Literature

Copper, The Loch Ness Monster

BIBLIOGRAPHY

For the Teacher

Fuller, Barbara. *Britain.* Cavendish, 1994.

Gan, Delice. *Sweden.* Cavendish, 1992.

John Birmingham's France. Dorling Kindersley, 2001.

Symynkywicz, Jeffrey B. *Germany: United Again.* Dillon, 1995.

For the Student

Easy

Powell, Jillian. *A History of France Through Art.* Thomson, 1996.

Average

Munro, Rosie. *The Inside-Outside Book of Paris.* Dutton, 1992.

Challenging

Hoobler, Dorothy, and Thomas Hoobler. *Italian Portraits.* Raintree, 1994.

Literature Connection

Devlin, Polly. *The Far Side of the Lough: Stories from an Irish Childhood.* O'Brien, 2001.

Ingpen, Robert, and Barbara Hayes. *Folk Tales and Fables of Europe.* Chelsea House, 1994.

Take It to the NET

The World Explorer companion Web site, found on **phschool.com**, offers activities for exploring geographical, historical, and cultural resources on the Internet. It also provides on-line links for key content and all Section and Chapter Assessment activities.

The **Teacher site** also provides teachers with regional data and ideas for student research and activities.

Students can use the **Student site** to find chapter-by-chapter Internet resource links and to access Self-Tests.

CHAPTER 17

Connecting to the Guiding Questions

In this chapter, students will read about countries in Western Europe. Content in this chapter corresponds to the following Guiding Questions outlined at the beginning of the unit.

- How has the geography of Europe and Russia influenced, economic, political, and cultural differences in the region?
- What are some cultural traits that European nations share, and what are some traits that make each nation unique?
- What are some economic advantages of participating in the European Union?
- How can people take advantage of new technologies and still maintain links to more traditional ways of life?

Using the Art Activities

As a class, list as many details as students can find that describe the painting, including color, facial expressions, clothing, and light.

- Students should find similarities and differences between the Mona Lisa and a portrait painting they have chosen from a library book.
- Students' self-portraits should reveal some personal details.

Heterogeneous Groups

The following activities are suitable for heterogeneous groups.

Interdisciplinary Connections

Art, p. 321

Cooperative Learning

The Wall, p. 317

eTeach

Be sure to check out this month's discussion with a Master Teacher. Go to **phschool.com**.

CHAPTER 17

WESTERN EUROPE: Exploring the Region Today

A Masterpiece of the Renaissance

USING ART

This painting is the *Mona Lisa* by Italian Renaissance painter Leonardo da Vinci. The *Mona Lisa* is one of the world's most famous paintings. The subject is the wife of an Italian merchant named Giocondo. The artist managed to capture a slight smile and eyes that seem to follow the viewer. Images of the *Mona Lisa* appear in modern art and her name is mentioned in literature and music throughout the world.

Comparing Portraits

Da Vinci painted the *Mona Lisa* with oil paints in a style that was popular in his time. Visit the library and find examples of more modern portrait paintings. Choose one and compare and contrast it with the painting of the *Mona Lisa*. How is the style different? What does each painting reveal about its subject?

Creating a Self-Portrait

In da Vinci's time, portraits were often used to capture and preserve an image of a person for history. Think about the ways that painters may reveal things about their subjects' lives. They may paint the subject with a certain facial expression, certain clothing, or certain way of sitting and show other objects or symbols in the painting. Draw or paint a self-portrait that says something about who you are.

Resource Directory

Teaching Resources

Primary Sources and Literature Readings extend content with a selection related to the concepts in this chapter.

Other Print Resources

DK Atlas

Technology

Case Study: Germany Reunites, from the World Video Explorer, enhances students' understanding of German reunification.

Student Edition on Audio CD, Ch. 17

SECTION 1

Great Britain and Ireland

Historic Roots of Modern Conflict

BEFORE YOU READ

READING FOCUS

1. How did democracy develop in Britain?
2. What key issues and events have contributed to the conflict in Northern Ireland?

KEY TERMS

Parliament
representative
constitutional monarchy
persecution

KEY PEOPLE AND PLACES

Northern Ireland
King John
Queen Elizabeth II
King Henry VIII

MAIN IDEA

Ireland has fought for unity and independence from Great Britain for centuries, though Great Britain has a long history of colonial and democratic rule.

NOTE TAKING

Copy the cause and effect chart below. As you read the section, fill in the chart with information about conflicts throughout Ireland's history.

Cause
1.
2.
3.
Event: Conflict in Ireland
Effects
1.
2.
3.

Setting the Scene

The United Kingdom is made up of England, Scotland, Wales, and **Northern Ireland.** The four countries have their own histories and cultures but are ruled by a single government. Though *United Kingdom of Great Britain and Northern Ireland* is the country's official name, people often call this region *Britain* or *Great Britain* instead. This is because most of the people live on the island of Great Britain. The government of the United Kingdom is a constitutional monarchy that is headed by a king or queen—a symbol of Britain's past and its customs.

A Democratic History

The roots of British democracy go back many hundreds of years. During the Middle Ages, British kings could not take major actions without the approval of a group of rich nobles. Over time, the power of this group grew. In 1215, the group forced one English monarch, **King John,** to sign a document called the Magna Carta, or "Great Charter." The Magna Carta strengthened the power of the nobles and limited the power of the king.

St. Edward's Crown

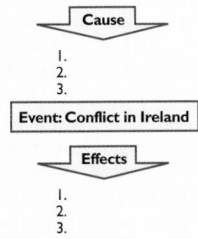

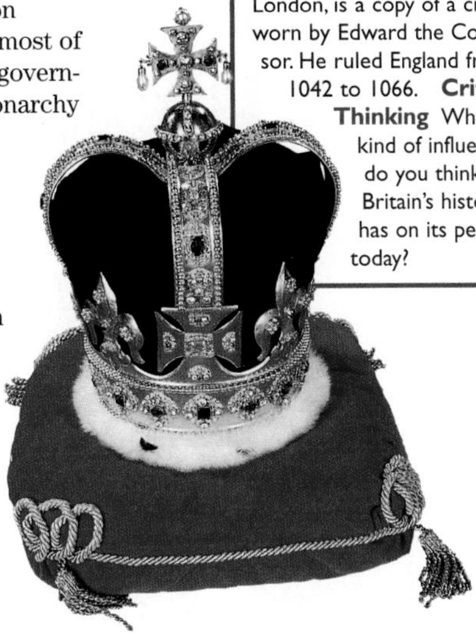

HISTORY St. Edward's crown, one of several crowns kept at the Tower of London, is a copy of a crown worn by Edward the Confessor. He ruled England from 1042 to 1066. **Critical Thinking** What kind of influence do you think Britain's history has on its people today?

SECTION 1

Lesson Objectives

1. Identify the historical events that led to the development of democracy in Great Britain.
2. Describe the key issues and events that have contributed to the conflict in Northern Ireland.

Lesson Plan

1 Engage

Warm-Up Activity

Point out to students that most of the world's nations were formed hundreds of years before the United States. Thus, their traditions are more established and less likely to change. Invite students to discuss traditions from established countries that students might or might not like to see in the United States. For instance, should we have a monarchy? Should we have a state religion?

Activating Prior Knowledge

Lead the class in a discussion about some United States traditions associated with public education (for instance, that it is universal, free, and common). Encourage students to identify British traditions that are similar to or different from other American traditions as they read through the section.

Resource Directory

Teaching Resources

Classroom Manager in the Unit 4 Teaching Resources, p. 50

Guided Reading and Review in the Unit 4 Teaching Resources, p. 51

Guide to the Essentials, p. 71

Technology

Section Reading Support Transparencies

Answers to...

CRITICAL THINKING

Students may mention the fact that not only buildings and other historic sites but also the monarchy connects Britain's past to its citizens today.

Lesson Plan continued

❷ Explore

Have students read through Section 1 and discuss Great Britain's democratic as well as imperial traditions. Why was the existence of powerful nobles important to the rise of democracy? Why was it important for Great Britain to build an empire? Invite students to make inferences about how Great Britain's democratic tradition may have affected that of the United States.

❸ Teach

Have students make cause-and-effect charts similar to the one shown for the democratic and imperialistic traditions of Great Britain.

	Cause	Effect
Empire		
Democracy		

Have students use the *Effect* column to identify facts from the section about the British Empire and British democracy, and record the corresponding causes in the *Cause* column. Use the completed charts as the basis for a discussion about change in Britain. This activity should take about 30 minutes.

Questions for Discussion

HISTORY Why do you think Britain holds onto its monarchy even though the monarchy has very little power?

The monarchy represents a strong tradition that helps to unify the British people.

CULTURE Why did Protestant landowners in Ireland oppose the idea of "Home Rule"?

Even though these landowners were in the majority, they would be outnumbered in a unified Irish nation and voted out of power.

In time, the group of nobles became known as the **Parliament.** This word comes from the French word *parler* (PAHR lay), which means "to talk." The Parliament later gained more power. It helped to decide the kinds of taxes paid by citizens and elected people from areas of the country to serve as **representatives.** A representative represents, or stands for, a group of people. In time, the people themselves elected these representatives.

Limited Power Britain's **Queen Elizabeth II** was crowned in 1953. The Queen may approve or reject laws passed by Parliament, but no British monarch has rejected a law since the 1700s. The Queen and members of her family may also sponsor charity events, participate in important national ceremonies and parades, and represent Britain on trips to other countries.

However, Britain's monarchs today do not have the power to make laws or collect taxes because Great Britain is now a **constitutional monarchy.** A constitution is a set of laws that describes how a government works. In a constitutional monarchy, the power of kings and queens is limited. The laws state what they can and cannot do. This is very different from the absolute monarchies of the past. British laws are made by Parliament, not by the king or queen.

Ireland: One Island, Two Nations

Ireland's struggle for independence goes back centuries. Originally the island was divided into small settlements controlled at different times by Irish chiefs, Catholic bishops, Viking invaders, Norman conquerors, and British planters. There was no unified central govern-

British Parliament, Present and Past

GOVERNMENT

The modern Parliament consists of the House of Commons, whose members actually make the nation's laws, and the House of Lords. The Prime Minister is the chief executive. **Critical Thinking** How do the houses of Parliament compare to the U.S. Congress?

Answers to...

CRITICAL THINKING

Both the U.S. Congress and the British Parliament are composed of two houses. Both institutions are legislative bodies. The U.S. Congress and one house of Parliament are elected bodies.

Resource Directory

Teaching Resources

Social Studies and Geography Skills, Identifying the Main Idea, p. 39

Technology

Color Transparencies 71 Western Europe: Political Map; **78** *The Tower of London with London Bridge Behind* Fine Art

How People Live Transparencies, Unit 4

United Kingdom

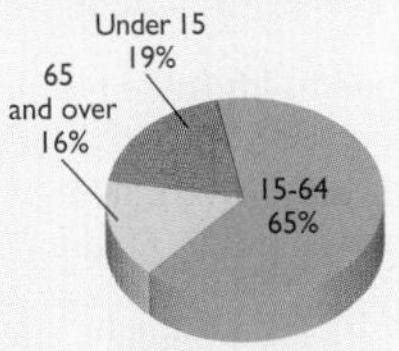

Age Structure (in years)

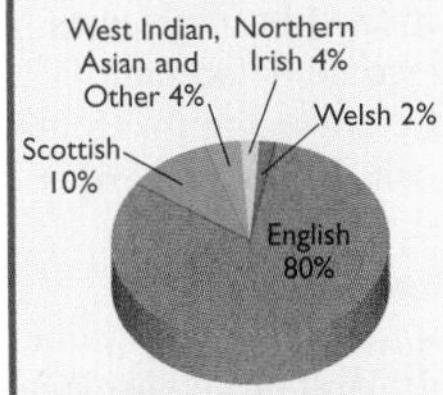

Ethnic Makeup

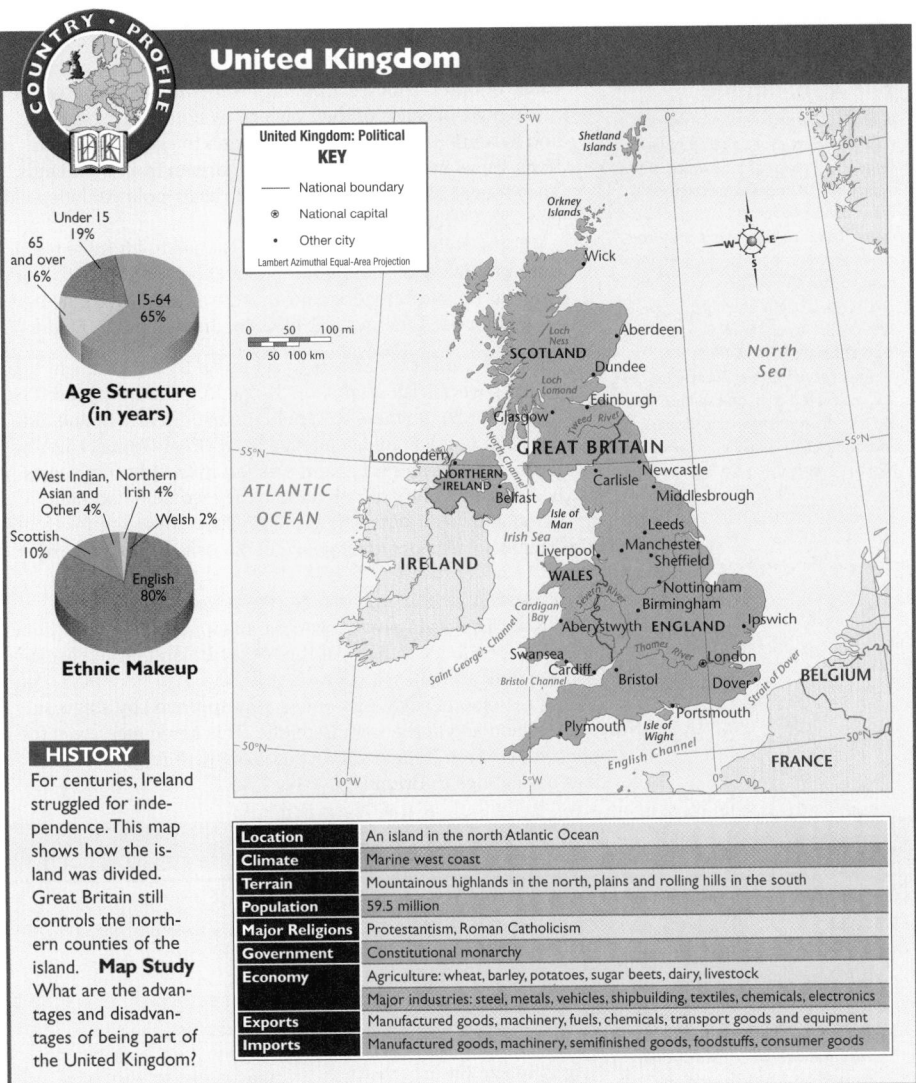

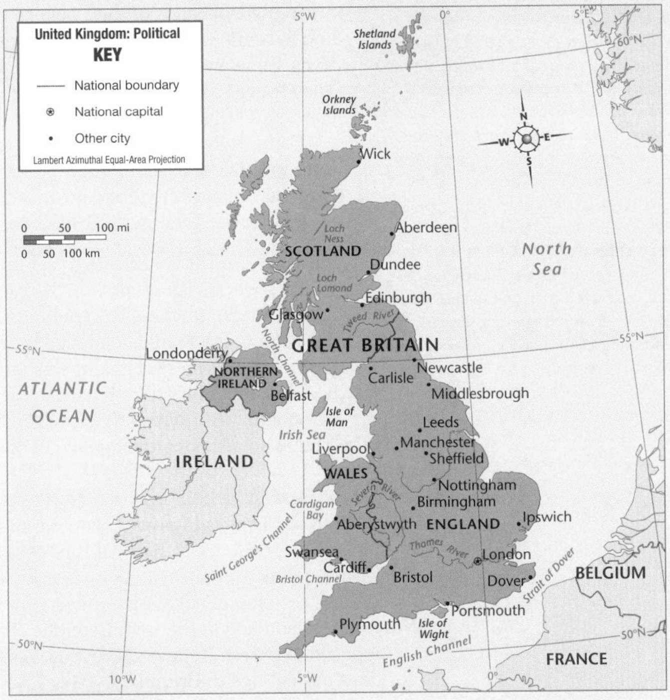

Location	An island in the north Atlantic Ocean
Climate	Marine west coast
Terrain	Mountainous highlands in the north, plains and rolling hills in the south
Population	59.5 million
Major Religions	Protestantism, Roman Catholicism
Government	Constitutional monarchy
Economy	Agriculture: wheat, barley, potatoes, sugar beets, dairy, livestock
	Major industries: steel, metals, vehicles, shipbuilding, textiles, chemicals, electronics
Exports	Manufactured goods, machinery, fuels, chemicals, transport goods and equipment
Imports	Manufactured goods, machinery, semifinished goods, foodstuffs, consumer goods

HISTORY

For centuries, Ireland struggled for independence. This map shows how the island was divided. Great Britain still controls the northern counties of the island. **Map Study** What are the advantages and disadvantages of being part of the United Kingdom?

ment so these individual settlements were easy prey. At the same time, the scattered settlements made it difficult for an outside force to take complete control of the island. In 1541, England's **King Henry VIII** declared himself King of Ireland and head of the Church. The colonization of Ireland by the English began.

SKILLS MINI LESSON

Identifying Central Issues

In order to **introduce** the skill, indicate to students that they can better understand their reading if they identify the central issue, or main idea. To help students **practice** the skill, offer the following steps: (1) Look for something that identifies the central issue. (2) Look for an idea that all the sentences or paragraphs have in common. (3) State the central issue in your own words. Work with students as they use these steps to identify the central issue in the paragraphs following *A Democratic History.* Ask volunteers to state the central issue of the section in their own words. Suggest that students **apply** the skill by working in pairs to find the central issue of the section *Ireland: One Island, Two Nations.*

4 Assess/Reteach

See the answers to the Section 1 Assessment. You may also use students' completed charts as an assessment.

Acceptable charts include at least one cause-and-effect relationship each for Democracy and Empire.

Commendable charts identify three cause-and-effect relationships for each topic.

Outstanding charts will include cause-and-effect relationships implied in the text.

BIOGRAPHY

Another Elizabeth

Queen Elizabeth I (1533–1603) reigned as queen of England from 1558 to 1603. Her reign marked one of England's greatest eras. During her rule, England became a major power in Europe, building a navy formidable enough to defeat the great Spanish Armada. England also experienced a cultural golden age during her reign, as exemplified by the writings of William Shakespeare.

ACTIVITY

Interdisciplinary Connections

Music Bring in recorded examples of traditional music from Ireland, Scotland, Wales, and England. Do the differences in musical styles help define the different cultures in the United Kingdom? What do the similarities in style (for instance, the use of English) say about life in the United Kingdom?

Musical/Rhythmic

Answers to...

MAP STUDY

An advantage would be having ties to Britain's power, economic resources, imported resources, trade partners, and protection. A disadvantage would be a lack of independence.

SECTION 1 ASSESSMENT

AFTER YOU READ

1. (a) partitioned part of Ireland that is part of the United Kingdom and ruled by Great Britain. (b) English monarch who signed the Magna Carta (c) Great Britain's current ruling monarch (d) English monarch who declared himself King of Ireland and head of the church
2. (a) representative body that makes the law in Great Britain (b) one who represents, or stands for, a group of people (c) government in which the power of kings and queens is limited by law (d) oppression
3. The House of Commons and the House of Lords comprise Britain's parliament.
4. The Republic of Ireland was established, and there have been many conflicts between Catholics and the Protestant majority in Northern Ireland.
5. Paragraphs will vary. Encourage students to express their ideas about democracy.
6. Responses will vary. Students might find out the latest developments and base their predictions on current events.
7. Encourage students to shed light on how the Great Famine affected life in Ireland as well as emigration from Ireland.

HISTORY

The Irish Famine

By 1841, the population of Ireland had grown to more than 8 million. Only small plots of land were available, and rents were high. Farm families lived on a diet of potatoes because they were easy to grow and did not take a lot of time to tend. Then, between 1845 and 1849, a blight rotted the potato crop creating a famine, or food shortage.

As a result of the Great Famine, it is estimated that one million people died from hunger and disease, and one million people emigrated to North America.

Religious Conflict Over the centuries, Ireland's religious heritage and ties to the Roman Catholic Church have been the cause of bitter disputes. Catholics were often **persecuted,** or mistreated, because of their beliefs, by both the government and by settlers sent over from England to establish plantations. Time and again the Irish were driven from their lands. They fought back, demanding equal rights, political independence, and religious freedom.

For a while, the British government had to lift trade restrictions on Irish goods and grant political power to the Irish parliament. Ireland's freedom, however, was short lived. In 1801, England passed the Act of Union, joining Ireland to England.

Political Conflict Efforts to set up an Irish parliament that would govern Irish affairs, or "Home Rule," were opposed by Protestant landowners who held the majority there and did not want political independence from Great Britain. Cutting ties to the British Parliament was not in their best interests because, in a unified Irish nation, they would be outnumbered and voted out of power. The Irish movement for Home Rule took many forms, including peaceful opposition, political force, and war.

A treaty signed in 1922 said that Northern Ireland, where the Protestants of Ulster held power, would remain part of Great Britain. It granted independence to most of the rest of Ireland, which became the Irish Republic in 1949.

In 1998, the Good Friday Agreement was approved by voters in Northern Ireland and in the Irish Republic. This agreement gives the Catholics in Northern Ireland a stronger voice in their government but does not cut ties to Britain.

SECTION 1 ASSESSMENT

AFTER YOU READ

RECALL

1. Identify: (a) Northern Ireland, (b) King John, (c) Queen Elizabeth II, (d) King Henry VIII
2. Define: (a) Parliament, (b) representative, (c) constitutional monarchy, (d) persecution.

COMPREHENSION

3. What two houses comprise Britain's Parliament?
4. What happened after Ireland was partitioned?

CRITICAL THINKING AND WRITING

5. **Exploring the Main Idea** Review the Main Idea statement at the beginning of this section. Then, write a paragraph about the importance of fair political representation in Parliament.
6. **Making Predictions** Imagine that it is the year 2025. Write a newspaper article describing life in Northern Ireland. Has the first quarter of the 21st century been peaceful? Why or why not?

ACTIVITY

7. **Researching the Great Famine** Visit the library or the Internet to learn more about Ireland's Great Famine. Write a short report that provides important details about the famine and how it affected life in Ireland.

Resource Directory

Teaching Resources

Section Quiz in the Unit 4 Teaching Resources, p. 52

SECTION 2

Belgium and the Netherlands

Changing Economies

BEFORE YOU READ

READING FOCUS

1. What are the main products and industries of Belgium and the Netherlands?
2. How might the European Union affect the relationship between Belgium and the Netherlands?

KEY TERMS

polders
Flemish

KEY PLACES

Flanders
Wallonia
Walloons
Brussels
Amsterdam
Rotterdam

NOTE TAKING

Copy the concept web below. As you read the section, fill in the web with information about Belgium and the Netherlands.

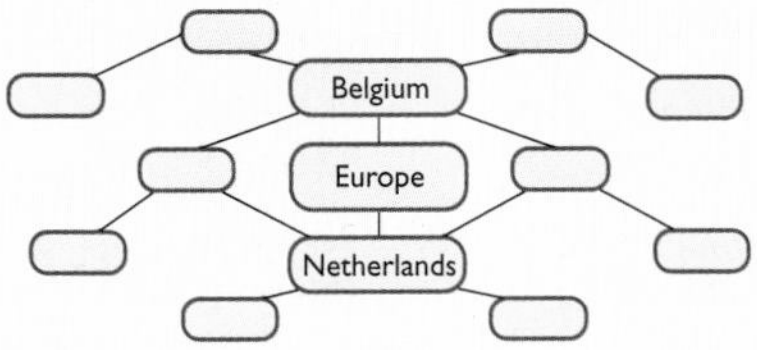

MAIN IDEA

Belgium and the Netherlands share borders and ties with neighboring countries, but they have unique economies and cultures.

Setting the Scene

Much of the region that makes up Belgium and the Netherlands is below sea level. To reclaim the land that would normally be under water, long walls called dikes were built to hold it back. Excess water is pumped into canals that empty into the North Sea. The reclaimed patches of land are called **polders** (POHL durz), and they are home to farmland and large cities.

Resources and Industry

For hundreds of years, control of the region that is now Belgium and the Netherlands was passed down from one European ruler to the next. In 1648, the Dutch occupying the Northern Netherlands, known as Holland, were granted independence from Spain. They rapidly built a strong economy through shipping, the spice trade, and colonization. In 1794, the Southern Netherlands, known as Belgium, was annexed to France. Industries developed and manufacturing centers flourished. In 1814, the provinces of the Northern and Southern Netherlands were combined to form one kingdom. But by 1830, differences in religion and language caused Belgium to break away from the Netherlands, and two separate nations were formed.

Reclaimed Land

GEOGRAPHY Polders like the one beside this canal add 3,000 square miles (7,770 sq km) of land to the Netherlands. In the crowded conditions of the Netherlands, this land that was once underwater is home to 3.5 million people. **Critical Thinking** How has the need for polders, and their uses, changed over the centuries?

Resource Directory

Teaching Resources

Classroom Manager in the Unit 4 Teaching Resources, p. 53

Guided Reading and Review in the Unit 4 Teaching Resources, p. 54

Guide to the Essentials, p. 72

Technology

Section Reading Support Transparencies

SECTION 2

Lesson Objectives

1. Identify the main products and industries of Belgium and the Netherlands.
2. Describe how the European Union might affect the relationship between Belgium and the Netherlands.

Lesson Plan

1 Engage

Warm-Up Activity

Point out to students that although Belgium and the Netherlands are geographically close to one another, they were ruled for many years by different European nations, and their cultures and economies developed independently of each other. Ask students to think about the relationship between the United States and Canada, or the United States and Mexico. Explain that both of these countries share borders with the U.S. Discuss similarities and differences between the United States and Canada and Mexico, including cultural customs, and industries and economies.

Activating Prior Knowledge

Ask students if they are familiar with dams or reservoirs that are used to control water supply, or with irrigation techniques in agricultural areas. Discuss the ways that these scientific innovations allow people to use land that might otherwise be too dry or too wet.

Answers to...

CRITICAL THINKING

Polders were first developed for farmland. Later, the land may have been used to build factories that were close to ocean ports and river transportation. Now the land may be used more often to support growing urban areas.

Lesson Plan continued

❷ Explore

Have students read through Section 2 and discuss the events that led to the independent countries of Belgium and the Netherlands, and the economies, industries and products of those regions. What are the main exports of each country? How will their participation in the European Union affect the strength of their economies in the future, and their relationship to one another?

❸ Teach

Have students create a chart with three columns listing the natural resources, industries and goods produced by Belgium and the Netherlands. As they work, have students think about the ways that each country's natural resources influences their industries and products, and have them write a brief summary of the chart findings that explains this relationship. This activity should take 30 minutes.

Questions for Discussion

GEOGRAPHY How did the use of polders allow Belgium and the Netherlands to have strong agricultural economies?

The polders increased the amount of land that could be used for farming.

HISTORY What caused Belgium to break away from the Netherlands in 1830?

Differences in religion and language caused Belgium's break with the Netherlands.

COUNTRY PROFILE: Belgium and the Netherlands

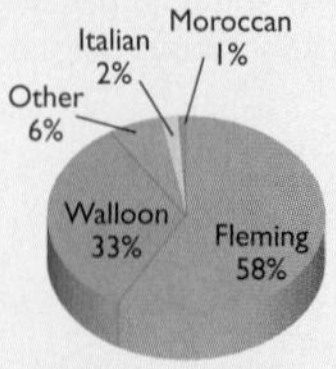

Ethnic Makeup (Belgium)

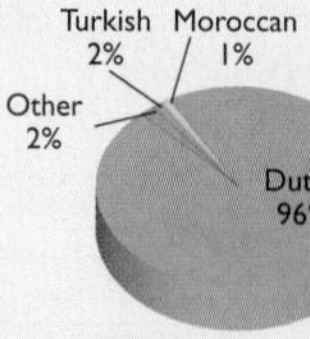

Ethnic Makeup (Netherlands)

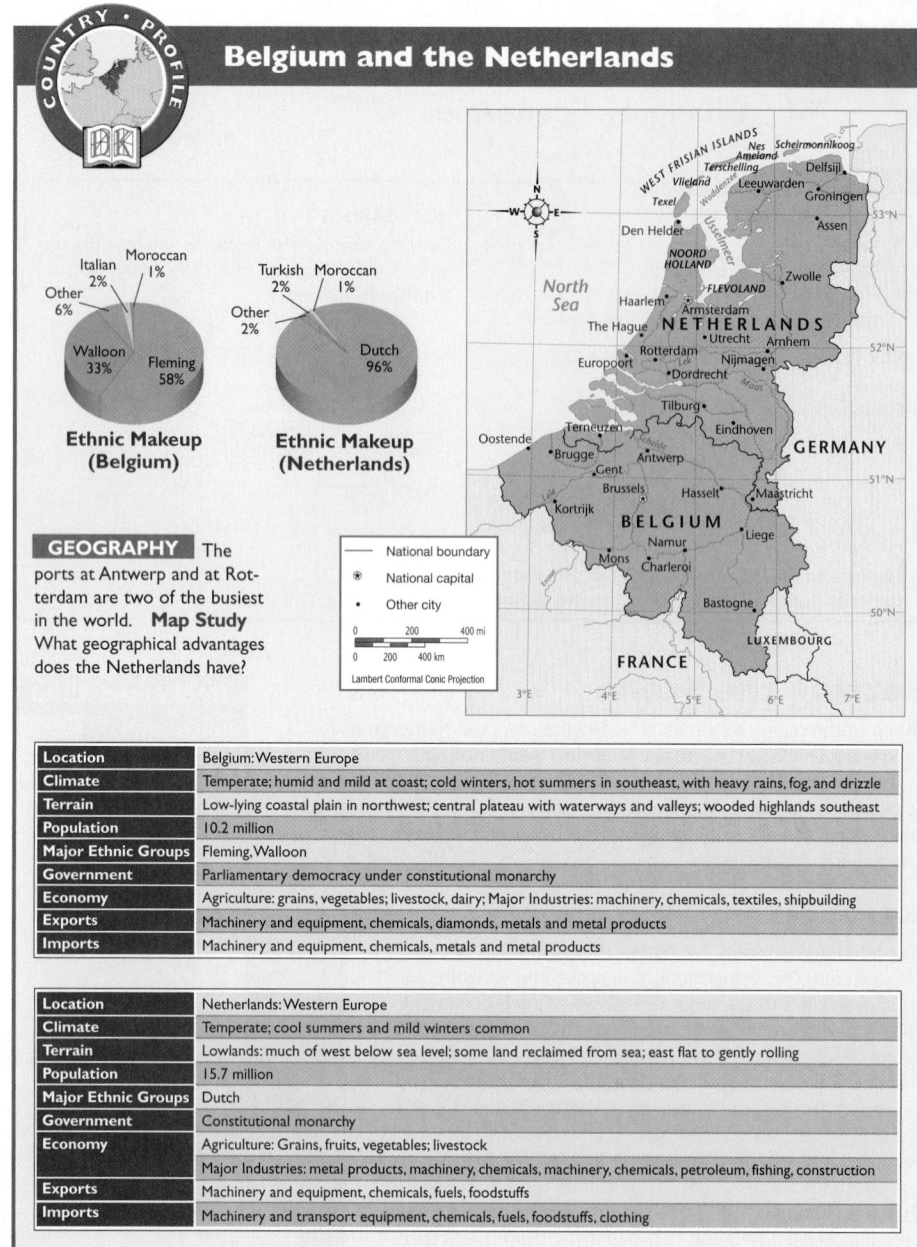

GEOGRAPHY The ports at Antwerp and at Rotterdam are two of the busiest in the world. **Map Study** What geographical advantages does the Netherlands have?

Location	Belgium: Western Europe
Climate	Temperate; humid and mild at coast; cold winters, hot summers in southeast, with heavy rains, fog, and drizzle
Terrain	Low-lying coastal plain in northwest; central plateau with waterways and valleys; wooded highlands southeast
Population	10.2 million
Major Ethnic Groups	Fleming, Walloon
Government	Parliamentary democracy under constitutional monarchy
Economy	Agriculture: grains, vegetables; livestock, dairy; Major Industries: machinery, chemicals, textiles, shipbuilding
Exports	Machinery and equipment, chemicals, diamonds, metals and metal products
Imports	Machinery and equipment, chemicals, metals and metal products

Location	Netherlands: Western Europe
Climate	Temperate; cool summers and mild winters common
Terrain	Lowlands: much of west below sea level; some land reclaimed from sea; east flat to gently rolling
Population	15.7 million
Major Ethnic Groups	Dutch
Government	Constitutional monarchy
Economy	Agriculture: Grains, fruits, vegetables; livestock
	Major Industries: metal products, machinery, chemicals, machinery, chemicals, petroleum, fishing, construction
Exports	Machinery and equipment, chemicals, fuels, foodstuffs
Imports	Machinery and transport equipment, chemicals, fuels, foodstuffs, clothing

Resource Directory

Teaching Resources

Outline Maps Western Europe: Political, p. 18

Answers to...

MAP AND CHART STUDY

The Netherlands has an extensive coastline with many port cities and access to major rivers.

Harvesting Crops

ECONOMICS

These Belgian farmers are cutting and bundling crops during the harvest season in West Flanders. **Critical Thinking** Why is it important that Belgium's agricultural production has became more efficient?

Belgium's Industries in the South Belgium is made up of three distinct regions. In the north, the people of **Flanders** speak Dutch, or **Flemish.** In the south, the people of **Wallonia,** called **Walloons,** speak French. The region around the capital, **Brussels,** at the center of the country and at the heart of Europe, is bilingual.

For hundreds of years, the region of Wallonia supported the primary industry of coal mining. Coal was used to power factories throughout the country. However, the reserves of coal, a nonrenewable resource, eventually ran out. Most coal mines closed down in the 1960s, and all coal mining had stopped by 1992. Coal now must be imported to keep the factories going and to provide heating.

The steel and textile industries that were located in the coal mining region went into a decline as mining ceased. The government has stepped in with reforms designed to help strengthen these industries, but regaining a healthy balance of trade has been slow.

Belgium's Industries in the North Industry in the more heavily populated region of Flanders has continued to grow. A strong transportation network supports the export of products. Over time, manufacturing has steadily replaced agriculture as a major industry, but agricultural production has become more efficient. Better use is made of the land and the crops that are grown have higher yields. These crops include cereals, potatoes, sugar beets, fruits, and vegetables.

Industry in the Netherlands Like Belgium, the Netherlands is not rich in natural resources. Exceptions include coal mining, and natural gas and petroleum exploration. The Netherlands has a successful dairy and cheese industry, and flower bulbs generate an important source of agricultural income.

4 Assess/Reteach

See the answers to the Section 2 Assessment. You may also use students' completed charts as an assessment.

Acceptable charts list at least two resources, industries, and goods per country. Summary reflects general knowledge of the influence of resources on industries and products.

Commendable charts list more than four resources, industries, and goods per country. Summary describes relationship between resource and resulting industries and products.

Outstanding charts list more than four resources, industries, and goods per country. Summary describes relationship between several specific resources and resulting industries and products.

ACTIVITY

Cooperative Learning

Investing in Industries Organize students into two groups. One group should represent Belgium, and the other the Netherlands. Have students in each group choose five industries from a list, that they will invest their country's money in developing. Have each group make a list of the products that will result from these industries, and decide what percentage they will keep, and what percentage they will export. Allow the two "countries" to discuss trade with each other, and have them draw up a trade agreement.

Verbal/Linguistic

Resource Directory

Technology

Color Transparencies 74–76 Historical Maps: Europe Today with Eastern Europe Updated (base maps with overlay)

Answers to...

CRITICAL THINKING

Efficiency is especially vital since Belgium has a limited amount of land available for farming.

SECTION 2 ASSESSMENT

AFTER YOU READ

1. (a) northern region of Belgium (b) southern region of Belgium (c) people who live in Wallonia (d) capital of Belgium (e) capital of the Netherlands (f) key Dutch seaport
2. (a) lands reclaimed from below sea level (b) language spoken in northern Belgium.
3. Belgium: cement, glass, pottery, steel, textiles, agricultural products; Netherlands: cheese, banking, textiles, electrical machinery, electronics, transport equipment, iron and steel, refined petroleum, ships, processed foods, plastics, chemicals, agricultural products
4. Sharing a common currency may increase trade between the two countries.
5. Similarities include many similar industries and products, use of polders to reclaim land, participation in the European Union. Differences include different histories and cultures.
6. Answers will vary, but should reflect an understanding that without polders, these two countries would not have been able to farm as much land; farmland would not have been as fertile and productive; and there would have been less space available for the construction or expansion of cities.
7. Students' reports will vary but should reflect an understanding of the histories of Belgium and the Netherlands, and their relationship to each other.

A Petro-Chemical Plant

ECONOMICS The Netherlands is not a country rich in natural resources. However, petroleum exploration and Holland's international ports support industries like the petro-chemical plant above. **Critical Thinking** How might a petro-chemical plant benefit and burden the communities nearby?

Raw materials are imported to the Netherlands to support industries that concentrate on manufacturing products. These include the production of textiles, metals, processed foods, plastics, and chemicals.

The city of **Amsterdam** is a major financial center for international banking. The busy port of **Rotterdam** supports the merchant marine and foreign trade with worldwide destinations for Amsterdam's many exports including machinery, textiles, petroleum products, fruits and vegetables, and meat.

Tourism is also an important part of the economy, and the careers of many people in Amsterdam are devoted to sharing Dutch history and culture with visitors.

The European Union

During the 1950s, six European countries, including the Netherlands, agreed to form a common market. Now, the number of countries involved in this union, called the European Union, has risen to fifteen. Both Belgium and the Netherlands have been leaders in the European Union. The growth of the union paves the way for more international activities that will cross the national and economic borders of the countries of Europe. A single currency, called the euro, is shared by all of the countries in the union. The European Union may help Belgium and the Netherlands to overcome cultural and historical disputes that have kept them apart in years past.

SECTION 2 ASSESSMENT

AFTER YOU READ

RECALL

1. Identify: (a) Flanders, (b) Wallonia, (c) Walloons, (d) Brussels, (e) Amsterdam, (f) Rotterdam
2. Define: (a) polders, (b) Flemish

COMPREHENSION

3. Name three industries that are important to Belgium, and three industries that are important to the Netherlands.
4. How might the European Union bring Belgium and the Netherlands closer together?

CRITICAL THINKING AND WRITING

5. **Exploring the Main Idea** Review the Main Idea statement at the beginning of this section. Then write a paragraph describing some of the similarities and differences between Belgium and the Netherlands.
6. **Draw Conclusions** Reclaimed patches of land in Belgium and the Netherlands would normally be under the North Sea, if not for polders. Without the polders, how might life be different in this region?

ACTIVITY

7. **Writing a Report** Find out more details about the unification, conflict, and separation that mark the history of Belgium and the Netherlands. What role did cultural identity play in the differences and disagreements between the Dutch, the Belgians, the Flemish, and the Walloons? Organize the information you collect into a brief report.

Resource Directory

Teaching Resources

Section Quiz in the Unit 4 Teaching Resources, p. 55

Answers to...

CRITICAL THINKING

Such a plant might provide jobs and lower taxes, yet it also might contribute to pollution and reduce the area's natural beauty.

SECTION 3

Germany

Political and Economic Reunion

BEFORE YOU READ

READING FOCUS

1. Why was Germany divided and how did it become reunited?
2. How are Germans dealing with the issues of a reunited nation?

KEY TERMS

Holocaust
genocide
reunification

KEY PEOPLE

Adolf Hitler

NOTE TAKING

Copy the table below. As you read the section, fill in the table with comparisons about Germany before and after reunification.

Germany before Reunification	Germany after Reunification

MAIN IDEA

The United States, Great Britain, France, and the Soviet Union divided Germany and its capital city, Berlin, into two parts at the end of World War II, and West Germany prospered, the East German economy collapsed, paving the way for political reunification in 1990.

Setting the Scene

In 1961, a policeman named Conrad Schumann stood guard at a barbed wire fence separating East Berlin from West Berlin. At that time, East Berlin was part of the communist government of East Germany and the fence was built to prevent people from escaping to West Berlin. Schumann had orders to shoot anyone who tried. Schumann thought about the colorful culture of West Berlin. He thought about political freedom and economic opportunities in the democracy of West Germany. So he jumped over the barbed wire fence separating East and West Berlin. Soon after Schumann's escape, the Berlin Wall was built to replace the fence, dividing the city in half.

Germany's Tragic History

To understand the importance of the Berlin Wall, you need to understand part of Germany's past. After losing World War I in 1918, the German government had to pay billions of dollars as punishment for attacking other countries. To make things even worse, the German economy collapsed. Prices soared. Germans everywhere felt desperate.

A Leap to Freedom

CITIZENSHIP

Conrad Schumann's responsibility was to prevent his fellow citizens from escaping into West Berlin. From West Berlin, people could reach democratic West Germany. **Critical Thinking** What might you have done if you were in Schumann's position?

315

SECTION 3

Lesson Objectives

1. Explain the historical causes for the division and reunification of Germany.
2. Describe how the traditional ways of former East Germany and West Germany are changing under the pressure of modern times.

Lesson Plan

1 Engage

Warm-Up Activity

Point out to students that in the former East Germany, the average citizen did not have freedom of movement within the country. Ask students to describe how they would feel if movement was restricted in the United States. What would they do if they were not allowed to visit relatives or find a job in another state? Would they live with the restrictions or try to oppose them?

Activating Prior Knowledge

Retell the end of the story of Rip Van Winkle—how he recognized the town and some of the people, but so many years had passed, everything seemed strange. Discuss the changes they would expect after a 25-year separation from friends and family.

Resource Directory

Teaching Resources

Classroom Manager in the Unit 4 Teaching Resources, p. 56

Guided Reading and Review in the Unit 4 Teaching Resources, p. 57

Guide to the Essentials, p. 73

Technology

Section Reading Support Transparencies

Answers to...

CRITICAL THINKING

Answers will vary. Encourage students to discuss their ideas about breaking rules that they believe are wrong or harmful to others.

Lesson Plan continued

2 Explore

Have students read through Section 3 and discuss the events leading to a divided Germany and the consequences of reunification. Why was Germany divided? Why was the Berlin Wall built? Why were both East Germans and West Germans dissatisfied following reunification?

3 Teach

Have students create a news program about the recent history of Germany. Direct students to include, in chronological order, the major historical events mentioned in this chapter. Suggest that students follow the news program with a commentary on Germany's possible future. This activity should take 30 minutes.

Questions for Discussion

HISTORY **What do you think East Berliners thought and felt the night the Berlin Wall was torn down?**

Students may speculate that they felt excitement, hope, and joy.

GOVERNMENT **How did the governments of East Germany and West Germany differ? How did this affect the lives of people in East Germany compared to those in West Germany?**

East Germany was communist, while West Germany was democratic. People in East Germany had fewer rights and did not live as well as people in West Germany.

COUNTRY PROFILE: Germany

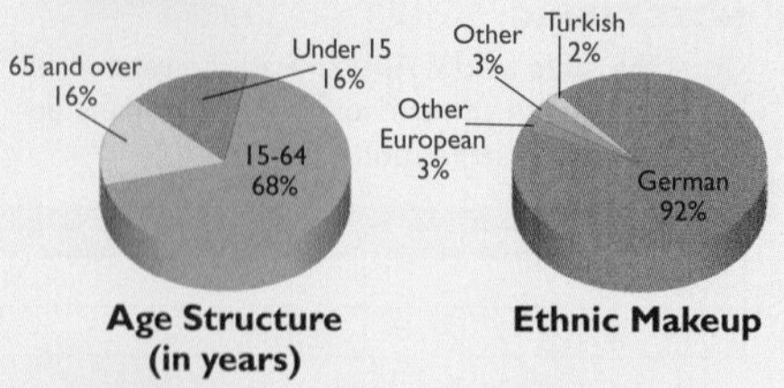

Location	Central European country to the east of France
Climate	Marine west coast
Terrain	Flat in the north, hilly in the central and western portions, mountainous in Bavaria
Population	82.1 million
Major Religions	Protestantism, Roman Catholicism
Goverment	Federal republic
Economy	Agriculture: grains, potatoes, sugar beets, fruit Major industries: steel, ships, vehicles, machinery, electronics, coal, chemicals, iron
Exports	Precision tools, chemicals, motor vehicles, steel, agricultural products, raw materials, fuels
Imports	Manufactured products, agricultural products, fuels, raw materials

GEOGRAPHY This map shows Germany's borders and major cities. It also shows the network of rivers that flow through the country. **Map Study** How are the locations of Bonn, Bremen, Hamburg, and Dresden similar?

Hitler and World War II Adolf Hitler (AY dahlf HIT lur), a young German soldier, had wept bitterly in 1918 when he learned that Germany had lost the war. He promised himself that his country would never suffer such a defeat again. Hitler became deeply involved in politics. In speech after speech, he promised to make Germany great again. By 1933, this once unknown soldier was dictator of Germany.

Hitler blamed Germany's economic problems on the Jews. He spread hateful theories about Jews, gypsies, and other ethnic groups in Germany. He claimed they were inferior to, or not as good as, other Germans. He claimed that true Germans were a superior ethnic group—and believed that this superior group deserved a larger country.

Resource Directory

Technology

Color Transparencies 71 Western Europe: Political Map; **88** *Stadium Tribune, Nuremberg, Germany* Fine Art

Passport to the World CD-ROM This interactive CD-ROM allows students to explore each region of the world. Students view regional videos, take a photo tour, and explore a historical timeline. Students record their travels in an Explorer's Journal, and receive passport stamps when they pass regional quizzes.

Answers to...

MAP STUDY

Location They all are located on rivers.

Many people did not believe Hitler's threats. But Hitler was deadly serious. He ordered attacks on neighboring countries and forced them under German rule. His actions led to the start of World War II in 1939. Great Britain, the Soviet Union, and the United States joined other nations to stop Hitler and the Germans. By the end of the war, Europe was in ruins. People around the world learned that the Germans had forced countless Jews, Gypsies, Slavs, and others into death prison camps. Millions of people were systematically murdered in these camps. Most of those killed in the camps were Jews. This horrible mass murder of six million Jews is called the **Holocaust** (HAHL uh kawst). The deliberate murder of a racial, political, or ethnic group is called **genocide.**

The Cold War At the end of the war, the Americans, the British, the French, and the Soviets divided Germany. The American, British, and French sections were joined into a democratic country called West Germany. The Soviet Union created communist East Germany.

Berlin was in the Soviet part of Germany. But the western half of it, called West Berlin, became part of democratic West Germany. This turned the western half of Berlin into an island of democracy in the middle of communism. The Berlin Wall separated the two halves of the city. But it divided more than Berlin. It was a symbol of a divided world. Little wonder that some people called it the "Wall of Shame."

East Germans led far different lives than West Germans. The communist government required people to obey without asking questions. It even encouraged people to spy on family members and neighbors. Children were taught to respect only those things that helped communism. Things from the West—including movies, music, books, and magazines—were seen as harmful to communism.

The Communists Weaken In time, communist rule started to change. One reason was that the East German economy was falling further behind the West German economy. The average West German had a much better life than the average East German. To keep East Germans happy, the government softened its rules and let some East Germans visit West Germany. Conrad Schumann's mother, who was then in her late seventies, was allowed to see him. But he still was not allowed to go to East Berlin to see her. If he crossed the border, he would be arrested and put in prison.

In the late 1980s, changes in the Soviet Union helped to cause the collapse of East Germany. Soviet leader Mikhail Gorbachev made it clear that he would not use force to protect communism in Eastern Europe. Fear of the Soviets had helped keep the East German government in power. Now this fear was gone and East Germany's government collapsed.

Free at Last!

HISTORY In the summer of 1989, many East Germans crossed into West Germany to begin new lives. **Critical Thinking** Why do you think that no efforts were made to prevent East Germans from fleeing to the West?

SKILLS MINI LESSON

Locating Information

You might **introduce** the skill by indicating to students that the fall of the Berlin Wall was an event of both historic and symbolic significance. Ask students how they might investigate some of the events associated with the fall of the wall. Help students **practice** the skill by working with them to make a list of possible sources of information from the general to the specific (for instance, encyclopedias, atlases, almanacs, periodical articles, and interviews with people who were present as the wall was destroyed). Record students' suggestions on the chalkboard. To **apply** the skill, have partners choose one question about fall of the Berlin Wall that they would like to have answered. Direct students to keep track of where they look for information and which locations supply the information they need. Invite students to share their questions and answers.

4 Assess/Reteach

See the answers to the Section 3 Assessment. You may also use students' completed news programs as an assessment.

Acceptable programs list in chronological order at least five major events and their causes.

Commendable programs list more than five major events and the causes of selected events.

Outstanding programs also include causes that resulted in more than one effect.

ACTIVITY

Cooperative Learning

The Wall Organize students into two groups on separate sides of the classroom. Tell students that you have constructed an imaginary wall dividing the two groups. Construct your "wall" so that one group has more advantages (for instance, exit access). Have students write about how it feels to be on their side of the wall. Then, "reunify" the two groups and have students share their observations.

Verbal/Linguistic

HISTORY

Music Marks the Moment

Many spontaneous celebrations surrounded the fall of the Berlin Wall. One of the most remarkable was the Berlin Celebration Concert, a performance of Beethoven's Symphony No. 9, given by Leonard Bernstein on Christmas Day, December 25, 1989. The same symphony had been used to mark the last days of the Third Reich. The celebration performance included musicians from East and West Germany as well as muscians from several European countries and the United States.

Answers to...

CRITICAL THINKING

East Germany's government collapsed after Soviet leaders withdrew their support of communism in Europe.

SECTION 3 ASSESSMENT

AFTER YOU READ

1. (a) German leader whose actions led to World War II and the Holocaust
2. (a) mass murder of millions of Jews and others by Germans during World War II (b) the deliberate murder of a racial, political, or ethnic group (c) process of Germany's becoming unified again
3. defeat of Germany in World War II and the beginning of the Cold War; weak East German economy and the loss of military support from the Soviet Union
4. Answers will vary, but students should indicate that people have access to more material goods and improved roads, but that there are fewer jobs, a higher cost of living, and fewer social welfare benefits.
5. Answers will vary. Students can express appreciation for the freedoms that they enjoy and the improvements to their quality of life, even if life is still more difficult than it is for relatives living in the west.
6. Answers will vary, but students should indicate that West Germans enjoyed more wealth and personal freedom.
7. Answers will vary, but students should include facts relating to the causes for this event.

The Wall Comes Down

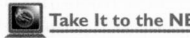

HISTORY Crowds began to destroy the Berlin Wall on November 9, 1989. They held a huge party on and around the wall, while people from both sides helped each other up and over. **Critical Thinking** Judging from the behavior of the crowds, how do you think Germans felt about the Berlin Wall?

The Berlin Wall collapsed as well. On November 9, 1989, crowds of Germans began scrambling over the wall. Some people raced to see friends and relatives. Others just wanted to enjoy a different life. People helped each other over the top of the wall to the other side. Crowds tore at the wall and took it apart block by block. Less than a year later, the governments of East and West Germany united. Germany had become a single country again.

Germany Reunited

Most Germans were thrilled about the fall of the Berlin Wall. The cultures of East and West Germany had remained similar in many ways. People in both Germanys spoke the same language and ate the same foods. They knew the same German composers, writers, and painters. Still, the process of becoming unified again, called **reunification** (ree yoo nuh fih KAY shun), would not be easy.

Germans spent millions of dollars to rebuild the economy of what was East Germany. For the first time since World War II, East Germans are enjoying modern televisions, cars, and washing machines. They have new shopping malls and better roads.

Easterners may have more televisions and cars since the reunification, but they have fewer jobs. In communist East Germany, people were guaranteed a job and food to eat. There are no such guarantees under the Western democratic system. This is one of the prices of freedom, and most former East Germans are willing to pay it.

When Germany was reunited in 1990, so was Berlin. The next year, the German legislature restored this city to its traditional role as the nation's capital. By 1999, most government offices had moved back to Berlin from the West German capital of Bonn.

SECTION 3 ASSESSMENT

AFTER YOU READ

RECALL

1. Identify: (a) Adolf Hitler
2. Define: (a) Holocaust, (b) genocide, (c) reunification

COMPREHENSION

3. Describe the events that led to the division of Germany and the events that led to its reunification.
4. How has the reunification of Germany affected life in the former East Germany?

CRITICAL THINKING AND WRITING

5. **Exploring the Main Idea** Review the Main Idea statement at the beginning of this section. Then, imagine that you are living in East Berlin. Write a letter to a relative in Bonn, describing how your life has changed since reunification.
6. **Making Comparisons** Compare personal freedom in East and West Germany during the Cold War.

ACTIVITY

Take It to the NET

7. **Reporting on the Berlin Wall** Choose a significant event related to the rise of the Berlin Wall. Imagine you are a newspaper reporter and write an article reporting on the event. Visit the World Explorer: People, Places, and Cultures section of **phschool.com** for help in completing this activity.

Resource Directory

Teaching Resources

Section Quiz in the Unit 4 Teaching Resources, p. 58

Answers to...

CRITICAL THINKING

Students may say that they saw the wall as an unwelcome barrier to their happiness.

SECTION 4

France and Italy

Cultural Influence on the World

BEFORE YOU READ

READING FOCUS

1. How is contemporary French culture connected to the past?
2. What cultural traits help to define the people of France?
3. What role does religion play in Italy?
4. What are the cultural characteristics of Italy?

KEY TERMS

manufacturing
emigrate

KEY PLACES

Aix-en-Provence
Paris
Vatican
Rome
Milan
Locorotondo

NOTE TAKING

Copy the Venn diagram below. As you read the section, fill in the diagram with comparisons about the cultures of France and Italy.

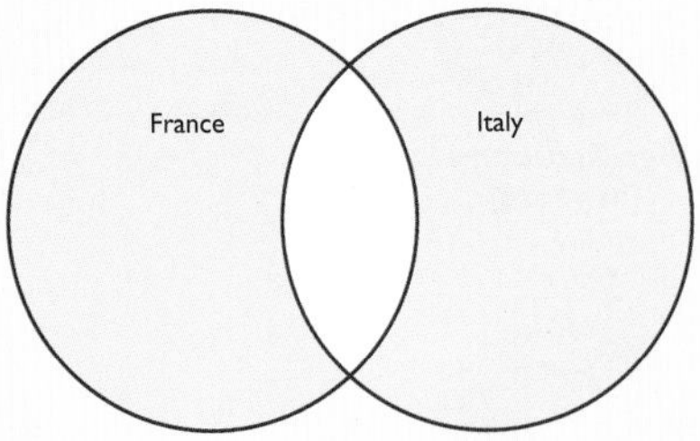

MAIN IDEA

Cultural traditions and institutions in France and Italy can be traced back through the centuries.

Setting the Scene

Catherine and Victoire are sisters. Both are in their 20s—just one year apart in age. The two look so much alike that some people think they are twins. They grew up in the south of France, in a city called **Aix-en-Provence** (EKS ahn praw VAHNS). It is a quiet, pretty town, a trading center for olives, almonds, and wine.

Catherine and Victoire are very different. Catherine still lives in Aix. She is married and has two children. Her husband works as a pastry chef, making cakes and other desserts. He follows French recipes that were created 150 years ago.

Victoire is single and lives in **Paris,** the capital of France. She works for a publisher. Her job is to get American books translated into French.

French Influence

CULTURE These girls are carrying baguettes, which are long, crusty loaves of bread. This type of bread is known throughout the world as "French bread." **Critical Thinking** What other familiar things are described using the adjective "French?"

SECTION 4

Lesson Objectives

1. Explain how the past informs contempoary French culture.
2. Identify some of the traditions and traits of French culture.
3. Explain the importance of religion to Italian culture.
4. Describe some of the cultural characteristics that define Italy.

Lesson Plan

1 Engage

Warm-Up Activity

Tell students that in most European countries today, popular music, television programs, and movies are dominated by American products and/or influences. Explain that while many Europeans welcome Americanization, others are wary of it. Ask students how they would feel if the stores in their community began to offer for sale only items made in other countries.

Activating Prior Knowledge

Ask students to think about things they like to do. Who are their favorite clothing designers? What sports do they like? What music do they like best? What food? What dances? How many of these activities have links to other cultures.

2 Explore

Have students read through Section 4 and discuss the different expressions of French culture. Why do the French and Italians take so much pride in their cultures? Why do they hold on to traditions?

Resource Directory

Teaching Resources

Classroom Manager in the Unit 4 Teaching Resources, p. 59

Guided Reading and Review in the Unit 4 Teaching Resources, p. 60

Guide to the Essentials, p. 74

Technology

Section Reading Support Transparencies

Answers to...

CRITICAL THINKING

Responses with vary. Possible answers include French doors, dressing, fries, horn, and pastry.

Lesson Plan continued

❸ Teach

Organize students into two groups. Have student pairs in one group write an article for a travel magazine promoting Aix-en-Provence or Locorotondo based on facts in the section. Students in the second group should produce a similar article for Paris or Milano. Point out that the rural articles should be geared toward travelers seeking the "old ways" and that the urban articles should emphasize a modern, changing society. Use the articles as the basis for a discussion of the conflicting cultural values in today's society. This activity should take about 30 minutes.

Questions for Discussion

CULTURE How has Catherine shown pride in French culture? How has Victoire shown that she is open to new ideas from outside of France?

Catherine talks about her proud feelings regarding French culture, such as the language, which has remained unchanged since the seventeenth century. Victoire's job is to translate American books into French, which shows she is interested in new ideas from different cultures.

ECONOMICS How do the major industries in northern and southern Italy differ?

Manufacturing is the main industry in northern Italy, while farming and fishing are the main industries in the south.

❹ Assess/Reteach

See the answers to the Section 4 Assessment. You may also use students' completed articles as an assessment.

Acceptable articles include at least three facts about the city and why these facts make it a desirable place to visit.

Commendable articles base their discussions on the desires of a traditionalist or modernist traveler.

Outstanding articles compare the merits of the profiled city with those of the other.

COUNTRY PROFILE

France

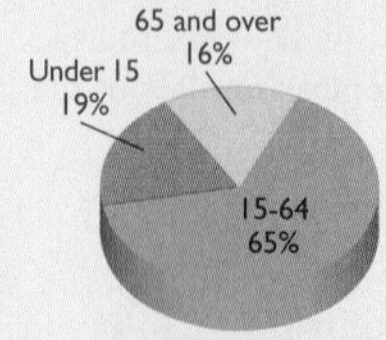

Age Structure (in years)

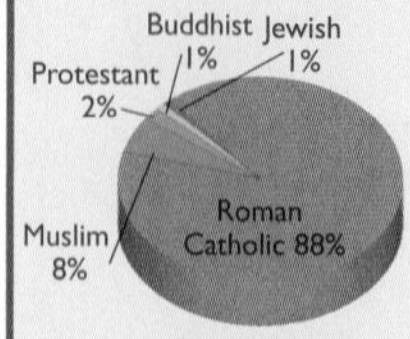

Religious Persuasion

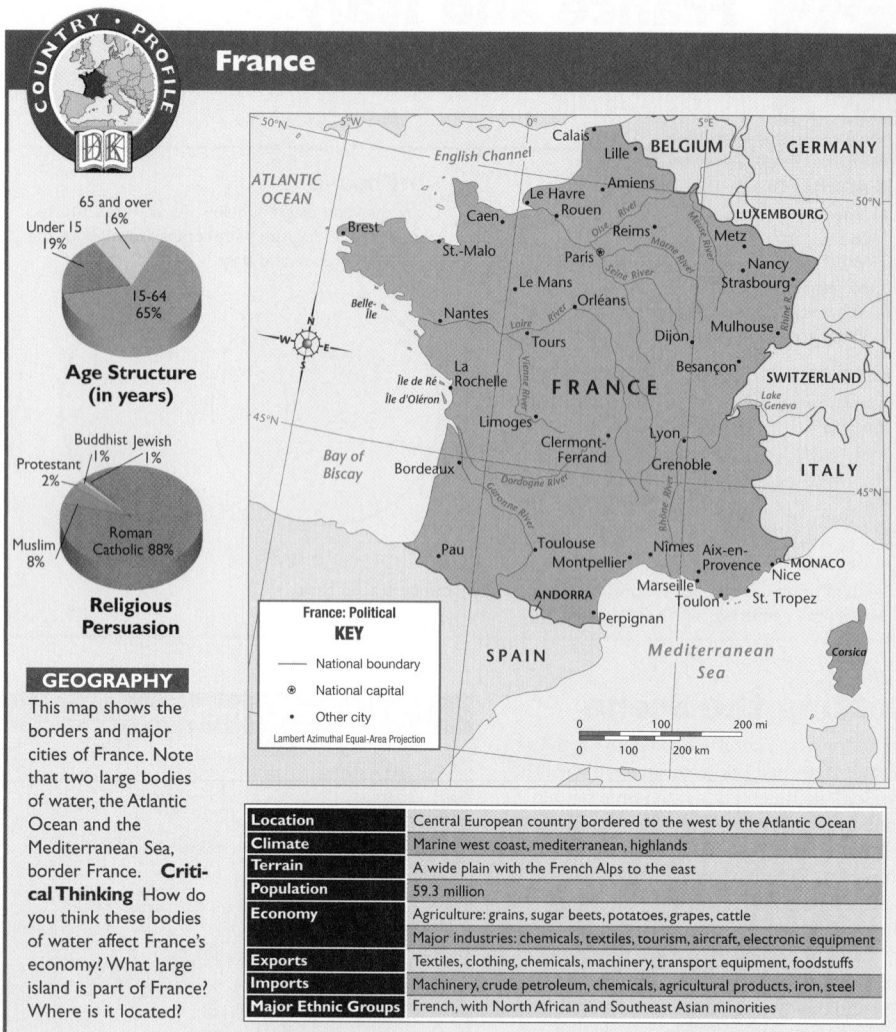

GEOGRAPHY This map shows the borders and major cities of France. Note that two large bodies of water, the Atlantic Ocean and the Mediterranean Sea, border France. **Critical Thinking** How do you think these bodies of water affect France's economy? What large island is part of France? Where is it located?

Location	Central European country bordered to the west by the Atlantic Ocean
Climate	Marine west coast, mediterranean, highlands
Terrain	A wide plain with the French Alps to the east
Population	59.3 million
Economy	Agriculture: grains, sugar beets, potatoes, grapes, cattle
	Major industries: chemicals, textiles, tourism, aircraft, electronic equipment
Exports	Textiles, clothing, chemicals, machinery, transport equipment, foodstuffs
Imports	Machinery, crude petroleum, chemicals, agricultural products, iron, steel
Major Ethnic Groups	French, with North African and Southeast Asian minorities

Contemporary Culture in France

The cultural traditions of France can be traced back for centuries. Despite rapid change in industrial centers and large cities, particularly over the last century, long-standing traditions and customs are still practiced in the more rural provinces and towns throughout the countryside. These traditions provide a cultural foundation that the French are proud to share with the rest of the world.

Answers to...

MAP AND CHART STUDY

These bodies of water make it easier for France to ship products into and out of the country; Corsica; in the Mediterranean Sea to the east of mainland France

Resource Directory

Technology

Passport to the World CD-ROM This interactive CD-ROM allows students to explore each region of the world. Students view regional videos, take a photo tour, and explore a historical timeline. Students record their travels in an Explorer's Journal, and receive passport stamps when they pass regional quizzes.

Traits that Define

Catherine and Victoire show us two sides of the French character. Each side values French culture differently. Catherine sums up her attitude this way:

> "We French are as modern as anyone else. But there is something very special about our culture. Take our language. It's very exact. In the seventeenth century [we] invented a standard for speaking correct French. Since then, an organization called the French Academy has tried to keep our language as correct as possible. We French love our traditions."

Catherine is right about the Academy. Since 1635, it has published dictionaries that give all the words accepted in the French language. The Academy makes rules about how these words should be used. This is an example of how the French work to preserve their culture.

Highlights of French Culture French culture has always had a lasting influence on the rest of the world. France has produced world-famous poets, philosophers, visual artists, and politicians, and the great city of Paris has been at the center of many of the major artistic and literary movements of the twentieth century.

In the 1920s, soon after the end of World War I, artists from all over the world flocked to Paris because they felt the city offered them the freedom to experiment with different forms of art, literature, and music. While living in Paris, writers such as Ernest Hemingway, F. Scott Fitzgerald, T. S. Eliot, Gertrude Stein, and James Joyce produced many of their most famous literary works. The Spanish painter, Pablo Picasso, the American photographer Man Ray, and France's own Jean Cocteau and André Breton were major figures in the visual arts.

France is also known for its cooking. In 1805, a French pastry chef named Marie-Antoine Carême (MUH ree ahn twahn kuh REM) began making desserts for rich and powerful people in France.

In 1833, Carême wrote a book on the art of French cooking. It set strict standards of excellence. Ever since Carême's book was published, French cooking has been one of the most respected kinds of cooking in the world.

Religion in Italy

The vast majority of French and Italian citizens are Roman Catholic and the world headquarters of the Roman Catholic Church are in the tiny nation called the **Vatican** (VAT ih kun). It is an independent city-state located within **Rome,** and its leader is the pope. Roman Catholicism unites about one billion people around the world, and it especially unites Italians. Not every Italian is Catholic, but Italy's history is closely tied to the history of Catholicism. Until recently, Catholicism was the official religion of the country.

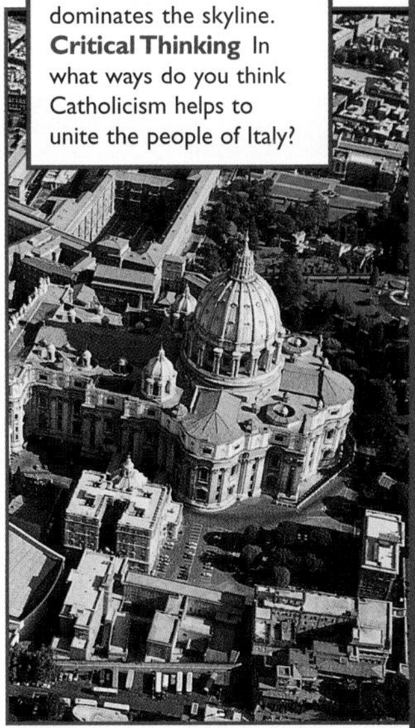

Vatican City

CULTURE This aerial view of Vatican City shows the grand dome of St. Peter's Church, which dominates the skyline. **Critical Thinking** In what ways do you think Catholicism helps to unite the people of Italy?

ACTIVITY

Interdisciplinary Connections

Art Explain to students that Michelangelo painted the ceiling of the Sistine Chapel by lying for months on his back atop a scaffold. Help students appreciate the difficulties faced by the artist by having each student first draw a picture sitting at a table or desk. Then, have them try to duplicate their efforts by drawing the same picture while lying on their backs. (Students might tape their papers to the bottoms of chairs or desks.) Have students compare their two drawings.

Visual/Spatial

ACTIVITY

Journal Writing

Go North, Young Man Inform students that in the years since World War II, millions of southern Italians have migrated to the north seeking better jobs. Even though the newcomers are citizens of the same country, these recent arrivals are not well integrated. They live in segregated areas and continue to follow their own traditions. Have students write a diary entry in their journal about a day in the life of a southern Italian who has relocated to northern Italy.

Verbal/Linguistic

HISTORY

A Papal Division

The establishment of the Holy Roman Empire in the early 800s is linked to the division of north and south evidenced in Italy today. The pope was given political power over central Italy, and the papal states effectively separated northern and southern Italy. The separation was heightened by the influence France, Spain, and Austria exerted on northern Italy. These associations led northern city-states to create great commercial and financial empires. Italy was unified in 1870.

Resource Directory

Technology

Color Transparencies 71 Western Europe: Political Map; *The Eiffel Tower* Fine Art; **84–85** *The Cathedral at Reims* (exterior and interior) Fine Art; *Eritrean Sibyl from the Sistine Chapel* Fine Art

Answers to...

CRITICAL THINKING

Students may note that Catholicism is closely tied to the nation's history.

SECTION 4 ASSESSMENT

AFTER YOU READ

1. (a) quiet city in the south of France (b) capital city of France (c) tiny nation that is the world headquarters of the Roman Catholic Church (d) capital city of Italy (e) city in northern Italy (f) small town in southernmost part of Italy.
2. (a) to move away from a homeland to another country (b) process of turning raw materials into finished products.
3. Answers will vary but may include French food, cars, music, clothes, films, art, and literature.
4. Italy is home to Vatican City, which draws many tourists to the country, and much of Italy's history, architecture, and art has been influenced by religion.
5. Answers will vary but may include manufacturing versus farming, modernity versus tradition, large versus small, and urban versus rural.
6. Answers will vary, but lists should include French and Italian foods, literature, language, art, and religion.
7. Answers will vary, but may include the importance of maintaining links to the past, the way in which language unifies people in different parts of the nation, and the way that language provides a unique identification in French culture.

Galleria Vittorio Emanuele

CULTURE This building was designed by Giuseppe Mengoni in 1861. It consists of a domed area, creating a covered shopping mall. **Critical Thinking** In what ways does this photograph show how Milan is a mix of the old and the new?

Cultural Differences in Northern and Southern Italy

Life in the North **Milan** (mih LAN) is typical of northern Italy. It is one part of a triangle of cities—with the cities of Turin and Genoa—that are home to most of Italy's manufacturing industries. **Manufacturing** is the process of turning raw materials into finished products. It also caters to international business.

Milan has a flashier side, too. Every season, people interested in fashions crowd into Milan to see collections from clothing designers. Italian fashion has become so important that Milan is second only to Paris as a fashion capital. Milan's factories also produce cars, planes, leather goods, and plastics.

Rural Culture in Southern Italy Southern Italy is very different from Milan. **Locorotondo** (loh koh roh TAWN doh) is a typical town located on the "heel" of the Italian "boot." Farming is the way most people here make a living, and wheat, olives, and fruits are grown here. Fishing is also an important industry. Southern Italian traditions and the family still rule everyday life.

Changing Cultures The cultures of both France and Italy will keep changing. As more and more people **emigrate,** or move in from other parts of the world, the cultures will become more diverse. At the same time, institutions and traditions that make each nation unique will be preserved and will continue to influence people all over the world for generations to come.

SECTION 4 ASSESSMENT

AFTER YOU READ

RECALL

1. Identify: (a) Aix-en-Provence, (b) Paris, (c) Vatican, (d) Rome, (e) Milan, (f) Locorotondo
2. Define: (a) emigrate, (b) manufacturing

COMPREHENSION

3. What are some cultural traditions of France that have influenced people around the world?
4. How has the Catholic religion influenced life in Italy?
5. What are three differences between life in Milan and life in a southern Italian village?

CRITICAL THINKING AND WRITING

6. **Exploring the Main Idea** Review the Main Idea statement at the beginning of this section. Work with a partner to make a list of ways in which cultural traditions in France and Italy can be traced back to these countries' pasts.

ACTIVITY

7. **Holding a Debate** It is important to the French to maintain certain standards in the French language. Hold a class debate about why preserving language is important and how it provides a link to cultural traditions.

Resource Directory

Teaching Resources

Section Quiz in the Unit 4 Teaching Resources, p. 61

Chapter Summary in the Unit 4 Teaching Resources, p. 62

Vocabulary in the Unit 4 Teaching Resources, p. 63

Reteaching in the Unit 4 Teaching Resources, p. 64

Enrichment in the Unit 4 Teaching Resources, p. 65

Critical Thinking in the Unit 4 Teaching Resources, p. 66

Answers to...

CRITICAL THINKING

The old building is complemented by modern architectural details.

Solving Problems

Problem

Swedish automobile makers can't compete with firms from other countries because they cannot make cars as quickly and cheaply as other countries

Possible Solutions

1. Look for economic growth in other areas, such as natural resources.
2. Make cars of less quality to increase production.
3. Partner with an American company and use their methods to increase production.
4. Hire more workers and allow less time for vacations.

Learn the Skill

Many countries today face problems. The problems are often economic—how to increase growth or reduce taxes so people have more money to spend and save. You probably face problems as well—how to earn spending money, get good grades, or make new friends.

One way to solve problems is to study how other people have solved the same problem. For example, governments can study successful solutions that other governments have come up with.

Another way to solve problems is to make a list of possible solutions and choose the best alternative. To solve problems, you can use a Problem-Solution Chart such as the one shown on this page. To complete the chart, follow these steps:

A. Identify the problem. Write it in the first box in the chart. In the sample chart, the problem is one faced by automobile makers in Sweden. They aren't able to sell many cars, because they cannot make them fast enough or cheap enough. How can the automobile makers and the government work together to increase sales and thereby boost Sweden's economy?

B. List possible solutions. Brainstorm and write down as many ideas as you can, even if you think the solution is not a good one, as it might lead to a better idea. Talk to others and get their ideas as well. Many governments have found solutions by studying what was done to correct a similar problem in another country. This is a time to call on experts and get as many ideas to choose from as possible.

C. Choose the best solution. Study each possible solution carefully. Think about the long-term effects of each. If you are with others, talk with them to find out if they are willing to help, and come up with a plan for working together. Then, choose the best solution and circle it. The solution that Sweden chose was to work with an American firm and learn how to increase production. Sweden was able to solve its problem.

D. Put the solution you chose into action.

E. Evaluate the results. If you aren't satisfied, build on your experiences and try another solution. Keep working with the problem until you are successful.

Practice the Skill

Working in a small group, make a list of problems facing your community or city. Choose one of the problems and create a Problem-Solution Chart like the one shown. First, define the problem. Then, work with your group to brainstorm several solutions. Discuss each solution thoroughly to determine if it will yield the results you want. Choose the solution that you think will work the best, and circle it. Explain your process and your chart to another small group.

Apply the Skill

See the Chapter Review and Assessment at the end of this chapter for more questions on solving problems.

Lesson Objectives

1. Understand how to use a Problem-Solution Chart to solve problems.
2. Solve a problem using a Problem-Solution Chart.

Lesson Plan

1 Engage

To introduce the skill, read the opening text under "Learn the Skill" aloud. Have students think about how they have solved problems in the past. Discuss how filling out a chart might be helpful. Invite students to share experiences in which someone helped them find a solution to a problem.

2 Explore

Direct students to read the steps under "Learn the Skill." Point out how the steps relate to the chart. Read the possible solutions and discuss the results of various ideas. Which solution do they think is best, and why?

3 Teach

Have students work together to solve problems using a Problem-Solution Chart. Provide newspaper and magazine articles on problems facing your community or country, and have students choose one of the problems to focus on.

For additional reinforcement, students can exchange problems with another group and try to add other solution suggestions to their charts.

4 Assess/Reteach

Charts should state the problem and provide several thoughtful options for solutions. Each group should choose one solution and be able to give reasons for their choice.

To further assess students' understanding of solving problems, have them complete the "Applying Your Skills" part of the Chapter Review and Assessment at the end of the chapter.

Resource Directory

Technology

Social Studies Skills Tutor CD-ROM

Answers to...

PRACTICE THE SKILL

Answers will vary. Students may list such problems with city parks, transportation, road repair, education, crime, and so forth.

CHAPTER 17

Review and Assessment

Creating a Chapter Summary

Student summaries will vary.

Sample summaries:

Section 2 Netherlands—leader in banking and manufacturing; Belgium—three regions maintain distinct cultural traditions, and try to keep pace with demands of world markets.

Section 3 Germany and Berlin divided into two parts after World War II. As the West prospered, the East German economy collapsed, resulting in political reunification.

Section 4 Cultures of France and Italy great influence on world. Both preserve cultural traditions. Italian culture influenced by Catholicism, and by distinct northern and southern regions.

Reviewing Key Terms

1. e **2.** a **3.** g **4.** f **5.** b **6.** c **7.** d

Reviewing the Main Ideas

1. Important symbol of Britain's past; provides source of shared pride
2. Home Rule is not in the best interests of the Protestants of Northern Ireland, because they would have to give up the powerful position as the colonial majority in the region.
3. The Netherlands has few natural resources and must import raw materials to be manufactured into goods for export.
4. The economy of Wallonia in southern Belgium depended on coal mining to fuel its steel manufacturing plants. The prosperity of the country has moved north to Flanders, where the majority of the population lives.
5. At the end of World War II, the victorious Allies divided Germany among themselves. The American, French, and British sections became democratic West Germany and the Soviet Union section became communist East Germany. Communist rule began to weaken as the East German economy lagged behind West Germany's. The Soviet Union withdrew its military support, and the unpopular government collapsed.
6. Cultural characteristics such as language, food, artists and writers, and a shared history linked Germans before reunification.
7. The French take pride in the purity of their language to preserve the traditions of the past.
8. Roman Catholicism unites the people of Italy, whether they are living in the cities or in the rural countryside.

CHAPTER 17

Review and Assessment

Creating a Chapter Summary

On a separate piece of paper, draw a diagram like this one, and include the information that summarizes the first section of the chapter. Then fill in the remaining boxes with summaries of Sections 2, 3, and 4.

WESTERN EUROPE

Section 1	Section 2	Section 3	Section 4
Great Britain is a constitutional monarchy whose laws are set by Parliament. As part of the United Kingdom, Northern Ireland is also governed by the British parliament. The Republic of Ireland is an independent nation.			

Reviewing Key Terms

Match the definitions in Column I with the key terms in Column II.

Column I	Column II
1. polders	a. oppression
2. persecution	b. government in which the power of kings and queens is limited by law
3. reunification	c. Dutch-speaking Belgian
4. Parliament	d. mass murder of millions of Jews and others by Germans during World War II
5. constitutional monarchy	e. land reclaimed from the sea
6. Flemish	f. representative body that makes the law in Great Britain
7. Holocaust	g. process of Germany's becoming unified again

Reviewing the Main Ideas

1. How does the monarchy help to unify Great Britain? (Section 1)
2. Why do the Protestants of Northern Ireland oppose Home Rule? (Section 1)
3. How does the Netherlands get raw materials for manufacturing? (Section 2)
4. What are some of the differences between northern and southern Belgium? (Section 2)
5. How was Germany divided and why was it reunified? (Section 3)
6. What kept Germans unified in their thinking even when their country was divided? (Section 3)
7. How do the French keep their cultural traditions? (Section 4)
8. Why is religion an important part of Italian culture? (Section 4)

324 UNIT 4 EUROPE AND RUSSIA

Map Activity

Western Europe

For each place listed below, write the letter from the map that shows its location.

1. Aix-en-Provence
2. London
3. The Netherlands
4. Italy
5. Berlin
6. Brussels

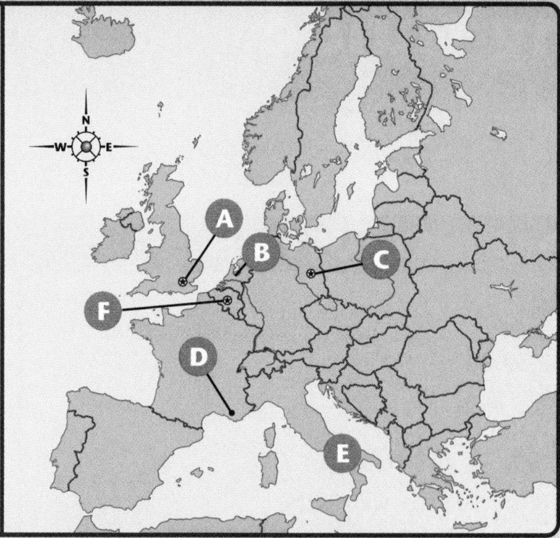

Take It to the NET

Enrichment For more map activities using geography skills, visit the social studies section of **phschool.com.**

Writing Activity

1. **Using Primary Sources** News about the current events described throughout this chapter can be researched at your school or local library. Use primary sources such as journal accounts, autobiographies, letters, and first-hand accounts to write a press release that gives an update on a current event in Great Britain, Ireland, Belgium, the Netherlands, Germany, France, or Italy.
2. **Writing a Travel Journal** Imagine that you have traveled to each country mentioned in this chapter. Write a journal entry describing some of the cultural or historical sites you visited, traditions you learned about, or experiences you enjoyed. Visit the library or Internet to help you complete the activity.

Critical Thinking

1. **Making Comparisons** Compare the partitioning of Germany with the partitioning of Ireland and the separation of the Netherlands from Belgium. What factors are similar? What factors are different?
2. **Drawing Conclusions** How do you think Germany will change in the future? How might Germans react to these changes?

Applying Your Skills

Turn to the Skills Activity on p. 323 to complete the following activity.

Think of a problem that you are having in your own life, and then create a Problem-Solution Chart to find the best solution.

Take It to the NET

Activity Take a virtual tour of Paris using the interactive map. Create a travel guide for your own town or city. Include photos or illustrations of sights, a map, and information about each point of interest. Visit the World Explorer: People, Places, and Cultures section of **phschool.com** for help in completing this activity.

Chapter 17 Self-Test As a final review activity, take the Chapter 17 Self-Test and get instant feedback on your answers. To take the test, visit the Social Studies section of **phschool.com.**

Map Activity

1. D **2.** A **3.** B **4.** E **5.** C **6.** F

Writing Activities

1. Students should use current sources to find out developments in the conflict in Ireland, or issues in Belgium, the Netherlands, Germany, or France.
2. Students' journal entries should reflect various details described in the text.

Critical Thinking

1. The partitioning of Germany was a result of World War II and was not a choice that the German people were offered. When Belgium broke away from the Netherlands, they waged a civil war to gain their independence, and their religious beliefs played a role. The partitioning of Ireland granted independence to the Catholic majority in the Republic of Ireland and left the Protestants in control of Northern Ireland as part of the United Kingdom. Efforts to reunite Ireland continue to this day.
2. Answers will vary. Possible answer: Many resources will be spent in order to help East Germany. The lifestyles of both groups will suffer in the short term, but the industrious German spirit will prevail, and Germans will work together to overcome their difficulties.

Applying Your Skills

Students' charts will vary, but should contain clear, detailed information in both sections.

Resource Directory

Teaching Resources

Cooperative Learning Activity in the Unit 4 Teaching Resources, pp. 122–125

Chapter Tests Forms A and B in the Unit 4 Teaching Resources, pp. 156–161

Guide to the Essentials, Ch. 17 Test, p. 25

Other Print Resources

Chapter Tests with ExamView® Test Bank, Ch. 17

Technology

ExamView® Test Bank CD-ROM, Ch. 17

Resource Pro® CD-ROM

Chapter 18 Planning Guide

Resource Manager

	CORE INSTRUCTION	READING/SKILLS
Chapter-Level Resources	**Teaching Resources** Program Overview Pacing Charts **Technology** Resource Pro® CD-ROM Companion Web site, phschool.com • eTeach	**Technology** Social Studies Skills Tutor CD-ROM Student Edition on Audio CD, Ch. 18
1 Poland: The Growth of Free Enterprise 1. Explain the dynamic changes in the Polish economy. 2. Describe the various challenges facing present-day Poland.	**Teaching Resources** **Unit 4** Classroom Manager, p. 68 Guided Reading and Review, p. 69	**Teaching Resources** Guide to the Essentials, p. 76 Social Studies and Geography Skills, p. 62 **Technology** Section Reading Support Transparencies
2 The Balkans: Cultural and Political Power Struggles 1. Explain how the geography of the Balkans has contributed to the distinct cultures in the region. 2. Explain how differences among various ethnic groups in the Balkans have led to conflicts.	**Teaching Resources** **Unit 4** Classroom Manager, p. 71 Guided Reading and Review, p. 72	**Teaching Resources** Guide to the Essentials, p. 77 Social Studies and Geography Skills, p. 60 **Technology** Section Reading Support Transparencies
3 The Czech Republic: An Economic Success Story 1. Explain how democratic traditions helped the Czech Republic make the transition to a democratic society after the fall of communism. 2. Describe the challenges of building a free enterprise economy.	**Teaching Resources** **Unit 4** Classroom Manager, p. 74 Guided Reading and Review, p. 75	**Teaching Resources** Guide to the Essentials, p. 78 Social Studies and Geography Skills, p. 93 **Technology** Section Reading Support Transparencies
4 Russia: New Democracy, Unstable Economy 1. Describe the changes that have taken place in Siberia since the fall of communism. 2. Describe the changes that have taken place in Moscow since the fall of communism.	**Teaching Resources** **Unit 4** Classroom Manager, p. 77 Guided Reading and Review, p. 78 Chapter Summary, p. 80 Vocabulary, p. 81 Reteaching, p. 82	**Teaching Resources** **Unit 4** Critical Thinking, p. 84 Guide to the Essentials, p. 79 Social Studies and Geography Skills, p. 50 **Technology** Section Reading Support Transparencies

ENRICHMENT / PRE-AP

Teaching Resources
Primary Sources and Literature Readings

Other Print Resources
DK Atlas

Technology
World Video Explorer: Making a Living; A New Business in Moscow, Daily Life; Russia Today
Companion Web site, phschool.com

Teaching Resources
Outline Maps, p. 24

Teaching Resources
Outline Maps, p. 22–23

Technology
Color Transparencies 74–76

Teaching Resources
Outline Maps, p. 22–23

Teaching Resources
Unit 4
Enrichment, p. 83
Cooperative Learning Activity, pp. 126–128

Technology
Color Transparencies 74–76
Passport to the World CD-ROM

ASSESSMENT

Prentice Hall Assessment System

Core Assessment
Chapter Tests with ExamView® Test Bank, Ch. 18
ExamView® Test Bank CD-ROM, Ch. 18

Standardized Test Preparation
Diagnose and Prescribe
Diagnostic Tests for Middle Grades Social Studies Skills
Review and Reteach
Review Book for World Studies
Practice and Assess
Test-taking Strategies with Transparencies for Middle Grades Test Prep Book
Test-taking Strategies Posters

Teaching Resources
Unit 4
Section Quizzes, pp. 70, 73, 76, and 79
Chapter Tests, pp. 162–167

Technology
Companion Web site, phschool.com
Ch. 18 Self-Test

World Video Explorer
Each region of the world is explored through regional flyovers and investigative field trips. Case study segments give students an in-depth view of the history, economy, government, and culture of a key place in each region. Case studies include Nigeria, Mexico, China, British Columbia, and the Czech Republic.

In Your Classroom

CUSTOMIZE FOR INDIVIDUAL NEEDS

Gifted and Talented

Teacher's Edition
- Committees on Goals, p. 332

Teaching Resources
- Enrichment, p. 83
- Primary Sources and Literature Readings

Honors/Pre-AP

Teacher's Edition
- Drawing Conclusions, p. 339

Teaching Resources
- Critical Thinking, p. 84
- Primary Sources and Literature Readings

ESL

Teacher's Edition
- Drawing Conclusions, p. 339

Teaching Resources
- Guided Reading and Review, pp. 69, 72, 75, and 78
- Vocabulary, p. 81
- Reteaching, p. 82
- Guide to the Essentials, pp. 76–79
- Social Studies and Geography Skills, pp. 50, 60, 62, 93

Technology
- Social Studies Skills Tutor CD-ROM
- Section Reading Support Transparencies

Less Proficient Readers

Teacher's Edition
- Drawing Conclusions, p. 339

Teaching Resources
- Guided Reading and Review, pp. 69, 72, 75, and 78
- Vocabulary, p. 81
- Reteaching, p. 82
- Guide to the Essentials, pp. 76–79
- Social Studies and Geography Skills, pp. 50, 60, 62, 93

Technology
- Social Studies Skills Tutor CD-ROM
- Section Reading Support Transparencies

Less Proficient Writers

Teacher's Edition
- Drawing Conclusions, p. 339

Teaching Resources
- Guided Reading and Review, pp. 69, 72, 75, and 78
- Vocabulary, p. 81
- Guide to the Essentials, pp. 76–79
- Social Studies and Geography Skills, p. 50, 60, 62, 93

Technology
- Social Studies Skills Tutor CD-ROM
- Section Reading Support Transparencies

DORLING KINDERSLEY

At the end of each unit, you will find information adapted from Dorling Kindersley's *Illustrated Children's Encyclopedia* that connects to the region being studied and to one of the seven content strands. In addition, your resources include Dorling Kindersley's *Atlas*, which contains valuable information about countries from around the world.

TEACHER'S EDITION INDEX

Activities committees on goals, p. 332; drawing conclusions, p. 339

Skills Mini Lessons Expressing Problems Clearly, p. 328; Recognizing Bias, p. 332; Assessing Your Understanding, p. 339

CHAPTER 18 PACING SUGGESTIONS

For 90-minute Blocks

See suggestions in the Teaching Resources Pacing Charts for Chapter 18. Use Color Transparencies 74–76.

Running Out of Time?

See the Guide to the Essentials, pp. 76–79.

INTERDISCIPLINARY LINKS

Middle Grades Math: Tools for Success

Course 1, Lesson 1-3, **Spreadsheets and Data Displays**

Course 2, Lesson 8-7, **Use Logical Reasoning**

Science Explorer

Environmental Science, Lesson 3-1, **Environmental Issues;** Lesson 4-1, **Conserving Land and Soil;** Lesson 4-2, **Solid Waste;** Lesson 4-3, **Hazardous Waste**

Prentice Hall Literature

Copper, Overdoing It, Zlateh the Goat

BIBLIOGRAPHY

For the Teacher

DK *DK Concise Atlas of the World.* Dorling Kindersley, 2001.

Otfinoski, Steven. *Poland.* Facts on File, 1995.

Schomp, Virginia. *Russia: New Freedoms, New Challenges.* Benchmark, 1995.

Ukraine. Lerner, 1993.

For the Student

Easy

Ganeri, Anita. *I Remember Bosnia.* Raintree, 1994.

Average

Morris, Ann. *On Their Toes: A Russian Ballet School.* Atheneum, 1991.

DK *Russia* (*Eyewitness* series). Dorling Kindersley, 2001.

Challenging

Cheney, Glenn Alan. *Chernobyl: The Ongoing Story of the World's Deadliest Nuclear Disaster.* New Discovery, 1993.

Literature Connection

Dommermuth-Costa, Carol. *Nikola Tesla: A Spark of Genius.* Lerner, 1994.

Filipovič, Zlata. *Zlata's Diary: A Child's Life in Sarajevo.* Viking, 1994.

Pausewang, Gundrun. *Fall-Out.* Viking, 1995.

Take It to the NET

The World Explorer companion Web site, found on **phschool.com**, offers activities for exploring geographical, historical, and cultural resources on the Internet. It also provides on-line links for key content and all Section and Chapter Assessment activities.

The **Teacher site** also provides teachers with regional data and ideas for student research and activities.

Students can use the **Student site** to find chapter-by-chapter Internet resource links and to access Self-Tests.

CHAPTER 18

Connecting to the Guiding Questions

In this chapter, students will read about the regions of Eastern Europe and Russia today. Content in this chapter corresponds to the following Guiding Questions outlined in the beginning of the unit.

- How are people's lives changing with the freedom of the newly formed democracies of Eastern Europe?
- Why is it important for people in democratic societies to exercise their responsibilities as citizens?
- How can people take advantage of new technologies and still maintain links to more traditional ways of life?

Using the Literature Activities

As a class, read aloud the entry from Zlata's diary. Make sure that students understand that Zlata is writing in her diary during a time of war.

- Zlata's diary reveals some of the hardships of war, including fear, sadness, and a longing for peace.
- Students' diaries should be kept for one week and should include details about both happy and sad events.

Heterogeneous Groups

The following activities are suitable for heterogeneous groups.

Cooperative Learning

Committees on Goals, p. 332

Critical Thinking

Drawing Conclusions, p. 339

eTeach

Be sure to check out this month's discussion with a Master Teacher. Go to **phschool.com**.

CHAPTER 18

EASTERN EUROPE AND RUSSIA: Exploring the Region Today

Peace, Not War

Thursday, December 3, 1992
Dear Mimmy,

Today is my birthday. My first wartime birthday. Twelve years old. Congratulations. Happy birthday to me!

As usual there was no electricity. Auntie Melica came with her family (Kenan, Naida, Nihad) and gave me a book.... The whole neighborhood got together in the evening. I got chocolate, vitamins, a heart shaped soap, a key chain, a pendant made of a stone from Cyprus, a ring (silver) and earrings.

The table was nicely laid, with little rolls, fish and rice salad, cream cheese (with Feta), canned corned beef, a pie, and of course—a birthday cake. Not how it used to be, but there's a war on. Luckily, there was no shooting, so we could celebrate.

It was nice, but something was missing. It's called peace!
Your Zlata

Using Literature

This letter was written by Zlata Filipovic, a young girl who lived through the civil war in the country of Bosnia. She wrote the letter in her diary, which she called "Mimmy." During the war in Bosnia, Zlata and her family spent their days in the basement to avoid gunfire. Schools closed. Food and water became scarce.

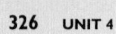

Using a Diary or Journal
Many people write in a diary or journal what they would tell no other person. Diaries can give people hope and courage, especially during hard times. What does this diary entry tell you about war? How do you think the experience of living through a war affected Zlata?

Keeping a Diary
Keep a diary for a week, writing one entry each day. Write about what makes you happy as well as things that bother or upset you. At the end of the week, write an entry telling what you think about keeping a diary.

326 UNIT 4 EUROPE AND RUSSIA

Resource Directory

Teaching Resources

Primary Sources and Literature Readings extend content with a selection related to the concepts in this chapter.

Other Print Resources

DK Atlas

Technology

Making a Living: A New Business in Moscow, from the World Video Explorer, enhances understanding of the challenges and rewards of starting a business in Moscow.

Daily Life: Russia Today, from the World Video Explorer, enhances understanding of daily life in Russia through the eyes of two Russian teenagers.

Student Edition on Audio CD, Ch. 18

SECTION 1

Poland

The Growth of Free Enterprise

BEFORE YOU READ

READING FOCUS

1. How is Poland's economy changing?
2. What are some of the challenges faced by all Polish citizens?

KEY TERMS

free enterprise

KEY PEOPLE

Pope John Paul II

MAIN IDEA

In Poland, communism once controlled people's lives and livelihood. Now, Poles are learning about freedom's rewards and responsibilities.

NOTE TAKING

Copy the table below. As you read the section, fill in the table with information about Poland's changing economy.

Changes in the Cities	Changes in the Countryside

Setting the Scene

After World War II, Poland was dominated by the Soviet Union. The Polish people were made to follow strict rules governing the economy, education, and free speech, but they would not give up their language or their strong connection to the Roman Catholic Church. **Pope John Paul II,** a Polish citizen, was made head of the Church in 1978. His leadership helped to reinforce traditional beliefs and to gain support for the Polish bid for freedom. In 1989, the communist government in Poland came to an end. The Polish people were committed to democracy and were ready to meet the challenges of freedom.

Cultural Traditions

CULTURE Christians across the world make decorated eggs at Easter. These brightly colored eggs are similar to those that Polish people exchange at Easter. **Critical Thinking** Why was it so important to many Polish people to maintain their religious customs during communist rule?

Changes in the Towns and Economy

Ever since the fall of communism, Poland has undergone rapid change in its economy. Under communism, the government owned and ran all of the businesses. Now the Poles have adopted a **free enterprise** system like that of the United States. In a free enterprise system, businesses can compete with each other for profit, with little government control.

Small businesses soon blossomed all over Poland's capital, Warsaw. Traders set up booths on the streets where they sold everything from American blue jeans to old Soviet army uniforms. Some traders earned enough money to take over stores that the government had once owned. Poland's economy

SECTION 1

Lesson Objectives

1. Explain the dynamic changes in the Polish economy.
2. Describe the various challenges facing present-day Poland.

Lesson Plan

1 Engage

Warm-Up Activity

Ask students to imagine how they would feel if a foreign country invaded the United States and took control of every aspect of their lives—including what their school could teach and the kind of government they could have. How would their lives change? What could they do to free the United States? What kinds of risks would they be willing to take?

Activating Prior Knowledge

Have students diiscuss changes they would expect to see in their hometown 20 years from now. Which changes do they think would be beneficial? Harmful? Which changes would be hard to get used to? Which would be easy to get used to?

Answers to...

CRITICAL THINKING

Maintaining ties to the church during communist rule allowed many Polish people to feel that they were holding on to one of their valued cultural traditions.

Resource Directory

Teaching Resources

Classroom Manager in the Unit 4 Teaching Resources, p. 68

Guided Reading and Review in the Unit 4 Teaching Resources, p. 69

Guide to the Essentials, p. 76

Technology

Section Reading Support Transparencies

Lesson Plan continued

❷ Explore

Have the students read the section and explore why there is such a great difference between the lives of people in cities and people in the countryside. Ask which of the two seemed to benefit more from communism and who lives better now than they would have under communism. Ask what traditions people still follow even after Poland became free of communism.

❸ Teach

Have students create a chart similar to the following.

Poland Yesterday and Today

	Life Under Communism	Life Under Free Enterprise
Type of Polish Citizen		
Farmer		
Business-person		
All Poles		

Have students fill in the chart with facts from the section. Use the chart as a basis for a discussion on how life has changed in Poland in recent years. Allow 30 minutes for this activity.

Question for Discussion

ECONOMICS **What do you predict will happen to the Polish economy in the future?**

Possible answers: The economy will continue to grow; good economic times will end if the global economy falters.

Answers to...

MAP STUDY

People in cities are likely to work in manufacturing and trade.

COUNTRY PROFILE

Poland

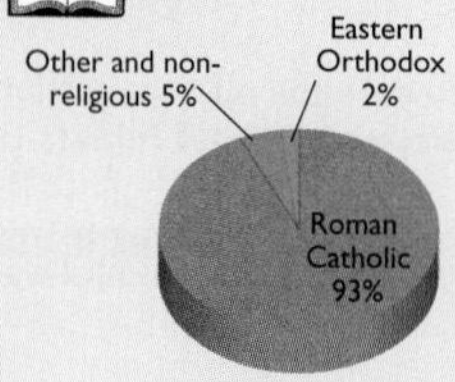

Religious Persuasion

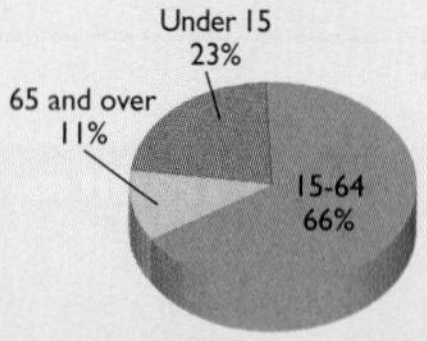

Age Structure (in years)

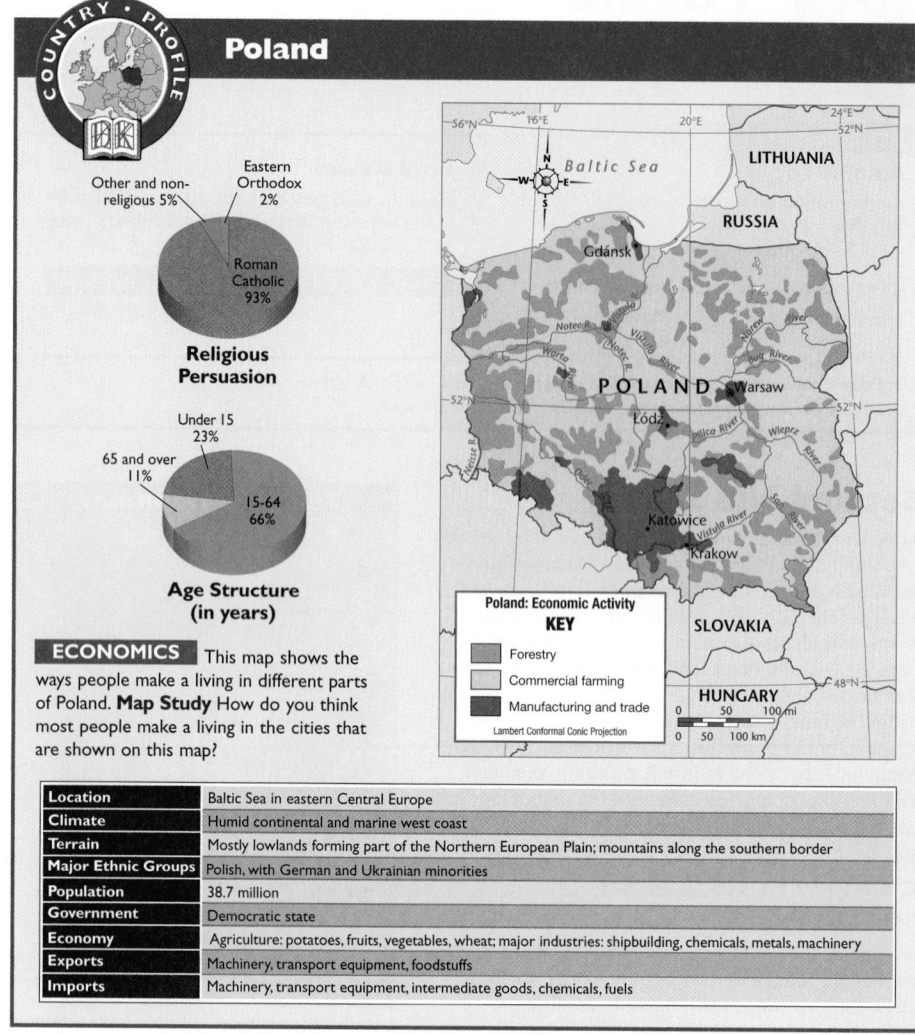

ECONOMICS This map shows the ways people make a living in different parts of Poland. **Map Study** How do you think most people make a living in the cities that are shown on this map?

Location	Baltic Sea in eastern Central Europe
Climate	Humid continental and marine west coast
Terrain	Mostly lowlands forming part of the Northern European Plain; mountains along the southern border
Major Ethnic Groups	Polish, with German and Ukrainian minorities
Population	38.7 million
Government	Democratic state
Economy	Agriculture: potatoes, fruits, vegetables, wheat; major industries: shipbuilding, chemicals, metals, machinery
Exports	Machinery, transport equipment, foodstuffs
Imports	Machinery, transport equipment, intermediate goods, chemicals, fuels

began growing faster than any other in Eastern Europe. Today, the standard of living of its people is growing stronger every day.

Challenges for the Future

Merchants and industrial workers are benefiting from their hard work. But people in rural areas are working harder and are not benefiting. Farmers, with no government support, find it hard to compete

SKILLS MINI LESSON

Expressing Problems Clearly

To **introduce** the skill, point out that defining and expressing a problem clearly are keys to understanding and solving the problem. As students consider the challenges facing people in Poland, engage them in a discussion about the differences between the opportunities offered in cities and those offered in urban areas. Ask students to **practice** defining the problem by generating a list of three benefits and three drawbacks of life in urban areas.

The items on the list should be events or conditions that have occurred or existed only since Poland adopted a free market economy. To **apply** the skill, have students summarize the information contained in their lists in a concise statement. For example: Some merchants in Polish cities have been able to improve their lives by opening their own stores. However, many people in Poland's cities remain unemployed.

Standard of Living in Eastern European Countries

Country	Percent of Population with Televisions	Percent of Population with Telephones
Albania	10%	2%
Czech Republic	33%	33%
Hungary	50%	20%
Poland	25%	14%
Serbia	17%	20%
United States	83%	77%

ECONOMICS One way to study a country's economic health is to take a look at its basic services, such as communications. This chart shows the percentage of people that have TVs and telephones in several European countries, as well as in the United States. **Chart Study** Based on this information, which country probably has the weakest economy?

in the European market. Many young people in rural areas feel that they have little chance to make a decent living. Some have moved to the city in the hope of finding jobs.

Migration to the cities, however, can cause overcrowding. Today, 60 percent of all Poles live in towns or cities, a huge increase from just 50 years ago. In response, the government is building apartment buildings and expanding suburban areas.

The new life is good in some ways and hard in others. Many Poles have things they never had before. For these people, the new way of life is good.

However, you can also see people with nothing to do. This, too, is a change. There are more people without jobs than there were under communism. The Poles will have to find ways to deal with such challenges. The Polish people are ready to do whatever is needed because, for the first time in many years, their future is in their own hands.

SECTION I ASSESSMENT

AFTER YOU READ

RECALL

1. Identify: (a) Pope John Paul II
2. Define: (a) free enterprise

COMPREHENSION

3. What economic changes have taken place in Poland since the end of communist rule?
4. What challenges have people in Poland's cities and towns had to face in recent times?

CRITICAL THINKING AND WRITING

5. **Exploring the Main Idea** Review the Main Idea statement at the beginning of this section. Then, write a paragraph describing the changes in Poland after communist rule.
6. **Comparing and Contrasting** Many Polish people left farms to move to cities like Warsaw in order to earn a better living. How was life in the city different from life in rural areas?

ACTIVITY

7. **Creating an Advertisement** Imagine that you are a business owner in Warsaw. Decide what your business is and then think of a way to promote it. Create a magazine advertisement for your business.

Resource Directory

Teaching Resources

Section Quiz in the Unit 4 Teaching Resources, p. 70

Outline Maps Poland, p. 24

Social Studies and Geography Skills, Analyzing Statistics, p. 62

4 Assess/Reteach

See the answers to the Section 1 Assessment. You may wish to use the students' completed charts as an assessment.

Acceptable charts contain at least three factually correct entries.

Commendable charts contain more than three factually correct entries.

Outstanding charts contain at least one factually correct entry in each cell and indicate an understanding of the changes brought about by adopting a free enterprise system.

SECTION I ASSESSMENT

AFTER YOU READ

1. (a) a Pole who became pope, the head of the Roman Catholic Church
2. (a) an economic system that allows people to own businesses privately with little government control
3. Among the economic changes are the development of a free enterprise system, the growth of independent small businesses, and a rise in the standard of living for some people living in cities.
4. Times are hard for farmers who do not have government support and are having trouble competing in the European market.
5. Answers will vary. Students should describe the changes discussed in the section.
6. People moving to Warsaw from rural areas might experience overcrowding, new technology, and competition for jobs.
7. Advertisements will vary, but should promote a business in a positive way.

Answers to...

CHART STUDY

Albania probably has the weakest economy because it has the lowest percent of population with televisions and telephones.

SECTION 2

Lesson Objectives

1. Explain how the geography of the Balkans has contributed to the distinct cultures in the region.
2. Explain how differences among various ethnic groups in the Balkans have led to conflicts.

Lesson Plan

1 Engage

Warm-Up Activity

Discuss with students how they would feel if neighbors with whom they had been friendly (and among whom they had lived and worked for many years) suddenly refused to talk to them and even made insulting remarks about them. Would they feel they could trust them?

Activating Prior Knowledge

Have students explore how they might feel if the country in which they and their families live broke apart, and different groups in the country began to fight one another.

SECTION 2

The Balkans

Cultural and Political Power Struggles

BEFORE YOU READ

READING FOCUS

1. How has the geography of the Balkans created cultural differences among people?
2. How have cultural differences in the Balkans led to war?

KEY TERMS

United Nations

KEY PLACES

Balkans
Kosovo

NOTE TAKING

Copy the concept web below. As you read the section, fill in the web with information about the Balkans.

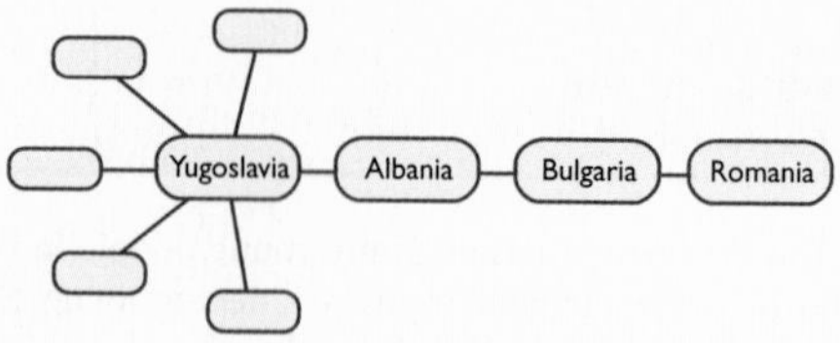

MAIN IDEA

Cultural differences have been the cause of violent conflict in the Balkans region and threaten the future of the people who live there.

Mostar, Bosnia-Herzegovina

CULTURE This bridge in Mostar, Bosnia-Herzegovina, stood for more than 400 years. It was destroyed in 1993 during a war between ethnic groups. **Critical Thinking** In what ways might war damage the culture of a particular region?

Setting the Scene

The **Balkans** is a region made up of several countries, including Yugoslavia. The region is located south of the Danube River and gets its name from the Turkish word for "mountain." The land here features rugged mountains, which form natural barriers around fertile valleys and isolated alpine villages. To the west of the Balkan Peninsula is the Adriatic Sea, to the southwest is the Ionian Sea, and to the east is the Black Sea.

A centuries-old clash of cultures divides the states that once were part of Yugoslavia. The area has been devastated by years of war and, for many people in the Balkans, the future is uncertain.

Geographic Barriers Lead to Cultural Differences

For centuries, the Ottoman Empire controlled the Balkans region. The people living there were cut off from the west until after World War I, when the countries of the Balkans region were finally established. These new countries were poor and unstable, and could not stand up to

Resource Directory

Teaching Resources

Classroom Manager in the Unit 4 Teaching Resources, p. 71

Guided Reading and Review in the Unit 4 Teaching Resources, p. 72

Guide to the Essentials, p. 77

Technology

Section Reading Support Transparencies

Answers to...

CRITICAL THINKING

During wars, the architecture and art of a culture might be damaged or destroyed. Cultural traditions and customs, such as religious practices or languages might be suppressed.

their more powerful neighbors. One of those neighbors, the Soviet Union, dominated the region after World War II.

Under a Soviet-influenced communist government, people gave up freedom in an effort to develop stronger industries and a more stable economy.

Distinct Cultural Groups The mountains of the Balkan region form natural barriers. Cultural groups developed without interference from each other, forming strong traditions and beliefs. Bringing these different groups together has had tragic results.

Many of the people in the Balkans share a Slavic background even though they belong to different ethnic groups. The largest groups in Yugoslavia are the Serbs, Croats (KROH atz), and Muslims, also called Bosniaks. Smaller groups are the Slovenes, Macedonians (mas uh DOH nee unz), and Montenegrins (mahn tuh NEH grins). Although these groups were unified under the communist government, they each have distinct languages and cultural identities.

Cultural Profile of the Balkan Countries

Country	Major Ethnic Groups	Major Religions	Languages
Albania	Albanian 95% Greek 3% Other 2%	Muslim 70% Albanian Orthodox 20% Roman Catholic 10%	Albanian Greek
Bosnia-Herzegovina	Serb 31% Bosniak 44% Croat 17% Other 8%	Muslim 40% Orthodox 31% Roman Catholic 15% Other 14%	Croatian Serbian Bosnian
Bulgaria	Bulgarian 83% Other 17%	Bulgarian Orthodox 84% Muslim 13% Other 3%	Bulgarian
Croatia	Croat 78% Serb 12% Other 10%	Roman Catholic 76% Orthodox 11% Muslim 1% Other 12%	Croatian Other
Former Yugoslav Republic of Macedonia	Macedonian 67% Albanian 23% Other 10%	Macedonian Orthodox 67% Muslim 30% Other 3%	Macedonian Albanian Turkish Serbo-Croatian
Romania	Romanian 89% Other 11%	Romanian Orthodox 87% Roman Catholic 5% Protestant 4% Other 4%	Romanian Hungarian German
Yugoslavia (Serbia and Montenegro)	Serb 62% Albanian 17% Montenegrin 5% Bosniak 3% Hungarian 3% Other 10%	Orthodox 65% Muslim 19% Roman Catholic 4% Protestant 1% Other 11%	Serbian Albanian
Slovenia	Slovene 88% Croat 3% Serb 2% Bosniak 1% Other 6%	Roman Catholic 71% Lutheran 1% Muslim 1% Atheist 4% Other 23%	Slovenian Serbo-Croatian

CULTURE This chart shows the ethnic, religious, and language groups of the people in the Balkan countries. **Chart Study** Which countries would you expect to be the most stable? Which countries would you expect to be the least stable? Give reasons for your answers.

Differences in Language Serbs and Croats both speak the Serbo-Croatian language, but they do not use the same alphabet to write. Slovenian, Macedonian, and Bulgarian languages are related to Serbo-Croatian, but they are not identical to it. Albanians and Romanians speak languages that are not closely related to those of their Slavic neighbors. Differences in language set the people in each group apart from each other.

Differences in Religion In the Balkans, the majority of the people are Christian Orthodox, Roman Catholic, or Muslim. People who want to live, work, and socialize only with people who share their religious beliefs have tried to rid their communities, often through the use of violence, of those people who do not share the same beliefs.

2 Explore

Have students read the section and discuss the reasons for instability in the Balkans. Discuss the roles that different religions and writing systems in the region played and what the former nations of Yugoslavia sought to gain from the war.

3 Teach

Ask each student to prepare a list of all the groups in former Yugoslavia that were involved in one way or another in armed conflict. Ask volunteers to read their lists aloud. Record the groups' names on the chalkboard. Then discuss the role of each group in either starting or contributing to the conflict. Allow 30 minutes for this activity.

Questions for Discussion

HISTORY How has the war in the former Yugoslavia affected the people there?

The war has been marked by much bloodshed, and people have been mistreated by their enemies. Large areas of Sarajevo have been destroyed.

SOCIAL STUDIES SKILLS Look at the Cultural Profile on this page. What conclusions can you draw about the religious persuasion of the largest ethnic group in Albania?

Albanian is the largest of the three ethnic groups, and 70 percent of the country are Muslim. Therefore, the vast majority of Albanians are Muslim. The other 25 percent are either Albanian Orthodox or Roman Catholic.

Resource Directory

Teaching Resources

Outline Maps, Eastern Europe, pp. 22–23

Social Studies and Geography Skills, Reading a Table, p. 60

Technology

Color Transparencies 74–76 Europe Today with Eastern Europe Updated (base maps with overlay)

Answers to...

CHART STUDY

The most stable countries are likely to be Albania, Bulgaria, Croatia, and Slovenia because they present fewer cultural conflicts in terms of ethnic groups, religion, and language. Least stable are likely to be Bosnia-Herzegovina, and Serbia and Montenegro.

Lesson Plan continued

4 Assess/Reteach

See the answers to the Section 2 Assessment. You may also direct students to refer to the list of groups written on the chalkboard or on the chart. Have them write a brief statement about each group's role in the current conflicts in the Balkans. Rate the students' statements on their accuracy and completeness.

ACTIVITY

Cooperative Learning

Committees on Goals Organize students into committees and ask each committee to represent one of the groups involved in the Bosnian conflict. Make sure that all the Yugoslavian peoples are covered. Have each committee discuss its reasons for joining the conflict. Also, have each committee identify what it hopes to gain through fighting. Allow for class discussion of each presentation.

Bodily/Kinesthetic

The Balkans: Political

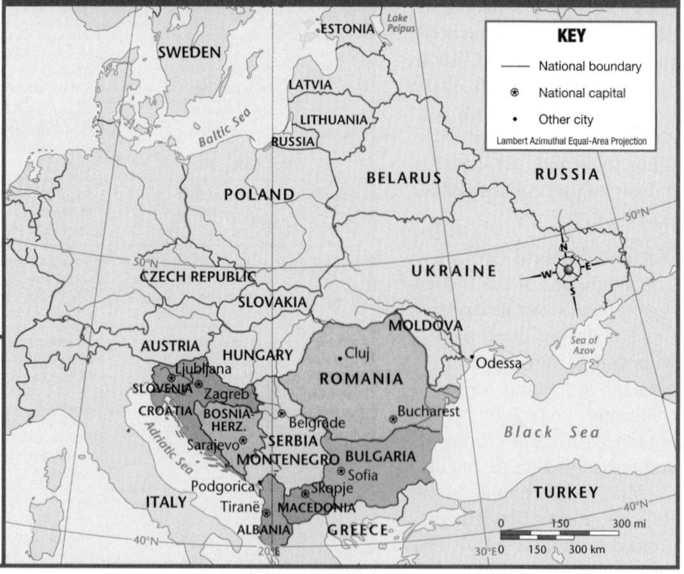

GEOGRAPHY
Map Study The Balkans are located between Western Europe and Russia. **Critical Thinking** How do you think these countries' locations have affected their histories?

Cultural Division and Destruction

In 1991, tensions among the Serbs, the Croats, and other groups in Yugoslavia came to a breaking point. The Serbs controlled the government of Yugoslavia, and some provinces did not want to live under Serbian rule.

Slovenia, Croatia, the Former Yugoslavian Republic of Macedonia, and Bosnia-Herzegovina all declared their independence and drew up borders to form their own countries.

Under communism, industries were concentrated in large factories near the natural resources needed for raw materials. The formation of independent countries divided the natural resources, industries, and transportation corridors in the region. The newly independent countries faced great challenges as they tried to build their new economies.

Adding to these challenges were cultural differences and disagreements over boundaries. Serbs wanted to keep control of the entire region, but only Montenegro joined Serbia. Serbs living in Croatia and Bosnia-Herzegovina, and Croats living outside of Croatia were worried about living under these new governments.

Eventually, these cultural conflicts resulted in bitter warfare. In Bosnia-Herzegovina, fighting broke out among the three main ethnic groups—Serbs, Croats, and Bosnian Muslims. Hundreds of thousands

SKILLS MINI LESSON

Recognizing Bias

You might **introduce** the skill by indicating to students that a biased piece of writing has a particular point of view. Point out that unless students can recognize bias in writing, they cannot judge the accuracy of a statement. Have students bring in several newspaper and periodical articles about the conflict in Bosnia-Herzegovina. Work with them to **practice** the skill by helping them find and identify opinions (beliefs that cannot be proved), loaded words and phrases (those that convey a hidden meaning), and what is missing. You might also encourage students to describe the tone of the articles they read. To **apply** the skill, suggest that students find three articles on Bosnia-Herzegovina and highlight any biased statements they find. Suggest that students exchange their articles with one another and discuss their findings.

Answers to...

CRITICAL THINKING

Students may note that these countries are surrounded by nations stronger than themselves. Thus other nations have meddled in the Balkans' affairs.

of lives were lost, and the capital city of Sarajevo was destroyed. Troops were sent in by the **United Nations,** a group of 189 countries that work together to bring about peace and cooperation among the nations of the world. They brought food and medicine to people cut off from supplies by Serbian forces. A peace treaty was finally signed in 1995 to divide Bosnia and Herzegovina into the Federation of Bosnia and Herzegovina and the Bosnian Serb Republika Srpska.

In 1999, fighting broke out again when Serbs fought against Albanians seeking independence in **Kosovo.** The international community was quick to respond with the bombing of Serbia and with the presence of peacekeeping troops. By 2001, the conflict had spilled over the border into Macedonia, putting thousands of civilians in danger and jeopardizing peace efforts.

These ongoing conflicts have prevented economic development in the Balkans region. Refugees fleeing from one part of the region to another have put huge financial burdens on poor countries. Bombing raids have destroyed bridges, communication lines, railways, and roads. Some countries, however, that have been able to avoid conflict and concentrate their efforts on establishing industries, building the economy, and lowering unemployment, are beginning to get results. Slovenia, Bulgaria, and Romania are all working toward becoming members of the European Union.

The Long War in Bosnia

HISTORY The war in Bosnia claimed about 200,000 lives and reduced cities to rubble. One relief worker there said, "Everyone in this city has memories of . . . when they had no water or electricity and they couldn't go out on the streets without fear of being shot." **Critical Thinking** What do you think would be some of the challenges of living in a country destroyed by war?

SECTION 2 ASSESSMENT

AFTER YOU READ

RECALL

1. Identify: (a) Balkans, (b) Kosovo

2. Define: (a) United Nations

COMPREHENSION

3. How has physical geography contributed to the separation of cultural groups in the Balkans?

4. What are the main cultural differences that have led to the conflicts in countries of the former Yugoslavia?

CRITICAL THINKING AND WRITING

5. Exploring the Main Idea Review the Main Idea statement at the beginning of this section. Then, write a paragraph describing the causes leading to the conflict in the Balkans, and how these conflicts might have been avoided.

6. Making Predictions What do you think will happen in the Balkan countries that were once part of Yugoslavia? Write an update for the year 2015.

ACTIVITY

Take It to the NET

7. Writing to a Pen Pal Establish a pen pal relationship with a student in Bosnia and ask questions that will help you to understand what life is like there. Share with your pen pal what life is like for you in the United States. Visit the World Explorer: People, Places, and Cultures section of **phschool.com** for help in completing this activity.

SECTION 2 ASSESSMENT

AFTER YOU READ

1. (a) countries located on the peninsula south of the Danube River and bordered by the Adriatic, Ionian, and Black seas (b) country that declared independence from former Yugoslavia
2. (a) an organization of countries working together to bring about peace and cooperation among the nations of the world
3. The rugged mountains in the Balkans region create a natural barrier that allowed cultures to develop separately.
4. Bosnians, Croatians, and Serbians speak the same language, but Serbs write the language differently. Most Bosnians are Muslims, whereas people of the other groups are Christians who have somewhat different religious practices.
5. Paragraphs should include mention of differences in language and religion leading to the conflicts. Students should mention the importance of tolerance and of finding a way to build communities that benefit from diversity.
6. Answers will vary. Some will show an optimistic view that cultural conflicts can be resolved; others will note that the cultural differences will continue to prevent the countries from building strong, stable economies and governments.
7. Questions and descriptions of American life will vary.

Resource Directory

Teaching Resources

Section Quiz in the Unit 4 Teaching Resources, p. 73

Answers to...

CRITICAL THINKING

Answers will vary, but students should mention such difficulties associated with traveling and getting food and supplies.

SECTION 3

Lesson Objectives

1. Explain how democratic traditions helped the Czech Republic make the transition to a democratic society after the fall of communism.
2. Describe the challenges of building a free enterprise economy.

Lesson Plan

1 Engage

Warm-Up Activity

Have students brainstorm a list of natural resources they might expect to find in a nation that has mountains and rivers but no coastline. Then, have them list industries that could be developed using these resources or combining them with raw materials imported from other countries. List jobs that might be available in urban or rural areas in keeping with these resources and industries.

Activating Prior Knowledge

Have students discuss some of the problems that have arisen as countries have declared their independence in the Balkans. How can these problems be avoided? What factors make these problems easier to resolve?

Answers to...

CRITICAL THINKING

Students may say that living without basic rights of free speech would be deeply unsettling or intolerable.

SECTION 3

The Czech Republic

An Economic Success Story

BEFORE YOU READ

READING FOCUS

1. How did the history of the Czech Republic prepare it for independence?
2. What economic challenges does the Czech Republic face?

KEY TERMS

privatization

KEY PLACES

Slovakia

MAIN IDEA

Before World War II, Czechoslovakia was a democratic nation with a strong economy, and now the Czech Republic is using its experience to rebuild the economy and compete in worldwide markets.

NOTE TAKING

Copy the outline below. As you read the section, fill in the outline with information about the Czech Republic.

I. Czechoslovakia to 1989
- A. World War I
  - 1.
  - 2.
- B. World War II
  - 1.
  - 2.
  - 3.
  - 4.
- C. Communist Takeover
  - 1.
  - 2.

II. Czechoslovakia since 1989
- A. Communist Collapse
  - 1.
  - 2.
- B. Czech Republic
  - 1.
  - 2.

The Struggle for Independence

HISTORY After decades of Societ domination, Czechs demanded freedom and independence in 1989. **Critical Thinking** What would it be like to live in a country where you were punished for protesting and speaking your mind?

Setting the Scene

In 1918 the Czechs and Slovaks joined together to form a single independent nation that enjoyed rapid growth and prosperity.

By 1939, when the German army began its occupation of the country during World War II, Czechoslovakia was one of the ten most developed nations in the world.

The Road Back to Independence

After World War II, the Czechoslovakian Republic and its democratic government were re-established, until a communist takeover in 1948. All private property was seized for the state. Political freedom and human rights were taken away from the Czech people.

Over the years, Czechoslovakians tried to keep their commitment to freedom alive even in a totalitarian state. The Soviet Union sent troops

Resource Directory

Teaching Resources

Classroom Manager in the Unit 4 Teaching Resources, p. 74

Guided Reading and Review in the Unit 4 Teaching Resources, p. 75

Guide to the Essentials, p. 78

Technology

Section Reading Support Transparencies

Czech Republic

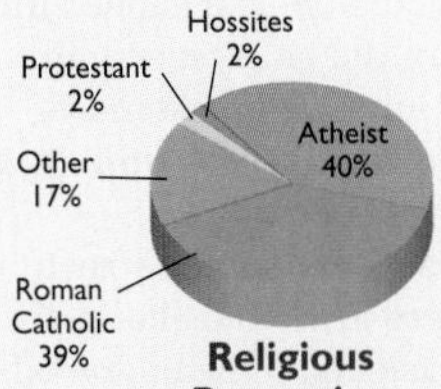

Religious Persuasion

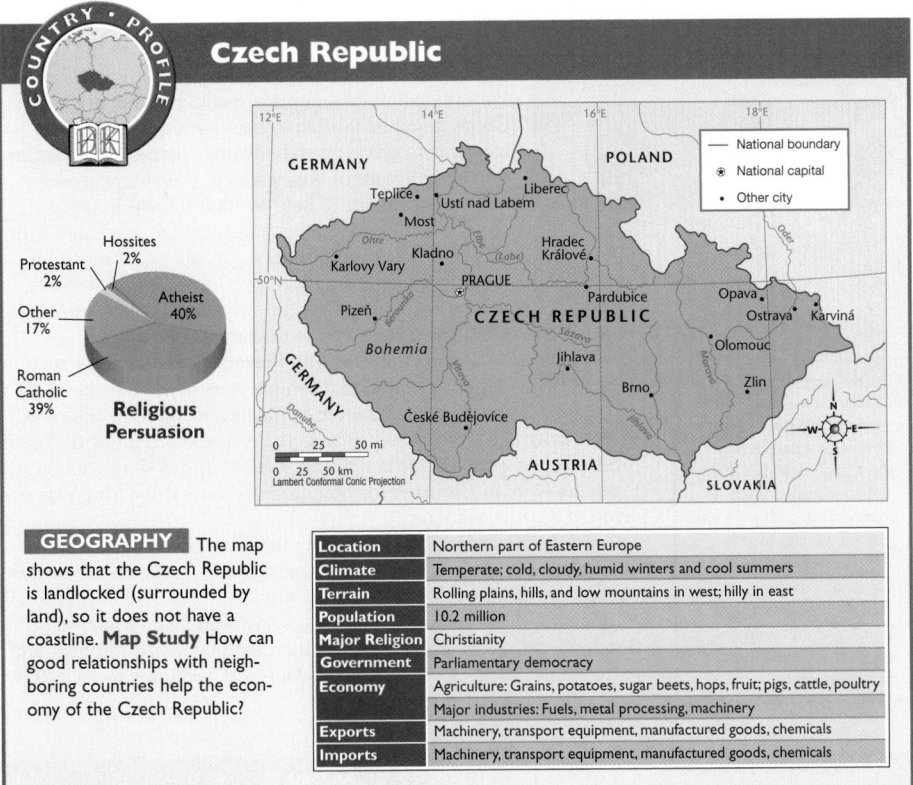

GEOGRAPHY The map shows that the Czech Republic is landlocked (surrounded by land), so it does not have a coastline. **Map Study** How can good relationships with neighboring countries help the economy of the Czech Republic?

Location	Northern part of Eastern Europe
Climate	Temperate; cold, cloudy, humid winters and cool summers
Terrain	Rolling plains, hills, and low mountains in west; hilly in east
Population	10.2 million
Major Religion	Christianity
Government	Parliamentary democracy
Economy	Agriculture: Grains, potatoes, sugar beets, hops, fruit; pigs, cattle, poultry
	Major industries: Fuels, metal processing, machinery
Exports	Machinery, transport equipment, manufactured goods, chemicals
Imports	Machinery, transport equipment, manufactured goods, chemicals

to keep strict control of the people. When the citizens rose up to protest, they were suppressed with harsh punishments.

Restoring a Free Enterprise System When the Soviet Union collapsed in 1989, Czechoslovakia regained its freedom. Within a few years, the Czech Republic peacefully separated from **Slovakia** to form its own nation.

Under communism, almost all goods manufactured in Czechoslovakia were sold only to the Soviet Union or other countries under Soviet control. Most manufacturers did not compete in world markets, and products did not have to meet the demands of the international marketplace. Even so, companies whose goods were exported built up strong reputations. The quality of the glassware, vehicles, planes, motorcycles, and textile machinery earned loyal customers and worldwide respect.

2 Explore

Have students read the section to find out how the Czech people have been able to use their historical experience to build a strong economy and regain control of their government as a democratic state. Students can compare the experiences of the Czech people to those of other people in the Balkans.

3 Teach

Have students create an annotated timeline to show how Czech history has helped the people establish independence today. This activity should take 20 minutes.

Questions for Discussion

ECONOMICS What steps has the Czech Republic taken in order to strengthen trade with other countries?

The government limited imports, increased exports, and improved marketing strategies for selling products.

CITIZENSHIP Under communism, were Czech citizens able to influence the political process?

No. Czech citizens lived in a totalitarian state and could not even protest.

4 Assess/Reteach

See the answers to the Section 3 Assessment. You may use students' completed timelines as an assessment.

Acceptable timelines contain at least 4 dates with brief notes.

Commendable timelines contain at least 5 dates with complete notes.

Outstanding timelines contain at least 6 dates with extensive notes.

Resource Directory

Teaching Resources

Outline Maps, Eastern Europe, pp. 22–23

Technology

World Video Explorer See the Czech Republic's case study for an overview of the Czech Republic's history, economy, government, and culture. Discussion questions are included.

Answers to...

MAP STUDY

The Czech Republic will have to cooperate with neighboring countries to help establish transportation corridors and shipping sites to build international trade.

SECTION 3 ASSESSMENT

AFTER YOU READ

1. A now-independent nation that was part of the former Czechoslovakia
2. The act of returning businesses to private ownership and management
3. The Czech Republic has a history of democratic rule; prior to World War II, it enjoyed freedom and independence.
4. Answers include upgrading manufacturing plants, increasing productivity, improving quality of goods, modernizing products, shutting down some factories, discontinuing some products, decreasing imports and increasing exports, developing marketing strategies, and opening transportation corridors.
5. Answers will vary. Students should mention the Czech Republic's efforts to increase trade and exports and to modernize and streamline its industries.
6. Answers will vary. Students might mention pride in workmanship, sharing in success, wage incentives, and so on.
7. Directories will vary. Accept all reasonable responses.

Better Factories, Better Products

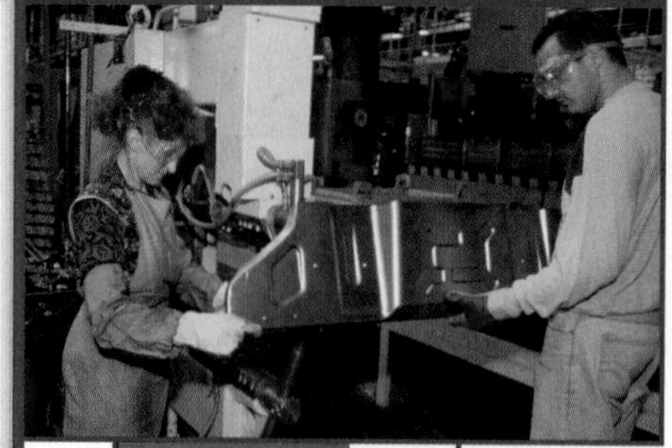

ECONOMICS These workers are on an assembly line at a car factory in the Czech Republic. Many Czech factories were modernized and improved to help improve the country's economy. **Critical Thinking** How would this car factory's modernization help improve the Czech Republic's economy?

Meeting New Economic Challenges

With the fall of communism, manufacturing in the Czech Republic needed to be restructured. The first step was to privatize state-owned businesses. **Privatization** is the return of businesses to private ownership and management. To help do this, citizens bought coupon booklets. The coupons could be exchanged for shares in companies. In this way, the citizens bought the companies from the state. Only the largest industries are still owned by the state, and little by little they are being transferred to the private sector.

During the split with Slovakia, some of the Czech Republic's industrial centers were lost. To make up for this loss, manufacturing plants needed to be upgraded. Productivity needed to increase and quality needed to improve. Some product lines were discontinued, and some factories were shut down. Products were modernized to compete with state-of-the-art goods developed by other nations.

In order to strengthen trade with other countries, imports were decreased, sales of exports were increased, and marketing strategies were developed in order to win contracts.

Meeting these economic challenges has been an enormous task. But each step in the process makes the Czech economy stronger and more stable. Today, Czech-made products are becoming more visible in the international marketplace.

SECTION 3 ASSESSMENT

AFTER YOU READ

RECALL

1. Identify: Slovakia
2. Define: privatization

COMPREHENSION

3. How has past experience helped the Czech Republic build an independent nation?
4. What are some of the economic challenges the Czech Republic has faced since the return of free enterprise?

CRITICAL THINKING AND WRITING

5. **Exploring the Main Idea** Review the Main Idea statement at the beginning of this section. Then make a list of the strategies the Czech Republic is using to strengthen its economy.
6. **Draw Inferences** Imagine that you are a worker in the Czech Republic. How has the free enterprise system changed your ideas about what you do? How do you feel about improving the quality of the products you help to manufacture? How can you benefit from the free enterprise system?

ACTIVITY

7. **Creating a Business Directory** Use library and Internet sources to find out about businesses and products that are being developed in the Czech Republic. Use the information you gather to create business profile cards that describe goods being developed and marketed around the world.

Resource Directory

Teaching Resources

Section Quiz in the Unit 4 Teaching Resources, p. 76

Social Studies and Geography Skills, Using the Library, p. 93

Answers to...

CRITICAL THINKING

Modernizing the factory would improve productivity; this could improve sales and thus the Czech Republic's economy.

SECTION 4

Russia

New Democracy, Unstable Economy

BEFORE YOU READ

READING FOCUS

1. How has life in Siberia changed since the fall of communism?
2. How has life in Moscow changed since the fall of communism?

KEY TERMS

investor

KEY PLACES

Kemerovo
Moscow

NOTE TAKING

Copy the table below. As you read the section, fill in the table with comparisons about life in Russia during and after communism.

	During Communism	After Communism
Life in Siberia		
Life in Moscow		

MAIN IDEA

The change to a free enterprise system after years of communist rule has been difficult for Russians, but the new system allows them to pursue economic opportunities that were once impossible.

Setting the Scene

Inessa Krichevskaya (in es UH kree chev SKY uh) has surprising feelings about change in Russia. "You know," she says, "it's a very difficult period in our country right now, but we will just have to live through it, because this is the right direction.... We can never go back to what was before."

Why are Inessa's feelings so surprising? For more than 30 years, she was a loyal communist. She lived and worked in the city of Moscow as an engineer. Like all other Russians, she always expected that the government would send her monthly checks when she grew too old to work. That was part of the communist system. But then Russia switched to the free enterprise system. Now Inessa is in her 60s and is retired. The amount she receives from the government is much less than she expected. Inessa gets about 1,300 rubles a month—only about $8.

The change from communism to democracy and a free enterprise system has not been easy. From Moscow to Siberia, Russian people have suffered many hardships to gain freedom.

Life in Siberia

During the Soviet years, the government tried to change Siberia, the huge region of eastern Russia. It built factories to take advantage of the region's rich reserves of

The Voice of Democracy

GOVERNMENT In countries like the United States, it is easy to take freedom for granted. Only after the collapse of communism were Russians able to speak freely about politics.

Critical Thinking How do you think the Russian people feel about being able freely to voice their ideas and beliefs?

Resource Directory

Teaching Resources

Classroom Manager in the Unit 4 Teaching Resources, p. 77

Guided Reading and Review in the Unit 4 Teaching Resources, p. 78

Guide to the Essentials, p. 79

Technology

Section Reading Support Transparencies

SECTION 4

Lesson Objectives

1. Describe the changes that have taken place in Siberia since the fall of communism.
2. Describe the changes that have taken place in Moscow since the fall of communism.

Lesson Plan

1 Engage

Warm-Up Activity

Ask students to imagine coming to school and being told that everything they have learned about the United States must be changed. A new kind of government has taken over in their town. Suddenly they find that the economy is entirely different. Ask students how they would feel if something like this happened in their town.

Activating Prior Knowledge

Have students keep in mind as they study this lesson that Russia is a very large and diverse country.

2 Explore

Have the students read the section and try to focus on the differences between the old ways of life that still remain and the changes that have taken place in recent years, both in Kemerovo and in Moscow. Suggest that students also think about shortcomings in Russian life that the country's leaders have to address.

Answers to...

CRITICAL THINKING

Students should recognize that citizens probably feel good about their right to stand up for their beliefs and to speak freely.

Lesson Plan continued

❸ Teach

Have students create a two-column chart similar to the following.

Old and New Ways in Russia

	Old Ways	New Ways
Kemerovo		
Moscow		

As students read the section, have them fill in the cells in the chart. You may use the chart as the basis for a class discussion. Allow about 30 minutes for this activity.

Questions for Discussion

CULTURE **Would you expect to find Moscow a very cosmopolitan city? Why or why not?**

Yes, because business opportunities have brought many international investors to the city.

ECONOMICS **Why was the middle class able to rise in Russia only after the fall of communism?**

Under communism, all businesses and farms were owned by the state, and people earned very little. When communism collapsed, new investments poured into Russia and people were encouraged to open their own small businesses. Workers could now earn more in their jobs, travel, and own goods that were once unavailable and unaffordable.

COUNTRY • PROFILE

Russia

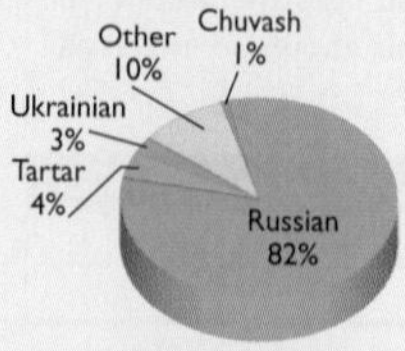

Ethnic Groups

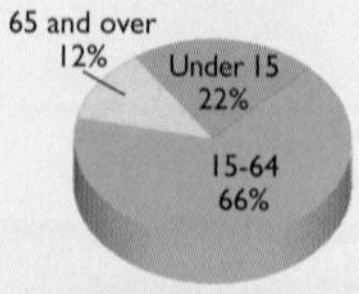

Age Structure (in years)

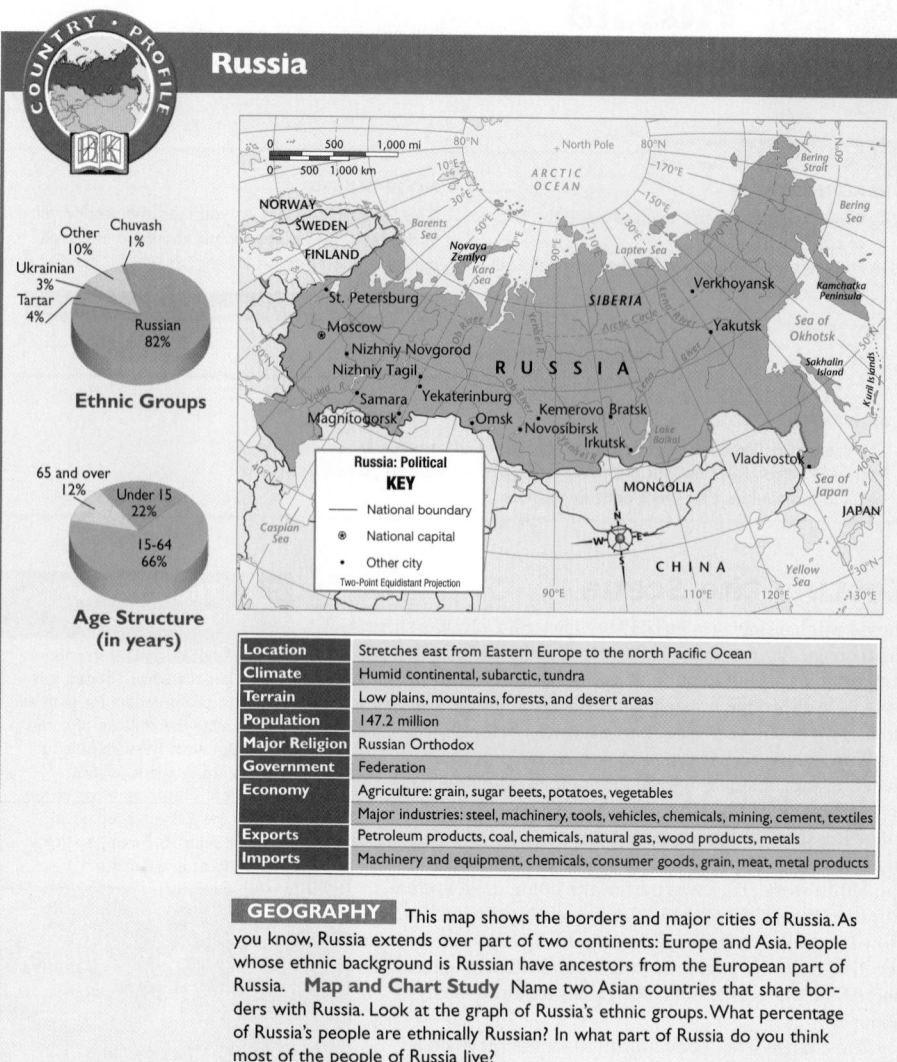

Location	Stretches east from Eastern Europe to the north Pacific Ocean
Climate	Humid continental, subarctic, tundra
Terrain	Low plains, mountains, forests, and desert areas
Population	147.2 million
Major Religion	Russian Orthodox
Government	Federation
Economy	Agriculture: grain, sugar beets, potatoes, vegetables
	Major industries: steel, machinery, tools, vehicles, chemicals, mining, cement, textiles
Exports	Petroleum products, coal, chemicals, natural gas, wood products, metals
Imports	Machinery and equipment, chemicals, consumer goods, grain, meat, metal products

GEOGRAPHY This map shows the borders and major cities of Russia. As you know, Russia extends over part of two continents: Europe and Asia. People whose ethnic background is Russian have ancestors from the European part of Russia. **Map and Chart Study** Name two Asian countries that share borders with Russia. Look at the graph of Russia's ethnic groups. What percentage of Russia's people are ethnically Russian? In what part of Russia do you think most of the people of Russia live?

coal, gold, iron, oil, and natural gas. The government took advantage of the Trans-Siberian Railroad to transport materials to and from Siberia. But today, many of the factories are outdated. In the Siberian city of **Kemerovo** (KEM uh roh voh), factories still release black smoke into the air. Other buildings in the town are crumbling. Rusty cars move slowly down the muddy streets.

Resource Directory

Teaching Resources

Outline Maps Russia, p. 27

Technology

Passport to the World CD-ROM This interactive CD-ROM allows students to explore each region of the world. Students view regional videos, take a photo tour, and explore a historical timeline. Students record their travels in an Explorer's Journal, and receive passport stamps when they pass regional quizzes.

Color Transparencies 74–76 Europe Today with Eastern Europe Updated (base mape with overlay)

Answers to...

MAP AND CHART STUDY

Mongolia and China; 82 percent; the European part

Traditional ways still continue in Siberia. Change is slow, especially in rural villages. But the fall of communism and the arrival of free enterprise are starting to affect life in the region. Under the communist system, everyone was guaranteed a job. Now Siberians who work in factories and coal mines must worry about losing their jobs. On the other hand, for the first time in more than 70 years, Siberians are able to buy their own homes. Before, they had to live in houses that belonged to the state. People can also now buy stock in the companies where they work.

Siberian Industry: A Mixed Blessing

SCIENCE AND TECHNOLOGY

Black smoke belches into the cool air in the Siberian town of Ulan Ude (oo LAHN oo DAY) along the Trans-Siberian Railroad. The railroad, completed in 1916, helped to link Siberia's rich natural resources to more densely populated areas of Europe. When towns along the tracks of this railroad became industrial centers, the number of available jobs increased, but so did pollution. **Critical Thinking** What are some ways that these industrial centers can deal with the problem of pollution?

Life in Moscow

In **Moscow,** where Inessa lives, buying shares in businesses is a big business in itself. Investors from everywhere, including the United States, have come to Moscow to make money. An **investor** is someone who spends money on improving a business in the hope of getting more money when the business succeeds. Some investors have become very wealthy. When the first American fast-food chain in Russia opened in Moscow, people lined up in the streets to try it out. The restaurant served 30,000 people on the first day.

A New Middle Class In big cities like Moscow, investors have brought big changes. Just outside the city, a new skyscraper reaches the sky. At its top is a fine restaurant, enclosed in stone and glass. The building is the world headquarters of Gazprom (GAHS prahm), Russia's only natural gas company. Started by a former communist official, it makes a huge amount of money.

The head of Gazprom is one of Russia's richest people. Many other former government leaders have become wealthy in the new Russian democracy. Another group of newly rich Russians leads criminal gangs. Both of these groups worry ordinary Russians—neither rich nor poor—who are members of the new middle class.

New investment and the creation of businesses, restaurants, and services have contributed to the rise of a middle class in Russia. Members of this middle class have been working hard since the collapse of communism in Russia. They dream of starting their own new business or opening a small factory. They have been studying Western ways of doing business and gaining knowledge from the Internet, which has

4 Assess/Reteach

See the answers to the Section 4 Assessment. You may use the students' completed charts as an assessment.

Acceptable charts contain at least four fact-based entries.

Commendable charts contain fact-based entries in each cell.

Outstanding charts contain at least two fact-based entries in each cell and show an understanding of how a successful economy affects the quality of life wherever you are.

ACTIVITY

Critical Thinking

Drawing Conclusions Tell students that there are 11 time zones in Russia, compared with only four in the continental United States. Have students use this information and a political map of Russia to conclude what activity might be taking place in St. Petersburg when it is dinnertime in Vladivostok. (The cities are approximately 4,500 miles apart. People in St. Petersburg are just waking up when it is dinnertime in Vladivostok.) Students may refer to the World Time Zones map on page 40.

Visual/Spatial

SKILLS MINI LESSON

Assessing Your Understanding

You might **introduce** the skill by suggesting that students will become better learners by pausing after reading the text under each heading rather than reading straight through from the beginning of the section to the end. In pausing, they should ask themselves whether they understand what they have just read.

To **practice** the skill, ask students to read the text under the heading *A New Middle Class* and have them give two examples of new wealth in Moscow. To **apply** the skill, have students read the section *Tradition and Change.* Then, have students choose partners and ask each other questions about the section.

Answers to...

CRITICAL THINKING

Students might mention ideas ranging from updating and upgrading machinery to levying stiff fines on industries that create pollution.

SECTION 4 ASSESSMENT

AFTER YOU READ

1. (a) a factory town in Siberia
   (b) the capital of Russia
2. (a) person who spends money on improving a business in the hope of gaining more money when the business succeeds
3. Under the communist system, everyone was guaranteed a job. Now Siberians who worked in factories and coal mines worry about losing their jobs. On the other hand, Siberians now are able to buy their own homes, as well as stock in the companies where they work.
4. Now investors from all over the world come to Moscow to make money. There are new buildings and new businesses, a rise in the middle class, as well as an increase in criminal gangs.
5. Answers will vary, but should include mention of competition among businesses, and an unstable economy.
6. Students' charts will vary but should include details from the section about life in Siberia and in Moscow.
7. Reports will vary but should include information about products, customers, employees, and how the business will succeed.

Building Anew in Moscow

ECONOMICS Since the fall of communism, people in Moscow, Russia's capital, have started over. They have constructed new buildings and started many new businesses. The number of cars in Russia has tripled, and the streets of the capital, once empty, are always busy. **Critical Thinking** How does starting a new business create jobs?

become popular in Russia. More than during Soviet times, ordinary Russians can own appliances and can sometimes afford to travel.

Like middle classes in other countries in the world, ordinary Russians are at a disadvantage when the economy does not thrive. Though Russians work hard to make capitalism succeed, they have had a lot of challenges to overcome. In 1998, the value of the ruble fell, causing prices of goods to skyrocket and bringing heavy inflation. In addition, Russia faced a severe food shortage, forcing Russians to change their diets and to seek food aid from the United States. President Boris Yeltsin was often blamed for Russia's problems.

Tradition and Change Free enterprise is changing Moscow, but old Russian ways survive alongside the new. After all, Russia is a huge country with many different ways of life. Russia faces many challenges in the future. Can a country with many different ethnic groups and an area of more than 6 million square miles (9 million sq km) hold itself together? Will the old ways and new ways become one common way for everyone? The answers to these questions are not yet clear. But Russians are united in the hope for a better future for all.

SECTION 4 ASSESSMENT

AFTER YOU READ

RECALL

1. Identify: (a) Kemerovo, (b) Moscow
2. Define: (a) investor

COMPREHENSION

3. How has the fall of communism affected life in Siberia?
4. How have the fall of communism and the growth of free enterprise affected life in Moscow?

CRITICAL THINKING AND WRITING

5. **Exploring the Main Idea** Review the Main Idea statement at the beginning of this section. Then, write an account of some of the biggest hardships you might face as a new business owner in Moscow.
6. **Comparing and Contrasting** Create a chart that shows the similarities and differences between life in Siberia, and life in Moscow.

ACTIVITY

7. **Writing a Business Report** Write a business report for a store that you have opened in Moscow. Explain what the business is, where you get your products, who your customers are, how many employees have, and why you think the business will succeed.

Resource Directory

Teaching Resources

Section Quiz in the Unit 4 Teaching Resources, p. 79

Chapter Summary in the Unit 4 Teaching Resources, p. 80

Vocabulary in the Unit 4 Teaching Resources, p. 81

Reteaching in the Unit 4 Teaching Resources, p. 82

Enrichment in the Unit 4 Teaching Resources, p. 83

Critical Thinking in the Unit 4 Teaching Resources, p. 84

Answers to...

CRITICAL THINKING

New businesses need employees. New businesses also need people to provide services to them, such as constructing buildings, fixing plumbing problems, or preparing taxes. In addition, people who are employed by a new business help to create jobs by using the money they earn to buy goods and services.

Drawing Inferences

Facts	Inferences
During communism the people in Yugoslavia got along. After communism, civil war erupted.	Communist rule kept the people from expressing ethnic tensions.
Ukraine means "border-land." Ukraine is surrounded by many countries. Ukraine has vast natural resources. The Ukraine has been invaded many times.	Other countries invade the Ukraine to gain its natural resources.
Six months after a nuclear accident at Chernobyl, people returned to work at the nuclear plant. But no one lived in the area.	
When the first American fast-food chain in Russia opened in Moscow, people lined up in the streets to try it out. The restaurant served 30,000 people on the first day.	

Learn the Skill

Writers do not always state everything directly. Sometimes when you read, you have to "read between the lines" in order to figure out what is not directly stated. When you read between the lines, you are drawing inferences. To help you draw inferences when you read, follow these steps:

A. Study what is stated, and look for facts. Knowing the facts when you read is an essential first step to drawing inferences. For example, you know from reading the first fact in the chart that the people in Yugoslavia got along during communism. After communism, civil war erupted. These are facts.

B. Draw inferences from the facts by using what you already know. Ask yourself, "What does this information suggest?" "What conclusions can I draw from these facts?" Use prior knowledge and common sense. Think about what is an obvious conclusion that is not stated in the material. Regarding what you know about Yugoslavia, you can conclude that below the surface during communism, serious differences existed between the people. Communist rule must have kept the people from expressing their tensions.

C. Read the facts in the second row of the chart about Ukraine. The facts are that Ukraine has lots of natural resources and has been taken over many times by other countries. To draw an inference, think about why the country is invaded. It's because the other countries want the natural resources. When you come to this conclusion as you read, you are drawing an inference.

Practice the Skill

The chart shown is incomplete. Make your own two-column chart. Label the first column "Facts." Label the second column "Inferences." Copy the information into your chart. Then, draw inferences to complete the last two rows of the chart. To do so, use your common sense and prior knowledge about people to figure out why no one lived near the Chernobyl plant and why so many Russians were interested in trying American fast food.

Apply the Skill

See the Chapter Review and Assessment at the end of this chapter for more questions on drawing inferences.

Lesson Objectives

1. Understand what drawing inferences means.
2. Draw inferences based on given facts.

Lesson Plan

1 Engage

Students probably draw inferences every day. Encourage them to give some examples from their everyday life and challenge them to draw inferences about why events happened as they did, or why people took certain actions.

2 Explore

Direct students to read the steps under "Learn the Skill." When finished, have them explain the two steps in their own words. Discuss with them why getting the facts straight first is so important.

3 Teach

Challenge students to complete the chart on their own. If students need more help, you might refer them to specific sections of the chapter. When finished, have students compare their answers. If they do not agree, they can discuss their reasons and try to come to some conclusions.

4 Assess/Reteach

Students' charts should be well-organized and easy to read.

To further assess students' understanding of drawing inferences, have them complete the "Applying Your Skills" part of the Chapter Review and Assessment at the end of the chapter.

Resource Directory

Teaching Resources

Social Studies and Geography Skills, Drawing Conclusions, p. 50

Technology

Social Studies Skills Tutor CD-ROM

Answers to...

PRACTICE THE SKILL

Students should be able to draw accurate inferences from the facts stated. Answers: 3) It was not safe to work at or live near the plant. 4) Russians are interested in American food and culture.

CHAPTER 18

Review and Assessment

Creating a Chapter Summary

Student summaries will vary.

Sample summaries:

Section 2 The new nations of the Balkans will have to overcome a history of cultural differences and religious conflicts in order to establish lasting order and peace.

Section 3 The Czech Republic has been able to call upon its past as it works to establish a new democratic government and free enterprise economy.

Section 4 The people of Russia are adjusting to the changes and challenges of their new government and economy following the fall of communism.

Reviewing Key Terms

1. d **2.** a **3.** c **4.** b

Reviewing the Main Ideas

1. devotion to Roman Catholic religion, Polish language, rural life
2. The free enterprise system and a government that no longer gives financial help to farmers are changing parts of Polish life.
3. conflicts among Serbians, Croatians, and Bosnians over who should rule different parts of the country
4. Sample answers: (a) language (b) writing systems, religions, branches of Christianity
5. Citizens have tried to purchase businesses from the state.
6. In Siberia, there are many factories—some of which are outdated. There are few cars and poor streets, and traditional ways continue. Moscow has tall buildings. The streets are busy with cars and visitors from all over the world.
7. The fall of communism has led to free enterprise, and to the establishment of privately owned businesses. Some people have become rich; crime has flourished; and retired people's pensions are very small.

CHAPTER 18

Review and Assessment

Creating a Chapter Summary

On a separate piece of paper, draw a diagram like this one, and include the information that summarizes the first section of the chapter. Then fill in the remaining boxes with summaries of Sections 2, 3, and 4.

EASTERN EUROPE AND RUSSIA

Section 1	Section 2	Section 3	Section 4
Since the fall of communism, the people of Poland are adjusting to a new way of life, while retaining their long-standing cultural traditions.			

Reviewing Key Terms

Match the definitions in Column I with the key terms in Column II.

Column I

1. person who spends money to help improve business in the hope of getting more money in return
2. a system that allows private businesses to compete with one another for profit, and with little government control
3. the return of businesses to private ownership and management
4. an international organization of countries that work together to bring about peace and cooperation worldwide

Column II

a. free enterprise
b. United Nations
c. privatization
d. investor

Reviewing the Main Ideas

1. What parts of Polish life have not changed? (Section 1)
2. What forces are changing some basic parts of Polish town life and country life? (Section 1)
3. What conflicts led to the breakup of Yugoslavia? (Section 2)
4. Name some things that Bosnians, Croats, and Serbs in the Balkans region have in common. Name some differences. (Section 2)
5. What challenges have the citizens of the Czech Republic faced in the change to a free enterprise system? (Section 3)
6. What are some differences between life in Siberia and life in Moscow? (Section 4)
7. How have recent events affected the people of Russia in different ways? (Section 4)

Map Activity

Eastern Europe

For each place listed below, write the letter from the map that shows its location.

1. Czech Republic
2. Poland
3. Sarajevo
4. Bosnia-Herzegovina
5. Serbia and Montenegro
6. Warsaw

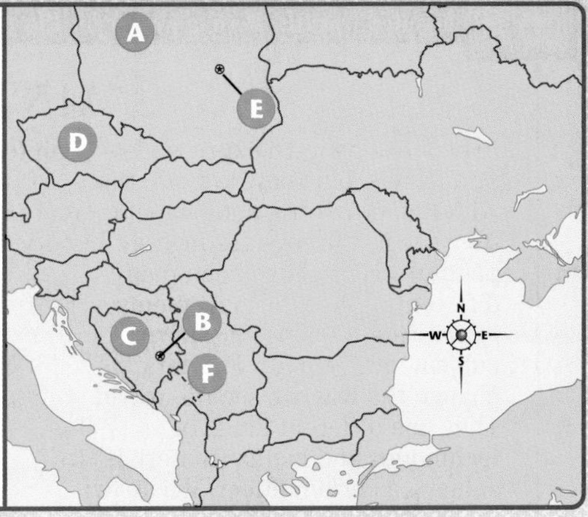

Take It to the NET

Enrichment For more map activities using geography skills, visit the social studies section of **phschool.com.**

Writing Activity

1. **Using Primary Sources** Nations are trying to work together to help resolve the conflicts between people in the Balkans. Visit your school or local library and use primary sources such as newspaper and magazine articles to find additional information on the events. Diaries, letters, and autobiographies of people who are involved in these conflicts may also be available. Write a character sketch to describe what life is like for a student, an athlete, a political leader, or some other citizen living in the region. Use your character sketch to introduce the person to your classmates.
2. **Writing an Advertisement** Write an advertisement for a hat shop in Warsaw. In the advertisement, explain why people should buy from new shops instead of from older stores that used to be run by the government.

Critical Thinking

1. **Making Comparisons** Compare Poland's change to a free enterprise system after the fall of communism to that in Russia. What similarities and differences are there in the way that their rural populations have been affected?
2. **Identifying a Problem** What do you think would help bring lasting peace to the Balkans? Explain your answer.

Applying Your Skills

Turn to the Skills Activity on p. 341 to help you draw inferences from the following facts.

1. For centuries, the Ottoman Empire controlled the Balkans region. After World War I, the countries of the Balkans region were established.
2. Under communism, industries in Yugoslavia were concentrated in large factories near the natural resources needed for raw materials. After the fall of communism, Yugoslavia broke apart into independent countries.

Take It to the NET

Activity Read about the dissolution of the USSR and life in Russia today. Choose one of the interactive activities found under "A Nation in Transition" or "Russia Today." Visit the World Explorer: People, Places, and Cultures section of **phschool.com** for help in completing this activity.

Chapter 18 Self-Test As a final review activity, take the Chapter 18 Self-Test and get instant feedback on your answers. To take the test, visit the Social Studies section of **phschool.com.**

Map Activity

1. D **2.** A **3.** B **4.** C **5.** F **6.** E

Writing Activity

1. Student character sketches should identify the cultural background of the subject and how that influences his or her interaction with those in power, how it affects his or her daily life, and how it will likely affect his or her future. The subject may also express his or her concern, fear, frustration, and personal opinion of the conflict and how it may be resolved.
2. Students' advertisements will vary, but most will mention that buying at a privately owned store will help improve the Polish economy. Students might also mention that because the store is owned by an individual, the customer may expect better service.

Critical Thinking

1. Students should list similarities such as these: Farm people lead a simple life, wear simple clothes, and have not benefited from changes of government. Differences listed should include the following: Polish farmers faced an abrupt change to free enterprise, whereas change has come more slowly to Siberian country life.
2. Accept any reasonable answer.

Applying Your Skills

1. Sample answer: The Ottoman Empire lost control of the region as a result of World War I.
2. Sample answer: Not all regions of the former Yugoslavia may be able to support industries, given a lack of natural resources.

Resource Directory

Teaching Resources

Cooperative Learning Activity in the Unit 4 Teaching Resources, pp. 126–128

Chapter Tests Forms A and B in the Unit 4 Teaching Resources, pp. 162–167

Unit Tests Forms A and B in the Unit 4 Teaching Resources, pp. 168–173

Guide to the Essentials, Ch. 18 Test, p. 80

Other Print Resources

Chapter Tests with ExamView® Test Bank, Ch. 18

Technology

ExamView® Test Bank CD-ROM, Ch. 18

Resource Pro® CD-ROM

UNIT 4

Introduction

The introduction on the student page on the right provides key facts and general information about painters.

- Students should read the introduction first to gain a basic knowledge of the subject before reading on.
- Have students read all of the subentries, which provide further information on painters, particularly focussing on their influence on culture as a whole, and on other painters. Have students also read the annotations that accompany and explain the photos and illustrations.
- When students have finished reading all of the information, discuss the connections between the information on these pages and what they have learned about Europe and Russia. Students may want to review Chapter 15.

ACTIVITY

Artistic Movements

Have students copy the style of an artistic movement, such as classicism, impressionism, post-impressionism, or cubism, to create a painting of their own. Allow students to choose the medium they want to paint in, and encourage them to use the techniques of the painters who painted in the particular style they have chosen. You may wish to have students construct and paint a still life, go outside and paint a local landscape, or copy the work of a master. Organize students' finished paintings by style to create a classroom gallery.

Visual/Spatial

Adapted from the Dorling Kindersley Illustrated Children's Encyclopedia

PAINTERS

Artists use paint to express ideas. Painters can capture the likeness of a face or a flower, but they do more than just paint realistic images. They also work with color, texture, and shape to create eye-catching images of the world as they see it. Cultures throughout history have produced their own great painters. There have been many different groups, or movements, in painting, such as classicism, cubism, and pop art. Painters change the way we see the world. They use different kinds of techniques and media (materials) to achieve a certain effect. Whatever the medium or the style, the work of any painter reflects his or her cultural traits.

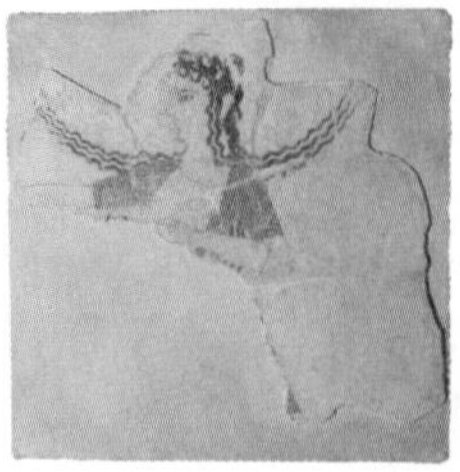

EARLY PAINTERS
The artists of ancient Egypt decorated the walls of tombs with scenes of gods and goddesses and of hunting and feasting. The Minoan people of early Greece painted their houses and palaces with pictures of dancers, birds, and flowers. Roman artists painted gods and goddesses and scenes from classical mythology.

? How is art used to express ideas and beliefs in a culture?

RENAISSANCE

One of the greatest periods of European painting was the Renaissance, which reached its height in Italy in the early part of the 16th century. During the Renaissance, painters studied perspective to develop a more realistic style of painting landscapes and portraits.

MICHELANGELO
Italian Michelangelo Buonarroti (1475–1564) is one of the best known painters of the Renaissance. He painted the ceiling of the Sistine Chapel at the Vatican in Rome between 1508 and 1512.

MEDIEVAL PAINTERS
In medieval times, most artists in Europe and Russia painted only subjects from Christianity. Painters used rich colors and thin layers of gold on wood panels for altarpieces or directly onto church walls. This style may look somewhat flat to us, but the images are powerful and reflect the deep religious feelings in western culture at that time.

REMBRANDT
Like Michelangelo, the Dutch artist Rembrandt van Rijn (1606–1669) is widely known by only his first name. Rembrandt's famous portraits, such as the self-portrait shown here, are powerful and full of expression.

344 UNIT 4 EUROPE AND RUSSIA

CULTURE

Painting and Culture

Painting has been a form of creative and cultural expression since the cave paintings of prehistoric times. Cultures express themselves in unique ways that reflect traditions, customs, shared experiences, and common beliefs. Styles of artistic expression, particularly in painting, developed and spread across the European continent and beyond, crossing geographic and political boundaries. Artistic style provides a concrete example of how cultures borrow from and influence one another.

CULTURE

Romantic Movement

During the late 18th and early 19th centuries, a new style of painting became known as the romantic movement. The romantics flooded their paintings with light and color. This is a detail from a painting called *The Swing* by a French romantic artist Fragonard (1732–1806).

Impressionism

The artists of the impressionist movement painted dabs of color to create the effect of light and shade that defines objects. Artists of the impressionist movement include Claude Monet, Camille Pissarro, Pierre Auguste Renoir, Edgar Degas, Mary Cassatt, and Alfred Sisley.

MONET
Claude Monet (1840–1926) was the leader of the impressionist movement. He painted many pictures of his garden and of the French countryside, including The Poppy Field *shown here. Up close, the painting consists of many brushstrokes of different colors. From a distance, the dabs of color come together to form a field of red flowers.*

PICASSO
Spanish painter Pablo Picasso (1881–1973) was one of the most creative and influential artists of the 20th century. His restless personality led him to paint in many different styles at different times of his life. His pictures of people painted using distorted shapes and sharp angles led to a movement called cubism.

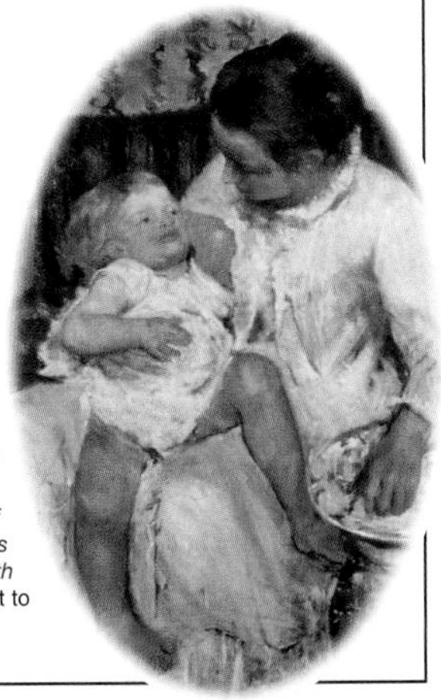

MARY CASSATT
Mary Cassatt (1845–1926) was born in the United States but spent much of her life in France. Like many artists of the day, she painted in the style of the French impressionists. Many of Mary Cassatt's paintings show the daily lives of women, often with their children. This painting is called Mother About to Wash her Sleepy Child, *1880.*

ACTIVITY

Exploring European Art

Have students work with partners to explore art across Europe. Have them begin by each choosing a different country to focus on. Then use library and Internet resources to find examples of paintings or decorative arts from that country. Encourage students to explore art over a long period of time to get an overview of the culture of that region. Bring pairs together in a forum to explore and compare artistic expression.

Verbal/Linguistic

CULTURE

The Impressionists

The artists that comprise the impressionist movement were influenced by each other and by the artists who had come before them. But they also brought their own individual experience to their work. The impressionist painter Pissarro was the son of a Portuguese Jew who owned a general store in St. Thomas, Virgin Islands. His Dominican mother was Spanish. Pissarro traveled back and forth to Paris, developing his early gifts and pursuing his lifelong love of art. His intense response to nature and desire to capture its essence form the cornerstone of the impressionist movement. An understanding of his background provides insight into his vision as an artist.

UNIT 5

Introducing the Unit

This unit was developed around eight strands of essential knowledge and skills that relate to the study of the people, places, and cultures of the contemporary world. These strands include **History, Geography, Economics, Government, Citizenship, Culture,** and **Science, Technology, and Society.** These seven strands, and the related Guiding Questions on the next pages, are intended as an organizational focus for the unit. All of the chapter content, activities, questions, and assessments relate to the seven skill areas.

Using the Pictures

Invite students to discuss the photographs and captions on these pages. Use them as a prompt for a discussion of what students know about history, geography, economics, government, citizenship, culture, and science and technology.

- You may want to begin a K-W-L chart on the chalkboard with the headings What We **K**now About Africa, What We **W**ant to Know About Africa, and What We **L**earned About Africa.
- Have students fill in the first column with several things they agree they already know. Then, ask them to brainstorm for what they would like to know about Africa to add to the second column.
- Students can fill in the third column as they work through the unit.

eTeach

Be sure to check out this month's discussion with a Master Teacher. Go to **phschool.com**.

UNIT 5

Welcome to Africa

GOVERNMENT

Witness the election of a new president ...

CULTURE

Listen to tales from the past ...

CITIZENSHIP

Work towards equal rights in South Africa ...

Resource Directory

Teaching Resources

Program Overview includes a guide to the Prentice Hall World Explorer program. You may wish to refer to the overview as you plan your instruction.

Pacing Charts for Unit 5 offer a variety of course configurations.

What do you want to learn?

ECONOMICS
Tend crops on a farm in Tanzania ...

HISTORY
Explore the ruins of Great Zimbabwe ...

SCIENCE, TECHNOLOGY, AND SOCIETY
Explore modern farming methods ...

GEOGRAPHY
Watch the sun set on the African plains ...

A journal can be your personal record of discovery. As you learn about Africa, you can create journal entries about what you read, write, think, and create. For your first entry, think about the history of Africa. What are some of the ways that history is passed down from one generation to the next in Africa? Compare how history is passed down in your culture.

UNIT 5 WELCOME TO AFRICA **347**

Resource Directory

 Technology

Social Studies Skills Tutor CD-ROM provides two levels of interactive instruction and practice in 20 core social studies skills.

Resource Pro® CD-ROM allows you to create customized lesson plans and print all resources directly from the CD-ROM.

Using the Explorer's Journal

Have students begin their Explorer's Journal as the paragraph on the student book page suggests. If at all possible, encourage students to use a separate small notebook for their Explorer's Journal entries. They can add to this journal as they learn more about Africa.

Project Possibilities

The projects in this book are designed to provide students with hands-on involvement in the content area. Write the following project ideas on the chalkboard and have students preview them and discuss which they might want to do. Students should work in small groups or in pairs to complete the activities.

Africa on Stage

Create a play about growing up in an African country. Choose characters, plan a plot, write the script, and present your play for an audience.

Africa in Art

Prepare a mini-museum of traditional African mask-making. Research different kinds of masks, how they are made, and what they mean.

Africa in the Future

What will life be like in Africa throughout the 21st century? Hold a conference with speakers, African foods, and press coverage.

Introducing

Guiding Questions

The seven Guiding Questions that appear on the reduced student edition pages to the right should act as a guide for learning about Africa, and for encouraging students to relate what they learn to their own experience. The Guiding Questions that relate to the content of each chapter in the unit also appear on the Chapter Opener pages in this teacher's edition.

- You may wish to add your own Guiding Questions to the list in order to tailor them to your particular course. Or, as a group activity, ask your class to develop its own Guiding Questions.

ACTIVITY

Guiding Questions Activity

Ask a volunteer to read aloud the Guiding Questions to the class.

- Have students write the seven headings on a separate piece of paper or in their Explorer's Journal. Have them think about what information they would like to learn about Africa, and write a question that relates to each heading.
- Have students share their questions with the rest of the class, and discuss any similarities.
- Create a master list of questions grouped under the seven headings. As students read about Africa, have them answer the questions on the list.
- At the end of the unit, if any questions remain unanswered, have students research and find the answers to those questions.

Guiding Questions

What questions do I need to ask to understand Africa?

Asking questions is a good way to learn. Think about what information you would want to know if you were visiting a new place, and what questions you might ask to find out. The questions on these pages can help guide your study of Africa. You might want to try adding a few of your own!

GEOGRAPHY

African cultures have been shaped by the need to survive in nearly every type of land on the Earth. The giant continent has people-packed cities, mountaintop coffee farms, and grasslands where zebras gallop. The geography of Africa presents huge barriers to movement, such as giant deserts and thick rain forests. Yet, from early times, Africans discovered ways to overcome these barriers.

1 How has geography affected the way African societies have developed?

HISTORY

Africa gave birth to some of the world's oldest civilizations. Early Africans traded widely beyond their borders, but much of the continent, especially beyond the coasts, was little known to the outside world until modern times. In myths, poetry, and stories, Africans passed down their history, telling of great kingdoms, family customs, and human wisdom. These histories shape Africans' sense of identity today.

2 How have Africans been affected by their history?

CULTURE

A culture is the set of beliefs and customs shared by a group of people. There is no single African "culture" because Africa has hundreds of cultures. Some are the unique traditions of people who lived in isolation. Yet more often ideas, customs, and inventions spread across Africa, varying as they passed from region to region.

3 How do Africa's many cultures differ from place to place?

GOVERNMENT

Africa's history includes powerful kingdoms, empires, and nations. Until recent times, though, Africans usually ruled themselves in smaller clans, villages, or towns. Today, many African national governments give their citizens American-style freedoms, such as the right to vote, to worship freely, and to choose where they live and work.

4 How do African governments compare with the United States government?

ECONOMICS

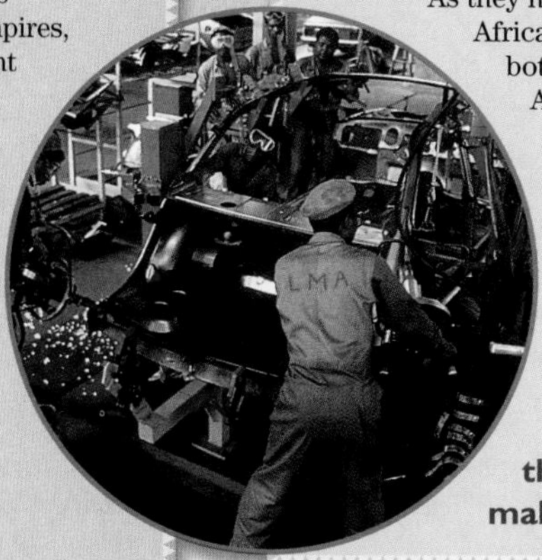

As they have for generations, many Africans raise crops and livestock, both to consume and to sell. Yet Africa's economy is becoming more industrialized. People work in everything from factories to restaurants to road construction. World demand for African products—oil, gold, coffee, and cocoa—provides jobs to millions of workers.

5 What are some of the ways that Africans make a living?

CITIZENSHIP

The nature of citizenship varies among the different regions of Africa. Citizens have different roles and responsibilities, and they participate in the political process in different ways. In some countries, citizens have fought hard to participate in their government's political process, and in other countries, they have brought about change using different methods.

6 How have Africans struggled to participate in their government's political processes?

SCIENCE, TECHNOLOGY, AND SOCIETY

Africa has an economy largely based on agriculture and the raising of livestock. Scientific innovations in farming are beginning to improve the economy in many African countries, and advances in technology and science are making Africa's economy increasingly industrialized.

7 How has Africa's relative isolation from the rest of the world affected the use of science and technology?

Take It to the NET

For more information on Africa, visit the World Explorer: People, Places, and Cultures companion Web site at **phschool.com.**

ACTIVITY

Using Primary and Secondary Sources

Ask students to think about their own daily routines and the foods, traditions, and special celebrations that have been passed down through their families. Discuss what life might be like in some countries in Africa for a family that belongs to a certain ethnic group.

- Have students work in pairs to create an outline that shows the different cultural features of an American family of a particular ethnicity or religion. (Volunteers can offer to be a group leader if they have a knowledge of or interest in a particular ethnicity or religion.)
- Then, have each pair choose a country from Africa and research that country to try to find information on the daily activities and cultural aspects of the people who live there.
- Encourage students to use primary and secondary resources in their research, including letters, interviews, biographies, and Internet sources.

Verbal/Linguistic

ACTIVITY ATLAS

Lesson Objectives

1. Describe the relative location and size of Africa.
2. Identify some key physical features of Africa.
3. Summarize the effect of deforestation on African lands and peoples.

Lesson Plan

1 Engage

Warm-Up Activity

Show students a U.S. weather map from a daily newspaper. Ask them to describe the weather in various parts of the country. As the class recognizes the climate variations among different regions of the country, discuss other ways in which these regions are different or the same.

Activating Prior Knowledge

Building on the previous discussion, ask students what characteristics Africa may share with the United States. What are some issues facing regions of the United States that may also face parts of Africa?

ACTIVITY ATLAS

Africa

Learning about Africa means being an explorer and a geographer. No explorer would start out without first checking some facts. Begin by exploring the maps of Africa on the following pages.

Relative Location

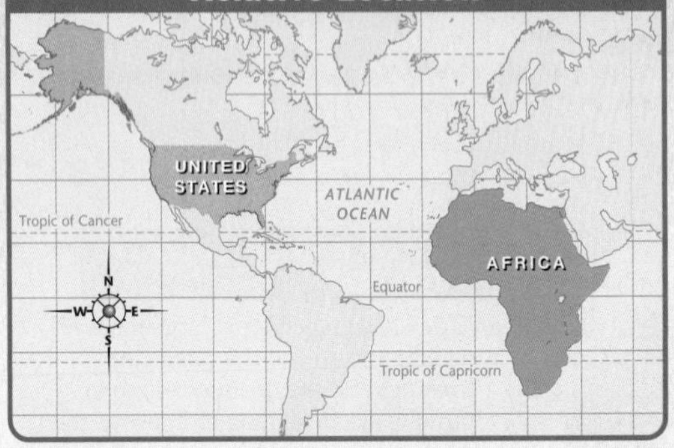

Relative Size

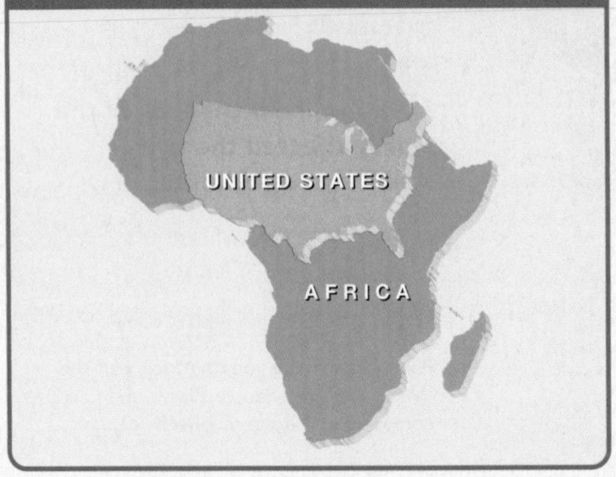

1. LOCATION

Explore Africa's Location One of the first questions a geographer asks about a place is "Where is it?" Use the map to describe Africa's location relative to the United States. What ocean lies between Africa and the United States? Note that the Equator extends through Africa. What role might their location on the Equator play in the climates of nearby countries? How do you think climates of the United States might differ from the climates of Africa?

2. REGIONS

Explore Africa's Size How big is Africa compared to the United States? On a separate sheet of paper, trace the map of the United States and cut it out. How many times can you fit it inside the map of Africa?

Take It to the NET

Items marked with this logo are periodically updated on the Internet. To get current information about the geography of Africa, go to **phschool.com.**

Answers to...

LOCATION

1. The Atlantic Ocean lies between Africa and the United States. Students may say that countries near the Equator probably have hot climates. Students may suggest that Africa's climates are hotter than those of the United States.

REGIONS

2. Africa is about three times larger than the United States.

Resource Directory

Teaching Resources

Activity Atlas in the Unit 5 Teaching Resources, pp. 97–103

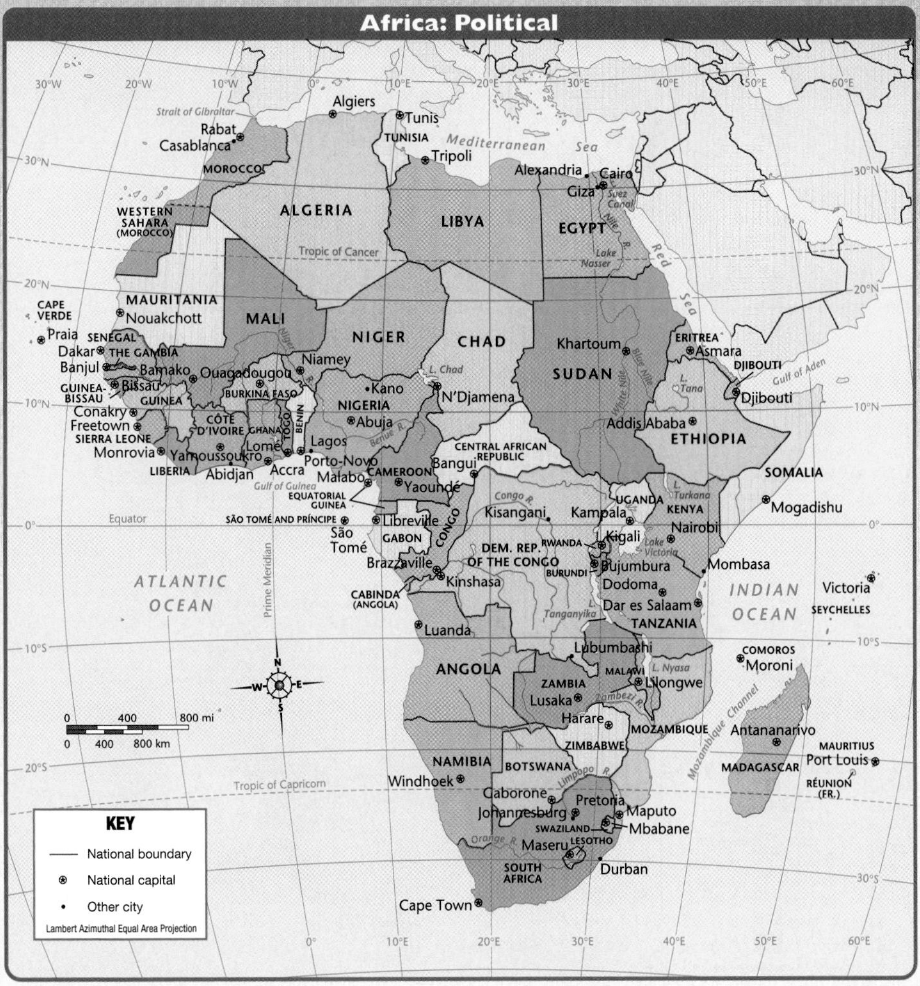

3. MOVEMENT

Explore the Influence of Geography on the Economy Fifteen African nations are landlocked. That is, they do not border any ocean. Point to them on the map. Make a list of them. Landlocked nations are often poor. How do you think being landlocked might affect a nation's economy?

2 Explore

Have students read the Activity Atlas carefully. Suggest that they create African Explorers' Logs for recording answers to the questions.

3 Teach

Ask students to create a fact sheet for Africa. Headings should include *Location, Major Physical Features, Key Political Elements*, and *Challenges*.

4 Assess/Reteach

Fact sheets should note Africa's location between the Atlantic and Indian Oceans and its nearness to the Equator. They should also note that the continent is mostly covered by a huge plateau with narrow coastal plains, limited vegetation, rivers, and some rain forests. The continent faces challenges such as deforestation and poverty.

Resource Directory

Teaching Resources

Outline Maps Africa, p. 32

Technology

Color Transparencies 97 Africa: Political Map

Answers to...

MOVEMENT

3. Landlocked nations: Mali, Niger, Chad, Ethiopia, Burkina Faso, Central African Republic, Uganda, Rwanda, Burundi, Democratic Republic of Congo, Zambia, Malawi, Zimbabwe, Botswana, Swaziland; a landlocked nation lacks access to oceans, which makes it more difficult and costly to transport goods in and out of the nation.

Practice in the Themes of Geography

Ask students to use the physical map and the natural vegetation map of Africa to find answers to the following questions concerning the five themes of geography.

Location Challenge students to name the major bodies of water that surround Africa. (Indian Ocean, Atlantic Ocean, Mediterranean Sea, Red Sea)

Place Prompt students to locate the Serengeti Plain and Lake Victoria on the map. Then, ask students to complete the following sentence: *The Serengeti Plain and Lake Victoria are both in the nation of ________.* (Tanzania)

Regions Ask students to name some African nations that have tropical rain forests. (Answers may include Côte d'Ivoire, Ghana, Cameroon, Gabon, Republic of Congo, and Congo.)

Movement Challenge students to identify the key physical feature that makes it difficult for people from Niger, Mali, and Chad to reach the Mediterranean Sea. (the world's largest desert—the Sahara)

Interaction Point out the Suez Canal to students, explaining that it was completed in 1869. Ask students how the canal might affect the economies of the African nations along the Red Sea. (Students should note that the canal gives these nations access to Mediterranean shipping routes.)

ACTIVITY ATLAS

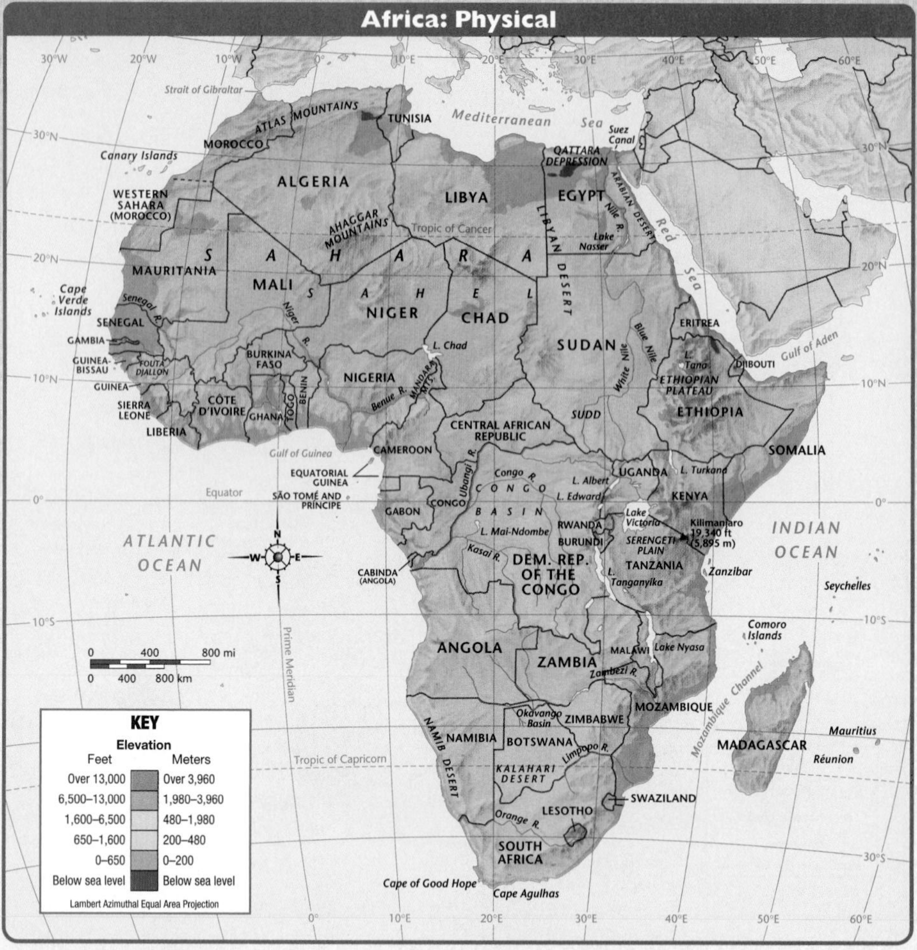

4. PLACE

Describe Africa's Physical Features Find Southern Africa on the map above. It extends south of 10°S. Steep cliffs rise up from the narrow coastal plains, where the dark green areas meet the lighter green. Trace these cliffs north with your finger. Inside this line of cliffs, how would you describe the physical features of the interior of Southern Africa?

352 UNIT 5 AFRICA

Resource Directory

Teaching Resources

Outline Maps Africa, p. 33

Technology

Color Transparencies 96 Africa: Political-Physical Map

Answers to...

PLACE

4. Inside the line of cliffs is a plateau ranging from 1,600 to 6,500 feet. The plateau is higher in the southeast and has some mountains.

5. REGIONS

Identify Africa's Physical Features An adventurous friend has flown off to Africa, but she hasn't told anyone where she is going. She sends you clues. Use the maps on pages 351, 352, and 353 to find her location.

A. *I've landed in a city in Ethiopia. It's in a region of tall grasses and few trees. The city is near 10°N and 40°E. What city am I in?*

B. *The area around me has Mediterranean vegetation. But I'm not anywhere near the Mediterranean Sea! I am flying over a city on a very narrow coastal plain. Nearby are steep cliffs. What city is below me?*

C. *Today, I flew above tropical rain forests along the Equator. Going north, the forests changed into savanna. I'm in a city north of where the Benue River meets the Niger River. Where am I?*

Africa: Natural Vegetation

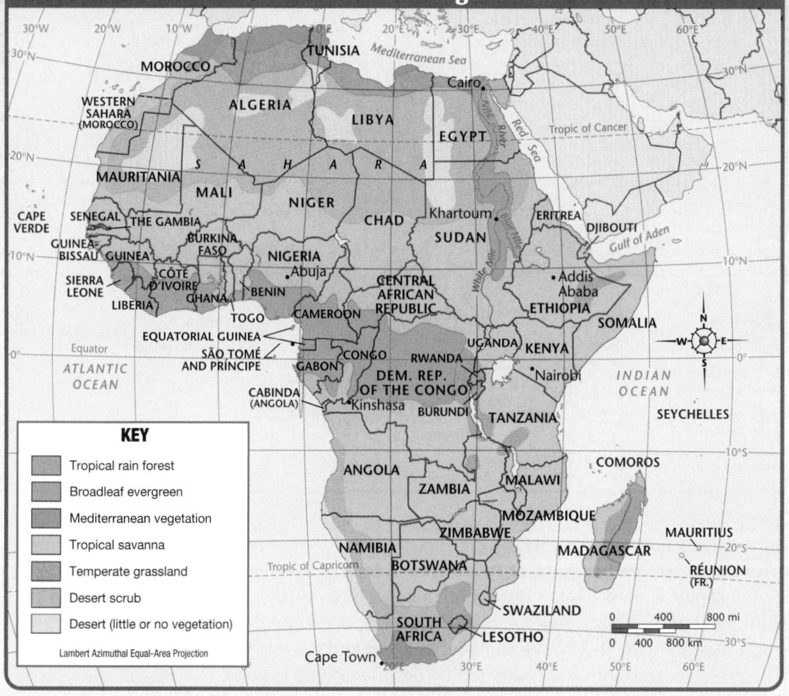

HISTORY

Sir Henry Morton Stanley (1841–1904)

During the 1800s, European interest in Africa's natural resources grew. A number of European explorers went to Africa to map the continent and assess how Europeans could benefit from Africa's resources. Henry Morton Stanley remains one of the best known of these explorers. Stanley first visited Africa in 1866 as a journalist. He had been hired to find the famous explorer Dr. David Livingstone, who had vanished somewhere in Africa's interior. Stanley succeeded, and upon finding Livingstone near Lake Tanganyika, he uttered the famous greeting, "Dr. Livingstone, I presume." Stanley spent many years exploring and mapping central Africa in the service of British and Belgian interests. Stanley wrote accounts of his discovery of the source and the path of the Congo River as well as several other books about his Central African expeditions.

Resource Directory

Teaching Resources

Social Studies and Geography Skills, Reading a Natural Vegetation Map, p. 23

Answers to...

REGIONS

5. a. Addis Ababa

b. Cape Town

c. Abuja

ACTIVITY ATLAS

ACTIVITY

Interdisciplinary Connections

Art Organize students into groups and assign each group a region of Africa to study. You may define regions by climate, physical features, or political boundaries. Challenge each group to generate a list of their region's physical features. Then, have groups design a home in which local people might live. Tell students to consider climate, landforms, available materials, and the need for protection. Invite groups to draw and then build models of their homes. Work as a whole class to compare and contrast the different homes.

Visual/Spatial

ACTIVITY ATLAS

Take It to the NET

Africa: Deforestation

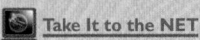

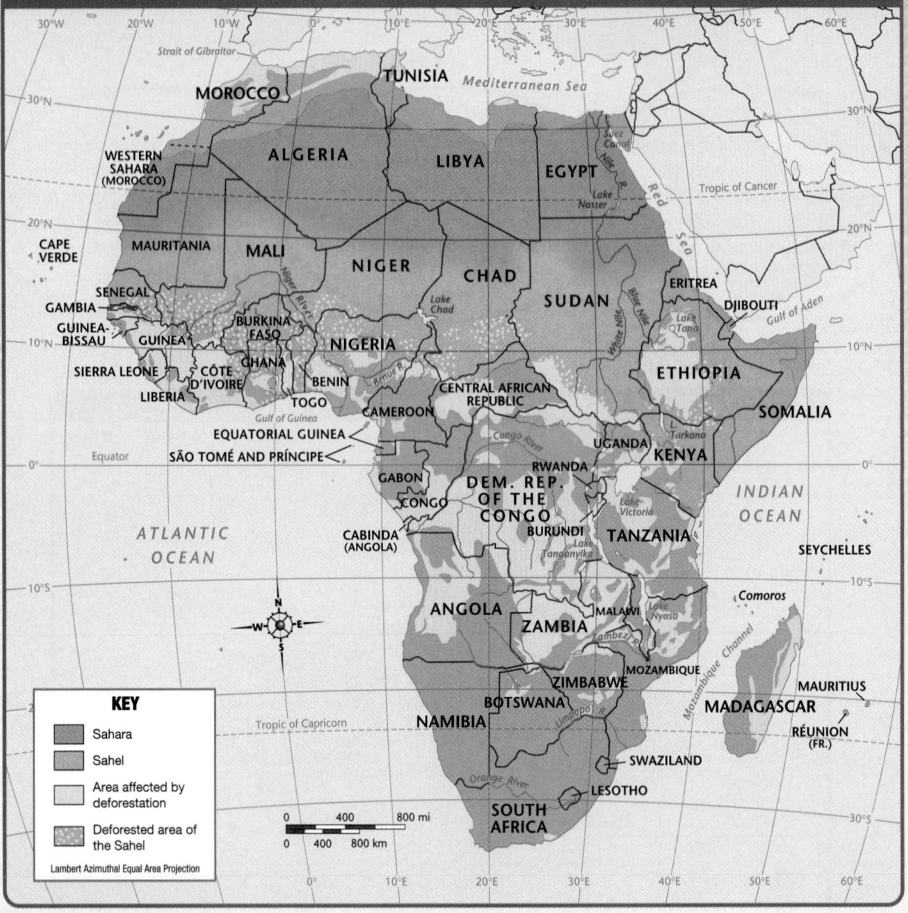

6. HUMAN-ENVIRONMENT INTERACTION

Explore the Effects of Physical Processes A loss of trees and forest is called deforestation. It causes droughts, raises temperatures, reduces animal life, and helps create deserts. Deforestation comes mainly from farmers and herders who clear trees to make farming and grazing land. On the map above, which regions are affected by deforestation? How can you tell?

Answers to...

HUMAN-ENVIRONMENT INTERACTION

6. East Africa, Central Africa, and the lands near 10°N latitude in west Africa are most affected by deforestation. The map key indicates by color where deforestation is affecting an area.

354 UNIT 5 AFRICA

Africa's Deepest, Largest, Tallest, and Longest . . .

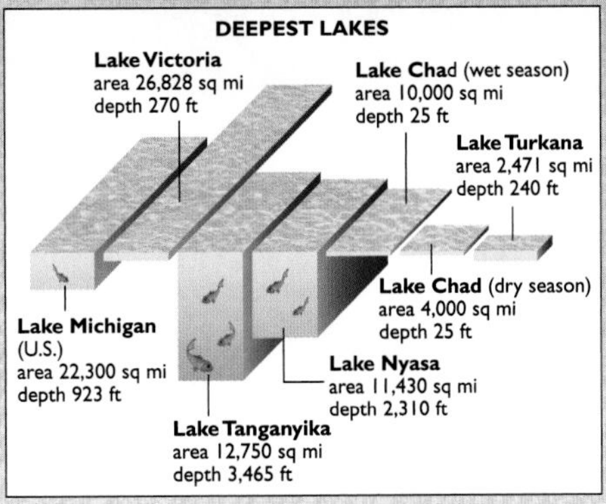

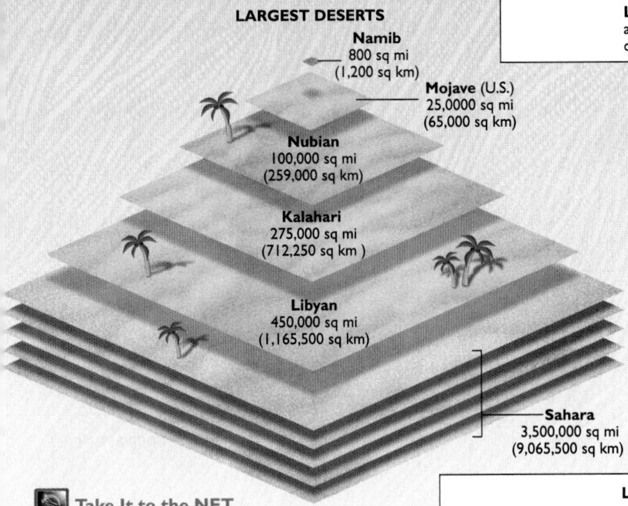

7. PLACE

Compare Physical Features Study the diagrams on this page. Using the maps in this Activity Atlas, locate each of the African features shown. What part of Africa—northern, southern, eastern, western, or central—has the (a) tallest mountain; (b) longest river; (c) deepest lake; (d) largest desert?

Take It to the NET

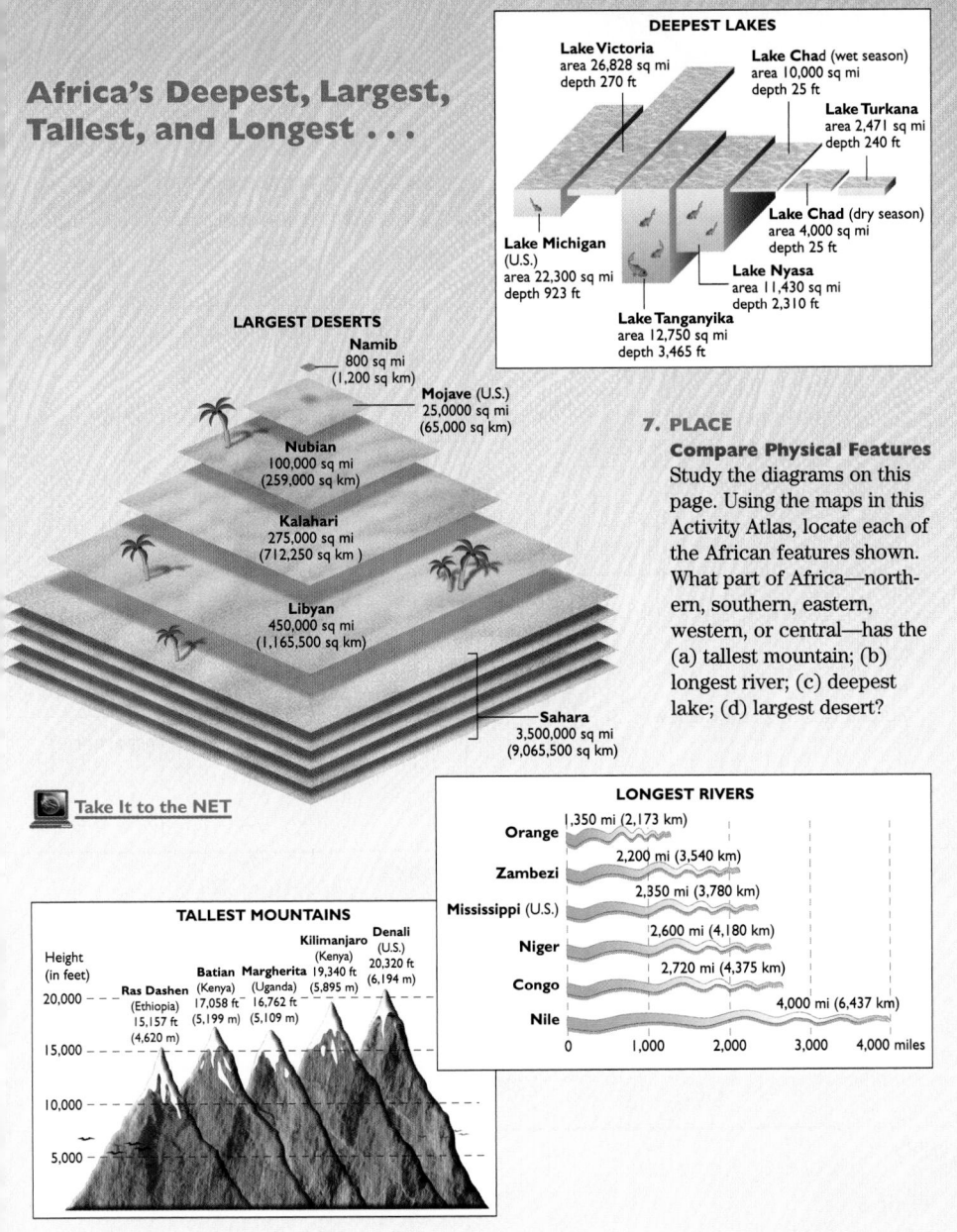

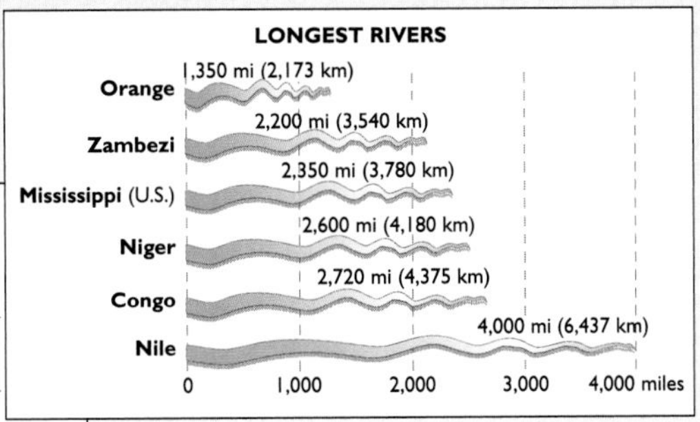

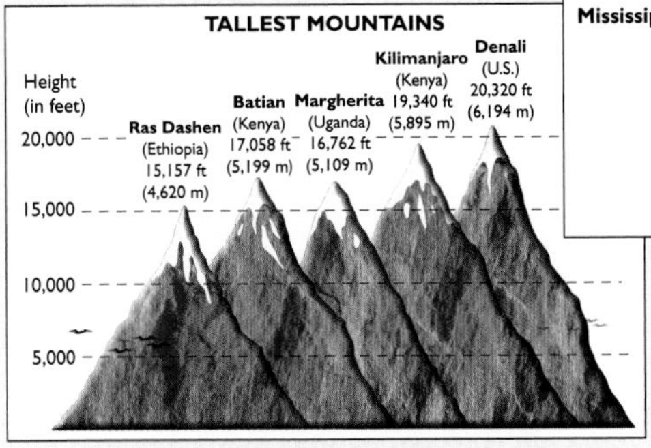

ACTIVITY

Discovery Learning

African City Hop Display a large map of Africa and ask students to review the different maps in the Activity Atlas. Then, assign each student an African city. Challenge students to come to the displayed map and trace a path from their assigned city to another designated African city. While tracing, each student should describe the physical features, climate and vegetation regions, and political boundaries that would be crossed during a journey between the two cities.

Visual/Spatial

ACTIVITY

Interdisciplinary Connections

Science Provide students with photos and information about a selection of African plants. This information can be found in encyclopedias, books about African vegetation, and on the Internet. Then, challenge students to makes some hypotheses about whether each of these plants could survive in your hometown. If you wish, work with students to verify hypotheses.

Logical/Mathematical

Answers to...

PLACE

7. **a.** eastern

b. eastern or northern

c. central

d. northern

Chapter 19 Planning Guide

Resource Manager

	CORE INSTRUCTION	READING/SKILLS
Chapter-Level Resources	**Teaching Resources** Program Overview Pacing Charts **Technology** Resource Pro® CD-ROM Companion Web site, phschool.com • eTeach	**Technology** Social Studies Skills Tutor CD-ROM Student Edition on Audio CD, Ch. 19
1 Physical Features 1. Identify Africa's major regions and describe their geographic features. 2. Describe Africa's major landforms. 3. Identify the effects that Africa's rivers have on the land and people.	**Teaching Resources** **Unit 5** Classroom Manager, p. 2 Guided Reading and Review, p. 3	**Teaching Resources** Guide to the Essentials, p. 81 **Technology** Section Reading Support Transparencies
2 Humans and the Physical Environment 1. Describe the major climate regions of Africa and the factors that influence climate. 2. Identify how humans understand and adapt to their environment.	**Teaching Resources** **Unit 5** Classroom Manager, p. 5 Guided Reading and Review, p. 6	**Teaching Resources** Guide to the Essentials, p. 82 **Technology** Section Reading Support Transparencies
3 Geographic Factors and Natural Resources 1. Identify some of Africa's key agricultural resources. 2. Identify some of Africa's key mineral and energy resources. 3. Describe some of the challenges facing Africans in balancing the development of their natural resources.	**Teaching Resources** **Unit 5** Classroom Manager, p. 8 Guided Reading and Review, p. 9 Chapter Summary, p. 11 Vocabulary, p. 12 Reteaching, p. 13	**Teaching Resources** **Unit 5** Critical Thinking, p. 15 Guide to the Essentials, p. 83 **Technology** Section Reading Support Transparencies

ENRICHMENT / PRE-AP

Teaching Resources
Primary Sources and Literature Readings

Other Print Resources
DK Atlas

Technology
World Video Explorer: Journey Over Africa, Geography: The Great Rift Valley
Companion Web site, phschool.com

Technology
Color Transparencies 101

Teaching Resources
Social Studies and Geography Skills, p. 24

Teaching Resources
Unit 5
Enrichment, p. 14
Cooperative Learning Activity, pp. 104–107

ASSESSMENT

Prentice Hall Assessment System

Core Assessment
Chapter Tests with ExamView® Test Bank, Ch. 19
ExamView® Test Bank CD-ROM, Ch. 19

Standardized Test Preparation
Diagnose and Prescribe
Diagnostic Tests for Middle Grades Social Studies Skills
Review and Reteach
Review Book for World Studies
Practice and Assess
Test-taking Strategies with Transparencies for Middle Grades Test Prep Book
Test-taking Strategies Posters

Teaching Resources
Unit 5
Section Quizzes, pp. 4, 7, and 10
Chapter Tests, pp. 130–135

Technology
Companion Web site, phschool.com
Ch. 19 Self-Test

World Video Explorer
Each region of the world is explored through regional flyovers and investigative field trips. Case study segments give students an in-depth view of the history, economy, government, and culture of a key place in each region. Case studies include Nigeria, Mexico, China, British Columbia, and the Czech Republic.

In Your Classroom

CUSTOMIZE FOR INDIVIDUAL NEEDS

Gifted and Talented

Teacher's Edition
- Language Arts, p. 359

Teaching Resources
- Enrichment, p. 14
- Primary Sources and Literature Readings

Honors/Pre-AP

Teacher's Edition
- Language Arts, p. 359

Teaching Resources
- Critical Thinking, p. 15
- Primary Sources and Literature Readings

ESL

Teacher's Edition
- Language Arts, p. 359

Teaching Resources
- Guided Reading and Review, pp. 3, 6, and 9
- Vocabulary, p. 12
- Reteaching, p. 13
- Guide to the Essentials, pp. 81–83

Technology
- Social Studies Skills Tutor CD-ROM
- Section Reading Support Transparencies

Less Proficient Readers

Teacher's Edition
- Language Arts, p. 359

Teaching Resources
- Guided Reading and Review, pp. 3, 6, and 9
- Vocabulary, p. 12
- Reteaching, p. 13
- Guide to the Essentials, pp. 81–83

Technology
- Social Studies Skills Tutor CD-ROM
- Section Reading Support Transparencies

Less Proficient Writers

Teacher's Edition
- Language Arts, p. 359

Teaching Resources
- Guided Reading and Review, pp. 3, 6, and 9
- Vocabulary, p. 12
- Guide to the Essentials, pp. 81–83

Technology
- Social Studies Skills Tutor CD-ROM
- Section Reading Support Transparencies

TEACHER'S EDITION INDEX

Activities language arts, p. 359

Connections early Egyptian civilization, p. 359

Skills Mini Lessons: Previewing, p. 359

CHAPTER 19 PACING SUGGESTIONS

 For 90-minute Blocks
See suggestions in the Teaching Resources Pacing Charts for Chapter 19. Use Color Transparencies 101.

 Running Out of Time?
See the Guide to the Essentials, pp. 81–83.

INTERDISCIPLINARY LINKS

Middle Grades Math: Tools for Success
Course 1, Lesson 1-1, **Organizing and Displaying Data;** Lesson 1-2, **Make a Table**

Science Explorer
Environmental Science, Lesson 2-4, **Earth's Biomes**

DORLING KINDERSLEY

At the end of each unit, you will find information adapted from Dorling Kindersley's *Illustrated Children's Encyclopedia* that connects to the region being studied and to one of the seven content strands. In addition, your resources include Dorling Kindersley's *Atlas*, which contains valuable information about countries from around the world.

BIBLIOGRAPHY

For the Teacher

Africa. National Geographic, 1991. Videocassette.

Brandenburg, Jim. *Sand and Fog: Adventures in Southern Africa.* Walker, 1994.

Kreikemeir, Gregory Scott. *Come with Me to Africa: A Photographic Journey.* Golden, 1994.

DK *Wild Africa: Exploring the African Habitats.* Dorling Kindersley, 2001.

For the Student

Easy

DK *DK Geography of the World.* Dorling Kindersley, 2001.

Kessler, Cristina. *All the King's Animals: The Return of Endangered Wildlife to Swaziland.* Boyds Mills, 1995.

Average

DK *Gorilla, Monkey & Ape* (*Eyewitness* series). Dorling Kindersley, 2001.

Challenging

Campbell, Eric. *The Year of the Leopard Song.* Harcourt Brace Jovanovich, 1992.

Literature Connection

Campbell, Eric. *The Place of Lions.* Harcourt Brace Jovanovich, 1991.

Weir, Bob, and Wendy Weir. *Panther Dream: A Story of the African Rainforest.* Hyperion, 1991.

Take It to the NET

The World Explorer companion Web site, found on **phschool.com**, offers activities for exploring geographical, historical, and cultural resources on the Internet. It also provides on-line links for key content and all Section and Chapter Assessment activities.

The **Teacher site** also provides teachers with regional data and ideas for student research and activities.

Students can use the **Student site** to find chapter-by-chapter Internet resource links and to access Self-Tests.

CHAPTER 19

Connecting to the

Guiding Questions

In this chapter, students will read about the physical geography of Africa. Content in this chapter corresponds to the following Guiding Questions outlined at the beginning of the unit.

- How has geography affected the way African societies have developed?
- What are some of the ways that Africans make a living?

Using the Map Activities

Have students first study the key and the map before they complete the activities. Make sure that students understand the symbols on the key and what the map shows.

- The map shows the Nile River valley. The Nile River defines the region.
- There are mountains to the east and plains to the west of the valley. Most cities are in the northern part of the valley.
- The Nile is used for irrigation and transportation. Most cities are located close to the Nile.
- Most cities are located near the river, which indicates the importance of water to the people, probably for irrigating crops and transporting goods and people.

Heterogeneous Groups

The following activity is suitable for heterogeneous groups.

Using Primary Sources

Language Arts, p. 359

eTeach

Be sure to check out this month's discussion with a Master Teacher. Go to **phschool.com**.

CHAPTER 19

AFRICA: Physical Geography

SECTION 1
Physical Features

SECTION 2
Humans and the Physical Environment

SECTION 3
Geographic Factors and Natural Resources

Nile River Valley

Using Maps

Because they cover such a large area, world maps lack the detail to show much about a specific part of the world. That is why people use regional maps. Regional maps focus on one part of the world, showing it in greater detail. This map shows the region in Africa known as the Nile River valley.

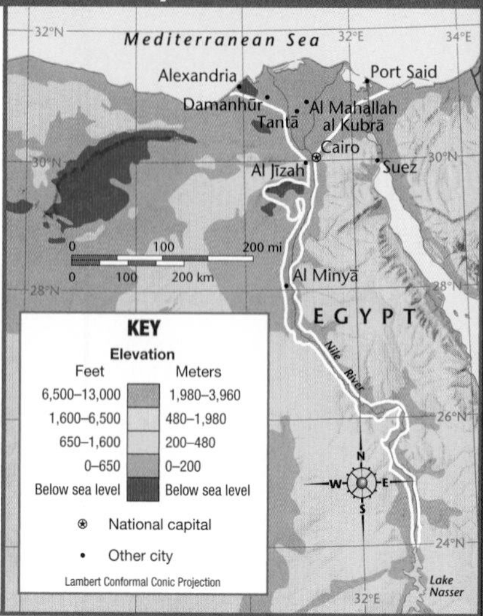

Understanding Regional Maps

A region is an area of the Earth that shares some common characteristics. What region is shown on this map? What defines the region? What landforms can be found on either side of the Nile River valley? Where are most of the cities in the Nile River valley located? Why might the Nile River be important to people in Egypt?

Exploring the Nile River Valley

Why would this map be useful in learning about the ways of life in this region? How might it help you to understand the history of the region? Use the library or the Internet to gather more information about the Nile River valley. Write a brief report describing the ways that the Nile River has shaped people's lives in this region.

Resource Directory

Teaching Resources

Primary Sources and Literature Readings extend content with a selection related to the concepts in this chapter.

Other Print Resources

DK Atlas

Technology

Journey Over Africa, from the World Video Explorer, introduces students to major landforms and climate regions of Africa.

Geography: The Great Rift Valley, from the World Video Explorer, enhances students' understanding of the geographic factors that make the Great Rift Valley an important location for archaeological study.

Student Edition on Audio CD, Ch. 19

SECTION 1

Africa

Physical Features

BEFORE YOU READ

READING FOCUS

1. What are the four regions of Africa and how do they differ geographically?
2. What are Africa's three major landforms?
3. What effects do Africa's rivers have on the land and people?

KEY TERMS

plateau
elevation
escarpment
rift
cataract
transportation barrier
silt
fertile
tributary

KEY PLACES

Sahara
Great Rift Valley
Nile River
Congo River
Niger River
Zambezi River

NOTE TAKING

Copy the chart below. As you read the section, fill in the chart by noting the regions in which each physical feature is located.

Physical Features	North	West	East	Central/South
Sahara				
Plateaus				
Great Rift Valley				
Nile River				
Congo River				
Niger River				
Zambezi River				

MAIN IDEA

Africa is a huge continent with a variety of regions and physical features that affect how people live and work in different regions.

Setting the Scene

Africa is a giant. More than three times bigger than the United States, it covers close to 11,700,000 square miles (more than 30,000,000 sq km). That is about one fifth of all of the land in the world. If you drove across Africa at its widest point going 65 miles (105 km) per hour, without stopping for gas or sleep, it would take you about 72 hours. Traveling north-to-south, the trip would take about 77 hours.

Africa's Contrasting Geography

Africa can be divided into four regions: 1) North, 2) West, 3) East, and 4) Central and Southern. Each region contains many different climates and physical features.

North Africa is marked by rocky mountains and the world's largest desert, the **Sahara.** The Sahara is almost the size of the United States.

Life in the Sahara

GEOGRAPHY The Sahara covers about 3 1/2 million square miles (9 million square km). It has a poulation of less than 2 million people. **Critical Thinking** What are some of the difficulties that people might face living in the Sahara?

SECTION 1

Lesson Objectives

1. Identify Africa's major regions and describe their geographic features.
2. Describe Africa's major landforms.
3. Identify the effects that Africa's rivers have on the land and people.

Lesson Plan

1 Engage

Warm-Up Activity

Give each student a ball of modeling clay (or demonstrate the following activity yourself). Mold the clay inside a pie plate or a flat-bottomed bowl. Turn the resulting shape so that the flat side is on top. Explain that this shape approximates the contours of the African continent. Ask students what they can learn about Africa's lands from studying its contours. For example, how might rivers flow?

Activating Prior Knowledge

Ask students to share with the class what they know about the geography of Africa. If necessary, prompt students with questions about rivers, mountains, deserts, and lakes. Record students' responses on the board.

Resource Directory

Teaching Resources

Classroom Manager in the Unit 5 Teaching Resources, p. 2

Guided Reading and Review in the Unit 5 Teaching Resources, p. 3

Guide to the Essentials, p. 81

Technology

Section Reading Support Transparencies

Answers to...

CRITICAL THINKING

Difficulties include the climate, lack of water, and lack of fertile soil for crops.

Lesson Plan continued

2 Explore

Help students understand Africa's geography by asking them to think about the following questions as they read the section: How might geographic factors influence how people live in different parts of Africa? In what ways might travel be difficult in Africa? Why are rivers an important physical feature?

3 Teach

Have students create a table with four side labels: *North, West, East, Central* and *Southern.* Top labels should be landforms such as *Plateaus, Rivers,* and *Mountains.* Students should check boxes to correlate side and top categories. Ask students to use their completed tables to write a summary of Africa's main geographic features. This activity should take about 30 minutes.

Question for Discussion

GEOGRAPHY Look at the physical map of Africa on p. 352. Locate a variety of physical features, including mountains and rivers, that form natural boundaries between countries. What are some benefits to having natural boundaries form political boundaries? What are some disadvantages?

Benefits include protection from neighboring countries; disadvantages include difficulties in traveling to and trading with neighboring countries.

4 Assess/Reteach

See the answers to the Section 1 Assessment. Completed tables can also be an assessment.

Acceptable tables include valid top and side labels.

Commendable tables correctly correlate features and regions.

Outstanding tables include summary statements that outline the variety of landforms in Africa.

West Africa, the continent's most populated region, consists mostly of grasslands. The soil in the grasslands is good for farming.

East Africa contains many mountains, and **plateaus**, which are large raised areas of mostly flat land. The East also has areas of grasslands and hills.

Much of Central and Southern Africa is flat or rolling grassland. The region also contains thick rain forests, mountains, and swamps. The Namib (NAHM eeb) Desert of the country of Namibia and the Kalahari (kal uh HAHR ee) Desert of Botswana are in this region.

Africa's Major Landforms

Africa can be described as an upside-down pie. If you were to slice Africa in half from east to west, you would see that much of the continent is a plateau that drops off sharply near the sea.

Plateaus Africa is often called the "plateau continent," because the elevation of much of the land area is high. **Elevation** is the height of land above sea level.

Each of Africa's four regions has mountains, but the highest are in East Africa. Mount Kilimanjaro is Africa's tallest mountain, rising to a height of 19,341 feet (5,895 m).

Coastal Plains Along much of Africa's coast is a strip of coastal plain. This strip of land is dry and sandy at some points, and marshy and moist at other places. In the city of Accra, in the West African

Africa's Coastal Plains

ECONOMICS

Narrow coastal plains line much of Africa's coast, like this one at Cape Coast, Ghana. **Critical Thinking** Based on this photograph, how do you think people living on Africa's coastal plains might make a living?

358 UNIT 5 AFRICA

Answers to...

CRITICAL THINKING

Answers may include fishing and tourism.

Resource Directory

Technology

Color Transparencies 101 Africa's Size Relative to Several Countries Map country of Ghana (GAHN uh), the coastal strip is only 16 miles (25 km) wide. It ends at a long **escarpment**, or steep cliff, that is about as high as a 100-story skyscraper.

The Great Rift Valley Mount Kilimanjaro is located on the edge of the **Great Rift Valley** in East Africa. The Great Rift Valley was formed millions of years ago, when the continents pulled apart. A **rift** is a deep trench. The rift that cuts through East Africa is 4,000 miles (6,400 km) long. Most of Africa's major lakes are located in or near the Great Rift Valley.

The Rivers of Africa

Four large rivers carry water from the mountains of Africa's plateaus to the sea. They are the **Nile,** the **Congo,** the **Niger** (NI jur) and the **Zambezi.** The rivers are useful for traveling but they are broken in places by **cataracts,** or rock-filled rapids. These cataracts act as transportation barriers because they make it impossible for ships to sail from Africa's interior to the sea. **Transportation barriers** are physical features that make it difficult to travel or transport goods from one region to another.

The Nile River The Nile is the longest river in the world. Its length, more than 4,000 miles (6,400 km), is more than the width of the United States. The sources of the Nile are the White Nile in the country of Uganda and the Blue Nile in the highlands of Ethiopia. From these two sources, the river flows north and spills into the Mediterranean Sea.

People have farmed the land surrounding the Nile for thousands of years. At one time, the Nile flooded its banks regularly. Farmers planted their crops to match the flood cycle of the river. The floods provided water for the crops and left behind a layer of **silt**, which is the tiny bits of rock and dirt that build up on the bottoms of rivers and lakes. Silt helps make soil **fertile**, containing substances that plants need in order to grow well.

In 1960, Egypt's government began building the Aswan High Dam to control the flooding of the Nile. As the water backed up behind the dam, it created Lake Nasser. Lake waters are channeled to water crops that grow in the desert, while water rushing through the dam makes electricity.

The Great Rift Valley

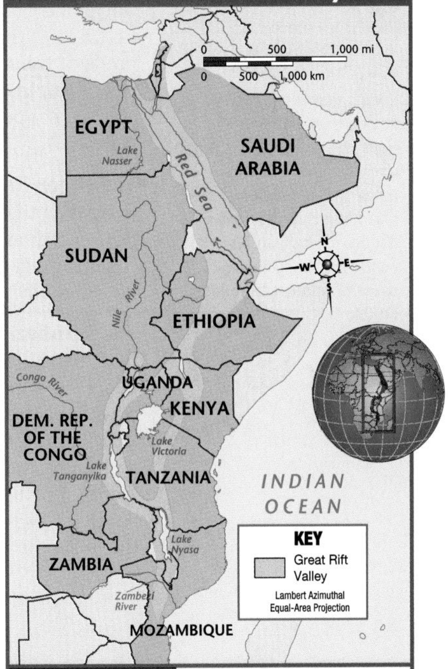

GEOGRAPHY The Great Rift Valley is so large that more than 30 Grand Canyons could fit inside it. Some of Africa's most spectacular mountains, volcanoes, and waterfalls can be found here. **Map Study** What sea is part of the Great Rift Valley? What bodies of water in the Great Rift Valley form natural borders between countries?

CULTURE

Early Egyptian Civilization

The Nile River was at the center of the ancient Egyptian civilization that flourished between 4000 B.C. and 2000 B.C. The river's floods enriched the soil and made farming possible. The proximity of land to the river also determined land values. Lands that flooded every year were worth more and taxed more heavily than those that flooded irregularly. One of the seasons was even called "flooding." Each year, the Egyptians would try to predict the flood's magnitude. They used special gauges called "nilometers" to measure the rising waters far upstream and then predict how high waters would rise downstream.

ACTIVITY

Using Primary Sources

Language Arts Provide students with some firsthand accounts of current and historical travel in Africa. Some current examples include *Come With Me to Africa*, by Gregory Scott Kreikemeir, and *From Cape Town to Cairo*, by David E. Duncan. As a historical example, you might choose selections from *Narrative of an Expedition to the Zambezi and Its Tributaries* (1865), by the Scottish explorer David Livingstone. Ask students what these accounts suggest about the difficulty of travel in Africa, both today and in the past. Have them cite specific examples in their responses.

Verbal/Linguistic

SKILLS MINI LESSON

Previewing

To **introduce** the skill, tell students that previewing what they are about to read can help them develop some expectations about it. List some previewing techniques on the chalkboard: (1) Note the head and subheads. (2) Study the pictures and captions. (3) Relate the subject matter to your own life. Have students **practice** and **apply** the skill using the text and pictures contained in the subsection *Africa's Rivers.* You might suggest that students develop a one- or two-sentence preview of the text similar to a capsule movie review. (A possible preview might read as follows: This section is about four of Africa's rivers—the Nile, Congo, Niger, and Zambezi—and some of their major features.)

Answers to...

MAP STUDY

The Red Sea is part of the Great Rift Valley. Lake Tanganyika and Lake Nyasa form natural borders for several countries.

SECTION I ASSESSMENT

AFTER YOU READ

1. (a) the world's largest desert, located in North Africa, (b) a huge valley that was formed millions of years ago when the continents pulled apart, (c) the longest river in the world, (d) Africa's second-longest river, (e) Africa's third-longest river, (f) Africa's fourth-longest river.
2. (a) large, raised area of mostly level land, (b) the height of land above sea level, (c) a steep cliff, (d) a deep trench, (e) rock-filled rapids, (f) tiny bits of rock and dirt that build up on the bottoms of rivers and lakes, (g) obstacles to movement through or along a route, (h) a type of soil that is able to grow a lot of plants, (i) a small river or stream that flows into a larger river.
3. North Africa is marked by rocky mountains and the world's largest desert, the Sahara. West Africa consists mostly of grasslands, East Africa contains many mountains and plateaus, as well as hills and grasslands, and much of Central and South Africa is flat or rolling grassland.
4. because the elevation of much of the land area is high
5. People fish in the rivers. Rivers are also used for travel, irrigation, and creating electricity. Cataracts make it impossible for ships to sail from Africa's interior to the sea.
6. Answers will vary. Students should list different landforms from the four regions of Africa, such as the Sahara, the coastal plain, and the Great Rift Valley. Students should explain why they would like to visit these specific landforms, and what they would do there.
7. Answers will vary. Students will probably conclude that more people would live in the area because they would have access to the resources necessary to establish permanent settlements.
8. Answers will vary. Students should include a description of each of the four regions, and a description of different sights they might expect to see while there.

LINKS TO **Science**

A River Without a Delta The Congo River's current is so strong that the river does not empty into the ocean at ground level (known as a *delta*). Instead, the river has cut a deep, wide canyon beneath the sea for a distance of about 125 miles (200 km).

The Congo River The Congo River flows through the rain forest of the country of Congo (KAHNG oh) in Central Africa. At 2,720 miles (4,375 km), the Congo is Africa's second-longest river. It is fed by hundreds of **tributaries**, or small rivers and streams that flow into a larger river. People in this region grow grains and cassava, a starchy plant similar to a potato. They also catch fish in the Congo with basket traps.

The Niger River Africa's third-longest river, the Niger, begins its journey in the West African country of Guinea (GIN ee). The river flows north and then bends south for 2,600 miles (4,180 km). The Niger provides water for farms in the river valley. People make a living catching fish in the river.

The Zambezi River The fourth-longest of Africa's rivers, the Zambezi, is in Southern Africa. It runs through or forms the borders of six countries: Angola, Zambia, Namibia, Botswana, Zimbabwe (zim BAHB way), and Mozambique (moh zam BEEK). The Zambezi is 2,200 miles (3,540 km) long. People have used the Zambezi's strong current to make electricity. About halfway to its outlet in the Indian Ocean, the Zambezi plunges into a canyon, creating Victoria Falls. The African name for Victoria Falls is "the smoke that thunders." People can see the mist and spray from 40 miles away.

SECTION I ASSESSMENT

AFTER YOU READ

RECALL

1. Identify: (a) Sahara, (b) Great Rift Valley, (c) Nile River, (d) Congo River, (e) Niger River, (f) Zambezi River
2. Define: (a) plateau, (b) elevation, (c) escarpment, (d) rift, (e) cataract, (f) transportation barrier, (g) silt, (h) fertile, (i) tributary

COMPREHENSION

3. Describe a major geographic feature from each of Africa's four regions.
4. Why is Africa called "the plateau continent?"
5. How do people use the rivers of Africa? What makes the rivers difficult to use?

CRITICAL THINKING AND WRITING

6. **Exploring the Main Idea** Review the Main Idea statement at the beginning of this section. Then, select 3 landforms in Africa that you would like to visit. Explain why you would like to go there and what you would do during your visit.
7. **Drawing Conclusions** Most of North Africa's population lives north of the Sahara near the Mediterranean Sea. If the Sahara were a grassland region with rivers and forests, would this change where people in North African countries live? Why?

ACTIVITY

8. **Writing a Journal** Imagine that you are traveling across each of Africa's four regions, and keeping a journal of your adventure. Write an entry for each region describing where you are and what sights you are seeing.

Resource Directory

Teaching Resources

Section Quiz in the Unit 5 Teaching Resources, p. 4

SECTION 2

Humans and the Physical Environment

BEFORE YOU READ

READING FOCUS

1. What physical features affect Africa's climate?
2. How have people in Africa learned to adapt to their environment?

KEY TERMS:

irrigate
oasis
savanna
nomad

NOTE TAKING

Copy the chart below. As you read the section, fill in the chart with information about the physical features of Africa and the ways that people in those regions have adapted to the environment.

	Rain Forest	Savanna	Desert
Physical Features			
Ways people adapt			

MAIN IDEA

Different climate regions in Africa have different weather patterns and physical features, affecting the way people live.

Setting the Scene

Visualize the continent of Africa with all of its different physical features: mountains, plateaus, rivers, forests, grasslands, and deserts. Now visualize people living and working in all of those different places. They must adapt the ways that they live and work in order to make the best use of their physical environment.

Ways People Adapt

GEOGRAPHY

In Botswana during the rainy season, floods like this one, on the Okavango River Delta, are common. **Critical Thinking** How does the climate in your region affect the way you live?

Physical Features and Climate

Look at the climate map on the following page. Find the Tropic of Cancer and the Tropic of Capricorn. Much of Africa lies between these two lines of latitude, which means that most of Africa is in a tropical climate region. The Equator runs through this midsection of the continent. These regions are usually hot.

Location near the Equator is not the only influence on climate. The climate of a place may depend on how close it is to large bodies of water. Major landforms and elevation also affect climate.

Living near the Equator A place's location in relation to the Equator influences the seasons. North of the Equator, winter and summer occur at the same time as in the

Resource Directory

Teaching Resources

Classroom Manager in the Unit 5 Teaching Resources, p. 5

Guided Reading and Review in the Unit 5 Teaching Resources, p. 6

Guide to the Essentials, p. 82

Technology

Section Reading Support Transparencies

SECTION 2

Lesson Objectives

1. Describe the major climate regions of Africa and the factors that influence climate.
2. Identify how humans understand and adapt to their environment.

Lesson Plan

1 Engage

Warm-Up Activity

Ask students to suppose that they have traveled two or three states' distance in any direction from your community. Have them describe the land and climate in the new location and then compare it with the land and climate in your community. Have students hypothesize about why any differences exist. Ask students whether they think both places are in the same climate region.

Activating Prior Knowledge

Have students consider the Reading Focus Questions and what the answers might be. Then, have them think about and discuss how their answers might be different if the same questions were asked about the United States. What are the similarities between the two regions? What are the differences?

2 Explore

As students read the section, encourage them to refer to the climate map. Ask students to look for answers to questions such as the following: How does a place's location in relation to the Equator affect seasons? What effect does elevation have on climate?

Answers to...

CRITICAL THINKING

Answers will vary. Students should give specific examples of the influence of climate on their lives.

Lesson Plan continued

❸ Teach

Have students create picture postcards that show four distinct climate and/or vegetation regions of Africa. Students should include descriptive caption text with each postcard. This activity should take about 30 minutes.

Question for Discussion

GEOGRAPHY Compare the physical map of Africa on p. 352 with the natural vegetation map on p. 353. Based on this information, where do you think the earliest civilizations would have developed in Africa? Why?

Students' responses will vary, but should show an awareness of physical features that would provide benefits to a growing civilization, including access to water and fertile land.

❹ Assess/Reteach

See the answers to the Section 2 Assessment. You may also use students' completed postcards for assessment.

Acceptable postcards illustrate four different climate or vegetation regions and include captions that identify each illustration.

Commendable postcards illustrate four different climate or vegetation regions and include captions that identify and locate each illustration.

Outstanding postcards show people engaged in an activity in some of the four different climate or vegetation regions. Captions link climate with human activities.

Africa: Climate Regions

GEOGRAPHY In some of Africa's deserts, it rains so rarely that children who live there may never have seen rain before. In tropical wet regions, it rains almost all the time. But most other regions of Africa have two seasons—rainy and dry. **Map Study** What climate is most common in Africa along the Equator? What climate is most common near the Tropics of Cancer and Capricorn?

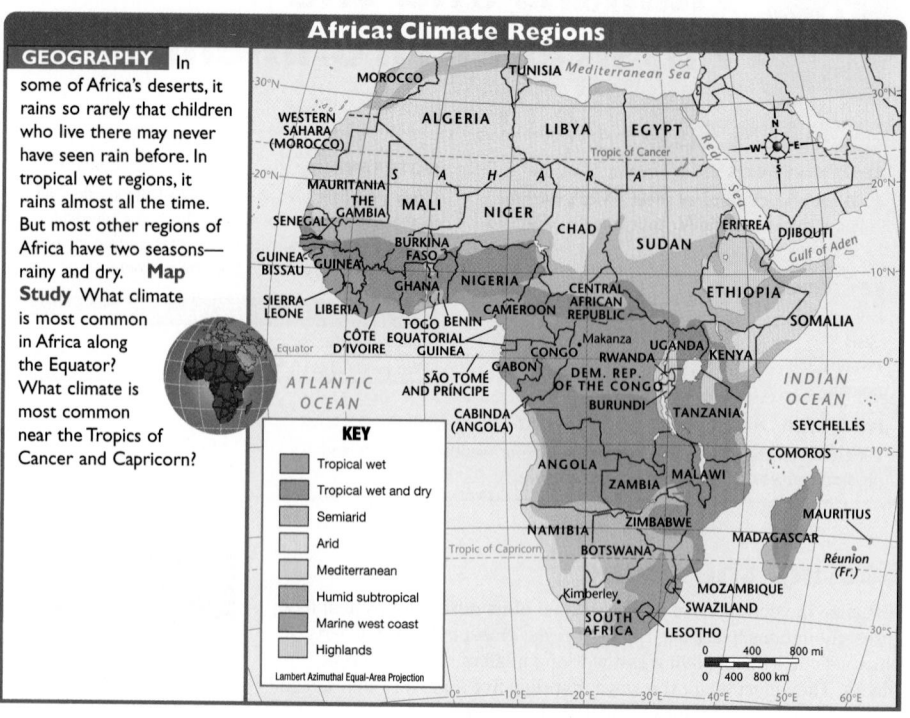

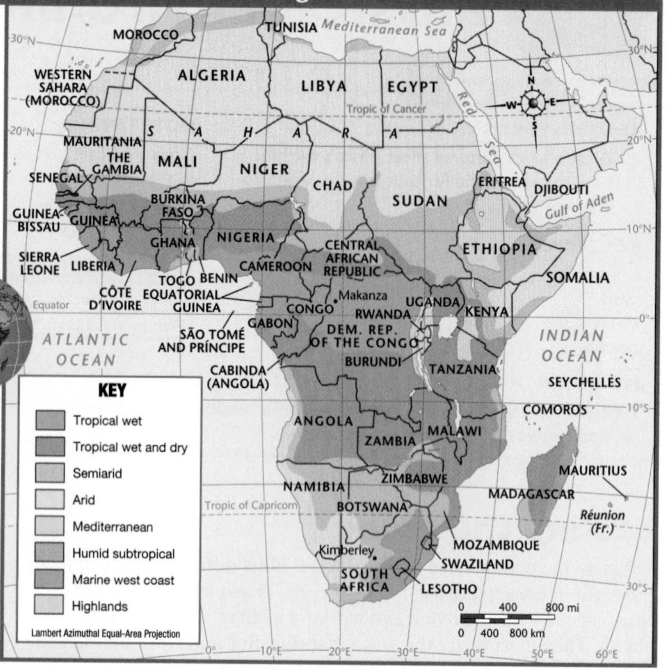

United States. South of the Equator, the seasons are reversed, with winter beginning in June.

Climate and Farming Elevation, or height above sea level, also affects climate. The higher the elevation, the cooler a place tends to be. The countries of Ethiopia and Somalia are about the same distance from the Equator, yet they have different climates. Ethiopia is on a very high plateau and has mild temperatures and much rain. Farmers can grow a wide range of crops—including bananas, coffee, dates, and oats. Because Ethiopia usually gets plenty of rain, many farmers there do not **irrigate**, or artificially water their crops.

Somalia, at a much lower elevation than Ethiopia, is hot and dry. Farming is possible only in or near an **oasis,** where crops can be irrigated. An oasis is a place where springs and fresh underground water make it possible to support life in a region that gets little rain.

Adapting to the Land

The land in Africa's different regions is varied. People in these different regions understand how to adapt to the seasons and to the land in order to make a living.

Resource Directory

Teaching Resources

Social Studies and Geography Skills, Reading a Climate Map, p. 24

Answers to...

MAP STUDY

A tropical wet climate is most common in equatorial Africa. An arid/semiarid climate is most common near the tropics of Cancer and Capricorn.

Tropical Rain Forests Tropical rain forests are regions where it rains nearly all the time. The moisture supports a rich environment of trees, plants, and animals. This region used to be much larger. It covered much of Central Africa. Through the years, people cut trees from the forest for wood or to clear land for farming. Once the trees were cut, heavy rains washed away the nutrients that make soil fertile.

Tropical Savannas Much of Africa north and south of the rain forest is tropical **savanna**. The savanna is a region of tall grasses. The climate of the savanna is tropical wet and dry. The savanna has two seasons: dry and wet. During the dry season, farming is impossible. People trade, build houses, and visit friends. In the wet season, the land turns green and farmers plant their crops.

Deserts in Africa Beyond the savanna lie the deserts. In the south lie the Kalahari and the Namib. The immense Sahara extends across most of North Africa. **Nomads** make their living in the Sahara. Nomads move to various places to make a living. Some nomads are traders, and others hunt game and gather food. Most nomads are herders. They travel to where they can get water and food for their goats, camels, or sheep.

The southern edge of the Sahara meets the savanna in a region called the Sahel (SAH hel), which is the Arab word for shore or border. The Sahel is very hot and dry. It receives only 4 to 8 inches (10 to 20 cm) of rain per year. Small shrubs, grass, and some trees grow there.

AS YOU READ

Monitor Your Reading Picture the rain forest. What might it look like and sound like? Feel like? Smell like?

SECTION 2 ASSESSMENT

AFTER YOU READ

RECALL

1. Define: (a) irrigate, (b) oasis, (c) savanna, (d) nomad

COMPREHENSION

2. How do physical features affect the climate in Africa?
3. What are some of the ways that people have adapted to the climate in different regions of Africa?

CRITICAL THINKING AND WRITING

4. **Exploring the Main Idea** Review the Main Idea statement at the beginning of this section. Then, imagine that you are taking a trip to Africa where you will be visiting several different climate regions. Make a packing list for your trip and explain why you are bringing each item.
5. **Summarizing** Africans face many environmental challenges because of their varied climate. Write a paragraph in which you summarize the major climate-related problems and solutions discussed in this section.

ACTIVITY

Take It to the NET

6. **Life in the Desert** Use the information on the web site to write a brief report about how humans and animals have adapted to life in the Sahara. Visit the World Explorer: People, Places, and Cultures section of **phschool.com** for help in completing this activity.

Resource Directory

Teaching Resources

Section Quiz in the Unit 5 Teaching Resources, p. 7

Answers to...

AS YOU READ

Answers will vary.

SECTION 2 ASSESSMENT

AFTER YOU READ

1. (a) to artificially water crops, (b) a place that gets little rain but where springs and underground water make it possible to support life, (c) a region of tall grasses, (d) a member of a people who move from place to place in order to make a living.
2. The physical features of Africa are varied, and so are its different climates. Tropical rain forests are regions where it rains nearly all of the time. The climate of the tropical savanna is tropical wet and dry, which means there is a dry season and a wet season. The desert regions are hot and dry and receive very little rainfall each year.
3. Answers will vary. Some of the ways that Africans have adapted to their environment are adapting their farming methods, relying on economic activities which are suited to the climate and physical features of the land, such as herding, trading, and hunting and gathering.
4. Answers will vary. Students' lists should show that they have thought about the different climate regions of Africa, and what clothing would be appropriate to bring to each region, and why.
5. Answers will vary. Sample summary: Africans must face the challenges of living in areas with very little rainfall (the desert) where farming is nearly impossible, and in areas with wet and dry seasons where farming must follow the beginning of the wet season (the Savanna). Farming is also difficult in rain forest areas, because once the land is cleared of trees, heavy rains wash away the nutrients that make the soil fertile.
6. Students' reports should provide information about humans' cultural adaptations and animals' physical adaptations to the environment. Encourage students to use photographs and illustrations in their reports.

SECTION 3

Lesson Objectives

1. Identify some of Africa's key agricultural resources.
2. Identify some of Africa's key mineral and energy resources.
3. Describe some of the challenges facing Africans in balancing the development of their natural resources.

Lesson Plan

1 Engage

Warm-Up Activity

Have students list hobbies and activities at which they excel. Discuss what each requires—for instance, time, money, equipment, or physical effort. Ask students whether they see any conflicts between the various interests. For example, there may be time conflicts or one activity may take the student away from home during an important family activity. Ask students how such conflicts might be resolved.

Activating Prior Knowledge

Introduce the saying "Don't put all of your eggs in one basket," and discuss its meaning with students. How do they think a saying like this might apply to a country's economy? Discuss why it might be important for a country to have a variety of economic resources.

Answers to...

CRITICAL THINKING

Students may say that the beans are a valuable crop because chocolate is a very popular food and in great demand.

SECTION 3

Geographic Factors and Natural Resources

BEFORE YOU READ

READING FOCUS

1. What are Africa's agricultural resources?
2. What are Africa's mineral and energy resources?
3. How is Africa preparing for the economic future?

KEY TERMS

subsistence farming
cash crop

NOTE TAKING

Copy the chart below. As you read the section, fill in the chart with information about Africa's crops and mineral resources.

Crops	Minerals
• cacao beans	• copper
• yams	• diamonds
•	•
•	•

MAIN IDEA

Geographic factors influence how Africa's natural resources are used and who benefits from them.

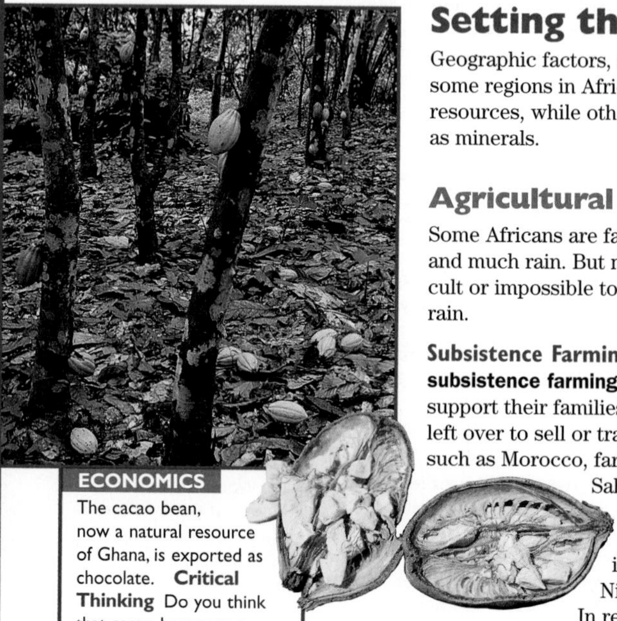

ECONOMICS The cacao bean, now a natural resource of Ghana, is exported as chocolate. **Critical Thinking** Do you think that cacao beans are a valuable crop? Why?

Setting the Scene

Geographic factors, such as climate, limit the ability of some regions in Africa to develop adequate natural resources, while other regions are rich in resources, such as minerals.

Agricultural Resources

Some Africans are farmers living in areas with fertile soil and much rain. But many Africans have land that is difficult or impossible to farm because of poor soil or too little rain.

Subsistence Farming Most of Africa's land is used for **subsistence farming**. Subsistence farmers raise crops to support their families. Generally, they have little or nothing left over to sell or trade. In northern African countries such as Morocco, farmers raise barley and wheat. Farms at Saharan oases in Egypt produce dates and small crops of barley and wheat. In the dry, tropical savannas of Burkina Faso (bur KEE nuh FAH soh) and Niger, subsistence farmers grow grains. In regions with more rainfall, farmers also grow vegetables, fruits and roots such as yams and cassava. In West Africa, corn and rice are important crops.

Resource Directory

Teaching Resources

Classroom Manager in the Unit 5 Teaching Resources, p. 8

Guided Reading and Review in the Unit 5 Teaching Resources, p. 9

Guide to the Essentials, p. 83

Technology

Section Reading Support Transparencies

Africa: Mineral and Energy Resources

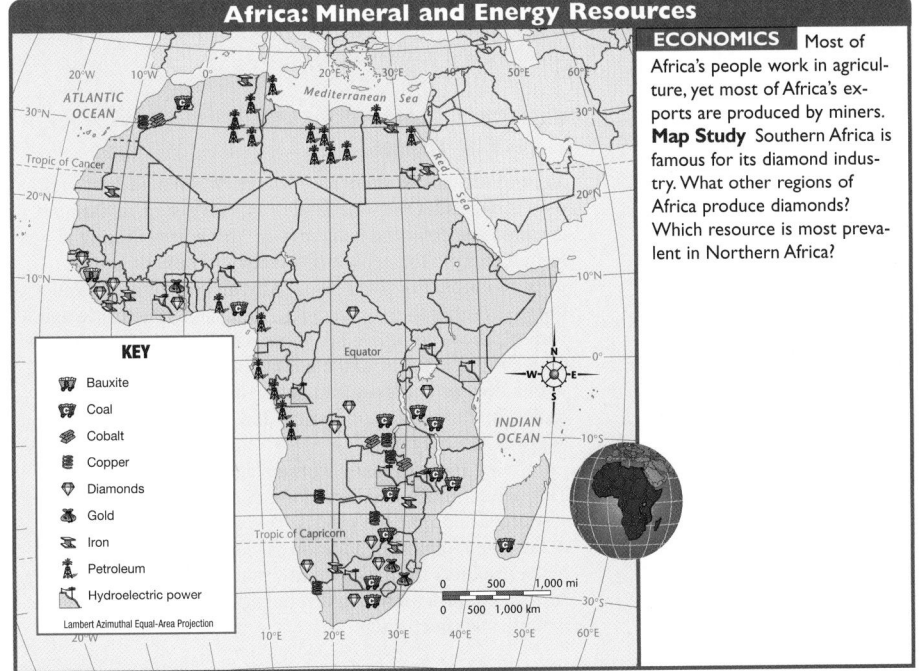

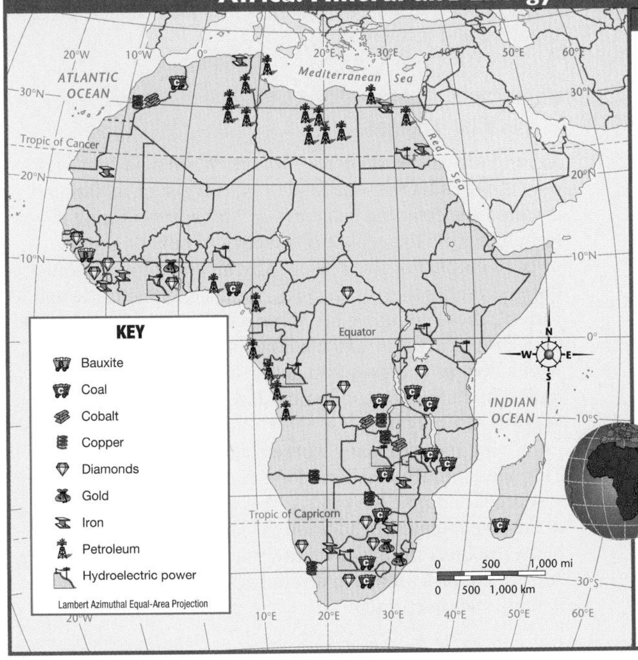

ECONOMICS Most of Africa's people work in agriculture, yet most of Africa's exports are produced by miners. **Map Study** Southern Africa is famous for its diamond industry. What other regions of Africa produce diamonds? Which resource is most prevalent in Northern Africa?

Cash Crops

In all regions of Africa, farmers raise crops to sell. These are called **cash crops**. Farmers in Côte d'Ivoire (koht deev WAR), Ghana, and Cameroon grow cash crops of coffee and cacao. Farmers in Kenya, Tanzania, Malawi, Zimbabwe, and Mozambique grow tea as a cash crop.

In recent years, more and more farmers have planted cash crops. As more land is used for cash crops, less land is planted with crops to feed families. In some regions, this has led to food shortages when cash crops have failed.

AS YOU READ

Summarize What are some examples of cash crops in Africa?

Mineral and Energy Resources

An economy is a system for producing, distributing, consuming, and owning goods, services, and wealth. Farming is the major part of Africa's economy. Mining is also important to Africa's economy.

Parts of Africa are rich in mineral resources. In North Africa, nations such as Libya and Algeria have large amounts of petroleum, which is used to make oil and gasoline. In West Africa, the country of Nigeria is a major oil producer. Ghana was once called the Gold

Answers to...

MAP STUDY

The western and central parts of Africa produce diamonds. Petroleum is the most prevalent resource in North Africa.

AS YOU READ

Examples include coffee, cacao, and tea.

2 Explore

Direct students to read the section. Stop them at intervals to discuss the following questions: How is subsistence farming different from raising cash crops? Why might Africans want to raise cash crops? What are the benefits of a diversified economy?

3 Teach

Have students work in small groups to create a cause-and-effect diagram concerning economic activities in Africa. Allow about 30 minutes for this activity.

Question for Discussion

ECONOMICS **How do you think farming to provide food for your family is different from farming cash crops?**

Subsistence farmers and cash crop farmers plant different crops, and cash crop farmers must grow much more than subsistence farmers do.

4 Assess/Reteach

See the answers to the Section 3 Assessment. You may also assess groups' cause-and-effect diagrams.

Acceptable diagrams accurately identify a minimum of three economic activities and the natural resources the activities require.

Commendable diagrams accurately identify four or more economic activities and the natural resources the activities require.

Outstanding diagrams accurately identify four or more economic activities and the natural resources the activities require. Diagrams include positive and negative effects of development.

SECTION 3 ASSESSMENT

AFTER YOU READ

1. (a) raising only enough crops to support a family (b) a crop that is raised to be sold
2. Answers will vary. Some of Africa's agricultural resources are cocoa, coffee, wheat, barley, tea, and fruits and vegetables.
3. Answers will vary. Some of Africa's mineral and energy resources are petroleum, oil, gold, diamond and copper.
4. Africans are trying to diversify their economy by producing a wider variety of crops, raw materials, and manufactured goods.
5. Paragraphs will vary. Sample paragraph: Subsistence farmers raise crops to support their families, and trade a few of their crops for other items they need to live. Cash crop farmers are farmers who raise crops in order to sell them. In recent years, more and more farmers have raised cash crops.
6. It is important for countries to diversify their economies so that they don't become too dependent on just one industry, such as farming. This protects their economy against the failure of a major cash crop or drop in world prices for an important mineral export.
7. Students may list cocoa, coffee, wood, and oil. Accept all reasonable responses.

SCIENCE, TECHNOLOGY AND SOCIETY

Mining a Natural Resource

South Africa is the world's leading supplier of gold, providing about 500 metric tons a year, more than half of the world's supply. A gold miner in South Africa works more than two miles underground in a huge mine, which operates both night and day. The gold from these mines is used to make jewelry, coins and even teeth for people around the world.

A modern underground mine uses vehicles, railroad cars, elevators that hold dozens of workers at a time, a power supply, and a ventilation shaft which pumps clean air into the mine. Safety is an important issue in the mining process, and most mines try hard to protect the workers and their equipment.

Critical Thinking Compare working in a gold mine to working on a cash crop farm in Africa. Which would you prefer and why?

Coast because it was a leading exporter of African gold. Other mineral resources from Africa include copper, silver, uranium, and diamonds.

Africa's Future Economic Development

Most of Africa's workers are farmers. When a nation's economy is dependent on one kind of industry, such as farming, it is called a specialized economy. In Africa, specializing in just farming makes the economy sensitive to rainfall and the price of crops. For this reason, African countries are now trying to diversify their economies. To diversify means to add variety. These countries are working to produce a variety of crops, raw materials, and manufactured goods. A country with a diverse economy will not be hurt as much if a major cash crop fails or if world prices for one of its major mineral exports suddenly drop.

Mining requires many workers and costly equipment. Throughout much of Africa, foreign companies mine African resources and take the profits. This system does little to help African economies. In addition, Africa has few factories to make products from its own raw materials. Therefore, many African countries want to diversify their economies to include manufacturing.

SECTION 3 ASSESSMENT

AFTER YOU READ

RECALL

1. Define: (a) subsistence farming, (b) cash crop

COMPREHENSION

2. What are Africa's agricultural resources?
3. What are Africa's mineral and energy resources?
4. How are Africans preparing for their economic future?

CRITICAL THINKING

5. **Exploring the Main Idea** Review the Main Idea statement at the beginning of this section. Then, write a paragraph describing and comparing subsistence farming and farming for cash crops.
6. **Identifying Central Issues** Why is it important for countries in Africa to diversify their economies?

ACTIVITY

7. **Writing to Learn** List some of Africa's natural resources that you and your family use. Then, write a paragraph that explains which you would miss most if you did not have it—and why you would miss it.

Resource Directory

Teaching Resources

Section Quiz in the Unit 5 Teaching Resources, p. 10

Chapter Summary in the Unit 5 Teaching Resources, p. 11

Vocabulary in the Unit 5 Teaching Resources, p. 12

Reteaching in the Unit 5 Teaching Resources, p. 13

Enrichment in the Unit 5 Teaching Resources, p. 14

Critical Thinking in the Unit 5 Teaching Resources, p. 15

Answers to...

CRITICAL THINKING

Students' responses will vary. Make sure students provide details to support their answers.

Comparing and Contrasting

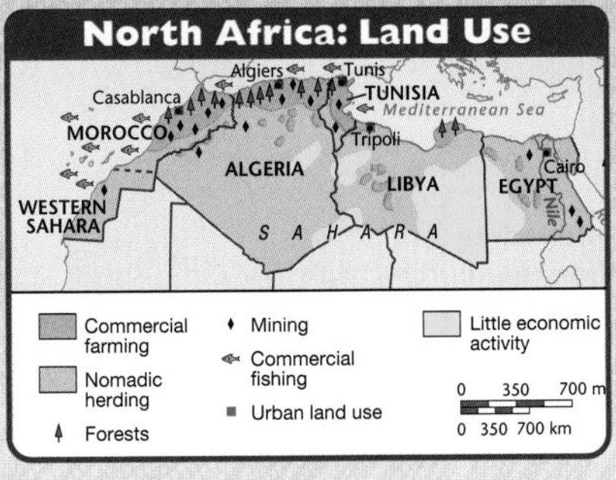

Learn the Skill

When you compare and contrast, you look for similarities and differences between or among objects and ideas. Finding these similarities and differences can help you organize, understand, and draw conclusions from the information you read.

The map above shows land use in North Africa. Using the map, you can compare and contrast land use in Algeria and Libya. To compare and contrast, follow these steps:

A. Determine the purpose for comparing and contrasting. What are you being asked to compare and contrast? In this case, you are being asked to compare and contrast land use in Algeria with land use in Libya.

B. Examine the information carefully. First, locate each country on the map. Then, read the information in the map key. Using the key, identify each type of land use in each country. From the map, you can see that land is used in Algeria primarily for nomadic herding, with areas in the north of the country used for commercial farming and mining. There are a few areas where there is little economic activity. In Libya, most of the land is used for nomadic herding, with some areas used for commercial farming. Almost half of the country has little economic activity.

C. Identify the similarities between or among the objects or ideas. Both countries use a majority of the land for nomadic herding, with smaller areas of commercial farming. In addition, both countries have areas with little economic activity.

D. Identify the differences. Algeria uses a larger percentage of the land for both nomadic herding and commercial farming than Libya. Algeria also uses land for mining, which Libya does not. Libya has a larger amount of land with little economic activity than Algeria.

E. Summarize these similarities and differences in order to draw conclusions. From the map, you can conclude that Algeria uses more of its land for a wider variety of economic activities than Libya does.

Practice the Skill

Continue to study the map to learn more about land use in North Africa. Follow the steps you learned to compare and contrast land use in Morocco and Egypt.

Apply the Skill

See the Chapter Review and Assessment at the end of this chapter for more questions on comparing and contrasting.

Lesson Objectives

1. Understand how to read and use a land use map.
2. Compare and contrast information on a land use map for different countries.

Lesson Plan

1 Engage

Ask students to discuss examples from their own experiences in which they had to compare and contrast information. Examples might include shopping for a particular project or deciding on where to go on a family vacation.

2 Explore

Remind students that they have seen land use maps earlier in their textbook. Ask them to recall the purpose of these kinds of maps. Then, ask them to read the map. What countries are shown? What do the colored areas on the map represent?

3 Teach

Direct students to read the steps under "Learn the Skill." Encourage students to use a graphic organizer, such as a Venn diagram, to help them record and compare the information about each country's use of land.

4 Assess/Reteach

To further assess students' understanding of comparing and contrasting, have them complete the "Applying Your Skills" part of the Chapter Review and Assessment at the end of the chapter.

Resource Directory

Technology

Social Studies Skills Tutor CD-ROM

Answers to...

PRACTICE THE SKILL

Students should note that both Morocco and Egypt use their land for mining. In addition, Egypt has a sizable area with little or no economic activity, while Morocco does not.

CHAPTER 19

Review and Assessment

Creating a Chapter Summary

Physical Features Africa is made up of four regions. Major landforms include plateaus, coastal plains, and the Great Rift Valley.

Humans and the Physical Environment Africa has many different climate regions affected by nearness to the Equator and landforms and bodies of water.

Natural Resources agricultural, mineral, and energy resources. Land is one of Africa's most valuable resources, and many Africans earn a living farming. Some countries like Africa are now developing policies and strategies to diversify, or expand, their economies.

Reviewing Key Terms

1. rift
2. irrigate
3. nomads
4. cash crop
5. savanna

Reviewing the Main Ideas

1. the plateau, coastal plains, Great Rift Valley, rivers
2. They are at high elevations.
3. because these areas are mostly desert and cannot be farmed
4. Subsistence farmers grow only enough crops to support their families. Cash crop farmers grow enough crops to sell.
5. Cacao beans and coffee are grown in Cote d'Ivoire, Ghana, and Cameroon; tea is grown in Kenya, Tanzania, Malawi, Zimbabwe, and Mozambique. Gold is mined in Ghana.
6. Diversification will help African countries protect themselves against problems caused by the failure of a major cash crop or a drop in world prices for an important export.

CHAPTER 19

Review and Assessment

Creating a Chapter Summary

On a separate piece of paper, draw a web like this one, and include the information that summarizes the information in each of the sections of the chapter. Add more ovals to the web as necessary.

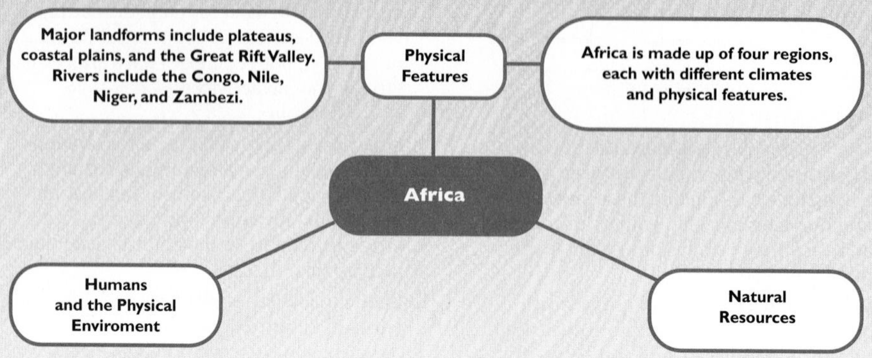
Major landforms include plateaus, coastal plains, and the Great Rift Valley. Rivers include the Congo, Nile, Niger, and Zambezi.
Physical Features
Africa is made up of four regions, each with different climates and physical features.
Africa
Humans and the Physical Enviroment
Natural Resources

Reviewing Key Terms

Use the following key terms to complete the sentences below.

cash crop nomads savanna rift irrigate

1. A ________ is a deep trench.
2. Because Ethiopia receives adequate rainfall, most farmers do not ________ their crops.
3. ________ are people who move from place to place to earn a living.
4. A crop sold for a profit is known as a ________.
5. A ________ is a region of tall grasses.

Reviewing the Main Ideas

1. List four major physical features of Africa. (Section 1)
2. Why might some parts of Africa have a cool climate even though they are near the Equator? (Section 2)
3. Explain why there is little or no farming in much of North Africa and parts of Southern Africa. (Section 2)
4. How is subsistence farming in Africa different from farming to raise cash crops? (Section 3)
5. List three cash crops grown in Africa, and where they are grown. Name one mineral resource found in Africa, and where it is found. (Section 3)
6. Explain why many African nations are trying to diversify their economies. (Section 3)

368 UNIT 5 AFRICA

Map Activity

Africa

For each place listed, write the letter from the map that shows its location.

1. Nile River
2. Congo River
3. Sahara
4. Zambezi River
5. Niger River
6. Great Rift Valley

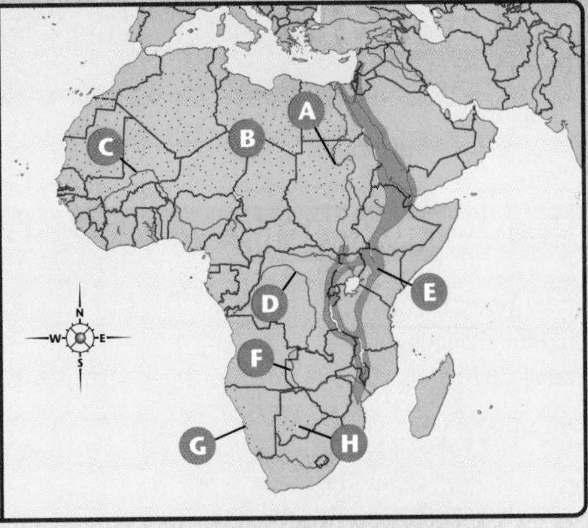

Take It to the NET

Enrichment For more map activities using geography skills, visit the social studies section of **phschool.com.**

Writing Activity

1. **Writing a Report** Describe some challenges Africans face that are caused by Africa's landforms or climate. Give examples of how Africans overcome, or are working to overcome, these challenges.
2. **Writing a Letter** Imagine that you have just returned from a trip to Africa. Write a letter to a friend describing some of the physical features and climates that you encountered in several different regions of Africa. Describe how the landscape and climate were similar to or different from the landscape and climate where you live.

Critical Thinking

1. **Identifying Central Issues** Explain the meaning of this statement. Give an example to support it. "People in Africa tend to live in grassland regions."
2. **Recognizing Cause and Effect** How did the yearly flooding of the Nile affect farmers in the Nile Valley? How did the building of the Aswan Dam affect the farmers?

Applying Your Skills

Study the map of Africa's mineral and energy resources on page 365. Refer to the Skills for Life activity on page 367 to help you complete the following activity.

Compare and contrast the resources of North Africa with those of Southern Africa.

Take It to the NET

Activity Create a map of Africa and include major geographical features, climate, and natural resources. Visit the World Explorer: People, Places, and Cultures section of **phschool.com** for help in completing this activity.

Chapter 19 Self-Test As a final review activity, take the Chapter 19 Self-Test and get instant feedback on your answers. To take the test, visit the Social Studies section of **phschool.com.**

Map Activity

1. A **2.** D **3.** B **4.** F **5.** C **6.** E

Writing Activity

1. Reports will vary. Accept reports that describe some of the following: difficulties traveling or transporting goods because of mountains or deserts, food or water shortages due to poor soil or unpredictable rainfall, crop failure due to lack of rain or the destruction of rain forests. Students may mention that Africans are working to overcome these problems by diversifying their economy, and may describe ways that Africans adapt to the physical environment.
2. Letters will vary. Accept letters that contain accurate details about the features of the landscape and climate in several different regions of Africa, and compare and contrast these features with those found in your region of the world.

Critical Thinking

1. People cannot live as easily in extreme climate areas such as deserts and rain forests. The soil in grassland areas is good for farming, so people can grow food for themselves.
2. Yearly Nile flooding brought water and fertile soil to farmlands, enabling farmers to grow crops. The Aswan Dam controls the flooding of the Nile. Water contained in a lake created by the dam is channeled to crops in the desert.

Applying Your Skills

North Africa's resources are mostly made up of petroleum, with coal, cobalt, and copper to a lesser extent. Southern Africa's resources are much more varied and include diamonds, coal, gold, cobalt, and copper.

Resource Directory

Teaching Resources

Cooperative Learning Activity in the Unit 5 Teaching Resources, pp. 104–107

Chapter Tests Forms A and B in the Unit 5 Teaching Resources, pp. 130–135

Guide to the Essentials, Ch. 19 Test, p. 84

Other Print Resources

Chapter Tests with ExamView® Test Bank, Ch. 19

Technology

ExamView® Test Bank CD-ROM, Ch. 19

Resource Pro® CD-ROM

CHAPTER 19 REVIEW AND ASSESSMENT 369

Chapter 20 Planning Guide

Resource Manager

	CORE INSTRUCTION	READING/SKILLS
Chapter-Level Resources	**Teaching Resources** Program Overview Pacing Charts **Technology** Resource Pro® CD-ROM Companion Web site, phschool.com • eTeach	**Technology** Social Studies Skills Tutor CD-ROM Student Edition on Audio CD, Ch. 20
1 Africa's First People 1. Explain how early Africans lived and got food. 2. Identify effects of farming and herding on early Africans. 3. Summarize the features of the civilizations along the Nile River. 4. Describe the possible causes and effects of the Bantu migration.	**Teaching Resources** **Unit 5** Classroom Manager, p. 17 Guided Reading and Review, p. 18	**Teaching Resources** Guide to the Essentials, p. 85 Social Studies and Geography Skills, p. 59 **Technology** Section Reading Support Transparencies
2 Kingdoms and Empires 1. Identify the ways that trade influenced kingdoms and civilizations in East Africa. 2. Trace the spread of Islam across Africa. 3. Identify key trade routes from East African city-states.	**Teaching Resources** **Unit 5** Classroom Manager, p. 20 Guided Reading and Review, p. 21	**Teaching Resources** Guide to the Essentials, p. 86 **Technology** Section Reading Support Transparencies
3 European Influence and African Independence 1. Describe the effects of colonization of Africa by European nations. 2. Summarize how African countries regained independence. 3. Explain some of the challenges African leaders faced after gaining independence.	**Teaching Resources** **Unit 5** Classroom Manager, p. 23 Guided Reading and Review, p. 24 Chapter Summary, p. 26 Vocabulary, p. 27 Reteaching, p. 28	**Teaching Resources** Guide to the Essentials, p. 87 **Technology** Section Reading Support Transparencies

NRICHMENT / PRE-AP

Teaching Resources
Primary Sources and Literature Readings

Other Print Resources
DK Atlas

Technology
World Video Explorer: Africa's Early Trading Empire
Companion Web site, phschool.com

Teaching Resources
Unit 5
Enrichment, p. 29
Cooperative Learning Activity, pp. 108–11

Technology
Color Transparencies 102, 104–106

ASSESSMENT

Prentice Hall Assessment System

Core Assessment
Chapter Tests with ExamView® Test Bank, Ch. 20
ExamView® Test Bank CD-ROM, Ch. 20

Standardized Test Preparation
Diagnose and Prescribe
Diagnostic Tests for Middle Grades Social Studies Skills
Review and Reteach
Review Book for World Studies
Practice and Assess
Test-taking Strategies with Transparencies for Middle Grades Test Prep Book
Test-taking Strategies Posters

Teaching Resources
Unit 5
Section Quizzes, pp. 19, 22, and 25
Chapter Tests, pp. 136–141

Technology
Companion Web site, phschool.com
Ch. 20 Self-Test

World Video Explorer
Each region of the world is explored through regional flyovers and investigative field trips. Case study segments give students an in-depth view of the history, economy, government, and culture of a key place in each region. Case studies include Nigeria, Mexico, China, British Columbia, and the Czech Republic.

In Your Classroom

CUSTOMIZE FOR INDIVIDUAL NEEDS

Gifted and Talented

Teacher's Edition
- Exploring History Through Literature, p. 372
- Write a Tribute, p. 376

Teaching Resources
- Enrichment, p. 29
- Primary Sources and Literature Readings

Honors/Pre-AP

Teacher's Edition
- Write a Tribute, p. 376
- Pan-Africanism, p. 379

Teaching Resources
- Critical Thinking, p. 30
- Primary Sources and Literature Readings

ESL

Teacher's Edition
- Amazing Grace, p. 379
- Mural of the Slave Trade, p. 379

Teaching Resources
- Guided Reading and Review, pp. 18, 21, and 24
- Vocabulary, p. 27
- Reteaching, p. 28
- Guide to the Essentials, pp. 85–87
- Social Studies and Geography Skills, p. 59

Technology
- Social Studies Skills Tutor CD-ROM
- Section Reading Support Transparencies

Less Proficient Readers

Teacher's Edition
- Mural of the Slave Trade, p. 379
- Pan-Africanism, p. 379

Teaching Resources
- Guided Reading and Review, pp. 18, 21, and 24
- Vocabulary, p. 27
- Reteaching, p. 28
- Guide to the Essentials, pp. 85–87
- Social Studies and Geography Skills, p. 59

Technology
- Social Studies Skills Tutor CD-ROM
- Section Reading Support Transparencies

Less Proficient Writers

Teacher's Edition
- Exploring History Through Literature, p. 372
- Mural of the Slave Trade, p. 372
- Amazing Grace, p. 372

Teaching Resources
- Guided Reading and Review, pp. 18, 21, and 24
- Vocabulary, p. 27
- Guide to the Essentials, pp. 85–87
- Social Studies and Geography Skills, p. 59

Technology
- Social Studies Skills Tutor CD-ROM
- Section Reading Support Transparencies

DORLING KINDERSLEY

At the end of each unit, you will find information adapted from Dorling Kindersley's *Illustrated Children's Encyclopedia* that connects to the region being studied and to one of the seven content strands. In addition, your resources include Dorling Kindersley's *Atlas*, which contains valuable information about countries from around the world.

TEACHER'S EDITION INDEX

CHAPTER 20 PACING SUGGESTIONS

For 90-minute Blocks

See suggestions in the Teaching Resources Pacing Charts for Chapter 20. Use Color Transparencies 102, 104–106.

Running Out of Time?

See the Guide to the Essentials, pp. 85–87.

INTERDISCIPLINARY LINKS

Middle Grades Math: Tools for Success
Course 1, Lesson 1-2 **Make a Table**

Science Explorer
Cells and Heredity, Chapter 5, **Changes over Time**

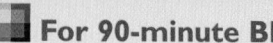

BIBLIOGRAPHY

For the Teacher

Halliburton, Warren J. *African Industries; Africa's Struggle to Survive; City and Village Life* (*Africa Today* series). Crestwood, 1993.

Ibazebo, Isimeme. *Exploration into Africa.* New Discovery, 1994.

Koslow, Philip. *The Kingdoms of Africa.* Chelsea House, 1995.

McIntosh, Jane, and Clint Twist. *Civilizations: Ten Thousand Years of Ancient History.* Dorling Kindersley, 2001.

For the Student

Easy

Wisniewski, David. *Sundiata: Lion King of Mali.* Clarion, 1992.

Average

Africa (*Eyewitness* series). Dorling Kindersley, 2001.

Challenging

Feelings, Tom. *The Middle Passage: White Ships, Black Cargo.* Dial, 1995.

Literature Connection

Hensen, Joyce. *The Captive.* Scholastic, 1994.

Rupert, Janet E. *The African Mask.* Clarion, 1994.

Take It to the NET

The World Explorer companion Web site, found on **phschool.com**, offers activities for exploring geographical, historical, and cultural resources on the Internet. It also provides on-line links for key content and all Section and Chapter Assessment activities.

The **Teacher site** also provides teachers with regional data and ideas for student research and activities.

Students can use the **Student site** to find chapter-by-chapter Internet resource links and to access Self-Tests.

CHAPTER 20

Connecting to the
Guiding Questions

In this chapter, students will read about the history of Africa. Content in this chapter corresponds to the following Guiding Questions outlined at the beginning of the unit:

- How have Africans been affected by their history?
- How has geography affected the way African societies have developed?

Using the Time Line Activities

Explain to students that this time line shows a period in history from 1450 to 1950. Make sure students understand how to read the time line.

- Portugal was the first European county to become involved in Africa. The first Europeans came to Africa to build trading posts, and later to trade slaves. Britain, France, Belgium, and Portugal controlled nearly all of Africa by 1918. Resistance against colonization was not successful because Europeans had greater military power.
- Students should choose eight significant events from African history after the 1920s, and create a time line showing these events and the dates during which they occurred.

Heterogeneous Groups

The following activities are suitable for heterogeneous groups.

Culture

Mural of the Slave Trade, p. 379

Journal Writing

Pan-Africanism, p. 379

eTeach

Be sure to check out this month's discussion with a Master Teacher. Go to **phschool.com**.

CHAPTER 20

AFRICA: Shaped by History

Europeans in Africa

1450 | 1550 | 1650 | 1750 | 1850 | 1950

- **1400s** Portugal begins building trading posts in West Africa.
- **1500s–1800s** Europeans trade slaves across the Atlantic Ocean.
- **1500s–1800s** Portuguese, Dutch, French, and English set up trading posts all along Africa's coasts.
- **1652** The Dutch establish a colony at the Cape of Good Hope.
- **1884** The Berlin Conference carves up control of Africa among colonial powers.
- **1912** South Africans form the African National Congress to protest laws that treated Africans unfairly.
- **1918** Britain, France, Belgium, and Portugal control nearly all of Africa.
- **1920s** Pan-African movement begins to form, with the slogan, "Africa for Africans."

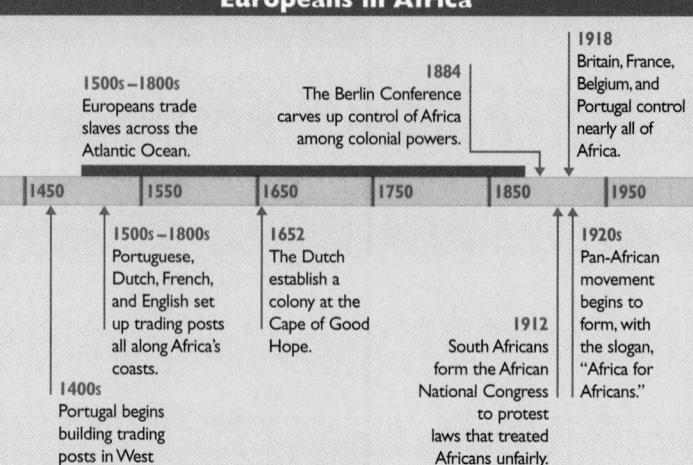

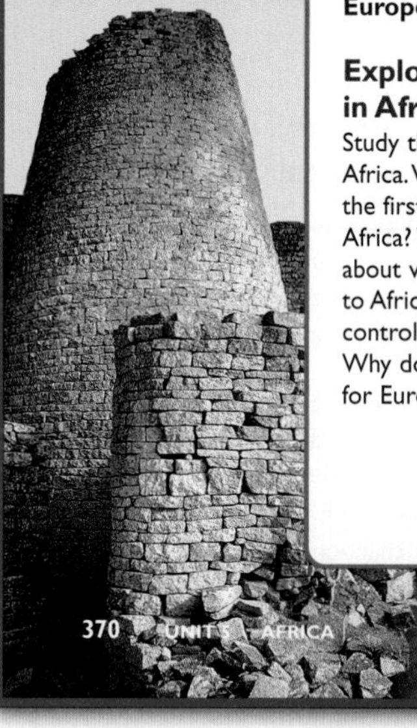

USING TIME LINES

Africans resisted European colonization, but as this time line shows, Europe slowly took control of more and more of Africa.

Exploring Europeans in Africa

Study the time line of Europeans in Africa. Which European country was the first to become involved with Africa? What does the time line reveal about why the first Europeans came to Africa? What European countries controlled most of Africa by 1918? Why do you think it was possible for Europeans to colonize Africa?

Making a Time Line

The last entry on the time line is for the 1920s. What happened next in African history? Use the library and the Internet to research major events in Africa's history from the 1920s to the present. Choose eight significant events from this period and create a time line showing the dates and events that you chose.

370 UNIT 5 AFRICA

Resource Directory

Teaching Resources

Primary Sources and Literature Readings extend content with a selection related to the concepts in this chapter.

Other Print Resources

DK Atlas

Technology

Africa's Early Trading Empire, from the World Video Explorer, enhances students' understanding of the trading empires of Ghana, Mal, and Songhai.

Student Edition on Audio CD, Ch. 20

SECTION 1

Africa's First People

BEFORE YOU READ

READING FOCUS

1. How did early Africans adapt to their environment?
2. How did the emergence of farming and herding change life for early Africans?
3. What are the features of a civilization?
4. How did important ideas and discoveries spread throughout Africa?

KEY TERMS

hunter-gatherer
domesticate
fertile
surplus
civilization
migrate
ethnic group

KEY PEOPLE AND PLACES

Louis Leakey
Egypt
Nubia
Bantu-speakers

NOTE TAKING

Copy this chart. As you read the section, complete the chart to show important facts or new ideas and discoveries of early Africans.

Stone Age	Farmers	Nile Civilizations

MAIN IDEA

Africa's first peoples survived by developing tools and techniques for farming and herding, and they later spread out and settled into societies.

Setting the Scene

Today the dry sands of the Sahara cover most of North Africa. Until about 4,000 years ago, however, this large area held enough water to support many people and animals. Scientists think that Africa's first farmers lived there. Paintings on cliffs and cave walls tell their story.

But the continent's first people lived in East Africa. We know this because of the stones and bones they left behind.

Hunter-Gatherers

The earliest humans probably survived by gathering wild fruits, nuts, and roots. These **hunter-gatherers** also hunted animals for meat and clothing. They made tools out of wood, animal bones, and then stone. The first use of stone tools marks the beginning of a period scientists call the Stone Age.

These stone tools worked very well. The scientist **Louis Leakey** found some of the first evidence of early people in East Africa. He also taught himself to make and use tools he had discovered.

CULTURE This painting was originally found in Algeria. **Critical Thinking** Do you think the horns on this woman's helmet suggest that the Sahara may once have supported animal life? Why?

Resource Directory

Teaching Resources

Classroom Manager in the Unit 5 Teaching Resources, p. 17

Guided Reading and Review in the Unit 5 Teaching Resources, p. 18

Guide to the Essentials, p. 85

Technology

Section Reading Support Transparencies

SECTION 1

Lesson Objectives

1. Explain how early Africans lived and got food.
2. Identify effects of farming and herding on early Africans.
3. Summarize the features of the civilizations along the Nile River.
4. Describe the possible causes and effects of the Bantu migration.

Lesson Plan

1 Engage

Warm-Up Activity

Ask students to imagine that a thousand years from now, archaeologist are studying some of the items in your classroom. Challenge students to speculate on what the scientists might learn about them by studying various items, such as pencils, a globe, student desks, a U.S. flag, and so on.

Activating Prior Knowledge

Ask students to think about how they know about events that occurred when they were too young to remember. Have they heard them described by family members? Have they seen photographs or home videos? Discuss with the class why people need to remember.

2 Explore

Ask students to consider the following questions as they read: What have scientists learned about the daily lives of early humans? Why did early Africans begin to farm? What were some characteristics of the civilizations along the Nile?

Answers to...

CRITICAL THINKING

Yes, because they are animal horns, suggesting that animals would have lived there.

Lesson Plan continued

3 Teach

Organize the class into five teams to compose some answers to the questions given in the Explore part of the Lesson Plan. Observe individual participation. After teams have completed their discussions, call on a member from each team to share their answer to one of the questions. This activity should take about 20 minutes.

Question for Discussion

ECONOMICS **Why would food surpluses allow some people in a community to do work other than farming?**

People would have food to eat without having to grow it, thereby allowing them time to do other kinds of work.

4 Assess/Reteach

See the answers to the Section 1 Assessment. You may also use team discussions as a basis for assessment.

Acceptable participation includes volunteering some correct information and ideas to the team discussion.

Commendable participation is demonstrated by taking an equal part in group discussions.

Outstanding participation includes insightful contributions to the group and class discussions.

ACTIVITY

Interdisciplinary Connections

Exploring History Through Literature Giuseppe Verdi's opera *Aïda* tells about the love between a Nubian princess, who is a slave in Egypt, and an Egyptian general during the period when the two kingdoms were at war. The opera provides insights into the personal conflicts and tensions that existed between the two cultures. Leontyne Price retells this story in the book *Aïda* (Harcourt, 1990). You might direct students in performing the Price version as a dramatic reading.

Musical/Rhythmic

Early Farming
SCIENCE AND TECHNOLOGY

When hunter-gatherers settled down in one area and became farmers, they spent many hours tilling, planting by hand, harvesting crops, and caring for domesticated animals. They used only tools that they could make by hand. Farmers used axes, like this one, to clear the land.

Critical Thinking
Would it be more difficult being a farmer, or a hunter-gatherer? Why do you think a hunter-gatherer would choose to become a farmer?

Farming and Herding

When hunter-gatherers began to farm and to herd animals, they probably planted wild grains such as wheat, barley, sorghum, and millet. At first, gatherers just protected the areas where these grains grew best. Then, they began to save some seed to plant for the next year's crop.

Later, people began to **domesticate** plants, or adapt them for their own use. People also domesticated animals by taming them and developing ways to use them.

Domesticating plants and animals meant people could plant their own crops. They did not have to travel to places where grains were already growing. As a result, they could settle in a certain place, usually where the land was **fertile,** or productive. Some communities produced a food **surplus,** or more than they needed. Surpluses allowed some people in the community to do work other than farming.

LINKS TO Math

The Thirst Zone
Africa's first farmers probably lived in Algeria, in North Africa. Thousands of years ago, more rain fell in this region. But today, much of North Africa is known as the "Thirst Zone." People need to drink about 2.5 quarts (2.4 liters) of water per day. People also use water for washing and farming. All in all, each person needs at least 21 quarts (20 liters) of water per day. In the Thirst Zone, only about five quarts (5 liters) of water per person is available.

Civilizations on the Nile

A **civilization** is a society with cities, a government, and social classes. Social classes form when people do a variety of jobs. Civilizations also have architecture, writing, and art. One civilization arose on the Nile River about 5,000 years ago.

Egypt Each summer, the Nile River flooded its banks. It left a layer of fertile silt that was ideal for farming. People began farming along the banks of the Nile by around 4000 B.C. They settled in scattered villages. Over the centuries, these villages grew into the civilization of ancient **Egypt.**

Ancient Egypt was ruled by kings and queens called pharaohs (FAY rohz). The people believed the pharaohs were gods as well as kings. When some pharaohs died, they were buried in pyramids. People painted murals and picture-writings called hieroglyphics (hy ur oh GLIF iks) on the walls in these pyramids.

Egyptian civilization included more than just the pyramids. The Egyptians were advanced in paper-making, architecture, medicine, and mathematics.

Nubia Starting in about 6000 B.C., several civilizations arose south of Egypt. This area was called **Nubia.** The final and greatest Nubian kingdom arose in the city of Meroë (MER oh ee) during the 500s B.C. It thrived until about the middle of the A.D. 300s. Meroë was probably the first place in Africa where iron was made.

Answers to...

CRITICAL THINKING

Students may say that it would be more difficult being a hunter-gatherer because the food supply would not always be constant. This is why a hunter-gatherer might choose to become a farmer.

Resource Directory

Teaching Resources

Social Studies and Geography Skills,
Reading a Time Line, p. 59

Ancient Art

CULTURE

This Egyptian wall painting shows Nubian princes arriving in Egypt. At first, Egypt ruled Nubia, but later, Nubia conquered much of Egypt.

Critical Thinking
What objects are the figures walking behind the princes carrying? Why do you think they are carrying these items?

The Bantu Migrations

By about 500 B.C., West Africans had learned to heat and shape iron. They used it to form parts of tools such as arrowheads, ax heads, and hoe blades. The strong iron tools made farming easier and created food surpluses. As a result, West Africa's population increased.

Around 2,000 years ago, a group of people who spoke Bantu (BAN too) languages began to **migrate,** or move, out of West Africa, perhaps looking for new land to farm. Over hundreds of years, these **Bantu-speakers** settled in Central and Southern Africa. They introduced farming, herding, and iron tools to these regions. Today, people in this part of Africa belong to hundreds of **ethnic groups,** or groups that share languages, religions, family ties, and customs. But almost all of these ethnic groups speak Bantu languages.

SECTION I ASSESSMENT

AFTER YOU READ

RECALL

1. Identify: (a) Louis Leakey, (b) Egypt, (c) Nubia, (d) Bantu-speakers
2. Define: (a) hunter-gatherer, (b) domesticate, (c) fertile, (d) surplus, (e) civilization, (f) migrate, (g) ethnic group

COMPREHENSION

3. What techniques did the earliest Africans use to work and feed themselves?
4. What caused early Africans to begin settling in permanent communities?
5. What were two important early civilizations in Africa?
6. How did the Bantu-speakers contribute to the development of Africa?

CRITICAL THINKING AND WRITING

7. **Exploring the Main Idea** Review the Main Idea statement at the beginning of this section. Then, create a time line showing dates and the sequence of some important developments from the earliest people in East Africa leading up to the civilizations along the Nile.
8. **Identifying Central Issues** Write a paragraph describing some of the important contributions of early Africans.

ACTIVITY

9. **Writing to Learn** Imagine you are in ancient Egypt. Write a message that might be found in hieroglyphics on a pyramid wall about an important event that you want to record for history.

SECTION I ASSESSMENT

AFTER YOU READ

1. (a) scientist who studied early humans in Africa (b) area along the Nile River where one of the first civilizations developed (c) area south of Egypt where several civilizations arose (d) West Africans who spoke Bantu languages and who migrated to Central and South Africa
2. (a) a person who hunted animals for meat and clothing and gathered wild fruits, nuts, and roots (b) to adapt plants and animals for use (c) productive (d) more than is needed (e) society with cities, government, and social classes (f) to move to a new land (g) a group that shares language, religion, family ties, and customs
3. The earliest Africans hunted animals and gathered food, and used stone tools.
4. They learned to domesticate plants and to herd and raise animals.
5. The Egyptian and Nubian civilizations that developed along the Nile are important early civilizations in Africa.
6. The Bantu brought tools, agricultural methods, and their language with them as they migrated.
7. Information on time lines will vary. Time lines should show Stone Age (25,000 years ago), Farmers and Herders (10,000–6,000 years ago), Nubian and Egyptian civilizations (8,000–6,000 years ago).
8. Paragraphs will vary. Possible contributions might include: cities, government, social classes, papermaking, mural painting, melting and shaping iron.
9. Messages will vary, but should be in pictograph form and should include relevant details about ancient Egyptian life.

Resource Directory

Teaching Resources

Section Quiz in the Unit 5 Teaching Resources, p. 19

Answers to...

CRITICAL THINKING

The figures are carrying gifts to present to the Egyptians, possibly as a peace offering.

CHAPTER 20 AFRICA: SHAPED BY HISTORY 373

SECTION 2

Lesson Objectives

1. Identify the ways that trade influenced kingdoms and civilizations in East Africa.
2. Trace the spread of Islam across Africa.
3. Identify key trade routes from East African city-states.

Lesson Plan

1 Engage

Warm-Up Activity

Ask students to look carefully at a physical map of Africa and to identify places on the map where they think ancient civilizations might have arisen. Suggest that they begin by listing the things that are needed to build a civilization, such as water and fertile land. Explain that they will be reading about some ancient African civilizations in this section. Encourage them to check their accuracy in predicting where civilizations were established.

Activating Prior Knowledge

Have the students think about what things they own or have at home that were made and came to the United States from other countries and what things were made in the United States. Ask them to make a short list and share it with a classmate. Then, combine students' lists and record the most frequently mentioned items on the chalkboard.

Answers to...

CRITICAL THINKING

Trade allowed people from different cultures to meet and interact with one another.

SECTION 2

Kingdoms and Empires

BEFORE YOU READ

READING FOCUS

1. Why was trade so significant to East Africa's kingdoms?
2. How did the Islamic religion spread from East Africa to other parts of Africa?
3. What were the important trade routes within and outside of East Africa?

NOTE TAKING

Copy these webs. As you read the section add information in the empty ovals about the important features of East Africa and West Africa.

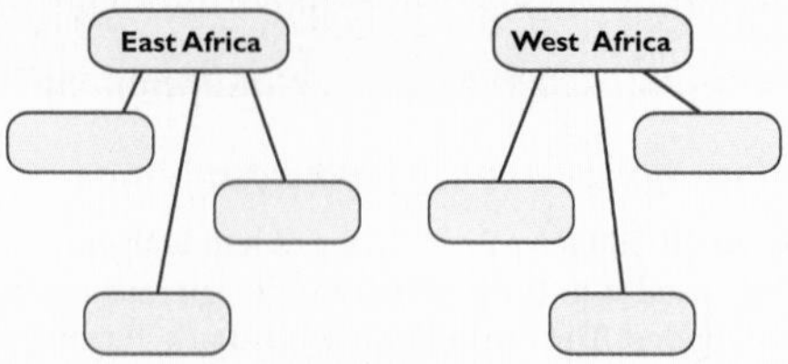

KEY TERMS	KEY PEOPLE AND PLACES	
Quran	Aksum	Songhai
pilgrimage	Ghana	Mansa Musa
Swahili	Mali	Tombouctou
city-state		Kilwa

MAIN IDEA

African societies were influenced by traders from other cultures who brought not only goods, but also new religions and languages.

Trade in East Africa

ECONOMICS As early as A.D. 1100, traders in East Africa bought and sold goods from many parts of the world. Traders bought animal skins, gold, and ivory, or elephant tusks (shown) from Africa and sold them in India and China. **Critical Thinking** How did trade help people in East Africa to learn about other cultures?

Setting the Scene

Adulis was the most important city in Aksum, a bustling trade center along the Red Sea. In the year A.D. 1, a Greek writer made a list of things you could buy there:

"Cloth made in Egypt…and brass, which is used for ornament and cut pieces instead of coin; sheets of soft copper, used for cooking utensils and cut up for bracelets and anklets for the women; iron, which is made into spears.…"

An East African Kingdom

Aksum was located in East Africa, in what is now Ethiopia and Eritrea. Around 1000 B.C., African and Arab traders began settling along the west coast of the Red Sea. These were the ancestors of the people of Aksum. Over time, Aksum came to control trade in the Red Sea. In time, Aksum would control a trade network that stretched from the Mediterranean Sea to India.

Ideas, as well as goods, traveled along these trade routes. The Christian religion traveled to Aksum along these routes. In fact, Aksum became a center of the early Ethiopian Christian Church. But Aksum began to decline in the 600s. Then, Arabs took control of much of the region's trade.

Resource Directory

Teaching Resources

Classroom Manager in the Unit 5 Teaching Resources, p. 20

Guided Reading and Review in the Unit 5 Teaching Resources, p. 21

Guide to the Essentials, p. 86

Technology

Section Reading Support Transparencies

374 UNIT 5 AFRICA

West African Kingdoms

As Aksum declined, great kingdoms arose on the other side of the continent, in West Africa. The power of these kingdoms was based on the trade of salt and gold. People need salt to survive, especially in hot areas like West Africa, but the people there had no local sources of salt. However, they had plenty of gold. For the people of North Africa, the opposite was true; they had salt, but no gold.

A brisk trade between North Africa and West Africa quickly grew. Control of this trade brought power and riches to three West African kingdoms—**Ghana** (GAH nuh), **Mali** (MAH lee), and **Songhai** (SAWNG hy).

Ghana The kingdom of Ghana was located between the Senegal and Niger rivers. From this location Ghana controlled trade across West Africa. Ghana's kings grew rich from the taxes they charged on the salt, gold, and other goods that flowed through their land. The flow of gold was so great that Arab writers called Ghana "land of gold." But in time, Ghana lost control of the trade routes. It gave way to a new power, the kingdom of Mali.

Mali and the Spread of Islam The kingdom of Mali arose in the mid-1200s in the Upper Niger Valley. Mali's powerful kings controlled both the gold mines of the south and the salt supplies of the north. In Mali, the king was called Mansa, which means "emperor."

Mali's most famous king, **Mansa Musa,** brought peace and order to the kingdom during his 25-year reign. He based his laws on the **Quran** (koo RAHN), the holy book of the religion of Islam. Over the centuries, Muslim traders had spread their religion into many parts of Africa.

In 1324, Mansa Musa made a **pilgrimage**—a religious journey—to the Arabian city of Mecca, a Muslim holy place where Muhammad, the prophet who first preached Islam, was born. Mansa Musa brought 60,000 people and eighty camels with him. Each camel carried 300 pounds (136 kg) of gold, which Mansa Musa gave to people along the way.

Mansa Musa's pilgrimage brought about new trading ties with other Muslim states. It also displayed Mali's wealth. Hearing the reports, Europe's rulers grew interested in African gold.

Songhai In time, Songhai became West Africa's most powerful kingdom. Its rulers controlled important trade routes and wealthy trading cities, such as **Tombouctou** (tohm book TOO), also a great Muslim learning center.

Songhai people still live near the Niger River, and Islam remains important in the region.

The Kingdom of Mali

CULTURE This image, showing Mansa Musa on his throne, is a detail from an old map of trading routes in Europe, Africa, and Asia. After Mansa Musa's pilgrimage to Mecca, Mali began to appear on maps throughout Asia and Europe. **Critical Thinking** Why do you think other countries in Asia and Europe became so interested in Mali?

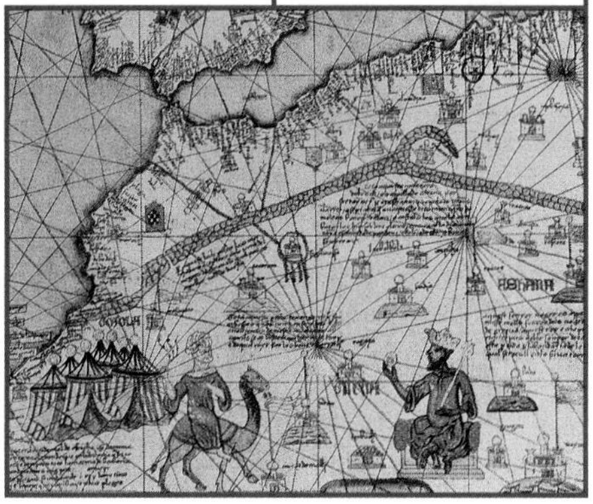

2 Explore

As students read the section, urge them to look for specific reasons for the success of each of the kingdoms and empires. Ask them to name some achievements of each, to explain which depended upon trade, and to identify which lasted the longest.

3 Teach

Have students create a chart that lists the kingdoms and city-states in rows. Have them label three columns: Time Period, Location, and Characteristics. Urge students to use the chart to compare and contrast the kingdoms and city-states. This activity should take about 25 minutes.

Question for Discussion

ECONOMICS **How did Ghana, Mali, and Songhai become wealthy from gold and salt even though they did not mine either one?**

They were powerful empires and trading centers that dominated nearby areas by controlling trade.

4 Assess/Reteach

See the answers to the Section 2 Assessment. You may also assess students' charts.

Acceptable work should include at least one detail in each cell of the chart.

Commendable work will have more than one specific detail in each cell of the chart.

Outstanding charts will provide a comprehensive comparison of the kingdoms and city-states.

SKILLS MINI LESSON

Locating Information

To **introduce** the skill, mention to students that they are surrounded by a sea of information. In order to locate the information they need, they will need to plan a route through that sea. Help students **practice** the skill by working with them to locate information about the kingdoms or city-states of ancient Africa. Have them clearly define the information they are seeking by formulating a question, for example: *Which goods were most important to traders in Mali?* Discuss with students the best sources for the information they are seeking. Have students **apply** the skill by researching the topic they chose and presenting the information they find in the form of a written report. Be sure students include a list of the sources they used.

Answers to...

CRITICAL THINKING

Mali had valuable resources, especially gold, which other countries would have been interested in.

ACTIVITY

Using Primary Sources

Write a Tribute It was said of Tombouctou: "Salt comes from the north, gold from the south, and the silver from the city of white men. But the word of God and the treasures of wisdom are only to be found in Tombouctou." Read aloud the quotation. Then, have students use the quotation as a model for writing a similar tribute to their school, community, or state. Encourage students to use literary devices such as rhythm, meter, and alliteration to make their tributes memorable.

Verbal/Linguistic

SECTION 2 ASSESSMENT

AFTER YOU READ

1. (a) ancient East African kingdom (b) kingdom between Senegal and Niger Rivers (c) kingdom that arose in the Upper Niger Valley (d) West Africa's most powerful kingdom (e) Muslim emperor of Mali (f) wealthy Songhai city and center of learning (g) East African city-state
2. (a) holy book of the religion of Islam (b) a religious journey (c) Bantu language with some Arab words mixed in (d) city with its own government, which often controlled surrounding land
3. The wealth and power of East African kingdoms was based primarily on trade.
4. Ideas, religions, and languages also spread along with trade.
5. East Africa traded across the Red Sea, the Mediterranean Sea, and to India and China.
6. Lists will vary, but may include: religion of Islam, Christianity, cotton, silk, porcelain, and Swahili language.
7. Students' journal entries should reflect the perspective of a young child in ancient Egypt.

East African Trade Routes

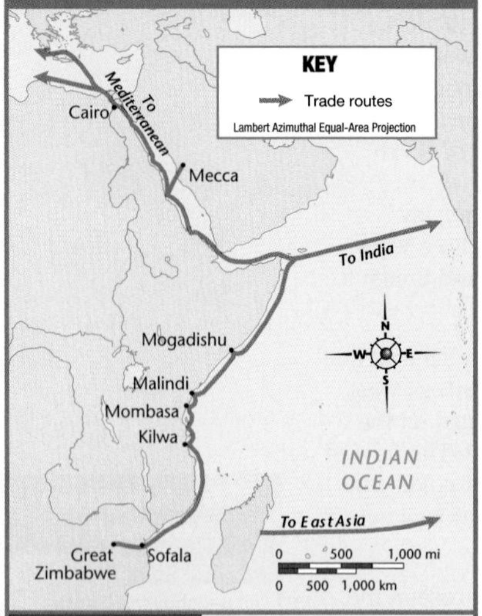

GEOGRAPHY Traders visiting East African city-states could buy gold from Africa, cotton from India, and porcelain from China. **Map Study** How were the East African city-states ideally located to become centers of trade?

East African City-States

As in West Africa, trade helped East African cities to develop. Around the time that Aksum declined, trading cities arose along East Africa's coast. Traders from these cities carried animal skins, ivory, and gold and other metals to India and China. The traders brought back many different goods.

Some of the traders who visited the area were Arab Muslims. In time, a new language called **Swahili** (swah HEE lee), developed in the area. It was a Bantu language with some Arab words mixed in. Today, many East Africans speak Swahili.

Some East African cities grew into powerful **city-states.** A city-state has its own government and controls much of the surrounding land. Among the greatest of these city-states were Malindi (muh LIN dee), Mombasa (mahm BAH suh), and **Kilwa** (KIL wah). These city-states grew rich from trade and huge taxes traders paid on goods they brought into the city.

Kilwa Ibn Batuta (ihb UHN ba TOO tah), a Muslim traveler from North Africa, visited Kilwa in 1331. He had seen great cities in China, India, and West Africa, but he wrote that Kilwa was "one of the most beautiful and best-constructed towns in the world." There, people lived in three-and four-story houses made of stone and sea coral.

SECTION 2 ASSESSMENT

AFTER YOU READ

RECALL

1. Identify: (a) Aksum, (b) Ghana, (c) Mali, (d) Songhai, (e) Mansa Musa, (f) Tombouctou, (g) Kilwa
2. Define: (a) Quran, (b) pilgrimage, (c) Swahili, (d) city-state

COMPREHENSION

3. What were the wealth and power of East African kingdoms based on?
4. In addition to goods, what else spread over West African trade routes?
5. What were the main trade routes of East Africa?

CRITICAL THINKING AND WRITING

6. **Exploring the Main Idea** Review the Main Idea statement at the beginning of this section. Then, make a list of the things introduced into African culture, past and present, by traders from other cultures.

ACTIVITY

Take It to the NET

7. **Exploring Daily Life in Ancient Egypt** Using the information on the Web site, write several journal entries from the perspective of a young child, including what you eat, how you live, and what you wear. Visit the World Explorer: People, Places, and Cultures section of **phschool.com** for help in completing this activity.

Answers to...

CRITICAL THINKING

They were located along waterways that could be used for transportation. They were at a crossroads of three trade routes.

Resource Directory

Teaching Resources

Section Quiz in the Unit 5 Teaching Resources, p. 22

SECTION 3

European Influence and African Independence

BEFORE YOU READ

READING FOCUS

1. What were the effects of European rule in Africa?
2. How did African nations win independence from European rule?
3. What challenges did African leaders face after independence?

KEY TERMS

colonize
nationalism
Pan-Africanism
boycott

KEY PEOPLE

Leopold Sedar Senghor
Kwame Nkrumah

NOTE TAKING

Copy this chart. As you read the section, complete the chart to show the events leading from the 1400s to Africa's independence.

1400s	
1500s	
1600s	
1700s	
1800s	
1900s	
1920	
1950s–1990s	

MAIN IDEA

For many centuries, Africans suffered the loss of their freedom, their land, and many of their traditions; many African countries have fought and succeeded in regaining their independence, and have faced the challenges of self-government.

Setting the Scene

On the island of Gorée (gaw RAY), off the coast of the West African country of Senegal, stands a museum called the House of Slaves. It honors over 20 million Africans who were enslaved and shipped across the Atlantic Ocean. Many Africans passed through this building. Their last view of Africa was an opening called "The Door of No Return." Beyond it lay the ocean and the slave ships bound for the Americas.

The Door of No Return

CULTURE The Door of No Return in Senegal led to a pier, where slave ships were waiting to sail to the Americas.
Critical Thinking Why is it important to have monuments like this one? What do they represent?

Trade with Europeans

Contact between Europeans and Africans began in North Africa with Europeans trading for gold and salt by bringing copper, clothing, and crops such as corn from the Americas.

Resource Directory

Teaching Resources

Classroom Manager in the Unit 5 Teaching Resources, p. 23

Guided Reading and Review in the Unit 5 Teaching Resources, p. 24

Guide to the Essentials, p. 87

Technology

Section Reading Support Transparencies

SECTION 3

Lesson Objectives

1. Describe the effects of colonization of Africa by European nations.
2. Summarize how African countries regained independence.
3. Explain some of the challenges African leaders faced after gaining independence.

Lesson Plan

1 Engage

Warm-Up Activity

Ask students what they would like to do when they grow up. Then, ask how they would feel if they were told they couldn't do any of those things. Instead, they would be assigned a job. If they refused to do what they were told, they could be severely punished. Urge students to discuss how they would feel about this future, and how they might go about changing this situation.

Activating Prior Knowledge

Begin a discussion with students about peoples' different ideas about independence. For some, it means having the freedom to make their own decisions. Ask students what independence means to them.

2 Explore

Have students read the section. Tell them to look for answers to these questions as they read: In what ways do contact with Europeans change Africa? Why did the slave trade develop? What were the causes that led to the African independence movement?

Answers to...

CRITICAL THINKING

Monuments allow people to remember past events and stand as testimony to the lives of people no longer alive.

Lesson Plan continued

3 Teach

Have students create a concept web for each of these four terms: European contact, slavery, colonization, and independence. Have them complete the webs with facts from the section. Have students use their webs to contribute to a follow-up class discussion. You may wish to create master webs on the chalkboard. This activity should take about 25 minutes.

Questions for Discussion

CULTURE **Why would the political boundaries drawn up in Africa by the Europeans cause conflict among Africans?**

The boundaries ended up dividing some ethnic groups and forcing other groups together. This would cause conflicts between different groups that had not been forced to live together and deal with each other before.

HISTORY **How do you think fighting in World War II affected Africans' feelings about democracy and independence?**

Because Africans were fighting for these ideals in other lands, it probably made them want these things even more for themselves.

4 Assess/Reteach

See the answers to the Section 3 Assessment. You may also want to assess students' completed concept webs.

Acceptable webs include at least six correct key ideas.

Commendable webs include at least 10 correct key ideas.

Outstanding webs include at least 10 correct key ideas plus additional terms or ideas linked to the key ideas.

Protecting Trade

HISTORY In 1482, the Portuguese built this fort, Elmina Castle, in Ghana to protect and supply their trade with West Africa. **Critical Thinking** Why do you think the Portuguese would need a fort to protect their trade in this region?

The Atlantic Slave Trade

Even before the arrival of the Europeans, slavery was common in Africa, but slaves usually won their freedom after a few years. However, the Europeans viewed slaves as property, and freedom in the future was not considered possible. They began transporting Africans across the Atlantic to work on the plantations and mines in North and South America. The effects of slavery, especially for West Africans, were disastrous. Families and societies were torn apart until it ended in the 1800s.

The Effects of Colonization

Many Europeans wanted to **colonize** Africa, or settle it and take over its governments. When the slave trade ended, some Europeans saw Africa's natural resources as a new way to build wealth and empires. Africans fiercely resisted European colonization, but the leaders of several European countries joined forces and set up rules for how they could claim African land. By 1900, many parts of Africa were colonized. Though not all were ruled in the same way, in most cases, the African people had little power in the governments that ruled them.

Europeans had gained power in part by encouraging Africans to fight each other. They also took the best land to farm and, in some areas, forced Africans to work under terrible conditions. The new political boundaries drawn up by the Europeans divided some ethnic groups and forced others together. This caused much conflict, some of which continues in Africa today.

Answers to...

CRITICAL THINKING

The Portuguese needed to protect their trade from other European powers as well as African peoples.

Resource Directory

Technology

Color Transparencies 102 Africa: Colonial Rule and Independence Map; **104–106** Scramble for Africa, 1850–1914 Map with overlays

The Growth of African Independence

Many Africans dreamed of independence in the late 1800s. Mankayi Sontanga (mun KY ee suhn THAN guh) put this dream to music. His song, called "Bless, O Lord, Our Land of Africa," expressed the growing nationalism of Africans. **Nationalism** is a feeling of pride in one's homeland. African leaders saw that to end colonial rule, they would have to build a spirit of togetherness among many ethnic groups.

In 1912, a political party was formed in South Africa and its members protested laws that limited the rights of black South Africans. Today this party is the African National Congress (ANC). In British West Africa, African lawyers formed the West African National Congress, a group that worked to gain Africans the right to vote.

The First President of Senegal

HISTORY Leopold Sedar Senghor, shown here with his wife at a celebration marking his 90th birthday, served as president of Senegal for 20 years. **Critical Thinking** What kind of challenges do you think Senghor faced when he became president of the newly-independent Senegal?

The Pan-African Movement

A movement called **Pan-Africanism** was formed in the 1920s. Unity and cooperation among all Africans, whether they live in Africa or not, was stressed and their motto was "Africa for Africans." One of the greatest leaders of Pan-Africanism was **Leopold Sedar Senghor** (SAN gawr) of Senegal. Senghor, a poet and political leader, encouraged Africans to study their traditions and to be proud of their culture. Senghor became the first president when Senegal became independent in 1960.

Paths to Independence

A major boost to African independence came in the 1930s and 1940s when some African countries joined with Great Britain, France, and the United States to fight the armies of Germany, Italy, and Japan. African soldiers, drivers, and transportation workers took part in the war effort. When World War II was over, Africans wanted their own freedom. Some European countries let go peacefully, as when Ghana won its independence from Britain. But Algeria had to fight for its freedom against France.

Ghana: From Past to Present In the British West African colony of the Gold Coast, **Kwame Nkrumah** organized protests against British rule in the early 1950s. These protests took the peaceful form of strikes and **boycotts.** In a boycott, people refuse to buy or use certain products or services. The British put Nkrumah in jail for his actions, but the protests continued without him. In 1957, he achieved his goal: independence for the Gold Coast. The country took the new name of Ghana, after the great trading kingdom that lasted until the 1200s. It was a name that recalled Africa's earlier greatness. Nkrumah became Ghana's first president in 1960.

HISTORY

Amazing Grace

While many ship captains became rich from the slave trade, at least one, John Newton, came to believe that the slave trade was abominable. Newton stopped trading in slaves and began to work to ban slavery in Great Britain. He put his feelings of regret and his hope for forgiveness into words in his hymn *Amazing Grace*, which begins:

Amazing grace, how sweet the sound
That saved a wretch like me,
I once was lost, but now I'm found,
Was blind, but now I see.

ACTIVITY

Culture

Mural of the Slave Trade Assign students to work in groups of four, with each group choosing an aspect of the slave trade as a topic. They might choose the journey across the Atlantic Ocean, the slave auction, or family separation. Have students create a mural depicting this topic. Suggest that students divide the work, assigning research to one member, planning the mural to a second member, and creating and presenting the mural to the third and fourth members. Have groups display their murals and share what they learned with the class.

Visual/Spatial

Answers to...

CRITICAL THINKING

Challenges possibly included economic and social problems caused by colonization.

ACTIVITY

Journal Writing

Pan-Africanism Tell students to suppose that they have just attended a rally of a Pan-African movement. It is the evening before they return home, and they are still very excited over all they have heard from speakers like Léopold Sédar Senghor. Ask students to record their feelings in their journal so that they will remember this great event.

Verbal/Linguistic

SECTION 3 ASSESSMENT

AFTER YOU READ

1. (a) Pan-Africanism political leader and first president of Senegal (b) Ghanaian boycott leader and the nation's first president
2. (a) to settle an area and take over its government (b) a feeling of pride in one's homeland (c) a political movement stressing unity and cooperation among all Africans (d) refusing to buy or use certain products or services
3. At first, Africans and Europeans benefited from mutual trade. Later, Europeans began to enslave Africans and divided Africa into European colonies.
4. Ghana gained independence from Great Britain through peaceful strikes and boycotts.
5. Decisions about how to divide up Africa were made without considering existing cultures and ethnic groups. As a result, modern African nations often include ethnic groups that traditionally have been enemies. National boundaries also often divide ethnic groups.
6. Answers will vary, but may include ongoing wars between ethnic groups over land, divided ethnic groups, and difficulties learning how to self-govern.
7. Answers will vary, but should demonstrate an understanding of unity and cooperation, the key ideas of the movement, reasons for feelings of growing nationalism due to past history, and future benefits for Africans.
8. Answers will vary. Articles should include the history of that country's colonization and events leading up to independence.

Gambians Celebrate Independence

HISTORY Gambia won its independence from Great Britain through peaceful elections in 1965. Schoolchildren celebrate Gambian independence every year. **Critical Thinking** How is this celebration similar to Fourth of July celebrations in the United States?

The Challenges of Independence Africa's new leaders had spent many years working for independence. But they had little experience actually governing a country. As a result, some new governments in Africa were not very stable.

In some African countries, military leaders took control of the government by force. Military governments are not always fair since the people often have few rights, and citizens may be jailed if they protest. But this form of government has held together some African countries that otherwise would have been torn apart by war.

Other African countries have a long history of democracy. In a democracy, citizens help to make governmental decisions. Some countries have made traditional ways a part of democratic governing. For example, in Botswana, lively political debates take place in "freedom squares." These outdoor meetings are like the traditional kgotla (KUHT luh), in which people talk with their leaders.

Most African countries are less than 40 years old. In contrast, the stable, democratic country of the United States is over 200 years old. Many Africans feel that building stable countries will take time. One leader commented, "Let Africa be given the time to develop its own system of democracy."

SECTION 3 ASSESSMENT

AFTER YOU READ

RECALL

1. Identify: (a) Leopold Sedar Senghor, (b) Kwame Nkrumah
2. Define: (a) colonize, (b) nationalism, (c) Pan-Africanism, (d) boycott

COMPREHENSION

3. How did relations between Africa and Europe change between the 1400s and the 1900s?
4. Describe Ghana's road to independence.
5. In what ways did colonial rule cause problems for African countries after independence?

CRITICAL THINKING AND WRITING

6. **Exploring the Main Idea** Review the Main Idea statement at the beginning of this section. Then, describe some of the challenges that African countries have faced after gaining their independence.
7. **Supporting a Point of View** Write a brief speech that a leader in the Pan-Africanism movement might give to persuade others to join the movement.

ACTIVITY

8. **Writing to Learn** Choose one African country that won its independence after 1950. Write a headline and a brief article for a newspaper that might have appeared on the day that country became independent.

Resource Directory

Teaching Resources

Section Quiz in the Unit 5 Teaching Resources, p. 25

Chapter Summary in the Unit 5 Teaching Resources, p. 26

Vocabulary in the Unit 5 Teaching Resources, p. 27

Reteaching in the Unit 5 Teaching Resources, p. 28

Enrichment in the Unit 5 Teaching Resources, p. 29

Critical Thinking in the Unit 5 Teaching Resources, p. 30

Answers to...

CRITICAL THINKING

Both commemorate gaining independence from Great Britain.

Organizing by Sequence and Category

Learn the Skill

Being able to follow a sequence of events and being able to categorize are skills that will help you when you read. Sequence is simply another name for the order of events. Categorizing is sorting items into groups.

Organizing by Sequence. You may have noticed in reading your textbook that some historical events are told in the order in which the events occurred. For example, war against the colonizers usually occurred before independence. You will probably read first about the steps that led to war, the war itself, and, finally, the new government. To find the sequence of events when reading, follow these steps:

A. Look for dates. They are usually included when you need to be able to follow a sequence of events. If you find a date that is missing the year, read the information that comes before it. Writers may refer to several dates in the same year without repeating the year.

B. Find clue words that refer to time, such as day, week, month, or year. These clues will help you keep the sequence of events clear.

Organizing by Category. When you read about economic issues, note how the topics are categorized. For example, you will probably read a section about farming, then a section on mining. This kind of text is organized by category. In this case, the categories are economic categories. Each topic might be further categorized. The section on mining might first address copper mining, then silver mining. You can also categorize information as you read. To do this, follow these steps:

A. Read the information and decide what topics are covered. Think about what the text is about and how the information could be sorted into categories.

B. Decide what categories you will use. For example, if reading about trade in ancient Africa, you might think of each type of good as a separate category. You could develop separate categories for food, clothing, jewelry, and tableware.

C. Once you have decided on the categories, you can sort information into them. Under food, for example, you might list: salt, oil, sugar, grain.

Practice the Skill

The chart below lists several countries in Africa and tells where they are found and the year in which they gained independence. Use the information in the chart to create two more charts. First, list the countries in a particular sequence. You decide what the sequence should be. Then, organize the countries into several categories. You decide what the categories should be. When finished, compare your two charts with the chart in your book. Which one(s) are the easiest to read and understand? How are sequencing and categorizing useful?

Country	Location	Year of Independence
Egypt	North Africa	1922
Kenya	East Africa	1963
Ghana	West Africa	1957
Somalia	East Africa	1960
South Africa	South Africa	1910
Algeria	North Africa	1962
Congo	Central Africa	1960
Tanzania	East Africa	1961
Nigeria	West Africa	1960
Ethiopia	East Africa	1941

Apply the Skill

See the Chapter Review and Assessment at the end of this chapter for more questions on organizing by sequence and category.

Resource Directory

Technology

Social Studies Skills Tutor CD-ROM

Answers to...

PRACTICE THE SKILL

Students should see that organizing by sequence and category help make information easier to understand.

Lesson Objectives

1. Identify sequence in written text.
2. Categorize information in written text.

Lesson Plan

1 Engage

To introduce the skill, read the opening text under "Learn the Skill" aloud. Point out to students that they will learn two different ways to organize writing and ideas: sequence and category. Have students give definitions for the two ways in their own words.

2 Explore

Direct students to read the steps for Organizing by Sequence. Have them summarize how to organize by sequence in their own words.

Direct students to read the steps for Organizing by Category. When finished, have them summarize that information as well.

3 Teach

You may want to allow students to work in pairs to complete the two charts. Instead of directing students on how to make the charts, have them brainstorm ways in which they can reorganize the information.

4 Assess/Reteach

Students should be able to organize the information in the chart both by sequence and by category.

To further assess students' understanding of organizing by sequence and by category, have them complete the "Applying Your Skills" part of the Chapter Review and Assessment at the end of the chapter.

CHAPTER 20

Review and Assessment

Creating a Chapter Summary

Section 2 Sample summary: When traders arrived in Africa, they brought not only goods, but also new ideas. Trade helped Africa's kingdoms to become powerful and wealthy.

Section 3 Sample summary: Europeans started out as equal trading partners with Africa, but over time began to enslave Africans, and acquire Africa's land and natural resources. Africa was divided into colonies by different European nations, but eventually, Africans won their independence from Europe. In more recent times, African governments have been faced with the challenges of self-government.

Reviewing Key Terms

1. d **2.** e **3.** h **4.** a **5.** f **6.** c **7.** b **8.** g

Reviewing the Main Ideas

1. hunting and gathering, farming and herding
2. They had cities, governments, social classes, architecture, writing, and art.
3. They became wealthy by controlling trade.
4. traders brought and exchanged not only goods, but also ideas and beliefs
5. The relationship between Europeans and Africans began as trade between equals, but Europeans began enslaving Africans and forcing millions of Africans to leave their homeland.
6. Families and societies were torn apart.
7. The growth of nationalism and World War II helped lead to independence for many African nations.

CHAPTER 20

Review and Assessment

Creating a Chapter Summary

On a separate piece of paper, draw a diagram like this one, and include the information that summarizes the first section of the chapter. Then, fill in the remaining boxes with a summary of sections 2 and 3.

AFRICA

Section 1
The continent's first people lived in East Africa. They survived by developing tools of stone and iron, and by becoming farmers and hunter-gatherers.

Section 2

Section 3

Reviewing Key Terms

Match the definitions in Column I with the key terms in Column II.

Column I

1. a society with cities
2. a movement that stressed unity among all Africans
3. a city that controls much of the land around it and has its own government
4. person who gathers wild food and hunts animals to survive
5. to settle in an area and take over or create a government
6. the holy book of the religion Islam.
7. a feeling of pride in one's homeland
8. a government in which citizens have power through their elected representatives

Column II

a. hunter-gatherer
b. nationalism
c. Quran
d. civilization
e. Pan-Africanism
f. colonize
g. democracy
h. city-state

Reviewing the Main Ideas

1. List some of the ways in which early Africans made a living. (Section 1)
2. What were Africa's earliest civilizations like? (Section 1)
3. How did Africa's kingdoms and city-states become wealthy? (Section 2)
4. How did trade help the spread of ideas among different cultures and regions? (Section 2)
5. How did relationship between Africans and Europeans change over time? (Section 3)
6. What were some of the effects of the Atlantic slave trade on Africa? (Section 3)
7. What factors helped lead to independence for many African countries? (Section 3)

Resource Directory

Teaching Resources

Cooperative Learning Activity in the Unit 5 Teaching Resources, pp. 108–111

Chapter Tests Forms A and B in the Unit 5 Teaching Resources, pp. 136–141

Guide to the Essentials Ch. 20 Test, p. 88

Map Activity

Africa

For each place listed below, write the letter from the map that shows its location.

1. Senegal
2. Tombouctou
3. Kilwa
4. Kingdom of Mali
5. Nubia
6. Aksum

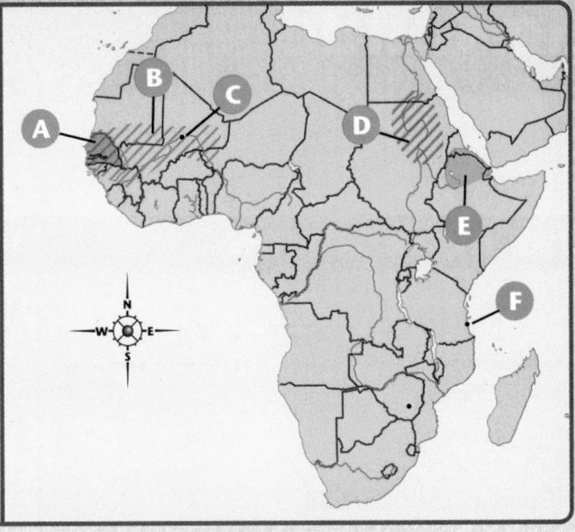

Take It to the NET

Enrichment For more map activities using geography skills, visit the social studies section of **phschool.com.**

Writing Activity

1. **Writing a Speech** In the 1800s, many people in the United States spoke out against slavery. They were called abolitionists because they wanted to abolish, or put an end to, slavery. Pretend that you are an abolitionist living in the 1800s. Use what you have learned about the slave trade to write a speech that will help persuade people that slavery is wrong.
2. **Writing a Letter** Today is Independence Day in your country. It is a day to remember those who fought for the freedom to govern themselves. Write a letter to your ancestors and tell them how you feel today.

Applying Your Skills

Turn to the Skills for Life activity on p. 381 to answer the following questions.

1. Reread pp. 374–376. How is the information about African kingdoms organized—by sequence or by category?
2. Reread pp. 378–380. How is most of this information organized? How can you tell?

Critical Thinking

1. **Recognizing Cause and Effect** Many of Africa's cities and countries are located along trade routes. How has trade affected Africa's history?
2. **Expressing Problems Clearly** The Atlantic slave trade lasted from the 1500s to the 1800s. How did the slave trade and the colonization of Africa affect traditional African cultures?
3. **Drawing Conclusions** How do you think most Africans feel about their hard-won independence? Explain your answer.

Take It to the NET

Activity Read about Africa's history. Choose a specific area to focus on and prepare a presentation of what you learned. Visit the World Explorer: People, Places, and Cultures section of **phschool.com** for help in completing this activity.

Chapter 20 Self-Test As a final review activity, take the Chapter 20 Self-Test and get instant feedback on your answers. To take the test, visit the Social Studies section of **phschool.com.**

Resource Directory

Other Print Resources

Chapter Tests with ExamView® Test Bank, Ch. 20

Technology

ExamView® Test Bank CD-ROM, Ch. 20

Resource Pro® CD-ROM

Map Activity

1. A **2.** C **3.** F **4.** B **5.** D **6.** E

Writing Activity

1. Speeches will vary, but will probably cite the inhuman conditions on slave ships, the moral wrongness of slavery, and the damage done to Africa as a result of the loss of its best workers to slavery.
2. Letters will vary, but should include reference to specific events from the independence movement mentioned in this chapter.

Critical Thinking

1. The early kingdoms and city-states of Africa grew wealthy through the trade of various natural resources. Later, Europeans came to Africa and began enslaving Africans. The slave traders grew rich and deprived Africa of some of its most capable people.
2. Enslaved Africans were taken to unfamiliar, faraway lands where it was difficult to maintain traditions. Europeans drew boundaries in Africa that did not reflect traditional boundaries. The new boundaries caused, and continue to cause, much conflict in Africa.
3. Answers will vary but should predict that Africans are proud of their accomplishments in their struggle for independence and may be cautious about outside influences based on their history.

Applying Your Skills

1. The information is organized by category (the specific kingdom), with some information about the specific kingdoms organized by sequence.
2. The information is organized by sequence.

Chapter 21 Planning Guide

Resource Manager

	CORE INSTRUCTION	READING/SKILLS
Chapter-Level Resources	**Teaching Resources** Program Overview Pacing Charts **Technology** Resource Pro® CD-ROM Companion Web site, phschool.com • eTeach	**Technology** Social Studies Skills Tutor CD-ROM Student Edition on Audio CD, Ch. 21
1 The Cultures of North Africa **1.** Define the word *culture* and explain how it unites people in North Africa. **2.** Describe some beliefs of Islam and its effect on life in North Africa. **3.** Explain how North Africa's Mediterranean location has influenced its cultures.	**Teaching Resources** **Unit 5** Classroom Manager, p. 32 Guided Reading and Review, p. 33	**Teaching Resources** Guide to the Essentials, p. 89 **Technology** Section Reading Support Transparencies
2 The Cultures of West Africa **1.** Describe aspects of cultural diversity in West Africa. **2.** Explain the role of the family in West African culture. **3.** Summarize how West Africans preserve cultural traditions.	**Teaching Resources** **Unit 5** Classroom Manager, p. 35 Guided Reading and Review, p. 36	**Teaching Resources** Guide to the Essentials, p. 90 **Technology** Section Reading Support Transparencies
3 The Cultures of East Africa **1.** Describe the influence of East Africa's location on its cultures. **2.** Summarize the role of the Swahili language in East African cultures. **3.** Explain how ideas about land ownership in East Africa have changed.	**Teaching Resources** **Unit 5** Classroom Manager, p. 38 Guided Reading and Review, p. 39	**Teaching Resources** Guide to the Essentials, p. 91 **Technology** Section Reading Support Transparencies
4 The Cultures of South Africa **1.** Describe the influence of South Africa on both the region of Southern Africa and on the entire continent. **2.** Explain how migrant labor and the formation of the mineworker's unions led to a new group identity among the peoples of Southern Africa.	**Teaching Resources** **Unit 5** Classroom Manager, p. 41 Guided Reading and Review, p. 42 Chapter Summary, p. 44 Vocabulary, p. 45 Reteaching, p. 46	**Teaching Resources** **Unit 5** Critical Thinking, p. 48 Guide to the Essentials, p. 92 **Technology** Section Reading Support Transparencies

ENRICHMENT / PRE-AP

Teaching Resources
Primary Sources and Literature Readings

Other Print Resources
DK Atlas

Technology
World Video Explorer: Cultures of Africa
Passport to the World CD-ROM
How People Live Transparencies, Unit 5
Companion Web site, phschool.com

Teaching Resources
Outline Maps, pp. 28–29

Teaching Resources
Outline Maps, p. 34

Teaching Resources
Unit 5
Enrichment, p. 47
Cooperative Learning Activity, pp. 112–115

ASSESSMENT

Prentice Hall Assessment System

Core Assessment
Chapter Tests with ExamView® Test Bank, Ch. 21
ExamView® Test Bank CD-ROM, Ch. 21

Standardized Test Preparation
Diagnose and Prescribe
Diagnostic Tests for Middle Grades Social Studies Skills
Review and Reteach
Review Book for World Studies
Practice and Assess
Test-taking Strategies with Transparencies for Middle Grades Test Prep Book
Test-taking Strategies Posters

Teaching Resources
Unit 5
Section Quizzes, pp. 34, 37, 40, and 43
Chapter Tests, pp. 142–147

Technology
Companion Web site, phschool.com
Ch. 21 Self-Test

World Video Explorer
Each region of the world is explored through regional flyovers and investigative field trips. Case study segments give students an in-depth view of the history, economy, government, and culture of a key place in each region. Case studies include Nigeria, Mexico, China, British Columbia, and the Czech Republic.

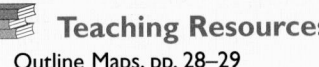

In Your Classroom

CUSTOMIZE FOR INDIVIDUAL NEEDS

Gifted and Talented

Teacher's Edition
- The Maasai, p. 392
- Culture, p. 393

Teaching Resources
- Enrichment, p. 47
- Primary Sources and Literature Readings

Honors/Pre-AP

Teacher's Edition
- The Maasai, p. 392

Teaching Resources
- Critical Thinking, p. 48
- Primary Sources and Literature Readings

ESL

Teacher's Edition
- Culture, p. 393

Teaching Resources
- Guided Reading and Review, pp. 33, 36, 39, and 42
- Vocabulary, p. 45
- Reteaching, p. 46
- Guide to the Essentials, pp. 89–92
- Outline Maps 28, 29, 34

Technology
- Social Studies Skills Tutor CD-ROM
- Section Reading Support Transparencies

Less Proficient Readers

Teacher's Edition
- Culture, p. 393

Teaching Resources
- Guided Reading and Review, pp. 33, 36, 39, and 42
- Vocabulary, p. 45
- Reteaching, p. 46
- Guide to the Essentials, pp. 89–92
- Outline Maps 28, 29, 34

Technology
- Social Studies Skills Tutor CD-ROM
- Section Reading Support Transparencies

Less Proficient Writers

Teacher's Edition
- The Maasai, p. 392

Teaching Resources
- Guided Reading and Review, pp. 33, 36, 39, and 42
- Vocabulary, p. 45
- Guide to the Essentials, pp. 89–92

Technology
- Social Studies Skills Tutor CD-ROM
- Section Reading Support Transparencies

TEACHER'S EDITION INDEX

Activities culture, p. 393

Connections the maasai, p. 392

Skills Mini Lessons Writing for a Purpose, p. 389; Identifying Central Issues, p. 395

CHAPTER 21 PACING SUGGESTIONS

 For 90-minute Blocks
See suggestions in the Teaching Resources Pacing Charts for Chapter 21.

 Running Out of Time?
See the Guide to the Essentials, pp. 89–92.

INTERDISCIPLINARY LINKS

Middle Grades Math: Tools for Success
Course 1, Lesson 1-3 **Mean, Median and Mode**

Prentice Hall Literature
Copper, **Why the Tortoise's Shell is Not Smooth**

 ## DORLING KINDERSLEY

At the end of each unit, you will find information adapted from Dorling Kindersley's *Illustrated Children's Encyclopedia* that connects to the region being studied and to one of the seven content strands. In addition, your resources include Dorling Kindersley's *Atlas,* which contains valuable information about countries from around the world.

BIBLIOGRAPHY

For the Teacher

Ayo, Yvonne. *Africa.* Knopf, 1995.

Haskins, Jim, and Joann Biondi. *From Afar to Zulu: A Dictionary of African Cultures.* Walker, 1995.

Islam: There Is No God But God. Time/Life, 1996. Videocassette.

Moore, Reavis. *Native Artists of Africa.* Muir, 1994.

For the Student

Easy

Angelou, Maya, and Margaret Courtney-Clark. *My Painted House, My Friendly Chicken, and Me.* Clarkson Potter, 1996.

Average

Children's History of the 20th Century. Dorling Kindersley, 2001.

Kipsigis; Maasai; Pokot; Rendille; (Heritage Library of African People series). Rosen, 1994.

Challenging

Knappert, Jan. *Kings, Gods, and Spirits from African Mythology.* Bedrick, 1994.

Literature Connection

Dupre, Rick. *Agassu: Legend of the Leopard King.* Carolrhoda, 1993.

Medlicott, Mary, editor. *The River That Went to the Sky: Twelve Tales by African Storytellers.* Kingfisher, 1995.

Take It to the NET

The World Explorer companion Web site, found on **phschool.com**, offers activities for exploring geographical, historical, and cultural resources on the Internet. It also provides on-line links for key content and all Section and Chapter Assessment activities.

The **Teacher site** also provides teachers with regional data and ideas for student research and activities.

Students can use the **Student site** to find chapter-by-chapter Internet resource links and to access Self-Tests.

CHAPTER 21

Connecting to the Guiding Questions

In this chapter, students will read about the cultures of Africa. Content in this chapter corresponds to the following Guiding Questions outlined at the beginning of the unit.

- How do Africa's many different cultures differ from place to place?
- What are some of the ways Africans make a living?
- How has Africa's relative isolation from the rest of the world affected the use of science and technology?

Using the Music Activities

Discuss with students what some of their favorite kinds of music are. As a class, determine, if possible, which kinds of music contain drum sounds. Ask students whether they have ever heard music that featured African drums.

- Students should use library and Internet sources to gather information about African drums.
- Students should use the information they gather to build a drum of their own, using materials that replicate those used to make an African drum, if possible.

Heterogeneous Groups

The following activity is suitable for heterogeneous groups.

Journal Writing
Culture, p. 393

eTeach
Be sure to check out this month's discussion with a Master Teacher. Go to **phschool.com**.

CHAPTER 21

AFRICA: Rich in Culture

Drums Go Drumming

Using Music

Music has many roles in the cultures of African countries—to send messages, tell a story, organize work, or celebrate a special occasion. People in African countries rarely play music by itself. Most often, they combine music with dance, theater, words, games, or visual art.

Exploring Musical Instruments

In many African cultures, drums play an important role in traditional and modern music. Use the library and the Internet to find out more about traditional African drums and how they differ. When you do research, look under subject headings such as African Arts, African Music, and Musical Instruments.

Making an African Drum

As you gather information about African drums, choose one as a model for making your own. Learn as much as you can about this kind of drum. Build your own drum using this information. If possible, use materials that are similar to the materials the traditional drums are made from. Experiment with different methods to see which sounds best.

384 UNIT 5 AFRICA

Resource Directory

Teaching Resources

Primary Sources and Literature Readings extend content with a selection related to the concepts in this chapter.

Other Print Resources

DK Atlas

Technology

Cultures of Africa, from the World Video Explorer, enhances students' understanding of the many factors of African culture.

How People Live Transparencies, Unit 5

Student Edition on Audio CD, Ch. 21

Passport to the World CD-ROM This interactive CD-ROM allows students to explore each region of the world. Students view regional videos, take a photo tour, and explore a historical timeline. Students record their travels in an Explorer's Journal, and receive passport stamps when they pass regional quizzes.

SECTION 1

The Cultures of North Africa

BEFORE YOU READ

FOCUS QUESTIONS

1. What is culture?
2. What are the major influences on the culture of North Africa?
3. How has their Mediterranean location affected the cultures of North Africa?

KEY TERMS

culture
cultural diffusion

MAIN IDEA

The culture, or way of life, in a society is influenced by different ethnic groups that may share common bonds, such as religion, language, and the influence of neighboring societies.

NOTE TAKING

Copy this web diagram. As you read the section, complete the web by adding the institutions and characteristics that are basic to all societies and which help to define culture.

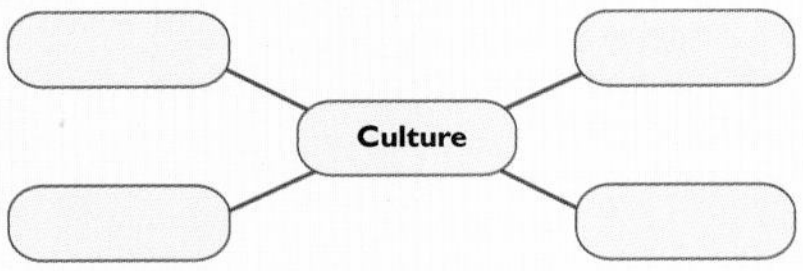

Setting the Scene

Thirteen-year-old Meena lives in the city of Marrakech (muh rah kehsh) in Morocco, a country in North Africa. Every morning she works in a factory, weaving carpets. She learned to weave carpets from her mother, who learned the skill from her mother. Carpets play an important role in Moroccan life. In some Moroccan homes, they serve as more than just floor coverings, and are used as chairs, beds, and prayer mats. They are also important exports for the country. In the afternoon, Meena leaves the factory to attend school. Her day ends at sunset, when she hears the crier who calls out from the nearby mosque, a Muslim house of worship. Muslims are followers of the religion of Islam. When she hears the call, Meena recites this prayer in Arabic: "There is no God but Allah, and Muhammad is His prophet."

Moroccan Carpets

CULTURE Moroccan weavers decorate their carpets with intricate designs. **Critical Thinking** Why are carpets an important part of Moroccan culture? What similar traditions do we have in the United States?

What Is Culture?

When a group of people share similar beliefs and customs they are said to share a **culture.** Culture has many elements, including food, clothing, homes, jobs, and language. It can also be shared ideas, such as how people view the world and practice a religion. In some cultures, for example, people take time to pray every day. Culture shapes the way people behave.

SECTION 1

Lesson Objectives

1. Define the term *culture* and explain how it unites people in North Africa.
2. Describe some beliefs of Islam and its effect on life in North Africa.
3. Explain how North Africa's Mediterranean location has influenced its cultures.

Lesson Plan

1 Engage

Warm-Up Activity

Ask students to name a cultural characteristic that they think most Americans share. For example, most Americans speak English. List and discuss some of the students' ideas, leading them to the conclusion that Americans have very diverse cultural characteristics. Ask students what they think it would be like to live in a place where almost everyone shares the same religion and many people share the same heritage.

Activating Prior Knowledge

Have students answer the following questions: What is a day in your life like? What is your school like? What is your home like? Invite students to discuss how they get to school, the subjects they study, their extracurricular activities, and other aspects of their daily lives.

Resource Directory

Teaching Resources

Classroom Manager in the Unit 5 Teaching Resources, p. 32

Guided Reading and Review in the Unit 5 Teaching Resources, p. 33

Guide to the Essentials, p. 89

Technology

Section Reading Support Transparencies

Answers to...

CRITICAL THINKING

In some Moroccan homes, carpets are used as chairs, beds, and prayer mats. They are also important exports for the country. Students' responses about similar traditions in the United States will vary.

Lesson Plan continued

2 Explore

As students read the section text, pause to discuss and answer the following questions: What is the main religion of North Africa and what are some important aspects of that religion? How can the influences of different cultures be seen in North Africa? What are some of the ways North Africans make a living?

3 Teach

Invite students to create a web with *Culture of North Africa* at the center. Secondary circles can contain details about the culture, and tertiary circles can identify cultural influences. Students may explain these influences using supporting facts from the section. This activity should take about 20 minutes.

Question for Discussion

GEOGRAPHY What effect has North Africa's location on the Mediterrean Sea had on the culture of the region?

Because of its location, North Africa has been the center of trade with Europe, Asia, and the rest of Africa. The culture of the region has been influenced by the other cultures with which it has come into contact.

4 Assess/Reteach

See the answers to the Section 1 Assessment. You may also use students' webs as an assessment.

Acceptable webs include a minimum of two details in secondary circles and two influences in tertiary circles.

Commendable webs include a minimum of three details in secondary circles and three influences in tertiary circles.

Outstanding webs include a minimum of three details in secondary circles and three influences in tertiary circles and show how the details and influences are related.

Community Centers

CULTURE Muslims often build a large, empty space into the middle of their mosques. Why? The empty space can be used for many different kinds of activities, including education. **Critical Thinking** How are religious buildings in your town or city used? Do they look like this one?

How Culture is Influenced

Religion is an important part of North African culture. More than 95 percent of North Africans practice Islam and are Muslims. Like Jews and Christians, Muslims believe in one God. Allah is the Arabic word for God.

The Influence of Islam In North Africa, many aspects of daily life are affected by the sacred book of Islam, the Quran. Like the Hebrew Torah and the Christian Bible, the Quran provides a guide to life and forbids lying, stealing, and murder. The Quran also prohibits gambling, eating pork, and drinking alcohol. North African countries use some Islamic laws to govern family life, business practices, banking, and government.

Religion and Language Unify The People In North Africa, the religion of Islam and the Arabic language unify people of many different ethnic backgrounds and ways of life. These people live in a large region that includes the countries of Egypt, Libya, Tunisia, Algeria, and Morocco. People here have many different backgrounds and ways of life.

An ethnic group is a group of people who share language, religion, and cultural traditions. Most North Africans are Arabs but the region has other ethnic groups, too. The largest of these is the Berbers, who live mainly in Algeria and Morocco. Most Berbers speak Arabic as well as Berber. Some live in cities, but most live in small villages in rugged mountain areas and make their living by herding and farming.

Answers to...

CRITICAL THINKING

Students may say that religious buildings are used for religions services and other community activities.

Resource Directory

Teaching Resources

Outline Maps, Southwest Asia: Physical, p. 28; Southwest Asia: Political p. 29

The Tuareg (TWAH reg) are a group of Berbers who live in the Sahara and make their living by herding camels and goats.

In large cities like Cairo (KY roh), Egypt and Tunis, Tunisia, people live with a mix of the traditional and modern ways of life. Some weave carpets or sell baskets. Others are scientists or sell computers in modern stores. The peoples of North Africa live vastly different lives, yet almost all consider themselves to be Muslims.

How Culture Spreads

Cultures are constantly changing as people and ideas move from one place to another. This movement of customs and ideas is called **cultural diffusion.** The word *diffuse* means "to spread out."

North Africa has been part of the diffusion process because of its Mediterranean location. Throughout history, it has been a hub of trade with Europe, Asia, and other parts of Africa. Wars, too, affected culture as one empire would conquer another. Thus, North Africans have influenced, and been influenced by, the cultures of many different places.

Contemporary North African Culture One of the more recent influences on North Africa is Western culture. Some North Africans are concerned that their countries are becoming too Western. More people are wearing Western clothes, buying Western products, seeing Western films, and adapting Western ideas. All over Africa, people face the challenge of how to preserve the traditions they value as their countries modernize.

AS YOU READ

Monitor Your Reading
What sights might you see if you were walking through a city in North Africa? How would these sights be different from what you might see walking through a city in the United States?

SECTION 1 ASSESSMENT

AFTER YOU READ

RECALL

1. Define: (a) culture, (b) cultural diffusion

COMPREHENSION

2. How does a common culture bind people together?
3. How does Islam affect everyday life in North Africa?
4. How has North Africa's location contributed to cultural diffusion?

CRITICAL THINKING AND WRITING

5. **Exploring the Main Idea** Review the Main Idea statement at the beginning of this section. Then, make a list of the common bonds that North Africans share. Which ones are common bonds in your culture?
6. **Comparing and Contrasting** Visualize a map of the United States. Which regions do you think have been culturally influenced by neighboring countries and in what ways? How is this similar to the influences on North Africa by other cultures? Write a paragraph to explain your thinking.

ACTIVITY

7. **Writing an Essay** What traditions in your culture do you think are worth preserving? Write an essay describing the customs you value most.

SECTION 1 ASSESSMENT

AFTER YOU READ

1. (a) way of life for people sharing customs and beliefs (b) movement or spreading of customs and ideas
2. People who share a common culture share similar beliefs and customs, as well as foods, languages, and sometimes clothing styles.
3. Followers of Islam must take time from their regular activities to pray several times a day. Islamic law also forbids gambling, eating pork, or drinking alcohol.
4. Location on the Mediterranean Sea has made interaction with Europe and Asia easier, aiding cultural diffusion.
5. The religion of Islam and the Arabic language are common bonds that North Africans share. In the United States, the English language is a common bond.
6. Sample answer: The southwest states have been influenced by Mexican culture. The northern states have been influenced by Canadian culture. The similarities in influences include people migrating from nearby countries, the introduction of new foods and clothing, and the inclusion of words from their languages.
7. Essays will vary, but students should identify specific traditions and give reasons for their preservation.

Resource Directory

Teaching Resources

Section Quiz in the Unit 5 Teaching Resources, p. 34

Answers to...

AS YOU READ

Answers will vary. Students may say that they would see a mix of traditional and modern ways of life, and that cities in the United States are similar in this respect.

SECTION 2

Lesson Objectives

1. Describe aspects of cultural diversity in West Africa.
2. Explain the role of the family in West African culture.
3. Summarize how West Africans preserve cultural traditions.

Lesson Plan

1 Engage

Warm-Up Activity

Have students imagine that they are creating a community newspaper. Ask them what languages should be represented in order to reach most readers. Elicit ideas for articles to help readers who speak different languages live, work, and communicate together.

Activating Prior Knowledge

Have students think about what they know about different ethnic groups in the United States. Have them choose one group and make notes about that group's culture, the language its people speak (in addition to English), and any special customs or beliefs. Pool students' contributions to make a class fact sheet about different ethnic groups and their cultures, languages, and customs.

2 Explore

Ask students to keep the following questions in mind as they read: Why is West Africa so culturally diverse? Why are young men going to the cities to work? How is life in West African cities different than life in the villages? What problems may result from West Africa's cultural diversity?

Answers to...

CRITICAL THINKING

The people who buy and sell the fish also benefit.

SECTION 2

The Cultures of West Africa

BEFORE YOU READ

READING FOCUS

1. Why does West Africa have such a variety of cultures?
2. What effects do family ties have on West African culture?
3. How has urbanization affected the cultures of West Africa?

KEY TERMS

cultural diversity
kinship
nuclear family
extended family
lineage
clan
griot

NOTE TAKING

Copy this chart. As you read the section, complete the chart by filling in information you read that helps to define kinship.

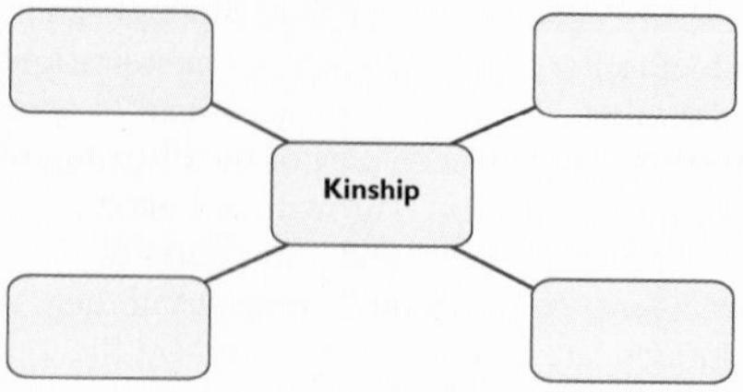

MAIN IDEA

Since West Africa has a wide variety of cultures and ethnic groups, West Africans are not united by a single religion or a common language.

A Market in Dakar, Senegal

ECONOMICS At this open-air market in Dakar, Senegal, customers can buy many kinds of groceries, including fresh fish. Senegal has built up its fishing industry so much that fish are its most important export. **Critical Thinking** Besides the people who catch the fish, who benefits from Dakar's fishing industry?

Setting the Scene

Like North Africans, West Africans see themselves as members of a number of groups. Just as you belong to a family, an ethnic group, and a country, so do West Africans. The culture of West Africa is created both by the similarities and by the differences of its people and their ways of life. There are 17 countries in this region with hundreds of ethnic groups. West Africa is famous for its **cultural diversity**—it has a wide variety of cultures.

Cultural Differences

With so many ethnic groups in West Africa, most West Africans learn to speak more than one lan-

Resource Directory

Teaching Resources

Classroom Manager in the Unit 5 Teaching Resources, p. 35

Guided Reading and Review in the Unit 5 Teaching Resources, p. 36

Guide to the Essentials, p. 90

Technology

Section Reading Support Transparencies

guage. Many can communicate in four or five languages and use these languages to conduct business or when traveling. This ability is an important way that a culturally diverse country can be unified in spite of its differences.

AS YOU READ
Draw Inferences How do you think the cultural diversity of West Africa affects the lives of its people?

Different Ways of Making a Living

The working life of West Africans can be as different as herding camels across the Sahara or working in a hotel in a large city. Most West Africans live in a village surrounded by farmland and grow cash crops. But, in some countries, such as Cote d'Ivoire, almost half of the people live and work in cities.

Cultural Ties

One of the strongest bonds West Africans have is the bond of **kinship,** which refers to a family relationship. The first level of kinship is the **nuclear family,** which consists of parents and their children. The next level is the **extended family,** which includes all other relatives. West Africans often live as an extended family, all working together and taking care of each other. This custom is reflected in the well-known African proverb, "It takes a village to raise a child."

In many rural areas, a group of families may trace their descent back to a common ancestor. Such a group forms a **lineage.** Several lineages form a **clan,** all with roots back to an even earlier ancestor.

Life in West Africa

ECONOMICS
Ways of making a living in West Africa vary from country to country. Most people in Mali make a living growing crops such as grains, corn, potatoes, yams, and cassava.
Critical Thinking Judging from the equipment these boys are using, how much work do you think is involved in raising crops on a typical farm in West Africa?

Preserving Culture

Family ties remain strong in West Africa, but with more people moving from rural villages to urban areas, or cities, family life is changing. This trend, called urbanization, is occurring in Africa and in the world. Often the young men go to the cities to find jobs, while the women stay to raise the children and farm the land. The men return to visit and share what they have earned.

One way for West Africans to adapt, change, and keep their family ties strong, is to pass on their history, values, and traditions to their children. They do this through storytelling, usually spoken rather than written. A storyteller called a **griot** (GREE oh) passes this oral tradition from one generation to the next.

3 Teach

Encourage students to develop an ad inviting people to visit West Africa for business and pleasure. Ads may include artwork, poetry, or mock quotations or testimonials if their content is plausible. Post the ads in the classroom and use them to begin a discussion about the cultures of West Africa. This activity should take about 30 minutes.

Questions for Discussion

ECONOMICS In what ways might rural family life in West Africa be affected by urbanization?

With men moving to the cities in search of work, the remaining family members would all have to take on extra responsibilities, from caring for children to performing household chores.

CULTURE What are some of the benefits of living with an extended family rather than with a nuclear family?

With more members of a family living together, there would be more people to help with household responsibilities.

4 Assess/Reteach

See the answers to the Section 2 Assessment. You may assess students' ads with the following criteria.

Acceptable ads include accurate data about West African culture.

Commendable ads use factual data in creative and original formats.

Outstanding ads show an understanding of the changes occurring in West Africa.

SKILLS MINI LESSON

Writing for a Purpose

To **introduce** the skill, explain that one reason people write is to communicate important facts and information. On the board under the heading *Writing to Inform*, list the following steps: 1) Decide what facts and data to communicate. 2) Identify the audience and assess the most effective examples and format to use.

Then, clarify and discuss these two steps in the context of the West African griot tradition, explaining that although griots do not write down their information, they still communicate to inform. Ask students to **practice** using the skill to identify what information a griot communicates (West African traditions). Then, have students identify the griot's audience and format (young people; histories, stories, fables, proverbs, riddles, and songs). Have students **apply** the skill to write informatively on a subject of their choosing.

Answers to...

AS YOU READ

West Africans often have to learn several languages in order to live and work among the many diverse cultures.

CRITICAL THINKING

Most students will say that the primitive equipment the boys are using indicates that a lot of work is needed to raise crops on a typical West African farm.

SECTION 2 ASSESSMENT

AFTER YOU READ

1. (a) wide variety of cultures (b) refers to a family relationship (c) parents and their children (d) relatives such as grandparents, aunts, uncles, and cousins (e) group of families who trace their descent to a common ancestor (f) several lineages who can trace their descent to the same early ancestor (g) a West African storyteller
2. West Africa includes 17 nations and hundreds of ethnic groups.
3. Family members help one another with personal issues, business matters, and decision making.
4. Urbanization has separated men from their families and weakened people's dependence on their extended families.
5. Similarities could include: living in a village surrounded by farmland and growing cash crops; speaking several languages, one of which might be the same; having a griot pass through or live in the village. The differences might include: different ethnic customs or traditions; different religious practices; having a different lineage and clan.
6. Shared responsibility makes members of an extended family aware of and connected to the community.
7. Have students read their myths and fables to the class when they have completed the activity.

A Griot Tells a Tale

CULTURE When a griot tells a story, it can take all night or even several days. The audience does not mind, because the stories are usually scary, funny, or exciting. This griot, from Côte d'Ivoire, is telling these children a legend from their history. The children pay careful attention, because the griot acts out parts of the story as he goes along. **Critical Thinking** How is griot storytelling similar to storytelling you have seen?

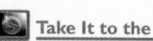

The Influence of West African Culture

West African traditions have greatly influenced other cultures, especially American culture. Enslaved West Africans brought their ideas, stories, dances, music, and customs to the United States. The stories of Brer Rabbit as well as blues and jazz music have their roots in West Africa. In recent years, three Nobel Prize winners for literature have been African. One of them, Wole Soyinka (WHO lay shaw YING kah) is from the West African country of Nigeria.

SECTION 2 ASSESSMENT

AFTER YOU READ

RECALL

1. Define: (a) cultural diversity, (b) kinship, (c) nuclear family, (d) extended family, (e) lineage, (f) clan, (g) griot

COMPREHENSION

2. In what ways is West Africa culturally diverse?
3. Describe the importance of family ties to West Africans.
4. How has urbanization changed the lives of West Africans?

CRITICAL THINKING AND WRITING

5. **Exploring the Main Idea** Review the Main Idea statement at the beginning of this section. Imagine that you live in a small village in an extended family in West Africa. Make a list of what you might have in common with someone in the next village, and what differences you might have.
6. **Drawing Conclusions** How has the extended family helped to develop a sense of community among West Africans? Write a paragraph explaining your answer.

ACTIVITY

Take It to the NET

7. **Writing a Myth or Fable** Read the myths and fables on the Web site. Using these stories as a guide, write your own myth or fable. Visit the World Explorer: People, Places, and Culture section of **phschool.com** for help in completing this activity.

Resource Directory

Teaching Resources

Section Quiz in the Unit 5 Teaching Resources, p. 37

Answers to...

CRITICAL THINKING

Answers will vary. Most stories are a way of passing information along from generation to generation. Many stories relate the history of families and communities.

SECTION 3

The Cultures of East Africa

BEFORE YOU READ

1. How has location affected the development of East African cultures?
2. What role does the Swahili language play in East African cultures?
3. How and why are ideas about land ownership changing in East Africa?

KEY TERMS

plantation

NOTE TAKING

Copy the diagram below. As you read the section, complete the diagram by filling in the information that shows the common characteristics shared by the cultures of East and West Africa.

East Africa | Bantu Language | West Africa

MAIN IDEA

East Africa is a region of great cultural diversity where the migration of people from other continents has influenced cultural development and the current society.

Setting the Scene

Alemeseged Taddesse Mekonnen (ah lem uh SEH ged TAH day say meh KOH nen) is an Ethiopian who works in a bakery in St. Louis, Missouri.

Mekonnen misses life with his close-knit family in Ethiopia. "At home we ate every meal together. If anyone was missing, we waited until they came home," he says. Mekonnen hopes to return home someday. He lives in the United States, but his heart is in Ethiopia.

Location Leads to Cultural Borrowing

Like West Africa, East Africa has many ethnic groups who speak different languages. In Ethiopia, alone, more than 70 languages are spoken. East Africa's diversity is the result of its location and people have been migrating to it for at least 2,000 years, when the Bantu-speaking people of West Africa arrived. From across the Indian Ocean, explorers from Arab countries, from India, and from China arrived and settled along East Africa's long coastline.

A Kenyan Family

CULTURE Shown below is a family from Kenya. Families in East Africa traditionally eat their meals together, using one bowl or plate. **Critical Thinking** What foods do people in the United States share from one plate or bowl? Why?

391

SECTION 3

Lesson Objectives

1. Describe the influence of East Africa's location on its cultures.
2. Summarize the role of the Swahili language in East African cultures.
3. Explain how ideas about land ownership in East Africa have changed.

Lesson Plan

1 Engage

Warm-Up Activity

Ask students who they think "owns" the Rocky Mountains, or parks in your community. Discuss who can use these places. Then, ask students who they think owns the building in which they live and who can use it. Tell students that in East Africa, traditional views about land ownership are similar to American views about public land.

Activating Prior Knowledge

Ask students to to make a list of words that come from other languages. Examples to offer would be: *banjo*, *canyon*, and *succotash*. *Banjo* comes from an African language; *canyon* comes from Spanish; and *succotash* comes from Narragansett, a Native American language.

2 Explore

Instruct students to read the section. Discuss with students why peoples from India, Europe, and Southwest Asia came together in East Africa. Ask: What is Swahili culture? How does it unify countries in East Africa? How did European ideas about land use differ from those of the East Africans?

Answers to...

CRITICAL THINKING

Answers may include popcorn and potato chips.

Resource Directory

Teaching Resources

Classroom Manager in the Unit 5 Teaching Resources, p. 38

Guided Reading and Review in the Unit 5 Teaching Resources, p. 39

Guide to the Essentials, p. 91

Technology

Section Reading Support Transparencies

Lesson Plan continued

3 Teach

Ask students to create three bookmarks commemorating a lecture series about East Africa. Students should use information from the section to add text or illustrations to the bookmarks that provide information about issues facing the region. This activity should take about 35 minutes.

Question for Discussion

ECONOMICS **Should land be owned or should it be used by all people according to their changing needs, as it was in traditional African culture?**

Students' responses will vary, but make sure they support their opinions with details from the text.

4 Assess/Reteach

See the answers to the Section 3 Assessment. You may also use students' bookmarks as an assessment tool.

Acceptable bookmarks are linked to the lesson objectives.

Commendable bookmarks are each linked to one of the lesson objectives and include decorations or text that illustrate a theme or issue.

Outstanding bookmarks are each linked to one of the lesson objectives and include text or several related decorations that illustrate or explain a theme or issue.

CULTURE

The Maasai

One of East Africa's many ethnic groups is the Maasai of Tanzania and Kenya. Maasai jewelry and hairstyles are quite striking. Women wear dozens of necklaces, bracelets, and earrings made of beaded copper and iron wire. Though the women shave their heads, the Maasai men groom their long hair with clay and grease. Then they braid their hair in tiny braids and loop or drape it about their heads in intricate designs.

A Family Farm in Rwanda

CULTURE On his family farm in Rwanda, this farmer grows potatoes, corn, beans, and cabbage. East Africans sometimes move away from their farms, but they almost always hope to return to them one day.
Critical Thinking What ties people to the places that they call home? Put your answer in the form of a chart with three headings: People, Ideas, Things.

Blended Cultures

Along the east coast of Africa from Somalia to Mozambique live Africans who have mixed African and Arab ancestry. They are the Swahili. The Swahili language, with its mixture of Bantu and Arabic words, is widely used for business and communication throughout the region. It is the official language of Kenya and Tanzania, although children here are also educated in English. By promoting the continuation of this language, these nations of blended cultures are trying to preserve their African heritage.

Like languages, religious beliefs in East Africa reflect its diversity. Islam was introduced into the region by Arab traders. Christianity spread to the region from North Africa and, later, through European influence. Traditional religions and practices also remain alive in East Africa and throughout the continent.

Changing Ideas About Land

The ways in which East Africans view and work the land form an important part of their culture. Traditionally, Africans did not own their

Answers to...

CRITICAL THINKING

Answers will vary. Possible answers might include family, friends, a sense of familiarity, and a sense of belonging.

Resource Directory

Teaching Resources

Outline Maps, West and Central Africa: Political, p. 34

own land. The idea of buying or selling the land did not exist. Extended families farmed plots of land near the village and produced crops for the whole group. Men cleared the land, women planted and harvested, and, meanwhile, men herded livestock or traded goods.

European settlers brought with them the idea of privately owned land. The British set up **plantations,** large farms where cash crops were grown. With independence, many countries broke up the old colonial plantations and the land was sold to individual Africans.

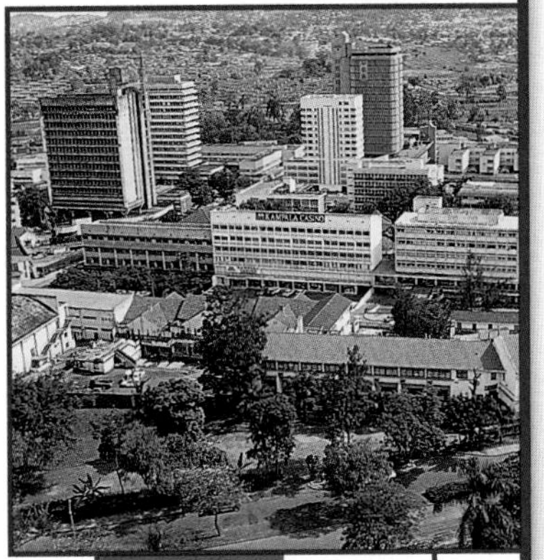

CULTURE Kampala is Uganda's largest city and leading trade center. It is a religious center as well. You can find Muslim mosques, Hindu temples, and Christian churches here. **Critical Thinking** What does the presence of these religious buildings tell you about the religious makeup of Uganda?

Increasing Urbanization

Like the rest of Africa, East Africa is becoming increasingly urban. Yet even people who spend most of their time in a city do not call it home. If asked where home is, an East African will name the village of his or her family or clan. Most people consider their life in the city to be temporary. They expect to return to their villages some day.

Some land in East Africa is still available to buy. But much of it is poor farmland in areas where few people live. In fertile areas like the Ethiopian Highlands and the Rift Valley, land for farming is scarce. Many people live in these areas where the farmland is fertile. In densely populated countries, such as Rwanda and Burundi, conflicts have developed over land.

SECTION 3 ASSESSMENT

AFTER YOU READ

RECALL

1. Define: (a) plantation

COMPREHENSION

2. Describe some ways in which East Africa's location along the Indian Ocean has affected its cultures.
3. Why is Swahili spoken by so many people in East Africa?
4. Explain the changes in ideas about land ownership in East Africa.

CRITICAL THINKING AND WRITING

5. **Exploring the Main Idea** Review the Main Idea statement at the beginning of this section. Think about the many people who migrated to East Africa and choose the group that you think had the most lasting influence. Use examples to support your choice.
6. **Making Comparisons** How did traditional East African ideas about land differ from the ideas of Europeans who took over parts of Africa?

ACTIVITY

7. **Writing a Descriptive Paragraph** Write a paragraph describing one of the cultural institutions in your society, such as your school or church. Explain why this institution is important to you and your family.

ACTIVITY

Journal Writing

Culture Challenge students to answer the question: Where is home? Explain that students should describe a place where they feel at home, which does not necessarily have to be where they currently live. They may use drawings, poetry, or a narrative to describe the place. Remind students that their journals are private and that no one else will read their entries.

Verbal/Linguistic

SECTION 3 ASSESSMENT

AFTER YOU READ

1. a large farm where cash crops are grown
2. East Africa's location on the Indian Ocean made it relatively easy for traders from Arab nations, India, and China to reach. They brought elements of their culture to East Africa.
3. Many people speak Swahili as a second language in order to communicate with others in a region where many different languages are spoken.
4. European settlers introduced the idea of ownership of land. Traditionally, Africans did not buy or sell land.
5. Answers will vary. Some students may say the West Africans who brought Bantu languages to East Africa had the most lasting influence. Others may say the Arab traders who brought Islam and the Arabic language which contributed to the Swahili language had the most lasting influence.
6. East Africans did not view land as a commodity to be bought and sold. They farmed land to grow food for their immediate needs. Europeans viewed the ownership of land as a way to earn money. They grew cash crops.
7. Descriptions will vary. Students should understand the concept of such institutions being basic to all societies.

Resource Directory

Teaching Resources

Section Quiz in the Unit 5 Teaching Resources, p. 40

Answers to...

CRITICAL THINKING

The diversity of the religious buildings reflects the religions diversity of the people.

SECTION 4

Lesson Objectives

1. Describe the influence of South Africa on both the region of Southern Africa and on the entire continent.
2. Explain how migrant labor and the formation of the mineworker's unions led to a new group identity among the peoples of Southern Africa.

Lesson Plan

1 Engage

Warm-Up Activity

Tell students that during the 1960s, black Americans joined together to win full political and civil rights. Ask students how they think this fight for rights affected black Americans' sense of community.

Activating Prior Knowledge

Ask the students to think of a goal that required hard work to achieve at home or at school. Suggest they think about why it was an important goal, and identify the plan they made and the strategies they used to achieve the goal. What obstacles did they have to overcome and how did they feel when they finally succeeded? Invite volunteers to share with the class some of this information.

Answers to...

CRITICAL THINKING

The Civil Rights movement in the United States was similar to the fight for equal rights in South Africa. Minorities fought for the right to vote and for other basic human rights. A leader in that movement was Martin Luther King, Jr. who, like Nelson Mandela, was arrested for his protest actions.

SECTION 4

The Cultures of South Africa

BEFORE YOU READ

READING FOCUS

1. How has the country of South Africa influenced the entire region of Southern Africa?
2. How did migrant labor give rise to a new group identity among the peoples of Southern Africa?

KEY TERMS	KEY PLACES AND PEOPLE
migrant worker	Republic of South Africa Nelson Mandela

MAIN IDEA

The culture of South Africa has developed around two issues, the conflict over basic rights between black South Africans and white South Africans, and the influence of the organized mine workers who also seek equal rights.

NOTE TAKING

Copy the outline below. As you read the section, complete the outline to show important events in the recent history of South Africa.

I. Modern History of the Nation of South Africa
- A. European minority rule
  - 1. separation of people into categories
  - 2.
- B.
  - 1.
  - 2.
- C.
  - 1.
  - 2.

The Fight for Equal Rights

GOVERNMENT South African blacks organized the African National Congress (ANC) to fight for equality. The ANC used boycotts, rallies, and work strikes to protest the government. **Critical Thinking** Do similarities exist between the fight for equal rights in South Africa, and the fight for equal rights in the United States? If so, why?

Setting the Scene

The African National Congress (ANC), a political party in the **Republic of South Africa,** played a key role in gaining political and civil rights for all South Africans. Until 1991, white South Africans had denied equal rights to blacks, who make up a majority of the population. Three countries—Tanzania, Zambia, and Zimbabwe—adopted the ANC anthem for their national anthem. Here are the words to the ANC anthem:

> "Bless, O Lord, our land of Africa
> Lift its name and make its people free.
> Take the gifts we offer unto Thee
> Hear us, faithful sons.
> Hear us, faithful sons."

The Influence of South Africa

South Africa is just one country in Southern Africa, but it has had, by far, the greatest impact on the region. Its influence has touched the lives of millions of people.

Resource Directory

Teaching Resources

Classroom Manager in the Unit 5 Teaching Resources, p. 41

Guided Reading and Review in the Unit 5 Teaching Resources, p. 42

Guide to the Essentials, p. 92

Technology

Section Reading Support Transparencies

Political Influence

Until the 1990s, a minority group of white people ruled South Africa, and everything in the country was separated into categories by skin color. People of African descent were classified as black, people of European descent as white, people of mixed ancestry as colored, with Asians forming a fourth category. Only people considered to be white were allowed to vote and have other basic rights of citizenship.

GOVERNMENT

A New South Africa

South Africa's first one-person one-vote election took place April 26–29, 1994. Millions of people waited patiently in mile-long lines to vote for the first time in their lives. The election was won by the African National Congress (ANC) with nearly two-thirds of the vote. Under a new South African flag, ANC president Nelson Mandela, freed after 27 years as a political prisoner, was inaugurated as president of the republic and head of a government of national unity. He invited the former president, F.W. de Klerk, to become a deputy president as a way to bring all South Africans together under a new government.

Growing Sense of Nationalism

White settlers, not blacks, had established the nation of South Africa. But as black South Africans struggled to gain political rights they began to think of themselves as full members of the nation. Soon there was a sense of nationalism that led eventually to black South Africans winning the rights of equal citizenship and, as the majority, the right to rule the nation.

In 1912, South African blacks organized the African National Congress (ANC) to fight for equality. Many ANC members, including **Nelson Mandela,** were jailed for their actions. Mandela spent almost 30 years in jail. The struggle finally paid off. In the 1990s, South Africa ended its discriminatory laws and gave nonwhite South Africans the right to vote for the first time. Mandela became South Africa's president. The struggle for majority rule inspired similar movements elsewhere in the region.

Economic Influence

South Africa is the richest and most industrialized country on the continent of Africa. Its economic power has affected all of

A South African Gold Miner

ECONOMICS This miner crawls through cramped tunnels until he reaches this "room," where he does not have space to stand up. **Critical Thinking** What do you think a work day for this gold miner would be like? Why do you think a worker would choose to leave his country to work in the mines?

❷ Explore

Draw a cause-and-effect diagram on the board. After students read the section, have volunteers fill in the diagram. You may prompt students by having them think of causes for these effects: *blacks began to view themselves as citizens; transportation links were built in South Africa; migrant workers forged a group identity.* Urge students to answer the question "why" as they identify corresponding causes.

❸ Teach

After students have read the section, have them develop a Venn diagram showing what things are traditional, modern, and a combination of modern and traditional. This activity should take about 20 minutes.

Question for Discussion

CULTURE **Why do you think group identity is so important in Africa? Is it important in other areas of the world?**

It is important for people to feel connected to a larger group. This sense of belonging is the basis of all cultures.

❹ Assess/Reteach

See the answers to the Section 4 Assessment. Students' completed diagrams can also be assessed.

Acceptable diagrams include two facts in each cell.

Commendable diagrams include three facts in each cell.

Outstanding diagrams include more than three facts in each cell.

SKILLS MINI LESSON

Identifying Central Issues

To **introduce** the skill, tell students that one way to understand their reading more fully is to identify main ideas, or central issues, in the text. Suggest the following strategies to help students identify central issues: 1) Check titles and headings for main ideas. 2) Read opening and closing sentences. 3) Think about an idea that all sections of text have in common. 4) Use your own words to restate the central issue. As a class, **practice** and **apply** these steps to the text under the heading *The Pull of South Africa.* Invite volunteers to write on the board their responses to each strategy. Then have students write one or two sentences stating the central issue of the text. (Possible answer: South Africa has had more influence than any other Southern African nation on the politics and economics of the region.)

Answers to...

CRITICAL THINKING

A work day for this miner would involve a great deal of hard, dangerous work. The need for an income would motivate a worker to leave his country and work in the mines.

SECTION 4 ASSESSMENT

AFTER YOU READ

1. (a) most industrialized country in Southern Africa (b) leader of South African equal rights movement and the nation's first black president.
2. someone who moves from place to place to find work
3. The struggle for majority rule in South Africa inspired and encouraged similar movements in nearby countries. South Africa has also drawn laborers from the entire region.
4. Their new group identity was based on a common experience as workers, not on kinship or ethnicity.
5. Answers will vary. Paragraphs should include the growth of nationalism, and the formation of a mining workers union.
6. Possible answers: Neighboring economies may have benefited from the income earned in South African industry. Nearby countries' economies may have suffered labor shortages.
7. Songs will vary. Song verses should demonstrate the miners' desire for political acknowledgement and representation.

Southern Africa because of its demand for labor, especially for mining workers. A huge work force of hundreds of thousands of **migrant workers,** people who move from place to place to find work, was soon created.

Migrant Workers Form a New Group Identity

Mine workers in South Africa were from many countries. They lived together in compounds, or fenced-in groups of homes. They were far from their families, clans, and ethnic groups. They worked long hours in dangerous conditions for low wages.

They began to think of themselves as a group—as workers. This kind of group identity was new for southern Africans. It was not based on family or ethnic group. Group identity is very important in Africa. This is reflected in the African proverb "A person is a person because of people." It means that a person is who he or she is because of his or her relationships with other people. The migrant workers formed a new identity based on how they related to each other as workers.

AS YOU READ
Summarize How did South Africa's mines affect its culture?

Mine Workers Form a Union In the 1980s, the mine workers in South Africa formed a union—the National Union of Mineworkers. This union was illegal at the time, but it played a leading role in the drive for equal rights. The union workers sometimes went on strike in support of their causes. Thus, the new identity of the mine workers led them to take group action.

SECTION 4 ASSESSMENT

AFTER YOU READ

RECALL

1. Identify: (a) Republic of South Africa, (b) Nelson Mandela
2. Define: (a) migrant worker

COMPREHENSION

3. Describe the political and economic effects South Africa has had on the entire region of Southern Africa.
4. What was unusual about migrant workers in South Africa forming a group identity as workers?

CRITICAL THINKING AND WRITING

5. **Exploring the Main Idea** Review the Main Idea statement at the beginning of this section. Then, write a paragraph summarizing the information in this section that supports this main idea.
6. **Recognizing Cause and Effect** What positive and/or negative effects might South Africa's labor needs have had on the economies of nearby countries?

ACTIVITY

7. **Writing a Song** Consider the life of a mine worker in a South African gold mine in the 1970s. Write the first verse of a song about miners' living and working conditions and wages.

Resource Directory

Teaching Resources

Section Quiz in the Unit 5 Teaching Resources, p. 43

Chapter Summary in the Unit 5 Teaching Resources, p. 44

Vocabulary in the Unit 5 Teaching Resources, p. 45

Reteaching in the Unit 5 Teaching Resources, p. 46

Enrichment in the Unit 5 Teaching Resources, p. 47

Critical Thinking in the Unit 5 Teaching Resources, p. 48

Answers to...

AS YOU READ

Mine workers began to form a group identity, which is very important in Africa.

Finding the Main Idea

supporting details

Music in Africa may be used to send messages or to a story. Horns, bells, and drums may be used to organize work. Xylophones, lutes, harps, flutes, and clarinets may be used to celebrate a special occasion. Music has many roles in the cultures of African countries.

main idea

Main Idea
Music has many roles in the cultures of African countries.
Supporting Details
Music can be used to send messages, tell a story, organize work, or celebrate a special occasion.
Supporting Details
Instruments include horns, bells, drums, xylophones, lutes, harps, flutes, and clarinets.

Learn the Skill

Each paragraph in a textbook contains a main idea and supporting details. The main idea is the most important idea about the paragraph's topic. Locating the main idea will help you figure out what the paragraph is about. To locate the main idea and supporting details in a paragraph, follow these steps:

A. Read the paragraph carefully.

B. Search the paragraph for the main idea. The main idea is often stated in the paragraph's first or last sentence. Reread the first and last sentences to see if they contain the main idea. Note that the last contains the main idea in the sample paragraph above. If neither the first or last sentence states the main idea, look for a main idea sentence in the middle of the paragraph. A main idea can also be unstated. When the main idea is not stated, readers must figure it out on their own, and state it in their own words.

C. After you have found the main idea, look for details that support the main idea. Supporting details are small pieces of information that tell more about the main idea. Some details may be more interesting than others, but all details tell about the topic. You should be able to find several supporting details in each paragraph.

Practice the Skill

Using what you have learned, find the main idea and supporting details of the paragraph on the Dogon people of Mali. Then, make a Main Idea-Supporting Details chart like the one shown on this page.

> The Dogon people of Mali use granaries to store grain. The granaries are made of twigs and mud but have stylized wooden doors. The Dogon believe the tree from which the wooden door was made contains a spirit that protects the stored grain. Although the rain and sun often wear down the granaries, the Dogon transfer the symbolic door from one granary to another.

Apply the Skill

See the Chapter Review and Assessment at the end of this chapter for more questions on finding the main idea.

CHAPTER 21 SKILLS FOR LIFE 397

Lesson Objectives

1. Locate the main idea in a paragraph.
2. Identify details that support the main idea.

Lesson Plan

1 Engage

To introduce the skill, read the opening text under "Learn the Skill" aloud. Point out that in this activity, they will focus on finding main idea and supporting details for paragraphs only.

2 Explore

Direct students to read the steps under "Learn the Skill." Make sure that students understand that the main idea can be either stated or unstated. When looking for the main idea, students should try to find a sentence that sums up the biggest point or idea in that paragraph. Have them read the sample paragraph and note the location of the main idea.

3 Teach

Have students read the paragraph and determine the main idea on their own. Check their main ideas before they complete the chart. Tell students they must list at least two supporting details.

4 Assess/Reteach

Students should be able to accurately locate the main idea of a paragraph. They should be able to find at least two supporting details.

To further assess students' understanding of main idea, have them complete the "Applying Your Skills" part of the Chapter Review and Assessment at the end of the chapter.

Resource Directory

Teaching Resources

Social Studies and Geography Skills, Identifying the Main Idea, p. 39

Technology

Social Studies Skills Tutor CD-ROM

Answers to...

PRACTICE THE SKILL

The main idea is stated in the first sentence.

CHAPTER 21

Review and Assessment

Student summaries will vary.

Sample summary:

Section 2 Seventeen countries make up the region of West Africa, and the result is great diversity in culture. There is no one language or religion, but ties to family and tradition are strong and help to unify people.

Section 3 The culture of East Africa has been influenced by Arab traders and explorers from China and India. The language, religion and customs of the region reflect the migration of people from West Africa and other countries over thousands of years.

Section 4 South Africa has had a great deal of influence over the entire region of Southern Africa. The fight for equal rights in South Africa came about as the result of a growing sense of nationalism among black South Africans, and the formation of a mining workers union.

Reviewing Key Terms

1. h **2.** f **3.** b **4.** g **5.** c **6.** a **7.** e **8.** d

Reviewing the Main Ideas

1. Islam unified the peoples of North Africa, creating a bond of common religion.
2. North Africa's location just across the Mediterranean Sea from Europe and Southwest Asia has aided cultural diffusion.
3. West Africa has hundreds of ethnic groups that speak different languages.
4. Members of extended families live together, sharing responsibility for one another.
5. East Africa's location along the Indian Ocean encouraged Arab traders to settle, spreading Arab culture along the coast.

CHAPTER 21

Review and Assessment

Creating a Chapter Summary

On a separate piece of paper, draw a diagram like this one, and include the information that summarizes the first section of the chapter. Then, fill in the remaining boxes with summaries of Sections 2, 3, and 4.

THE CULTURES OF AFRICA

Section 1	Section 2	Section 3	Section 4
North Africa's location on the Mediterranean, and its history as a trading center have greatly influenced its culture, which is a blend of African, European, and Southwest Asian elements. The religion of Islam plays an important role in North African life.			

Reviewing Key Terms

Match the definitions in Column I with the key terms in Column II.

Column I	Column II
1. parents and their children	a. cultural diffusion
2. people who move in order to find work	b. culture
3. shared beliefs and customs	c. kinship
4. large farms of cash crops	d. cultural diversity
5. a family relationship	e. clan
6. a spreading of culture	f. migrant worker
7. several lineages with a common ancestor	g. plantation
8. a wide variety of cultures	h. nuclear family

Reviewing the Main Ideas

1. Describe how Islam has influenced the culture of North Africa. (Section 1)
2. What factor has greatly aided cultural diffusion in North Africa? (Section 1)
3. In what ways is West Africa culturally diverse? (Section 2)
4. What role do family ties play in West African culture? (Section 2)
5. Explain how location has affected East African cultures. (Section 3)
6. How does the language of Swahili help unite the people of East Africa? (Section 3)
7. How has South Africa affected the cultures of the entire region of Southern Africa? (Section 4)
8. What major effect did migrant labor have on the people of southern Africa? (Section 4)

6. Swahili aids communication, because it serves as a second language for millions of people speaking various first languages.
7. South Africa has drawn workers from throughout the region of Southern Africa. The struggle for majority rule in South Africa inspired similar movements in nearby countries.
8. It caused them to develop a new group identity as workers.

Map Activity

Africa

For each place listed below, write the letter from the map that shows its location.

1. Mediterranean Sea
2. North Africa
3. West Africa
4. East Africa
5. Southern and Central Africa

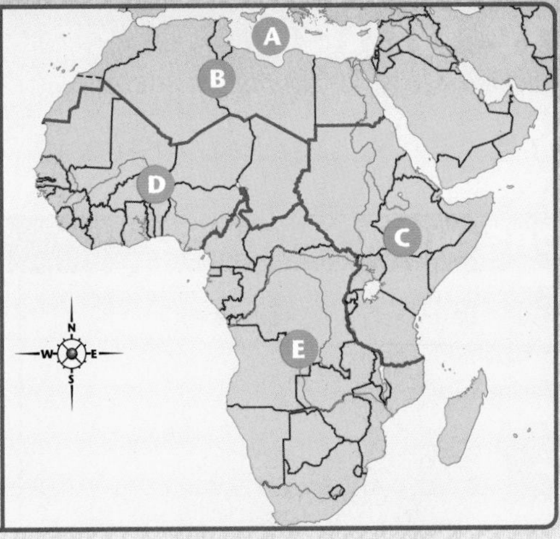

Take It to the NET

Enrichment For more map activities using geography skills, visit the social studies section of **phschool.com.**

Writing Activity

1. **Writing a Dialogue** An exchange student from an African country has come to stay at your home for six weeks. You and your family are sharing your first dinner with the visitor. Write a dialogue in which you ask your visitor about African culture. Use what you have learned in this chapter to write your visitor's answers.
2. **Writing a Newspaper Article** You are a news reporter in South Africa and you have the opportunity to interview Nelson Mandela. Prepare a list of the questions you would most want to ask him, and then visit your school or local library to try to find the answers to your questions. When you are finished with your research, write a newspaper article based on the information you have gathered.

Applying Your Skills

Read the first paragraph under the heading "Cultural Ties" on p. 389. Create a chart like you did on p. 397 to identify the main idea of the paragraph and the details used to support this main idea.

Critical Thinking

1. **Identifying Central Issues** Explain why the proverb "A person is a person because of people" is particularly suited to African culture.
2. **Making a Valid Generalization** What benefits and problems have come with modernization in Africa?
3. **Drawing Conclusions** Which organization founded in the 20th century do you think has had the greatest effect on the events of modern Africa? Explain your answer.

Take It to the NET

View art and personal objects from Africa. Think about art and personal objects you've seen from your region of the world. What do these things reflect about your region's culture and history? Visit the **phschool.com** for help in completing this activity.

Chapter 21 Self-Test As a final review activity, take the Chapter 21 Self-Test and get instant feedback on your answers. To take the test, visit the Social Studies section of **phschool.com.**

Map Activity

1. A **2.** B **3.** D **4.** C **5.** E

Writing Activity

1. Dialogues will vary, but should show a clear grasp of the facts and issues presented in the chapter.
2. Articles will vary, but questions and answers should reflect an understanding of the important issues in the fight for equal rights in South Africa, Nelson Mandela's contribution, and the significance of the changes that resulted.

Critical Thinking

1. Students might note that relations with other people, particularly family members, are very important in Africa. People are more group-oriented and less individualistic.
2. Students might identify a higher standard of living for some people as a possible benefit. As a drawback, students might cite the loss of close ties among members of extended families.
3. Answers will vary. Possible answer: The African National Congress (ANC). It brought an end to the discriminatory laws regarding equal rights, the right to vote, and the right to form unions. It helped establish majority rule in South Africa.

Applying Your Skills

Students should identify the main idea of the paragraph as the first sentence.

Resource Directory

Teaching Resources

Cooperative Learning Activity in the Unit 5 Teaching Resources, pp. 112–115

Chapter Tests Forms A and B in the Unit 5 Teaching Resources, pp. 142–147

Guide to the Essentials, Ch. 21 Test, p. 93

Other Print Resources

Chapter Tests with ExamView® Test Bank, Ch. 21

Technology

ExamView® Test Bank CD-ROM, Ch. 21

Resource Pro® CD-ROM

Chapter 22 Planning Guide

Resource Manager

	CORE INSTRUCTION	READING/SKILLS
Chapter-Level Resources	**Teaching Resources** Program Overview Pacing Charts **Technology** Resource Pro® CD-ROM Companion Web site, phschool.com • eTeach	**Technology** Social Studies Skills Tutor CD-ROM Student Edition on Audio CD, Ch. 22
1 Egypt: A Nation Shaped by Islam 1. Explain the influence of Islam on Egyptian culture. 2. Compare and contrast the lives of urban and rural Egyptians.	**Teaching Resources** **Unit 5** Classroom Manager, p. 50 Guided Reading and Review, p. 51	**Teaching Resources** Guide to the Essentials, p. 94 **Technology** Section Reading Support Transparencies
2 Algeria: Urban and Rural Ways of Life 1. Describe the differences and similarities between the Berbers and the Arabs of Algeria. 2. Compare and contrast rural and city life in Algeria.	**Teaching Resources** **Unit 5** Classroom Manager, p. 53 Guided Reading and Review, p. 54	**Teaching Resources** Guide to the Essentials, p. 95 **Technology** Section Reading Support Transparencies
3 Nigeria: One Country, Many Ethnic Groups 1. Trace historic factors leading to a multi-ethnic Nigeria. 2. Describe the ways of life for Nigeria's three main ethnic groups.	**Teaching Resources** **Unit 5** Classroom Manager, p. 56 Guided Reading and Review, p. 57	**Teaching Resources** Guide to the Essentials, p. 96 **Technology** Section Reading Support Transparencies
4 Ghana: Origins of a Democratic Government 1. Identify the circumstances that led to Ghana's gaining its independence. 2. Describe economic and political setbacks and successes following Ghana's independence.	**Teaching Resources** **Unit 5** Classroom Manager, p. 59 Guided Reading and Review, p. 60 Chapter Summary, p. 62 Vocabulary, p. 63 Reteaching, p. 64	**Teaching Resources** **Unit 5** Critical Thinking, p. 66 Guide to the Essentials, p. 97 Social Studies and Geography Skills, pp. 17 and 53 **Technology** Section Reading Support Transparencies

ENRICHMENT / PRE-AP

Teaching Resources
Primary Sources and Literature Readings

Other Print Resources
DK Atlas

Technology
World Video Explorer: Daily Life: Cairo, A Trip to Coastal West Africa
Companion Web site, phschool.com

Technology
Color Transparencies 97, 100

Teaching Resources
Unit 5
Enrichment, p. 65
Cooperative Learning Activity, pp. 116–119

Technology
Color Transparencies 96

ASSESSMENT

Prentice Hall Assessment System

Core Assessment
Chapter Tests with ExamView® Test Bank, Ch. 22
ExamView® Test Bank CD-ROM, Ch. 22

Standardized Test Preparation
Diagnose and Prescribe
Diagnostic Tests for Middle Grades Social Studies Skills
Review and Reteach
Review Book for World Studies
Practice and Assess
Test-taking Strategies with Transparencies for Middle Grades Test Prep Book
Test-taking Strategies Posters

Teaching Resources
Unit 5
Section Quizzes, pp. 53, 55, 58, and 61
Chapter Tests, pp. 148-153

Technology
Companion Web site, phschool.com
Ch. 22 Self-Test

World Video Explorer
Each region of the world is explored through regional flyovers and investigative field trips. Case study segments give students an in-depth view of the history, economy, government, and culture of a key place in each region. Case studies include Nigeria, Mexico, China, British Columbia, and the Czech Republic.

In Your Classroom

CUSTOMIZE FOR INDIVIDUAL NEEDS

Gifted and Talented

Teacher's Edition
- Language Arts, p. 406

Teaching Resources
- Enrichment, p. 65
- Primary Sources and Literature Readings

Honors/Pre-AP

Teacher's Edition
- Language Arts, p. 406

Teaching Resources
- Critical Thinking, p. 66
- Primary Sources and Literature Readings

ESL

Teacher's Edition
- Identifying Central Issues, p. 403
- Language Arts, p. 413

Teaching Resources
- Guided Reading and Review, pp. 51, 54, 57, and 60
- Vocabulary, p. 63
- Reteaching, p. 64
- Guide to the Essentials, pp. 94–97
- Social Studies and Geography Skills, p. 17 and 53

Technology
- Social Studies Skills Tutor CD-ROM
- Section Reading Support Transparencies

Less Proficient Readers

Teacher's Edition
- Identifying Central Issues, p. 403
- Language Arts, p. 413

Teaching Resources
- Guided Reading and Review, pp. 51, 54, 57, and 60
- Vocabulary, p. 63
- Reteaching, p. 64
- Guide to the Essentials, pp. 94–97
- Social Studies and Geography Skills, p. 17 and 53

Technology
- Social Studies Skills Tutor CD-ROM
- Section Reading Support Transparencies

Less Proficient Writers

Teacher's Edition
- Identifying Central Issues, p. 403
- Language Arts, p. 413

Teaching Resources
- Guided Reading and Review, pp. 51, 54, 57, and 60
- Vocabulary, p. 63
- Guide to the Essentials, pp. 94–97
- Social Studies and Geography Skills, p. 17 and 53

Technology
- Social Studies Skills Tutor CD-ROM
- Section Reading Support Transparencies

DORLING KINDERSLEY

At the end of each unit, you will find information adapted from Dorling Kindersley's *Illustrated Children's Encyclopedia* that connects to the region being studied and to one of the seven content strands. In addition, your resources include Dorling Kindersley's *Atlas*, which contains valuable information about countries from around the world.

TEACHER'S EDITION INDEX

CHAPTER 22 PACING SUGGESTIONS

For 90-minute Blocks

See suggestions in the Teaching Resources Pacing Charts for Chapter 22. Use Color Transparencies 96, 97, 100.

Running Out of Time?

See the Guide to the Essentials, pp. 94–97.

INTERDISCIPLINARY LINKS

Middle Grades Math: Tools for Success
Course 1, Lesson 1-5 **Reading and Understanding Graphs**

Science Explorer
Earth's Waters, Lesson 2-1, **Streams and Rivers;** Lesson 2-3, **Wetland Environments**

BIBLIOGRAPHY

For the Teacher

Adeeb, Hassan, and Bonnetta Adeeb. *Nigeria: One Nation, Many Cultures.* Benchmark, 1996.

Ayoub, Abderrahman, Jamila Binous, Ali Mtimet, and Hedi Slim. *Umm El Madayan: An Islamic City Through the Ages.* Houghton Mifflin, 1994.

King, John. *Bedouin.* Raintree, 1993.

Knight, Khadijah. *Islam.* Thomson, 1995.

For the Student

Easy

Onyefulu, Ifeoma. *Ogbo: Sharing Life in an African Village.* Gulliver/Harcourt Brace Jovanovich, 1996.

Average

Algeria in Pictures. Lerner, 1992.

Brace, Steve. *Ghana.* Thomson, 1995.

Challenging

Hermes, Jules. *The Children of Morocco.* Carolrhoda, 1995.

World Desk Reference. Dorling Kindersley, 2001.

Literature Connection

Angelou, Maya, and Margaret Courtney-Clark. *Kofi and His Magic.* Clarkson Potter, 1996.

Olaleye, Isaac. *The Distant Talking Drum: Poems from Nigeria.* Wordsong, 1995.

Take It to the NET

The World Explorer companion Web site, found on **phschool.com**, offers activities for exploring geographical, historical, and cultural resources on the Internet. It also provides on-line links for key content and all Section and Chapter Assessment activities.

The **Teacher site** also provides teachers with regional data and ideas for student research and activities.

Students can use the **Student site** to find chapter-by-chapter Internet resource links and to access Self-Tests.

CHAPTER 22

Connecting to the Guiding Questions

In this chapter, students will read about countries in North and West Africa. Content in this chapter corresponds to the following Guiding Questions outlined at the beginning of the unit.

- How have Africans been affected by their history?
- How do Africa's many cultures differ from place to place?
- How do African governments compare with the United States government?

Using the Art Activities

Explain to students that Islam is a major religion in Africa and the official religion of many countries in the world.

- Students should be able to conclude that the Muslims had studied comets. They knew that the moon was round, and that it was partially blocked by the shadow of the Earth at certain times of the month, as the sliver of the moon in the illustration shows.
- Students should list what they know about space and astronomy without referring to any sources, and should represent what they know in an illustration of their own.

Heterogeneous Groups

The following activities are suitable for heterogeneous groups.

Critical Thinking

Identifying Central Issues, p. 403

Culture

Language Arts, p. 413

eTeach

Be sure to check out this month's discussion with a Master Teacher. Go to **phschool.com**.

CHAPTER 22

NORTH AND WEST AFRICA: Exploring the Region Today

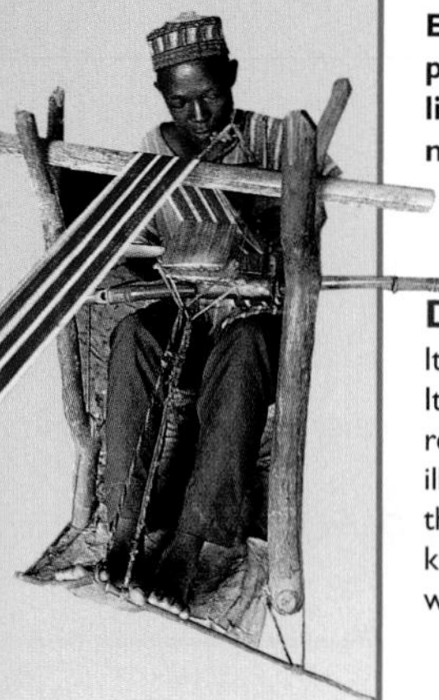

Heavenly Bodies

USING ART

Education is a priority in the religion of Islam, one of the major religions practiced in Africa. From the 600s on, Muslims have studied art, literature, philosophy, math, astronomy, and medicine. Muslim mathematicians invented algebra, and Muslim astronomers accurately mapped the locations of the stars. A Muslim astronomer drew this comet in the 1500s.

Drawing Conclusions

It wasn't until the 1500s that Galileo, an Italian, discovered that the planets revolve around the sun. Study the illustration carefully. Think about what the Muslim astronomer might have known about the heavens. Make a list of what you think he knew, and why.

Exploring Science through Art

Make a list of the facts you can recall about astronomy and outer space. Then use the facts to create an illustration that reveals what you know. Compare your drawing to the Muslim illustration. How are they alike? How are they different?

Resource Directory

Teaching Resources

Primary Sources and Literature Readings extend content with a selection related to the concepts in this chapter.

Other Print Resources

DK Atlas

Technology

Daily Life: Cairo, from the World Video Explorer, enhances students' understanding of daily life in Cairo, including the impact of overcrowding on the city's inhabitants.

A Trip to Coastal West Africa, from the World Video Explorer, enhances students' understanding of the history and culture of coastal West Africa.

Student Edition on Audio CD, Ch. 22

SECTION 1

Egypt
A Nation Shaped by Islam

BEFORE YOU READ

READING FOCUS
1. How does religion affect Egypt's culture?
2. How does life differ for Egyptians living in rural and urban areas?

KEY TERMS
bazaar
fellaheen

KEY PLACES
Cairo

NOTE TAKING
Copy this chart. As you read the section, complete the chart to show the aspects of daily Egyptian life that help define Muslim culture.

MAIN IDEA
Even though some Egyptians live in modern cities and others live in rural areas, most are unified by their faith in Islam.

Setting the Scene

At noon, the restaurants in Cairo stand empty. It's the Muslim holiday of Ramadan (RAM uh dahn) and for a month followers of Islam will fast, or go without food, from dawn to dusk. Muslim culture is one of the strongest elements that unify Egyptian society.

Egypt's Religious Culture

Egypt is across the Red Sea from Saudi Arabia, where the messenger of Islam, Muhammad, was born. Like most countries in North Africa, Islam is now the major religion in Egypt. In fact, it is the country's official religion.

Cairo's Busy Streets

GEOGRAPHY

More people live in Cairo than in any other city in Africa. Most of the people who live here are Muslim Arabs. **Critical Thinking** What similarities and differences do you see between this busy street in Cairo, and cities in the United States? Make a list.

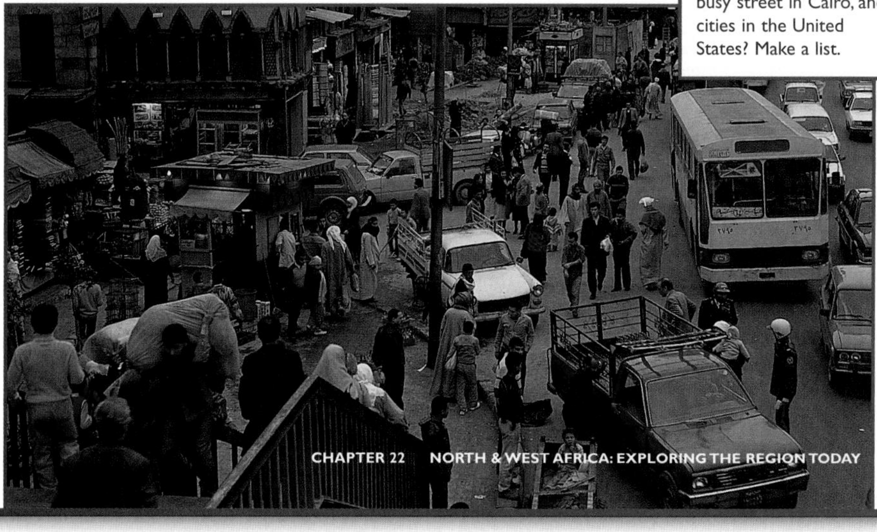

SECTION 1

Lesson Objectives

1. Explain the influence of Islam on Egyptian culture.
2. Compare and contrast the lives of urban and rural Egyptians.

Lesson Plan

1 Engage

Warm-Up Activity

Have students list the differences between living in a city and living in a rural area in the United States. Ask them to compare and contrast the kinds of jobs and the types of housing found in the two areas. Record students' responses on the chalkboard.

Activating Prior Knowledge

Invite volunteers to name their favorite holidays and describe how they celebrate them. Encourage discussion about special foods, songs and traditions related to the holiday. Ask them to share why their family celebrates on that holiday and whether it is one shared by most Americans or is specific to certain groups of Americans.

2 Explore

Have students read the section and explore questions such as these: What are some important teachings and practices of Islam? How has Islam affected the way Egyptians live? Why do some Egyptian women wear veils? Why have many people moved from rural areas to cities?

Resource Directory

Teaching Resources

Classroom Manager in the Unit 5 Teaching Resources, p. 50

Guided Reading and Review in the Unit 5 Teaching Resources, p. 51

Guide to the Essentials, p. 94

Technology

Section Reading Support Transparencies

Answers to...

CRITICAL THINKING

Students' lists will vary but should include similarities such as shopping, traffic, and population density. Differences may include the clothing people wear and the types of shops.

Lesson Plan continued

3 Teach

Ask students to write a letter from the point of view of a rural Egyptian visiting Cairo for the first time. Tell students to include in their letters observations of things that a rural person would find unfamiliar as well as things familiar. This activity should take about 20 minutes.

Question for Discussion

ECONOMICS **Do you think the Egyptian government was right to provide the "suburban" graveyards with electricity? Why?**

Students' responses will vary, but they may say that the government was wrong because it did nothing to help overcrowding and housing shortages in the city.

4 Assess/Reteach

See the answers to the Section 1 Assessment. You may also use students' letters as an assessment.

Acceptable letters identify one familiar thing or situation, such as the practice of Islam, and one thing unfamiliar, such as crowds.

Commendable letters identify at least one familiar thing or situation and at least two things unfamiliar.

Outstanding letters identify at least two familiar things or situations, such as the practice of Islam and the scarcity of land, and at least two things unfamiliar, such as crowds and apartment buildings.

COUNTRY PROFILE

Egypt

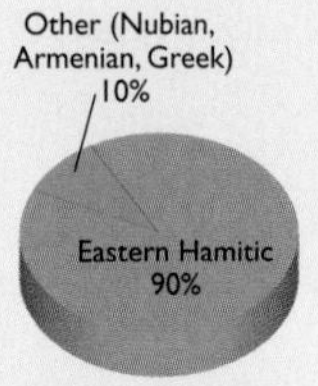

Ethnic Makeup

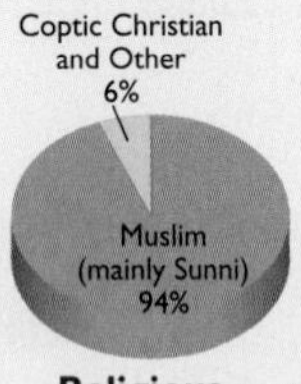

Religious Persuasion

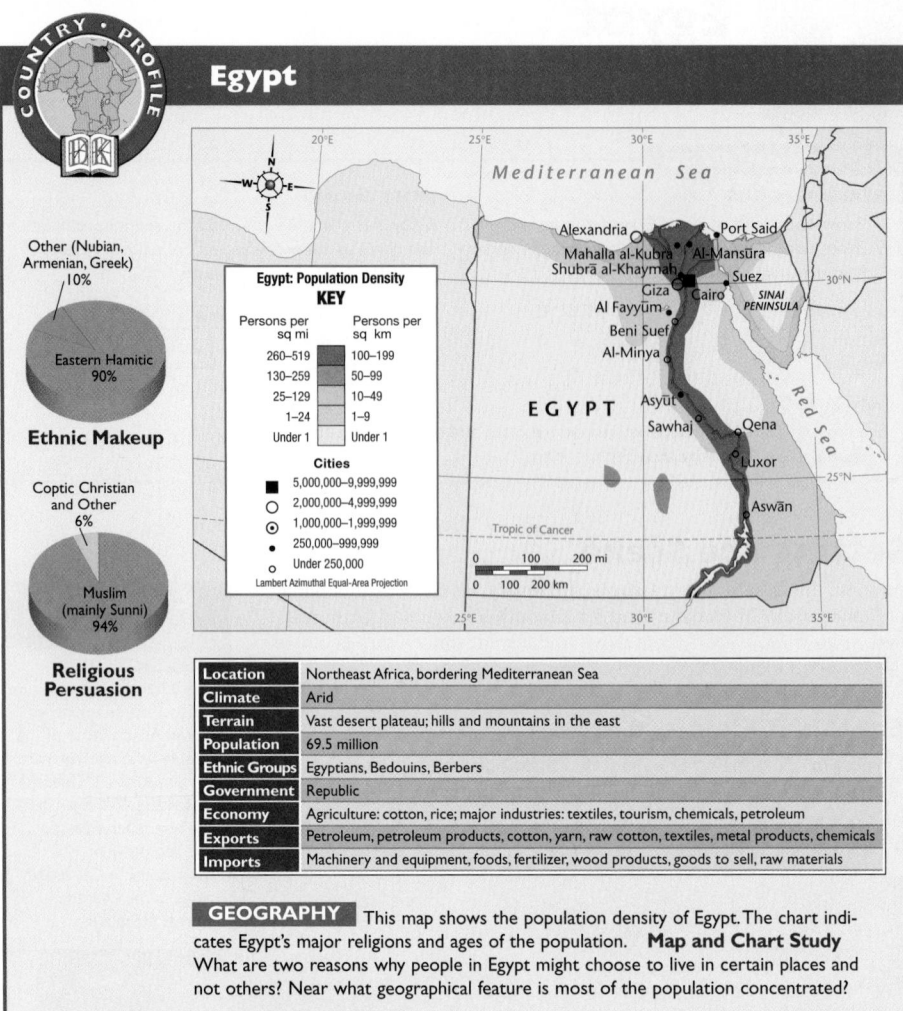

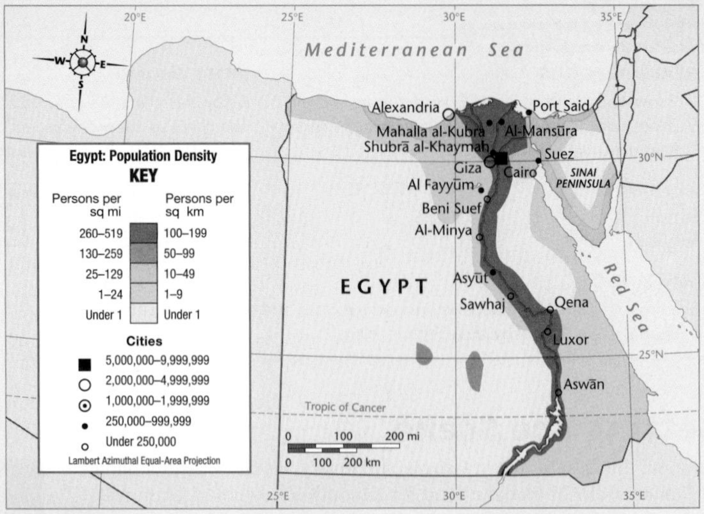

Location	Northeast Africa, bordering Mediterranean Sea
Climate	Arid
Terrain	Vast desert plateau; hills and mountains in the east
Population	69.5 million
Ethnic Groups	Egyptians, Bedouins, Berbers
Government	Republic
Economy	Agriculture: cotton, rice; major industries: textiles, tourism, chemicals, petroleum
Exports	Petroleum, petroleum products, cotton, yarn, raw cotton, textiles, metal products, chemicals
Imports	Machinery and equipment, foods, fertilizer, wood products, goods to sell, raw materials

GEOGRAPHY This map shows the population density of Egypt. The chart indicates Egypt's major religions and ages of the population. **Map and Chart Study** What are two reasons why people in Egypt might choose to live in certain places and not others? Near what geographical feature is most of the population concentrated?

Muslim Beliefs

Muslims believe that the Quran, their holy book, contains the words of God and that they were revealed to Muhammad during the month of Ramadan. They also believe that the Jewish Torah and the Christian Bible are the word of God.

Muslims pray five times a day, often in a mosque, a building used for worship. They face in the direction of Mecca, the city in Saudi Arabia, where Islam's holiest shrine is located.

Resource Directory

Technology

Color Transparencies 97 Africa: Political Map; **100** Africa: Political Map

Answers to...

MAP AND CHART STUDY

Reasons include climate and access to water. Most of the population is concentrated around the Nile River.

An Islamic Renewal

Praying and fasting are two ways that Egyptian Muslims have brought their religion into their daily lives. But many other teachings in the Quran, such as the importance of honesty, honor, giving to others, and having love and respect for their families, govern their daily lives.

While most Muslims believe that the laws of Egypt should be based on Islamic law, there is some disagreement among Egyptians. One area of disagreement is the public behavior of women. Muhammad taught that men and women are equal in the eyes of God. Both are required by Islamic law to dress modestly in public. One part of the debate is whether women should be required to cover their faces with a veil. Some people feel women should be covered except for their eyes. Other Egyptians feel that women should have the right to choose in this case.

Diversity of Life in Egypt

While the people of Egypt share the common bond of their religious practice, their lives differ greatly depending on whether they live in a city or a rural village.

Urban Life About half of all Egyptians live in cities. **Cairo,** the nation's capital and largest city has more than 13 million people, more people than live in Los Angeles and Chicago combined.

It is Africa's largest city. Some parts of the city are more than 1,000 years old, while other parts look like a modern western city. Apartment buildings with air-conditioning are common. Shopping takes place in open-air markets called **bazaars.**

Many people move to the cities from rural areas. They hope to find jobs and better education. As a result, Cairo is very crowded. There are traffic jams and housing shortages. Some people live in tents that they have set up on rowboats on the Nile. Others live in homes they have built in the huge graveyards on the outskirts of Cairo. So many people live in the graveyards that they are considered suburbs of the city, and the government has provided the graveyards with electricity.

A Traffic Jam in Cairo

CULTURE Some people think that Cairo is the loudest city in the world because of its honking horns and roar of car engines. More than 7 million people live in the city, but millions more drive or take buses and trains in from the suburbs during the day. **Critical Thinking** What are some ways that the city of Cairo could help reduce this kind of traffic?

CULTURE

Feast of Eid-ul-Fitr

This feast is celebrated at the end of Ramadan. On this day, which varies from year to year depending on when Ramadan occurs, Muslim families throughout the world celebrate *eid* (happiness). This celebration marks not only the end of a fast, but also the bond that has been created through shared hardship. Muslims celebrate by exchanging gifts with friends and relatives and sharing holiday meals.

HISTORY

Women in Ancient Egypt

The women of ancient Egypt had higher status than women in other parts of the ancient world. Women at the top of the social hierarchy could own and dispose of property as they saw fit, free slaves, and bring about lawsuits.

ACTIVITY

Critical Thinking

Identifying Central Issues *Suitable as a whole class activity.* Discuss with students ways of identifying central issues as they read. You might point out that central issues are sometimes stated indirectly and sometimes stated directly. Have students work with a partner to identify the central issue of the last paragraph of the section. "Despite their differences, however, most Egyptians are unified by one thing—their faith in Islam." Invite students to restate the central issue in their own words.

Verbal/Linguistic

SKILLS MINI LESSON

Read Actively

You might **introduce** the skill by asking students to connect their own knowledge of American urban and rural areas to the information given in the text. Point out to students that their own knowledge and experiences can help them understand what they are reading. Tell students that to read actively, they may also ask *questions* about what they are reading, *visualize* something described, and predict what will happen as they read. Have students **practice** and **apply** the skill by using one of the four strategies as they read the material under the heading *Urban Life.* Invite students to discuss the strategies they used and to explain how the strategies helped them engage in their reading.

Answers to...

CRITICAL THINKING

Students' responses will vary but may include persuading people to use public transportation or carpool.

SECTION 1 ASSESSMENT

AFTER YOU READ

1. Egypt's capital
2. (a) traditional open-air market (b) rural farmers
3. Possible answers: Muslims must pray five times a day. During Ramadan, Muslims must fast from dawn to dusk.
4. Most urban dwellers live in apartment buildings and have electricity. Cities are crowded. Most rural dwellers are farmers and typically live in homes made of mud bricks or stone.
5. Answers will vary, but may include: prayer, fasting, honesty, honor, giving to others, having love and respect for their families, and dressing modestly.
6. Possible entry: In Egypt, people dress modestly in accordance with Islamic law. People also listen to recordings of the Quran. In the United States, some religious leaders dress a certain way, but most people do not dress in a way that reflects their beliefs.

A Farm in Egypt

ECONOMICS With power from a water buffalo, a fellaheen woman runs a traditional machine that separates the seeds of grain from the plants. **Critical Thinking** What conclusions about farming as a way of life in Egypt can you draw based on this photograph?

Rural Life In the rural areas of Egypt, most people live in villages along the Nile or the Suez Canal. Most villagers make their living by farming. These farmers are called **fellaheen** (fel uh HEEN) and, because land is scarce along the river banks, most have small, rented plots of land. Others work in the fields of rich landowners. Fellaheen live in homes built of mud bricks or stones, with one to three rooms and a courtyard that is shared with the animals.

Whether living in a city or in a rural area, most Egyptians hope that renewing their Muslim faith every day will help them to maintain traditional values and customs in a modern age.

SECTION 1 ASSESSMENT

AFTER YOU READ

RECALL

1. Identify: (a) Cairo
2. Define: (a) bazaar, (b) fellaheen

COMPREHENSION

3. Give two examples of how Islam affects everyday life in Egypt.
4. Compare the lives of city and village dwellers in Egypt.

CRITICAL THINKING AND WRITING

5. **Exploring the Main Idea** Review the Main Idea statement at the beginning of this section. Then, write a paragraph about the ways that Egyptians are united by their Islamic faith.

ACTIVITY

6. **Writing to Learn** In a journal entry, describe how the clothes people wear and the music they listen to may reflect their beliefs. Use examples from your own experience as well as from this section.

Resource Directory

Teaching Resources

Section Quiz in the Unit 5 Teaching Resources, p. 53

Answers to...

CRITICAL THINKING

Answers will vary. Students may say that farming in Egypt involves a great deal of physical labor.

SECTION 2

Algeria

Urban and Rural Ways of Life

BEFORE YOU READ

READING FOCUS

1. What are some differences and similarities between the Berbers and the Arabs of Algeria?
2. How is life in Algerian cities different from life in the villages?

KEY TERMS
terrace
souq
casbah

KEY PEOPLE AND PLACES
Berber
Arab

NOTE TAKING
Copy this chart. As you read the section, complete the chart by filling in information on Algeria and its people. Add more circles to the web as you go.

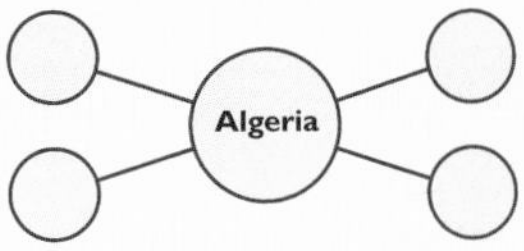

MAIN IDEA
While Algeria's two main ethnic groups, the Berbers and the Arabs, have similar cultural traditions, important aspects of their cultures set them apart.

Setting the Scene

Like many people in many parts of the world, Algerians adapt to their climate by resting during the hottest hours of the day. If you were visiting Adrar, an oasis city in the Algerian Sahara, during midday, the temperature outside would be about 124 degrees F (51 degrees C). To survive in that heat, people must drink enough water to produce 2 to 4 gallons (7.6 to 15.2l) of perspiration a day.

Algeria's Ethnic Groups

The Sahara covers all of Algeria south of the Atlas Mountains and water is in short supply in this area. For this reason, fewer than three percent of Algeria's people live here. But because of their resourcefulness, **Berber** and **Arab** nomads have survived in the Sahara for hundreds of years.

The Berbers and Arabs The Berbers and the Arabs are Algeria's two main ethnic groups. The Berbers have lived in North Africa since at least 3000 B.C. Many historians think they migrated from Southwest Asia. They settled in the Atlas Mountains and on plains near Algeria's coast. Most Berbers live in villages in rural areas and continue to follow traditional ways of life. Their households form an extended family, but each married couple in a family has its own home opening onto the family courtyard. In this way, grandparents, parents, sons, daughters, and cousins can all live close together.

A Desert Lifestyle

CULTURE These men live in the Sahara's Ahaggar Mountains. Even in the mountains, the sun is so hot that people must wear clothes that cover most of their skin.
Critical Thinking
How do the clothes these men are wearing help them adapt to living in the desert?

405

Resource Directory

Teaching Resources

Classroom Manager in the Unit 5 Teaching Resources, p. 53

Guided Reading and Review in the Unit 5 Teaching Resources, p. 54

Guide to the Essentials, p. 95

Technology

Section Reading Support Transparencies

SECTION 2

Lesson Objectives

1. Describe the differences and similarities between the Berbers and the Arabs of Algeria.
2. Compare and contrast rural and city life in Algeria.

Lesson Plan

1 Engage

Warm-Up Activity

Ask students to brainstorm a list of the many ethnic groups that have come to the United States. Encourage students to think of foods, music, dances, art, words, and other contributions various ethnic groups have made to American culture.

Activating Prior Knowledge

Ask students to think about how they adapt to their climate. Ask them to brainstorm some ideas about how they change their schedule or choose their clothing based on the weather. What items would people need to survive in a desert climate?

2 Explore

As students read the section, have them consider questions such as the following: Where do most Algerians live? What is a typical Berber household like? How do most people who live in Berber villages make their livings? How have the Arabs influenced Berber life? What are some features of Algerian cities?

Answers to...

CRITICAL THINKING

Their clothes cover most of their skin, protecting them from the sun.

Lesson Plan continued

❸ Teach

Ask students to work in groups of four to make a Venn diagram showing similarities and differences between the Berbers and the Arabs of Algeria. Use the diagrams as a basis for discussion of the section. This activity should take about 20 minutes.

Question for Discussion

CULTURE **Considering that rural Berbers make a living by farming and herding, do you think an extended family household is a benefit or a disadvantage? Why?**

An extended family would be a benefit for farmers and herders because there would be more people to farm the crops and herd the animals. That, in turn, would probably result in more profits for the family.

❹ Assess/Reteach

See the answers to the Section 2 Assessment. You may also use students' Venn diagrams as an assessment.

Acceptable diagrams show one similarity and one difference between Berbers and Arabs.

Commendable diagrams show two similarities and two differences between Berbers and Arabs.

Outstanding diagrams show at least two similarities and two differences between Berbers and Arabs and indicate that city-dwelling Berbers and Arabs have the most in common.

COUNTRY • PROFILE

Algeria

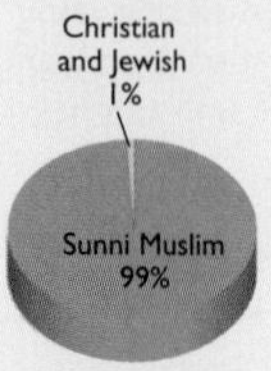

Religious Persuasion

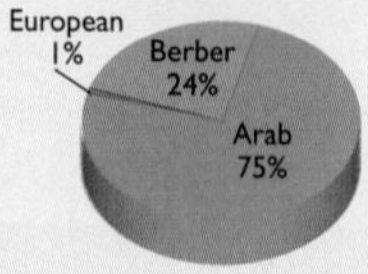

Ethnic Makeup

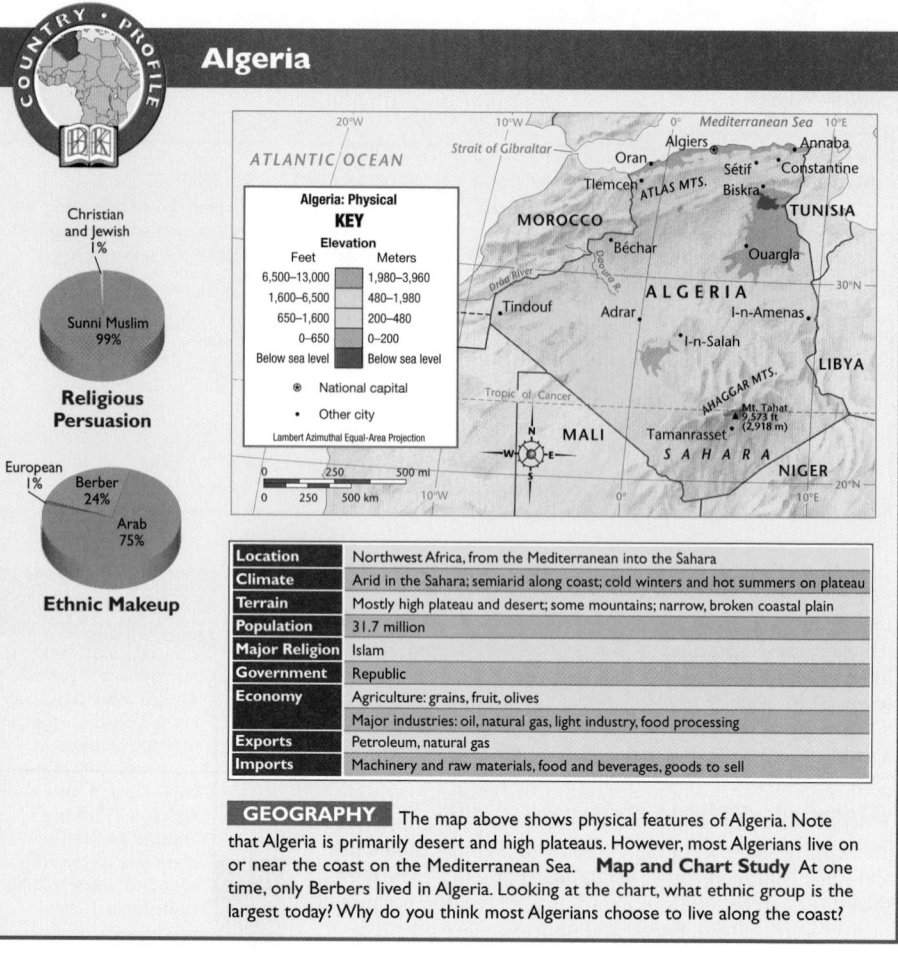

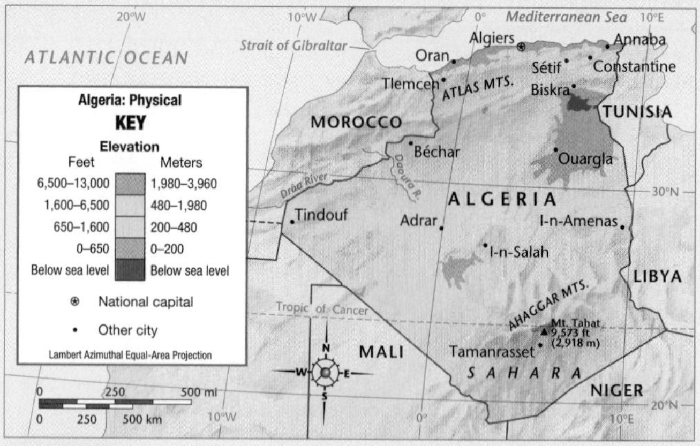

Location	Northwest Africa, from the Mediterranean into the Sahara
Climate	Arid in the Sahara; semiarid along coast; cold winters and hot summers on plateau
Terrain	Mostly high plateau and desert; some mountains; narrow, broken coastal plain
Population	31.7 million
Major Religion	Islam
Government	Republic
Economy	Agriculture: grains, fruit, olives
	Major industries: oil, natural gas, light industry, food processing
Exports	Petroleum, natural gas
Imports	Machinery and raw materials, food and beverages, goods to sell

GEOGRAPHY The map above shows physical features of Algeria. Note that Algeria is primarily desert and high plateaus. However, most Algerians live on or near the coast on the Mediterranean Sea. **Map and Chart Study** At one time, only Berbers lived in Algeria. Looking at the chart, what ethnic group is the largest today? Why do you think most Algerians choose to live along the coast?

Family is so important to the Berbers that their village governments are based on it. The head of each family is a member of the village assembly, which makes laws for the village.

Most rural Berbers make a living by farming and herding. They get up as soon as it is light and work until the sun is hottest. Then, people rest for several hours before going back to work until dark. In the mountains, the Berbers build **terraces,** or platforms cut into the mountainside, for their crops. The terraces increase farmland and keep the soil in place when it rains.

Arabs in Algeria The Berber way of life changed in the A.D. 600s, when Arabs spread across North Africa. The Arabs conquered North

406 UNIT 5 AFRICA

SKILLS MINI LESSON

Distinguishing Facts From Opinions

You might **introduce** the skill by asking students to look at the information in the Country Profile. Point out that the Country Profile contains *facts* about Algeria. Tell students that facts can be proved. *Opinions* are the beliefs or ideas of a person or a group and cannot be proved. Words such as *believe* or *think* often signal the statement of an opinion. To **practice** the skill, have students read the first paragraph under the heading ***The Berbers***. Ask students to identify one sentence that is a fact and one that is an opinion. (Fact: "The Berbers and the Arabs are Algeria's two main ethnic groups." Opinion: "No one knows exactly where they came from, but many historians think they migrated from Southwest Asia.") Ask students to **apply** the skill by writing two statements about themselves: one that is factual and one that is an opinion.

Answers to...

MAP AND CHART STUDY

Arabs are the largest ethnic group. The temperatures are cooler.

Africa gradually, over hundreds of years. Peace in the region came about when most Berbers accepted the religion of Islam.

Arab traditions are like Berber traditions in many ways. For example, both Arabs and Berbers often live with extended families. However, Arabs and Berbers do differ.

Arabs created a central government in Algeria that is based on Islam. The Berber tradition is for each village to govern itself. But Berbers adapted to Arab rule by keeping their own governments along with the new one.

Most Arabs were nomads. They usually camped near a well or stream in the summer and herded animals across the desert during the rest of the year. As a result of Arab influence, many Berbers changed from a farming to a nomadic lifestyle. However, most Berbers today are farmers, while some Berber nomads still migrate.

Life in the Cities About half of Algeria's people live in cities where mosques and open-air marketplaces called **souqs** (sooks) are common. Older parts of the cities are called **casbahs** (KAHZ bahz). The houses and stores here are close to each other on narrow, winding streets. Newer parts of the cities look like cities in Europe and the United States, with tall buildings and wide streets.

Berbers and Arabs Today

Berbers and Arabs have mixed over the centuries. Both groups are Muslim, and most Berbers speak Berber and Arabic. Because France ruled Algeria for part of its history, many Berbers and Arabs also speak French. The Berbers and the Arabs of Algeria have had many conflicts in the past. However, there have also been long periods during which they learned from each other peacefully. Algeria's future will continue to mix Berber and Arab, old and new.

SECTION 2 ASSESSMENT

AFTER YOU READ

RECALL

1. Identify: (a) Berber, (b) Arab
2. Define: (a) terrace, (b) souq, (c) casbah

COMPREHENSION

3. How did Arabs change the Berber way of life?
4. How are Arabs and Berbers similar today?

CRITICAL THINKING AND WRITING

5. **Exploring the Main Idea** Review the Main Idea statement at the beginning of this section. Then, write a paragraph about differences between Berbers and Arabs.
6. **Recognizing Cause and Effect** Why do you think that the Berbers maintained their language and traditions after Arabs came to Algeria?

ACTIVITY

Take It to the NET

7. **Creating a Guidebook** Create a guidebook for your region. Include the same categories of information that you found on the Web site. Visit the World Explorer: People, Places, and Cultures section of **phschool.com** for help in completing this activity.

Resource Directory

Teaching Resources

Section Quiz in the Unit 5 Teaching Resources, p. 55

SECTION 2 ASSESSMENT

AFTER YOU READ

1. (a) a member of one of the main ethnic groups of Algeria, a group that has lived in North Africa since at least 3000 B.C. (b) a member of one of the main ethnic groups of Algeria, a group that conquered North Africa beginning in the A.D. 600s.
2. (a) a platform cut into a mountainside that aids farmers by keeping soil from washing away when it rains (b) an open-air marketplace (c) an older part of an Algerian city
3. The Arabs created a central government in Algeria based on Islam, and many Berbers converted to Islam.
4. Possible answer: They practice the same religion.
5. Students may suggest that conflicts were caused by different ideas about how to use land. The Berbers usually farmed, and the Arabs were nomadic herders. Berbers and Arabs worked out compromises.
6. The traditional Berber way is to live in households of extended families. This would make it easier to keep language and historical traditions alive. Living in rural villages and making a living by farming or herding, it was not necessary for them to blend with another group, for example, through trading. With Arabs settling primarily along Algeria's coast, the rural Berber villages would not have felt a major influence except from the Arabs who traveled through as nomads.
7. Before students begin creating their guidebooks, they should create a plan for what they want to include in it. You may want to create a classroom display when students have finished their guidebooks.

SECTION 3

Lesson Objectives

1. Trace historic factors leading to a multiethnic Nigeria.
2. Describe the different ways of life for Nigeria's three main ethnic groups.

Lesson Plan

1 Engage

Warm-Up Activity

Have students suppose that they are visiting a country where people speak a different language and have different customs. Ask students what difficulties they might encounter. Would they feel like outsiders? Would they try to find someone who spoke their language?

Activating Prior Knowledge

Ask students to think about ways in which they use language in daily life. Have them estimate the number of people they have communicated with so far today. Then, have them consider how they would have communicated with these people if many of them did not share their language.

2 Explore

Ask students to keep the following questions in mind as they read the section: What are Nigeria's three main ethnic groups? What changes occurred when Europeans arrived? How did the three main ethnic groups and other ethnic groups form the country of Nigeria?

Answers to...

CRITICAL THINKING

Answers will vary, but students should recognize that the presence of many different ethnic groups might mean that Nigeria has a mix of traditions in its music, art, crafts, and other cultural areas.

SECTION 3

Nigeria

One Country, Many Ethnic Groups

BEFORE YOU READ

READING FOCUS

1. How have events in history led to a multiethnic Nigeria?
2. How are Nigeria's main ethnic groups similar to and different from each other?

KEY TERMS

multiethnic
census

KEY PLACES

Lagos
Abuja
Kano

NOTE TAKING

Copy this chart. As you read the section, complete the chart with information about each of Nigeria's three main ethnic groups.

Hausa-Fulani	Yoruba	Ibo

MAIN IDEA

Nigeria is Africa's most populated country, with many ethnic groups that have learned to cooperate and unify as one independent nation.

Calabash Carver in Kurmi Market

CULTURE A carver decorates a calabash, or empty gourd, at his stall in Kano's Kurmi Market. At this market, people can buy goods from many African countries. **Critical Thinking** How might Nigeria's culture be influenced by the presence of so many different ethnic groups?

Setting the Scene

The language of Nigeria is not Nigerian because there is no such language. Nigerians speak more than 250 languages!

The languages of Nigeria match its ethnic groups. Nigeria's three most widely spoken languages are Hausa, Yoruba, and Ibo and there are places called Hausaland, Yorubaland, and Iboland. But these places are not countries. In fact, Hausaland and Yorubaland both lie partly in Nigeria and partly in other countries. Look at the map in the Country Profile on the next page. You can see that Nigeria's borders do not match the borders of any one ethnic group. Nigeria is **multiethnic,** which means that many ethnic groups live within its borders.

Nigeria's History

Why are there so many ethnic groups and languages within one country? Before Europeans arrived, what is now Nigeria was ruled by many ethnic groups, including the Hausa, the Yoruba, and the Ibo. But when Europeans drew Nigeria's borders, they did not think about ethnic groups.

By 1914, Great Britain had taken over the government of Nigeria. The borders of the British colony of Nigeria included part of Hausaland, part of Yorubaland, and Iboland. When Nigeria became independent in 1960, ethnic groups that had always lived separately became part of one nation. To help unify the country, in 1991 the government moved the nation's capital from **Lagos,** in the south, to **Abuja** (ah BOO jah) in the central portion of the country.

Resource Directory

Teaching Resources

Classroom Manager in the Unit 5 Teaching Resources, p. 56

Guided Reading and Review in the Unit 5 Teaching Resources, p. 57

Guide to the Essentials, p. 96

Technology

Section Reading Support Transparencies

World Video Explorer See the Nigeria case study for an overview of Nigeria's history, economy, government, and culture. Discussion questions are included.

Passport to the World CD-ROM This interactive CD-ROM allows students to explore each region of the world. Students view regional videos, take a photo tour, and explore a historical timeline. Students record their travels in an Explorer's Journal and receive passport stamps when they pass regional quizzes.

Nigeria

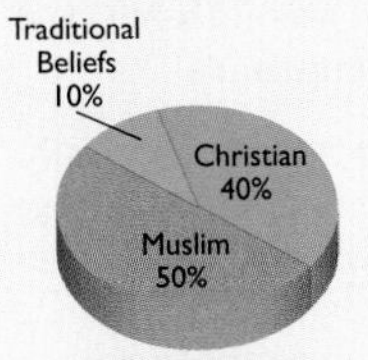

Religious Persuasion

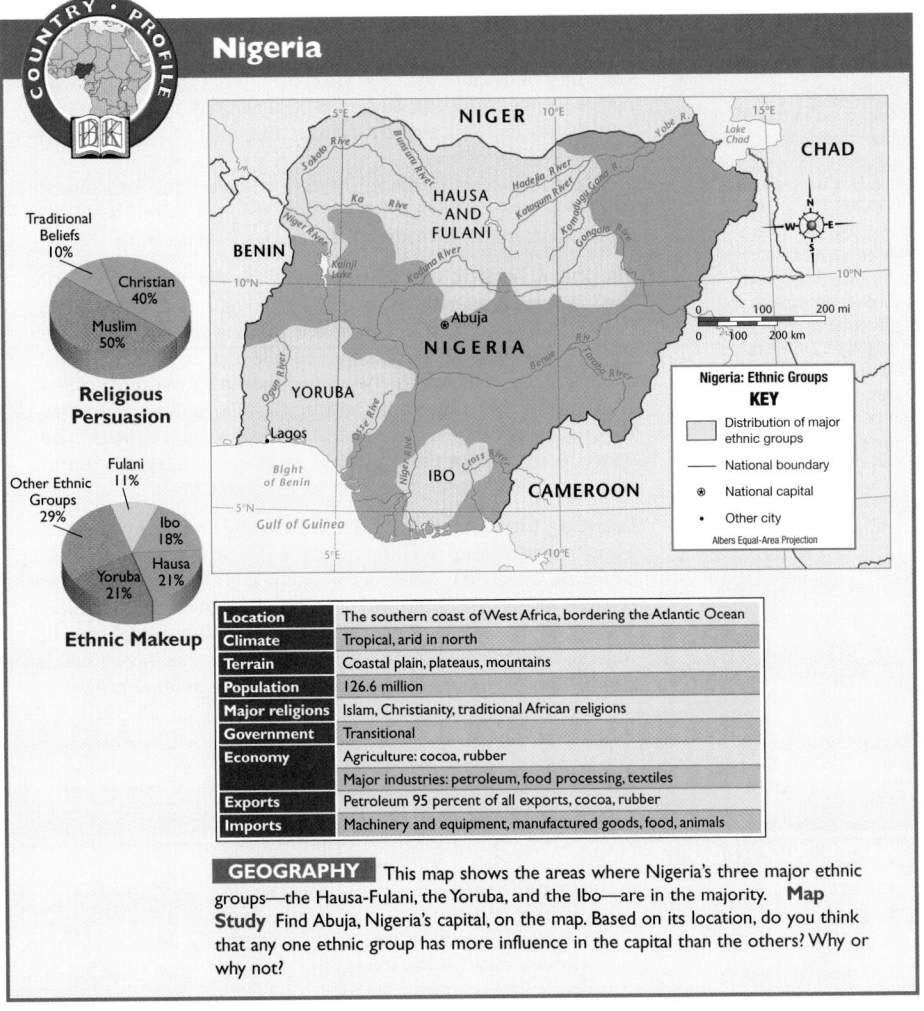

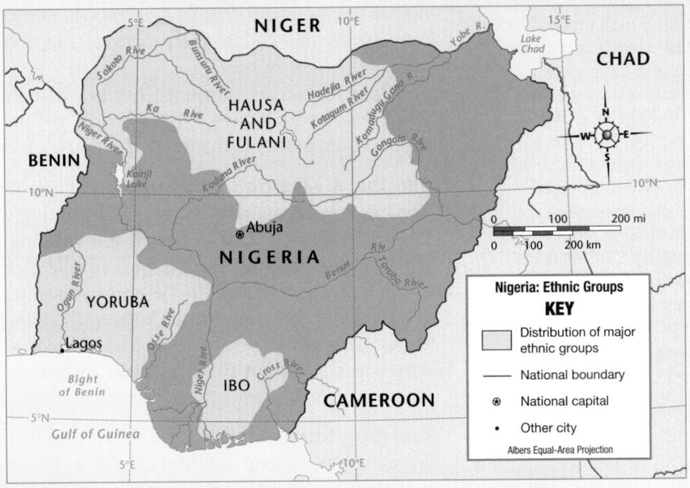

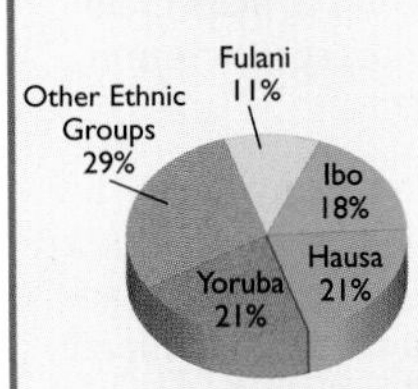

Ethnic Makeup

Location	The southern coast of West Africa, bordering the Atlantic Ocean
Climate	Tropical, arid in north
Terrain	Coastal plain, plateaus, mountains
Population	126.6 million
Major religions	Islam, Christianity, traditional African religions
Government	Transitional
Economy	Agriculture: cocoa, rubber
	Major industries: petroleum, food processing, textiles
Exports	Petroleum 95 percent of all exports, cocoa, rubber
Imports	Machinery and equipment, manufactured goods, food, animals

GEOGRAPHY This map shows the areas where Nigeria's three major ethnic groups—the Hausa-Fulani, the Yoruba, and the Ibo—are in the majority. **Map Study** Find Abuja, Nigeria's capital, on the map. Based on its location, do you think that any one ethnic group has more influence in the capital than the others? Why or why not?

Three Different Cultures

The Hausa and the Fulani make up about 33 percent of Nigeria's people and most are Muslims. For hundreds of years, the Hausa-Fulani have made an important part of their living by trading goods from as far away as Spain, Italy, and Egypt. The Hausa-Fulani built cities at the crossroads of trade routes. Each of these cities had its own ruler, was enclosed by walls, and had a central market. **Kano,** the oldest city in West Africa, is a Hausa city and has been a center of trade for over 1,000 years.

3 Teach

Have students create a chart with three rows labeled: *Ibo*, *Hausa-Fulani*, and *Yoruba*, and three columns labeled: *Region*, *Culture*, and *History*. Ask students to fill in the chart with facts from the section. Use the completed chart as the basis for a discussion of the differences and the similarities between these groups. This activity should take about 20 minutes.

Question for Discussion

CULTURE In what ways is the culture of Nigeria similar to those of Egypt and Algeria? In what ways is it different?

Nigeria's culture is much more multiethnic than that of Egypt and Algeria, although Algeria does have a sizable Berber population. Also, while both Egypt and Algeria are predominantly Muslim countries, Nigeria has almost as many Christians as Muslims.

4 Assess/Reteach

See the answers to the Section 3 Assessment. You may also use students' completed charts as an assessment.

Acceptable charts include a correct entry in each cell.

Commendable charts include two or more entries in some of the cells.

Outstanding charts demonstrate an awareness of larger cultural and historical issues, such as the fact that colonialism affected the groups differently.

SKILLS MINI LESSON

Reading Tables and Analyzing Statistics

Allow students a few moments to study the table shown in the Country Profile, and then **introduce** the skill by telling them that this table shows statistics, or numerical data, and other important data about Nigeria. Point out that the numerical data is presented in the form of pie graphs. Together, these data in the Country Profile provide information about Nigeria's geography, economy, and people. Work with students to **practice** reading the table, identifying how the data are related. For example, the information about climate and terrain can help students visualize what Nigeria's land looks like. Have students **apply** the skill by asking them to write a statement that explains the relationship between two or more pieces of data in the table.

Answers to...

MAP STUDY

Students may guess that Abuja's location in the central part of Nigeria helps ensure that no ethnic group has more influence in the capital.

SECTION 3 ASSESSMENT

AFTER YOU READ

1. (a) Nigeria's former capital, located in the south of the country (b) Nigeria's new capital, located in the central part of the country (c) the oldest city in West Africa, built by the Hausa-Fulani
2. (a) made up of many ethnic groups (b) a count of all the people in a country
3. When Europeans first arrived, many people were sold into slavery, especially members of the Yoruba ethnic group. Moreover, when Europeans drew Nigeria's borders, they did not match the borders of any one ethnic group. So, when Nigeria became an independent country in 1960, ethnic groups that had always lived separately became part of one nation.
4. The Hausa-Fulani live in the north. The Yoruba live in the southwest. The Ibo live in the southeast.
5. Nigeria has a history of finding ways to bring its many ethnic groups closer. Abuja was chosen as the capital because of its proximity to more than one ethnic group. Some groups, like the Ibo, have traditionally held democratic forms of self-rule, such as a council of elders. Having been a center of the European slave trade, Nigerians would value freedom.
6. A census reveals which ethnic group is the largest, and therefore determines which group will hold the majority of political power.
7. Possible answer: Nigerians should have one national language because then the different ethnic groups could communicate better. Better communication could help people solve problems and misunderstandings.

LINKS TO Language Arts

Pidgin How do people talk to each other when they speak different languages? One way is to create a language that includes a little of each language. This kind of language is called pidgin. Nigerian pidgin mixes English words with the grammar of Nigerian languages. Enslaved Africans and their captors may have been the first people in Africa to use pidgin.

The Yoruba: Farmers Near the Coast About 20 percent of Nigeria's people are Yoruba and many of them still live in Lagos, the city-state they built more than 500 years ago. In the 1800s, Lagos was a center for the European slave trade where many Yoruba were sold into slavery and sent to the Americas. But, today, Lagos is a more peaceful center of trade.

Most Yoruba are farmers. They live with their families in large compounds which have several houses grouped around a big yard. A Yoruba community is made up of many such compounds.

The Ibo: A Tradition of Democracy The Ibo have traditionally lived as rural farmers in the southeast and have not built any large cities like Kano or Lagos. They live in farming villages. Unlike the Hausa-Fulani and the Yoruba, the Ibo rule themselves with a democratic council of elders who work together to solve problems.

Tensions sometimes arise between the Ibo and the other two major groups. In 1967, the Ibo tried to leave Nigeria to start their own country and for two and a half years the country was torn by war. In the end, however, Nigeria stayed united.

Counting Citizens It is hard to tell exactly how many people are in each ethnic group. A count of all the people in a country is called a **census.** In Nigeria, whenever a census is taken, it causes debate because the largest group will have the most power in government.

In 1991, the census showed that over 88 million people live in Nigeria, and that the Hausa-Fulani are the country's largest ethnic group. This gives them more political power than other groups.

SECTION 3 ASSESSMENT

AFTER YOU READ

RECALL

1. Identify: (a) Lagos, (b) Abuja, (c) Kano
2. Define: (a) multiethnic, (b) census

COMPREHENSION

3. How did the arrival of Europeans in the region affect the ethnic groups that live in the region?
4. What are the three largest ethnic groups in Nigeria, and where does each group live?

CRITICAL THINKING AND WRITING

5. **Exploring the Main Idea** Review the Main Idea statement at the beginning of this section. Then, write a paragraph summarizing some of the reasons why Nigeria was able to bring together many ethnic groups to work together in self-government. Think about past influences and contributions of modern leaders.
6. **Cause and Effect** Why is taking a census so important to different ethnic groups in Nigeria?

ACTIVITY

7. **Writing to Learn** Currently, Nigeria does not have one national language. Based on what you have learned, do you think a national language might be useful for Nigeria? Why or why not? Write a paragraph explaining your opinion.

Resource Directory

Teaching Resources

Section Quiz in the Unit 5 Teaching Resources, p. 58

Ghana
Origins of a Democratic Government

BEFORE YOU READ

READING FOCUS

1. What changes did Kwame Nkrumah, bring to Ghana?
2. How has life in Ghana changed since independence?

KEY TERMS

sovereignty
coup

KEY PEOPLE

Kwame Nkrumah
Jerry Rawlings

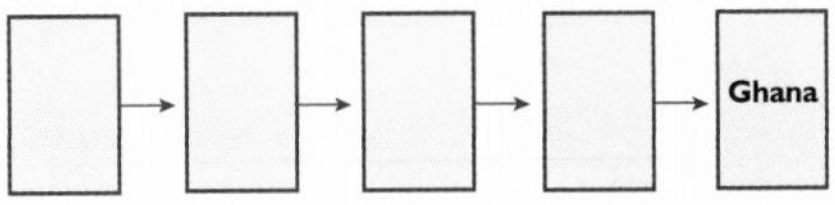

MAIN IDEA

While facing many challenges, the people of Ghana strive to maintain a democratic government.

NOTE TAKING

Copy this chart. As you read the section, complete the chart showing the events that led to Ghana's independence.

☐ → ☐ → ☐ → ☐ → Ghana

Setting the Scene

In 1935, **Kwame Nkrumah,** a 26-year-old student, sailed from Ghana to the United States. At that time, Ghana was called the Gold Coast and it had been ruled by Great Britain for over 60 years. Nkrumah was well aware that the people of his country did not have true freedom or equality, and when he saw the Statue of Liberty for the first time, it made him determined to bring freedom not only to his country, but to the whole continent.

Moving Toward Independence

In 1947, Nkrumah returned to the Gold Coast. The Gold Coast was named for its gold, which is one of the country's most important natural resources. The Country Profile on the next page shows the country's other important resources.

While the Gold Coast had many resources, most of its people were poor. Nkrumah believed that the people should benefit from the wealth of their own country, so he began traveling all over the country to convince the people to demand independence from Great Britain.

Independent Ghana

HISTORY Kwame Nkrumah, the first leader of independent Ghana, showed his respect for African traditions by wearing traditional clothing. **Critical Thinking** What African traditions do you think Kwame Nkrumah might have felt were most important to maintain in Ghana? Why?

Resource Directory

 Teaching Resources

Classroom Manager in the Unit 5 Teaching Resources, p. 59

Guided Reading and Review in the Unit 5 Teaching Resources, p. 60

Guide to the Essentials, p. 97

 Technology

Section Reading Support Transparencies

Lesson Objectives

1. Identify the circumstances that led to Ghana's gaining its independence.
2. Describe economic and political setbacks and successes following Ghana's independence.

Lesson Plan

1 Engage

Warm-Up Activity

Ask students to think about what an ideal form of government would be. Have them consider what kind of person or persons would lead the government and make decisions.

Activating Prior Knowledge

Ask students to think about a turning point in their lives, such as moving to a new community or beginning a new school. Explain that a turning point is a situation that triggers change. What was different for them after that turning point? What remained the same?

2 Explore

As students read the section, ask them the following questions: Why did Nkrumah want his country to be independent? How did the British benefit from the Gold Coast's economy? What are Ghana's economy and culture like today?

Answers to...

CRITICAL THINKING

African traditions might include hard work, care of natural resources, pride in history, and respect for differences among ethnic groups.

Lesson Plan continued

3 Teach

Have students make a time line of events in Nkrumah's life. Important moments in Ghana's history should also be included. This activity should take about 20 minutes.

Question for Discussion

CITIZENSHIP **Why did Kwame Nkrumah believe that Ghana should be independent? Do you agree or disagree with his reason? Why?**

He believed that the people of Ghana, not Great Britain, should benefit from the wealth of the country. Most students will agree with his reason because the people who do the work should benefit from it.

4 Assess/Reteach

See the answers to the Section 4 Assessment. You may also assess students' time lines.

Acceptable time lines show two key events each in Nkrumah's life and in Ghana's history.

Commendable time lines show at least three key events each in Nkrumah's life and in Ghana's history.

Outstanding time lines show all key events in Nkrumah's life and highlight Ghana's most significant historical events.

HISTORY

The End of Colonialism

Ghana's independence was achieved peacefully, but some African countries fought wars to gain their freedom. The Algerians, for example, fought the French for eight years before becoming an independent nation. Angola and Mozambique battled the Portuguese before winning independence in 1975. Britain didn't recognize Zimbabwe's independence until 1980, after years of fighting.

COUNTRY • PROFILE

Ghana

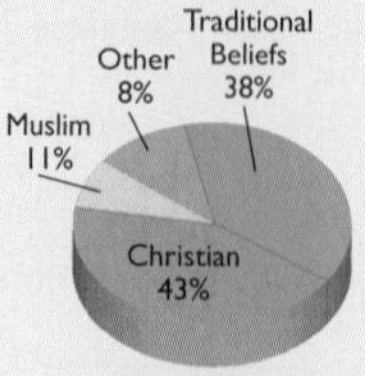

Religious Persuasion

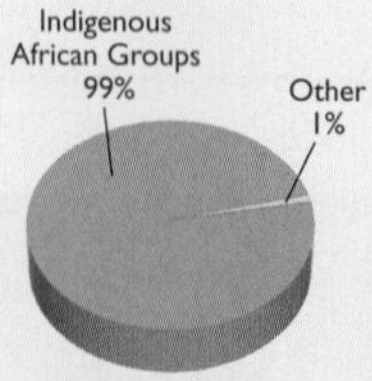

Ethnic Group

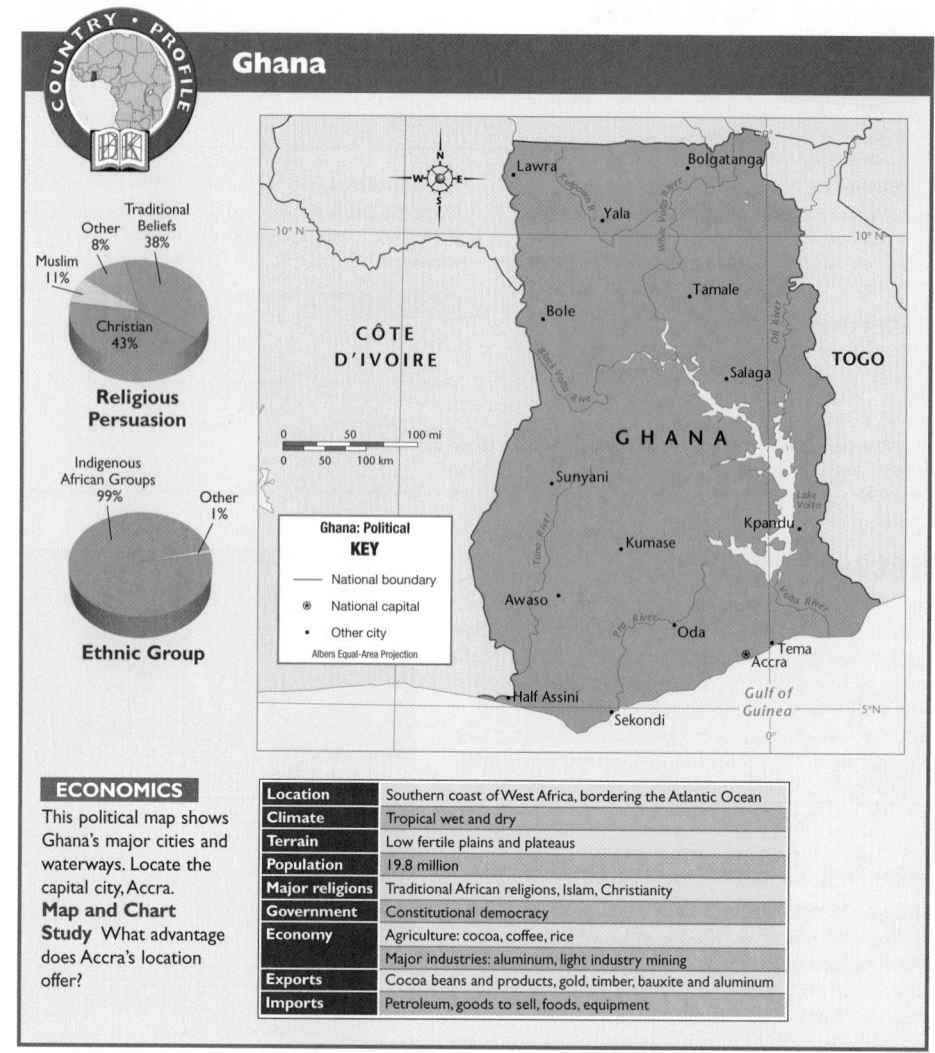

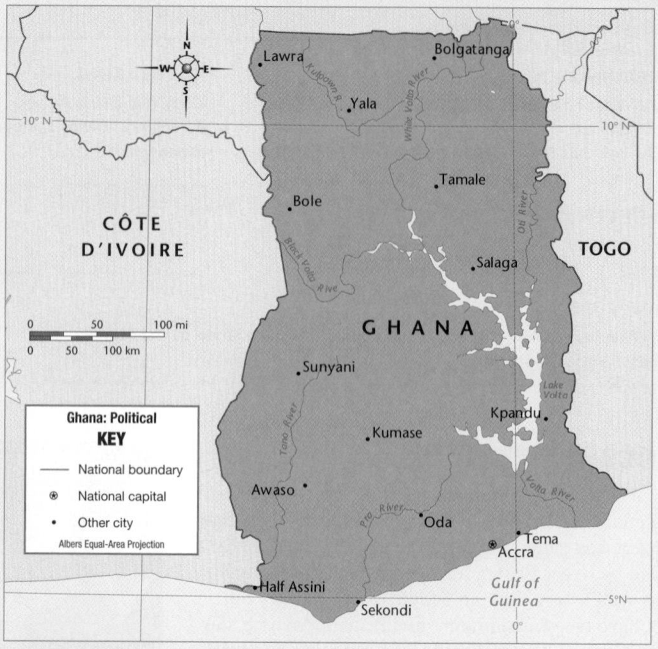

ECONOMICS

This political map shows Ghana's major cities and waterways. Locate the capital city, Accra.

Map and Chart Study What advantage does Accra's location offer?

Location	Southern coast of West Africa, bordering the Atlantic Ocean
Climate	Tropical wet and dry
Terrain	Low fertile plains and plateaus
Population	19.8 million
Major religions	Traditional African religions, Islam, Christianity
Government	Constitutional democracy
Economy	Agriculture: cocoa, coffee, rice
	Major industries: aluminum, light industry mining
Exports	Cocoa beans and products, gold, timber, bauxite and aluminum
Imports	Petroleum, goods to sell, foods, equipment

Traditional Government in Ghana

The Akan are the largest ethnic group in Ghana. When the Akan give power to a new leader, they also give a warning: If the leader does not rule fairly, the people can give power to a new ruler. In this way, the Akan are democratic since the people have control over who rules them.

412 UNIT 5 AFRICA

Answers to...

MAP AND CHART STUDY

Accra is located on the Gulf of Guinea, so it is a seaport.

Resource Directory

Program Resources

Social Studies and Geography Skills, Reading a Political Map, p. 17; Reading a Circle Graph, p. 53

Technology

Color Transparencies 96 Africa, South of the Sahara: Physical-Political Map

While the Europeans were trading in gold and slaves on the coast, some Akan groups formed the Asante kingdom. This kingdom became very rich from trade and controlled parts of the northern savanna and the coastal south. The Asante used all their power to try to stop the Europeans from taking over west Africa.

The Influence of Colonialism In 1874, Great Britain made the Gold Coast a colony and tried to control the economy. It encouraged farmers to grow cocoa for British chocolate factories and exported timber and gold. As these raw materials left the country, goods from other countries were shipped in. People grew fewer food crops because growing cash crops like cocoa brought in more money and food had to be imported. People also spent more time on farming and less on traditional crafts. The British sold food and factory-made goods to the people of the Gold Coast. Soon, the Gold Coast began to depend on these imports.

The British also built schools in the Gold Coast. Foreign missionaries ran the schools and Christianity began to replace traditional religions. By the time Ghana became independent in 1957, many new ideas and lifestyles had come to traditional communities. Kwame Nkrumah, for example, was a Christian. But he also believed in parts of the traditional African religion. Nkrumah's respect for old and new ways helped him govern when Ghana became independent.

AS YOU READ

Draw Inferences How does your community blend traditional ways of life with modern ways?

ECONOMICS Since colonization, many Ghanaian women purchase machine-made cotton fabrics, instead of traditional Kente cloth, for everyday dresses and head scarves. **Critical Thinking** Do you think this effect of colonization is positive or negative? Why?

Independence

In 1957, Nkrumah gave a moving speech to his people. Great Britain, he said, had finally agreed to grant them **sovereignty** (SAHV run tee), or political independence. Cheering, the people carried Nkrumah through the streets. Crowds sang victory songs to celebrate a dream come true.

Nkrumah became the leader of the new country and later, the president. The government changed the country's name to Ghana, after an African kingdom that had ruled the region hundreds of years ago. Ghana was the first African colony south of the Sahara to become independent.

Since independence, Ghana has worked to balance new technology with traditional culture. Modern health care, electricity, transportation, and education are things that most Ghanaians want.

SKILLS MINI LESSON

Recognizing Cause and Effect

To **introduce** the skill, tell students that a cause is the reason an event or development occurs. An effect is the result of the event or development. The words *because*, *since*, and *as* often indicate causes. The words *therefore*, *led*, and *as a result* often signal effects. Have students **practice** the skill by looking for cause-and-effect relationships in the text under the heading *The Influence of Colonialism*. Point out that sometimes an effect may become the cause of another effect. Students may **apply** the skill by looking for other cause-and-effect relationships as they read the rest of the section.

ACTIVITY

Culture

Language Arts Traditionally, the Akan name their children according to the day of the week on which a child is born. For example, Kwame Nkrumah's first name is the Akan day-name for a boy born on Saturday. Allow students to use the information in the table below to discover and pronounce their Akan day-name. Invite students to make decorated name tags with their day-names.

Day	Girls	Boys
Sun.	Akosua (ah KOS OO uh)	Kwasi (KWAH see)
Mon.	Adwoa (AD joh uh)	Kodwo (KOO joh)
Tues.	Abena (AH beh nuh)	Kwabena (KWAH beh nuh)
Wed.	Akua (ah KOO uh)	Kweku (KWAY koo)
Thurs.	Yaa (yah)	Yaw (YAH OO)
Fri.	Afua (AF OO uh)	Kofi (KOO fee)
Sat.	Amma (AH muh)	Kwame (KWAH mee)

Verbal/Linguistic

CULTURE

Education

All children in Ghana are required to attend elementary and junior high school. Students start learning English in first grade. From fourth grade onward, all classes are taught in English, which is the official language of Ghana.

Answers to...

CRITICAL THINKING

Students may say that the effect is negative because it represents a loss of tradition.

SECTION 4 ASSESSMENT

AFTER YOU READ

1. (a) first leader of independent Ghana (b) president of Ghana who established economic reforms
2. (a) political independence (b) a takeover
3. The British encouraged farmers to grow cash crops instead of food crops. Food and factory-made goods had to be imported, and the people became dependent on these imports.
4. They have faced economic debt, struggles for power between military and democratic government, and the need to combine modern convenience with cultural preservation.
5. Answers will vary. May include: the Ghanaian people expect their leaders to be trustworthy and to respond to the peoples' opinions; they value independence; they strive for cooperation among over seventy-five ethnic groups; they value education and health care; they try to blend modern technology with traditional culture. Important beliefs and traditions would include: democracy; honesty from their leaders; hard work and sacrifice; religion; art and African traditional culture.
6. Nkrumah tried to rush change and spent too much money in the process. This caused the Ghanaian economy to suffer. After Nkrumah's downfall, the country was headed by few successful governments. When Nkrumah died in 1972, he was hailed as a national hero because people felt he had done his best to help the country.
7. Answers will vary. Students should write about solutions to one or two community problems, name some possible obstacles, and suggest ways to overcome those obstacles.

GOVERNMENT

Pulled down by angry citizens, the headless statue of Kwame Nkrumah lies on the grounds of the central police station in Accra. Nkrumah was out of the country when the government was overthrown, in February 1966. He never returned to Ghana, but lived in exile in the nearby country of Guinea.

Nkrumah's Government Is Overthrown Nine years after being carried through the streets as a hero, Nkrumah was thrown out of office by a military **coup** (koo), or takeover. Most Ghanaian citizens did not protest. In fact, many celebrated. People pulled down statues of Nkrumah.

How did this hero become an enemy? Nkrumah had big plans for Ghana. He borrowed huge amounts of money to make those plans happen fast. But when world prices fell for cocoa, the country's chief export, Ghana could not pay back its loans. Many people blamed Nkrumah for the country's economic problems.

Nkrumah's downfall did not end Ghana's problems. The country alternated between military and democratically elected governments. Few were successful. In the meantime, people began to think better of Nkrumah. Many felt that he had done his best to help the country. When he died in 1972, he was hailed as a national hero.

Ghana's Economy and Culture Today In the 1980s, Ghana's president, **Jerry Rawlings,** tried to reform Ghana's politics and economy. Rawlings was a military officer who had taken part in some of the earlier coups. Rawlings stressed the traditional African values of hard work and sacrifice. Ghanaians supported Rawlings, and as a result, Ghana's economy began to grow.

Ghana is still dependent on the sale of cocoa. Even so, the economy has grown so much that Ghana has been able to build better roads and irrigation systems. The government plans to improve education and health care. People have formed groups so they can voice concerns about issues that affect their lives.

Ghana's culture, as well as its economy, has benefited from Rawlings's renewal of traditional values. Ghana has special centers that have been set up to keep the country's traditional culture alive.

SECTION 4 ASSESSMENT

AFTER YOU READ

RECALL

1. Identify: (a) Kwame Nkrumah, (b) Jerry Rawlings
2. Define: (a) sovereignty, (b) coup

COMPREHENSION

3. How did colonization affect Ghana's economy and its push for independence?
4. What challenges have leaders of independent Ghana faced?

CRITICAL THINKING AND WRITING

5. **Exploring the Main Idea** Review the Main Idea statement at the beginning of this section. Then, write a paragraph describing the beliefs and traditions Ghanaians drew on to successfully form an independent democracy.
6. **Recognizing Cause and Effect** Kwame Nkrumah went from being a Ghanaian hero to an unpopular figure to a hero again. What caused this change in people's attitudes?

ACTIVITY

7. **Writing an Essay** Write an essay about one or two changes you would like to see in your country or community. Describe the obstacles that might stand in the way of this change, and how these obstacles could be overcome.

414 UNIT 5 AFRICA

Resource Directory

Teaching Resources

Section Quiz in the Unit 5 Teaching Resources, p. 61

Chapter Summary in the Unit 5 Teaching Resources, p. 62

Vocabulary in the Unit 5 Teaching Resources, p. 63

Reteaching in the Unit 5 Teaching Resources, p. 64

Enrichment in the Unit 5 Teaching Resources, p. 65

Critical Thinking in the Unit 5 Teaching Resources, p. 66

Using Models

What You Need

To make a model showing the desertification process, you will need:

- a three-sided box
- blow-dryer
- piece of sod as wide as the box
- sand
- goggles

Learn the Skill

A model is a small copy of something, used to represent an object or a process. For example, a globe is a model of the Earth. Models are useful because they make it easier to see and understand the object or process being represented.

In this activity, you will make a model that will help you explore and understand one cause of desertification. Desertification occurs when land that was once fertile becomes a desert. The land becomes dry and salty, underground water dries up, erosion occurs, and plant life dies.

The Sahara is expanding into the edge of the savanna, or the Sahel. The desertification of the Sahel affects not only the environment, but also the people living there.

A. Set up your model. Place the box so that the open end is in front of you. Put on your goggles. Lay the sod in the box, with some space between the sod and the back of the box. Pour the sand in a pile across the open end of the box, directly in front of the sod. Hold the blow-dryer at the open end of the box so that it will blow across the sand toward the sod.

B. Create a windstorm by using the blow-dryer to create wind. Lift handfuls of sand and let it sift through your fingers in front of the blow-dryer, so that the sand is blown across the grass. This represents the sandy winds that blow across the desert and over grassy lands. Do this for about one minute, holding the blow-dryer no higher than the top of the sod. Note how much sand gets caught in the grass.

C. Begin the desertification process. Thin the vegetation by removing about half of the grass in the sod. This is similar to what happens when vegetation is grazed or dies from climate change. Use the blow-dryer and handfuls of sand to create another windstorm, again for one minute. How much sand is in the sod this time? How does the grass look?

D. Continue the desertification process. This time remove almost all of the grass in the sod. This represents more overgrazing and the death of vegetation. Make a final one-minute windstorm. How much sand is in the sod now? How does the sand affect the soil?

Practice the Skill

Record your observations from the activity. What happened to the sand as it blew across the grass? What happened to the remaining grass and topsoil as the sand blew across the "overgrazed" sod? Imagine you are a cattle herder who needs to feed your cattle. You know that if you let your animals graze, you might contribute to desertification. But if your animals do not eat, they will die. What would you do?

Apply the Skill

See the Chapter Review and Assessment at the end of this chapter for more questions on using models.

Resource Directory

Technology

Social Studies Skills Tutor CD-ROM

Answers to...

PRACTICE THE SKILL

Students' responses will vary. Accept all reasonable answers.

Lesson Objectives

1. Understand how using models can enhance learning.
2. Make a model that shows how desertification affects land and its productivity.

Lesson Plan

1 Engage

To introduce the skill, read aloud the opening text under "Learn the Skill." Show students a globe. Ask them how being able to see and use the globe helps their understanding when they are learning about world geography.

2 Explore

Direct students to read and follow the steps under "Learn the Skill." Have them work in small groups. Choose an area of the classroom for making the model, or have students work outside.

3 Teach

Have students discuss what they learned from making and using the model. Students should have a better working understanding of the process of desertification.

4 Assess/Reteach

Students should be able to make the model and draw accurate conclusions from it. They should be able to explain the process they used, and the conclusions they drew.

To further assess students' understanding of making models, have them complete the "Applying Your Skills" part of the Chapter Review and Assessment at the end of the chapter.

CHAPTER 22 SKILLS FOR LIFE 415

CHAPTER 22

Review and Assessment

Creating a Chapter Summary

Summaries will vary.

Sample summary:

Algeria Algeria's two main ethnic groups, the Berbers and the Arabs, have a long history of conflict. However, they have found ways to live together and learn from each other.

Nigeria More people live in Nigeria than any other African country. Many ethnic groups worked together towards independence for Nigeria.

Ghana Ghana led the movement in African countries from colonial rule to independence. Today, the people of Ghana are working toward building an even stronger democratic government and country.

Reviewing Key Terms

Students' sentences should show an understanding of each term.

Reviewing the Main Ideas

1. by praying five times a day, as required by the Quran and by living according to its teachings
2. The cities are crowded and most people live in apartments. Most rural people are farmers and live in mud-brick or stone houses.
3. Most Berbers and Arabs are Muslims, and many speak Arabic and live with their extended families. Traditionally, Arabs were nomads and Berbers were farmers. Arabs created a central government based on Islam, while each Berber village had its own government.
4. The Sahara covers more than 85 percent of Algeria. A small number of Berber and Arab nomads live in the desert. Berbers who farm in the mountains construct terraces to keep soil from washing away.

CHAPTER 22

Review and Assessment

Creating a Chapter Summary

On a separate piece of paper, draw a chart like this one, and include the information that summarizes what you learned about Eygpt. Then, fill in the remaining boxes by summarizing the information you learned about the other three countries.

Egypt	Egyptians are a diverse people, but they are unified by their Islamic beliefs. The religion of Islam affects all aspects of Egyptian life.
Algeria	
Nigeria	
Ghana	

Reviewing Key Terms

Use each of the following words in a sentence that explains its meaning.

1. fellaheen (p. 404)
2. souq (p. 407)
3. census (p. 410)
4. bazaar (p. 403)
5. multiethnic (p. 408)
6. casbah (p. 407)
7. coup (p. 414)
8. sovereignty (p. 413)

Reviewing the Main Ideas

1. How do Egyptians show their faith in Islam in their daily lives? (Section 1)
2. How does life in Egypt's cities differ from life in Egypt's rural areas? (Section 1)
3. What do Berbers and Arabs have in common and what sets them apart? (Section 2)
4. How does Algeria's geography affect the people who live there? (Section 2)
5. What are Nigeria's three largest ethnic groups? (Section 3)
6. How are politics in Nigeria affected by its census? (Section 3)
7. What role did Kwame Nkrumah play in Ghana's move to independence? (Section 4)
8. How has Ghana changed since it became independent? (Section 4)

416 UNIT 5 AFRICA

5. The Yoruba, the Ibo, and the Hausa-Fulani
6. A census shows which ethnic group is the largest. The largest group will have the most political power.
7. He traveled all over the country to convince people that they should demand independence from Great Britain. He became the first leader of the new country of Ghana.
8. Its economy has grown. The government has been able to build better roads and irrigation systems and has addressed the concerns of the people.

Map Activity

North Africa

For each place listed below, write the letter from the map that shows its location.

1. Cairo
2. Algeria
3. Mediterranean Sea
4. Egypt
5. Sahara
6. Nigeria
7. Ghana
8. Lagos
9. Abuja
10. Algiers

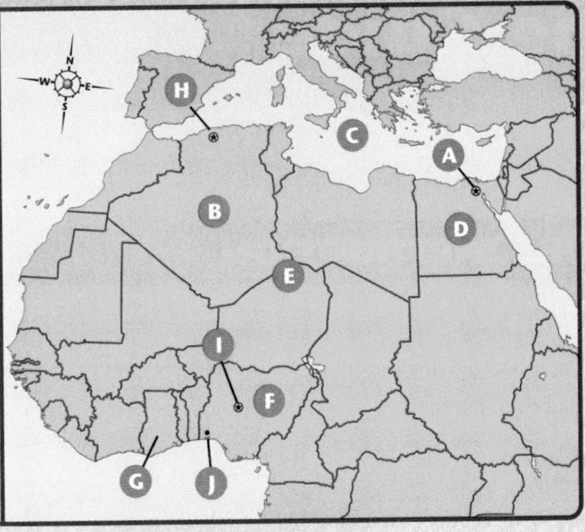

Take It to the NET

Enrichment For more map activities using geography skills, visit the social studies section of **phschool.com.**

Writing Activity

1. **Writing a News Report** Choose one of the recent events described in this chapter and write a news report about it. Remember to describe these five things for your readers: who, what, when, where, and why.
2. **Writing a Poem** The Berber languages are rarely written down. Most Berber history is preserved by professional poets. Pretend that you are a professional poet living in the 600s, when Arabs first came to North Africa. Write a poem explaining some of the differences and similarities between Arabs and Berbers.

Critical Thinking

1. **Making Comparisons** Compare Egypt's geography to that of Ghana. How do you think each country's geography affected its history?
2. **Making Valid Generalizations** Choose one feature or aspect of culture that best portrays the country and its people for each of the four countries studied in this chapter.

Applying Your Skills

Turn to the Skills for Life activity on p. 415 to answer the following questions.

1. Explain how using models helps you to learn about an object or process.
2. How did using the desertification model help you understand the process of desertification? Do you think you would have understood the process as well if you had only read about it and not used the model? Why?

Take It to the NET

Activity Read about the people, history, and culture of Ghana. How is life in Ghana different from life in the United States? Visit the World Explorer: People, Places, and Cultures section of **phschool.com** for help in completing this activity.

Chapter 22 Self-Test As a final review activity, take the Chapter 22 Self-Test and get instant feedback on your answers. To take the test, visit the Social Studies section of **phschool.com.**

Resource Directory

Teaching Resources

Cooperative Learning Activity in the Unit 5 Teaching Resources, pp. 116–119

Chapter Tests Forms A and B in the Unit 5 Teaching Resources, pp. 148–153

Guide to the Essentials, Ch. 22 Test, p. 98

Other Print Resources

Chapter Tests with ExamView® Test Bank, Ch. 22

Technology

ExamView® Test Bank CD-ROM, Ch. 22

Resource Pro® CD-ROM

Map Activity

1. A **2.** B **3.** C **4.** D **5.** E **6.** F **7.** G **8.** J **9.** I **10.** H

Writing Activity

1. Reports will vary, but should identify an event covered in the chapter, such as the census taken in Nigeria.
2. Poems will vary. Students may mention differences in language, religion, and style of government.

Critical Thinking

1. Egypt borders on the Mediterranean Sea, but much of its terrain is covered by a vast desert. Most of the population lives along the Nile River, or on the Mediterranean Coast. Because of its location across the Red Sea from Saudi Arabia, the religion of Islam was brought by Arab traders and its population is now mostly Muslim. Land is scarce for farming so overpopulation affects the major cities today. Ghana borders on the Atlantic Ocean, has a tropical climate with mostly low fertile plains and plateaus. It is rich in agricultural products because of the good land for farming, especially the growing of cocoa. The economy also benefits from the natural resources of gold, timber and minerals. These resources attracted foreign settlers and colonial rule.
2. Answers will vary. Sample: Egypt: Islamic faith; Algeria: a mix of Berber and Arab cultures; Nigeria: the most populated African country; Ghana: hard-working, independent people.

Applying Your Skills

1. Making models allows you to see first-hand the effects of a process like desertification.
2. Student responses should reflect the results of their experiments with the model.

Chapter 23 Planning Guide

Resource Manager

	CORE INSTRUCTION	READING/SKILLS
Chapter-Level Resources	**Teaching Resources** Program Overview Pacing Charts **Technology** Resource Pro® CD-ROM Companion Web site, phschool.com • eTeach	**Technology** Social Studies Skills Tutor CD-ROM Student Edition on Audio CD, Ch. 23
1 Rwanda and Burundi: Torn by Ethnic Conflict 1. Identify the ethnic groups that populate Rwanda and Burundi and their origins. 2. Understand the history of the conflict between the Hutu and the Tutsi and the current crisis that exists in Rwanda and Burundi.	**Teaching Resources** **Unit 5** Classroom Manager, p. 68 Guided Reading and Review, p. 69	**Teaching Resources** Guide to the Essentials, p. 99 Social Studies and Geography Skills, p. 18 **Technology** Section Reading Support Transparencies
2 Kenya: Diverse Cultures, Shared Goals 1. Identify the cultural values of the Kenyans and the ways they have worked to preserve these values. 2. Describe some of the reasons why Kenyans are moving to urban areas and how they maintain family ties once there.	**Teaching Resources** **Unit 5** Classroom Manager, p. 71 Guided Reading and Review, p. 72	**Teaching Resources** Guide to the Essentials, p. 100 Social Studies and Geography Skills, p. 89 **Technology** Section Reading Support Transparencies
3 The Democratic Republic of the Congo: A Government in Turmoil 1. Describe the significance of natural resources in the Congo's history. 2. Summarize the Congo's economic challenges since independence.	**Teaching Resources** **Unit 5** Classroom Manager, p. 74 Guided Reading and Review, p. 75	**Teaching Resources** Guide to the Essentials, p. 101 **Technology** Section Reading Support Transparencies
4 South Africa: The End of Apartheid 1. Describe the policies and legacy of apartheid. 2. Identify the challenges that face post-apartheid South Africa.	**Teaching Resources** **Unit 5** Classroom Manager, p. 77 Guided Reading and Review, p. 78 Chapter Summary, p. 80 Vocabulary, p. 81 Reteaching, p. 82	**Teaching Resources** **Unit 5** Critical Thinking, p. 84 Guide to the Essentials, p. 102 **Technology** Section Reading Support Transparencies

ENRICHMENT / PRE-AP

Teaching Resources
Primary Sources and Literature Readings

Other Print Resources
DK Atlas

Technology
World Video Explorer: Case Study: Ecotourism and Spotlight on: Apartheid
Companion Web site, phschool.com

Teaching Resources
Outline Maps, p. 34

Technology
Color Transparencies 98

Teaching Resources
Outline Maps, p. 35

Technology
Color Transparencies 93 and 99
Passport to the World CD-ROM

Teaching Resources
Outline Maps, p. 35

Technology
Color Transparencies 93 and 99
Passport to the World CD-ROM

Teaching Resources
Unit 5
Enrichment, p. 83
Cooperative Learning Activity, pp. 120–123
Outline Maps, p. 35

Technology
Color Transparencies 93 and 99

ASSESSMENT

Prentice Hall Assessment System

Core Assessment
Chapter Tests with ExamView® Test Bank, Ch. 23
ExamView® Test Bank CD-ROM, Ch. 23

Standardized Test Preparation
Diagnose and Prescribe
Diagnostic Tests for Middle Grades Social Studies Skills
Review and Reteach
Review Book for World Studies
Practice and Assess
Test-taking Strategies with Transparencies for Middle Grades Test Prep Book
Test-taking Strategies Posters

Teaching Resources
Unit 5
Section Quizzes, pp. 70, 73, 76, and 79
Chapter Tests, pp. 154–159

Technology
Companion Web site, phschool.com
Ch. 23 Self-Test

World Video Explorer
Each region of the world is explored through regional flyovers and investigative field trips. Case study segments give students an in-depth view of the history, economy, government, and culture of a key place in each region. Case studies include Nigeria, Mexico, China, British Columbia, and the Czech Republic.

In Your Classroom

CUSTOMIZE FOR INDIVIDUAL NEEDS

Gifted and Talented

Teacher's Edition

- Letter Writing, p. 421
- Ngugi wa Thiong'o, p. 425
- Drawing Conclusions, p. 429

Teaching Resources

- Enrichment, p. 83
- Primary Sources and Literature Readings

Honors/Pre-AP

Teacher's Edition

- Conducting Electricity, p. 429
- Nadine Gordimer, p. 433

Teaching Resources

- Critical Thinking, p. 84
- Primary Sources and Literature Readings

ESL

Teacher's Edition

- Art, p. 425
- Congolese Cuisine, p. 429
- In Protest, p. 433

Teaching Resources

- Guided Reading and Review, pp. 69, 72, 75, and 78
- Vocabulary, p. 81
- Reteaching, p. 82
- Guide to the Essentials, pp. 99–102
- Social Studies and Geography Skills, pp. 18, 89

Technology

- Social Studies Skills Tutor CD-ROM
- Section Reading Support Transparencies

Less Proficient Readers

Teacher's Edition

- Letter Writing, p. 421
- In Protest, p. 433
- Conducting Electricity, p. 429

Teaching Resources

- Guided Reading and Review, pp. 69, 72, 75, and 78
- Vocabulary, p. 81
- Reteaching, p. 82
- Guide to the Essentials, pp. 99–102
- Social Studies and Geography Skills, pp. 18, 89

Technology

- Social Studies Skills Tutor CD-ROM
- Section Reading Support Transparencies

Less Proficient Writers

Teacher's Edition

- Protecting the Mountain Gorillas, p. 421
- Art, p. 425
- Congolese Cuisine, p. 429

Teaching Resources

- Guided Reading and Review, pp. 69, 72, 75, and 78
- Vocabulary, p. 81
- Guide to the Essentials, pp. 99–102
- Social Studies and Geography Skills, pp. 18, 89

Technology

- Social Studies Skills Tutor CD-ROM
- Section Reading Support Transparencies

DORLING KINDERSLEY

At the end of each unit, you will find information adapted from Dorling Kindersley's *Illustrated Children's Encyclopedia* that connects to the region being studied and to one of the seven content strands. In addition, your resources include Dorling Kindersley's *Atlas*, which contains valuable information about countries from around the world.

TEACHER'S EDITION INDEX

CHAPTER 23 PACING SUGGESTIONS

For 90-minute Blocks

See suggestions in the Teaching Resources Pacing Charts for Chapter 23. Use Color Transparencies 93, 98, and 99.

Running Out of Time?

See the Guide to the Essentials, pp. 99–102.

INTERDISCIPLINARY LINKS

Middle Grades Math: Tools for Success

Course 1, Lesson 1-5 **Reading and Understanding Graphs**

Course 1, Lesson 3-8 **Metric Units of Length**

Science Explorer

Environmental Science, Lesson 2-4, **Earth's Biomes**

Earth's Waters, Lesson 2-1, **Streams and Rivers;** Lesson 2-3, **Wetland Environments**

Animals, Lesson 4-4, **Diversity of Mammals**

From Bacteria to Plants, Lesson 1-3; **Classifying Organisms,** Lesson 1-4; **The Six Kingdoms**

Prentice Hall Literature

Copper, Why Monkeys Lie in Trees

BIBLIOGRAPHY

For the Teacher

African Religions: Zulu Zion. Time/Life, 1996. Videocassette.

DK *DK Concise Atlas of the World.* Dorling Kindersley, 2001.

Langley, Myrtle. Religion. Knopf, 1996.

Pratt, Paula Bryant. *The End of Apartheid in South Africa.* Lucent, 1995.

For the Student

Easy

DK *Africa* (*Eyewitness* series). Dorling Kindersley, 2001.

Average

Nicholson, Robert. *The Zulus.* Chelsea House, 1994.

Wilkes, Sybella. *One Day We Had to Run! Refugee Children Tell Their Stories in Words and Paintings.* Millbrook, 1995.

Challenging

Otfinoski, Steven. *Nelson Mandela: The Fight Against Apartheid.* Millbrook, 1992.

Literature Connection

Grimsdell, Jeremy. *Kalinzu: A Story from Africa.* Kingfisher, 1993.

Kurtz, Jane. *Pulling the Lion's Tail.* Simon & Schuster, 1995.

Take It to the NET

The World Explorer companion Web site, found on **phschool.com**, offers activities for exploring geographical, historical, and cultural resources on the Internet. It also provides on-line links for key content and all Section and Chapter Assessment activities.

The **Teacher site** also provides teachers with regional data and ideas for student research and activities.

Students can use the **Student site** to find chapter-by-chapter Internet resource links and to access Self-Tests.

CHAPTER 23

Connecting to the Guiding Questions

In this chapter, students will read about countries in East, Central, and Southern Africa. Content in this chapter corresponds to the following Guiding Questions outlined at the beginning of the unit.

- How do Africa's many cultures differ from place to place?
- What are some of the ways that Africans make a living?
- How have African's struggled to participate in their governments' political processes?

Using the Autobiographies Activities

Explain to students that Nelson Mandela earned a Nobel Peace Prize for negotiating a peaceful transition of power in South Africa.

- Mandela says that he did not have one single moment of realization, but rather, that it was "a thousand slights" and "a thousand indignities" that made him fight for the end of apartheid. The excerpt reveals Mandela to be a man of great determination and courage.
- Students should make a list of six questions revealing what additional information they would like to learn about Mandela. Reports should sufficiently answer all of their questions.

Heterogeneous Groups

The following activities are suitable for heterogeneous groups.

Journal Writing

Writing a Letter, p. 421

In Protest, p. 433

eTeach

Be sure to check out this month's discussion with a Master Teacher. Go to **phschool.com**.

CHAPTER 23

EAST, CENTRAL, AND SOUTH AFRICA: Exploring the Region Today

A Lifetime of Struggle

"I cannot pinpoint a moment when I became politicized, when I knew that I would spend my life in the liberation struggle. I had no epiphany, no singular revelation, no moment of truth, but a steady accumulation of a thousand slights, and a thousand indignities produced in me an anger, a desire to fight the system that imprisoned my people."

—Nelson Mandela from *Mandela: An Illustrated Autobiography*

USING AUTOBIOGRAPHIES

This excerpt is from an autobiography written by Nelson Mandela. An autobiography is a book written about a person's life, by that person. Nelson Mandela was elected president of South Africa in 1994, after spending 28 years in prison for fighting apartheid.

Understanding the Author

Use a dictionary to find the meaning of the words, *politicized, epiphany, revelation, slight,* and *indignity.* What does Nelson Mandela say was the cause of his efforts to fight apartheid? What does this excerpt reveal about Nelson Mandela? What does it reveal about his struggle to fight apartheid?

Learning More about the Author

This is only a brief excerpt from Nelson Mandela's autobiography. What else would you like to know about his life? Make a list of six questions about Mandela's life that you would like to have answered. Use the library and the Internet to find the answers, and then write a brief report on Mandela that you can share with the rest of the class.

Resource Directory

Teaching Resources

Primary Sources and Literature Readings extend content with a selection related to the concepts in this chapter.

Other Print Resources

DK Atlas

Technology

Case Study: Ecotourism, from the World Video Explorer, enhances understanding of the ways in which East Africa, like other regions worldwide, protects wildlife while benefiting from tourism.

Spotlight On: Apartheid, from the World Video Explorer, enhances understanding of the political and social changes resulting from the demise of apartheid in South Africa.

Student Edition on Audio CD, Ch. 23

SECTION 1

Rwanda and Burundi

Torn By Ethnic Conflict

BEFORE YOU READ

READING FOCUS

1. What are the three main ethnic groups in Rwanda and Burundi and how did they arrive in the region?
2. What has been the history of conflict between two of the major ethnic groups in these countries?

KEY TERMS

aristocratic
mwami
ganwa
vassal
refugee

KEY PEOPLE

Hutu
Tutsi
Twa

NOTE TAKING

Copy this chart. As you read the section, complete the chart with information on the Hutu and Tutsi people of Rwanda and Burundi.

	Hutu	Tutsi
• Orgin		
• Place in Society		
• Religion		
• Occupation		

MAIN IDEA

Since independence in the 1960s, both Rwanda and its neighboring country, Burundi, have experienced civil war between two major ethnic groups, the Hutu and the Tutsi.

Setting the Scene

The kingdoms of Rwanda and Burundi date back to the 15th and 16th centuries.

Both countries have rich and varied wildlife including elephants, antelopes, zebras, and buffalo. Rare mountain gorillas live in one of the last remaining sanctuaries in Rwanda's Volcanoes National Park. The people of this region, primarily **Hutu** and **Tutsi,** share common social structures and religious beliefs. Rwanda and Burundi are neighbors but they have a long and unhappy history of conflict that has not yet been resolved.

Mountain Gorillas of Rwanda

CULTURE Over the years, many people have fought to protect Rwanda's dwindling gorilla population. **Critical Thinking** Do you think it is important for countries to protect endangered species? Why?

Cultural Origins

The first inhabitants of both Rwanda and Burundi were the **Twa,** a Pygmy people, who were hunters and pottery makers. Today, the Pygmies live in areas near the Equator.

SECTION 1

Lesson Objectives

1. Identify the ethnic groups that populate Rwanda and Burundi and their origins.
2. Understand the history of the conflict between the Hutu and the Tutsi and the current crisis that exists in Rwanda and Burundi.

Lesson Plan

1 Engage

Warm-Up Activity

Have students do a quick write about what they think the cause of the conflict between different ethnic groups in Rwanda and Burundi might be about. Have them think about how geography and history might impact on the conflict, and then share their ideas in a class discussion.

Activating Prior Knowledge

Ask students to think of a time when they have been neutral observers of a conflict between two people or two groups of people. Have them suppose that they have been asked to bring about a resolution to the conflict. What problems would they be most concerned about resolving? How would they try to be fair to both sides? What problems might they encounter in trying to find a fair resolution?

Resource Directory

Teaching Resources

Classroom Manager in the Unit 5 Teaching Resources, p. 68

Guided Reading and Review in the Unit 5 Teaching Resources, p. 69

Guide to the Essentials, p. 99

Technology

Section Reading Support Transparencies

Answers to...

CRITICAL THINKING

Students may say that it is important because the animals cannot protect themselves.

CHAPTER 23 EAST, CENTRAL, AND SOUTH AFRICA: EXPLORING THE REGION TODAY 419

Lesson Plan continued

2 Explore

Have students read the section and then discuss questions such as: What common bonds between the Hutu and Tutsi might eventually help bring them together?

3 Teach

Have students begin two concept webs. They should label one *Rwanda* and one *Burundi.* Encourage students to suggest words or phrases that describe these countries, their histories, and their people. Aspects common to both countries can be connected to both webs. This activity should take about 20 minutes.

Questions for Discussion

CULTURE **Why do you think the Hutus accepted their roles as vassals of the Tutsi landowners?**

The Tutsi had superior military skills, so even though there were many more Hutus than Tutsis, they probably felt powerless and did not fight back.

GOVERNMENT **What was the form of government established by Tutsis? How do you think this form of government helped to create tensions between the Hutus and Tutsis?**

The Tutsis established an aristocracy, in which a minority rules. Because the Hutus were such a large majority, this would have created tension because there was no Hutu representation in the political system.

Answers to...

CRITICAL THINKING

In Rwanda there are about 11 Hutus for every Tutsi. In Burundi, there are about 6 Hutus for every Tutsi.

COUNTRY • PROFILE

Rwanda and Burundi

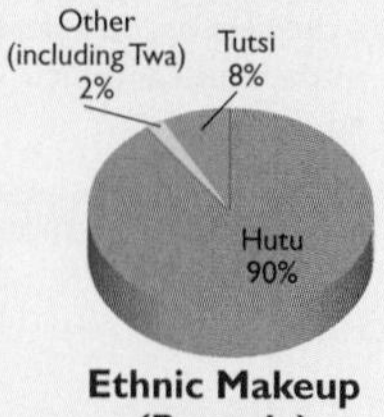

Ethnic Makeup (Rwanda)

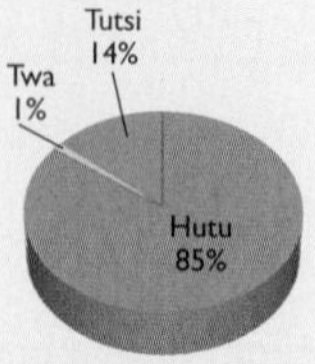

Ethnic Makeup (Burundi)

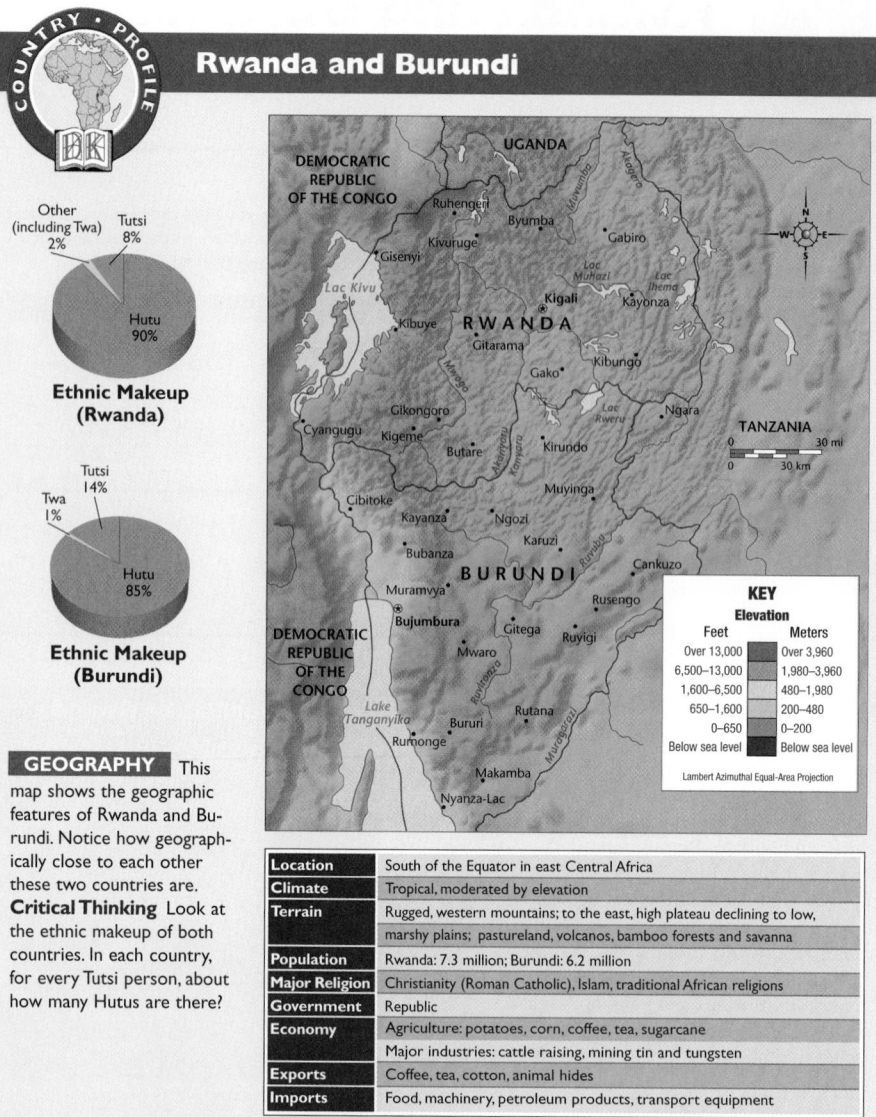

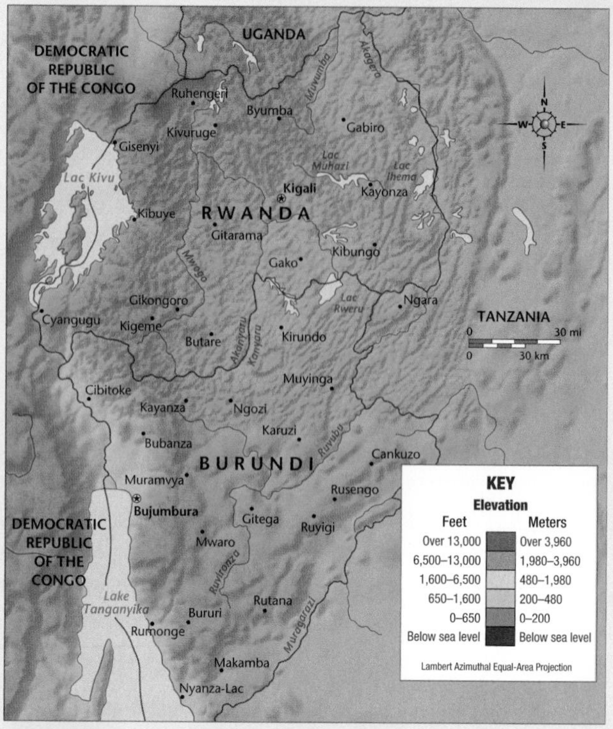

GEOGRAPHY This map shows the geographic features of Rwanda and Burundi. Notice how geographically close to each other these two countries are. **Critical Thinking** Look at the ethnic makeup of both countries. In each country, for every Tutsi person, about how many Hutus are there?

Location	South of the Equator in east Central Africa
Climate	Tropical, moderated by elevation
Terrain	Rugged, western mountains; to the east, high plateau declining to low, marshy plains; pastureland, volcanos, bamboo forests and savanna
Population	Rwanda: 7.3 million; Burundi: 6.2 million
Major Religion	Christianity (Roman Catholic), Islam, traditional African religions
Government	Republic
Economy	Agriculture: potatoes, corn, coffee, tea, sugarcane Major industries: cattle raising, mining tin and tungsten
Exports	Coffee, tea, cotton, animal hides
Imports	Food, machinery, petroleum products, transport equipment

The Hutu arrived next. They were Bantu-speakers who migrated to the region from West Africa. Finally, the Tutsi settled here, and are believed to have come from either the Nile River Valley or from Ethiopia.

Resource Directory

Teaching Resources

Social Studies and Geography Skills, Elevation on a Map, p. 18

Outline Maps, West and Central Africa, p. 34

Technology

Color Transparencies 98 West and Central Africa: Political Map

The ethnic makeup of both Rwanda and Burundi is similar. The Hutu account for 85–90% of the population. The Tutsi form the other significant portion of the population, while the Twa comprise just a tiny fraction. Despite this, it is the Tutsi who have always held a dominant place in both societies.

The Aristocratic Minority

When the Tutsi arrived in this region, the Hutu were well established and made their living as subsistence farmers. But the Hutu were soon under the control of the Tutsi, who had superior military skills. The Tutsi, who were herdsmen, gained control of the land. They became **aristocratic** rulers, those who are in the minority but are considered a privileged, upper class. A political system developed headed by a **mwami** (king) who divided the land among his **ganwa** (princes or lords). This Tutsi form of government continued until both countries gained independence from Belgium in 1962.

Life for the Hutu Majority

The Hutus in these societies were considered to be **vassals,** or servants, of the Tutsi landowners.

The Hutus' task was to safeguard the cattle herds, but they also raised crops of plantains, corn, and yams. The Tutsi lords, who in modern times were called chiefs and military captains, required the Hutu to support them through their labor. The Hutu accepted this role until civil war erupted in 1959 and, then again, after independence in 1962.

Cultures at War

Belgium had occupied both Rwanda and Burundi after World War I but its influence was declining in the late 1950s. It was then that the Hutu majority began to demand a more equal role in society. In Rwanda, the Hutu succeeded in overthrowing the ruling Tutsi king, and thousands of Tutsis were killed, while others were driven into exile in neighboring countries. By 1994, the Tutsi were again in power. This time, as many as 2 million Hutu fled the region and became **refugees,** people who seek safety in another country.

In Burundi, rebellions by the Hutu were brutally put down by the Tutsi, who controlled the country until the 1993 elections gave power to the Hutu.

AS YOU READ

Summarize How did the role of the Hutu in society differ from that of the Tutsi?

Refugees Return Home

CULTURE Thousands of Hutu refugees returned to Rwanda after fleeing the country for their safety.
Critical Thinking Why do you think these refugees wanted to return to Rwanda after facing so much danger and violence?

4 Assess/Reteach

See the answers to the Section 1 Assessment. You may also use students' completed webs as an assessment.

Acceptable webs identify three unique facts about each country and one common aspect.

Commendable webs identify four unique facts about each country and two common aspects.

Outstanding webs identify more than four unique facts about each country and two or more common aspects.

HISTORY

Protecting the Mountain Gorillas

In 1966, a young woman named Dian Fossey climbed up 10,000 feet into the Virunga Volcanoes of Rwanda and first glimpsed the gentle giants she would spend the rest of her life studying. There were an estimated 480 mountain gorillas at that time. She would later write a book about them called *Gorillas in the Mist.* After 20 years, the gorillas were at risk for extinction because of poachers who would hunt and kill them. Dian Fossey was killed trying to protect the great apes from poachers. Her grave marker says: "No one loved gorillas more…"

ACTIVITY

Journal Writing

Letter Writing Ask students to write a personal letter in their journal to someone associated with the Rwanda/Burundi region from the past or present. For example, you may tell them that former South African President Nelson Mandela is heading up a delegation of representatives working towards peace in the region. Or they may wish to ask questions in a letter to anthropologist Dian Fossey. If they are interested in the explorers who passed through this region, they might write to them.

Verbal/Linguistic

Answers to…

AS YOU READ

The Hutus were servants of the Tutsi landowners.

CRITICAL THINKING

Students may say that the desire to be at home in Rwanda was greater than the fear of danger and violence.

SECTION 1 ASSESSMENT

AFTER YOU READ

1. (a) the majority ethnic group, arriving originally from Bantu-speaking regions of West Africa, (b) the minority ethnic group, probably originally from Ethiopia, considered to historically have been in control of governing this region, (c) the Pygmy race of people making up a very small percentage of the population
2. (a) ruling upper class in a society, (b) king, (c) princes or lords, (d) servants, (e) people forced from their country due to war or other conditions that require they find safety in another country.
3. The Twa have lived in Rwanda and Burundi the longest. Today, they live in areas near the equator. The Hutu migrated from West Africa. Most recently, the Tutsi came from either the Nile River Valley or Ethiopia.
4. They used their superior military strength.
5. Answers should show an understanding of the origins and aspects that differentiate the two groups.
6. Answers should relate to the difficulties each group will face in maintaining a stable government, as well as rebuilding the economy and industry; attracting skilled workers and professionals to rebuild the education and health care systems; the loss of generations of family members; and environmental issues from years of neglect and abuse of the land and natural resources.
7. If necessary, review with students how to construct a timeline. Suggest that students first identify the events that they will put on their timelines so that they have an idea how large to make them timelines.

GOVERNMENT In 2000, President Bill Clinton traveled to Tanzania to take part in the Burundi Peace Talks. **Critical Thinking** Why do you think international leaders intervened in the conflicts in Rwanda and Burundi?

World Leaders Intervene

Both Rwanda and Burundi have experienced continual upheaval as a result of military coups, assassinations, and outbreaks of ethnic violence. In 1994, the rest of the world began to recognize the desperate situation in these countries. In April of that year, the presidents of both Rwanda and Burundi were killed when their airplane was shot down. In the turmoil that followed, extreme Hutu soldiers in Rwanda killed hundreds of thousands of civilians, most of them Tutsi. World leaders, including South African President Nelson Mandela and United States President Bill Clinton, began organizing peace talks in hopes of ending the violence.

Contemporary Issues

The way to peace has not yet been found in either Rwanda or Burundi. Because of war, many other problems have developed for the people of both countries. Health conditions are extremely poor with few doctors, very little medicine, and shortages of food. Children often die very young and although education is free, many children cannot attend school. The effects of war will cause suffering in these countries even after the struggles end.

SECTION 1 ASSESSMENT

AFTER YOU READ

RECALL

1. Identify: (a) Tutsi, (b) Hutu, (c) Twa
2. Define: (a) aristocratic, (b) mwami, (c) ganwa, (d) vassal, e) refugee

COMPREHENSION

3. Who were the first inhabitants of both Rwanda and Burundi? Where do they live now?
4. How did the minority Tutsi people first gain and keep control over the majority Hutu?

CRITICAL THINKING AND WRITING

5. **Exploring the Main Idea** Review the Main Idea statement at the beginning of this section. Then, write a paragraph comparing and contrasting the Hutu and Tutsi peoples, and discussing each group's historic role in the region.
6. **Making Predictions** How will the years of war affect life in Rwanda and Burundi even after the fighting stops? What problems would you predict for education, culture, families, the environment, and the economies?

ACTIVITY

7. **Creating a Timeline** Using the information you learned in this section, create a timeline that shows the major events in the history of Rwanda and Burundi.

Answers to...

CRITICAL THINKING

International leaders may have felt that outside intervention was necessary to help stop the conflict. They may have feared further loss of life in the area.

Resource Directory

Teaching Resources

Section Quiz in the Unit 5 Teaching Resources, p. 70

SECTION 2

Kenya

Diverse Cultures, Shared Goals

BEFORE YOU READ

READING FOCUS:

1. How have Kenyans worked together to preserve the things they value most?
2. How do Kenyans who move to Nairobi from rural areas maintain ties to their homes and families?

KEY TERMS

harambee

KEY PEOPLE AND PLACES

Mount Kenya
Jomo Kenyatta
Nairobi

NOTE TAKING

Copy this chart. As you read the section, complete the chart with information about the values, traditions, and natural resources that contribute to Kenya's economy.

Values and Traditions	Natural Resources

MAIN IDEA

Kenya's diverse people belong to more than 40 different ethnic groups, but they are all loyal to their homeland and work together to preserve their values and families.

Setting the Scene

"Where is your shamba?" This is a question that two Kenyans usually ask each other when they first meet. A shamba is a small farm owned and run by a Kenyan family. Even Kenyans who live in the city think of the piece of land where they were born as home and return to it throughout their lives. Land is very important to Kenyans.

A Kenyan Shamba

CULTURE This series of buildings is part of a shamba. It was built by a family that is part of Kenya's Kikuyu ethnic group. The whole shamba is considered the family home. **Critical Thinking** What do you think "home" means to the Kenyan people?

Kenya's Geography and People

Kenya is a country in central East Africa. **Mount Kenya,** Kenya's highest mountain, lies just south of the Equator, but its twin peaks are covered with snow all year. Southwest of Mount Kenya is a region of highlands. Its average temperature is 67°F (19°C). The area also gets plenty of rain, so the land is good for farming. Most of Kenya's people are farmers, who live in shambas dotting the countryside in the highlands.

The land near the coast is warmer but also has good farmland. Farther inland, plains stretch across Kenya, and here there is little rainfall so the plains can support only bushes, small trees, and grasses. North of the plains lie deserts, where the temperature can sometimes climb as high as 135°F (57°C).

Resource Directory

Teaching Resources

Classroom Manager in the Unit 5 Teaching Resources, p. 71

Guided Reading and Review in the Unit 5 Teaching Resources, p. 72

Guide to the Essentials, p. 100

Technology

Section Reading Support Transparencies

SECTION 2

Lesson Objectives

1. Identify the cultural values of the Kenyans and the ways they have worked to preserve these values.
2. Describe some of the reasons why Kenyans are moving to urban areas and how they maintain family ties once there.

Lesson Plan

1 Engage

Warm-Up Activity

Ask students to think of ways in which groups sometimes "pull together" to achieve a common goal, such as organizing a neighborhood cleanup. Record students' ideas on the board. Then, ask why teamwork is necessary for these activities to be successful.

Activating Prior Knowledge

Discuss with students some of the ways that they stay in touch with friends and family members when someone moves away. Then, ask students how they cope with feeling homesick when they are away from home.

2 Explore

Have students read the section and then discuss questions such as the following: What are the features of rural and urban life in Kenya? What is *harambee*, and what are some examples of it? What kinds of work do women do?

Answers to...

CRITICAL THINKING

"Home" to the Kenyan people usually means the piece of land where they were born.

Lesson Plan continued

❸ Teach

Have students begin two concept webs. They should label one web *Females* and the other *Males*. Encourage students to suggest words or phrases that describe differences and similarities between the ways men and women in Kenya live. Aspects common to both sexes can be connected to both webs. This activity should take about 25 minutes.

Questions for Discussion

GEOGRAPHY **Look at the information about Kenya's economy on this page. What parts of the country might be suited to agriculture?**

Areas in the south part of Kenya, especially the southwest, are suited to agriculture because there are desert regions in the north.

CULTURE **How is the population of Kenya similar to those in Rwanda and Burundi? How is it different?**

Kenya's people are indigenous Africans, as are the people of Rwanda and Burundi. However, there are only two major ethnic groups in both Rwanda and Burundi, while there are over 40 ethnic groups in Kenya.

❹ Assess/Reteach

See the answers to the Section 2 Assessment. You may also use students' completed webs as an assessment.

Acceptable webs identify three unique facts each for males and females and three they share.

Commendable webs identify four unique facts each for males and females and three they share.

Outstanding webs identify more than four unique facts each for males and females and more than three they share.

Answers to...

MAP AND CHART STUDY

The western part of Kenya has the highest elevation. The eastern part has the lowest elevation.

COUNTRY PROFILE

Kenya

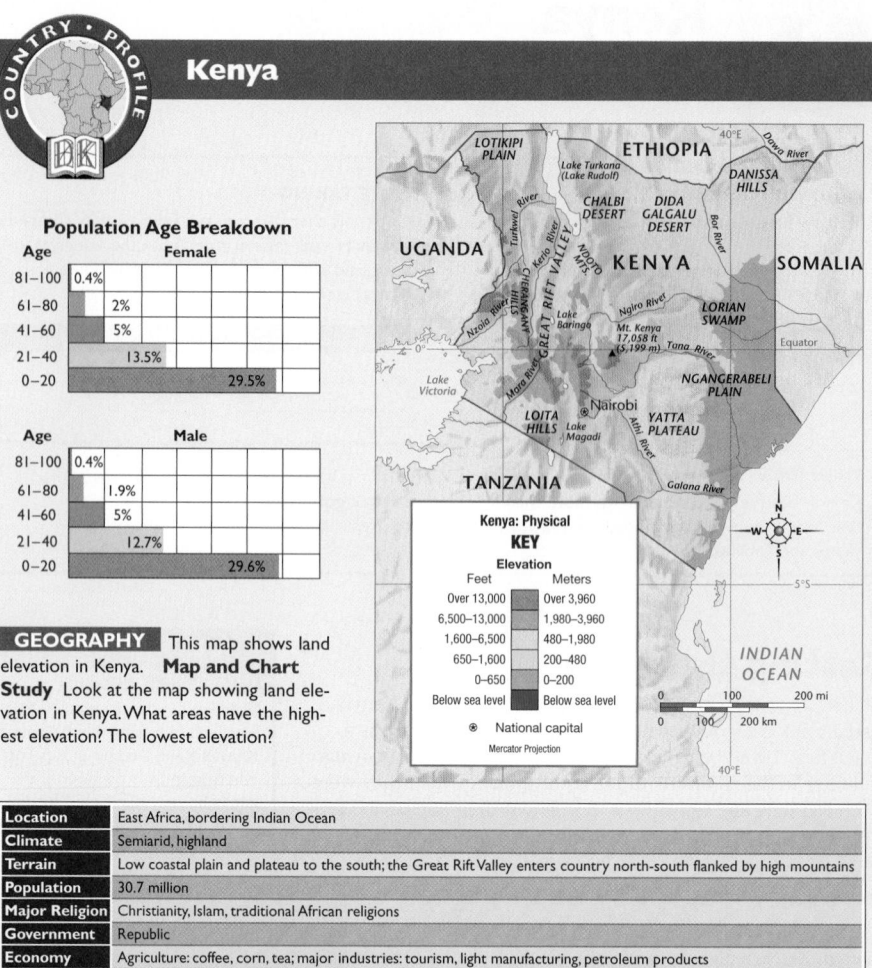

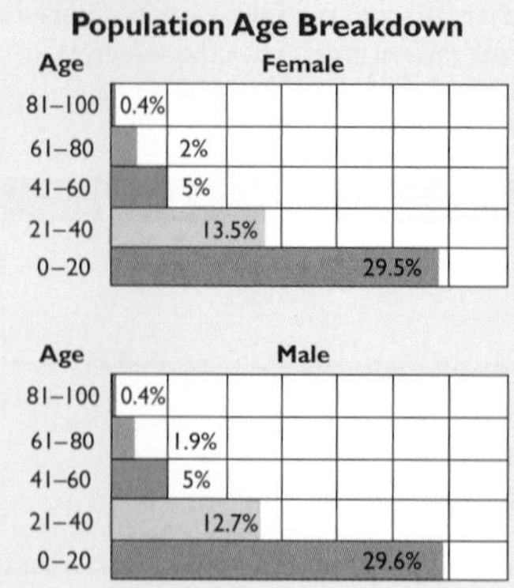

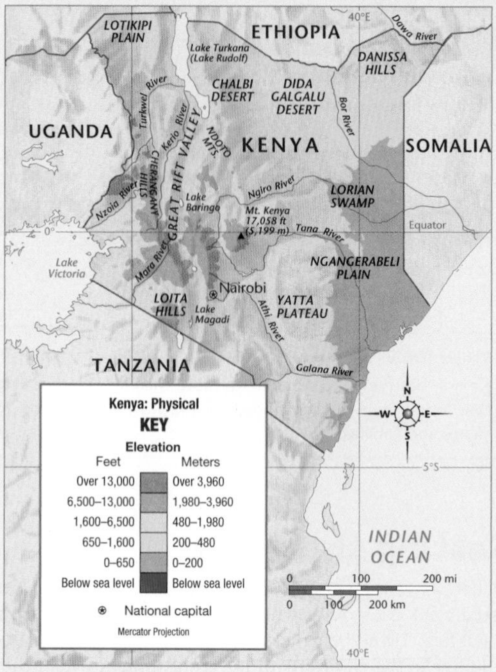

GEOGRAPHY This map shows land elevation in Kenya. **Map and Chart Study** Look at the map showing land elevation in Kenya. What areas have the highest elevation? The lowest elevation?

Location	East Africa, bordering Indian Ocean
Climate	Semiarid, highland
Terrain	Low coastal plain and plateau to the south; the Great Rift Valley enters country north-south flanked by high mountains
Population	30.7 million
Major Religion	Christianity, Islam, traditional African religions
Government	Republic
Economy	Agriculture: coffee, corn, tea; major industries: tourism, light manufacturing, petroleum products
Exports	Tea, coffee, petroleum products
Imports	Machinery and equipment, petroleum and petroleum products, iron and steel, raw materials, food, goods to sell

The Diversity of Kenya's People Nearly all of Kenya's people are indigenous Africans who belong to more than 40 different ethnic groups, each with its own culture and language. Most Kenyans are Christian or Muslim.

Despite the differences among Kenya's people, they have many things in common. As they value the land, Kenyans also value their families, which often have six or more children. People consider their cousins to be almost like brothers and sisters.

Resource Directory

Teaching Resources

Outline Maps, East and Southern Africa, p. 35

Technology

Passport to the World CD-ROM This interactive CD-ROM allows students to explore each region of the world. Students view regional videos, take a photo tour, and explore a historical timeline. Students record their travels in an Explorer's Journal and receive passport stamps when they pass regional quizzes.

Color Transparencies 93 Africa South of the Sahara: Physical Political Map; **99** East and Southern Africa: Political Map

Harambee—Working Together After Kenya gained independence in 1963, the new president, **Jomo Kenyatta** (JOH moh ken YAH tuh), began a campaign he called **harambee** (hah RAHM bay). The word is Swahili for "let's pull together." One example is Kenyatta's approach to education in which the government pays for some of a child's education, but the people work together to build and support schools.

AS YOU READ

Summarize What is the concept behind harambee? What is an example of this campaign?

Kenya's Labor Moves to the Cities

The people who live in the rural areas of Kenya are farmers. Like farmers all over Africa, most are women, who grow fruits and vegetables to eat and herd livestock. Men also farm, but they usually raise cash crops, such as coffee and tea.

Farming in the Highlands The Kikuyu (ki KOO yoo) are Kenya's largest ethnic group. Many Kikuyu live on the highlands near Mount Kenya. The Kikuyu grow food and cash crops such as coffee and sisal, which is used to make rope.

Children in a farming village have more responsibilities than most children in the United States. To see what a typical day is like for a Kenyan child, look at the schedule below.

City Life The way of life of many Kenyans is changing. As the population increases, people are moving to the city to find work. Most women and children, however, stay in the rural areas. It is expensive for them to move to the city and easier to support their families by farming.

Nairobi: Kenya's Capital City Every day, new residents arrive in **Nairobi** (ny ROH bee) by train, bus, or matatu (muh TAH too)—a minibus. Nairobi's population grew from one million in 1985 to three

A Typical Day for Some Young Kenyans

5:45 A.M.	Get up, wash, and dress.	**10:20 A.M.**	Break	**5:30 P.M.**	Reach home. Wash uniforms. Lock up goats and sheep. Help prepare supper.
6:15 A.M.	Eat breakfast.	**11:00 A.M.**	Lessons	**7:00 P.M.**	Eat supper.
6:30 A.M.	Start walking to school.	**12:45 A.M.**	Lunch break. Children bring their own lunch.	**7:30 P.M.**	Wash up.
7:00 A.M.	Arrive at school. Help clean the school.	**1:00 P.M.**	Play.	**8:00 P.M.**	Do homework every night.
7:30 A.M.	Prepare for lessons.	**2:00 P.M.**	Lessons start.	**8:30 P.M.**	Wash and prepare for bed.
7:45 A.M.	Assembly. Sing national anthem.	**4:00 P.M.**	Lessons end. Help clean the school or work on the school shamba.	**9:00 P.M.**	Go to bed.
8:00 A.M.	Lessons start.	**5:00 P.M.**	Start walking home.		

CULTURE Like you, many Kenyan children spend most of each day in school. **Chart Study** Compare your schedule with this one. How might your day be different if you lived in Kenya? How might it be similar?

ACTIVITY

Culture

Art The Maasai are well known for the beautiful beaded jewelry they make. Organize students into two or three large groups to make a collection of Maasai jewelry. Show students photographs of the Maasai for guidance. Provide each group with wire and colored beads. Students may make necklaces, bracelets, headbands, or earrings.

Bodily/Kinesthetic

CULTURE

Ngugi wa Thiong'o (born 1938)

Kenya's best-known writer, Ngugi wa Thiong'o, was born into a Kikuyu community in the highlands of Kenya. He attended a colonial school and earned degrees from universities in Uganda and Great Britain. In 1964, he wrote his first novel, *Weep Not, Child.* Though Ngugi wrote in English, the novel tells the story of a Kikuyu family during Kenya's struggle for independence. In his other works, he often deals with the social, moral, and racial issues that confront a young nation. After 1977, Ngugi began publishing works in Swahili or in his native Kikuyu language. This made his writing much more accessible to most Kenyans. Whether writing in English, Swahili, or Kikuyu, however, Ngugi's novels and plays have always been part of the African tradition that calls upon the power of literature to combat injustice.

SKILLS MINI LESSON

Drawing Conclusions

To **introduce** the skill, explain that when people draw a conclusion they are making an educated guess, which is based upon available clues and knowledge they already have. Tell students that they may **practice** drawing some conclusions about life in Nairobi as they read the text under the heading *Nairobi: Kenya's Capital City.* Have students look for clues about the size of the population and the distance people travel to get to work and to relate the clues to what they already know about cities. Then ask students to **apply** the skill by writing a short paragraph about what challenges Nairobi will probably need to address in the early 2000s. (Students may conclude that Nairobi will need to build new housing and roads and may need to expand its public transportation system. The country might also need to find ways to provide social services to a large and fairly poor population.)

Answers to...

AS YOU READ

The concept behind harambee is cooperation. An example is people working together to build and support schools for their children.

CHART STUDY

Answers will vary. Students will probably recognize similarities in school schedules and note differences in home chores.

SECTION 2 ASSESSMENT

AFTER YOU READ

1. (a) Kenya's highest mountain (b) the first president of the independent nation of Kenya (c) Kenya's capital city
2. the Swahili word for "let's pull together," exemplary of the Kenyan characteristic of working together
3. Children may begin their day by carrying water to their village. They may milk cattle or goats and clean their homes before going to school.
4. They move to find work in the city.
5. Kenyans support harambee, or pulling together, to preserve their values. Harambee has led to success in self-government, improved educational systems, and support for rural Kenyan families and their men working in the cities.
6. Women must take on all the work of raising children. They also often work as farmers to support the household.
7. Entries will vary, but should discuss the need to find work and earn a living. Problems to overcome might include being separated from his home and family.

ECONOMICS Residents enjoy a stroll in downtown Nairobi, an important business center and one of the largest cities in East Africa. Many products are manufactured here. In addition, much of East African banking and trade is centered in Nairobi. **Critical Thinking** What in the picture looks familiar to you? What, if anything, looks unfamiliar?

million in 1995, making it bigger than the city of Chicago in the United States. By the year 2000, the city had more than four million residents.

Many men move to Nairobi in order to earn money to support their families. When men move to the city without their families, they often feel homesick for their loved ones in rural villages. Meanwhile, the women who are left behind must do twice as much work. Many people have responded to this situation in the spirit of harambee—working together.

Women's Self-Help Groups One of the best examples of harambee in rural Kenya are women's self-help groups, which women in rural areas all over Kenya have formed to solve problems in their communities. In addition to the crops they grow for their families to eat, the women grow cash crops, sell them, and save the money as a group. The women then meet to decide what to do with the money they have saved.

In Mitero, a village in the mountains north of Nairobi, Kikuyu women's groups have built a nursery school and installed water pipes for the community. They also loan money to women who want to start small businesses. Sometimes, they give money to women who need to buy such things as a cow or a water tank.

Men in the City Moses Mpoke (MOH zuz uhm POHK ay) is from a Maasai village and he traditionally made a living farming and herding. Mpoke finished high school and now works in Nairobi. He has land in his home village, but the land is too dry for farming and he could not find good grazing for his livestock. He left the village to find work.

Men who move to the city work hard. Men in Nairobi who are from the same ethnic group often welcome each other, share rooms, and help each other.

SECTION 2 ASSESSMENT

AFTER YOU READ

RECALL

1. Identify: (a) Mount Kenya, (b) Jomo Kenyatta, (c) Nairobi
2. Define: (a) harambee

COMPREHENSION

3. Describe a typical day in the life of a young Kenyan.
4. Why do so many Kenyan men move to Nairobi?

CRITICAL THINKING AND WRITING

5. **Exploring the Main Idea** Review the Main Idea statement at the beginning of this section. Then, write a paragraph that discusses how Kenyans work together to preserve their values and families.
6. **Expressing Problems Clearly** How are women in rural villages affected when men move to the city?

ACTIVITY

7. **Journal Writing** Write a journal entry from the point of view of a Kenyan man who has just left his home and moved to the city. What new opportunities have brought him there and what problems must he overcome?

Resource Directory

Teaching Resources

Section Quiz in the Unit 5 Teaching Resources, p. 73

Social Studies and Geography Skills, Writing to Describe, p. 89

Answers to...

CRITICAL THINKING

Students' responses will vary.

SECTION 3

The Democratic Republic of the Congo

A Government in Turmoil

BEFORE YOU READ

READING FOCUS

1. Why have minerals long been important to the Congo's economy?
2. What economic challenges has the Congo faced since independence?

KEY TERMS

authoritarian
nationalize

KEY PEOPLE AND PLACES

Shaba
Mobutu Sese Seko

NOTE TAKING

Copy this chart. As you read the section, fill in the information that shows some of the problems and turmoil that have affected the Congo throughout its history.

Portuguese Arrive for Gold → [ ] → [ ] → [ ] → [ ]

MAIN IDEA

The Democratic Republic of the Congo is a mineral-rich country with a long history of unrest.

Setting the Scene

Since the 1930s, the Democratic Republic of the Congo (often called the Congo) has become one of the world's main sources of copper. The Congo also has supplies of many other resources, including gold, diamonds, forests, water, and wildlife which have played an important role in the nation's history. Even so, a small part of the country's natural resources have been developed.

Copper Mining in the Congo

ECONOMICS In the Congo, miners take copper out of the ground in layers, leaving an open pit behind. **Critical Thinking** How might a country's natural resources affect its history?

Mining and Other Natural Resources

The Democratic Republic of the Congo is located in west Central Africa and is equal in size to the United States east of the Mississippi River. It is Africa's third largest country.

Although about two-thirds of the Congo's people work as farmers, mining produces most of the country's wealth. The Congo has huge copper deposits in the southern province of **Shaba** (SHAB uh), the Swahili word for copper. The country also has reserves of gold and other minerals and produces more diamonds than any other country, except Australia.

Resource Directory

Teaching Resources

Classroom Manager in the Unit 5 Teaching Resources, p. 74

Guided Reading and Review in the Unit 5 Teaching Resources, p. 75

Guide to the Essentials, p. 101

Technology

Section Reading Support Transparencies

SECTION 3

Lesson Objectives

1. Describe the significance of natural resources in the Congo's history.
2. Summarize the Congo's economic challenges since independence.

Lesson Plan

1 Engage

Warm-Up Activity

Tell students that developing countries often rely upon loans from wealthier countries to finance the building of transportation systems, communications systems, hospitals, and other services. Ask students to discuss the effect that paying back large loans might have on the country's economy.

Activating Prior Knowledge

Ask students to think about what resources a country needs to provide a good life for its people. Suggest that they make a list and rank each resource according to its importance. Invite them to share their lists with the class.

2 Explore

As students read the section, have them look for answers to the following questions: What are the Congo's most important natural resources? How have the Congo's abundant natural resources affected the lives of the Congolese? What have been some of the results of rebellion and changes in leadership?

Answers to...

CRITICAL THINKING

Students should recognize that a country's natural resources make it a more desirable place to live, draw people from other regions, and support a healthier economy.

Lesson Plan continued

3 Teach

Ask students to make timelines that describe important dates and time periods in the economic and political histories of the Congo. This activity should take about 25 minutes.

Questions for Discussion

GEOGRAPHY Look at the map of natural resources on this page. How many hydroelectric power sites are located close to mineral deposits? Why would it be useful to have a power plant near a mine?

All four plants are located near mineral deposits. Mining processes and operations require large amounts of electrical power.

ECONOMICS Once peace returns to the Congo, how do you think the Congolese can restore their country's economy?

They can focus on mining resources for which there is a demand, and also expand the export of agricultural crops.

4 Assess/Reteach

See the answers to the Section 3 Assessment. You may also use students' completed timelines as an assessment.

Acceptable timelines include descriptions of political or economic conditions during three different time periods.

Commendable timelines include descriptions of political or economic conditions during more than three different time periods.

Outstanding timelines include descriptions of political or economic conditions during more than three time periods and indicate that the establishment of control over natural resources is a common thread in the Congo's history.

COUNTRY PROFILE: The Democratic Republic of the Congo

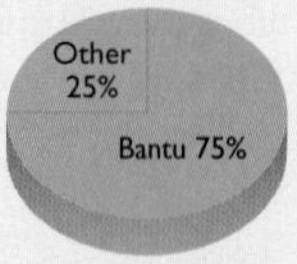

Ethnic Makeup

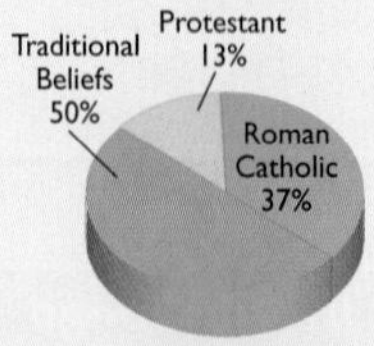

Religious Persuasion

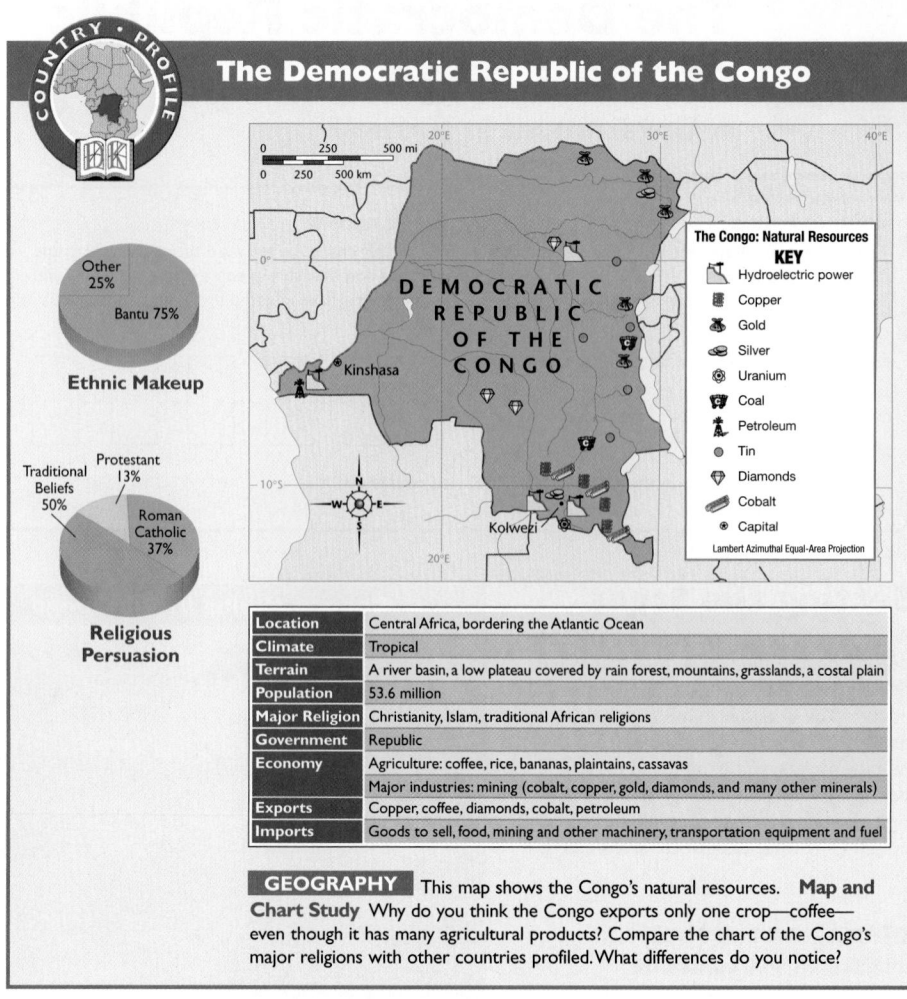

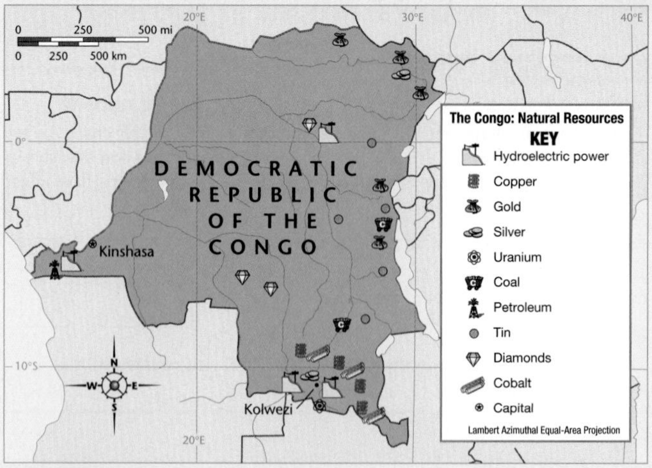

Location	Central Africa, bordering the Atlantic Ocean
Climate	Tropical
Terrain	A river basin, a low plateau covered by rain forest, mountains, grasslands, a costal plain
Population	53.6 million
Major Religion	Christianity, Islam, traditional African religions
Government	Republic
Economy	Agriculture: coffee, rice, bananas, plaintains, cassavas
	Major industries: mining (cobalt, copper, gold, diamonds, and many other minerals)
Exports	Copper, coffee, diamonds, cobalt, petroleum
Imports	Goods to sell, food, mining and other machinery, transportation equipment and fuel

GEOGRAPHY This map shows the Congo's natural resources. **Map and Chart Study** Why do you think the Congo exports only one crop—coffee—even though it has many agricultural products? Compare the chart of the Congo's major religions with other countries profiled. What differences do you notice?

Natural Resources in the Congo's History

Events relating to natural resources dominate the history of the Congo. The power of the ancient kingdoms of Kongo, Luba, and Lunda was based on their knowledge of ironworking. In the 1480s, the Portuguese came to the Congo in search of gold. When Belgium colonized the area 400 years later, it forced Africans to harvest wild rubber, but later was interested only in the Congo's other resources, especially its copper and diamonds.

Answers to...

MAP AND CHART STUDY

The Congo receives enough income from its major industries of mining copper, gold, diamonds and other minerals. Therefore, it does not have to sell its food as cash crops.

Fifty percent of Congo's people practice traditional beliefs, while other African countries profiled were primarily Muslim. The Protestant religion is also a major religion here, unlike in other African countries.

The Challenges of Independence

In the Congo's first years of independence, various groups fought each other for power. The foreign companies that controlled many of the country's industries feared this unrest would hurt their businesses. In 1965, they helped a military leader, **Mobutu Sese Seko** (muh BOO too SAY say SAY koh) take power.

Mobutu tried to restore order through an **authoritarian** government. An authoritarian government is one in which a single leader or small group of leaders has all the power. This type of government is not democratic. First, Mobutu renamed the country Zaire. Then, he **nationalized,** or put under government control, the foreign-owned companies. But this economic decision failed when government officials ran the companies poorly. When the world price of copper fell sharply in the 1970s, Zaire's export income fell and the nation could not pay back its debts.

Agriculture in Eastern Congo

GEOGRAPHY

Although the Congo is rich in natural resources, not all Congolese make a living as miners. Many Congolese work as farmers. They grow bananas, plantains, cassavas, corn, peanuts, and rice for their families. Others make a living growing cash crops such as cocoa, coffee, cotton, and tea. **Critical Thinking** The fields shown in this photograph are in a hilly area of the Congo. How do you think the shape of the land here creates challenges for farmers?

SKILLS MINI LESSON

Expressing Problems Clearly

To **introduce** the skill, point out that defining and expressing a problem clearly is the first step in understanding and solving the problem. As students consider the relentless poverty in the Congo, engage them in a discussion about why the country remains so poor, despite its wealth of natural resources. Students may **practice** defining the problem by writing a list of three obstacles to the Congo's economic health. The obstacles should be events or conditions that have occurred or existed only since the Congo became independent. To **apply** the skill, have students summarize the information contained in their lists in a concise statement. For example: Poor management of nationalized industries, a drop in earnings from copper, and a large amount of foreign debt led to the collapse of the Congo's economy.

CULTURE

Congolese Cuisine

The Congolese eat starchy foods such as corn, cassava, sorghum, and rice. Women and older children pound these foods into meal and then cook the meal with sweet potatoes, yams, or bananas.

ACTIVITY

Critical Thinking

Drawing Conclusions Write *Democratic System* and *Authoritarian System* on the chalkboard. Give students the following list of events and have them decide whether each event could or could not occur under each of the two types of government systems:

(1) the cancellation of elections

(2) open criticism of political leaders

(3) the impeachment of a high government official

(4) being arrested without a warrant.

Verbal/Linguistic

ACTIVITY

Interdisciplinary Connection

Conducting Electricity Copper is heavily used in electrical industries because it is an excellent conductor of electricity. Students can observe copper's conductivity by doing the following demonstration with a flashlight battery, a flashlight bulb, and a 6-inch segment of copper wire. Tell students to wrap the copper wire around the metal base of the bulb, and then to experiment with making contact between the bulb, the wire, and the two ends of the battery until the bulb lights.

Bodily/Kinesthetic

Answers to...

CRITICAL THINKING

Soil erosion could be a big problem for farmers.

SECTION 3 ASSESSMENT

AFTER YOU READ

1. (a) southern province of the Congo that has abundant copper deposits (b) the authoritarian leader who ruled the Congo (then Zaire) from 1965 to 1997
2. (a) a form of government in which a single leader or a small group of leaders have all the power (b) to put under the control of the national government
3. Copper, gold, and diamonds are some of the Congo's mineral resources. The Congo's economy relies heavily upon mining industries. A drop in copper prices in the 1970s was one of the factors that led to the collapse of the economy.
4. He nationalized industries and borrowed money from foreign countries. The changes were not successful; the industries were badly managed and the Congo could not pay back its loans.
5. War and political unrest use valuable people, time, money and resources that are, therefore, not spent in developing a country's resources and building on its strengths.
6. Possible answer: If a country's economy collapses, as the Congo's did, it affects the financial condition of all of the people in the country. Cuts in government spending on social services have negatively affected living conditions.
7. Possible title: "The History of the Congo." Students may describe the part that natural resources have played in the precolonial, colonial, and postcolonial histories of the Congo.

Answers to...

CRITICAL THINKING

Students' responses will vary, but most students will say that he did not have the well being of his country in mind because he seemed to want complete control for himself.

GOVERNMENT While Mobutu was successful in encouraging a sense of nationhood, he accumulated a large personal fortune through exploitation and corruption. **Critical Thinking** Considering the changes that Mobutu made when he took power, do you think he had the well being of his country in mind? Why?

Economic Collapse Leads to Conflict

When Zaire's economy collapsed, Mobutu cut government spending. This hit the poor people of Zaire especially hard. Unemployment rose and political groups began forming to challenge Mobutu's policies.

Throughout the 1980s, Mobutu continued to rule harshly, and Zaire's economy continued to decline. Calls for reform came from inside and outside Zaire. In the early 1990s, Mobutu's grip on the country weakened. He began to promise major changes, but failed to carry through on any of them. In 1996, a minor uprising began in a region of eastern Zaire. A small ethnic group, with the help and support of neighboring countries, grew into a rebel army. Within months, they took control of eastern Zaire and, in 1997, took over the capital city of Kinshasa. Mobutu was expelled from the country and later died in Morocco.

A New Government and Continued Conflict

The rebels renamed the country the Democratic Republic of the Congo and promised to establish a new constitution and hold national elections. However, rebel groups with differing ideas continued fighting until 1999. The United Nations tried to arrange a cease fire among the rebel groups, and urged the armies of neighboring countries who had joined the fighting to withdraw. A cease fire was called in July 1999, but outbreaks of fighting still occur.

SECTION 3 ASSESSMENT

AFTER YOU READ

RECALL

1. Identify: (a) Shaba, (b) Mobutu Sese Seko
2. Define: (a) authoritarian, (b) nationalize

COMPREHENSION

3. What are some of the Congo's mineral resources? What role have they played in the Congo's development as a nation?
4. What economic changes did Mobutu Sese Seko make when he took power? How successful were these changes?

CRITICAL THINKING AND WRITING

5. **Exploring the Main Idea** Review the Main Idea statement at the beginning of this section. Then, write a paragraph about the relationship that might exist between the Congo's political turmoil and the fact that the country has not fully developed its natural resources.
6. **Drawing Conclusions** Why do you think Congolese people's wages and living conditions have declined since independence?

ACTIVITY

7. **Writing a Description** Write a title and a short description for a book about the history of the Congo. Design a cover by deciding what images best represent the Congo's history.

Resource Directory

Teaching Resources

Section Quiz in the Unit 5 Teaching Resources, p. 76

SECTION 4

South Africa

The End of Apartheid

BEFORE YOU READ

READING FOCUS

1. How did apartheid develop into the law of the land in the Republic of South Africa? How did the people of South Africa finally change the apartheid system?
2. How has life changed for the people of South Africa in the years since the end of apartheid?

KEY TERMS

apartheid
discriminate
homeland

KEY PEOPLE AND PLACES

Cape Town
F.W. de Klerk
Nelson Mandela

NOTE TAKING

Copy this chart. As you read the section, complete the chart with information about some of the effects of apartheid on black South Africans.

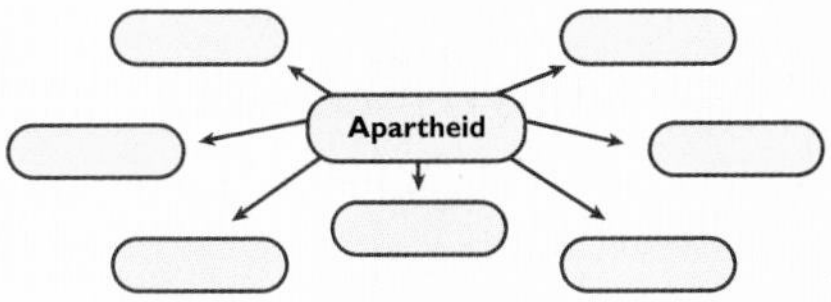

MAIN IDEA

The history of the Republic of South Africa is marked by racial division and social inequality, which only recently ended when black South Africans gained full citizenship rights and majority control of the government.

Setting the Scene

The Republic of South Africa lies at the southern tip of Africa and is larger than the states of Texas and California combined. Like the United States, South Africa has seacoasts on two oceans—the Atlantic Ocean and the Indian Ocean. South Africa is one of the wealthiest African countries. Yet, until recently, white people controlled almost all its riches because society was divided by law along racial and ethnic lines. How did such a system come to be?

Rule by Few

The ancestors of most black South Africans arrived some 1,500 years ago during the Bantu migrations. White Europeans first arrived about 400 years ago when Dutch settlers set up a colony at Cape Town. In time, they thought of themselves as Africans. They called themselves Afrikaners (af rih KAHN erz) and spoke their own language, Afrikaans. British, French, and German settlers arrived later and, by the late 1800s, these white settlers had forced black South Africans off of the best farmlands.

Divided Society

GOVERNMENT

Under apartheid, blacks and whites were even forced to sit separately at sports events. **Critical Thinking** Does any historical situation in the United States parallel South African apartheid?

Resource Directory

Teaching Resources

Classroom Manager in the Unit 5 Teaching Resources, p. 77

Guided Reading and Review in the Unit 5 Teaching Resources, p. 78

Guide to the Essentials, p. 102

Technology

Section Reading Support Transparencies

SECTION 4

Lesson Objectives

1. Describe the policies and legacy of apartheid.
2. Identify the challenges that face post-apartheid South Africa.

Lesson Plan

1 Engage

Warm-Up Activity

Ask students how they would react to a new school policy that says all right-handed people can occupy only the basement of the school and must always carry special passes. Ask students whether they think such a policy would be fair. What would they do to oppose it?

Activating Prior Knowledge

Begin a discussion by asking students if they have ever experienced being left out when they wanted to be included. Ask them to think about how they dealt with the experience of being unfairly left out and invite them to write about it in their journal.

2 Explore

Have students read the section. Ask them to consider questions such as the following: What was apartheid? During apartheid, why did black families and white families live so differently? What changes were made in South Africa after Nelson Mandela became president?

Answers to...

CRITICAL THINKING

Students may mention racial segregation in the United States.

Lesson Plan continued

3 Teach

Have students create a chart with three columns: *Life Under Apartheid, Life After Apartheid,* and *Reasons for Change.* Ask students to fill in the chart with facts from the section. Use the completed charts as the basis for a discussion of predictions about South Africa's future. This activity should take about 25 minutes.

Questions for Discussion

CITIZENSHIP Why was it difficult for black families in South Africa to improve their lives?

Apartheid kept blacks in low-paying jobs and poor schools, and forced them to live in areas that were not fertile. It was difficult for them to improve their situation, especially because they did not have the right to vote.

CULTURE Although apartheid has ended, how are people still divided by race in South Africa?

White people have already been well educated and still have a good deal of economic power. Most black people have not been well educated and do not yet have the skills they need to rise out of poverty.

4 Assess/Reteach

See the answers to the Section 4 Assessment. You may also use students' completed charts as an assessment.

Acceptable charts include three factual entries in each column.

Commendable charts include at least four factual entries in each column.

Outstanding charts include at least four factual entries in each column, some of which are opinions supported by facts from the section.

Answers to...

MAP AND CHART STUDY

Blacks form the majority of South Africa's population. The homelands were created to keep blacks and whites separate.

COUNTRY PROFILE

South Africa

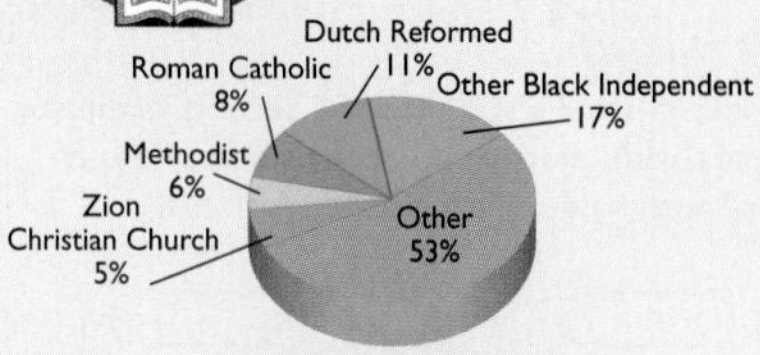

Religious Persuasion

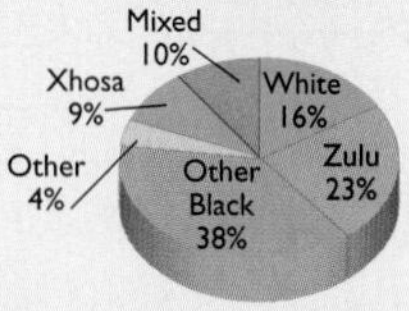

Ethnic Makeup

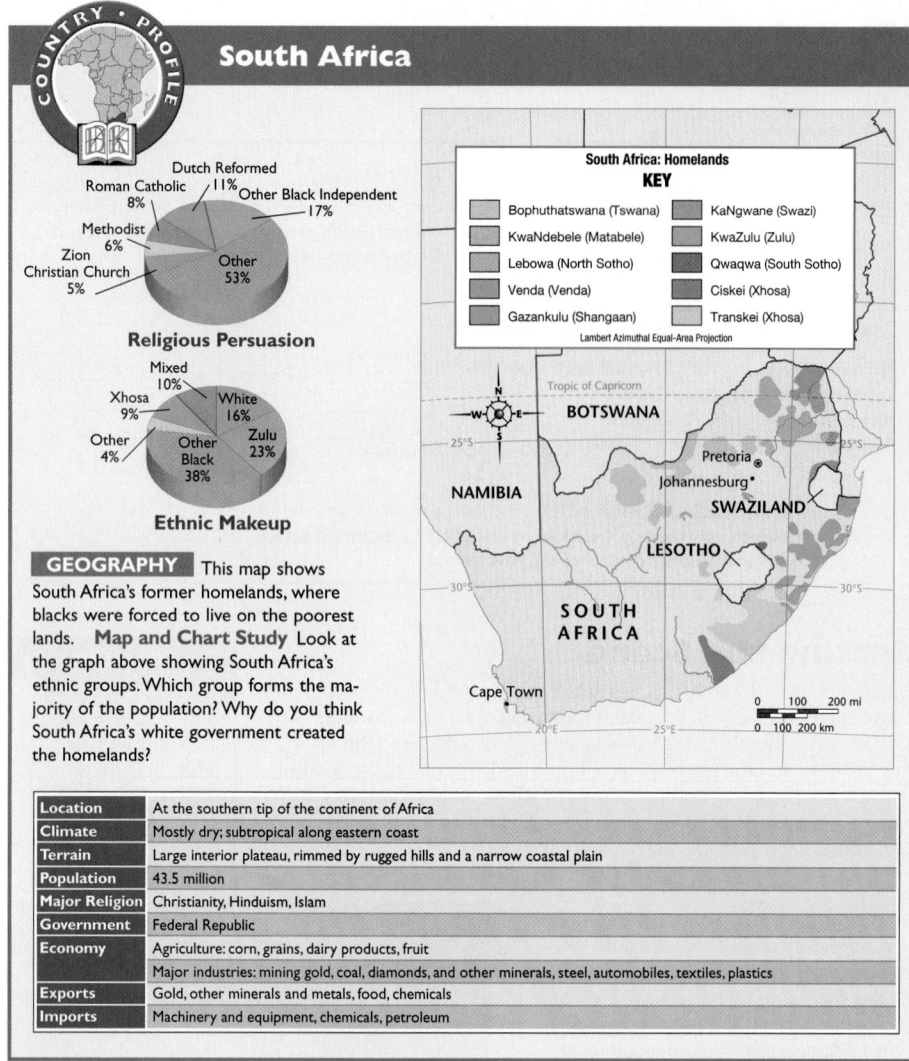

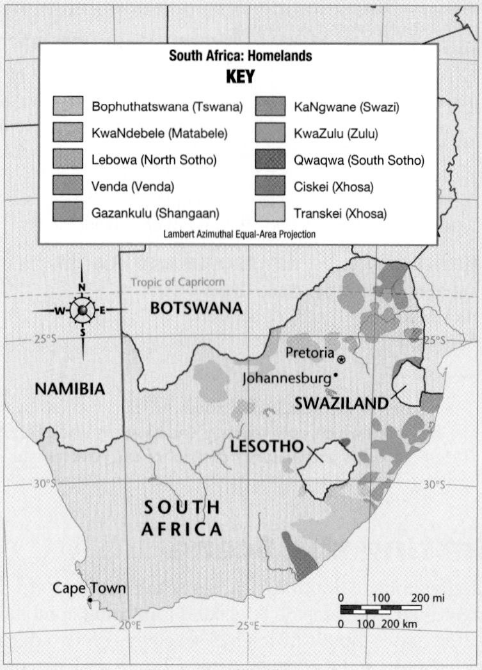

GEOGRAPHY This map shows South Africa's former homelands, where blacks were forced to live on the poorest lands. **Map and Chart Study** Look at the graph above showing South Africa's ethnic groups. Which group forms the majority of the population? Why do you think South Africa's white government created the homelands?

Location	At the southern tip of the continent of Africa
Climate	Mostly dry; subtropical along eastern coast
Terrain	Large interior plateau, rimmed by rugged hills and a narrow coastal plain
Population	43.5 million
Major Religion	Christianity, Hinduism, Islam
Government	Federal Republic
Economy	Agriculture: corn, grains, dairy products, fruit
	Major industries: mining gold, coal, diamonds, and other minerals, steel, automobiles, textiles, plastics
Exports	Gold, other minerals and metals, food, chemicals
Imports	Machinery and equipment, chemicals, petroleum

The British and Afrikaners eventually fought each other for control of South Africa. To get away from the British, the Afrikaners founded their own states, Transvaal (tranz VAHL) and Orange Free State. Soon, however, diamonds and gold were discovered in the Transvaal. British prospectors pushed Afrikaners off their farms. The British and the Afrikaners fought for three years over the territory. Britain finally won, and declared South Africa an independent country in 1910.

432 UNIT 5 AFRICA

Resource Directory

Teaching Resources

Outline Maps, East and Southern Africa, p. 35

Technology

Passport to the World CD-ROM This interactive CD-ROM allows students to explore each region of the world. Students view regional videos, take a photo tour, and explore a historical timeline. Students record their travels in an Explorer's Journal and receive passport stamps when they pass regional quizzes.

Color Transparencies 93 Africa South of the Sahara: Physical Political Map; **99** East and Southern Africa: Political Map

Minority White Rule in South Africa The government of the new country passed laws to keep land and wealth under control of the white population. Blacks could not own land. They could work in white areas, but the best jobs and the highest pay were reserved for whites.

In 1948, the Afrikaners political party, the National Party, was elected to run the country. New laws were added to the system of white power. The system was called **apartheid** (uh PAHR tayt), Afrikaans for "separateness." Apartheid laws placed every South African into one of four categories based on race and made it legal to discriminate in this way.

To **discriminate** means to treat people differently, and often unfairly, based on race, religion, or sex. The four racial categories were black, white, colored, and Asian.

Coloreds, or people of mixed race, and Asians, usually people from India, had a few rights but blacks were denied citizenship rights, including the right to vote. The system kept them in low-paying jobs, poor schools, and kept them out of white restaurants and hospitals. In addition they were forced to move to 10 poor rural areas called **homelands.** These homelands had the driest and least fertile land.

A Country Unites Against Apartheid

Many South Africans, black and white, fought apartheid through peaceful and organized protests. The well-armed South African government responded with deadly force, resulting in many deaths and jailings. But the demonstrations kept growing.

Countries around the world joined the movement against apartheid. Many nations stopped trading with South Africa. Its athletes were banned from the Olympic games and other international sporting events.

In 1990, faced with a weakening economy and continuing protests, South Africa's president, **F. W. de Klerk,** helped pass laws to end apartheid. South Africans of all colors peacefully elected a president, for the first time, in April of 1994 when they chose **Nelson Mandela,** a black leader who had spent many years in prison for fighting apartheid.

First Multiracial Elections, 1994

CITIZENSHIP Women in Johannesburg joyously displayed the identification papers that allowed them to vote in the historic election on April 26, 1994. Blacks had to wait in line for as long as eight hours to cast ballots for the first time in their lives. **Critical Thinking** How do you think black people felt voting for the first time in this historic election? Is this different from or similar to the way people think about voting in the United States?

SKILLS MINI LESSON

Organizing Information

To **introduce** the skill, explain that it is often helpful to organize information in a graphic such as a chart, table, or time line. Organizing information in one of these ways is useful when studying for a test or writing a report. Have students **practice** the skill by asking them to extract and paraphrase separately the histories of black Africans, the Dutch (Afrikaners), and the British. Then, have students **apply** the skill by making a timeline for each of the three groups, using the same scale, beginning in the year A.D. 500 (the period of the Bantu migration) and ending in 1994. Students should then compare their three timelines. Ask them to identify how political power has shifted over time among the three.

ACTIVITY

Journal Writing

In Protest Music and poetry were two ways in which black South Africans expressed their opposition to apartheid. Invite students to record their own ideas about the unfairness of apartheid or of a similar aspect of American society in the form of a protest song or poem. Remind students that their journals are private and will not be graded or judged by others.

Verbal/Linguistic

CULTURE

Nadine Gordimer (born 1923)

Though novelist and short-story writer Nadine Gordimer is a member of the South African white minority, she has always been adamantly against the policy of apartheid. From an early age, she supported outlawed black political groups that sought the end of apartheid and enforced racism. Gordimer voiced opposition to her country's racial policies in her novels and stories, and the South African government responded by banning her books. Elsewhere, however, Gordimer's writing has been crucial in drawing international attention to the destructive effects of apartheid on the lives of all South Africans. In 1991, Gordimer was awarded the Nobel Prize for Literature; during that same year, as South Africa took its first tentative steps toward ending apartheid, the government lifted its ban on Gordimer's books.

Answers to...

CRITICAL THINKING

Students should recognize the sense of victory and happiness that black people in South Africa would have felt having finally won the right to vote. Students might contrast this with voting in the United States, which many people now take for granted.

SECTION 4 ASSESSMENT

AFTER YOU READ

1. (a) city on the southern tip of Africa where Dutch settlers established a colony in 1652 (b) president of South Africa who helped bring about the end of apartheid (c) South Africa's first black president, who spent many years in prison for fighting apartheid
2. (a) the legal policy of racial separation (b) to treat people differently based upon their race, religion, or sex (c) a poor, rural area where black South Africans were forced to live
3. The system kept blacks and coloreds in low-paying jobs and inferior schools. Whites had control of the government and the economy. National and international pressure on the government finally ended apartheid.
4. Legal racial discrimination has ended.
5. Answers will vary. Paragraphs should include recognition of the great limitations placed on the lives of black South Africans, and should convey hopefulness about the opportunities an end to apartheid would bring.
6. Possible answer: The government must find ways of reassuring whites that the new system can work, while making sure that blacks have an equal chance for a good life.
7. Remind students that they should support their positions with facts, examples, and details.

Answers to...

AS YOU READ

Students may mention that South Africans might learn more about the challenge facing them now, as well as realizing that progress will be slow, but possible.

AS YOU READ

Draw Inferences What do you think South Africans could learn from people who remember integration efforts in the United States?

Building a New Nation

Despite the end of apartheid under Mandela's government and new opportunities for millions of blacks, South Africa remained a divided society. The white population still held a lot of power and many did not like the changes in South Africa. Mandela's government had to find ways to reassure whites while making certain that blacks had an equal chance for a good life.

To help heal South Africa, Nelson Mandela's government set up a Truth and Reconciliation Commission which was to examine the crimes of the apartheid era. In 1998, the commission issued its final report. It condemned human rights abuses by both white and black South Africans. It also granted amnesty, or forgiveness, to some people who had committed crimes.

In June 1999, South Africa held its second election open to all races. Mandela's party stayed in power, but Nelson Mandela ended his political career. Thanks to his leadership, South Africans are working together to build a peaceful and prosperous nation.

SECTION 4 ASSESSMENT

AFTER YOU READ

RECALL

1. Identify: (a) Cape Town, (b) F.W. de Klerk, (c) Nelson Mandela
2. Define: (a) apartheid, (b) discriminate, (c) homeland

COMPREHENSION

3. How did apartheid affect South Africans? How did the system of apartheid ultimately end?
4. What changes have taken place in South Africa since the collapse of apartheid?

CRITICAL THINKING AND WRITING

5. **Exploring the Main Idea** Review the Main Idea statement at the beginning of this section. Then, write a paragraph from the point of view of a black South African fighting apartheid laws. Explain how discrimination affects that person and what equality will mean for them.
6. **Expressing Problems Clearly** What challenges must the South African government meet in order to build a new nation based on equality for all?

ACTIVITY

Take It to the NET

7. **Understanding Apartheid** Gather information on apartheid from the web site, and then write a position paper in which you discuss your views and thoughts about the subject. Visit the World Explorer: People, Places, and Cultures section of **phschool.com** for help in completing this activity.

Resource Directory

Teaching Resources

Section Quiz in the Unit 5 Teaching Resources, p. 79

Chapter Summary in the Unit 5 Teaching Resources, p. 80

Vocabulary in the Unit 5 Teaching Resources, p. 81

Reteaching in the Unit 5 Teaching Resources, p. 82

Enrichment in the Unit 5 Teaching Resources, p. 83

Critical Thinking in the Unit 5 Teaching Resources, p. 84

Drawing Conclusions

Clues from your reading
+
What you already know
↓
Conclusion

Learn the Skill

You probably draw conclusions several times a day in your daily activities. Drawing conclusions is a skill that will help you get the most out of what you read. Drawing conclusions means making sensible decisions or forming reasonable opinions after thinking about the facts and details in what you are reading. To draw conclusions, follow these steps:

A. When you read look for clues, or evidence, that can lead to more understanding. For example, you might see a picture of Somali women wearing hajeebs—long, plain gowns with veils that completely cover their hair and neck. This clothing can serve as a clue to Somali culture.

B. Use what you already know. From reading about life in Egypt in an earlier chapter, for example, you might already know that Muslim women wear this type of clothing.

C. Add the clues that you found and what you already know, and then draw a conclusion. When you add the appearance of the Somali women to your knowledge of the way Muslim women dress, you can conclude that the Somali women are Muslims.

D. Stop to evaluate the decision you made. Ask yourself if the conclusion make sense. Is it the only reasonable alternative? Is it based on inaccurate facts or false assumptions? If you think the conclusion is faulty, try again to draw a conclusion that makes sense.

Practice the Skill

Read each of the following short pieces of information. Use clues from them and what you already know to write at least one conclusion. Then evaluate your conclusion by giving reasons why it makes sense. The first one is done for you.

1. Lake Victoria in East Africa is named after Queen Victoria of England.
Conclusion: This area was previously colonized by the British.
Evaluation: It makes sense, because East Africans or colonizers from another country would not have named their lake after Queen Victoria of England.

2. As a tourist, you find both Muslim mosques and Christian churches in Addis Ababa, the capital of Ethiopia.

3. Swahili is a language that contains a mix of African and Arab words. Swahili has become the language of East African trade.

Apply the Skill

See the Chapter Review and Assessment at the end of this chapter for more questions on drawing conclusions.

Lesson Objectives

1. Explain the steps used to draw conclusions.
2. Draw conclusions in context.

Lesson Plan

1 Engage

Have students give examples of drawing conclusions in their everyday lives. If students need help, pose different scenarios from daily life and guide them to recognize the conclusions they draw from these events.

2 Explore

Direct students to read the steps under "Learn the Skill" and to study the graphic organizer. Point out that not all conclusions drawn are accurate. Tell students that they may have to revise their conclusions as they read more information about a topic.

3 Teach

Group students to answer the practice questions.

For additional reinforcement, have students draw two appropriate conclusions about a familiar celebrity or political leader. Each conclusion should be outlined in equation format, modeled after the illustration in the text.

4 Assess/Reteach

To assess, create a drawing-conclusions equation diagram on the chalkboard. Evaluate students' contributions by noting how they identify clues, relate existing knowledge to the clues, and combine knowledge and clues to draw conclusions.

To further assess students' understanding of drawing conclusions, have them complete the "Applying Your Skills" part of the Chapter Review and Assessment at the end of the chapter.

Resource Directory

Teaching Resources

Social Studies and Geography Skills, Drawing Conclusions, p. 50

Technology

Social Studies Skills Tutor CD-ROM

Answers to...

PRACTICE THE SKILL

Students may conclude: 2) Both Muslims and Christians live in Ethiopia; 3) East Africans speak both African and Arab languages. Since Swahili contains words from both languages, it is a good choice as a common, uniting language.

CHAPTER 23

Review and Assessment

Creating a Chapter Summary

Student summaries will vary.

Sample summary:

Section 2 In Kenya, taking care of one's family and maintaining the family land are valued highly. Individuals and communities share in the spirit of harambee, or pulling together to achieve a goal.

Section 3 The Democratic Republic of Congo is a country very rich in mineral resources such as diamonds, copper, and gold. Ongoing civil war and instability in the government affect the quality of life.

Section 4 South Africa has developed into one of Africa's wealthiest countries because of its abundant natural resources. However, only in the last ten years has the nation begun to correct the wrongs of racial discrimination during years of apartheid.

Reviewing Key Terms

1. e **2.** f **3.** b **4.** a **5.** g **6.** d **7.** c

Reviewing the Main Ideas

1. Hutu, Tutsi, and Twa
2. The minority Tutsi took control of the land and resources from the majority Hutu through superior military power and ability to negotiate contracts. They kept the Hutu in a subordinate position and, when the Hutu rebelled, the Tutsi handled the uprisings in a brutal way.
3. Harambee was necessary for individual families to survive when the men had to leave the villages for the cities in search of work. This concept was demonstrated by the women who, on their own, cared for the land and the children. Over 40 different ethnic groups came together to achieve independence and to work under the leadership of the government facing the challenges of independence.
4. The Congo has reserves of precious metals and minerals including copper, gold, silver, uranium, coal, tin, petroleum, and diamonds.
5. The promise of mining these reserves first brought colonial settlers to the Congo and they sought to develop the resources for their own benefit. Foreign companies became involved in domestic policy in order to protect their financial interests.
6. European settlers created apartheid in order to gain and keep control of South Africa's land and wealth.
7. South Africans, blacks and many whites, fought apartheid for forty years. International pressure and leadership from people like Nelson Mandela and F.W. de Klerk finally brought apartheid to an end in the 1990s.

CHAPTER 23

Review and Assessment

Creating a Chapter Summary

On a separate piece of paper, draw a diagram like this one and include the information that summarizes the first section of the chapter. Then, fill in the remaining boxes with summaries of Sections 2, 3, and 4.

EAST, CENTRAL, AND SOUTH AFRICA

Section 1	Section 2	Section 3	Section 4
The Central African countries of Rwanda and Burundi have been devastated by the war between both countries' two major ethnic groups, the Hutu and the Tutsi. Hundreds of thousands of people have died in fighting.			

Reviewing Key Terms

Match the definitions in Column I with the key terms in Column II.

Column I

1. under government control
2. system of laws legalizing racial discrimination
3. Swahili word for "let's pull together"
4. person seeking safety outside their country
5. when a single leader or group has all the power
6. rural areas where black South Africans were forced to live
7. to treat people in a different way based on race, religion, or sex

Column II

a. refugee
b. harambee
c. discriminate
d. homelands
e. nationalize
f. apartheid
g. authoritarian

Reviewing the Main Ideas

1. Identify the three ethnic groups populating Rwanda and Burundi. (Section 1)
2. What is the source of conflict between the two largest ethnic groups in Rwanda and Burundi? (Section 1)
3. Why has the concept of harambee been important to individual Kenyans and to Kenya as a country? (Section 2)
4. What are Congo's greatest natural resources? (Section 3)
5. How has mining played a role in Congo's past and present? (Section 3)
6. What were the beginnings of the apartheid system in South Africa? (Section 4)
7. What people and events finally brought an end to the apartheid system? (Section 4)

Map Activity

Location

For each place listed below, write the letter from the map that shows its location.

1. Nairobi
2. Kenya
3. Cape Town
4. Johannesburg
5. Kinshasa
6. Democratic Republic of the Congo
7. South Africa

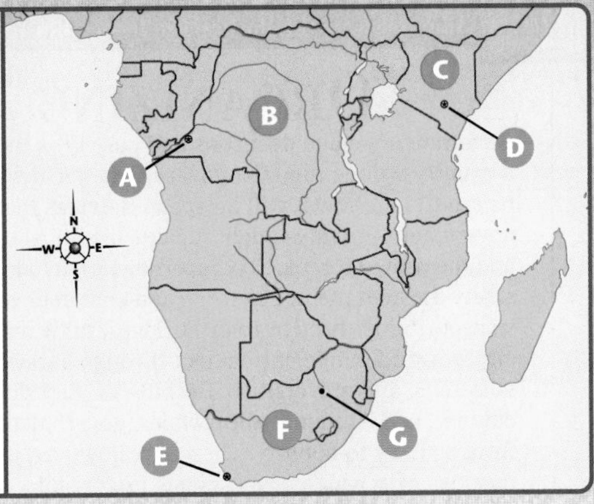

Take It to the NET

Enrichment For more map activities using geography skills, visit the social studies section of **phschool.com.**

Writing Activity

1. **Writing Interview Questions** Choose either South Africa or the Congo. Write a list of five interview questions you would ask someone who has been elected president of the country. Consider the challenges the new president faces. Then exchange questions with a partner. Pretend that you are the president. Write answers to your partner's questions.
2. **Writing a Journal Entry** The countries currently experiencing civil wars—the Congo, Rwanda, and Burundi—share similar histories and consequences of war. Write a journal entry that explores some of these similarities.

Critical Thinking

1. **Drawing Conclusions** South Africa's new government is trying to persuade skilled white workers to remain in the country. Based on what you know about apartheid, why do you think the country faces a shortage of skilled workers?
2. **Recognizing Cause and Effect** The people of Kenya believe in large, extended families working together. How did this attitude benefit the country in its struggle for independence and solving problems after independence?

Applying Your Skills

Turn to the Skills for Life activity on p. 435 to answer the following questions.

1. Explain why drawing conclusions is an important skill to use when reading.
2. Read the following excerpt from p. 433. What conclusion about the demonstrators can you draw from this information?

   Many South Africans, black and white, fought apartheid through peaceful and organized protests. The well-armed South African government responded with deadly force, resulting in many deaths and jailings. But the demonstrations kept growing.

Take It to the NET

Activity Compare and contrast city life in Kenya to city life in America, as well as rural life in both countries. Visit the World Explorer: People, Places, and Cultures section of **phschool.com** for help in completing this activity.

Chapter 23 Self-Test As a final review activity, take the Chapter 23 Self-Test and get instant feedback on your answers. To take the test, visit the Social Studies section of **phschool.com.**

Map Activity

1. D **2.** C **3.** E **4.** G **5.** A **6.** B **7.** F

Writing Activity

1. Students' lists of questions will vary, but should reflect an understanding of the current political and economic issues facing the Congo and South Africa.
2. Students' journal entries will vary but should outline some of the major similarities and show an understanding of why these similarities exist.

Critical Thinking

1. Only the white population was offered good educational opportunities and good jobs. The majority of South Africans will need training and education to become highly skilled workers.
2. The new president, Jomo Kenyatta promoted a campaign of harambee and this helped bring together over 40 different ethnic groups in the country to work for common goals. One of these involved education. The government pays for a portion of the cost but people in villages must work together to build and support schools.

Applying Your Skills

1. It is important to form opinions and make decisions about what you read.
2. Students should conclude that, although they faced death and prison, demonstrators felt strongly about protesting apartheid.

Resource Directory

Teaching Resources

Cooperative Learning Activity in the Unit 5 Teaching Resources, pp. 120–123

Chapter Tests Forms A and B in the Unit 5 Teaching Resources, pp. 154–159

Guide to the Essentials, Ch. 23 Test, p. 103

Unit Tests Forms A and B in the Unit 5 Teaching Resources, pp. 160–165

Other Print Resources

Chapter Tests with ExamView® Test Bank, Ch. 23

Technology

ExamView® Test Bank CD-ROM, Ch. 23

Resource Pro® CD-ROM

UNIT 5

Introduction

The introduction on the student page on the right provides key facts and general information about government and how it can be organized.

- Students should read the introduction first to gain a basic knowledge of the subject before reading on.
- Have students read all of the subentries, which provide further information on government and governing institutions. Have students also read the annotations that accompany and explain the photos and illustrations.
- When students have finished reading all of the information, discuss the connections between the information on these pages and what they have learned about Africa. Students may want to review Chapters 22 and 23.

ACTIVITY

Planning a Web Site

Have students work in small groups to plan a web site that will provide information on an African country's history, government, cultural traditions, economic resources, and challenges for the future. Groups should create a flow chart that will show the home page and links to other relevant topics. Invite students to share their site plans with the rest of the group in an oral presentation.

Visual/Spatial

Adapted from the Dorling Kindersley Illustrated Children's Encyclopedia

Organizing To Govern

Governments make decisions and pass laws that determine how a country will be run. The government decides how money will be raised and how it will be spent. Services that the government provides might include health, education, welfare, and the armed forces. The government may also see to public safety through the police force and civil defense; public transportation through roads, bridges, railways, and airports; and public enrichment through libraries, museums, and universities. Because of historical, cultural, and economic differences, governments vary from country to country. There are, however, three main ways in which governments are organized: republic, monarchy, and dictatorship. In a republic, the people limit the power of the head of state. They vote in an election to choose their government and chief executive. In a monarchy, the head of the royal family is the head of state, though a parliament may be elected to set policy and pass laws. In a dictatorship, a single ruler has unlimited power, and the people do not have any say in the affairs of state.

MONARCHY

In a monarchy, a king or queen rules the country. For centuries, the monarchs of Europe made laws and collected taxes. Today only a few monarchs, such as the king of Swaziland, have political power.

? How have conflicts between different forms of government influenced world history?

PLATO

More than 2,000 years ago, the Greek philosopher Plato wrote the first book about governments and how they rule people—what today we call politics. His book, The Republic, *set out ideas for how to organize a democracy, which means "government by the people."*

PRESIDENCY

In a republic, the people vote to choose the head of state. In South Africa, for example, the president holds real political power and is responsible for the administration of the country and for its foreign policy. To the left, Thabo Mvuyelwa Mbeki is sworn in as president of the Republic of South Africa in 1998.

GOVERNMENT

African Independence

The nations of Africa share a legacy of struggle, first to gain independence from European colonial rule, and then to establish democratic governments. In many of the developing nations of Africa civil and ethnic strife, corrupt leaders, famine, disease, extreme poverty, and natural disasters have conspired against the best efforts of those who would champion freedom and social reform. Economic aid and support from the nations of the west can help to ease suffering, mediate disputes, and strengthen emerging democracies as African leaders strive to create a united Africa.

In the United States, the seat of government is Washington, D.C. In the Capitol Building, members of Congress (made up of the Senate and the House of Representatives) meet to discuss policies and pass laws.

SEATS OF POWER

Every government has a meeting place that is the seat of power. In the seat of power, federal laws are passed to provide a structure for the entire country. State or provincial governments and local governments carry out the federal laws and set policies according to federal guidelines outlined in the constitution.

INDEPENDENCE

The coming of independence to much of Africa after 1956 did not always bring peace or prosperity to the new nations. Many were weakened by famines and droughts or torn apart by civil wars. Few have managed to maintain civilian governments without periods of military dictatorships.

BENIN
The west African Kingdom of Benin reached the height of its power between the 14th and 17th centuries. Above is a Benin bronze mask.

NELSON MANDELA
In 1994, Nelson Mandela, a leader of the ANC, became the president of South Africa.

APARTHEID

In 1948, the National Party came to power in South Africa. Years of segregation, known as apartheid, followed. The policy gave white people power but denied black people many rights, including the vote. In 1990 the African National Congress (ANC), a banned black nationalist movement led by Nelson Mandela, was legalized, and the apartheid laws began to be dismantled. In 1994, the first-ever free elections were held.

ACTIVITY

Creating a Timeline

Have students work with partners to create timelines that show colonial rule, independence, and other events in Africa's history that lead to the current governing bodies of the various nations of Africa. Each pair of students should choose a different country to explore. Have them use library and Internet resources to find information that focuses on both the history of government in their chosen country, and how the current government was established.

Verbal/Linguistic

GOVERNMENT

Nelson Mandela

Since stepping down as president of South Africa, Nelson Mandela has not stopped working towards unity and freedom in the countries of Africa. His efforts to negotiate a peace settlement between the ancient rival tribes of Burundi have led to a compromise that may finally bring civil strife and unrest in that region to an end. Hutu and Tutsi leaders have agreed to serve jointly in a transitional government that will share governing responsibilities.

UNIT 6

Introducing the Unit

This unit was developed around seven strands of essential knowledge and skills that relate to the study of people, places, and cultures of the contemporary world. These strands include **History, Geography, Economics, Government, Citizenship, Culture,** and **Science, Technology, and Society.** These seven strands, and the related Guiding Questions on the next pages, are intended as an organizational focus for the unit. All of the chapter content, activities, questions, and assessments relate to the seven strands, which act as an umbrella under which all of the material falls.

Using the Pictures

Use the photographs on the reduced student pages as a prompt for a discussion of what students know about history, geography, economics, government, citizenship, culture, and science and technology of Asia.

- You may want to begin a **K-W-L** chart on the chalkboard for Asia, with the headings What We **K**now About Asia, What We **W**ant to Know About Asia, and What We **L**earned About Asia.
- Have students fill in the first column with several things they agree they already know. Then, ask them to brainstorm what they would like to know about Asia to add to the second column.
- Students can fill in the third column as they work through the text.

eTeach

Be sure to check out this month's discussion with a Master Teacher. Go to **phschool.com**.

UNIT 6

Welcome to Asia

GEOGRAPHY

Climb the steep sides of Mount Fuji ...

SCIENCE, TECHNOLOGY, AND SOCIETY

Explore innovations in computer technology ...

HISTORY

Visit the ancient Taj Mahal ...

Resource Directory

Teaching Resources

Program Overview includes a guide to the Prentice Hall World Explorer program. You may wish to refer to the overview as you plan your instruction.

Pacing Charts for Unit 6 offer a variety of course configurations.

What do you want to learn?

GOVERNMENT

Witness a handshake for peace ...

ECONOMICS

Increase productivity at a Japanese seafood plant ...

CULTURE

Act out China's traditional myths and legends ...

CITIZENSHIP

Demonstrate for better wages in South Korea ...

A journal can be your personal record of discovery. As you learn about Asia, you can create journal entries about what you read, write, think, and create. For your first entry, think about the geography of Asia. What are some of Asia's most distinctive geographic features? Compare and contrast them to geographic features in the place where you live.

Resource Directory

Technology

Social Studies Skills Tutor CD-ROM provides two levels of interactive instruction and practice in 20 core social studies skills.

Resource Pro® CD-ROM allows you to create customized lesson plans and print all resources directly from the CD-ROM.

Using the Explorer's Journal

Have students begin their Explorer's Journal as the paragraph on the student book page suggests. If at all possible, encourage students to use a separate small notebook for their Explorer's Journal entries. They can add to this journal as they learn more about Asia.

Project Possibilities

The projects in this book are designed to provide students with hands-on involvement in the content area. Write the following project ideas on the chalkboard and have students preview them and discuss which they might want to do. You may assign projects as cooperative activities, whole-class projects, or individual projects.

Agricultural Center

Build an information center about agriculture in Asia. Draw a large map of the region and hang it on your classroom wall. Then, as you read about different kinds of farming, mark them on the appropriate region of your map. Design a small poster for each major type of agriculture. On the poster, write about the location of this type of agriculture, the land, climate, products, and how the farms work.

Independence Biography

Choose an Asian country that was once ruled by colonists from another country. Find a person who played a major role in this country's struggle for independence. Write a biography for this person and his or her part in the end of colonialism.

Travel Log

As you read this unit, keep a journal of experiences of a journey through Asia. Write an entry for each country you read about. Focus on a part of the country or culture that most interests you.

Introducing

Guiding Questions

The seven Guiding Questions that appear on the reduced student edition pages to the right should act as a guide for learning about Asia, and for encouraging students to relate what they learn to their own experience. The Guiding Questions that relate to the content of each chapter in the unit also appear on the Chapter Opener pages in the student edition.

- You may wish to add your own Guiding Questions to the list in order to tailor them to your particular course. Or, as a group activity, ask your class to develop its own Guiding Questions.

ACTIVITY

Using the Guiding Questions

Ask a volunteer to read aloud the Guiding Questions to the class.

- Have students write the seven headings on a separate piece of paper or in their Explorer's Journal. Have them think about what information they would like to learn about Asia and write a question that relates to each heading.
- Have students share their questions with the rest of the class, and discuss any similarities. Create a master list of questions grouped under the seven headings. As you read about Asia, try to answer the questions on the list.
- At the end of the unit, if any questions remain unanswered, have students research and find the answers to those questions.

Guiding Questions

What questions do I need to ask to understand Asia?

Asking questions is a good way to learn. Think about what information you would want to know if you were visiting a new place, and what questions you might ask to find out. The questions on these pages can help guide your study of Asia. You might want to try adding a few of your own!

GEOGRAPHY

Asia is a region of extremes, with some of the driest deserts, longest rivers, and highest mountains in the world. The giant continent has cities crowded with people, small villages where people struggle to adapt to their physical environment, busy shipping ports, and a region of volcanic islands. Bodies of water such as the Pacific Ocean and the Indus River shape the lives of people who live near their shores.

1 How has geography affected the way Asian societies have developed?

HISTORY

Some of the world's first great civilizations arose in Asia. Traders, explorers, and travelers passed through the region bringing new ideas that Asians borrowed and adapted. Architectural treasures, traditional art forms, and a diversity of languages reflect the region's rich history. This history continues to shape Asians' sense of identity today.

2 How have history and the achievements of historic figures influenced life in Asia today?

CULTURE

Many of the world's religions began in Asia. Today, religious beliefs and practices help to define the many cultures of this vast region. In Southwest Asia, religious law and civil law are often the same. In South Asia and East Asia, religious observances and celebrations play a major part in daily life.

3 How has religion affected the way Asian societies have developed?

GOVERNMENT

Asian governments in the past have included powerful dynasties and empires, as well as periods of foreign rule. Today the governments of Asia vary widely. They include the communist governments of China and North Korea, and the more democratic governments of Japan and South Korea. In the Southwest Asian country of Israel, democracy prevails, but old conflicts still threaten the stability of the region.

4 How do Asian governments compare with each other and with the government of the United States?

ECONOMICS

As they have for generations, many Asians raise crops both to support their families, and to sell or export for profit. Many Asian nations are industrialized, while others are becoming more so. The industries that support the people of Asia range from small-scale production of traditional crafts, to large-scale factory production of auto parts. World demand for oil has brought great wealth to some countries in Southwest Asia.

5 How do physical geography and natural resources affect the ways that Asians earn a living?

CITIZENSHIP

The nature of citizenship in the different regions of Asia is largely defined by the history of those regions. Some Asian countries have only recently gained independence from colonial rule. Their governments face great challenges in building a political process that is acceptable to all, and in which citizens can participate in the decision-making process.

6 How does participation in the political process differ in Asia and in the United States?

SCIENCE, TECHNOLOGY, AND SOCIETY

Asia has long been a region defined by excellence in scientific and technological innovation, and it maintains that distinction today. Israelis have devised irrigation methods to help develop important agricultural areas in desert land. Farmers in Saudi Arabia have used technology to adapt to a climate of hot summers and cold winters. Japan has become a world leader in computer technology.

7 How have geographic factors affected the development of science and technology in Asia?

Take It to the NET

For more information on Asia, visit the World Explorer: People, Places, and Cultures companion Web site at **phschool.com.**

ACTIVITY

Using Primary and Secondary Sources

Goals for the Future Ask students to think about their own goals for the future and how their goals are affected by job opportunities where they live. Discuss what a young person's work goal might be in some Asian countries, and how it may be different from that of a young person in the United States.

- Have students work in pairs, sharing jobs they might like to hold or careers they might like to pursue.
- Have each pair choose a country from Asia and research that country to try to find information on the job opportunities awaiting young people who live there.
- Encourage students to use primary and secondary resources in their research, including letters, interviews, biographies, and Internet sites.

Verbal/Linguistic

ACTIVITY ATLAS

Lesson Objectives

1. Describe the relative location and size of Asia.
2. Identify countries of Asia.
3. Identify key physical features of Asia.
4. Explain some effects of climate on land use.

Lesson Plan

1 Engage

Warm-Up Activity

Ask students to describe the role older family members or neighbors play in their lives. Have them list some lessons older people have taught them.

Activating Prior Knowledge

Ask students what they know about Asia. For example, which nations are part of Asia? Point out that Asia's cultures are much older than most of those in the United States. Discuss with students why learning about the lands and cultures of Asia is useful to a young nation such as the United States.

ACTIVITY ATLAS

Asia

Learning about Asia means being an explorer and a geographer. No explorer would start out without first checking some facts. Begin by exploring the maps of Asia on the following pages.

Relative Location

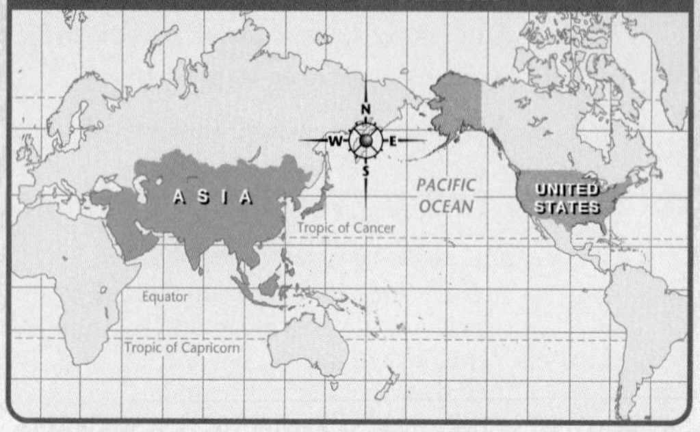

Relative Size

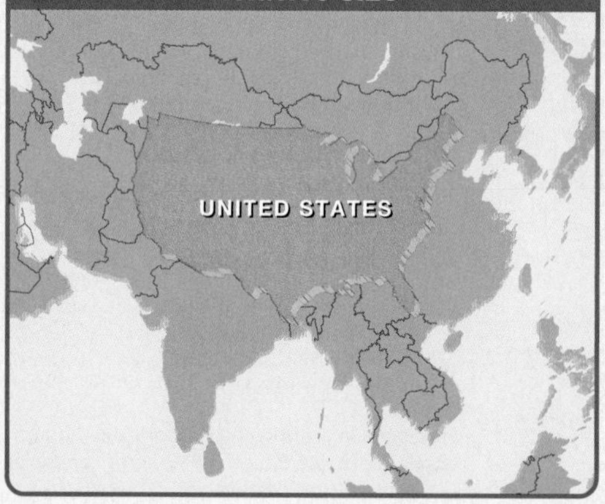

1. LOCATION

Locate Asia and the United States Look at the map at left. The land that is colored green is Asia. What ocean lies between Asia and the United States? If you lived on the west coast of the United States, in which direction would you travel to reach Asia?

2. REGIONS

Estimate Asia's Size The Relative Size map on the left shows the United States superimposed over the southern part of the Asian continent. How large is this part of Asia compared to the continental United States? Use a ruler to measure the greatest distance across this portion of Asia from east to west. Now make the same measurement for the United States. About how many times wider is this portion of Asia east to west than the United States?

Take It to the NET

Items marked with this logo are periodically updated on the Internet. To get current information about the geography of Asia, go to **phschool.com.**

Resource Directory

Teaching Resources

Activity Atlas in the Unit 6 Teaching Resources, pp. 99–106

Answers to...

LOCATION

1. The Pacific Ocean lies between Asia and the United States. You would travel west.

REGIONS

2. Asia is about two and one-half times as wide as the United States from east to west.

Asia: Political

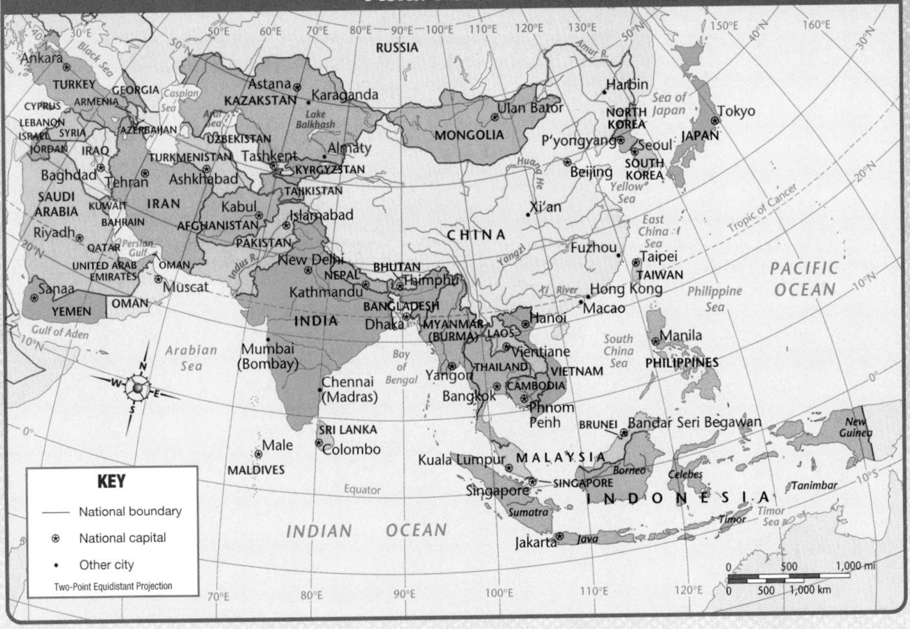

3. PLACE

Identify Countries in Asia Asia is the largest continent on the Earth. The map above shows countries in Asia. Which Asian country on the map do you think is the biggest? Asia also includes many countries that are located on islands. Find three island countries on the map. What are their names? Asia extends far to the west and east. One country in the western part of Asia is Saudi Arabia. Name three countries that are near Saudi Arabia.

The continent of Asia also includes part of the country of Russia. Russia is such a big country that it is a part of two continents—Europe and Asia. Notice the location of Russia on the map. Most of Russia lies in Asia. Most Russians, however, live in the European part of Russia. For this reason, geographers often include Russia in discussions of Europe, rather than in discussions of Asia.

2 Explore

Prompt students to read the Activity Atlas materials carefully. Have small groups of students ask and answer questions about the material. Any questions still unanswered should be posted in the classroom for discussion during and after the class's study of Asia.

3 Teach

Have students create a brochure profiling Asia. They can use a single piece of paper folded into thirds. Their profiles should contain vital statistics, a description of the region, and an illustration. This activity should take about 25 minutes.

4 Assess/Reteach

Brochures should locate Asia relative to the United States. They should note the region's huge size, enormous mountains, monsoon climate areas, and commercial and farming activities.

Resource Directory

Teaching Resources

Outline Maps Southwest Asia, pp. 28–29; South Asia, pp. 36–37; East Asia, pp. 39–40; Southeast Asia, p. 43

Technology

Color Transparencies 116 East Asia: Political Map; **123** Southeast Asia: Political Map; **125** South Asia: Political Map; **134** Southwest Asia and North Africa: Political Map

Answers to...

PLACE

3. China is the largest Asian country. Island countries include Indonesia, Malaysia, the Philippines, Sri Lanka, Taiwan, Japan, Singapore, and Brunei. Countries near Saudi Arabia include the United Arab Emirates, Oman, Yemen, Jordan, Iraq, Kuwait, Bahrain, and Qatar.

ACTIVITY ATLAS

Practice in the Themes of Geography

Ask students to use the maps in the Activity Atlas to answer the following questions about the five themes of geography.

Place Ask students in which countries the Gobi Desert is located. (China and Mongolia)

Regions Ask students which region of Asia, northern or southern, is most affected by monsoons. (southern)

Movement Ask students to identify Asian rivers that could be used to transport people and goods to an ocean. (Huang He, Indus, Chang Jiang, and Xi)

Human-Environment Interaction Have students describe how most of the land in Kazakstan is used. (for livestock raising)

Location Ask students to use the political map and identify the Asian country that lies directly on the Equator. (Indonesia)

ACTIVITY ATLAS

Asia: Physical

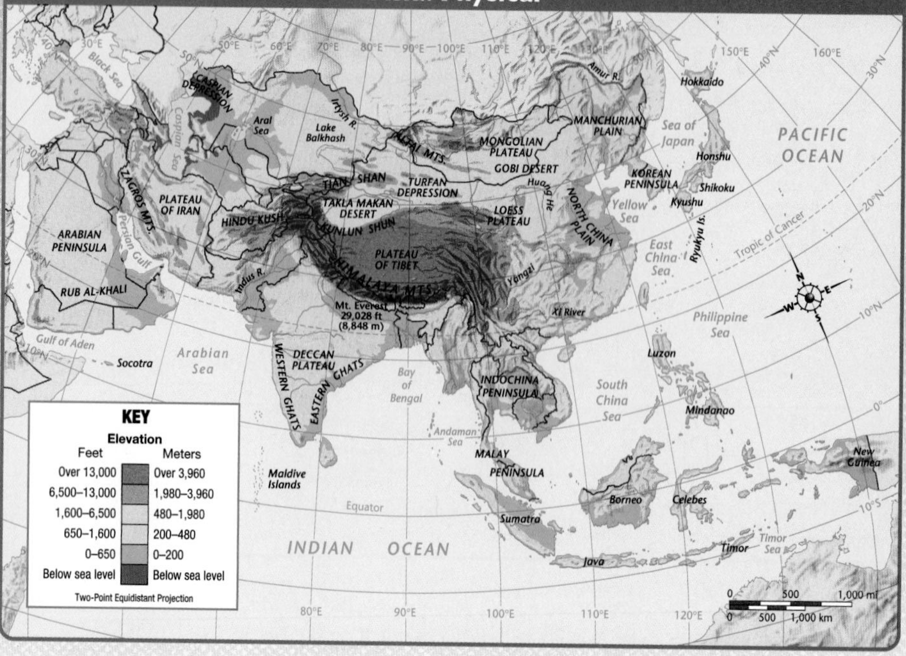

4. MOVEMENT

Analyze the Influence of Geography on the Economy The Himalaya Mountains are the highest mountains in the world. Asia has other high mountain ranges as well, and large, barren deserts. Find these physical features on the map. What effect do you think these barriers to transportation have on the economies of countries in Asia?

5. LOCATION

Identify Bodies of Water and Peninsulas in Asia Asia is surrounded by water on most sides. Use the map above to locate and name the bodies of water from the eastern side of Asia to the western side. Asia also has four major peninsulas. A peninsula is an area of land that is connected to a larger land and is surrounded by water on most sides. Asia's four major peninsulas are labeled on the map. What are their names?

Answers to...

MOVEMENT

4. The mountains and deserts are formidable barriers and will hinder the ability of countries to import or export goods. The barriers may hurt their economies.

LOCATION

5. Surrounding water: Sea of Japan, Yellow Sea, East China Sea, Philippine Sea, Timor Sea, South China Sea, Andaman Sea, Bay of Bengal, Arabian Sea, Persian Gulf, and Gulf of Aden. Peninsulas: the Korean, the Malay, the Indochina, and the Arabian.

Resource Directory

Teaching Resources

Outline Maps Southwest Asia, pp. 28–29; South Asia, pp. 36–37; East Asia, pp. 39–40; Southeast Asia, p. 43

Technology

Color Transparencies 115 East Asia: Physical-Political Map; **122** Southeast Asia: Physical-Political Map; **124** South Asia: Physical-Political Map; **133** Southwest Asia and North Africa: Physical-Political Map

6. HUMAN-ENVIRONMENT INTERACTION

Examine the Effect of Physical Processes Monsoons are great winds that blow across Southeast Asia and India every winter and summer. Winter monsoons blow dry air across the land and push clouds away from land toward the oceans. Summer monsoons blow clouds and moist air across the land, creating great rains. The map below shows the land use and monsoons in Asia. Read the following descriptions. Then use the map to answer the questions.

A. *This country is on a peninsula that juts out into the Indian Ocean. The Bay of Bengal borders its east coast. What's the name of this country? What is most of the land used for in this country?*

B. *This is a large country with a long eastern coast. Nomadic herding takes place in the western half of the country. Wet monsoons blow from the south, affecting the southeastern coast. What is the name of the country?*

C. *Find Southeast Asia on the map. Much of this area has a tropical wet climate. What kind of monsoon affects this area the most? What two types of farming take place in this region?*

Asia: Land Use and Monsoons

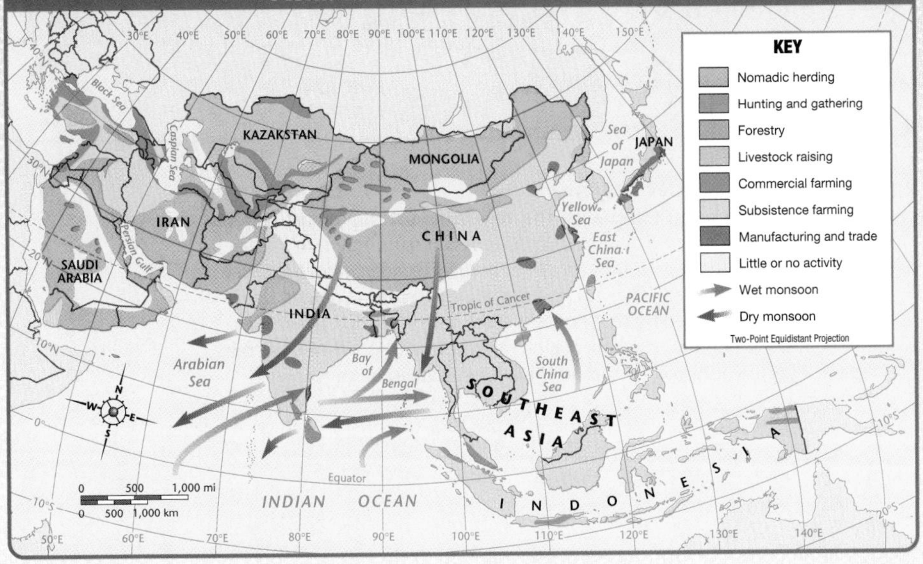

GEOGRAPHY

Rainfall in Asia

Precipitation varies dramatically in different parts of Asia, affecting agricultural activities, transportation, and the survival of people, plants, and animals. In Thailand, which is subject to monsoon rains, precipitation can vary from 35–120 inches (890–3,050 mm) each year. Yet in Hami, at the edge of the Gobi Desert in China, or in Riyadh, located in Saudi Arabia's Rub al-Khali Desert, only about 1 inch (25 mm) or less of rain may fall in a year.

Resource Directory

Teaching Resources

Social Studies and Geography Skills,
Reading a Wind Map, p. 36

Answers to...

HUMAN-ENVIRONMENT INTERACTION

6. A. The country is India, and most of its land is used for subsistence farming.

B. China

C. Southeast Asia is most affected by wet monsoons. Subsistence and commercial farming take place in the area.

ACTIVITY ATLAS

ACTIVITY

Interdisciplinary Connections

Science Ask students to use an atlas or almanac to identify some environmental challenges facing the nations of Asia. (flooding, water pollution and shortage, air pollution, desertification, habitat destruction, deforestation) Direct students to research and present a brief oral report on one of these problems, including its causes and some possible solutions.

Verbal/Linguistic

Answers to...

HUMAN-ENVIRONMENT INTERACTION

7. Vietnam, Cambodia, and the Philippines have lost all their rain forests. New Guinea has the largest remaining rain forest.

ACTIVITY ATLAS

Take It to the NET

Rainforests in Asia

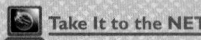

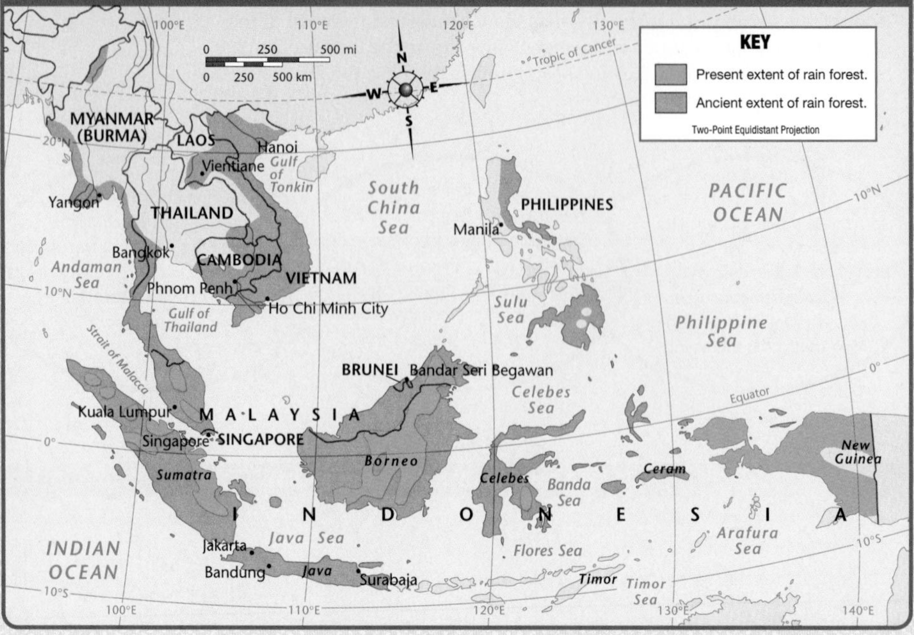

7. HUMAN-ENVIRONMENT INTERACTION

Examine the Impact of People on the Environment Southeast Asia has high rainfall and is located near the Equator. As a result, much of the region was once covered with rain forest. In recent decades, many of these forests have disappeared. They are cut down by farmers who need land. Other forests are cleared by timber companies seeking wood for sale to other countries. Look at the map. Which nations have lost all of their rain forests? Where would you go to find the largest remaining rain forest?

Asia's Biggest

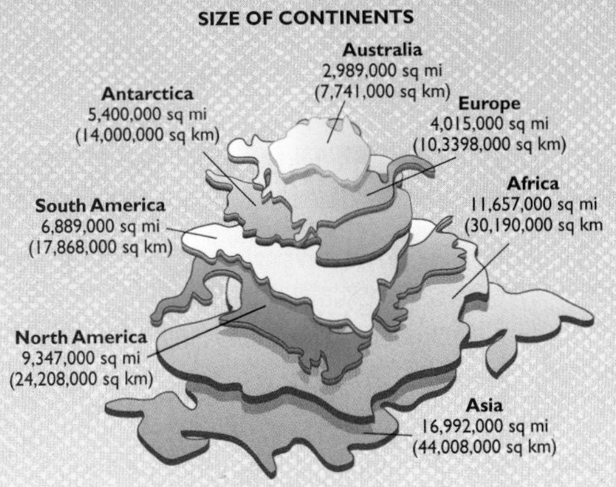

8. PLACE

Compare Physical Features Study these charts and diagrams. They compare features of Asia with those of the rest of the world. How many of the world's seven longest rivers are in Asia? What is Asia's longest river? What percentage of the world's population lives in Asia? How many of the world's five highest mountains are in Asia? Where is Mount Everest located? List the three largest continents from largest to smallest.

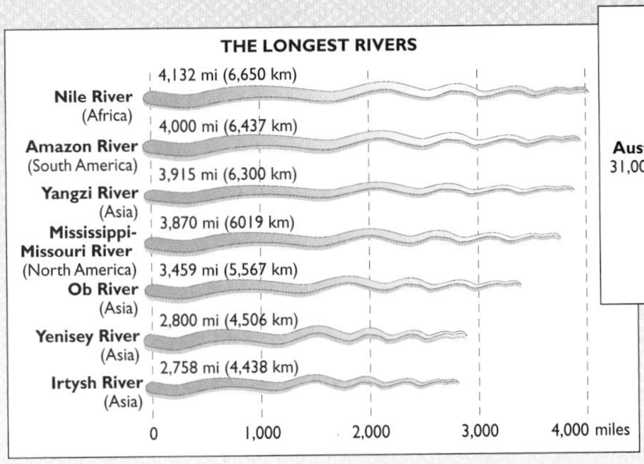

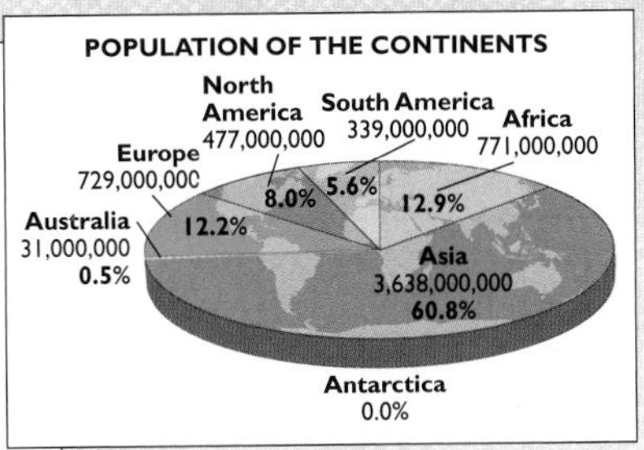

Take It to the NET

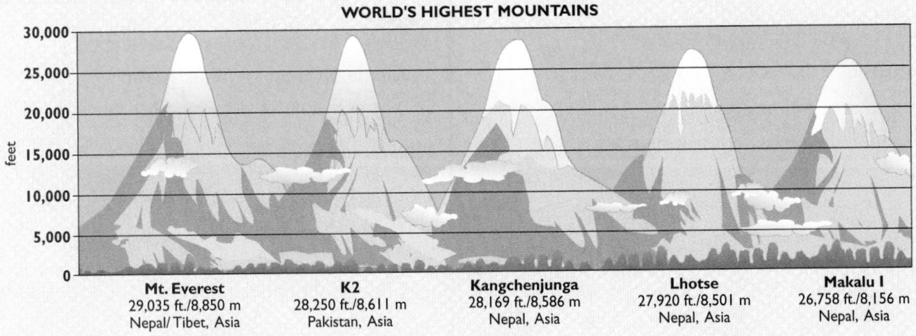

ACTIVITY

Discovery Learning

The Nations of Asia Use a wall map of Asia, clear, static-cling plastic sheeting affixed to a window, and permanent markers. Divide the nations of Asia among students, and have each student trace, color, and cut out his or her countries. Have students label each country with three key facts. Then, direct students to take turns adding their nations to the window map. Before adding their nations, students should hold up each cutout and read the key facts. Once the class identifies the countries, students should label the countries with their names and fit them in the correct location on the window map.

Visual/Spatial, Bodily/Kinesthetic

Resource Directory

Teaching Resources

Social Studies and Geography Skills, Reading a Bar Graph, p. 51; Reading a Circle Graph, p. 53

Answers to...

PLACE

8. Of the world's seven longest rivers, four are in Asia. The longest is the Yangzi River. About 61 percent of the world's population lives in Asia. All of the world's five highest mountains are in Asia. Mount Everest is located on the border of Nepal and Tibet in Asia. The three largest continents are Asia, Africa, and North America.

Chapter 24 Planning Guide

Resource Manager

	CORE INSTRUCTION	READING/SKILLS
Chapter-Level Resources	**Teaching Resources** Program Overview Pacing Charts **Technology** Resource Pro® CD-ROM Companion Web site, phschool.com • eTeach	**Technology** Social Studies Skills Tutor CD-ROM Student Edition on Audio CD, Ch. 24
1 Physical Features 1. Identify some physical processes that have shaped the landscape of Asia. 2. Explain why rivers are important natural resources in Asia. 3. Describe ways geographic factors affect population density in Asia.	**Teaching Resources** **Unit 6** Classroom Manager, p. 2 Guided Reading and Review, p. 4	**Teaching Resources** Guide to the Essentials, p. 104 Social Studies and Geography Skills, p. 31 **Technology** Section Reading Support Transparencies
2 Humans and the Physical Environment 1. Explain how the physical environment affects people's lives in Southwest Asia. 2. Explain how the physical environment affects people's lives in East Asia. 3. Explain how the physical environment affects people's lives in South and Southeast Asia.	**Teaching Resources** **Unit 6** Classroom Manager, p. 5 Guided Reading and Review, p. 6	**Teaching Resources** Guide to the Essentials, p. 105 Social Studies and Geography Skills, p. 35 **Technology** Section Reading Support Transparencies
3 Geographic Factors and Natural Resources 1. Explain how people in South and Southeast Asia use land and water resources to make a living. 2. Explain how people in East Asia use the Pacific Ocean as a resource for food. 3. Explain how oil wealth affects people and economic development in Southwest Asia.	**Teaching Resources** **Unit 6** Classroom Manager, p. 8 Guided Reading and Review, p. 9 Chapter Summary, p. 11 Vocabulary, p. 12 Reteaching, p. 13	**Teaching Resources** **Unit 6** Critical Thinking, p. 15 Guide to the Essentials, p. 106 Social Studies and Geography Skills, p. 32 **Technology** Section Reading Support Transparencies

ENRICHMENT / PRE-AP

Teaching Resources
Primary Sources and Literature Readings

Other Print Resources
DK Atlas

Technology
World Video Explorer: Journey Over Asia and the Pacific, Making a Living: Thailand, and Case Study: Living in a Dry Land
Companion Web site, phschool.com

Teaching Resources
Outline Maps, pp. 36–37, 39–40, and 43

Technology
Color Transparencies 115, 122, 126, and 133

Technology
Color Transparencies 177, 118, 127, and 128

Teaching Resources
Unit 6
Enrichment, p. 14
Cooperative Learning Activity, pp. 107–109

ASSESSMENT

Prentice Hall Assessment System

Core Assessment
Chapter Tests with ExamView® Test Bank, Ch. 24
ExamView® Test Bank CD-ROM, Ch. 24

Standardized Test Preparation
Diagnose and Prescribe
Diagnostic Tests for Middle Grades Social Studies Skills
Review and Reteach
Review Book for World Studies
Practice and Assess
Test-taking Strategies with Transparencies for Middle Grades Test Prep Book
Test-taking Strategies Posters

Teaching Resources
Unit 6
Section Quizzes, pp. 4, 7, and 10
Chapter Tests, pp. 134–139

Technology
Companion Web site, phschool.com Ch. 24 Self-Test
Ch. 24 Self-Test

World Video Explorer
Each region of the world is explored through regional flyovers and investigative field trips. Case study segments give students an in-depth view of the history, economy, government, and culture of a key place in each region. Case studies include Nigeria, Mexico, China, British Columbia, and the Czech Republic.

In Your Classroom

CUSTOMIZE FOR INDIVIDUAL NEEDS

Gifted and Talented

Teacher's Edition
- Exploring Asia, p. 453
- Creating Charts, p. 460

Teaching Resources
- Enrichment, p. 14
- Primary Sources and Literature Readings

Honors/Pre-AP

Teacher's Edition
- All Earth, p. 453
- Interpreting Data p. 456

Teaching Resources
- Critical Thinking, p. 15
- Primary Sources and Literature Readings

ESL

Teacher's Edition
- Exploring Asia, p. 453

Teaching Resources
- Guided Reading and Review, pp. 4, 6, and 9
- Vocabulary, p. 12
- Reteaching, p. 13
- Guide to the Essentials, pp. 104–106
- Social Studies and Geography Skills, pp. 31, 32, and 35

Technology
- Social Studies Skills Tutor CD-ROM
- Section Reading Support Transparencies

Less Proficient Readers

Teacher's Edition
- Exploring Asia, p. 453
- Creating Charts, p. 460

Teaching Resources
- Guided Reading and Review, pp. 4, 6, and 9
- Vocabulary, p. 12
- Reteaching, p. 13
- Guide to the Essentials, pp. 104–106
- Social Studies and Geography Skills, pp. 31, 32, and 35

Technology
- Social Studies Skills Tutor CD-ROM
- Section Reading Support Transparencies

Less Proficient Writers

Teacher's Edition
- All Earth, p. 453
- Interpreting Data, p. 456

Teaching Resources
- Guided Reading and Review, pp. 4, 6, and 9
- Vocabulary, p. 12
- Guide to the Essentials, pp. 104–106
- Social Studies and Geography Skills, pp. 31, 32, and 35

Technology
- Social Studies Skills Tutor CD-ROM
- Section Reading Support Transparencies

DORLING KINDERSLEY

At the end of each unit, you will find information adapted from Dorling Kindersley's *Illustrated Children's Encyclopedia* that connects to the region being studied and to one of the seven content strands. In addition, your resources include Dorling Kindersley's *Atlas*, which contains valuable information about countries from around the world.

TEACHER'S EDITION INDEX

CHAPTER 24 PACING SUGGESTIONS

For 90-minute Blocks

See suggestions in the Teaching Resources Pacing Charts for Chapter 24. Use Color Transparencies 115, 118, 122, 126–128, 133, and 177.

Running Out of Time?

See the Guide to the Essentials, pp. 104–106.

INTERDISCIPLINARY LINKS

Middle Grades Math: Tools for Success

Course 1, Lesson 11-4, **Theoretical Probability**

Course 2, Lesson 5-1, **Estimating with Fractions and Mixed Numbers**

Course 1, Lesson 1-2, **Make a Table;** Lesson 1-6, **Making Bar and Line Graphs; Math Toolbox, Other Methods of Displaying Data**

Course 2, Lesson 10-1, **Number Patterns;** Lesson 10-5, **Using Tables, Rules, and Graphs**

Science Explorer

Environmental Science, Lesson 3-1, **Environmental Issues**

Inside Earth, Chapter 2, **Earthquakes;** Chapter 3, **Volcanoes**

Weather and Climate, Lesson 2-3, **Winds**

Environmental Science, Lesson 6-1, **Fossil Fuels**

Inside Earth, Chapter 4, **Minerals**

Prentice Hall Literature

Copper, Breaker's Bridge

Copper, A Crippled Boy

BIBLIOGRAPHY

For the Teacher

Knapp, Ronald G., ed. *Chinese Landscapes: The Village As Place.* University of Hawaii, 1992.

Macquitty, Miranda. *Desert.* Knopf, 1994.

DK Taylor, Tim, and Mick Aston. *Atlas of Archaeology.* Dorling Kindersley, 2001.

Wilkinson, Philip. *The Lands of the Bible.* Chelsea House, 1994.

For the Student

Easy

DK *Everest: Reaching the World's Highest Peak* (*Discoveries* series). Dorling Kindersley, 2001.

Lewin, Ted. *Sacred River.* Clarion, 1995.

Average

Kalman, Bobbie. *Vietnam: The Land.* Crabtree, 1996.

Challenging

DuBois, Jill. *Korea.* Cavendish, 1993.

Heinrichs, Ann. *Nepal.* Children's Press, 1996.

Literature Connection

Buck, Pearl. *The Big Wave.* John Day, 1947.

Huynh, Quang Nhuong. *The Land I Lost: Adventures of a Boy in Vietnam.* Harper, 1982.

Schlein, Miriam. *The Year of the Panda.* Crowell, 1990.

Take It to the NET

The World Explorer companion Web site, found on **phschool.com**, offers activities for exploring geographical, historical, and cultural resources on the Internet. It also provides on-line links for key content and all Section and Chapter Assessment activities.

The **Teacher site** also provides teachers with regional data and ideas for student research and activities.

Students can use the **Student site** to find chapter-by-chapter Internet resource links and to access Self-Tests.

CHAPTER 24

Connecting to the Guiding Questions

In this chapter, students will read about the physical geography of Asia. Content in this chapter corresponds to the following Guiding Questions outlined in the beginning of the unit.

- How has geography affected the way Asian societies have developed?
- How do physical geography and natural resources affect the ways that Asians earn a living?
- How have geographic factors affected the development of science and technology in Asia?

Using the Picture Activities

Students may be unaware that a large area of China is desert. Have them locate the Gobi desert on a physical map of China. Ask them to name other deserts with which they are familiar.

- Students should find a map of the Gobi Desert, trace the map onto another piece of paper, and draw a dotted line showing their intended route. Accept any reasonable answers to questions about how long the trip might take, and what factors might slow their travel.
- Students should base their journal entries on the information they find about the Gobi desert.

Heterogeneous Groups

The following activities are suitable for heterogeneous groups.

Journal Writing

Exploring Asia, p. 453

Geography

Interpreting Data, p. 456

eTeach

Be sure to check out this month's discussion with a Master Teacher. Go to **phschool.com**.

CHAPTER 24

ASIA: Physical Geography

Dry Land

Using Pictures

The Gobi is Asia's largest desert. Barren lands stretch for approximately 500,000 square miles across China and Mongolia. Very little rain falls here. The word "Gobi" is a Mongolian word meaning "place without water." Yet even with harsh weather and little water, people, plants, and animals manage to survive in this desert.

Charting a Trip across the Desert

Find and trace a map of the Gobi. Draw a dotted line on the map to chart the path of a trip you might take by truck through it. Use the map scale to determine how many miles you are planning to travel. To decide how many miles to travel each day, first answer these questions:

- How many miles an hour do you think your truck can travel across the desert sand?
- What might slow you down? How much time will you plan for emergencies and rest?

Keeping a Travel Journal

People who live in desert climates have devised ways of preserving water and staying cool during the day and warm at night. Research the Gobi's animals, plants, people, land, and weather. Then, use the information you find to write a journal about your desert travel. Describe what you think it feels like to spend nights and days in the desert. What discoveries, setbacks, or dangers might you encounter? Give details using all of your senses—sight, sound, smell, taste, and touch.

450 UNIT 6 ASIA

Resource Directory

Teaching Resources

Primary Sources and Literature Readings extend content with a selection related to the concepts in this chapter.

Other Print Resources

DK Atlas

Technology

Journey Over Asia and the Pacific, from the World Video Explorer, introduces students to the major landforms of Asia.

Making a Living: Thailand, from the World Video Explorer, enhances understanding of the ways in which Thailand's economy is tied to its geography and natural resources.

Case Study: Living in a Dry Land, from the World Video Explorer, enhances understanding of life in regions of the world with few water resources.

Student Edition on Audio CD, Ch. 24

SECTION 1

Physical Features

BEFORE YOU READ

READING FOCUS

1. How have physical processes shaped the landscape of Asia?
2. Why are rivers important natural resources in Asia?
3. How do geographic factors affect where people live in Asia?

KEY TERMS

subcontinent

KEY PLACES

Himalaya Mountains
Yangzi
Huang He
Ganges River
Indus River
Tigris River
Euphrates River

NOTE TAKING

Copy the chart below. As you read the section, fill in the chart with information about Asia's physical features and population distribution.

	Major Landforms or Vegetation Regions	Major Bodies of Water	Major Areas of Population
Indian Subcontinent			
Southeast Asia			
Southwest and Central Asia			

MAIN IDEA

Asia's natural resources include rivers that provide water and transportation, and fertile valleys where it is easiest for people to live and grow food.

Setting the Scene

Two hundred million years ago, the land now called the Indian **subcontinent,** in the region of South Asia, was attached to the east coast of Africa. A subcontinent is a large landmass that is a major part of a continent. Scientists believe that at one time, all of the Earth's continents were joined.

About 200 million years ago, the land shifted and cracked and the continents began to break apart. The Indian subcontinent split off from Africa and crept slowly toward Asia. The landmass moved so slowly that it took about four years to travel the length of an average pencil.

About 40 million years ago, the Indian subcontinent collided with Asia. Just as the front ends of cars crumple in a traffic accident, northern India and southern Asia crumpled where they met. This area is the huge **Himalayan Mountain** range, which contains the tallest peaks in the world.

The Himalaya Mountains

GEOGRAPHY A stream fed by melting snow zigzags down through the rugged Himalaya Mountains in the Lahaul Valley of northern India. **Critical Thinking** Using the map on page 452, name two rivers whose sources are in the Himalaya Mountains.

SECTION 1

Lesson Objectives

1. Identify some physical processes that have shaped the landscape of Asia.
2. Explain why rivers are important natural resources in Asia.
3. Describe ways geographic factors affect population density in Asia.

Lesson Plan

1 Engage

Warm-Up Activity

Have students discuss movies or stories in which geographic factors are an important part of the plot. You might prompt students by mentioning stories of pioneers crossing the plains and mountains of the American West. Discuss how people confront the challenges of their environment and how geographic features affect where people settle.

Activating Prior Knowledge

Invite students who have visited another part of your state to describe the physical features of the area.

Resource Directory

Teaching Resources

Classroom Manager in the Unit 6 Teaching Resources, p. 2

Guided Reading and Review in the Unit 6 Teaching Resources, p. 3

Guide to the Essentials, p. 104

Technology

Section Reading Support Transparencies

Answers to...

MAP STUDY

Two rivers are the Indus River and the Ganges River.

Lesson Plan continued

2 Explore

Have students think about the following questions as they read Section 1. What are some major physical features of Asia? In which of these places do large numbers of people live and why? In which of these places do few people live and why?

3 Teach

After they read the section, direct students to work in pairs as they combine information from the physical and population density maps of East Asia to create a single map. Have them first trace the physical map, copy its labels, and indicate areas of high population density by shading with a colored pencil. Then, have students choose two physical features and explain why they attract so many people. Suggest that students also mention two sparsely populated areas and explain what keeps people away. This activity should take about 35 minutes.

Questions for Discussion

GEOGRAPHY Where do most people in Southwest and Central Asia live, and why?

Because the region possesses some of the largest deserts in the world, most people live in the river valleys where they can farm and raise livestock.

GEOGRAPHY Why is the Shatt-al-Arab Channel in Iraq important to the country?

It provides Iraq with its only transportation outlet to the Persian Gulf.

East Asia: Physical

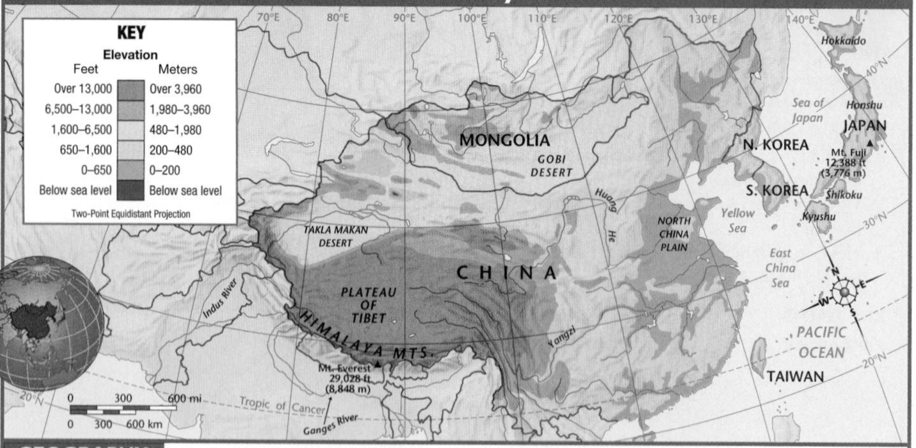

GEOGRAPHY Notice the variety of Asia's landforms. For example, the Himalaya Mountains, whose name means "Snowy Range," border the Plateau of Tibet. Much of this plateau is flat, but its elevation is high. Many rivers of East Asia and other regions of Asia begin in this area. **Map Study** How can you tell just by looking at the map that China's greatest rivers, the Huang He and the Yangzi, flow toward the east?

Powerful Physical Processes

Mountain ranges in China, northeast of India, also were formed by the collision of these two landmasses. This ancient mountain-building process continues today. Scientists estimate that Mount Everest is "growing" about 2 inches (5 cm) each year. Everest, the world's tallest mountain, rises 29,035 feet (8,850 m), or about five and a half miles high!

Farther east of China, natural forces also shaped the islands of Japan as earthquakes forced some parts of the earth to rise and others to sink. Erupting volcanoes piled up mountains of lava and ash, forming new mountains. Today, in many parts of Asia, earthquakes and volcanoes are still changing the landscape. Most of the islands here are mountainous because they are the peaks of underwater volcanoes.

Life Giving Rivers

Asia has many rivers which are natural resources providing not only water, but also means of transportation. One is China's **Yangzi** (yang ZEE), which flows 3,915 miles (6,300 km) to the East China Sea and is the only river in East Asia that is deep enough for cargo ships to sail on. More than 400 million people live along the banks of another river, the **Huang He** (hwahng hay), which runs through a fertile region called the North China Plain.

Resource Directory

Teaching Resources

Social Studies and Geography Skills, Reading a Population Distribution Map, p. 31

Outline Maps, South Asia, pp. 36–37; East Asia, pp. 39–40; Southeast Asia, p. 43

Technology

Color Transparencies 115 East Asia: Phsyical-Political Map; **122** Southeast Asia: Physical-Political Map; **126** South Asia: Physical-Political Map; **133** Southwest Asia and North Africa: Physical-Political Map

Answers to...

MAP STUDY

Rivers can only flow downhill, which in this case is eastward.

Mountain Beginnings The two most important rivers in the region of South Asia—the **Ganges** and the **Indus**—begin high in the Himalaya Mountains.

The Ganges River flows in a wide sweeping arc across northern India while the Indus flows westward from the Himalaya Mountains into the country of Pakistan.

Rivers carry from the mountains the water and minerals necessary for good farming. The plains around the rivers, therefore, are quite fertile and, as a result, heavily populated.

Rivers in the Dry World The regions of Southwest and Central Asia are nicknamed "the Dry World" because they contain some of the largest deserts on Earth. The Rub al-Khali is almost as big as the state of Texas. The Kara Kum covers 70 percent of Turkmenistan (turk men ih STAHN). While few plants grow in Southwest and Central Asian deserts, some of the most fertile soil in the world lies along the **Tigris, Euphrates** (yoo FRAYT eez), and Ural rivers. When these rivers flood, they deposit rich soil along their banks, soil that is good for growing crops. So, more people live in river valleys than anywhere else in the region.

Rivers are not only important as sources of water. They also provide means of transportation. The Tigris and Euphrates rivers, for example, both begin in Turkey and make their way south. They combine to form the Shatt-al-Arab Channel, in Iraq. This channel empties into the Persian Gulf, and gives Iraq its only outlet to the sea.

East Asia: Population Density

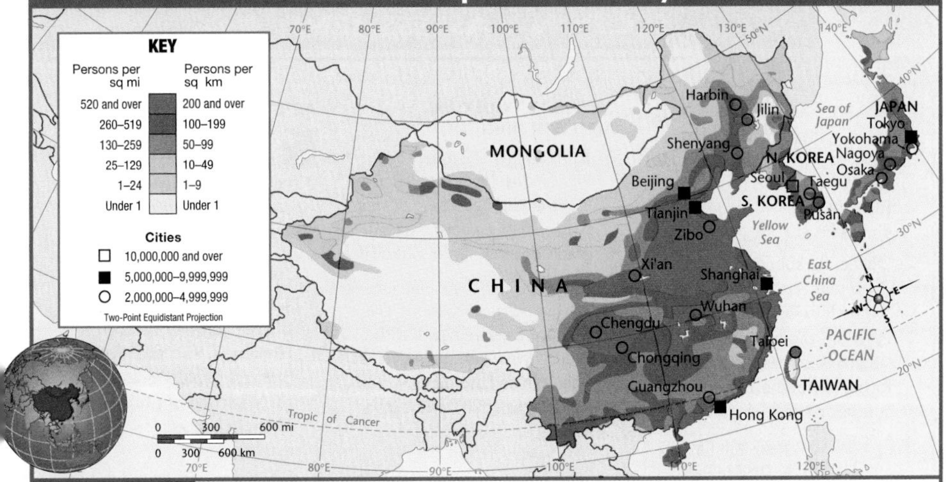

GEOGRAPHY As you can see, the largest number of China's people is found in the east central part of the country. **Map Study** Why do you think the population density is the way it is?

4 Assess/Reteach

See the answers to the Section 1 Assessment. You may also use students' maps and explanations for assessment.

Acceptable maps and explanations fulfill the minimum requirements listed.

Commendable maps display an understanding of how physical features support or inhibit economic activity.

Outstanding maps and explanations draw parallels with population densities in other parts of the world.

ACTIVITY

Journal Writing

Exploring Asia Invite students to choose an outstanding physical feature of Asia such as the Himalaya Mountains or the Huang He. Tell them to use what they have read in this section and their own research to write an entry about a visit to one of these features.

Verbal/Linguistic

GEOGRAPHY

All Earth

Pangaea (a Greek word meaning "all earth") is the name scientists proposed for the huge landmass composed of all the Earth's continents. Scientists think that the area that is now the United States once lay near the Equator. India was near the South Pole. Such locations affected climate. Geological evidence suggests that part of India was once covered by a glacier.

SKILLS MINI LESSON

Organizing Information

As a way to **introduce** the skill to students, explain that it is often useful to organize information in a graphic such as a chart or table. Organizing information in such a way is helpful when studying for a test or writing a report. Have students **practice** the skill by asking them to organize information about the landforms of Asia in a chart. Suggest that students use *East Asia*, *South Asia*, *Southwest* and *Southeast Asia* as column labels and *Mountains* and *Bodies of Water* as row labels. Have students **apply** the skill by instructing them to use their completed charts to write two or more sentences about the landforms of each region in Asia. Invite volunteers to read their sentences aloud.

Answers to...

MAP STUDY

The population density of the North China Plain is very high, probably because the land is good farmland.

SECTION I ASSESSMENT

AFTER YOU READ

1. (a) mountain range containing Mount Everest and forming a barrier between South Asia and the rest of the continent (b) only river in East Asia deep enough for cargo ships to sail on (c) runs through one of the most fertile regions of China and supports more than 400 million people living along its banks (d) important river in South Asia carrying from the mountains the minerals necessary for farming (e) flows westward through India from the Himalayas bringing minerals and water to farmland in the hottest and driest part of the Indian subcontinent (f) and (g) rivers that flow southward from Turkey, and flooding and depositing rich soil along their banks, and also providing a means of transportation
2. (a) large landmass that is a major part of a continent
3. The collision of northern India and southern Asia formed the Himalaya Mountains.
4. The Tigris and Euphrates are important sources of water for people and crops in a dry land. These rivers also provide a means of transportation: they combine to form the Shatt-al-Arab Channel, which empties into the Persian Gulf and gives Iraq an outlet to the sea.
5. Responses will vary, but paragraphs should include specific mention of a wide variety of Asia's physical features, such as mountains and rivers.
6. Responses will vary, but students should identify physical features discussed in the section and describe their appeal.
7. Encourage students to be descriptive in their journal accounts.

Answers to...

CRITICAL THINKING

The mountains prevent the population from spreading evenly across the land.

GEOGRAPHY

Seoul, seen here at dusk, is one of East Asia's most densely populated cities.
Critical Thinking Judging from this photograph, how do you think geographic factors affect population density in Seoul?

Geography and Population

As you can see on the map on the previous page, the population of East Asia is not spread evenly across the land because few people live in the deserts, highlands, and mountains. Yet, almost 1.5 billion people make their homes in China, North Korea, South Korea, and Japan. This means that people crowd into the lowland and coastal areas and these parts of East Asia have a very high population density, or average number of people living in a square mile (or square km).

In East Asia, level ground is scarce and must be shared by cities, farms, and industries. For example, almost half the population of Japan is crowded on less than 3 percent of the country's total land. Most of the population of China is located in the east.

Although East Asia is largely a rural region, and about 75 percent of China's people live in rural areas, East Asia also has some of the largest cities in the world. In Japan, 80 percent of the people live in cities, and in South Korea, Seoul, the capital city, has a population of more than 10 million.

Mainland Southeast Asia The nations of mainland Southeast Asia are Vietnam, Cambodia, Laos (LAH ohs), Myanmar (MY AHN mar), and Thailand (TY land). Southeast Asia is about one-fifth the size of the United States. Much of this area is covered by forested mountains but most people live in the narrow river valleys between mountain ranges. Just as on the Indian subcontinent, rivers flow from the north and provide river valleys with the water and minerals necessary to grow crops.

SECTION I ASSESSMENT

AFTER YOU READ

RECALL

1. Identify: (a) Himalaya Mountains, (b) Yangzi, (c) Huang He, (d) Ganges River, (e) Indus River, (f) Tigris River, (g) Euphrates River
2. Define: (a) subcontinent

COMPREHENSION

3. How did the collision of two landmasses shape the landforms of northern India and southern Asia?
4. In what two ways are the Tigris and Euphrates rivers important natural resources for people in Southwest Asia?

CRITICAL THINKING AND WRITING

5. **Exploring the Main Idea** Review the Main Idea statement at the beginning of this section. Then, write a paragraph describing the physical features of Asia.
6. **Supporting a Point of View** You are a travel agent with a client who wants to visit East Asia. Which landforms would you suggest that your client visit?

ACTIVITY

Take It to the NET

7. **Journeying through the Himalayas** Imagine that you are a traveler who has come to explore the Himalayas. Use the information on the web site to write a journal account of your journey through the Himalayas. Visit the World Explorer: People, Places, and Cultures section of **phschool.com** for help in completing this activity.

Resource Directory

Teaching Resources

Section Quiz in the Unit 6 Teaching Resources, p. 4

SECTION 2

Humans and the Physical Environment

BEFORE YOU READ

READING FOCUS

1. How does the physical environment affect people's lives in Southwest Asia?
2. How does the physical environment affect people's lives in East Asia?
3. How does the physical environment affect people's lives in South and Southeast Asia?

KEY TERMS

arable land
monsoon

NOTE TAKING

Copy the outline below. As you read the section, fill in the outline with information about how the physical environment affects people's lives in Asia.

I. **Aspects and effects of the physical environment**
   A.
      1. Dry climate - People must adapt farming methods
      2. Limited arable land —
   B. East, South, and Southeast Asia
      1.
      2. Tropical climate (Southeast Asia) —

MAIN IDEA

Throughout Asia, humans must adapt to difficult, and sometimes dangerous, physical environments.

Setting the Scene

Muhammad bin Abdallah Al Shaykh (MOO ham ud BIN ub dul LAH AL SHAYK) and his family raise crops on what was once a huge, sandy plain in Saudi Arabia. Only thornscrub, a kind of short, stubby shrub, grows here. Before Muhammad and his family could grow any crops on their land, they had to drill a well more than 600 feet (183 m) deep.

Muhammad's family also dug irrigation canals throughout their 20 acres (8 hectares) of farmland. After they planted trees to help protect the farm from the fierce desert winds, they planted date palms. Dates are an important crop in Southwest Asia because the palms survive well in desert conditions.

Dates are not the only crop grown by Muhammad's family. They also grow cucumbers, tomatoes, corn, and large crops of alfalfa. The extremely long roots of alfalfa plants can find moisture deeper in the ground. Growing plants with long roots is one way that farmers adapt to a climate of hot summers and cool winters.

The Date Palm

ECONOMICS

Muhammad bin Abdallah Al Shaykh inspects one of the date palms on his farm. These trees produce a sweet, nourishing fruit. In addition, the trunk provides timber, and leaves provide fuel and the makings of baskets and rope. **Critical Thinking** Why is the date palm a good plant to raise for sale?

SECTION 2

Lesson Objectives

1. Explain how the physical environment affects people's lives in Southwest Asia.
2. Explain how the physical environment affects people's lives in East Asia.
3. Explain how the physical environment affects people's lives in South and Southeast Asia.

Lesson Plan

1 Engage

Warm-Up Activity

Have students describe the conditions on the coldest and hottest days they can recall. Ask how the weather affected what they did.

Activating Prior Knowledge

Give students the following list: bananas, coconuts, oranges, and apples. Ask them to identify which, if any, of these can be grown in their climate. Invite students to describe the climate they associate with each of these fruits.

2 Explore

As students read the section, have them look for answers to the following question: Why are bodies of water so important to Southwest Asia? When they have finished, discuss monsoons and typhoons and why they occur in East, South, and Southwest Asia.

Resource Directory

Teaching Resources

Classroom Manager in the Unit 6 Teaching Resources, p. 5

Guided Reading and Review in the Unit 6 Teaching Resources, p. 6

Guide to the Essentials, p. 105

Technology

Section Reading Support Transparencies

Answers to...

CRITICAL THINKING

Date palms provide several products that can be sold or used by those who raise them.

Lesson Plan continued

3 Teach

Have students make two word webs: one with the phrase *benefits associated with climate* at the center and another with the phrase *difficulties associated with climate* at the center. Have students complete the webs with facts and examples from the section. This activity should take about 15 minutes.

Question for Discussion

GEOGRAPHY How are the lives of people living along the Huang He affected by climate?

During the summer months, they may be flooded out of their homes and farms by the heavy rains of the monsoons. The river also provides water needed for agriculture.

4 Assess/Reteach

See the answers to the Section 2 Assessment. You may also assess students' webs.

Acceptable Webs contain at least two benefits and two difficulties associated with climate.

Commendable Webs contain three or more benefits and difficulties associated with climate.

Outstanding Webs contain three or more benefits and difficulties associated with climate and include data about the climate's effect on people and vegetation.

AS YOU READ

Use Prior Knowledge What parts of the United States have plenty of arable land?

Adapting to Harsh Conditions

Southwest Asia is a region of huge climate extremes. It has scorching summers followed by bitterly cold winters. In some places, temperatures change drastically every day. Winter or summer, however, one thing remains the same: Southwest Asia is among the largest dry regions on the Earth.

Most workers in Southwest Asia work on farms. In Turkey and Syria, agriculture is the most important economic activity. But the amount of **arable land,** or land that can produce crops, is limited. In some places, the soil is not fertile. Sometimes there is not enough water to go around. In other places, mountains make it hard to farm. Under such conditions, people have a hard time making a living.

A River in Flood

GEOGRAPHY Like the Huang He, the Yangzi, China's other great river, sometimes floods. A 1998 flood was the worst in 44 years, killing 4,100 people and causing about $30 billion in damage. Here, three workers in Wuhan visit their store by rowboat. **Critical Thinking** How might a river like the Yangzi be both a blessing and a curse for the people living along its banks?

The Influence of Climate

Climate greatly affects life in East Asia. In China, the region around the Huang He, or Yellow River, is a good example. The river gets its name from the brownish yellow dirt that is blown by the desert winds. The river picks up the dirt and deposits it to the east on the North China Plain. The plain is a huge 125,000 square mile (32,375,000 hectare) area around the river and one of the best farming areas in China.

The river, nicknamed "China's Sorrow," is both a blessing and a curse for Chinese farmers who live along its banks because the Huang He can overflow its banks during the monsoons. **Monsoons** are winds that blow across the region at certain times of the year. In summer, Pacific Ocean winds blow west toward the Asian continent. They cause hot, humid weather and heavy rain.

In winter, the winds blow toward the east and bring cooler, drier air to the continent. In parts of China, the winter monsoons produce dust storms that last for days. Where they cross warm ocean waters, such as those of the South China Sea, these monsoons pick up moisture that later drops as rain or snow.

ACTIVITY

Geography

Interpreting Data Using weather data from a major newspaper, have students locate high and low temperatures for several cities in Southwest Asia. Ask students to calculate the difference between each city's high and low temperatures and list the cities in order, from that with the greatest to that with the smallest temperature range. Have students do this for several days and determine the average temperature range over a week.

Logical/Mathematical

Answers to...

AS YOU READ

Students should identify the Southeast and the Midwest.

CRITICAL THINKING

The river can provide water for drinking, transportation, and irrigation, but when it floods, it brings destruction.

Resource Directory

Teaching Resources

Social Studies and Geography Skills, Reading a Climate Map, p. 35

Technology

Color Transparencies 177 China: Climate Regions Map; **118** China: Agricultural Regions Map

Stormy Asia

The monsoon rains in Asia provide water for half the world's population. But they affect life in South Asia in other ways as well. In India, students start school in June, after the first rains have fallen. Their long vacation comes during the spring, when hot, stifling temperatures make it hard to concentrate at school.

In Nepal, fierce monsoon rains can bring mudslides that destroy entire villages. The mud comes from hills that have been stripped of their trees. In Bangladesh, swollen rivers can overflow and flood two-thirds of the land.

Much of Southeast Asia has a tropical wet climate and is covered with rain forests. Vietnam owes its lush coastal rain forests to the winter monsoons. As these winter winds blow south from China toward Vietnam, they cross the South China Sea. The air picks up moisture, which falls as rain when the air reaches the coast.

The rain forests of Southeast Asia are lush and thick. However, there are disadvantages to living in the tropical climate of Southeast Asia—typhoons. When typhoons hit land, the high winds and heavy rain often lead to widespread property damage and loss of life.

Mumbai—A Monsoon City

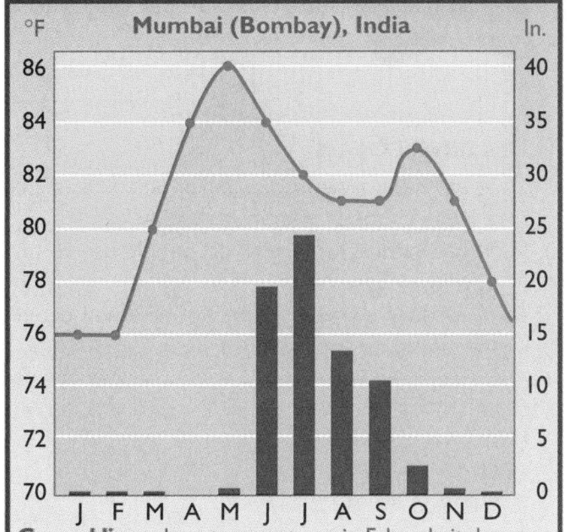

Curved lines show temperatures in Fahrenheit degrees.
Bars show precipitation in inches.

GEOGRAPHY This climate graph shows the average monthly temperature and precipitation for Mumbai (Bombay), India. As you can see on the graph, heavy rainfall starts in June. This marks the beginning of the summer monsoons. **Chart Study** What effect do the summer monsoon winds have on the temperature in Mumbai?

SECTION 2 ASSESSMENT

AFTER YOU READ

RECALL

1. Define: (a) arable land, (b) monsoon

COMPREHENSION

2. How does the physical environment affect farmers in Southwest Asia?
3. How do monsoons affect people's lives in South Asia?
4. What is one disadvantage to living in the tropical climate of Southeast Asia?

CRITICAL THINKING AND WRITING

5. **Exploring the Main Idea** Review the Main Idea statement at the beginning of this section. Then, make a list of different features of the physical environment in Asia, and how these features affect people's lives.
6. **Recognizing Cause and Effect** The climate of South Asia, and the lives of the people who live there, are greatly affected by the presence of the Himalaya Mountains. How might the climate and lives of the people of South Asia be different if the Himalaya Mountains were not there? Write a paragraph to answer.

ACTIVITY

7. **Writing a Letter** You are traveling through Asia with a tour group. Write a letter to a friend or family member at home describing the different climates and vegetation where you have visited, and how they compare to the climate and vegetation where you live.

SECTION 2 ASSESSMENT

AFTER YOU READ

1. (a) land that can produce crops (b) winds that blow across a region at certain times of the year
2. A harsh physical environment challenges farmers in Southwest Asia to make adaptations such as growing plants with long roots and digging irrigation canals.
3. Monsoons provide water for the many people of South Asia but can cause injury or death in mudslides and flooding.
4. Typhoons are one disadvantage to living in the tropical climate of Southeast Asia
5. Responses will vary, but lists should include a variety of features, such as monsoons and different climate features.
6. Sample response: During the winter, the Himalaya Mountains block the cold air coming from the north, which keeps South Asia from having cold winters. Without the shielding effect of these mountains, winters in South Asia would be much colder. People would need warmer clothing and shelter.
7. Letters will vary, but should include descriptions of different climates and vegetation in Asia, and a comparison to climate and vegetation in the region where the student lives.

Resource Directory

Teaching Resources

Section Quiz in the Unit 6 Teaching Resources, p. 7

Technology

Color Transparencies 127 South Asia: Precipitation and Monsoons, November to April Map; **128** South Asia: Precipitation and Monsoons, May to October Map

Answers to...

CHART STUDY

Monsoon winds make Mumbai a little cooler.

SECTION 3

Lesson Objectives

1. Explain how people in South and Southeast Asia use land and water resources to make a living.
2. Explain how people in East Asia use the Pacific Ocean as a resource for food.
3. Explain how oil wealth affects people and economic development in Southwest Asia.

Lesson Plan

1 Engage

Warm-Up Activity

Work with students to develop a list of natural resources found in your area. Include renewable resources such as water. After the list is completed, discuss with students how people use the resources.

Activating Prior Knowledge

Take a quick poll of students to find out how many would have trouble getting to school on time if gasoline were not available.

2 Explore

Have students read the section and explore the following questions: How do most people in South and Southeast Asia make their living? How do people use water resources in East Asia? How is oil wealth distributed throughout Southwest Asia?

Answers to...

CRITICAL THINKING

A drop in tea prices would probably mean that tea workers would earn much lower wages and might have trouble buying food and other necessities.

SECTION 3

Geographic Factors and Natural Resources

BEFORE YOU READ

READING FOCUS

1. What natural resources do people use to make a living in South and Southeast Asia?
2. What natural resources do people use to make a living in East Asia?
3. How does oil wealth affect people and economic development in Southwest Asia?

KEY TERMS

cash crop
aquaculture
standard of living

NOTE TAKING

Copy this diagram. As you read the section, complete the diagram to show key resources in Asia and the problems involved in using these resources.

	Key Resources	Problems in Using Resources
South & Southeast Asia	cash crops such as tea and rubber	
East Asia	Precious metals & mineral resources	
Southwest Asia		

MAIN IDEA

Land and water resources, along with oil, contribute to the way most people in South and Southeast Asia make their living.

Harvesting Tea

ECONOMICS Tea is an important cash crop in the island nation of Sri Lanka. These workers can pick about 40 pounds (18 kg) of tea a day. **Critical Thinking** What might happen to the people of Sri Lanka if tea prices fell very low?

Setting the Scene

If you had been born in a small village in Thailand, you would probably live in a bamboo house built on stilts near a river. During the monsoon rains, the river might flood, and you would paddle home after school in a small boat. During the dry season, your family's prized possession, a water buffalo, would live between the stilts under your house. There it would be safe from wild animals.

Most of your time would be spent growing rice. Soon after planting seeds in boxes, you would transplant the sprouts to the fields just before the rains. Throughout the growing season, you would keep the fields flooded. You would carefully weed between the rice plants, using a knife or a sickle. All this is hard but necessary work. In Thailand, as in much of Asia, rice is the most important part of all meals.

Resource Directory

Teaching Resources

Classroom Manager in the Unit 6 Teaching Resources, p. 8

Guided Reading and Review in the Unit 6 Teaching Resources, p. 9

Guide to the Essentials, p. 106

Technology

Section Reading Support Transparencies

East Asia: Natural Resources

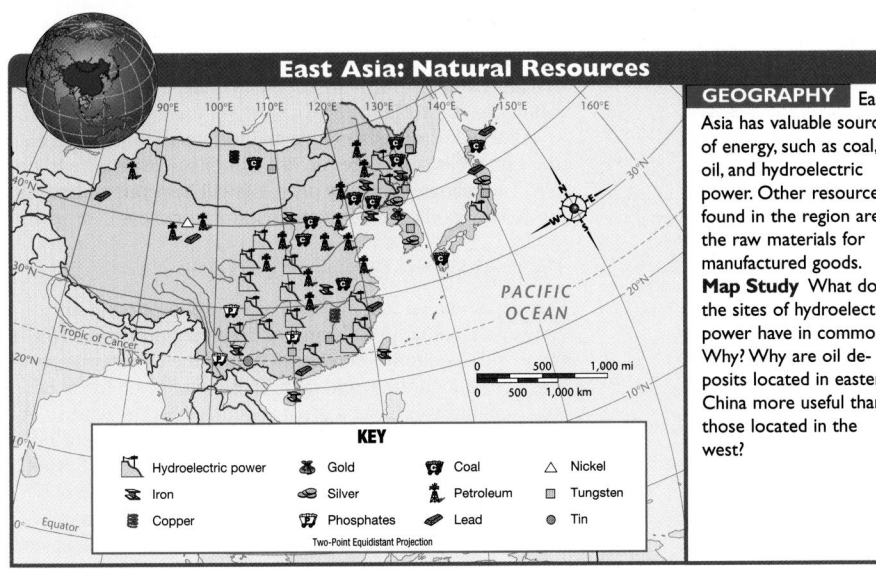

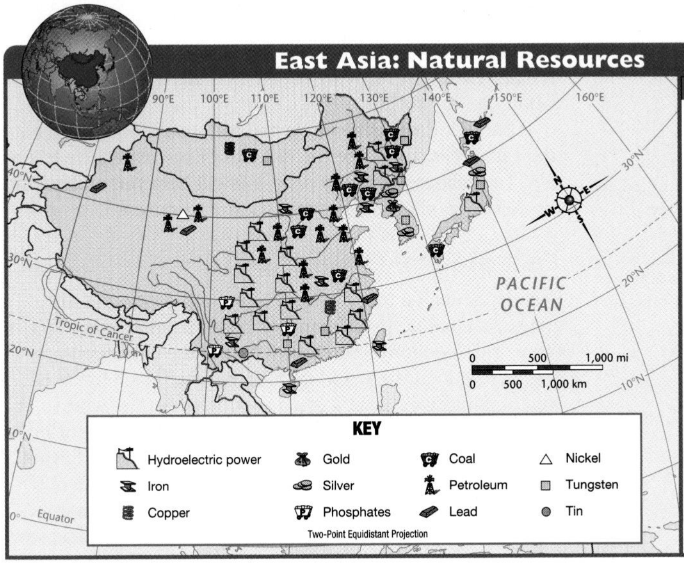

GEOGRAPHY East Asia has valuable sources of energy, such as coal, oil, and hydroelectric power. Other resources found in the region are the raw materials for manufactured goods.

Map Study What do the sites of hydroelectric power have in common? Why? Why are oil deposits located in eastern China more useful than those located in the west?

Land and Water: Precious Resources

Most of the people of South and Southeast Asia make their living from the land. They live in small villages clustered along the fertile valleys of the region's mighty rivers where they build their own homes, often from bamboo, and grow their own food. Some use the same building and farming methods that their ancestors relied upon thousands of years ago.

Some countries of South and Southeast Asia produce cash crops such as tea, cotton, and rubber. A **cash crop** is one that is raised to be sold for money on the world market.

Cash crops often bring in a great deal of money, but they may also cause problems by making the economies of a region dependent on world prices for the crops. When prices are high, the people who produce the crops are able to buy food. But when world prices fall, the cash crops do not bring in enough money. Because they cannot eat tea or rubber, the people who produce these crops sometimes go hungry.

LINKS TO Science

India's Salt Lake
During the hot months, the 90-square-mile (230-sq-km) Sambhar Lake in northwestern India is dry. Oddly, during this time the lake bed looks as though it is covered in snow. The white blanket is not snow but a sheet of salt. This salt supply was harvested as far back as the 1500s. It is an important resource for the region even today.

Using East Asia's Resources

The Pacific Ocean is an important resource for food in East Asia. Some people in East Asia catch fish using poles, nets, and even trained birds, called cormorants. But fishing is also a big business. Huge boats owned by corporations catch large numbers of fish and shellfish.

East Asians also practice **aquaculture,** or sea farming. In shallow bays throughout the area, people raise fish in huge cages and artificial reefs provide beds for shrimp and oysters. The lakes and rivers of

3 Teach

Have students make a chart with the column headings *Natural Resources* and *Uses.* Along the side, have them label rows *South Asia, Southeast Asia, East Asia,* and *Southwest Asia.* They should fill in the chart with facts from the section. This activity should take about 10 minutes.

Questions for Discussion

ECONOMICS How are cash crops a potential problem for the countries that depend on them?

Cash crops are dependent on world prices. Therefore, when world prices fall for a particular crop, that crop is often unable to bring in enough money to its producer.

GEOGRAPHY Why do East Asians practice aquaculture?

East Asia's geographic location, near many bays along the shore, makes it suitable for aquaculture.

4 Assess/Reteach

See the answers to the Section 3 Assessment. You may also use students' completed charts as an assessment.

Acceptable charts have at least two examples in each cell.

Commendable charts have at least three examples in each cell.

Outstanding charts are thorough and accurate and demonstrate a firm grasp of the main ideas of the section.

Resource Directory

Teaching Resources

Social Studies and Geography Skills, Reading a Natural Resources Map, p. 32

Answers to...

MAP STUDY

All hydroelectric plants are near rivers because hydroelectric power is generated by moving water. Students may note that the oil deposits in eastern China are closer to China's most populated areas. Oil from eastern China is also closer to the ocean and could be exported less expensively.

ACTIVITY

Cooperative Learning

Creating Charts Have students work in pairs to create charts with the following column labels: *Oil*, *Water*, and *Importance*. Students should label the rows *Turkey*, *Kuwait*, *Saudi Arabia* and *Jordan*. Ask students to use the charts to find and organize information about the condition of Southwest Asian nations lacking or possessing these resources.

Verbal/Linguistic, Logical/Mathematical

SECTION 3 ASSESSMENT

AFTER YOU READ

1. (a) a crop raised to be sold for money on the world market (b) a cultivation of the sea (c) the material quality of life
2. People in South and Southeast Asia use land and water resources to make a living by farming the region's rich river valley.
3. In East Asia, people catch fish from the Pacific Ocean, and also practice aquaculture, setting up fish farms in shallow bays.
4. Southwest Asian countries might collaborate by sharing the equipment, training, and funding needed to access all the region's oil.
5. Responses will vary, but students' paragraphs should include mention of different natural resources and how the availability or scarcity of those resources affects the standard of living in different regions.
6. Reports should cite specific suggestions such as limiting driving to conserve oil and using less water when cleaning and cooking.
7. You may wish to have students work in groups. Each group can research the mineral wealth of a particular South and Southeast Asian country.

CITIZENSHIP

Working Together

During the Persian Gulf War of 1991, after the Iraqi Army set fire to Kuwait's oil wells, a group of brave oil-firefighters from Texas, led by a man named Red Adair, saved the day. Working with Kuwaitis, they smothered the fires with nitrogen. The work was dangerous; firefighters breathed smoke; the heat melted desert sands into glass. It took eight months to put out the fires.

China are also important sources of food. In fact, almost twice as many freshwater fish are caught in China as in any other country in the world.

Although East Asia's lands and waters are filled with natural resources, some are too difficult or too expensive to obtain. The resource map on page 459 will help you understand the distribution of this region's natural resources.

Petroleum: Black Gold

Petroleum can be found in only a few places around the globe. As a result, petroleum-rich countries play a key role in the world's economy. Southwest Asia is the largest oil-producing region in the world and is greatly affected by its oil wealth. Southwest Asia has more than half of the world's oil reserves, but some countries in the region have little or no oil. These countries tend to have a lower **standard of living,** or quality of life, than their oil-rich neighbors because they do not have the income that petroleum brings. However, these countries benefit from oil wealth income another way. When their citizens work in oil-rich nations, they bring money home.

Kazakstan is one of three Central Asian countries that contain large oil reserves. Uzbekistan (ooz BEK ih stan) and Turkmenistan are the others. They have developed less of their petroleum reserves than other nations in Southwest Asia. Many countries want to help Kazakstan and its neighbors develop a larger oil industry. They offer equipment, training, and loans, in return for a share in the wealth.

SECTION 3 ASSESSMENT

AFTER YOU READ

RECALL

1. Define (a) cash crop, (b) aquaculture, (c) standard of living

COMPREHENSION

2. How do people in South and Southeast Asia use land and water resources?
3. How do people in East Asia use the Pacific Ocean as a resource for food?
4. How might Southwest Asian countries work together to best use the oil reserves of the region?

CRITICAL THINKING AND WRITING

5. **Exploring the Main Idea** Review the Main Idea statement at the beginning of this section. Then, write a paragraph explaining how natural resources affect the standard of living in different regions.
6. **Writing to Learn** The economy of Southwest Asia depends on oil and on water. (There are few permanent water sources in the region.) Write a 1-page report explaining ways in which water and oil can be conserved.

ACTIVITY

7. **Learning about Gems** The mineral wealth of South and Southeast Asia includes valuable gems. Myanmar, Thailand, Sri Lanka, and India are the source of fine rubies and sapphires. Do research in the library or on the Internet to find out more about the kinds of gems found in Asia and how the resources contribute to the various countries' economies. Share your findings in a class presentation.

Resource Directory

Teaching Resources

Section Quiz in the Unit 6 Teaching Resources, p. 10

Chapter Summary in the Unit 6 Teaching Resources, p. 11

Vocabulary in the Unit 6 Teaching Resources, p. 12

Reteaching in the Unit 6 Teaching Resources, p. 13

Enrichment in the Unit 6 Teaching Resources, p. 14

Critical Thinking in the Unit 6 Teaching Resources, p. 15

Analyzing Images

Learn the Skill

You encounter images every day in your life—on television, in newspapers and magazines, and on the Internet. These images convey information, communicate ideas, and influence attitudes. It is important to know how to read these images, just as it is to know how to read the words on this page. Follow these steps to learn how to analyze images:

A. Identify the content of the image. Pay careful attention to all of the elements that make up the image. Which elements are the most important?

B. Identify the emotional elements in the image. Artists and photographers often use color and form to communicate their ideas and emotions. What feelings are conveyed by the elements of the image?

C. Identify and read any text that appears with the image. Often, an image will have a title, caption, or other text that can help you to analyze it. What does the text tell you about the image?

D. Identify the purpose of the image. Images are created for many different reasons. Some provide information, some try to persuade, and others are meant to entertain. Thinking about why an image was created can help you better understand it.

E. Respond to the image. Identify the emotions the image causes you to feel. Think about how these emotions relate to the purpose of the image. How effective is the image in its intended purpose?

Practice the Skill

Practice analyzing the image "Mount Haruna" by reviewing the steps you learned and answering the questions that follow.

Mount Haruna

View of Mount Haruna Under the Snow, Japanese print, early 1800's

- What are some of the important elements in this print? Which element is the most important? Why?
- How does the artist use color to convey emotion in this print?
- What information about the print does the caption provide?
- Why do you think this print was created? What is its purpose?
- What emotions and feelings does this print convey?

Apply the Skill

See the Chapter Review and Assessment at the end of this chapter for more questions on analyzing images.

Lesson Objectives

1. Understand how to analyze images.
2. Practice analyzing images.

Lesson Plan

1 Engage

To introduce the skill, read the opening text under "Learn the Skill" aloud. You may wish to have volunteers look up the word *analyze* and read the different definitions to the class. Then, have students choose the definition that best fits what they do when they look at text, such as a paragraph, to see how the different words and sentences work together.

2 Explore

Have students read the steps under "Learn the Skill." Point out that steps A through D have them identifying different aspects of the image, and that their response to the image is the last step in the process. Help them to see that an analytical response can only result from careful consideration of the elements that make up images.

3 Teach

Have students look at the Japanese print. Then, have them analyze the image by answering the questions.

For additional reinforcement, have students pick another image from the chapter and analyze it, using the five steps listed under "Learn the Skill."

4 Assess/Reteach

Students should be able to analyze the painting by using the five steps listed.

To further assess students' understanding, have them do the activity under the "Applying Your Skills" part of the Chapter Review and Assessment.

Resource Directory

Technology

Social Studies Skills Tutor CD-ROM

Answers to...

PRACTICE THE SKILL

Students' responses will vary, but should take into account all the elements of the image.

CHAPTER 24 SKILLS FOR LIFE 461

CHAPTER 24

Review and Assessment

Creating a Chapter Summary

Student summaries will vary.

Sample summaries:

Section 2 Southwest Asia is a very dry region with little arable land and climate extremes—hot summers and very cold winters. East Asia is also affected by climate. Monsoons blow across the South Asian continent causing hot, humid weather and heavy rain in the summer and cooler, drier weather in the winter. Southeast Asia has a tropical, wet climate and is covered by rain forests.

Section 3 South and Southeast Asia have many natural resources. With much fertile land, most people make their living as farmers. Many of them grow cash crops, such as tea, cotton and rubber. Using the resources of the Pacific Ocean, many East Asians have fishing businesses and practice aquafarming. Petroleum is the major resource of Southwest Asia. It is the largest oil-producing region in the world.

Reviewing Key Terms

1. A country's standard of living refers to its quality of life.
2. T
3. T
4. East Asians practice aquaculture, which is sea farming.
5. T

Reviewing the Main Ideas

1. colliding landmasses, volcanoes
2. water, transportation, and hydroelectricity
3. Geographical factors such as nearness to freshwater make it easier for people to make a living.
4. Farmers have a hard time making a living in Southwest Asia because of limited arable land.
5. Monsoons bring extreme weather conditions, such as long dust storms and floods. They bring life–giving water but can destroy lives.
6. wealth and a higher standard of living
7. land and water

CHAPTER 24

Review and Assessment

Creating a Chapter Summary

On a separate piece of paper, draw a diagram like this one, and include the information that summarizes the first section of the chapter. Then, fill in the remaining boxes with summaries of Sections 2 and 3.

ASIA: PHYSICAL GEOGRAPHY

Section 1	Section 2	Section 3
Natural forces have shaped Asia's physical landscape and continue to do so today. The world's tallest mountains and some of the world's largest deserts are found in Asia. There are also many important rivers.		

Reviewing Key Terms

Read each statement below. Decide whether it is true or false. If it is false, rewrite the underlined portion to make the statement true.

1. A country's standard of living refers to the size of its population.
2. A subcontinent is a large landmass that is a major part of a continent.
3. If land is arable, it can produce crops.
4. East Asians practice aquaculture, which raises crops to be sold for money.
5. Monsoons are winds that blow across East Asia at certain times of the year.

Reviewing the Main Ideas

1. Name two natural forces that shaped Asia's landscape. (Section 1)
2. What do rivers provide for people in Asia? (Section 1)
3. Why is population density high in areas such as coastal lowlands and river valleys? (Section 1)
4. How does limited arable land affect the lives of people in Southwest Asia? (Section 2)
5. How do monsoons affect the lives of people in East and South Asia? (Section 2)
6. What benefits has Southwest Asia gained from its oil reserves? (Section 2)
7. What are two natural resources that people in South, Southeast, and East Asia use to make their living? (Section 3)

Map Activity

Asia

For each place listed below, write the letter from the map that shows its location.

1. Ganges River
2. Indus River
3. Thailand
4. Himalaya Mountains
5. Yangzi
6. Huang He
7. Sri Lanka

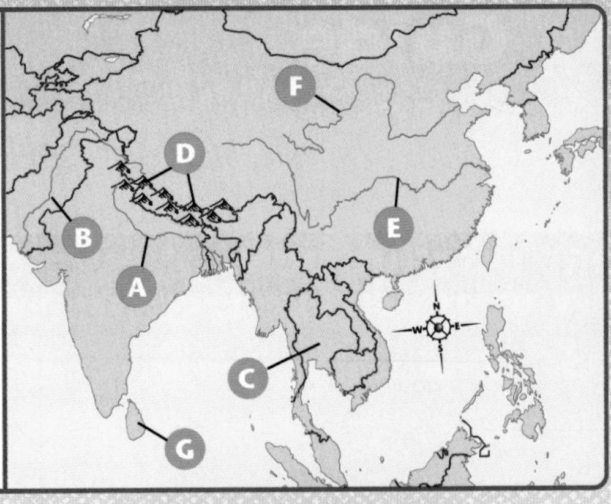

Take It to the NET

Enrichment For more map activities using geography skills, visit the social studies section of **phschool.com.**

Writing Activity

1. **Writing a Report** China's Huang He has created rich soil for the surrounding lands. This makes these lands the best agricultural areas in China. However, China's monsoon season causes the river to overflow frequently. Do some research to find out how people protect fields from flood damage. Write a report that contains suggestions for the farmers who live along the banks of the Huang He to protect their crops.
2. **Writing a Pamphlet** In order to have enough water to meet the needs of the population, irrigation systems must be used throughout Southwest Asia. Sometimes these irrigation systems can cause environmental problems or deprive other countries of water. Select a country in Southwest Asia. Write a pamphlet that describes the advantages a dam might bring to this country. Also, mention possible problems the dam might bring and offer solutions to those problems.

Critical Thinking

1. **Drawing Conclusions** The Yangzi is the only river in East Asia that is deep enough for cargo ships to sail on. How might this affect the population density of the lands surrounding the river? Of East Asia?
2. **Recognizing Cause and Effect** Most of Southwest Asia has an arid or semi-arid climate. What are two effects of this lack of water?

Applying Your Skills

Turn to the Skills for Life activity on p. 461 to help you complete the following activity.

Choose an image from a newspaper or magazine and analyze it. Record your analysis on a sheet of paper.

Take It to the NET

Activity Explore Asia's vast and diverse physical features. Create a map of Asia that includes major geographical features such as mountain ranges, rivers, lakes, and forest areas. Visit the World Explorer: People, Places, and Cultures section of **phschool.com** for help in completing this activity.

Chapter 24 Self-Test As a final review activity, take the Chapter 24 Self-Test and get instant feedback on your answers. To take the test, visit the Social Studies section of **phschool.com.**

Map Activity

1. A **2.** B **3.** C **4.** D **5.** E **6.** F **7.** G

Writing Activity

1. Suggestions might include reforestation to slow erosion and the construction of dams or dikes to prevent flooding. Reports should demonstrate awareness of audience and purpose.
2. Pamphlets should list increased agricultural production as well as possible hydroelectric production as advantages. Disadvantages might include the drawing of water from other lands, the drying up of lakes, and a loss of fertility in lands that formerly benefited from annual flooding.

Critical Thinking

1. Students should conclude that if cargo ships sail on the river, port cities and towns will attract people who make their living in shipping, trade, and related jobs. Population will be unevenly distributed.
2. Possible response: a need for irrigation to produce food, high population density near water sources.

Applying Your Skills

Make sure the students' images are appropriate for the activity. Have students present their image and thoughts on the image to the rest of the class.

Resource Directory

Teaching Resources

Cooperative Learning Activity in the Unit 6 Teaching Resources, pp. 107–109

Chapter Tests Forms A and B in the Unit 6 Teaching Resources, pp. 134–139

Guide to the Essentials, Ch. 24 Test, p. 107

Other Print Resources

Chapter Tests with ExamView® Test Bank, Ch. 24

Technology

ExamView® Test Bank CD-ROM, Ch. 24

Resource Pro® CD-ROM

Chapter 25 Planning Guide

Resource Manager

	CORE INSTRUCTION	READING/SKILLS
Chapter-Level Resources	**Teaching Resources** Program Overview Pacing Charts **Technology** Resource Pro® CD-ROM Companion Web site, phschool.com • eTeach	**Technology** Social Studies Skills Tutor CD-ROM Student Edition on Audio CD, Ch. 25
1 East Asia 1. List several achievements of East Asian civilizations. 2. Explain how culture traits spread in East Asia and from East Asia to the West. 3. Trace the rise of communism in East Asia, including the influence of Western trade in the region.	**Teaching Resources** **Unit 6** Classroom Manager, p. 17 Guided Reading and Review, p. 18	**Teaching Resources** Guide to the Essentials, p. 108 Social Studies and Geography Skills, p. 59 **Technology** Section Reading Support Transparencies
2 Southeast Asia 1. Explain how culture traits spread from China, India, Southwest Asia, and Europe to Southeast Asia. 2. Identify the effects of colonial rule on Southeast Asia.	**Teaching Resources** **Unit 6** Classroom Manager, p. 20 Guided Reading and Review, p. 21	**Teaching Resources** Guide to the Essentials, p. 109 **Technology** Section Reading Support Transparencies
3 South Asia 1. Describe how the Aryan invasion affected South Asia. 2. List contributions of some important groups and people in South Asian history.	**Teaching Resources** **Unit 6** Classroom Manager, p. 23 Guided Reading and Review, p. 24	**Teaching Resources** Guide to the Essentials, p. 110 Social Studies and Geography Skills, p. 1 **Technology** Section Reading Support Transparencies
4 Southwest Asia 1. Identify achievements of individuals and groups in ancient Southwest Asia. 2. Give examples of how political boundaries have influenced conflicts between different groups in Southwest Asia.	**Teaching Resources** **Unit 6** Classroom Manager, p. 26 Guided Reading and Review, p. 27 Chapter Summary, p. 29 Vocabulary, p. 30 Reteaching, p. 31	**Teaching Resources** **Unit 6** Critical Thinking, p. 33 Guide to the Essentials, p. 111 **Technology** Section Reading Support Transparencies

ENRICHMENT / PRE-AP

Teaching Resources
Primary Sources and Literature Readings

Other Print Resources
DK Atlas

Technology
World Video Explorer: Cultures of Asia and the Pacific, Daily Life: India, and A Trip to: Jerusalem
Companion Web site, phschool.com

Technology
Color Transparencies, 129–131
Passport to the World CD-ROM

Teaching Resources
Unit 6
Enrichment, p. 32
Cooperative Learning Activity, pp. 111–113
Outline Maps, pp. 28–29

Technology
Color Transparencies 134–135

ASSESSMENT

Prentice Hall Assessment System

Core Assessment
Chapter Tests with ExamView® Test Bank, Ch. 25
ExamView® Test Bank CD-ROM, Ch. 25

Standardized Test Preparation
Diagnose and Prescribe
Diagnostic Tests for Middle Grades Social Studies Skills
Review and Reteach
Review Book for World Studies
Practice and Assess
Test-taking Strategies with Transparencies for Middle Grades Test Prep Book
Test-taking Strategies Posters

Teaching Resources
Unit 6
Section Quizzes, pp. 19, 22, 25, and 28
Chapter Tests, pp. 141–145

Technology
Companion Web site, phschool.com
Ch. 25 Self-Test

World Video Explorer
Each region of the world is explored through regional flyovers and investigative field trips. Case study segments give students an in-depth view of the history, economy, government, and culture of a key place in each region. Case studies include Nigeria, Mexico, China, British Columbia, and the Czech Republic.

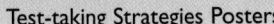

In Your Classroom

CUSTOMIZE FOR INDIVIDUAL NEEDS

Gifted and Talented

Teacher's Edition
- Declaration of Independence, p. 471
- Writing a Law, p. 474

Teaching Resources
- Enrichment, p. 32
- Primary Sources and Literature Readings

Honors/Pre-AP

Teacher's Edition
- Korean Contributions, p. 467
- Writing a Law, p. 474

Teaching Resources
- Critical Thinking, p. 33
- Primary Sources and Literature Readings

ESL

Teacher's Edition
- The Civil Rights Movement, p. 474
- Peace Talks, p. 478

Teaching Resources
- Guided Reading and Review, pp. 18, 21, 24, and 27
- Vocabulary, p. 30
- Reteaching, p. 31
- Guide to the Essentials, pp. 108–111
- Social Studies and Geography Skills, pp. 1 and 59

Technology
- Social Studies Skills Tutor CD-ROM
- Section Reading Support Transparencies

Less Proficient Readers

Teacher's Edition
- Declaration of Independence, p. 471
- Peace Talks, p. 478

Teaching Resources
- Guided Reading and Review, pp. 18, 21, 24, and 27
- Vocabulary, p. 30
- Reteaching, p. 31
- Guide to the Essentials, pp. 108–111
- Social Studies and Geography Skills, pp. 1 and 59

Technology
- Social Studies Skills Tutor CD-ROM
- Section Reading Support Transparencies

Less Proficient Writers

Teacher's Edition
- Buddhism, p. 467
- Korean Contributions, p. 467
- Peace Talks, p. 478

Teaching Resources
- Guided Reading and Review, pp. 18, 21, 24, and 27
- Vocabulary, p. 30
- Guide to the Essentials , pp. 108–111
- Social Studies and Geography Skills, pp. 1 and 59

Technology
- Social Studies Skills Tutor CD-ROM
- Section Reading Support Transparencies

DORLING KINDERSLEY

At the end of each unit, you will find information adapted from Dorling Kindersley's *Illustrated Children's Encyclopedia* that connects to the region being studied and to one of the seven content strands. In addition, your resources include Dorling Kindersley's *Atlas*, which contains valuable information about countries from around the world.

TEACHER'S EDITION INDEX

CHAPTER 25 PACING SUGGESTIONS

For 90-minute Blocks

See suggestions in the Teaching Resources Pacing Charts for Chapter 25. Use Color Transparencies 129–131, 134–135.

Running Out of Time?

See the Guide to the Essentials, pp. 108–111.

INTERDISCIPLINARY LINKS

Middle Grades Math: Tools for Success

Course 1, Lesson 11-6, **Independent Events**
Course 2, Lesson 5-2, **Adding and Subtracting Fractions**
Course 1, Lesson 10-1, **Using a Number Line**
Course 2, Lesson 7-8, **Circle Graphs**
Course 1, Lesson 1-2, **Make a Table**
Course 2, Lesson 11-7, **Symmetry and Reflections**

Science Explorer

Cells and Heredity, Lesson 4-3, **Advances in Genetics**

Prentice Hall Literature

Copper, Haiku
Bronze, Ribbons; Three Haiku by Basho
Bronze, The Hummingbird that Lived Through Winter

BIBLIOGRAPHY

For the Teacher

Collins, Michael, and Matthew Price. *The Story of Christianity.* Dorling Kindersley, 2001.

Galvin, Irene Flum. *Japan: A Modern Land with Ancient Roots.* Benchmark, 1996.

Reid, Straun. *The Silk and Spice Routes: Inventions and Trade.* New Discovery, 1994.

For the Student

Easy

Major, John S. *The Silk Route: Seven Thousand Miles of History.* HarperCollins, 1995.

Average

Ancient China. Time-Life, 1996.

Fisher, Leonard Everett. *Gandhi.* Atheneum, 1995.

King, Dr. John. *Kurds.* Thomson, 1994.

Challenging

Timelines of the Ancient World: A Visual Chronology from the Origins of Life to AD 1500. Dorling Kindersley, 2001.

Sheehan, Sea. *Cambodia.* Cavendish, 1996.

Literature Connection

Bosse, Malcolm. *Tusk and Stone.* Front Street, 1995.

Kipling, Rudyard. *The Complete Just So Stories.* Viking, 1993.

Take It to the NET

The World Explorer companion Web site, found on **phschool.com**, offers activities for exploring geographical, historical, and cultural resources on the Internet. It also provides on-line links for key content and all Section and Chapter Assessment activities.

The **Teacher site** also provides teachers with regional data and ideas for student research and activities.

Students can use the **Student site** to find chapter-by-chapter Internet resource links and to access Self-Tests.

CHAPTER 25

Connecting to the Guiding Questions

In this chapter, students will read about the history of Asia. Content in this chapter corresponds to the following Guiding Questions outlined at the beginning of the unit.

- How has history and the achievements of historic figures influenced life in Asia today?
- How has religion affected the way Asian societies have developed?
- How do Asian governments compare with each other and with the government of the United States?

Using the Speech Activities

In preparation for these activities, you might want to provide background information on Gandhi. Students may be interested to know that America's great civil rights leader, Dr. Martin Luther King, adopted Gandhi's principles of nonviolence.

- Students should learn from their research that the Indian people were divided by religion and ethnicity. Gandhi's death was discouraging because he was a beloved leader who inspired action and social change.
- Speeches should reflect the student's strong feelings about the topic, and should use repetition as a device for emphasizing key points.

Heterogeneous Groups

The following activities are suitable for heterogeneous groups.

Government

Declaration of Independence, p. 471

Citizenship

Writing a Law, p. 474

eTeach

Be sure to check out this month's discussion with a Master Teacher. Go to **phschool.com**.

CHAPTER 25

ASIA: Shaped by History

Mohandas K. Gandhi

"He was perhaps the greatest symbol of the India of the past, and of the future.... We stand on this perilous edge of the present, between the past and the future, and we face all manner of perils. And the greatest peril is sometimes the lack of faith which comes to us, the sense of frustration that comes to us, the sinking of the heart and of the spirit that comes to us when we see ideals go overboard, when we see the great things that we talked about somehow pass into empty words, and life taking a different course. Yet, I do believe that perhaps this period will pass soon enough."

—*Jawaharlal Nehru*

USING SPEECHES

Mohandas K. Gandhi (1869–1948) was a greatly beloved spiritual and political leader in India who played an important role in India gaining its freedom from Great Britain in 1947. Jawaharlal Nehru, India's first Prime Minister, delivered this speech in 1948 after Gandhi's death.

Understanding the Speech

In his speech, Nehru speaks of the perils, or dangers, that face the new nation of India, and "the sinking of the heart and spirit" that comes when ideals are lost. Do research to find out what some of the perils faced by India were, and what happened after Gandhi's death. Why do you think people felt discouraged at Gandhi's death?

Writing a Speech

Great speechmakers often use repetition of phrases to create a sense of rhythm when they talk. Examine Nehru's speech for words or phrases that are repeated. Read the speech aloud, listening for the repetition. Then, prepare a short speech on a topic that you feel strongly about, using repetition to emphasize key points in your speech. Present your speech to the class.

Resource Directory

Teaching Resources

Primary Sources and Literature Readings extend content with a selection related to the concepts in this chapter.

Other Print Resources

DK Atlas

Technology

Cultures of Asia and the Pacific, from the World Video Explorer, enhances understanding of the many cultures of Asia.

Daily Life: India, from the World Video Explorer, enhances understanding of daily life in rural and urban India.

A Trip to: Jerusalem, from the World Video Explorer, enhances understanding of Jerusalem as the birthplace of three world religions.

Student Edition on Audio CD, Ch. 25

SECTION 1

East Asia

BEFORE YOU READ

READING FOCUS

1. What are some of ancient East Asia's major achievements?
2. How did culture traits spread within East Asia and from East Asia to the West?
3. How did Western trade pressure contribute to the rise of communist nations in East Asia after World War II?

KEY TERMS

civilization
emperor
dynasty
migration
clan
cultural diffusion

NOTE TAKING

Copy the diagram below. As you read the section, fill in the diagram to show causes and effects in East Asian history.

Cause	Effects
• Chinese wanted to keep rest of the world out	• Built Great Wall of China

MAIN IDEA

Discoveries and advances in science, technology, and the arts spread within East Asia and to Western nations before conflicts within and beyond East Asia erupted during World War II.

Setting the Scene

Over two thousand years ago, Confucius (kun FYOO shus), one of the most important thinkers of ancient times, advised his pupils:

"Let the ruler be a ruler and the subject be a subject."

"A youth, when at home, should act with respect to his parents, and, abroad, be respectful to his elders."

Confucius taught that everyone has duties and responsibilities. If a person acts correctly, the result will be peace and harmony. Confucius' ideas helped both China's government run smoothly for years and Chinese culture to last for centuries.

Statue of Confucius

CULTURE This statue of Confucius stands in the Chinatown section of New York City. **Critical Thinking** Why do you think that Chinese people all over the world still admire Confucius?

East Asia's Achievements

A **civilization** has cities, a central government, workers who do specialized jobs, and social classes. Of the world's early civilizations, only China's has survived. This makes it the oldest continuous civilization in the world.

The Glory That Was China For much of its history, China had little to do with the rest of the world. The Great Wall of China—started before 206 B.C.—is a symbol of China's desire to keep the

SECTION 1

Lesson Objectives

1. List several achievements of East Asian civilizations.
2. Explain how culture traits spread in East Asia and from East Asia to the West.
3. Trace the rise of communism in East Asia, including the influence of Western trade in the region.

Lesson Plan

1 Engage

Warm-Up Activity

Ask students what they consider to be the main achievements of American culture. Stimulate students' responses by writing these words on the chalkboard: *democracy, civil rights, space exploration, inventions, music.*

Activating Prior Knowledge

Have students identify and discuss different cultures that they have contact with in daily life. Encourage students to consider foods, words, clothing, entertainers, sports, and types of music from other countries. Prime the discussion by offering examples such as pizza, spaghetti, and soccer.

Resource Directory

Teaching Resources

Classroom Manager in the Unit 6 Teaching Resources, p. 17

Guided Reading and Review in the Unit 6 Teaching Resources, p. 18

Guide to the Essentials, p. 108

Technology

Section Reading Support Transparencies

Passport to the World CD-ROM This interactive CD-ROM allows students to explore each region of the world. Students view regional videos, take a photo tour, and explore a historical timeline. Students record their travels in an Explorer's Journal and receive passport stamps when they pass regional quizzes.

Answers to...

CRITICAL THINKING

Possible response: Chinese people admire Confucius because they appreciate his contributions to Chinese culture.

Lesson Plan continued

2 Explore

Have student partners create K-W-L charts entitled *East Asian Achievements.*

East Asian Achievements		
Know	Want to Know	Learned

Invite students to discuss any important achievements of China and Japan with which they are familiar. After discussion, have students fill in the first two columns of the chart. As students read the section, have them fill in the third column of their K-W-L charts with the major achievements of China and Japan.

3 Teach

Ask students to create a web showing how Chinese culture influenced the Koreans and the Japanese. Have students discuss why Chinese civilization is considered one of the world's most important. Ask them to evaluate the achievements of East Asian cultures. This activity should take about 20 minutes.

Questions for Discussion

HISTORY How did East Asian countries interact with the West before the 1800s? How did this interaction change?

East Asian countries remained relatively isolated from the West until Europeans aggressively sought to trade with and learn from these civilizations.

SOCIAL STUDIES SKILLS How were the goals of the Nationalists and the Communists in China similar? How were they different?

Both groups wanted less foreign influence in China. The Nationalists wanted to make the country stronger so it would not have to rely on other countries, while the Communists seemed to want a complete change in Chinese society by breaking the power of the wealthy classes and driving out all foreign influences.

AS YOU READ

Monitor Your Reading Think of two questions you might ask about the achievements of China.

world at a distance. Chinese leaders named their country the Middle Kingdom because to them, it was the center of the universe.

The Chinese had reason to be proud. They invented paper, gunpowder, silk weaving, the magnetic compass, the printing press, clockwork, the spinning wheel, and the water wheel. Chinese engineers were experts at digging canals, building dams and bridges, and setting up irrigation systems.

Ancient China was governed by an **emperor**—a ruler of widespread lands and groups of people. A series of rulers from the same family was a **dynasty.** Chinese history is described by dynasties.

Migration Influences Korea Around 1200 B.C., during a time of troubles in China, some Chinese migrated to the Korean Peninsula. A **migration** is a movement of people from one country or region to another to make a new home. Later, other Chinese settled in the southern part of the peninsula. These migrations led to a transfer of Chinese knowledge and customs to the Koreans.

Years of Japanese Isolation For much of Japan's history, **clans,** or groups of families who claimed a common ancestor, fought each other for land and power. Around A.D. 500, one clan, the Yamato (yah mah toh), became powerful. Claiming descent from the sun goddess, Yamato leaders took the title of "emperor." Many emperors sat on Japan's throne. For a long time they had little power. Instead, shoguns (SHOH gunz), or "emperor's generals," made the laws. Warrior nobles, the samurai (SAM uh rye), enforced these laws. Together, the shoguns and samurai ruled Japan for more than 700 years.

Japanese leaders came to believe that isolation, or separation, was the best way to keep the country united. Thus, Japan was isolated from the outside world from 1640 to 1853.

HISTORY The time line highlights some important events and cultural contributions of several dynasties.
Chart Study Under which dynasty do you think China made the most important achievements? Why?

Major Dynasties of China

1500 B.C. | 1000 B.C. | 500 B.C. | A.D. 1 | A.D. 500 | A.D. 1000 | A.D. 1500

Shang
1700 B.C.–1100 B.C.
- Writing
- Wheeled chariots

Zhou
1100 B.C.–256 B.C.
- Confucius lived
- First canals built

Qin
221 B.C.–206 B.C.
- China took its name from this dynasty
- Great Wall built
- Standard weights and measures

Han
206 B.C.–A.D. 220
- Chinese trace their ancestry to this dynasty
- Paper, compass, seismograph invented
- Buddhism comes to China from India

Tang
A.D. 618–A.D. 907
- Art and poetry flourish
- Chinese goods flow to Southwest Asia and Europe
- First book printed

Song
A.D. 960–A.D. 1279
- Block printing and paper money

Ming
A.D. 1368–A.D. 1644
- Artists and philosophers make China a highly civilized country

Qing
A.D. 1644–A.D. 1911
- Last dynasty ends with Emperor Pu Yi

466 UNIT 6 ASIA

Answers to...

AS YOU READ

Students' questions will vary, but should focus on Chinese achievements.

CHART STUDY

Answers will vary. Students may say that China made the most important achievements under the Han because under that dynasty, inventions that greatly advanced communication, navigation, and seismology were made.

Resource Directory

Teaching Resources

Social Studies and Geography Skills, Reading a Timeline, p. 59

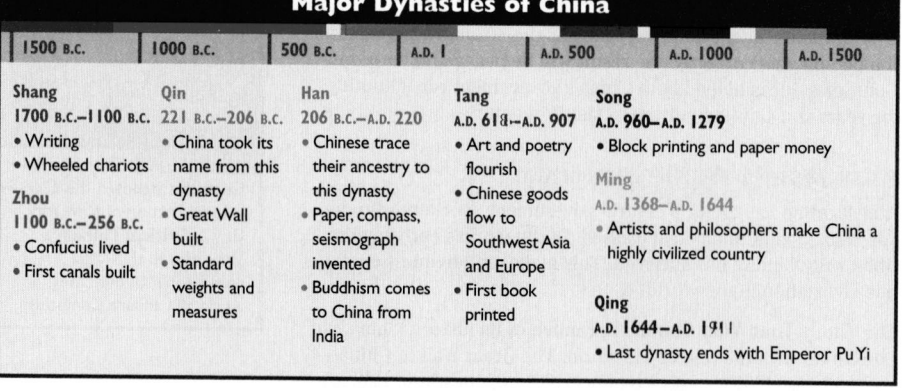

Events in Japanese History

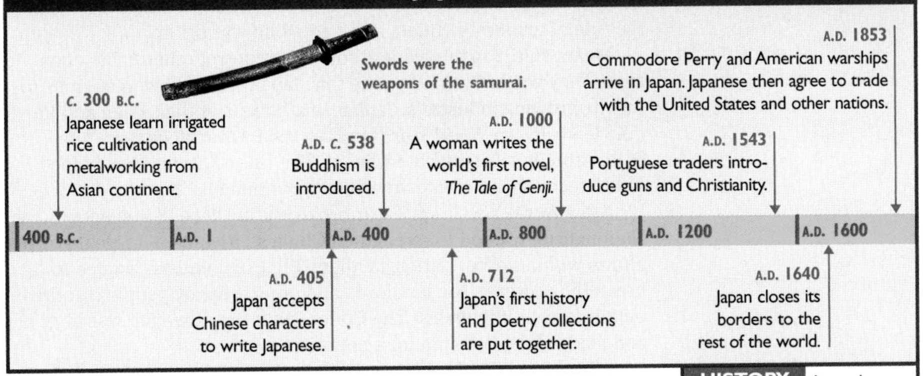
Swords were the weapons of the samurai.
c. 300 B.C. Japanese learn irrigated rice cultivation and metalworking from Asian continent.
A.D. c. 538 Buddhism is introduced.
A.D. 1000 A woman writes the world's first novel, The Tale of Genji.
A.D. 1543 Portuguese traders introduce guns and Christianity.
A.D. 1853 Commodore Perry and American warships arrive in Japan. Japanese then agree to trade with the United States and other nations.
400 B.C.
A.D. 1
A.D. 400
A.D. 800
A.D. 1200
A.D. 1600
A.D. 405 Japan accepts Chinese characters to write Japanese.
A.D. 712 Japan's first history and poetry collections are put together.
A.D. 1640 Japan closes its borders to the rest of the world.

HISTORY Japan has interacted with outside nations except for one period in it history.
Chart Study Name three examples of cultural diffusion shown in the time line.

Culture Traits Spread

In ancient times, China led the world in inventions and discoveries. Many Chinese discoveries then spread to Korea and Japan. This **cultural diffusion,** or spreading of ideas, happened early and the teachings of Confucius were among the first ideas to be passed along. The religion of Buddhism (BOOD izm), which China had adopted from India, later spread to Korea and Japan.

Cultural diffusion was not always friendly. For example, Korean potters so impressed the Japanese that they were captured and taken back to Japan in 1598. East Asian culture owes much to early exchanges among China, Japan, and Korea. The countries changed what they borrowed until the tradition became their own.

Trade Pressure and Communism

Although at times East Asia was not interested in the rest of the world, the world was interested in East Asia. In the 1800s, Europeans and Americans began to produce great amounts of manufactured goods. East Asia seemed like a good place to sell these products, so Western trading ships sailed to Asian ports.

In 1853, U.S. Commodore Matthew Perry sailed with four warships to Japan to force it to grant trading rights to the United States. The Japanese adapted Western ways and inventions that were useful to them, helping Japan to become the strongest nation in Asia.

The opening up of China was different. Foreign countries wanted to control parts of China and its wealth and it became clear that the country was not strong enough to protect itself as the British, French, Dutch, Russians, and Japanese gained control over parts of China. The United States feared losing the opportunity to share in China's riches and, in 1899, announced a policy opening China for trade with all nations equally. For a while, this halted efforts to divide up China.

4 Assess/Reteach

See the answers to the Section 1 Assessment. You may also assess students' webs.

Acceptable Webs show at least two ways in which China influenced its neighbors.

Commendable Webs show additional influences and historical ties.

Outstanding Webs include both positive and negative aspects of China's influence and demonstrate an understanding of cultural diffusion.

CULTURE

Buddhism

Buddhism began in India around 500 B.C. with the teachings of Siddhartha Gautama, called "The Enlightened One." Once Buddhism had spread to China, it became a major force in the culture. A form of Chinese Buddhism spread to Japan, where it became known as Zen Buddhism. Since the 1950s, Zen has become a popular form of Buddhism in the United States. Buddhism has about 325 million followers worldwide.

SCIENCE, TECHNOLOGY, AND SOCIETY

Korean Contributions

Koreans made significant cultural contributions to East Asia and the wider world. In A.D. 647, Koreans built the first astronomical observatory in Asia. In the 1400s A.D., Koreans invented the rain gauge, barometer, iron hanging bridge, ironclad warship, and metal moving type.

SKILLS MINI LESSON

Using a Timeline

You may introduce the skill by explaining that a timeline is a kind of map of the past—it organizes important dates in chronological order and shows the relationships and "distances" between events. Allow students to practice the skill by directing them to answer the following questions about the Major Dynasties of China timeline on the opposite page. *Did the Tang dynasty rule before or after the Zhou dynasty? (after) During which dynasty did the Chinese standarize weights and measures?* (Qin) *Did they do this before or after they invented paper?* (before) *How many years passed between the beginning of the Qin dynasty and the end of the Han dynasty?* (440) Direct students to the Events in Japanese History timeline on this page. Suggest that student pairs apply the skill by devising three questions that can be answered using the timeline.

Answers to...

CHART STUDY

Possible response: Chinese characters, Buddhism, and guns enter Japan from other countries.

SECTION I ASSESSMENT

AFTER YOU READ

1. 1. (a) a society that has cities, a central government, workers who do specialized jobs, and social classes (b) ruler of widespread lands and groups of people (c) a series of rulers from the same family (d) movement of people from one country or region to make a new home (e) group of families who claim a common ancestor (f) spreading of ideas and culture through the movement of people
2. Ancient East Asian civilizations were responsible for inventions and innovations, such as clockwork, the spinning wheel, and the printing press.
3. Both China and North Korea became communist nations after World War II, partly in reaction to Western influences.
4. Possible response: The magnetic compass could allow seafarers to navigate in foggy weather beyond sight of the shoreline. It could increase people's ability to explore the world.
5. By remaining isolated, a country could develop and promote a unique culture with which all residents could identify.
6. You may want to have students work in pairs to complete this activity. Remind students to include a key and compass rose on their maps.

Conflict and Communism Many Chinese blamed the emperor for the growing foreign influence. In 1911, revolution broke out in China, the rule of emperors ended, and a republic was set up.

Meanwhile, Japan's leaders sought to control other Asian countries. They wanted to make sure that Japan would have resources to fuel its growing industries. Japanese attacks on other Asian and Pacific lands led to World War II in East Asia. Ultimately, the United States and its allies defeated Japan. The United States then helped Japan recover and create an elected government.

After World War II, civil war broke out in China. Some people, the Nationalists, wanted to strengthen China so it could manage its own affairs without other nations. Others, the Communists, wanted to break the power of the landlords and other wealthy people and drive out all foreign influences. The Communists won the civil war in 1949 and made China a communist nation.

After World War II, Korea was split in two. Communists ruled North Korea and South Korea turned to Western nations for support. In 1950, the two Koreas exploded into a bloody civil war when North Korea invaded South Korea. The United States and other United Nations countries sent 480,000 troops to help South Korea, while China sent troops to help North Korea. The war dragged on for three years, killing about 54,000 U.S. soldiers and as many as 1.8 million Korean soldiers and civilians. Neither side won. The battle line at the end of the war, in 1953, remains the border between the two Koreas today.

SECTION I ASSESSMENT

AFTER YOU READ

RECALL

1. Define: (a) civilization, (b) emperor, (c) dynasty, (d) migration, (e) clan, (f) cultural diffusion

COMPREHENSION

2. What are some major achievements of ancient East Asian civilizations?
3. How did China and North Korea change in the years after Western trade opened up with East Asia?

CRITICAL THINKING AND WRITING

4. **Exploring the Main Idea** Review the Main Idea statement at the beginning of this section. Then, choose an invention of the Chinese. Write a paragraph explaining why the invention is important or the difference that the invention might make in people's lives.
5. **Making Inferences and Drawing Conclusions** Write one or two sentences explaining why isolating a country from its neighbors might help keep it united.

ACTIVITY

Take It to the NET

6. **Mapping the Silk Road** The ancient trade route known as the Silk Road was actually several routes connecting the cities and cultures of the east and west. Create a map outlining the Silk Road. Visit the World Explorer: People, Places, and Cultures section of **phschool.com** for help in completing this activity.

Resource Directory

Teaching Resources

Section Quiz in the Unit 6 Teaching Resources, p. 19

468 UNIT 6 ASIA

SECTION 2

Southeast Asia

BEFORE YOU READ

READING FOCUS

1. How did culture traits spread from China, India, Southwest Asia, and Europe to Southeast Asia?
2. How did colonial rule influence Southeast Asia?

KEY PLACES

Angkor Wat

MAIN IDEA

Culture traits spread from other countries to Southeast Asia through conquest, trade, missions, and colonization.

NOTE TAKING

Copy the word web below. As you read the section, fill in the word web with information about how culture traits spread from other countries to Southeast Asia.

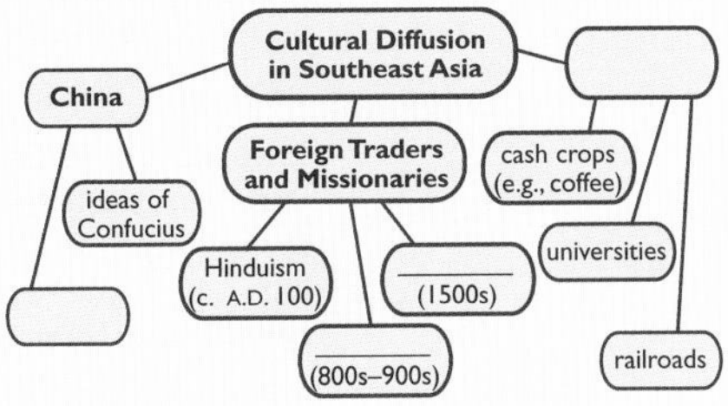

Setting the Scene

Deep in the rain forests of Cambodia lies the Hindu temple **Angkor Wat**—the largest temple in the world. It was built in the A.D. 1100s by the Khmer (kuh MEHR), whose empire included Cambodia and much of Laos, Thailand, and Vietnam. The empire enjoyed great wealth and it is said that the king, wearing gold and pearls, rode on an elephant whose tusks were wrapped in gold. The remains of Angkor Wat stand today as proof of the great civilization.

Culture and Conquest

From time to time, Chinese armies swept into Southeast Asia. In 111 B.C., the Chinese took over Vietnam and they ruled the country for more than 1,000 years. During that time, the Vietnamese began using Chinese ways of farming. They also began using the ideas of Confucius to run their government.

Angkor Wat

CULTURE Angkor Wat is almost one square mile (2.6 sq km) in area. Its inner walls are covered with carvings of figures from Hindu myths.

Critical Thinking Why do you think the Khmer built such a grand structure?

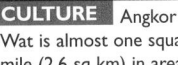

SECTION 2

Lesson Objectives

1. Explain how culture traits spread from China, India, Southwest Asia, and Europe to Southeast Asia.
2. Identify the effects of colonial rule on Southeast Asia.

Lesson Plan

1 Engage

Warm-Up Activity

Ask students to discuss how they would feel if a foreign country made laws for the people of our country, told us what kinds of crops we could raise, and then stationed their troops here to make sure we obeyed their laws. How might the people of our country respond?

Activating Prior Knowledge

Ask students to identify and describe some of the contributions made by people from various cultures who have immigrated to the United States.

2 Explore

Have students read the section and explore the following questions: What religions do Southeast Asians practice? Why did colonial powers wish to control Southeast Asia? Why did Southeast Asian nations seek independence?

Resource Directory

Teaching Resources

Classroom Manager in the Unit 6 Teaching Resources, p. 20

Guided Reading and Review in the Unit 6 Teaching Resources, p. 21

Guide to the Essentials, p. 109

Technology

Section Reading Support Transparencies

Answers to...

CRITICAL THINKING

Possible answer: The Khmer built the temple as a display of their strength and wealth.

Lesson Plan continued

3 Teach

Have students make timelines that show important events and time periods related to the cultures of Southeast Asia. Students should record dates and information related to religion, colonial rule, and independence. This activity should take about 25 minutes.

Questions for Discussion

HISTORY Why were many Southeast Asians hopeful when the Japanese invaded the region in World War II? Why were they disappointed?

They hoped that a Japanese victory would end colonialism. They were disappointed because Japanese authority was just as harsh as colonial rule.

CULTURE What were some of the challenges facing Southeast Asian countries after gaining independence?

Student should mention the difficulties of establishing new democratic governments and improving economies hurt by colonialism.

4 Assess/Reteach

See the answers to the Section 2 Assessment. You may also use students' completed timelines as an assessment.

Acceptable timelines include one important date related to each of the categories of religion, colonial rule, and independence.

Commendable timelines have entries for several countries and include important dates related to religion, colonial rule, and independence.

Outstanding timelines have entries for several countries; include important dates related to religion, colonial rule, and independence; and identify specific time periods and their cultural significance.

Religion The Indians were another influence on Southeast Asia. For example, around A.D. 100, Indians introduced Hinduism to the region and, today, there are Hindus in Bali and parts of Malaysia. Buddhists eventually outnumbered Hindus in the region and today there are many Buddhists in Myanmar, Thailand, Laos, and Cambodia.

During the 800s and 900s, Arab traders introduced Islam to Southeast Asia. Today, Islam is the religion of millions in Malaysia, Indonesia, the southern Philippines, and other Asian countries.

European missionaries brought Christianity to the area in the 1500s. Today, most Filipinos are Christian and there are groups of Christians in other Southeast Asian countries, too.

From Colonial Rule to Independence

Europeans brought more than Christianity to Southeast Asia. Traders from Europe first arrived in the region in the 1500s. To gain control of the rich trade in silks, iron, silver, pearls, and spices, they built trading posts in the region. By the 1800s, European nations had gained control of most of Southeast Asia.

Colonial Rule in Southeast Asia, 1914

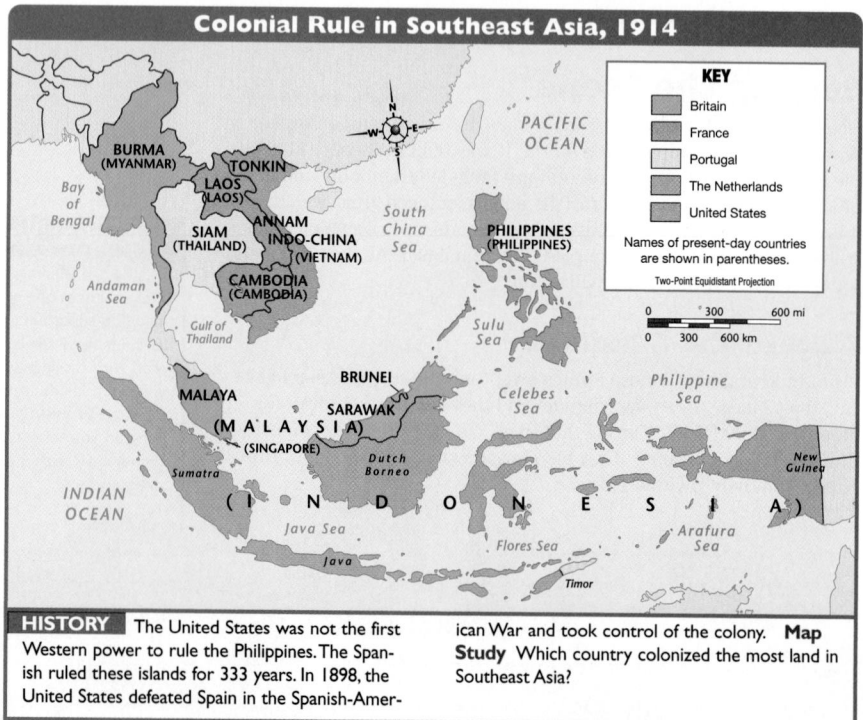

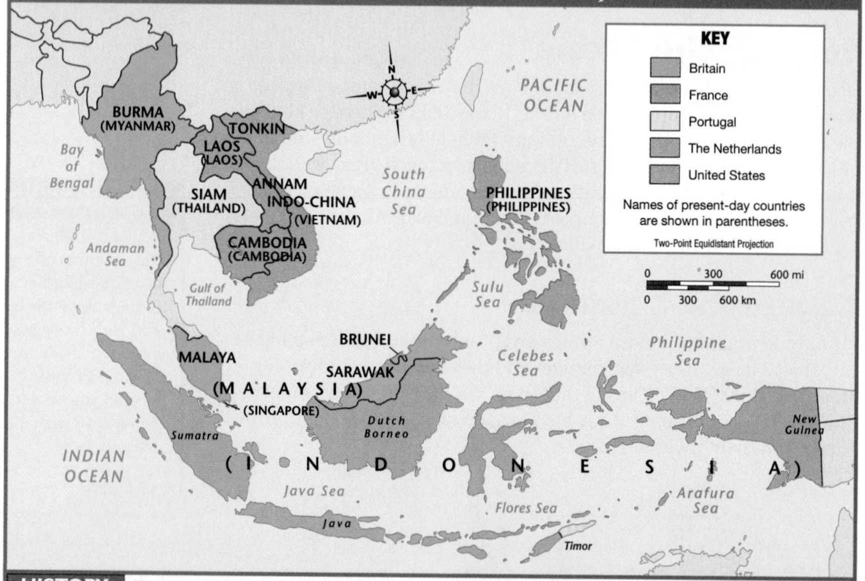

HISTORY The United States was not the first Western power to rule the Philippines. The Spanish ruled these islands for 333 years. In 1898, the United States defeated Spain in the Spanish-American War and took control of the colony. **Map Study** Which country colonized the most land in Southeast Asia?

Answers to...

MAP STUDY

The Netherlands colonized the most land.

470 UNIT 6 ASIA

Effects of Colonial Rule Outside nations gained control of the Southeast Asian economy and forced their colonies to grow cash crops. On the island of Java, the Dutch forced farmers to grow and sell coffee. This caused rice production to fall, which meant that there was not enough food for people to eat.

Colonial rulers built a network of roads, bridges, and railroads in Southeast Asia making it easier to move people and goods across the region. The colonial powers also built schools and universities, which helped to produce skilled workers for colonial industries. These educated Southeast Asians would eventually lead the struggle for freedom.

Fighting for Freedom By the early 1900s, nationalists were organizing independence movements throughout Southeast Asia. During World War II, invading Japanese drove out European colonial powers and many Southeast Asians hoped that a Japanese victory would end colonialism in the region. However, Japanese rule proved to be as harsh as, or harsher than that of the former colonial powers.

After the Japanese were defeated in World War II, Western nations hoped to regain power in Southeast Asia. But Southeast Asians had other hopes; they wanted independence. In fact, most Southeast Asian countries did gain independence, though some, like Malayasia and Indonesia had to fight for it.

After independence, the nations of Southeast Asia worked to create new governments. Some were democratic but others were controlled by dictators, leaders who have absolute power.

CITIZENSHIP

Working Together For Freedom

East Timor takes up half of a small island several hundred miles from the capital of Indonesia, Jakarta. A former Portuguese colony, East Timor was invaded by Indonesia in 1975 and ruled harshly. Some people, however, fought back. Carlos Filipe Ximenes Belo, a Roman Catholic bishop, and José Ramos-Horta, a politician, worked peacefully on behalf of the Timorese people. They were awarded the 1996 Nobel Peace Prize for their efforts. In 1999, East Timor voted to become an independent nation.

SECTION 2 ASSESSMENT

AFTER YOU READ

RECALL

1. Identify: (a) Angkor Wat

COMPREHENSION

2. Name four ways that culture spread from other countries to Southeast Asia.

3. How did colonial rule affect the economies of Southeast Asia?

CRITICAL THINKING AND WRITING

4. Exploring the Main Idea Review the Main Idea statement at the beginning of this section. Then, write a paragraph describing cultural diffusion in Southeast Asia.

5. Hypothesizing Imagine that the Southeast Asian countries did not gain independence from the colonial powers. How would life in these countries be different today?

ACTIVITY

6. Delivering a Speech Write a speech urging Southeast Asians to support independence from European rule. Make sure your speech has a persuasive argument. When you are finished, deliver your speech to your class.

ACTIVITY

Government

Declaration of Independence
Have student pairs develop a "Declaration of Independence" for a Southeast Asian country that was under colonial rule. Allow research time so that students can identify issues that triggered the independence movement. Students may wish to use the American Declaration of Independence as a model. You might remind them that it begins with a general statement of principles and then lists specific grievances.

Verbal/Linguistic

SECTION 2 ASSESSMENT

AFTER YOU READ

1. (a) located in Cambodia; the world's largest religious temple complex
2. trade, conquests, missions, colonization
3. Colonial rulers took control over the economy, forcing people to grow cash crops.
4. Students' paragraphs should mention that culture traits spread from China, India, Europe, and Arab countries through conquest, trade, and colonialization.
5. Possible answer: Citizens of Southeast Asian countries probably would have little or no voice in governing and making decisions about their lives, such as how to earn a living.
6. Speeches should give some specific reasons why the people wanted to be free of European rule.

Resource Directory

Teaching Resources

Section Quiz in the Unit 6 Teaching Resources, p. 22

SECTION 3

Lesson Objectives

1. Describe how the Aryan invasion affected South Asia.
2. List contributions of some important groups and people in South Asian history.

Lesson Plan

1 Engage

Warm-Up Activity

Ask students whether they have ever had an experience that triggered a major change in their lives or their way of thinking. Tell students that in this section, they will learn about some singular experiences that had major effects on the history of both South Asia and the world.

Activating Prior Knowledge

Ask students to list groups and people who have made an important contribution to U.S. history. Have students identify or describe the contributions. Record all responses on the chalkboard.

2 Explore

Have students read the section and explore the following questions: How did Aryan invaders influence life in the Indus Valley? What great empires affected life in India? What role did Great Britain play in India's history?

Answers to...

CRITICAL THINKING

Ancient peoples built settlements near rivers, which provided water for drinking and irrigation for crops.

SECTION 3

South Asia

BEFORE YOU READ

READING FOCUS

1. How did the Aryan invasion affect South Asia?
2. What are some important groups and people in the history of South Asia?

KEY TERMS

caste
colony
partition

KEY PEOPLE

Asoka
Mohandas K. Gandhi

MAIN IDEA

South Asia, a region originally influenced by the Aryan invasion, has had a number of important leaders in its long history.

NOTE TAKING

Copy the chart below. As you read the section, fill in the chart with information about key groups and individuals in the history of South Asia.

Group or Individual	Approx. Dates of Influence	Contribution
Aryans		
Maurya–Chandragupta		
Maurya–Asoka		
Mughal–Akbar		
Mughal–Shan Jahan		
Mohandas K. Gandhi		

Mohenjo-Daro

GEOGRAPHY The people of Mohenjo-Daro built their city on mounds of earth to protect it from the floods of the Indus River. **Critical Thinking** Why was the Indus River valley a likely place for scientists to come across the ruins of an ancient civilization?

Setting the Scene

In 1922, scientists digging near the Indus River came upon the ruins of an ancient city they called Mohenjo-Daro (moh HEN joh DAH roh). The city had wide, straight streets and large buildings. It had a sewer system and a large walled fortress. Mohenjo-Daro was part of a civilization that developed about 4,500 years ago.

The people who lived there were part of one of the world's oldest civilizations. Over the centuries, many other people moved into the region. Some came peacefully. Others marched in with swords in their hands.

The Aryan Invasion

Between 2000 B.C. and 1500 B.C., invaders known as Aryans (AIR ee unz) swept down on the people of the Indus Valley. The Indus Valley farmers were no match for the Aryan soldiers in horse-drawn chariots, and the Aryans took control of the area. In time, they moved eastward to the Ganges River, laying claim to much of northern India.

The Aryans ruled northern India for more than 1,000 years. They introduced new ways of living. For instance, they divided people into three classes—priests, warriors, and ordinary working people. This division grew out of Aryan religious writings called the Vedas (VAY duz). In time, the Aryans drew the

Resource Directory

Teaching Resources

Classroom Manager in the Unit 6 Teaching Resources, p. 23

Guided Reading and Review in the Unit 6 Teaching Resources, p. 24

Guide to the Essentials, p. 110

Technology

Section Reading Support Transparencies

The Early History of India

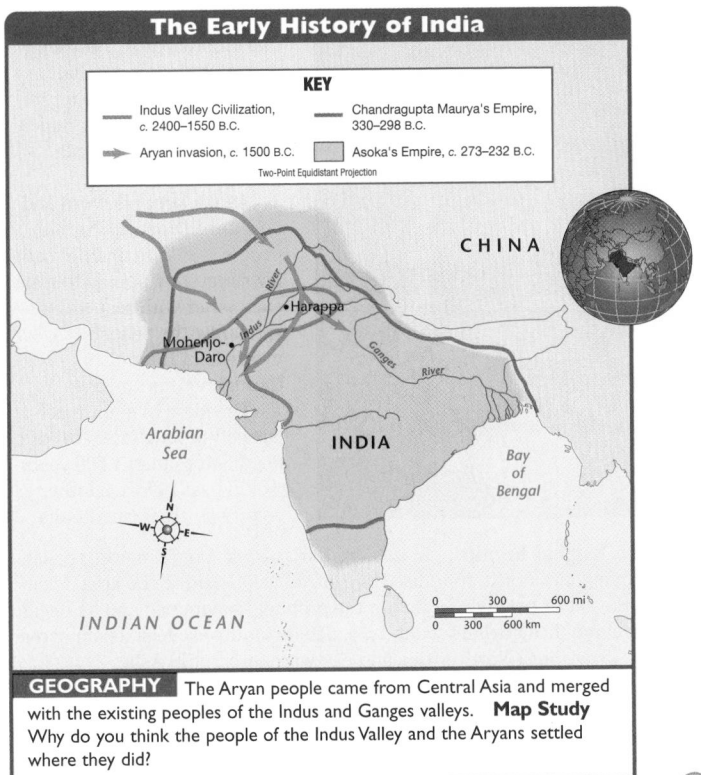

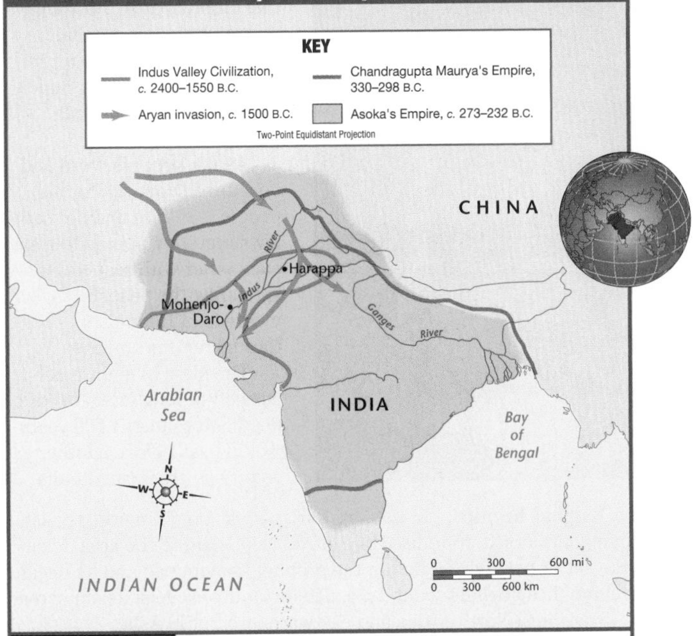

GEOGRAPHY The Aryan people came from Central Asia and merged with the existing peoples of the Indus and Ganges valleys. **Map Study** Why do you think the people of the Indus Valley and the Aryans settled where they did?

conquered people into their class system. By 500 B.C., there was a strict division of classes. Europeans later called it the **caste** system. Each caste, or class, had special duties and work.

The caste system became a central part of a new system of belief that also emerged from Aryan religious ideas and practices. This system of beliefs, Hinduism, is the world's oldest living religion.

Important Groups and People

For hundreds of years, India was divided into many small kingdoms. No one ruler emerged to unite them.

The Maurya Empire Around 330 B.C., a fierce leader named Chandragupta Maurya (CHUN druh gup tuh MAH ur yuh) conquered many kingdoms. By the time of his death in 298 B.C., he ruled an empire that covered much of the subcontinent.

Maurya's grandson, **Asoka** (uh SOH kuh), continued the conquests,

LINKS TO **Math**

Decimal Numbers By A.D. 600, Indian astronomers were using the decimal system—a numbering system based on tens. Their system also had place values and a zero. This made it easy to add, subtract, multiply, and divide. Europeans were using Roman numerals at this time. They later switched to this decimal, or Hindu-Arabic, system. It is used worldwide today.

Resource Directory

Teaching Resources

Social Studies and Geography Skills, Using the Map Key, p. 1

3 Teach

Have students develop a card game based on this section. Give each student four index cards. Have them write one question on the front and three multiple-choice answers on the back of each card. Tell students to use the following categories for their questions: the Aryans, Great Empires, and Gandhi. If time permits, collect all the cards and allow groups to play the game. This activity should take about 30 minutes.

Questions for Discussion

CULTURE Why was the Indian subcontinent divided into two countries in 1947?

After independence, the Muslim minority in India feared that their rights would not be protected by the Hindu majority, so Pakistan was formed as a Muslim nation.

HISTORY What important influence did Asoka have on the Maurya empire?

Asoka brought peace to the empire. He gave up war and violence and passed laws requiring people to treat each other with respect.

4 Assess/Reteach

See the answers to the Section 3 Assessment. You may also use students' question cards as an assessment.

Acceptable cards include a question related to each of the categories.

Commendable cards include a question that tests knowledge of a main idea in each category.

Outstanding cards include a question that demonstrates a thorough understanding of a main idea in each category.

Answers to...

MAP STUDY

The rivers provided water for people and crops as well as a means of transportation.

CITIZENSHIP

The Civil Rights Movement

American Civil Rights leader Martin Luther King, Jr., was influenced by Gandhi's methods of nonviolent resistance. He adopted some of Gandhi's techniques in his efforts to end racial inequality in the United States. Like Gandhi, King organized a boycott to gain recognition of injustice. African Americans boycotted the Birmingham, Alabama, public bus service in protest of laws that restricted African Americans to certain seats on buses. The boycott was successful and led to new laws that ended racial segregation in the South.

ACTIVITY

Citizenship

Writing a Law Mention to students that after Asoka renounced violent conquest, he traveled his empire in order to serve his subjects and relieve suffering when he could. His guiding principles were honesty, mercifulness, consideration, and respect. Throughout India, he erected huge pillars on which were inscriptions urging the people to treat one another justly and humanely. Invite students to write a statement or law in the spirit of Asoka's principles. Students may write and decorate their law or statement by hand or may use a computer and choose a typeface. Post students' inscriptions around the classroom.

Visual/Spatial, Verbal/Linguistic

The Taj Mahal

CULTURE It took 20,000 workers 22 years to finish the Taj Mahal, the stunning monument Shah Jahan built to his wife. **Critical Thinking** How does the architecture of the Taj Mahal reflect its builder's Islamic religion?

but this soon changed. After one bloody battle, Asoka gave up war and violence and freed his prisoners. Later he changed his beliefs to Buddhism and vowed to rule peacefully.

Asoka kept his word and he showed concern for his people's welfare and he made laws requiring people to treat each other with respect, spreading the peaceful message of Buddhism throughout his empire.

The Maurya empire collapsed not long after Asoka's death. More than 1,500 years would pass before another empire as great ruled India.

The Mughal Empire In the A.D. 700s, people from the north began moving into northern India. They introduced Islam to the area. Islam is the set of beliefs revealed to the prophet Muhammad and he began teaching these beliefs around A.D. 610 in Southwest Asia. Islam spread westward into North Africa and eastward into South Asia.

The Mughals (MOO gulz) were among these Muslims, or followers of Islam, who settled in India. They arrived in the 1500s and established an empire ruled by Akbar (AK bar), from 1556 to 1605 who allowed all people to worship freely, regardless of their religion. He also supported the arts and literature.

Akbar's grandson, Shah Jahan (SHAH juh HAHN), built many grand buildings. Perhaps the greatest is the Taj Mahal (TAHZH muh HAHL), built as a magnificent tomb for Mumtaz (mum TAHZ) Mahal, his wife. But the cost of this and other of Jahan's building projects was enormous. It drained the empire of money and, eventually, helped to cause the empire's collapse in the 1700s.

AS YOU READ
Monitor Your Reading What questions do you have about how India won its freedom from Britain?

Colonization and Resistance During the 1700s, 1800s, and 1900s, European nations established many colonies in Asia, Africa, and the Americas. A **colony** is a territory ruled by another nation, usually one very far away. Through trade and war, the nations of Europe made colonies of most of South Asia. Britain took over most of the region, including India, and because of the riches it produced, the British called India the "jewel in the crown" of their empire.

While Britain treasured its empire, many Indians treasured their freedom and a strong independence movement grew up. Its greatest

Resource Directory

Technology

Color Transparencies 129–131 South Asia, 1945–Present (base map with overlays)

Answers to...

CRITICAL THINKING

Possible response: The Taj Mahal resembles an Islamic mosque.

AS YOU READ

Students' questions will vary, but will probably ask if India's independence was gained through violence or peacefully.

leader was **Mohandas K. Gandhi** (GAHN dee) who called for people to resist British rule. However, Gandhi stressed that they should do this through nonviolent means. For example, he urged a boycott of British goods. A boycott means a refusal to buy or use goods and services. Gandhi was jailed many times for opposing British rule, but this only made him a greater hero to his people. Gandhi's efforts played a major part in forcing Britain to grant India its freedom in 1947.

Past Conflicts Shape Current Conditions Independence was soon followed by the horror of religious warfare. During the struggle for freedom, Hindus and Muslims had worked together. However, Muslims were a minority. Many feared that their rights would not be protected in a land with a Hindu majority. In 1947, Hindus and Muslims agreed on the **partition,** or division, of the subcontinent into two nations. India would be mainly Hindu. Muslims would be the majority in Pakistan.

This did not stop the fighting, and more than 500,000 people were killed. Gandhi himself was murdered, and conflict between the two nations continued. In 1971, for example, Indian troops helped East Pakistan break away from Pakistan to form the nation of Bangladesh (bahn gluh DESH). Even today, India and Pakistan continue to view each other with distrust.

Strength without Violence

HISTORY Mohandas K. Gandhi urged Indians to resist the British by following Hindu traditions. He preached the Hindu idea of *ahimsa,* or nonviolence and respect for all life. Because of his nonviolent approach, Indians call him *Mahatma,* or "Great Soul." **Critical Thinking** Why do you think Gandhi's nonviolent methods proved so successful?

SECTION 3 ASSESSMENT

AFTER YOU READ

RECALL

1. Identify: (a) Asoka, (b) Mohandas K. Gandhi
2. Define: (a) caste, (b) colony, (c) partition

COMPREHENSION

3. What social system did the Aryans introduce in South Asia?
4. Name two important people in South Asian history and tell one contribution of each.

CRITICAL THINKING AND WRITING

5. **Exploring the Main Idea** Review the Main Idea statement at the beginning of this section. Then, write a paragraph that describes some of the important influences that the Aryan invasion brought to South Asia.
6. **Comparing and Contrasting** Consider how the horse-drawn chariot enabled the Aryans to take control of the area where the Indus Valley farmers lived. What technological innovations have given particular regions, countries, or groups power over others in recent times?

ACTIVITY

7. **Writing to Learn** Write a journal entry in which you discuss why you think Gandhi's being jailed made him more of a hero to the people of India.

SECTION 3 ASSESSMENT

AFTER YOU READ

1. (a) ruler of the Maurya empire who gave up war, converted to Buddhism, and vowed to rule peacefully (b) leader of the Indian independence movement against British Rule Based
2. (a) class of people that perform special duties and work (b) territory ruled by another nation (c) divison
3. The Aryans introduced the caste system.
4. Possible response: The Maurya emperor Chandragupta conquered many kingdoms and established a vast empire on the subcontinent. The Mughal emperor Shah Jahan built many grand buildings, including the Taj Mahal.
5. Possible response: People or groups important to the history of a region make a contribution to its culture that lasts for many years. For example, the Maurya united many separate kingdoms of northern India in a single empire that lasted about 100 years.
6. Possible responses: the steam engine, submarine, combustion engine, hydrogen bomb, computer
7. Students may say that people saw Gandhi as a courageous person, willing to suffer for what he believed; his standing up to the British encouraged others to follow his example.

Resource Directory

Teaching Resources

Section Quiz in the Unit 6 Teaching Resources, p. 25

Answers to...

CRITICAL THINKING

Possible answer: The people respected Gandhi for not resorting to violence.

SECTION 4

Lesson Objectives

1. Identify achievements of individuals and groups in ancient Southwest Asia.
2. Give examples of how political boundaries have intensified conflicts between different groups in Southwest Asia.

Lesson Plan

1 Engage

Warm-Up Activity

Ask volunteers to share their feelings about their community. What do they like about the community? What makes it special to them? Discuss actions students have taken to advance the community's causes, defend it from criticism, or demonstrate its strengths.

Activating Prior Knowledge

Point out that every society has rules. Ask students what rules they must follow at school, at home, and in their community. Ask what would happen if these rules were not followed. Then, ask students how societies communicate their rules to the people. Work with students to help them identify means such as the media, religious texts and services, signs, handbooks, oral transmission, and so forth.

Answers to...

CRITICAL THINKING

Answers will vary. Students may say that the people used a system of writing for recording important events, record keeping, or keeping a calendar for crop planting.

SECTION 4

Southwest Asia

BEFORE YOU READ

READING FOCUS

1. What achievements did individuals and groups make in ancient Southwest Asia?
2. How have political boundaries intensified conflicts between different groups in Southwest Asia?

KEY PLACES

Mesopotamia
Palestine

MAIN IDEA

In modern times, political boundaries and ethnic differences have intensified regional conflicts between groups and countries in Southwest Asia.

NOTE TAKING

Copy the diagram below. As you read the section, complete the diagram with information about two ongoing conflicts in Southwest Asia.

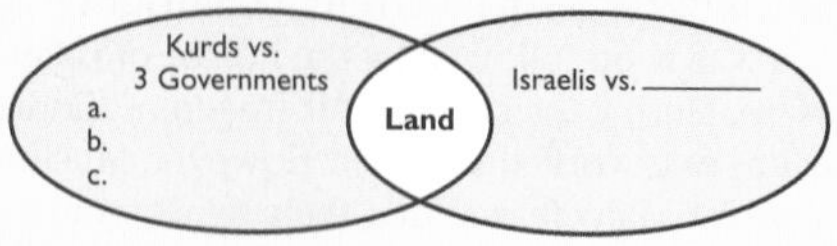

Ancient Writing System

CULTURE The people of Mesopotamia used a writing system made up of wedge-shaped marks. This tablet shows the calculations for the area of a piece of land. **Critical Thinking** What other uses would this early civilization have had for a system of writing?

Setting the Scene

Hammurabi's Code was written about 3,800 years ago in Southwest Asia. People have described its laws as demanding "an eye for an eye." But there was more to the code than that:

"If the robber is not caught, the man who has been robbed shall formally declare whatever he has lost...and the city and the mayor...shall replace whatever he has lost for him."

The code punished people for wrong doings, but also offered justice to those hurt through no fault of their own.

Mesopotamia

Hammurabi ruled the city of Babylon from about 1800 B.C. to 1750 B.C. and he united the region along the Tigris and Euphrates rivers. This region is called **Mesopotamia,** which means "between the rivers."

People have lived in Mesopotamia for thousands of years, long before Hammurabi united it, and by 3500 B.C., the people made the area a center of farming and trade. The Tigris and Euphrates rivers flooded every year, leaving fertile soil along their banks. People dug irrigation ditches to bring water to fields that lay far from the river. Irrigation helped them to produce a crop surplus, or more than they needed.

Resource Directory

Teaching Resources

Classroom Manager in the Unit 6 Teaching Resources, p. 26

Guided Reading and Review in the Unit 6 Teaching Resources, p. 27

Guide to the Essentials, p. 111

Technology

Section Reading Support Transparencies

Political Boundaries Intensify Conflicts and Challenges

For many centuries, Southwest Asia has been a crossroads for Asia, Africa, and Europe. As a result, many different religious and ethnic groups live here. These differences, along with conflicts over political boundaries, have led to violent disputes.

Aswir Shawat is a Kurd from the town of Halabja, Iraq. Kurds are an ethnic group whose people live in many parts of Southwest Asia and who have their own language and culture. However, they do not have a country of their own. Their desire for a country has led to conflicts between Kurds and the governments of Iran, Iraq, and Turkey. Shawat describes what happened to him when the Iraqi army attacked his hometown in 1991:

> "Over 5,000 Kurdish people were killed at Halabja, and thousands were injured. . . .We had to go with thousands of people towards the border to Iran. I walked with my grandmother and brother. Nobody took anything with them. We left all our things in Halabja. When we got to Iran, they took us to a camp and gave us a tent. At the camp, we found our mother and grandfather."

Ancient Southwest Asia

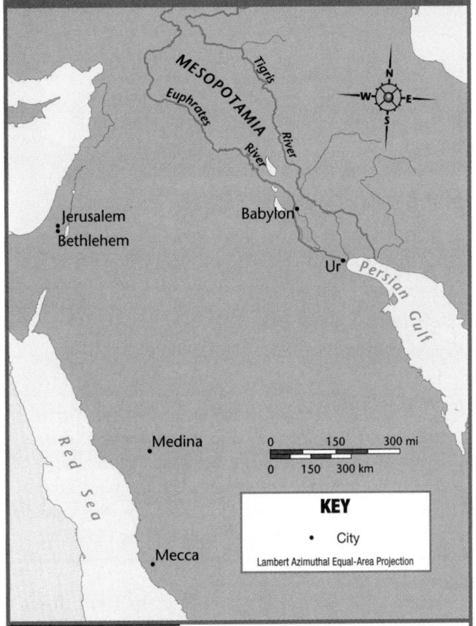

GEOGRAPHY Southwest Asia was the location of some of the world's earliest civilizations. It is also the birthplace of Judaism, Christianity, and Islam. Jerusalem, Bethlehem, Mecca, and Medina all have religious connections. **Map Study** Between which two rivers is Mesopotamia located?

After World War I, a conflict broke out between Arabs and Jews in Southwest Asia. Judaism has its roots in Southwest Asia. Over the centuries, a few Jews continued to live in their homeland, but many had settled in other parts of the world. In the late 1800s, Jews from around the world began to dream of returning to Palestine, an area along the eastern shore of the Mediterranean Sea. This alarmed the Arabs who lived there. **Palestine** was their homeland, too. When some Jews began moving to Palestine at the end of World War I, tensions rose.

Jews continued to migrate to Palestine during the 1930s. During World War II, millions of Jews in Europe were killed solely because they were Jewish. After the war, many of those who had survived decided to go to Palestine. The United Nations voted to divide Palestine into separate Arab and Jewish states. Arabs were unhappy with the borders chosen, and were determined to fight. The result was war.

2 Explore

While reading the section text, urge students to seek answers to questions such as the following: What were some of the achievements of Mesopotamian civilizations? What conflicts exist in Southwest Asia?

3 Teach

Have students create an annotated timeline of Southwest Asia's history. Ask them to add brief summaries or examples to explain the events. This activity should take about 30 minutes.

Questions for Discussion

HISTORY **What aspect of Mesopotamian culture still affects people today?**

The idea that all citizens must obey the same set of laws still affects us today.

CULTURE **Why is conflict usually a result of dividing land among different cultures and groups?**

When more than one group or culture seeks to control a single area, conflicts will develop.

4 Assess/Reteach

See the answers to the Section 4 Assessment. You may also assess student's timelines.

Acceptable timelines include accurate dates for all the events mentioned in this section.

Commendable timelines provide explanatory data for at least two events.

Outstanding timelines provide explanatory data for most events.

Resource Directory

Teaching Resources

Outline Maps, Southwest Asia, pp. 28–29

Technology

Color Transparencies 135 The U.N. Partition of Palestine, 1947 and Israel, 1949 Map; **134** Israel and the Occupied Territories, 1967 and 1994 Map

Answers to...

MAP STUDY

On the map, Mesopotamia is between the Tigris and Euphrates rivers.

ACTIVITY

Cooperative Learning

Peace Talks Discuss the conflicts facing both the Arabs and Jews—the desire to live in and control the same lands. Stress that both groups have legitimate historical links to the disputed area. Organize students into groups, and ask them to research the conflict and the various attempts to come to an agreement. Groups should use their research and the material presented in the section to role-play peace talks.

Verbal/Linguistic

SECTION 4 ASSESSMENT

AFTER YOU READ

1. (a) region along the Tigris and Euphrates rivers whose name means "between the rivers" (b) area along the eastern shore of the Mediterranean, important to Arabs and Israelis.
2. Hammurabi united Mesopotamia and established a legal code; before Hammurabi, ancient Mesopotamians made the region a center of farming and trade.
3. Kurds have been isolated and oppressed by the governments of Turkey, Iran, and Iraq. Arabs and Jews have fought over control of land.
4. Paragraphs should explain the conflict between the Kurds and the governments of Iran, Iraq, and Turkey, and the conflict between the Arabs and the Israelis.
5. Writing may have enabled Hammurabi to record his laws for future civilizations to understand.
6. The quote from Aswir Shawat is a primary source. The remaining text is a secondary source. A primary source gives firsthand information. A secondary source gives an explanation or interpretation.

Answers to...

CRITICAL THINKING

Because it seemed like a step toward peace in the Middle East.

HISTORY Former Israeli Prime Minister Yitzhak Rabin (left) shook hands with Yasser Arafat (right), chairman of the Palestine Liberation Organization (PLO). In 1993 U.S. President Bill Clinton invited the two leaders to the White House, where they signed a peace agreement between Israel and the PLO. This event paved the way for the Wye agreement of 1998, which called for Israel to give Palestinians more land, and to release some Palestinian prisoners from Israeli jails. **Critical Thinking** Why do you think that many people considered the 1993 meeting a historic occasion?

In 1948, Jews formed their own state, Israel. Their state was recognized by the United Nations. Since then, the Arabs of Palestine have lived as refugees in other Arab nations or in Israel, under Israeli rule. Israel and the Arab nations that border it have fought a number of bloody wars. Arabs and Israelis continue to work toward peace, but progress is slow.

SECTION 4 ASSESSMENT

AFTER YOU READ

RECALL

1. Identify: (a) Mesopotamia, (b) Palestine

COMPREHENSION

2. Name two achievements of Hammurabi and one achievement of more ancient people in Mesopotamia.
3. How has the drawing of political boundaries caused conflicts for Kurds, Arabs, and Jews in Southwest Asia?

CRITICAL THINKING AND WRITING

4. **Exploring the Main Idea** Review the Main Idea statement at the beginning of this section. Write a paragraph explaining the ongoing conflicts in Southwest Asia and describing the parties involved.
5. **Drawing Conclusions** Write a paragraph explaining how writing may have helped Mesopotamia leave its mark on the world.

ACTIVITY

6. **Writing to Learn** Review the first three paragraphs on page 477. Then, write a paragraph identifying a primary source and a secondary source and telling what is different about these two types of sources.

Resource Directory

Teaching Resources

Section Quiz in the Unit 6 Teaching Resources, p. 28

Chapter Summary in the Unit 6 Teaching Resources, p. 29

Vocabulary in the Unit 6 Teaching Resources, p. 30

Reteaching in the Unit 6 Teaching Resources, p. 31

Enrichment in the Unit 6 Teaching Resources, p. 32

Critical Thinking in the Unit 6 Teaching Resources, p. 33

Identifying Cause and Effect

Learn the Skill

A cause is something that makes something else happen. The effect is what happens. Cause and effect can explain the relationship between events. History is full of causes and effects. A single event can have more than one cause or more than one effect. Also, an effect can in turn become the cause of more effects. Learning to correctly recognize causes and effects will help you to understand history.

To understand how cause-effect relationships work, make a cause-effect diagram of the information about Jewish people in Europe moving to Palestine after World War II. To make your cause-effect diagram, complete the following steps:

A. Identify the event. Jews left different European countries to move to Palestine after World War II. Write the event in the middle of a sheet of paper and circle it.

B. Identify the causes. What caused them to move to Palestine? You should be able to identify at least two causes. Not only did they move because they were being persecuted in Europe, but also because they believed Palestine to be their ancient homeland and Jerusalem their holy city. Write these causes to the left of the event, and draw a circle around each one. Then, draw an arrow from each cause to the event in the center.

C. Identify the effects. One effect was discord between Arabs and Jews. Another was the establishment of Israel as a nation. Write the effects to the right of the event, and circle each one. Then, draw an arrow from the event to each effect.

Now look your diagram over to see how it works. By following the arrows, you can trace the causes and effects of events.

Practice the Skill

Read the paragraph below. Look for cause-and-effect relationships between the events. Words and phrases such as "as a result" will give you clues that a cause-and-effect relationship exists. Make a list of the cause-effect relationships you find.

Sui Wendi

Sui Wendi ruled China as emperor from A.D. 581 to 604. As a young worker for the northern Chou dynasty, he helped the emperor gain control of most of northern China. As a result, he became a valued official.

As emperor, Sui Wendi invaded southern China. It had been divided from the rest of China for about 300 years. In 589, Sui Wendi became ruler of all of China. Long after his death, China remained united and powerful.

Sui Wendi also began reconstruction of the Grand Canal, which connects China's two greatest rivers. This improved transportation of goods in China. And he reformed the ways in which government officials were chosen by requiring civil service tests. The result is that he created a talented and skilled group of officials.

Apply the Skill

See the Chapter Review and Assessment at the end of this chapter for more questions on cause and effect.

Lesson Objectives

1. Define the terms cause and effect.
2. Recognize cause and effect in context.

Lesson Plan

1 Engage

To introduce the skill, read aloud the opening text under "Learn the Skill". Ask students to define cause and effect in their own words. Give examples and ask students to identify them as examples of cause or effect. Help students read the cause-effect diagram by following the arrows.

2 Explore

Ask students to read the steps under "Learn the Skill" on their own. Point out that the event of Jews moving to Palestine is used as an example in the steps. Have students pay attention to which events are causes and which are effects. Remind students that an effect can serve as the cause of another event.

3 Teach

Challenge students to read the information about Sui Wendi and find several cause-effect relationships.

For additional reinforcement, ask students to fill out a cause-effect diagram using the above information.

4 Assess/Reteach

Students should be able to identify causes and effects when they read.

To further assess students' understanding of comparing maps have them complete the "Applying Your Skills" part of the Chapter Review and Assessment.

Resource Directory

Teaching Resources

Social Studies and Geography Skills, Recognizing Cause and Effect, p. 47

Technology

Social Studies Skills Tutor CD-ROM

Answers to...

PRACTICE THE SKILL

Causes and effects include: Because Sui Wendi helped the emperor gain control of most of northern China, he became a valued official; reconstruction of the Grand Canal improved the transportation of goods; government reform resulted in a skilled group of government officials.

CHAPTER 25

Review and Assessment

Creating a Chapter Summary

Student summaries will vary.

Sample summaries:

Section 2 Culture traits spread from other countries to Southeast Asia via conquest, trade, missions, and colonization. European nations ruled most of Southeast Asia for many years, provoking widespread rebellion in the 1900s.

Section 3 Important groups in the history of South Asia include the Aryans, Mauryans, and Mughals. Important individuals include the Maura emperor Asoka and the Indian leader Mohandas K. Gandhi.

Section 4 Ancient people made Mesopotamia a center of farming and trade. Hammurabi united the region about 1800 B.C. and established one of the earliest known legal codes. Today, the region is the site of long-standing conflicts over land.

Reviewing Key Terms

1. b **2.** d **3.** g **4.** a **5.** f **6.** c **7.** e

Reviewing the Main Ideas

1. Possible answer: silk weaving, clockwork, the printing press, the water wheel
2. Migration, invasion, and trade led to the spread of ideas and culture within East Asia and to Western nations through a process known as cultural diffusion.
3. through conquest, trade, colonization, and missions
4. By the early 1900s, Southeast Asian nationalists were organizing independence movements in an attempt to break free of European rule.
5. The Aryans established a caste system, which divided people into classes that performed specialized work.
6. Possible answer: the Maurya emperor Asoka, the independence leader Mohandas K. Gandhi
7. Hammurabi's Code
8. Political boundaries leave Palestinians without a homeland of their own.

CHAPTER 25

Review and Assessment

Creating a Chapter Summary

On a separate piece of paper, draw a diagram like this one, and include the information that summarizes the first section of the chapter. Then, fill in the remaining boxes with summaries of Sections 2, 3, and 4.

ASIA: SHAPED BY HISTORY

Section 1	Section 2	Section 3	Section 4
The many achievements of East Asian civilizations spread to other regions via migration, invasion, and trade. Conflicts within the region helped spark World War II, after which China and North Korea became communist nations.			

Reviewing Key Terms

Match the key terms in Column I with the definitions in Column II.

Column I

1. dynasty
2. colony
3. boycott
4. caste
5. migration
6. dictator
7. cultural diffusion

Column II

a. class of people that performs special work
b. series of rulers from the same family
c. leader who has absolute power
d. territory ruled by another nation
e. spreading of ideas and culture through the movement of people
f. movement of people from one region to another
g. refusal to buy or use goods and services

Reviewing the Main Ideas

1. Name several discoveries made by early East Asian civilizations. (Section 1)
2. What was the effect of migration, invasion, and trade within East Asia and, ultimately, on Western nations? (Section 1)
3. How did culture traits spread from other countries to Southeast Asia? (Section 2)
4. By the early 1900s, what was Southeast Asians' growing response to colonization? (Section 2)
5. What new way of life did the Aryans establish in South Asia? (Section 3)
6. Identify two important leaders in the history of South Asia. (Section 3)
7. Identify one achievement of early Southwest Asia. (Section 4)
8. How do political boundaries in Southwest Asia affect Palestinians? (Section 4)

Map Activity

Asia

For each place listed below, write the letter on the map that shows the location. Use the Atlas at the back of the book to complete the exercise.

1. India
2. Vietnam
3. Pacific Ocean
4. China
5. Japan

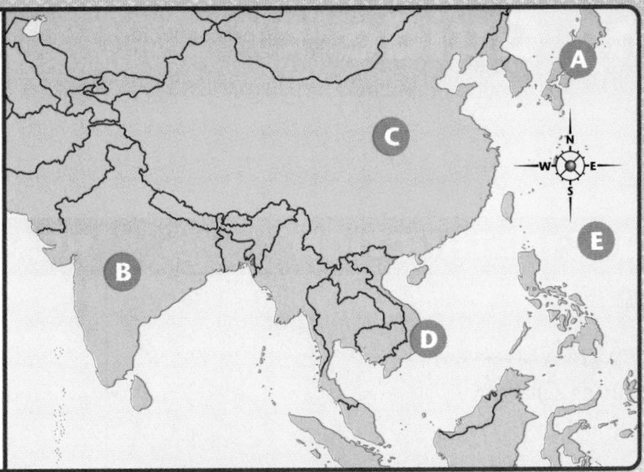

Writing Activity

1. **Writing a Newspaper Editorial** Choose one conflict that you read about in this chapter. Write a newspaper editorial that gives your point of view on the conflict.
2. **Writing a Progress Report** Choose one of the countries discussed in this chapter and write a progress report about it. Do additional research, using primary or secondary sources, to find more information. Remember to address the problems the nation faces and the solutions being put forward to address those problems.

Critical Thinking

1. **Drawing Conclusions** Both ancient China and Japan attempted to isolate themselves from foreign influences. How did this affect both countries?
2. **Drawing Inferences** What sorts of conflicts might erupt in a very young country such as Israel?

Applying Your Skills

Turn to the Skills for Life activity on page 479 to answer the following questions.

1. What is a cause?
2. What is an effect?
3. How are causes and effects related?
4. What were the causes of so many Jewish people moving to Palestine after World War II?
5. What were the effects of this move?

Take It to the NET

Activity Read about the Qin, Han, and Ming dynasties and the contributions they made to the world. Where do you see these contributions in society today? Visit the World Explorer: People, Places, and Cultures section of **phschool.com** for help in completing this activity.

Chapter 25 Self-Test As a final review activity, take the Chapter 25 Self-Test and get instant feedback on your answers. To take the test, visit the Social Studies section of **phschool.com.**

Map Activity

1. B **2.** D **3.** E **4.** C **5.** A

Writing Activity

1. Responses will vary. Students should correctly identify the nations engaged in the conflict and demonstrate an understanding of the issues underlying the conflict.
2. Reports should clearly outline problems. Solutions should be supported by facts.

Critical Thinking

1. Possible answer: During China's years of isolation, the Chinese developed a unique civilization and produced many important inventions and innovations. Japanese leaders believed that they kept their country united through isolation.
2. Possible answer: Conflicts might erupt over who should govern the country and how it should be governed.

Applying Your Skills

1. A cause is something that makes something else happen.
2. An effect is what happens.
3. An effect is the result of a cause.
4. The Jews moved because they were being persecuted in Europe, and also because they believed Palestine to be their ancient homeland and Jerusalem their holy city.
5. One effect was discord between Arabs and Jews. Another was the establishment of Israel as a nation.

Resource Directory

Teaching Resources

Cooperative Learning Activity in the Unit 6 Teaching Resources, pp. 111–113

Chapter Tests Forms A and B in the Unit 6 Teaching Resources, pp. 141–145

Guide to the Essentials, Ch. 25 Test, p. 112

Other Print Resources

Chapter Tests with ExamView® Test Bank, Ch. 25

Technology

ExamView® Test Bank CD-ROM, Ch. 25

Resource Pro® CD-ROM

Chapter 26 Planning Guide

Resource Manager

	CORE INSTRUCTION	READING/SKILLS
Chapter-Level Resources	**Teaching Resources** Program Overview Pacing Charts **Technology** Resource Pro® CD-ROM Companion Web site, phschool.com • eTeach	**Technology** Social Studies Skills Tutor CD-ROM Student Edition on Audio CD, Ch. 26
1 East Asia 1. Describe how the traditions of the past live on in modern East Asia. 2. Identify the similarities and differences in the populations of East Asian nations.	**Teaching Resources** **Unit 6** Classroom Manager, p. 35 Guided Reading and Review, p. 36	**Teaching Resources** Guide to the Essentials, p. 113 **Technology** Section Reading Support Transparencies
2 Southeast Asia 1. Explain how the cultural heritage of Southeast Asia is reflected in religion and the arts. 2. Explain how mineral wealth is used to support an Islamic heritage in Southeast Asia.	**Teaching Resources** **Unit 6** Classroom Manager, p. 38 Guided Reading and Review, p. 39	**Teaching Resources** Guide to the Essentials, p. 114 **Technology** Section Reading Support Transparencies
3 South Asia 1. Identify two religions that have roots in South Asia. 2. Describe the challenges of religious diversity in South Asia. 3. Explain how many languages spoken in South Asia are related.	**Teaching Resources** **Unit 6** Classroom Manager, p. 41 Guided Reading and Review, p. 42	**Teaching Resources** Guide to the Essentials, p. 115 Social Studies and Geography Skills, p. 60 **Technology** Section Reading Support Transparencies
4 Southwest Asia 1. Explain why there are so many cultures in Southwest Asia. 2. Identify three religions that have roots in Southwest Asia	**Teaching Resources** **Unit 6** Classroom Manager, p. 44 Guided Reading and Review, p. 45 Chapter Summary, p. 47 Vocabulary, p. 48 Reteaching, p. 49	**Teaching Resources** **Unit 6** Critical Thinking, p. 51 Guide to the Essentials, p. 116 **Technology** Section Reading Support Transparencies

ENRICHMENT / PRE-AP

Teaching Resources
Primary Sources and Literature Readings

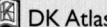

Other Print Resources
DK Atlas

Technology
World Video Explorer: Cultures of Asia and the South Pacific, Daily Life: India, A Trip to Jerusalem
Companion Web site, phschool.com

Teaching Resources
Outline Maps, pp. 39–40, 41–42

Technology
Color Transparencies 115, 137-140
Passport to the World CD-ROM

Teaching Resources
Outline Maps, p. 43

Technology
Color Transparencies 122

Teaching Resources
Outline Maps, pp. 36–37, 38

Technology
Color Transparencies 126, 144, 145

Teaching Resources
Unit 6
Enrichment, p. 50
Cooperative Learning Activity, pp. 115–117
Outline Maps, pp. 28–29

Technology
Color Transparencies 133

ASSESSMENT

Prentice Hall Assessment System

Core Assessment
Chapter Tests with ExamView® Test Bank, Ch. 26
ExamView® Test Bank CD-ROM, Ch. 26

Standardized Test Preparation
Diagnose and Prescribe
Diagnostic Tests for Middle Grades Social Studies Skills
Review and Reteach
Review Book for World Studies
Practice and Assess
Test-taking Strategies with Transparencies for Middle Grades Test Prep Book
Test-taking Strategies Posters

Teaching Resources
Unit 6
Section Quizzes, pp. 37, 40, 43, and 46
Chapter Tests, pp. 146–151

Technology
Companion Web site, phschool.com
Ch. 26 Self-Test

World Video Explorer
Each region of the world is explored through regional flyovers and investigative field trips. Case study segments give students an in-depth view of the history, economy, government, and culture of a key place in each region. Case studies include Nigeria, Mexico, China, British Columbia, and the Czech Republic.

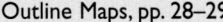

In Your Classroom

CUSTOMIZE FOR INDIVIDUAL NEEDS

Gifted and Talented

Teacher's Edition
- Past and Present, p. 489

Teaching Resources
- Enrichment, p. 50
- Primary Sources and Literature Readings

Honors/Pre-AP

Teacher's Edition
- Past and Present, p. 489

Teaching Resources
- Critical Thinking, p. 51
- Primary Sources and Literature Readings

ESL

Teacher's Edition
- Language Arts, p. 492

Teaching Resources
- Guided Reading and Review, pp. 36, 39, 42, and 45
- Vocabulary, p. 48
- Reteaching, p. 49
- Guide to the Essentials, pp. 113–116
- Social Studies and Geography Skills, p. 60

Technology
- Social Studies Skills Tutor CD-ROM
- Section Reading Support Transparencies

Less Proficient Readers

Teacher's Edition
- Language Arts, p. 492

Teaching Resources
- Guided Reading and Review, pp. 36, 39, 42, and 45
- Vocabulary, p. 48
- Reteaching, p. 49
- Guide to the Essentials, pp. 113–116
- Social Studies and Geography Skills, p. 60

Technology
- Social Studies Skills Tutor CD-ROM
- Section Reading Support Transparencies

Less Proficient Writers

Teacher's Edition
- Language Arts, p. 492

Teaching Resources
- Guided Reading and Review, pp. 36, 39, 42, and 45
- Vocabulary, p. 48
- Guide to the Essentials, pp. 113–116

Technology
- Social Studies Skills Tutor CD-ROM
- Section Reading Support Transparencies

DORLING KINDERSLEY

At the end of each unit, you will find information adapted from Dorling Kindersley's *Illustrated Children's Encyclopedia* that connects to the region being studied and to one of the seven content strands. In addition, your resources include Dorling Kindersley's *Atlas*, which contains valuable information about countries from around the world.

TEACHER'S EDITION INDEX

CHAPTER 26 PACING SUGGESTIONS

For 90-minute Blocks

See suggestions in the Teaching Resources Pacing Charts for Chapter 26. Use Color Transparencies 115, 122, 126, 133, 137–140, 144–145.

Running Out of Time?

See the Guide to the Essentials, pp. 113–116.

INTERDISCIPLINARY LINKS

Middle Grades Math: Tools for Success

Course 1, Lesson 1-2, **Make a Table**
Course 2, Lesson 10-1, **Using a Number Line**
Course 1, Lesson 11-6, **Independent Events**
Course 2, Lesson 5-2, **Adding and Subtracting Fractions**
Course 2, Lesson 7-8, **Circle Graphs**
Course 2, Lesson 11-7, **Symmetry and Reflections**

Science Explorer

Cells and Heredity, Lesson 4-3, **Advances in Genetics**

Prentice Hall Literature

Copper, Haiku
Bronze, Ribbons; Three Haiku by Basho
Bronze, The Hummingbird that Lived Through Winter

BIBLIOGRAPHY

For the Teacher

Goldman, Elizabeth. *Believers: Spiritual Leaders of the World.* Oxford University, 1996.

Illustrated Dictionary of Religions. Dorling Kindersley, 2001.

Stepanchuk, Carol. *Red Eggs and Dragon Boats: Celebrating Chinese Festivals.* Pacific View, 1994.

Vuong, Lynette Dyer. *Sky Legends of Vietnam.* HarperCollins, 1993.

For the Student

Easy

Reynolds, Jan. *Mongolia: Vanishing Cultures.* Harcourt, 1994.

Average

O'Connor, Karen. *A Kurdish Family.* Lerner, 1996.

Challenging

Stewart, Whitney. *The Fourteenth Dalai Lama: Spiritual Leader of Tibet.* Lerner, 1996.

Wilson, Colin. *Atlas of Holy Places & Sacred Sites.* Dorling Kindersley, 2001.

Literature Connection

Singer, Isaac Bashevis. *Zlateh the Goat, and Other Stories.* HarperCollins, 1996.

Yep, Laurence. *The Shell Woman and the King: A Chinese Folktale.* Dial, 1993.

Take It to the NET

The World Explorer companion Web site, found on **phschool.com**, offers activities for exploring geographical, historical, and cultural resources on the Internet. It also provides on-line links for key content and all Section and Chapter Assessment activities.

The **Teacher site** also provides teachers with regional data and ideas for student research and activities.

Students can use the **Student site** to find chapter-by-chapter Internet resource links and to access Self-Tests.

CHAPTER 26

Connecting to the Guiding Questions

In this chapter, students will read about the cultures of Asia. Content in this chapter corresponds to the following Guiding Questions outlined in the beginning of the unit.

- How has history and the achievements of historic figures influenced life in Asia today?
- How has religion affected the way Asian societies have developed?
- How do Asian governments compare with each other and with the government of the United States?
- How does participation in the political process differ in Asia and in the United States?

Using the Literature Activities

The author of *Sadako and the Thousand Paper Cranes* was living in Japan when she heard Sadako's story and decided to retell it in a story for American children.

- Students' stories should be based on Japanese legends and should be updated with modern characters and plots.
- Allow students to experiment with different origami shapes and figures.

Heterogeneous Groups

The following activities are suitable for heterogeneous groups.

Class Discussion

Past and Present, p. 489

Interdisciplinary Connections

Language Arts, p. 492

eTeach

Be sure to check out this month's discussion with a Master Teacher. Go to **phschool.com**.

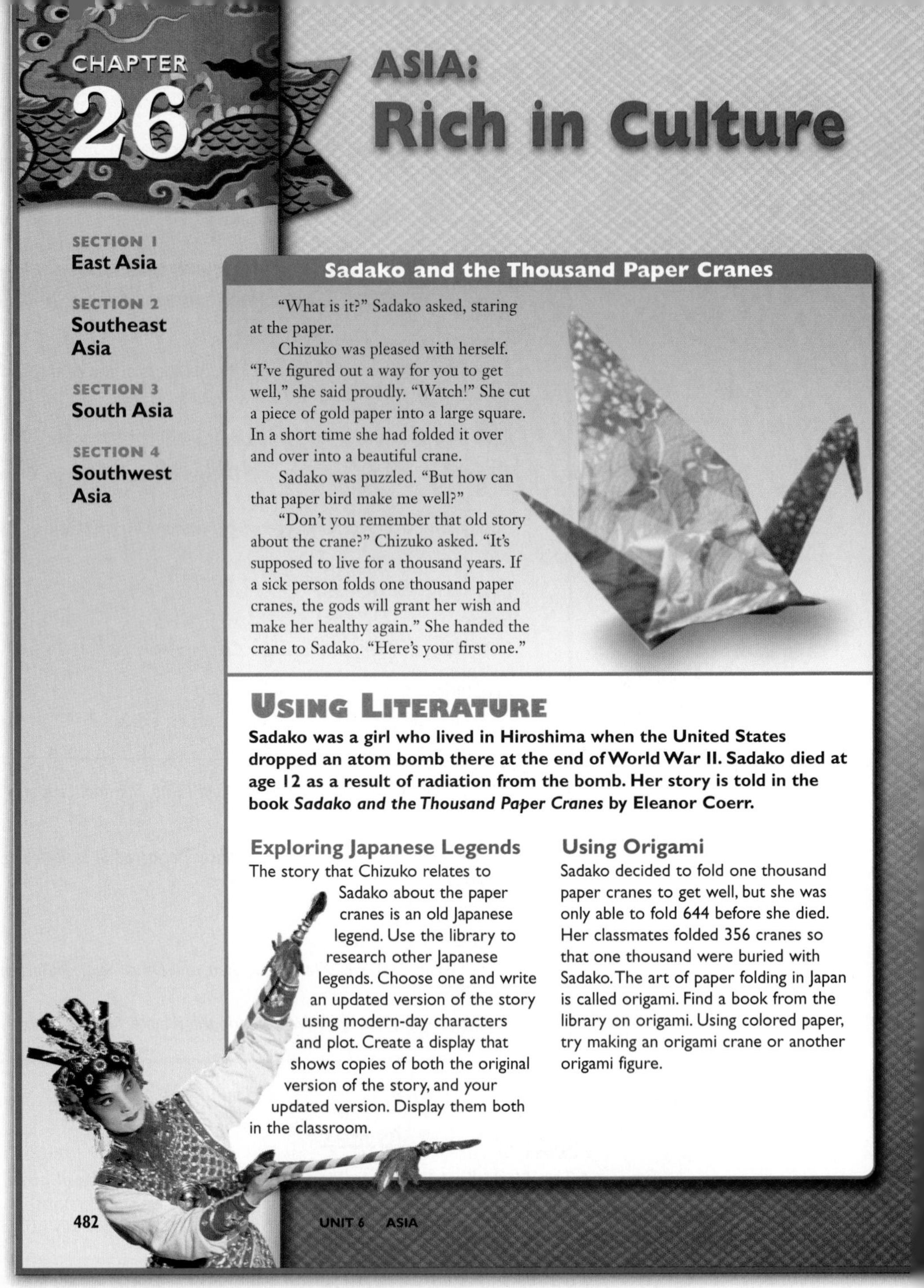

CHAPTER 26

ASIA: Rich in Culture

Sadako and the Thousand Paper Cranes

"What is it?" Sadako asked, staring at the paper.

Chizuko was pleased with herself. "I've figured out a way for you to get well," she said proudly. "Watch!" She cut a piece of gold paper into a large square. In a short time she had folded it over and over into a beautiful crane.

Sadako was puzzled. "But how can that paper bird make me well?"

"Don't you remember that old story about the crane?" Chizuko asked. "It's supposed to live for a thousand years. If a sick person folds one thousand paper cranes, the gods will grant her wish and make her healthy again." She handed the crane to Sadako. "Here's your first one."

USING LITERATURE

Sadako was a girl who lived in Hiroshima when the United States dropped an atom bomb there at the end of World War II. Sadako died at age 12 as a result of radiation from the bomb. Her story is told in the book *Sadako and the Thousand Paper Cranes* by Eleanor Coerr.

Exploring Japanese Legends

The story that Chizuko relates to Sadako about the paper cranes is an old Japanese legend. Use the library to research other Japanese legends. Choose one and write an updated version of the story using modern-day characters and plot. Create a display that shows copies of both the original version of the story, and your updated version. Display them both in the classroom.

Using Origami

Sadako decided to fold one thousand paper cranes to get well, but she was only able to fold 644 before she died. Her classmates folded 356 cranes so that one thousand were buried with Sadako. The art of paper folding in Japan is called origami. Find a book from the library on origami. Using colored paper, try making an origami crane or another origami figure.

482 UNIT 6 ASIA

Resource Directory

Teaching Resources

Primary Sources and Literature Readings extend content with a selection related to the concepts in this chapter.

Other Print Resources

DK Atlas

Technology

Cultures of Asia and the Pacific, from the World Video Explorer, enhances understanding of the many cultures of Asia.

Daily Life: India, from the World Video Explorer, enhances understanding of daily life in rural and urban India.

A Trip to: Jerusalem, from the World Video Explorer, enhances understanding of Jerusalem as the birthplace of three world religions.

Student Edition on Audio CD, Ch. 26

SECTION 1

East Asia

BEFORE YOU READ

READING FOCUS

1. How does East Asia's past affect modern-day culture?
2. What similarities and differences in population exist within East Asia?

KEY TERMS

commune
dialect
nomad
homogeneous

NOTE TAKING

Copy the chart below. As you read the section, fill in the chart with details of how each nation blends tradition with modern practice.

Country	Mix of Old and New
China	
Korea	
Japan	

MAIN IDEA

In East Asia, the past influences modern-day expressions of culture, whether in Communist China or technology-based Japan, and similarities and differences among nations are shown in the ethnic make-up of their populations.

Setting the Scene

The Chinese game *weiqi* (way chee) has ancient cultural roots. One player has 180 black stones standing for night. The other has 180 white stones standing for day. The goal is to surround and capture the opponent's stones. But to the Chinese, *weiqi* is more than a game. For centuries, Buddhists have used it to discipline the mind and study behavior. Masters can look at a game record to see exactly when players became too greedy and doomed themselves to defeat. Today, you can see people playing this ancient game in any park in China.

Tradition Amid Change

In East Asia, tradition mixes with change. Businesspeople in Western suits greet each other with a bow. Ancient palaces stand among skyscrapers. In Japan, China, and the Koreas, reminders of the past mingle with activities of the present.

The Ideal Family

CULTURE The Chinese government uses billboard advertising to encourage people to limit the size of their families. **Critical Thinking** Why do you think the Chinese government wants people to have small families?

CHAPTER 26 ASIA: RICH IN CULTURE 483

Resource Directory

Teaching Resources

Classroom Manager in the Unit 6 Teaching Resources, p. 35

Guided Reading and Review in the Unit 5 Teaching Resources, p. 36

Guide to the Essentials, p. 113

Technology

Section Reading Support Transparencies

Passport to the World CD-ROM This interactive CD-ROM allows students to explore each region of the world. Students view regional videos, take a photo tour, and explore a historical timeline. Students record their travels in an Explorer's Journal, and receive passport stamps when they pass regional quizzes.

SECTION 1

Lesson Objectives

1. Describe how the traditions of the past live on in modern East Asia.
2. Identify the similarities and differences in the populations of East Asian nations.

Lesson Plan

1 Engage

Warm-Up Activity

Remind students that the United States has influenced many countries around the world by exporting its movies, TV programs, music, clothing, technology, and business methods. Have students discuss how these phenomena can change life in other countries.

Activating Prior Knowledge

Discuss some of the ways in which students keep connections with their families' pasts. Prompt the discussion by mentioning items such as photographs, home movies, letters, and mementos. Discuss why people desire a link with their pasts.

Answers to...

CRITICAL THINKING

China wants to limit population growth.

Lesson Plan continued

❷ Explore

Have students read Section 1 and make a chart contrasting the traditional and the modern in China, Japan, and the two Koreas. Discuss the long-standing traditions in East Asia and what value they have today. Point out that of all the countries in East Asia, China has made the greatest break with its past. Have students list some ways in which China, under the Communists, has broken with its past political, economic, and social systems. Discuss why the communist leaders want their people to make a break with the past.

❸ Teach

Invite students to work with a partner to create a quiz of five questions on the main ideas in Section 1. Then have pairs exchange their quizzes with another pair and answer the questions in writing. Suggest that they return papers to the quiz writers for grading. The quiz takers should note whether the questions were fair and clear and covered the main ideas. This activity should take about 25 minutes.

Questions for Discussion

HISTORY How did the Han dynasty affect the ethnic make-up of China?

The Han dynasty existed throughout central and eastern China. About 19 of every 20 Chinese people can trace their ancestry to the Han. The minority ethnic groups live mainly in the western parts of China.

CULTURE What are some of the ways the Japanese preserve their cultural heritage?

Many Japanese follow traditional customs at home, such as wearing kimonos and sitting on floor mats to have their dinner. Traditional arts and crafts are also preserved through governmental programs.

CULTURE This woman from Tibet, in the western part of China, reflects the tradition of her ethnic group in her headdress, jewelry, and the way she carries her baby. **Critical Thinking** In what ways do the clothes you wear reflect the traditions of your culture or ethnic group?

Communism Brings Change to China When the Communists came into power in 1949, they made major changes in the Chinese way of life. To begin with, the government created **communes,** communities in which land is held in common and where members live and work together. Chinese farmers were accustomed to living in family groups that worked together in small fields, so they resisted the communes. Food production fell, and China suffered terrible food shortages. Only when the government allowed some private ownership did food production grow.

The Communists also tried to slow China's population growth by attacking the idea of large families. Here, they had more success. Chinese couples are supposed to wait until their late twenties to marry. They are not supposed to have more than one child per family. Chinese families with only one child receive special privileges.

The mixture of old and new affects the lives of all Chinese. Even the cities retain aspects of the old China, as the streets are filled with three-wheeled cabs pedaled like tricycles. Tiny shops sell traditional cures made from herbs and exist alongside modern hospitals.

Changing Korea In Korea, daily life is affected by long-standing traditions. A family looks after the welfare of all its members. In rural areas, grandparents, parents, aunts, and uncles may live in one household. In the cities, a family is usually just parents and children.

As in China, modern ways are more popular in urban areas. Most Koreans wear modern clothes and save their traditional dress of trousers or a long skirt with a long jacket for holidays. Earlier, Korean women had few opportunities. Today, they can work and vote.

Japan's Blend of Old and New Japanese work at computers in skyscrapers and ride home on speedy trains. Once they reach home, however, they may follow traditional customs and change into kimonos, or robes and sit on mats at a low table to have dinner. Japanese students dress like students in the United States, though some wear the headbands of samurai warriors to show that they are getting ready for a challenge.

Answers to...

CRITICAL THINKING

Answers will vary. Encourage students to give specific examples of the clothes and the culture or ethnic group they reflect.

Resource Directory

Teaching Resources

Outline Maps, East Asia, pp. 39–40; China, p. 41; Japan and Korea, p. 42

Technology

Color Transparencies 115 East Asia: Physical-Political; **137–140** Fine Arts from East Asia

The Japanese try hard to preserve the past. For example, some years ago, the Japanese saw that traditional arts and crafts were dying out, so the government began offering lifetime salaries to some artists. Their main task is to teach young people who will keep the ancient arts alive.

Similarities and Differences in Population

One culture dominates within each East Asian country. Distinct subcultures persist in different regions of China because of its tremendous ethnic diversity.

China: The Han and Others About 19 of every 20 Chinese people trace their ancestry to the Han, the people of China's second dynasty. As you can see on the map below, the Han live mostly in eastern and central China. Although they have a common language, they speak different **dialects,** or forms of a single language, from region to region. The other Chinese come from 55 different minority groups who live mainly in the western parts of China.

China: Ethnic Groups

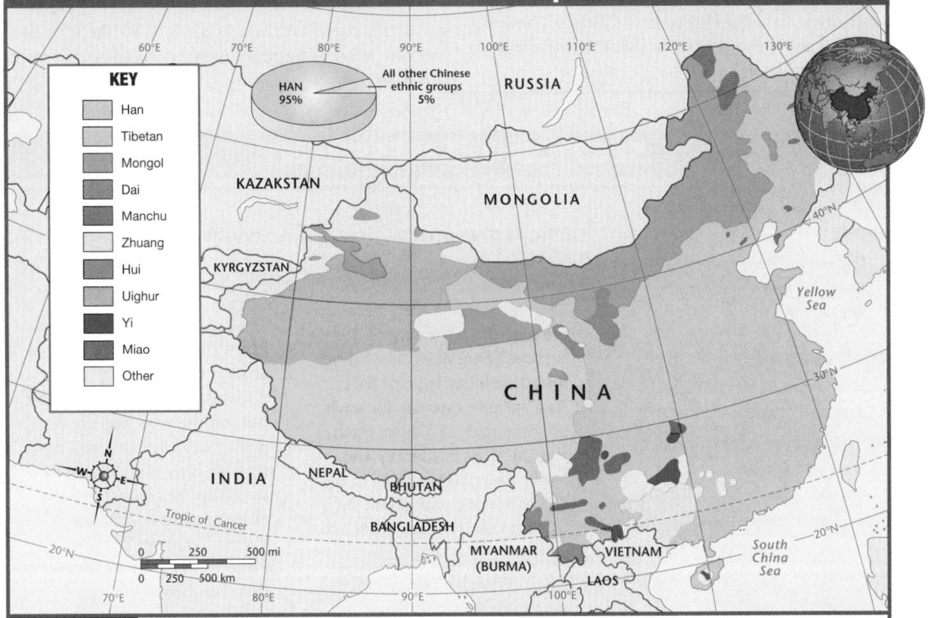

CULTURE China is one of the most ethnically diverse nations in the world. Even so, 95 percent of the Chinese people are from the Han ethnic group.

Map Study Where do most Mongols live? Which group do you think has more political power in China, the Tibetans or the Han? Explain.

❹ Assess/Reteach

See the answers to the Section 1 Assessment. You may also use students' quizzes for assessment.

Acceptable quizzes cover the main points of the section.

Commendable quizzes cover the main points of the section and contain at least one critical thinking question.

Outstanding quizzes show originality and contain several critical thinking questions.

HISTORY

Mongols

Under the leadership of Genghis Khan, the Mongols invaded China from the north during the early 1200s. They were disciplined and fierce fighters who conquered China and much of Asia. The conquest of China was completed by Genghis Khan's grandson Kublai Khan, who established the Yuan dynasty that ruled China for more than a century. Mongol rule ended in 1368, when the Chinese restored rule under the Ming emperors. The Mongols were the first foreigners to control China.

SKILLS MINI LESSON

Recognizing Bias

You might **introduce** the skill by telling students that biased materials tell a story from only one point of view. In order to know whether what they are reading presents a fair picture, students need to be able to recognize bias in writing. To help students **practice** the skill, provide several news articles and editorials about Japan, China, and Korea. Assist students as they work in pairs to find

- opinions that cannot be proved;
- words and phrases that carry a hidden meaning or give a positive or negative impression;
- information that might present a second or different perspective; and
- the overall tone of the writing—positive, negative, or neutral.

Encourage students to **apply** this skill as they read materials for research projects.

Answers to...

MAP STUDY

Most Mongols live in the part of China that borders eastern and southern Mongolia. The Han are probably more politically powerful because they are more numerous than the Tibetans.

SECTION I ASSESSMENT

AFTER YOU READ

1. (a) community in which land is held in common and where members live and work together (b) form of a language (c) person who has no settled home (d) very similar
2. Students' answers should include the idea that in Japan and South Korea traditional dress, food, holidays, forms of art and music, medicine, and religion exist side-by-side with more recent influences from the West. In China, an effort has been made to turn away from the past and to adopt a modern lifestyle that differs from the West in its political and economic system (communism).
3. Historians believe that Koreans are descended from groups of Mongolian nomads who eventually lost their separate traditions and formed a homogeneous group. Japan's population is homogeneous because the country isolated itself from the rest of the world for a long time.
4. Outlines should accurately identify ethnic distribution in each nation, along with examples of traditional and modern life practices.
5. Students should recognize that China is the most populous country in the world. The Chinese government wishes to control population growth so that there will be enough food and jobs for all citizens.
6. You may wish to let students choose a particular Asian country to do their essays or posters on.

AS YOU READ

Draw Inferences What do you think it would be like to live in a country with a homogeneous population?

Korea and Japan: Few Minorities Historians believe that the ancient Koreans were descended from many different groups of **nomads** from Mongolia. Nomads are people who have no settled home.

They move from place to place in search of water and grazing for their herds. Over centuries, these groups lost their separate traditions. They formed one **homogeneous** (hoh muh JEE nee us) group. That is, the group's members were very similar. Today, even with the division of Korea into two countries, the population is homogeneous. There are few minority groups.

Because it was an island nation and it isolated itself from the world for part of its history, Japan has one of the most homogenous populations on the Earth. Nearly all of the people belong to the same ethnic group, a group that shares language, religion, and cultural traditions. Minority groups are few. One notable minority group is the Ainu (EYE noo), who may have been Japan's first inhabitants. Small numbers of Koreans and Chinese also live in Japan. However, Japan has strict rules on immigration. It is hard for anyone who is not Japanese by birth to become a citizen.

CULTURE These Ainu women are performing together in traditional dress. They have painted their lips in a traditional style as well. The Ainu live in parts of the Japanese island of Hokkaido. **Critical Thinking** What are some challenges that the Ainu might face as a minority group in Japan?

SECTION I ASSESSMENT

AFTER YOU READ

RECALL

1. Define: (a) commune, (b) dialect, (c) nomad, (d) homogeneous

COMPREHENSION

2. How does East Asia reflect past and present traditions?
3. Why are the populations of Korea and Japan homogeneous?

CRITICAL THINKING AND WRITING

4. **Exploring the Main Idea** Review the Main Idea statement at the beginning of this section. Then, write an outline for a three-day tour of East Asia. Include one day for each of these nations: China, Japan, and the Koreas. Identify and briefly describe elements of old and new along with ethnic distribution that visitors might see.
5. **Identifying Cause and Effect** Write a paragraph explaining why you think the Communists wanted to slow China's population growth.

ACTIVITY

Take It to the NET

6. **Understanding Buddhism** More than 300 million people around the world practice Buddhism. Using the information on the web site, create a poster or write an essay describing how the philosophy of Buddhism has influenced the cultures of Asia. Visit the World Explorer: People, Places, and Cultures section of **phschool.com** for help in completing this activity.

Answers to...

AS YOU READ

Answers will vary. Students may say that it would not be as interesting as living a country with cultural diversity.

CRITICAL THINKING

Students may say that the Ainu might experience prejudice and oppression as a minority group in Japan.

Resource Directory

Teaching Resources

Section Quiz in the Unit 6 Teaching Resources, p. 37

SECTION 2

Southeast Asia

BEFORE YOU READ

READING FOCUS

1. How is Southeast Asia's cultural heritage reflected in religion and the arts?
2. How is mineral wealth used to support an Islamic heritage in Southeast Asia?

KEY TERMS

The Ramayana

KEY PLACES

Brunei

MAIN IDEA

Religion, architecture, and the arts reflect a mix of tradition and change in Southeast Asia.

NOTE TAKING

Copy the chart below. As you read the section, fill in the chart to give examples of how the cultural heritage of Southeast Asia is reflected in modern-day life.

	Seen in
Cultural Heritage	
Religious Heritage	

Setting the Scene

Water puppet shows started in Vietnam centuries ago. With the pond for a stage, a puppeteer guides wooden figures so that they appear to wade through the water. The puppets are attached to rods and strings hidden under water. Audiences sit at the water's edge and stage settings of trees and clouds are placed on the pond.

At the same time, people in Southeast Asia enjoy the thrill of modern conveniences, like motorbikes, while retaining the beauty of traditional arts, like water puppet shows. Religion and architecture, like the arts, reflect a mix of tradition and change in Southeast Asia.

Modern Conveniences

CULTURE These young Vietnamese women enjoy traveling by motorbike. These vehicles are cheaper than cars and speedier than bicycles. **Critical Thinking** Use the description of water puppet shows and the photograph to identify one contrast that a visitor to Vietnam might observe. Can you think of others?

Arts and Religion in Cambodia

Most Cambodians are Buddhists, yet the cultural heritage of Hinduism is reflected in Cambodian arts. In the capital city of Phnom Pen, Cambodia's Royal Ballet has performed ***The Ramayana,*** a Hindu epic poem, since the 1700s. In Cambodian villages, this poem often is read aloud or acted out by shadow puppets.

Resource Directory

Teaching Resources

Classroom Manager in the Unit 6 Teaching Resources, p. 38

Guided Reading and Review in the Unit 6 Teaching Resources, p. 39

Guide to the Essentials, p. 114

Technology

Section Reading Support Transparencies

SECTION 2

Lesson Objectives

1. Explain how the cultural heritage of Southeast Asia is reflected in religion and the arts.
2. Explain how mineral wealth is used to support an Islamic heritage in Southeast Asia.

Lesson Plan

1 Engage

Warm-Up Activity

Ask students whether the girls in the picture look like their image of teens in Southeast Asia. Discuss ways in which these girls' lives compare to the lives of teenagers in the United States.

Activating Prior Knowledge

Ask students to think about ways in which their lives reflect their heritage, perhaps their religious heritage or the culture in which their grandparents were born. Lead a discussion about how traditions, customs, and religious practices in a family reflect its cultural heritage.

2 Explore

Distribute outline maps of Asia. Ask students to draw a compass rose on the map. Have them look to the southeast and locate Myanmar, Thailand, Laos, Cambodia, Vietnam, Malaysia, the Philippines, and Indonesia. Have students label these countries. Suggest that, as they read Section 2, students use their maps to locate the countries discussed. This activity should take about 15 minutes.

Answers to...

CRITICAL THINKING

A visitor to Vietnam might observe the contrast between old and new.

Lesson Plan continued

3 Teach

Ask students to suppose that they have just spent a week in Southeast Asia. Ask them to write an essay about the experience. Emphasize to students that they should include in their essays examples of the cultural and religious heritage of the people of this region. Encourage students to include specific examples from the text. This activity should take about 30 minutes.

Questions for Discussion

CULTURE **How is Hinduism reflected most in Cambodian society?**

Hinduism is reflected in Cambodian arts.

CITIZENSHIP **In return for free health care and free education, what are the citizens of Brunei expected to do?**

They are expected to obey the government ruled by decree of Sir Hassanal Bolkiah.

4 Assess/Reteach

See answers to the Section 2 Assessment. You may also assess the students' essays.

Acceptable essays include accurate descriptions of the cultural and religious heritage of the people of Southeast Asia.

Commendable essays include accurate descriptions and examples of the cultural and religious heritage of the people of Southeast Asia.

Outstanding essays include accurate descriptions and specific examples of the cultural and religious heritage of the people of the region to create a vivid picture of Southeast Asia.

Answers to...

CRITICAL THINKING

Possible answer: By providing food, clothing, teachers, health-care workers, and opportunities for immigration

Displaced by War

HISTORY In the mid-1970s, civil war forced thousands of Cambodians to leave their homes and move to refugee camps near the border of Thailand and Cambodia. These children are in a refugee camp in Thailand.

Critical Thinking How can nations such as the United States help refugees like these children who were displaced by war?

Hindus believe that *The Ramayana*, completed in about 4 A.D., was revealed to its author by Brahma, the god of creation. The epic tells of a prince named Rama, who is ousted from his throne, and his beloved wife Sita, who is kidnapped by a demon king. *The Ramayana* is told and retold, in many different versions, throughout India and Southeast Asia. A tale of intrigue, betrayal, love, and loss, it goes beyond the boundaries of societies and conveys universal themes.

Today many Cambodians—about 90 percent—practice Buddhism, although at one time the Cambodian government discouraged the practice of religion. Two key ideas of Buddhism are that life includes suffering and that people live, die, and are reborn. These ideas may have helped Cambodians make sense of their recent history, during which many innocent people suffered and died.

Resource Directory

Teaching Resources

Outline Maps, Southeast Asia, p. 43

Technology

Color Transparencies 122 Southeast Asia: Physical-Political Map

A Heritage Maintained

The nations of Southeast Asia are rich in minerals. Indonesia, Myanmar, and the small kingdom of **Brunei** contain large deposits of oil. Brunei, on the northwestern coast of the island of Borneo, is only about the size of the state of Delaware. Yet this tiny nation boasts the world's biggest palace, the home of the Sultan of Brunei. This building covers 50 acres (20 hectares)—about the area of 36 football fields—and has 1,788 rooms.

Although not all of its people are Muslims, Brunei is an Islamic nation. It has used its oil wealth to sustain its people and to support Islamic traditions. The people of Brunei receive free health care, free education, and high wages on which they do not pay taxes. In return, they are expected to obey the government ruled by decree of Sultan Sir Hassanal Bolkiah.

Brunei's religious heritage is reflected in the sultan's government, which strictly enforces Islamic customs and traditions, and in its architecture, which reflects the nation's adherence to Islam.

The Sultan Omar Ali Saifuddin Mosque

CULTURE This mosque in Brunei, completed in 1958, is a modern-day example of classical Islamic architecture. With its distinctive gold dome, the mosque dominates the city skyline. **Critical Thinking** Give an example of a building in your state or community that reflects an aspect of Americans' cultural heritage.

SECTION 2 ASSESSMENT

AFTER YOU READ

RECALL

1. Identify: Brunei
2. Define: *The Ramayana*

COMPREHENSION

3. How have key ideas of Buddhism helped Cambodians make sense of their recent history?
4. Give an example of how Brunei uses its mineral wealth to support its Islamic heritage.

CRITICAL THINKING AND WRITING

5. **Exploring the Main Idea** Review the Main Idea statement at the beginning of this section. Then, imagine that you are visiting a country in Southeast Asia. Write a journal entry describing sights that reflect a cultural mix of past and present.
6. **Making Inferences and Drawing Conclusions** Why do you think the Hindu epic *The Ramayana* is so popular in Cambodia, an overwhelmingly Buddhist country?

ACTIVITY

7. **Writing a Poem** Imagine that you have been displaced from your home by war. Write a poem describing your feelings about your present life and your hopes for the future.

Resource Directory

Teaching Resources

Section Quiz in the Unit 6 Teaching Resources, p. 40

ACTIVITY

Class Discussion

Past and Present Have students research and find additional examples of how past and present mingle in Southeast Asian cultures that are not treated in the text. You might assign topics such as Philippine music and literature, Malaysian decorative art, Laotian dance, Thai dance and music, Myanmar architecture, and the classical dance traditions of Java and Bali (in Indonesia). Suggest that students consult a print or CD-ROM encyclopedia. Have students share the information that they find in a class discussion.

Verbal/Linguistic

SECTION 2 ASSESSMENT

AFTER YOU READ

1. Brunei is a small kingdom on the northwestern coast of the island of Borneo.
2. A Hindu epic told throughout India and Southeast Asia.
3. Buddhism leads them to expect suffering.
4. The use of oil revenues to support Brunei's Islamic heritage can be seen in architectural projects such as the Sultan Omar Ali Saifuddin Mosque.
5. Answers will vary but should include examples such as bicycles and motorbikes in Vietnam or modern buildings with classical Islamic design in Brunei.
6. Hindu culture took root in Cambodia during the Khmer empire.
7. Answers will vary. Accept all poems that indicate students have reflected thoughtfully on the subject matter.

Answers to...

CRITICAL THINKING

Answers will vary. Students will probably mention houses of worship, sectarian schools, courthouse, and so on.

CHAPTER 26 ASIA: RICH IN CULTURE 489

SECTION 3

Lesson Objectives

1. Identify two religions that have roots in South Asia.
2. Describe the challenges of religious diversity in South Asia.
3. Explain how many languages spoken in South Asia are related.

Lesson Plan

1 Engage

Warm-Up Activity

Have students pick one of the people in the photograph "A Religious Festival." Have them write a short description of the person addressing these questions: What is the person wearing? Where does he or she live? What language do you think the person speaks? What do you think he or she is doing?

Activating Prior Knowledge

Ask students to think about religions practiced by people in the United States. Pose these questions for discussion: Does religion affect culture in the United States? What religious holidays are also national holidays? What do the words "in God we trust," on U.S. currency, reveal about the nation's cultural heritage? Do Americans' religious beliefs affect their political views?

Answers to...

CRITICAL THINKING

Students may mention that religion seems to have a very public role in everyday life.

SECTION 3

South Asia

BEFORE YOU READ

READING FOCUS

1. What two religions have roots in South Asia?
2. What challenges does religious diversity present in South Asia?
3. How are many languages in South Asia related?

KEY PEOPLE

Siddhartha Gautama

MAIN IDEA

Many religions, including Islam and Sikhism, and languages are important in the politics and culture of South Asia.

NOTE TAKING

Copy this chart. As you read the section, complete the chart to show details about language and religion in South Asia. Add more ovals to the web as you go.

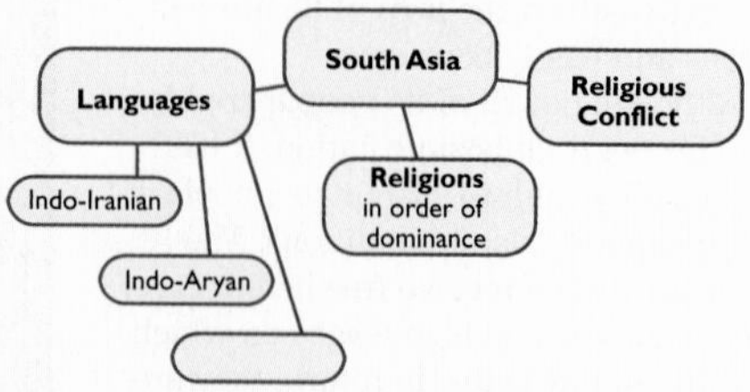

A Religious Festival

CULTURE The picture shows a religious festival in India. **Critical Thinking** What does the picture tell you about the role of religion in everyday life in South Asia?

Setting the Scene

When the Aryans invaded the Indus Valley between 2000 B.C. and 1500 B.C., they brought with them new ways of living. One of these divided people into three classes—priests, warriors, and ordinary working people. This system, known as the caste system, was based on Aryan religious writings called the Vedas (VAY duz). It became a central part of a new system of belief that also emerged from Aryan religious ideas and practices. This system of beliefs, Hinduism, is the world's oldest living religion.

Religions of South Asia

Of the two major world religions that developed in India, Hinduism by far has the most followers in the region today. Buddhism had its greatest following in India in the 200s B.C.

Resource Directory

Teaching Resources

Classroom Manager in the Unit 6 Teaching Resources, p. 41

Guided Reading and Review in the Unit 6 Teaching Resources, p. 42

Guide to the Essentials, p. 115

Technology

Section Reading Support Transparencies

Buddhism in India

HISTORY The religion founded by the Buddha (left) had its greatest following during the time of the Indian ruler Asoka. The stone lions (right) topped one of the pillars that Asoka set up all over India. Asoka had Buddhist writings carved on these pillars. After Asoka's death, Buddhism nearly died out in India, but missionaries carried the religion to Japan, Korea, China, and Vietnam.
Critical Thinking How is the spread of Buddhism a good example of cultural diffusion?

Hinduism Hinduism is unlike other major world religions. It does not have one single founder. However, it has many great religious thinkers. Also, Hindus worship many gods and goddesses, but they believe in a single spirit. To Hindus, the various gods and goddesses represent different parts of this spirit. As an old Hindu saying states: "God is one, but wise people know it by many names." Today, Hinduism is the national religion of India and has 700 million followers there.

Buddhism Buddhism, like Hinduism, developed in India. According to Buddhist tradition, its founder was a prince named **Siddhartha Gautama** (shid DAHR tuh goh TUH MUH). He was born in about 560 B.C., in present-day Nepal. Gautama was a Hindu of high caste who lived a privileged life, safe from hunger and disease.

When he was 29 years old, Gautama left home to learn about his kingdom. For the first time, he saw people who were hungry, sick, and poor. He became so unhappy that he gave up his wealth and pledged his life to finding the causes for people's suffering.

Eventually, Gautama found what he believed was the solution. He taught that people can be free of suffering if they give up selfish desires for power, wealth, and pleasure. He then became known as the Buddha, or "Enlightened One." People of all backgrounds, princes and ordinary people alike, flocked to hear his sermons.

For a while after the Buddha's death, Buddhism had a huge following in India. Over time, however, it almost completely died out there.

AS YOU READ
Monitor Your Reading Think of three questions you might ask about the teaching of the Buddha.

2 Explore

As they read the section text, have students trace on a world map the spread of Buddhism from Nepal to India and from India to East and Southeast Asia. Have them locate on the map the countries identified in the chart, Languages of South Asia, on page 493.

3 Teach

After reading the section text, urge students to formulate one question about an additional aspect of South Asian culture that interests them. (Possibilities include arts such as music, theater, dance, and film.) Have students find, read, and summarize an encyclopedia article that addresses their question. This activity should take about 30 minutes.

Questions for Discussion

CULTURE **What lasting effect did the Aryan invasion have on South Asia?**

The Aryans brought Hinduism to India, and the religion eventually spread to other parts of South Asia.

HISTORY **What did Siddhartha Gautama believe was the solution to people's suffering?**

He believed that people would be free from suffering if they gave up their selfish desires for power, wealth, and pleasure.

Resource Directory

Teaching Resources

Outline Maps, South Asia, pp. 36–37; India, p. 38

Technology

Color Transparencies 126 South Asia: Physical-Political Map

Answers to...

CRITICAL THINKING

Buddhism is a good example of cultural diffusion because it was spread from South Asia to other parts of Asia by Buddhist missionaries.

AS YOU READ

Questions will vary.

Lesson Plan continued

4 Assess/Reteach

See the answers to the Section 3 Assessment. You may also assess students' summaries.

Acceptable summaries include a clearly stated main idea and three details.

Commendable summaries show a link between the student's question and the summarized answer, while also providing succinct information on the topic.

Outstanding summaries incorporate vivid details and an eloquently stated main idea, along with a clear statement of how the information answers the student's original question.

ACTIVITY

Interdisciplinary Connections

Language Arts Remind students that, rather than the four seasons found in temperate climates, much of South Asia has a monsoon climate. Ask students to do research and then make a calendar showing the dry seasons and rainy seasons of India. Have them also find out how daily life is altered during the monsoon season. How do people dress? Store food? Keep appointments? Travel from one place to another? Students may present their information in an oral report, photo essay, or poster.

Verbal/Linguistic, Visual/Spatial

HISTORY

Tenzing Norgay (1914–1986)

On May 29, 1953 Tenzing Norgay of Nepal and Edmund Hillary of New Zealand were the first people to reach the summit of Mount Everest, the world's highest peak. Owing to the scarcity of oxygen at such high elevation, the celebration was brief. Tenzing ate a piece of cake, took a few photos, and—being a dutiful Buddhist—left an offering of food before he descended.

GOVERNMENT

India Welcomes Exiles

In 1950, Communist China invaded Tibet. Up until that time, Tibet had been an independent country ruled by the 14th Dalai Lama. Tibetan Buddhists consider the Dalai Lama to be the reincarnation of the first Dalai Lama and therefore the true spiritual and temporal ruler of Tibet. In 1959, the Dalai Lama and 100,000 followers fled Tibet and established a government-in-exile in India in an effort to preserve Tibet's religion and culture. In 1989, the Dalai Lama received the Nobel Prize for Peace for his nonviolent campaign to end Chinese occupation of Tibet.

The Challenge of Diversity

Today, about 80 percent of Indians are Hindus. Yet other religions remain important in Indian politics and culture. For example, Muslim traders brought Islam to India during the 700s A.D. and today about 14 percent of Indians are Muslim. Christianity and Sikhism are small but significant religious minorities in present-day India.

Armed conflict between religious groups endangers many people in India and presents a constant challenge to its government. Muslims and Hindus fight to control Kashmir, on the border between Pakistan and India. Sikhs have expressed their desire for more control of the Punjab area with terrorist attacks that are met by severe, sometimes brutal, reprisals by the Hindu-dominated government.

One Root, Many Languages

Just as two religions of South Asia—Buddhism and Hinduism—have common roots, so do many South Asian languages. They belong to a very large group of related

Indira Gandhi

HISTORY Indira Gandhi served as prime minister of India from 1966 to 1984. Conflict between the Indian government and Sikhs, a religious minority, led to Gandhi's death in 1984. She was assassinated after she ordered an attack on a temple held by armed Sikhs. **Critical Thinking** How does the experience of India reflect the problems and possibilities of a large nation with a diverse population? What similarities and differences can you identify between India and the United States?

Answers to...

CRITICAL THINKING

Possible answers: Because their country is so large and diverse in population, many Indians identify with their cultural and religious background much more strongly than with their nationality. Like India, the United States is a large and culturally diverse nation. Fewer languages are spoken in the United States than in India, and the United States has been an independent nation almost two hundred years longer.

Resource Directory

Teaching Resources

Social Studies and Geography Skills, Reading a Table, p. 60

Technology

Color Transparencies 144 *Buddha and Shiva Nataraja, Lord of the Dance* Fine Art; **145** Krishna Student Art

Languages of South Asia

Country	Major Languages
Afghanistan	Pashtu, Dari Persian, Turkic
Bangladesh	Bengali (official), English
Bhutan	Dzongkha (official), Gurung, Assamese
India	Hindi (official), Bengali, English, and 13 other languages
Nepal	Nepali (official) and many others
Pakistan	Urdu (official), English (official), Punjabi, Sindhi
Sri Lanka	Sinhalese (official), Tamil

CULTURE This chart shows the major languages spoken in South Asia. In India, for example, over 1,000 different languages and dialects are spoken. An official language is one chosen by a nation and used for government business. **Critical Thinking** Why do you think English is a major language in several South Asian countries?

languages which make up the Indo–Iranian branch of the Indo–European language group. Study the chart above to learn more about the languages spoken in South Asia.

Hindi, which is spoken mainly by South Asian Hindus, and Urdu, spoken mainly by South Asian Muslims, are dialects of this group.

More South Asian literature has been written in Bengali than in any other modern Indian language. Bengali is spoken in West Bengal, India, and throughout Bangladesh.

SECTION 3 ASSESSMENT

AFTER YOU READ

RECALL

1. Identify: Siddhartha Gautama

COMPREHENSION

2. Name two religions that have roots in South Asia.
3. Describe how religious diversity presents challenges to people who live in South Asia.
4. Explain how many languages spoken in South Asia are related.

CRITICAL THINKING AND WRITING

5. **Exploring the Main Idea** Review the Main Idea statement at the beginning of this section. Then, write a statement describing cultural heritage and diversity in South Asia, including specific examples.
6. **Making Predictions** Do you think the conflicts between different religious groups in South Asia will intensify or be resolved over time? Explain your thinking in a brief written prediction.
7. **Identifying Cause and Effect** Why do you think so many languages in South Asia have common roots? Write a paragraph to answer.

ACTIVITY

8. **Time Traveling** Locate your town on a map of the world showing time zones. Then, locate a city in South Asia such as Kathmandu, Nepal, or Kabul, Afghanistan. List that city's name and what time it is there when it is a) midnight, b) noon, and c) 5:00 p.m. in your town.

SECTION 3 ASSESSMENT

AFTER YOU READ

1. founder of Buddhism
2. Hinduism, Buddhism
3. Differing religious beliefs have led to different cultural identities and armed conflicts over control of territory within existing nations.
4. Many languages spoken in South Asia are part of the Indo–European language group.
5. South Asia is diverse in religion and language. Hinduism, Islam, Buddhism, and Sikhism are four of the religions practiced in South Asia. The many languages spoken in this region include Urdu and Hindi.
6. Possible answers: The conflicts will intensify as people's frustration increases; for example, as the dispute over Kashmir continues unresolved; The conflicts will find resolution as people get tired of fighting and want, even more than winning, to secure a peaceful future for their children.
7. Possible answer: South Asia has been invaded, conquered, settled, and inhabited by many different peoples over many years.
8. Answers will vary depending on the time zone in which students live.

Resource Directory

Teaching Resources

Section Quiz in the Unit 6 Teaching Resources, p. 43

Answers to...

CHART STUDY

English is a major language because much of South Asia was colonized by the British.

SECTION 4

Lesson Objectives

1. Explain why there are so many cultures in Southwest Asia.
2. Identify three religions that have roots in Southwest Asia.

Lesson Plan

1 Engage

Warm-Up Activity

Show students a large regional map of Southwest Asia. Have them focus on the countries and physical features that border the region. Discuss with students which cultures might have influenced the cultures of Southwest Asia. How might people from other areas have traveled to Southwest Asia?

Activating Prior Knowledge

Ask students to think about how they are affected by their culture, education, and part of the country in which they live. Pose these questions for discussion: How does your history affect the person you are today? How does your history make you a unique individual? Then, ask volunteers to list some ways to learn about a person's history.

2 Explore

While reading the section text, urge students to seek answers to questions such as the following: How do the location and size of Southwest Asia affect the cultures represented by its people? What religions link many cultures in the region?

Answers to...

CRITICAL THINKING

Answers will vary. Students may say that it would offer a welcome break to reflect and meditate; others may say it would be very intrusive.

SECTION 4

Southwest Asia

BEFORE YOU READ

1. Why are there so many cultures in Southwest Asia?
2. What three religions have roots in Southwest Asia?

KEY TERMS

muezzin
minaret

KEY PEOPLE AND PLACES

Abraham
Jerusalem
Jesus of Nazareth
Bethlehem
Muhammad
Mecca

MAIN IDEA

Three world religions—Christianity, Judaism, and Islam—and many different cultures have their roots in Southwest Asia, an area of great cultural diversity.

NOTE TAKING

Copy the diagram below. As you read the section, fill in the diagram to show some similarities and differences in three religions that have roots in Southwest Asia.

	Judaism	Islam	Christianity
birthplace			
holy city			
founder			
country of origin			
sacred text			

The Blue Mosque

CULTURE The mosque in the background is known as the Blue Mosque because of the blue tile decorating its interior. It is located in Istanbul, Turkey. The tall towers visible are the minarets, from which the muezzin calls Muslims to prayer. **Critical Thinking** What do you think it would be like to live in a place where everything stopped for prayer five times a day?

Setting the Scene

The sights and sounds of Islam are present everywhere in Southwest Asia. One sound is the call of the **muezzin** (moo EZ in), a person whose job it is to summon Muslims to pray from high atop the mosque in a **minaret.** Five times a day, wherever they are, Muslims stop what they are doing and pray.

Cultural Diversity

Southwest Asia's location has always made it an important link between Asia, Africa, and Europe. As a result, this region became a crossroad and hub of civilization. Throughout history, many empires have successively dominated the region. Most of these empires, such as the Hittite and Persian empires, originated in Southwest and Central Asia and they made lasting cultural contributions to the area. In addition, many of the people in this region were traders and traveled extensively throughout Asia, Africa, and Europe, which further promoted the cultural diffusion of ideas and traditions.

Resource Directory

Teaching Resources

Classroom Manager in the Unit 6 Teaching Resources, p. 44

Guided Reading and Review in the Unit 6 Teaching Resources, p. 45

Guide to the Essentials, p. 116

Technology

Section Reading Support Transparencies

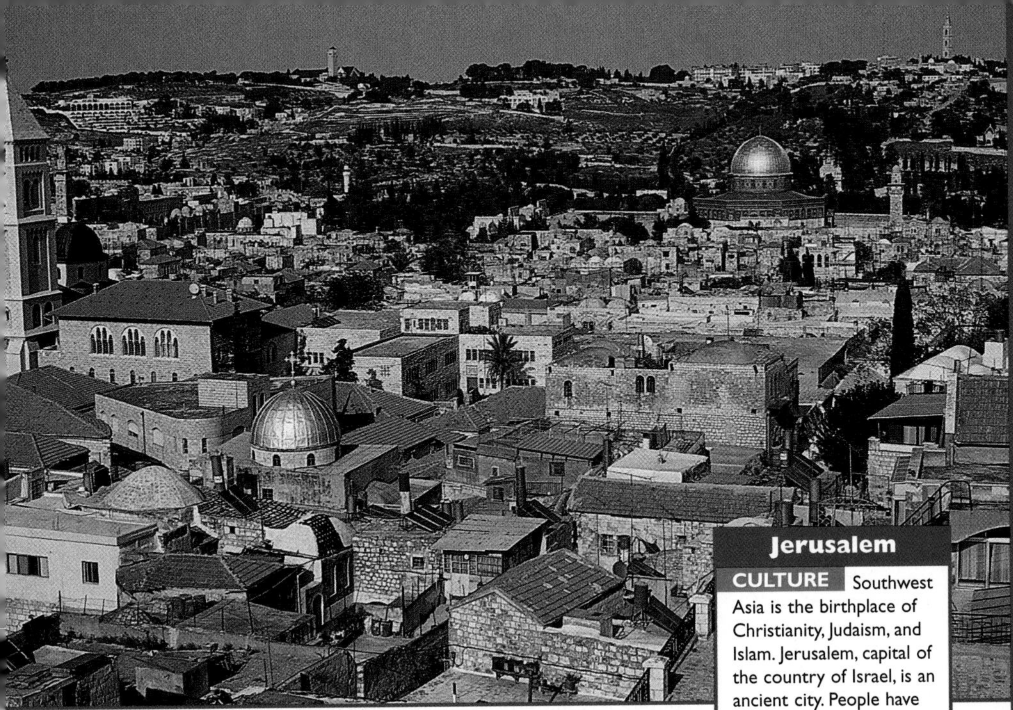

Jerusalem

CULTURE Southwest Asia is the birthplace of Christianity, Judaism, and Islam. Jerusalem, capital of the country of Israel, is an ancient city. People have been living there since 1800 B.C. Jerusalem is holy to Christians, Jews, and Muslims because events important to their religions took place there. To the left is the silver dome of a Christian church. The golden-domed building is called the Dome of the Rock. It stands over the rock from which Muslims believe the prophet Muhammad rose into heaven to speak with God.
Critical Thinking Do you think it is easy for three religions to share a holy city? Why or why not?

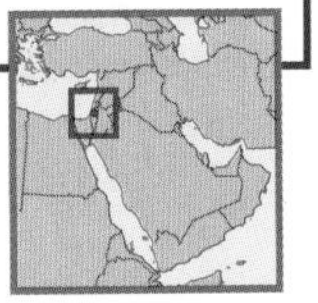

Birthplace of Three Religions

Christianity, Judaism, and Islam all developed in Southwest Asia. Judaism is believed to have started with **Abraham** over 3,000 years ago. Abraham and his family lived in Mesopotamia. According to the Torah, the collection of writings sacred to the Jews, God told Abraham to take his family west to another land called Canaan (present-day Israel). God promised Abraham that he would make him the father of a great nation. In return, Abraham promised that he and his descendants would worship only God. Today, **Jerusalem,** the capital of Israel, is a holy city for Jews.

The Rise of Christianity Christianity began as a movement within Judaism. Around 30 A.D., a young man called **Jesus of Nazareth** began preaching to his fellow Jews, encouraging people to turn to God and lead moral lives.

Christian teachings tell that Jesus was born in **Bethlehem,** a town just outside of Jerusalem considered to be holy for Christians. Some people believed that he was the messiah, and they followed him until he was arrested, tried, and executed in Jerusalem. Accounts of Jesus's life were later written down by his followers and now form an important part of the New Testament in the Christian Bible.

After the death of Jesus, his followers began to form small communities, living and praying together. They began referring to Jesus

Resource Directory

Teaching Resources

Outline Maps, Southwest Asia, pp. 28–29

Technology

Color Transparencies 133 Southwest Asia and North Africa: Physical-Political Map

3 Teach

Have students create two concept webs for Southwest Asia. One web shoud have religion at the center and the other, culture. Students should add features of each topic to the webs, drawing links if appropriate. This activity should take about 20 minutes.

Questions for Discussion

CULTURE How does cultural diversity affect Southwest Asia today?

More than 30 languages are spoken in the region today. It is home to three major religions. Also, the region has been marred by much violence and conflict between the different cultures.

CULTURE How did the ideas and traditions of different cultures spread throughout Southwest Asia?

Many people in this region were traders and traveled a great deal throughout Asia, Africa, and Europe. This allowed different cultural ideas and traditions to spread.

4 Assess/Reteach

See the answers to the Section 4 Assessment. You may also assess students' webs.

Acceptable Webs include accurate additions to each web.

Commendable Webs include accurate additions, some of which note the importance of trade and political systems.

Outstanding Webs include accurate additions and recognize several links between cultural influences and challenges.

Answers to...

CRITICAL THINKING

Answers will vary. Some students may say that it is not easy because issues are bound to arise over the rights to the sacred land and places of worship.

SECTION 4 ASSESSMENT

AFTER YOU READ

1. (a) a person whose job it is to summon Muslims to prayer (b) a place high atop a mosque where the muezzin calls Muslims to prayer
2. (a) city in Israel that Jews, Christians, and Muslims consider holy (b) founder of Judaism (c) founder of Christianity (d) a town outside of Jerusalem where Jesus was born (e) founder of Islam (f) holy city for Muslims located in Saudi Arabia
3. Southwest Asia's location made it an important link between Asia, Africa, and Europe. Many different empires successfully dominated the region, leaving a lasting cultural impression.
4. Judaism, Christianity, and Islam
5. Answers will vary. Students may mention that the three religions are linked by place but separated by beliefs, practices, and ethnicity.
6. You may wish to have students work with a partner or in groups to research and create their country profiles.

West Bank Neighbors

CULTURE Israel has occupied the West Bank area since the late 1960s. In this picture, Israeli soldiers in the West Bank town of Hebron watch as two mothers, one Israeli (on the left), one Palestinian, walk with their children. **Critical Thinking** Why might cultural differences lead to conflict?

as Christ, which means "messiah." These followers were known as Christians. Gradually, these Christians began traveling along the ancient trade routes and preached the teachings of Jesus along the way. Soon, these small communities spread throughout the Roman Empire. Despite the persecution of its followers, Christianity would come to be the major religion of the Roman Empire, which helped the religion to flourish around the Mediterranean.

Muhammad and Islam **Muhammad,** the prophet of Islam, was born in the Arabian city of **Mecca** in approximately 570 A.D. Mecca, which is now a holy city for Muslims, is located in what is now Saudia Arabia. In the early 600s, Muhammad had a vision in which the angel Gabriel appeared to him and told him that he was to be the messenger of God, known as Allah in Arabic. Muhammad began teaching what he had learned. He taught the people of Mecca that Allah alone was God and that people would be judged by their actions and deeds, not by their wealth or power. These teachings form the basis of Islam's holy book, the Quran.

The Region Today

Southwest Asia is still a region of great cultural diversity. Dozens of different ethnic groups call this area home, and together they speak more than 30 languages, including Arabic, Turkish, Persian, Hebrew, and Armenian. However, with this cultural diversity has come conflict and violence—both within many of the countries and between many countries in this area.

SECTION 4 ASSESSMENT

AFTER YOU READ

RECALL

1. Define: (a) muezzin, (b) minaret
2. Identify: (a) Abraham, (b) Jerusalem, (c) Jesus of Nazareth, (d) Bethlehem, (e) Muhammad, (f) Mecca

COMPREHENSION

3. Describe the factors that account for the great cultural diversity of Southwest Asia.
4. Name the three religions that have their roots in Southwest Asia.

CRITICAL THINKING AND WRITING

5. **Exploring the Main Idea** Review the Main Idea statement at the beginning of this section. Then, write a paragraph describing some of the factors that link the three major religions in Southwest Asia.

ACTIVITY

6. **Creating a Country Profile** Create a country profile for one of the following Southwest Asian countries: Turkey, Iran, or Lebanon. Visit the library or the Internet to find out about the ethnic groups and religions in the country, and create a suitable chart that shows this information. Draw a map of the country, indicating the capital as well as important land forms to display along with the charts you create.

Resource Directory

Teaching Resources

Section Quiz in the Unit 6 Teaching Resources, p. 46

Chapter Summary in the Unit 6 Teaching Resources, p. 47

Vocabulary in the Unit 6 Teaching Resources, p. 48

Reteaching in the Unit 6 Teaching Resources, p. 49

Enrichment in the Unit 6 Teaching Resources, p. 50

Critical Thinking in the Unit 6 Teaching Resources, p. 51

Answers to...

CRITICAL THINKING

Answers will vary. Some students may say that the cultural difference might lead to conflicts because what is acceptable to one group may not be acceptable to another.

Explaining Points of View

Learn the Skill

A point of view is the position from which a person looks at something. Throughout history, various individuals and groups have held varying points of view. To recognize and explain varying points of view as you read, you must look closely at a person's argument to understand the reasons behind that belief. Understanding the viewpoints of groups of people and historical leaders will help you better understand what you read. To explain points of view, follow these steps:

A. Be on the lookout as you read for information on a person or group's point of view. This may be in the form of a statement within the text in which a viewpoint is given. Or a point of view may be revealed through the actions of people. The following sentences give the opposing religious viewpoints of the Soviet Union and ethnic Kazaks:

> When the Soviet Union took control of Kazakstan in the 1920s, they banned the practice of Islam and tried to stamp out Muslim culture. After the Cold War, ethnic Kazaks rebuilt the mosques and began celebrating their culture and religion once again.

B. Look for reasons why each side has a certain position, and analyze those reasons. The following sentences explain why the Soviets restricted the practice of religion in the Soviet Union:

> Wherever they went, the Soviets restricted the practice of religion, believing it was an "opium" of the people. The Soviets wanted people to celebrate communism, not religion. They believed the absence of religion would make their rule stronger.

C. Be able to explain both sides of the argument by giving reasons why different people take various positions on the same issue. To explain the practice of religion in Kazakstan, for example, you might write:

> The Kazaks were proud of their heritage and wanted the freedom to worship as they pleased and follow the religions of their ancestors.

Practice the Skill

Read the following information. Then follow the steps to write a summary to explain the two points of view.

The Soviet Union in Kazakstan

Ethnic Kazaks lived a nomadic lifestyle, taking their livestock to places where they could find food and water. But the Soviets believed it would be better for the Kazaks to become farmers and give up their nomadic lifestyle. They forced the Kazaks to work on collective farms. The Kazaks bitterly opposed plowing under their grazing land for crops. Then, the Soviets diverted so much water for irrigation from the Aral Sea, which the Kazaks live close to, that the sea shrunk in size, grounding many ships on what used to be the bottom of the sea. The irrigation has ended, but the Kazaks believe it will take 30 years for the Aral Sea to return to its normal size.

Apply the Skill

Turn to the Applying Your Skills section of the Chapter Review and Assessment for more questions on explaining points of view.

Lesson Objectives

1. Define point of view.
2. Identify points of view when reading.

Lesson Plan

1 Engage

To introduce the skill, read aloud the opening text under "Learn the Skill." Ask students to give a definition for point of view in their own words. Explain to them that understanding a point of view can help them to better understand people from other cultures.

2 Explore

Instruct students to read the steps and examples under "Learn the Skill." For A, ask them to find an example in which a point of view is given in a statement and another which is revealed through the groups' actions. Point out that they will better understand history when they know the reasons why each side took a certain position.

3 Teach

Students should read the paragraph and write a short summary, stating two different opinions. Remind them to follow the steps and try to understand the arguments for both sides.

For additional reinforcement, ask students to explain points of view when reading about other countries or cultures.

4 Assess/Reteach

Students should be able to find two different points of view in the selection titled "Kazakstan and the Soviet Union."

To further assess students' understanding of recognizing points of view, have them complete the "Applying Your Skills" part of the Chapter Review and Assessment.

Resource Directory

Technology

Social Studies Skills Tutor CD-ROM

Answers to...

PRACTICE THE SKILL

Students may conclude that the Soviets believed farming was a better lifestyle than grazing cattle or sheep. They may conclude that the Soviets did not care about the land in the same way that the Kazaks did.

CHAPTER 26

Review and Assessment

Creating a Chapter Summary

Student summaries will vary.

Sample summaries:

Section 2 A mixture of tradition and change, manifest in religious practices, architecture, and arts, characterizes the nations of Southeast Asia. Wealth in the oil-rich kingdom of Brunei is used to benefit people and to reinforce the heritage of Islam.

Section 3 South Asia is the birthplace of two religions, Hinduism and Buddhism. Religious diversity presents significant political and social challenges in the region. South Asia is also characterized by a diversity of languages, many of which are Indo-Iranian.

Section 4 Many cultures are represented in the vast region of Southwest Asia, the birthplace of Judaism, Christianity, and Islam.

Reviewing Key Terms

1. h **2.** c **3.** g **4.** e **5.** a **6.** b **7.** d **8.** f

Reviewing the Main Ideas

1. Past and present intermingle in modern-day culture.
2. Japan and the Koreas have homogeneous populations. China is ethnically diverse.
3. The past and present mix in Southeast Asia.
4. Oil wealth is used to support the people of Brunei and to reinforce the heritage of Islam.
5. Hinduism and Buddhism have roots in South Asia. Islam and Sikhism are two additional religions that are important in the region today.
6. Indo-Iranian
7. Judaism, Christianity, and Islam

CHAPTER 26

Review and Assessment

Creating a Chapter Summary

On a separate piece of paper, draw a diagram like this one, and include the information that summarizes the first section of the chapter. Then, fill in the remaining boxes with summaries of Sections 2, 3, and 4.

ASIA: RICH IN CULTURE

Section 1	Section 2	Section 3	Section 4
History influences modern-day culture in East Asia. Countries in this region differ in the make-up of their populations. Japan and the Koreas have homogeneous populations, whereas China is one of the most ethnically diverse nations in the world.			

Reviewing Key Terms

Match the key terms in Column I with the definitions in Column II.

Column I	Column II
1. Jesus	**a.** very similar
2. dialects	**b.** founder of Buddhism
3. nomad	**c.** forms of a single language
4. deity	**d.** founder of Judaism
5. homogeneous	**e.** a god
6. Siddhartha Gautauma	**f.** founder of Islam
7. Abraham	**g.** person who has no settled home
8. Muhammad	**h.** founder of Christianity

Reviewing the Main Ideas

1. How do past and present blend in East Asia? (Section 1)
2. Which East Asian nations have homogeneous populations? Which is ethnically diverse? (Section 1)
3. What do religious practices, architectural style, and arts reveal about the relationship between past and present in Southeast Asia? (Section 2)
4. How is oil wealth used in Brunei? (Section 2)
5. What religions have roots in South Asia, and what other religions are important in the region today? (Section 3)
6. In what group of related languages are many languages of South Asia? (Section 3)
7. What three religions have their roots in Southwest Asia? (Section 4)

Resource Directory

Teaching Resources

Cooperative Learning Activity in the Unit 6 Teaching Resources, pp. 115–117

Chapter Tests Forms A and B in the Unit 6 Teaching Resources, pp. 146–151

Guide to the Essentials, Ch. 26 Test, p. 117

Map Activity

For each place below, write the letter from the map that shows its location. Use the maps in the Activity Atlas at the front of the book to help you.

1. China
2. Brunei
3. Japan
4. Vietnam
5. Israel
6. India
7. Nepal
8. North Korea
9. South Korea
10. Cambodia

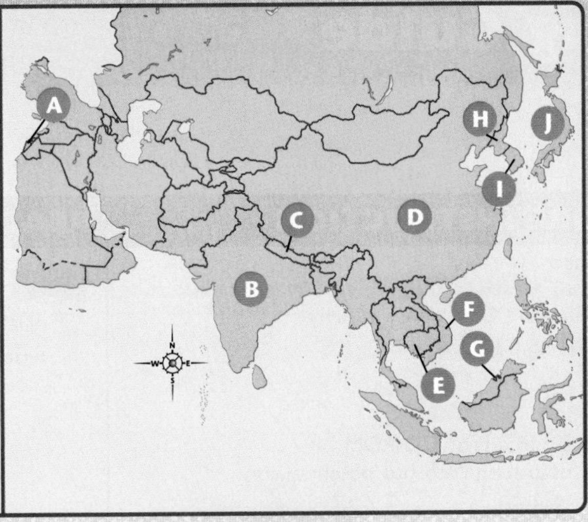

Take It to the NET

Enrichment For more map activities using geography skills, visit the Social Studies section of **phschool.com.**

Writing Activity

1. **Writing Sentences** Based on what you have read in this chapter, write five sentences describing how tradition and change exist together in Asia. Then, write five sentences describing how tradition and change exist together in the United States.
2. **Writing a Letter** You are visiting Asia to observe how the past and present intermingle in everyday life. Write a letter to a teacher describing your observations.

Critical Thinking

1. **Comparing and Contrasting** How do cultures in Southwest Asia compare to other Asian cultures you have studied?
2. **Generalizing** Each country in Asia is unique. However, many Asian countries have certain similarities in relation to their cultural heritage. What relationship to their heritages do many Asian countries share?

Applying Your Skills

Turn to the Skills for Life activity on p. 497 to answer the following questions.

1. Write a definition for point of view.
2. What did the ethnic Kazaks do after the Cold War that lets the reader know that they value their Islamic religion?

Take It to the NET

Activity Examine some of the ceramic pieces in this exhibit. What do you learn about ancient Asian culture from looking at these objects? Visit the World Explorer: People, Places, and Cultures section of **phschool.com** for help in completing this activity.

Chapter 26 Self-Test As a final review activity, take the Chapter 26 Self-Test and get instant feedback on your answers. To take the test, visit the Social Studies section of **phschool.com.**

Map Activity

1. D **2.** G **3.** J **4.** F **5.** A **6.** B **7.** C **8.** H **9.** I **10.** E

Writing Activity

1. Accept all reasonable answers that are adequately supported by references to information in the text.
2. Encourage students to use detailed descriptions in their observations.

Critical Thinking

1. Answers will vary. Some studetns may note that the cultures in this region, like cultures in other Asian countries, have been there for thousands of years.
2. Many Asian countries appreciate their cultural heritage and wish to preserve it even as they adopt foreign practices and modern ways.

Applying Your Skills

1. A point of view is the position from which a person looks at something.
2. The Kazaks rebuilt the mosques.

Resource Directory

Other Print Resources

Chapter Tests with ExamView® Test Bank, Ch. 26

Technology

ExamView® Test Bank CD-ROM, Ch. 26

Resource Pro® CD-ROM

Chapter 27 Planning Guide

Resource Manager

	CORE INSTRUCTION	READING/SKILLS
Chapter-Level Resources	**Teaching Resources** Program Overview Pacing Charts **Technology** Resource Pro® CD-ROM Companion Web site, phschool.com • eTeach	**Technology** Social Studies Skills Tutor CD-ROM Student Edition on Audio CD, Ch. 27
1 China: Political and Economic Changes 1. Summarize the impact of Communism and the rule of Mao Zedong on China. 2. Evaluate changes taking place in China in the 1990s.	**Teaching Resources** **Unit 6** Classroom Manager, p. 53 Guided Reading and Review, p. 54	**Teaching Resources** Guide to the Essentials, p. 118 **Technology** Section Reading Support Transparencies
2 Japan: A Thriving Market Economy 1. Describe Japan's economic growth and recent setbacks. 2. Explain how tradition hampers change in modern-day Japan.	**Teaching Resources** **Unit 6** Classroom Manager, p. 56 Guided Reading and Review, p. 57	**Teaching Resources** Guide to the Essentials, p. 119 **Technology** Section Reading Support Transparencies
3 The Koreas: Different Ways of Governing 1. Explain how South Korea became an economic success. 2. Determine the reasons why North Korea has developed more slowly than South Korea.	**Teaching Resources** **Unit 6** Classroom Manager, p. 59 Guided Reading and Review, p. 60	**Teaching Resources** Guide to the Essentials, p. 120 **Technology** Section Reading Support Transparencies
4 Vietnam: Rebuilding the Economy 1. Explain Vietnam's struggle to shed colonial rule and the effects of civil war on the country. 2. Describe how the Vietnamese are rebuilding their country.	**Teaching Resources** **Unit 6** Classroom Manager, p. 62 Guided Reading and Review, p. 63 Chapter Summary, p. 65 Vocabulary, p. 66 Reteaching, p. 67	**Teaching Resources** **Unit 6** Critical Thinking, p. 69 Guide to the Essentials, p. 121 Social Studies and Geography Skills, p. 45 **Technology** Section Reading Support Transparencies

ENRICHMENT / PRE-AP

Teaching Resources
Primary Sources and Literature Readings

Other Print Resources
DK Atlas

Technology
World Video Explorer: Cultures of Asia and the Pacific, Spotlight on: Baseball in Japan
Companion Web site, phschool.com

Teaching Resources
Outline Maps, p. 41

Technology
Color Transparencies 116, 117, 118, 119, 138
Passport to the World CD-ROM

Teaching Resources
Outline Maps, p. 42

Technology
Color Transparencies 120,121,143

Teaching Resources
Outline Maps, p. 42

Technology
Color Transparencies 115, 116

Teaching Resources
Unit 6
Enrichment, p. 68
Cooperative Learning Activity, pp. 119–122

Technology
Color Transparencies 123
Passport to the World CD-ROM

ASSESSMENT

Prentice Hall Assessment System

Core Assessment
Chapter Tests with ExamView® Test Bank, Ch. 27
ExamView® Test Bank CD-ROM, Ch. 27

Standardized Test Preparation
Diagnose and Prescribe
Diagnostic Tests for Middle Grades Social Studies Skills
Review and Reteach
Review Book for World Studies
Practice and Assess
Test-taking Strategies with Transparencies for Middle Grades Test Prep Book
Test-taking Strategies Posters

Teaching Resources
Unit 6
Section Quizzes, pp. 55, 58, 61, and 64
Chapter Tests, pp. 152–157

Technology
Companion Web site, phschool.com
Ch. 27 Self-Test

World Video Explorer
Each region of the world is explored through regional flyovers and investigative field trips. Case study segments give students an in-depth view of the history, economy, government, and culture of a key place in each region. Case studies include Nigeria, Mexico, China, British Columbia, and the Czech Republic.

In Your Classroom

CUSTOMIZE FOR INDIVIDUAL NEEDS

Gifted and Talented

Teacher's Edition
- Research to express Ideas Orally, p. 507
- Vietnam and the United States, p. 513

Teaching Resources
- Enrichment, p. 68
- Primary Sources and Literature Readings

Honors/Pre-AP

Teacher's Edition
- Research to express Ideas Orally, p. 507
- Vietnam and the United States, p. 513

Teaching Resources
- Critical Thinking, p. 69
- Primary Sources and Literature Readings

ESL

Teacher's Edition
- Recognizing Cause and Effect, p. 503

Teaching Resources
- Guided Reading and Review, pp. 54, 57, 60, and 63
- Vocabulary, p. 66
- Reteaching, p. 67
- Guide to the Essentials, pp. 118–121
- Social Studies and Geography Skills, p. 45

Technology
- Social Studies Skills Tutor CD-ROM
- Section Reading Support Transparencies

Less Proficient Readers

Teacher's Edition
- Recognizing Cause and Effect, p. 503

Teaching Resources
- Guided Reading and Review, pp. 54, 57, 60, and 63
- Vocabulary, p. 66
- Reteaching, p. 67
- Guide to the Essentials, pp. 118–121
- Social Studies and Geography Skills, p. 45

Technology
- Social Studies Skills Tutor CD-ROM
- Section Reading Support Transparencies

Less Proficient Writers

Teacher's Edition
- Recognizing Cause and Effect, p. 503
- Vietnam and the United States, p. 513

Teaching Resources
- Guided Reading and Review, pp. 54, 57, 60, and 63
- Vocabulary, p. 66
- Guide to the Essentials, pp. 118–121

Technology
- Social Studies Skills Tutor CD-ROM
- Section Reading Support Transparencies

DORLING KINDERSLEY

At the end of each unit, you will find information adapted from Dorling Kindersley's *Illustrated Children's Encyclopedia* that connects to the region being studied and to one of the seven content strands. In addition, your resources include Dorling Kindersley's *Atlas*, which contains valuable information about countries from around the world.

TEACHER'S EDITION INDEX

CHAPTER 27 PACING SUGGESTIONS

For 90-minute Blocks

See suggestions in the Teaching Resources Pacing Charts for Chapter 27. Use Color Transparencies 116–119, 120–121, 123, 138, and 143.

Running Out of Time?

See the Guide to the Essentials, pp. 118–121.

INTERDISCIPLINARY LINKS

Middle Grades Math: Tools for Success

Course 1, Lesson 10-1, **Using a Number Line**

Course 1, Lesson 11-6, **Independent Events**

Course 2, Lesson 5-2, **Adding and Subtracting Fractions**

Course 2, Lesson 7-8, **Circle Graphs**

Science Explorer

Cells and Heredity, Lesson 4-3, **Advances in Genetics**

Prentice Hall Literature

Copper, Haiku

Bronze, Ribbons; Three Haiku by Basho

BIBLIOGRAPHY

For the Teacher

Marrin, Albert. *America and Vietnam: The Elephant and the Tiger.* Viking, 1992.

Viesti, Joe, and Diane Hall. *Celebrate! In Southeast Asia.* Lothrop, 1996.

Vuong, Lynette Dyer. *The Golden Carp and Other Tales of Vietnam.* Lothrop, 1993.

For the Student

Easy

Hermes, Jules. *The Children of India.* Carolrhoda, 1994.

Average

DK *DK Compact World Atlas.* Dorling Kindersley, 2001.

Downer, Lesley. *Japan.* Thomson (Modern Industrial World series), 1995.

Kalman, Bobbie. *Vietnam: The People.* Crabtree, 1996.

Challenging

Langone, John. *In the Shogun's Shadow: Understanding a Changing Japan.* Little, Brown, 1994.

Zhang, Song Nan. *The Children of China: An Artist's Journey.* Tundra, 1995.

Literature Connection

Baillie, Allan. *Little Brother.* Viking, 1992.

Bateson-Hill, Margaret. *Lao Lao of Dragon Mountain.* De Agostini, 1996.

San Souci, Robert. *The Samurai's Daughter.* Dial, 1992.

Take It to the NET

The World Explorer companion Web site, found on **phschool.com**, offers activities for exploring geographical, historical, and cultural resources on the Internet. It also provides on-line links for key content and all Section and Chapter Assessment activities.

The **Teacher site** also provides teachers with regional data and ideas for student research and activities.

Students can use the **Student site** to find chapter-by-chapter Internet resource links and to access Self-Tests.

CHAPTER 27

Connecting to the Guiding Questions

In this chapter, students will read about the region in East and Southeast Asia today. Content in this chapter corresponds to the following Guiding Questions outlined in the beginning of the unit.

- How has history and the achievements of historic figures influenced life in Asia today?
- How do Asian governments compare with each other and with the government of the United States?
- How does participation in the political process differ in Asia and in the United States?

Using the Picture Activities

Tell students that about one-fourth of China's foreign trade passes through Shanghai, one of the world's most crowded urban areas.

- Students should identify urban elements from the picture such as crowded streets, heavy traffic, and tall buildings. Trade has resulted in the increased urbanization of Shanghai, and growth in its businesses.
- Students should make logical predictions based upon the information they gather about China's natural resources.

Heterogeneous Groups

The following activities are suitable for heterogeneous groups.

Critical Thinking

Recognizing Cause and Effect, p. 503

Science and Technology

Research to Express Ideas Orally, p. 507

eTeach

Be sure to check out this month's discussion with a Master Teacher. Go to **phschool.com**.

CHAPTER 27

EAST AND SOUTHEAST ASIA: Exploring the Region Today

City Life

Using Pictures

Shanghai, located near the mouth of the Yangzi River, is China's leading port. With a population of 8 million people, it is the largest city in China.

Exploring Shanghai

Shanghai is a modern city. What are some of the details in the picture that show this? What effect do you think trade has had on the growth of the city of Shanghai? What effect do you think trade has had on culture in the city of Shanghai?

Making Predictions

China exports many goods to other countries around the world. Use an encyclopedia to gather information on China's natural resources. Make a list of the resources, and then brainstorm a list of products you think China might export to other countries, based on your list of resources. Use library and Internet sources to gather information and make a list of China's major exports. Check to see if your predictions about China's exports were accurate.

Resource Directory

Teaching Resources

Primary Sources and Literature Readings extend content with a selection related to the concepts in this chapter.

Other Print Resources

DK Atlas

Technology

Cultures of Asia and the Pacific, from the World Video Explorer, enhances students' understanding of the many cultures of Asia and the Pacific.

Spotlight on: Baseball in Japan, from the World Video Explorer, enhances students' understanding of cultural diffusion through a look at how baseball is played in Japan.

Student Edition on Audio CD, Ch. 27

SECTION 1

China

Political and Economic Changes

BEFORE YOU READ

READING FOCUS

1. How has communism changed the lives of many Chinese?
2. What steps has China recently taken to improve its economy?

KEY TERMS
radical
free enterprise

KEY PEOPLE AND PLACES
Mao Zedong
Red Guard
Taiwan

NOTE TAKING
Copy the diagram below. As you read the section, fill in the diagram to show similarities and differences—from 1949 to the present—between China and Taiwan.

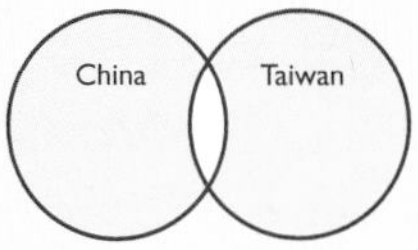

MAIN IDEA
China has undergone tremendous political and economic change since 1949.

Setting the Scene

During the early 1980s, the streets of large Chinese cities were fairly quiet. Most people traveled by bicycle—200 million of them. At this time, the total number of vehicles in all of China was 100,000. In 1996, 670,000 cars, buses, and trucks crowded the streets of major cities. In the early 1980s, most houses were cramped, single-story dwellings made of clay and brick. Few had running water or flush toilets. Today, China's major cities have high-rise apartment and office buildings. New roads connect rural areas to the cities. Change is speeding up as China works to become an industrial nation.

Busy Modern Streets

CULTURE China's streets are no longer packed with bicycles. In modern Shanghai, throngs of walkers share the streets with buses and other motor vehicles. **Critical Thinking** What are some advantages and disadvantages of motor vehicles displacing bicycles?

Unlimited Government

When Chinese Communists took power from the Nationalists in 1949, they had few friends among the major nations of the world. The United States had backed the Nationalists, and the Soviet Union had been on the Communists' side, but later withdrew its support because it disagreed with China about how a communist society should be run.

The Communists faced enormous problems when they took control. China had not had peace for almost a century. Most Chinese were extremely poor. Their methods of farming and manufacturing were out of date.

SECTION 1

Lesson Objectives

1. Summarize the impact of Communism and the rule of Mao Zedong on China.
2. Evaluate changes taking place in China in the 1990s.

Lesson Plan

1 Engage

Warm-Up Activity

Have students read the introduction and discuss what it might be like to live in China during this period of rapid change. Elicit their reactions to the changes described. What might be some positive and negative results of these changes?

Activating Prior Knowledge

Ask students to think about the ways in which their community has changed during their lifetimes. What new highways and buildings have been built? Are there new places for entertainment? Is there more traffic today? Lead a discussion about how these changes have or have not affected students' everyday lives.

Resource Directory

Teaching Resources

Classroom Manager in the Unit 6 Teaching Resources, p. 53

Guided Reading and Review in the Unit 6 Teaching Resources, p. 54

Guide to the Essentials, p. 118

Technology

Section Reading Support Transparencies

Answers to...

CRITICAL THINKING

Possible answer: Motor vehicles enable people to get where they need to go and carry what they need to carry more quickly and easily. However, motor vehicles create air pollution and do not provide the physical exercise of pedaling a bicycle.

CHAPTER 27 EAST AND SOUTHEAST ASIA: EXPLORING THE REGION TODAY 501

Lesson Plan continued

❷ Explore

Have students read Section 1. Discuss the problems the Communists faced when they took power. What actions did they take? How did the actions help solve the problems? What actions could have been better planned? Discuss Mao's reasons for launching the Cultural Revolution. What is China's economy like now?

❸ Teach

Invite students to write a 5-minute "I Was There" documentary script chronicling the changes in China from the 1950s, when the Communists came to power, to the 1990s, when free enterprise was added to the economic system. Documentaries should be written in the first person. This activity should take about 30 minutes.

Questions for Discussion

ECONOMICS Why did the rush to increase factory and farm production during the early years of communist China fail?

The communists lacked the planning and experience to successfully increase industrial and agricultural output.

SOCIAL STUDIES SKILLS Look at the Country Profile of China on this page. What does the religious persuasion of most Chinese citizens tell you about communist governments?

Most Chinese are non-religious or atheists—59%. One aspect of communism is that it discourages religious belief and does not support religious institutions.

Answers to...

MAP AND CHART STUDY

Most cities are in the eastern part of China. The graph indicates that most workers have jobs in agriculture and forestry, so it is likely that more workers work in rural areas.

COUNTRY • PROFILE

China

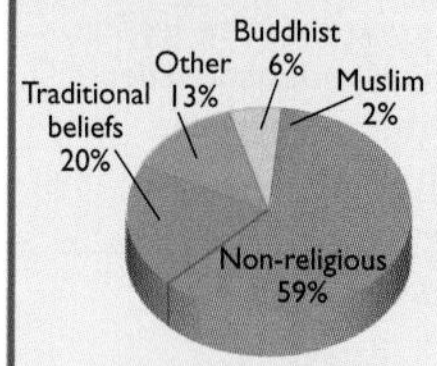

Religious Persuasion

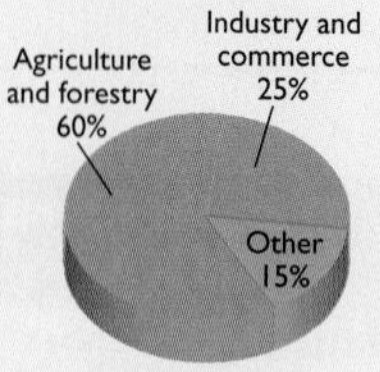

Labor Force

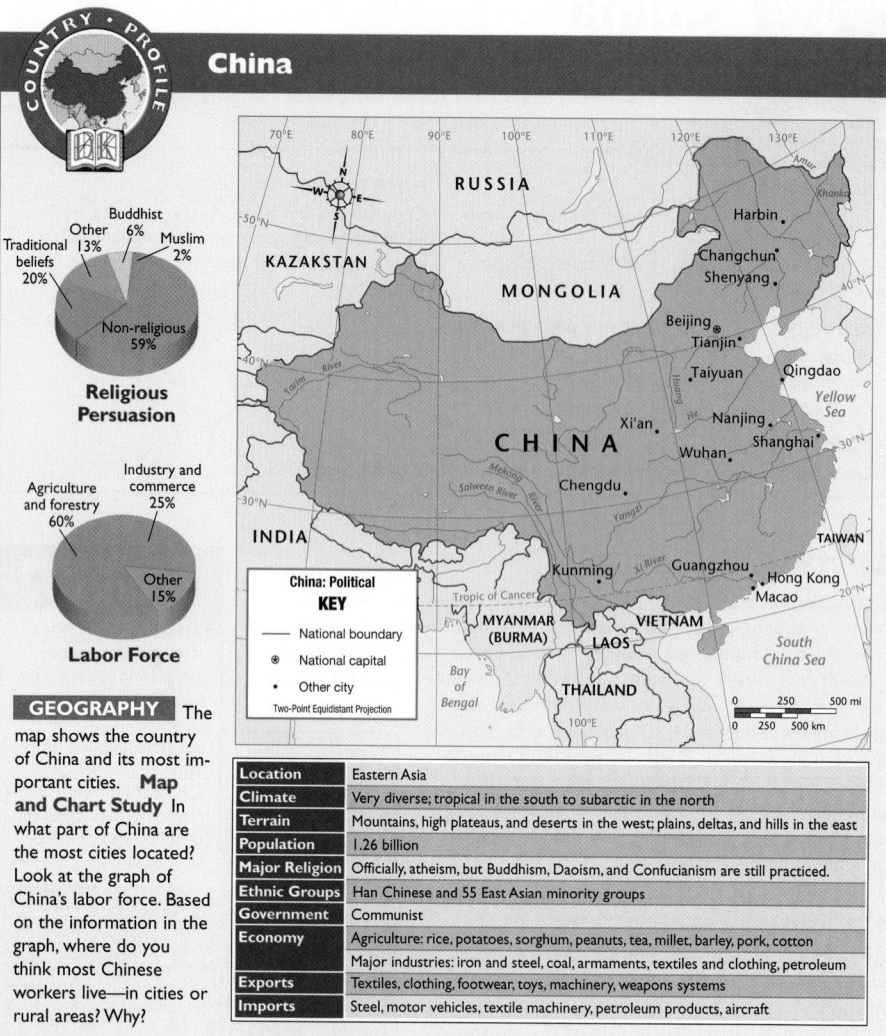

GEOGRAPHY The map shows the country of China and its most important cities. **Map and Chart Study** In what part of China are the most cities located? Look at the graph of China's labor force. Based on the information in the graph, where do you think most Chinese workers live—in cities or rural areas? Why?

Location	Eastern Asia
Climate	Very diverse; tropical in the south to subarctic in the north
Terrain	Mountains, high plateaus, and deserts in the west; plains, deltas, and hills in the east
Population	1.26 billion
Major Religion	Officially, atheism, but Buddhism, Daoism, and Confucianism are still practiced.
Ethnic Groups	Han Chinese and 55 East Asian minority groups
Government	Communist
Economy	Agriculture: rice, potatoes, sorghum, peanuts, tea, millet, barley, pork, cotton
	Major industries: iron and steel, coal, armaments, textiles and clothing, petroleum
Exports	Textiles, clothing, footwear, toys, machinery, weapons systems
Imports	Steel, motor vehicles, textile machinery, petroleum products, aircraft

Under the leadership of **Mao Zedong** (MOW zuh DUNG), China made huge changes. The government seized land from large landowners, as well as taking over all factories and businesses. But Mao was not satisfied. Economic growth was too slow.

In the 1950s, Mao began a policy of **radical,** or extreme change. This policy, called the "Great Leap Forward," turned out to be a giant step backward. The Communists rushed to increase production on

Resource Directory

Teaching Resources

Outline Maps, China: Political, p. 41

Technology

Color Transparencies 118 China: Agricultural Regions Map overlay; **119** China: Population Density Map overlay

World Video Explorer See the China case study for an overview of China's history, economy, government, and culture. Discussion questions are included.

Passport to the World CD-ROM This interactive CD-ROM allows students to explore each region of the world. Students view regional videos, take a photo tour, and explore a historical timeline. Students record their travels in an Explorer's Journal, and receive passport stamps when they pass regional quizzes.

farms and in factories. But they ignored the need for experience and planning. For example, they ordered a huge increase in steel production. Thousands of untrained workers built furnaces for steel-making that never worked.

In 1966, Mao introduced another radical policy called the Cultural Revolution. His aim was to create a society with no ties to the past. Mao urged students to rebel against teachers and families. Students formed bands of radicals called the **Red Guard.** These bands destroyed some of China's most beautiful ancient buildings and beat up and imprisoned many Chinese artists and professionals such as lawyers and doctors.

Then, the Red Guard began to threaten Mao's government, and they were imprisoned, too. Mao ended the Cultural Revolution in 1969. The ill-conceived policy had left China in a shambles, with hundreds of thousands of citizens dead.

LINKS TO
Language Arts

Writing Chinese To write their language, the Chinese use characters, or symbols. Each one stands for a word or part of a word. To read and write, people must learn thousands of characters. Since 1949, the government has tried to make it easier to read and write Chinese. It adopted simpler forms of some characters. Schools use a system called *pinyin* to help teach Chinese. Pinyin uses the English alphabet to write Chinese words.

Improvement through Entrepreneurship

During the late 1970s, the Communists realized that their policies had hurt China. After Mao's death in 1976, more moderate Communists gained power. Over the next 20 years, they gradually introduced a limited form of **free enterprise.** Under this economic system, people are allowed to choose their own jobs, start private businesses, and make a profit. The new system also includes farming. Farmers can grow extra crops on private plots of land and can sell the crops for a profit.

Today, both the government and private citizens act as entrepreneurs. They form and manage small businesses, such as jade carving, porcelain making, and silk weaving. In addition, privately owned Chinese factories make cars, elevators, electronic equipment, watches, cameras, and bicycles.

The Growth of Taiwan

After their defeat by the Communists in 1949, the Nationalists

Taiwan: Physical

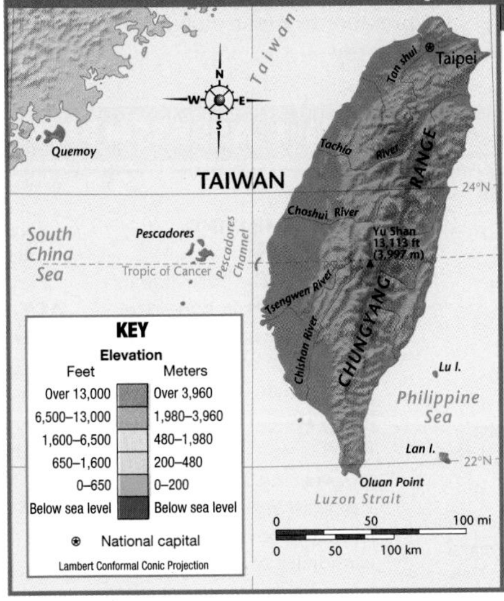

GEOGRAPHY The island of Taiwan has an area of 13,900 square miles (35,980 sq km). This makes it almost twice the size of the state of New Jersey. Like much of East Asia, Taiwan is mountainous. Its farmers often build terraces for growing crops. **Map Study** Find Taiwan on the Country Profile map of China on page 502. How does Taiwan compare with mainland China in size? Now study this map. In what areas of Taiwan do you think most of the island's people live? Why?

4 Assess/Reteach

See the answers to the Section 1 Assessment. You may also use students' documentaries for assessment.

Acceptable documentaries correctly describe the historical events mentioned in the section.

Commendable documentaries display an understanding of how these events affected individuals.

Outstanding documentaries reveal the character of the writer and his or her reactions to various political and economic events.

HISTORY

Jiang Qing (1914?–1991)

One of the most influential women in Mao's government was his wife, Jiang Qing. In 1963, she took charge of a cultural reform movement that reworked traditional Chinese drama and ballet so that they contained proletarian motifs. By 1966, Mao had granted Jiang sweeping powers, which she used to almost completely eliminate many long-standing cultural traditions. Jiang fell out of favor after Mao's death and was convicted with three others—the Gang of Four—of causing the mass civil unrest that occurred during the Cultural Revolution. Jiang died in prision, reportedly a suicide.

ACTIVITY

Critical Thinking

Recognizing Cause and Effect
Suitable as a whole class activity. Make a two-column chart on the chalkboard with the headings *Causes* and *Effects.* Write *Great Leap Forward* in the *Effects* column and challenge students to complete the *Causes* column by identifying the problems China faced that led to Mao's institution of the policy.

Visual/Spatial

Resource Directory

Technology

Color Transparencies 116 East Asia: Political Map; **138** *Wedding Group* Fine Art

Answers to...

MAP STUDY

Taiwan is much smaller than mainland China. Most people live on the western coast where the land is flattest and can be most easily farmed.

SECTION 1 ASSESSMENT

AFTER YOU READ

1. (a) Chinese communist leader (b) band of radicals urged by Mao to do away with old ideas, customs, and traditions (c) island nation off the coast of southern China that has a free enterprise economy
2. (a) extreme, as in extreme change (b) economic system in which people are free to choose their own jobs, start private businesses, and make a profit
3. Possible answer: Privately owned land, factories, and businesses were seized by the government. During the Cultural Revolution, there was great turmoil, and many people died.
4. Since the 1970s, there has been a move toward some free enterprise. China is now becoming a world economic force, and there is a growing middle class.
5. The Chinese government seized land from large landowners and took over all factories and businesses. Mao instituted a radical policy called the "Great Leap Forward," which called for increased production in factories and on farms. Mao also introduced the Cultural Revolution, a radical policy that aimed to create a society with no ties to the past.
6. Responses may vary, but should indicate that China is a communist country that is just beginning to allow free enterprise, while Taiwan has had a free enterprise system since the 1950s. China is now enjoying a booming economy while Taiwan has had one since the 1970s.
7. Students' letters should be supported by information from the text and their own knowledge.

The Three Gorges Dam

ECONOMICS

The construction of the Three Gorges Dam on China's Yangzi River is the largest hydroelectric project in the world. Begun in 1994, the project will generate up to one-ninth of China's power when completed around 2009. **Critical Thinking** How might the dam benefit the farmers who live and work along the banks of the Yangzi River? How might it harm them?

fled to **Taiwan,** an island 100 miles (161 km) off China's southeast coast. Here they set up a government they called the Republic of China.

Even in the 1950s, Taiwan's free enterprise economy was one of Asia's strongest. The Chinese on Taiwan started a program that allowed farmers to buy land at low prices. This increased farm output and brought in more money to the government. This money helped Taiwan build new ports and modern railroads, and with aid from the United States, Taiwan also built roads and helped industries. The Taiwanese then increased their trade with foreign nations. They sell computer chips, computers, and other electronic products to the rest of the world.

Challenges in China

Today, China is becoming a world economic force. Money to develop industry and business is pouring into the country, and China's middle class is growing. Yet progress has created some challenges. Rural areas of China have not prospered as much as urban areas. Farmers sometimes have trouble getting their crops to markets.

China is working on these problems. The government has built new communities in rural areas. Like tiny towns, they have schools, parks, and libraries. The government is encouraging the growth of business and industry in these communities and throughout rural China.

Another challenge China faces is its poor human rights record. With foreign investment and trade on the rise, China is under increasing pressure from the global community to foster civil rights among its citizenry.

SECTION 1 ASSESSMENT

AFTER YOU READ

RECALL

1. Identify: (a) Mao Zedong, (b) Red Guard, (c) Taiwan
2. Define: (a) radical, (b) free enterprise

COMPREHENSION

3. How did early communist policies affect the people of China?
4. In what ways has China's economy changed in recent years?

CRITICAL THINKING AND WRITING

5. **Exploring the Main Idea** Review the Main Idea statement at the beginning of this section. List some of the changes that China underwent after Mao Zedong came to power.
6. **Comparing and Contrasting** Explain the differences between the economies of China and Taiwan. In your discussion, give the reasons for the differences.

ACTIVITY

7. **Writing to Learn** Write a letter giving economic advice to a developing nation. Use what you have learned about China to suggest ways for the country to build a strong economy.

Answers to...

CRITICAL THINKING

Farmers might benefit from the dam because it will ensure that they have enough water to irrigate their crops and will decrease the danger of flooding. The water held behind the dam will cover many villages and existing farmland.

Resource Directory

Teaching Resources

Section Quiz in the Unit 6 Teaching Resources, p. 55

SECTION 2

Japan

A Thriving Market Economy

BEFORE YOU READ

READING FOCUS

1. How did Japan become one of the most successful developed nations in the world?
2. How do traditions inhibit change in Japan?

KEY TERMS

robot
subsidize
incentive
discrimination

MAIN IDEA

After World War II, Japan regained its status as an important manufacturing country and became a prosperous industrial nation.

NOTE TAKING

Copy the diagram below. As you read the section, fill in the diagram to show what caused Japan to develop a thriving market economy and to identify some of the current threats to this economy.

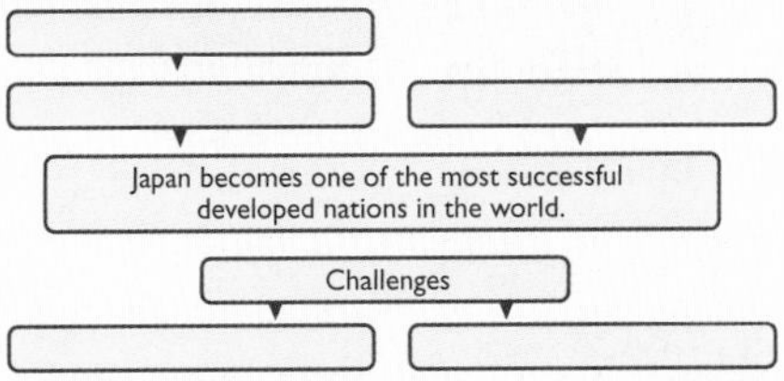
Japan becomes one of the most successful developed nations in the world.
Challenges

Setting the Scene

A Japanese company that makes **robots,** computer-driven machines that do tasks once done by humans, holds an Idea Olympics each year. Employees compete in thinking up ideas to improve the company. Nearly half of the employees work on these ideas on their own time.

Reorganizing Economic Systems

Some of Japan's ideas have come from outside the nation. Once Japan opened its ports to other countries in the 1800s, it welcomed new inventions from the West. For years, the Japanese worked to build major industries. By the 1920s, Japan had become an important manufacturing country. Its economy depended on importing natural resources and exporting manufactured goods.

A Uniform Work Ethic

CULTURE Workers in neat uniforms exercise in unison at a seafood plant. The Japanese believe that such group activities make workers more productive. **Critical Thinking** Why do you think group activities would make these workers more productive? Explain your answer.

SECTION 2

Lesson Objectives

1. Describe Japan's economic growth and recent setbacks.
2. Explain how tradition hampers change in modern-day Japan.

Lesson Plan

1 Engage

Warm-Up Activity

Have students tell a partner what kind of job they would like when they finish their education and why they want that particular job.

Activating Prior Knowledge

Ask students what makes a good job. Ask them what things a person should consider when looking for a job. Record their ideas on the chalkboard. Students may refer to the list as they read the section.

Resource Directory

Teaching Resources

Classroom Manager in the Unit 6 Teaching Resources, p. 56

Guided Reading and Review in the Unit 6 Teaching Resources, p. 57

Guide to the Essentials, p. 119

Technology

Section Reading Support Transparencies

Answers to...

CRITICAL THINKING

Possible answers: Students may say that such activities increase production because workers will get to know their co-workers better and identify with the group.

CHAPTER 27 EAST AND SOUTHEAST ASIA: EXPLORING THE REGION TODAY 505

Lesson Plan continued

2 Explore

Help students examine the map and Country Profile of Japan. Have students read the section to find answers to the Assessment questions. After reading, ask students to list several reasons for Japan's economic success. Ask students to consider to what extent the Japanese attitude toward work is a factor in this success. Then, ask students to describe Japan's recent economic problems. Urge them to support their opinions with examples from the text.

3 Teach

Have students write a brief essay on this topic: Are there any aspects of Japanese employment that you think American companies should adopt? Have them give reasons for their suggestions. Allow volunteers to share their essays with the class and discuss ideas. This activity will take about 30 minutes.

Questions for Discussion

CULTURE **When did Japan open its ports to the West, and how did it change the country?**

Japan opened its ports to other countries in the 1800s. New ideas and inventions from the West were welcomed, and Japanese industry was able to grow and compete globally.

SCIENCE, TECHNOLOGY, AND SOCIETY

What Japanese technological inventions have had a global impact?

The Japanese people invented personal stereos and small, hand-held electronic games. They have also contributed significantly to computer technology.

Answers to...

MAP AND CHART STUDY

The sea provides easy transportation between the countries, which aids the exchange of ideas. Service jobs include teaching, practicing medicine or law, serving food, nursing, and cleaning houses and buildings.

COUNTRY PROFILE

Japan

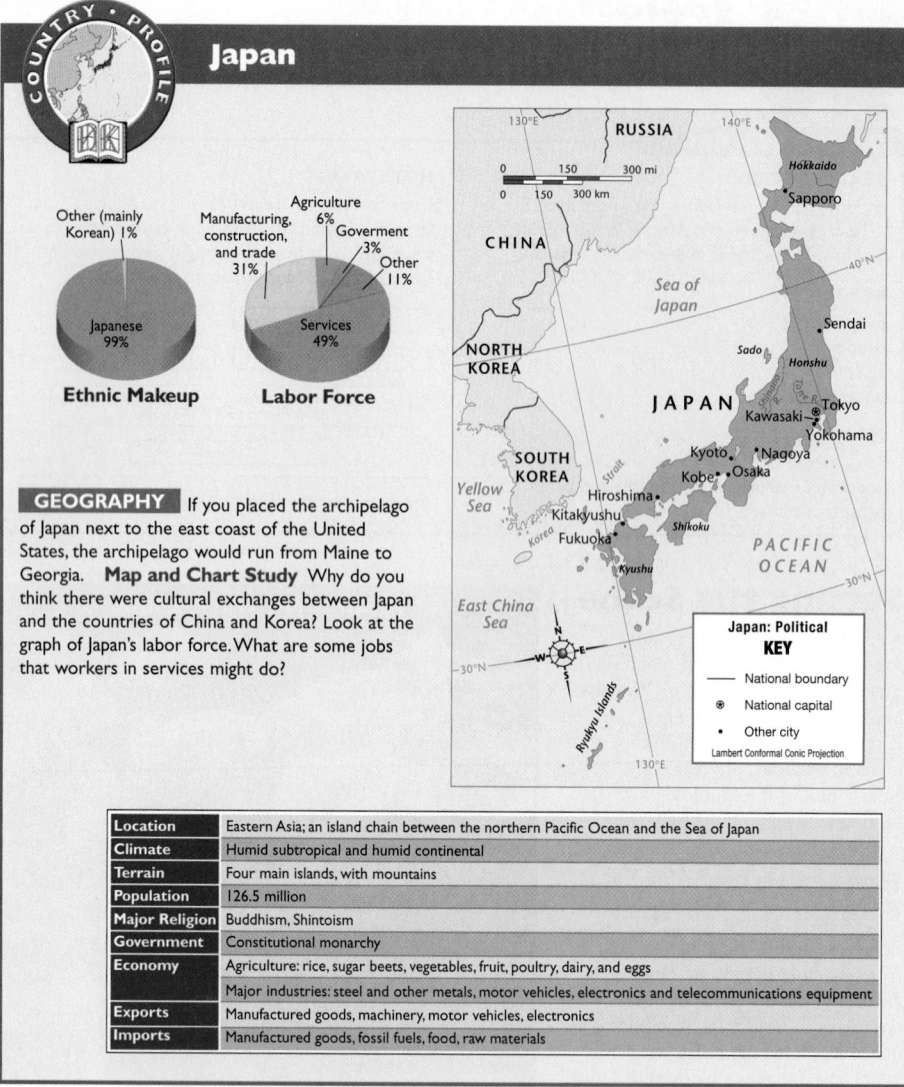

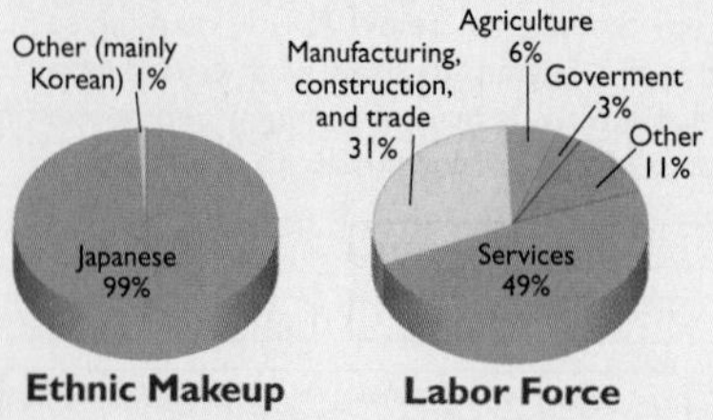

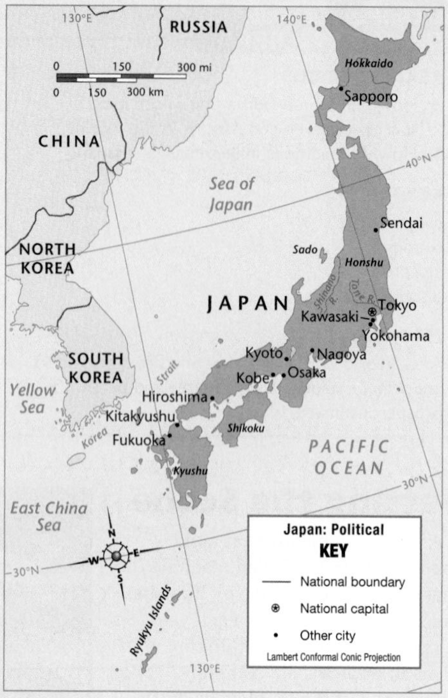

GEOGRAPHY If you placed the archipelago of Japan next to the east coast of the United States, the archipelago would run from Maine to Georgia. **Map and Chart Study** Why do you think there were cultural exchanges between Japan and the countries of China and Korea? Look at the graph of Japan's labor force. What are some jobs that workers in services might do?

Location	Eastern Asia; an island chain between the northern Pacific Ocean and the Sea of Japan
Climate	Humid subtropical and humid continental
Terrain	Four main islands, with mountains
Population	126.5 million
Major Religion	Buddhism, Shintoism
Government	Constitutional monarchy
Economy	Agriculture: rice, sugar beets, vegetables, fruit, poultry, dairy, and eggs
	Major industries: steel and other metals, motor vehicles, electronics and telecommunications equipment
Exports	Manufactured goods, machinery, motor vehicles, electronics
Imports	Manufactured goods, fossil fuels, food, raw materials

World War II and Beyond After World War II, Japan was in ruins. Only a few factories were still running. They made shoes from scraps of wood, and kitchen pots and pans from soldiers' steel helmets. The idea that the Japanese might soon be able to compete with the industrial giants of the West seemed impossible.

506 UNIT 6 ASIA

Resource Directory

Teaching Resources

Outline Maps, Japan and the Koreas: Political, p. 42

Technology

Color Transparencies 120 Japan and the United States: Political Map; **121** Japan and the United States: Climate Regions Map

Financial aid from the United States helped rebuild industry. Another reason Japan became a prosperous industrial nation was its ability to change and grow. The Japanese government helped industries by **subsidizing,** or financially supporting, them. This allowed companies to build large factories and buy modern machines. With more goods to sell, manufacturers could earn more money. Workers also earned more money, so they were able to spend more. This raised the demand for Japanese goods within Japan itself.

Since the 1960s, Japan has produced some of the world's most modern industrial robots. By the 1970s, the Japanese were making more watches and cameras than the Swiss and the Germans, and by the 1980s, Japan made and sold a large share of the world's cars, electronic goods, skiing gear, and bicycles. Japan also produced huge amounts of steel and many ships. You are probably familiar with personal stereos and small, hand-held electronic games. These were invented by the Japanese.

Japan's Workers

Japan has enjoyed great economic success. Employees work hard. Japanese workers view themselves as members of a group, all working toward one goal. They work long hours and take few vacations.

Japanese companies tend to be loyal to their workers. Large companies offer **incentives,** or benefits, that attract workers and keep them happy. These incentives include free housing, education, and medical care. As a result, Japanese workers produce more goods than any other workers in the world.

Limiting Government's Role In Japan, there has always been a close cooperation between business and government. In the past, this has helped businesses to thrive. In recent years, however, it has hurt Japan's economy.

The Japanese government has always supported its citizens, no matter what the cost. Workers are rarely laid off, even when the companies they work for make no profits and cannot pay their salaries. The government has always stepped in to make companies and people happy. One way that it has been able to do this is by taking a strong role in Japan's banks and stock markets. The government controls bank loans, encourages consumers to save their money in banks, and regulates the stock market to expand and strengthen Japan's economy and create a high standard of living. In recent years, however, the economy has suffered. The government has not provided a banking system to regulate loans, and its control of the stock market has discouraged healthy competition.

Tiny Computer Chips

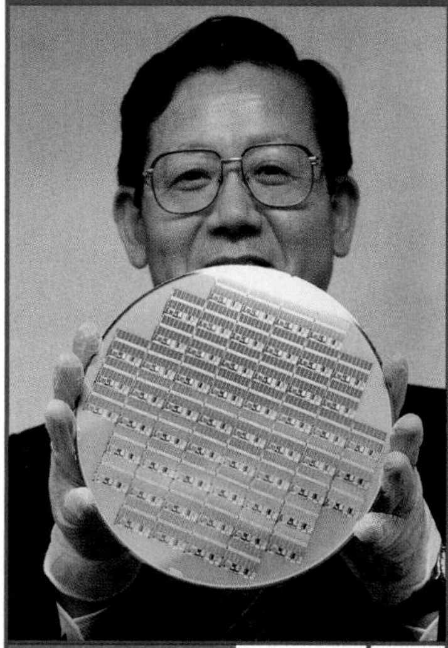

SCIENCE AND TECHNOLOGY In recent years, Japan has become a leader in computer technology. Here, a manager of a Japanese computer company displays dynamic random access memory, or DRAM, chips. These tiny chips, which measure about 0.5 inches (1 cm) by 0.75 inches (2 cm), are the "brains" of a computer. **Critical Thinking** How did the Japanese government help computer technology and other industries to grow?

4 Assess/Reteach

See the answers to the Section 2 Assessment. You may also use students' essays for assessment.

Acceptable essays list at least one valid reason for each suggestion.

Commendable essays show a deeper understanding of why certain practices should be adopted.

Outstanding essays highlight the importance of the relationship of mutual respect between employer and employee.

ACTIVITY

Science and Technology

Research to Express Ideas Orally Explain that robots are widely used in many industries around the world. Suggest that students work in groups of four to find out what kinds of robots exist and choose one kind as the subject of a presentation, detailing what it does and how it works. Allow groups to choose either of the following forms of presentation: a skit showing the robot in action, with researchers explaining how it works; or a model of the robot with an audiotape explanation. Remind students that they can assign roles to group members, for instance, researcher, animator or artist, scriptwriter, and reporter.

Bodily/Kinesthetic

Resource Directory

Technology

Color Transparencies 143 *Ladies With Western Musical Instruments* Fine Art

Answers to...

CRITICAL THINKING

Japanese government subsidies allowed companies to build large factories and buy modern machines.

SECTION 2 ASSESSMENT

AFTER YOU READ

1. (a) computer-driven machine that does tasks once done by humans (b) to economically support (c) benefit that makes a person want to do something (d) unequal treatment of certain people or groups
2. Students' reasons for success should include the productivity of Japanese workers, the Japanese ability to improve technological inventions, and company incentives. Reasons for downturn should include too much government support of unprofitable businesses, too much government control of the stock market, and the lack of banking regulations.
3. Japanese women often work outside the home until they marry. They may also return to work after raising their children. However, traditional Japanese views limit salaries and opportunities for women.
4. Students' paragraphs should be supported by information from the text and their own knowledge.
5. Students' answers should note that workers take pride in doing jobs well and working as a team that contributes to a company's success. The incentives of free housing, education, and medical care also inspire loyalty and gratitude to a company.
6. Students' essays should show the results of research on this topic. They should compare American and Japanese workers' attitudes toward their employers, their job satisfaction, and their satisfaction with benefits and incentives offered by employers.
7. Make sure students limit their graphs or charts only to information regarding Japan's economy.

Women in the Labor Force

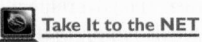

ECONOMICS

Employees of an American computer firm discuss a technical problem at the company's Japan headquarters. **Critical Thinking** What do you predict will happen to the role of Japanese women in economic life?

Tradition Inhibits Change

As elsewhere in East Asia, traditions are important in Japan. Times are changing, but change comes slowly. The role of women is one example. As in the past, being married is the most acceptable position for a Japanese woman. Large companies often have marriage bureaus to introduce their single employees.

Japan's hard-working wives and mothers support the economy and are in charge of their households. They make schooling decisions, handle the family finances, and take care of major purchases.

Japanese women often work before marriage. In the past, many worked in rice fields, fisheries, and factories, or as nurses or teachers. Today, though, some married women are venturing outside the home in a new direction—as part-time workers.

In the 1980s, the largest group of working women in Japan was the army of "office ladies." They served tea, did light cleaning, held doors, and answered the phone. Today, office ladies are rare. Instead, women are crowding the workplace, often working long hours beside male workers—who get higher salaries and good benefits.

At present, few women become managers in Japanese businesses and even when they do, they may meet with job **discrimination,** or unequal treatment. For this reason, many young women are not willing to join Japanese firms. Instead, they look for jobs with foreign businesses in Japan. They are also finding jobs in newer fields where there is less discrimination.

SECTION 2 ASSESSMENT

AFTER YOU READ

RECALL

1. Define: (a) robot, (b) subsidize, (c) incentive, (d) discrimination

COMPREHENSION

2. What are some reasons for Japan's economic success and for its recent downturn?
3. Do the roles played by women illustrate how tradition and change affect Japan today?

CRITICAL THINKING AND WRITING

4. **Exploring the Main Idea** Review the Main Idea statement at the beginning of this section. Then, imagine you are a Japanese grandparent. Write a descriptive paragraph for your grandchildren describing the economic changes you have seen since World War II.
5. **Making Inferences and Drawing Conclusions** Why does their view of work and incentives help Japanese employees produce more?
6. **Writing an Essay** Question several friends or people about their attitudes toward their jobs. Do they feel part of a team? Do they take pride in their work? What incentives do their employers offer? Write a short essay comparing American views with Japanese views.

ACTIVITY

Take It to the NET

7. **Graphing Japan's Economy** Create a graph or chart to organize the information found on the Web site. Visit the World Explorer: People, Places, and Cultures section of **phschool.com** for help in completing this activity.

508 UNIT 6 ASIA

Answers to...

CRITICAL THINKING

Possible answer: Large numbers of Japanese women will eventually become managers in Japanese companies because Japanese companies will realize that they are losing valuable talent to foreign firms.

Resource Directory

Teaching Resources

Section Quiz in the Unit 6 Teaching Resources, p. 58

SECTION 3

The Koreas

Different Ways of Governing

BEFORE YOU READ

READING FOCUS

1. How has South Korea become an economic success?
2. Why has North Korea been slower to develop?

KEY TERMS

demilitarized zone
diversify
famine

NOTE TAKING

Copy the chart below. As you read the section, fill in the diagram to show differences in the economies and governments of the Koreas.

South Korea	North Korea

MAIN IDEA

South Korea, a democracy with a strong economy based on free enterprise, and North Korea, a communist country with a command economy, comprise a heavily divided region in East Asia.

Setting the Scene

DMZ stands for **"demilitarized zone."** In the Koreas, it is a border area between North and South Korea in which no weapons are allowed. The DMZ holds back more than weapons and troops, however. It keeps all people, supplies, and communication from passing between the countries. It also divides two countries that are on very different economic paths.

In the DMZ

GOVERNMENT

South Korean troops patrol a section of the barbed-wire fence that extends along the demilitarized zone. North and South Korea each fear they will be attacked by the other. **Critical Thinking** What do you think it would be like to live right next to an enemy nation?

South Korea: An Asian Economic Tiger?

In the mid-1900s, South Korea had agricultural resources but few industries. A half-century later, South Korea has become a leading economic power.

South Korea is a democracy with an economy based on free enterprise. After World War II, South Korea's factories focused on making cloth and processed foods. Later, it developed heavy industry. In the 1970s, South Korea—along with Thailand, Hong Kong, the Philippines, and some other Asian nations—experienced an economic boom. People dubbed these nations "Asian Tigers." Today, South Korea is among the world's top shipbuilders. It has a growing electronics industry that exports radios, televisions, and computers. It has large refineries, or factories that process oil, used to make plastics, rubber, and other products.

South Korea's change from a farming to an industrial economy has created a building boom. Factories, office and apartment

Resource Directory

Teaching Resources

Classroom Manager in the Unit 6 Teaching Resources, p. 59

Guided Reading and Review in the Unit 6 Teaching Resources, p. 60

Guide to the Essentials, p. 120

Technology

Section Reading Support Transparencies

SECTION 3

Lesson Objectives

1. Explain how South Korea became an economic success.
2. Determine the reasons why North Korea has developed more slowly than South Korea.

Lesson Plan

1 Engage

Warm-Up Activity

Discuss the concept of economic freedom—the freedom to start your own business offering a product or service that people want or need. Ask students how they think economic freedom can help make businesses successful.

Activating Prior Knowledge

Ask students to discuss how they react when limits are imposed on their activities.

2 Explore

Have students read Section 3 and discuss the following questions: What is the DMZ and what is its purpose? How and why did South Korea become an industrial success? How did the political system in North Korea keep the country from industrial and agricultural success? What stands in the way of reunification of the two Koreas? How could reunification help both Koreas?

Answers to...

CRITICAL THINKING

Accept all reasonable responses.

Lesson Plan continued

3 Teach

Review material in this section and the chapter by having a "quiz show." Organize the class into two teams. Prepare questions covering key terms and main ideas from the first three sections or use questions from the Section Assessments. Alternate questions between the two teams. If a "contestant" cannot answer, give the question to the other team. This activity should take about 30 minutes.

Questions for Discussion

SOCIAL STUDIES SKILLS Look at the Country Profile on this page. Why is the North Korean position on religion similar to that of the Chinese?

Both North Korea and China are communist countries.

ECONOMICS How did South Korea become an economic power, or "Asian Tiger," in the 1970s?

South Korea developed industry, effectively changing from a farming economy to an industrial economy.

4 Assess/Reteach

See the answers to the Section 3 Assessment. You may also use the "quiz show" for assessment and assign the section assessment accordingly.

COUNTRY • PROFILE

North Korea and South Korea

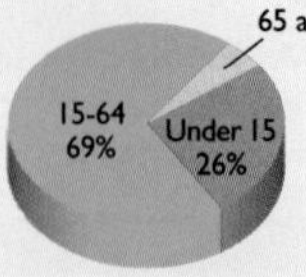

Age Structure (in years)

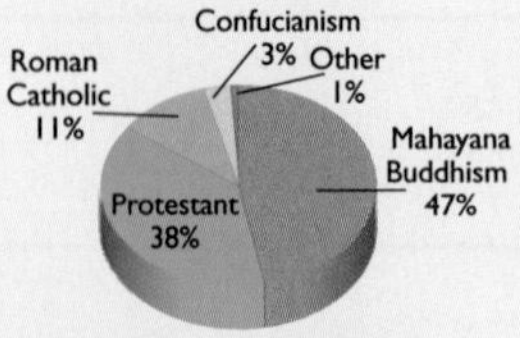

Religious Persuasion

Religion is not widely practiced in North Korea because the government discourages it.

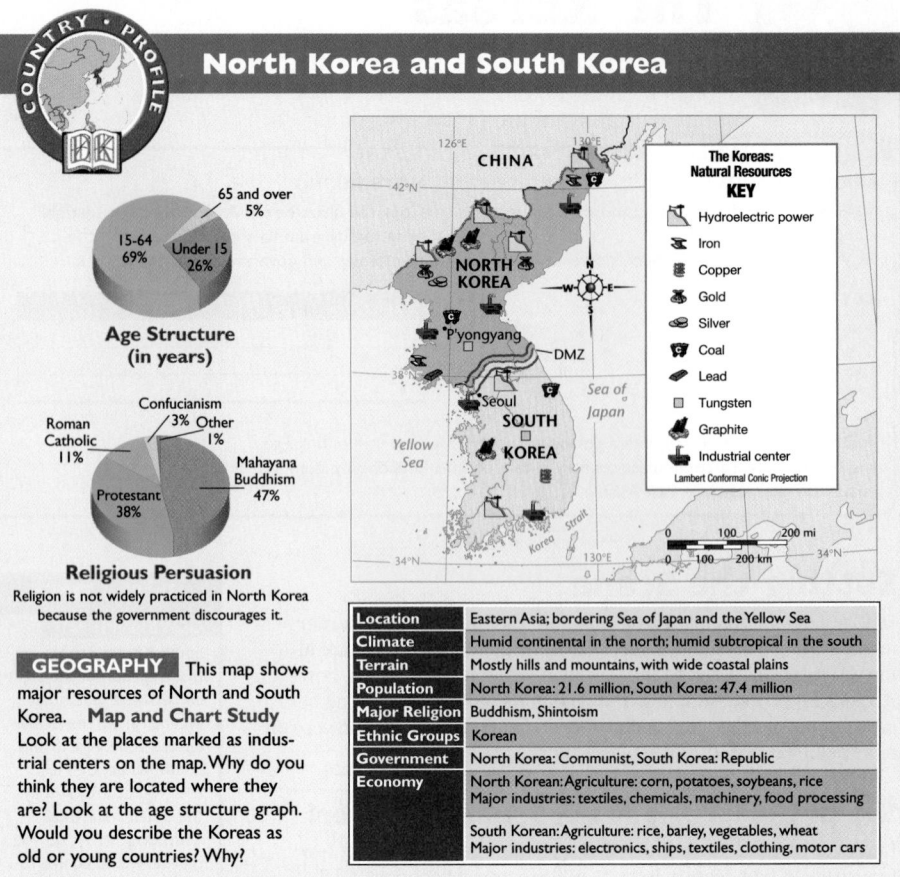

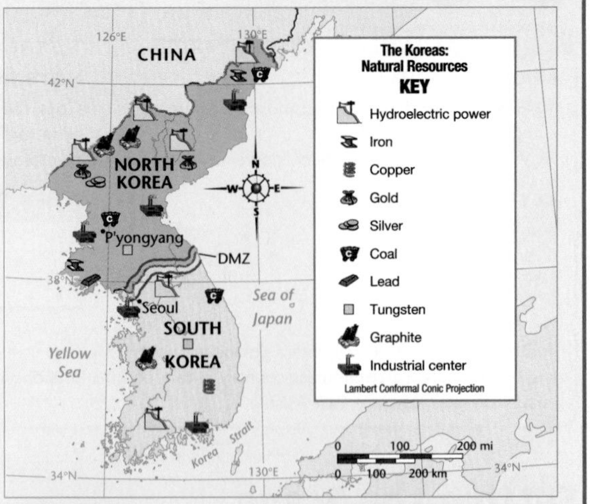

GEOGRAPHY This map shows major resources of North and South Korea. **Map and Chart Study** Look at the places marked as industrial centers on the map. Why do you think they are located where they are? Look at the age structure graph. Would you describe the Koreas as old or young countries? Why?

Location	Eastern Asia; bordering Sea of Japan and the Yellow Sea
Climate	Humid continental in the north; humid subtropical in the south
Terrain	Mostly hills and mountains, with wide coastal plains
Population	North Korea: 21.6 million, South Korea: 47.4 million
Major Religion	Buddhism, Shintoism
Ethnic Groups	Korean
Government	North Korea: Communist, South Korea: Republic
Economy	North Korean: Agriculture: corn, potatoes, soybeans, rice Major industries: textiles, chemicals, machinery, food processing South Korean: Agriculture: rice, barley, vegetables, wheat Major industries: electronics, ships, textiles, clothing, motor cars

AS YOU READ

Find Main Ideas How does South Korea's economy differ from North Korea's economy?

buildings, and roads have sprung up to meet the needs of modern society.

Despite its successes, South Korea faces a number of challenges. Like Japan, it lacks natural resources and it must import large amounts of raw materials to keep industry running. Major imports are oil, iron, steel, and chemicals. The cost of living has grown, and wages often cannot keep up.

In addition, like the other Asian Tigers, South Korea has faced severe economic difficulties in the past few years. Corruption in government has been widespread, and huge debts have piled up. South Korea hopes to restructure its political and financial systems. If it succeeds in turning the crisis into opportunity, it can become a Tiger once again.

Answers to...

MAP AND CHART STUDY

All the marked industrial centers are located on or near coasts. Their location makes it easy to get raw materials and to transport finished goods. Young. The majority of the Koreas' population is between the ages of 15 and 64.

AS YOU READ

South Korea's economy is based on free enterprise. North Korea is a communist country with government-owned factories, farms, and businesses.

Resource Directory

Teaching Resources

Outline Maps, Japan and the Koreas: Political, p. 42

Technology

Color Transparencies 115 East Asia: Physical-Political Map; **116** East Asia: Political Map

North Korea: A Command Economy

North Korea is a communist country that has kept itself closed to much of the rest of the world. This has kept out new technology and fresh ideas. Yet North Korea is rich in mineral resources. Until the end of World War II, it was the industrial center of the Korean Peninsula.

Today, however, North Korea cannot compete with South Korea. It still manufactures goods in government-owned factories and these factories produce poor-quality goods. Little has been done to **diversify,** or add variety to, the economy.

Farming methods, too, are outdated in the north. Many farmers burn hillsides to prepare for planting crops. After a few years of destroying vegetation, the good soil can be washed away by rain. Then, the fields can no longer be farmed. In 1996, North Koreans faced **famine,** or a huge food shortage, and starvation. For the first time, they asked noncommunist countries for aid.

Why don't the two sides get together? They share a common heritage and language. Many families have members living on both sides of the DMZ. North Korea has great need of the food raised in the south. Its industries would also benefit from the technology of the south. South Korea's needs are fewer. It could make good use of the mineral resources of the north. But South Korea can easily buy what it needs with the money from exports. It is mainly political differences that keep the two countries from joining peacefully. Probably only the end of communism in the north will allow Korea to be unified again.

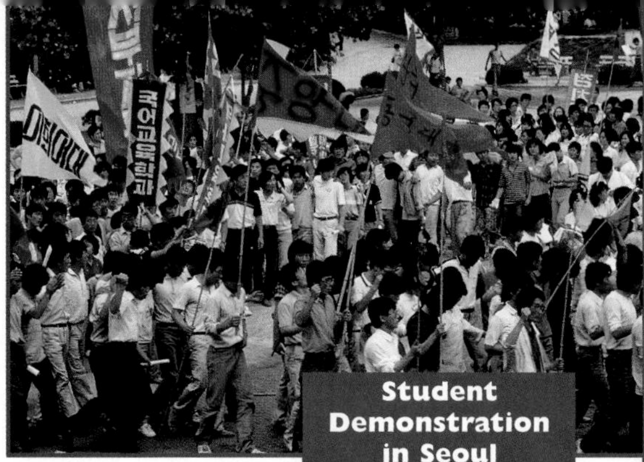

Student Demonstration in Seoul

CITIZENSHIP

In South Korea, groups often take to the streets to demand higher wages, better working conditions, new government programs, or friendlier relations with North Korea. Here, a group of college students march in such a parade, or demonstration, in Seoul. Sometimes, marchers clash with police. **Critical Thinking** What kinds of slogans do you think might be written on the colorful banners carried by the students?

SECTION 3 ASSESSMENT

AFTER YOU READ

RECALL

1. Define (a) demilitarized zone, (b) diversify, (c) famine

COMPREHENSION

2. Discuss the reasons for South Korea's economic success and recent downturn.
3. Why has North Korea's economy lagged behind South Korea's?

CRITICAL THINKING AND WRITING

4. **Exploring the Main Idea** Review the Main Idea statement at the beginning of this section. Then, list the industries and resources in South Korea and North Korea.
5. **Comparing and Contrasting** How do the governments of North and South Korea affect their economies?

ACTIVITY

6. **Writing to Learn** The division between North and South Korea has cut you off from family members. It has also influenced the way you live. Write a journal entry describing what it is like to live in either North or South Korea.

Resource Directory

Teaching Resources

Section Quiz in the Unit 6 Teaching Resources, p. 61

SECTION 3 ASSESSMENT

AFTER YOU READ

1. (a) border area between North and South Korea in which no weapons are allowed (b) to add variety (c) severe food shortage
2. Students' reasons for success should include the fact that South Korea has had the economic freedom to industrialize and that the government has encouraged industry and farming. Reasons for downturn should include corruption in government and increasing debt.
3. Students' answers should show awareness of the fact that, as a communist country, North Korea has been cut off from outside aid and new technology. The goods produced by government-owned factories cannot compete in the world market, and there has been little diversification. Poor farming methods have resulted in a famine.
4. South Korea has oil refineries and industries in shipping and electronics. South Korea lacks natural resources and must import large amounts of raw material to keep industry running. North Korea has mineral resources, but no longer has a viable industrial center because the communist government has kept out the fresh ideas and new technology necessary to keep industry running.
5. Students' answers should show awareness of the contrasting results when a government controls the economy, as in North Korea, and when a government allows economic freedom, as in South Korea.
6. Students' journal entries should accurately describe political and economic life in one of the two Koreas. Students might also mention that they miss relatives in the other Korea.

Answers to...

CRITICAL THINKING

The slogans probably refer to the students' demands.

SECTION 4

Lesson Objectives

1. Explain Vietnam's struggle to shed colonial rule and the effects of civil war on the country.
2. Describe how the Vietnamese are rebuilding their country.

Lesson Plan

1 Engage

Warm-Up Activity

Refresh students' memories concerning the events of the American Civil War and the struggle to hold the North and the South together as one nation. Remind students that most of the fighting took place in the South. Ask students how the war affected the economy of the South. How did the South rebuild following the war?

Activating Prior Knowledge

Have students write down two or three things they know about the Vietnam War. Ask volunteers to share their knowledge of the Vietnam War era with the class.

2 Explore

As students read, have them consider the following questions: What roles did France and the United States play in Vietnam? Why was Vietnam divided in half? How are the Vietnamese working to rebuild their country and develop their economy?

Answers to...

CRITICAL THINKING

Students may say the women learned to make pottery the way their mothers and grandmothers made pottery: by hand. Students may also say that the women are too poor to afford a potter's wheel.

SECTION 4

Vietnam

Rebuilding the Economy

BEFORE YOU READ

READING FOCUS

1. What conflicts have divided Vietnam?
2. How are the Vietnamese rebuilding their economy?

KEY TERMS

refugee

KEY PEOPLE AND PLACES

Ho Chi Minh
Ho Chi Minh City

MAIN IDEA

After decades of conflict and war devastated Vietnam, a reunited country has struggled to rebuild its economy.

NOTE TAKING

Copy the diagram below. As you read the section, fill in the diagram to show what caused a long and devastating war in Vietnam, and to identify some of the problems war left behind.

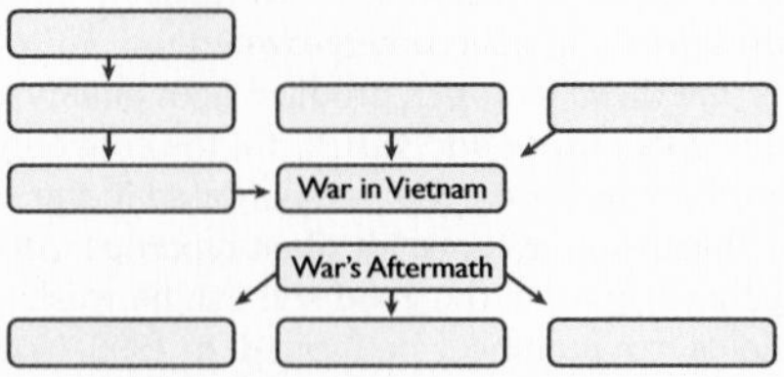

CULTURE These Vietamese women are making dishes and bowls in a traditional way. It takes great skill to form smooth, round pots from clay without using a potter's wheel. **Critical Thinking** Why do you think these women are not using a potter's wheel to make their pottery?

Setting the Scene

It is summer in northern Vietnam. Villagers cut, harvest, and plow rice fields just as their parents and grandparents did. Unlike their parents and grandparents, however, these villagers are making money. Rice farmers in the village of Phu Do return from the fields to a second job: noodle-making. Farmers in Son Dong carve religious statues from wood in their free time. Potters in Bat Trang, goldsmiths in Dong Sam, embroiderers in Thuong Tin—all are earning money from age-old crafts. Their success helps to rebuild the economy of Vietnam.

Decades of Conflict and War

In the mid-1800s, France took over Vietnam as a colony. The Vietnamese people resented French rule. They wanted to have their own government on their own soil. In 1946, many Vietnamese heeded the call to arms of independence leader **Ho Chi Minh** (hoh chee min).

Under Ho Chi Minh, the Vietnamese Communists defeated the French. The United States did not want Vietnam to become a communist country. After the French defeat, a treaty divided Vietnam into two nations. The northern nation was controlled by Communists. Under Ho Chi Minh, they tried to take over the south by force. In 1959, Ho Chi Minh's forces, the Viet Cong, launched a war to achieve this goal. As they threatened South Vietnam, the United States took an active role in the war.

Resource Directory

Teaching Resources

Classroom Manager in the Unit 6 Teaching Resources, p. 62

Guided Reading and Review in the Unit 6 Teaching Resources, p. 63

Guide to the Essentials, p. 121

Technology

Section Reading Support Transparencies

Vietnam

COUNTRY • PROFILE

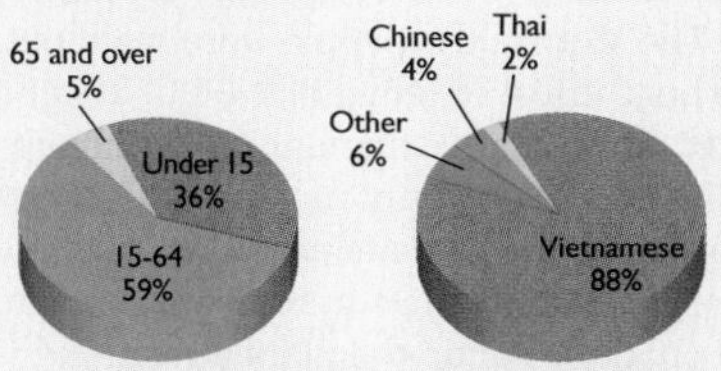

Age Structure (in years)   **Ethnic Makeup**

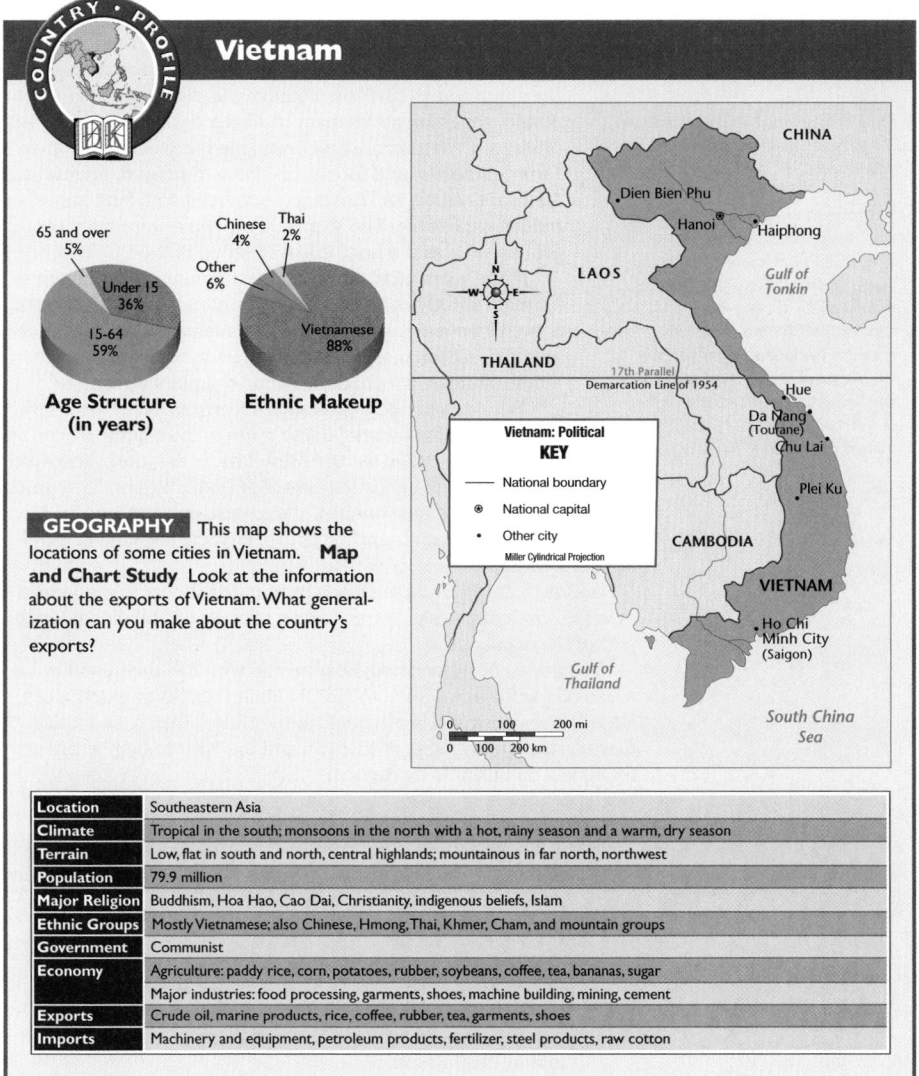

GEOGRAPHY This map shows the locations of some cities in Vietnam. **Map and Chart Study** Look at the information about the exports of Vietnam. What generalization can you make about the country's exports?

Location	Southeastern Asia
Climate	Tropical in the south; monsoons in the north with a hot, rainy season and a warm, dry season
Terrain	Low, flat in south and north, central highlands; mountainous in far north, northwest
Population	79.9 million
Major Religion	Buddhism, Hoa Hao, Cao Dai, Christianity, indigenous beliefs, Islam
Ethnic Groups	Mostly Vietnamese; also Chinese, Hmong, Thai, Khmer, Cham, and mountain groups
Government	Communist
Economy	Agriculture: paddy rice, corn, potatoes, rubber, soybeans, coffee, tea, bananas, sugar
	Major industries: food processing, garments, shoes, machine building, mining, cement
Exports	Crude oil, marine products, rice, coffee, rubber, tea, garments, shoes
Imports	Machinery and equipment, petroleum products, fertilizer, steel products, raw cotton

By the 1970s, Vietnam had been at war for more than 30 years. The United States government realized it was fighting a war it would never win. In addition, thousands of people in the United States were calling for an end to the war. By 1973, the United States finally ended its part in the war.

3 Teach

Have students make an outline of the key ideas in this section, including at least one detail for each key idea. This activity should take about 20 minutes.

Questions for Discussion

SOCIAL STUDIES SKILLS **Look at the map in Country Profile on this page. Why do you think North Vietnam was communist and South Vietnam was not before the two were unified under a communist government after the Vietnam War?**

North Vietnam borders communist China and was probably influenced by Chinese communist ideology.

CITIZENSHIP **How did the Trung sisters fulfill the role of responsible citizens?**

They helped free their people and establish independence.

4 Assess/Reteach

See the answers to the Section 4 Assessment. You may also use students' completed outlines as an assessment.

Acceptable outlines include one detail for each key idea.

Commendable outlines include at least two supporting details from each key idea.

Outstanding outlines include many significant points covered in this section, each with two or more supporting details.

Resource Directory

Technology

Color Transparencies 123 Southeast Asia: Political Map

Passport to the World CD-ROM This interactive CD-ROM allows students to explore each region of the world. Students view regional videos, take a photo tour, and explore a historical timeline. Students record their travels in an Explorer's Journal, and receive passport stamps when they pass regional quizzes.

Answers to...

MAP AND CHART STUDY

Vietnam exports mainly manufactured goods.

CHAPTER 27 EAST AND SOUTHEAST ASIA: EXPLORING THE REGION TODAY 513

ACTIVITY

Culture

Vietnam and the United States
Assign small groups to research ways in which the Vietnam War and Vietnamese culture have influenced the United States. Groups may research and present oral reports on the history and significance of the Vietnam War Memorial in Washington, D.C.; interview a Vietnam War veteran or an immigrant from Vietnam and present the interview to the class; or contact or visit a Vietnamese cultural organization and report on how Vietnamese immigrants celebrate holidays here in the United States.

Verbal/Linguistic

SECTION 4 ASSESSMENT

AFTER YOU READ

1. (a) Vietnamese communist leader (b) Vietnam's most prosperous city, located in the southern part of the country
2. (a) person who flees his or her country because of war
3. After Vietnam defeated France, the country was divided into North and South Vietnam: North Vietnam fought to take over South Vietnam.
4. Vietnam has allowed some free enterprise, which has helped some people improve their lives.
5. Possible response: Challenges: repairing the damage to cities and fields wrought by bombs and land mines, recovering from the loss of family and friends; Rebuilding: establishing new businesses, hotels, restaurants, and factories; making use of returning refugees' knowledge and experience gained in other countries.
6. Possible response: The government wanted to honor Ho Chi Minh because he defeated the French and led the Vietnamese fight for unification.
7. Responses will vary but should reflect an understanding of the role that Ho Chi Minh played in Vietnam and of what he meant to the Vietnamese.

CITIZENSHIP

The Trung Sisters

Long before France, China ruled Vietnam for approximately 1,000 years. In A.D. 39, two sisters named Trung-Trac and Trung-Nhi led a Vietnamese army in freeing 65 towns from the Chinese. The sisters established an independent state, declared themselves queens, and ruled for three years. Although the Chinese eventually crushed the independent nation, the Vietnamese continue to honor the Trung sisters, as attested by the street in Ho Chi Minh City named for them.

The Vietnamese Rebuild

After the United States pulled out, North Vietnam conquered the south and in 1976, the country was reunited under a communist government. Vietnam had been devastated by the war. Millions of Vietnamese had been killed or wounded, homes, farms, factories, and forests had been destroyed, bombs had torn cities apart, and fields were covered with land mines, or hidden explosives. The Vietnamese people were worn out. Still ahead was the huge effort of rebuilding.

In the years after the war, the communist government in Vietnam strictly controlled the lives of its citizens. Although it is still a communist country, Vietnam now allows some free enterprise. Still, most Vietnamese live in rural areas where whole families live on a few hundred dollars a year.

Vietnam's greatest economic successes have been in rebuilding its cities. Hanoi in the north is the capital. Saigon (sy GAHN), now called **Ho Chi Minh City,** is the most prosperous city in Vietnam and is the center of trade. Well-off Vietnamese buy designer clothing and watches, stereo systems, and jewelry. Many of these people run restaurants or hotels, buy and sell land or buildings, or own factories.

Although northern Vietnam has been much slower to modernize than the south, the desire for economic success has taken hold in that part of the country, too.

Thousands of former **refugees,** people who flee their country because of war, have returned to Ho Chi Minh City. Some ex-refugees attended business and law schools in the United States, and today they use their knowledge of Vietnam and the West to help wealthy foreigners do business in Vietnam.

SECTION 4 ASSESSMENT

AFTER YOU READ

RECALL

1. Identify: (a) Ho Chi Minh, (b) Ho Chi Minh City
2. Define: (a) refugee

COMPREHENSION

3. What conflicts have divided Vietnam?
4. What successes has Vietnam had in rebuilding its economy?

CRITICAL THINKING AND WRITING

5. **Exploring the Main Idea** Review the Main Idea statement at the beginning of this section. Then, list two challenges that Vietnam faced after the war and two ways that Vietnam is rebuilding its economy.
6. **Identifying Frame of Reference and Point of View** Why do you think Saigon was renamed Ho Chi Minh City after the war?

ACTIVITY

7. **Writing a Letter to the Editor** Imagine that you are a Vietnamese living in Saigon in 1954. Write a letter to a newspaper expressing your attitude towards Ho Chi Minh.

Resource Directory

Teaching Resources

Section Quiz in the Unit 6 Teaching Resources, p. 64

Chapter Summary in the Unit 6 Teaching Resources, p. 65

Vocabulary in the Unit 6 Teaching Resources, p. 66

Reteaching in the Unit 6 Teaching Resources, p. 67

Enrichment in the Unit 6 Teaching Resources, p. 68

Critical Thinking in the Unit 6 Teaching Resources, p. 69

Recognizing Bias

Learn the Skill

Being biased means leaning toward a particular point of view. Sometimes, people who write about something only know one side of the story. Other people leave out information on purpose to give their own viewpoint. Biased writing takes a side, even if at first it seems not to. You need to be able to recognize bias in writing in order to know whether you're getting a fair picture of a situation. When you read, you can look for certain clues that will point out a writer's bias. To determine whether a writer is biased, do the following:

A. Look for opinions. Opinions are beliefs that cannot be proven. They are the opposite of facts, which can be proven. Biased writing often contains opinions disguised as facts. For example, the statement, "Life in South Vietnam was better than life in North Vietnam," may sound like a fact, but it is an opinion. It doesn't matter whether you agree with the opinion or think that it makes sense.

B. Look for loaded words and phrases that carry a hidden meaning. These words may give a positive or a negative impression. Read this sentence: "Vietnam's low flat deltas create picture perfect shorelines." The words "picture perfect" are loaded. They give a very positive impression. However, this hidden meaning cannot be proved. It is not fact.

C. Look for what isn't there. Biased writers often leave out information that does not support their bias. For example, the writer might tell you that "South Vietnam's president Ngo Dinh Diem distributed land among more farmers and built new factories during the 1950s," but leave out any negative actions of Diem's or any positive actions of North Vietnam's leader.

D. Think about the tone. Tone is the overall feeling of a piece of writing. It shows the writer's attitude toward the subject: "Water puppets became a crude form of entertainment." This sentence gives you the clear impression that the writer has negative feelings about Vietnamese forms of entertainment. Unbiased writing provides the facts and lets the reader form his or her own conclusions.

Practice the Skill

The selection in the box is a biased description of Vietnam today. To identify the bias, follow steps A through D. Consider these questions: Are there any opinions disguised as facts in the selection? What words give a positive or negative impression of Vietnam? What important facts about Vietnam does the writer fail to include? How would you describe the tone of the writing? Is it positive or negative? After you have finished, describe Vietnam today in one paragraph without bias.

Vietnam Today

It is unfortunate that Vietnam became a communist country. Today it is one of the poorest nations in Asia. Most houses have no indoor toilets or running water. The government of Vietnam would do well to model itself after the United States.

Apply the Skill

See the Chapter Review and Assessment at the end of this chapter for more questions on recognizing bias.

Lesson Objectives

1. Define the term bias.
2. Identify important clues to bias.
3. Recognize bias in context.

Lesson Plan

1 Engage

To introduce the skill, ask volunteers to give a definition for the word "bias" and write these definitions on the board. Then read the opening text under "Learn the Skill" aloud. Discuss with students the meaning of bias in written text. Ask students to brainstorm reasons why a writer might use bias.

2 Explore

Students can read the steps and examples about Vietnam under "Learn the Skill" to practice recognizing bias. Encourage students to record their questions as they read. Then, work through each step as a class. After each step, challenge students to identify clues for recognizing bias.

3 Teach

Have students read the paragraph titled "Vietnam Today" and use the steps to look for bias. If students have difficulty, have them work with a partner and discuss their reasons for deciding whether or not a statement includes bias.

4 Assess/Reteach

They should recognize the word "unfortunate" in the first sentences as a loaded word. Students will probably conclude that the writer has a bias toward the United States and against communism.

To further assess students' understanding of recognizing bias, have them complete the "Applying Your Skills" part of the Chapter Review and Assessment.

Resource Directory

Teaching Resources

Social Studies and Geography Skills, Recognizing Bias, p. 45

Technology

Social Studies Skills Tutor CD-ROM

Answers to...

PRACTICE THE SKILL

The first and last sentences are disguised as facts. The word *unfortunate* gives a negative impression of Vietnam. The writer fails to include any positive aspects about Vietnam. The tone of the description is negative.

CHAPTER 27

Review and Assessment

Creating a Chapter Summary

Student summaries will vary.

Sample summaries:

Section 2 A prosperous industrial nation, Japan faces new economic challenges such as revamping the relationship between business and government and the role of women in economic life.

Section 3 The Koreas are divided in two countries, North Korea and South Korea. North Korea is a communist country with a weak, command economy. South Korea is a democracy with a strong, free-enterprise economy.

Section 4 In the 20th century, conflict and war devastated Vietnam. Since the Vietnam War ended in 1976, the reunited nation has been struggling to rebuild its economy. Its greatest successes are in its cities. Rural areas remain very poor.

Reviewing Key Terms

1. c **2.** b **3.** f **4.** e **5.** d **6.** a **7.** g

Reviewing the Main Ideas

1. Mao Zedong's hard–line communist policies devastated China's economy.
2. The introduction of some free enterprise has strengthened China's economy in recent years.
3. Its free enterprise system has helped Taiwan to become and remain economically strong.
4. The Japanese government subsidized industry, and Japanese employees worked very hard.
5. The relationship between government and business; the role of women in economic life
6. North Korea is a communist country with a command economy. South Korea is a republic or democratic republic with a free-enterprise economy.
7. Vietnam was divided into two nations, South Vietnam and North Vietnam.
8. The allowance of some free enterprise is helping some Vietnamese attain a higher standard of living.

CHAPTER 27

Review and Assessment

Creating a Chapter Summary

On a separate piece of paper, draw a diagram like this one, and include the information that summarizes the first section of the chapter. Then, fill in the remaining boxes with summaries of Sections 2, 3, and 4.

EAST AND SOUTHEAST ASIA TODAY

Section 1	Section 2	Section 3	Section 4
In recent years, China has begun to repair its economy, which was devastated during the long rule of Mao Zedong. Taiwan has a free enterprise economy that, since the nation's founding, has been one of the strongest in Asia.			

Reviewing Key Terms

Match the key terms in Column I with the definitions in Column II.

Column I	Column II
1. subsidize	a. extreme
2. diversify	b. add variety
3. incentive	c. support financially
4. refugee	d. economic system that allows people to choose jobs, start private businesses, make a profit
5. free enterprise	e. person who flees his or her country because of war
6. radical	f. benefit that inspires people to work hard
7. discrimination	g. unequal treatment

Reviewing the Main Ideas

1. How did the policies of Mao Zedong affect China's economy? (Section 1)
2. What change has strengthened China's economy in recent years? (Section 1)
3. What has helped Taiwan to become and remain economically strong? (Section 1)
4. How did Japan regain economic strength after World War II? (Section 2)
5. What issues must Japan address to maintain a strong economy? (Section 2)
6. What political and economic differences divide North and South Korea? (Section 3)
7. How was Vietnam divided after it gained independence from France? (Section 4)
8. What change in economic policy is helping some Vietnamese attain a higher standard of living? (Section 4)

516 UNIT 6 ASIA

Map Activity

East and Southeast Asia

For each place listed below, write the letter from the map that shows its location. Use the Atlas in the back of your book to help you.

1. Japan
2. China
3. Taiwan
4. South Korea
5. North Korea
6. Hong Kong

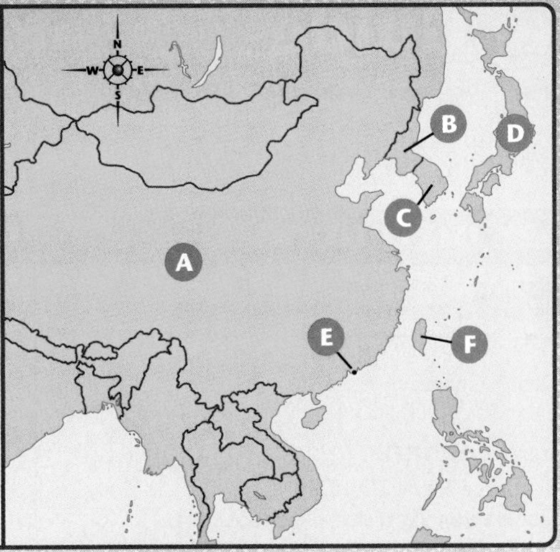

Take It to the NET

Enrichment For more map activities using geography skills, visit the social studies section of **phschool.com.**

Writing Activity

1. **Writing a Newspaper Editorial** Choose one conflict that you read about in this chapter. Write a newspaper editorial that gives your point of view on the conflict.
2. **Using Primary Sources** Choose one of the places discussed in the chapter to research. Visit your school library and use primary sources such as interviews found in newspaper or magazine articles and memoirs to find additional information on the place. Write a travel article that provides information and suggestions for what to see and how to act in the place.

Critical Thinking

1. **Comparing and Contrasting** Compare the policies of the communist government of China before and after the late 1970s.
2. **Identifying the Main Ideas and Supporting Details** Why are Japan's people sometimes called its only natural resources?

Applying Your Skills

Look through a current newspaper or magazine to find a short article that interests you. Review the steps you learned to recognize bias. Read your chosen article and determine whether the writer is biased. Record your thoughts on a separate sheet of paper, making sure to support your decision with details from the article.

Take It to the NET

Activity Read the news article about the current state of Vietnam's economy and government. Who controls the economy in Vietnam? How is it different from the economy in the United States? Visit the World Explorer: People, Places, and Cultures section of **phschool.com** for help in completing this activity.

Chapter 27 Self-Test As a final review activity, take the Chapter 27 Self-Test and get instant feedback on your answers. To take the test, visit the Social Studies section of **phschool.com.**

Map Activity

1. D **2.** A **3.** F **4.** C **5.** B **6.** E

Writing Activity

1. Responses will vary. Students should correctly identify the nations engaged in the conflict and demonstrate an understanding of the issues underlying the conflict.
2. Students' articles should be supported by information from the text and their own research.

Critical Thinking

1. During the 1950s and 1960s, the government tried without much success to force rapid economic and political change. After Mao's death, the government allowed limited free enterprise, which helped improve the economy.
2. Japan has few natural resources, and much of its economic success is due to the Japanese people's dedicated work ethic and high productivity.

Applying Your Skills

Have students pair up and review each other's work. Then, have students share their article and thoughts on the article with the rest of the class.

Resource Directory

Teaching Resources

Cooperative Learning Activity in the Unit 6 Teaching Resources, pp. 119–122

Chapter Tests Forms A and B in the Unit 6 Teaching Resources, pp. 152–157

Guide to the Essentials, Ch. 27 Test, p. 122

Other Print Resources

Chapter Tests with ExamView® Test Bank, Ch. 27

Technology

ExamView® Test Bank CD-ROM, Ch. 27

Resource Pro® CD-ROM

Chapter 28 Planning Guide

Resource Manager

	CORE INSTRUCTION	READING/SKILLS
Chapter-Level Resources	**Teaching Resources** Program Overview Pacing Charts **Technology** Resource Pro® CD-ROM Companion Web site, phschool.com • eTeach	**Technology** Social Studies Skills Tutor CD-ROM Student Edition on Audio CD, Ch. 28
1 Pakistan: Making Economic Progress 1. Identify how the Indus River intensifies conflict between Pakistan and India. 2. Describe the importance of irrigation to Pakistan's agricultural economy. 3. Explain how Pakistan is making economic progress.	**Teaching Resources** **Unit 6** Classroom Manager, p. 71 Guided Reading and Review, p.72	**Teaching Resources** Guide to the Essentials, p. 123 **Technology** Section Reading Support Transparencies
2 India: A Democracy Rooted in Tradition 1. Identify opportunities for Untouchables that have arisen since independence. 2. Describe how women influence the political process in India.	**Teaching Resources** **Unit 6** Classroom Manager, p. 74 Guided Reading and Review, p. 75	**Teaching Resources** Guide to the Essentials, p. 124 **Technology** Section Reading Support Transparencies
3 Saudi Arabia: Islam and the Oil Industry 1. Explain how the discovery of oil has affected the lives of Saudi Arabians. 2. Describe how Islam structures the lives of women in Saudi Arabia.	**Teaching Resources** **Unit 6** Classroom Manager, p. 77 Guided Reading and Review, p. 78	**Teaching Resources** Guide to the Essentials, p. 125 **Technology** Section Reading Support Transparencies
4 Israel: Building Its Economy 1. Describe how Israel's geography influences its economy. 2. Identify ways in which people work together economically in Israel. 3. Understand why Israel has had to cooperate with neighboring countries.	**Teaching Resources** **Unit 6** Classroom Manager, p. 80 Guided Reading and Review, p. 81 Chapter Summary, p. 83 Vocabulary, p. 84 Reteaching, p. 85	**Teaching Resources** **Unit 6** Critical Thinking, p. 87 Guide to the Essentials, p. 126 Social Studies and Geography Skills, p. 48 **Technology** Section Reading Support Transparencies

ENRICHMENT / PRE-AP

Teaching Resources
Primary Sources and Literature Readings

Other Print Resources
DK Atlas

Technology
World Video Explorer: Daily Life: India
Companion Web site, phschool.com

Technology
Color Transparencies 125

Teaching Resources
Outline Maps, p. 37

Technology
Color Transparencies 126, 129–131
Passport to the World CD-ROM

Teaching Resources
Outline Maps, p. 30

Technology
Color Transparencies 134

Teaching Resources
Unit 6
- Enrichment, p. 86
- Cooperative Learning Activity, pp. 123–126
- Outline Maps, pp. 28, 29

ASSESSMENT

Prentice Hall Assessment System

Core Assessment
Chapter Tests with ExamView® Test Bank, Ch. 28
ExamView® Test Bank CD-ROM, Ch. 28

Standardized Test Preparation
Diagnose and Prescribe
Diagnostic Tests for Middle Grades Social Studies Skills
Review and Reteach
Review Book for World Studies
Practice and Assess
Test-taking Strategies with Transparencies for Middle Grades Test Prep Book
Test-taking Strategies Posters

Teaching Resources
Unit 6
- Section Quizzes, pp. 73, 76, 79, and 82
- Chapter Tests, pp. 158–163

Technology
Companion Web site, phschool.com
Ch. 28 Self-Test

World Video Explorer
Each region of the world is explored through regional flyovers and investigative field trips. Case study segments give students an in-depth view of the history, economy, government, and culture of a key place in each region. Case studies include Nigeria, Mexico, China, British Columbia, and the Czech Republic.

In Your Classroom

CUSTOMIZE FOR INDIVIDUAL NEEDS

Gifted and Talented

Teacher's Edition
- Art, p. 529
- Identifying Central Issues, p.533

Teaching Resources
- Enrichment, p. 86

Other Print Resources
- Primary Sources and Literature Readings

Honors/Pre-AP

Teacher's Edition
- Art, p. 529
- Identifying Central Issues, p.533

Teaching Resources
- Critical Thinking, p. 87
- Primary Sources and Literature Readings

ESL

Teacher's Edition
- Science, p. 521
- Art, p. 529

Teaching Resources
- Guided Reading and Review, pp. 72, 75, 78, and 81
- Vocabulary, p. 84
- Reteaching, p. 85
- Guide to the Essentials, pp. 123–126
- Social Studies and Geography Skills, p. 48

Technology
- Social Studies Skills Tutor CD-ROM
- Section Reading Support Transparencies

Less Proficient Readers

Teacher's Edition
- Science, p. 521
- Art, p. 529

Teaching Resources
- Guided Reading and Review, pp. 72, 75, 78, and 81
- Vocabulary, p. 84
- Reteaching, p. 85
- Guide to the Essentials, pp. 123–126
- Social Studies and Geography Skills, p. 48

Technology
- Social Studies Skills Tutor CD-ROM
- Section Reading Support Transparencies

Less Proficient Writers

Teacher's Edition
- Science, p. 521
- Art, p. 529

Teaching Resources
- Guided Reading and Review, pp. 72, 75, 78, and 81
- Vocabulary, p. 84
- Guide to the Essentials, pp. 123–126
- Social Studies and Geography Skills, p. 48

Technology
- Social Studies Skills Tutor CD-ROM
- Section Reading Support Transparencies

DORLING KINDERSLEY

At the end of each unit, you will find information adapted from Dorling Kindersley's *Illustrated Children's Encyclopedia* that connects to the region being studied and to one of the seven content strands. In addition, your resources include Dorling Kindersley's *Atlas*, which contains valuable information about countries from around the world.

TEACHER'S EDITION INDEX

CHAPTER 28 PACING SUGGESTIONS

For 90-minute Blocks

See suggestions in the Teaching Resources Pacing Charts for Chapter 28. Use Color Transparencies 125, 126, 129–131, 134.

Running Out of Time?

See the Guide to the Essentials, pp. 123–126.

INTERDISCIPLINARY LINKS

Middle Grades Math: Tools for Success

Course 1, Lesson 1-2, **Make a Table;** Lesson 10-1, **Using a Number Line**

Course 2, Lesson 7-8, **Circle Graphs;** Lesson 11-7, **Symmetry and Reflections**

Science Explorer

Cells and Heredity, Lesson 4-3, **Advance in Genetics**

Prentice Hall Literature

Bronze, The Hummingbird that Lived Through Winter

BIBLIOGRAPHY

For the Teacher

DuBois, Jill. *Israel.* Cavendish, 1992.

Ghose, Vijaya. *India.* Cavendish, 1994.

Wakin, Edward. *Contemporary Political Leaders of the Middle East.* Facts on File, 1996.

World Desk Reference. Dorling Kindersley, 2001.

For the Student

Easy

Ghazi, Suhaib Hamid. *Ramadan.* Holiday House, 1996.

Average

Ali, Sharifah Enayat. *Afghanistan.* Cavendish, 1996.

Margolies, Barbara A. *Kanu of Kathmandu: A Journey in Nepal.* Four Winds, 1992.

Challenging

Mozeson, I. E., and Lois Stavsky. *Jerusalem Mosaic: Young Voices from the Holy City.* Four Winds, 1994.

Literature Connection

Perkins, Mitali. *The Sunita Experiment.* Joy Street/Little, Brown, 1993.

Westall, Robert. *Gulf.* Scholastic, 1996.

Take It to the NET

The World Explorer companion Web site, found on **phschool.com**, offers activities for exploring geographical, historical, and cultural resources on the Internet. It also provides on-line links for key content and all Section and Chapter Assessment activities.

The **Teacher site** also provides teachers with regional data and ideas for student research and activities.

Students can use the **Student site** to find chapter-by-chapter Internet resource links and to access Self-Tests.

CHAPTER 28

Connecting to the Guiding Questions

In this chapter, students will read about countries in South and Southwest Asia. Content in this chapter corresponds to the following Guiding Questions outlined at the beginning of the unit.

- How has geography affected the way Asian societies have developed?
- How has history and the achievements of historic figures influenced life in Asia today?
- How has religion affected the way Asian societies have developed?
- How do physical geography and natural resources affect the way that Asians earn a living?
- How have geographic factors affected the development of science and technology in Asia?

Using the Picture Activities

The Shah named the building after his wife, Mumtaz-i-Mahal, which means, "pride of the palace."

- Students should calculate that the mausoleum was finished in 1643 and the complex was completed in 1654.
- Students should use the dimensions from the text to help them create an accurate model representation of the Taj Mahal.

Heterogeneous Groups

The following activities are suitable for heterogeneous groups.

Interdisciplinary Connections,

Art, p. 529

Critical Thinking

Identifying Main Issues, p. 525

eTeach

Be sure to check out this month's discussion with a Master Teacher. Go to **phschool.com**.

CHAPTER 28

SOUTH AND SOUTHWEST ASIA
Exploring the Region Today

A Tribute to Beauty

Using Pictures

The Taj Mahal was built by Shah Jahan, a Muslim ruler from northern India. It represents the throne of God in paradise, but also served as a mausoleum (tomb) for the Shah and his wife when they died.

Taj Mahal Math

Construction of the Taj Mahal began in 1632. It took 20,000 workers eleven years to complete the mausoleum, and another eleven years to finish the entire complex. In what year was the mausoleum finished? How many years did it take to finish the entire complex?

Making a Model of the Taj Mahal

The Taj Mahal is made of white marble. The mausoleum rises about 120 feet into the air and covers an area of about 300 square feet. The minarets are 133 feet high. Notice the large dome in the center as well as other smaller domes. The large dome is 70 feet in diameter. Work with a partner. Use clay, a piece of cardboard for a base, and the photo on this page to create a model of the Taj Mahal.

Resource Directory

Teaching Resources

Primary Sources and Literature Readings extend content with a selection related to the concepts in this chapter.

Other Print Resources

DK Atlas

Technology

Daily Life: India, from the World Video Explorer, enhances students' understanding of daily life in rural and urban India.

Student Edition on Audio CD, Ch. 28

SECTION 1

Pakistan

Making Economic Progress

BEFORE YOU READ

READING FOCUS

1. How does the Indus River influence the relationship between Pakistan and India?
2. What has Pakistan done to help its farmers?
3. What economic growth has taken place in Pakistan?

KEY TERMS
drought

KEY PLACE
Kashmir

NOTE TAKING

Copy the outline below. As you read the section, add to the outline to show how Pakistan is making economic progress.

I. **Geographical Issues**
  A. Indus River is vital to Pakistan's economy
  B.
II. **Agriculture**
III. **Industrial Growth**

MAIN IDEA

Most Pakistanis are farmers, but economic growth is taking place through the development of agricultural and other industries.

Setting the Scene

Many of us take water for granted. We turn on the tap, and water pours out. But many countries in the world lack water resources. **Drought,** or a long period without rain, is a major problem in Pakistan. It is one cause of the conflict over the region of **Kashmir** (KAZH mihr).

Geography Influences Politics

Kashmir is a land of high mountains and beautiful lakes. The Indus River flows from the high mountains of Kashmir. Therefore, whoever controls Kashmir, controls the water flow of the Indus River. Farmers need this water to irrigate crops because without the Indus River, Pakistan would be a dry, hot desert.

Kashmir is bordered by Pakistan, India, China, and Afghanistan. Both Pakistan and India claim Kashmir and want to control the waters of the Indus. The conflict over Kashmir has led to battles between India and Pakistan. This is how important water is to the region.

Terraced Farming

GEOGRAPHY Only about 6 percent of Kashmir's land is good for growing crops. Here, farmers have built terraces so they can grow crops on sloping land. **Critical Thinking** How does the snow on the mountain tops affect the river?

Resource Directory

Teaching Resources

Classroom Manager in the Unit 6 Teaching Resources, p. 71

Guided Reading and Review in the Unit 6 Teaching Resources, p. 72

Guide to the Essentials, p. 123

Technology

Section Reading Support Transparencies

SECTION 1

Lesson Objectives

1. Identify how the Indus River intensifies conflict between Pakistan and India.
2. Describe the importance of irrigation to Pakistan's agricultural economy.
3. Explain how Pakistan is making economic progress.

Lesson Plan

1 Engage

Warm-Up Activity

Mention to students that many people rely on rivers to irrigate crops, but that rivers also may play a part in producing large quantities of electricity. Electricity can be generated from energy produced by moving water. Explain that in Pakistan, harnessing the waterpower of the Indus River has helped industry grow.

Activating Prior Knowledge

Have students jot down several goals that they have achieved. Tell them to put a star beside those that required the help of other people. Ask them to think about how people often work together to achieve a goal desired by a group.

2 Explore

Have students read the section and explore the following questions: Why is the Indus River so important to Pakistan? How is Pakistan's industrial output related to the crops it grows? What do Pakistan's small workshops produce?

Answers to...

CRITICAL THINKING

Snow melt from the mountaintops increases the flow of the river and, therefore, the amount of water available for irrigation.

Lesson Plan continued

❸ Teach

Have students develop a quiz based on the agricultural and industrial sectors of Pakistan's economy. Ask students to write four questions and to provide an answer key. Then, have students exchange quizzes with a partner. This activity should take about 20 minutes.

Questions for Discussion

ECONOMICS How do Pakistan's steel mills help the country to save money?

Because Pakistan can produce all the steel it needs, it does not have to buy it from another country.

SOCIAL STUDIES SKILLS Look at the circle graph of the age structure of Pakistanis on this page. How does the number of adults (age 15–64) compare with the number of children? What conclusions can you draw based on this information?

There are almost as many children as adults in Pakistan. This could mean that families have many children.

❹ Assess/Reteach

See the answers to the Section 1 Assessment. You may also use students' completed quizzes as an assessment.

Acceptable quizzes include four questions with correct answers.

Commendable quizzes include four questions with correct answers that demonstrate a grasp of the main ideas of the section.

Outstanding quizzes include four questions with correct answers and indicate an understanding of how the parts of Pakistan's economy are linked.

Answers to...

MAP AND CHART STUDY

Most of Pakistan's crops are grown along the Indus and its tributaries.

COUNTRY • PROFILE

Pakistan

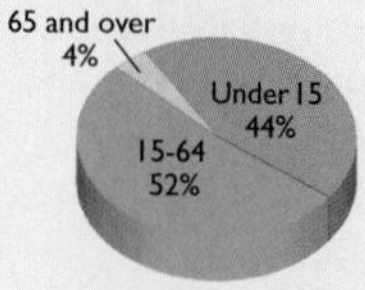

Age Structure (in years)

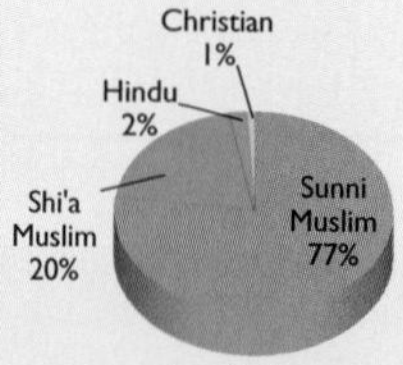

Religious Persuasion

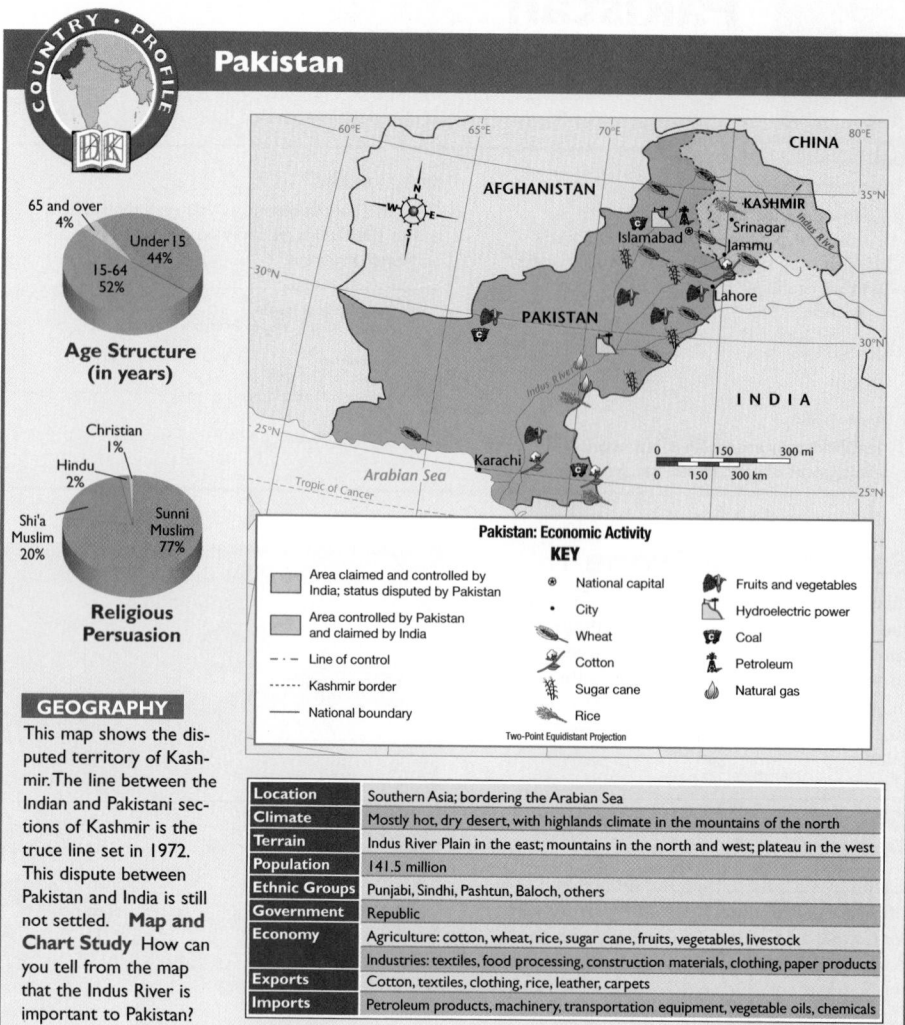

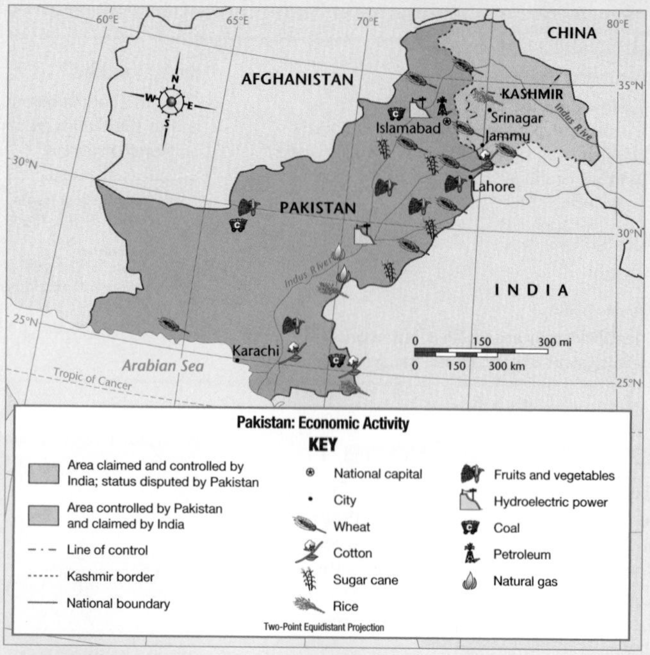

GEOGRAPHY This map shows the disputed territory of Kashmir. The line between the Indian and Pakistani sections of Kashmir is the truce line set in 1972. This dispute between Pakistan and India is still not settled. **Map and Chart Study** How can you tell from the map that the Indus River is important to Pakistan?

Location	Southern Asia; bordering the Arabian Sea
Climate	Mostly hot, dry desert, with highlands climate in the mountains of the north
Terrain	Indus River Plain in the east; mountains in the north and west; plateau in the west
Population	141.5 million
Ethnic Groups	Punjabi, Sindhi, Pashtun, Baloch, others
Government	Republic
Economy	Agriculture: cotton, wheat, rice, sugar cane, fruits, vegetables, livestock
	Industries: textiles, food processing, construction materials, clothing, paper products
Exports	Cotton, textiles, clothing, rice, leather, carpets
Imports	Petroleum products, machinery, transportation equipment, vegetable oils, chemicals

An Agricultural Nation

Through hard work and clever farming methods, Pakistani farmers grow large amounts of wheat, cotton, and sugar cane. They also grow so much rice that they can export it to other countries. The great advances the country has made in agriculture could easily be lost without the much-needed water.

SKILLS MINI LESSON

Using Distribution Maps

To **introduce** the skill, explain that a distribution map shows where something is located. Have students look at the map and the map key in the Country Profile, and ask a volunteer to identify what this distribution map shows (economic activity in Pakistan). Ask students to **practice** using the map by having them answer the following questions: *Which of the following is not a crop produced in Pakistan: wheat, corn, or rice?* (corn) *Near which large city is coal mined and hydroelectricity produced?* (Islamabad) *Are more crops grown in the eastern or the western part of Pakistan?* (eastern) Pairs of students may **apply** the skill by devising a true-and-false quiz about the products of Pakistan. Tell students that all questions should be able to be answered using the distribution map. When pairs have completed their quiz questions, have them challenge another pair to take their quiz.

Irrigation Produces Larger Crops Pakistanis on the Indus Plain have built thousands of canals and ditches to move water to their fields. In this way, farmers maintain a steady flow of water, even during droughts. As more land is irrigated, more acres are farmed. This has increased the amount of crops.

At harvest time, the bright yellow flowers of Pakistan's five kinds of mustard blanket the fields. Improved farming methods allow Pakistani farmers to grow lentils, beans used in a spicy dish called dhal (dahl). Farmers also grow fruits, such as apricots and mangoes, and vegetables, such as chilis and peas.

Problems and Solutions Irrigation solves many farming problems, but it creates others. For example, river water contains small amounts of salts which, over time, build up in the soil and slow plant growth. Pakistani scientists are trying to find a way to treat the salt-damaged soil.

Pakistanis have another water problem. During the monsoon season, damaging floods occur. One solution is the large dams built by the government. The dams catch and hold monsoon rains. The waters are then released as needed, into irrigation canals.

Economic Development

In addition to helping farmers, dams speed industrial growth. Dams can release rushing water to create hydroelectric energy. In Pakistan, hydroelectric power plants produce energy to run mills and factories. Most industry is located near the sources of hydroelectric power, on the Indus Plain.

Wheat Harvest in Pakistan

ECONOMICS These Pakistani farmers are removing the husks from wheat grains by tossing the wheat into the air. In addition to such age-old practices, they also use modern farming methods. For example, they plant seeds developed by scientists that produce bigger crops. Since farmers started doing this in the 1960s, wheat production has doubled. Pakistan now grows more wheat than Kansas and Nebraska combined.
Critical Thinking Why do you think some Pakistani farmers still rely on age-old agricultural practices even today?

HISTORY

Nuclear Testing

In May 1998, a nuclear arms race threatened to start in South Asia. First, India conducted three underground nuclear tests. Then, Pakistan answered with five underground explosions—its first nuclear tests ever. Suddenly the two countries' conflicts over Kashmir became much more serious. In 1999, that conflict intensified when Muslim soldiers crossed into India's zone of control in Kashmir, and Indian troops battled to drive them out. The potential for either side to use nuclear arms brought calls from leaders around the world for a quick resolution of the crisis.

ACTIVITY

Interdisciplinary Connections

Science Dams built for purposes of irrigation and to generate hydroelectric power have helped Pakistan build its economy, but dams sometimes have some serious environmental effects. Have students work with a partner to prepare an oral report that outlines the effects of dams on the environment. Encourage students to develop visual elements for their reports, such as graphs, charts, maps, and pictures.

Verbal/Linguistic, Visual/Spatial

Resource Directory

Technology

Color Transparencies 125 South Asia: Political Map

Answers to...

CRITICAL THINKING

Students may say that these farmers are familiar with these age-old practices or that they do not have the money to buy new agricultural technology.

CHAPTER 28 SOUTH AND SOUTHWEST ASIA: EXPLORING THE REGION TODAY 521

HISTORY

U.S. Invasion of Afghanistan

In 2001, the uneasy alliance between Pakistan and the United States in the wake of the terrorist attacks on September 11, 2001 created a difficult situation for the government of Pakistan. The government supported the air strikes by the United States in Afghanistan, but needed to suppress protests from some of its fundamentalist citizens.

SECTION 1 ASSESSMENT

AFTER YOU READ

1. region through which the Indus River flows, claimed by both Pakistan and India
2. long period without rain
3. Farmers need water from the Indus to irrigate their crops; without irrigation, the land would be a desert.
4. Pakistanis have built canals for irrigation and dams to store water. Scientists are looking for ways to treat salt-damaged soil.
5. Since independence, Pakistan has established industries based on agriculture.
6. Students will say that Pakistan's industrial growth should help improve its economy.
7. Paragraphs should explain that The Indus River flows through Kashmir. Both India and Pakistan claim the region and want to have control over the waters of the Indus River.
8. Encourage students to review the section before they write their letters. You may want to have volunteers read aloud their letters to the class.

Answers to...

CRITICAL THINKING

Pakistan can earn money by exporting the crafts.

Traditional Crafts

ECONOMICS Many people in Pakistan work in small workshops producing traditional crafts. This worker from Karachi makes wooden trays and boxes that are inlaid with metal designs. Other traditional craft items produced in Pakistan include lace, carpets, pottery, and leather goods. **Critical Thinking** How might the development of traditional crafts help Pakistan's economy?

Industries Based on Agriculture At independence, Pakistan had few factories. Pakistan has worked hard to build its economy through agriculture and industry. Today, Pakistan is one of the more prosperous countries in Asia. Even so, only a few Pakistanis can afford such things as refrigerators, telephones, and cars.

Pakistan began its industrial growth by building on what its people knew best: farming. More than half of Pakistan's industrial output comes from turning crops such as cotton into manufactured goods such as socks.

Industries: From Steel to Crafts The nation also has other industries. The chemical industry produces paint, soap, and dye. Several steel mills allow Pakistan to make almost all the steel it needs, helping the country to save money.

Millions of Pakistanis work in small workshops, instead of in large factories. Workshops produce field hockey sticks, furniture, knives, saddles, and carpets. Pakistan is famous for its beautiful carpets. Some sell for as much as $25,000 in Pakistan—and $50,000 in New York or London.

Pakistanis are working hard to improve their future. By building industries and modernizing agriculture, they hope to raise their quality of life.

SECTION 1 ASSESSMENT

AFTER YOU READ

AFTER YOU READ

1. Identify: Kashmir
2. Define: drought

COMPREHENSION

3. Why is the Indus River crucial to Pakistani farmers?
4. What steps has Pakistan taken to improve its agriculture?
5. What industries have emerged since Pakistan became a nation?

CRITICAL THINKING AND WRITING

6. **Exploring the Main Idea** Review the Main Idea statement at the beginning of this section. Then, write a short paragraph discussing the impact you think Pakistan's industrial growth will have on its economy.
7. **Identifying a Problem** Write a paragraph explaining why Kashmir is important to both India and Pakistan.

ACTIVITY

8. **Write a Letter** You are a Pakistani farmer. Write a letter to your cousin or friend in the United States describing your crops and the hardships you face to keep your farm productive.

Resource Directory

Teaching Resources

Section Quiz in the Unit 6 Teaching Resources, p. 73

SECTION 2

India

A Democracy Rooted in Tradition

BEFORE YOU READ

READING FOCUS

1. How have opportunities for Untouchables increased since independence?
2. How do Indian women influence the political process?

KEY TERMS

caste
quota
purdah
parliament

MAIN IDEA

Since independence, opportunities for more Indians to participate in and influence the political process have widened tremendously, though change has occurred faster in the cities than in more tradition-bound rural areas.

NOTE TAKING

Copy the chart below. As you read the section, fill in the chart to show how Untouchables and women are becoming full citizens in India.

Untouchables	Women

Setting the Scene

The whole village had turned up for the Hindu religious service—everyone from members of the highest caste to those of no caste, the Untouchables. After the service, the people sat down to a meal. No one seemed to mind who was sitting next to them. At the end of the meal, lower caste members and Untouchables began to clean up the dining room. Some higher caste members told them to stop, then did the work themselves. Stunned, an Untouchable said, "This is the first time in my life to see such a sight."

Busy Streets

CULTURE An Indian barber shaves a customer. Many barbers in India work in the open air. **Critical Thinking** What are economic reasons why a barber would want to work outside?

Opportunity for All Citizens

Why did the Untouchable express surprise? Because of the ancient traditions, such as the caste system, in which Indian culture is rooted.

The Caste System Traditional Hindu society divides its followers into four **castes,** or social groups. The castes put people in order from the bottom of society to the top. Below the lowest caste are the Untouchables. They are a "casteless" or outcast Hindu group.

Resource Directory

Teaching Resources

Classroom Manager in the Unit 6 Teaching Resources, p. 74

Guided Reading and Review in the Unit 6 Teaching Resources, p. 75

Guide to the Essentials, p. 124

Technology

Section Reading Support Transparencies

SECTION 2

Lesson Objectives

1. Identify opportunities for Untouchables that have arisen since independence.
2. Describe how women influence the political process in India.

Lesson Plan

1 Engage

Warm-Up Activity

Ask student volunteers to explain what kinds of work their grandfathers and grandmothers did. Do their parents do the same kind of work? Ask whether they plan to do the same work their fathers or mothers do. If not, why not?

Activating Prior Knowledge

Ask students to imagine that they were expected to work in the same occupation as the rest of their family—an occupation that their family has worked at for hundreds of years. Have them write a few sentences explaining how they would feel about this situation. Ask volunteers to share their sentences with the rest of the class.

2 Explore

Have students read the section and explore the following questions: What is the caste system? How has the caste system changed in recent years? How have women's roles changed since independence?

Answers to...

CRITICAL THINKING

Students may say that the barber does not have to pay rent or that he might get more clients because he is more visible outside.

Lesson Plan continued

3 Teach

Have students write a brief essay about the changes that have taken place in India since independence. Students should focus on how the caste system has evolved and how the roles of women have changed. This activity should take about 20 minutes.

Questions for Discussion

CITIZENSHIP **How do you think India's independence from Britain affected women's rights? Do you think women will gain more rights in Indian society?**

Many women played an active role in the fight against Britain, which would have shown that they were just as important as men in the fight for independence. It would be difficult for a country that won its independence to not treat all its citizens as equals. Women are likely to gain more rights in the future.

ECONOMICS **Look at the table of information in the Country Profile on this page. Why do you think India is able to export clothing?**

Cotton is a major crop and textile manufacturing is an important industry.

Answers to...

MAP AND CHART STUDY

Most Hindus live in the main part of the country that extends from the northern border south to the Indian Ocean. The far northern section is mainly Islamic. Seventeen percent of India's population practices religions other than Hinduism.

COUNTRY PROFILE

India

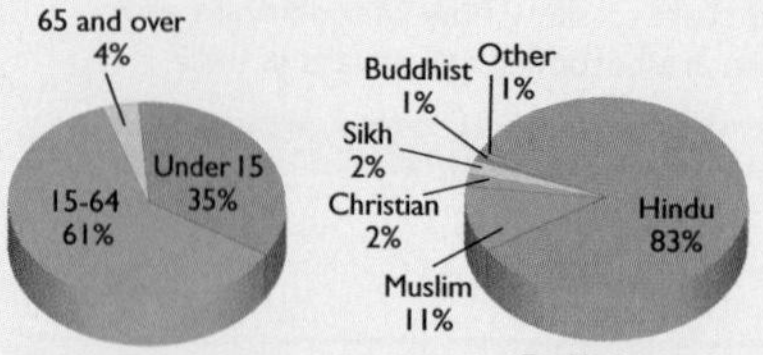

Age Structure (in years)

Religious Persuasion

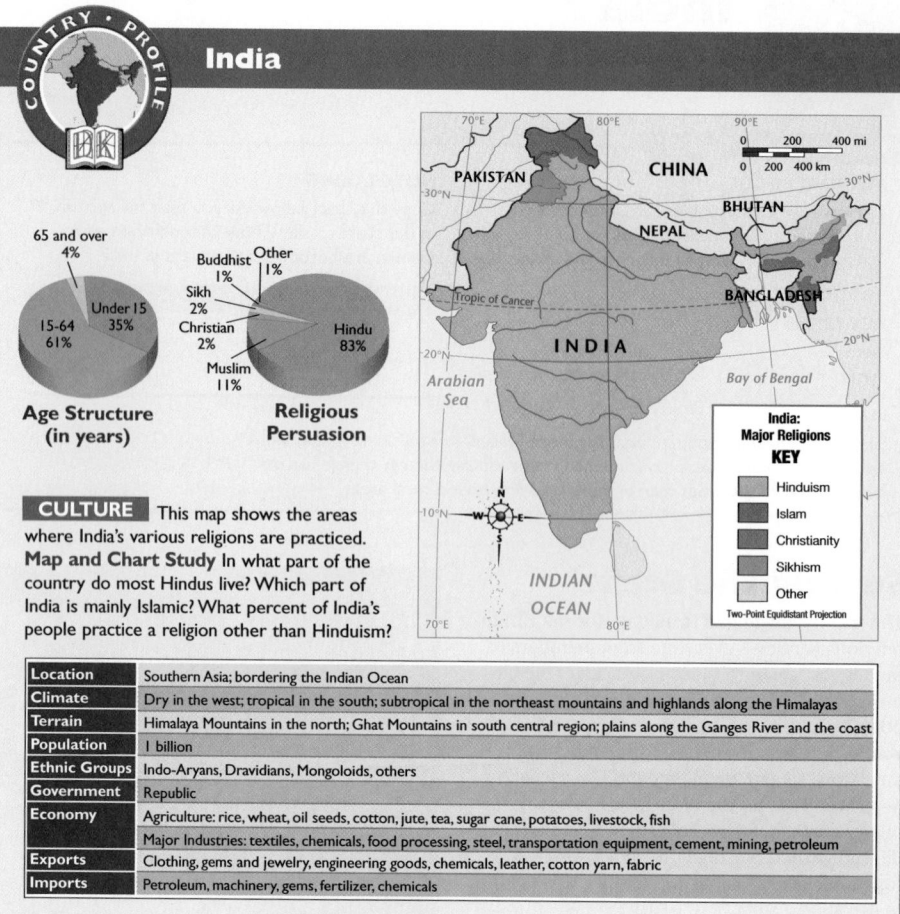

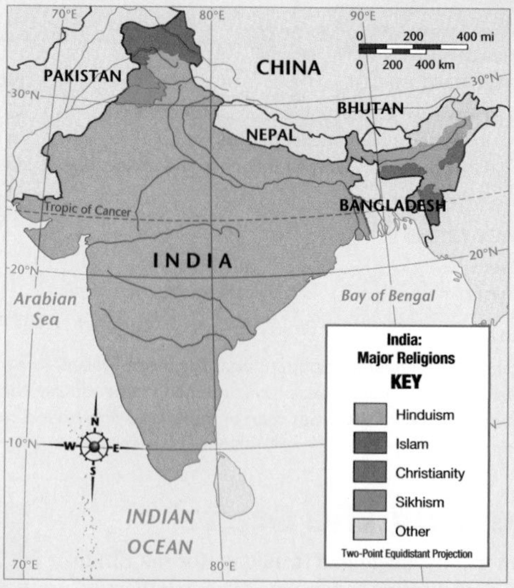

CULTURE This map shows the areas where India's various religions are practiced. **Map and Chart Study** In what part of the country do most Hindus live? Which part of India is mainly Islamic? What percent of India's people practice a religion other than Hinduism?

Location	Southern Asia; bordering the Indian Ocean
Climate	Dry in the west; tropical in the south; subtropical in the northeast mountains and highlands along the Himalayas
Terrain	Himalaya Mountains in the north; Ghat Mountains in south central region; plains along the Ganges River and the coast
Population	1 billion
Ethnic Groups	Indo-Aryans, Dravidians, Mongoloids, others
Government	Republic
Economy	Agriculture: rice, wheat, oil seeds, cotton, jute, tea, sugar cane, potatoes, livestock, fish
	Major Industries: textiles, chemicals, food processing, steel, transportation equipment, cement, mining, petroleum
Exports	Clothing, gems and jewelry, engineering goods, chemicals, leather, cotton yarn, fabric
Imports	Petroleum, machinery, gems, fertilizer, chemicals

Over thousands of years, the caste system grew complex. The main castes divided into hundreds of groups, or subcastes. The people in each subcaste had the same job. Shopkeepers, barbers, and weavers, for example, each had their own subcaste. The caste system gave Hindus a sense of order. But for the Untouchables, life was hard. Untouchables could do only the dirtiest work. They were not allowed to mix with people of higher castes.

The System Weakens Today, however, the caste system is weakening. During India's struggle for independence, Mohandas Gandhi began to fight for the rights of Untouchables. He took Untouchables as his pupils. He called them *Harijans*, or children of God.

SKILLS MINI LESSON

Reading Tables and Analyzing Statistics

allow students a few moments to study the table and charts shown in the Country Profile. Then **introduce** the skill by telling them that the table and charts show statistics, or numerical data, and other important data about India. Point out that some of the numerical data is presented in the form of pie graphs. Together, these data provide information about India's geography, economy, and people. Have students **practice** and **apply** the skill by asking them to study the information related to India's economy. Then, ask them the following questions: *Why do you think India doesn't import food?* (India grows food crops such as rice, wheat, and potatoes. Livestock and fish are also an important part of the economy.) *What export is linked to India's cotton crop?* (cotton yarn; clothing and fabric may also be made from cotton.)

Urban and Rural Life

GEOGRAPHY This street scene in Jaipur (JY poor), northern India (inset), illustrates well the hustle and bustle of Indian city life. In the countryside outside Jaipur (above), however, life is much quieter. **Critical Thinking** What other differences do you think exist between rural and urban life in India?

After independence from Britain in 1947, India became the world's largest democracy. In the spirit of democracy, India passed laws to protect the rights of Untouchables and to help them improve their lives. The government uses quotas to guarantee jobs to Untouchables. A **quota** is a certain portion of something, such as jobs, that is set aside for a group. Universities must also accept a quota of Untouchables as students.

The caste system is slower to change in rural areas. Here, it is hard to enforce laws to protect Untouchables. In a small village, everyone knows everyone else's caste. In some villages, Untouchables are still forbidden to draw water from the public well. Also, they may be allowed only certain jobs. However, some villages have loosened the rules. For example, Untouchables now are able to worship at village temples and, through India's public school system, the children of Untouchables are able to go to school.

In crowded cities, however, it is easier for Untouchables to blend into society. People there tend to be more tolerant.

4 Assess/Reteach

See the answers to the Section 2 Assessment. You may also use students' completed essays as an assessment.

Acceptable essays note the weakening of the caste system and an increase in rights for women.

Commendable essays note the weakening of the caste system by providing specific examples and name some of the rights gained by women.

Outstanding essays note the weakening of the caste system by providing specific examples and name political and economic rights gained by women.

ACTIVITY

Critical Thinking

Identifying Main Issues *Suitable as an individual activity.* Ask students to address the following questions in a news brief about the decline of the caste system in India.

- What are castes?
- What effect has the caste system had on society?
- What measures have weakened the caste system?

Verbal/Linguistic

Resource Directory

Teaching Resources

Outline Map South Asia: Political, p. 37

Technology

Color Transparencies 126 South Asia: Physical-Political Map; **129–131** South Asia: 1945–Present (map and overlays)

Passport to the World CD-ROM This interactive CD-ROM allows students to explore each region of the world. Students view regional videos, take a photo tour, and explore a historical timeline. Students record their travels in an Explorer's Journal, and receive passport stamps when they pass regional quizzes.

Answers to...

CRITICAL THINKING

Students may mention differences in living quarters, jobs, and forms of recreation.

SECTION 2 ASSESSMENT

AFTER YOU READ

1. (a) social classes (b) certain portion of something, such as jobs, set aside for a group (c) custom for women to cover their heads and faces with veils (d) law making body
2. In cities, people are more tolerant and ready to change the caste system; in rural areas, everyone knows everyone else's caste, and change is slower.
3. They can vote and engage in business. They are also free to enter public life and government service.
4. Paragraphs will vary. Students may observe that the spirit of democracy can be seen in the increased rights of Untouchables and the growing role of women in the political process.
5. Possible reasons: The Untouchables have been unfairly treated for a very long time. The government wants to end the injustice.
6. Letters will vary. Letters may ask Mistry about the representation of women in the Indian government or about job opportunities for women.

CITIZENSHIP

Mother Teresa of Calcutta (1910–1997)

The Roman Catholic nun Mother Teresa dedicated her life to serving the poor. Mother Teresa founded a religious order called the Missionaries of Charity. It operates centers for people who have no money but have disabilities or diseases, such as leprosy. The order has saved the lives of many thousands of poverty-stricken Indians. For her work, Mother Teresa was awarded the Padma Shri ("Lord of the Lotus") from the Indian government and the Nobel Peace Prize.

Women in India

Like belief about castes, beliefs about men and women are changing in modern India. For many years, the roles of men and women were rigid. Women had few rights. They were expected to marry and have children.

Women Gain Rights Gandhi urged women to play an active part in India's fight against Britain. Women took part in boycotts and prepared leaflets. Since independence, Indian women have gained many rights. They can now vote and engage in business. They are now free to take part in public life, as well. In 1966, a woman, Indira Gandhi, became prime minister. She was the daughter of Jawaharlal Nehru (juh WA hur lal NAY roo), India's first prime minister.

Changing Roles for Indian Women In addition to gaining legal rights, women have changed their roles in other ways. Many Muslim women no longer follow the custom of **purdah,** or covering their heads and faces with veils. Many Indian women today have careers and work outside the home. More and more women are entering the fields of science and health care. In fact, India has a higher percentage of women doctors than the United States.

Also, more Indian women than American women hold high government positions. For example, Roda Mistry, who lives in the city of Hyderabad, in central India, is president of the Indian Council on Social Welfare. Before reaching this position, Mistry was a member of the Indian **parliament,** or lawmaking body. She also served as Minister of Tourism and Minister of Women's and Children's Welfare in the Indian government. Mistry is a well-respected political leader, showing how far women have come in India.

SECTION 2 ASSESSMENT

AFTER YOU READ

RECALL

1. (a) caste, (b) quota, (c) purdah, (d) parliament

COMPREHENSION

2. How is the caste system different in cities and rural villages?
3. How have women's roles in the political process changed since independence?

CRITICAL THINKING AND WRITING

4. **Exploring the Main Idea** Review the Main Idea statement at the beginning of this section. Then, write a paragraph explaining how the spirit of democracy can be seen in changes that have occurred in India.
5. **Making Inferences** List some reasons why you think the Indian government has taken the lead in helping Untouchables.

ACTIVITY

6. **Writing a Letter** Write a letter to Roda Mistry. Include some questions about the roles of women in India.

Resource Directory

Teaching Resources

Section Quiz in the Unit 6 Teaching Resources, p. 76

SECTION 3

Saudi Arabia

Islam and the Oil Industry

BEFORE YOU READ

READING FOCUS

1. How has oil wealth changed Saudi Arabia?
2. How do Islamic beliefs affect women in Saudi Arabia?

KEY TERMS

hajj

KEY PLACES

Mecca
Riyadh

MAIN IDEA

Oil wealth has allowed Saudi Arabia to modernize its cities, build networks of transportation and communication, and educate its people, though at the same time maintaining tradition.

NOTE TAKING

Copy the diagram below. As you read the section, complete the diagram to show some outgrowths of Saudi Arabia's oil wealth and its traditional Islamic values. Add more circles to the web as you go.

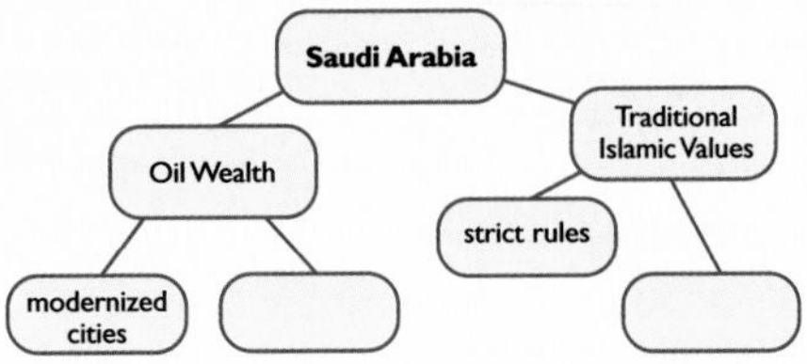

Setting the Scene

For more than a thousand years, Muslims from all over the world have been making pilgrimages to **Mecca,** Saudi Arabia. By going to Mecca, they honor the memory of Abraham, who is said to have built the first house of worship here. The pilgrimage is called the **hajj** (hahj). Muslims must make the hajj once in their lifetime if they can.

Holy Pilgrimage

CULTURE Each year, over two million Muslims make the hajj to Mecca. Here, huge crowds worship at the Kabah, the holiest site in all of Islam. The Kabah is the cube-shaped structure to the left in the picture. **Critical Thinking** How do you think making the hajj in the past compares to making this pilgrimage today? Use the photograph to help you.

Oil and the Economy

In 1900, Mecca was a small and very poor town and the area known as Saudi Arabia was one of the poorest countries in the world. Many of its people made a living by herding livestock through the desert.

But in the 1930s, everything changed. People discovered oil on the Arabian Peninsula. Oil reserves changed the fortunes of Saudi Arabia and several other countries in the region. It made them rich.

Resource Directory

Teaching Resources

Classroom Manager in the Unit 6 Teaching Resources, p. 77

Guided Reading and Review in the Unit 6 Teaching Resources, p. 78

Guide to the Essentials, p. 125

Technology

Section Reading Support Transparencies

SECTION 3

Lesson Objectives

1. Explain how the discovery of oil has affected the lives of Saudi Arabians.
2. Describe how Islam structures the lives of women in Saudi Arabia.

Lesson Plan

1 Engage

Warm-Up Activity

Have students suppose that a valuable resource such as oil was discovered in your community. Discuss with students how the local government might use the new revenues to make improvements in public services. How would the new wealth affect individuals? How would it affect the community as a whole?

Activating Prior Knowledge

Ask students what petroleum products they use every day. You might mention to students that petroleum derivatives are an ingredient in almost all plastics.

2 Explore

Discuss the following questions with students after they read the section text: What was life like in Saudi Arabia before and after the discovery of oil? How is the life of a Saudi woman different from that of a Saudi man? What does the government do to encourage and maintain traditional values?

Answers to...

CRITICAL THINKING

Accept all reasonable responses. Students might infer that to reach Mecca in earlier times, Muslims had to travel across mountains and deserts by foot, horse, or camel and camp nearby. Today, many Muslims may travel by airplane and stay in a modern hotel.

Lesson Plan continued

③ Teach

Ask students to suppose that they have just spent the day in Saudi Arabia. Ask them to write a letter about the experience. Emphasize to students that they should include in their letters evidence of how the oil economy and Islam shape daily life. Encourage students to include specific examples from the text. This activity should take about 25 minutes.

Questions for Discussion

ECONOMICS Why do buildings in Riyadh go up at a rapid pace when oil prices are high?

Oil is a huge international business and when oil prices are high, there is more money to spend on building projects in the city.

ECONOMICS Why do many Saudi leaders think their country depends too much on oil?

The Saudi economy would be more stable if it had income from other industries to rely on when oil prices are down.

④ Assess/Reteach

See the answers to the Section 3 Assessment. You may also assess students' letters.

Acceptable letters include accurate descriptions of how the oil economy and Islam shape daily life.

Commendable letters include accurate descriptions and examples of how the oil economy and Islam shape daily life.

Outstanding letters include accurate descriptions and specific examples related to the influence of Islam and the oil economy to create a vivid picture of Saudi Arabia.

COUNTRY PROFILE

Saudi Arabia

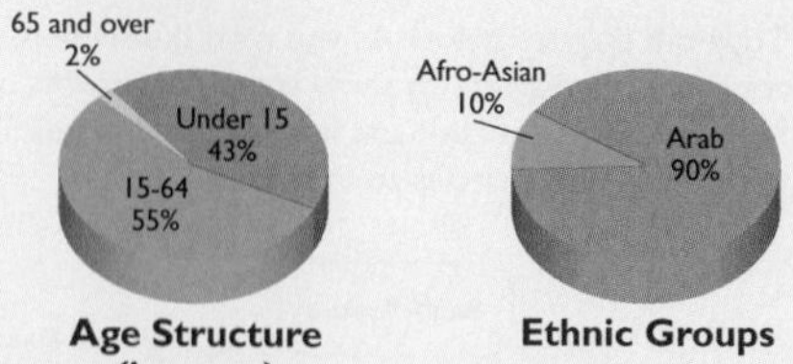

Age Structure (in years) **Ethnic Groups**

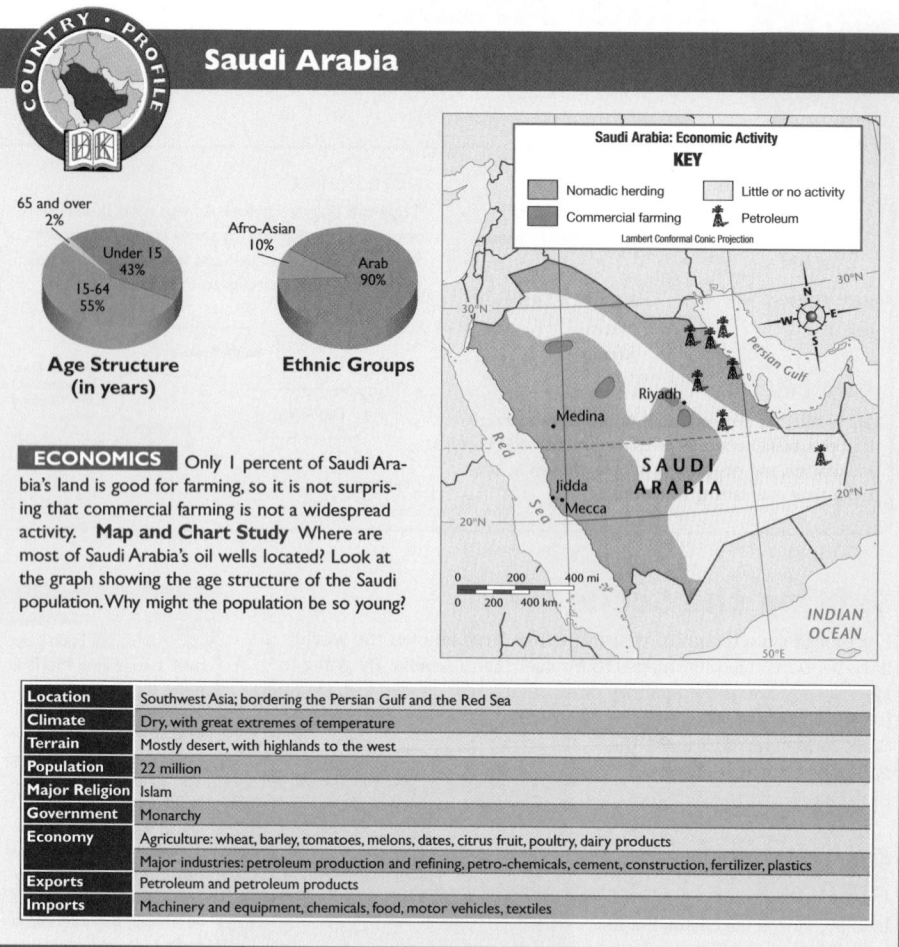

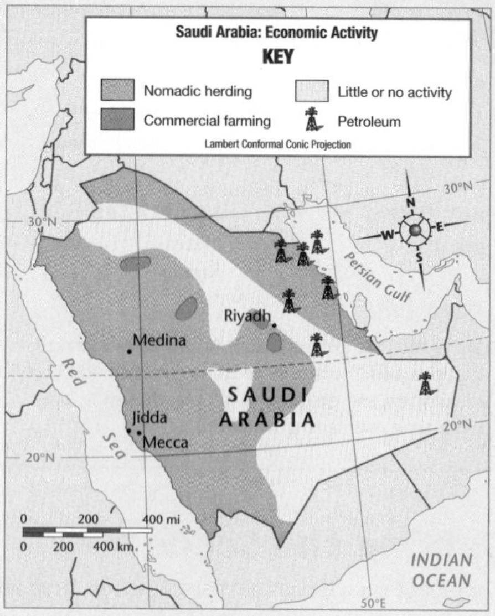

ECONOMICS Only 1 percent of Saudi Arabia's land is good for farming, so it is not surprising that commercial farming is not a widespread activity. **Map and Chart Study** Where are most of Saudi Arabia's oil wells located? Look at the graph showing the age structure of the Saudi population. Why might the population be so young?

Location	Southwest Asia; bordering the Persian Gulf and the Red Sea
Climate	Dry, with great extremes of temperature
Terrain	Mostly desert, with highlands to the west
Population	22 million
Major Religion	Islam
Government	Monarchy
Economy	Agriculture: wheat, barley, tomatoes, melons, dates, citrus fruit, poultry, dairy products
	Major industries: petroleum production and refining, petro-chemicals, cement, construction, fertilizer, plastics
Exports	Petroleum and petroleum products
Imports	Machinery and equipment, chemicals, food, motor vehicles, textiles

Boom and Bust When night falls in **Riyadh** (ree AHD), Saudi Arabia's capital, the skyline begins to glow. The lights of the many apartment and office buildings flicker on. Large buildings line the city streets. When oil prices are high, buildings go up at a rapid pace. Money pours in, allowing communities like Riyadh to modernize. But when oil prices are down, the economy of the entire country is shaken. Many large building projects grind to a stop.

Saudi Arabia has the most important oil economy in the world. Under its deserts lie more than 250 billion barrels of oil, about one fourth of the world's supply. No other country on the Earth exports more petroleum.

Answers to...

MAP AND CHART STUDY

Most oil wells are near or off of Saudi Arabia's eastern coast. Families might have many children making for a young population, or, there is a short life expectancy.

Resource Directory

Teaching Resources

Outline Maps Saudi Arabia, p. 30

Technology

Color Transparencies 134 Southwest Asia: Political Map

Many Saudi leaders think that Saudi Arabia depends too much on oil, so the Saudis are trying to diversify their economy. They want to create many different ways for the country to earn money. But today, oil exports are still Saudi Arabia's main source of income.

Meanwhile, projects paid for with oil money have changed the lives of all Saudi Arabians. Before the oil boom, there were few roads in Saudi Arabia. Now roads link all parts of the country. In the past, people often lived without electricity and telephones. Now these luxuries are common in Saudi Arabia.

The nation's wealth has also made it possible to develop a good school system by building thousands of schools. In 1900, many Saudi Arabians could not read or write. But today, Saudi students are becoming doctors, scientists, and teachers.

Traditional Values In Saudi Arabia, Islam regulates most people's lives. For example, cities like Riyadh contain department stores, hotels, and universities, but they have no movie theaters or nightclubs. The Sunni branch of Islam, which most Saudi Arabians follow, forbids this kind of entertainment.

Also, alcohol and pork are illegal in Saudi Arabia and all shops must close during the five times a day when Muslims pray. Saudi Arabians use Western inventions to improve their lives. But they make sure these inventions do not interfere with their traditions.

The Role of Women in Saudi Arabia

Many laws in Saudi Arabia deal with the role of women, protecting them in certain ways, but also forbidding them to do some things. The role of women is changing, but traditional values remain strong.

Old Ways and New Professions In Riyadh, women who go out in public cover themselves with a full-length black cloak. Even their faces are usually covered. This is one of the rules of the country. Another rule is that women may not drive cars. At home, women stay in the part of the house designated for them if guests are visiting.

Samira Al Tuwaijri (suh MIH ruh al tuh WAY zhree), a young woman who lives in Riyadh, follows these rules. Tuwaijri is also a doctor in the King Fahd Hospital. She is studying to become a surgeon.

Dual Lives

CULTURE This doctor in Riyadh (above) wears Western-style clothes in her office. In the street, she wears a traditional full-length black cloak similar to the ones worn by these women in the Saudi city of Jidda (left).
Critical Thinking What can you tell about the women in each of these photographs?

CULTURE

Women Behind the Wheel

For many years in Saudi Arabia, an unofficial ban on women drivers went unchallenged. During the time of military mobilization in anticipation of the Persian Gulf War, some women believed it was time such restrictions ended. In November 1990, 49 Saudi Arabian women drove down a main thoroughfare in Riyadh. The protest gained the attention of the international press but failed to achieve the desired effect in Saudi Arabia where the unofficial ban quickly became official.

ACTIVITY

Interdisciplinary Connections

Art Representational art of humans or animals is forbidden in Saudi Arabia, because Islamic convention holds that only God can create life. However, the visual arts are a vital part of Saudi life. Saudi artists make use of patterns, symbols, and geometric shapes in their artistic endeavors, which include painting and sculpture, woven baskets, and patterned rugs. If possible, show students photos of Saudi art forms. Then, provide students with a variety of art materials and allow them to make their own nonrepresentational art.

Visual/Spatial, Bodily/Kinesthetic

SKILLS MINI LESSON

Writing for a Purpose

To **introduce** the skill, ask students to identify an aspect of Saudi Arabia's history or culture that they would like to learn more about. Point out that writing a report can serve the dual purpose of informing yourself as well as others. To **practice** the skill, help students list some key elements of informative writing. You might post the following steps on the board: 1) choose a topic; 2) identify the audience and its current knowledge of the topic; 3) conduct necessary research; 4) organize ideas in an outline. Students may **apply** the skill by following the above steps and writing a report on their chosen topic.

Answers to...

CRITICAL THINKING

Students may say that the doctor's clothes represent more modern values than the women in traditional dress.

SECTION 3 ASSESSMENT

AFTER YOU READ

1. (a) city in western Saudi Arabia that Muslims regard as holy (b) Saudi Arabia's capital city
2. Muslim pilgrimage to Mecca
3. Possible answers: cities became modernized, people grew wealthy, the school system was expanded and improved
4. They work only with other women; they respect traditions such as veils for women when in public; they follow family dictates without question.
5. Students should describe ways in which their lives have improved, perhaps through better education, better roads, or electrical lighting. Students writing from a woman's perspective may note that their daughters and granddaughters have greater educational and employment opportunities than they did.
6. Al Tuwaijri accepts most of the limitations on her freedom but believes women's roles will gradually change.
7. Saudi Arabia is a large country with access to important waterways. Some of the land is used for herding and farming, but there is a considerable amount with little or no economic activity. Because of the rich oil fields in the country, the country's economy ends up relying a great deal on oil.

"Traditionally, women have always...stayed at home to cook and look after the family. Working for a living was just not done," says Tuwaijri.

But when Saudi Arabia built new schools, women became better educated. "Women are no longer content to just stay at home....We are able to compete in a man's world," Tuwaijri says.

Despite the changes, women and men usually still remain separate. Boys and girls go to different schools and do not socialize with one another. Women choose careers where they will not have to work closely with men. Tuwaijri's patients are all women. "I could have entered general medicine, but I have been brought up strictly and it was difficult to adjust to examining male patients," she says.

Religion Shapes Culture Most of the rules governing women's behavior in Saudi Arabia come from the Quran, the holy book of Islam. It requires fair treatment of women. Muslim women could own property long before Western women had that right. However, not all Muslims agree on how to apply the Quran to modern life.

"I suppose it is difficult for those who live in the West to understand why I am not allowed to be photographed," Tuwaijri says. "In Islam, the family is very important and a family decision is accepted by all members without question....Even if I disagreed with it, I would still abide by it."

Like many Saudi women, Tuwaijri is content with her role in a Muslim society. She does not want to live as Western women live. "There are many things in our culture which limit our freedom, but I would not want change overnight," she says. "It is important that we move into the future slowly and with care."

SECTION 3 ASSESSMENT

AFTER YOU READ

RECALL

1. Identify: (a) Mecca, (b) Riyadh
2. Define: hajj

COMPREHENSION

3. Name three changes that occurred in Saudi Arabia as the country grew wealthy from oil.
4. How do Saudi Arabian women keep a traditional Muslim way of life even with the changes brought by their oil wealth?

CRITICAL THINKING AND WRITING

5. **Exploring the Main Idea** Review the Main Idea statement at the beginning of this section. Then, pretend you are an older man or woman in Saudi Arabia. Write a journal entry describing what has changed in your life and what has stayed the same since the discovery of oil in the 1930s.
6. **Identifying Frame of Reference and Point of View** What is Samira Al Tuwaijri's point of view about the place of women in her culture?

ACTIVITY

7. **Making Observations** Using the map on page 528, make a list of observations about Saudi Arabia's geographic setting and the influence of this setting on the country. Include in your list observations about Saudi Arabia's neighbors, relative size, and access to water.

Resource Directory

Teaching Resources

Section Quiz in the Unit 6 Teaching Resources, p. 79

SECTION 4

Israel

Building Its Economy

BEFORE YOU READ

READING FOCUS

1. How does geography affect Israel's economy?
2. How do people in Israel work together?
3. Why has Israel had to cooperate with neighboring countries?

KEY TERMS

moshavim
kibbutz

KEY PLACE

Negev Desert

NOTE TAKING

Copy the chart below. As you read the section, fill in the chart to show how the people of Israel have made it possible to farm in the desert.

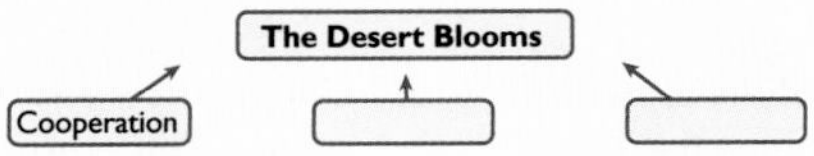

MAIN IDEA

By means of agricultural technology, the people of Israel have transformed a desert region to grow fruits and vegetables sold around the world.

Setting the Scene

Picture a land of rock and sand that is the lowest point on the Earth—1,310 feet (399 m) below sea level. Barely an inch of rain falls each year. Daytime temperatures can exceed 120°F (49°C). This is the **Negev Desert,** which makes up the southern two thirds of the country of Israel.

Technology Alters Geography

Israel's geography is similar to the rest of Southwest Asia and two thirds of the country is covered by desert. Throughout history, people in desert regions have made a living by herding animals across the desert, not by farming. In Israel, that has changed.

The people of Israel have used technology, new ideas, and hard work to make desert farming possible. Today, fruits and vegetables grown here are sold around the world as agriculture has become an important part of Israel's economy.

Kalman Eisenmann grows fruits and vegetables on Negev land that was once barren and dry. He uses an irrigation system that is controlled by a computer. It moves water underground through plastic tubes straight to the roots of the plants. This way of irrigating crops was invented in Israel. When it was developed, few people lived in this desert, but now half a million people live here.

Desert Farming

ECONOMICS With the sands of Israel's Negev Desert rising behind them, workers harvest strawberries.
Critical Thinking Why do you suppose this crop is grown under protective plastic sheeting?

Resource Directory

Teaching Resources

Classroom Manager in the Unit 6 Teaching Resources, p. 80

Guided Reading and Review in the Unit 6 Teaching Resources, p. 81

Guide to the Essentials, p. 126

Technology

Section Reading Support Transparencies

SECTION 4

Lesson Objectives

1. Describe how Israel's geography influences its economy.
2. Identify ways in which people work together economically in Israel.
3. Understand why Israel has had to cooperate with neighboring countries.

Lesson Plan

1 Engage

Warm-Up Activity

Ask students to estimate the amount of water they consume each day in food and drinks. Together, estimate the class's total daily water consumption. Then, tell students to suppose that the amount of water available is only three quarters of that needed. Challenge students to suggest how the water can be shared. Explain that for Israel and its neighbors, managing a limited water supply is a critical issue.

Activating Prior Knowledge

Ask students to think of a time when they were faced with a nearly impossible challenge. How did they react? Solicit ideas from volunteers about strategies they use for tackling difficult tasks.

Answers to...

CRITICAL THINKING

The plastic sheeting keeps water from evaporating into the hot desert air.

Lesson Plan continued

2 Explore

Have students consider the following questions as they read: What innovation allows Israelis to farm in the desert? What is life like on a kibbutz?

3 Teach

Organize students into groups of six to plan a kibbutz. Ask groups to determine a) what industry the kibbutz will use to support itself, b) how people will obtain food and other necessities, and c) how people not directly involved in farming or manufacturing could benefit the kibbutz. Have groups present the results of their discussion by writing a mission statement. This activity should take about 30 minutes.

Question for Discussion

GEOGRAPHY Look at the map of Israel in the Country Profile on this page. Why is Israel called "The Garden in the Desert"?

Israel is located in a dry, barren region. However, because of technological advances in crop-growing and irrigation, the country has been able to grow a number of different agricultural products.

4 Assess/Reteach

See the answers to the Section 4 Assessment. You may also assess the student's mission statements.

Acceptable mission statements provide answers for the three questions presented above.

Commendable mission statements answer each of the three questions and reflect a clear understanding of the function and purpose of a kibbutz.

Outstanding mission statements address each of the questions and reflect an appreciation for the challenges and benefits of life on a kibbutz.

COUNTRY PROFILE

Israel

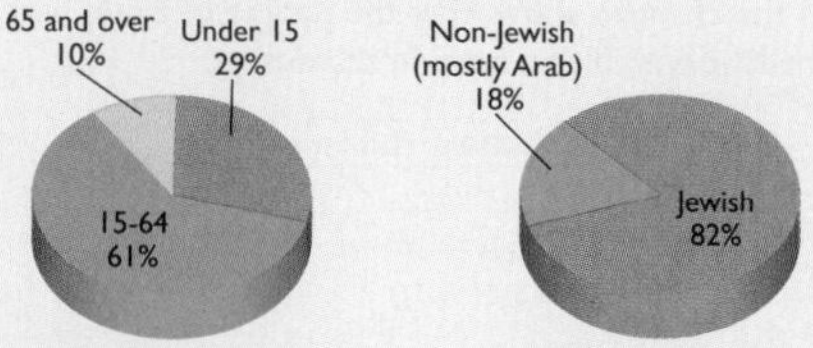

Age Structure (in years)

Ethnic Groups

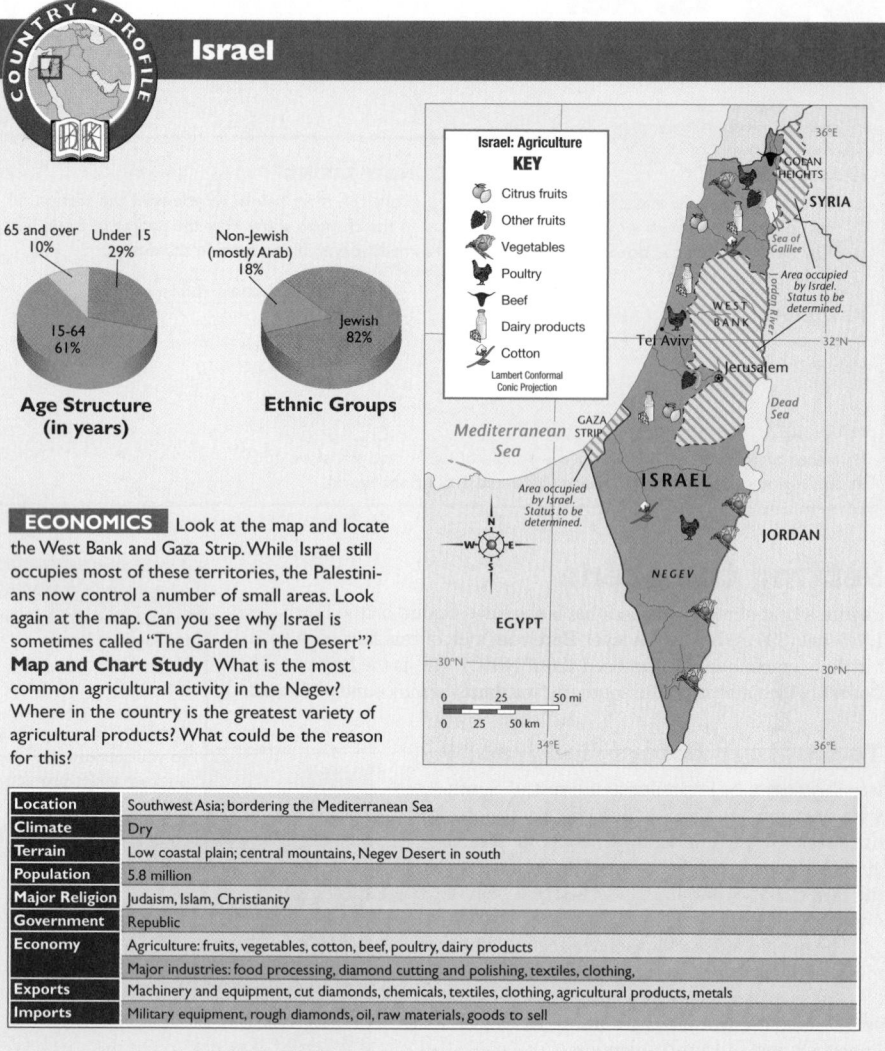

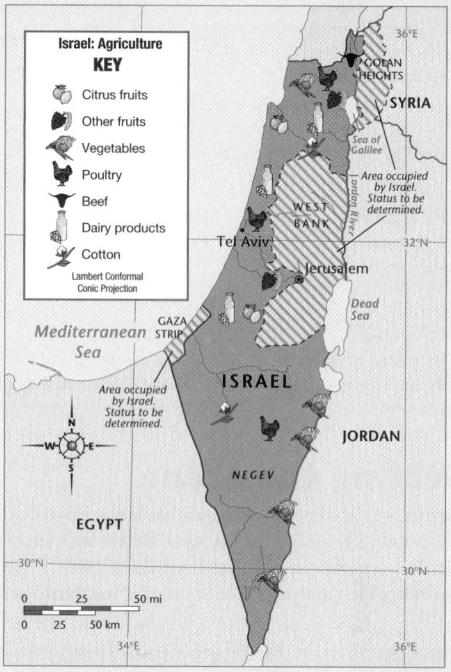

ECONOMICS Look at the map and locate the West Bank and Gaza Strip. While Israel still occupies most of these territories, the Palestinians now control a number of small areas. Look again at the map. Can you see why Israel is sometimes called "The Garden in the Desert"?
Map and Chart Study What is the most common agricultural activity in the Negev? Where in the country is the greatest variety of agricultural products? What could be the reason for this?

Location	Southwest Asia; bordering the Mediterranean Sea
Climate	Dry
Terrain	Low coastal plain; central mountains, Negev Desert in south
Population	5.8 million
Major Religion	Judaism, Islam, Christianity
Government	Republic
Economy	Agriculture: fruits, vegetables, cotton, beef, poultry, dairy products
	Major industries: food processing, diamond cutting and polishing, textiles, clothing,
Exports	Machinery and equipment, cut diamonds, chemicals, textiles, clothing, agricultural products, metals
Imports	Military equipment, rough diamonds, oil, raw materials, goods to sell

Working Together

Israel became a nation in 1948. Since then, it has almost doubled the amount of farmland within its borders. One reason for this success has been cooperation among farmworkers. In Israel, most people who do not live in cities live in **moshavim** (moh shah VEEM), small farming villages. The workers here cooperate. They combine their money to buy

Answers to...

MAPS AND CHART STUDY

Growing vegetables is the most common agricultural activity in the Negev. The greatest variety of products is in the north, because there is better access to water.

Resource Directory

Teaching Resources

Outline Maps Southwest Asia: Physical, p. 28; Southwest Asia: Political, p. 29

Life on a Kibbutz

ECONOMICS On an Israeli kibbutz, all able-bodied adults work. While some adults tend crops such as oranges, others are busy cooking, doing the laundry, or teaching school. Children on a kibbutz may live with their parents, or they may stay in a Children's House, where they eat, sleep, and attend school. This kibbutz kindergarten class (right) is learning how to bake bread. **Critical Thinking** How is life for children on a kibbutz similar to your life? How is it different?

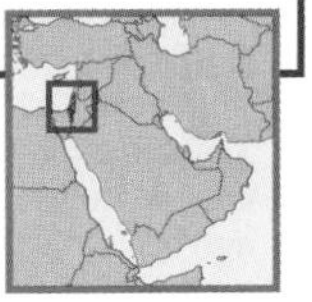

equipment and they tell each other about new methods of farming. They also pool their crops to get a better price.

The **kibbutz** (kih BOOTS) is another kind of cooperative settlement found in Israel. People who live on a kibbutz cooperate in all parts of life. They eat together, work together, and share profits equally. The people on a kibbutz do not earn any money while they work there, but the kibbutz provides their housing, meals, education, and health care.

On a kibbutz, people do more than farm. They may also work in factories, some of which make products such as electronic equipment and clothing. Manufacturing is an important part of Israel's economy since it exports products to many nations.

Israel and Its Neighbors

Israel has succeeded in making its dry lands come to life. However, like all countries in Southwest Asia, it must continue to manage its water carefully. To do this, Israel must cooperate with its neighbors.

Sharing the Jordan River Galilee, in northern Israel, is a land of rolling green hills and valleys covered with wildflowers. Farmers pick bananas for market. Picnickers sit near the Sea of Galilee and toss scraps of bread to seagulls. Tourists who come to this fertile region may forget that Israel is a dry land. They may also find it hard to believe that Galilee has been the site of conflict between Israel and its Arab neighbors. The Jordan River, which runs through Galilee, is important both to Israel and to its Arab neighbors.

The Jordan River runs along Israel's borders with Syria and Jordan. It flows into the Dead Sea. In many places, this river is small and muddy. However, in Southwest Asia, the Jordan River is a vital resource. Israel, Syria, and Jordan each irrigate their crops with water

CITIZENSHIP

Golda Meir (1898–1978)

Golda Meir ranks as one of the most influential women of the century. Meir was born in Ukraine but moved to the United States to escape anti-Jewish sentiment. As a young adult, she became active in the Jewish movement to establish a homeland and moved to a kibbutz in Palestine. Once Israel became a nation, Meir held several important government posts, and in 1969 was elected prime minister. As prime minister, she pushed for diplomatic rather than military settlement of disputes between Israel and neighboring Arab countries.

SKILLS MINI LESSON

Expressing Problems Clearly

To **introduce** the skill, explain that defining and expressing a problem clearly is the first step in understanding and possibly solving that problem. As students consider the conflict between Jordan and Israel over how to share the Jordan River, engage them in a discussion about why both countries need to use the river. Ask students to **practice** defining the problem by making a chart that shows examples of how each country wants to use the river and describes how certain plans would affect both countries. Have students **apply** the skill by asking them to summarize the information contained in the chart in a concise statement.

Answers to...

CRITICAL THINKING

Most students will probably mention that communal living is the biggest difference between their lives and those of children on a kibbutz.

CHAPTER 28 SOUTH AND SOUTHWEST ASIA: EXPLORING THE REGION TODAY 533

SECTION 4 ASSESSMENT

AFTER YOU READ

1. desert occupying southern two thirds of Israel
2. (a) small farming villages (b) cooperative settlement
3. dry lands, water shortages
4. Israelis pool resources and knowledge. They also work cooperatively on kibbutzim.
5. The Jordan River is located along national boundaries and since water is a precious resource, Israel must cooperate with its neighbors to manage it carefully.
6. Students' answers should include technological innovations such as underground irrigation.
7. Students' answers should demonstrate that they understand that working on a kibbutz requires a high degree of cooperative effort.
8. Israel's population is mainly Jewish and a majority of people are between the ages of 15 and 64.

GEOGRAPHY The Jordan River is the lowest river in the world. It begins in the springs of Mount Hermon in Syria and empties into the Dead Sea, approximately 1,310 feet (399m) below sea level. **Critical Thinking** How does the Jordan River's location affect the conflict between Israel and its Arab neighbors?

from the Jordan. For example, Israel uses water from this river to irrigate part of the Negev Desert.

Each country's use of Jordan River water affects its neighbors. The long conflict between Israel and the Arab states makes it hard for these neighbors to trust each other. Therefore, they watch each other's use of the Jordan River closely. When Israel began building a national irrigation system in the 1950s, Syria tried to stop the project. In the 1960s, Israel tried to stop Syria from channeling some of the river's waters. Today, the country of Jordan worries that it does not have enough water to meet its needs. It plans to build a dam near the Sea of Galilee. No building has begun, because if Jordan starts without Israel's approval, war could result.

SECTION 4 ASSESSMENT

AFTER YOU READ

RECALL

1. Identify: Negev Desert
2. Define: (a) moshavim, (b) kibbutz

COMPREHENSION

3. What geographical problems has Israel overcome to build a healthy economy?
4. How have Israelis worked together to overcome obstacles?
5. Why must Israel cooperate with its neighbors to manage its water resources?

CRITICAL THINKING AND WRITING

6. **Exploring the Main Idea** Review the Main Idea statement at the beginning of this section. Then, imagine you are a visitor in Israel. Write a postcard describing how the people of Israel grow crops on land that once was barren and dry.
7. **Comparing and Contrasting** What do you think would be some advantages and disadvantages of life on a kibbutz?

ACTIVITY

8. **Writing a Description** Using the information in the Country Profile on page 532, write a brief description of Israel's population.

Answers to...

CRITICAL THINKING

The Jordan River is located right along the borders of Israel, Jordan, and Syria. All countries use the Jordan River's water. Conflict can arise over the amount of water used by each country.

Resource Directory

Teaching Resources

Section Quiz in the Unit 6 Teaching Resources, p. 82

Chapter Summary in the Unit 6 Teaching Resources, p. 83

Vocabulary in the Unit 6 Teaching Resources, p. 84

Reteaching in the Unit 6 Teaching Resources, p. 85

Enrichment in the Unit 6 Teaching Resources, p. 86

Critical Thinking in the Unit 6 Teaching Resources, p. 87

Making Predictions

A. What I already know: Trees are sometimes planted to stop erosion.

B. Patterns: When other farmers have planted trees, the erosion has stopped.

C. List Possible Outcomes:

1) Farmland is more attractive.

2) Trees bear fruit.

3) Trees stop the wind from producing erosion.

D. Make a Prediction: The trees will stop the erosion.

E. Evaluation: The trees did not stop the erosion, but they did slow it down. Perhaps Dad planted the wrong kinds of trees, or not enough trees.

Learn the Skill

Imagine that you live in the Negev Desert in Israel where rainfall often erodes the desert soil. One day, your father plants trees where the erosion usually takes place. Can you predict what might happen as a result? When you make a prediction, you determine what the logical consequences of certain actions or decisions will be. Follow these steps to make predictions:

A. Think about what you already know, and write it down on paper. You might recall, for example, that trees are sometimes planted to stop erosion. This prior information will help you make a prediction.

B. Look for patterns. Maybe you have seen other farmers plant trees in eroded areas. Perhaps you noted that the erosion stopped or slowed. Think about what these patterns reveal. Write down any patterns that you've noted.

C. Make a list of possible outcomes. Brainstorm as many ideas as you can without thinking about how valid they are. Write all of your ideas down. When you see trees planted in the desert, your list might look like the one shown on this page.

D. Use what you have learned from doing steps A, B, and C to make a prediction. First, analyze each outcome to determine which one is the most likely outcome. You will probably choose the most likely outcome.

E. Evaluate the results. Even though your prediction might be likely, things may not turn out as you had expected. You don't know yet whether the trees your father planted will actually stop the erosion. Only time will tell if your prediction was accurate.

Practice the Skill

Read each of the events listed below. Then, follow the steps to make a prediction.

1. Israel, Syria, and Jordan all need water from the Jordan River, which borders all three countries, to irrigate their crops. Predict the result.

2. Saudi Arabia improves transportation and lodging to make it easier for Muslim pilgrims to come to Mecca. Predict the result.

3. Saudi Arabian leaders think that Saudi Arabia depends too much on oil. Predict the result.

4. More and more women in Saudi Arabia are receiving a higher education. Predict the result.

Apply the Skill

See the Chapter Review and Assessment at the end of this chapter for more questions on making predictions.

Resource Directory

Teaching Resources

Social Studies and Geography Skills, Predicting Consequences, p. 48

Technology

Social Studies Skills Tutor CD-ROM

Answers to...

PRACTICE THE SKILL

Students will probably predict: 1) conflict; 2) more pilgrims will come; 3) Saudi Arabia diversifies their exports; 4) Women's roles gradually change.

Lesson Objectives

1. Explain the meaning of making predictions.
2. Make predictions about world events.

Lesson Plan

1 Engage

Students are probably familiar with making predictions when they read fiction in reading class. Have them recall how they predict what will happen next when reading a story. Discuss how predicting real-life events throughout the world might be similar to that.

2 Explore

Invite students to study the chart. As you read each example from each step, have students point to the corresponding information on the chart. Provide other events and help students make a prediction based on the steps. For example, you might ask students to predict what results of trying to grow crops in the desert.

3 Teach

Students will read each event and follow the steps to make a prediction. Alternately, you might want to allow students to choose one event, or assign a single event to each. Students may work together to make predictions.

For additional reinforcement, pause when reading about world events and ask students to use the steps to predict the results.

4 Assess/Reteach

Students should be able to follow the steps to make predictions about world events.

To further assess students' understanding of comparing maps have them complete the "Applying Your Skills" part of the Chapter Review and Assessment at the end of the chapter.

CHAPTER 28

Review and Assessment

Creating a Chapter Summary

Student summaries will vary.

Sample summaries:

Section 2 Since India attained independence, Untouchables and women have achieved greater rights and greater access to the political process. Social changes such as these have occurred faster in the cities than in the countryside.

Section 3 With its newfound oil wealth, Saudi Arabia has modernized its cities, built networks of transportation and communication, and educated its people. In the midst of change, Saudi Arabia remains a traditional Islamic nation.

Section 4 The people of Israel have used technology, new ideas, and hard work to transform a desert into an economically–important farming region. Like many groups in Israel, farmers cooperate to share possessions and knowledge.

Reviewing Key Terms

1. b **2.** a **3.** c **4.** d **5.** f **6.** e

Reviewing the Main Ideas

1. the Indus River
2. Pakistan is achieving economic growth through industrial development.
3. Untouchables and women
4. in the cities
5. Islamic values and traditions can be seen in laws regulating food, drink, and entertainment and in the roles of women.
6. The desert has made it hard for Israel to achieve its goal of developing agriculture.
7. Most farmers in Israel live in moshavim, where they combine money to buy equipment, share knowledge of new farming methods, and pool their crops to get a better price.

CHAPTER 28

Review and Assessment

Creating a Chapter Summary

On a separate piece of paper, draw a diagram like this one, and include the information that summarizes the first section of the chapter. Then, fill in the remaining boxes with summaries of Sections 2, 3, and 4.

SOUTH AND SOUTHWEST ASIA TODAY

Section 1	Section 2	Section 3	Section 4
The conflict between India and Pakistan has been influenced by control of the Indus River, but Pakistan, a nation of farmers, is achieving economic growth through industrial development.			

Reviewing Key Terms

Match the key terms in Column I with the definitions in Column II.

Column I	Column II
1. moshavim	**a.** social group
2. caste	**b.** small cooperative farming villages in Israel
3. drought	**c.** long period without rain
4. hajj	**d.** Islamic pilgrimage to Mecca
5. kibbutz	**e.** law-making body
6. parliament	**f.** cooperative settlement

Reviewing the Main Ideas

1. What geographical factor influences the conflict between Pakistan and India? (Section 1)
2. How is Pakistan achieving economic growth? (Section 1)
3. What two groups have attained greater rights and access to the political process since Indian independence? (Section 2)
4. Where has social change occurred faster, in India's cities or its countryside? (Section 2)
5. How are Islamic values and traditions reflected in Saudi Arabia? (Section 3)
6. What challenge has the desert posed to Israel's economy? (Section 4)
7. How do farmers in Israel work together? (Section 4)

536 UNIT 6 ASIA

Map Activity

South and Southwest Asia

For each place or geographical feature listed below, write the letter from the map that shows its location.

1. Pakistan
2. Riyadh
3. Negev Desert
4. Mecca
5. Indus River
6. India

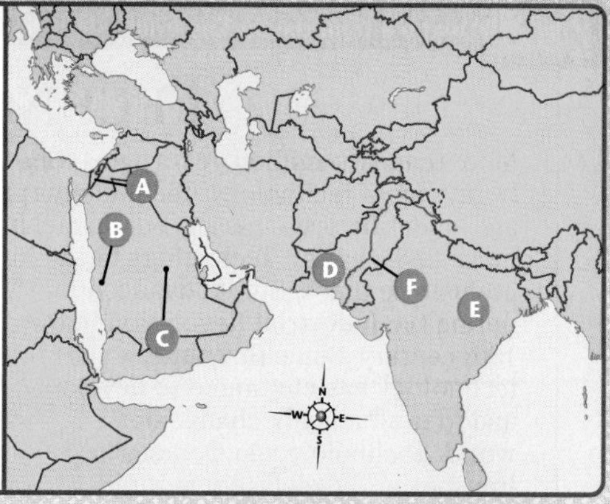

Take It to the NET

Enrichment For more map activities using geography skills, visit the social studies section of **phschool.com**.

Writing Activity

1. **Writing a Briefing Paper** Find out about the political issues that have connected one of the following countries—Saudi Arabia or Israel—to the United States. Write a briefing paper for an incoming U.S. Senator or Representative summarizing your findings about involvement of the United States with this country.
2. **Writing a Speech** Choose one current issue discussed in the chapter to research. (Possibilities include the conflict over Kashmir or women's roles in Muslim society.) Visit your school or local library and use primary sources such as newspaper and magazine articles to find additional information about the issue. Write a speech that provides information about the issue and gives your opinion on how to address it.

Critical Thinking

1. **Making Comparisons** Compare the lives of women in India with those of women in Saudi Arabia.
2. **Recognizing Cause and Effect** What are some ways that low levels of rainfall might affect life in Southwest Asia?
3. **Drawing Conclusions** Explain why oil is such a valuable resource to Saudi Arabia.

Applying Your Skills

Turn to the Skills for Life activity on page 535 to answer the following questions.

1. Jordan builds a dam on the Jordan River. Predict the reaction of Syria and Israel.
2. India gains control over all of Kashmir. Predict the reaction of Pakistan.

Take It to the NET

Activity Read about the histories, governments, and cultures of South Asia. How is democracy in India similiar to and different from democracy in the United States? Visit the World Explorer: People, Places, and Cultures section of **phschool.com** for help in completing this activity.

Chapter 28 Self-Test As a final review activity, take the Chapter 28 Self-Test and get instant feedback on your answers. To take the test, visit the Social Studies section of **phschool.com**.

Map Activity

1. D **2.** C **3.** A **4.** B **5.** F **6.** E

Writing Activity

1. Briefing papers should provide correct and relevant information and offer insights based on past involvement and current challenges.
2. Speeches should clearly outline problems. Opinions should be supported by facts.

Critical Thinking

1. Possible answer: Women in both countries are working hard to gain equality. However, women in India seem to enjoy more rights and freedom than do women in Saudi Arabia.
2. Low precipitation might limit the kinds of crops that can be grown and limit the number of people who can settle in dry regions of Southwest Asia.
3. Sample response: Oil can be used to generate energy, which is important to industry, agriculture, transportation, and the daily lives of people who live in the industrialized world. Because energy is so important, oil can be sold for a lot of money.

Applying Your Skills

1. Syria and Israel would object because the dam might interfere with their access to the water.
2. Pakistan would object because it would jeopardize their access to the Indus River.

Resource Directory

Teaching Resources

Cooperative Learning Activity in the Unit 6 Teaching Resources, pp. 123–126

Chapter Tests Forms A and B in the Unit 6 Teaching Resources, pp. 158–163

Guide to the Essentials, Ch. 28 Test, p. 127

Unit Test Forms A and B in the Unit 6 Teaching Resources, pp. 164–169

Other Print Resources

Chapter Tests with ExamView® Test Bank, Ch. 28

Technology

ExamView® Test Bank CD-ROM, Ch. 28

Resource Pro® CD-ROM

UNIT 6

Introduction

The introduction on the student page on the right provides key facts and general information about technology.

- Students should read the introduction first to gain a basic knowledge of the subject before reading on.
- Have students read all of the subentries, which provide further information on technology, particularly focussing on how it impacts the global community. Have students also read the annotations that accompany and explain the photos and illustrations.
- When students have finished reading all of the information, discuss the connections between the information on these pages and what they have learned about Asia. Students might want to review sections on economic development in Chapters 27 and 28.

ACTIVITY

Inventing Solutions

Have students work in small groups to define a challenge or obstacle that exists in their daily lives, and to propose a technological solution or aid to that challenge. Once groups have defined the challenge, have them brainstorm ideas for an invention that might help solve it, or make it easier to deal with. Then have groups choose one of their ideas and draw a design for it, outlining a plan with the materials that will be needed to build it, and how it will work. Have groups present their invention to the rest of the class.

Visual/Spatial

Adapted from the Dorling Kindersley Illustrated Children's Encyclopedia

TECHNOLOGY

More than two million years ago, stone tools were invented, marking the beginning of technology. Technology is the way in which people use ideas and scientific principles to build machines that make tasks easier. Technology began in prehistoric times, but it advanced rapidly during the Industrial Revolution in the 18th century. Since that time, technology has continued to develop and to dramatically change our world. Technological advances in transportation, electronics, and communications have made the world a smaller place. Even the most isolated cultures of the world are accessible. Cooperation between cultures means that shared knowledge and ideas can benefit people worldwide.

Threshing machines help farmers separate the heads from the stalks of rice plants. Previously this job had to be done by hand.

? How have science and technology helped to shape the world?

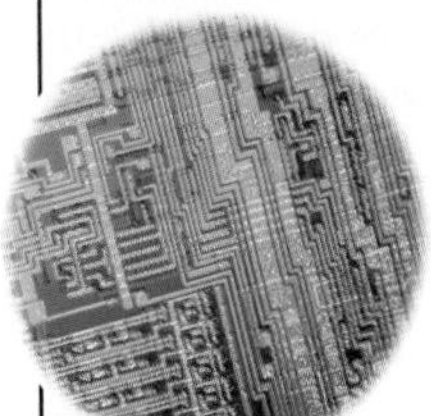

Microchips lie at the heart of a computer. These tiny devices store and process huge amounts of information at high speed.

COMPUTERS

The development of computers has been one of the most important recent advances in technology. The invention of the microchip changed the emphasis of producing goods from mechanical to electronic. Many tasks that were once done manually are now automated.

Disabled members of the community can participate in more activities because of advanced technology and specially designed equipment.

SCIENCE, TECHNOLOGY, AND SOCIETY

Facing Technological Challenges

Technological innovations have created a need for worldwide policies and global agencies to oversee and administer them. One such agency is the Common Agenda for Cooperation in Global Perspective. The Common Agenda was formed in 1993 by the U.S. and Japan to address the technological challenges of the 21st century. The partnership has brought together scientists and researchers who work to solve economic, social, and environmental problems.

COMMUNICATIONS

Today, people around the globe can communicate instantly with each other no matter where they are. Speech, pictures, and text are turned into signals and are transmitted to telephones, fax machines, computers, radios, and televisions. The signals travel via wires, cables, fiber optics, radio waves, and satellites.

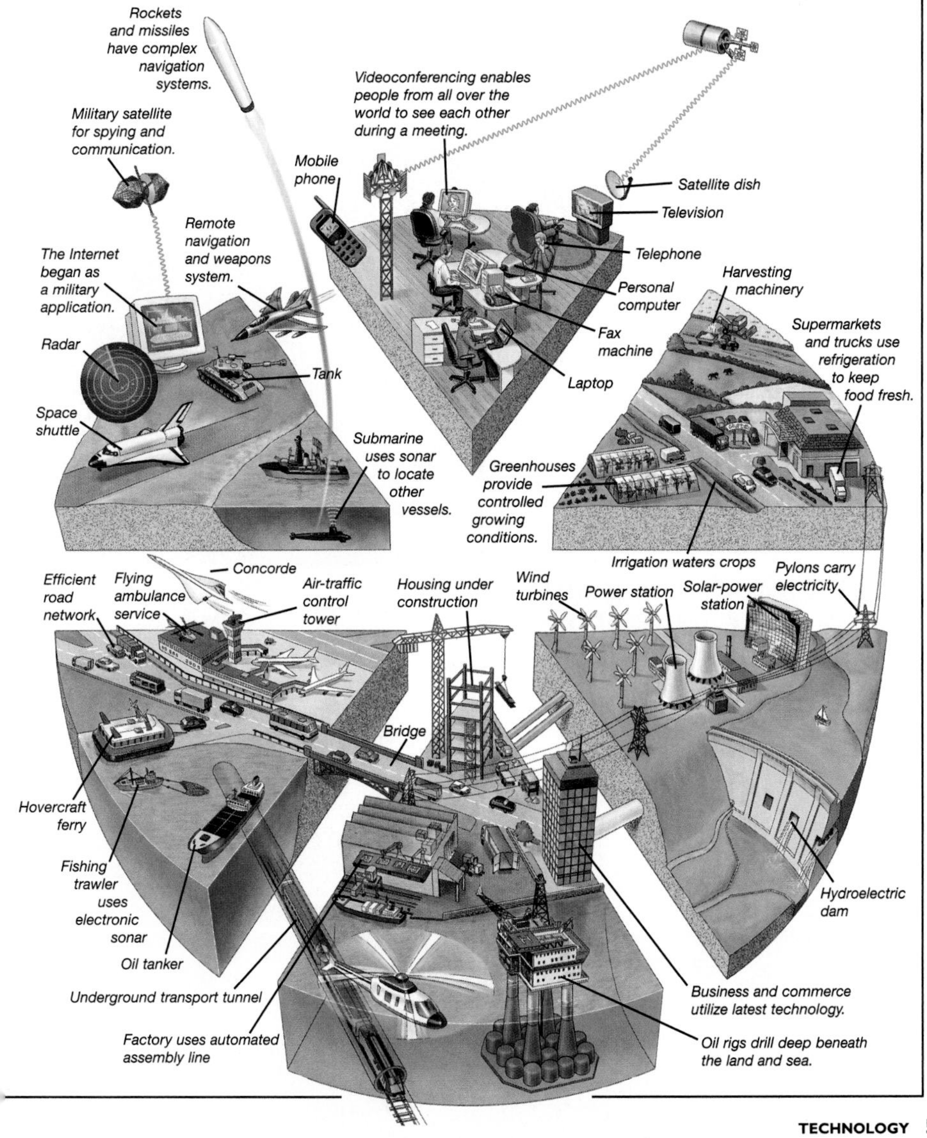

ACTIVITY

Charting the Use of Technology

Have students create a chart that shows how technology influences their daily lives. First, have students predict how many times a day they use technology. Have them keep a journal for one week, recording each activity they do that requires the use of technology, such as setting the alarm of a digital clock, or using a microwave to heat their dinner. When they have collected all of the data for the week, have them create a chart that shows the days of the week, and lists the activities for each day that use technology. As a class, discuss whether students' predictions were accurate.

Verbal/Linguistic

SCIENCE, TECHNOLOGY, AND SOCIETY

Akio Morita

Akio Morita was one of the founders of the Sony Corporation. Morita had a lifelong interest in mathematics and physics, and from an early age spent his spare time exploring electronics. Following World War II, Morita met Masaru Ibuka. The two decided to go into business together, and the seeds of Sony Corporation were sown. Technologies such as the Walkman and the VCR, help define how we spend our leisure time, and are examples of Morita's extraordinary creativity and vision.

UNIT 7

Introducing the Unit

This unit was developed around seven strands of essential knowledge and skills that relate to the study of people, places, and cultures of the contemporary world. These strands include **History, Geography, Economics, Government, Citizenship, Culture,** and **Science, Technology, and Society.** These seven strands, and the related Guiding Questions on the next pages, are intended as an organizational focus for the unit. All of the chapter content, activities, questions, and assessments relate to the seven strands, which act as an umbrella under which all of the material falls.

Using the Pictures

Use the photographs on the reduced student pages as a prompt for a discussion of what students know about history, geography, economics, government, citizenship, culture, and science and technology of the Pacific Realm.

- You may want to begin a **K-W-L** chart on the chalkboard for the Pacific Realm, with the headings What We **K**now About the Pacific Realm, What We **W**ant to Know About the Pacific Realm, and What We **L**earned About the Pacific Realm.
- Have students fill in the first column with several things they agree they already know. Then, ask them to brainstorm what they would like to know about the Pacific Realm to add to the second column.
- Students can fill in the third column as they work through the text.

eTeach

Be sure to check out this month's discussion with a Master Teacher. Go to **phschool.com**.

UNIT 7

Welcome to The Pacific Realm

GOVERNMENT

Learn about parliamentary democracies ...

HISTORY

Study the giant statues of Easter Island ...

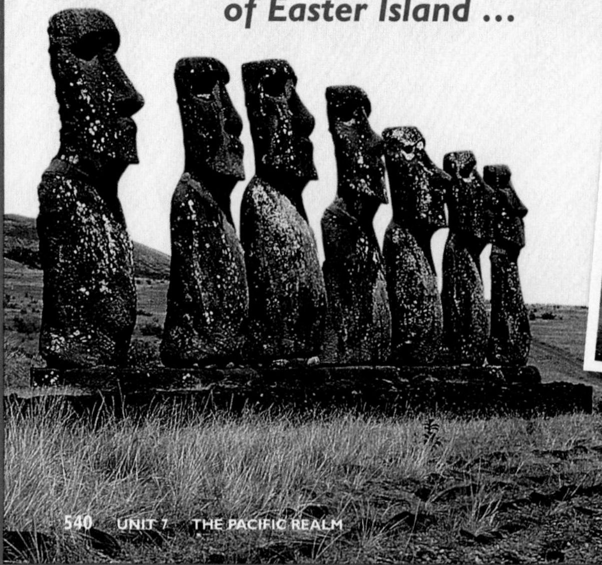

SCIENCE, TECHNOLOGY, AND SOCIETY

Herd cattle in the Outback ...

Resource Directory

Teaching Resources

Program Overview includes a guide to the Prentice Hall World Explorer program. You may wish to refer to the overview as you plan your instruction.

Pacing Charts for Unit 7 offer a variety of course configurations.

What do you want to learn?

GEOGRAPHY
Explore the volcanic islands of Polynesia ...

ECONOMICS
Visit a busy city in New Zealand ...

CULTURE
Create a traditional painting ...

CITIZENSHIP
Meet Australia's young citizens ...

A journal can be your personal record of discovery. As you learn about the Pacific Realm, you can create journal entries about what you read, write, think, and create. For your first entry, think about the different cultures of the Pacific Realm. How have these cultures helped to define life in this region?

Resource Directory

Technology

Social Studies Skills Tutor CD-ROM provides two levels of interactive instruction and practice in 20 core social studies skills.

Resource Pro® CD-ROM allows you to create customized lesson plans and print all resources directly from the CD-ROM.

Using the Explorer's Journal

Have students begin their Explorer's Journal as the paragraph on the student book page suggests. If at all possible, encourage students to use a separate small notebook for their Explorer's Journal entries. They can add to this journal as they learn more about the Pacific Realm.

Project Possibilities

The projects in this book are designed to provide students with hands-on involvement in the content area. Write the following project ideas on the chalkboard and have students preview them and discuss which they might want to do. You may assign projects as cooperative activities, whole-class projects, or individual projects.

Trade Fair

Plan a trade fair for the countries of the Pacific Realm. Choose a country to research. Find out about its major products and trade partners. Set up a booth to show and tell visitors about trade in your country. Bring books about the country and make posters, pamphlets, and charts for your booth.

Pacific Realm History

Choose an important political or cultural event in the history of one Pacific Realm nation. Write a report that describes the event and explains its influence on the rest of the nation.

Geography of the Pacific

Create a topographical model of a country in the Pacific Realm. Visit the library or use the Internet to gather information on the physical features and landforms of the country you have chosen. Make a list of the materials you'll need to build your model, and make a sketch of the model before you begin. When the model is complete, present an oral report on how physical geography affects the way people live in this country.

Introducing

Guiding Questions

The seven Guiding Questions that appear on the reduced student edition pages to the right should act as a guide for learning about the Pacific Realm, and for encouraging students to relate what they learn to their own experience. The Guiding Questions that relate to the content of each chapter in the unit also appear on the Chapter Opener pages in the student edition.

- You may wish to add your own Guiding Questions to the list in order to tailor them to your particular course. Or, as a group activity, ask your class to develop its own Guiding Questions.

ACTIVITY

Using the Guiding Questions

Ask a volunteer to read aloud the Guiding Questions to the class.

- Have students write the seven headings on a separate piece of paper or in their Explorer's Journal. Have them think about what information they would like to learn about the Pacific Realm and write a question that relates to each heading.
- Have students share their questions with the rest of the class, and discuss any similarities. Create a master list of questions grouped under the seven headings. As you read about the Pacific Realm, try to answer the questions on the list.
- At the end of the unit, if any questions remain unanswered, have students research and find the answers to those questions.

Guiding Questions

What questions do I need to ask to understand the Pacific Realm?

Asking questions is a good way to learn. Think about what information you would want to know if you were visiting a new place, and what questions you might ask to find out. The questions on these pages can help guide your study of the Pacific Realm. You might want to try adding a few of your own!

GEOGRAPHY

Chains of islands lie in the Pacific Ocean, east of the Asian continent. Geography greatly affects the lives of people who live on these islands. The high islands have rich volcanic soil that is good for growing crops. Low islands have poor soil and a scarcity of natural resources, which makes earning a living difficult.

1 How has physical geography affected economic development in the Pacific Realm?

HISTORY

Colonization and settlement have greatly affected the history of the Pacific Realm. Australia entered the world of nations as a penal colony. New Zealand attracted British settlers with its fine harbors and fertile soil. The Pacific islands appealed to Europeans as a site for trading posts and naval bases. Most nations in the Pacific Realm have attained freedom from colonial rule only within the last 125 years.

2 What characteristics of life in the Pacific Realm resulted from colonization?

CULTURE

The diverse culture of the Pacific Realm is the result of its vibrant history, and a blending of the customs and heritages of its many peoples. The cultural traditions of indigenous peoples, early explorers and colonists, and more recent immigrants influence the arts, religion, language, and customs of the region.

3 How does the past influence contemporary expressions of culture in the Pacific Realm?

GOVERNMENT

The governments of Australia and New Zealand are greatly influenced by the early colonization and settlement of these regions by the British. European governmental traditions continue to shape the governing institutions and laws, but increasingly, the indigenous peoples of the region are demanding and gaining a voice in government.

4 How do the governments of Australia and New Zealand compare with the government of Great Britain?

ECONOMICS

As they have for generations, many people in the Pacific Realm raise crops to sell. Australia and New Zealand are world leaders in wool production. A lack of natural resources poses economic challenges on many of the Pacific islands, where people are increasingly turning to the tourist industry to strengthen their economies.

5 What are some of the ways that people in the Pacific Realm earn a living?

CITIZENSHIP

The rights of citizenship vary among cultural groups in the Pacific Realm. In recent years, indigenous peoples have been fighting for, and gaining more rights. They are working hard to improve the quality of their lives, while still preserving the important traditions of their cultures.

6 How does the nature of citizenship vary among the different cultures of the Pacific Realm?

SCIENCE, TECHNOLOGY, AND SOCIETY

Scientific innovations in farming and ranching practices have contributed to the strong economies in Australia and New Zealand. New research into the potential health and medical benefits of coconut oil may bring increased prosperity to the Pacific islands.

7 How have geographical factors affected the use of science and technology in the Pacific Realm?

Take It to the NET

For more information on the Pacific Realm, visit World Explorer: People, Places, and Cultures companion Web site at **phschool.com.**

ACTIVITY

Using Primary and Secondary Sources

Families Ask students to think about relationships within their extended families and how maintaining those relationships is affected by the geography (size and location) and economy (job opportunities) in the part of the world where they live. Discuss what relationships within extended families might be like in the Pacific Realm. Talk about how maintaining such relationships may be easier or harder than in the United States.

- Have students choose a country from the Pacific Realm. Tell them to locate primary and secondary sources that give information on the importance of family relationships there.
- Encourage students to use computer software, online data bases, print material, and oral material (if available) to acquire information.

Verbal/Linguistic

ACTIVITY ATLAS

Lesson Objectives

1. Describe the relative location and size of the Pacific Realm.
2. Identify countries and regions of the Pacific Realm.
3. Describe key physical features and physical processes of the Pacific Realm.
4. Explain some effects of geography on land use.

Lesson Plan

1 Engage

Warm-Up Activity

Ask students what would happen if they threw a handful of stones of different sizes into the air. Guide them in understanding how they will bounce and scatter over a wide area.

Activating Prior Knowledge

Ask students what they know about the Pacific Ocean. If necessary, remind them that it is the world's largest ocean. Tell them that although it is vast, it is not empty. Scattered over it, like the stones they threw in the air, are many large and small islands. Invite them to name some of these islands.

ACTIVITY ATLAS

The Pacific Realm

Learning about the Pacific Realm means being an explorer and a geographer. No explorer would start out without first checking some facts. Begin by exploring the maps of the Pacific Realm on the following pages.

Relative Location

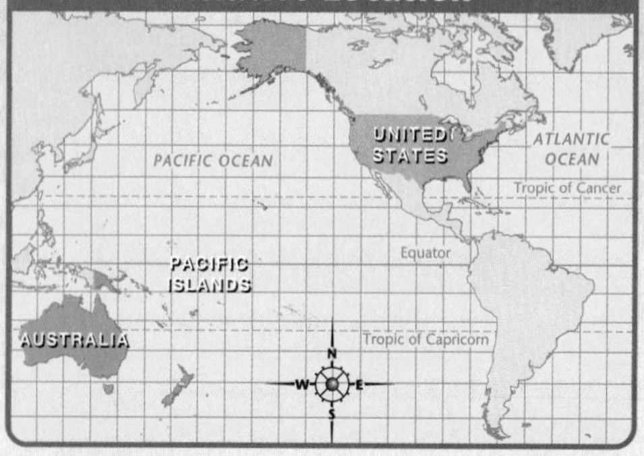

1. LOCATION

Locate Australia and the Pacific Islands Use the map at the left to describe the location of Australia and the Pacific islands relative to the United States. What ocean would you cross to reach Australia from the west coast of the United States? In what direction would you travel? On which side of the Equator is Australia located? Where are the Pacific islands located relative to the Equator?

Relative Size

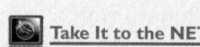

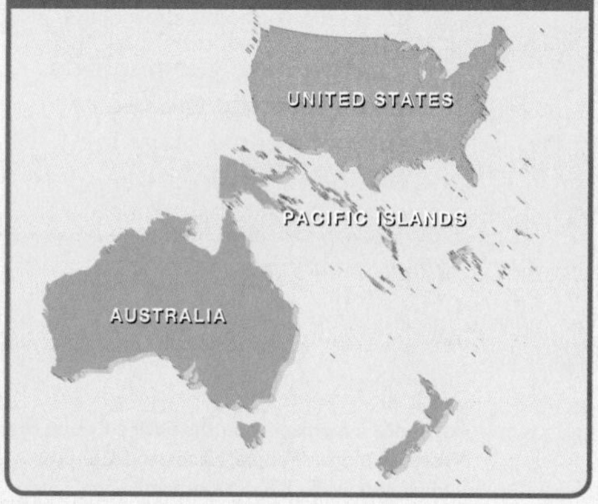

2. PLACE

Compare the Size of Australia, the Pacific Islands, and the United States Look at the map to the left. How large is Australia compared to the continental United States? Now compare the United States to the area covered by the Pacific islands. How do they compare east-to-west? North-to-south?

Take It to the NET

Items marked with this logo are periodically updated on the Internet. To get current information about the geography of the Pacific Realm, go to **phschool.com.**

Answers to...

LOCATION

1. You would cross the Pacific Ocean. You would travel to the southwest. Australia is south of the Equator. Australia and most of the Pacific islands are south of the Equator, with a few to the north.

PLACE

2. Australia is about the same size as the U.S. The east-west extent of the Pacific Islands area is about twice that of the U.S. The north-south extent of the Pacific islands area is about five times that of the U.S.

Resource Directory

Teaching Resources

Activity Atlas in the Unit 7 Teaching Resources, pp. 37–46

Australia and the Pacific Islands: Political

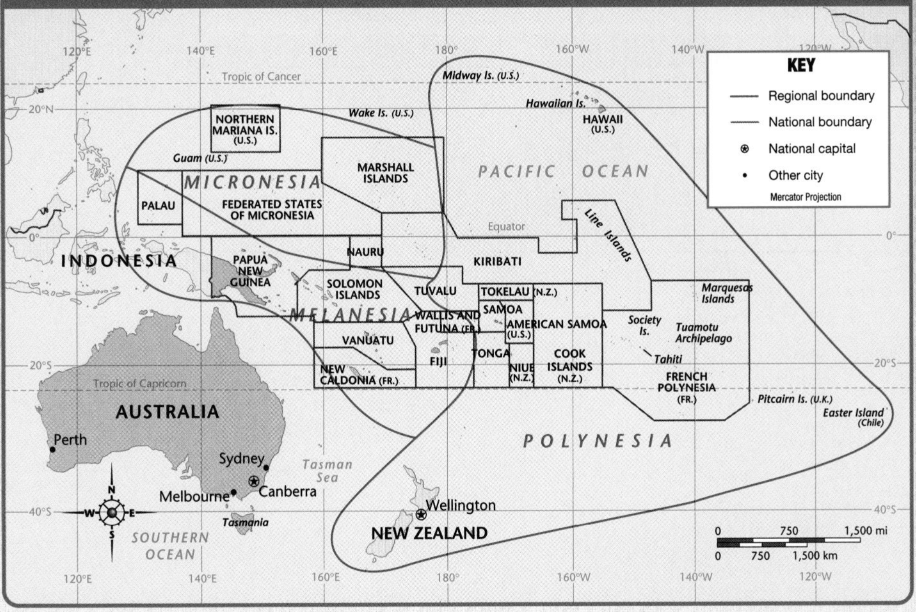

3. **PLACE**
Explore the Pacific Realm Australia is both a continent and a country. Find it on the map. What is Australia's national capital? Most of the Pacific islands are tiny. Two of the larger islands make up the country of New Zealand. Where is New Zealand relative to Australia? The Pacific islands are divided into three groups. They are Micronesia, Melanesia, and Polynesia. These are regions, not countries. Each region is shown on the map above. In which region is Hawaii? Hawaii is also one of the fifty United States.

4. **MOVEMENT**
Analyze the Movement of Historical Societies The first people to live on the Pacific islands settled in New Guinea about 30,000 years ago. From there, they traveled across the Pacific Ocean by canoe. They reached Micronesia first. In what general direction did they travel? Then they traveled on to Polynesia. About how far did they travel from New Guinea to reach the Hawaiian Islands? How far to Easter Island?

❷ Explore

Have students work in pairs and preview the chapter by looking at the maps, reading the map titles, and the headings of each paragraph. Then, ask them to write three or four questions they would like to have answered about the material. Tell them to look for answers as they read.

❸ Teach

Have students create a web diagram for the Pacific Realm. Get them started by writing Pacific Realm on the chalkboard and drawing a circle around it. Draw two more circles for Australia and Pacific Islands. Instruct students to add more circles with details about each of these categories.

❹ Assess/Reteach

Cluster diagrams should locate Australia and the Pacific Islands relative to the United States and to the Equator. They should note the physical features of Australia and New Zealand and the volcanic history of the region. They should also include details about land use in Australia.

Resource Directory

Teaching Resources

Outline Maps Australia and New Zealand, pp. 44–45; Pacific Islands, p. 46

Technology

Color Transparencies 150 Australia and the Pacific Islands: Political Map

Answers to...

PLACE

3. Australia's capital is Canberra. New Zealand is east of Australia. Hawaii is in Polynesia.

MOVEMENT

4. They traveled to the north or northeast. They traveled about 4,100 miles to reach the Hawaiian Islands. They traveled about 6,500 miles to reach Easter Island.

ACTIVITY ATLAS

Practice in the Themes of Geography

Place Ask students which oceans surround Australia. (The Pacific and Indian Oceans)

Regions Ask students where they would go to find the highest mountains in the Pacific Realm. (New Zealand)

Movement Have students discuss some of the obstacles the first people to inhabit the Pacific Realm would have faced. (Students should note the vast distances across open water that the first settlers would have had to cross. They should be aware that they only had small canoes and that storms and lack of navigation instruments would have made their journeys dangerous.)

Human-Environment Interaction Ask students what they can conclude about the geography of Australia by the way in which people use the land. (Much of Australia is dry and harsh. The lands that are more suitable for development are in the east and near the coasts.)

Location Ask students to use compass directions to describe the location of Easter Island in relation to the rest of Polynesia. (It is farther east than any other Polynesian island.)

ACTIVITY ATLAS

Take It to the NET

Ring of Fire

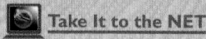

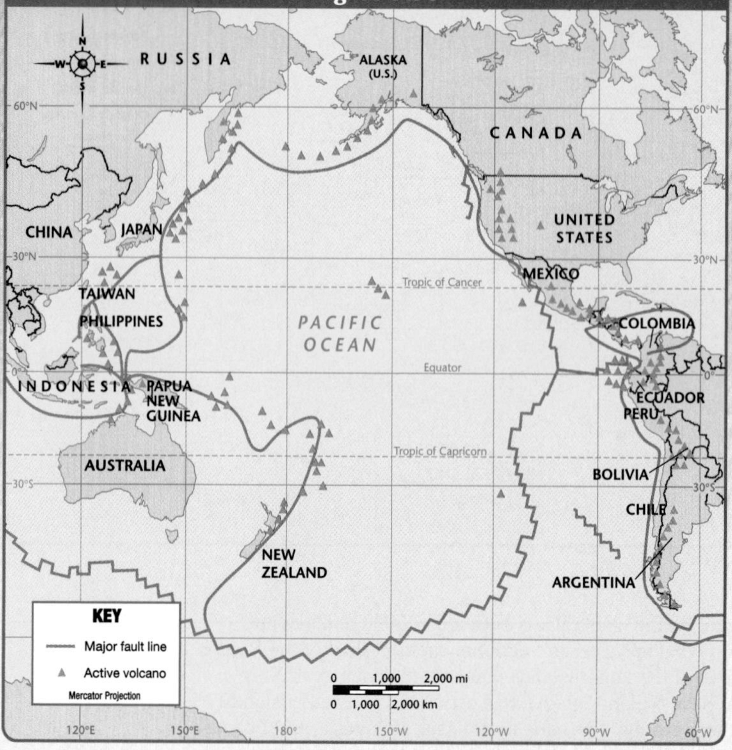

5. REGIONS

Explore Physical Processes in the Pacific Active volcanoes surround the Pacific Ocean. Many occur on the Pacific islands. Others are found in parts of North and South America. Use the map to name countries with several volcanoes. Now trace these strings of volcanoes with your finger. Why do you think this region is called the Ring of Fire?

6. REGIONS

Analyze Physical Processes Fault lines are breaks in the Earth's crust, where beneath lies hot, liquid rock. Find the fault lines on the map and trace them with your finger. Where do you find volcanoes in relation to fault lines? During earthquakes, the Earth's crust briefly opens, and sometimes liquid rock, or lava, escapes. What might this have to do with volcanoes?

Answers to...

REGIONS

5. Countries with many active volcanoes include the United States, Mexico, Colombia, Bolivia, Argentina, and Chile. The region is called the Ring of Fire because the chain of volcanoes forms a ring.

REGIONS

6. Volcanoes are usually very near fault lines. Students should recognize that earthquakes and volcanoes are related seismic events.

Resource Directory

Technology

Color Transparencies 153 Tectonic Plate Boundaries Map

7. PLACE

Locate Physical Features of Australia and New Zealand A favorite uncle has invited you to join him on a visit to Australia and New Zealand. You will be traveling widely and exploring the physical features of the region. Use the map below to plan your visit.

A. *Your first stop will be New Zealand. You want to see the Southern Alps. Which island will you visit?*

B. *From New Zealand, you will be flying to Australia by the shortest route. Then the plane heads north, following the coast to the Great Barrier Reef. What mountain range is to your west?*

C. *You end up in the Kimberley Plateau, and then fly south to the Nullarbor Plain. What deserts will you pass over?*

BONUS

Your trip is planned for July. What clothing should you pack for your visit to the Southern Alps? For the area around the Great Barrier Reef?

Australia and New Zealand: Physical

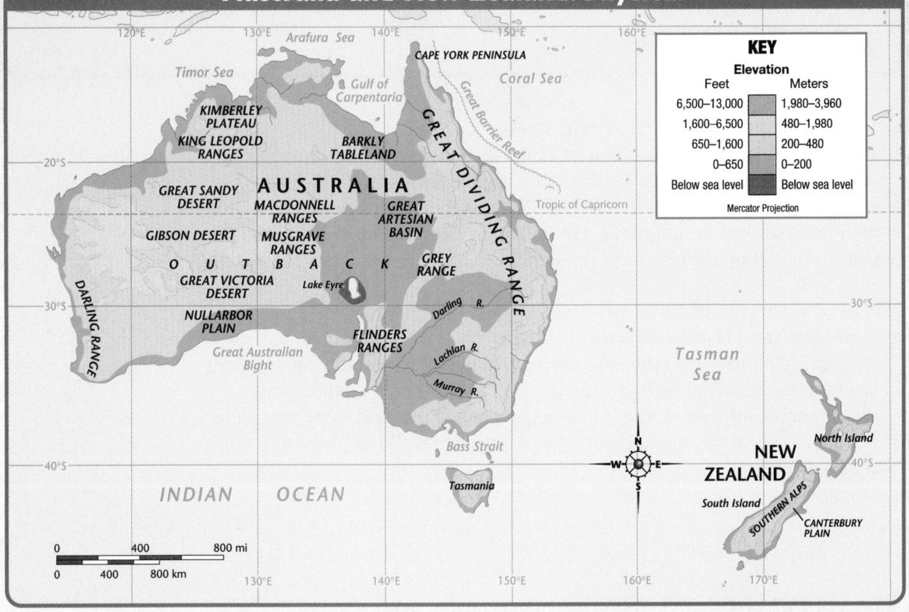

GEOGRAPHY

Climate and the Equator

How far north or south of the Equator that a place is located is an important factor in determining how hot or cold it is. Many of the Pacific islands are very near the Equator. They are warm and plants grow year round. Other parts of the region can become cold and have snow. New Zealand's South Island extends to nearly 48° S latitude. Only the extreme border of the continental United States reaches this far north. Ask students what winters are like in northern Maine, Minnesota, or Washington. Point out, however, that the surrounding oceans do moderate the temperatures of New Zealand.

Resource Directory

Teaching Resources

Outline Maps Australia and New Zealand, pp. 44–45

Technology

Color Transparencies 151 Australia and New Zealand: Physical-Political Map

Answers to...

PLACE

7. **A.** South Island
   B. The Great Dividing Range
   C. Great Sandy Desert, Gibson Desert, Great Victoria Desert

BONUS

South of the Equator, seasons are the reverse of those north of the Equator, so it will be winter. Students should suggest heavy winter clothing for the Southern Alps. The Great Barrier Reef is north of the Tropic of Capricorn, so it is in the tropics. Students should bring lighter clothing.

ACTIVITY

Discovery Learning

Where Am I? Have students choose a place in Australia or the Pacific islands and write it on a piece of paper. Then have students work in groups of five or six and take turns being "it." Students in the group must ask the person who is it questions to discover what place he or she has chosen. The questions must have yes or no answers. The person who is it must answer all questions honestly. Have students take turns being "it" until everyone has had a turn.

Logical/Mathematical, Verbal/Linguistic

ACTIVITY ATLAS

Take It to the NET

Land Use of Australia

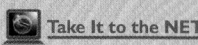

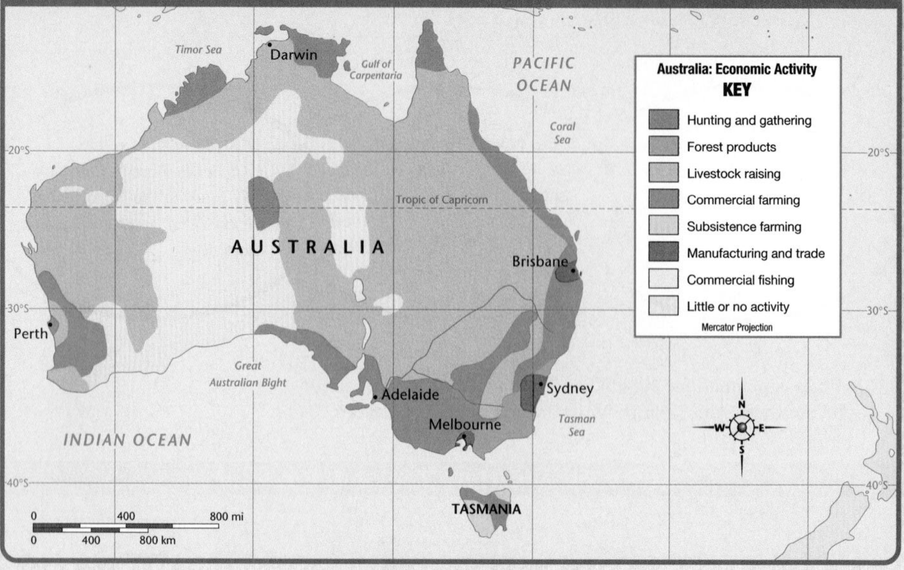

8. **HUMAN-ENVIRONMENT INTERACTION**
Examine Ways People Use the Physical Environment How people use the land is one of the main features of a region. How many different types of land use are identified on the map? What is the most widespread use of land in Australia? Compare the use of land in eastern and western Australia. What conclusions can you reach?

9. **HUMAN-ENVIRONMENT INTERACTION**
Compare Land Use to Physical Features Look at the physical map on page 547. Compare it to the land use map above. What relationship do you see between physical features and the way people use the land? What areas receive little or no use? How do people use the land in mountainous regions? Look at the manufacturing and trade areas. What physical feature is close to them?

548 UNIT 7 PACIFIC REALM

Answers to...

HUMAN-ENVIRONMENT INTERACTION

8. Eight land uses are shown, including areas with little or no activity. The most widespread use of land is for livestock raising. Students might conclude that the eastern half of Australia is better suited for agriculture, fishing, and manufacturing and trade.

HUMAN-ENVIRONMENT INTERACTION

9. Students may note a relationship between agriculture and lower elevations that have rivers. Deserts receive little or no use. In mountainous regions, land is most often used for livestock raising. Manufacturing and trade areas are located near the ocean.

Resource Directory

Teaching Resources

Outline Maps Australia and New Zealand, pp. 44–45

Technology

Color Transparencies 151 Australia and New Zealand: Physical-Political Map

Comparing the Pacific Realm's Longest, Highest, and Biggest

10. PLACE

Compare Physical Features What is the highest mountain in New Zealand? How much higher is the highest mountain in the world? About how many times larger is Australia's largest desert than the Mojave Desert? What is the longest river in Australia?

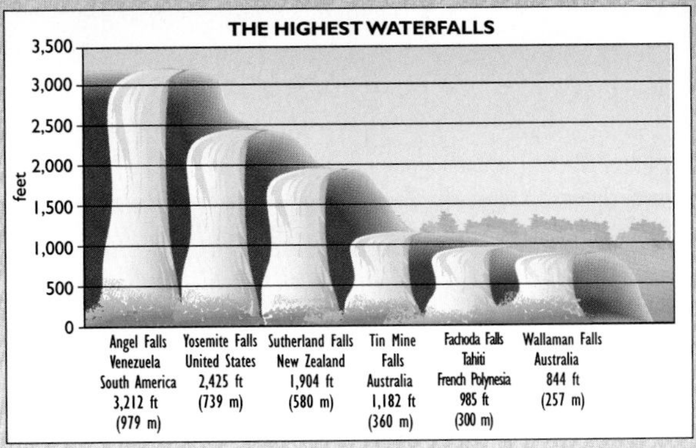

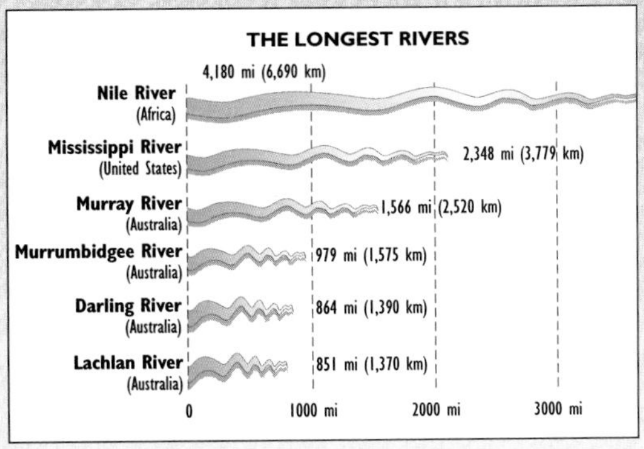

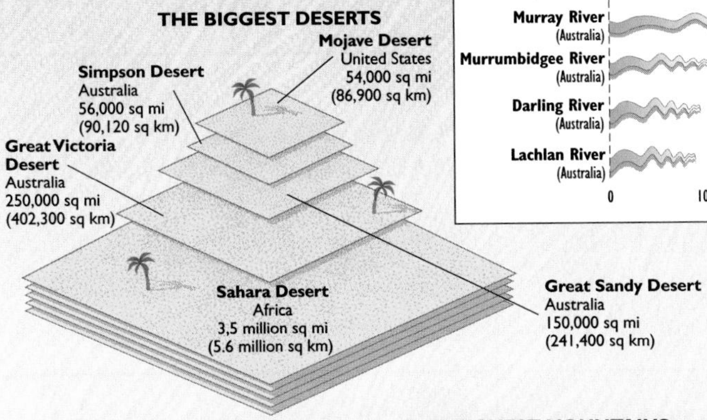

ACTIVITY

Interdisciplinary Connections

Art Have students work individually or in pairs and do research to learn about one island group in the Pacific Realm. You might instruct them to use library, Internet, or classroom resources. Have them create drawings to illustrate important landforms or features of the islands. They might also download images from the Internet. Then, have students present their findings to the class.

Visual/Spatial, Verbal/Linguistic

Resource Directory

Teaching Resources

Social Studies and Geography Skills, Reading a Bar Graph, p. 51; Reading a Diagram, p. 54

Answers to...

PLACE

10. The highest mountain in New Zealand is Mount Cook. Mount Everest is almost 17,000 feet higher than Mount Cook. Great Victoria Desert is about five times the size of the Mojave Desert. The Murray River is the longest river in Australia.

Chapter 29 Planning Guide

Resource Manager

	CORE INSTRUCTION	READING/SKILLS
Chapter-Level Resources	**Teaching Resources** Program Overview Pacing Charts **Technology** Resource Pro® CD-ROM Companion Web site, phschool.com • eTeach	**Technology** Social Studies Skills Tutor CD-ROM Student Edition on Audio CD, Ch. 29
1 Physical Features 1. Explain how plate movement has affected the physical geography of Australia and New Zealand. 2. Identify the major physical features of New Zealand. 3. Contrast high islands and low islands.	**Teaching Resources** **Unit 7** Classroom Manager, p. 2 Guided Reading and Review, p. 3	**Teaching Resources** Guide to the Essentials, p. 128 Social Studies and Geography Skills, p. 54 **Technology** Section Reading Support Transparencies
2 Humans and the Physical Environment 1. Identify geographic factors that explain where most people in Australia live. 2. Explain how the geysers of New Zealand's North Island are used as an energy resource. 3. Compare and contrast Australia and New Zealand.	**Teaching Resources** **Unit 7** Classroom Manager, p. 5 Guided Reading and Review, p. 6	**Teaching Resources** Guide to the Essentials, p. 129 **Technology** Section Reading Support Transparencies
3 Geographic Factors and Natural Resources 1. Describe the physical geography of the Pacific islands. 2. Identify some of the natural resources of the Pacific islands.	**Teaching Resources** **Unit 7** Classroom Manager, p. 8 Guided Reading and Review, p. 9 Chapter Summary, p. 11 Vocabulary, p. 12 Reteaching, p. 13	**Teaching Resources** **Unit 7** Critical Thinking, p. 15 Guide to the Essentials, p. 130 **Technology** Section Reading Support Transparencies

ENRICHMENT / PRE-AP

Teaching Resources
Primary Sources and Literature Readings

Other Print Resources
DK Atlas

Technology
World Video Explorer: Geography: Australia and New Zealand
Companion Web site, phschool.com

Teaching Resources
Outline Maps, pp. 44–45

Technology
Color Transparencies 151 and 156
Passport to the World CD-ROM

Teaching Resources
Unit 7
- Enrichment, p. 14
- Cooperative Learning Activity, pp. 47–50
- Outline Maps, p. 46

Technology
Color Transparencies 150

ASSESSMENT

Prentice Hall Assessment System

Core Assessment
Chapter Tests with ExamView® Test Bank, Ch. 29
ExamView® Test Bank CD-ROM, Ch. 29

Standardized Test Preparation
Diagnose and Prescribe
Diagnostic Tests for Middle Grades Social Studies Skills
Review and Reteach
Review Book for World Studies
Practice and Assess
Test-taking Strategies with Transparencies for Middle Grades Test Prep Book
Test-taking Strategies Posters

Teaching Resources
Unit 7
- Section Quizzes, pp. 4, 7, and 10
- Chapter Tests, pp. 65–67

Technology
Companion Web site, phschool.com
Ch. 29 Self-Test

World Video Explorer
Each region of the world is explored through regional flyovers and investigative field trips. Case study segments give students an in-depth view of the history, economy, government, and culture of a key place in each region. Case studies include Nigeria, Mexico, China, British Columbia, and the Czech Republic.

In Your Classroom

CUSTOMIZE FOR INDIVIDUAL NEEDS

Gifted and Talented

Teacher's Edition
- Coral Reefs, p. 553

Teaching Resources
- Enrichment, p. 14
- Primary Sources and Literature Readings

Honors/Pre-AP

Teacher's Edition
- A New Hawaiian Island, p. 553

Teaching Resources
- Critical Thinking, p. 15
- Primary Sources and Literature Readings

ESL

Teacher's Edition
- Uluru, p. 557

Teaching Resources
- Guided Reading and Review, pp. 3, 6, and 9
- Vocabulary, p. 12
- Reteaching, p. 13
- Guide to the Essentials, pp. 128–130
- Social Studies and Geography Skills, p. 54

Technology
- Social Studies Skills Tutor CD-ROM
- Section Reading Support Transparencies

Less Proficient Readers

Teacher's Edition
- Coral Reefs, p. 553

Teaching Resources
- Guided Reading and Review, pp. 3, 6, and 9
- Vocabulary, p. 12
- Reteaching, p. 13
- Guide to the Essentials , pp. 128–130
- Social Studies and Geography Skills, p. 54

Technology
- Social Studies Skills Tutor CD-ROM
- Section Reading Support Transparencies

Less Proficient Writers

Teacher's Edition
- A New Hawaiian Island, p. 553

Teaching Resources
- Guided Reading and Review, pp. 3, 6, and 9
- Vocabulary, p. 12
- Guide to the Essentials, pp. 128–130
- Social Studies and Geography Skills, p. 54

Technology
- Social Studies Skills Tutor CD-ROM
- Section Reading Support Transparencies

DORLING KINDERSLEY

At the end of each unit, you will find information adapted from Dorling Kindersley's *Illustrated Children's Encyclopedia* that connects to the region being studied and to one of the seven content strands. In addition, your resources include Dorling Kindersley's *Atlas*, which contains valuable information about countries from around the world.

TEACHER'S EDITION INDEX

Activities coral reefs, p. 553; uluru, p. 557
Connections a new hawaiian island, p. 553
Skills Mini Lessons Recognizing Cause and Effect, p. 556

CHAPTER 29 PACING SUGGESTIONS

For 90-minute Blocks

See suggestions in the Teaching Resources Pacing Charts for Chapter 29. Use Color Transparencies 150-151 and 156.

Running Out of Time?

See the Guide to the Essentials, pp. 128–130.

INTERDISCIPLINARY LINKS

Middle Grades Math: Tools for Success
Course 1, Lesson 1-4, **Using Spreadsheets to Organize Data**
Course 2, Lesson 1-1, **Reporting Frequency**

Science Explorer
Animals, Lesson 4-4, **Diversity of Mammals**
Earth's Changing Surface, Chapter 3, **Erosion and Deposition**

BIBLIOGRAPHY

For the Teacher

Animal: The Definitive Visual Guide to the World's Wildlife. Dorling Kindersley, 2001.

Australia. National Geographic 51444, 1991. Videocassette.

World Desk Reference. Dorling Kindersley, 2001.

For the Student

Easy

Eversole, Robyn. *Flood Fish*. Crown, 1995.

Ocean (*Eye Wonder* series). Dorling Kindersley, 2001.

Average

Coral Reef (*Look Closer* series). Dorling Kindersley, 2001.

Pringle, Laurence. *Coral Reefs: Earth's Undersea Treasures*. Simon & Schuster, 1995.

Wood, Jenny. *The Children's Atlas of People and Places*. Millbrook, 1993.

Literature Connection

Fagan, Andrew. *Swirly World: The Solo Voyages*. HarperCollins, 2001.

Hill, Anthony. *The Burnt Stick*. Houghton Mifflin, 1995.

Take It to the NET

The World Explorer companion Web site, found on **phschool.com**, offers activities for exploring geographical, historical, and cultural resources on the Internet. It also provides on-line links for key content and all Section and Chapter Assessment activities.

The **Teacher site** also provides teachers with regional data and ideas for student research and activities.

Students can use the **Student site** to find chapter-by-chapter Internet resource links and to access Self-Tests.

CHAPTER 29

Connecting to the Guiding Questions

In this chapter, students will read about the physical geography of Australia, New Zealand, and the Pacific islands. Content in this chapter corresponds to the following Guiding Questions outlined at the beginning of the unit.

- How has the physical geography affected economic development in the Pacific Realm?
- What are some of the ways that people in the Pacific Realm earn a living?
- How have geographical factors affected the use of science and technology in the Pacific Realm?

Using the Map Activities

Point out the inset globe that accompanies the map and help students determine where the Pacific region is in relation to the other continents.

- The maps shows that regional boundaries include not only the islands but ocean as well. The three large groups of Pacific islands are Micronesia, Melanesia, and Polynesia.
- You may wish to have students list possible reasons why so few people live in this area. Students might suggest lack of arable land and natural resources, and too few industries.

Heterogeneous Groups

The following activities are suitable for heterogeneous groups.

Locating Information

Coral Reefs, p. 553

Cooperative Learning

Uluru, p. 557

eTeach

Be sure to check out this month's discussion with a Master Teacher. Go to **phschool.com**.

CHAPTER 29

AUSTRALIA, NEW ZEALAND, AND THE PACIFIC ISLANDS: Physical Geography

SECTION 1
Physical Features

SECTION 2
Humans and the Physical Environment

SECTION 3
Geographic Factors and Natural Resources

The Pacific Region

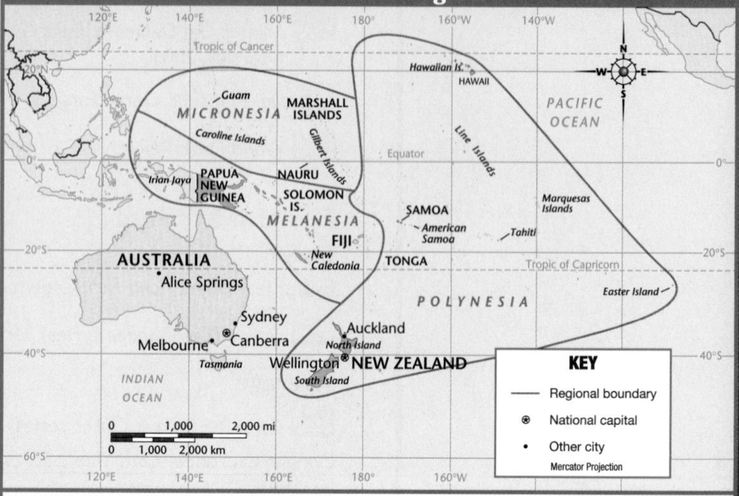

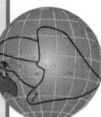

USING MAPS

The Pacific region includes the continent of Australia and many islands. The largest islands are those that make up New Guinea and New Zealand, but there are thousands of others.

Understanding the Pacific Islands Region

Look at the map scale. What important fact does the map scale tell you about the Pacific region? Name the three large groups of Pacific islands. Why isn't Australia included in one of the regional boundaries? Locate the Pacific region on another map or globe.

Making Connections

The Pacific region is one of the largest in the world. But only about 29 million people live there. That is less than 1 percent of the world's population. Why do you think so few people live in this region? Write a short description, telling what you think life on a small island in the Pacific might be like.

Resource Directory

Teaching Resources

Primary Sources and Literature Readings extend content with a selection related to the concepts in this chapter.

Other Print Resources

DK Atlas

Technology

Geography: Australia and New Zealand, from the World Video Explorer, enhances understanding of how geography influences the lives of people in New Zealand and in the Australian Outback.

Student Edition on Audio CD, Ch. 29

SECTION 1

Physical Features

BEFORE YOU READ

READING FOCUS

1. How has plate movement affected the environments of Australia and New Zealand?
2. What are the major physical features of New Zealand?
3. What is the difference between high islands and low islands?

KEY TERMS

marsupial
tectonic plate
geyser
fiord
atoll
coral

NOTE TAKING

Copy the table below. As you read the section, mark the correct box or boxes beside each area in the Pacific realm to show some features of its physical geography.

Physical Geography				
	Reefs and Atolls	Unique Animal Life	Geysers and Fiords	Volcanoes
Australia				
New Zealand				
Pacific islands				

MAIN IDEA

Earth movement and location have caused unique and diverse plant and animal life in both Australia and New Zealand.

Setting the Scene

What strange-looking bird has a long bill, does not fly, and only comes out at night to hunt? If you said a kiwi, you are right. The people of New Zealand are so proud of this unusual bird that they have made it their national symbol. They even call themselves "Kiwis." The bird is just one of many unique animals found in New Zealand and its neighbor to the west, Australia.

The Amazing Kiwi Bird

GEOGRAPHY The kiwi has no tail, and it is the only bird with nostrils at the tip of its beak. These help it sniff out insects and berries.
Critical Thinking Why do you think the people of New Zealand would call themselves "Kiwis"?

Unique Environments

Australia and New Zealand lie between the Pacific Ocean and the Indian Ocean. Both are in the Southern Hemisphere, south of the Equator. This means that their seasons are the opposite of those in the United States. They are far from other landmasses, which has made them unique.

New Zealand and Australia are so far from other large landmasses that many of their plants and animals are found nowhere else on the Earth. Only in New Zealand can you find kiwis

Resource Directory

Teaching Resources

Classroom Manager in the Unit 7 Teaching Resources, p. 2

Guided Reading and Review in the Unit 7 Teaching Resources, p. 3

Guide to the Essentials, p. 128

Technology

Section Reading Support Transparencies

Passport to the World CD-ROM This interactive CD-ROM allows students to explore each region of the world. Students view regional videos, take photo tours, and explore a historical timeline. Students record their travels in an Explorer's Journal, and receive passport stamps when they pass regional quizzes.

SECTION 1

Lesson Objectives

1. Explain how plate movement has affected the physical geography of Australia and New Zealand.
2. Identify the major physical features of New Zealand.
3. Contrast high islands and low islands.

Lesson Plan

1 Engage

Warm-Up Activity

Point out Australia, New Zealand, and the Pacific Islands on a globe. Ask students to describe the location of these places in relation to the location of the United States.

Activating Prior Knowledge

Ask students to think about the physical features in the place where they live. Do they live near mountains? Forests? Farmland? Do they live in a desert, or near the ocean? Discuss with students what they like most and least about living in their physical environment.

2 Explore

Have students read the section and examine the map and photos to find answers to the following questions: How has location affected the plant and animal life of Australia and New Zealand? How were the landforms on the North Island of New Zealand formed? Why are some Pacific islands called high islands and some called low islands?

Answers to...

CRITICAL THINKING

Possible answer: New Zealanders are proud of animals like the Kiwi, which make their country unique.

Lesson Plan continued

❸ Teach

Have students prepare a travel guide for New Zealand and the Pacific Islands. The guide should describe the physical features of the two areas, focusing on features that are unique to them. This activity should take about 20 minutes.

Questions for Discussion

GEOGRAPHY **What geographic event is responsible for the unique vegetation and animal life in Australia and New Zealand?**

When the Indo-Australian plate broke away as a separate landmass several hundred million years ago, it enlarged the distance between Australia and New Zealand and Asia.

GEOGRAPHY **Why do Australia and New Zealand have their seasons opposite to those in the United States?**

Their location below the Equator in the Southern Hemisphere causes their seasons to be opposite to those in the United States.

❹ Assess/Reteach

See the answers to the Section 1 Assessment. You may also use students' completed travel guides as an assessment.

Acceptable travel guides include two to three facts about each country.

Commendable travel guides include at least four facts about each country and focus on unique aspects of the countries.

Outstanding travel guides include five or more facts about each country and focus on unique aspects of the countries.

Answers to...

MAP STUDY

Most of Australia's deserts are in the west. New Zealand's South Island is more mountainous.

Australia and New Zealand: Physical

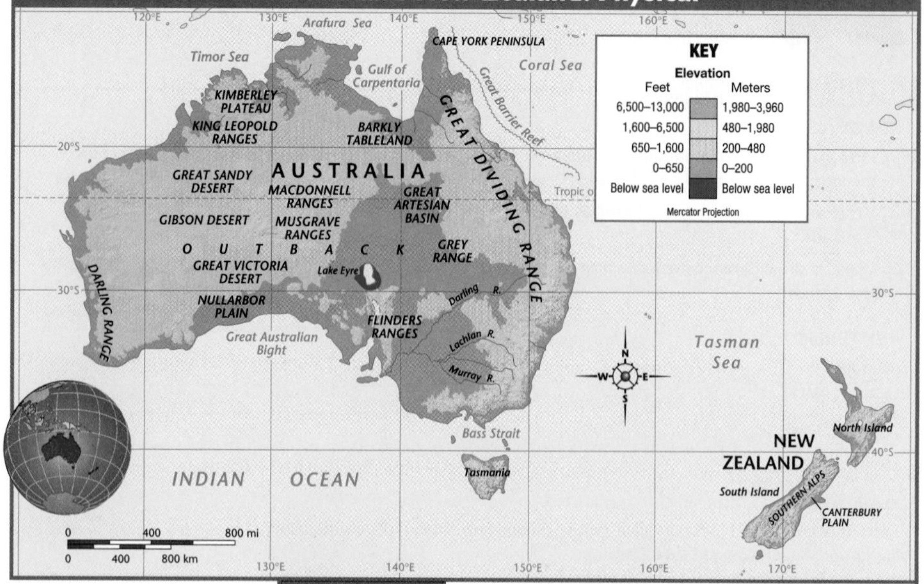

GEOGRAPHY Apart from the Great Dividing Range, most of Australia is quite flat. The huge area to the west of the Great Dividing Range is made up of plains or low plateaus. In contrast, New Zealand is mountainous or hilly.
Map Study Where are most of Australia's deserts located? Which of New Zealand's two islands is more mountainous?

and yellow-eyed penguins. Eighty-four percent of the vegetation in New Zealand's forests grows nowhere else. Australia has many unique creatures, such as the kangaroo and the koala. These animals are biologically unique, too. They are **marsupials** (mar SOO pea ulz), or animals that carry their young in a body pouch. Marsupials are found elsewhere in the world. The opossum of North America, for instance, is a marsupial. But in Australia, almost all mammals are marsupials. This is not true anywhere else on the Earth.

The uniqueness of New Zealand and Australia results from forces beneath the Earth's surface. The outer "skin" of the Earth, or the crust, is broken into huge pieces called **tectonic plates.** Australia, New Zealand, and the Pacific islands are all part of the Indo-Australian plate. Once that plate was part of a landmass that included Asia. Then, several hundred million years ago, the plate broke away. Slowly—only an inch or two each year—it moved southeast in the Pacific Ocean.

As the plate moved, the distance between the islands and Asia increased. Over the centuries, small changes occurred naturally in the

552 UNIT 7 THE PACIFIC REALM

Resource Directory

Teaching Resources

Outline Maps, Australia and New Zealand, pp. 44–45

Technology

Color Transparencies 151 Australia and New Zealand: Physical-Political Map

islands' animals and plants. For instance, many birds have lost the ability to fly, even though they still have small wings. Because of the islands' isolation, these living things did not spread to other regions.

Physical Features

Australia is the Earth's largest island and smallest continent. It is about as large as the continental United States. That means the part of the United States located between Canada and Mexico.

Look at the map on page 552 and find New Zealand, which lies about 1,200 miles (1,900 km) southeast of Australia. Made up of two islands, North Island and South Island, New Zealand is much smaller than Australia. Yet it is one of the largest countries in the Pacific region—about the size of the state of Colorado.

Here, the land forms have been shaped by volcanoes. They, in turn, were caused by the movement of tectonic plates. Like other island groups, New Zealand's North and South Islands were formed by volcanoes when these plates collided.

Both North and South Island have highlands, forests, lakes, and rugged, snowcapped mountains. In the middle of North Island lies a volcanic plateau. Three of the volcanoes are active. North of the volcanoes, **geysers** (GY zurz), or hot springs, shoot scalding water over 100 feet (30.5 m) into the air.

South Island has a high mountain range called the Southern Alps. Mount Cook, the highest peak in the range, rises to 12,349 feet (3,764 m). Glaciers cover the mountainsides. Below, crystal-clear lakes dot the landscape. **Fiords** (fyordz), or narrow inlets, slice the southwest coastline. Here, the mountains reach the sea. To the southeast lies a flat fertile land called the Canterbury Plain.

LINKS TO Science

Steam Heat Geysers are found in three places in the world: the northwestern United States, Iceland, and New Zealand. In these places, movements of tectonic plates have created deep cracks in the Earth's crust. Water seeps down into the cracks until it reaches very hot rocks. The heat raises the temperature of the water until it is so hot that it bursts upward in a shower of water and steam.

Changing the Earth

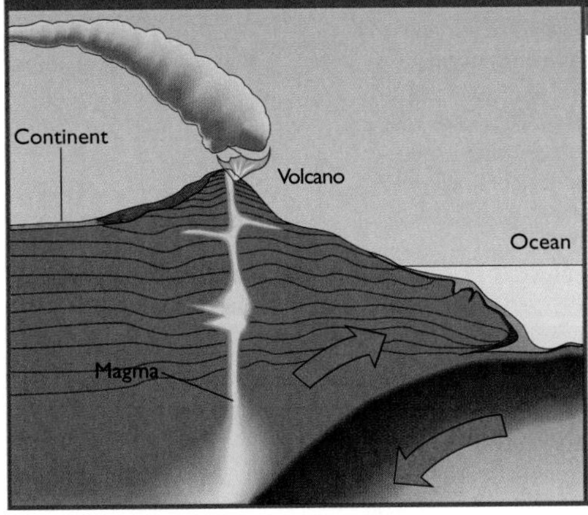

GEOGRAPHY New Zealand and its volcanoes were formed when the Pacific and Indo-Australian plates crashed together. The Pacific plate slid downwards into the Earth, forcing the edge of the Indo-Australian plate upwards. Friction and heat from inside the Earth melted the rock at the edges of the two plates. This molten rock, or magma, rose to the surface, causing volcanic eruptions. **Chart Study** Which is the Pacific plate, the one on the left of the diagram or the one on the right? What do the two arrows indicate?

ACTIVITY

Locating Information

Coral Reefs Encourage groups of students to investigate the state of coral reefs around the world. Suggest that they present their findings in a news documentary titled *Coral Reefs Today*. Indicate that students can each report on a different facet of the topic, including worldwide locations of coral reefs, the different types of coral, and animals that live in or near coral. One student can then give an overview of the natural and human-caused hazards that threaten the fragile environment of coral reefs.

Verbal/Linguistic

GEOGRAPHY

A New Hawaiian Island

Researchers are anticipating another Hawaiian island! The existing islands, formed over the last five million years, are each the result of an ocean-floor volcano whose repeated eruptions built up a lava cone tall enough to reach above the surface of the ocean. Now, using satellites and sophisticated radar techniques, researchers have found evidence of another volcano, 0.6 mile (1 km) below the surface of the ocean and 18 miles (30 km) off the southeastern coast of the island of Hawaii. The island, already named Loihi, is expected to break the surface of the ocean in about 50,000 years.

Resource Directory

Teaching Resources

Social Studies and Geography Skills, Reading a Diagram, p. 54

Technology

Color Transparencies 156 Types of Volcanoes Diagram

Answers to...

CHART STUDY

The Pacific plate is on the right. The arrows indicate the opposite motions of the Pacific and Indo-Australian plates.

SECTION I ASSESSMENT

AFTER YOU READ

1. (a) animals that carry their young in a body pouch (b) huge piece of the Earth's crust (c) hot spring that shoots scalding water into the air (d) narrow inlet (e) small coral island in the shape of a ring (f) rocklike material made up of the skeletons of tiny sea creatures
2. Plate movement isolated Australia and New Zealand from other large landmasses, causing many of their animals and plants to be unique on the Earth.
3. New Zealand has glaciers, volcanic mountains, forests, geysers, fiords, and lakes.
4. High islands are formed by volcanoes and usually have mountains. Low islands are reefs or atolls.
5. Postcards should include some of the major physical features noted in the section.
6. Possible answer: One advantage might be the natural beauty of the environment. One disadvantage might be the threat of a volcanic eruption.
7. Reports should focus on the uniqueness of Australia's and New Zealand's plant and animal life.
8. Encourage them to use explanatory notes and diagrams to explain the formation of a volcano.

Answers to...

CHART STUDY

The islands are made of coral, a rocklike substance; crops need fertile soil to grow.

A Coral Atoll

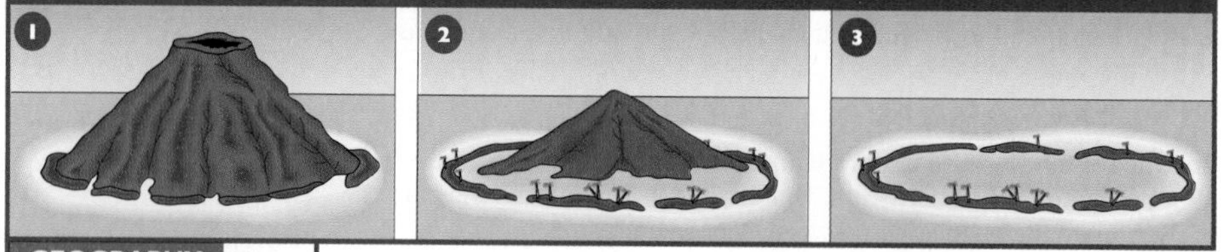

GEOGRAPHY The diagrams above show how a coral atoll is formed. It begins as a "fringe" of coral around a volcanic island. This coral reef continues to build as the island is worn away. Eventually, only the coral reef is left. **Chart Study** Why do you think coral islands cannot support much agriculture?

The Pacific Islands: High and Low

Geographers divide the Pacific islands into high islands and low islands. Volcanoes form high islands. They usually have mountains and the soil, which consists of volcanic ash, is very fertile.

Low islands are reefs or atolls. An **atoll** (a TAWL) is a small coral island in the shape of a ring which encloses a shallow pool of ocean water called a lagoon. Often the lagoon has at least one opening to the sea. An atoll often rises only a few feet above the Pacific. Low islands have this shape and low elevation because they are built on coral reefs. **Coral** is a rocklike material made up of the skeletons of tiny sea creatures. A reef expands until it nears the surface. Then sand and other debris accumulate on the reef's surface, raising the island above the level of the water.

SECTION I ASSESSMENT

AFTER YOU READ

AFTER YOU READ

1. Define (a) marsupial, (b) tectonic plate, (c) geyser, (d) fiord, (e) atoll, (f) coral

COMPREHENSION

2. How has plate movement affected the environments of Australia and New Zealand?
3. What are some physical features of New Zealand?
4. What is the difference between high islands and low islands?

CRITICAL THINKING AND WRITING

5. **Exploring the Main Idea** Review the Main Idea statement at the beginning of this section. Then, imagine you are visiting Australia, New Zealand, or the Pacific islands. Write a postcard to a friend describing some of the physical features that you see.
6. **Drawing Conclusions** What might be one advantage and one disadvantage of living in a region where there are volcanic mountains?

ACTIVITY

7. **Writing a Report** Find out more about the unique plants and animals of Australia and New Zealand. Choose one that interests you. Write and illustrate a report about it.

Take It to the NET

8. **Creating a Model Volcano** Using the information on the web site, create a model of a volcano and label its major parts. Write a short report describing how a volcano is formed and what causes an eruption. Visit the World Explorer: People, Places, and Cultures section of **phschool.com** for help in completing this activity.

Resource Directory

Teaching Resources

Section Quiz in the Unit 7 Teaching Resources, p. 4

SECTION 2

Humans and the Physical Environment

BEFORE YOU READ

READING FOCUS

1. What geographic factors help explain where most people in Australia live?
2. What is one energy resource found on North Island and how is it used?
3. How are Australia and New Zealand similar and different?

KEY PLACES

Great Dividing Range
Outback

MAIN IDEA

There are many similarities and differences in the topography and climates of New Zealand and Australia.

NOTE TAKING

Copy the diagram below. As you read the section, complete the diagram to show ways in which people in Australia and New Zealand have responded to their physical environment.

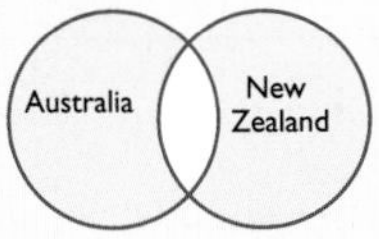

Setting the Scene

Although Australia is about as large as the continental United States, Australia has a much smaller population. Most Australians live on narrow plains along Australia's eastern and southeastern coasts. Australia's physical geography reveals why.

Australia: Climate and Population

Find the region along Australia's east coast on the map on page 552. This plain has Australia's most fertile farmland and receives ample rain. Winds flowing westward across the Pacific Ocean pick up moisture. As the winds rise to cross the **Great Dividing Range**—mountains just to the west of the coastal plain—the moisture falls as rain. These winds also help make the climate mild and pleasant. Australia's most important rivers, the Murray and the Darling,

Uluru

GEOGRAPHY Uluru, once known as Ayers Rock, is 1.5 miles (2.4 km) long and 1,000 feet (305 m) high. This huge red monolith, or rock mass, is a major landmark in Australia's Outback. Rock paintings, made thousands of years ago, cover the walls of many caves in Uluru. In 1985 the Australian government returned the land where the monolith stands to native people who live in the region. **Critical Thinking** Why do you think Uluru is so important to the native people who live there? What could have been the purpose of the rock paintings?

Resource Directory

Teaching Resources

Classroom Manager in the Unit 7 Teaching Resources, p. 5

Guided Reading and Review in the Unit 7 Teaching Resources, p. 6

Guide to the Essentials, p. 129

Technology

Section Reading Support Transparencies

SECTION 2

Lesson Objectives

1. Identify geographic factors that explain where most people in Australia live.
2. Explain how the geysers of New Zealand's North Island are used as an energy resource.
3. Compare and contrast Australia and New Zealand.

Lesson Plan

1 Engage

Warm-Up Activity

Have students compare and contrast their own state with a neighboring state. Guide the discussion so that students focus on geographic features and the effects of those features on how people earn a living and where people live.

Activating Prior Knowledge

Ask students to think of a natural resource found in the region where they live. Discuss how people in the area use this natural resource.

2 Explore

Have students think about the following questions as they read Section 2. How is Australia similar to and different from the United States? How is Australia similar to and different from New Zealand? How does a rain shadow like the one west of the Great Dividing Range affect vegetation?

Answers to...

CRITICAL THINKING

Students' answers should reflect an understanding of Uluru's spiritual significance for the Aboriginal people living in the area.

Lesson Plan continued

3 Teach

Have students make two word webs: one with the phrase *Australia's regional climates* at the center and another with the phrase *Geographical factors influencing Australia's climate* at the center. Have students complete the webs with facts from the section. This activity should take about 15 minutes.

Questions for Discussion

GEOGRAPHY What aspect of Australia's physical geography explains why most people live on the plains along the country's eastern and southeastern coasts?

Australia's east and southern coasts receive ample rain. The rest of Australia is either semiarid or desert. Since rain rarely falls here and there are few rivers, habitation is more difficult.

GEOGRAPHY What geographic factors make farming and ranching suitable economic activities for New Zealand?

New Zealand has a mild climate, and it receives abundant rain. These factors make the land suitable for farming and ranching.

4 Assess/Reteach

See the answers to the Section Assessment. You may also want to assess students' word webs.

Acceptable webs include at least two facts each.

Commendable webs include at least three facts each and state how at least one of the geographical factors listed influences the climate of Australia.

Outstanding webs include at least three facts and state how each of the geographical factors listed influences the climate of Australia.

Answers to...

CRITICAL THINKING

They have access to trade, resources from the ocean, and mild coastal climates.

New Zealand's Population

GEOGRAPHY The picture above shows towering Mount Cook on New Zealand's South Island. Sheep, like these grazing in the hills below Mount Cook, far outnumber New Zealand's human inhabitants. **Critical Thinking** Why do you think that most of the country's people live in harbor cities, like Auckland on New Zealand's North Island? (Shown on the left)

flow through the region. Most Australians live here, in cities.

The rest of Australia is very different. Just west of the Great Dividing Range is a rain shadow. This is a region that gets little precipitation because of the mountain range and is made up of semiarid plateaus and desert lands. Since rain seldom falls here, and there are few rivers, people depend on wells for fresh water. Farther west, the huge central plain called the **Outback** is desert and dry grassland.

New Zealand: Climate and Energy

Although New Zealand is more than 1,000 miles (1,600 km) long, no place is more than 80 miles (129 km) from the sea. The country's mild climate and abundance of rainfall help support farming and ranching. Farmers produce most of New Zealand's crops in the fertile

SKILLS MINI LESSON

Recognizing Cause and Effect

You might **introduce** the skill by telling students that a cause is any condition or event that makes something happen. What happens as a result of the cause is the effect. Help students **practice** the skill by asking them to find examples of cause-and-effect relationships in the text. For example, much of Australia is dry desert; much of Australia is sparsely populated. To **apply** the skill, have students create a cause-and-effect graphic organizer. Suggest that students use the graphic organizer to show what factors, or causes, are responsible for Australia's population-distribution patterns.

Canterbury Plain. Ranchers also raise sheep and cattle there. New Zealand's climate is not as hot as Australia's because New Zealand is farther from the Equator.

Recall from Section 1 that hot springs called geysers are found on North Island in New Zealand. New Zealanders use steam from these geysers as a source of electricity. To harness energy from geysers, workers drill into them and insert pipes. The pipes transport the steam in geysers to generators that use steam power to produce electricity.

Comparing Australia and New Zealand

Although Australia and New Zealand are often spoken of together, they are completely different countries separated by some 1,200 miles (1,900 km) of ocean. They do have some similarities: both are located in the South Pacific, both have important natural resources, and both raise sheep and cattle and grow similar crops. In both countries, most of the population lives in cities along the coast.

Australia, however, is mostly flat, while most of New Zealand is mountainous with some active volcanoes. Part of Australia has a tropical climate while about half of it has an arid climate. New Zealand's temperature is mild with plenty of rainfall.

CITIZENSHIP

Sir Edmund Hillary

The mountains of his native New Zealand had a defining influence on Sir Edmund Hillary's life. On May 29, 1953, he and Tenzing Norgay became the first people to reach the summit of Mount Everest, the highest spot on Earth. Hillary used the fame that came with this mountaineering "first" to help the people of Nepal, one of the world's poorest countries. He played a leading role in building clinics, hospitals, and seventeen schools. In addition, Hillary helped persuade the Nepalese government to pass laws protecting the country's mountains and forests. He also persuaded the government of New Zealand to provide assistance to make the area around Mount Everest a national park.

SECTION 2 ASSESSMENT

AFTER YOU READ

RECALL

1. Identify: (a) Great Dividing Range, (b) Outback

COMPREHENSION

2. Why do most people in Australia live along the coast?
3. How do New Zealanders use the geysers on North Island?
4. What are some differences and similarities between Australia and New Zealand?

CRITICAL THINKING AND WRITING

5. **Exploring the Main Idea** Review the Main Idea statement at the beginning of this section. Then, draw a thematic map that shows the population distribution in Australia and New Zealand. You can use the information in this section and in a reference source, such as an atlas, to help you.
6. **Identifying Cause and Effect** How has Australia's physical geography affected where people live?
7. **Making Inferences** Since they can use geysers to generate electricity, can people on North Island use all the energy that they want, without thinking about conservation?

ACTIVITY

8. **Writing to Learn** Find out more about the natural resources of Australia and New Zealand. Write a brief report about these resources.

Resource Directory

Teaching Resources

Section Quiz in the Unit 7 Teaching Resources, p. 7

ACTIVITY

Cooperative Learning

Uluru Have students work in small groups of three or four to research Uluru. Students can consider some of the following questions: How was the rock formed? What is the rock made of? How did Uluru figure into the culture of the native people of Australia? Students can present their findings in a class presentation.

Verbal/Linguistic

SECTION 2 ASSESSMENT

AFTER YOU READ

1. (a) mountains located to the east of Australia's central plain or mountains located to the west of Australia's eastern coastal plains (b) central Australian plain made up of desert and dry grassland
2. Most people in Australia live along the coast because the climate is mild and pleasant there.
3. New Zealanders use these energy resources to produce electricity.
4. Australia and New Zealand are both located in the South Pacific, have important natural resources, and raise similar crops. Population distribution, concentrated along the coasts, is similar in both countries. The physical features and climate of the two nations vary.
5. Students' maps should contain a key and should indicate that population distribution is much greater along the coasts than in the interiors.
6. The fertile farmland and ample rainfall along the eastern and southeastern coasts, contrasted with the arid and desert lands in the interior, have concentrated Australia's population on a narrow plain along the eastern and southeastern coasts.
7. Students' answers will vary, but should reflect an understanding that geothermal energy resources will run out if they are used more quickly than they can be renewed by physical processes.
8. Encourage students to find pictures to illustrate their reports.

CHAPTER 29 AUSTRALIA, NEW ZEALAND, AND THE PACIFIC ISLANDS: PHYSICAL GEOGRAPHY 557

SECTION 3

Lesson Objectives

1. Describe the physical geography of the Pacific islands.
2. Identify some of the natural resources of the Pacific islands.

Lesson Plan

1 Engage

Warm-Up Activity

Write the following terms on the chalkboard: *Hawaii*, *Tahiti*, and *Fiji*. Ask students to describe in writing the images that come to mind when they hear these terms. Call on volunteers to share their images with the class. Tell students that these three places are part of the region known as the Pacific islands.

Activating Prior Knowledge

Ask students who have visited a tropical island to describe their experiences. Discuss with students why such locations are so desirable as vacation destinations.

2 Explore

Have students read the section and then ask them the following questions. What are some physical features of each of the three regions of the Pacific islands? What is the climate and vegetation like?

Answers to...

CRITICAL THINKING

Students might mention tourism as a possible industry, or might discuss ways that Nauru can protect its remaining phosphate resources.

SECTION 3

Geographic Factors and Natural Resources

BEFORE YOU READ

READING FOCUS

1. What is the physical geography of the Pacific islands?
2. What are some natural resources of the Pacific islands?

KEY PLACES

Melanesia
Micronesia
Polynesia
Papua New Guinea

NOTE TAKING

Copy the chart below. As you read the section, fill in the chart with important facts about the Pacific islands.

The Pacific Islands		
Melanesia	Micronesia	Polynesia
• mostly high islands		

MAIN IDEA

Geographic factors such as location and physical features help determine the climate and vegetation of the Pacific islands.

Nauru's Natural Resources

ECONOMICS This picture shows a phosphate mine on Nauru. Phosphate is Nauru's only natural resource. **Critical Thinking** What kinds of industry might the people of Nauru develop instead of mining?

Setting the Scene

Luana Bogdan lives in Nauru (nah OO roo), the smallest country in the world. Tomorrow, she will be 12 years old. She is very excited, but she is also sad. Luana knows her family may soon have to leave Nauru.

Nauru's economy depended on its phosphate mines. But now the phosphate, used to make fertilizer, is almost gone. Even worse, mining has stripped the tiny island of its trees and vegetation. Nauru's leaders are trying to restore the island's ruined environment. If they fail, the Nauruans will have to find a new homeland.

The Pacific Islands: Physical Geography

The islands of the Pacific are geographically diverse. If you visited a high island, you might see three types of forests: mangrove forests ringing the coast, palm forests further inland, and monsoon forests in the center. If you visited a typical coral atoll, you would see much less plant life—only shrubs, small trees, grasses, and coconut palm trees.

Resource Directory

Teaching Resources

Classroom Manager in the Unit 7 Teaching Resources, p. 8

Guided Reading and Review in the Unit 7 Teaching Resources, p. 9

Guide to the Essentials, p. 130

Technology

Section Reading Support Transparencies

Three Regions The region known as the Pacific islands is divided into three areas. **Melanesia** (mel uh NEE zhuh) means "black islands." **Micronesia** (my kruh NEE zhuh) means "small islands." **Polynesia** (pahl uh NEE zhuh) means "many islands." Any island that falls inside the boundaries of a particular region belongs to that group.

The island region with the most people is Melanesia, which is north and east of Australia. Most of Melanesia's large islands are high islands. New Guinea, for example, has two ranges of high mountains and is divided into two countries. The western half of the island is called Irian Jaya (IHR ee ahn JAH yuh). It is part of the country of Indonesia. The eastern half is **Papua New Guinea** (PAP yuh wuh noo GIN ee), the largest and most populated Melanesian country. Some smaller Melanesian islands are Fiji, the Solomon Islands, and New Caledonia.

Most of the islands of Micronesia lie north of the Equator. Made up largely of low islands, Micronesia covers an area of the Pacific as large as the continental United States. Some of Micronesia's 2,000 islands are less than 1 square mile (2.6 sq km) in area. The largest is Guam, which is just 210 square miles (544 sq km). Most of Micronesia's islands are divided into groups. The largest are the Caroline, Gilbert, Marshall, and Mariana islands. Guam is part of the Marianas.

Polynesia is the largest island region in the Pacific. It includes our fiftieth state, Hawaii. Polynesia consists of a great many high islands, such as Tahiti and Samoa. Dense jungles cover their high volcanic mountains. Along the shores are palm-fringed, sandy beaches. The Tuamotus and Tonga are examples of Polynesia's few low islands and atolls.

GOVERNMENT

The Pacific islands include ten independent nations, three political units of larger nations (such as Hawaii), six nations closely associated with their former colonial power, and seven territories administered by other nations. The last group includes American Samoa and Guam, which are administered by the United States. The seven territories can generally act independently in matters that concern their own internal affairs. Yet, because the territories depend economically on the mainland government, they cannot afford to oppose its decisions. For example, until 1996 France tested nuclear bombs on uninhabited atolls in French Polynesia—despite widespread protests by French Polynesians.

Climate, Vegetation, and Natural Resources

The Pacific islands lie in the tropics with warm temperatures year-round. Daytime temperatures reach between the 80s and mid-90s in degrees Fahrenheit (around 32°C) and nighttime temperatures average about 75°F (24°C). The ocean and the winds keep the temperatures from getting too high. The amount of rainfall marks the change from one season to another.

Some Pacific islands have wet and dry seasons. Most islands, however, receive heavy rainfall all year long. In Hawaii, for example, volcanic peaks such as Mauna Kea (MOW nuh KAY uh) receive 100 inches of rain each year, usually in brief, heavy downpours. Some low islands, however, receive only scattered rainfall.

GEOGRAPHY

Mauna Kea is the tallest volcano on the island of Hawaii. It stands more than 5.6 mi (9km) from the sea floor to its summit. **Critical Thinking** Is the temperature at the volcano's summit lower or higher than the temperture at its base on land? Why?

3 Teach

Ask students to make a chart that compares the three regions of the Pacific islands. Columns should be labeled *Melanesia, Micronesia,* and *Polynesia.* Rows should be labeled *Meaning of Name, Types of Islands,* and *Major Islands.* This activity should take about 20 minutes.

Questions for Discussion

GEOGRAPHY Which of the fifty states is located in a Pacific island region?

Hawaii is located in Polynesia, the largest island region in the Pacific.

ECONOMICS What natural resource provides stability to Nauru's economy?

Naturally-occurring phosphate is a chief source of Nauru's economy.

4 Assess/Reteach

See the answers to the Section 3 Assessment. You may also assess students' charts.

Acceptable charts include at least six facts.

Commendable charts include facts for each category of the chart and list at least one island for the category titled *Major Islands.*

Outstanding charts include facts for each category of the chart and list more than one island for the category titled *Major Islands.*

Resource Directory

Teaching Resources

Outline Maps, Pacific Islands, p. 46

Technology

Color Transparencies 150 Australia and the Pacific Islands: Political Map

Answers to...

CRITICAL THINKING

The temperature at the volcano's summit is lower than the temperature at its base on land because air is colder at high altitudes.

SECTION 3 ASSESSMENT

AFTER YOU READ

1. (a) island group in the Pacific made up largely of high islands, located north and east of Australia (b) island group in the Pacific made up largely of low islands, located mostly north of the Equator (c) largest island region in the Pacific, consisting mostly of high islands and a few low islands (d) largest and most populated Melanesian country
2. Melanesia, Micronesia, Polynesia. Most of Melanesia's islands are high islands; most of Micronesia's islands are small, low islands. Polynesia is the largest of the three island regions. Its high volcanic mountains are covered with jungles. Sandy beaches and palm trees dot the shores.
3. tropical rain forest plants, coconut palms, grasses
4. Students' graphic organizers should contain at least one geographic factor and one natural resource.
5. High islands have much rainfall, fertile soil, and rich vegetation, which can provide various ways of making a living. Low islands, on the other hand, have little vegetation and poor soil. They are usually much smaller than high islands.
6. Students' paragraphs should explain the reason for the move and specific ways to meet the challenges of living on the island.

Answers to...

CRITICAL THINKING

Heat is the source of energy for tropical storms.

Dangerous Storms

GEOGRAPHY The wet season in the Pacific often brings violent weather. Here, high winds and driving rain bend the coconut palms on Palmerston Atoll in the Cook Islands. **Critical Thinking** The most violent tropical storms occur when the weather is hot. Why do you suppose that is?

Because of high temperatures, much rainfall, and fertile soil, high islands like Papua New Guinea and the Hawaiian Islands have rich vegetation. Tropical rain forests cover the hills and savanna grasses grow in the lowlands. Low islands, on the other hand, have little vegetation. The poor soil supports only palm trees, grasses, and small shrubs.

The Pacific island region has few natural resources. The coconut palm is the most important resource because it provides food, clothing, and shelter. Islanders export dried coconut meat, which is used in margarine, cooking oils, and luxury soaps. Some low islands, like Nauru, have phosphate deposits that can be exported. But the Pacific islands' most valuable resource may be their beauty. Tourism is gaining importance in the region and providing a new source of income.

SECTION 3 ASSESSMENT

AFTER YOU READ

RECALL

1. Identify: (a) Melanesia, (b) Micronesia, (c) Polynesia, (d) Papua New Guinea

COMPREHENSION

2. What are the three main regions of the Pacific islands? Briefly describe the geography of each region.
3. Describe some of the vegetation of the Pacific islands.

CRITICAL THINKING AND WRITING

4. **Exploring the Main Idea** Review the Main Idea statement at the beginning of this section. Then, choose one of the three regions in the Pacific islands. Create a graphic organizer that shows some of its geographic features and natural resources.
5. **Identifying Cause and Effect** Higher islands often have a better standard of living than low islands. Write a paragraph explaining why this is so.

ACTIVITY

6. Suppose you have decided to live on one of the Pacific islands. Write a paragraph explaining why you have decided to move. How will you handle the challenges of island life?

Resource Directory

Teaching Resources

Section Quiz in the Unit 7 Teaching Resources, p. 10

Chapter Summary in the Unit 7 Teaching Resources, p. 11

Vocabulary in the Unit 7 Teaching Resources, p. 12

Reteaching in the Unit 7 Teaching Resources, p. 13

Enrichment in the Unit 7 Teaching Resources, p. 14

Critical Thinking in the Unit 7 Teaching Resources, p. 15

Distinguishing Fact and Opinion

Kiwis can only be found in New Zealand.

New Zealand has the most unusual creatures on the Earth.

Learn the Skill

Distinguishing fact from opinion is something you will need to do almost every day of your life, and it is a valuable skill when you read as well. To help you learn the difference between fact and opinion, follow these steps:

A. To determine if a statement is a fact, decide if it can be proven true or false. A fact can always be proven true or false. The first statement above is a fact because you can prove that it is true. You can find evidence to prove that kiwis are not found anywhere else on the Earth other than New Zealand.

B. To determine if a statement is an opinion, decide if it is a belief that cannot be proven true or false. Opinions are often indicated by words and phrases such as "I think," "I believe," "should," or "ought to." An opinion may be based on fact, but it still cannot be proven true or false. The second statement above is an opinion because there is no way to prove that the most unusual creatures on the Earth live on New Zealand. The statement is an expression of the writer's belief.

Practice the Skill

Now distinguish facts from opinions in a real case. First, read the paragraph in the box once or twice until you are sure you understand its meaning. Then, read each sentence one at a time. Ask yourself: Is this a fact that can be proven true or false, or is this an opinion, a belief that cannot be proven true or false? Identify which statements are facts and which are opinions.

Hawaii

Hawaii is a part of the island region in the Pacific called Polynesia. It is also one of the 50 United States. If you want to visit an island in Polynesia, the best island to visit is Hawaii. Its balmy weather is perfect all year. You should avoid the volcanic peaks, though. They receive as much as 100 inches of rain each year. The warm weather and rainfall create lush vegetation, including palm trees, grasses, and shrubs. Hawaii is indeed the most beautiful island in Polynesia.

Apply the Skill

See the Chapter Review and Assessment at the end of this chapter for more questions on distinguishing fact from opinion.

Lesson Objectives

1. Define the terms "fact" and "opinion."
2. Identify facts and opinions from context.

Lesson Plan

1 Engage

Have students define the terms "fact" and "opinion" in their own words. You may wish to have them write their definitions on a piece of paper first. Encourage them to use what they have already learned about these terms when they write their definitions. Then, allow volunteers to read their definitions to the class.

2 Explore

Direct students to read the steps under "Learn the Skill." Have students provide examples of facts and opinions by making statements and telling whether it is a fact or an opinion.

3 Teach

You might want to have students copy each sentence in the paragraph on Hawaii and then give their reasons for determining whether it is a fact or an opinion. When finished, students can compare and discuss answers.

4 Assess/Reteach

Students should be able to determine whether each sentence contains a fact or an opinion. They should be able to give reasons for their answers.

To further assess students' understanding of comparing maps have them complete the "Applying Your Skills" part of the Chapter Review and Assessment.

Resource Directory

Teaching Resources

Social Studies and Geography Skills, Distinguishing Fact and Opinion, p. 41

Technology

Social Studies Skills Tutor CD-ROM

Answers to...

PRACTICE THE SKILL

Sentences 1, 2, 6, and 7 are facts. The rest contain opinions.

CHAPTER 29

Review and Assessment

Creating a Chapter Summary

Student summaries will vary.

Sample summaries:

Section 2 In both Australia and New Zealand, population distribution is greatest along the coast. These two countries have both similarities, including their location in the South Pacific, and the types of crops that they raise, and differences, including topography and climate.

Section 3 Geographic factors strongly influence the climate and vegetation of the Pacific islands. Rain forests, fertile soil, and coconut palms are some of the natural resources found on high islands in the region.

Reviewing Key Terms

1. a **2.** e **3.** d **4.** f **5.** c **6.** b

Reviewing the Main Ideas

1. Because Australia and New Zealand are isolated from other large landmasses, many of their animals and plants are found nowhere else on the Earth.
2. New Zealand
3. mountains
4. Most people live along the coast, where the climate is mild.
5. to produce electricity
6. Possible answer: The crops raised are similar; the climate is different.
7. Possible answer: location and topography
8. Possible answer: Rain forests and fertile soil are found on the high islands and in coastal areas.

CHAPTER 29

Review and Assessment

Creating a Chapter Summary

On a separate piece of paper, draw a diagram like this one, and include the information that summarizes the first section of the chapter. Then, fill in the remaining boxes with summaries of Sections 2 and 3.

THE PACIFIC REALM: PHYSICAL GEOGRAPHY

Section 1	Section 2	Section 3
Australia and New Zealand were formed by the breaking and drifting of the Indo-Australian plate. The movement of that plate resulted in the region's unique plant and animal life.		

Reviewing Key Terms

Match the definitions in Column I with the key terms in Column II.

Column I

a. rocklike material formed by the skeletons of tiny sea creatures

b. animals that carry their young in a body pouch

c. huge piece of the Earth's crust

d. small coral island in the shape of a ring

e. narrow inlet

f. hot spring that shoots scalding water into the air

Column II

1. coral

2. fiord

3. atoll

4. geyser

5. tectonic plate

6. marsupials

Reviewing the Main Ideas

1. How does geographic isolation affect plant and animal life in Australia and New Zealand? (Section 1)
2. What country in the Pacific realm is characterized by diverse physical features such as volcanic mountains, forests, lakes, glaciers, geysers, and fiords? (Section 1)
3. What physical feature would you expect to find on a high island? (Section 1)
4. How does climate affect where people live in Australia? (Section 2)
5. How do New Zealanders use the geysers on North Island? (Section 2)
6. Describe one similarity and one difference between Australia and New Zealand. (Section 2)
7. What geographic factors help determine the climate and vegetation of the Pacific islands? (Section 3)
8. What natural resources are found on the high islands and in coastal areas? (Section 3)

Resource Directory

Teaching Resources

Cooperative Learning Activity in the Unit 7 Teaching Resources, pp. 47–50

Chapter Tests Forms A and B in the Unit 7 Teaching Resources, pp. 65–67

Guide to the Essentials, Ch. 29 Test, p. 131

Map Activity

The Pacific Realm

For each place listed below, write the letter from the map that shows its location.

1. Micronesia
2. South Island
3. New Zealand
4. Australia
5. Polynesia
6. Melanesia
7. North Island

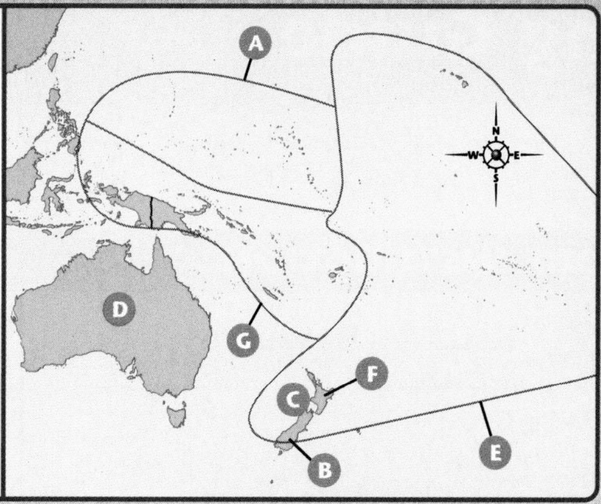

Take It to the NET

Enrichment For more map activities using geography skills, visit the social studies section of **phschool.com.**

Writing Activity

1. **Writing a Travel Itinerary** Choose one country that you read about in this chapter. Then do some research to learn more about it. If you spent a week there, what would you see? Write a list describing the things you would most want to see and do in a week. Then organize your list in a day-by-day plan.
2. **Writing a Book Report** Find and read a traditional story or folk tale from Australia, New Zealand, or the Pacific islands. Think about how the story reflects the geography and culture of the country it comes from. Write a four-or-five-sentence book report similar to one that might be used on a television program like *Reading Rainbow.*

Critical Thinking

1. **Recognizing Cause and Effect** How does the shape of New Zealand affect its climate?
2. **Comparing and Contrasting** What are two differences between high islands and low islands? What is one similarity?

Applying Your Skills

Turn to the Skills for Life activity on p. 561 to complete the following activity.

Using ten note cards, write five facts and five opinions about the Pacific region. On the back of each card, write FACT if you wrote a fact and OPINION if you wrote an opinion. Choose a partner and shuffle your cards. Challenge your partner to identify each statement as a fact or an opinion. For each statement, explain how you decided if it was a fact or an opinion.

Take It to the NET

Activity Australia, New Zealand, and some of the Pacific islands are collectively known as Australasia. Create a map of Australasia. Include major geographic features, natural resources, and climate. Visit the World Explorer: People, Places, and Cultures section of **phschool.com** for help in completing this activity.

Chapter 29 Self-Test As a final review activity, take the Chapter 29 Self-Test and get instant feedback on your answers. To take the test, visit the Social Studies section of **phschool.com.**

Map Activity

1. A **2.** B **3.** C **4.** D **5.** E **6.** G **7.** F

Writing Activity

1. Students should include a list of things they would most want to see and do, and incorporate this list in a realistic plan for a week-long visit.
2. Students' reports should identify the country that the story comes from. Students should use information from Chapter 29 to explain how the story reflects the geography and culture of that country.

Critical Thinking

1. New Zealand's shape is such that no place in the country is more than 80 miles from the sea. As a result, the climate is mild and the country gets plenty of rain.
2. High islands are formed from volcanoes; low islands are made of coral. High islands have rich vegetation; low islands have little vegetation. Both kinds of islands can be found in the Pacific island region.

Applying Your Skills

Students should use information they have learned from all sections of Chapter 29 to create their Pacific fact and opinion cards.

Resource Directory

Other Print Resources

Chapter Tests with ExamView® Test Bank, Ch. 29

Technology

ExamView® Test Bank CD-ROM, Ch. 29

Resource Pro® CD-ROM

Chapter 30 Planning Guide

Resource Manager

	CORE INSTRUCTION	READING/SKILLS
Chapter-Level Resources	**Teaching Resources** Program Overview Pacing Charts **Technology** Resource Pro® CD-ROM Companion Web site, phschool.com • eTeach	**Technology** Social Studies Skills Tutor CD-ROM Student Edition on Audio CD, Ch. 30
1 Historical and Cultural Traditions 1. Explain how people settled Australia and New Zealand. 2. Identify the groups that shaped the cultures of Australia and New Zealand. 3. Describe how Pacific island nations have been influenced by other cultures.	**Teaching Resources** **Unit 7** Classroom Manager, p. 17 Guided Reading and Review, p. 18	**Teaching Resources** Guide to the Essentials, p. 132 **Technology** Section Reading Support Transparencies
2 Australia and New Zealand: Trade and Agriculture 1. Identify key aspects of Australia's economy. 2. Explain how New Zealand's climate affects its economy.	**Teaching Resources** **Unit 7** Classroom Manager, p. 20 Guided Reading and Review, p. 21	**Teaching Resources** Guide to the Essentials, p. 133 Social Studies and Geography Skills, pp. 25 and 88 **Technology** Section Reading Support Transparencies
3 The Pacific Islands: Scarcity of Natural Resources 1. Explain how a scarcity of natural resources has affected the people of the Pacific islands. 2. Identify important industries in the Pacific islands.	**Teaching Resources** **Unit 7** Classroom Manager, p. 23 Guided Reading and Review, p. 24 Chapter Summary, p. 26 Vocabulary, p. 27 Reteaching, p. 28	**Teaching Resources** **Unit 7** Critical Thinking, p. 30 Guide to the Essentials, p. 134 **Technology** Section Reading Support Transparencies

ENRICHMENT / PRE-AP

Teaching Resources
Primary Sources and Literature Readings

Other Print Resources
DK Atlas

Technology
Companion Web site, phschool.com

Technology
How People Live Transparencies, Unit 7

Technology
Color Transparencies 151
Passport to the World CD-ROM

Teaching Resources
Unit 7
Enrichment, p. 29
Cooperative Learning Activity, pp. 51–54
Outline Maps, p. 46

ASSESSMENT

Prentice Hall Assessment System

Core Assessment
Chapter Tests with ExamView® Test Bank, Ch. 30
ExamView® Test Bank CD-ROM, Ch. 30

Standardized Test Preparation

Diagnose and Prescribe
Diagnostic Tests for Middle Grades Social Studies Skills

Review and Reteach
Review Book for World Studies

Practice and Assess
Test-taking Strategies with Transparencies for Middle Grades Test Prep Book
Test-taking Strategies Posters

Teaching Resources
Unit 7
Section Quizzes, pp. 19, 22, and 25
Chapter Tests, pp. 68–73

Technology
Companion Web site, phschool.com
Ch. 30 Self-Test

World Video Explorer
Each region of the world is explored through regional flyovers and investigative field trips. Case study segments give students an in-depth view of the history, economy, government, and culture of a key place in each region. Case studies include Nigeria, Mexico, China, British Columbia, and the Czech Republic.

In Your Classroom

CUSTOMIZE FOR INDIVIDUAL NEEDS

Gifted and Talented

Teacher's Edition
- Interdependence Among Societies, p. 571
- Travel Article, p. 571

Teaching Resources
- Enrichment, p. 29
- Primary Sources and Literature Readings

Honors/Pre-AP

Teacher's Edition
- Pineapple Politics, p. 575
- Making a Country Profile, p. 575

Teaching Resources
- Critical Thinking, p. 30
- Primary Sources and Literature Readings

ESL

Teacher's Edition
- Huge Monuments, p. 567

Teaching Resources
- Guided Reading and Review, pp. 18, 21, and 24
- Vocabulary, p. 27
- Reteaching, p. 28
- Guide to the Essentials, pp. 132–134
- Social Studies and Geography Skills, pp. 25 and 88

Technology
- Social Studies Skills Tutor CD-ROM
- Section Reading Support Transparencies

Less Proficient Readers

Teacher's Edition
- Travel Article, p. 571
- Making a Country Profile, p. 575

Teaching Resources
- Guided Reading and Review, pp. 18, 21, and 24
- Vocabulary, p. 27
- Reteaching, p. 28
- Guide to the Essentials, pp. 132–134
- Social Studies and Geography Skills, pp. 25 and 88

Technology
- Social Studies Skills Tutor CD-ROM
- Section Reading Support Transparencies

Less Proficient Writers

Teacher's Edition
- Work or Starve, p. 567
- Making a Country Profile, p. 575

Teaching Resources
- Guided Reading and Review, pp. 18, 21, and 24
- Vocabulary, p. 27
- Guide to the Essentials, pp. 132–134
- Social Studies and Geography Skills, pp. 25 and 88

Technology
- Social Studies Skills Tutor CD-ROM
- Section Reading Support Transparencies

DORLING KINDERSLEY

At the end of each unit, you will find information adapted from Dorling Kindersley's *Illustrated Children's Encyclopedia* that connects to the region being studied and to one of the seven content strands. In addition, your resources include Dorling Kindersley's *Atlas*, which contains valuable information about countries from around the world.

TEACHER'S EDITION INDEX

CHAPTER 30 PACING SUGGESTIONS

For 90-minute Blocks

See suggestions in the Teaching Resources Pacing Charts for Chapter 30. Use Color Transparencies 151.

Running Out of Time?

See the Guide to the Essentials, pp. 132–134.

INTERDISCIPLINARY LINKS

Middle Grades Math: Tools for Success

Course 1, Lesson 1-4, **Using Spreadsheets to Organize Data**

Course 2, Lesson 1-1, **Reporting Frequency**

Science Explorer

Animals, Lesson 4-4, **Diversity of Mammals**

Earth's Changing Surface, Chapter 3, **Erosion and Deposition**

BIBLIOGRAPHY

For the Teacher

Dolce, Laura. *Australia.* Chelsea House, 1990.

McIntosh, Jane, and Clint Twist. *Civilizations: Ten Thousand Years of Ancient History.* Dorling Kindersley, 2001.

Tanaki, Ronald. *Raising Cane: The World of Plantation Hawaii.* Chelsea House, 1994.

Ultimate Pocket Book of the World Atlas & Factfile. Dorling Kindersley, 2001.

For the Student

Easy

Duder, Tessa, and Anton Petrov. *A Book of Pacific Lullabies.* HarperCollins, 2001.

MacDonald, Robert. *Maori.* Thomson, 1994.

Average

Margolies, Barbara A. *Warriors, Wigmen, and the Crocodile People: Journeys in Papua New Guinea.* Four Winds, 1993.

Challenging

Blumberg, Rhoda. *The Remarkable Voyages of Captain Cook.* Atheneum, 1991.

Literature Connection

Lattimore, Deborah Nourse. *Punga: The Goddess of Ugly.* Harcourt, 1993.

Winitana, Chris, and Andy Reisinger. *Legends of Aotearoa.* HarperCollins, 2001.

Take It to the NET

The World Explorer companion Web site, found on **phschool.com**, offers activities for exploring geographical, historical, and cultural resources on the Internet. It also provides on-line links for key content and all Section and Chapter Assessment activities.

The **Teacher site** also provides teachers with regional data and ideas for student research and activities.

Students can use the **Student site** to find chapter-by-chapter Internet resource links and to access Self-Tests.

CHAPTER 30

Connecting to the Guiding Questions

In this chapter, students will read about the history, culture, and economics of Australia, New Zealand, and the Pacific islands. Content in this chapter corresponds to the following Guiding Questions outlined at the beginning of the unit.

- What characteristics of life in the Pacific Realm resulted from colonialization?
- How does the past influence contemporary expressions of culture in the Pacific Realm?
- How do the governments of Australia and New Zealand compare with the government of England?
- What are some of the ways that people in the Pacific Realm earn a living?
- How does the nature of citizenship vary among the different cultures of the Pacific Realm?

Using the Picture Activities

Discuss with students why historians and artists value cave and rock paintings. How do they think these paintings can be preserved?

- Students will note that the two figures are a fish and two people, perhaps an adult and a child. Stories should incorporate these figures in some way.
- Students should complete a drawing or painting that depicts some aspect of contemporary life.

Heterogeneous Groups

The following activities are suitable for heterogeneous groups.

Interdisciplinary Connections

Travel Article, p. 571

Cooperative Learning

Making a Country Profile, p. 575

CHAPTER 30

AUSTRALIA, NEW ZEALAND, AND THE PACIFIC ISLANDS: History, Culture, Economics

Telling the Story of Dreamtime

USING PICTURES

According to Aboriginal tradition, in the "Dreamtime" before humans walked the Earth, mythical ancestors formed the world's mountains, rivers, plants, and animals. Aborigines passed on their traditions orally from generation to generation. Aborigine artists also used carvings and rock paintings like this ancient one in northern Australia, to record stories and history. Aborigines still use such ancient practices to keep their traditions alive.

Writing a Story

Take a close look at the figures in the rock painting. What do you see? What are these figures, and what do you think they symbolize? Write a brief story that might go along with the figures and events shown in this painting.

Making a Rock Painting

If you were to leave behind a drawing to show what life is like at the beginning of the 21st century, what would you draw? Write down several ideas. You might want to brainstorm with a friend. Then, use either a drawing or painting to illustrate an event or activity from life in the 21st century.

eTeach

Be sure to check out this month's discussion with a Master Teacher. Go to **phschool.com**.

Resource Directory

Teaching Resources

Primary Sources and Literature Readings extend content with a selection related to the concepts in this chapter.

Other Print Resources

DK Atlas

Technology

Student Edition on Audio CD, Ch. 30

SECTION 1

Historical and Cultural Traditions

BEFORE YOU READ

READING FOCUS

1. How did people settle Australia and New Zealand?
2. What groups shaped the cultures of Australia and New Zealand?
3. How have the Pacific island nations been influenced by other cultures?

KEY TERMS

penal colony
station

NOTE TAKING

Copy the chart below. As you read the section, complete the chart with information about the history and cultures of Australia, New Zealand, and the Pacific islands.

Australia	New Zealand	Pacific Islands
earliest people were Aborigines		

MAIN IDEA

The strong, unique cultures of the earliest people in Australia, New Zealand, and the Pacific islands were greatly influenced by the arrival of Europeans in the 1700s and 1800s.

Setting the Scene

Hundreds of giant stone statues dot the landscape of Easter Island. Made of solid volcanic rock, each statue stands 10 to 40 feet (3 to 12 m) tall. Some weigh more than 50 tons (46 metric tons).

Easter Island's statues still impress people. Scientists also wonder how people first came to other parts of the Pacific region.

Early Settlers in Australia and New Zealand

Scientists think that the Aborigines (ab uh RIJ uh neez), the earliest settlers in Australia, came from Asia about 40,000 years ago. For thousands of years, they hunted and gathered food along the coasts and river valleys and learned to live in the Outback.

During this time, the Aboriginal population stayed at a stable, even level. People lived in small family groups that moved from place to place in search of food and water. All had strong religious beliefs about nature and the land. Such beliefs played a key role in their way of life.

Easter Island's Mysterious Statues

CULTURE Eyeless stone giants dot the landscape of Easter Island. No one knows for sure how the ancient islanders carved and erected these statues. **Critical Thinking** Why do you think these huge stone images were built?

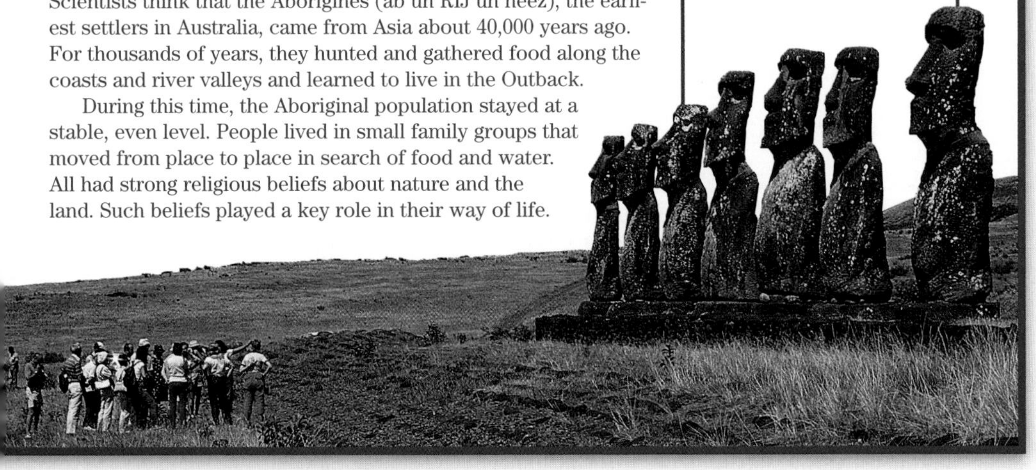

Resource Directory

Teaching Resources

Classroom Manager in the Unit 7 Teaching Resources, p. 17

Guided Reading and Review in the Unit 7 Teaching Resources, p. 18

Guide to the Essentials, p. 132

Technology

Section Reading Support Transparencies

SECTION 1

Lesson Objectives

1. Explain how people settled Australia and New Zealand.
2. Identify the groups that shaped the cultures of Australia and New Zealand.
3. Describe how Pacific island nations have been influenced by other cultures.

Lesson Plan

1 Engage

Warm-Up Activity

Write the following on the board: *My traditions and way of life have been influenced by* ________. Ask students to complete the statement with the name of a particular culture. Discuss with students how their ways of life have been influenced by the particular group.

Activating Prior Knowledge

Discuss with students how they determine what things to take when going on a trip or a vacation. Ask volunteers to share their ideas with the class. Point out that the people who settled in the Pacific islands region had to make similar decisions about what to bring along.

2 Explore

Ask students to skim the section and note the main headings. Have them find answers to the following questions: Who were the early settlers in Australia and in New Zealand? Why does the Pacific region have a variety of cultures?

Answers to...

CRITICAL THINKING

The islanders built the enormous stone sculptures to mark burial places, to commemorate an important event, or to honor their gods.

Lesson Plan continued

3 Teach

Have students write an essay answering the following question: How have various groups of people affected the cultures of Australia, New Zealand, and the Pacific islands? Students should use the information in the section for their essays. This activity should take about 25 minutes.

Questions for Discussion

HISTORY **Which explorer claimed Australia and New Zealand for Britain, and when did he accomplish this feat?**

British captain James Cook explored New Zealand in 1769 and Australia in 1770.

GEOGRAPHY **Why was the colony of New Zealand attractive to many British settlers?**

The colony of New Zealand had fine harbors and fertile soil, conditions that were attractive to British settlers.

4 Assess/Reteach

See the answers to the Section 1 Assessment. You may also assess students' essays.

Acceptable essays include facts about the early peoples who settled in the Pacific region.

Commendable essays include details about the early peoples as well as about European influence in either Australia or New Zealand.

Outstanding essays show an understanding of how early peoples and Europeans influenced the modern cultures of Australia, New Zealand, and the Pacific islands.

Answers to...

CRITICAL THINKING

Europeans were the first to colonize Australia.

AS YOU READ

The sudden discovery of gold might cause a sudden influx of people.

A Country With European Roots

CULTURE These students from Sydney illustrate Australia's ethnic makeup—95 percent European. **Critical Thinking** What factors account for this ethnic mix?

AS YOU READ

Monitor Your Reading How might the discovery of a resource like gold affect the population of a country?

Cultural Influences

The Maori of New Zealand The earliest people in New Zealand were the Maori (MAH oh ree). Their ancestors first traveled from Asia to Polynesia. Then, about 1,000 years ago, the Maori traveled across the ocean to New Zealand and settled in villages, making a living as hunters and farmers. But the Maori also prized fighting and conquering their enemies and used storytelling to pass on their beliefs.

The Arrival of Europeans European explorers heard about a mysterious continent that lay to the south of Asia and in the 1600s, several ships reached either Australia or New Zealand. In 1769, British captain James Cook explored New Zealand and the next year, the east coast of Australia. He claimed both lands for Britain.

In 1788, the British founded the first colony in Australia as a **penal colony.** This is a place settled by convicts, or prisoners. Soon, other colonists settled in Australia, some of whom worked for the prison facilities. Others went to find new land. Then, in 1851, gold was discovered, and the population soared. Not long after, Britain stopped sending convicts to Australia. Some 50 years later, in 1901, Australia gained independence.

New Zealand was settled by Europeans at about the same time as Australia and in 1840, the British took control of New Zealand. The colony, with its fine harbors and fertile soil, attracted many British settlers. New Zealand gained independence in 1907.

Present-Day Cultures of Australia and New Zealand

Today, most Australians and New Zealanders are descendants of British settlers. They share British culture, holidays, and customs, and most express pride in their British heritage, especially their parliamentary system of government and belief in freedom and democracy.

However, Australia and New Zealand are not exactly alike. Each has its own unique culture. For example, Australians have added many new words to the language. These include "mate," which means "close friend," and "fair go," which means "equal opportunity." New Zealanders are deeply opposed to nuclear warfare. No ships carrying nuclear arms are allowed to use New Zealand harbors.

The Aborigines Today Today, about 200,000 Aborigines live in Australia. Since the arrival of Europeans, the Aborigines have suffered

Resource Directory

Technology

How People Live Transparencies, Unit 7

great hardships. In the colonial period, settlers forced these native peoples off their lands. Tens of thousands died of European diseases and others were forced to work on sheep and cattle **stations,** which are extremely large ranches. The settlers demanded that the Aborigines adopt European ways. As a result, they began to lose their own customs and traditions. Recently, however, life for Aborigines has begun to improve a little.

The Maori Way of Life When New Zealand became a British colony, Britain promised to protect Maori land. Settlers, however, broke that promise. For many years, the settlers and the Maori clashed violently. The settlers finally defeated the Maori in 1872.

After their defeat, the Maori were forced to adopt English ways. Maori culture seemed in danger of being destroyed. Slowly, however, Maori leaders gained more power and recovered some traditional lands. New laws now allow the Maori to practice their customs and ceremonies.

Today, there are more than 300,000 Maori in New Zealand. They make up about 9 percent of the country's population. Many Maori now live in cities and work in businesses, factories, and offices. But they still honor their Maori heritage. Many speak both Maori and English. Thanks to their artists, writers, and singers, Maori culture is an important part of the lives of all New Zealanders.

A Traditional Way of Life

CULTURE At Rotorua, where many Maori people live, a woman in traditional dress heats her food in the sizzling hot springs. **Critical Thinking** How is this Maori woman making use of a natural resource? What technologies might we use today instead of resources like this?

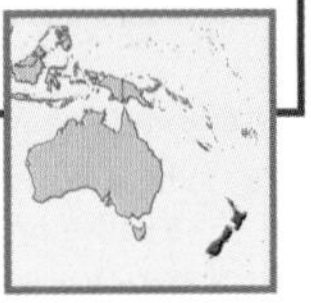

The Cultures of the Pacific Islands

Scientists believe that the first people to inhabit the Pacific islands came from Southeast Asia more than 30,000 years ago. First, these people settled on New Guinea, Melanesia's largest island. Then, over thousands of years, they traveled across the Pacific by canoe to Micronesia and later Polynesia.

A Variety of Cultures As people settled the Pacific region, they developed many different cultures. Because of the distances between islands, groups could not communicate with each other and each group developed its own language, customs, and religious beliefs. However, the people did have things in common since they lived in an ocean environment. They used the ocean to obtain food and for transportation. Most built their lives around their small villages or farms.

From Colonies to Independence The arrival of Europeans in the 1800s had a great impact on the Pacific islands. Britain, France, and Germany set up trading posts and naval bases on many islands. Japan and the United States soon joined the race for control of the Pacific region. In the late 1800s, these nations turned the islands into colonies and for the next 100 years, ruled the people of the Pacific.

CULTURE

Work or Starve

The British government made clear that it did not intend to feed or house convicts transported to Australia. Newly arrived convicts had two choices—to work or to starve. However, when the first ships landed, many convicts were already starving. For five years convicts, sailors, and guards all existed on the brink of starvation. The first crops fell to wind and salt. There were a few vegetable gardens, but rats, cutworms, caterpillars, and parrots helped themselves to the colonists' vegetables. The only abundant food was a fishy-tasting bird named "Bird of Providence." More than 170,000 of these birds were killed between April and July 1790. By 1804, these birds had nearly disappeared.

CULTURE

Huge Monuments

Megalithic monuments, such as the ones on Easter Island and on other islands of the Pacific region, can be found in all parts of the world. The monuments are generally stone structures erected as burial places or as memorials of significant events. One of the most famous sites of megalithic monuments is Stonehenge, England. The purpose of these monuments has been debated. One theory suggests that they were used as an astronomical tool to predict seasons or as a simple daily calendar. Significant numbers of megaliths exist in western France, the British Isles, Spain, Portugal, Africa, and India.

SKILLS MINI LESSON

Organizing Your Time

You might **introduce** the skill by indicating to students that organizing their time is especially important when completing a school project. Point out that a task list, which indicates the tasks that need to be done in order to complete a project, is a useful tool for time management. Students may **practice** the skill by generating a task list for completing the Take It to the Net activity in the Section Review. To **apply** the skill, have students rank and prioritize the tasks and estimate the amount of time each task will take. After students have completed the activity, invite volunteers to discuss how the task list helped them complete the assignment.

Answers to...

CRITICAL THINKING

The Maori woman is using the heat from the hot springs to heat her food. Students might mention the use of gas and electric stoves, and microwave ovens as technology we use today.

SECTION 1 ASSESSMENT

AFTER YOU READ

1. (a) place settled by convicts, or prisoners (b) extremely large ranch
2. Asia
3. The Europeans took over the land of the native peoples. In Australia, Aborigines were forced into labor. Many died from European diseases. In New Zealand, Europeans and Maoris clashed over land, and the Europeans won. The Maori were forced to adopt European ways.
4. Students' charts will vary, but should reflect an understanding that both peoples were from Asia, and both groups' ancestral lands were eventually claimed and settled by the British. However, the Aborigines and the Maori each have a unique culture.
5. People on an island are less likely to come into contact with other cultures because they are isolated by a body of water. Therefore, they are more likely to develop and maintain their own unique culture.
6. Students should develop their entries using information in the section.
7. Students may want to work in groups to prepare their oral presentations.

Life in the Pacific Islands

CULTURE Most of Papua New Guinea's four million residents still farm, fish, and build their houses in the traditional way. **Critical Thinking** Why do you suppose residents of this village build their houses on stilts?

After World War II, most Pacific islands gained independence. By then, traditional island cultures had blended with cultures from Europe, America, and other countries. Most governments were democratic, and most churches were Christian. Many Pacific islanders read and spoke English. Foreign companies operated businesses and large farms here. Since independence, the lives of most island people have improved, but incomes are still low. Many depend on fishing or on growing such crops as taro and yams to make a living.

SECTION 1 ASSESSMENT

AFTER YOU READ

RECALL

1. Define: (a) penal colony, (b) station

COMPREHENSION

2. Where do scientists believe the native peoples of Australia, New Zealand, and the Pacific islands came from?
3. What happened to Native peoples when Europeans arrived in Australia and New Zealand?

CRITICAL THINKING AND WRITING

4. **Exploring the Main Idea** Review the Main Idea statement at the beginning of this section. Then, create a chart that compares the histories of the Aborigines and the Maori. In what ways are they similar? In what ways are they different?
5. **Making Inferences** Why might people who live on an island be able to preserve their culture for a long period of time without change?

ACTIVITY

6. **Making a Timeline** Create a timeline with ten brief entries tracing the history of Australia, New Zealand, and the Pacific islands.

Take It to the NET

7. **Exploring Aboriginal Culture** Using the information on the web site, choose one aspect of aboriginal culture or history that interests you and create an oral presentation that includes visual aids. Visit the World Explorer: People, Places, and Cultures section of **phschool.com** for help in completing this activity.

Resource Directory

Teaching Resources

Section Quiz in the Unit 7 Teaching Resources, p. 19

Answers to...

CRITICAL THINKING

They use stilts to prevent damage from flooding due to storms or high tides.

SECTION 2

Australia and New Zealand

Trade and Agriculture

BEFORE YOU READ

READING FOCUS

1. What are some key aspects of Australia's economy?
2. How does New Zealand's climate influence its economy?

KEY TERMS

artesian well

KEY PLACES

Sydney
Alice Springs

MAIN IDEA

The economies of Australia and New Zealand are dependent upon agriculture and trade, and both countries have close economic ties with Pacific Rim nations.

NOTE TAKING

Copy the table below. As you read the section, complete the table to show some similarities between the economies of Australia and New Zealand.

	Australia	New Zealand
Ranching		
Farming		
Trade with Pacific Rim nations		

Setting the Scene

Michael Chang owns a successful trading company in **Sydney,** Australia's largest city. From his office in a modern glass skyscraper, he sometimes watches Sydney's busy harbor. What interests him most are the large cargo ships.

John Koeyers and his family own a huge cattle ranch in northwest Australia. He uses a Jeep to round up the herds on his ranch. The Koeyers sell most of their cattle to companies that supply fast-food restaurants in Asian nations.

Lyle Sansbury is chairman of the Board of Directors of the Nurungga Farming Company. He is very proud of the farm. It produces barley, wheat, cattle, and sheep. Lyle is full of plans for expanding the company into other activities, such as fish farming. The Nurungga Farm is one of the successful businesses owned and run by Aborigines.

The Sydney Opera House

CULTURE The Sydney Opera House was completed in 1973. The building's white concrete arches look like the sails of a huge ship. **Critical Thinking** How does the architecture of the Opera House relate to its environment?

Resource Directory

Teaching Resources

Classroom Manager in the Unit 7 Teaching Resources, p. 20

Guided Reading and Review in the Unit 7 Teaching Resources, p. 21

Guide to the Essentials, p. 133

Technology

Section Reading Support Transparencies

SECTION 2

Lesson Objectives

1. Identify key aspects of Australia's economy.
2. Explain how New Zealand's climate affects its economy.

Lesson Plan

1 Engage

Warm-Up Activity

Ask students to list some of the ways that people in the United States make a living. Call on volunteers, and write their responses on the chalkboard. Then ask students to speculate on some of the ways that people in Australia make a living. After students have read Section 2, have them compare their responses with the information in the section.

Activating Prior Knowledge

Encourage students to think about what happened to Native American lands and ways of life when settlers moved west in the United States. Ask students to compare the conflicts between Native Americans and settlers in the United States with the conflicts between the Aborigines and European settlers in Australia.

2 Explore

After students read the section, have them find answers to the following questions. Which countries does Australia trade with? What crops and animals are raised on Australia's farms and ranches? How has New Zealand achieved great agricultural productivity?

Answers to...

CRITICAL THINKING

The Opera House is designed to look like a sailing ship, which fits with the ocean harbor environment where it is located.

Lesson Plan continued

❸ Teach

Ask students to use the information in this section to create a captioned mural titled *Ways of Life in Australia and New Zealand*. Students might work individually or with a partner. The mural should provide facts and visuals about each nation's economy: trading, farming, and ranching. Display and discuss completed murals. This activity should take about 30 minutes.

Questions for Discussion

ECONOMICS How have Japan, the United States, and other Pacific Rim nations contributed to Australia's economy?

These countries have invested large amounts of money in Australia's economy, and they have set up banks, insurance companies, and other businesses in Australia.

GEOGRAPHY Where is Australian farmland located? Why is it located there?

Australian farmland is in southeastern Australia and along the east coast near the country's few rivers. Geographical factors, such as landforms and climate, make the area suitable for farming.

COUNTRY PROFILE Australia

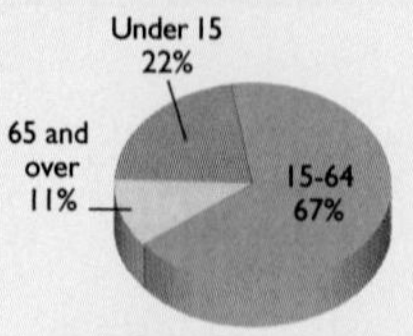

Age Structure (in years)

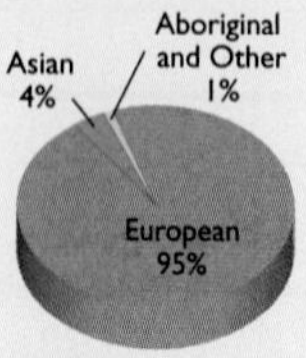

Ethnic Groups

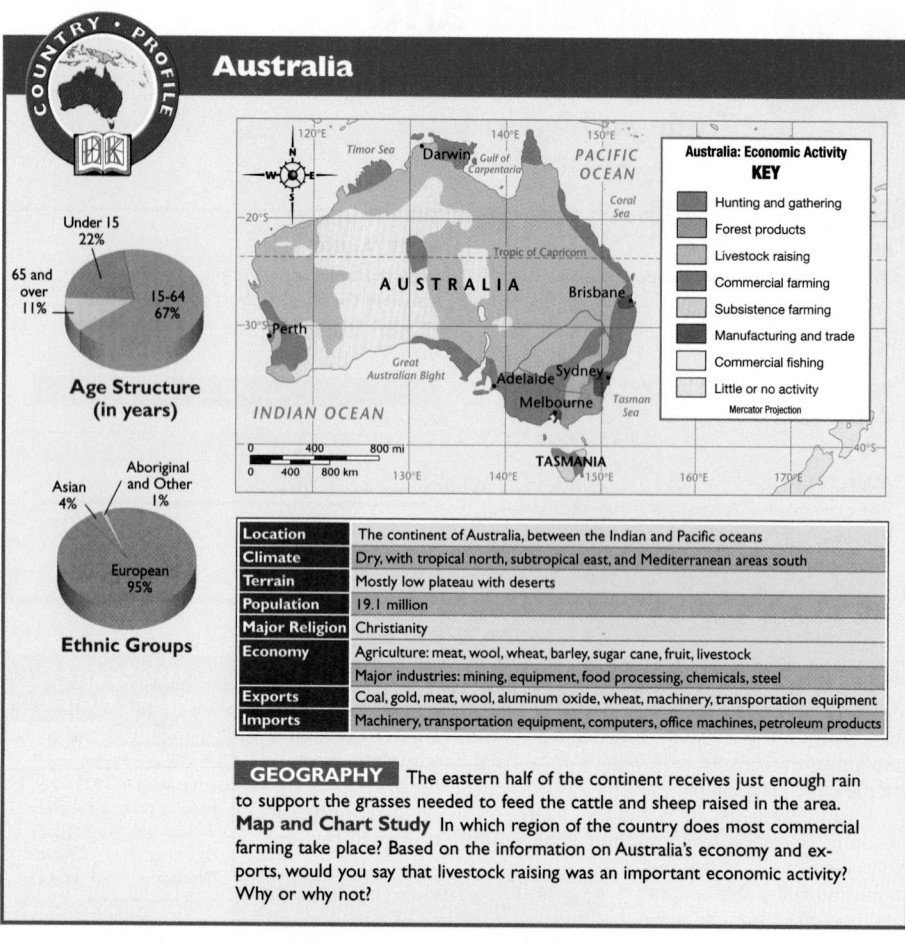

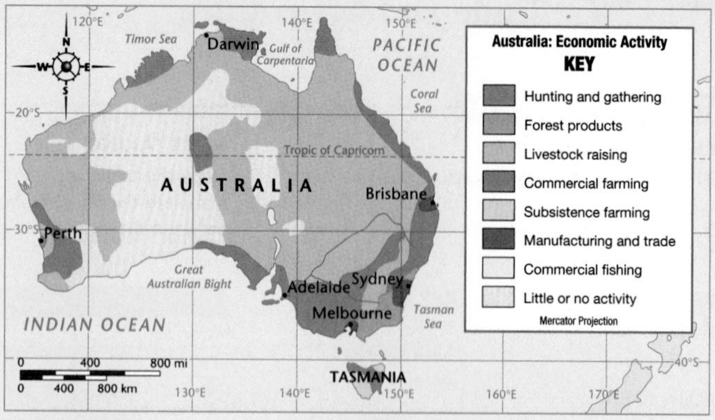

Location	The continent of Australia, between the Indian and Pacific oceans
Climate	Dry, with tropical north, subtropical east, and Mediterranean areas south
Terrain	Mostly low plateau with deserts
Population	19.1 million
Major Religion	Christianity
Economy	Agriculture: meat, wool, wheat, barley, sugar cane, fruit, livestock
	Major industries: mining, equipment, food processing, chemicals, steel
Exports	Coal, gold, meat, wool, aluminum oxide, wheat, machinery, transportation equipment
Imports	Machinery, transportation equipment, computers, office machines, petroleum products

GEOGRAPHY The eastern half of the continent receives just enough rain to support the grasses needed to feed the cattle and sheep raised in the area. **Map and Chart Study** In which region of the country does most commercial farming take place? Based on the information on Australia's economy and exports, would you say that livestock raising was an important economic activity? Why or why not?

AS YOU READ
Monitor Your Reading What do all three people have in common? How do they contribute to Australia's economy?

A Trading Economy

Michael Chang, the Koeyers, and Lyle Sansbury are all Australians. The definition of Australian has changed since Australia achieved independence. It is no longer "British." It now reflects the diversity of Australia's people. Today, Australia has close ties with other nations of the Pacific Rim. These nations border the Pacific Ocean. They include Japan, South Korea, China, and Taiwan. The United States is another major Pacific Rim nation. It is one of Australia's key trading partners.

Japan, the United States, and other Pacific Rim nations have invested large amounts of money in Australia's economy. They also have set up banks, insurance companies, and other businesses in Aus-

Answers to...

MAP AND CHART STUDY

Most commercial farming is done in the southeastern part of Australia. Livestock raising is an important part of Australia's economy because meat, wool, and livestock make up a significant part of the economy. Australia also earns income from exporting meat and wool.

AS YOU READ

All three people are Australian. All three produce or trade goods for export.

Resource Directory

Teaching Resources

Social Studies and Geography Skills, Reading an Economic Activity Map, p. 25

Technology

Color Transparencies 151 Australia and New Zealand: Physical-Political Map

Passport to the World CD-ROM This interactive CD-ROM allows students to explore each region of the world. Students view regional videos, take a photo tour, and explore a historical timeline. Students record their travels in an Explorer's Journal, and receive passport stamps when they pass regional quizzes.

tralia. More and more, Australia's economy depends on trade with these Pacific Rim countries.

Michael Chang's trading company is just one of hundreds of companies that do business with Pacific Rim countries. He sends various products to many countries in Asia. John Koeyers is involved in trade, too. Large cargo ships transport his cattle to South Korea and Taiwan. Other cargo ships carry Australian wool, meat, and many other products to foreign markets. And even larger ocean tankers carry Australia's coal, zinc, lead, and other minerals to Japan.

Farming It seems strange that farm products are an important export, because only about 6 percent of Australia's land is good for farming. Most of this land is in southeastern Australia and along the east coast. The country's few rivers are in those areas. Farmers use the river water to irrigate their crops. Australian farmers raise barley, oats, and sugar cane. However, their most valuable crop is wheat. Australia is one of the world's leading wheat growers and exporters.

Ranching Ranching is another key part of Australia's economy. Australian sheep and cattle provide lamb, mutton, and beef for export. And Australia is the world's leading wool producer. Most cattle and sheep are raised on large stations. Some of the largest are in the Outback.

For example, the Koeyers' ranch is in a hot, dry area in northwest Australia. It covers 680,000 acres (275,196 hectares). Another Outback station, near **Alice Springs** in the center of Australia, is even larger. It covers 12,000 square miles (31,080 sq km)—about as much

Cattle Round-Up

ECONOMICS

Huge ranches in Australia's hot, dry Outback are ideal for grazing sheep and cattle. Some of these ranches, or stations, are bigger than some American states.

Critical Thinking Why is it necessary for ranchers to use technology, such as the helicopter shown above, on stations such as this one? What other kinds of technology might they use?

4 Assess/Reteach

See the answers to the Section 2 Assessment. You might also use students' completed murals as an assessment.

Acceptable murals indicate key parts of Australia's and New Zealand's economy through illustrations.

Commendable murals include illustrations as well as at least one fact for key parts of Australia's and New Zealand's economy.

Outstanding murals include illustrations and captions that provide several facts about key parts of Australia's and New Zealand's economy.

ACTIVITY

Interdisciplinary Connections

Travel Article Direct students to study the information in the Country Profile. Then, suggest that they use the information to write an article about Australia for a travel magazine. Indicate to students that the purpose of their articles should be to provide an overview of Australia that will be useful to people who are planning to visit the country. Before students publish their articles, have them work with their partners to edit and review one another's work. Invite volunteers to share their articles with the class.

Verbal/Linguistic

Resource Directory

Teaching Resources

Social Studies and Geography Skills, Writing to Present Information, p. 88

Answers to...

CRITICAL THINKING

Ranchers rely on technology like helicopters because they have to take care of such large amounts of land. They might also use cars or trucks or other motorized vehicles in order to cover as much ground as possible. They might use technology such as two-way radios to communicate with each other, and other technologies to keep track of their livestock.

SECTION 2 ASSESSMENT

AFTER YOU READ

1. (a) Australia's largest city (b) city in central Australia
2. well that is drilled deep into the Earth to tap porous rock filled with groundwater
3. Australian exports: cattle, wool, meat, coal, zinc, lead, wheat; trading partners: Japan, South Korea, China, Taiwan, United States
4. New Zealand's climate is mild, which means animals need less shelter and can find food more easily, even in winter.
5. Students should use the information in the section to write their descriptions of life on a cattle station near Alice Springs.
6. Paragraphs should reflect an understanding that Japan has a scarcity of mineral resources, and Australia has coal, zinc, and lead to sell.
7. Students should use the proper form for business correspondence. Encourage students to use persuasion in their letters and to base their letters on actual New Zealand products.

Harvesting Wheat

ECONOMICS New Zealand's agricultural productivity is one of the highest in the world. In the picture above, a farmer harvests wheat in Waikari, which is on New Zealand's South Island. **Critical Thinking** Why do you think such a small nation has such high agricultural production?

as the state of Maryland. Even with this much land, the cattle can barely find enough grass for grazing. Fresh water also is scarce. Rain falls rarely, and the region has only a few small streams. To supply water for their cattle, the Koeyers use underground **artesian wells,** holes drilled deep into the Earth to tap porous rock filled with groundwater.

Trade and Agriculture in New Zealand

With favorable climate and conditions, and the widespread use of modern farming methods and machinery, New Zealand has achieved tremendous productivity. Indeed, the agricultural productivity of this small nation is one of the highest in the world. New Zealand's farmers produce hundreds of thousands of metric tons of cereal crops, including wheat, barley, oats, and maize.

New Zealand's ranchers can raise dairy cows, sheep, and beef cattle relatively cheaply, thanks to the mild climate in which they live. Ranchers do not have to spend money building and maintaining winter livestock shelters.

Foreign Trade Like Australia, New Zealand has close ties with other nations of the Pacific Rim. Its key trading partners include Japan, South Korea, Hong Kong, the United States, and Taiwan. New Zealand also maintains a brisk trade with Australia, the United Kingdom, and Germany.

New Zealand exports more dairy products than any other nation. It also exports more wool than any other nation, except for Australia. Other important exports are cereal crops, kiwi fruit, beef, fish, mutton, and lamb.

SECTION 2 ASSESSMENT

AFTER YOU READ

RECALL

1. Identify: (a) Sydney, (b) Alice Springs
2. Define: (a) artesian well

COMPREHENSION

3. What are some important exports of Australia? Who are Australia's primary trading partners?
4. How is New Zealand's climate suited to ranching?

CRITICAL THINKING AND WRITING

5. **Exploring the Main Idea** Review the Main Idea statement at the beginning of this section. Suppose that you and your family lived on a huge cattle station near Alice Springs. Write a description of what you think your lives would be like. Include economic issues that affect your family.
6. **Drawing Conclusions** Write a brief paragraph explaining why Australia makes a good trading partner for Japan.

ACTIVITY

7. **Write to Learn** You are from New Zealand and setting up your own exporting company. Write a business letter to the owner of a Pacific Rim company explaining the items you plan to export and why he or she should do business with you.

Resource Directory

Teaching Resources

Section Quiz in the Unit 7 Teaching Resources, p. 22

Answers to...

CRITICAL THINKING

New Zealand's geography and climate make it well suited for agricultural activity.

SECTION 3

The Pacific Islands

Scarcity of Natural Resources

BEFORE YOU READ

READING FOCUS

1. How does a scarcity of natural resources affect life in the Pacific islands?
2. What industries are important in the Pacific islands?

KEY TERMS

copra
primary industry
secondary industry
tertiary industry
tourism

KEY PLACES

Fiji
Tahiti

NOTE TAKING

Copy the web diagram below. As you read the section, fill in the web with details about different industries in the Pacific islands. Add more circles as needed.

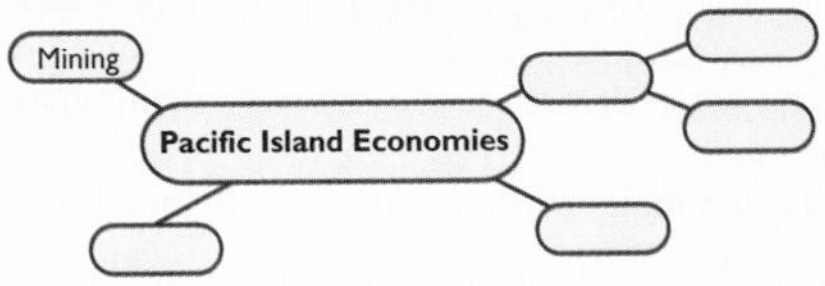

MAIN IDEA

The Pacific islands have few natural resources, and while most Pacific islanders earn a living farming or fishing, tourism is a fast-growing industry.

Setting the Scene

The Pacific Ocean covers nearly one-third of the Earth's surface. About 25,000 islands dot the Pacific. While many of those islands are high islands with fertile soil that allows the people living there to grow crops, other smaller, low islands have poor, sandy soil and little fresh water, which makes it difficult for people to grow crops. Some of these low islands have mineral deposits such as phosphate that can be exported. However, it is the beauty of the Pacific islands that is its top resource, fueling tourism and providing a new source of income for the islands' inhabitants.

A High Island in Polynesia

ECONOMICS Volcanoes created high islands like the Marquesas Islands in Polynesia. The Pacific islands' stunning beaches and exotic landscapes make them prime tourist attractions and aid in the economy of the region. **Critical Thinking** How do you think these tourist attractions aid in the economy of the region?

CHAPTER 30 AUSTRALIA, NEW ZEALAND, AND THE PACIFIC ISLANDS: HISTORY, CULTURE, ECONOMICS 573

Resource Directory

Teaching Resources

Classroom Manager in the Unit 7 Teaching Resources, p. 23

Guided Reading and Review in the Unit 7 Teaching Resources, p. 24

Guide to the Essentials, p. 134

Technology

Section Reading Support Transparencies

SECTION 3

Lesson Objectives

1. Explain how a scarcity of natural resources has affected the people of the Pacific islands.
2. Identify important industries in the Pacific islands.

Lesson Plan

1 Engage

Warm-Up Activity

Ask students to name three natural resources in the area where they live. List these resources on the board, and discuss how people use them. Ask students how their lives would be different if they did not have them.

Activating Prior Knowledge

Draw students' attention to the list on the board. Ask students whether they have ever been in a situation, such as a hiking or camping trip, or a vacation to another part of the world, where certain natural resources such as fresh water have been scarce or unavailable. Discuss how this scarcity of resources affected life in that place.

2 Explore

Encourage students to respond to the following questions as they read: How do most people in the Pacific islands earn a living? What is the most important natural resource of the Pacific islands? What secondary and tertiary industries are found on the Pacific islands? What are some benefits and challenges of the growing tourist industry?

Answers to...

CRITICAL THINKING

Tourist attractions help the local economy by drawing people from other parts of the world who vacation in these parts and spend money.

Lesson Plan continued

3 Teach

Have students write an economic development plan for the less-developed Pacific islands. Tell students to acknowledge the scarcity of natural resources and the need for people to earn a living while preserving the environment. This activity should take about 25 minutes.

Questions for Discussion

ECONOMICS **What are some of the primary industries of the Pacific islands?**

Primary industries of the Pacific islands include fishing, mining, and agriculture.

GEOGRAPHY **How does the natural beauty of the Pacific islands affect the population distribution and economy?**

The beauty of the Pacific islands fuels tourism and provides an important source of income for island inhabitants.

4 Assess/Reteach

See the answers to the Section 3 Assessment. You may also assess students' economic development plans.

Acceptable plans should acknowledge the scarcity of natural resources and the need for people to earn a living while preserving their environment.

Commendable plans should explain how a scarcity of natural resources affects the islands' economy and should suggest at least one way for islanders to earn a living in today's world economy.

Outstanding plans should do all of the above, identify the islands' beauty as potentially their greatest natural resource, and make recommendations for strengthening the islands' economy while preserving their beauty.

Answers to...

CHART STUDY

Coconut oil comes from copra. Coconut oil acts as a preservative in cookies, so they stay fresh longer.

SCIENCE, TECHNOLOGY, AND SOCIETY

Natural Resource Yields Medicine

Leading coconut-producing nations have joined together in an intergovernmental organization called the Asian and Pacific Coconut Community (APCC). Each year the APCC panel, also called "Cocotech," holds a meeting in which scientists, researchers, traders, processors, farmers, exporters, and policy makers exchange ideas. In a recent meeting, panelists applauded new research into the potential health and medical benefits of coconut oil. In ongoing clinical tests, researchers are using monolaurin, a fatty acid found in coconut oil, to treat patients with HIV or AIDS.

Adapting to Life with Few Natural Resources

The whole Pacific island region has few natural resources. The coconut palm is the most important one. It provides food, clothing, and shelter. Islanders export dried coconut meat or **copra,** which is used in margarine, cooking oils, and luxury soaps.

Pacific Island Industries

The economies of the Pacific islands, like those of many developing nations, are based on **primary industries** such as fishing, agriculture, and mining. These industries create or collect raw materials. Most Pacific islanders earn their living by farming or fishing. Many own their own farms, and some farms are owned collectively by entire villages. Besides coconut palm, farmers cultivate other crops that can grow easily in a tropical climate. Sugar cane and bananas are widely grown on the larger islands. Sugar production and export is a key industry on the island of **Fiji,** which also has its share of banana groves. In New Guinea, farmers grow coffee and cocoa for global export.

Mining and forestry employ people on some of the larger islands, including Fiji and Papua New Guinea. Pacific islanders are working hard to develop these other industries. Foreign investment is

Coconut Palm: One Resource, Many Uses

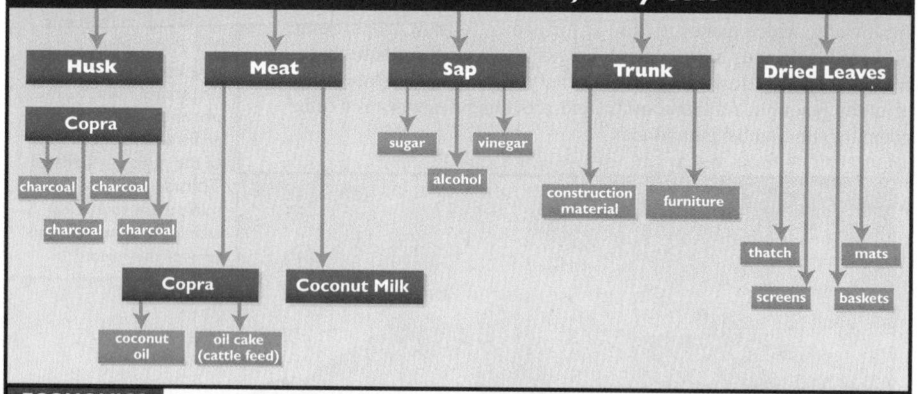

ECONOMICS Not only does the coconut palm provide food, clothing, and shelter—it also saves lives. During hurricanes, Pacific islanders can lash themselves to the trunk of the coconut palm to avoid being swept out to sea.

Chart Study Find coconut oil on the chart. (a) From what part of the plant does coconut oil come? (b) Coconut oil is high in lauric acid, which keeps it from spoiling. Why is coconut oil often used in factory-made cookies?

Resource Directory

Teaching Resources

Outline Maps, Pacific Islands, p. 46

helping to develop one of the world's largest copper mines on the island of Bougainville in Papua New Guinea.

Secondary industries, also known as manufacturing industries, take raw materials (such as sugar) produced by primary industries, and process them into consumer goods (such as candy). Secondary industry is uncommon in the Pacific islands, but there are some exceptions. For example, fishing boats and pleasure craft are built on Fiji. Paint is also manufactured on that island.

Fiji by Boat

ECONOMICS Many Pacific islanders work in the tourist industry. In this photograph, a group of tourists take in the sights of Fiji by boat.
Critical Thinking Do you think that such tours can help vacationers learn about different cultures?

Tourism: A Growing Industry

Service industries, also known as **tertiary industries,** do not produce goods, such as cloth or computers, but provide services, such as banking and communications. **Tourism** is the business of providing services for tourists and is a growing tertiary industry in the Pacific islands. Once remote and accessable only by boat or small plane, the Pacific islands became a prime tourist attraction in the 1950s with the availability of jet airplane travel.

More tourists visit Fiji than any other Pacific island nation. In recent years, tourism has outpaced sugar as Fiji's main source of foreign income. French Polynesia—specifically **Tahiti**—is another very popular tourist destination. Many travelers from Japan, the United States, Britain, France, Australia, and New Zealand visit the Pacific islands, reflecting ongoing ties between the region and the countries that once colonized it.

HISTORY

Pineapple Politics

Queen Liliuokalani, Hawaii's last reigning monarch, witnessed Hawaii's transition from an independent Pacific islands nation to a territory of the United States. By 1891, when Liliuokalani took the throne, sugar cane and pineapple interests had begun to erode the power of the monarchy. Native Hawaiians were alarmed as the island's wealth slipped into foreign hands. Liliuokalani tried to reverse the trend and reestablish the monarchy, but she was unsuccessful. In the end, American businessmen, led by Sanford B. Dole, took control of the islands' government. In 1900, the Hawaiian Islands became a U.S. territory.

ACTIVITY

Cooperative Learning

Making a Country Profile Have students work in small groups to create a country profile for a Pacific island nation. You may want to assign each group a specific nation. Students should locate physical maps of their nations, provide information about the country's location, climate, terrain, population, religions, and economy. Encourage students to make their profiles look like the ones in their text. Have students create a classroom display of their profiles when they have completed the activity.

Verbal/Linguistic, Visual/Spatial

Resource Directory

Teaching Resources

Vocabulary in the Unit 7 Teaching Resources, p. 27

Critical Thinking in the Unit 7 Teaching Resources, p. 30

Answers to...

CRITICAL THINKING

Answers will vary. Students should explain why tours of foreign places help vacationers learn more about different cultures and give specific examples.

SECTION 3 ASSESSMENT

AFTER YOU READ

1. (a) a Pacific island with more tourist visitors than any other Pacific island nation (b) an island in French Polynesia that is a popular tourist destination
2. (a) dried coconut meat (b) industries such as fishing, farming, and mining (c) manufacturing industries (d) service industries (e) the business of providing services for tourists
3. The Pacific island are trying to develop other industries, such as tourism.
4. Some of the important industries of the Pacific islands are fishing, farming, mining, and tourism.
5. Responses will vary, but should give examples of how the coconut palm is used for food, household goods, and building.
6. Answers will vary, but students might indicate that trade could be difficult because the Pacific islands do not have enough resources to trade for the manufactured goods they might want.
7. Journal entries should describe reasons for the move and specific benefits, such as warm temperatures, and drawbacks, such as meeting the challenge of earning a living on the island.

Snorkeling in the Pacific Islands

CULTURE

Surrounded by clear aquablue water and bathed in plenty of sunshine, the Pacific islands offer tourists excellent opportunities to explore the spectacular variety of marine life.

Critical Thinking
What other activities might tourists enjoy on a Pacific island vacation? Do you think tourism is harmful to island and marine ecosystems?

As tourism gains importance in the Pacific islands, it provides a new source of income. Yet tourism has a downside. Most tourist facilities, such as hotels and resorts, are owned not by Pacific islanders but by foreigners. This means that much of the industry's profit leaves the region. Moreover, many jobs in the tourist industry are not open to islanders. Those that are generally require little skill and pay low wages. Finally, many tourist activities can be harmful to the environment. Pacific islanders will need to plan carefully to protect their coral reefs, rain forests, and coastal areas.

SECTION 3 ASSESSMENT

AFTER YOU READ

RECALL

1. Identify: (a) Fiji, (b) Tahiti
2. Define: (a) copra, (b) primary industry, (c) secondary industry, (d) tertiary industry, (e) tourism

COMPREHENSION

3. How are the Pacific islands trying to compensate for a scarcity of natural resources?
4. What are some of the important industries of the Pacific islands?

CRITICAL THINKING AND WRITING

5. **Exploring the Main Idea** Review the Main Idea statement at the beginning of this section. Then, write a short speech in which a Pacific islander explains the value of the coconut palm. Use standard grammar, spelling, sentence structure, and punctuation.
6. **Understanding Cause and Effect** How might the scarcity of natural resources on the Pacific islands affect trade between these nations and other, more industrial nations around the world?

ACTIVITY

7. **Writing a Journal Entry** Suppose you have decided to live on one of the Pacific islands. Write a journal entry explaining your decision to relocate. What are the benefits of island life? What are the drawbacks?

Resource Directory

Teaching Resources

Section Quiz in the Unit 7 Teaching Resources, p. 25

Chapter Summary in the Unit 7 Teaching Resources, p. 26

Reteaching in the Unit 7 Teaching Resources, p. 28

Enrichment in the Unit 7 Teaching Resources, p. 29

Answers to...

CRITICAL THINKING

Students may list activities such as water-skiing, surfing, snorkeling, or swimming. Some may think these activities are harmful to marine life.

Identifying Frame of Reference

Learn the Skill

William Buckley escaped from a British penal colony in Australia in 1803. While wandering in the bush, he found a broken spear lying on a grave and picked it up. When the Aborigines found Buckley, they welcomed him warmly and took him to live with their tribe. Why did they do this?

To find the answer to this question, you would need to understand Aboriginal culture and the historical period in which this event happened. Doing this will help you understand the frame of reference of the Aborigines. When and where we grow up provides us with certain ways of looking at the world. This frame of reference influences the way a person thinks and behaves. In the case of William Buckley, the people noted that his pale skin was similar to that of their dead, whose skin turned white during cremation. Then, they recognized the spear he was carrying as one that belonged to a relative who had died recently. The Aborigines believed that the land was inhabited by many spirits. They welcomed Buckley because they thought he was their dead relative returning to them.

To identify a frame of reference when you read, follow these steps:

A. Read the information, paying attention to the groups of people or individuals involved and the event that occurs. Write this information on a sheet of paper.

B. Note the place and time in which the event takes place. This information may be revealed directly, but you might also find clues in the language and habits of the people described.

C. Look for evidence of different cultural values, attitudes, and beliefs. Write your evidence on the sheet of paper, being careful not to judge the culture by your own present-day values and attitudes.

D. Use the information you have collected to write a short paragraph describing the frame of reference.

Practice the Skill

Read the following journal entry written by a fictitious character adopted by the Aborigines of Australia. Then, follow the four steps to determine the frame of reference from which it is written.

Living with the Aborigines

I, James Carter, was sent to a penal colony in Australia in 1799 for stealing bread. Two years later I escaped and went to live with the Aborigines in the bush. The following information describes some of my experiences with them:

I arrived at the camp in bad shape, with a bad cut on my leg and a headache from the heat and lack of water. The hunters who found me took me immediately to a shelter. An old woman drew a few green tree ants from a gourd and boiled them to prepare a drink that took my headache away. Another woman examined my leg and then left, only to return a short time later with several large grubs. The grubs, I learned later, were witchety grubs, one of the staple foods of the aborigines. She crushed the worms and used the salve to heal my cut.

After my leg was healed, I attended a moth feast with the aborigines in the Bogong Mountains. Bogong moths covered rock crevices everywhere. The people gathered thousands of these moths and then cooked them in sand and hot ashes to remove their wings and legs. Then the moths were sifted with nets, which removed their heads. I found them to be surprisingly tasty.

Apply the Skill

See the Chapter Review and Assessment at the end of this chapter for more questions on identifying a frame of reference.

Lesson Objectives

1. Define frame of reference.
2. Identify frame of reference in context.

Lesson Plan

1 Engage

To introduce the skill, read aloud the opening text under "Learn the Skill." Ask students to define frame of reference. Point out that different cultures have different frames of reference, and that attitudes, values, and beliefs differ according to the times. Make sure students understand that the story of William Buckley is a true story.

2 Explore

Ask students to read the four steps under "Learn the Skill." On another sheet of paper have them list the items that they will write on a sheet of paper. You may wish to have them practice following the steps using the information about William Buckley.

3 Teach

Students should read the excerpt and follow the steps to write a description of the frame of reference.

For additional reinforcement, apply the four steps to other text, such as a primary source (letter, journal entry) from another time period.

4 Assess/Reteach

Students should note information pertaining to groups of people, the event, place, time, and cultural differences.

To further assess students' understanding of frame of reference, have them complete the "Applying Your Skills" part of the Chapter Review and Assessment.

Resource Directory

Technology

Social Studies Skills Tutor CD-ROM

Answers to...

PRACTICE THE SKILL

Students should understand that Carter is British and is a person in need of help. Given his different experiences, values, and beliefs, Carter might not have understood the kind of treatment he received from the Aborigines, and may have been surprised that he was well-received.

CHAPTER 30

Review and Assessment

Creating a Chapter Summary

Student summaries will vary.

Sample summaries:

Australia

Economics: trade and agriculture

New Zealand

Culture: influenced by traditional island and European cultures

Economics: trade and agriculture

Pacific Islands

History: settled by early travelers from Southeast Asia, later colonized by European countries, and gained independence after World War II

Culture: traditional island cultures

Economics: farming, fishing, and tourism

Reviewing Key Terms

1. True
2. True
3. False. Copra is the dried coconut meat.
4. False. An artesian well is a deep well drilled into the Earth to tap groundwater in porous rock.
5. True

Reviewing the Main Ideas

1. The Aborigines were the earliest inhabitants of Australia, and the Maori were the earliest inhabitants of New Zealand.
2. The ocean was a major source of food and the main means of transportation and trade for all the islands.
3. Ranching, farming, and trade are important parts of both nations' economies.
4. Australia maintains strong economic ties with other nations of the Pacific Rim, including Japan, China, Taiwan, and the United States.
5. A scarcity of natural resources makes it hard for many of the people of the Pacific islands to earn a living.
6. Farming, fishing, mining, and forestry are four primary industries found in the Pacific islands.

CHAPTER 30

Review and Assessment

Creating a Chapter Summary

On a separate piece of paper, draw a chart like this one, and include the information that summarizes the first section of the chapter. Then, complete the chart by summarizing the information in Sections 2 and 3.

	Australia	New Zealand	Pacific Islands
History	• Settled by Aborigines and then by the British	• Settled by Maori and then by the British	
Culture	• Influenced by traditional island and European cultures		
Economics			

Reviewing Key Terms

Read each sentence and decide if the definition is true or false. If it is false, rewrite the definition so that it is correct.

1. A penal colony is a place settled by convicts or prisoners.
2. A station is a very large sheep or cattle ranch.
3. Copra is the dried leaves of the coconut palm.
4. An artesian well is a shallow pool of water.
5. Secondary industries are those industries that manufacture goods and products.

Reviewing the Main Ideas

1. Who were the earliest inhabitants of Australia and New Zealand? (Section 1)
2. What similarities among the Pacific islands are caused by the ocean environment that the islands share? (Section 1)
3. What three important industries contribute to the economies of both Australia and New Zealand? (Section 2)
4. What ties does Australia maintain with other nations of the Pacific region? (Section 2)
5. Why is it difficult for many of the people of the Pacific islands to earn a living? (Section 3)
6. What are four primary industries found in the Pacific islands? (Section 3)

578 UNIT 7 THE PACIFIC REALM

Map Activity

Australia, New Zealand, and the Pacific Islands

For each place listed below, write the letter from the map that shows its location.

1. New Zealand
2. Papua New Guinea
3. Sydney
4. Pacific Ocean
5. Tasmania

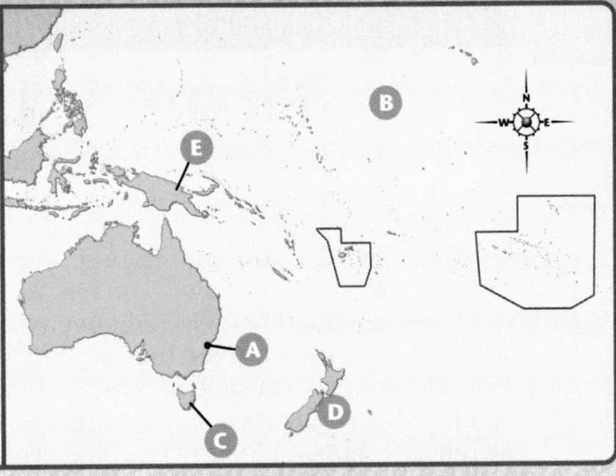

Take It to the NET

Enrichment For more map activities using geography skills, visit the social studies section of **phschool.com.**

Writing Activity

1. **Writing a Pamphlet** Write a pamphlet explaining how the history and culture of Australia, New Zealand, or the Pacific islands can be seen today. Draw pictures to illustrate your pamphlet, or use pictures clipped from travel brochures or photocopied from reference books or geography magazines. Write a caption for each picture, explaining what it shows and identifying the location shown.
2. **Writing an Article** Use the information in the Country Profile on page 570 to write an article about Australia for a travel magazine. In your article, provide an overview of the country for people who are planning to visit it.

Critical Thinking

1. **Comparing and Contrasting** Compare the European influences on Australia, New Zealand, and the Pacific islands. Draw a chart to show similarities and differences.
2. **Comparing and Contrasting** In American history, Native Americans were forcibly moved to reservations. How does this compare with the history of Aborigines?

Applying Your Skills

Turn to the Skills for Life activity on p. 577 to help you complete the following activity.

Write a brief essay in which you identify and explore some of the influences in your life that might shape your frame of reference.

Take It to the NET

Activity Read about the region known as Oceania, which includes the Pacific islands. Create a table or chart to organize the information contained in the Web site. Visit the World Explorer: People, Places, and Cultures section of **phschool.com** for help in completing this activity.

Chapter 30 Self-Test As a final review activity, take the Chapter 30 Self-Test and get instant feedback on your answers. To take the test, visit the Social Studies section of **phschool.com.**

Map Activity

1. D **2.** E **3.** A **4.** B **5.** C

Writing Activity

1. Responses will vary, but pamphlets should reflect what students learned in the chapter, and should include captioned illustrations that complement the text.
2. Students' articles should include information on the climate and geography of Australia. Students should use the Country Profile to provide an informative overview.

Critical Thinking

1. Charts may show as a similarity the establishment of European–style governments. Differences might include Australia's first colony being founded by the British as a penal colony, and the Pacific islands being colonized by other countries in addition to Britain.
2. Responses will vary and should include an understanding that, like the Native Americans, Aborigines were forced from their homelands.

Applying Your Skills

Students' essays should reflect the various forces that shaped their frames of reference, such as time period, groups of people, the nature of events occurring, and location.

Resource Directory

Teaching Resources

Cooperative Learning Activity in the Unit 7 Teaching Resources, pp. 51–54

Chapter Tests Forms A and B in the Unit 7 Teaching Resources, pp. 68–73

Guide to the Essentials, Ch. 30 Test, p. 135

Unit Test Forms A and B in the Unit 7 Teaching Resources, pp. 74–79

Other Print Resources

Chapter Tests with ExamView® Test Bank, Ch. 30

Technology

ExamView® Test Bank CD-ROM, Ch. 30

Resource Pro® CD-ROM

UNIT 7

Introduction

The introduction on the student page on the right provides key facts and general information about economics.

- Students should read the introduction first to gain a basic knowledge of the subject before reading on.
- Have students read all of the subentries, which provide further information on trade and industry, particularly focussing on how it influences where and how people live. Have students also read the annotations that accompany and explain the photos and illustrations.
- When students have finished reading all of the information, discuss the connections between the information on these pages and what they have learned about Australia and New Zealand. Students might want to review Chapter 30.

ACTIVITY

Creating Trade and Industry Maps

Have students work in small groups to create special purpose maps showing the natural resources, products, and industries of Australia and New Zealand. First, have groups collect information and compile a list of the natural resources, products, and industries of this region. Then have them list the various locations where these resources and industries are found, and where goods are produced. Finally, have them create a map of the region, and a map key with symbols representing the resources, products, and industries. Label the maps with the correct symbols. Display students' maps in the classroom.

Visual/Spatial

Adapted from the Dorling Kindersley Illustrated Children's Encyclopedia

TRADE AND INDUSTRY

Without trade and industry, people would have to create everything they needed in order to live. If you wanted a loaf of bread, you would have to grow the wheat, grind it into flour at the mill you built, mix the dough in bowls you carved with tools you made, and bake it in an oven that you built from your own bricks. Industry organizes the production of an item such as bread so that a small number of farmers, millers, bakers, and distributors supply enough bread for everyone. Similar industrial organization is used to supply us with everything we use, from water to automobiles. Trade is the process of buying and selling. Trade helps to supply raw materials to manufacturers and then distribute the goods that are made. Together, trade and industry combine to determine the economics of a nation.

SILK ROAD
Trade between different regions and peoples goes back to ancient times. The Silk Road was one of the earliest and most famous trade routes. Traders led horses and camels along this route between 300 B.C. and A.D. 1600, carrying silk and other goods from China to Europe.

? How do trade and industry influence where and how people live?

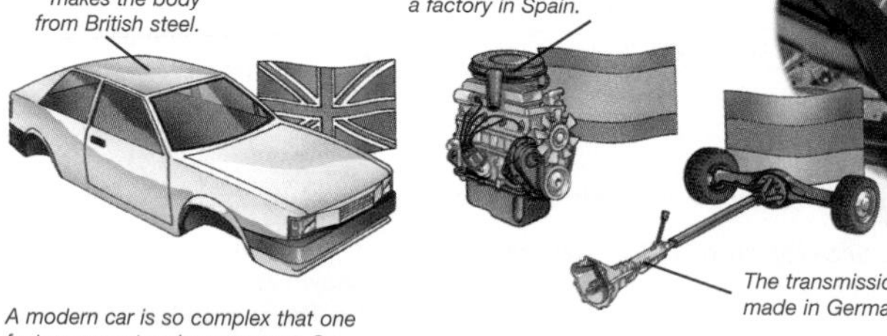

A French factory makes the body from British steel.

The engine comes from a factory in Spain.

The transmission is made in Germany.

A modern car is so complex that one factory cannot make every part. So, many factories build car components, and an assembly plant puts the behicle together.

Final assembly of the car may take place in Spain.

STRIP MINING
Australia has huge mineral wealth, and mining is an important industry. The country produces one third of the world's uranium, which is essential for nuclear power. In recent years, iron ore has been excavated in large strip mines where giant digging machines remove entire hills.

MANUFACTURING

The basic form of industry is manufacturing. This means working on materials to make a finished product. Almost everything we use is the product of manufacturing, and most manufacturing takes place in large factories. Some goods go through many stages of manufacturing. For example, workers making cars assemble manufactured parts which, in turn, have been made in many other factories, often in other countries.

580 UNIT 7 PACIFIC REALM

ECONOMICS

The Economies of Australia

For many years, Australia has depended on its natural resources and advanced agricultural and mining industries to build its economy. As a result, fuels and minerals account for about one third of the total exports per year. Production of wheat, wool, and meat are also strong industries, along with newer industries such as wine, dairy, and canola oil production. Australia continues to take advantage of its educated workforce, its commitment to innovation, and its ability to attract international business.

ECONOMICS

Sheep shearers work very quickly: some can clip a lamb in under a minute.

FARMING

New Zealand has a warm, moist climate which is ideal for many types of farming. Sheep and cattle ranching are the biggest businesses. There are two cattle and 13 sheep for every human in New Zealand. The country exports more dairy products and lamb than any other nation and is the second largest exporter of wool. Over the past 15 years production of other crops, such as kiwi fruit, oranges, and lemons, has increased. Newly built fishing boats have helped New Zealand's fleet increase its catch, and today the country is a major seafood exporter.

FACTORIES

Some industry takes place in people's homes, but workers in factories make most of the products that we buy. In a factory each person has a small task in the manufacturing process. He or she may operate a large machine or assemble something by hand. No one person makes an entire product. This process of mass production makes manufacturing cheaper and quicker. Most factories are owned by governments or large companies; a few factories are owned by the people who work in them.

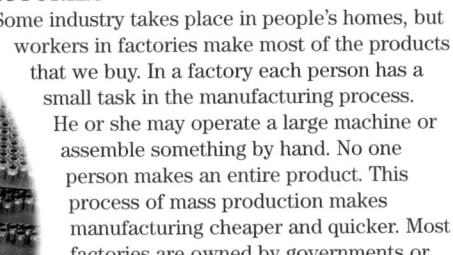

FILMMAKING

The Australian film industry produces a number of important films each year. Some, such as *Picnic at Hanging Rock* (1975), which tells of the mysterious disappearance of a group of Australian schoolgirls, have received international acclaim.

ACTIVITY

Tracing Trade Routes

Have students work with partners to create special purpose maps that show trade routes between Australia and its main trading partners, including Japan, Korea, Taiwan, China, Singapore, Hong Kong, Indonesia, the United States, New Zealand, and the United Kingdom. Have partners choose several export products, find out where they originate, whether land, sea, or air routes are used to transport them, and what their final destinations are. Have them mark the routes on a map of the region. Display maps in the classroom.

Verbal/Linguistic

ECONOMICS

Australian Trade Opportunities

Mark Vaile, Australia's Minister for Trade, has concentrated his efforts on expanding Australia's trade worldwide. He has supported policies and legislation aimed at encouraging exporters to find new opportunities and to take advantage of existing opportunities. As a result, economic forecasts for Australia for the year 2001 show record-breaking growth and increased exports at all levels of the economy, including production of raw wool and high-tech products.

582 REFERENCE TABLE OF CONTENTS

Reference

TABLE OF CONTENTS

REFERENCE TABLE OF CONTENTS 583

Atlas

The World: Political

180°
160°W
140°W
120°W
100°W
80°W
60°
80°N
60°N
40°N
20°N
0°
20°S
40°S
60°S
80°S
ALASKA (U.S.)
CANADA
NORTH AMERICA
Ottawa
UNITED STATES
Washington, D.C.
Azores
Bermuda (U.K.)
International Date Line
Tropic of Cancer
See Inset Below
MEXICO
Mexico City
HAWAII (U.S.)
PACIFIC OCEAN
Caracas
GUYANA
VENEZUELA
Paramaribo
Georgetown
SURINAME
Bogotá
Cayenne
COLOMBIA
FRENCH GUIANA (FR.)
Equator
Quito
Galápagos Is. (Ec.)
ECUADOR
POLYNESIA
Wallis and Futuna (Fr.)
KIRIBATI
TOKELAU (N.Z.)
AMERICAN SAMOA (U.S.)
COOK ISLANDS (N.Z.)
SAMOA
TONGA
FRENCH POLYNESIA (FR.)
SOUTH AMERICA
PERU
Lima
BRAZIL
La Paz
BOLIVIA
Brasília
Sucre
PARAGUAY
Tropic of Capricorn
Asunción
PITCAIRN IS. (U.K.)
CHILE
ARGENTINA
URUGUAY
Santiago
Buenos Aires
Montevideo
0 1,000 2,000 mi
0 1,000 2,000 km
Falkland Is. (U.K.)
Antarctic Circle

Central America and the Caribbean

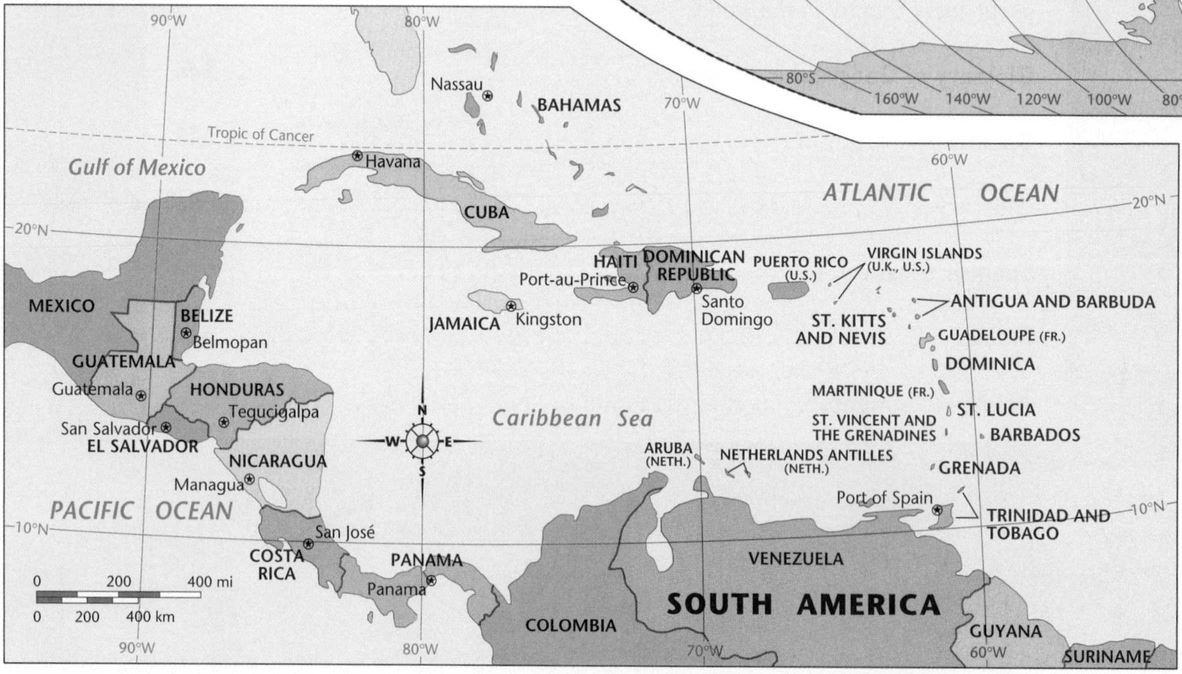
90°W
80°W
70°W
60°W
20°N
10°N
Nassau
BAHAMAS
Tropic of Cancer
Gulf of Mexico
Havana
ATLANTIC OCEAN
CUBA
HAITI
DOMINICAN REPUBLIC
PUERTO RICO (U.S.)
VIRGIN ISLANDS (U.K., U.S.)
Port-au-Prince
Santo Domingo
ANTIGUA AND BARBUDA
MEXICO
BELIZE
Belmopan
JAMAICA
Kingston
ST. KITTS AND NEVIS
GUADELOUPE (FR.)
DOMINICA
GUATEMALA
Guatemala
HONDURAS
Tegucigalpa
MARTINIQUE (FR.)
ST. LUCIA
San Salvador
EL SALVADOR
Caribbean Sea
ST. VINCENT AND THE GRENADINES
BARBADOS
NICARAGUA
Managua
ARUBA (NETH.)
NETHERLANDS ANTILLES (NETH.)
GRENADA
PACIFIC OCEAN
Port of Spain
TRINIDAD AND TOBAGO
San José
COSTA RICA
PANAMA
Panama
VENEZUELA
0 200 400 mi
0 200 400 km
SOUTH AMERICA
COLOMBIA
GUYANA
SURINAME
N
S
E
W

584 ATLAS

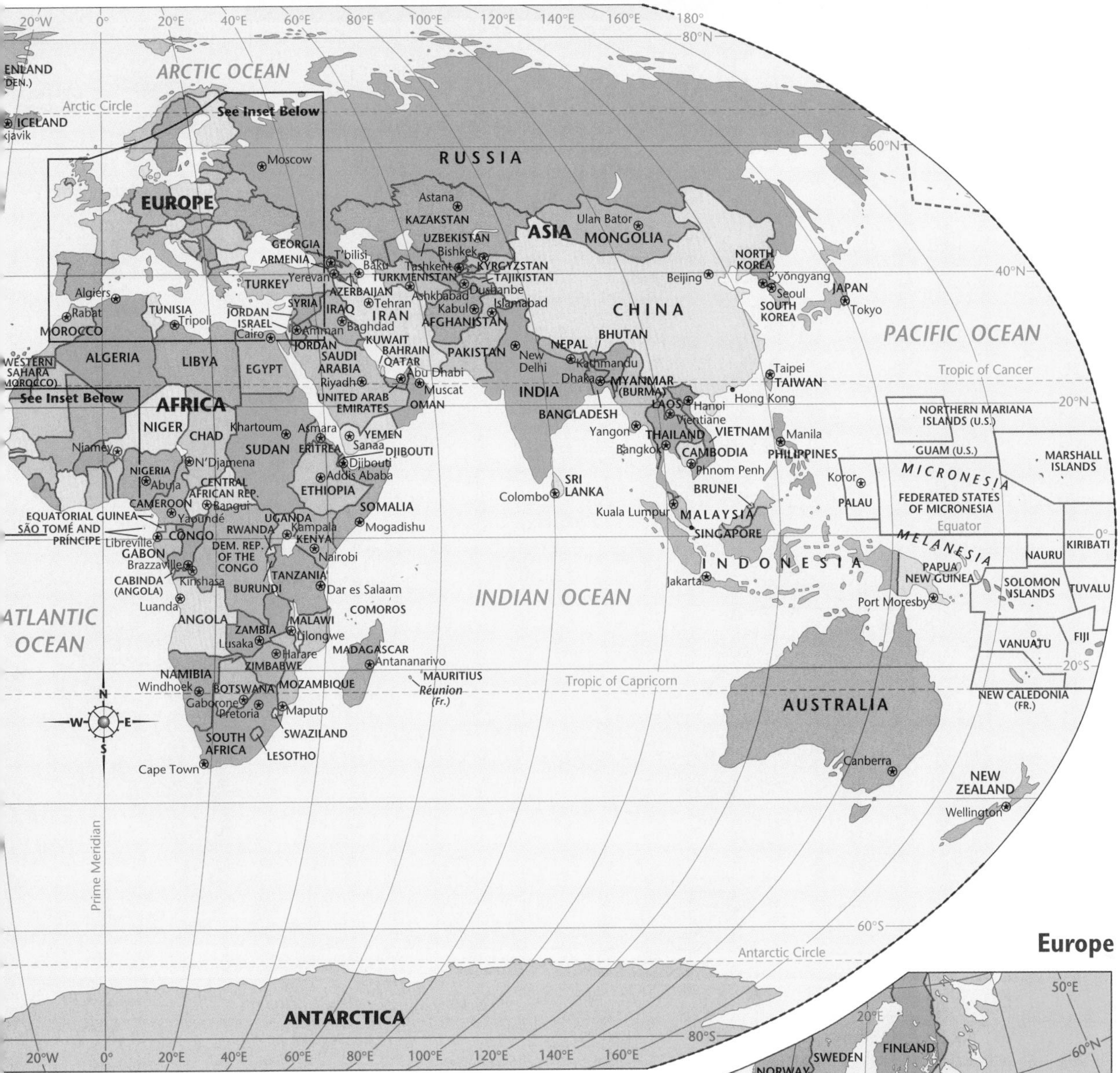

West Africa

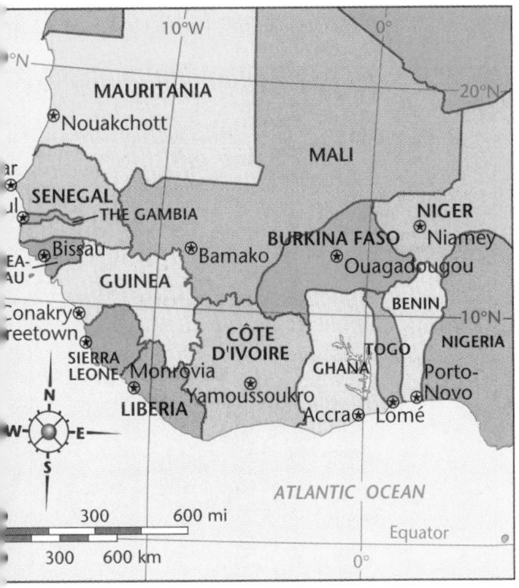

Europe

ATLAS 585

KEY

Elevation

Feet	Meters
Over 13,000	Over 3,960
6,500–13,000	1,980–3,960
1,600–6,500	480–1,980
650–1,600	200–480
0–650	0–200
Below sea level	Below sea level

Ice cap

Ice shelf

Robinson Projection

South Pole

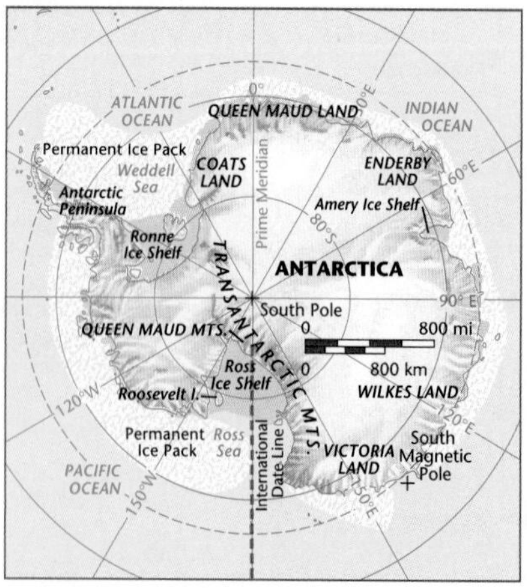

586 ATLAS

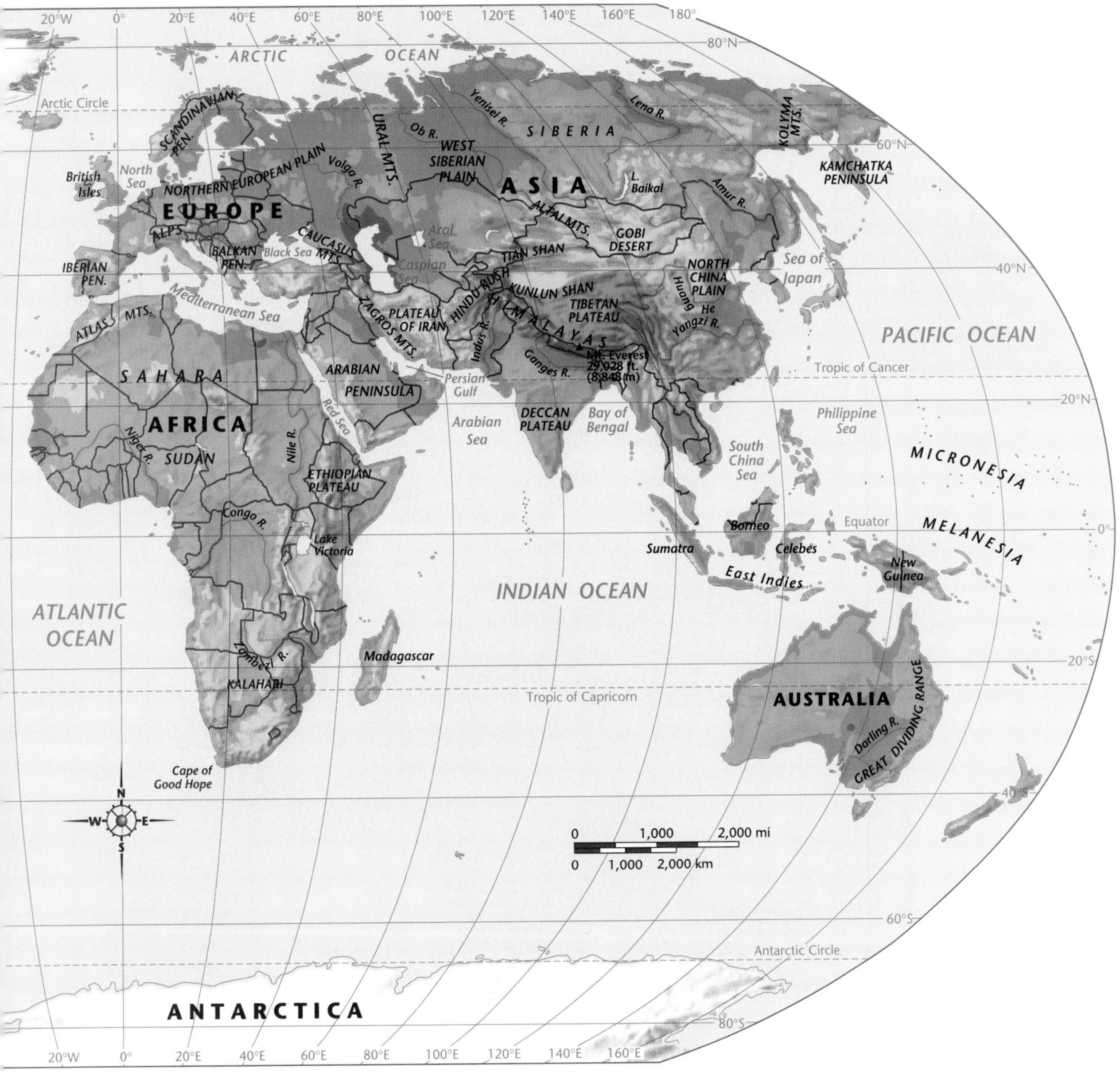
20°W
0°
20°E
40°E
60°E
80°E
100°E
120°E
140°E
160°E
180°
80°N
60°N
40°N
20°N
0°
20°S
40°S
60°S
80°S
ARCTIC OCEAN
Arctic Circle
SCANDINAVIAN PEN.
British Isles
North Sea
NORTHERN EUROPEAN PLAIN
Volga R.
URAL MTS.
Ob R.
Yenisei R.
WEST SIBERIAN PLAIN
SIBERIA
Lena R.
KOLYMA MTS.
KAMCHATKA PENINSULA
L. Baikal
Amur R.
ASIA
EUROPE
ALPS
CAUCASUS MTS.
Aral Sea
ALTAI MTS.
GOBI DESERT
BALKAN PEN.
Black Sea
Caspian Sea
TIAN SHAN
NORTH CHINA PLAIN
Sea of Japan
IBERIAN PEN.
Mediterranean Sea
HINDU KUSH
KUNLUN SHAN
TIBETAN PLATEAU
Huang He
Yangzi R.
ATLAS MTS.
PLATEAU OF IRAN
ZAGROS MTS.
HIMALAYAS
Indus R.
Mt. Everest 29,028 ft. (8,848 m)
Ganges R.
PACIFIC OCEAN
SAHARA
ARABIAN PENINSULA
Persian Gulf
Tropic of Cancer
Red Sea
DECCAN PLATEAU
Bay of Bengal
Philippine Sea
AFRICA
Arabian Sea
Niger R.
SUDAN
Nile R.
South China Sea
MICRONESIA
ETHIOPIAN PLATEAU
Congo R.
Borneo
Equator
MELANESIA
Lake Victoria
Sumatra
Celebes
New Guinea
East Indies
INDIAN OCEAN
ATLANTIC OCEAN
Madagascar
Zambezi R.
KALAHARI
Tropic of Capricorn
AUSTRALIA
GREAT DIVIDING RANGE
Darling R.
Cape of Good Hope
N
W
E
S
0
1,000
2,000 mi
0
1,000
2,000 km
Antarctic Circle
ANTARCTICA

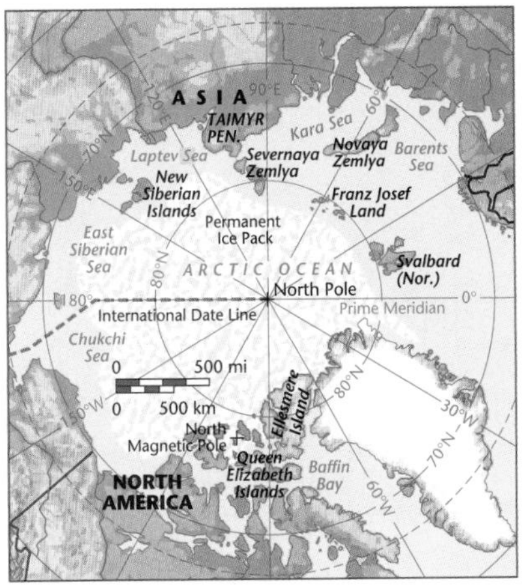
ASIA
TAIMYR PEN.
Kara Sea
Laptev Sea
New Siberian Islands
Severnaya Zemlya
Novaya Zemlya
Barents Sea
Franz Josef Land
Permanent Ice Pack
East Siberian Sea
ARCTIC OCEAN
Svalbard (Nor.)
North Pole
180°
0°
Prime Meridian
International Date Line
Chukchi Sea
0
500 mi
0
500 km
North Magnetic Pole
Ellesmere Island
Queen Elizabeth Islands
Baffin Bay
NORTH AMERICA
80°N
70°N
30°W
60°W
150°W
90°E
60°E

North Pole

ATLAS 587

United States: Political

588 ATLAS

CANADA
90°W
80°W
70°W
0 150 300 mi
0 150 300 km
Presque Isle
MAINE
Augusta
Portland
Montpelier
VERMONT
NEW HAMPSHIRE
Concord
Boston
NEW YORK
Albany
MASSACHUSETTS
Providence
Hartford
RHODE ISLAND
New Haven
CONNECTICUT
40°N
New York City
Trenton
NEW JERSEY
Philadelphia
Dover
DELAWARE
Baltimore
Annapolis
Washington, D.C.
MARYLAND
Richmond
Norfolk
VIRGINIA
PENNSYLVANIA
Harrisburg
Pittsburgh
Buffalo
Lake Ontario
Lake Erie
Lake Huron
Lake Superior
Lake Michigan
Sault Ste. Marie
MICHIGAN
Lansing
Detroit
Cleveland
OHIO
Columbus
Cincinnati
WEST VIRGINIA
Charleston
INDIANA
Indianapolis
Louisville
Frankfort
KENTUCKY
Ohio River
Tennessee River
ILLINOIS
Chicago
Springfield
St. Louis
WISCONSIN
Milwaukee
Madison
MINNESOTA
Duluth
Minneapolis
St. Paul
Mississippi River
Missouri River
IOWA
Des Moines
Cedar Rapids
Omaha
Lincoln
ORTH AKOTA
OUTH AKOTA
Topeka
Kansas City
ANSAS
Kansas River
Wichita
Jefferson City
MISSOURI
OKLAHOMA
Tulsa
Oklahoma City
ARKANSAS
Little Rock
Pine Bluff
Red River
Memphis
Nashville
TENNESSEE
Raleigh
NORTH CAROLINA
Charlotte
ATLANTIC OCEAN
Columbia
SOUTH CAROLINA
Charleston
Atlanta
GEORGIA
Savannah
Birmingham
ALABAMA
Montgomery
Columbus
MISSISSIPPI
Jackson
Hattiesburg
Dallas
Shreveport
EXAS
Austin
San Antonio
Houston
Baton Rouge
LOUISIANA
New Orleans
Tallahassee
Jacksonville
FLORIDA
Tampa
Lake Okeechobee
Miami
30°N
Gulf of Mexico
N
E
S
W
KEY
National boundary
State boundary
National capital
State capital
Other city
Transverse Mercator Projection

ATLAS 589

North and South America: Political

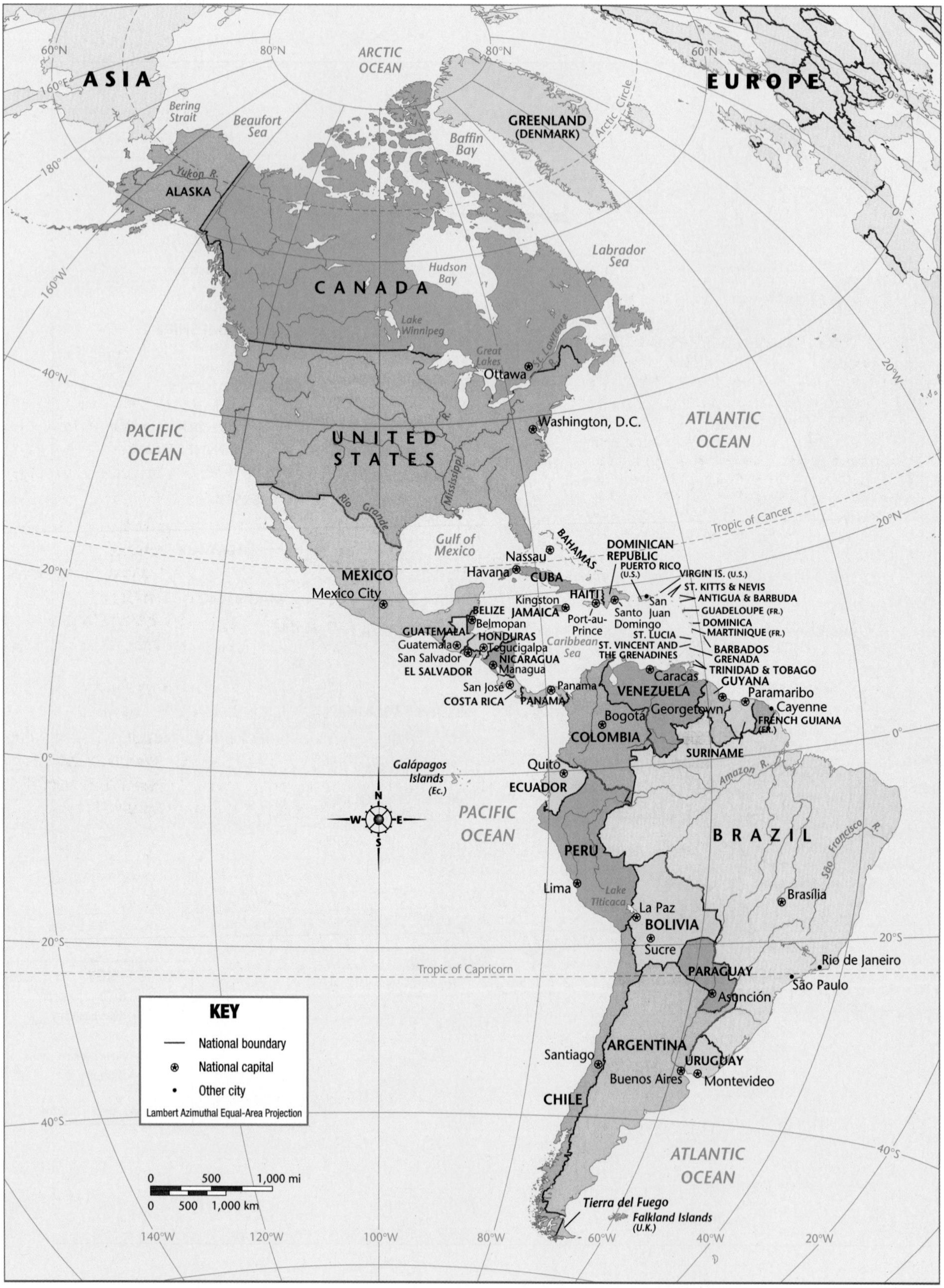
ASIA
EUROPE
ARCTIC OCEAN
Bering Strait
Beaufort Sea
GREENLAND (DENMARK)
Baffin Bay
Arctic Circle
Yukon R.
ALASKA
Labrador Sea
Hudson Bay
CANADA
Lake Winnipeg
Great Lakes
St. Lawrence R.
Ottawa
PACIFIC OCEAN
Washington, D.C.
ATLANTIC OCEAN
UNITED STATES
Mississippi R.
Rio Grande
Tropic of Cancer
Gulf of Mexico
BAHAMAS
Nassau
DOMINICAN REPUBLIC
PUERTO RICO (U.S.)
VIRGIN IS. (U.S.)
ST. KITTS & NEVIS
ANTIGUA & BARBUDA
GUADELOUPE (FR.)
DOMINICA
MARTINIQUE (FR.)
ST. LUCIA
ST. VINCENT AND THE GRENADINES
BARBADOS
GRENADA
TRINIDAD & TOBAGO
MEXICO
Mexico City
Havana
CUBA
HAITI
San Juan
Kingston
JAMAICA
Port-au-Prince
Santo Domingo
BELIZE
Belmopan
GUATEMALA
Guatemala
HONDURAS
Tegucigalpa
San Salvador
EL SALVADOR
NICARAGUA
Managua
Caribbean Sea
San José
COSTA RICA
Panama
PANAMA
Caracas
VENEZUELA
GUYANA
Georgetown
Paramaribo
Cayenne
FRENCH GUIANA (FR.)
SURINAME
Bogotá
COLOMBIA
Galápagos Islands (Ec.)
Quito
ECUADOR
Amazon R.
N
W
E
S
PACIFIC OCEAN
BRAZIL
São Francisco R.
PERU
Lima
Lake Titicaca
La Paz
BOLIVIA
Sucre
Brasília
Rio de Janeiro
São Paulo
Tropic of Capricorn
PARAGUAY
Asunción
KEY
National boundary
National capital
Other city
Lambert Azimuthal Equal-Area Projection
Santiago
ARGENTINA
URUGUAY
Buenos Aires
Montevideo
CHILE
ATLANTIC OCEAN
0 500 1,000 mi
0 500 1,000 km
Tierra del Fuego
Falkland Islands (U.K.)
60°N
80°N
80°N
60°N
160°E
180°
160°W
40°N
20°N
0°
20°S
40°S
20°W
20°N
0°
20°S
40°S
140°W
120°W
100°W
80°W
60°W
40°W
20°W

590 ATLAS

North and South America: Physical

ARCTIC OCEAN
ASIA
EUROPE
Bering Strait
Beaufort Sea
Baffin Bay
Arctic Circle
Yukon R.
Mackenzie R.
Labrador Sea
Hudson Bay
CANADIAN SHIELD
Lake Winnipeg
Great Lakes
St. Lawrence R.
ROCKY MOUNTAINS
GREAT PLAINS
CASCADES
Great Salt Lake
Missouri R.
Ohio R.
APPALACHIAN MTS.
Mississippi R.
Colorado R.
SIERRA NEVADA
PACIFIC OCEAN
ATLANTIC OCEAN
Rio Grande
BAJA CALIFORNIA
SIERRA MADRE OCCIDENTAL
SIERRA MADRE ORIENTAL
Gulf of Mexico
Tropic of Cancer
YUCATÁN PENINSULA
Hispaniola
Caribbean Sea
ISTHMUS OF PANAMA
Orinoco R.
Amazon R.
AMAZON BASIN
PACIFIC OCEAN
ANDES MOUNTAINS
Lake Titicaca
São Francisco R.
BRAZILIAN HIGHLANDS
Paraguay R.
Paraná R.
ATACAMA DESERT
PAMPAS
Tropic of Capricorn
PATAGONIA
ATLANTIC OCEAN
Tierra del Fuego
N
S
E
W
60°N
80°N
160°E
180°
160°W
40°N
20°N
0°
20°S
40°S
20°W
140°W
120°W
100°W
80°W
60°W
40°W
20°W
KEY
Elevation
Feet
Meters
Over 13,000
Over 3,960
6,500–13,000
1,980–3,960
1,600–6,500
480–1,980
650–1,600
200–480
0–650
0–200
Ice cap
Lambert Azimuthal Equal-Area Projection
0
500
1,000 mi
0
500
1,000 km

ATLAS 591

Europe: Political

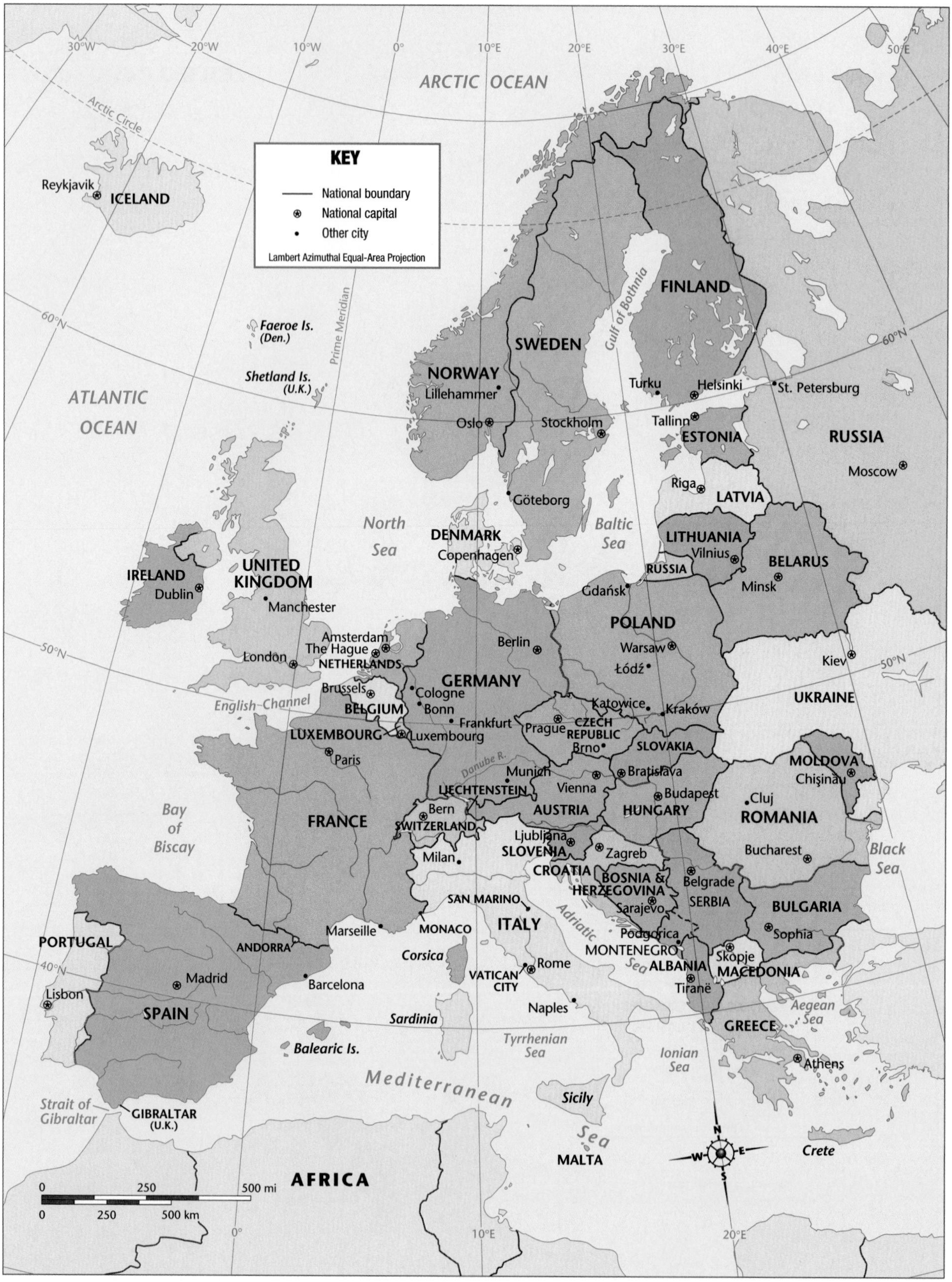

592 ATLAS

Europe: Physical

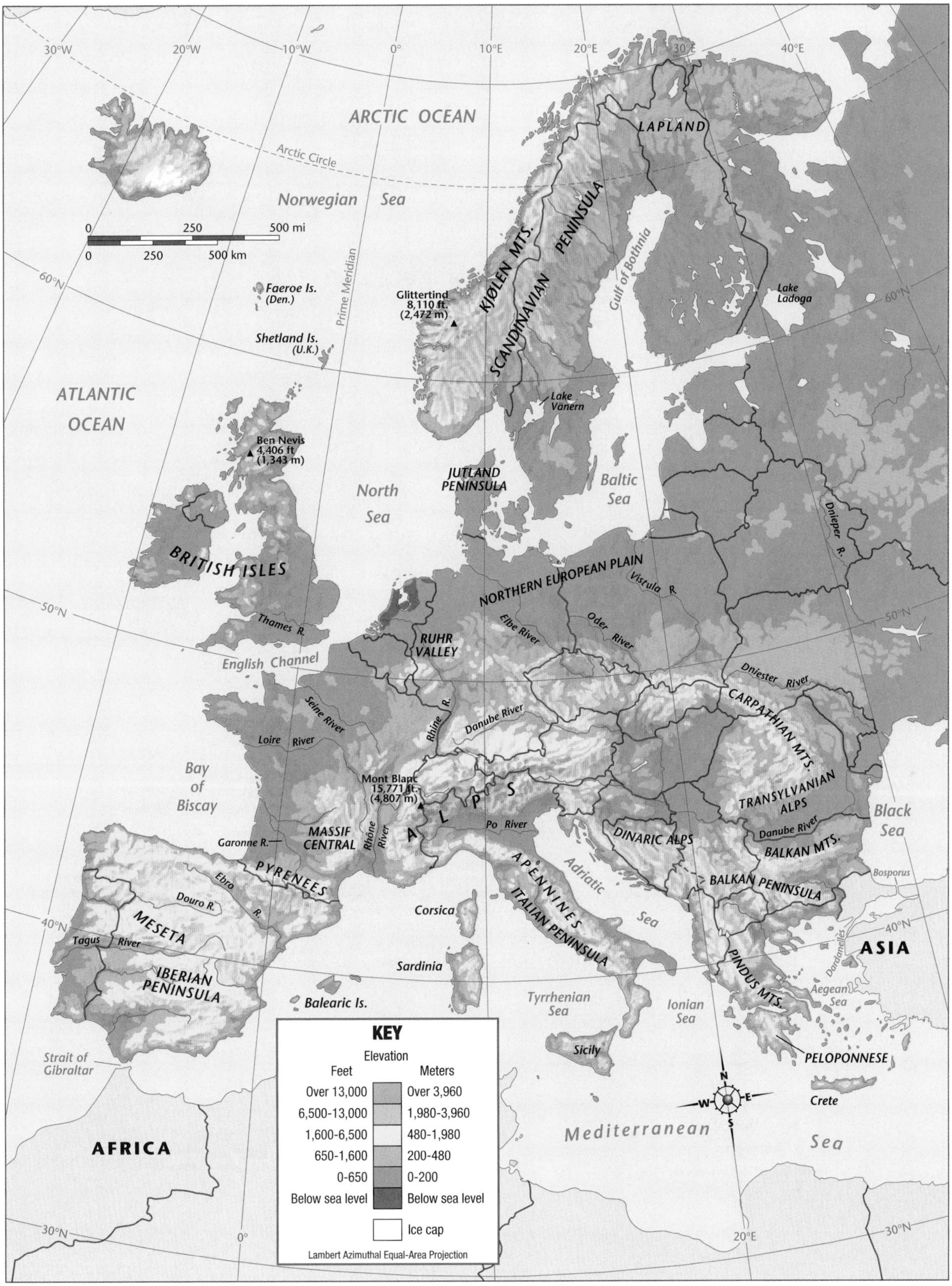
ARCTIC OCEAN
Arctic Circle
Norwegian Sea
ATLANTIC OCEAN
North Sea
Baltic Sea
Gulf of Bothnia
LAPLAND
SCANDINAVIAN PENINSULA
KJØLEN MTS.
Glittertind 8,110 ft. (2,472 m)
Lake Vanern
Lake Ladoga
Faeroe Is. (Den.)
Shetland Is. (U.K.)
Prime Meridian
Ben Nevis 4,406 ft (1,343 m)
BRITISH ISLES
Thames R.
English Channel
JUTLAND PENINSULA
NORTHERN EUROPEAN PLAIN
RUHR VALLEY
Elbe River
Oder River
Vistula R.
Dnieper R.
Dniester River
CARPATHIAN MTS.
TRANSYLVANIAN ALPS
Danube River
Rhine R.
Seine River
Loire River
Bay of Biscay
Garonne R.
MASSIF CENTRAL
Rhône River
Mont Blanc 15,771 ft. (4,807 m)
ALPS
Po River
DINARIC ALPS
BALKAN MTS.
BALKAN PENINSULA
Black Sea
Bosporus
PYRENEES
Ebro R.
Douro R.
MESETA
Tagus River
IBERIAN PENINSULA
APENNINES
ITALIAN PENINSULA
Adriatic Sea
Corsica
Sardinia
Balearic Is.
Tyrrhenian Sea
Ionian Sea
Sicily
PINDUS MTS.
Dardanelles
Aegean Sea
PELOPONNESE
Crete
ASIA
Strait of Gibraltar
AFRICA
Mediterranean Sea
30°W
20°W
10°W
0°
10°E
20°E
30°E
40°E
60°N
50°N
40°N
30°N
0 250 500 mi
0 250 500 km
N E S W
KEY
Elevation
Feet Meters
Over 13,000 Over 3,960
6,500-13,000 1,980-3,960
1,600-6,500 480-1,980
650-1,600 200-480
0-650 0-200
Below sea level Below sea level
Ice cap
Lambert Azimuthal Equal-Area Projection

ATLAS 593

Africa: Political

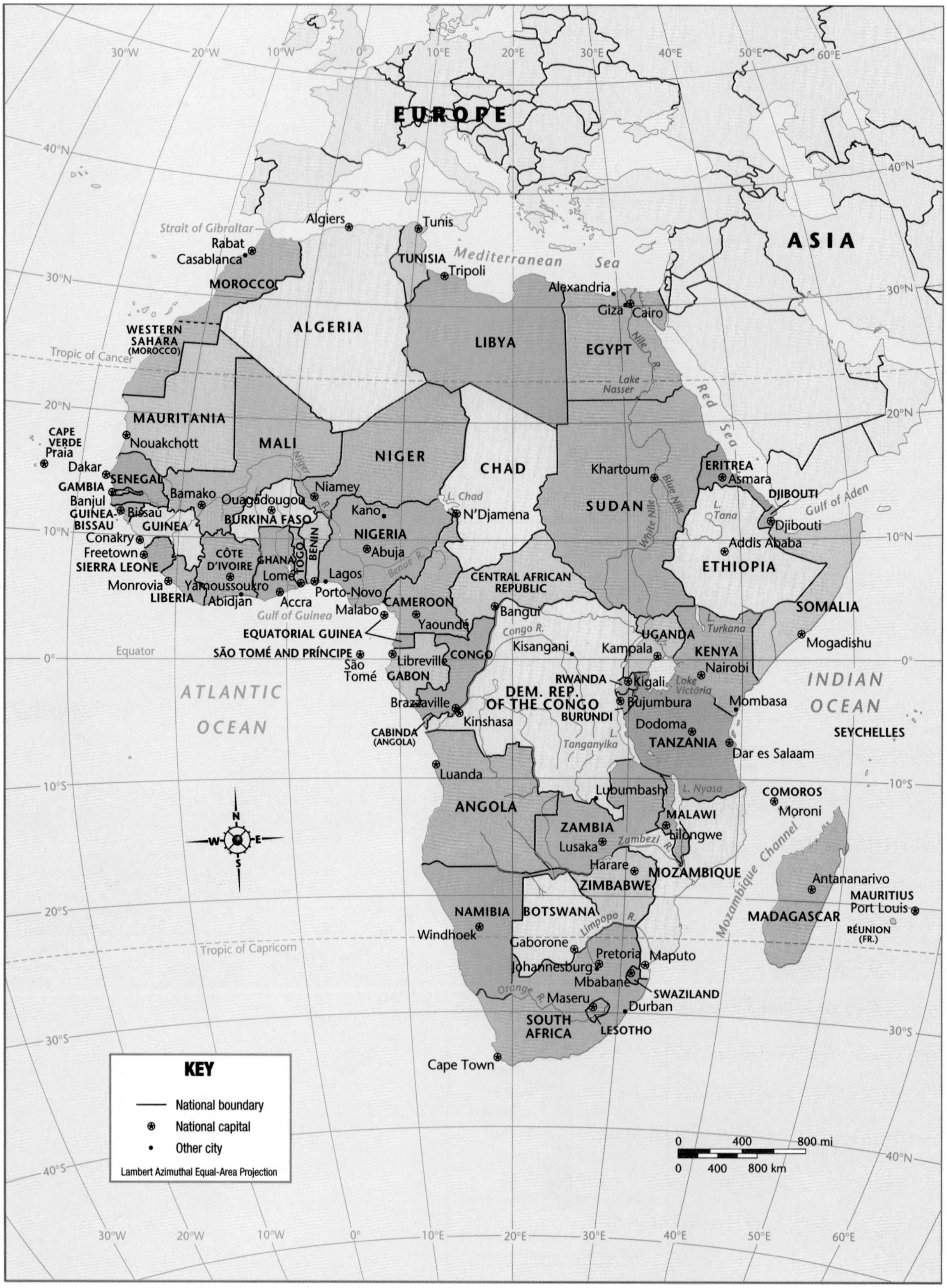

EUROPE
ASIA
Strait of Gibraltar
Algiers
Tunis
Rabat
Casablanca
TUNISIA
Mediterranean Sea
Tripoli
MOROCCO
Alexandria
Giza
Cairo
ALGERIA
WESTERN SAHARA (MOROCCO)
LIBYA
EGYPT
Tropic of Cancer
Nile R.
Lake Nasser
Red Sea
MAURITANIA
CAPE VERDE
Praia
Nouakchott
MALI
Niger R.
NIGER
CHAD
Khartoum
ERITREA
Asmara
Dakar
SENEGAL
GAMBIA
Banjul
GUINEA-BISSAU
Bissau
GUINEA
Conakry
Freetown
SIERRA LEONE
Monrovia
LIBERIA
Bamako
Ouagadougou
BURKINA FASO
Niamey
Kano
NIGERIA
Abuja
L. Chad
N'Djamena
SUDAN
Blue Nile
White Nile
L. Tana
DJIBOUTI
Djibouti
Gulf of Aden
Addis Ababa
ETHIOPIA
CÔTE D'IVOIRE
Yamoussoukro
Abidjan
GHANA
Accra
TOGO
Lomé
BENIN
Porto-Novo
Lagos
Benue R.
Gulf of Guinea
Malabo
CAMEROON
Yaoundé
CENTRAL AFRICAN REPUBLIC
Bangui
SOMALIA
Mogadishu
EQUATORIAL GUINEA
SÃO TOMÉ AND PRÍNCIPE
São Tomé
Libreville
GABON
CONGO
Congo R.
Kisangani
UGANDA
Kampala
L. Turkana
KENYA
Nairobi
Equator
ATLANTIC OCEAN
INDIAN OCEAN
RWANDA
Kigali
Lake Victoria
DEM. REP. OF THE CONGO
BURUNDI
Bujumbura
Mombasa
Brazzaville
Kinshasa
CABINDA (ANGOLA)
L. Tanganyika
Dodoma
TANZANIA
Dar es Salaam
SEYCHELLES
Luanda
Lubumbashi
L. Nyasa
COMOROS
Moroni
ANGOLA
MALAWI
Lilongwe
ZAMBIA
Lusaka
Zambezi R.
Mozambique Channel
Harare
MOZAMBIQUE
ZIMBABWE
Antananarivo
MAURITIUS
Port Louis
MADAGASCAR
RÉUNION (FR.)
NAMIBIA
BOTSWANA
Limpopo R.
Windhoek
Gaborone
Tropic of Capricorn
Pretoria
Maputo
Johannesburg
Mbabane
SWAZILAND
Orange R.
Maseru
Durban
SOUTH AFRICA
LESOTHO
Cape Town
N
S
E
W
KEY
National boundary
National capital
Other city
Lambert Azimuthal Equal-Area Projection
0
400
800 mi
0
400
800 km
30°W
20°W
10°W
0°
10°E
20°E
30°E
40°E
50°E
60°E
40°N
30°N
20°N
10°N
0°
10°S
20°S
30°S
40°S

594 ATLAS

Africa: Physical

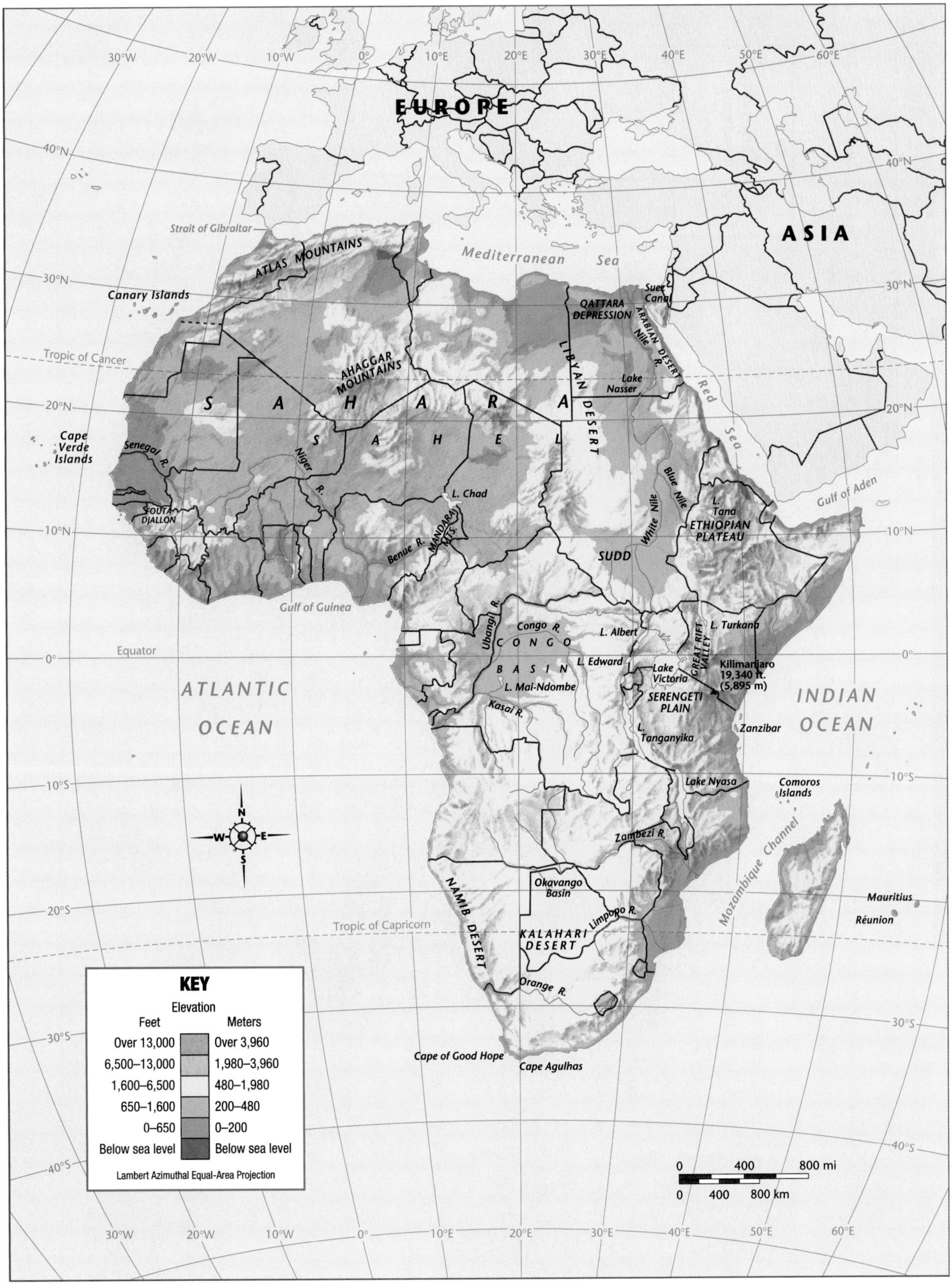
EUROPE
ASIA
Mediterranean Sea
Strait of Gibraltar
ATLAS MOUNTAINS
Canary Islands
Tropic of Cancer
AHAGGAR MOUNTAINS
S A H A R A
S A H E L
Cape Verde Islands
Senegal R.
Niger R.
FOUTA DJALLON
L. Chad
Benue R.
MANDARA MTS.
QATTARA DEPRESSION
Suez Canal
ARABIAN DESERT
Nile R.
LIBYAN DESERT
Lake Nasser
Red Sea
Gulf of Aden
Blue Nile
White Nile
L. Tana
ETHIOPIAN PLATEAU
SUDD
Gulf of Guinea
Equator
ATLANTIC OCEAN
Ubangi R.
Congo R.
CONGO BASIN
L. Mai-Ndombe
Kasai R.
L. Albert
L. Edward
Lake Victoria
GREAT RIFT VALLEY
L. Turkana
Kilimanjaro 19,340 ft. (5,895 m)
SERENGETI PLAIN
L. Tanganyika
Zanzibar
INDIAN OCEAN
Lake Nyasa
Comoros Islands
Zambezi R.
Mozambique Channel
Mauritius
Réunion
Okavango Basin
NAMIB DESERT
Tropic of Capricorn
Limpopo R.
KALAHARI DESERT
Orange R.
Cape of Good Hope
Cape Agulhas
30°W 20°W 10°W 0° 10°E 20°E 30°E 40°E 50°E 60°E
40°N 30°N 20°N 10°N 0° 10°S 20°S 30°S 40°S
N S E W
KEY
Elevation
Feet Meters
Over 13,000 Over 3,960
6,500–13,000 1,980–3,960
1,600–6,500 480–1,980
650–1,600 200–480
0–650 0–200
Below sea level Below sea level
Lambert Azimuthal Equal-Area Projection
0 400 800 mi
0 400 800 km

ATLAS 595

Asia: Political

596 ATLAS

Asia: Physical

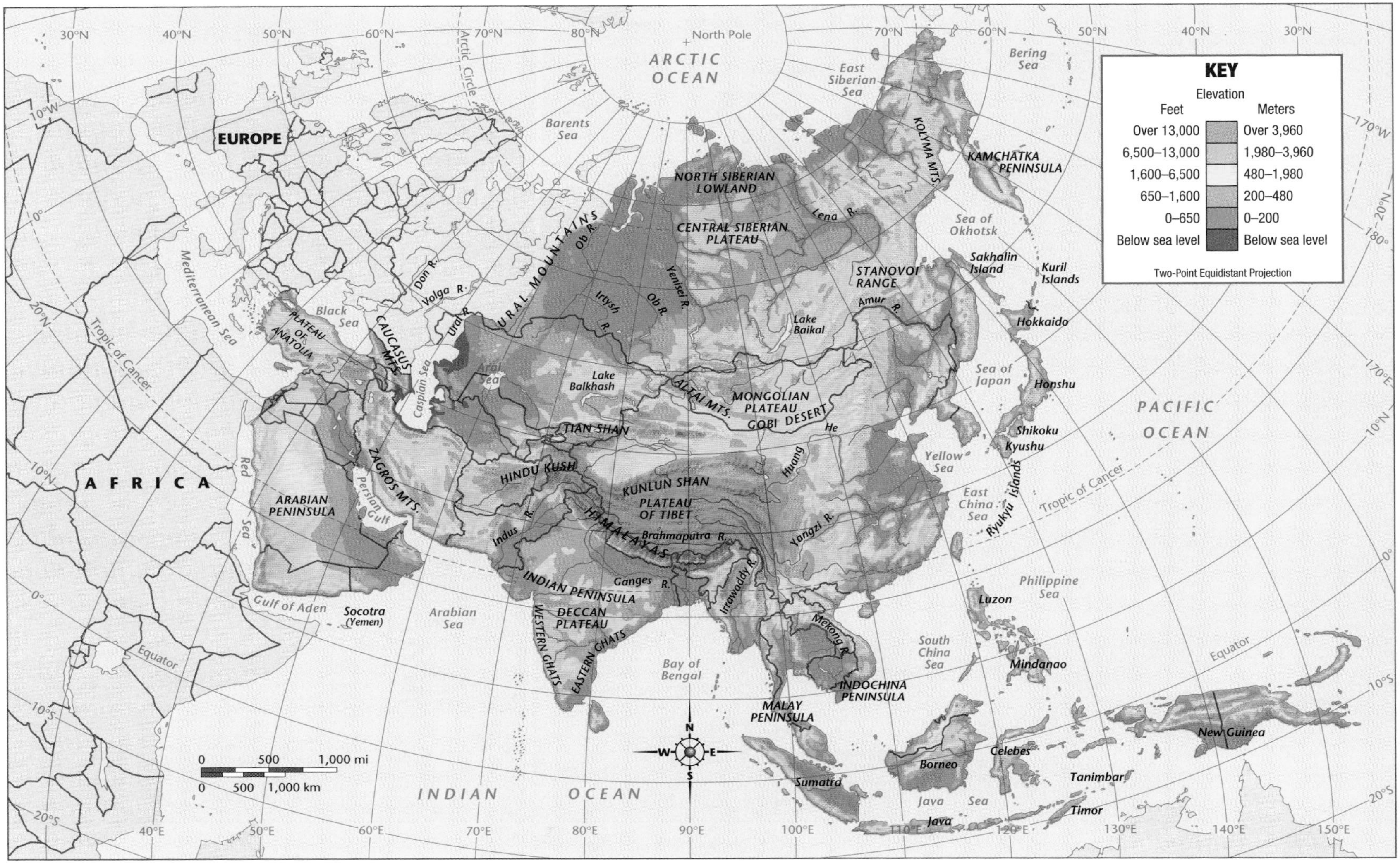

ATLAS 597

Australia, New Zealand, and the Pacific Islands: Physical–Political

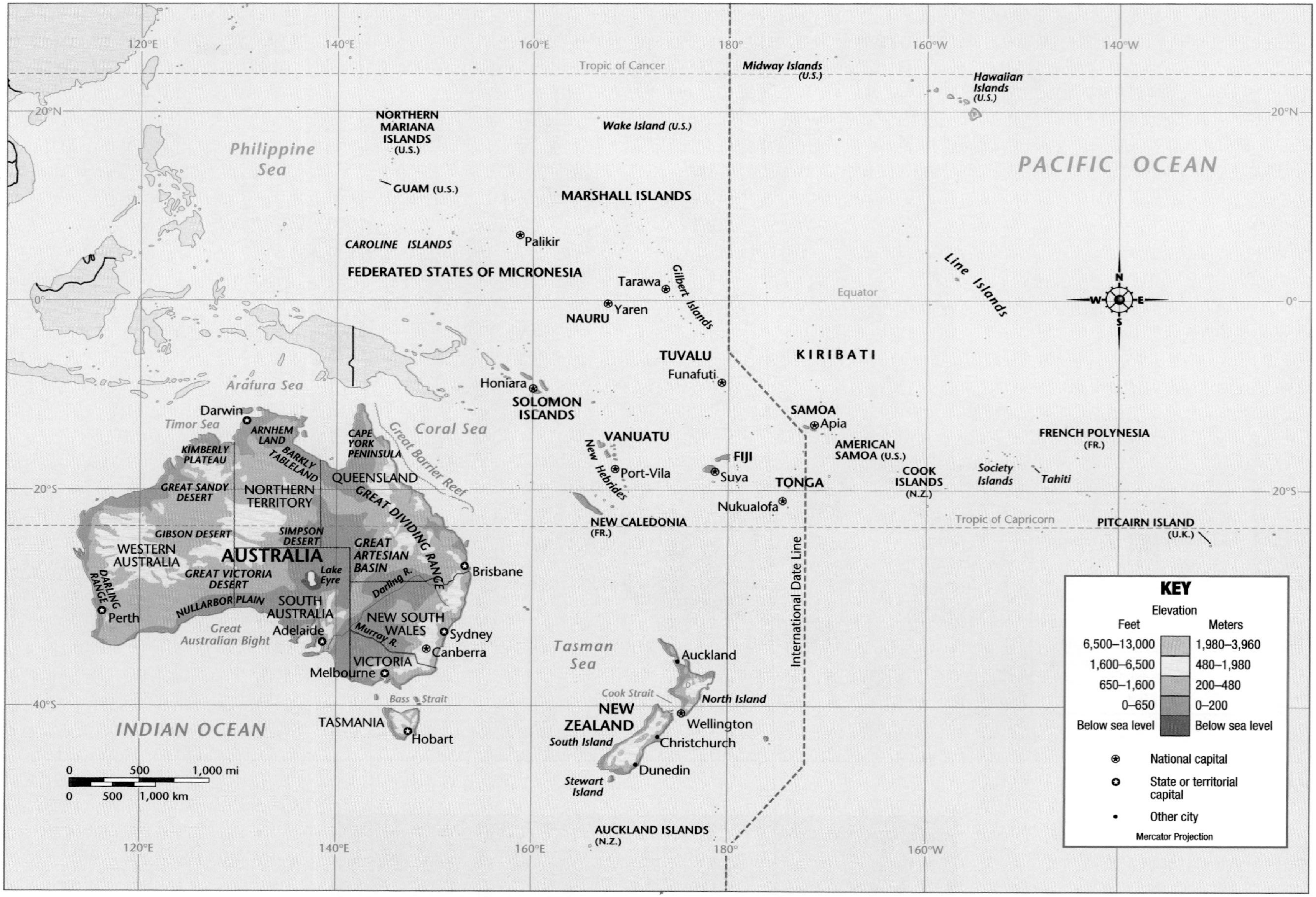

Philippine Sea
NORTHERN MARIANA ISLANDS (U.S.)
GUAM (U.S.)
CAROLINE ISLANDS
FEDERATED STATES OF MICRONESIA
Palikir
MARSHALL ISLANDS
Wake Island (U.S.)
Midway Islands (U.S.)
Hawaiian Islands (U.S.)
PACIFIC OCEAN
Tropic of Cancer
Equator
Tropic of Capricorn
Line Islands
Tarawa
Gilbert Islands
Yaren
NAURU
TUVALU
Funafuti
KIRIBATI
Honiara
SOLOMON ISLANDS
Arafura Sea
Coral Sea
Great Barrier Reef
Darwin
Timor Sea
ARNHEM LAND
KIMBERLY PLATEAU
BARKLY TABLELAND
CAPE YORK PENINSULA
QUEENSLAND
NORTHERN TERRITORY
GREAT SANDY DESERT
GREAT DIVIDING RANGE
GIBSON DESERT
SIMPSON DESERT
WESTERN AUSTRALIA
AUSTRALIA
GREAT ARTESIAN BASIN
Lake Eyre
GREAT VICTORIA DESERT
DARLING RANGE
Perth
NULLARBOR PLAIN
SOUTH AUSTRALIA
Darling R.
Brisbane
NEW SOUTH WALES
Murray R.
Sydney
Canberra
Adelaide
Great Australian Bight
VICTORIA
Melbourne
Bass Strait
TASMANIA
Hobart
INDIAN OCEAN
VANUATU
New Hebrides
Port-Vila
NEW CALEDONIA (FR.)
FIJI
Suva
SAMOA
Apia
AMERICAN SAMOA (U.S.)
TONGA
Nukualofa
COOK ISLANDS (N.Z.)
Society Islands
Tahiti
FRENCH POLYNESIA (FR.)
PITCAIRN ISLAND (U.K.)
International Date Line
Tasman Sea
Auckland
Cook Strait
North Island
NEW ZEALAND
Wellington
South Island
Christchurch
Dunedin
Stewart Island
AUCKLAND ISLANDS (N.Z.)
N
E
S
W
120°E
140°E
160°E
180°
160°W
140°W
20°N
0°
20°S
40°S
0
500
1,000 mi
0
500
1,000 km
KEY
Elevation
Feet
Meters
6,500–13,000
1,980–3,960
1,600–6,500
480–1,980
650–1,600
200–480
0–650
0–200
Below sea level
Below sea level
National capital
State or territorial capital
Other city
Mercator Projection

598 ATLAS

The Arctic and Antarctica

The Arctic

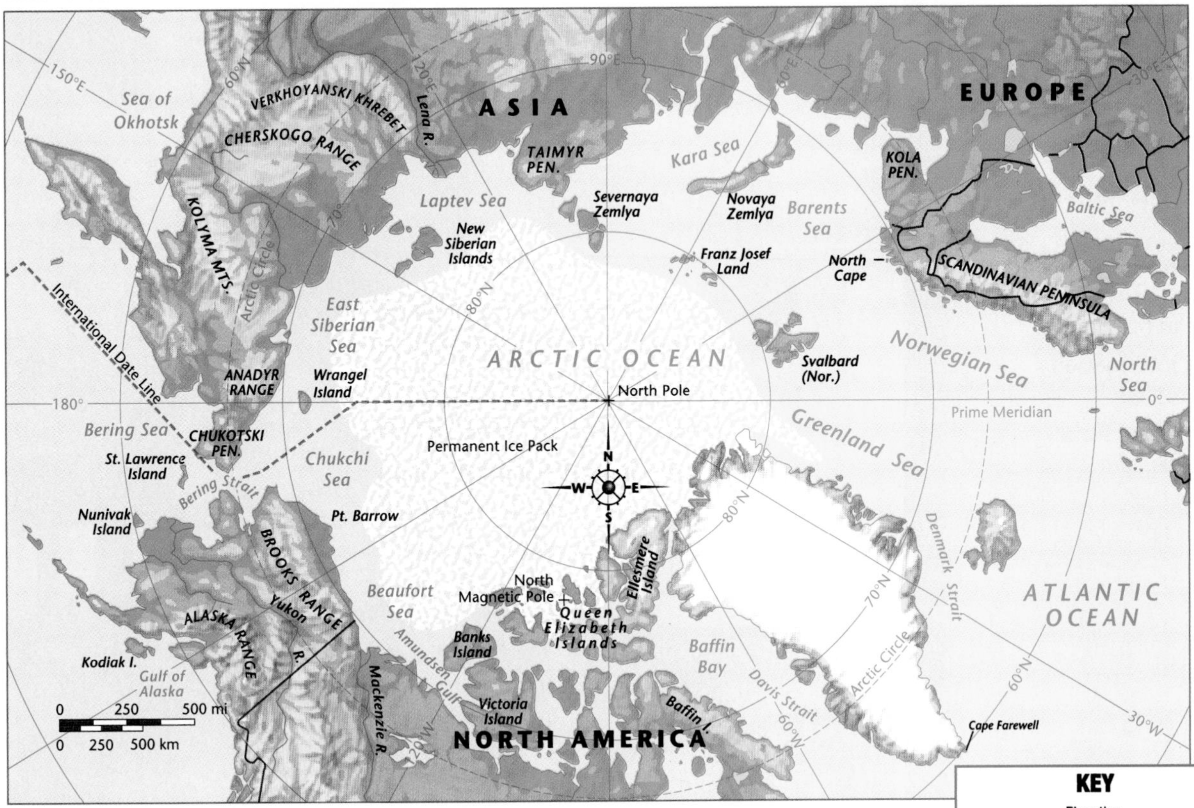

KEY		
Elevation		
Feet		Meters
Over 13,000		Over 3,960
6,500–13,000		1,980–3,960
1,600–6,500		480–1,980
650–1,600		200–480
0–650		0–200
		Ice cap
		Ice shelf

Orthographic Projection

Antarctica

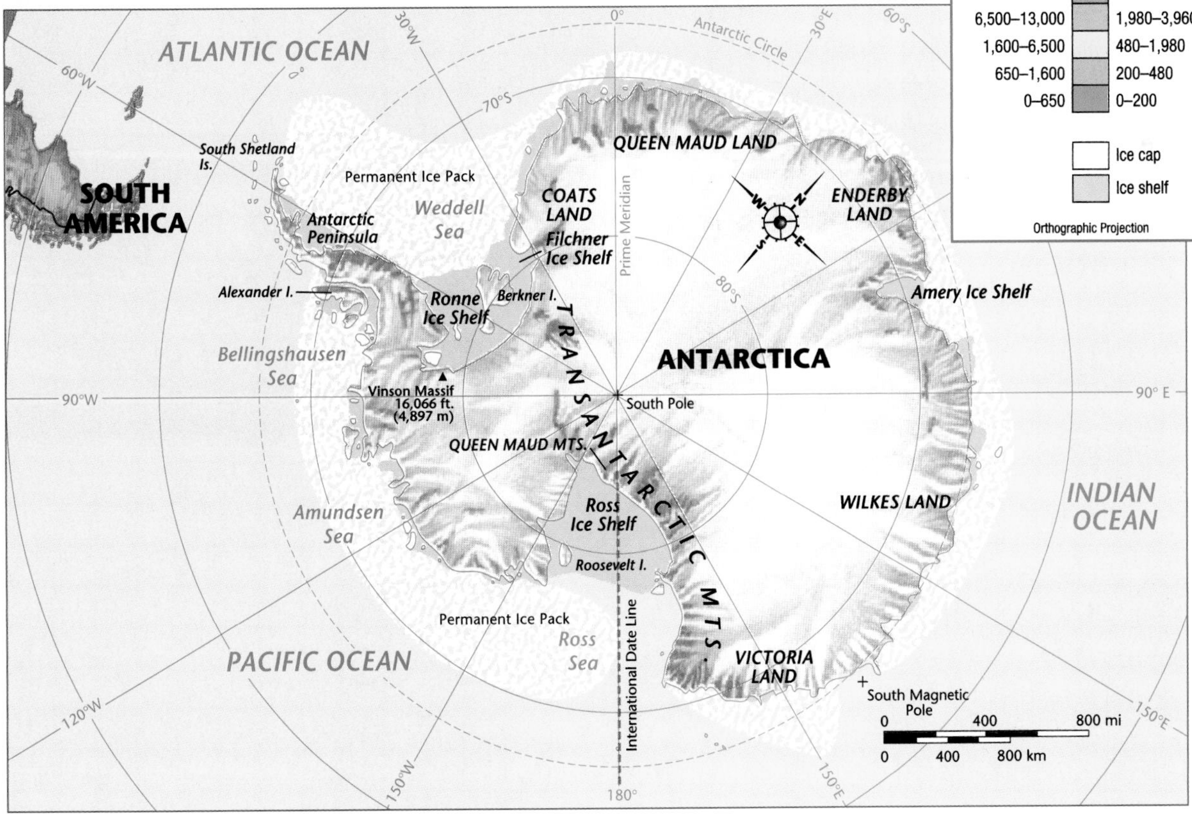

ATLAS 599

Regional Database

Using the Regional Database

The Regional Database can be used in the following ways:

- To provide a comprehensive study of all the world's countries, as well as all U.S. states and Canadian provinces
- To provide a source of information for student research projects
- To provide comparative data for a group of countries, states, and provinces under study

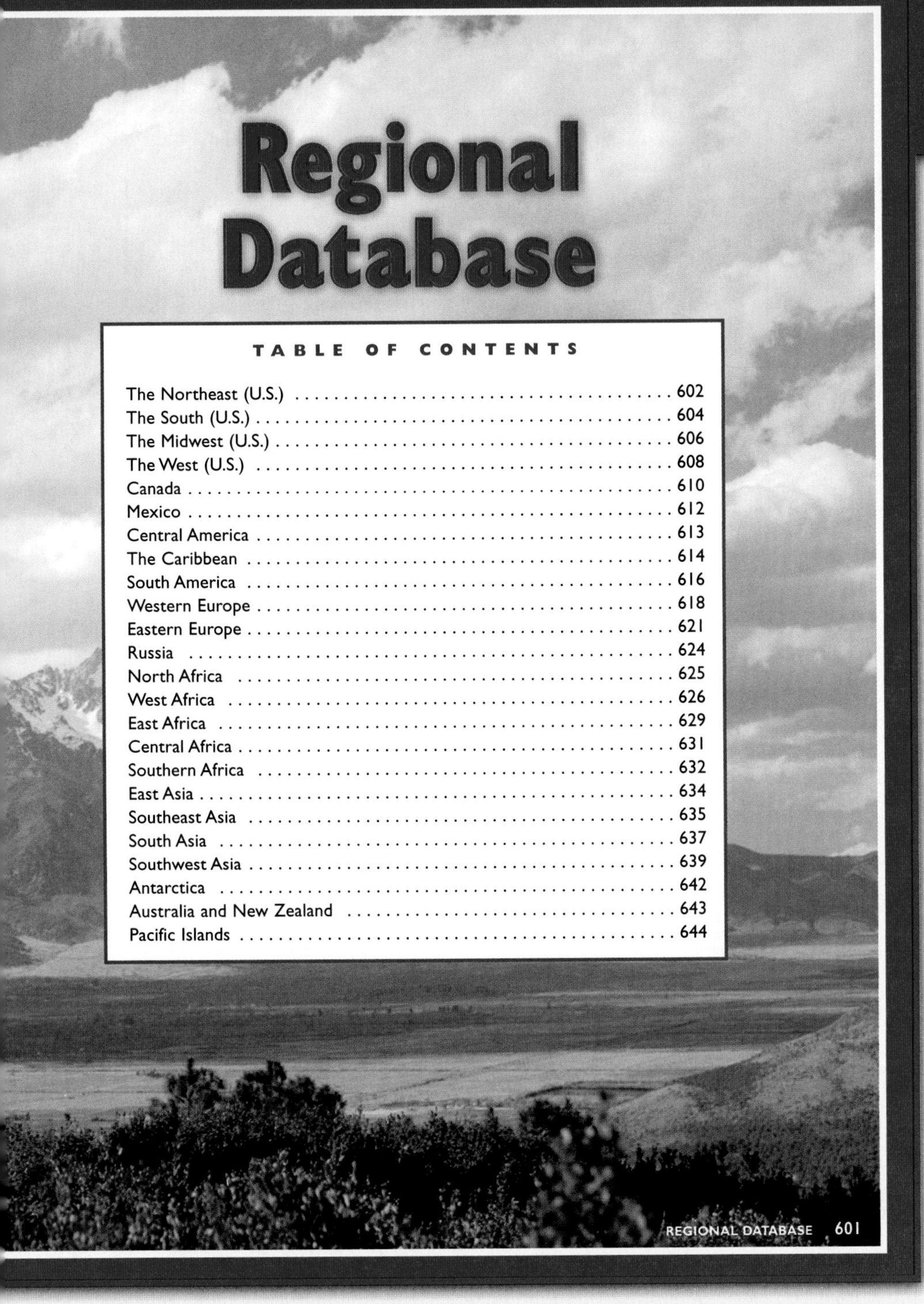

Regional Database

TABLE OF CONTENTS

Using Political Maps

Political maps in the Regional Database show every country in the world, as well as each of the U.S. states and Canadian provinces. Countries and states are grouped by geographic region. Within each region, the countries, states, or provinces are listed alphabetically. In addition, information is given for the following categories of data for each country:

- capital
- area
- climate
- population
- major ethnic groups
- major religions
- government
- currency
- leading exports
- major languages

And for each state or province:

- capital
- area
- climate
- population
- agriculture
- economic activities

Regional Database

Lesson Objectives

Gather, understand, and apply information about the northeastern United States.

Lesson Plan

1 Explore

Before students look at the map, ask them to volunteer the names of states that they think make up the Northeast. Once all the states have been named, ask students which country many of these states share a border with (*Canada*).

2 Teach

Explain that the Northeast was the first region of the United States to be heavily settled, and is also the most densely populated region today. Remind students that though the Northeast is limited in natural resources, its extensive coastlines have made fishing and trade important industries throughout the history of the region. Explain that the region's many harbors and large population helped the Northeast become a major commercial center.

The Northeast (U.S.): Political

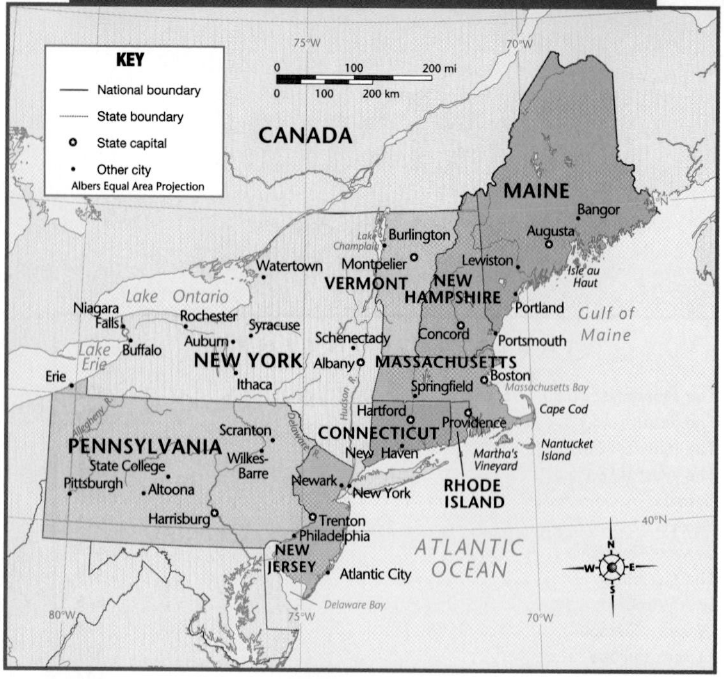

Connecticut

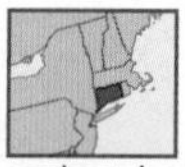

Capital: Hartford
Area: 5,544 sq mi; 14,359 sq km
Climate: Humid continental; cold winters and long, hot summers
Population: 3.4 million
Agriculture: Mushrooms, vegetables, sweet corn, tobacco, apples, hay; poultry, dairy products, livestock; nursery stock, Christmas trees
Economic Activities: Aircraft engines and parts, submarines, helicopters, machinery and computer equipment, electrical equipment, medical instruments, pharmaceuticals

Maine

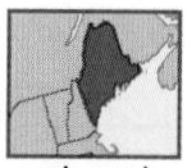

Capital: Augusta
Area: 35,387 sq mi; 91,652 sq km
Climate: Humid continental; cold winters and moderate summers; milder along coast
Population: 1.3 million
Agriculture: Potatoes, blueberries, apples; poultry, dairy products; fish; timber
Economic Activities: Pulp and paper, transportation equipment, wood products, food processing, tourism

Massachusetts

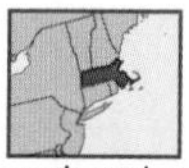

Capital: Boston
Area: 10,555 sq mi; 27,337 sq km
Climate: Humid continental; cold winters and long, hot summers; milder along coast
Population: 6.3 million
Agriculture: Cranberries, greenhouse and nursery plants, vegetables; fish
Economic Activities: Electrical, electronic, and industrial equipment, printing and publishing, metal products, food processing

New Hampshire

Capital: Concord
Area: 9,351 sq mi; 24,219 sq km
Climate: Humid continental; long, cold winters and cool summers; severe winters in northern mountains
Population: 1.2 million
Agriculture: Nursery and greenhouse products, hay, vegetables, fruit, maple syrup and sugar products; timber
Economic Activities: Tourism, machinery, electrical and electronic products, plastics

Resource Directory

Other Print Resources

DK Atlas

Technology

Color Transparencies 30 The United States: Northeast: Physical-Political Map; **41** The United States: Percent Changes in States Population Map; **42** The United States Agricultural Regions Map

New Jersey

Capital: Trenton
Area: 8,722 sq mi; 22,590 sq km
Climate: Humid continental; cold, snowy winters and hot, humid summers
Population: 8.4 million
Agriculture: Nursery plants, tomatoes, blueberries, peaches; dairy products; timber
Economic Activities: Chemicals, pharmaceuticals, electronic equipment, food processing, telecommunications, biotechnology, printing and publishing

New York

Capital: Albany
Area: 54,475 sq mi; 141,090 sq km
Climate: Humid continental; severely cold winters in north; mildest along coast
Population: 19 million
Agriculture: Potatoes, onions, cabbage, sweet corn, grapes, apples, strawberries, pears, maple syrup, hay, wheat, oats, dry beans; dairy products, cattle, poultry; timber
Economic Activities: Printing and publishing, food processing, textiles, pharmaceuticals, machinery, instruments, toys and sporting goods, electronic equipment, automotive and aircraft parts

Pennsylvania

Capital: Harrisburg
Area: 46,058 sq mi; 119,290 sq km
Climate: Humid continental; fairly wet; harsh winters and short summers in the plateaus and mountains; milder winters and longer summers in the lowlands, valleys, and coastal plain
Population: 12.3 million
Agriculture: Corn, hay, mushrooms, apples, potatoes, winter wheat, oats, vegetables, tobacco, grapes, peaches; dairy products, chickens, cattle, hogs; timber
Economic Activities: Food processing, metal products, industrial machinery and equipment, transportation equipment, rubber and plastics, electronic equipment, chemicals and pharmaceuticals, lumber and wood products, tourism, biotechnology, printing and publishing, mining (coal, limestone)

Rhode Island

Capital: Providence
Area: 1,545 sq mi; 4,002 sq km
Climate: Humid continental (moderated by Atlantic Ocean); fairly wet
Population: 1 million
Agriculture: Greenhouse and nursery products, turf, sweet corn, potatoes; dairy products; fish
Economic Activities: Costume jewelry and silverware, toys, machinery, textiles, electronics

Vermont

Capital: Montpelier
Area: 9,615 sq mi; 24,903 sq km
Climate: Humid continental; long, cold winters and short, warm summers; heavy snowfall in mountains
Population: 610,000
Agriculture: Apples, maple syrup and sugar; nursery and greenhouse products, vegetables, small fruits, hay; dairy products
Economic Activities: Electrical and electronic equipment, machine tools, furniture, scales, books, food processing, mining (granite, marble, limestone, slate), tourism

3 Assess/Reteach

Point out that the Northeast has one natural resource in abundance—forests. Ask students if they can name an industry that depended on forests in colonial times (*shipbuilding*). Have students refer to the agriculture and major industry descriptions and list all products or industries that depend on forests today. Guide them to include less obvious industries such as printing and maple syrup.

Resource Directory

Technology

Passport to the World CD-ROM This interactive CD-ROM allows students to explore each region of the world. Students view regional videos, take a photo tour, and explore a historical timeline. Students record their travels in an Explorer's Journal, and receive passport stamps when they pass regional quizzes.

REGIONAL DATABASE 603

Regional Database

Lesson Objectives

Gather, understand, and apply information about the southern United States.

Lesson Plan

1 Explore

Begin by having students use their map scales to assess the size of the South. Ask how many miles the South runs from its southernmost to northernmost points (*just over 900 miles*). Remind students that the nation's capital is located in the South.

2 Teach

Explain that all the states of the South share warm, humid climates. Ask students what two bodies of water border the southern states (*the Atlantic Ocean and the Gulf of Mexico*). Explain that weather systems developing in those waters bring much rain to the region. Ask what the combination of warm temperatures and rain is ideal for (*growing crops*). Point out that farming has always been important to the South; more recently, industry has boomed there.

3 Assess/Reteach

Tell students that farms and factories throughout the South have always been labor intensive

Ask them to draw conclusions about why certain industries have grown in the South.

The South (U.S.): Political

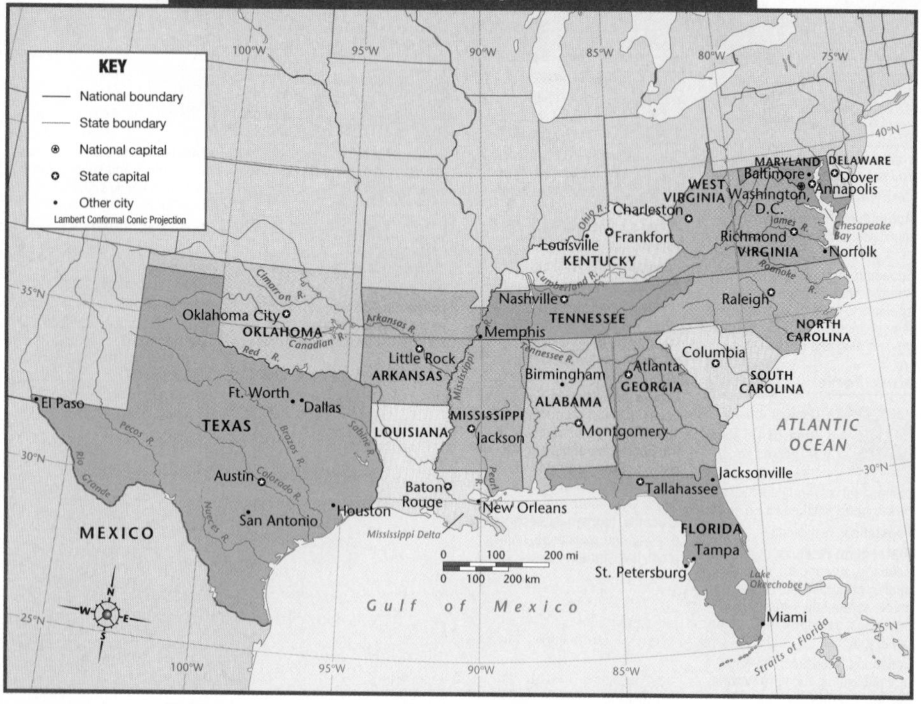

Alabama

Capital: Montgomery
Area: 52,423 sq mi; 135,775 sq km
Climate: Humid subtropical; short, mild winters and long, hot summers
Population: 4.4 million
Agriculture: Cotton, greenhouse and nursery products, peanuts, sweet potatoes; cattle, chickens; timber
Economic Activities: Pulp and paper, chemicals, electronics, clothing, textiles, mining (iron ore, limestone, coal), lumber and wood products, food processing, iron and steel

Arkansas

Capital: Little Rock
Area: 53,182 sq mi; 137,741 sq km
Climate: Mediterranean; mild, wet winters and long, hot summers; cooler and drier in north and west
Population: 2.7 million
Agriculture: Rice, soybeans, cotton, tomatoes, grapes, apples, peaches, wheat; chickens, cattle, hogs; timber
Economic Activities: Food processing, chemicals, lumber, paper, plastics, electric motors, furniture, auto parts, airplane parts, clothing, machinery, steel, tourism

Delaware

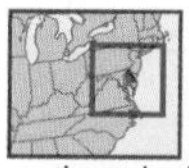

Capital: Dover
Area: 2,489 sq mi; 6,446 sq km
Climate: Humid continental; mild winters and hot, humid summers
Population: 780,000
Agriculture: Soybeans, potatoes, corn, mushrooms, lima beans, green peas, barley, cucumbers, wheat, corn, sorghum, nursery products; chickens, eggs
Economic Activities: Chemicals, tourism, auto assembly, food processing, transportation equipment, clothing

Florida

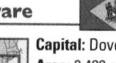

Capital: Tallahassee
Area: 65,758 sq mi; 170,313 sq km
Climate: Mostly humid subtropical; warm winters, hot summers; tropical in far south
Population: 16 million
Agriculture: Citrus fruits, vegetables, melons, nursery products, potatoes, sugarcane; chickens, cattle; fish
Economic Activities: Tourism, electrical, electronic, and transportation equipment, food processing, printing and publishing

Resource Directory

Other Print Resources

DK Atlas

Technology

Color Transparencies 37 The United States: South: Physical-Political Map; **42** The United States: Agricultural Region Map

Passport to the World CD-ROM This interactive CD-ROM allows students to explore each region of the world. Students view regional videos, take a photo tour, and explore a historical timeline. Students record their travels in an Explorer's Journal, and receive passport stamps when they pass regional quizzes.

Georgia

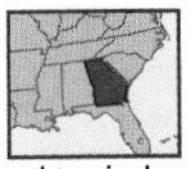

Capital: Atlanta
Area: 59,441 sq mi; 153,952 sq km
Climate: Humid subtropical; mild, humid winters and hot, humid summers; cooler in mountains
Population: 8.2 million
Agriculture: Peanuts, cotton, corn, tobacco, hay soybeans; cattle, hogs, chickens; timber
Economic Activities: Textiles, clothing, food processing, pulp and paper, transportation equipment, chemicals, printing and publishing, lumber

Kentucky

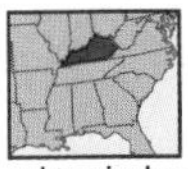

Capital: Frankfort
Area: 40,411 sq mi; 104,664 sq km
Climate: Humid subtropical; cool winters, warm or hot summers
Population: 4 million
Agriculture: Tobacco, corn, soybeans, hay; cattle, horses, hogs, chickens
Economic Activities: Transportation and industrial machinery, chemicals, clothing, printing and publishing, food processing, electrical and electronic equipment, mining (coal)

Louisiana

Capital: Baton Rouge
Area: 51,843 sq mi; 134,273 sq km
Climate: Humid subtropical; short, mild winters and long, hot, humid summers
Population: 4.5 million
Agriculture: Cotton, sugarcane, soybeans, rice, corn, sweet potatoes, pecans, sorghum; cattle; fish; timber
Economic Activities: Tourism, chemicals, food processing, transportation equipment, electronic equipment, petroleum and natural gas, lumber, pulp and paper, construction

Maryland

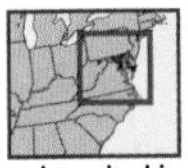

Capital: Annapolis
Area: 12,407 sq mi; 32,134 sq km
Climate: Humid subtropical in east; cool winters and hot, humid summers; continental in west, with colder winters and cooler summers
Population: 5.3 million
Agriculture: Greenhouse and nursery products, soybeans, corn, tobacco; chicken, dairy products; timber
Economic Activities: Electrical and electronic equipment, food processing, chemicals, printed materials, tourism, transportation equipment

Mississippi

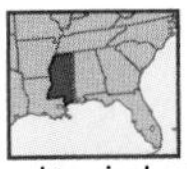

Capital: Jackson
Area: 48,434 sq mi; 125,444 sq km
Climate: Humid subtropical; mild winters and long, hot humid summers; cooler in highlands
Population: 2.8 million
Agriculture: Cotton, rice, soybeans, hay, corn; cattle, chickens; timber
Economic Activities: Transportation equipment, chemicals and plastics, food processing, furniture, lumber and wood products, electrical machinery

North Carolina

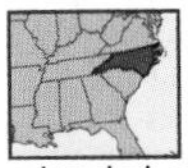

Capital: Raleigh
Area: 53,821 sq mi; 139,396 sq km
Climate: Humid subtropical; cool winters, hot summers; colder in mountains
Population: 8 million
Agriculture: Tobacco, greenhouse and nursery products, cotton, soybeans, corn, grains, wheat, peanuts, sweet potatoes; turkeys, hogs, chickens, eggs, cattle; fish, timber;
Economic Activities: Food processing, chemicals, textiles, industrial machinery and equipment, electrical and electronic equipment, furniture, tobacco products, pulp and paper, tourism

Oklahoma

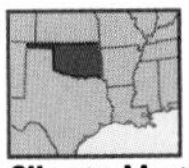

Capital: Oklahoma City
Area: 69,903 sq mi; 181,048 sq km
Climate: Mostly humid subtropical; moderate, short winters and very hot, long summers; dry subtropical in west
Population: 3.4 million
Agriculture: Wheat, cotton, hay, peanuts, grain sorghum, soybeans, corn, pecans; cattle, hogs, chickens
Economic Activities: Machinery, transportation equipment, food processing, metal products, mining (coal), petroleum and natural gas, tourism

South Carolina

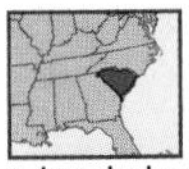

Capital: Columbia
Area: 32,007 sq mi; 82,898 sq km
Climate: Humid subtropical; mild winters, hot summers
Population: 4 million
Agriculture: Tobacco, greenhouse and nursery products, cotton, soybeans, corn, hay, wheat, peaches, tomatoes; chickens, eggs, turkeys; timber
Economic Activities: Textiles, tourism, chemicals, machinery and other metal products, clothing

Tennessee

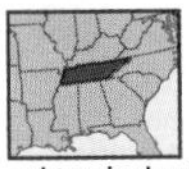

Capital: Nashville
Area: 42,146 sq mi; 109,158 sq km
Climate: Humid subtropical; mild winters, hot summers, and abundant rain; colder in mountains
Population: 5.7 million
Agriculture: Tobacco, cotton, soybeans, grain, corn; cattle, chickens, eggs, hogs; timber
Economic Activities: Chemicals, food processing, transportation equipment, industrial machinery and equipment, metal products, rubber and plastic products, pulp and paper, printing and publishing

Texas

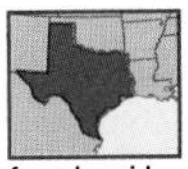

Capital: Austin
Area: 268,601 sq mi; 695,674 sq km
Climate: Varies from humid subtropical in east to semiarid in central area to arid in far west; mostly mild winters and hot summers
Population: 20.8 million
Agriculture: Cotton, wheat and other grains, vegetable, citrus and other fruits, greenhouse and nursery products, pecans, peanuts; cattle, chickens, sheep, hogs, dairy products, eggs; fish; timber
Economic Activities: Industrial machinery and equipment, food processing, electrical and electronic equipment, chemicals, clothing, petroleum and natural gas

Virginia

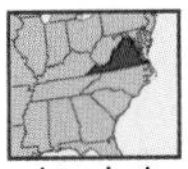

Capital: Richmond
Area: 42,769 sq mi; 110,771 sq km
Climate: Humid subtropical; mild, wet winters and hot, mostly humid summers; coldest in northwest
Population: 7 million
Agriculture: Tobacco, corn, soybeans, winter wheat, peanuts, cotton; chickens, dairy products, cattle, hogs; fish; timber
Economic Activities: Food processing, transportation equipment, printing, textiles, electrical and electronic equipment, industrial machinery and equipment, lumber and wood products, chemicals, rubber and plastics, furniture

West Virginia

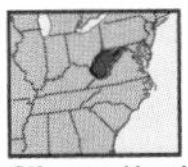

Capital: Charleston
Area: 24,231 sq mi; 62,758 sq km
Climate: Humid continental; cold, humid winters and warm, humid summers
Population: 1.8 million
Agriculture: Apples, peaches, hay, tobacco, corn, wheat, oats; dairy products, eggs, cattle, chickens, turkeys
Economic Activities: Machinery, plastic and hardwood products, metal products, chemicals, aluminum, automotive parts, steel, mining (coal)

Portfolio Assessment

Overview

The following activities help students explore, collect, and arrange the information they find in the Regional Database. You may wish to have students add these activities to a portfolio of information about the countries of the world. To assess student work, refer to the generic rubrics in the Assessment Handbook.

Main Activity

- Point out to students that the South has always had many diverse influences on its culture, foods and place names. The first European settlers borrowed heavily from the Native Americans who already lived there, and continued to do so from the African American slaves who worked for them. Hispanic influence has always been strong in parts of the South.
- Have groups of students select a southern state to explore. Using library materials or the Internet, students should research the cultural influences on the state they chose. They can compile their results into the form of an illustrated magazine article. When completed, all articles may be combined into a magazine.

Additional Activity

Students can include a map of their state with their article. They will draw the outline of the state, and then include only those cities or geographical features that have non-English place names. Next to the place names, they should include the language or origin for that name.

Resource Directory

Other Print Resources

Assessment Handbook Generic Rubrics 16 and 31

REGIONAL DATABASE 605

Regional Database

Lesson Objectives

Gather, understand, and apply information about the midwestern United States.

Lesson Plan

1 Explore

Ask students, before looking at the descriptions of the Midwest, to volunteer descriptions of their own from memory or from prior learning. Then, have them look at the map. Ask what geographical feature, prominent in the Northeast and South, is lacking in the Midwest (*ocean coastlines*).

2 Teach

Draw students' attention to the Great Plains on their maps. Explain that this is a huge region of flat grasslands on which grains are grown and cattle raised. Tell students that flat plains characterize much of the Midwest. Remind students that this region has historically been known as "the nation's breadbasket." Ask students to speculate on why it gained this name (*midwestern farms provide most of the nation's grains*).

The Midwest (U.S): Political

Illinois

Capital: Springfield
Area: 57,918 sq mi; 150,007 sq km
Climate: Humid continental; cold, snowy winters and hot summers
Population: 12.4 million
Agriculture: Corn, soybeans, wheat, sorghum, hay; hogs, cattle, dairy products, chickens
Economic Activities: Machinery, electrical and electronic equipment, primary metals (steel) and metal products, chemical products, printing and publishing, food processing, construction, mining (coal)

Indiana

Capital: Indianapolis
Area: 36,420 sq mi; 94,327 sq km
Climate: Humid continental; cool winters and long, warm summers; warmer; wetter in far south
Population: 6.1 million
Agriculture: Corn, soybeans, wheat, greenhouse and nursery products, tomatoes and other vegetables, popcorn, fruit, hay, tobacco, mint; hogs, chickens, cattle
Economic Activities: Primary metals (steel), transportation equipment, motor vehicles and equipment, industrial machinery and equipment, food processing, electrical and electronic equipment, pharmaceuticals

Iowa

Capital: Des Moines
Area: 56,276 sq mi; 145,754 sq km
Climate: Humid continental; cold winters and warm, moist summers
Population: 2.9 million
Agriculture: Corn, soybeans, oats, hay; hogs, chickens, cattle, dairy products
Economic Activities: Construction, food processing, tires, farm machinery, electronic equipment, appliances, furniture, chemicals, fertilizers, auto parts

Kansas

Capital: Topeka
Area: 82,282 sq mi; 213,110 sq km
Climate: Humid continental; cold winters, hot summers; drier in west
Population: 2.7 million
Agriculture: Wheat, sorghum, corn, hay, soybeans, sunflowers; cattle, hogs, dairy products
Economic Activities: Transportation equipment, machinery and computer equipment, food processing, printing and publishing, chemicals, natural gas, rubber and plastic products, clothing

Resource Directory

Other Print Resources

DK Atlas

Technology

Color Transparencies 38 The United States: Midwest: Physical-Political Map; **42** The United States: Agricultural Regions Map

Passport to the World CD-ROM This interactive CD-ROM allows students to explore each region of the world. Students view regional videos, take a photo tour, and explore a historical timeline. Students record their travels in an Explorer's Journal, and receive passport stamps when they pass regional quizzes.

Michigan

Capital: Lansing
Area: 96,810 sq mi; 250,736 sq km
Climate: Humid continental (moderated by Great Lakes); snowy, cold winters and moist, mild to hot summers
Population: 9.9 million
Agriculture: Corn, wheat, soybeans, dry beans, hay, potatoes, sweet corn, apples, cherries, sugar beets, blueberries, cucumbers, grapes; cattle, hogs, chickens, dairy products
Economic Activities: Automobiles, transportation equipment, machinery, metal products, food processing, plastics, pharmaceuticals, furniture, tourism, cement, mining (iron ore, limestone)

Minnesota

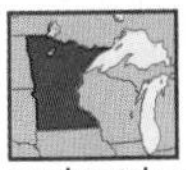

Capital: Saint Paul
Area: 86,943 sq mi; 225,182 sq km
Climate: Humid continental; cold winters, hot summers; dry in far west
Population: 4.9 million
Agriculture: Corn, soybeans, wheat, sugar beets, hay, barley, potatoes, sunflowers; chickens, turkeys, hogs, cattle, dairy products, eggs
Economic Activities: Mining (iron ore), food processing, chemical and paper products, industrial machinery, electrical and electronic equipment, computers, printing and publishing, scientific and medical instruments, metal products, forest products, tourism

Missouri

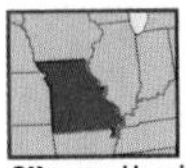

Capital: Jefferson City
Area: 69,709 sq mi; 180,546 sq km
Climate: Humid continental; mostly cold winters and hot summers
Population: 5.6 million
Agriculture: Soybeans, corn, wheat, hay, cotton, sorghum; cattle, hogs, dairy products, chickens, turkeys, eggs
Economic Activities: Transportation equipment, food processing, electrical and electronic equipment, chemicals, printing and publishing, tourism

Nebraska

Capital: Lincoln
Area: 77,358 sq mi; 200,356 sq km
Climate: Continental; cold winters, hot summers; dry in northwest
Population: 1.7 million
Agriculture: Corn, sorghum, soybeans, hay, wheat, dry beans, oats, potatoes, sugar beets; cattle, hogs, chickens
Economic Activities: Food processing, industrial machinery, printed materials, electrical and electronic equipment, mining (sand and gravel, limestone), metal products, transportation equipment

North Dakota

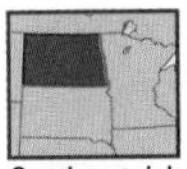

Capital: Bismarck
Area: 70,704 sq mi; 183,123 sq km
Climate: Continental; long, cold winters and hot summers; dry in west
Population: 640,000
Agriculture: Wheat, barley, flaxseed, oats, potatoes, dry beans, honey, soybeans, sugar beets, sunflowers, hay; cattle
Economic Activities: Petroleum and natural gas, mining (coal), food processing, farm equipment, metal products, electronic equipment

Ohio

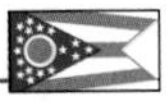

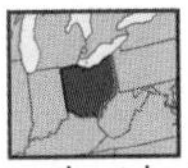

Capital: Columbus
Area: 44,828 sq mi; 116,104 sq km
Climate: Humid continental; mild to cold winters, warm to hot summers
Population: 11.3 million
Agriculture: Corn, hay, winter wheat, oats, soybeans, greenhouse and nursery products; dairy products, cattle, hogs, chickens
Economic Activities: Transportation equipment, machinery, steel and aluminum, metal products, rubber and plastics, food processing

South Dakota

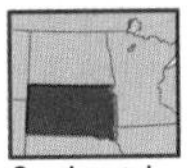

Capital: Pierre
Area: 77,121 sq mi; 199,743 sq km
Climate: Continental; cold winters, hot summers; low humidity; dry in west
Population: 750,000
Agriculture: Corn, soybeans, oats, wheat, sunflowers, sorghum; cattle, hogs, sheep, dairy products
Economic Activities: Food processing, machinery, electrical and electronic equipment, mining (gold), clothing

Wisconsin

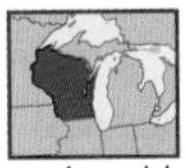

Capital: Madison
Area: 65,503 sq mi; 169,652 sq km
Climate: Humid continental; long, cold winters and short, warm summers (moderated by Great Lakes)
Population: 5.4 million
Agriculture: Corn, hay, soybeans, potatoes, cranberries, sweet corn, peas, oats, snap beans; cattle, dairy products, hogs, chickens
Economic Activities: Food processing, motor vehicles and equipment, paper products, medical instruments and supplies, printing, plastics

3 Assess/Reteach

Ask students to read the agriculture descriptions for the states of the Midwest. Ask them which two products are grown most commonly in the region (*corn, soybeans*). Have students make a list of products that are made from corn and soybeans.

REGIONAL DATABASE 607

Regional Database

Lesson Objectives

Gather, understand, and apply information about the western United States.

Lesson Plan

1 Explore

Have students volunteer names of states that make up the western United States. Ask which two western states do not border any others (*Alaska, Hawaii*). Point out that the part of this region lying in the contiguous United States stretches about 1,200 miles from north to south, and is the only region to border both Mexico and Canada.

2 Teach

Tell students that the West is a region of great contrasts. Explain that while most of the western states share an arid or semiarid climate, Hawaii's climate is tropical with rain forests, and northern Alaska is tundra. Point out that most of the West receives little rain; however, the northwestern states are known for continuous rainfall, and Hawaii includes the wettest spot on the Earth. Finally, explain that almost every kind of physical feature can be found in the West.

The West (U.S.): Political

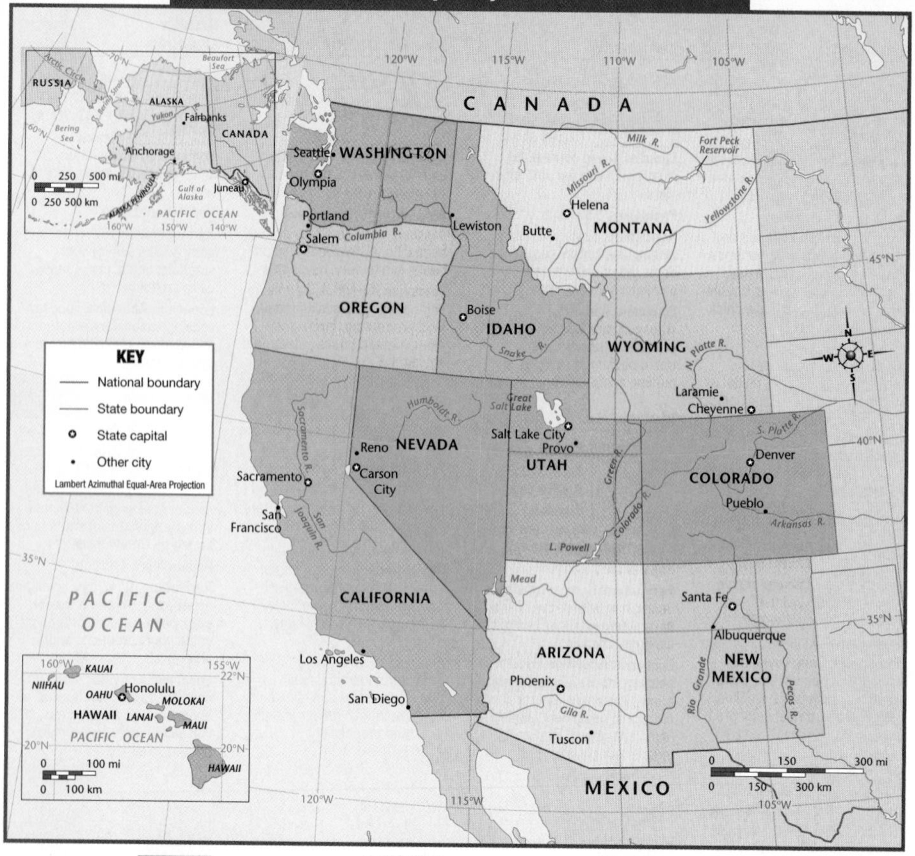

Alaska

Capital: Juneau
Area: 656,425 sq mi; 1,700,134 sq km
Climate: Maritime in southeast and southwest (moist and mild); much colder and drier in west; continental in central area; Arctic in north, with extremely cold winters and cool summers
Population: 630,000
Agriculture: Greenhouse products, barley, oats, hay, potatoes, lettuce; fish
Economic Activities: Petroleum, tourism, fish products, mining (zinc, lead, gold), lumber and pulp, transportation equipment, furs

Arizona

Capital: Phoenix
Area: 114,006 sq mi; 295,274 sq km
Climate: Semiarid; mild winters and searing hot summers in south; cold winters and mostly cool summers in the high plateau of the north
Population: 5.1 million
Agriculture: Cotton, lettuce, cantaloupe, cauliflower, broccoli, sorghum, barley, corn, wheat, citrus fruits; cattle
Economic Activities: Electrical and electronic equipment, printing and publishing, food processing, metal products, tourism, mining (copper)

California

Capital: Sacramento
Area: 163,707 sq mi; 423,999
Climate: Marine west coast along northern coast; semiarid in much of south, but extremely arid in desert areas; mostly cool to mild winters and warm to hot summers; cold, snowy winters in mountains
Population: 32.3 million
Agriculture: Grapes, cotton, flowers, citrus fruits, rice, nursery products, hay, tomatoes, lettuce, strawberries, almonds, asparagus; dairy products, cattle, sheep, chickens, eggs; fish; timber
Economic Activities: Tourism, clothing, electrical and electronic equipment, computers, food processing, industrial machinery, transportation equipment and instruments, petroleum

608 REGIONAL DATABASE

Resource Directory

Other Print Resources

DK Atlas

Technology

Color Transparencies 39 The United States: West: Physical-Political Map

Passport to the World CD-ROM This interactive CD-ROM allows students to explore each region of the world. Students view regional videos, take a photo tour, and explore a historical timeline. Students record their travels in an Explorer's Journal, and receive passport stamps when they pass regional quizzes.

Colorado

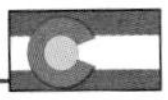

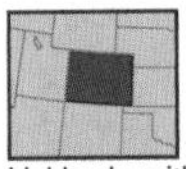

Capital: Denver
Area: 104,100 sq mi; 269,618 sq km
Climate: Mostly highlands, with varying temperatures and precipitation; alpine conditions in high mountains; cold, dry winters and hot, dry summers in eastern plains
Population: 4.3 million
Agriculture: Corn, wheat, hay, sugar beets, barley, potatoes, apples, peaches, pears, dry beans, sorghum, onions, oats, sunflowers; cattle, sheep, hogs, chickens
Economic Activities: Computer equipment and instruments, food processing, machinery, aerospace products, construction, tourism, natural gas

Hawaii

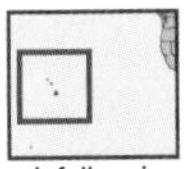

Capital: Honolulu
Area: 10,932 sq mi; 28,314 sq km
Climate: Tropical; rainfall varies greatly; snow on highest peaks in winter
Population: 1.2 million
Agriculture: Sugar cane, pineapples, macadamia nuts, fruits, coffee, vegetables, flowers; cattle; fish
Economic Activities: Tourism, food processing, clothing, printing and publishing

Idaho

Capital: Boise
Area: 83,574 sq mi; 216,456 sq km
Climate: Semiarid; cold winters, hot summers; cooler and wetter in mountains
Population: 1.3 million
Agriculture: Potatoes, wheat, peas, dry beans, sugar beets, alfalfa seeds, lentils, hops, barley, plums and prunes, mint, onions, corn, cherries, apples, hay; cattle, chickens; timber
Economic Activities: Electronic components, computer equipment, food processing, tourism, lumber and wood products, chemical products, metal products, machinery, mining (phosphate rock, gold)

Montana

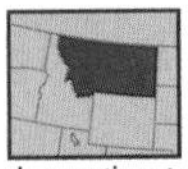

Capital: Helena
Area: 147,046 sq mi; 380,848 sq km
Climate: Mostly dry continental; cold winters, hot summers; milder winters, cooler summers, and more precipitation in west
Population: 900,000
Agriculture: Wheat, barley, sugar beets, hay, oats; cattle, sheep
Economic Activities: Food processing, wood and paper products, mining (copper, gold), printing and publishing, tourism, coal and petroleum

Nevada

Capital: Carson City
Area: 110,567 sq mi; 286,367 sq km
Climate: Mostly arid; mild winters and extremely hot summers in south; damper and cooler in mountains
Population: 2 million
Agriculture: Hay, alfalfa seeds, potatoes, onions, garlic, barley, wheat; cattle, dairy products
Economic Activities: Gaming, tourism, mining (gold, copper, silver), food processing, plastics, chemicals, aerospace products, printing and publishing, irrigation equipment

New Mexico

Capital: Santa Fe
Area: 121,593 sq mi; 314,925 sq km
Climate: Semiarid; mostly mild, sunny, and dry; cooler and wetter in mountains
Population: 1.8 million
Agriculture: Hay, onions, chiles, greenhouse and nursery products, pecans, cotton; cattle, dairy products, chickens
Economic Activities: Mining (coal, copper), natural gas, petroleum, food processing, machinery, clothing, lumber, printing and publishing, transportation equipment, electronic equipment

Oregon

Capital: Salem
Area: 98,386 sq mi; 254,819 sq km
Climate: Mostly marine west coast; mild winters and cool summers; highland in mountains, with severe winters; semiarid in east, with cold winters and warm summers
Population: 3.4 million
Agriculture: Greenhouse and nursery products, hay, wheat, grass seed, potatoes, onions, pears, mint; cattle, dairy products, chickens; timber
Economic Activities: Electrical and electronic equipment, lumber and wood products, metals, transportation equipment, food processing, pulp and paper, construction

Utah

Capital: Salt Lake City
Area: 84,904 sq mi; 219,901 sq km
Climate: Arid; mild, dry winters and hot, dry summers; colder winters in north; wetter and colder in mountains
Population: 2.2 million
Agriculture: Hay, corn, wheat, barley, apples, potatoes, cherries, onions, peaches, pears; cattle, dairy products, poultry, eggs
Economic Activities: Medical instruments, electronic components, food processing, metal products, transportation equipment, steel and copper

Washington

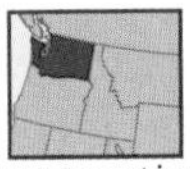

Capital: Olympia
Area: 71,303 sq mi; 184,674 sq km
Climate: Marine west coast in west, with mild, wet winters and cool summers; semiarid in east with cold winters and hot summers
Population: 5.6 million
Agriculture: Apples, potatoes, wheat, barley, hay, hops, mint, peas, corn; livestock, dairy products; fish; timber
Economic Activities: Transportation equipment, computer software, pulp and paper, lumber and plywood, aluminum, tourism

Wyoming

Capital: Chayenne
Area: 97,818 sq mi; 253,348 sq km
Climate: Continental; long, cold winters, and warm summers, little precipitation
Population: 490,000
Agriculture: Wheat, beans, barley, oats, sugar beets, hay; cattle, sheep
Economic Activities: Mining (coal), petroleum, natural gas, tourism, chemicals, wood products, food processing

3 Assess/Reteach

Write these words on the chalkboard: *Oceans*, *Coasts*, *Rivers*, *Lakes*, *Mountains*, *Deserts*, *Canyons*, *Basins*, and *Islands*. Ask students to write down these headings on a sheet of paper. Using the maps from their books, students should list states under each heading that have these features.

REGIONAL DATABASE 609

Regional Database

Lesson Objectives

Gather, understand, and apply information about the provinces of Canada.

Lesson Plan

1 Explore

Tell students they can make predictions about some of Canada's economic activities just by looking at the map. Ask them to predict where commercial fishing might be important (*British Columbia, New Brunswick, Newfoundland, Nova Scotia, Prince Edward Island*). Then, ask where commercial farming might be important (*Alberta, Manitoba, Ontario, Quebec, Saskatchewan*). Have students give reasons for their predictions.

2 Teach

Tell students they will test some of their predictions. Have them skim the data below the map to find out which provinces have fishing and farming and which have farming only.

3 Assess/Reteach

Remind students that commercial farming is a major economic activity in Canada. Ask students which factors related to physical geography would influence where commercial farming would be most likely to take place. *(Answers may vary, but should include climate, terrain, and soil quality.)*

Canada: Political

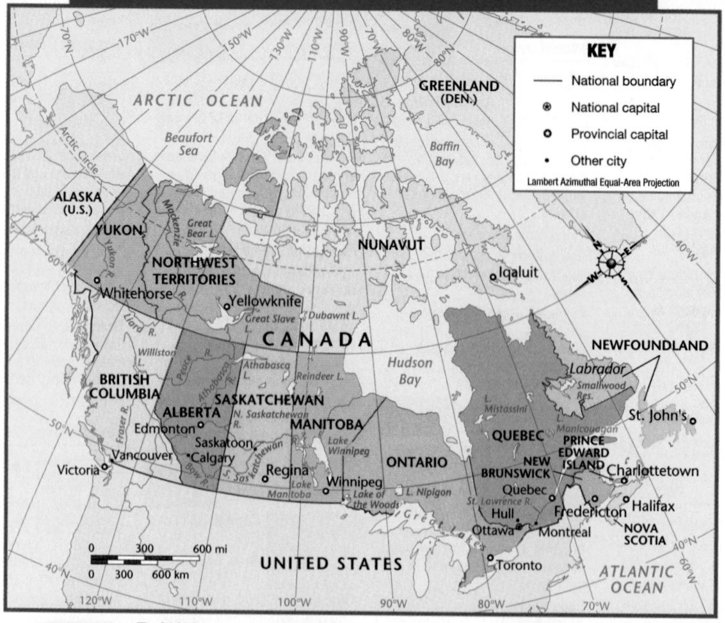

Alberta

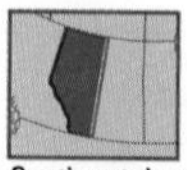

Capital: Edmonton
Area: 255,541 sq mi; 661,848 sq km
Climate: Continental; extremely cold winters and warm summers
Population: 3 million
Agriculture: Grains, oilseeds, wheat; cattle, hogs, dairy products, poultry; timber
Economic Activities: Food processing, chemicals, petroleum, refining, construction, paper products, wood products, machinery, metal products, electrical and electronic equipment

British Columbia

Capital: Victoria
Area: 364,764 sq mi; 944,735 sq km
Climate: Mostly continental; colder in mountains; marine west coast along coast, with mild temperatures and much rain
Population: 4.1 million
Agriculture: Peas, tomatoes, apples, cherries, plums, raspberries, strawberries, flowers; dairy products, poultry, cattle; fish, timber;
Economic Activities: Wood processing, pulp and paper, mining (copper, zinc, gold), food processing, tourism, petroleum and coal products, metal products, printed materials, chemicals

Manitoba

Capital: Winnipeg
Area: 250,116 sq mi; 647,797 sq km
Climate: Continental; extremely cold winters, warm summers
Population: 1.1 million
Agriculture: Wheat, canola, flax; hogs, cattle, dairy products
Economic Activities: Food processing, machinery, transportation equipment, printing and publishing, mining (nickel, copper, gold)

New Brunswick

Capital: Fredericton
Area: 28,150 sq mi; 72,908 sq km
Climate: Humid continental; maritime along coasts
Population: 760,000
Agriculture: Potatoes; livestock, poultry, dairy products; fish; timber
Economic Activities: Mining (zinc, lead), paper products, food processing, lumber, metal products

Newfoundland and Labrador

Capital: Saint John's
Area: 156,453 sq mi; 405,212 sq km
Climate: Ranges from subarctic in Labrador to humid continental in Newfoundland; heavy winter snowfalls common
Population: 540,000
Agriculture: Vegetables; dairy products, poultry; fish
Economic Activities: Mining (iron ore), food processing, newsprint

Northwest Territories

Capital: Yellowknife
Area: 519,734 sq mi; 1,346,106 sq km
Climate: Subarctic; extremely cold winters and relatively warm, but short, summers; dry
Population: 40,000
Agriculture: Very limited; some vegetables, dairy products, cattle
Economic Activities: Mining (zinc, gold, lead, silver), petroleum and natural gas, fur trapping

Resource Directory

Other Print Resources

DK Atlas

Technology

Color Transparencies 31 Canada: Physical-Political Map; **32** Canada: Political Map

Passport to the World CD-ROM This interactive CD-ROM allows students to explore each region of the world. Students view regional videos, take a photo tour, and explore a historical timeline. Students record their travels in an Explorer's Journal, and receive passport stamps when they pass regional quizzes.

Nova Scotia

Capital: Halifax
Area: 21,345 sq mi; 55,284 sq km
Climate: Humid continental; moderated by cool North Atlantic Ocean
Population: 940,000
Agriculture: Blueberries, vegetables; dairy products, poultry, livestock; fish
Economic Activities: Food processing, pulp and paper products, transportation equipment, iron and steel

Nunavut

Capital: Iqaluit
Area: 808,184 sq mi; 2,093,190 sq km
Climate: Subarctic on mainland, with continuous permafrost; arctic on northernmost islands, with no true summer; dry throughout; polar desert in northwest
Population: 30,000
Agriculture: Fish
Economic Activities: Mining (copper, lead, silver, zinc), tourism, hunting and trapping, arts and crafts products

Ontario

Capital: Toronto
Area: 415,598 sq mi; 1,076,395 sq km
Climate: Humid continental in south; subarctic in far north
Population: 11.7 million
Agriculture: Vegetables, grains, oilseeds; dairy products, livestock, poultry; timber
Economic Activities: Food processing, electrical and electronic equipment, chemicals, mining (nickel, gold, copper, zinc), metal products, transportation equipment, paper products, cement, construction

Prince Edward Island

Capital: Charlottetown
Area: 2,185 sq mi; 5,660 sq km
Climate: Humid continental; moderated by cool North Atlantic Ocean
Population: 140,000
Agriculture: Potatoes, other vegetables, tobacco; diary products, livestock; fish
Economic Activities: Food processing, tourism, fertilizer, commercial printed materials

Quebec

Capital: Quebec
Area: 595,391 sq mi; 1,542,056 sq km
Climate: Mostly continental, with severely cold winters and warm, humid summers; subarctic in north
Population: 7.4 million
Agriculture: Vegetables, grains; dairy products, livestock, poultry; timber
Economic Activities: Pulp and paper, transportation equipment, food processing, mining (gold, copper, zinc, asbestos), electrical and electronic equipment, chemicals, wood products, metal products

Saskatchewan

Capital: Regina
Area: 251,366 sq mi; 651,036 sq km
Climate: Continental; cold winters, warm to hot summers
Population: 1 million
Agriculture: Wheat, barley, oilseeds; cattle, hogs, dairy products
Economic Activities: Food processing, mining (potash, uranium, coal), petroleum, construction, chemicals, machinery, electrical and electronic equipment, printing and publishing, metal products

Yukon Territory

Capital: Whitehorse
Area: 186,272 sq mi; 482,443 sq km
Climate: Mostly subarctic; extremely cold winters and warm summers; dry; arctic in extreme north and mountains
Population: 30,000
Agriculture: Very limited; some potatoes, animal feed crops, and livestock
Economic Activities: Mining (gold, zinc, lead, silver), tourism

Resource Directory

Other Print Resources

Assessment Handbook Generic Rubrics 19 and 27

Portfolio Assessment

Overview

The following activities help students explore, collect, and arrange the information they find in the Regional Database. You may wish to have students add this activity to a portfolio of information about the countries of the world. To assess student work, refer to the generic rubrics in the Assessment Handbook.

Main Activity

Explain that Canada is a vast country that supports a variety of economic activities. Many of these industries have a great influence on the region of the country in which they are found.

- Have students do research to identify the main economic activities in Canada. They may use the Internet or various library resources, including atlases.
- Next, have students choose one economic activity and research how it has made an impact on Canada or on the region within the country where it is most often found.
- Ask students to write a report on the economic activity they have chosen. Their report should include the location or locations within Canada where this industry is most often found, and at least two examples of how it has made an impact on Canada.

Additional Activity

Students can create a chart showing the major imports and exports of Canada. Charts can include such facts as which countries Canada exports the most goods to, and which countries they import goods from.

Regional Database

Lesson Objectives

Gather, understand, and apply information about Mexico.

Lesson Plan

1 Explore

Ask students which country Mexico shares the largest border with (*the United States*). Remind them that Mexico is located on the continent of North America. Ask them to name other countries of North America.

2 Teach

Ask volunteers to read some of the descriptions of Mexico. Tell students that *mestizo* is a Spanish word, used to describe descendants of Spanish settlers and Native Americans. Explain that they make up about 60% of Mexico's total population. Ask students if they think the mestizo population in Mexico is alike or different from populations of ethnic groups in the United States today.

3 Assess/Reteach

Write *Similar to the United States* on the chalkboard. Prompt students to first list geographic features from the map or description of Mexico. (*both countries have large mountain ranges; both have dense forests and extensive coasts*). Then, have them list cultural features (*large non-white populations; both have Christianity as their main religion*).

Mexico: Political

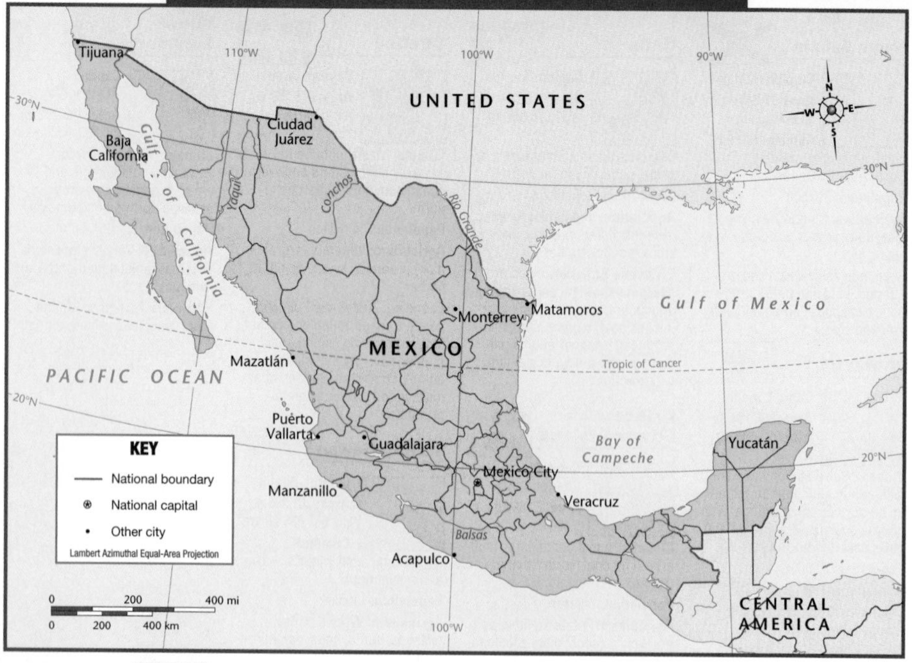

Mexico

Capital: Mexico City
Area: 761,632 sq mi; 1,972,550 sq km
Climate: Hot and dry north; temperate central; tropical south, with rainy and dry seasons
Population: 100.3 million
Major Ethnic Groups: Mestizo, European, Native American groups
Major Religions: Christianity
Government: Federal Republic
Currency: 1 New Mexican peso (Mex $) = 100 centavos
Leading Exports: Crude oil, oil products, coffee, and silver
Major Languages: Spanish and Mayan dialects

Resource Directory

Other Print Resources

DK Atlas

Technology

Color Transparencies 60 Mexico: Physical-Political Map; **61** Mexico: Political Map

Passport to the World CD-ROM This interactive CD-ROM allows students to explore each region of the world. Students view regional videos, take a photo tour, and explore a historical timeline. Students record their travels in an Explorer's Journal, and receive passport stamps when they pass regional quizzes.

612 REGIONAL DATABASE

Central America: Political

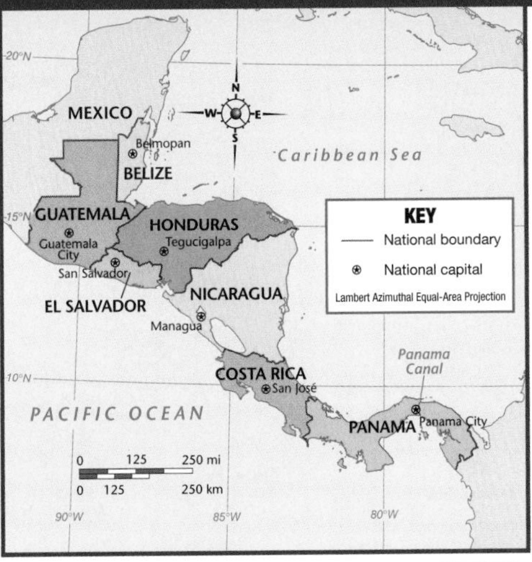

Belize

Capital: Belmopan
Area: 8,865 sq mi; 22,960 sq km
Climate: Subtropical; long rainy season
Population: 249,000
Major Ethnic Groups: African or part African; Native American, mainly Carib and Maya
Major Religions: Christianity
Government: Parliamentary democracy
Currency: 1 Belizean dollar (Bz $) = 100 cents
Leading Exports: Sugar, citrus fruits, bananas, and clothing
Major Languages: English (official), Spanish, Maya, and Garifuna

Costa Rica

Capital: San José
Area: 19,730 sq mi; 51,100 sq km
Climate: Tropical along coast; mild in interior; long rainy season
Population: 3.7 million
Major Ethnic Groups: European, mestizo
Major Religions: Christianity
Government: Democratic republic
Currency: 1 Costa Rican colon (C) = 100 centimos
Leading Exports: Coffee, bananas, textiles, and sugar
Major Languages: Spanish and English

El Salvador

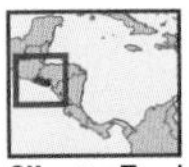

Capital: San Salvador
Area: 8,124 sq mi; 21,040 sq km
Climate: Tropical; very hot along coastal plain but cooler in mountains; rainy summers and dry winters
Population: 6.1 million
Major Ethnic Groups: Mestizo (mix of European with Maya and Nahuatl)
Major Religions: Christianity
Government: Republic
Currency: 1 Salvadoran colon (C) = 100 centavos
Leading Exports: Coffee, sugar cane, and shrimp
Major Languages: Spanish and Nahua

Guatemala

Capital: Guatemala
Area: 42,044 sq mi; 108,890 sq km
Climate: Ranges from hot and humid at coast to cold in mountains; rainy summers and dry winters
Population: 12.6 million
Major Ethnic Groups: Mestizo (mix of European and Native American called Ladino), Maya
Major Religions: Christianity, traditional Mayan
Government: Constitutional democratic republic
Currency: 1 quetzal (Q) = 100 centavos
Leading Exports: Coffee, sugar, bananas, cardamom, and beef
Major Languages: Spanish, Quiche, Cakchiquel, Kekchi, and various languages and dialects

Honduras

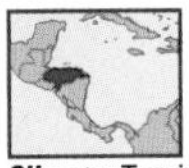

Capital: Tegucigalpa
Area: 43,280 sq mi; 112,090 sq km
Climate: Tropical; hot, humid coastal lowlands; rainy summers, dry winters
Population: 6.2 million
Major Ethnic Groups: Mestizo
Major Religions: Christianity
Government: Democratic constitutional republic
Currency: 1 lempira (L) = 100 centavos
Leading Exports: Bananas, coffee, shrimp, lobsters, and minerals
Major Languages: Spanish and various dialects

Nicaragua

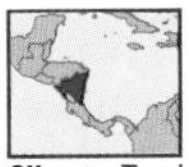

Capital: Managua
Area: 50,000 sq mi; 129,494 sq km
Climate: Tropical; hottest at coasts; rainy summers
Population: 4.8 million
Major Ethnic Groups: Mestizo
Major Religions: Christianity
Government: Republic
Currency: 1 gold cordoba (C$) = 100 centavos
Leading Exports: Meat, coffee, cotton, sugar, seafood, and gold
Major Languages: Spanish (official), English, and various languages

Panama

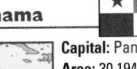

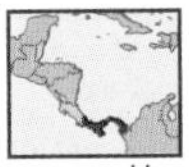

Capital: Panama
Area: 30,194 sq mi; 78,200 sq km
Climate: Tropical; warm and humid
Population: 2.8 million
Major Ethnic Groups: Mestizo, mixed European and African
Major Religions: Christianity
Government: Constitutional democracy
Currency: 1 balboa (B) = 100 centesimos
Leading Exports: Bananas, shrimp, sugar, clothing, and coffee
Major Languages: Spanish (official) and English

Lesson Objectives

Gather, understand, and apply information about the countries of Central America.

Lesson Plan

1 Explore

Refer to the political map of Central America. Remind students that this region, along with the islands of the Caribbean, the United States, and Canada, makes up the continent of North America. Have volunteers list the countries of this region.

2 Teach

Point out that Central America is a narrow piece of land connecting the continents of North and South America. It also separates the Pacific Ocean from the Caribbean Sea.

3 Assess/Reteach

Have a volunteer read the leading exports entries for several countries. As the volunteer reads, other students should note which kinds of exports appear most frequently. Then, ask students to make a connection between the climate of Central America (*Tropical, subtropical, rainy*) and the products that are grown there (*sugar, coffee, bananas, etc.*)

Resource Directory

Technology

Color Transparencies 63 Central America and the Caribbean: Political Map

Regional Database

Lesson Objectives

Gather, understand, and apply information about the countries of the Caribbean.

Lesson Plan

1 Explore

Refer to the political map of the Caribbean. Remind students that this region, along with Central America, the United States, and Canada, makes up the continent of North America. Have volunteers list the countries of this region.

2 Teach

Explain that the Caribbean includes many independent nations as well as islands that are affiliated with other countries (*Puerto Rico is a commonwealth of the United States; Martinique is a department of France, etc.*) Ask students why they think many islands of the region have ties to the United States and European nations.

3 Assess/Reteach

Have a volunteer read the leading exports entries for several countries. As the volunteer reads, other students should note which kinds of exports appear most frequently. Then, ask students to make a connection between the climate of the Caribbean (*Tropical, subtropical, rainy*) and the products that are grown there (*sugar, coffee, bananas, etc.*)

The Caribbean: Political

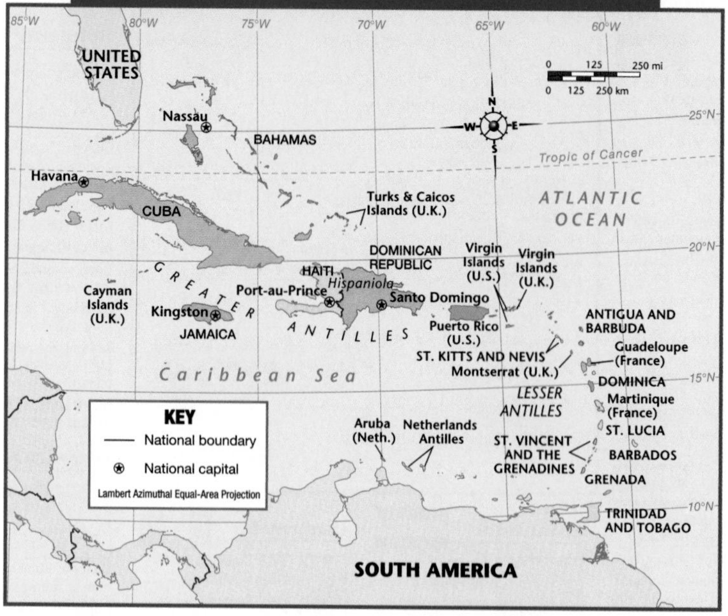

Antigua and Barbuda

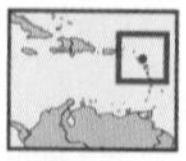

Capital: Saint John's
Area: 170 sq mi; 440 sq km
Climate: Tropical; dry
Population: 66,000
Major Ethnic Groups: African
Major Religions: Christianity
Government: Constitutional monarchy with Westminster-style parliament
Currency: 1 East Caribbean dollar (EC$) = 100 cents
Leading Exports: Petroleum products and manufactures
Major Languages: English (official) and various dialects

Bahamas

Capital: Nassau
Area: 5,382 sq mi; 13,940 sq km
Climate: Subtropical
Population: 295,000
Major Ethnic Groups: African
Major Religions: Christianity
Government: Constitutional parliamentary democracy
Currency: 1 Bahamian dollar (B$) = 100 cents
Leading Exports: Pharmaceuticals, cement, rum, and crawfish
Major Languages: English and Creole

Barbados

Capital: Bridgetown
Area: 166 sq mi; 430 sq km
Climate: Tropical; rainy season
Population: 275,000
Major Ethnic Groups: African
Major Religions: Christianity
Government: Parliamentary democracy, independent sovereign state within the Commonwealth
Currency: 1 Barbadian dollar (Bds$) = 100 cents
Leading Exports: Sugar and molasses, and rum
Major Languages: English

Cuba

Capital: Havana
Area: 42,805 sq mi; 110,860 sq km
Climate: Semitropical; rainy, hot summers
Population: 11.1 million
Major Ethnic Groups: European, mixed European and African
Major Religions: Christianity
Government: Communist state
Currency: 1 Cuban peso (Cu$) = 100 centavos
Leading Exports: Sugar, nickel, shellfish, and tobacco
Major Languages: Spanish

Resource Directory

Other Print Resources

DK Atlas

Technology

Color Transparencies 63 Central America and the Caribbean: Political Map

Dominica

Capital: Roseau
Area: 290 sq mi; 750 sq km
Climate: Tropical; rainy summers and dry winters
Population: 72,000
Major Ethnic Groups: African
Major Religions: Christianity
Government: Parliamentary democracy, republic within the Commonwealth
Currency: 1 East Caribbean dollar (EC$) = 100 cents
Leading Exports: Bananas, soap, bay oil, and vegetables
Major Languages: English and French patois

Dominican Republic

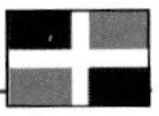

Capital: Santo Domingo
Area: 18,815 sq mi; 48,730 sq km
Climate: Semitropical; warm in lowlands, much cooler and wetter in highlands; rainy season
Population: 8.4 million
Major Ethnic Groups: Mixed European and African
Major Religions: Christianity
Government: Representative democracy
Currency: 1 Dominican peso (RD$) = 100 centavos
Leading Exports: Ferronickel, sugar, gold, coffee, and cocoa
Major Languages: Spanish

Grenada

Capital: Saint George's
Area: 131 sq mi; 340 sq km
Climate: Tropical; rainy season
Population: 89,000
Major Ethnic Groups: African
Major Religions: Christianity
Government: Constitutional monarchy with Westminster-style parliament
Currency: 1 East Caribbean dollar (EC$) = 100 cents
Leading Exports: Bananas, cocoa, and fruits and vegetables
Major Languages: English and French patois

Haiti

Capital: Port-au-Prince
Area: 10,714 sq mi; 27,750 sq km
Climate: Tropical; rainfall heavy in southwest, much lighter in northwest; hot in lowlands, much cooler in highlands
Population: 6.8 million
Major Ethnic Groups: African
Major Religions: Christianity, sometimes combined with African traditional beliefs
Government: Elected government
Currency: 1 gourde (G) = 100 centimes
Leading Exports: Light manufactures and coffee
Major Languages: French and Creole

Jamaica

Capital: Kingston
Area: 4,243 sq mi; 10,990 sq km
Climate: Tropical; hot and humid in coastal lowlands; rain heavy in northeast mountains
Population: 2.6 million
Major Ethnic Groups: African
Major Religions: Christianity
Government: Constitutional parliamentary democracy
Currency: 1 Jamaican dollar (J$) = 100 cents
Leading Exports: Alumina, bauxite, sugar, bananas, and rum
Major Languages: English and Creole

Saint Kitts and Nevis

Capital: Basseterre
Area: 104 sq mi; 269 sq km
Climate: Tropical; rainy season
Population: 39,000
Major Ethnic Groups: African
Major Religions: Christianity
Government: Constitutional monarchy with Westminster-style parliament
Currency: 1 East Caribbean dollar (EC$) = 100 cents
Leading Exports: Machinery, food, and electronics
Major Languages: English

Saint Lucia

Capital: Castries
Area: 239 sq mi; 620 sq km
Climate: Tropical; rainy season
Population: 156,000
Major Ethnic Groups: African
Major Religions: Christianity
Government: Westminster-style parliamentary democracy
Currency: 1 East Caribbean dollar (EC$) = 100 cents
Leading Exports: Bananas, clothing, cocoa, and vegetables
Major Languages: English and French patois

Saint Vincent and the Grenadines

Capital: Kingstown
Area: 150 sq mi; 388 sq km
Climate: Tropical; rainy season
Population: 115,000
Major Ethnic Groups: African
Major Religions: Christianity
Government: Parliamentary democracy, independent sovereign state within the Commonwealth
Currency: 1 East Caribbean dollar (EC$) = 100 cents
Leading Exports: Bananas, and eddoes and dasheen (taro)
Major Languages: English and French patois

Trinidad and Tobago

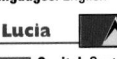

Capital: Port-of Spain
Area: 1,981 sq mi; 5,130 sq km
Climate: Tropical; rainy season
Population: 1.2 million
Major Ethnic Groups: African, East Indian
Major Religions: Christianity, Hinduism
Government: Parliamentary democracy
Currency: 1 Trinidad and Tobago dollar (TT$) = 100 cents
Leading Exports: Petroleum and petroleum products
Major Languages: English, Hindu, French, and Spanish

Portfolio Assessment

Overview

The following activities help students explore, collect, and arrange the information they find in the Regional Database. You may wish to have students add these activities to a portfolio of information about the countries of the world. To assess student work, refer to the generic rubrics in the Assessment Handbook.

Main Activity

- Explain to students that each of the countries in this region has a unique history shaped by the interaction between native peoples and European settlers or colonizers.
- Have students, working in small groups, choose one country from either Central America or the Caribbean. Students should use the library or the Internet to do research on the country they chose.
- Ask students to write a report on the history of that country. Their reports should pay special attention to where the people of that country came from, how the culture of the country has evolved, and how people have made a living in the past and today.

Additional Activity

Students can create a timeline of important events in the history of the country they chose. Ask students to illustrate their timelines with pictures that highlight important geographical features, agricultural products, or cultural artifacts of that country.

Resource Directory

Other Print Resources

Assessment Handbook Generic Rubrics 9, 19 and 26

Regional Database

Lesson Objectives

Gather, understand, and apply information about South America.

Lesson Plan

1 Explore

Point out that Brazil occupies almost the entire eastern half of South America, and is much larger than any of the continent's other countries. Ask a volunteer to name the largest river in Brazil (*the Amazon*).

Ask a volunteer to name the countries on the map of South America. Emphasize that many of these countries have extensive coastlines.

2 Teach

Have students locate the Equator on the map of South America. Explain that countries located south of the Equator have seasons opposite to those in the Northern Hemisphere. Ask students what season it would be right now in Brazil. Point out to students that many of the countries of this region have a variety of exports, which reflect an abundance of natural resources.

3 Assess/Reteach

Point out to students the different ethnic groups in the countries of this region. Have students read the ethnic group entries for Argentina and Uruguay. How do they differ from most of the other countries of South America? (*the major ethnic group for Argentina and Uruguay is European*).

South America: Political

Argentina

Capital: Buenos Aires
Area: 1,068,339 sq mi; 2,766,890 sq km
Climate: Mainly temperate; tropical area in northeast; cold in mountains; north wetter than south and west
Population: 37 million
Major Ethnic Groups: European
Major Religions: Christianity
Government: Republic
Currency: 1 peso = 100 centavos
Leading Exports: Edible oils, fuels and energy, cereals, feed, motor vehicles
Major Languages: Spanish (official), English, Italian, German, and French

Bolivia

Capital: La Paz
Area: 424,179 sq mi; 1,098,580 sq km
Climate: Varies with elevation, from hot and wet to cold and dry; rainy season
Population: 8.1 million
Major Ethnic Groups: Quechua, Aymara, mestizo
Major Religions: Christianity
Government: Republic
Currency: 1 boliviano ($B) = 100 centavos
Leading Exports: Soybeans, natural gas, zinc, gold, wood
Major Languages: Spanish, Quechua, and Aymara

Brazil

Capital: Brasília
Area: 3,286,600 sq mi; 8,511,965 sq km
Climate: Tropical to subtropical; north rainy, hot, and humid all year; central seasonal rains and temperatures; northeast long dry season; south more moderate temperatures and rainfall
Population: 172.9 million
Major Ethnic Groups: European, mixed European and African
Major Religions: Christianity
Government: Federative republic
Currency: 1 real (R$) = 100 centavos
Leading Exports: Manufactures, iron ore, soybeans, footwear, coffee
Major Languages: Portuguese, Spanish, English, and French

Chile

Capital: Santiago
Area: 292,269 sq mi; 756,950 sq km
Climate: Arid desert in north; mild, dry central; cool, rainy south
Population: 15.1 million
Major Ethnic Groups: Mestizo (mix of Spanish and mainly Araucanian)
Major Religions: Christianity
Government: Republic
Currency: 1 Chilean peso (Ch$) = 100 centavos
Leading Exports: Copper, fish, fruits, paper and pulp, chemicals
Major Languages: Spanish

Colombia

Capital: Bogotá
Area: 439,751 sq mi; 1,138,910 sq km
Climate: Tropical along coasts and river valleys; subtropical to cold in the mountains, rainy and dry periods alternate
Population: 39.7 million
Major Ethnic Groups: Mestizo, European
Major Religions: Christianity
Government: Republic; executive branch dominates government structure
Currency: 1 Colombian peso (Col$) = 100 centavos
Leading Exports: Petroleum, coffee, coal, and bananas
Major Languages: Spanish

Ecuador

Capital: Quito
Area: 109,487 sq mi; 283,560 sq km
Climate: Tropical along coast; hotter and more humid in rain forest; moderate in central region
Population: 12.9 million
Major Ethnic Groups: Mestizo, Native American
Major Religions: Christianity
Government: Republic
Currency: 1 sucre (S/) = 100 centavos
Leading Exports: Petroleum, bananas, shrimp, and cocoa
Major Languages: Spanish, Quechua, and various languages

Resource Directory

Other Print Resources

DK Atlas

Technology

Color Transparencies 53 South America: Physical-Political Map; **54** South America: Political Map

Passport to the World CD-ROM This interactive CD-ROM allows students to explore each region of the world. Students view regional videos, take a photo tour, and explore a historical timeline. Students record their travels in an Explorer's Journal, and receive passport stamps when they pass regional quizzes.

French Guiana

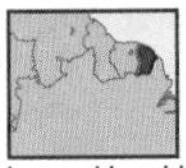

Capital: Cayenne
Area: 35,135 sq mi; 91,000 sq km
Climate: Tropical; hot and humid; dry summers, rainy winters
Population: 173,000
Major Ethnic Groups: African or mixed African and European (also known as Creole)
Major Religions: Christianity
Government: Overseas department of France
Currency: 1 French franc (F) = 100 centimes
Leading Exports: Shrimp, timber, gold, rum, rosewood essence, clothing
Major Languages: French

Guyana

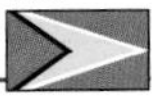

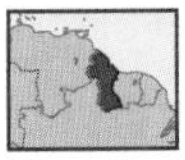

Capital: Georgetown
Area: 83,003 sq mi; 214,970 sq km
Climate: Tropical; rainy season
Population: 697,000
Major Ethnic Groups: East Indian, African
Major Religions: Christianity, Hinduism
Government: Republic within the Commonwealth
Currency: 1 Guyanese dollar (G$) = 100 cents
Leading Exports: Sugar, gold, bauxite/alumina, rice and shrimp
Major Languages: English and various dialects

Paraguay

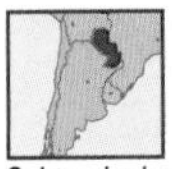

Capital: Asuncion
Area: 157,052 sq mi; 406,750 sq km
Climate: Subtropical; rainy in east; semi-arid in parts of west
Population: 5.6 million
Major Ethnic Groups: Mestizo
Major Religions: Christianity
Government: Constitutional republic
Currency: 1 guarani (G) = 100 centimos
Leading Exports: Soybeans, feed, cotton, meal, edible oils
Major Languages: Spanish (official) and Guarani

Peru

Capital: Lima
Area: 496,243 sq
Climate: Arid along coast; tropical in northeast; temperate to cold in the mountains, where rainfall varies
Population: 27 million
Major Ethnic Groups: Native American, mestizo
Major Religions: Christianity
Government: Constitutional republic
Currency: 1 nuevo sol (S/.) – 100 centimos
Leading Exports: Fish and fish products, copper, zinc, gold
Major Languages: Spanish (official), Quechua (official), and Aymara

Suriname

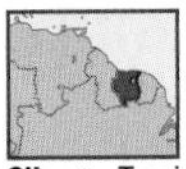

Capital: Paramaribo
Area: 63,041 sq mi; 163,270 sq km
Climate: Tropical; rainy season
Population: 431,000
Major Ethnic Groups: Asian (mainly from India and Indonesia), mixed African and Native American
Major Religions: Christianity, Hinduism, Islam
Government: Constitutional democracy
Currency: 1 Surinamese guilder, gulden, or florin (Sf.) = 100 cents
Leading Exports: Alumina, Aluminum, crude oil, lumber, shrimp and fish
Major Languages: Dutch (official), English, Sranang, Tongo, Hindustani, and Japanese

Uruguay

Capital: Montevideo
Area: 68,041 sq mi; 176,220 sq km
Climate: Temperate; ample rainfall all year
Population: 3.3 million
Major Ethnic Groups: European
Major Religions: Christianity
Government: Republic
Currency: 1 Uruguayan peso ($Ur) = 100 centesimos
Leading Exports: Meat, rice, leather products, vehicles, dairy products, wool
Major Languages: Spanish and Brazilero

Venezuela

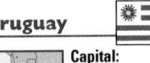

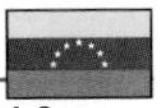

Capital: Caracas
Area: 352,156 sq mi; 912,050 sq km
Climate: Tropical along coast and in grasslands; milder in highlands
Population: 23.5 million
Major Ethnic Groups: Mestizo, European
Major Religions: Christianity
Government: Federal Republic
Currency: 1 bolivar (Bs) = 100 centimos
Leading Exports: Petroleum, bauxite and aluminum, steel
Major Languages: Spanish and various languages

Portfolio Assessment

Overview

The following activities help students explore, collect, and arrange the information they find in the Regional Database. You may wish to have students add these activities to a portfolio of information about the countries of the world. To assess student work, refer to the generic rubrics in the Assessment Handbook.

Main Activity

Explain that while the countries of South America share some characteristics, they also are quite distinct from each other. One difference, for example, is language. Point out that in Guyana, English is the official language, in Suriname it is Dutch, and in French Guiana it is French.

- Students will "visit" each country of the region, by means of reference materials or the Internet. Ask them to keep a travel journal, and to record at least one entry for each country.
- Entries should indicate dress, physical geography, and languages spoken. Students should also pay attention to how people work, and if the country appears to be wealthy or poor.

Additional Activity

Student pairs can record conversations that they have with citizens of the countries they visit.

Resource Directory

Other Print Resources

Assessment Handbook Generic Rubrics 21 and 30

Regional Database

Lesson Objectives

Gather, understand, and apply information about the countries of Western Europe.

Lesson Plan

1 Explore

List the countries of Western Europe on the chalkboard. Ask students which three nations in the region are the smallest (*Andorra, Liechtenstein, Monaco*). Point out that the Netherlands is also known by the name *Holland*. Point out that three of the countries in Western Europe are islands (*The United Kingdom, Ireland, and Iceland*). Help students to understand that these nations' geographic location isolates them somewhat from the other countries of Western Europe.

2 Teach

Have a volunteer read some of the climate entries. Explain that Western Europe is a region of geographical diversity. Point out that while Switzerland, Austria, and parts of France are dominated by the Alps and have cold, snowy winters, southern France has a semitropical climate.

The countries in the northern part of this region all share a proximity to water and an extensive coastline, which affects the climate.

Western Europe: Political

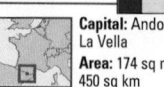

Andorra

Capital: Andorra La Vella
Area: 174 sq mi; 450 sq km
Climate: Temperate; snowy, cold winters and cool, dry summers
Population: 67,000
Major Ethnic Groups: Spanish, Andorran, Portuguese
Major Religions: Christianity
Government: Parliamentary democracy (since March 1993) that retains as its heads of state a coprincipality; the two princes are the president of France and biship of Seo de Urgel, Spain, who are represented locally by coprinces' representatives
Currency: 1 French franc (F) = 100 cenntimes; 1 peseta (Pta) = 100 centimos; the French and Spanish currencies are used
Leading Exports: Tobacco products and furniture
Major Languages: Catalan (official), French, and Castilian

Austria

Capital: Vienna
Area: 32,376 sq mi; 83,850 sq km
Climate: Temperate; cold, often severe winters in valleys; short summers
Population: 8.1 million
Major Ethnic Groups: German
Major Religions: Christianity
Government: Federal republic
Currency: 1 Austrian schilling (AS) = 100 groschen
Leading Exports: Machinery and equipment, and iron and steel, paper and paperboard
Major Languages: German

Belgium

Capital: Brussels
Area: 11,780 sq mi; 30,510 sq km
Climate: Temperate; humid and mild at coast; cold winters, hot summers in southeast, with heavy rains, fog, and drizzle common
Population: 10.2 million
Major Ethnic Groups: Fleming, Walloon
Major Religions: Christianity
Government: Federal parliamentary democracy under a constitutional monarch
Currency: 1 Belgian franc (BF) = 100 centimes
Leading Exports: Iron and steel, and transportation equipment, chemicals, diamonds
Major Languages: Dutch, French, and German

Denmark

Capital: Copenhagen
Area: 16,630 sq mi; 43,070 sq km
Climate: Temperate; humid; mild, windy winters and cool summers
Population: 5.3 million
Major Ethnic Groups: Scandinavian, Inuit, Faroese, German
Major Religions: Christianity
Government: Constitutional monarchy
Currency: 1 Danish drone (DKr) = 100 oere
Leading Exports: Machinery and instruments, meat and meat products, and dairy products
Major Languages: Danish, Faroese, Greenlandic, and German

Finland

Capital: Helsinki
Area: 130,132 sq mi; 337,030 sq km
Climate: Cold temperate (moderated by warm North Atlantic Current)
Population: 5.2 million
Major Ethnic Groups: Finn, Swede
Major Religions: Christianity
Government: Republic
Currency: 1 markka (FMk) or Finmark = 100 pennia
Leading Exports: Machinery and equipment, chemicals, metals, timber, paper and pulp
Major Languages: Finnish, Swedish, Lapp, and Russian

France

Capital: Paris
Area: 211,217 sq mi; 547,030 sq km
Climate: Mostly temperate; severe winters and hot summers in interior; more moderate on Atlantic coast; semitropical on Mediterranean coast
Population: 59.3 million
Major Ethnic Groups: French, Celtic
Major Religions: Christianity
Government: Republic
Currency: 1 French franc (F) = 100 centimes
Leading Exports: Machinery and transportation equipment, chemicals, iron and steel products
Major Languages: French and regional dialects and languages

Resource Directory

Other Print Resources

DK Atlas

Technology

Color Transparencies 71 Western Europe: Political Map

Passport to the World CD-ROM This interactive CD-ROM allows students to explore each region of the world. Students view regional videos, take a photo tour, and explore a historical timeline. Students record their travels in an Explorer's Journal, and receive passport stamps when they pass regional quizzes.

Germany

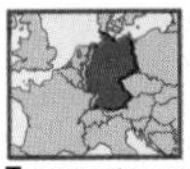

Capital: Berlin
Area: 137,808 sq mi; 356,910 sq km
Climate: Temperate; cool winters, warm summers; more rainy in south
Population: 82.8 million
Major Ethnic Groups: German
Major Religions: Christianity
Government: Federal republic
Currency: 1 deutsche mark (DM) = 100 pfennige
Leading Exports: Machines and machine tools, and chemicals, metals and manufactures
Major Languages: German

Greece

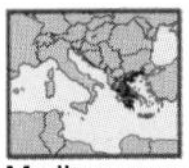

Capital: Athens
Area: 50,944 sq mi; 131,940 sq km
Climate: Mediterranean; hot, dry summers; rainy winters on west coast
Population: 10.6 million
Major Ethnic Groups: Greek
Major Religions: Christianity
Government: Parliamentary republic; monarchy rejected by referendum December 8, 1974
Currency: 1 drachma (Dr) = 100 lepta
Leading Exports: Manufactured goods, foodstuffs, fuels, and chemicals
Major Languages: Greek, English, and French

Holy See (Vatican City)

Capital: Vatican City
Area: 0.17 sq mi; 0.44 sq km
Climate: Temperate; mild, rainy winters; hot, dry summers
Population: 880
Major Ethnic Groups: Italian, Swiss, other
Major Religions: Christianity
Government: Monarchical-sacerdotal state
Currency: 1 Vatican lira (Vlit) = 100 centesimi
Leading Exports: None
Major Languages: Italian, Latin, and various languages

Iceland

Capital: Reykjavik
Area: 39,770 sq mi; 103,000 sq km
Climate: Temperate (moderated by North Atlantic Current)
Population: 276,000
Major Ethnic Groups: Mixed Norwegian and Celtic
Major Religions: Christianity
Government: Constitutional republic
Currency: 1 Icelandic krona (Ikr) = 100 aurar
Leading Exports: Fish and fish products, and animal products
Major Languages: Icelandic

Ireland

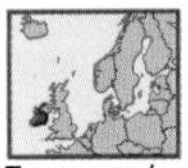

Capital: Dublin
Area: 27,136 sq mi; 70,280 sq km
Climate: Temperate (moderated by warm North Atlantic Current)
Population: 3.8 million
Major Ethnic Groups: Celtic, English
Major Religions: Christianity
Government: Republic
Currency: 1 Irish pound = 100 pence
Leading Exports: Machinery and equipment, computers, chemicals, pharmaceuticals
Major Languages: English and Irish Gaelic

Italy

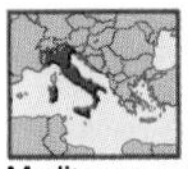

Capital: Rome
Area: 116,310 sq mi; 301,230 sq km
Climate: Mediterranean; Alpine in far north; hot, dry in south
Population: 57.6 million
Major Ethnic Groups: Italian
Major Religions: Christianity
Government: Republic
Currency: 1 Italian lira (Lit) = 100 centesimi
Leading Exports: Engineering products, textiles and clothing, production machinery, motor vehicles, transport equipment
Major Languages: Italian, German, French, and Slovene

Liechtenstein

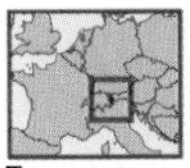

Capital: Vaduz
Area: 62 sq mi; 160 sq km
Climate: Temperate
Population: 32,000
Major Ethnic Groups: Allemanic, Italian, Turkish
Major Religions: Christianity
Government: Hereditary constitutional monarchy
Currency: 1 Swiss franc, franken, or franco (SFR) = 100 centimes, rappen, or centesimi
Leading Exports: Small specialty machinery and dental products
Major Languages: German and Alemannic

Luxembourg

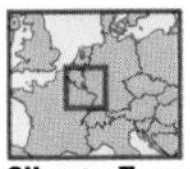

Capital: Luxembourg
Area: 998 sq mi; 2,586 sq km
Climate: Temperate
Population: 437,000
Major Ethnic Groups: Mix of Celtic, French, and German
Major Religions: Christianity
Government: Constitutional monarchy
Currency: 1 Luxembourg franc (LuxF) = 100 centimes
Leading Exports: Finished steel products and chemicals
Major Languages: Luxembourgian, German, French, and English

Malta

Capital: Valletta
Area: 124 sq mi; 320 sq km
Climate: Mediterranean; mild, rainy winters and hot, dry summers
Population: 392,000
Major Ethnic Groups: Maltese (descendants of ancient Carthaginians and Phoenicians, mixed with other Mediterranean groups)
Major Religions: Christianity
Government: Parliamentary democracy
Currency: 1 Maltese lira (LM) = 100 cents
Leading Exports: Machinery and transportation equipment, manufactures
Major Languages: Maltese and English

Monaco

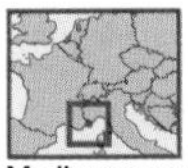

Capital: Monaco
Area: .73 sq mi; 1.9 sq km
Climate: Mediterranean; mild, wet winters and hot, dry summers
Population: 32,000
Major Ethnic Groups: French, Monegasque, Italian
Major Religions: Christianity
Government: Constitutional monarchy
Currency: 1 French franc (F) = 100 centimes
Leading Exports: Exports through France
Major Languages: French (official), English, Italian, and Monegasque

3 Assess/Reteach

Ask students to list the major languages of the countries in this region. Point out that while these countries are in close proximity to each other, their cultures are often quite different. Have students speculate about how these cultural differences might affect trade, travel, and communication amongst these countries.

Regional Database

Portfolio Assessment

Overview

The following activities help students explore, collect, and arrange the information they find in the Regional Data Bank. You may wish to have students add these activities to a portfolio of information about the countries of the world. To assess student work, refer to the generic rubrics in the Assessment Handbook.

Main Activity

Point out that tourism is an important industry for all the countries of Western Europe.

- Have groups of students use the descriptions of countries in the region to choose one that interests them. Then, have them prepare a tour guide for that country.
- Students may use reference books or the Internet to find information about the language, historical and cultural sites, foods, traditional dress, and geography of their country. Tell students to emphasize the things that would attract people to travel to that country.

Additional Activity

Students can illustrate their tour guides with pictures of souvenirs that a person might bring back from their country.

Netherlands

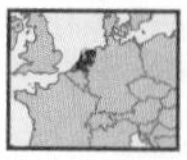

Capital: Amsterdam
Area: 16,036 sq mi; 41,532 sq km
Climate: Temperate; cool summers and mild winters
Population: 15.9 million
Major Ethnic Groups: Dutch
Major Religions: Christianity
Government: Constitutional monarchy
Currency: 1 Netherlands guilder, gulden or florin (f) = 100 cents
Leading Exports: Machinery and equipment, chemicals, fuels, foodstuffs
Major Languages: Dutch

Norway

Capital: Oslo
Area: 125,186 sq mi; 324,220 sq km
Climate: Temperate along coast (moderated by North Atlantic Current); colder inland; subarctic in far north; rainy all year on west coast
Population: 4.5 million
Major Ethnic Groups: Norwegian (Nordic, Alpine, Baltic), Lapps
Major Religions: Christianity
Government: Constitutional monarchy
Currency: 1 Norwegian Krone (NKr) = 100 oere
Leading Exports: Petroleum and petroleum products, machinery and equipment, metals, chemicals
Major Languages: Norwegian (official), Lapp, and Finnish

Portugal

Capital: Lisbon
Area: 35,553 sq mi; 92,080 sq km
Climate: Temperate; cool, rainy in north and warmer, drier in south
Population: 10 million
Major Ethnic Groups: Portuguese (mixed Mediterranean)
Major Religions: Christianity
Government: Parliamentary democracy
Currency: 1 Portuguese escudo (Esc) = 100 centavos
Leading Exports: Clothing and footwear, and machinery, chemicals
Major Languages: Portuguese

San Marino

Capital: San Marino
Area: 23 sq mi; 60 sq km
Climate: Mediterranean; mild winters and warm summers
Population: 27,000
Major Ethnic Groups: Sammarinese, Italian
Major Religions: Christianity
Government: Republic
Currency: 1 Italian lira (Lit) = 100 centesimi
Leading Exports: Building stone, lime, wood, and chestnuts
Major Languages: Italian

Spain

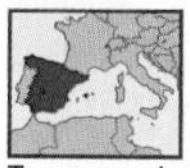

Capital: Madrid
Area: 194,892 sq mi; 504,750 sq km
Climate: Temperate; hot, dry summers in central area; cooler, wetter in north; subtropical along Mediterranean coast
Population: 40 million
Major Ethnic Groups: Spanish (mixed Mediterranean and Nordic)
Major Religions: Christianity
Government: Parliamentary monarchy
Currency: 1 peseta (Pta) = 100 centimos
Leading Exports: Machinery, motor vehicles, foodstuffs
Major Languages: Spanish, Catalan, Galician, and Basque

Sweden

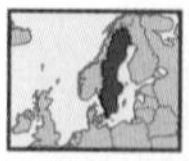

Capital: Stockholm
Area: 173,738 sq mi; 449,964 sq km
Climate: Temperate in south (moderated by North Atlantic Current); subarctic in north; rainfall low except in higher mountains; heavy snow in north and central regions
Population: 8.9 million
Major Ethnic Groups: Swedish
Major Religions: Christianity
Government: Constitutional monarchy
Currency: 1 Swedish krona (SKr) = 100 oere
Leading Exports: Machinery, motor vehicles, and paper products
Major Languages: Swedish, Lapp, and Finnish

Switzerland

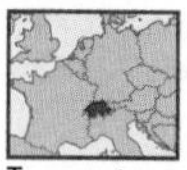

Capital: Bern
Area: 15,943 sq mi; 41,290 sq km
Climate: Temperate on plateau and in lower valleys; moderate rainfall; mountains colder and rainier; with heavy snow in winter
Population: 7.3 million
Major Ethnic Groups: German, French, Italian
Major Religions: Christianity
Government: Federal republic
Currency: 1 Swiss franc, franken, or franco (SFR) = 100 centimes, rappen, or centesimi
Leading Exports: Machinery, chemicals, metals, watches
Major Languages: German, French, Italian, Romansch, and various languages

United Kingdom

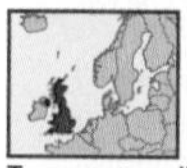

Capital: London
Area: 94,529 sq mi; 244,820 sq km
Climate: Temperate; mild, often wet and chilly; cooler, rainier in highlands
Population: 59.5 million
Major Ethnic Groups: English, Scottish, Irish, Welsh
Major Religions: Christianity
Government: Constitutional monarchy
Currency: 1 British pound = 100 pence
Leading Exports: Manufactured goods, fuels, chemicals, food, beverages
Major Languages: English, Welsh, and Scottish Gaelic

Resource Directory

Other Print Resources

Assessment Handbook Generic Rubrics 9 and 23

Eastern Europe: Political

Albania

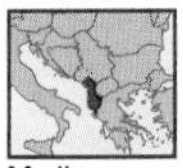

Capital: Tiranë
Area: 11,101 sq mi; 28,750 sq km
Climate: Mediterranean; rainy, mild winters and hot, dry summers at coast; more humid in north; more rainy in mountains
Population: 3.5 million
Major Ethnic Groups: Albanian
Major Religions: Islam, Christianity
Government: Emerging democracy
Currency: 1 lek (L) = 100 qintars
Leading Exports: Asphalt, metals and metallic ores, and electricity
Major Languages: Albanian, Tosk dialect, and Greek

Armenia

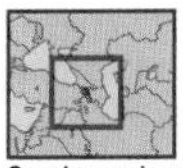

Capital: Yerevan
Area: 11,506 sq mi; 29,800 sq km
Climate: Continental; moderate winters and long, hot summers; arid on plains
Population: 3.3 million
Major Ethnic Groups: Armenian
Major Religions: Christianity
Government: Republic
Currency: 1 dram = 100 luma
Leading Exports: Diamonds, scrap metal, machinery and equipment
Major Languages: Armenian and Russian

Azerbaijan

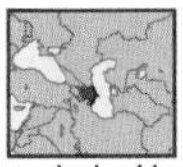

Capital: Baku
Area: 33,438 sq mi; 86,600 sq km
Climate: Dry subtropical, with mild winters and long, hot summers; colder in mountains
Population: 7.7 million
Major Ethnic Groups: Azeri
Major Religions: Islam
Government: Republic
Currency: 1 manat = 100 gopiks
Leading Exports: Oil and gas, machinery, cotton
Major Languages: Azeri, Russian, and Armenian

Belarus

Capital: Minsk
Area: 79,926 sq mi; 207,600 sq km
Climate: Continental; cold winters and cool summers, with high humidity
Population: 10.4 million
Major Ethnic Groups: Belarusian
Major Religions: Christianity
Government: Republic
Currency: Belarusian rubel (BR)
Leading Exports: Machinery and transportation equipment
Major Languages: Byelorussian and Russian

Bosnia and Herzegovina

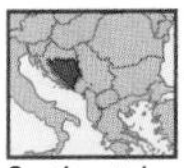

Capital: Sarajevo
Area: 19,782 sq mi; 51,233 sq km
Climate: Continental; cold winters, hot summers; cooler, harsher in mountains; mild, rainy winters along coast
Population: 3.8 million
Major Ethnic Groups: Serb, Croat
Major Religions: Islam, Christianity
Government: Emerging democracy
Currency: 1 convertible marka (KM) = 100 convertible pfenniga
Leading Exports: None
Major Languages: Croatian, Serbian, Bosnian

Bulgaria

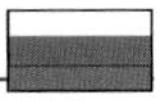

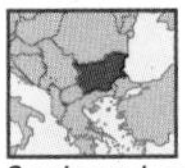

Capital: Sofia
Area: 42,824 sq mi; 110,910 sq km
Climate: Continental; cold winters, hot summers
Population: 7.8 million
Major Ethnic Groups: Bulgarian
Major Religions: Christianity
Government: Parliamentary democracy
Currency: 1 lev (Lv) = 100 stotinki
Leading Exports: Machinery and agricultural products
Major Languages: Bulgarian

Croatia

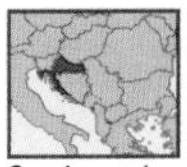

Capital: Zagreb
Area: 21,830 sq mi; 56,538 sq km
Climate: Continental; cold winters, hot summers; Mediterranean along coast, with mild winters and dry summers
Population: 4.3 million
Major Ethnic Groups: Croat, Serb
Major Religions: Christianity
Government: Presidential parliamentary democracy
Currency: 1 Croatian kuna (HRK) = 100 lipas
Leading Exports: Textiles, chemicals, foodstuffs, fuels
Major Languages: Croatian

Czech Republic

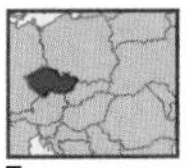

Capital: Prague
Area: 30,388 sq mi; 78,703 sq km
Climate: Temperate; cold, cloudy, humid winters and cool summers
Population: 10.3 million
Major Ethnic Groups: Czech
Major Religions: Christianity
Government: Parliamentary democracy
Currency: 1 koruna (Kc) = 100 haleru
Leading Exports: Machinery and transportation equipment, manufactured goods
Major Languages: Czech and Slovak

Lesson Objectives

Gather, understand, and apply information about the countries of Eastern Europe.

Lesson Plan

1 Explore

Name the countries of Eastern Europe that appear on this map. Ask students what continent Eastern Europe borders (*Asia*). Have students use the terrain and climate entries to offer descriptions of the countries of this region. Point out that unlike much of Western Europe, in this region most of the countries are landlocked and many of the countries are mountainous.

Resource Directory

Other Print Resources

DK Atlas

Technology

Color Transparencies 72 Eastern Europe: Political Map

REGIONAL DATABASE 621

Lesson Plan continued

2 Teach

Explain that the location of Eastern Europe between powerful nations in Europe and Russia has produced a complicated history for many nations of the region. Tell students that most of the countries of the region, with the exception of Poland, the Czech Republic, Slovakia, and Hungary, have been known historically as *the Balkans*—a term taken from the peninsula on which most of Eastern Europe is located. Explain that many of these nations were under Russian control in recent history, but in the past few decades have attained independence.

Estonia

Capital: Tallinn
Area: 17,414 sq mi; 45,100 sq km
Climate: Maritime; moderate, wet winters and cool summers
Population: 1.4 million
Major Ethnic Groups: Estonian, Russian
Major Religions: Christianity
Government: Parliamentary democracy
Currency: 1 Estonian kroon (EEK) = 100 sents
Leading Exports: Textiles, food products, vehicles, metals
Major Languages: Estonian, Latvian, Lithuanian, and Russian

Georgia

Capital: T'bilisi
Area: 26,912 sq mi; 69,700 sq km
Climate: Continental; cold, wet winters and cool summers in mountains; cold winters, hot summers in far east; subtropical on coast
Population: 5 million
Major Ethnic Groups: Georgian
Major Religions: Christianity
Government: Republic
Currency: 1 lari (GEL) = 100 tetry
Leading Exports: Citrus fruits, tea, and wine
Major Languages: Georgian, Russian, Armenian, Azeri, and various others

Hungary

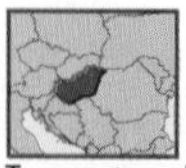

Capital: Budapest
Area: 35,920 sq mi; 93,030 sq km
Climate: Temperate; cold, humid winters and warm summers
Population: 10.1 million
Major Ethnic Groups: Hungarian
Major Religions: Christianity
Government: Parliamentary democracy
Currency: 1 forint (Ft) = 100 filler
Leading Exports: Machinery and equipment, manufactured goods, fuels and electricity
Major Languages: Hungarian and various others

Latvia

Capital: Riga
Area: 24,750 sq mi; 64,100 sq km
Climate: Maritime; mild winters and cool summers; humid
Population: 2.4 million
Major Ethnic Groups: Latvian, Russian
Major Religions: Christianity
Government: Parliamentary democracy
Currency: 1 Latvian lat (LVL) = 100 santims
Leading Exports: Wood and wood products, machinery and equipment, metals
Major Languages: Lettish, Lithuanian, Russian, and various others

Lithuania

Capital: Vilnius
Area: 25,175 sq mi; 65,200 sq km
Climate: Maritime; mild winters and cool summers
Population: 3.6 million
Major Ethnic Groups: Lithuanian
Major Religions: Christianity
Government: Parliamentary democracy
Currency: 1 Lithuanian litas = 100 centas
Leading Exports: Machinery and equipment, mineral products, textiles and clothing, chemicals, foodstuffs
Major Languages: Lithuanian, Polish, and Russian

Macedonia

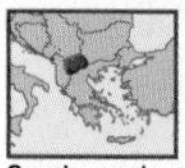

Capital: Skopje
Area: 9,781 sq mi; 25,333 sq km
Climate: Continental; cold, snowy winters and hot, dry summers; milder in valleys and river basins
Population: 2 million
Major Ethnic Groups: Macedonian Slav, Albanian
Major Religions: Christianity, Islam
Government: Emerging democracy
Currency: 1 Macedonian dinar (MKD) = 100 deni
Leading Exports: Manufactured goods and machinery
Major Languages: Macedonian, Albanian, Turkish, Serb, Gypsy, and various others

Moldova

Capital: Chisinau
Area: 13,012 sq mi; 33,700 sq km
Climate: Continental; mild winters, warm summers; light rainfall
Population: 4.4 million
Major Ethnic Groups: Moldovan, Ukranian, Russian
Major Religions: Christianity
Government: Republic
Currency: Moldovan leu (MLD) (plural lei)
Leading Exports: Foodstuffs, wine, and tobacco
Major Languages: Moldovan (official), Russian, and Gagauz dialect

Poland

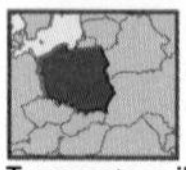

Capital: Warsaw
Area: 120,731 sq mi; 312,680 sq km
Climate: Temperate; mild, rainy summers and cold, snowy winters
Population: 38.6
Major Ethnic Groups: Polish
Major Religions: Christianity
Government: Republic
Currency: 1 zloty (Zl) = 100 groszy
Leading Exports: Manufactured goods and chemicals, machinery and equipment, food and live animals
Major Languages: Polish

Romania

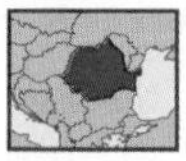

Capital: Bucharest
Area: 91,702 sq mi; 237,500 sq km
Climate: Temperate; cold, cloudy, snowy winters and warm, sunny summers
Population: 22.4 million
Major Ethnic Groups: Romanian
Major Religions: Christianity
Government: Republic
Currency: 1 leu (L) = 100 bani
Leading Exports: Textiles and footwear, metals and metal products, machinery and equipment, minerals and fuels
Major Languages: Romanian, Hungarian, and German

Serbia and Montenegro

Capital: Belgrade
Area: 39,436 sq mi; 102,350 sq km
Climate: Continental in north and north central region (cold winters and hot, humid summers); Mediterranean in south central region and along coast in south (mild winters and hot, dry summers); colder winters inland
Population: 10.7 million
Major Ethnic Groups: Serbian, Albanian, Montenegrin
Major Religions: Christianity, Islam
Government: Republic
Currency: 1 Yugoslav New Dinar (YD) = 100 paras; Montenegro made the German deutsche mark legal tender alongside the Yugoslav dinar
Leading Exports: Manufactured goods, food and live animals, raw materials
Major Languages: Serbian and Albanian

Slovakia

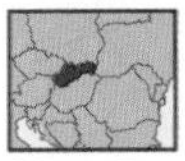

Capital: Bratislava
Area: 18,860 sq mi; 48,845 sq km
Climate: Temperate; cold winters, hot summers
Population: 5.4 million
Major Ethnic Groups: Slovak, Hungarian
Major Religions: Christianity
Government: Parliamentary democracy
Currency: 1 koruna (SK) = 100 halierov
Leading Exports: Machinery and transportation equipment, manufactured goods, chemicals
Major Languages: Slovak and Hungarian

Slovenia

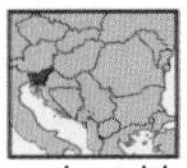

Capital: Ljubljana
Area: 7,837 sq mi; 20,296 sq km
Climate: Mostly continental; harsh winters, rainy summers in mountains; more moderate in east; Mediterranean along coast
Population: 1.9 million
Major Ethnic Groups: Slovene
Major Religions: Christianity
Government: Parliamentary democratic republic
Currency: 1 tolar (SIT) = 100 stotins
Leading Exports: Manufactured goods, machinery and transportation equipment, chemicals
Major Languages: Slovenian, Serbo-Croatian, and various others

Ukraine

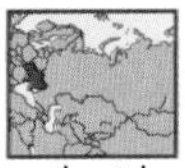

Capital: Kiev
Area: 233,098 sq mi; 603,700 sq km
Climate: Mostly continental; cold winters, warm summers; Mediterranean in far south
Population: 49.2 million
Major Ethnic Groups: Ukrainian, Russian
Major Religions: Christianity
Government: Republic
Currency: 1 hryvna = 100 kopiykas
Leading Exports: Metals, fuel and petroleum products, machinery and transport equipment, food products
Major Languages: Ukranian, Russian, Romanian, Polish, and Hungarian

3 Assess/Reteach

Ask students to read the major religions entries for each of the countries of Eastern Europe. Ask them what difference they notice from the entries for the regions of Europe they have already studied (*Islam is a major religion in several countries*)

Regional Database

Lesson Objectives

Gather, understand, and apply information about Russia.

Lesson Plan

1 Explore

Point out that Russia is not only the largest country in Europe, but the largest in the world. Have students note that it stretches from the Asian border well into the Arctic Circle, and its easternmost tip is separated from Alaska in the United States only by the narrow Bering Strait.

2 Teach

Tell students that throughout most of the twentieth century, the nations bordering Russia in the west, along with Russia, were all part of the United Soviet Socialist Republics (USSR). The USSR was dissolved in 1991, and these countries became independent republics. Explain that many of them retain close economic and military ties with Russia.

3 Assess/Reteach

Ask student volunteers to read aloud the climate entries for Russia. Explain that despite Russia's size, much of the land is not suitable for farming. Tell students that only a tiny percentage of Russians are engaged in agriculture. However, the country has vast mineral resources, including the world's largest oil and natural gas reserves. Have students find other countries in Europe with important mineral reserves.

Russia: Political

Russia

Capital: Moscow
Area: 6,952,996 sq mi; 17,075,200 sq km
Climate: Mostly humid continental; long, cold winters and short, cool summers; milder in south; subarctic in north; tundra in far north
Population: 146 million
Major Ethnic Groups: Russian, Tatar, Ukranian
Major Religions: Christianity, Islam
Government: Federation
Currency: 1 ruble (R) = 100 kopeks
Leading Exports: Petroleum and petroleum products, natural gas, wood and wood products
Major Languages: Russian and various languages

Resource Directory

Other Print Resources

DK Atlas

Technology

Color Transparencies 73 Northern Eurasia: Political Map

Passport to the World CD-ROM This interactive CD-ROM allows students to explore each region of the world. Students view regional videos, take a photo tour, and explore a historical timeline. Students record their travels in an Explorer's Journal, and receive passport stamps when they pass regional quizzes.

624 REGIONAL DATABASE

North Africa: Political

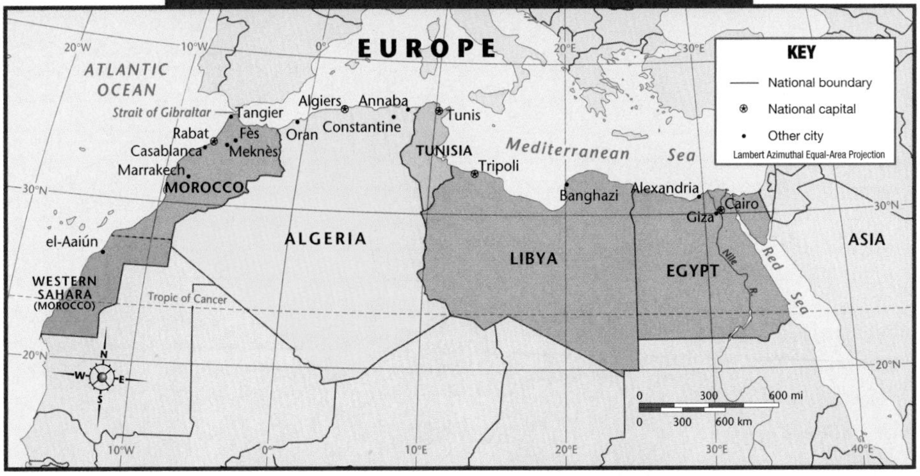

Algeria

Capital: Algiers
Area: 919,626 sq mi; 2,381,740 sq km
Climate: Arid in the Sahara; semiarid along coast; drier with cold winters and hot summers on high plateau
Population: 31.2 million
Major Ethnic Groups: Arab-Berber
Major Religions: Islam
Government: Republic
Currency: 1 Algerian dinar (DA) = 100 centimes
Leading Exports: Petroleum and petroleum products, natural gas
Major Languages: Arabic (official), French, and Berber dialects

Egypt

Capital: Cairo
Area: 386,675 sq mi; 1,001,450 sq km
Climate: Arid
Population: 68.3 million
Major Ethnic Groups: Egyptian, Bedouin, Berber
Major Religions: Islam
Government: Republic
Currency: 1 Egyptian pound = 100 piasters
Leading Exports: Crude oil, petroleum products, cotton, textiles
Major Languages: Arabic, English, and French

Libya

Capital: Tripoli
Area: 679,385 sq mi; 1,759,540 sq km
Climate: Moderate along coast; extremely hot, dry desert interior
Population: 5.1 million
Major Ethnic Groups: Berber, Arab
Major Religions: Islam
Government: Jamahiriya (a state of the masses) in theory, governed by the populace through local councils; in fact, a military dictatorship
Currency: 1 Libyan dinar (LD) = 1,000 dirhams
Leading Exports: Crude oil and refined petroleum products
Major Languages: Arabic, Italian, and English

Morocco

Capital: Rabat
Area: 172,420 sq mi; 446,550 sq km
Climate: Mediterranean; more extreme in interior
Population: 30.1 million
Major Ethnic Groups: Arab-Berber
Major Religions: Islam
Government: Constitutional monarchy
Currency: 1 Morooccan dirham (DH) = 100 centimes
Leading Exports: Phosphates and fertilizers, food and beverages, minerals
Major Languages: Arabic (official), Berber dialects, and French

Tunisia

Capital: Tunis
Area: 63,172 sq mi; 163,610 sq km
Climate: Temperate in north with mild, rainy winters and hot, dry summers; desert in south
Population: 9.6 million
Major Ethnic Groups: Arab
Major Religions: Islam
Government: Republic
Currency: 1 Tunisian dinar (TD) = 1,000 millimes
Leading Exports: Textiles, mechanical goods, phosphates and chemicals, agricultural products
Major Languages: Arabic and French

Lesson Objectives

Gather, understand, and apply information about the countries of North Africa.

Lesson Plan

1 Explore

Ask students which North African country is the largest. (*Algeria*) Next, ask which is the smallest. (*Tunisia*) Have students describe the relative location of Egypt. (*easternmost country in North Africa, bordered by the Mediterranean Sea and the Red Sea, directly east of Libya*) Have students find Western Sahara on the map. Explain that this territory belongs to the nation of Morocco.

2 Teach

Tell students that the Sahara extends across most of North Africa and influences many aspects of life in the region. Most North Africans live along the Mediterranean coast or along the Nile River valley because the Sahara cannot sustain a large population. People who live in the desert are nomads who make a living by herding. Have students read the country descriptions. Ask them what major religion the region shares. (*Islam*)

3 Assess/Reteach

Have students skim the entries for exports in the country descriptions. Ask them to name examples of crops. (*grains, cotton, olives, citrus fruits, dates, vegetables*) Ask how farmers are able to grow such a variety of crops in a region dominated by desert. (*Farming takes place along the coasts, the Nile River valley, and in desert oases.*)

Resource Directory

Other Print Resources

DK Atlas

Technology

Color Transparencies 97 Africa: Political Map

Passport to the World CD-ROM This interactive CD-ROM allows students to explore each region of the world. Students view regional videos, take a photo tour, and explore a historical timeline. Students record their travels in an Explorer's Journal, and receive passport stamps when they pass regional quizzes.

Regional Database

Lesson Objectives

Gather, understand, and apply information about the countries of West Africa.

Lesson Plan

1 Explore

Begin by pointing out that West Africa is a region of many countries. They range in size from The Gambia, a country smaller than the state of Connecticut, to Chad, the largest country in West Africa. Have students count the number of countries in West Africa. (*seventeen*)

2 Teach

Explain that five countries in West Africa are located in the Sahel, a broad band of semiarid land. The Sahel separates the Sahara to the north from the tropical rain forests along West Africa's coast. Have students locate these Sahel countries: Mauritania, Mali, Niger, Burkina Faso, and Chad. The remaining West African countries ring the coastline of West Africa. One, Cape Verde, is a small island nation.

West Africa: Political

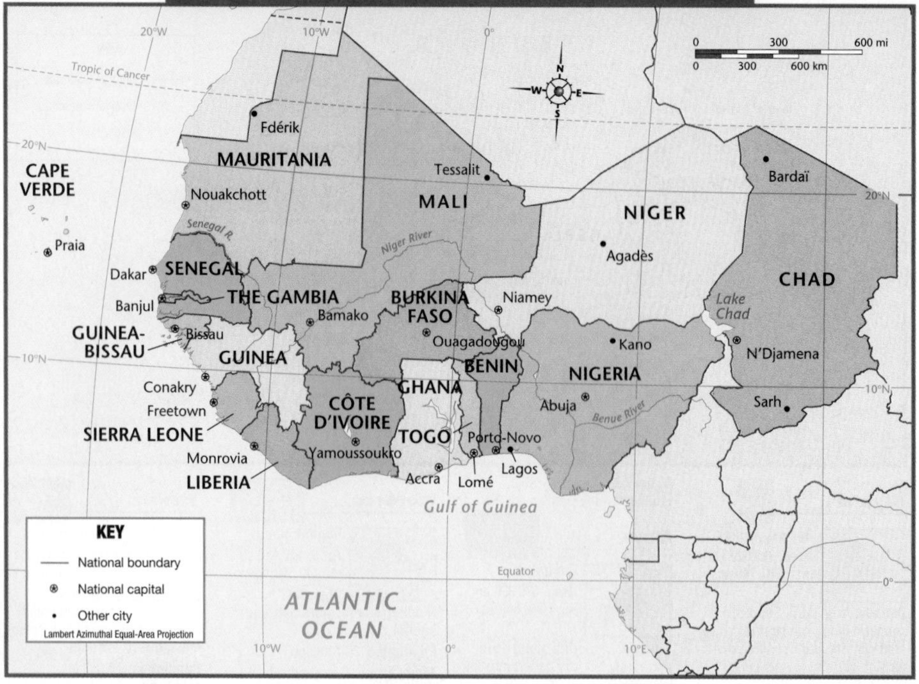

Benin

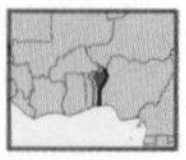

Capital: Porto-Novo
Area: 43,484 sq mi; 112,620 sq km
Climate: Tropical; hot, humid in south; semiarid in north
Population: 6.4 million
Major Ethnic Groups: Fon, Adja, Yoruba, Bariba
Major Religions: Traditional African religions
Government: Republic under multiparty democratic rule
Currency: 1 Communaute Financiere Africaine franc (CFAF) = 100 centimes
Leading Exports: Cotton, crude oil, palm products, and cocoa
Major Languages: French (official), Fon, Yoruba, and at least 6 various languages

Burkina Faso

Capital: Ouagadougou
Area: 105,873 sq mi; 274,200 sq km
Climate: Tropical; warm, dry winters and hot, wet summers
Population: 11.9 million
Major Ethnic Groups: Mossi, Gurunsi, Senufo, Lobi
Major Religions: Traditional African religions, Islam
Government: Presidential democracy, National assembly
Currency: 1 Communaute Financiere Africaine franc (CFAF) = 100 centimes
Leading Exports: Cotton, gold, and animal products
Major Languages: French (official) and Sudanic languages

Cape Verde

Capital: Praia
Area: 1,556 sq mi; 4,030 sq km
Climate: Tropical; warm, dry summer; little rainfall
Population: 400,000
Major Ethnic Groups: Mixed African and European
Major Religions: Mix of Christianity and traditional African religions
Government: Republic
Currency: 1 Cape Verdean escudo (CVEsc) = 100 centavos
Leading Exports: Fuel, shoes, garments, fish, bananas, hides
Major Languages: Portuguese and Crioulo

Chad

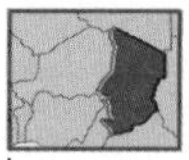

Capital: N'Djamena
Area: 495,772 sq mi; 1,284,000 sq km
Climate: Tropical in south; desert in north
Population: 8.4 million
Major Ethnic Groups: Arab, Toubou, Hadjerai, Sara, Ngambaye, Mbaye, other indigenous African groups
Major Religions: Islam, Christianity, traditional African religions
Government: Republic
Currency: 1 Communaute Financiere Africaine franc (CFAF) = 100 centimes
Leading Exports: Cotton, cattle, and textiles
Major Languages: French, Arabic, Sara, Sango, and over 100 various languages and dialects

Resource Directory

Other Print Resources

DK Atlas

Technology

Color Transparencies 98 West and Central Africa: Political Map

Passport to the World CD-ROM This interactive CD-ROM allows students to explore each region of the world. Students view regional videos, take a photo tour, and explore a historical timeline. Students record their travels in an Explorer's Journal, and receive passport stamps when they pass regional quizzes.

Côte D'Ivoire

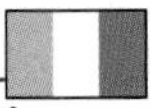

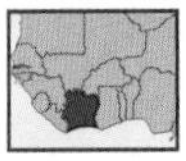

Capital: Yamoussoukro
Area: 124,507 sq mi; 322,460 sq km
Climate: Tropical along coast, semiarid in far north
Population: 16 million
Major Ethnic Groups: Baoule, Bete, Senoufou, Malinke
Major Religions: Islam, Christianity, traditional African religions
Government: Republic; multiparty presidential regime established 1960
Currency: 1 Communaute Financiere Africaine franc (CFAF) = 100 centimes
Leading Exports: Cocoa, coffee, tropical woods, and petroleum
Major Languages: French, Dioula, and 59 other dialects

The Gambia

Capital: Banjul
Area: 4,363 sq mi; 11,300 sq km
Climate: Subtropical; hot, rainy season; cooler, dry season
Population: 1.4 million
Major Ethnic Groups: Mandinka, Fula, Wolof, Jola, Serahuli
Major Religions: Islam
Government: Republic under multiparty democratic rule
Currency: 1 dalasi (D) = 100 butut
Leading Exports: Peanuts and peanut products, and fish
Major Languages: English, Mandinka, Wolof, Fula, and various languages

Ghana

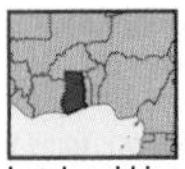

Capital: Accra
Area: 92,104 sq mi; 238,540 sq km
Climate: Tropical; hot, humid in southwest; hot, dry in north; warm, dry along southeast coast
Population: 19.5 million
Major Ethnic Groups: Akan, Moshi-Dagomba, Ewe, Ga
Major Religions: Traditional African religions, Islam, Christianity
Government: Constitutional democracy
Currency: 1 new cedi (C) = 100 pesewas
Leading Exports: Cocoa, gold, timber, tuna, and bauxite
Major Languages: English, Akan, Moshi-Dagomba, Ewe, and Ga

Guinea

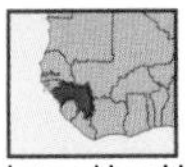

Capital: Conakry
Area: 94,930 sq mi; 245,860 sq km
Climate: Mostly hot and humid; monsoonal-type rainy season; dry season
Population: 7.5 million
Major Ethnic Groups: Peuhl, Malinke, Soussou
Major Religions: Islam
Government: Republic
Currency: 1 Guinean franc (FG) = 100 centimes
Leading Exports: Bauxite, alumina, diamonds, gold, and coffee
Major Languages: French and various languages

Guinea-Bissau

Capital: Bissau
Area: 13,946 sq mi; 36,210 sq mi
Climate: Tropical; mostly hot and humid; monsoonal-type rainy season; dry season
Population: 1.3 million
Major Ethnic Groups: Balanta, Fula, Manjaca, Mandinga, Papel
Major Religions: Traditional African religions, Islam
Government: Republic, multiparty since mid-1991
Currency: 1 Communaute Financiere Africaine franc (CFAF) = 100 centimes
Leading Exports: Cashews, shrimp, peanuts, and palm kernels
Major Languages: Portuguese, Crioulo, and various languages

Liberia

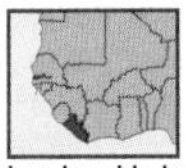

Capital: Monrovia
Area: 43,002 sq mi; 111,370 sq km
Climate: Tropical; hot, humid; dry winters; wet, cloudy summers
Population: 3.2 million
Major Ethnic Groups: Kpelle, Bassa, Gio, Kru
Major Religions: Traditional African religions, Christianity, Islam
Government: Republic
Currency: 1 Liberian dollar (L$) = 100 cents
Leading Exports: Diamonds, iron ore, rubber, timber, and coffee
Major Languages: English (official), some 20 ethnic group languages

Mali

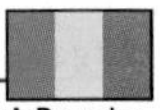

Capital: Bamako
Area: 478,783 sq mi; 1,240,000 sq km
Climate: Arid in north, semiarid in south
Population: 10.7 million
Major Ethnic Groups: Bambara, Malinke, Soninke, Peul, Valtaic
Major Religions: Islam
Government: Republic
Currency: 1 Communaute Financiere Africaine franc (CFAF) = 100 centimes
Leading Exports: Cotton, livestock, and gold
Major Languages: French, Bambara, and various languages

Mauritania

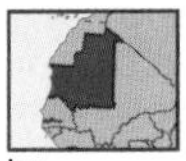

Capital: Nouakchott
Area: 397,969 sq mi; 1,030,700 sq km
Climate: Desert, always hot, dry, and dusty
Population: 2.7 million
Major Ethnic Groups: Mixed Maur and indigenous
Major Religions: Islam
Government: Republic
Currency: 1 ouguiya (UM) = 5 khoums
Leading Exports: Iron ore, and fish and fish products
Major Languages: Hasaniya Arabic, Wolof, Pular, and Soninke
Major Languages: English (official), Mende, Temne, and Krio

3 Assess/Reteach

Much of the Sahel is savanna. During periods of drought, large areas of the Sahel may lose all vegetation and turn from savanna to desert. Have students refer to the climate entries. Ask which countries in West Africa are affected by desertification. (*the Sahel countries of Mauritania, Mali, Niger, Burkina Faso, and Chad*)

Portfolio Assessment

Overview

The following activities help students explore, collect, and arrange the information they find in the Regional Database. You may wish to have students add these activities to a portfolio of information about the countries of the world. To assess student work, refer to the generic rubrics in the Assessment Handbook.

Main Activity

As students can see from the text descriptions, West Africa is a region of ethnic diversity.

- Have students choose a country in West Africa with at least three ethnic groups listed in the text description. Ask students to use the library or the Internet to do research on the country they choose.
- Students' research should focus on the people and cultures of the country. Have them locate the following: current population, number of official languages, economic activities, and ethnic traditions. Students should include at least one illustration of an ethnic group in their country.
- Ask students to compile their information in a written report. Encourage students to develop a creative format for their reports. For example, information could be presented as a data sheet for Americans planning to visit the country, or as a news magazine story.

Additional Activity

Extend the activity by asking students to compile a brief history of the country they have chosen. Ask students to include the country's date of independence and major events since independence.

Niger

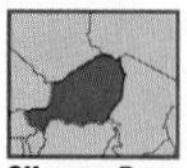

Capital: Niamey
Area: 489,208 sq mi; 1,267,000 sq km
Climate: Desert; mostly hot, dry, dusty; tropical in extreme south
Population: 10.1 million
Major Ethnic Groups: Hausa, Djerma
Major Religions: Islam
Government: Republic
Currency: 1 Communaute Financiere Africaine franc (CFAF) = 100 centimes
Leading Exports: Uranium ore and livestock products
Major Languages: French (official), Hausa, and Djerma

Nigeria

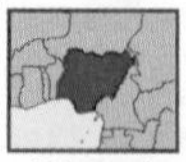

Capital: Abuja
Area: 356,682 sq mi; 923,770 sq km
Climate: Tropical; arid in north
Population: 123.3 million
Major Ethnic Groups: Hausa, Fulani, Yoruba, Igbo, Ijaw
Major Religions: Islam, Christianity
Government: Republic transitioning from military to civilian rule
Currency: 1 naira (N) = 100 kobo
Leading Exports: Petroleum and petroleum products
Major Languages: English (official), Hausa, Yoruba, Igbo, and Fulani

Senegal

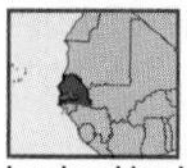

Capital: Dakar
Area: 75,752 sq mi; 196,190 sq km
Climate: Tropical; hot, humid; rainy season has strong southeast winds; dry season dominated by hot, dry wind
Population: 10 million
Major Ethnic Groups: Wolof, Pular, Serer
Major Religions: Islam
Government: Republic under multiparty democratic rule
Currency: 1 Communaute Financiere Africaine franc (CFAF) = 100 centimes
Leading Exports: Fish, ground nuts, and petroleum products
Major Languages: French (official), Wolof, Pulaar, Jola, and Mandinka

Sierra Leone

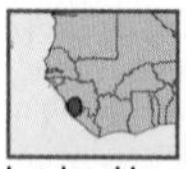

Capital: Freetown
Area: 27,700 sq mi; 71,740 sq km
Climate: Tropical; hot, humid; summer rainy season; winter dry season
Population: 5.2 million
Major Ethnic Groups: Temne, Mende
Major Religions: Islam, traditional African religions
Government: Constitutional democracy
Currency: 1 leone (Le) = 100 cents
Leading Exports: Diamonds, rutile, cocoa, coffee, and fish
Major Languages: English (official), Mende, Temne, and Krio

Togo

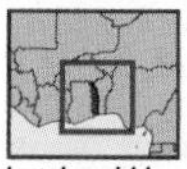

Capital: Lome
Area: 21,927 sq mi; 56,790 sq km
Climate: Tropical; hot, humid in south; semiarid in north
Population: 5 million
Major Ethnic Groups: Ewe, Mina, Kabre
Major Religions: Traditional African religions, Christianity
Government: Republic under transition to multiparty democracy
Currency: 1 Communaute Financiere Africaine franc (CFAF) = 100 centimes
Leading Exports: Phosphates, cotton, cocoa, and coffee
Major Languages: French, Ewe and Mina, Dagomba, and Kabye

Resource Directory

Other Print Resources

Assessment Handbook Generic Rubrics 27 and 31

East Africa: Political

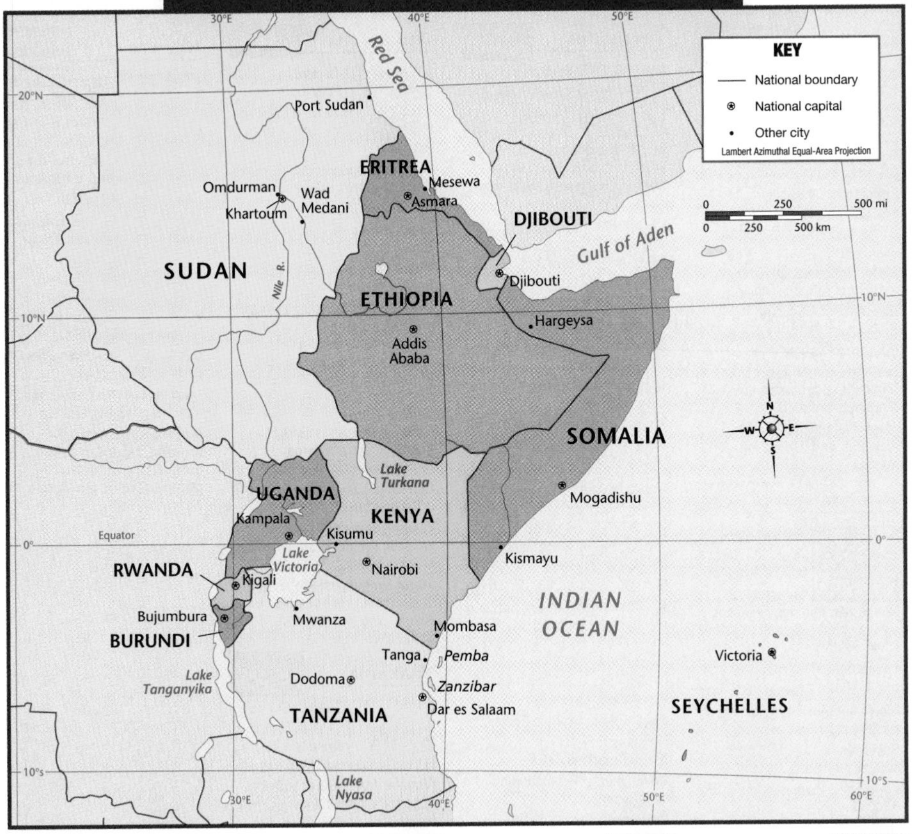

Burundi

Capital: Bujumbura
Area: 10,746 sq mi; 27,830 sq km
Climate: Tropical; temperature moderated by altitude; wet seasons alternate with dry seasons
Population: 6 million
Major Ethnic Groups: Hutu, Tutsi, Twa
Major Religions: Christianity, traditional African religions, Islam
Government: Republic
Currency: 1 Burundi franc (Fbu) = 100 centimes
Leading Exports: Coffee, tea, sugar, cotton, and hides
Major Languages: Kirundi, French, and Swahili

Djibouti

Capital: Djibouti
Area: 8,495 sq mi; 22,000 sq km
Climate: Desert; extremely hot and dry
Population: 451,000
Major Ethnic Groups: Somali, Afar
Major Religions: Islam
Government: Republic
Currency: 1 Djiboutian franc (DF) = 100 centimes
Leading Exports: Hides and skins, and coffee
Major Languages: French, Arabic, Somali, and Afar

Eritrea

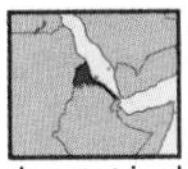

Capital: Asmara
Area: 46,844 sq mi; 121,320 sq km
Climate: Hot, dry desert strip along Red Sea coast; cooler and wetter in central highlands; semiarid in western hills and lowlands
Population: 4.1 million
Major Ethnic Groups: Tigrinya, Tigre, and Kunama
Major Religions: Islam, Christianity
Government: Transitional
Currency: 1 nafka = 100 cents
Leading Exports: Livestock, sorghum, textiles, food
Major Languages: Afar, Amharic, Arabic, Tigre, Kunama, Tigrinya and Cushitic dialects

Ethiopia

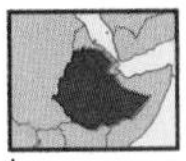

Capital: Addis Ababa
Area: 435,201 sq mi; 1,127,127 sq km
Climate: Subtropical on central plateau; varies with elevation
Population: 64.1 million
Major Ethnic Groups: Oromo, Amhara, Tigre, Sidamo, Shankella, and Somali
Major Religions: Islam, Christianity
Government: Federal republic
Currency: 1 birr (Br) = 100 cents
Leading Exports: Coffee, leather products, and gold
Major Languages: Amharic, Tigrinya, Orominga, Guaraginga, Somali, Arabic, English, and various languages

Lesson Objectives

Gather, understand, and apply information about the countries of East Africa.

Lesson Plan

1 Explore

Have students look at the map of East Africa. Ask volunteers to answer the following questions: Which countries in East Africa have coastlines? *(Sudan, Eritrea, Djibouti, Somalia, Kenya, Tanzania, Seychelles)* Which countries in East Africa are landlocked? *(Ethiopia, Uganda, Rwanda, Burundi)*

2 Teach

Point out that several East African countries have locations valuable for trade. Ethiopia, Somalia, Eritrea, and Djibouti are located on a landform known as the Horn of Africa. These countries are located near the oil supplies of the Middle East and the shipping lanes of the Red Sea and the Gulf of Aden.

Resource Directory

Other Print Resources

DK Atlas

Technology

Color Transparencies 99 East and Southern Africa: Political Map

Passport to the World CD-ROM This interactive CD-ROM allows students to explore each region of the world. Students view regional videos, take a photo tour, and explore a historical timeline. Students record their travels in an Explorer's Journal, and receive passport stamps when they pass regional quizzes.

Regional Database

Lesson Plan continued

3 Assess/Reteach

Have students practice the skill of relative location by asking them to match the following locations with the correct country: This country has coastlines along the Indian Ocean and the Gulf of Aden. (*Somalia*) The Equator extends through this landlocked country. (*Uganda*) This country shares a northern border with Ethiopia and a southern border with Tanzania. (*Kenya*) This country shares an eastern border with Eritrea and Ethiopia. (*Sudan*)

Kenya

Capital: Nairobi
Area: 224,970 sq mi; 582,650 sq km
Climate: Humid, wet along coast; dry on plateaus; temperate in highlands
Population: 30.3 million
Major Ethnic Groups: Kikuyu, Luhya, Luo, Kalenjin, Kamba, Kisii, Meru
Major Religions: Christianity, traditional African religions
Government: Republic
Currency: 1 Kenyan shilling (KSh) = 100 cents
Leading Exports: Tea, coffee, horticultural products, and petroleum products
Major Languages: English, Kiswahili, and various languages

Rwanda

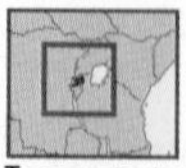

Capital: Kigali
Area: 10,170 sq mi; 26,340 sq km
Climate: Temperate; two rainy seasons; mild in mountains with frost and snow possible
Population: 7.2 million
Major Ethnic Groups: Hutu, Tutsi
Major Religions: Christianity, traditional African religions
Government: Republic; presidential, multiparty system
Currency: 1 Rwandan franc (RF) = 100 centimes
Leading Exports: Coffee, tea, hides, and tin ore
Major Languages: Kinyarwanda (official), French (official), English (official), and Kiswahili

Seychelles

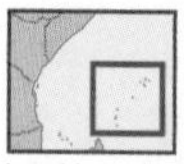

Capital: Victoria
Area: 176 sq mi; 455 sq km
Climate: Tropical; humid; cooler season during southeast monsoon; warmer season during northwest monsoon
Population: 79,000
Major Ethnic Groups: Seychellois (mix of Asian, African, and European)
Major Religions: Christianity
Government: Republic
Currency: 1 Seychelles rupee (Sre) = 100 cents
Leading Exports: Fish, cinnamon bark, and copra
Major Languages: English (official), French (official), and Creole

Somalia

Capital: Mogadishu
Area: 246,210 sq mi; 637,660 sq km
Climate: Mostly desert; hot; monsoon winds bring rainy season and dry season; little rainfall, hot and humid between monsoons
Population: 7.2 million
Major Ethnic Groups: Somali, Bantu
Major Religions: Islam
Government: No functioning government
Currency: 1 Somali shilling (SoSh) = 100 cents
Leading Exports: Livestock, bananas, fish, and hides
Major Languages: Somali (official), Arabic, Italian, and English

Sudan

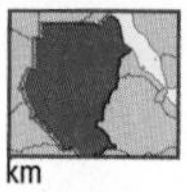

Capital: Khartoum
Area: 967,532 sq mi; 2,505,810 sq km
Climate: Tropical in south; arid desert in north; rainy season
Population: 35 million
Major Ethnic Groups: Azande, Dinka, Arab
Major Religions: Islam, traditional African religions
Government: Transitional; note: previously ruling military junta; presidential and National Assembly elections held in March 1996; new constitution drafted by Presidential Committee, went into effect on June 30, 1998 after being approved in nationwide referendum
Currency: 1 Sudanese dinar (SD) = 100 piastres
Leading Exports: Cotton, sesame, livestock, groundnuts, oil, gum arabic
Major Languages: Arabic (official), Nubian, Ta Bedawie, Nilotic, Nilo-Hamitic, and Sudanic dialects

Tanzania

Capital: Dar Es Salaam
Area: 364,914 sq mi; 945,090 sq km
Climate: Tropical wet and dry; temperate in highlands
Population: 35.3 million
Major Ethnic Groups: Bantu
Major Religions: Christianity, Islam, traditional African religions
Government: Republic
Currency: 1 Tanzanian shilling (TSh) = 100 cents
Leading Exports: Coffee, manufactured goods, cotton, cashew nuts, minerals
Major Languages: Kiswahili, Kiunguju, English, Arabic, and various languages

Uganda

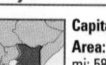

Capital: Kampala
Area: 91,139 sq mi; 236,040 sq km
Climate: Tropical; generally rainy with two dry seasons; semiarid in northeast
Population: 23.3 million
Major Ethnic Groups: Baganda, Karamojong, Basogo, Iteso, Langi, Rwanda
Major Religions: Christianity, Islam, traditional African religions
Government: Republic
Currency: 1 Ugandan shilling (Ush) = 100 cents
Leading Exports: Coffee, fish and fish products, and tea
Major Languages: English, Luganda, Niger-Congo languages, Nilo-Saharan languages, Swahili, and Arabic

Central Africa: Political

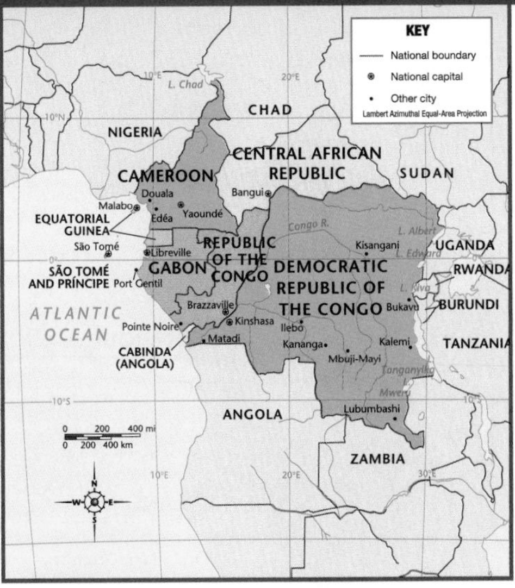

Cameroon

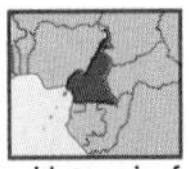

Capital: Yaounde
Area: 183,574 sq mi; 475,440 sq km
Climate: Varies with terrain, from tropical along coast to semiarid and hot in north; wet in mountains
Population: 15.4 million
Major Ethnic Groups: Cameroon Highlanders, Equatorial Bantu, Kirdi, Fulani
Major Religions: Traditional African religions, Christianity, Islam
Government: Unitary republic; multiparty presidential regime
Currency: 1 Communaute Financiere Africaine franc (CFAF) = 100 centimes
Leading Exports: Crude oil and petroleum products, lumber, cocoa beans, and aluminum
Major Languages: 24 various languages, English, and French

Central African Republic

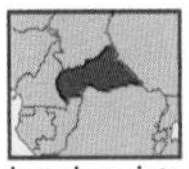

Capital: Bangui
Area: 240,542 sq mi; 622,980 sq km
Climate: Tropical; hot, dry winters; mild to hot, wet summers
Population: 3.5 million
Major Ethnic Groups: Baya, Banda, Mandjia, Sara
Major Religions: Christianity, traditional African religions, Islam
Government: Republic
Currency: 1 Communaute Financiere Africaine franc (CFAF) = 100 centimes
Leading Exports: Diamonds, timber, cotton, coffee, and tobacco
Major Languages: French, Sangho, Arabic, Hunsa, and Swahili

Congo, Democratic Republic of the

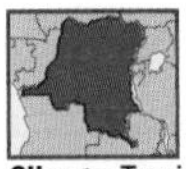

Capital: Kinshasa
Area: 905,599 sq mi; 2,345,410 sq km
Climate: Tropical; very hot and humid; cooler in highlands; rainy seasons north and south
Population: 52 million
Major Ethnic Groups: Mongo, Luba, Mangbetu-Azande, Kongo
Major Religions: Christianity, traditional African religions, Islam
Government: Dictatorship; presumably undergoing a transition to representative government
Currency: Congolese franc (CF)
Leading Exports: Diamonds, copper, coffee, cobalt, and crude oil
Major Languages: French, Lingala, Kingwana, Kikongo, and Tshiluba

Congo, Republic of the

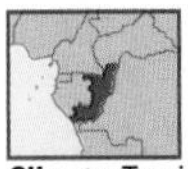

Capital: Brazzavile
Area: 132,051 sq mi; 342,000 sq km
Climate: Tropical; rainy and dry seasons; constantly high temperatures and humidity; particularly harsh near Equator
Population: 2.8 million
Major Ethnic Groups: Kongo, Sangha, M'Bochi, Teke
Major Religions: Christianity, traditional African religions
Government: Republic
Currency: 1 Communaute Financiere Africaine franc (CFAF) = 100 centimes
Leading Exports: Petroleum, lumber, plywood, sugar, and cocoa
Major Languages: French, Lingala, Monokutuba, Kikongo, and other languages

Equatorial Guinea

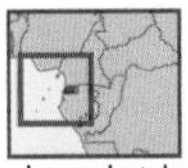

Capital: Malabo
Area: 10,831 sq mi; 28,050 sq km
Climate: Tropical; always hot, humid
Population: 474,000
Major Ethnic Groups: Bubi, Fernandinos, Fang
Major Religions: Christianity, traditional African religions
Government: Republic
Currency: 1 Communaute Financiere Africaine franc (CFAF) = 100 centimes
Leading Exports: Petroleum, timber, and cocoa beans
Major Languages: Spanish, French, pidgin English, Fang, Bubi, and Ibo

Gabon

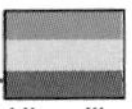

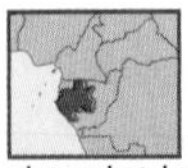

Capital: Libreville
Area: 103,351 sq mi; 267,670 sq km
Climate: Tropical; always hot, humid; rainy seasons alternate with dry seasons
Population: 1.2 million
Major Ethnic Groups: Fang, Eshira, Bapounou, Bateke
Major Religions: Christianity, traditional African religions
Government: Republic; multiparty presidential regime
Currency: 1 Communaute Financiere Africaine franc (CFAF) = 100 centimes
Leading Exports: Crude oil, timber, manganese, and uranium
Major Languages: French, Fang, Myene, Bateke, Bapounou/Eschira, and Bandjabi

São Tomé and Príncipe

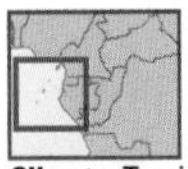

Capital: São Tomé
Area: 371 sq mi; 960 sq km
Climate: Tropical; hot, humid; rainy season
Population: 160,000
Major Ethnic Groups: Mestico (mix of European and Native American), angolares (descendants of Angolan slaves), forros (descendants of freed slaves), servicais (contract laborers from Angola, Mozambique, and Cape Verde), tongas (children of servicais born on the islands)
Major Religions: Christianity
Government: Republic
Currency: 1 dobra (Db) = 100 centimes
Leading Exports: Cocoa, copra, coffee, and palm oil
Major Languages: Portuguese (official)

Lesson Objectives

Gather, understand, and apply information about the countries of Central Africa.

Lesson Plan

1 Explore

Have students look at the map of Central Africa. Point out that the Equator extends through this region. Ask students to locate the largest country in Central Africa. (*the Democratic Republic of Congo, formerly Zaire*)

2 Teach

Ask students to locate the Congo River on the map. Most of it is located in the Democratic Republic of Congo. Explain to students that the Congo is the largest river of the region. Its length is 2,900 miles. Have students locate some of the Congo's many tributaries. The river and its tributaries total about 9,000 miles. This river system is a great waterway that provides transportation, food, and water for much of the region.

3 Assess/Reteach

Ask students to locate the capitals of the Congo Republic and the Democratic Republic of Congo. (*Brazzaville is the capital of the Congo Republic. Kinshasa is the capital of the Democratic Republic of the Congo.*) Ask students to describe the relative location of these two cities. (*Kinshasa and Brazzaville are located across from one another on the Congo River.*) What forms the national boundary between these two capitals? (*the Congo River*)

Resource Directory

Other Print Resources

DK Atlas

Technology

Color Transparencies 98 West and Central Africa: Political Map

Passport to the World CD-ROM This interactive CD-ROM allows students to explore each region of the world. Students view regional videos, take a photo tour, and explore a historical timeline. Students record their travels in an Explorer's Journal, and receive passport stamps when they pass regional quizzes.

Regional Database

Lesson Objectives

Gather, understand, and apply information about the countries of Southern Africa.

Lesson Plan

1 Explore

Write the words *landlocked, coastal,* and *island* on the chalkboard. Have students use the map to locate the landlocked countries of Southern Africa. Write them on the chalkboard under *landlocked.* Have students do the same for the coastal and island countries of South Africa. Write them on the chalkboard as well.

2 Teach

Have students look at the text descriptions. Ask them to find the most populated country in Southern Africa. (*South Africa*) Tell students that South Africa is the wealthiest and most developed country in Africa.

3 Assess/Reteach

Have students review the locations of the countries of Southern Africa. Divide the class into pairs. Have each pair of students take turns giving clues about the relative location of countries in Southern Africa. Model the activity by giving the following clue to a student: This country is entirely landlocked and is located north of South Africa. (*Botswana*) Students may refer to the map as they complete the activity.

Southern Africa: Political

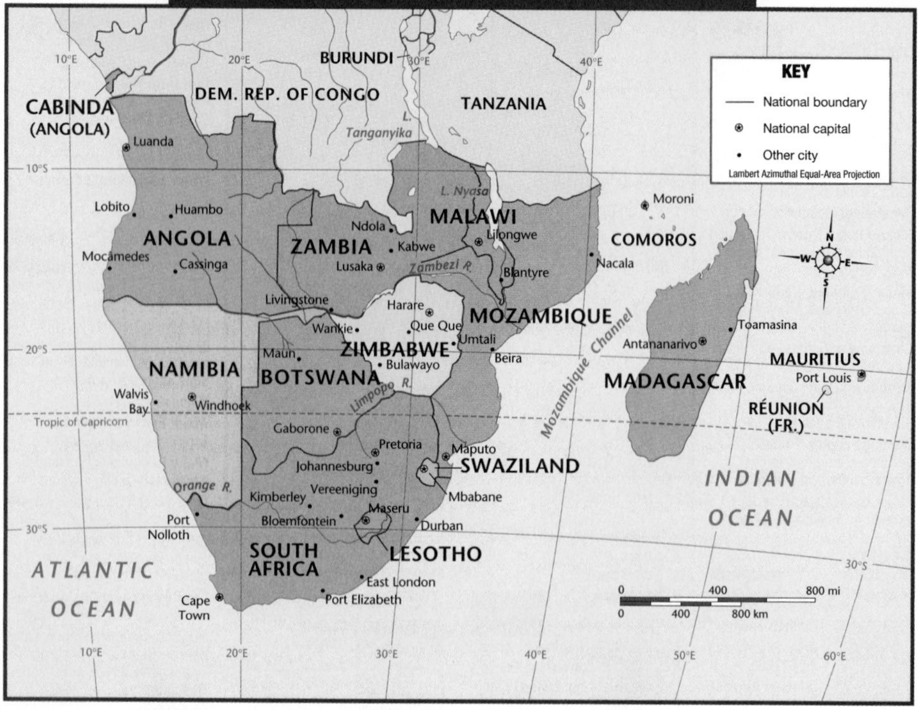

Angola

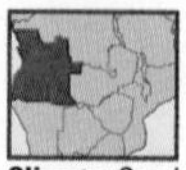

Capital: Luanda
Area: 481,370 sq mi; 1,246,700 sq km
Climate: Semiarid in south and along coast to Luanda; tropical in north with a cool, dry season and a hot, rainy season
Population: 10.1 million
Major Ethnic Groups: Ovimbundu, Kimbundu, Bakongo
Major Religions: Traditional African religions, Christianity
Government: Transitional government, nominally a multiparty democracy with a strong presidential system
Currency: 1 kwanza (NKz) = 100 lwei
Leading Exports: Crude oil, diamonds, and refined petroleum products
Major Languages: Portuguese (official), Bantu, and various languages

Botswana

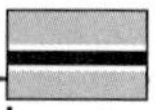

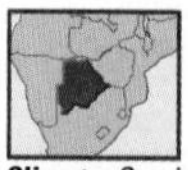

Capital: Gaborone
Area: 231,812 sq mi; 600,370 sq km
Climate: Semiarid; warm winters; hot summers
Population: 1.6 million
Major Ethnic Groups: Batswana
Major Religions: Traditional African religions, Christianity
Government: Parliamentary republic
Currency: 1 pula (P) = 100 thebe
Leading Exports: Diamonds, vehicles, copper and nickel, and meat
Major Languages: English and Setswana

Comoros

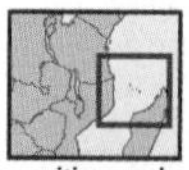

Capital: Moroni
Area: 838 sq mi; 2,170 sq km
Climate: Tropical maritime, rainy season
Population: 578,000
Major Ethnic Groups: Antalote, Cafre, Makoa, Oimatsaha, Sakalava
Major Religions: Islam
Government: Independent republic
Currency: 1 Comoran franc (CF) = 100 centimes
Leading Exports: Vanilla, ylang-ylang, cloves, and perfume oil
Major Languages: Arabic, French, and Comoran

Lesotho

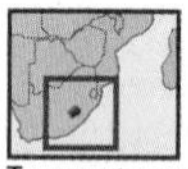

Capital: Maseru
Area: 11,719 sq mi; 30,350 sq km
Climate: Temperate; cool to cold, dry winters; hot, wet summers
Population: 2.1 million
Major Ethnic Groups: Sotho
Major Religions: Christianity, traditional African religions
Government: Parliamentary constitutional monarchy
Currency: 1 loti (L) = 100 lisente
Leading Exports: manufactures, wool, mohair, food and live animals
Major Languages: Sesotho, English, Zulu, and Xhosa

Resource Directory

Other Print Resources

DK Atlas

Technology

Color Transparencies 99 East and Southern Africa: Political Map

Passport to the World CD-ROM This interactive CD-ROM allows students to explore each region of the world. Students view regional videos, take a photo tour, and explore a historical timeline. Students record their travels in an Explorer's Journal, and receive passport stamps when they pass regional quizzes.

Madagascar

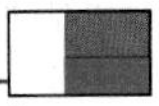

Capital: Antananarivo
Area: 226,665 sq mi; 587,040 sq km
Climate: Tropical along coast; temperate inland; arid in south
Population: 15.5 million
Major Ethnic Groups: Merina, Betsileo, Cotiers
Major Religions: Traditional African religions, Christianity
Government: Republic
Currency: 1 Malagasy franc (FMG) = 100 centimes
Leading Exports: Coffee, vanilla, cloves, shellfish, and sugar
Major Languages: French and Malagasy

Malawi

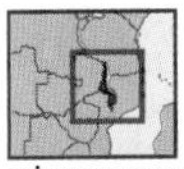

Capital: Lilongwe
Area: 45,747 sq mi; 118,480 sq km
Climate: Tropical; rainy season; cooler in highlands
Population: 10.4 million
Major Ethnic Groups: Chewa, Nyanja, other indigenous African groups
Major Religions: Christianity, Islam
Government: Multiparty democracy
Currency: 1 Malawian kwacha (MK) = 100 tambala
Leading Exports: Tobacco, tea, sugar, coffee, and peanuts
Major Languages: English, Chichewa, and various languages

Mauritius

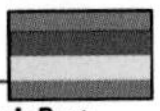

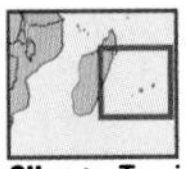

Capital: Port Louis
Area: 718 sq mi; 1,860 sq km
Climate: Tropical, modified by southeast trade winds; warm, dry winter; hot, wet humid summer
Population: 1.2 million
Major Ethnic Groups: Indo-Mauritian, Creole
Major Religions: Hinduism, Christianity, Islam
Government: Parliamentary democracy
Currency: 1 Mauritian rupee (MauR) = 100 cents
Leading Exports: Clothing, textiles, sugar, cut flowers, and molasses
Major Languages: English (official), Creole, French, Hindi, Urdu, Hakka, and Bojpoori

Mozambique

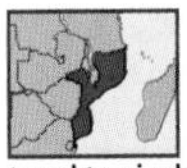

Capital: Maputo
Area: 309,506 sq mi; 801,590 sq km
Climate: Tropical to subtropical; dry season
Population: 19.1 million
Major Ethnic Groups: Shangaan, Chokwe, Manyika, Sena, Makua
Major Religions: Traditional African religions, Christianity, Islam
Government: Republic
Currency: 1 metical (Mt) = 100 centavos
Leading Exports: Shrimp, cashews, cotton, sugar, copra, and citrus
Major Languages: Portuguese and various dialects

Namibia

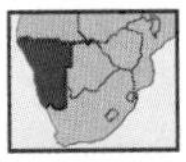

Capital: Windhoek
Area: 318,707 sq mi; 825,418 sq km
Climate: Desert; hot, dry; little rainfall
Population: 1.8 million
Major Ethnic Groups: Ovambo, Kavangos
Major Religions: Christianity, traditional African religions
Government: Republic
Currency: 1 Namibian dollar (N$) = 100 cents
Leading Exports: Diamonds, copper, gold, zinc, and lead
Major Languages: English (official), Afrikaans, German, Oshivambo, Herero, Nama

South Africa

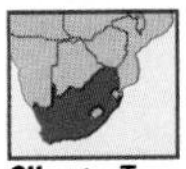

Capital: Pretoria
Area: 471,027 sq mi; 1,219,912 sq km
Climate: Temperate; mostly dry; subtropical along eastern coast
Population: 43.4 million
Major Ethnic Groups: Nguni, Caucasian
Major Religions: Christianity, traditional African religions
Government: Republic
Currency: 1 rand (R) = 100 cents
Leading Exports: Gold, diamonds, other minerals and metals
Major Languages: Afrikaans, English, Ndebele, Pedi, Sotho, Swazi, Tsonga, Tswana, Venda, Xhosa, and Zulu (all official)

Swaziland

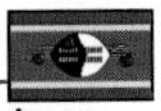

Capital: Mbabane
Area: 6,641 sq mi; 17,360 sq km
Climate: Mostly temperate; more tropical in east
Population: 1.1 million
Major Ethnic Groups: Swazi
Major Religions: Christianity, traditional African religions
Government: Monarchy, independent member of Commonwealth
Currency: 1 lilangeni (E) = 100 cents
Leading Exports: Sugar, edible concentrates, and wood pulp
Major Languages: English (official), siSwati (official)

Zambia

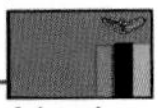

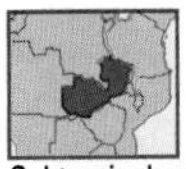

Capital: Lusaka
Area: 290,594 sq mi; 752,610 sq km
Climate: Subtropical; rainy season
Population: 9.6 million
Major Ethnic Groups: Bemba, Nyanja, Tonga
Major Religions: Christianity, Islam
Government: Republic
Currency: 1 Zambian kwacha (ZK) = 100 ngwee
Leading Exports: Copper, cobalt, electricity, and tobacco
Major Languages: English (official) and about 70 various languages

Zimbabwe

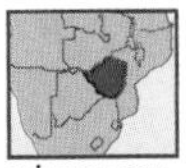

Capital: Harare
Area: 150,809 sq mi; 390,580 sq km
Climate: Tropical; rainy season
Population: 11.3 million
Major Ethnic Groups: Shona, Ndebele
Major Religions: Christian/traditional mix, Christianity, traditional African religions
Government: Parliamentary democracy
Currency: 1 Zimbabwean dollar (Z$) = 100 cents
Leading Exports: Tobacco, gold, ferroalloys, cotton
Major Languages: English, Shona, and Sindebele

Portfolio Assessment

Overview

The following activities help students explore, collect, and arrange the information they find in the Regional Data Bank. You may wish to have students add these activities to a portfolio of information about the countries of the world. To assess student work, refer to the generic rubrics in the Assessment Handbook.

Main Activity

Ask students to choose an African nation they would like to visit. Have them write a short paragraph explaining why they wish to visit that country. Then, have students use the library or the Internet to write an itinerary of their imaginary trip.

- Ask students to be sure to include a visit to the country's capital and one other major city. Students should also include a place where they can learn about the country's history.
- Students can display their itineraries on a bulletin board. If time allows, volunteers may present them to the class.

Additional Activity

Some of the crops grown in Africa may be unfamiliar to some students. Have students read the export entries in the text descriptions and note any crops that are unfamiliar to them. Students can do research to learn more about these crops. They may include cacao, copra, sisal, cassava, plantains, sorghum, and pulses.

Resource Directory

Other Print Resources

Assessment Handbook Generic Rubrics 23 and 27

Regional Database

Lesson Objectives

Gather, understand, and apply information about the countries of East Asia.

Lesson Plan

1 Explore

Have students look at the map of East Asia. Ask students which East Asian country is the largest (*China*). Next, ask students which East Asian country is the smallest (*Taiwan*). Ask students which East Asian country is made up of islands (*Japan*).

2 Teach

Ask students to locate the Huang He and the Yangzi Rivers in China. Both are major transportation routes in China. The Yangzi is China's east-west waterway. Ocean-going ships can travel about 700 miles inland to the city of Wuhan. Ask students to find Shanghai, located at the mouth of the Yangzi River. Shanghai is China's major port. It is also the largest city in China.

3 Assess/Reteach

Explain that China's physical location between eastern and western Asia has historically made it a crossroads of trade and ideas. Point out that Chinese art and culture heavily influenced that of its neighbors, Japan and the Koreas. Ask students what religion is common to all East Asian countries (*Buddhism*). Explain that Buddhism came to China from India, and then spread to the other East Asian countries.

East Asia: Political

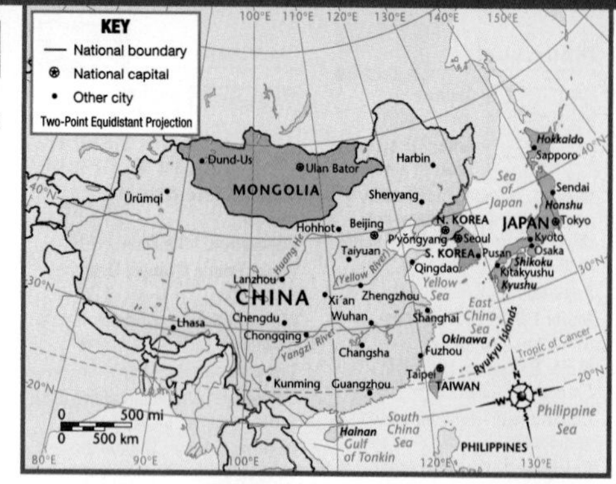

China

Capital: Beijing
Area: 3,705,533 sq mi; 9,596,960 sq km
Climate: Mostly continental; varies from tropical in far southeast to subarctic in far north; cold, dry winters and warm summers, with heavy rains along coast
Population: 1.2 billion
Major Ethnic Groups: Han Chinese
Major Religions: Daoism, Buddhism
Government: Communist state
Currency: 1 yuan = 10 jiao
Leading Exports: Textiles, garments, footwear, and toys
Major Languages: Mandarin, Putonghua, Yue, Wu, Minbei, Minnan, Xiang, and Gan and Hakka dialects

Japan

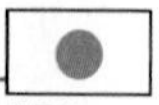

Capital: Tokyo
Area: 145,888 sq mi; 377,835 sq km
Climate: Ranges from subtropical in south to continental in north; mostly mild winters and hot, humid summers; severe, long winters in north
Population: 126.5 million
Major Ethnic Groups: Japanese
Major Religions: Buddhism, Shintoism
Government: Constitutional monarchy
Currency: yen
Leading Exports: Machinery, motor vehicles, and electronics
Major Languages: Japanese

Mongolia

Capital: Ulaanbaatar
Area: 604,270 sq mi; 1,565,000 sq km
Climate: Arid; extremely cold winters, mild summers
Population: 2.6 million
Major Ethnic Groups: Halh Mongol
Major Religions: Buddhism
Government: Republic
Currency: 1 tughrik (Tug) = 100 mongos
Leading Exports: Copper, livestock, animal products, and cashmere
Major Languages: Khalkha Mongol, Turkic, Russian, and Chinese

North Korea

Capital: P'yongyang
Area: 46,542 sq mi; 120,540 sq km
Climate: Humid continental; cold winters and wet, hot summers
Population: 21.7 million
Major Ethnic Groups: Korean
Major Religions: Ch'ondogyo (mix of Confucianism and Daoism), Buddhism
Government: Authoritarian socialist, one-man dictatorship
Currency: 1 North Korean won (Wn) = 100 chon
Leading Exports: Minerals and metallurgical products
Major Languages: Korean

South Korea

Capital: Seoul
Area: 38,025 sq mi; 98,480 sq km
Climate: Continental; cold, dry winters and hot, rainy summers
Population: 47.5 million
Major Ethnic Groups: Korean
Major Religions: Christianity, Buddhism
Government: Republic
Currency: 1 South Korean won (W) = 100 chun
Leading Exports: Electronic and electrical equipment
Major Languages: Korean and English

Taiwan

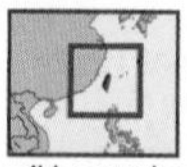

Capital: Taipei
Area: 13,892 sq mi; 35,980 sq km
Climate: Tropical; mild, wet winters and hot, humid summers; cloudy most of year
Population: 22.2 million
Major Ethnic Groups: Han Chinese
Major Religions: Buddhism, Daoism
Government: Multiparty democratic regime headed by popularly elected president
Currency: 1 New Taiwanese dollar (NT$) = 100 cents
Leading Exports: Electrical machinery and electronics
Major Languages: Mandarin Chinese (official), Taiwanese, and Hakka dialects

Resource Directory

Other Print Resources

DK Atlas

Technology

Color Transparencies 115 East Asia: Physical-Political Map; **116** East Asia: Political Map

Passport to the World CD-ROM This interactive CD-ROM allows students to explore each region of the world. Students view regional videos, take a photo tour, and explore a historical timeline. Students record their travels in an Explorer's Journal, and receive passport stamps when they pass regional quizzes.

Southeast Asia: Political

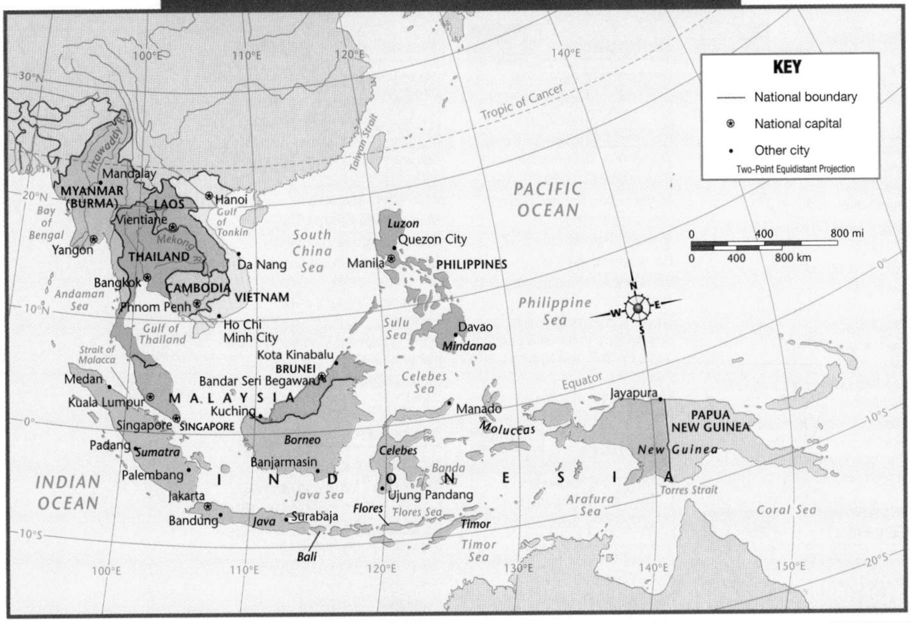

Brunei

Capital: Bandar Seri Begawan
Area: 2,228 sq mi; 5,770 sq km
Climate: Tropical wet; hot, humid; long rainy season
Population: 336,000
Major Ethnic Groups: Malay, Chinese
Major Religions: Islam
Government: Constitutional sultanate
Currency: 1 Bruneian dollar (B$) = 100 cents
Leading Exports: Crude oil and liquefied natural gas
Major Languages: Malay, English, and Chinese

Cambodia

Capital: Phnom Penh
Area: 69,902 sq mi; 181,040 sq km
Climate: Tropical; hot, humid; rainy season and dry season
Population: 12.2 million
Major Ethnic Groups: Khmer
Major Religions: Buddhism
Government: Multiparty liberal democracy under a constitutional monarchy established in September 1993
Currency: 1 new riel (CR) = 100 sen
Leading Exports: Timber, garements, rubber, rice, fish
Major Languages: Khmer and French

Indonesia

Capital: Jakarta
Area: 741,052 sq mi; 1,919,251 sq km
Climate: Tropical; hot, humid; cooler in upland areas; rainy season and dry season
Population: 224.8 million
Major Ethnic Groups: Javanese, Sundanese
Major Religions: Islam
Government: Republic
Currency: Indonesian rupiah (Rp) = 100 sen
Leading Exports: Oil and gas, plywood, textiles
Major Languages: Bahasa Indonesia, English, Dutch, Javanese, and various dialects

Laos

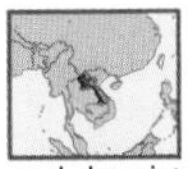

Capital: Vientiane
Area: 91,432 sq mi; 236,800 sq km
Climate: Tropical; cool, dry winters and hot, wet summers
Population: 5.5 million
Major Ethnic Groups: Lao Loum, Lao Theung
Major Religions: Buddhism, traditional beliefs
Government: Communist state
Currency: 1 new kip (NK) = 100 at
Leading Exports: Electricity, wood products, coffee, and tin
Major Languages: Lao, French, English, and various languages

Lesson Objectives

Gather, understand, and apply information about the countries of Southeast Asia.

Lesson Plan

1 Explore

Ask volunteers to name two landforms that make up much of Southeast Asia (*peninsulas and islands*). Have students find the country of Malaysia. Point out that part of Malaysia is located on a peninsula and the other part is located on the island of Borneo.

2 Teach

Have students find the Southeast Asian countries located entirely on islands (*Brunei, Philippines, Indonesia, Singapore*). The island of Singapore is located just off the tip of the Malay Peninsula. Point out the peninsula where the mainland Southeast Asian countries are located. Tell students this peninsula is called the Indochina Peninsula. Have them name the countries on it (*Myanmar, Laos, Thailand, Cambodia, Vietnam*).

3 Assess/Reteach

Have students practice the skill of relative location by asking them to match the following locations with the correct country: This country has a coastline along the South China Sea (*Vietnam*). The Mekong River forms part of the border of this landlocked country (*Laos*). This country is made up of islands, including the two islands of Luzon and Mindanao (*Philippines*).

Resource Directory

Other Print Resources

DK Atlas

Technology

Color Transparencies 122 Southeast Asia: Physical-Political Map; **123** Southeast Asia: Political Map

Passport to the World CD-ROM This interactive CD-ROM allows students to explore each region of the world. Students view regional videos, take a photo tour, and explore a historical timeline. Students record their travels in an Explorer's Journal, and receive passport stamps when they pass regional quizzes.

Regional Database

Portfolio Assessment

Overview

The following activities help students explore, collect, and arrange the information they find in the Regional Database. You may wish to have students add these activities to a portfolio of information about the countries of the world. To assess student work, refer to the generic rubrics in the Assessment Handbook.

Main Activity

Explain that Southeast Asia has historically been a cultural crossroads.

- Have small groups of students select one southeast Asian country to profile. Ask each group to use library and Internet resources to compile a historical profile of that country. Then, each group will teach a mini-lesson to the other groups in the class.
- Profiles should answer the following questions: What was this country's ancient culture? How did other cultures influence this country? What kinds of trade and other activities brought different peoples to this country? Has this country been ruled by another country sometime in its history?

Additional Activity

Groups can research historical or archaeological objects that have been found in their country. They can find photos of these objects, or create their own drawings of them. Then, they can conduct an "archaeological dig" with their classmates.

Malaysia

Capital: Kuala Lumpur
Area: 127,322 sq mi; 329,750 sq km
Climate: Tropical; hot, humid, and rainy; cooler and drier in highlands
Population: 21.8 million
Major Ethnic Groups: Malay, Chinese
Major Religions: Islam, Buddhism
Government: Constitutional monarchy
Currency: 1 ringgit (M$) = 100 sen
Leading Exports: Electronic equipment
Major Languages: Malay, English, Mandarin, Tamil, Chinese dialects, and various languages and dialects

Myanmar (Burma)

Capital: Rangoon
Area: 261,979 sq mi; 678,500 sq km
Climate: Tropical; dry, warm winters and rainy, hot, humid summers
Population: 41.7 million
Major Ethnic Groups: Burman
Major Religions: Buddhism
Government: Military regime
Currency: 1 kyat (K) = 100 pyas
Leading Exports: Pulses and beans, prawns, fish, rice; teak
Major Languages: Burmese

Philippines

Capital: Manila
Area: 115,834 sq mi; 300,000 sq km
Climate: Tropical; dry winters and rainy summers
Population: 81.1 million
Major Ethnic Groups: Filipino (Christian Malay)
Major Religions: Christianity
Government: Republic
Currency: 1 Philippine peso (P) = 100 centavos
Leading Exports: Electronics, machinery and transport equipment, textiles, and coconut products
Major Languages: Filipino and English (official)

Singapore

Capital: Singapore
Area: 244 sq mi; 633 sq km
Climate: Tropical; hot, humid, rainy all year
Population: 4.1 million
Major Ethnic Groups: Chinese
Major Religions: Buddhism
Government: Parliamentary republic
Currency: 1 Singapore dollar (S$) = 100 cents
Leading Exports: Machinery and equipment (including electronics
Major Languages: Chinese, Malay, Tamil, and English

Thailand

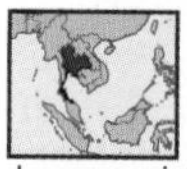

Capital: Bangkok
Area: 198,456 sq mi; 514,000 sq km
Climate: Tropical; dry, warm winters and hot, wet, summers
Population: 61.2 million
Major Ethnic Groups: Thai
Major Religions: Buddhism
Government: Constitutional monarchy
Currency: 1 baht (B) = 100 satang
Leading Exports: Machinery and manufactures
Major Languages: Thai and English

Vietnam

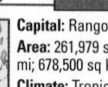

Capital: Hanoi
Area: 127,248 sq mi; 329,560 sq km
Climate: Mostly tropical; hot, dry winters and hot, rainy summers; cooler winters in North
Population: 78.8 million
Major Ethnic Groups: Vietnamese
Major Religions: Buddhism, Christianity
Government: Communist state
Currency: 1 new dong (D) = 100 xu
Leading Exports: Petroleum, rice, and agricultural products
Major Languages: Vietnamese, French, Chinese, English, Khmer, and various languages

Resource Directory

Other Print Resources

Assessment Handbook Generic Rubrics 17, 18, and 26

South Asia: Political

Afghanistan

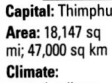

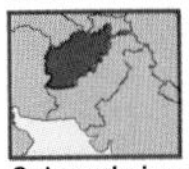

Capital: Kabul
Area: 251,738 sq mi; 652,000 sq km
Climate: Subarctic in mountains; arid in lowlands; cold, dry winters and hot summers
Population: 25.8 million
Major Ethnic Groups: Pashtun, Tajik, Hazara
Major Religions: Islam
Government: No functioning central government, administered by factions
Currency: 1 afghani (AF) = 100 puls
Leading Exports: Fruits and nuts, handwoven carpets, and wool
Major Languages: Pashtu, Afghan Persian, Turkic, and 30 various languages

Bangladesh

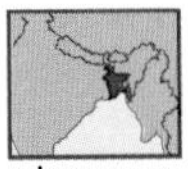

Capital: Dhaka
Area: 55,600 sq mi; 144,000 sq km
Climate: Tropical; rainy season
Population: 129.2 million
Major Ethnic Groups: Bengali
Major Religions: Islam
Government: Republic
Currency: 1 taka (TK) = 100 poisha
Leading Exports: Garments, jute and jute goods, and leather
Major Languages: Bangla and English

Bhutan

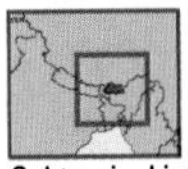

Capital: Thimphu
Area: 18,147 sq mi; 47,000 sq km
Climate: Subtropical in central valleys, with cool winters and hot summers; hotter and more humid in southern plains; highlands in mountains, with bitterly cold winters and cool summers
Population: 2 million
Major Ethnic Groups: Bhutia, Nepali
Major Religions: Buddhism, Hinduism
Government: Monarchy; special treaty relationship with India
Currency: 1 ngultrum (Nu) = 100 chetrum; note – Indian currency is also legal tener
Leading Exports: Cardamon, gypsum, timber and handicrafts
Major Languages: Dzongkha (official), Tibetan dialects, and Nepalese dialects

India

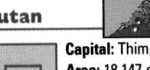

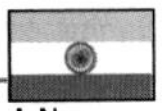

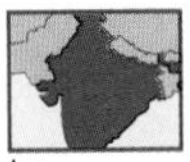

Capital: New Delhi
Area: 1,269,389 sq mi; 3,287,590 sq km
Climate: Mostly tropical in south; mostly subtropical in north; cool, dry winters and hot, dry summers, with heavy rain during monsoon; cold winters and cool summers in mountains; arid in West
Population: 1 billion
Major Ethnic Groups: Indo-Aryan, Dravidian
Major Religions: Hinduism
Government: Federal republic
Currency: 1 Indian rupee (Re) = 100 paise
Leading Exports: Clothing, and gems and jewelry
Major Languages: English, Hindi, Bengali, Telugu, Marathi, Tamil, Urdu, Gujarati, Malayam, Kannada, Oriya, Punjabi, Assamese, Kashmiri, Sindhi, Sanskrit, and Hindustani (all official)

Lesson Objectives

Gather, understand, and apply information about the countries of South Asia.

Lesson Plan

1 Explore

Have students look at the map of South Asia. Ask students to name the largest country in this region (*India*). Point out that the region of South Asia is a subcontinent, or large landmass, jutting out from Asia.

2 Teach

Have students name the remaining countries in South Asia (*Afghanistan, Pakistan, Nepal, Bhutan, Bangladesh, Maldives, Sri Lanka*). Be sure students include Maldives and Sri Lanka. Point out that Maldives is made up of nearly 2,000 islands. The nation of Sri Lanka is one large island.

Resource Directory

Other Print Resources

DK Atlas

Technology

Color Transparencies 124 South Asia: Physical-Political Map; **125** South Asia: Political Map

Passport to the World CD-ROM This interactive CD-ROM allows students to explore each region of the world. Students view regional videos, take a photo tour, and explore a historical timeline. Students record their travels in an Explorer's Journal, and receive passport stamps when they pass regional quizzes.

Regional Database

Lesson Plan continued

③ Assess/Reteach

Explain that India shares a border with all but three South Asian countries. Ask students to name these three countries (*Afghanistan, Sri Lanka, and Maldives*).

Maldives

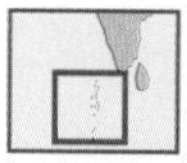

Capital: Male
Area: 116 sq mi; 300 sq km
Climate: Tropical; hot, humid; rainy season in summer
Population: 301,000
Major Ethnic Groups: mix of Sinhalese, Dravidian, Arabian, and Affrican
Major Religions: Islam
Government: Republic
Currency: 1 rufiyaa (Rf) = 100 laari
Leading Exports: Fish and clothing
Major Languages: Divehi dialect and English

Nepal

Capital: Kathmandu
Area: 54,365 sq mi; 140,800 sq km
Climate: Highlands in North, with cool summers and severe winters; subtropical in south, with hot, wet summers and mild, dry winters
Population: 24.7 million
Major Ethnic Groups: Newars, Indian, Tibetan
Major Religions: Hinduism
Government: Parliamentary democracy
Currency: 1 Nepalese rupee (NR) = 100 paisa
Leading Exports: Carpets, clothing, and leather goods
Major Languages: Nepali (official), and 20 various languages divided into numerous dialects

Pakistan

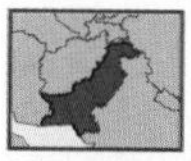

Capital: Islamabad
Area: 310,414 sq mi; 803,940 sq km
Climate: Mostly arid; cold winters in mountains; extremely hot summers in central valley
Population: 141.5 million
Major Ethnic Groups: Punjabi
Major Religions: Islam
Government: Federal republic
Currency: 1 Pakistani rupee (Pre) = 100 paisa
Leading Exports: Cotton, textiles, clothing, rice, and leather
Major Languages: Urdu (official), English (official), Punjabi, Sindhi, Pashtu, Urdu, Balochi, and other languages

Sri Lanka

Capital: Colombo
Area: 25,333 sq mi; 65,610 sq km
Climate: Tropical; hot, humid; cooler and less humid in mountains; wet in southwest; dry north of mountains
Population: 19.2 million
Major Ethnic Groups: Sinhalese, Tamil
Major Religions: Buddhism
Government: Republic
Currency: 1 Sri Lankan rupee (SLRe) = 100 cents
Leading Exports: Garments and textiles, teas, and diamonds
Major Languages: Sinhala (official) and Tamil

Southwest Asia: Political

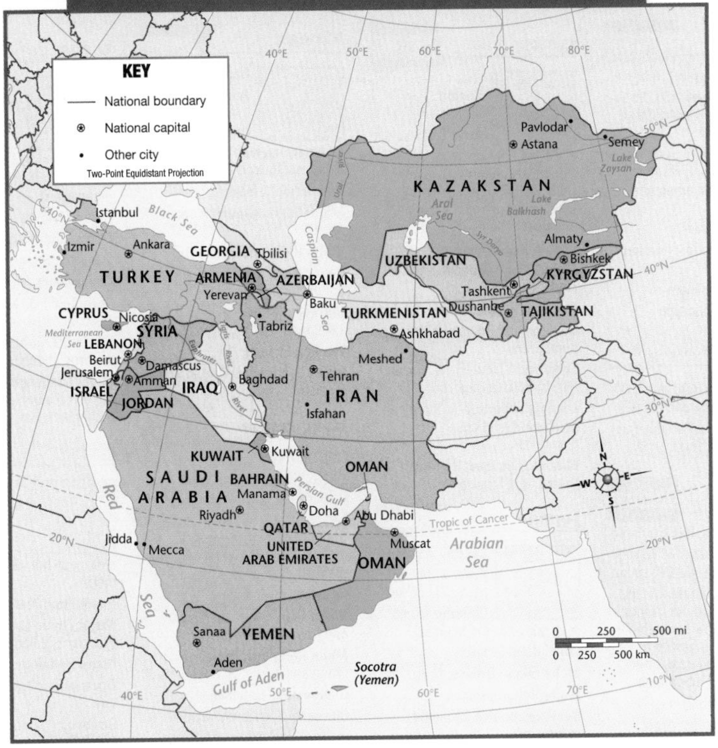

Armenia

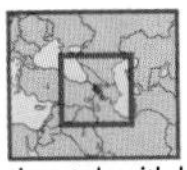

Capital: Yerevan
Area: 11,506 sq mi; 29,800 sq km
Climate: Dry continental, with hot summers and cold winters
Population: 3.3 million
Major Ethnic Groups: Armenian
Major Religions: Christianity
Government: Republic
Currency: 1 dram = 100 luma
Leading Exports: Diamonds, scrap metal, machinery and equipment
Major Languages: Armenian and Russian

Azerbaijan

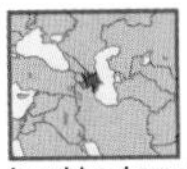

Capital: Baku
Area: 33,438 sq mi; 86,600 sq km
Climate: Dry to humid subtropical and dry to humid continental; moderate rainfall in south, tundra in mountains of north
Population: 7.7 million
Major Ethnic Groups: Azeri
Major Religions: Islam
Government: Republic
Currency: 1 manat = 100 gopiks
Leading Exports: Oil and gas, machinery, cotton
Major Languages: Azeri, Russian, Armenian

Bahrain

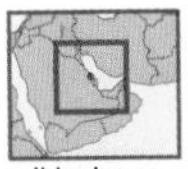

Capital: Manama
Area: 239 sq mi; 620 sq km
Climate: Arid; mild winters and very hot, humid summers
Population: 634,000
Major Ethnic Groups: Bahraini
Major Religions: Islam
Government: Traditional monarchy
Currency: 1 Bahraini dinar (BD) = 1000 fils
Leading Exports: Petroleum and petroleum products
Major Languages: Arabic, English, Farsi, and Urdu

Cyprus

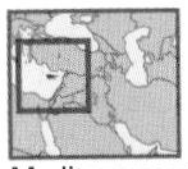

Capital: Nicosia
Area: 3,572 sq mi; 9,250 sq km
Climate: Mediterranean; cool, wet winters and hot, dry summers
Population: 758,000
Major Ethnic Groups: Greek, Turkish
Major Religions: Christianity, Islam
Government: Republic
Currency: Greek Cypriot area: 1 Cypriot pound = 100 cents; Turkish Cypriot area: 1 Turkish lira (TL) = 100 Kurus
Leading Exports: Citrus, potatoes, grapes, wines, and cement
Major Languages: Greek, Turkish, and English

Lesson Objectives

Gather, understand, and apply information about the countries of Southwest Asia.

Lesson Plan

1 Explore

Have students look at the map of Southwest Asia. Point out that this is a large area including many countries, several of which are strategically important to the United States. These include Iran, Iraq, Israel, Jordan, Lebanon, Saudi Arabia, and Syria.

Resource Directory

Other Print Resources

DK Atlas

Technology

Color Transparencies 133 Southwest Asia and North Africa: Physical-Political Map; **134** Southwest Asia and North Africa: Political Map

Passport to the World CD-ROM This interactive CD-ROM allows students to explore each region of the world. Students view regional videos, take a photo tour, and explore a historical timeline. Students record their travels in an Explorer's Journal, and receive passport stamps when they pass regional quizzes.

Regional Database

Lesson Plan continued

❷ Teach

Write *Southwest Asia* on the chalkboard. Using the map, work with students to classify the countries in this region. It includes the following countries: Turkey, Cyprus, Syria, Lebanon, Israel, Jordan, Iraq, Saudi Arabia, Yemen, Oman, Qatar, Bahrain, United Arab Emirates, Kuwait, Iran, Kazakstan, Uzbekistan, Kyrgyzstan, Tajikistan, Turkmenistan, Azerbaijan, Armenia, and Georgia. Point out that many southwest countries were formerly part of the Soviet Union. Have students skim the country descriptions, taking special note of major religions and leading exports.

Iran

Capital: Tehran
Area: 636,296 sq mi; 1,648,000 sq km
Climate: Mostly arid or semiarid; extremely hot along southern coast; subtropical along northern coast
Population: 65.6 million
Major Ethnic Groups: Persian, Azerbaijani
Major Religions: Islam
Government: Theocratic republic
Currency: 10 Iranian rials (IR) = 1 toman
Leading Exports: Petroleum, carpets, fruit, nuts, and hides
Major Languages: Persian and Persian dialects, Turkic and Turkic dialects

Iraq

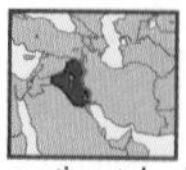

Capital: Baghdad
Area: 168,760 sq mi; 437,072 sq km
Climate: Mostly continental; mild to cool winters with dry, extremely hot summers in central and southern areas; cool summers and cold, often snowy winters in mountains
Population: 22.7 million
Major Ethnic Groups: Arab, Kurdish
Major Religions: Islam
Government: Republic
Currency: 1 Iraqi dinar (ID) = 1,000 fils
Leading Exports: Crude oil
Major Languages: Arabic, Kurdish, Assyrian, and Armenian

Israel

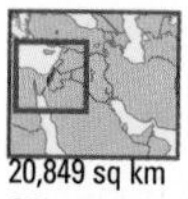

Capital: Jerusalem
Area: 8,019 sq mi; 20,849 sq km
Climate: Mediterranean; cool, rainy winters and warm, dry summers; hot and dry in south and east
Population: 5.8 million
Major Ethnic Groups: Jewish, Arab
Major Religions: Judaism, Islam
Government: Parliamentary democracy
Currency: 1 New Israeli shekel (NIS) = 100 new agorot
Leading Exports: Machinery and equipment, and cut diamonds
Major Languages: Hebrew, Arabic, and English

Jordan

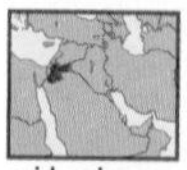

Capital: Amman
Area: 34,447 sq mi; 89,213 sq km
Climate: Mostly arid, rainy season in west
Population: 5 million
Major Ethnic Groups: Arab
Major Religions: Islam
Government: Constitutional monarchy
Currency: 1 Jordanian dinar (JD) = 1,000 fils
Leading Exports: Phosphates, fertilizers, and potash
Major Languages: Arabic and English

Kazakstan

Capital: Astana
Area: 1,049,191 sq mi; 2,717,300 sq km
Climate: Continental; ranges from arid to semiarid; cold, snowy winters and hot summers
Population: 16.7 million
Major Ethnic Groups: Kazakh, Russian
Major Religions: Islam, Christianity
Government: Republic
Currency: 1 Kazakhstani tenge = 100 tiyn
Leading Exports: Oil, and ferrous and nonferrous metals
Major Languages: Kazakh and Russian

Kuwait

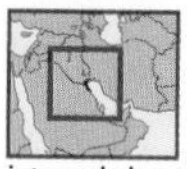

Capital: Kuwait
Area: 6,881 sq mi; 17,820 sq km
Climate: Arid; intensely hot summers and short, cool winters
Population: 2 million
Major Ethnic Groups: Kuwaiti, Arab
Major Religions: Islam
Government: Nominal constitutional monarchy
Currency: 1 Kuwaiti dinar (KD) = 1,000 fils
Leading Exports: Oil
Major Languages: Arabic and English

Kyrgyzstan

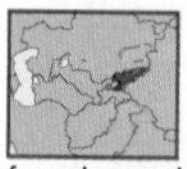

Capital: Bishkek
Area: 76,644 sq mi; 198,500 sq km
Climate: Varies from dry continental to polar in mountains; subtropical in southwest
Population: 4.7 million
Major Ethnic Groups: Kyrgyz and Russian
Major Religions: Islam, Christianity
Government: Republic
Currency: 1 Kyrgyzstani som (KGS) = 100 tyiyn
Leading Exports: Wool, meat, cotton, metals, and shoes
Major Languages: Kyrgyz and Russian

Lebanon

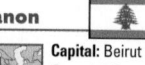

Capital: Beirut
Area: 4,016 sq mi; 10,400 sq km
Climate: Mediterranean; mild-to-cool, wet winters and hot, dry summers; snow in mountains
Population: 3.5 million
Major Ethnic Groups: Arab
Major Religions: Islam, Christianity
Government: Republic
Currency: 1 Lebanese pound = 100 piasters
Leading Exports: Agricultural products, chemicals, and textiles
Major Languages: Arabic, French, Armenian, and English

Oman

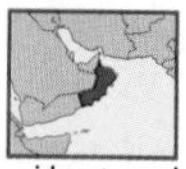

Capital: Muscat
Area: 82,034 sq mi; 212,460 sq km
Climate: Mostly arid; extremely hot and dry; less dry in mountains; hot and humid along coast
Population: 2.5 million
Major Ethnic Groups: Arab
Major Religions: Islam
Government: Monarchy
Currency: 1 Omani rial (RO) = 1,000 baiza
Leading Exports: Petroleum, reexports, and fish
Major Languages: Arabic, English, Baluchi, Urdu, and Indian dialects

Qatar

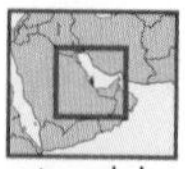

Capital: Doha
Area: 4,247 sq mi; 11,000 sq km
Climate: Arid; extremely hot, dry; humid summers
Population: 744,000
Major Ethnic Groups: Arab, Pakistani, Indian
Major Religions: Islam
Government: Traditional monarchy
Currency: 1 Qatari riyal (QR) = 100 dirhams
Leading Exports: Petroleum products, steel, and fertilizers
Major Languages: Arabic and English

Saudi Arabia

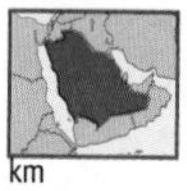

Capital: Riyadh
Area: 757,011 sq mi; 1,960,582 sq km
Climate: Arid; harsh, with warm winters and extremely hot summers; winter frost and snow possible in central area and mountains
Population: 22 million
Major Ethnic Groups: Arab
Major Religions: Islam
Government: Monarchy
Currency: 1 Saudi riyal (SR) = 100 halalah
Leading Exports: Petroleum and petroleum products
Major Languages: Arabic

Syria

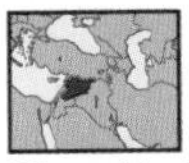

Capital: Damascus
Area: 71,501 sq mi; 185,180 sq km
Climate: Mostly semiarid; Mediterranean along coast, with mild, rainy winters and hot, dry summers; colder winters in mountains; colder and drier in southeast
Population: 16 million
Major Ethnic Groups: Arab
Major Religions: Islam
Government: Republic under military regime since March 1963
Currency: 1 Syrian pound = 100 piastres
Leading Exports: Petroleum, textiles, cotton, and fruits
Major Languages: Arabic, Kurdish, Armenian, Aramaic, Circassian, and French

Tajikistan

Capital: Dushanbe
Area: 55,253 sq mi; 143,100 sq km
Climate: Continental in lowland valleys, with cold winters and hot summers; extremely cold winters and cool summers in eastern mountains
Population: 6.4 million
Major Ethnic Groups: Tajik, Uzbek
Major Religions: Islam
Government: Republic
Currency: Tajikistani ruble (TJR) = 100 tanga
Leading Exports: Cotton, aluminum, fruits, and vegetable oil
Major Languages: Tajik and Russian

Turkey

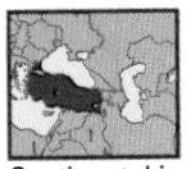

Capital: Ankara
Area: 301,394 sq mi; 780,580 sq km
Climate: Continental in central region, with cold winters and hot summers; harsher winters in mountains; mild, wet winters near coast
Population: 65.6 million
Major Ethnic Groups: Turkish, Kurdish
Major Religions: Islam
Government: Republican parliamentary democracy
Currency: Turkish lira (TL) = 100 kurus
Leading Exports: Manufactured products and foodstuffs
Major Languages: Turkish, Kurdish, and Arabic

Turkmenistan

Capital: Ashgabat
Area: 188,463 sq mi; 488,100 sq km
Climate: Dry continental; cold winters, very hot summers
Population: 4.5 million
Major Ethnic Groups: Turkmen
Major Religions: Islam
Government: Republic
Currency: 1 Turkmenmanat (TMM) = 100 tenesi
Leading Exports: Natural gas, cotton, and petroleum products
Major Languages: Turkmen, Russian, Uzbek, and various languages

United Arab Emirates

Capital: Abu Dhabi
Area: 32,000 sq mi; 82,880 sq km
Climate: Arid; mild winters, extremely hot summers; cooler in mountains
Population: 2.3 million
Major Ethnic Groups: South Asian, Emiri (native Arab peoples)
Major Religions: Islam
Government: Federation with specified powers delegated to the UAE federal governments and other powers reserved to member emirates
Currency: 1 Emirian dirham (Dh) = 100 fils
Leading Exports: Crude oil, natural gas, re-exports, and dried fish
Major Languages: Arabic, Persian, English, Hindi, and Urdu

Uzbekistan

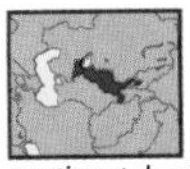

Capital: Tashkent
Area: 172,748 sq mi; 447,400 sq km
Climate: Harsh continental; mild winters and long hot summers; arid in north central desert region; semiarid in east
Population: 24.7 million
Major Ethnic Groups: Uzbek
Major Religions: Islam
Government: Republic; effectively authoritarian presidential rule, with little power outside the executive branch; executive power concentrated in the presidency
Currency: Uzbekistani som (UKS)
Leading Exports: Cotton, gold, natural gas, and minerals
Major Languages: Uzbek, Russian, Tajik, various languages

Yemen

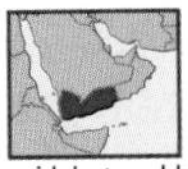

Capital: Sanaa
Area: 203,857 sq mi; 527,970 sq km
Climate: Mostly arid; hot and humid along coast; milder in highlands; extraordinarily hot, dry, harsh in east
Population: 17.5 million
Major Ethnic Groups: Arab
Major Religions: Islam
Government: Republic
Currency: Yemeni rial (YER) = 100 fils
Leading Exports: Crude oil, cotton, coffee
Major Languages: Arabic

❸ Assess/Reteach

Have students review the country descriptions. Then, ask students the following questions: What is the major religion in Southwest Asia? (*Islam*) In which countries does petroleum and oil production dominate as a major export? (*Azerbaijan, Bahrain, Iran, Iraq, Kuwait, Kazakstan, and Oman*).

Lesson Objectives

Gather, understand, and apply information about the continent of Antarctica.

Lesson Plan

1 Explore

Have students look at the map of Antarctica and identify the different countries that have claimed areas on the continent. *(The United States, Russia, Japan, Australia, Brazil, Argentina, France, Germany, South Africa, Chile, Poland.)*

2 Teach

Explain to students that the existence of land south of the Arctic Circle was not confirmed until the early 1820s. It was not until 1838 that Antarctica was known to be a continent, and not a group of islands. Ask students to name some geographic factors that make Antarctica unsuitable as a place to live. *(The extremely cold climate and icy terrain make it difficult to support plant and animal life. Transportation would also be very limited. People would not be able to support themselves with any kind of suitable economic activity on this continent.)*

3 Assess/Reteach

Ask students to speculate what life must be like for researchers who live on Antarctica during the winter months. Have them consider issues such as food, shelter, and transportation in their responses.

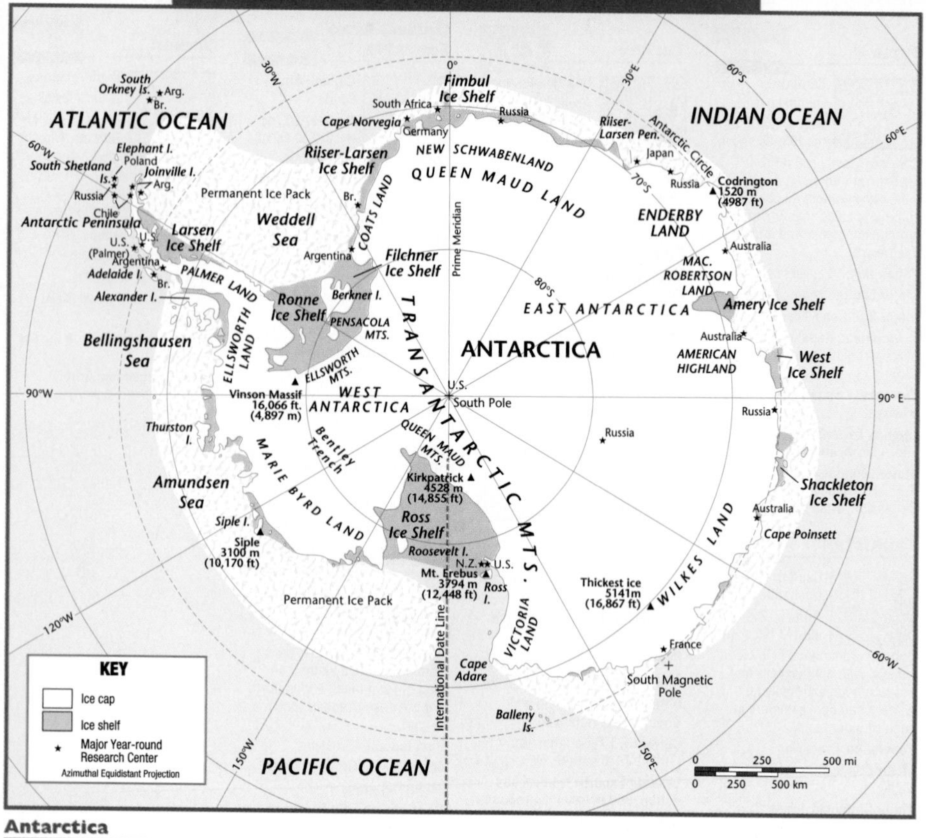

Antarctica

Capital: None
Area: 5,400,000 sq mi; 14,000,000 sq km
Climate: Ice Cap; dry, windy, extremely cold; coldest in the interior, where winter low temperature falls below –110°F (-80°C); warmest along coast of Antarctic Peninsula, where summer high temperature rises just above freezing
Population: (Staff of research stations) About 4,115 people in summer, about 1,046 in winter
Major Ethnic Groups: None
Major Religions: None
Government: Antarctic Treaty
Currency: None
Leading Exports: None
Major Languages: None

Australia and New Zealand: Political

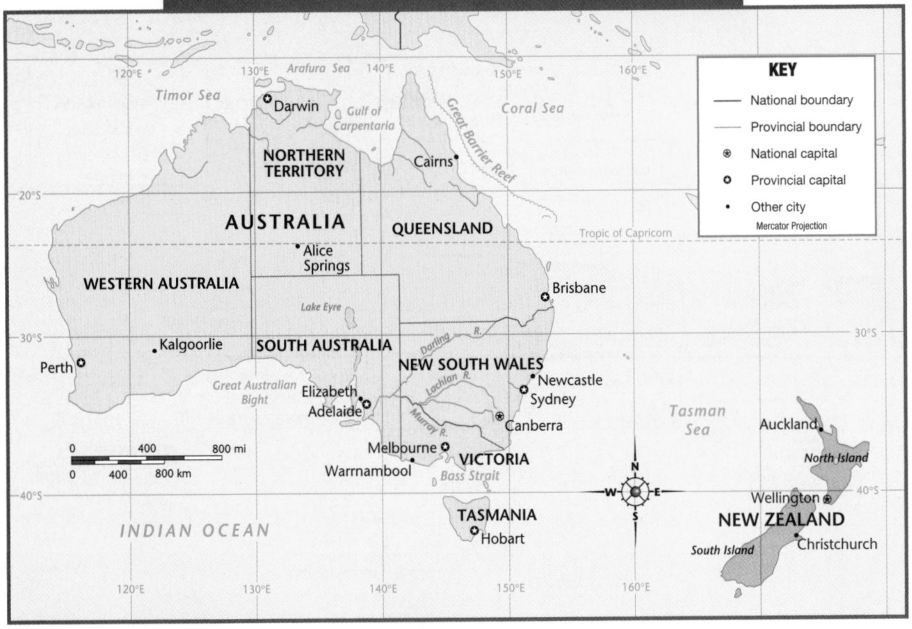

Australia

Capital: Canberra
Area: 2,968,010 sq mi; 7,686,850 sq km
Climate: Mostly arid to semiarid; tropical in north, with warm, dry winters and hot, wet summers; cool winters and warm summers in south and east
Population: 19.2 million
Major Ethnic Groups: European (British, Irish ancestry)
Major Religions: Christianity
Government: Democratic, federal-state system recognizing the British Monarch as Soverign
Currency: 1 Australian dollar ($A) = 100 cents
Leading Exports: Coal, gold, meat, wool, and alumina
Major Languages: English and various languages

New Zealand

Capital: Wellington
Area: 103,741 sq mi; 268,680 sq km
Climate: mostly temperate; generally mild all year, with moderate to abundant rainfall; warmest in far north; coldest in mountains of southwest
Population: 3.8 million
Major Ethnic Groups: European (British ancestry), Maori
Major Religions: Christianity
Government: Parliamentary democracy
Currency: 1 New Zealand dollar (NZ$) = 100 cents
Leading Exports: Wool, lamb, muton, beef, fish, and cheese
Major Languages: English and Maori

Lesson Objectives

Gather, understand, and apply information about the countries of Australia and New Zealand.

Lesson Plan

1 Explore

Have students compare the climates of New Zealand and Australia, and their major exports.

2 Teach

Tell students that Australia has nearly the same land area as the United States and is the world's sixth largest country. Yet just 18.5 million people live there—only about a million more people than live in the New York City metropolitan area. Explain that Australia's population is small because the continent was once considered remote and much of the climate is harsh. Ask students to describe the location of most of Australia's cities. (*Most are located near or along the coast.*) Discuss how New Zealand differs from other Pacific islands where the major ethnic groups are made up of native peoples. (*New Zealand has a long history of European influence, in both culture and government*).

3 Assess/Reteach

Australia is divided into seven states or provinces. Ask students to name each one and its provincial capital. Have students find and name Australia's capital. (*Canberra*) New Zealand is made up of two separate islands. Have students find the capital. (*Wellington, on North Island*).

Resource Directory

Other Print Resources

DK Atlas

Technology

Color Transparencies 150 The Pacific Islands: Political Map; **151** Australia and New Zealand: Physical-Political Map

Passport to the World CD-ROM This interactive CD-ROM allows students to explore each region of the world. Students view regional videos, take a photo tour, and explore a historical timeline. Students record their travels in an Explorer's Journal, and receive passport stamps when they pass regional quizzes.

Regional Database

Lesson Objectives

Gather, understand, and apply information about the Pacific Island nations.

Lesson Plan

1 Explore

Tell students that thousands of islands can be found in the southern Pacific Ocean. Today most are nations. Others are territories under the control of other nations. Have students locate the Northern Mariana Islands on the map. Point out the "(U.S.)" under the map label. This shows that these islands are a United States territory. Have students find other examples of territories (*New Caledonia and French Polynesia, both French territories*).

2 Teach

Have students locate the lines drawn around the various island groups on the map. Explain that these indicate national or territorial boundaries, and that a nation's territory can include water as well as land. Point out that because the scale of the map is very large, the islands appear as tiny dots. Direct students' attention to the country descriptions, and explain that the list includes only nations. Point out that each nation consists of many islands, not just a single one. For example, the nation of Fiji consists of more than 800 islands.

Pacific Islands: Political

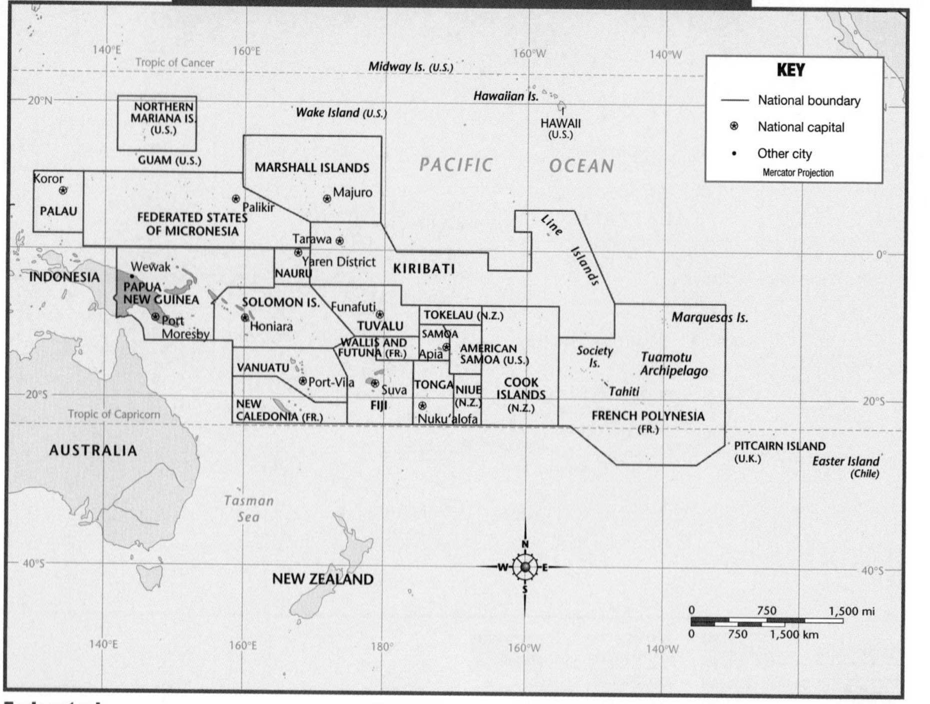

Federated States of Micronesia

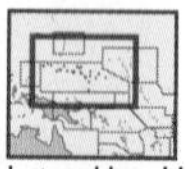

Capital: Palikir
Area: 271 sq mi; 702 sq km
Climate: Tropical; hot and humid, with heavy rainfall all year
Population: 133,000
Major Ethnic Groups: Micronesian
Major Religions: Christianity
Government: Constitutional government in free Association with the US; the Compact of Free Association entered into force November 3, 1986
Currency: 1 United States dollar (US$) = 100 cents
Leading Exports: Fish, copra, bananas, and black pepper
Major Languages: English, Turkese, Pohnpeian, Yapese, and Kosrean

Fiji

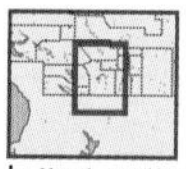

Capital: Suva
Area: 7,054 sq mi; 18,270 sq km
Climate: Tropical; hottest, wettest in summer
Population: 832,000
Major Ethnic Groups: Fijian, Indian
Major Religions: Christianity, Hinduism
Government: Republic
Currency: 1 Fijian dollar (F$) = 100 cents
Leading Exports: Sugar, clothing, gold, processed fish, and lumber
Major Languages: English, Fijian, and Hindustani

Kiribati

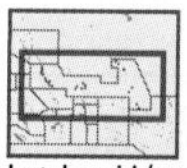

Capital: Tarawa
Area: 277 sq mi; 717 sq km
Climate: Tropical; hot, humid (moderated by trade winds)
Population: 92,000
Major Ethnic Groups: Micronesian
Major Religions: Christianity
Government: Republic
Currency: 1 Australian dollar ($A) = 100 cents
Leading Exports: Copra, seaweed, and fish
Major Languages: English and Gilbertese

Marshall Islands

Capital: Majuro
Area: 70 sq mi; 181.3 sq km
Climate: Tropical; hot, humid; rainy season
Population: 68,000
Major Ethnic Groups: Micronesian
Major Religions: Christianity
Government: Constitutional government in free Association with the US; the Compact of Free Association entered into force October 21, 1986
Currency: 1 United States dollar (US$) = 100 cents
Leading Exports: Coconut oil, fish, live animals, and trichus shells
Major Languages: English, Marshallese dialects, and Japanese

Resource Directory

Other Print Resources

DK Atlas

Technology

Color Transparencies 150 Australia and the Pacific Islands: Political Map

Passport to the World CD-ROM This interactive CD-ROM allows students to explore each region of the world. Students view regional videos, take a photo tour, and explore a historical timeline. Students record their travels in an Explorer's Journal, and receive passport stamps when they pass regional quizzes.

Nauru

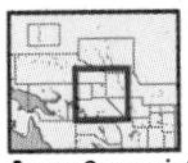

Capital: Government offices in Yaren District
Area: 8 sq mi; 21 sq km
Climate: Tropical; hot, humid; rainy season
Population: 12,000
Major Ethnic Groups: Nauruan, other Pacific Islander
Major Religions: Christianity
Government: Republic
Currency: 1 Australian dollar ($A) = 100 cents
Leading Exports: Phosphates
Major Languages: Nauruan and English

Palau

Capital: Koror – note: a new capital is being built about 20 Km northeast of Koror
Area: 177 sq mi; 458 sq km
Climate: Tropical; hot, humid; rainy season
Population: 19,000
Major Ethnic Groups: Palauan (mix of Polynesian, Malayan, and Melanesian)
Major Religions: Christianity, Modekngei (traditional Palauan religion)
Government: Constitutional government in free Association with the US; the Compact of Free Association entered into force October 1, 1994
Currency: 1 United States dollar (US$) = 100 cents
Leading Exports: Trochus, tuna, copra, and handicrafts
Major Languages: English (official), Sonsorolese, Angaur, Japanese, Tobi, and Palauan

Papua New Guinea

Capital: Port Moresby
Area: 178,704 sq mi; 462,840 sq km
Climate: Tropical; hot and humid in lowlands; cooler in mountains; heavy rain in most areas all year
Population: 4.9 million
Major Ethnic Groups: Melanesian, Papuan
Major Religions: Christianity, mix of Christian and traditional beliefs
Government: Parliamentary democracy
Currency: 1 kina (K) = 100 toea
Leading Exports: Gold, copper ore, oil, logs, and palm oil
Major Languages: English, pidgin English, and Motu

Samoa

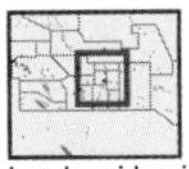

Capital: Apia
Area: 1,104 sq mi; 2,860 sq km
Climate: Tropical; hot, humid; rainy season
Population: 179,000
Major Ethnic Groups: Samoan
Major Religions: Christianity
Government: Constitutional monarchy under native chief
Currency: 1 tala (WS$) = 100 sene
Leading Exports: Coconut oil and cream, taro, copra, and cocoa
Major Languages: Samoan and English

Solomon Islands

Capital: Honiara
Area: 10,985 sq mi; 28,450 sq km
Climate: Tropical; hot, humid
Population: 466,000
Major Ethnic Groups: Melanesian
Major Religions: Christianity
Government: Parliamentary democracy
Currency: 1 Solomon Islands dollar (SI$) = 100 cents
Leading Exports: Fish, timber, palm oil, cocoa, and copra
Major Languages: Melanesian pidgin and English

Tonga

Capital: Nukualofa
Area: 289 sq mi; 748 sq km
Climate: Tropical; (modified by trade winds); very humid; warm season and cool season
Population: 102,000
Major Ethnic Groups: Polynesian
Major Religions: Christianity
Government: Hereditary constitutional monarchy
Currency: 1 pa'anga (T$) = 100 seniti
Leading Exports: Squash, vanilla, fish, root crops, and coconut oil
Major Languages: Tongan and English

Tuvalu

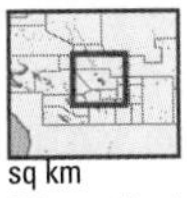

Capital: Fongafale, on Funafuti atoll
Area: 10 sq mi; 26 sq km
Climate: Tropical; warm, humid all year (moderated by trade winds); heavy summer rains
Population: 11,000
Major Ethnic Groups: Polynesian
Major Religions: Christianity
Government: Constitutional monarchy with a parliamentary democracy, began debating republic status in 1992
Currency: 1 Tuvaluan dollar ($T) or 1 Australian dollar ($A) = 100 cents
Leading Exports: Copra
Major Languages: Tuvaluan and English

Vanuatu

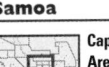

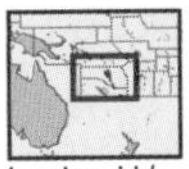

Capital: Port-Vila
Area: 5,699 sq mi; 14,760 sq km
Climate: Tropical; hot, humid (moderated by winter trade winds); wettest in northern islands
Population: 190,000
Major Ethnic Groups: Melanesian
Major Religions: Christianity
Government: Republic
Currency: 1 vatu (VT) = 100 centimes
Leading Exports: Copra, beef, cocoa, timber, and coffee
Major Languages: English, French, pidgin, and Bislama

3 Assess/Reteach

Have students look at the text description for Federated States of Micronesia. Ask how many islands make up this nation. (*more than 600 islands*) Have students find the nation on the map by giving them this location: between 140°E and 160° and just north of the equator. Then, have students name the capital. (*Palikir*)

Glossary of Basic Geographic Terms

basin
a depression in the surface of the land; some basins are filled with water

bay
a part of a sea or lake that extends into the land

butte
a small raised area of land with steep sides

▲ butte

canyon
a deep, narrow valley with steep sides; often has a stream flowing through it

cataract
a large waterfall; any strong flood or rush of water

◀ cataract

delta
a triangular-shaped plain at the mouth of a river, formed when sediment is deposited by flowing water

flood plain
a broad plain on either side of a river, formed when sediment settles on the riverbanks

glacier
a huge, slow-moving mass of snow and ice

hill
an area that rises above surrounding land and has a rounded top; lower and usually less steep than a mountain

island
an area of land completely surrounded by water

isthmus
a narrow strip of land that connects two larger areas of land

mesa
a high, flat-topped landform with cliff-like sides; larger than a butte

mountain
an area that rises steeply at least 2,000 feet (610 m) above surrounding land; usually wide at the bottom and rising to a narrow peak or ridge

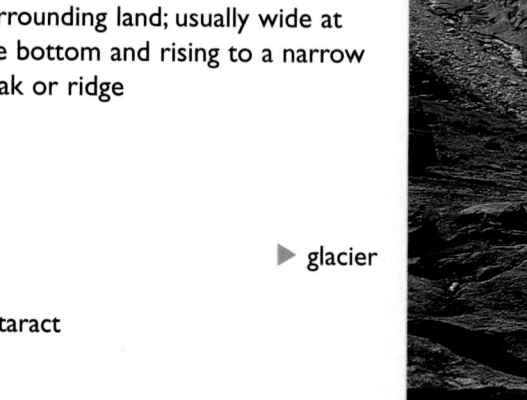

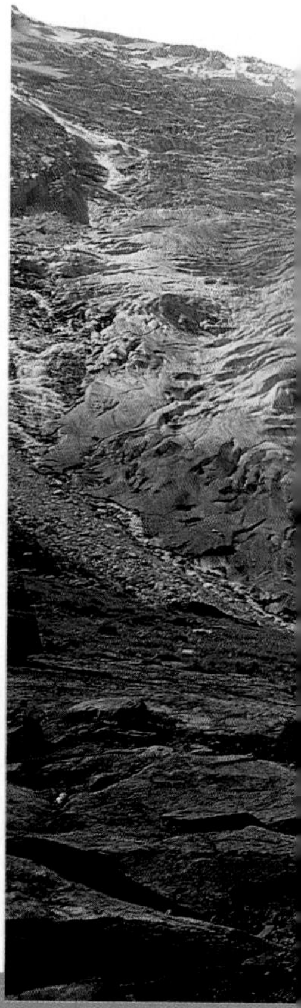

▶ glacier

646 GLOSSARY OF BASIC GEOGRAPHIC TERMS

◀ delta

mountain pass
a gap between mountains

peninsula
an area of land almost completely surrounded by water and connected to the mainland by an isthmus

plain
a large area of flat or gently rolling land

plateau
a large, flat area that rises above the surrounding land; at least one side has a steep slope

river mouth
the point where a river enters a lake or sea

strait
a narrow stretch of water that connects two larger bodies of water

tributary
a river or stream that flows into a larger river

volcano
an opening in the Earth's surface through which molten rock, ashes, and gasses from the Earth's interior escape

▶ volcano

Gazetteer

A

Abuja (9°N, 7°E) the federal capital of Nigeria, p. 408

Aix-en-Provence (43.32°N, 5.26°E) a city in the south of France, p. 319

Aksum an ancient city in northern Ethiopia, a powerful kingdom and trade center from about A.D. 200 to A.D. 600, p. 374

Alice Springs (23°S, 133°E) a town in Northern Territory, Australia, p. 571

Amazonian rain forest a large tropical rain forest occupying the drainage basin of the Amazon River in northern South America and covering an area of 2,700,000 square miles, p. 175

Amsterdam (52.22°N, 4.53°E) a major financial center of the Netherlands, p. 314

Andes Mountains (13°S, 75°W) a mountain system extending along the western coast of South America, pp. 175, 206

Angkor Wat (13°N, 103°E) an archaeological site in present-day Angkor, in northwest Cambodia; the world's largest religious temple complex, p. 469

Antarctic Circle (66°S) line of latitude around the Earth near the South Pole, p. 14

Appalachian Mountains a mountain system in eastern North America, p. 74

Arctic Circle (66°N) line of latitude around the Earth near the North Pole, p. 14

Atacama Desert (23.5°S, 69°W) a desert in Chile, South America; the driest place on the Earth, p. 175

Athens (38°N, 23.38°E) the capital city of modern Greece; the world's most powerful cultural center in the 400s B.C., p. 275

Atlanta (33°N, 84°W) the capital of the state of Georgia, p. 125

B

Balkans a region located south of the Danube River made up of several countries, including the former Yugoslavia, that gets its name from the Turkish word for "mountain," p. 330

Barcelona (41.25°N, 2.08°E) a city and seaport in northeastern Spain, p. 265

Berlin (51.31°N, 13.28°E) the capital city of Germany; divided into East Berlin and West Berlin between 1949 and 1989, pp. 291, 315

Bethlehem (31.43°N, 35.12°E) a town outside of Jerusalem considered to be holy by Christians as the town where Jesus was born, p. 495

Bosnia a Balkan country in which Croatian, Serbian, and Bosnian are spoken, and Muslim, Orthodox, and Roman Catholic faiths are practiced, p. 331

Boston (42°N, 71°W) the capital of the state of Massachusetts, p. 123

Brasilia (15.49°S, 47.39°W) the capital city of Brazil, p. 236

Brazil (9°S, 53°W) the largest country in South America, p. 177

Brunei a small kingdom on the northwestern coast of the island of Borneo with large deposits of oil, p. 489

Brussels (50°N, 4.22°E) capital of Belgium, p. 313

Buenos Aires (34.35°S, 58.22°W), capital of Argentina, p. 241

C

Cairo (30°N, 31°E) the capital of Egypt and most populous city in Africa, p. 403

Canal Zone a 10-mile strip of land along the Panama Canal, stretching from the Atlantic Ocean to the Pacific Ocean, p. 224

648 GAZETTEER

Cape Town (33°S, 18°E) the legislative capital of the Republic of South Africa; the capital of Cape Province, p. 431

Caracas (10.3°N, 66.58°W) the capital city of Venezuela, p. 240

Caribbean (14.3°N, 75.3°W) a part of the southern Atlantic Ocean, p. 169

Central America (10.45°N, 87.15°W) the part of Latin America that includes the seven republics of Guatemala, Honduras, El Salvador, Nicaragua, Costa Rica, Panama, and Belize, p. 171

Chicago (41°N, 87°W) a major city in the state of Illinois, on Lake Michigan, p. 132

Colombia (3.3°N, 72.3°W) a country in South America, p. 177

Congo River a river in Central Africa that flows into the Atlantic Ocean, p. 359

Copán (14.5°N, 89.1°W) a ruined ancient Mayan city in western Honduras, p. 183

Cuba (22°N, 79°W) the largest island country in the Caribbean Sea, p. 44, 204

Copán

Cuzco (13.36°S, 71.52°W) a city in Peru; capital of the Incan empire, p. 184

Czech Republic (50°N, 15°E) a country in Eastern Europe, p. 297

D

Death Valley (36°N, 117°W) the hottest, driest region of North America, located in southeastern California, p. 74

Detroit (42°N, 83°W) a city in the state of Michigan, p. 132

E

Egypt (26°S, 27°E) a country in North Africa, officially Arab Republic of Egypt, p. 372

Equator an imaginary line that circles the globe at its widest point (halfway between the North and South poles), dividing the Earth into two halves called hemispheres; used as a reference point from which north and south latitudes are measured, p. 13

Euphrates River a river that flows south from Turkey through Syria and Iraq; the ancient civilizations of Babylon and Ur were situated near its banks, p. 453

Eurasia the landmass that includes the European and Asian continents, p. 261

Europe (50°N, 15°E) the world's second-smallest continent; a peninsula of the Eurasian landmass bounded by the Arctic Ocean, the Atlantic Ocean, the Mediterranean Sea, and Asia; p. 261

F

Fiji a Pacific island nation popular with tourists, p. 575

Flanders region in north Belgium, p. 313

Fraser River a major river of western North America along the border between British Columbia and Alberta, p. 151

GAZETTEER 649

Himalaya Mountains

G

Ganges River a river in India and Bangladesh flowing from the Himalaya Mountains to the Bay of Bengal; considered by Hindus to be the most holy river in India, p. 453

Ghana (8°N, 2°W) a country in West Africa, officially Republic of Ghana, p. 375

Grand Coulee Dam (47°N, 119°W) a dam on the Columbia River in the state of Washington, p. 81

Great Dividing Range a series of plateaus and mountain ranges in eastern Australia, p. 555

Great Lakes a group of five large lakes in central North America: Lakes Superior, Michigan, Huron, Erie, and Ontario, p. 75

Great Rift Valley the major branch of the East African Rift System, p. 359

Greece an important civilization in the classical era; currently a modern country in Europe on the Mediterranean Sea, p. 275

Guatemala (15.45°N, 91.45°W) a country in Central America, p. 217

H

Himalaya Mountains the Central Asian mountain range extending along the India-Tibet border, through Pakistan, Nepal, and Bhutan, and containing the world's highest peaks, p. 451

Ho Chi Minh City (10°N, 106°E) the largest city in Vietnam, named for the President of North Vietnam; formerly Saigon, p. 514

Honduras a rural country in Central America, p. 200

Huang He the second-longest river in China; it flows across northern China to the Yellow Sea; also known as the Yellow River, p. 452

I

Iceland a geographically isolated island nation near the Arctic Circle, p. 266

650 GAZETTEER

Indus River a river rising in Tibet and flowing through India and Pakistan into the Arabian Sea, p. 453

Irkutsk (ihr KOOTSK) (52.16°N, 104°E) a city in east-central Russia, on the Central Siberian Plateau, p. 265

J

Jakarta (6°S, 106°E) the capital and largest city of the Republic of Indonesia, p. 46

Jamaica (17.45°N, 78°W) a tropical island country in the Caribbean Sea; pp. 177, 203

Jamestown the first permanent British settlement in North America, located in present-day Virginia; now a site of historic preservation, p. 88

Jerusalem (31.47°N, 35°E) the capital of Israel; a holy city for Christians, Jews, and Muslims, p. 495

K

Kano (12°N, 8°E) a city and the capital of Kano state in northern Nigeria; a historic kingdom in northern Nigeria, p. 409

Kashmir (39°N, 75°E) a disputed territory in northwest India, parts of which have been claimed by India, Pakistan, and China since 1947, p. 519

Kemerovo (55.31°N, 86.05°E) a city in south-central Russia, p. 338

Kilwa late tenth-century Islamic city-state located on an island off the coast of present-day Tanzania, p. 376

Kosovo the site of fighting in 1999 when Serbs fought against Albanians seeking independence, p. 333

L

Lagos (6°N, 3°E) a city and chief Atlantic port of Nigeria; a state in Nigeria, p. 408

Locorotondo (40.45°N, 17.20°E) a town located in southern Italy, p. 322

London (51.3°N, .07°W) the capital city of the United Kingdom, p. 291

M

Madrid (40.26°N, 3.42°W) the capital city of Spain, p. 291

Mali (15°N, 0.15°W) an early African empire; a present-day country in West Africa, officially Republic of Mali, p. 375

Mecca (21°N, 39°E) a city in western Saudi Arabia; birthplace of the prophet Muhammad and most holy city for Islamic people, pp. 496, 527

Mecca

Melanesia (13°S, 164°E) the most populous of the three groups of Pacific islands; includes Fiji, Papua New Guinea, and others, p. 559

Mesopotamia a historic region in western Asia between the Tigris and Euphrates rivers; one of the cradles of civilization, p. 476

Mexico (23.45°N, 104°W) a country in North America, p. 170

Mexico City (19.28°N, 99.09°W) the capital of and largest city in Mexico; one of the largest urban areas in the world, pp. 198, 213

Micronesia one of the three groups of Pacific islands; includes Guam, the Marshall Islands, and others, p. 559

Milan (45.27°N, 9.17°E) a city in northern Italy known for its fashion industry, p. 322

GAZETTEER 651

Mississippi River a large river in the central United States flowing south from Minnesota to the Gulf of Mexico, p. 76

Montreal (45°N, 73°W) the largest city in the province of Quebec, Canada, p. 142

Moscow (55.45°N, 37.37°E) the capital city of modern Russia; one of the largest cities in the world; the home of the czars, p. 339

Mount Kenya (0.10°S, 37°E) a volcano in central Kenya, p. 423

N

Nairobi (1°S, 36°E) the capital of Kenya, p. 425

Negev Desert a triangular, arid region in southwest Israel, touching the Gulf of Aquaba, p. 531

New York City (40°N, 73°W) a large city and port at the mouth of the Hudson River in the state of New York, p. 124

New York City

Nicaragua the largest country in Central America in area, but not the largest in population, p. 219

Niger River the river in West Africa that flows from Guinea into the Gulf of Guinea, p. 359

Nile River the longest river in the world, flows through northeastern Africa into the Mediterranean Sea, p. 359

Northern Ireland the largely Protestant region of Ireland governed by Great Britain, p. 319

North Sea (56.09°N, 3.16°E) an arm of the Atlantic Ocean between Great Britain and the European mainland, p. 269

Norway country in northwestern Europe occupying the western part of the Scandinavian peninsula, pp. 265–266

Nubia an ancient region in North Africa, p. 372

Nunavut a Canadian territory with its own government, p. 114

O

Ontario (50°N, 88°W) the second-largest province in Canada, p. 99

Ottawa (45.24°N, 75.43°W) national capital of Canada, p. 147

Outback in general, a remote area with few people; specifically, the arid inland region of Australia, p. 556

P

Pacific Northwest the region in the northwestern United States that includes Oregon, Washington, and part of Idaho, p. 135

Pacific Rim the countries bordering on the Pacific Ocean, p. 152

Palestine (31°N, 35°E) a historical region at the east end of the Mediterranean Sea, now divided between Israel and Jordan, pp. 276, 477

Pampas [PAHM puhs] a vast, flat grassland similar to the Great Plains in the United States, p. 241

652 GAZETTEER

Panama (9°N, 80°W) a country in Central America, p. 221

Panama Canal (9.2°N, 79.55°W) an important shipping canal across the Isthmus of Panama, linking the Caribbean Sea (and the Atlantic Ocean) to the Pacific Ocean, p. 221

Pangaea according to scientific theory, a single landmass that broke apart to form today's separate continents; thought to have existed about 180 million years ago, p. 28

Papua New Guinea (7°S, 142°E) an island country in the southwest Pacific; the eastern half of New Guinea, officially the Independent State of Papua New Guinea, p. 559

Papua New Guinea

Paris (48.51°N, 2.2°E) the capital city of France, p. 291

Patagonia (46.45°S, 69.3°W) desert in southern Argentia; the largest desert in the Americas, p. 174

Pennsylvania Colony a colony in America founded in 1680 by William Penn, who purchased land from the Native Americans, p. 88

Philadelphia (40°N, 75°W) a city and port in Pennsylvania on the Delaware River, p. 123

Polynesia largest of the three groups of Pacific islands, includes New Zealand, Hawaii, Easter, and Tahiti islands, p. 559

Portland (45°N, 122°W) the largest city in the state of Oregon, p. 136

Q

Quebec (51°N, 70°W) a province in southeastern Canada, p. 99

Quebec City (46°N, 71°W) the capital city of the province of Quebec, Canada, p. 141

R

Republic of South Africa (28°S, 24°E) southernmost country in Africa, p. 394

Rio de Janeiro (22.5°S, 43.2°W) a major city in Brazil, p. 236

Riyadh (24°N, 46°E) the capital of Saudi Arabia, p. 528

Rocky Mountains the major mountain range in western North America, extending south from Alberta, Canada, through the western United States to Mexico, p. 74

Rome (41.52°N, 12.37°E) the capital of modern Italy; one of the world's greatest ancient empires (753 B.C.–A.D. 476), p. 276

Ruhr Valley (51.18°N, 8.17°E) an area along a river in the major industrial region in western Germany, p. 269

Russia (61°N, 60°E) a country in northern Eurasia, p. 261

S

St. Lawrence Lowlands a major agricultural region in eastern Canada, p. 82

St. Lawrence River a river in eastern North America; the third-longest river in Canada, p. 76

St. Louis (38°N, 90°W) a major city in Missouri, on the Mississippi River, p. 132

St. Petersburg (59.57°N, 30.2°E) the second-largest city in Russia (previous names Petrograd, Leningrad), located on the Baltic Sea; founded by Peter the Great, p. 301

Sahara largest desert in the world, covers almost all of North Africa, p. 357

GAZETTEER 653

São Paulo (23°S, 46°W) the largest city in Brazil, p. 46

San Jose (37°N, 121°W) a city in western California, p. 136

Santiago (33.26°S, 70.4°W) the capital city of Chile, p. 238

Sarajevo (43.5°N, 18.26°E) the capital city of Bosnia-Herzegovina, p. 333

Saskatchewan (50.12°N, 100.4°W) province in central Canada, p. 152

Shaba [SHAB uh] a southern province in Zaire, p. 427

Siberia [Sy BIHR ee uh] (57°N, 97°E) a resource-rich region of Russia, extending east across northern Asia from the Ural Mountains to the Pacific Coast, p. 261

Sierra Nevada a mountain range in California in the western United States, p. 135

Silesia [sy LEE shuh] (50.58°N, 16.53°E) a historic region located in today's southwest Poland, p. 269

Slovakia (48.5°N, 20°E) a country in Eastern Europe, pp. 296, 335

Songhai an empire and trading state in West Africa founded in the 1400s, p. 375

South America (15°S, 60°W) the world's fourth-largest continent, bounded by the Caribbean Sea, the Atlantic Ocean, and the Pacific Ocean, and linked to North America by the Isthmus of Panama, p. 171

Stockholm (59.20°N, 18.03°E) capital of Sweden, p. 291

Sydney (33°S, 151°E) the capital of New South Wales, on the southeastern coast of Australia, p. 569

T

Tahiti a popular tourist destination in the Pacific islands, p. 575

Taiwan (23°N, 122°E) a large island country off the southeast coast of mainland China, formerly Formosa; since 1949, the Nationalist Republic of China, p. 504

Tenochtitlán Aztec capital city covering more than five square miles on a series of islands in Lake Texcoco; Spanish conquerors destroyed the city and built modern Mexico City atop its ruins, p. 184

Siberia

654 GAZETTEER

Tigris River a river that flows through Turkey, Iraq, and Iran to the Persian Gulf; the ancient civilizations of Nineveh and Ur were situated near its banks, p. 453

Tombouctou (16°N, 3°W) city in Mali near the Niger River; in the past an important center of Islamic education and a trans-Saharan caravan stop (also spelled Timbuktu), p. 375

Toronto (43.39°N, 79.23°W) capital of Ontario, p. 147

Trinidad and Tobago (11°N, 61°W) republic of the West Indies, on the two islands called Trinidad and Tobago, p. 205

Tropic of Cancer (23.5°N) the northern boundary of the tropics, or the band of Earth that receives the most direct light and heat energy from the sun; such a region lies on both sides of the Equator; p. 13

Tropic of Capricorn (23.5°S) the southern boundary of the tropics; see above, p. 13

U

Ukraine [yoo KRAYN] an independent country in Eastern Europe, formerly part of the Soviet Union, p. 269

Ural [YOOR uhl] **Mountains** (56.28°N, 58.13°E) a mountain system in northern Eurasia forming part of the border between Europe and Asia, p. 261

V

Valley of Mexico the area in Mexico where Lake Texcoco, Tenochtitlán, and modern Mexico City are located, p. 184

Vancouver (49°N, 123°W) a city in southwestern British Columbia, Canada, p. 149

Vatican an independent city-state located in Italy that is the world headquarters of the Roman Catholic Church, p. 321

Venezuela (8°N, 65°W) a country in South America, p. 177

Vatican

W

Wallonia region in southern Belgium, p. 313

Washington, D.C. (38°N, 77°W) the capital city of the United States, located between Maryland and Virginia on the Potomac River, pp. 128

Y

Yangzi the longest river in Asia, flowing through China to the East China Sea, p. 452

Z

Zambezi River a river in Central and Southern Africa that flows into the Indian Ocean, p. 360

GAZETTEER 655

Glossary

A

abolitionist a person who believed that enslaving people was wrong and who wanted to end the practice, p. 92

alliance a mutual agreement between countries to protect and defend each other, p. 283

alluvial relating to the fertile topsoil left by rivers after a flood, p. 80

apartheid [uh PAHR tayt] the South African system in which racial groups were separated and racial discrimination was legal, p. 433

aquaculture a cultivation of the sea; common crops are shrimp and oysters, p. 459

aqueduct a pipe or channel used to carry water from a distant source to dry areas, p. 185

arable land land that can produce crops, p. 456

aristocrats people who are in the minority but are considered a privileged, upper class, p. 421

artesian well a deep well drilled into the Earth to tap groundwater in porous rock, p. 572

atmosphere the multilayered band of gases that surrounds the Earth, p. 27

atoll [A tawl] a group of small coral islands in the shape of a ring that encloses a lagoon, p. 554

authoritarian controlled by one person or a small group, p. 429

axis an imaginary line around which a planet turns; the Earth turns around an axis which runs between its North and South poles, p. 12

B

bazaar a traditional open-air market with rows of shops or stalls, p. 403

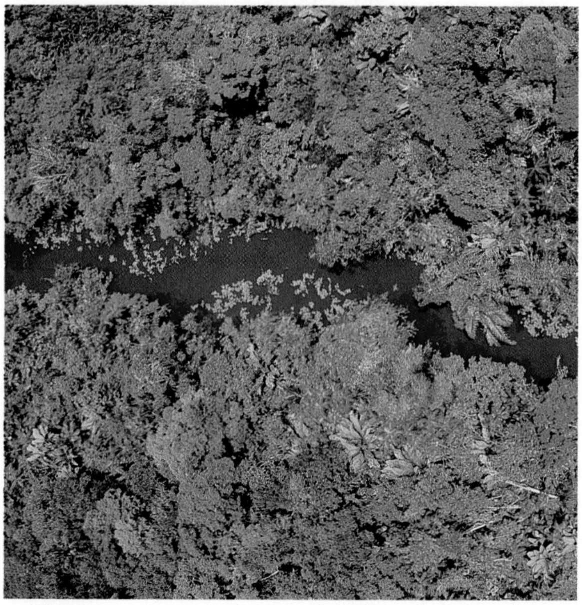

canopy

bilingual speaking two languages; having two official languages, p. 100

birthrate the number of live births each year per 1,000 people, p. 43

bolas [BOH lahs] a set of leather cords and three iron balls or stones thrown at the legs of animals to capture them, p. 244

boom a period of increased prosperity during which more of a product is produced and sold, p. 240

boomtown a settlement that springs up quickly, often to serve the needs of miners, p. 151

boycott a refusal to buy or use goods and services, pp. 89, 379

C

campesinos [kahm peh SEE nohs] landless peasants and poor farmers, pp. 198, 233

canopy a dense mass of leaves forming the top layer of a forest, p. 234

656 GLOSSARY

capital money used to expand a business, p. 131

capitalism an economic system in which people and privately owned companies own both basic and nonbasic businesses and industries, p. 53

cardinal direction one of the four compass points: north, south, east, and west, p. 21

Carnival an annual celebration in Latin America with music, dances, and parades, p. 205

casbah an old, crowded section of a North African city, p. 407

cash crop a crop raised to be sold for money on the world market, pp. 365, 459

caste a class of people in India, p. 473

cataract a rock-filled rapid, p. 359

caudillo [kow DEE yoh] a military officer who rules strictly, p. 191

census a count of the people in a country, p. 410

city-state a loose organization of people that has its own government and controls much of the surrounding land, p. 376

civilization a society with cities, a central government, social classes, and, usually, writing, art, and architecture, p. 372, 465

civil rights movement a large group of people who worked together in the United States beginning in the 1960s to end the segregation of African Americans and support equal rights for all minorities, p. 97

Civil War the war between the northern and southern states in the United States, which began in 1861 and ended in 1865, p. 93

clan a group of families who claim a common ancestor, pp. 389, 466

climate the weather patterns that an area typically experiences over a long period of time, p. 34

Cold War a period of great tension between the United States and the former Soviet Union, which lasted for more than 40 years after World War II, pp. 97, 286

colonize to settle an area and take over or create a government, p. 378

colony a territory ruled by another nation, usually one far away, p. 474

command economy an economy in which economic decisions are made by the government, p. 53

commonwealth a self-governing political unit with strong ties to a particular country, p. 232

commune a community in which land is held in common and where members live and work together, p. 484

Communism a theory of government in which property such as farms and factories is owned by the government for the benefit of all citizens; a political system in which the central government controls all aspects of citizens' lives, pp. 97, 285

commute to travel regularly to and from a place, particularly to and from a job, p. 121

compass rose a map feature that usually shows the four cardinal directions, p. 21

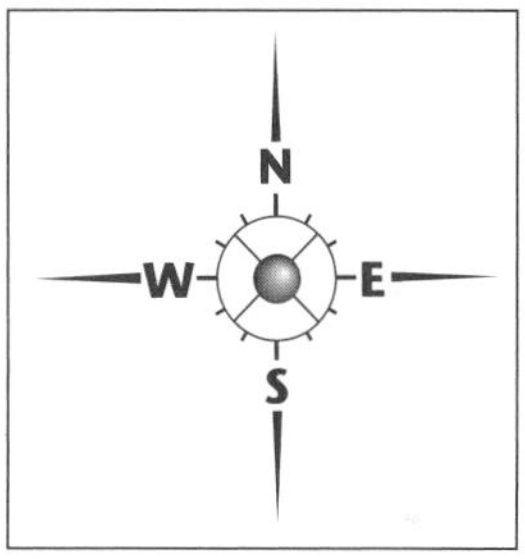

compass rose

Confederacy the Confederate States of America; a group of Southern states that seceded from the United States following Abraham Lincoln's 1860 election, p. 93

coniferous [koh NIF ur us] pertaining to cone-bearing trees, p. 267

conquistador [kon KEES ta dor] 16th-century conquerors working for the Spanish government who were in charge of gaining land and wealth in the Americas, p. 187

constitution a statement of a country's basic laws and values, pp. 55, 232

Constitution the document written in 1787 and approved in 1789 that established three branches of American government and protected the rights of individual citizens, p. 89

GLOSSARY 657

constitutional monarchy a government in which a king or queen is the head of state but has limited powers; for example, the present government of Great Britain, p. 308

consumer a person who buys goods and services, p. 52

Continental Divide the boundary that separates rivers flowing toward opposite sides of a continent; in North America, in the Rocky Mountains, p. 74

copra dried coconut meat used in margarine, cooking oils, and luxury soaps, p. 574

coral a rock-like substance formed from the skeletons of tiny sea animals, pp. 171, 554

corporate farm a large farm run by a corporation; may consist of many smaller farms once owned by families, p. 131

cosmopolitan characterized by ethnic or cultural diversity and sophistication, p. 241

coup [koo] the takeover of a government, often done by military force, p. 414

Creole a person, often of European and African descent, born in the Caribbean or other parts of the Americas, whose culture has strong French and African influence; a dialect spoken by Creoles, p. 219

coral

criollo [kree OH yoh] a person born of Spanish parents born outside Spain; often among the best-educated and wealthiest people in the Spanish colonies, p. 190

cultural diffusion a spreading of ideas and practices from one culture to another, pp. 387, 467

cultural diversity a wide variety of cultures, pp. 105, 388

cultural exchange a process in which different cultures share ideas and ways of doing things, p. 105

cultural landscape a landscape that has been changed by human beings and that reflects their culture, p. 48

cultural trait a behavioral characteristic of a people, such as a language, skill, or custom, passed from one generation to another, p. 48

culture language, religious beliefs, values, customs, and other ways of life shared by a group of people, p. 48, 385

culture region an area in which people share the same cultural traits, p. 48

czar [ZAR] title of Russian emperors before the formation of the Soviet Union, p. 285

D

death rate the number of deaths each year per 1,000 people, p. 43

deciduous [duh SID joo us] pertaining to trees that lose their leaves, p. 267

Declaration of Independence the document written by Thomas Jefferson in 1776 that explained American colonists' reasons for rejecting British rule; representatives from each of the thirteen colonies showed their for independence by signing the document, p. 89

degree a unit of measure used to determine absolute location; on globes and maps, latitude and longitude ar measured in degrees, p. 16

658 GLOSSARY

demilitarized zone a border area between countries in which no weapons are allowed; in the Koreas, it is the zone between South and North Korea, p. 509

democracy [dih MAHK ruh see] government of the people, by the people, pp. 55, 275

demographer a scientist who studies human populations, including their size; growth; density; distribution; and rates of births, marriages, and deaths, p. 41

dialect a version of a language found only in certain regions, p. 485

dictator a ruler of a country who has complete power, pp. 220, 231, 286

dictatorship a government in which one person, a dictator, governs, p. 56

direct democracy a system of government in which the people participate directly in decision-making, p. 55

discriminate to treat people unfairly based on race, religion, or gender, p. 433

discrimination unfair treatment, often based on race or gender, p. 508

distortion a misrepresentation of the true shape; each map projection used by a cartographer produces some distortion, p. 20

diversify to add variety; to expand, pp. 178, 511

diversity variety, p. 201

domesticate to adapt wild plants and animals for human use, p. 372

dominion a self-governing area subject to Great Britain, for example, Canada prior to 1939, p. 99

drought a long period without rain, p. 519

Duma a Russian congress established by Czar Nicholas whose members were elected by the people, p. 285

dynasty a series of rulers from the same family; Chinese history is described by dynasties, p. 466

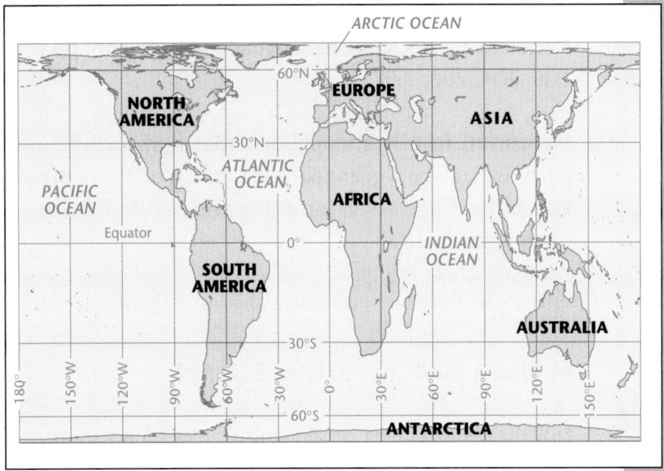

distortion

E

economy the ways that goods and services are produced and made available to people; pp. 52, 192

elevation height of land above sea level; pp. 174, 358

emigrate to move out of one country into another, p. 199, 319

emperor a ruler of widespread lands, p. 466

empire a large collection of people and lands ruled by a single government, p. 276

environment all of the surroundings and conditions that affect living things, such as water, soil, and air, p. 11

erosion a process by which water, wind, or ice wears away landforms and carries the material to another place, p. 29

escarpment a high, steep slope or cliff at the edge of a plateau or mountain range, p. 359

estancias [eh STAHN see yahs] estates owned privately by individuals, p. 242

ethics the standards or code of moral behavior that distinguishes between right and wrong for a particular person, religion, group, profession, and so on, p. 50

GLOSSARY 659

ethnic group a group of people who share the same ancestors, culture, language, or religion, pp. 106, 204, 296, 373

extended family a family unit that may include parents, children, grandparents, aunts, uncles, cousins, and other relatives, often living with or near each other, pp. 49, 389

F

famine a food shortage, pp. 310, 511

fellaheen peasants or agricultural workers in an Arab country, p. 404

fertile containing substances that plants need in order to grow well, pp. 359, 372

feudalism [FYOOD ul iz um] a kind of society in which people worked and sometimes fought for a local lord in return for protection and the use of land, p. 277

fiord [fyord] a narrow bay or inlet from the sea bordered by steep cliffs, p. 553

Flemish Dutch the language spoken by the people of Flanders in northern Belgium, p. 313

forty-niner one of the first miners of the California Gold Rush of 1849, p. 135

fossil fuel any one of several nonrenewable resources such as coal, oil, or natural gas, created from the remains of plants and animals, pp. 32, 268

Francophone a person who speaks French as his or her first language, p. 143

free enterprise an economic system in which individuals can start and run their own businesses, pp. 53, 327, 503

G

ganwa princes or lords, p. 421

gauchos [GOW chohz] nomadic cowboys of the mid-18th century who roamed the Pampas and later became hired farmhand on private estates, pp. 241–242

genocide deliberate murder of a racial, political, or ethnic group, p. 317

geography the study of the Earth's surface and the processes that shape it, the connections between places, and the relationships between people and their environment, p. 15

geyser [GY zur] a hot spring that shoots scalding water into the air, p. 553

glacier a huge, slow-moving sheet of ice that fills valleys between mountains, p. 74

globe a round model of the Earth that shows the continents and oceans in their true shapes, p. 19

Golden Horseshoe a manufacturing region in Ontario that includes the Toronto metropolitan area, p. 147

goods products that are made to be sold; cars, baskets, computers, and paper are all examples of goods, p. 52

government the system that establishes and enforces the laws and institutions of a society; some governments are controlled by a few people, and others are controlled by many, p. 54

Green Revolution changes in agriculture since the 1950s that have greatly increased the world's food supply; the Green Revolution's reliance on costly technologies and dangerous pesticides can be both financially and environmentally damaging to nations, p. 43

glacier

660 GLOSSARY

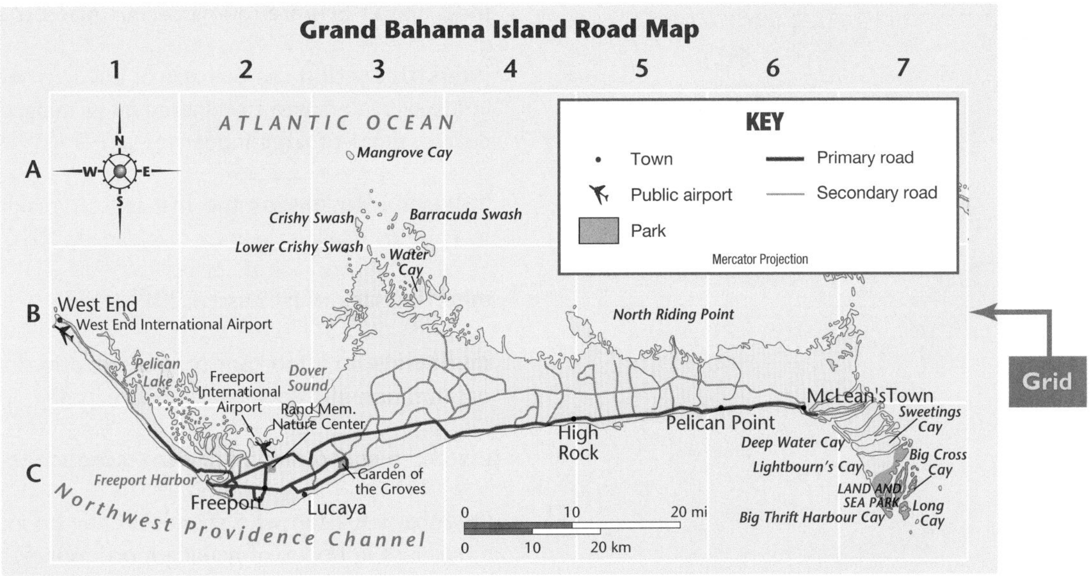

grid

grid a system used on maps to help locate places; some are based on longitude and latitude, while others are composed of letters and numbers, p. 22

griot [GREE oh] an African storyteller, p. 389

Group of Seven a group of Canadian painters in the 1920s and 1930s who developed bold techniques in their landscape works, p. 111

guerilla a person who takes part in irregular warfare as a member of an independent group, p. 220

H

hacienda [hah see EN duh] plantation owned by the Spanish settlers or the Catholic Church in Spanish America, p. 188

hajj the pilgrimage made by Muslims to Mecca, p. 527

harambee the Swahili word for "let's pull together"; the campaign in Kenya begun by President Jomo Kenyatta in 1963, after the country became independent, p. 425

heritage the customs and practices passed from one generation to the next, p. 299

hieroglyphics a system of writing using signs and symbols, used by the Maya and other cultures, p. 184

high latitudes the regions between the Arctic Circle and the North Pole and the Antarctic Circle and the South Pole, p. 14

hill a landform that rises above the surrounding land and that has a rounded top; a hill is lower and usually less steep than a mountain, p. 27

Holocaust the execution of 6 million Jews by German Nazis during World War II, pp. 96, 317

homeland South African lands where blacks were forced to live during apartheid; driest and least fertile parts of the country, p. 433

Homestead Act a law passed in 1862 giving 160 acres (65 hectares) of land on the Midwestern plains to any adult willing to live on and farm it for five years, p. 95

homogeneous having similar members, in reference to a group, p. 486

humanism an approach to knowledge that focused on worldly rather than religious values, p. 279

hunter-gatherer person who gathers wild food and hunts animals to survive, p. 371

hydroelectricity electric power produced by moving water, usually generated by releasing water from a dam across a river, pp. 81, 177

GLOSSARY 661

key

hydroelectric power the power generated by water-driven turbines, p. 270

I

immigrant a person who moves to a new country in order to settle there, pp. 44, 91

immunity a natural resistance to disease, p. 150

imperialism the control by one country of the political and economic life of another country or region, p. 282

import to bring products into one country from another to sell, p. 208

improvisation an element in jazz in which musicians spontaneously create music, p. 110

incentive a benefit often used by large companies to attract workers and keep them happy, p. 507

indentured servant a person who, in exchange for benefits received, must work for a period of years to gain freedom, p. 88

indigenous originating in a certain place, p. 114, 150

industrialization the process of building new industries in an area dominated by farming; the development of large industries, p. 127

Industrial Revolution the change from making goods by hand to making them by machine, pp. 91, 281

injustice lack of fairness, p. 201

institution an important practice, relationship, or organization in a society or culture, p. 49

invest to spend money to earn more money, p. 192

investor a person who spends money on improving a business in hopes of making more money, p. 339

irrigate to artifically water crops, p. 362

isthmus narrow strip of land that has water on both sides and joins two larger bodies of land, p. 171

K

key the section of a map that explains the symbols for the map features; also called a legend, p. 22

kibbutz a cooperative settlement found in Israel, p. 533

kinship a family relationship, p. 389

L

labor force the supply of workers, p. 95

ladino [lah DEE noh] in Guatemala, a mestizo, or descendant of Native Americans and Spaniards, p. 217

landform an area of the Earth's surface with a definite shape; mountains and hills are examples of landforms, p. 27

latitude an imaginary line, also called a parallel, that circles the Earth parallel to the Equator; used to measure a distance north or south of the Equator in degrees, p. 13

life expectancy the number of years that a person may be expected, on average, to live, p. 43

662 GLOSSARY

lineage a group of families with a common ancestor, p. 389

Line of Demarcation an imaginary line from the North Pole to the South Pole (at about 50° longitude) set forth in the 1494 Treaty of Tordesillas; Spain had the right to settle and trade west of the line and Portugal had the right to settle and trade east of the line, p. 187

lock a section of waterway in which ships are raised or lowered by adjusting the water level, p. 221

loess [LOH ess] a type of rich, dustlike soil found on the North European Plain, p. 270

longitude an imaginary line, also called a meridian, that runs north and south from one pole to another; used to measure a distance east or west of the Prime Meridian in degrees, p. 16

Louisiana Purchase the sale of land in 1803 by France to the United States; all the land between the Mississippi River and the eastern slope of the Rocky Mountains, p. 90

low latitudes the region between the Tropic of Cancer and the Tropic of Capricorn, p. 13

M

maize both the plant and the kernel of corn, p. 184

manufacturing the process of turning raw materials into a finished product, p. 319

market economy an economy in which most businesses are privately owned, p. 53

marsupial an animal, such as the kangaroo or the koala, that carries its young in a body pouch, p. 551

maquiladora [ma kee la DOR a] a factory, often near the U.S.-Mexico border, that assembles goods for export, p. 199

mass transit a system of subways, buses, and commuter trains used to transport large numbers of people to and from urban areas, p. 136

megalopolis a number of cities and suburbs that blend into one very large urban area, p. 121

meridian an imaginary line that circles the globe from north to south and runs through both the North and South poles; the lines of longitude on maps or globes are meridians, p. 16

mestizo a person of mixed Spanish and Native American ancestry, p. 188

Middle Ages the period in European history between ancient and modern times; approximately A.D. 500–1500, p. 277

middle class a group of people that included traders, merchants, and others who were economically between the poor and the very rich, p. 279

middle latitudes the regions between the Tropic of Cancer and the Arctic Circle and the Tropic of Capricorn and the Antarctic Circle, p. 14

migrant farmworker a laborer who travels from one area to another, picking crops that are in season, p. 213

migrant worker a person who moves from place to place to find work, p. 396

migrate to move from one place to another, p. 373

migration a movement from place to place, pp. 44, 295, 466

minaret a high tower attached to a mosque, with one or more balconies, p. 494

minaret

GLOSSARY 663

mixed-crop farm a farm that grows several different kinds of crops, p. 130

monarch the ruler of a kingdom or empire, such as a king or queen, p. 279

monarchy a system of authoritarian government headed by a monarch—usually a king or a queen—who inherits the throne by birth, p. 55

monsoons the winds that blow across East Asia at certain times of the year; in summer, they are very wet; in winter, they are generally dry unless they have crossed warm ocean currents, p. 456

moshavim small farming villages in Israel, p. 532

mountain usually, a landform that rises more than 2000 ft (610m) above sea level and is wide at the bottom and narrow at the peak, p. 27

mountain

muezzin [moo EZ in] a person who summons Muslims to pray by chanting, p. 494

multicultural influenced by many cultures, p. 293

multiethnic containing many ethnic groups, p. 408

mwami king, p. 421

N

nationalism a feeling of pride in one's own homeland; a group's identiy as members of a nation, pp. 283, 379

nationalist a person who is devoted to the interests of his or her country, p. 468

nationalize to put a once-private industry under national control, p. 429

natural resource any useful material found in the environment, p. 31

navigable [NAV ih guh bul] wide enough and deep enough for ships to travel through, p. 263

nonrenewable resource a resource that cannot be replaced once it is used; nonrenewable resources include fossil fuels such as coal and oil, and minerals such as iron, copper, and gold, pp. 32, 268

nomad a person who moves around to make a living, usually by herding animals, trading, hunting, or gathering food, pp. 363, 486

nuclear family a family unit that includes a mother, father, and their children, pp. 49, 389

O

oasis a fertile place in a desert where there is water and vegetation, p. 362

one-crop economy an economy in which only one crop provides a majority of a country's income, p. 230

orbit the path followed by an object in space as it moves around another, such as that of Earth as it moves around the sun, p. 12

P

Pan-Africanism a movement that stressed unity among all Africans, p. 379

parallel in geography, any of the imaginary lines that circle Earth parallel to the Equator; a latitude line, p. 16

parliament a lawmaking body, p. 525

Parliament a group of elected officials in Great Britain who help govern by deciding about taxes and other laws, pp. 280, 308

partition division, p. 475

partitioned divided, p. 309

664 GLOSSARY

prairie

Pax Romana Roman peace; a 200-year period of peace that began when Augustus, the first emperor of Rome, took power in 27 B.C., p. 276

penal colony a place settled by convicts or prisoners; the British founded the first colony in Australia as a penal colony, p. 566

peninsula land nearly surrounded by water, p. 264

permafrost permanently frozen layer of ground below the top layer of soil, pp. 79, 267

persecution harassment, often based on religious or ethnic intolerance, p. 310

petrochemical a substance, such as plastic, paint, or asphalt, that is made from petroleum, p. 127

photosynthesis [foht oh SIN thuh sis] the process by which green plants and trees produce their own food using water, carbon dioxide, and sunlight; oxygen is released as a result of photosynthesis, p. 234

pilgrimage a religious journey; for Muslims, the journey to Mecca, p. 375

plain a large area of flat or gently rolling land usually without many trees, p. 27

plantation a large, one-crop farm with many workers, common in the Southern United States before the Civil War, pp. 88, 393

plate in geography, a huge section of Earth's crust, p. 28

plate tectonics the theory that the Earth's crust is made of huge, slowly moving slabs of rock called plates, p. 28

plateau [pla TOH] a large, mostly flat area that rises above the surrounding land; at least one side has a steep slope; pp. 27, 170, 262, 358

polders new pieces of land reclaimed from the sea; in the Netherlands, land created by building dikes and draining water, p. 311

policies methods and plans governments use to do their work, p. 275

political movement a large group of people who work together to defend their rights or to change the leaders in power, p. 219

population the people living in a particular region; especially, the total number of people in an area, p. 41

population density the average number of people living in an area, pp. 42

population distribution how a population is spread over an area, p. 41

porteños Europeans who settled in and around Buenos Aires to trade, p. 243

prairie a region of flat or rolling land covered with tall grasses, pp. 79, 267

precipitation all the forms of water, such as rain, sleet, hail, and snow, that fall to the ground from the atmosphere, p. 34

GLOSSARY 665

primary industry the part of the economy that produces raw materials; examples include agriculture, fishing, mining, and forestry, pp. 52, 574

Prime Meridian an imaginary line of longitude, or meridian, that runs from the North Pole to the South Pole through Greenwich, England; it is designated 0° longitude and is used as a reference point from which east and west lines of longitude are measured, p. 16

privatization the return of businesses to private ownership and management, pp. 240, 336

producer a person who makes products that are used by other people, p. 52

projection a representation of the Earth's rounded surface on a flat piece of paper, p. 20

propaganda the spread of ideas designed to promote a specific cause, p. 299

"push-pull" theory a theory of migration that says people migrate because certain things in their lives "push" them to leave, and certain things in a new place "pull" them, p.45

Q

quaternary industry information technologies, including industries that provide Internet services, computer software, cable, and telephone service, p. 52

Quran [koo rahn] the holy book of the religion of Islam, p. 375

Quebecois literature French Canadian literature, p. 110

Quiet Revolution a peaceful change in the government of Quebec, Canada, in which the Parti Québécois won control of the legislature and made French the official language, p. 143

quota a certain portion of something, such as jobs, set aside for a group, pp. 55, 116

R

radical extreme, p. 502

rain shadow an area on the side of a mountain away from the wind that receives little rainfall, p. 78

refugees

The Ramayana an ancient Hindu epic poem that Hindus believe was revealed to its author by Brahma, the god of creation, pp. 487–488

raw material a material or resource that is still in its natural state, before being processed or manufactured into a useful product, p. 32

recession a downturn in business activity and economic prosperity, not as severe as a depression, p. 131

Reconstruction United States plan for rebuilding the nation after the Civil War, included a period when the South was governed by the United States Army, p. 93

recyclable resource a resource that cycles through natural processes in the environment; water, nitrogen, and carbon are recyclable resources, p. 32

referendum a ballot or vote in which voters decide for or against a particular issue, p. 143

refugees people who seek safety in another country, pp. 421, 514

666 GLOSSARY

religious diversity a variety of religious faiths coexisting in a single region, p. 107

Renaissance a period of European history that included a rebirth of interest in learning and art, peaking in the 1500s, p. 279

renewable resource a natural resource that the environment continues to supply or replace as it is used; trees, water, and wind are renewable resources, p. 32

repress to put down, keep from acting, p. 300

representative a person who represents, or stands for, a group of people, usually in government, p. 308

representative democracy a system of government in which the people elect representatives to run the affairs of the country, p. 55

reservation land set aside for a specific purpose, as by the Canadian government for indigenous peoples, p. 113

reunification the process of becoming unified again, p. 318

revolution one complete orbit of the Earth around the sun; the Earth completes one revolution every 365 days, or one year, p. 12

revolution a political movement in which people overthrow the existing government and set up another, pp. 189, 280

Revolutionary War the war in which the American colonies won their independence from Britain, fought from 1775–1781, p. 89

rift a deep crack in the Earth's surface, p. 359

robot a computer-driven machine that does tasks once done by humans, p. 505

rotation the spinning motion of Earth, like a top on its axis; Earth takes about 24 hours to rotate one time, p. 12

rural having to do with the countryside, p. 198

rural area an area with low population density, such as a village or the countryside, p. 46

S

savanna region of tall grasses, p. 363

scale the size of an area on a map as compared with the area's actual size, p. 19

Scientific Revolution a movement that took place during the 1600s and 1700s, when scientists began to base their study of the world on observable facts rather than on beliefs, p. 280

secondary industry manufacturing businesses that take materials from primary industries and other secondary industries and make them into goods, pp. 52, 575

segregate to set apart and force to use separate schools, housing, parks, and so on because of race and religion, p. 93

savanna

GLOSSARY 667

serf a person who lived on and farmed a lord's land in feudal times; he or she did not own land and depended on the lord for protection, p. 277

services work done or duties performed for other people, such as the work of a doctor or of a television repair person, p. 52

settlement house a community center for poor immigrants to the United States, p. 95

silt fine-grained sediment deposited by rivers, p. 359

social structure the relationship within a society (or a large group of people) that forms a basis for interaction among members of that society, p. 49

souq an open-air marketplace, p. 407

sovereignty [SAHV run tee] political independence, p. 413

squatter a person who settles on someone else's land without permission, p. 214

standard of living the material quality of life, p. 460

station in Australia, a very large sheep or cattle ranch, p. 567

steppes mostly treeless plains; in Russia, the steppes are grasslands of fertile soil suitable for farming, p. 267

strike work stoppage; a refusal to continue to work until certain demands of workers are met, p. 219

subcontinent a large landmass that is a major part of a continent; for example, the Indian subcontinent, p. 451

subsidize to economically support; some governments subsidize certain industries, p. 507

subsistence farmer one who grows just enough food to support one's family, p. 207

subsistence farming raising just enough crops to support one's family, p. 364

Sun Belt area of the United States stretching from the southern Atlantic Coast to the coast of California; known for its warm weather, p. 128

surplus more than is needed, p. 372

Swahili an African language that includes some Arabic words, p. 376

T

taiga [TY guh] an enormous Russian forest, covering more than four million square miles, p. 267

tariff a fee or tax that a government charges for goods entering the country, p. 294

technology tools and the skills that people need to use them; the practical use of scientific skills, especially in industry, p. 48

tectonic plate a large piece of the Earth's crust, p. 552

temperature the degree of hotness or coldness of something, such as water or air, usually measured with a thermometer, p. 34

terrace a platform cut into the side of a mountain, used for growing crops in steep places, p. 406

tertiary industry service activities such as banking, transportation, health care, and police protection, pp. 52, 575

textiles cloth products, p. 281

terrace

668 GLOSSARY

totem poles a tall, carved wooden pole containing symbols, found among Native Americans of the Pacific Northwest, p. 150

tourism the business of providing services for tourists, or visitors, to a region, p. 575

traditional economy an economy in which producing, buying, and selling goods operates by the customs, traditions, and habits of the group, pp. 52–53

transportation barrier physical features that make it difficult to travel or transport goods from one region to another, p. 359

transportation corridors routes through which people can travel by foot, vehicle, rail, ship, or airplane; pp. 76, 222

treaty an agreement in writing made between two or more countries, p. 187

Treaty of Tordesillas [tor day SEE yas] the 1494 treaty setting up the Line of Demarcation, giving Spain the right to settle and trade west of the line and Portugal the same rights east of the line, p. 187

tributary (TRIB yoo tehr ee) a stream that flows into a larger river or body of water, pp. 76, 172, 263, 360

tropics the area on Earth between the 23°N and 23°S lines of latitude, where the climate is almost always hot, p. 78

tundra a cold, dry region covered with snow for more than half the year; a vast, treeless plain where the subsoil is always frozen, p. 79, 267

turbines large spinning machines, often powered by water, that can generate electricity, p. 270

U

United Empire Loyalists American colonists loyal to Great Britain who relocated to Canada after the American Revolution, p. 145

vegetation

United Nations an organization of countries established in 1945 that works for peace and cooperation around the world, p. 333

urban having to do with the city, p. 198

urban area an area with a high population density; a city or a town, p. 46

urbanization the movement of populations toward cities and the resulting city growth, pp. 45, 292

V

vassals servants, p. 421

vegetation the plants in an area, p. 36

W

weather the condition of the bottom layer of the Earth's atmosphere in one place over a short period of time, p. 34

weathering the breaking down of rocks by wind, rain, or ice, p. 29

GLOSSARY 669

Spanish Glossary

A

abolitionist/abolicionista persona que consideraba a la esclavitud como un error y quería terminar con esta costumbre, p. 92

alliance/alianza acuerdo mutuo entre países para protegerse y defenderse uno al otro, p. 283

alluvial/aluvión relativo al suelo superficial fértil que dejan los ríos después de una inundación, p. 80

apartheid/apartheid sistema sudafricano en el que la población estaba separada por raza, y la discriminación racial era legal, p. 433

aquaculture/acuicultura cultivo marítimo; los cultivos más comunes son los de camarón y de ostras, p. 459

aqueduct/acueducto tubería o canal que sirve para transportar agua desde una fuente distante hasta regiones áridas, p. 185

arable land/tierras de cultivo terreno que puede producir cosechas, p. 456

aristocrats/aristócratas personas que son minoría, pero que se consideran una clase privilegiada y alta, p. 421

artesian well/pozo artesiano pozo profundo perforado en la roca porosa de la superficie terrestre para obtener el agua subterránea, p. 572

atmosphere/atmósfera franja de varias capas de gases que rodea a la Tierra, p. 27

atoll/atolón grupo de pequeñas islas de coral con forma de anillo que encierra a una laguna, p. 554

authoritarian/autoritario controlado por una persona o un pequeño grupo, p. 429

axis/eje línea imaginaria en torno a la cual gira un planeta; la Tierra gira en su propio eje, que va del Polo Norte al Polo Sur, p. 12

B

bazaar/bazar mercado tradicional al aire libre con hileras de tiendas o puestos, p. 403

bilingual/bilingüe que habla dos idiomas; que tiene dos idiomas oficiales, p. 100

birthrate/tasa de natalidad porcentaje por año de nacimientos con vida por cada 1,000 habitantes, p. 43

bolas/boleadoras conjunto de cordeles de cuero y tres esferas de hierro o piedras que se lanzan a las patas de los animales para capturarlos, p. 244

boom/auge periodo de prosperidad en aumento en el que se produce y se vende una mayor cantidad de cierto producto, p. 240

boomtown/pueblo en auge población que tiene un rápido crecimiento, con frecuencia para satisfacer las necesidades de los mineros, p. 151

boycott/boicoteo renuencia a comprar o usar bienes y servicios, pp. 89, 379

C

campesinos/campesinos aldeanos sin tierras y agricultores de pocos recursos, pp. 198, 233

canopy/dosel masa densa de hojas que forma la capa superior de un bosque, p. 234

capital/capital dinero que sirve para expandir un negocio, p. 131

capitalism/capitalismo sistema económico en que las personas y las compañías privadas son propietarias de negocios e industrias básicos y no básicos, p. 53

cardinal direction/punto cardinal uno de los cuatro puntos de la brújula: norte, sur, este y oeste, p. 21

670 SPANISH GLOSSARY

Carnival/carnaval celebración anual en América Latina que se lleva a cabo con música, danzas y desfiles, p. 205

casbah/casbah barrio antiguo y muy poblado de las ciudades de África del Norte, p. 407

cash crop/cultivo para la venta producto de cultivo que se cosecha para cambiarlo por dinero en el mercado mundial, pp. 365, 459

caste/casta una clase de personas en la India, p. 473

cataract/catarata rápido que corre sobre un lecho de rocas, p. 359

caudillo/caudillo oficial militar que gobierna estrictamente, p. 191

census/censo recuento de la población de un país, p. 410

city-state/ciudad-estado forma de organización en que las poblaciones tienen su propio gobierno y controlan gran parte del territorio que las rodea, p. 376

civilization/civilización sociedad con ciudades, un gobierno central, clases sociales y, por lo general, escritura, arte y arquitectura, pp. 372, 465

civil rights movement/movimiento por los derechos civiles grupo numeroso de personas que se unieron en Estados Unidos desde principios de la década de 1960 para acabar con la discriminación de los afroestadounidenses y para apoyar la igualdad de derechos para los grupos minoritarios, p. 97

Civil War/Guerra Civil guerra entre los estados del norte y del sur de Estados Unidos que empezó en 1861 y terminó en 1865, p. 93

clan/clan grupo de familias que mantienen un antecesor común, pp. 389, 466

climate/clima pautas atmosféricas típicas que experimenta una región durante un largo periodo, p. 34

Cold War/Guerra Fría periodo de gran tensión entre Estados Unidos y la antigua Unión Soviética, que duró más de 40 años después de la Segunda Guerra Mundial, pp. 97, 286

colonize/colonizar establecerse en un área y crear o apoderarse de un gobierno, p. 378

colony/colonia territorio gobernado por otra nación, por lo general lejana, p. 474

command economy/economía dirigida economía en que las decisiones económicas las toma el gobierno, p. 53

commonwealth/mancomunidad unidad política autogobernada y con fuertes lazos hacia un país en particular, p. 232

commune/comuna comunidad donde las tierras son comunes y los miembros viven y trabajan juntos, p. 484

Communism/comunismo teoría de gobierno en que las propiedades como las granjas y las fábricas son propiedad del gobierno para el beneficio de todos los ciudadanos; sistema político en que el gobierno central controla todos los aspectos de la vida de los ciudadanos, pp. 97, 285

commute/viajar a diario ir y regresar regularmente de un lugar a otro, particularmente de la casa al trabajo, p. 121

compass rose/rosa de los vientos figura de un mapa que por lo común muestra los cuatro puntos cardinales, p. 21

Confederacy/Confederación los Estados Confederados; conjunto de estados del sur que se separó de Estados Unidos después de la elección de Abraham Lincoln en 1860, p. 93

coniferous/coníferas pertenecientes a los árboles con frutos en forma de cono, p. 267

conquistador/conquistador soldado del siglo XVI que al mando del gobierno español tenía la misión de obtener tierras y riquezas en el continente americano, p. 187

constitution/constitución declaración de las leyes y los valores básicos de un país, pp. 55, 232

Constitution/Constitución documento escrito en 1787 y aprobado en 1789 que estableció los tres poderes del gobierno estadounidense y protegió los derechos individuales de los ciudadanos, p. 89

SPANISH GLOSSARY 671

constitutional monarchy/mornarquía constitucional gobierno en el que un rey o reina dirige el estado, pero que tiene poderes limitados; por ejemplo, el gobierno actual de Gran Bretaña, p. 308

consumer/consumidor persona que compra bienes y servicios, p. 52

Continental Divide/divisoria continental límite que separa a los ríos de un continente que corren en direcciones opuestas; en América del Norte, en las montañas Rocosas, p. 74

copra/copra pulpa de coco deshidratada que se usa para hacer margarina, aceites de cocina y jabones finos, p. 574

coral/coral sustancia que parece roca y está formada de esqueletos de pequeños animales marinos, pp. 171, 554

corporate farm/granja corporativa granja muy grande dirigida por una corporación; puede estar formada por varias granjas más pequeñas que alguna vez fueron propiedades familiares, p. 131

cosmopolitan/cosmopolita caracterizado por diversidad étnica o cultural y sofisticación, p. 241

coup/golpe de estado toma de un gobierno, generalmente por parte de las fuerzas militares, p. 414

Creole/*Creole* persona nacida en el Caribe o en otra parte de América, por lo general de descendientes europeos y africanos, cuya cultura tiene fuertes influencias francesas y africanas; dialecto que hablan los criollos, p. 219

criollo/criollo persona de padres españoles nacida fuera de España; por lo general perteneciente a la clase adinerada y mejor educada en las colonias españolas, p. 190

cultural diffusion/difusión cultural diseminación de ideas y costumbres de una cultura para otra, pp. 387, 467

cultural diversity/diversidad cultural extensa variedad de culturas, pp. 105, 388

cultural exchange/intercambio cultural proceso en el que culturas diferentes comparten ideas y formas de hacer las cosas, p. 105

cultural landscape/paisaje cultural paisaje modificado por los seres humanos y que refleja su cultura, p. 48

cultural trait/rasgo cultural comportamiento particular de una población, tales como idioma, destrezas y costumbres, que pasan de una generación a otra, p. 48

culture/cultura idioma, creencias religiosas, valores, costumbres y demás formas de vida que comparte un grupo de personas, pp. 48, 385

culture region/región cultural área donde las personas comparten los mismos rasgos culturales, p. 48

czar/zar título de los emperadores rusos antes de la formación de la Unión Soviética, p. 285

D

death rate/tasa de mortalidad número de muertes por año por cada 1,000 personas, p. 43

deciduous/caducifolio perteneciente a los árboles que pierden sus hojas, p. 267

Declaration of Independence/Declaración de Independencia documento escrito por Thomas Jefferson en 1776 que expuso las razones de los colonos estadounidenses para rechazar al gobierno británico; los representantes de cada una de las trece colonias firmaron el documento para mostrar su postura en favor de la independencia, p. 89

degree/grado unidad de medida para determinar la ubicación precisa; en globos terráqueos y mapas, la latitud y la longitud se miden en grados, p. 16

demilitarized zone/zona de tolerancia área de la frontera entre países donde no se permite el uso de armas; en Corea, es la zona entre Corea del Norte y Corea del Sur, p. 509

democracy/democracia gobierno del pueblo por el pueblo, pp. 55, 275

demographer/demógrafo científico que estudia las características de las poblaciones humanas, como su tamaño, crecimiento, densidad y distribución, así como sus tasas de nacimiento, matrimonios y mortandad, p. 41

672 SPANISH GLOSSARY

dialect/dialecto versión de un idioma que se habla sólo en ciertas regiones, p. 485

dictator/dictador gobernante de un país que tiene todo el poder, pp. 220, 231, 286

dictatorship/dictadura gobierno dirigido por una persona, por un dictador, p. 56

direct democracy/democracia directa sistema de gobierno en que el pueblo participa directamente en la toma de decisiones, p. 55

discriminate/discriminar tratar con injusticia a las personas por su raza, religión o género, p. 433

discrimination/discriminación trato injusto a menudo a causa de la raza o el género, p. 508

distortion/distorsión representación falsa de una forma verdadera; los mapas de proyección (planisferios) que usan los cartógrafos generan cierta distorsión, p. 20

diversify/diversificar variar; expandir, aumentar, pp. 178, 511

diversity/diversidad variedad, p. 201

domesticate/domesticar adaptar plantas silvestres y animales salvajes para el uso humano, p. 372

dominion/dominio zona de autogobierno sujeta a Gran Bretaña, por ejemplo, Canadá antes de 1939, p. 99

drought/sequía periodo largo sin lluvia, p. 519

Duma/Duma congreso ruso, establecido por el zar Nicolás, a cuyos miembros los elegía el pueblo, p. 285

dynasty/dinastía serie de gobernantes pertenecientes a la misma familia; la historia china se describe por medio de sus dinastías, p. 466

E

economy/economía manera de producir y poner al alcance del pueblo los bienes y servicios en un país, pp. 52, 192

elevation/altitud elevación del terreno sobre el nivel del mar, pp. 174, 358

emigrate/emigrar irse a vivir de un país a otro, p. 199, 319

emperor/emperador gobernante de un extenso territorio, p. 466

empire/imperio extenso grupo de personas y tierras regidas por un solo gobernante, p. 276

environment/medio ambiente todo el medio y las condiciones que afectan a los seres vivos, por ejemplo, el agua, el suelo y el aire, p. 11

erosion/erosión proceso mediante el cual el agua, el viento o el hielo desgasta el relieve del suelo y transporta la materia a otro sitio, p. 29

escarpment/escarpadura acantilado escarpado al borde de una meseta o cordillera, p. 359

estancias/estancias haciendas o fincas que son propiedad particular de un individuo, p. 242

ethics/ética estándares o código de comportamiento moral de una persona, una religión, un grupo, una profesión, etcétera, que permite distinguir entre el bien y el mal, p. 50

ethnic group/grupo étnico grupo de personas cuyos antepasados, cultura, idioma y religión les son comunes, pp. 106, 204, 296, 373

extended family/familia extendida unidad familiar que abarca padres, hijos, abuelos, tías, tíos, primos y demás parientes, que por lo general viven bajo el mismo techo o muy cerca uno de otro, pp. 49, 389

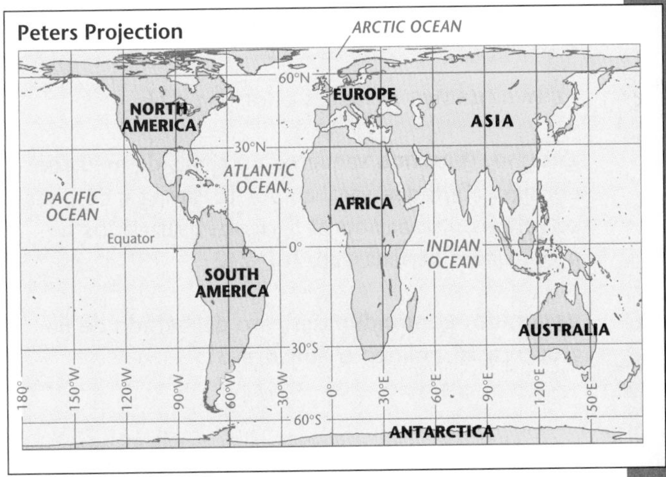

distortion/distorsión

SPANISH GLOSSARY 673

F

famine/hambruna insuficiencia de alimentos, pp. 310, 511

fellaheen/felá campesino o labrador agrícola de los países árabes, p. 404

fertile/fértil se dice del suelo que contiene las sustancias que las plantas necesitan para crecer bien, pp. 359, 372

feudalism/feudalismo clase de organización social en donde las personas trabajaban e incluso peleaban para un señor a cambio de protección y de permiso para usar la tierra , p. 277

fiord/fiordo bahía estrecha o entrada del mar, rodeado de acantilados escarpados, p. 553

Flemish Dutch/holandés flamenco idioma que se habla en Flandes, región del norte de Bélgica, p. 313

forty-niner/*forty-niner* uno de los primeros mineros de la Fiebre del Oro en 1849, p. 135

fossil fuel/combustible fósil cualquiera de los recursos no renovables como el carbón, el petróleo o el gas natural, que se formaron a partir de los restos de plantas y animales, pp. 32, 268

Francophone/francófono persona que habla el francés como primera lengua, p. 143

free enterprise/libre empresa sistema económico en el que los individuos establecen y dirigen su propio negocio, pp. 53, 327, 503

G

ganwa/ganwa príncipes o lores, p. 421

gaucho/gauchos vaqueros nómadas de mediados del siglo XVIII que vagaban por la Pampa y después se volvieron trabajadores agrícolas asalariados en propiedades privadas, pp. 241–242

genocide/genocidio asesinato deliberado de un grupo racial, político o étnico, p. 317

geography/geografía estudio de la superficie de la Tierra y de sus procesos de formación, las conexiones entre lugares y las relaciones entre las personas y su medio ambiente, p. 15

geyser/géiser manantial caliente que lanza agua hirviente al aire, p. 553

glacier/glaciar bloque de hielo enorme, de movimiento muy lento, que ocupa un valle entre dos montañas, p. 74

globe/globo terráqueo modelo redondo de la Tierra que muestra los continentes y océanos en sus formas reales, p. 19

Golden Horseshoe/*Golden Horseshoe* región manufacturera de Ontario que abarca el área metropolitana de Toronto, p. 147

goods/bienes de consumo productos que se fabrican para su venta; autos, cestos, computadoras y papel son ejemplos de bienes, p. 52

government/gobierno sistema que establece y hace cumplir las leyes e instituciones de una sociedad; algunos gobiernos están controlados por pocas personas y otros por muchas personas, p. 54

Green Revolution/Revolución verde cambios en la agricultura desde la década de 1950 que han aumentado en gran medida el abastecimiento de alimentos en el mundo; la sustentación de la Revolución verde en tecnología costosa y pesticidas peligrosos puede perjudicar tanto el medio ambiente como a las finanzas de las naciones, p. 43

grid/cuadrícula sistema para localizar lugares en los mapas; algunas se basan en la longitud y la latitud, y otras usan números y letras, p. 22

griot/griot contador de cuentos africano, p. 389

Group of Seven/Grupo de los Siete grupo de pintores canadienses en las décadas de 1920 y 1930 que desarrollaron técnicas audaces en sus obras paisajistas, p. 111

guerilla/guerrillero persona que participa en una guerra irregular como miembro de un grupo independiente, p. 220

674 SPANISH GLOSSARY

H

hacienda/hacienda plantación de colonos españoles o de la Iglesia católica en la América hispana, p. 188

hajj/hajj peregrinación que hacen los musulmanes a la Meca, p. 527

harambee/harambi palabra suajili que significa "hagámoslo juntos"; campaña en Kenya que inició el presidente Jomo Kenyatta en 1963, después de que el país se independizó, p. 425

heritage/herencia hábitos y costumbres que pasan de una generación a otra, p. 299

hieroglyphics/jeroglíficos sistema de escritura con signos y símbolos que usaron los mayas y otras culturas, p. 184

high latitudes/latitudes altas regiones entre el círculo polar Ártico y el polo Norte y el círculo polar Antártico y el polo Sur, p. 14

hill/colina formación del suelo más alta que el terreno que la rodea, con una cima redondeada; por lo general una colina es más baja y menos empinada que una montaña, p. 27

Holocaust/Holocausto ejecución de 6 millones de judíos por los nazis alemanes durante la Segunda Guerra Mundial, pp. 96, 317

homeland/tierra natal tierras de Sudáfrica donde eran forzadas a vivir las personas de raza negra durante el apartheid; zonas más áridas y menos fértiles del país, p. 433

Homestead Act/ley de colonización ley aprobada en 1862 que otorgaba 160 acres (65 hectáreas) de tierra de las llanuras del Medio Oeste a todo adulto que quisiera vivir en ella y cultivarla durante 5 años, p. 95

homogeneous/homogéneo que tiene elementos similares en relación con un grupo, p. 486

humanism/humanismo aproximación del conocimiento que se enfocó en los valores materiales más que en los valores religiosos, p. 279

hunter-gatherer/cazador-recolector persona que recolectaba alimentos silvestres y cazaba animales para sobrevivir, p. 371

hydroelectricity/hidroelectricidad energía eléctrica producida por agua en movimiento, por lo común es la que se genera al soltar el agua de una presa, pp. 81, 177

hydroelectric power/energía hidroeléctrica energía generada por turbinas impulsadas por agua, p. 270

I

immigrant/inmigrante persona que se muda a otro país para establecerse en él, pp. 44, 91

immunity/inmunidad resistencia natural a la enfermedad, p. 150

imperialism/imperialismo control que ejerce un país en la vida política y económica de otro país o región, p. 282

import/importar introducir productos de un país a otro para venderlos, p. 208

improvisation/improvisación recurso del jazz donde los músicos crean música espontáneamente, p. 110

incentive/incentivo prestación que las grandes empresas usan para atraer a sus empleados y mantenerlos contentos, p. 507

indentured servant/sirviente por contrato persona que, a cambio de un beneficio, trabaja por un periodo de años para liberarse, p. 88

indigenous/autóctono originario de cierto lugar, p. 114, 150

industrialization/industrialización proceso de establecimiento de nuevas industrias en una región donde predomina la agricultura; desarrollo de grandes industrias, p. 127

Industrial Revolution/Revolución Industrial cambio de elaborar productos a mano para producirlos con máquinas, pp. 91, 281

injustice/injusticia falta de equidad, p. 201

SPANISH GLOSSARY 675

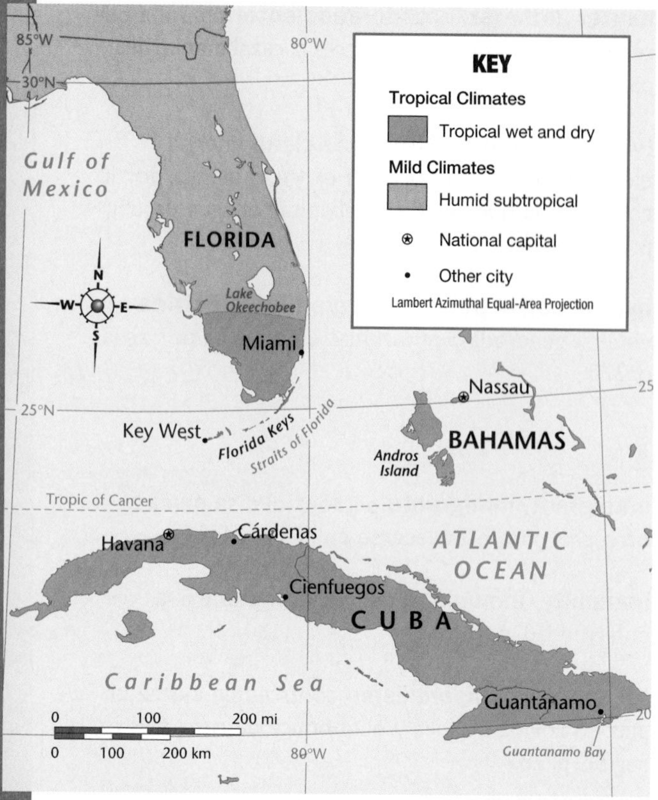

key/clave

institution/institución organización, relación o costumbre importante en una sociedad o cultura, p. 49

invest/invertir usar el dinero para obtener más dinero, p. 192

investor/inversionista persona que gasta dinero para mejorar un negocio con la esperanza de obtener más dinero, p. 339

irrigate/regar regar los cultivos de manera artificial, p. 362

isthmus/istmo franja estrecha de tierra con agua en ambos lados y unida a dos masas de tierra más grandes, p. 171

K

key/clave parte del mapa que explica la simbología de las características del mapa; también se llama leyenda, p. 22

kibbutz/kibutz asentamiento cooperativo que se encuentra en Israel, p. 533

kinship/parentesco relación familiar, p. 389

L

labor force/fuerza laboral trabajadores con que se cuenta, p. 95

ladino/ladino en Guatemala, mestizo o descendiente de indígenas americanos y de españoles, p. 217

landform/accidente geográfico área de la superficie terrestre con forma definida; las montañas y las colinas son ejemplos de accidentes geográficos, p. 27

latitude/latitud línea imaginaria, también llamada paralelo, que rodea a la Tierra y es paralela al ecuador; sirve para medir distancias en grados al norte y al sur del ecuador, p. 13

life expectancy/expectativa de vida cantidad de años que se espera que viva en promedio una persona, p. 43

lineage/linaje grupo de familias con un antepasado común, p. 389

Line of Demarcation/línea de demarcación línea imaginaria del polo Norte al polo Sur (aproximadamente a 50° de longitud) establecida en 1494 en el Tratado de Tordesillas; España tenía el derecho de colonizar y comerciar al oeste de la línea y Portugal al este de la línea, p. 187

lock/esclusa sección de vía marítima donde se eleva o se baja a los barcos ajustando el nivel del agua, p. 221

loess/loes clase de suelo nutritivo, de grano fino, que se encuentra en las planicies del norte de Europa, p. 270

longitude/longitud línea imaginaria, también llamada meridiano, que va de norte a sur, de un polo a otro; sirve para medir en grados la distancia de este a oeste del primer meridiano, p. 16

676 SPANISH GLOSSARY

Louisiana Purchase/Compra de Luisiana venta de tierra en 1803 de Francia a Estados Unidos; todo el terreno entre el río Mississippi y la ladera este de las montañas Rocosas, p. 90

low latitudes/latitudes bajas región entre el trópico de Cáncer y el trópico de Capricornio, p. 13

M

maize/maíz planta y grano del maíz, p. 184

manufacturing/manufactura proceso de convertir materia prima en productos terminados, p. 319

market economy/economía de mercado economía en la que la mayoría de los negocios son de propiedad privada, p. 53

marsupial/marsupial animal que, como el canguro o el koala, lleva a su cría en una bolsa de su cuerpo, p. 551

maquiladora/maquiladora fábrica de montaje de productos para la exportación, frecuentemente ubicada cerca de la frontera entre México y E.E. U.U., p. 199

mass transit/transporte masivo sistema de trenes subterráneos, autobuses y ferrocarriles de viaje por abono que transporta una gran cantidad de personas desde y hacia las áreas urbanas, p. 136

megalopolis/megalópolis conjunto de ciudades y de suburbios que mezclan en una gran área urbana, p. 121

meridian/meridiano línea imaginaria que rodea a la Tierra de norte a sur, y que pasa por los polos; las líneas de longitud en los mapas o globos terráqueos son los meridianos, p. 16

mestizo/mestizo persona que desciende de la mezcla entre españoles e indígenas americanos, p. 188

Middle Ages/Edad Media periodo de la historia europea entre la antigüedad y la era moderna; aproximadamente de los años 500 a 1500 D.C., p. 277

middle class/clase media grupo de personas, entre las que había comerciantes y mercaderes, que económicamente estaban entre los pobres y los muy ricos, p. 279

middle latitudes/latitudes medias regiones entre el trópico de Cáncer y el círculo polar Ártico, y el trópico de Capricornio y el círculo polar Antártico, p. 14

migrant worker/trabajador migratorio persona que se traslada de un lugar a otro para encontrar trabajo, p. 396

migrate/emigrar ir de un lugar a otro, p. 373

migration/migración trasladarse de un lugar a otro, pp. 44, 295, 466

minaret/minarete torre alta unida a una mezquita, con uno o más balcones, p. 494

mixed-crop farm/granja de cultivo mixto granja que produce diferentes clases de cultivo, p. 130

monarch/monarca gobernante de un reino o imperio, que puede ser un rey o una reina, p. 279

monarchy/monarquía sistema de gobierno autoritario encabezado por un monarca –por lo general un rey o una reina—que hereda el trono de nacimiento, p. 55

monsoons/monzón vientos que soplan por el este de Asia en ciertas épocas del año; en verano son muy húmedos; en invierno por lo general son secos, a menos que hayan cruzado las corrientes oceánicas cálidas, p. 456

moshavim/moshavim pequeñas aldeas de cultivo en Israel, p. 532

mountain/montaña por lo general, accidente geográfico que alcanza más de 2000 pies (610 m) por encima del nivel del mar, y es ancho en su base y angosto en su cima, p. 27

muezzin/muecín persona que convoca a los musulmanes por medio de cantos a orar, p. 494

multicultural/multicultural influido por varias culturas, p. 293

multiethnic/multiétnico que contiene varios grupos étnicos, p. 408

mwami/mwami rey, p. 421

SPANISH GLOSSARY 677

N

nationalism/nacionalismo sentimiento de orgullo hacia la tierra natal propia; identidad de un grupo como miembros de una nación, pp. 283, 379

nationalist/nacionalista persona dedicada a los intereses de su país, p. 468

nationalize/nacionalizar poner la industria que alguna vez fue privada bajo el control de la nación, p. 429

natural resource/recurso natural cualquier materia útil que se encuentre en el medio ambiente, p. 31

navigable/navegable lo suficientemente ancho y profundo para que los barcos lo puedan recorrer, p. 263

nonrenewable resource/recurso no renovable recurso que no puede reemplazarse después de usarse; algunos recursos no renovables son los combustibles fósiles como el carbón y el petróleo, y los minerales como el hierro, el cobre y el oro, pp. 32, 268

nomad/nómada persona que se traslada constantemente para ganarse la vida, casi siempre mediante el pastoreo de animales, el comercio, la caza y la recolección de alimentos, pp. 363, 486

nuclear family/familia nuclear unidad familiar formada por un padre, una madre y sus hijos, pp. 49, 389

O

oasis/oasis lugar fértil del desierto, donde hay agua y vegetación, p. 362

one-crop economy/economía de un solo cultivo economía en que un solo cultivo proporciona la mayor parte de los ingresos de un país, p. 230

orbit/órbita trayectoria que sigue un objeto en el espacio cuando se mueve alrededor de otro, como la Tierra que se mueve alrededor del Sol, p. 12

P

Pan-Africanism/panafricanismo movimiento que acentuó la unidad entre todos los africanos, p. 379

parallel/paralelo en geografía, cualquiera de las líneas imaginarias paralelas al ecuador que rodean la Tierra; cualquier línea de latitud, p. 16

parliament/parlamento organismo que hace las leyes, p. 525

Parliament/Parlamento grupo de funcionarios electos en Gran Bretaña que ayudan al gobierno a determinar los impuestos y a emitir otras leyes, pp. 280, 308

partition/separación división, p. 475

partitioned/separado dividido, p. 309

Pax Romana/Pax Romana paz romana; periodo de 200 años de paz que empezó cuando Augusto, el primer emperador romano, tomó el poder en al año 27 A.C., p. 276

penal colony/colonia penitenciaria lugar establecido por convictos o prisioneros; los británicos fundaron la primera colonia en Australia como colonia penitenciaria, p. 566

peninsula/península tierra rodeada por agua casi por completo, p. 264

permafrost/permafrost capa de tierra permanentemente congelada bajo la capa superior del suelo, pp. 79, 267

persecution/persecución acosamiento, con frecuencia basado en intolerancia religiosa o étnica, p. 310

petrochemical/producto petroquímico sustancia que se deriva del petróleo, como plástico, pintura o asfalto, p. 127

photosynthesis/fotosíntesis proceso por el que las plantas y los árboles verdes producen su propio alimento por medio de agua, dióxido de carbono y luz solar; el oxígeno se libera como consecuencia de la fotosíntesis, p. 234

678 SPANISH GLOSSARY

pilgrimage/peregrinación recorrido religioso; para los musulmanes, viaje a La Meca, p. 375

plain/llanura región grande de tierras llanas o ligeramente ondulantes sin muchos árboles, p. 27

plantation/plantación granja muy grande de un solo cultivo con muchos trabajadores, común en el sur de Estados Unidos antes de la Guerra Civil, pp. 88, 393

plate/placa en geografía, sección grande de corteza terrestre, p. 28

plate tectonics/placas tectónicas teoría de que la corteza terrestre está formada por enormes porciones de roca, de lento movimiento, llamadas placas, p. 28

plateau/meseta región grande, la mayor parte plana, que sobresale del terreno que la rodea; tiene al menos un lado de cuesta empinada, pp. 27, 170, 262, 358

polders/pólder terreno nuevo que se ha ganado al mar; en los Países Bajos, terreno que se forma al construir diques y drenar el agua del mar, p. 311

policies/políticas métodos y planes que usan los gobiernos para realizar sus proyectos, p. 275

political movement/movimiento político grupo grande de personas que trabajan juntas para defender sus derechos o cambiar a los líderes que están en el poder, p. 219

population/población personas que viven en una región particular; en especial la cantidad total de personas en una región, p. 41

population density/densidad de población cantidad promedio de personas que viven en una área, p. 42

population distribution/distribución de la población forma en que la población de una región está repartida, p. 41

porteños/porteños europeos que se establecieron en Buenos Aires y sus alrededores para comerciar, p. 243

prairie/pradera región de terreno plano u ondulante cubierto con pastos altos, pp. 79, 267

precipitation/precipitación todas las formas del agua, como lluvia, aguanieve, granizo y nieve, que cae de la atmósfera a la Tierra, p. 34

primary industry/industria primaria parte de la economía que produce materia prima; ejemplos de ella son la agricultura, la pesca, la minería y la silvicultura, pp. 52, 574

Prime Meridian/primer meridiano línea imaginaria de longitud, o meridiano, que va del polo Norte al polo Sur y pasa por Greenwich, Inglaterra; tiene designado el grado cero de longitud y se usa como punto de referencia para que puedan medirse las líneas de longitud del este y del oeste, p. 16

privatization/privatización restitución de los negocios a la propiedad y la administración privadas, pp. 240, 336

producer/productor persona que fabrica productos que usan otras personas, p. 52

projection/proyección representación de la superficie redonda de la Tierra en la superficie plana de un papel, p. 20

propaganda/propaganda difusión de ideas para promover una causa específica, p. 299

"push-pull" theory/teoría de "atracción y rechazo" teoría migratoria que afirma que las personas emigran por el rechazo a ciertas cosas en su vida y la atracción hacia ciertas cosas de un nuevo lugar, p. 45

Q

quaternary industry/industria cuaternaria tecnología de información, abarca las industrias que proveen servicios de Internet, software para computadoras, y servicios de cable y telefonía, p. 52

Quran/Corán libro sagrado de la religión islámica, p. 375

Quebecois literature/literatura de Quebec literatura canadiense en lengua francesa, p. 110

SPANISH GLOSSARY 679

refugees/refugiados

Quiet Revolution/Revolución silenciosa cambio pacífico del gobierno de Quebec, Canadá, en el que el Parti Québécois tomó el control de la legislatura e hizo del francés el idioma oficial, p. 143

quota/cuota cierta parte de algo, como un trabajo, que se reserva para un grupo, pp. 55, 116

R

radical/radical extremo, p. 502

rain shadow/sombra de lluvia área sin viento en un lado de la montaña, donde cae una lluvia ligera, p. 78

The Ramayana/el Ramayana poema épico hindú antiguo que los hindúes consideran una revelación de Brahma, el dios de la creación, para su autor, pp. 487–488

raw material/materia prima materia o recurso que aún se encuentra en su estado natural, antes de procesarse o manufacturarse como producto útil, p. 32

recession/recesión una baja en la actividad de los negocios y el crecimiento económico, no tan grave como una depresión, p. 131

Reconstruction/Reconstrucción plan de Estados Unidos para reconstruir la nación después de la Guerra Civil, abarca el periodo en que el ejército de Estados Unidos gobernó los estados del Sur, p. 93

recyclable resource/recurso cíclico recurso con un proceso cíclico natural en el medio ambiente; entre ellos el agua, el nitrógeno y el carbono, p. 32

referendum/referéndum boleta o voto con el que los votantes deciden a favor o en contra de un asunto en particular, p. 143

refugees/refugiados personas que buscan seguridad en otro país, pp. 421, 514

religious diversity/diversidad religiosa variedad de creencias religiosas que existen al mismo tiempo en una región, p. 107

Renaissance/Renacimiento periodo de la historia europea en el que surgió un nuevo interés en la enseñanza y el arte; culminó en el siglo XVI, p. 279

renewable resource/recurso renovable recurso natural que el medio ambiente continúa suministrando o que reemplaza al usarlo; los árboles, el agua y el viento son recursos renovables, p. 32

repress/reprimir sofocar, abstenerse de actuar, p. 300

representative/representante persona que representa o defiende a un grupo de personas, por lo general en el gobierno, p. 308

representative democracy/democracia representativa sistema de gobierno en el que las personas eligen a sus representantes para que resuelvan los asuntos del país, p. 55

reservation/reservación terreno que se reserva para un propósito específico, como lo hizo el gobierno de Canadá con los pueblos indígenas, p. 113

680 SPANISH GLOSSARY

reunification/reunificación proceso de volver a unirse, p. 318

revolution/traslación vuelta completa de la Tierra alrededor del Sol; la Tierra completa una revolución cada 365 días o cada año, p. 12

revolution/revolución movimiento político en el que el pueblo derroca el gobierno existente y establece otro, pp. 189, 280

Revolutionary War/Guerra de Independencia guerra entre los años 1775–1781 en que las colonias estadounidenses lograron su independencia de Gran Bretaña, p. 89

rift/grieta hendidura profunda en la superficie terrestre, p. 359

robot/robot máquina dirigida por computadora que realiza tareas que antes hacían los seres humanos, p. 505

rotation/rotación movimiento giratorio de la Tierra, como un trompo en su eje; la Tierra tarda 24 horas para hacer una rotación, p. 12

rural/rural relativo al campo, p. 198

rural area/área rural región con una densidad de población baja, como una villa o el campo, p. 46

savanna/sabana

S

savanna/sabana región de pastos altos, p. 363

scale/escala tamaño de una región en un mapa en relación con su tamaño real, p. 19

Scientific Revolution/Revolución científica movimiento que tuvo lugar durante los siglos XVII y XVIII, cuando los científicos basaron sus estudios sobre el mundo en hechos observables más que en creencias, p. 280

secondary industry/industria secundaria empresas de manufactura que elaboran productos con materiales de la industria primaria y de otras industrias secundarias, pp. 52, 575

segregate/segregar apartar y obligar a usar otras escuelas, casas, parques, etc., por la raza o la religión, p. 93

serf/siervo persona que vivió y trabajó las tierras de un señor feudal; no era propietaria de las tierras y dependía de la protección del señor feudal, p. 277

services/servicios trabajo o tarea que se realiza para otra persona, como la atención de un médico o la reparación del televisor por parte de otra persona, p. 52

settlement house/casa de establecimiento centro comunitario para inmigrantes pobres en Estados Unidos, p. 95

silt/cieno sedimento de grano fino depositado por los ríos, p. 359

social structure/estructura social forma en que las personas de una cultura se organizan en pequeños grupos; cada grupo pequeño desempeña un papel específico, p. 49

souq/souq mercado al aire libre, p. 407

SPANISH GLOSSARY 681

sovereignty/soberanía independencia política, p. 413

squatter/ocupante ilegal persona que se establece en el terreno de otro sin su permiso, p. 214

standard of living/estándar de vida calidad de vida material, p. 460

station/dehesa en Australia, un rancho muy grande de ovejas o ganado, p. 567

steppes/estepas llanuras en su mayor parte sin árboles; en Rusia, las estepas son praderas de suelo fértil apto para la agricultura, p. 267

strike/huelga interrupción del trabajo; renuencia a seguir trabajando hasta que se satisfagan ciertas demandas de los trabajadores, p. 219

subcontinent/subcontinente gran masa de tierra que forma la mayor parte de un continente; por ejemplo, el subcontinente de la India, p. 451

subsidize/subsidiar apoyar económicamente; algunos gobiernos subsidian ciertas industrias, p. 507

subsistence farmer/agricultor de subsistencia agricultor que produce sólo lo necesario para mantener a su familia, p. 207

subsistence farming/agricultura de subsistencia cultivar solo las cosechas suficientes para mantener a la familia, p. 364

Sun Belt/*Sun Belt* (franja del sol) región de Estados Unidos que se extiende desde el sur de la costa del Atlántico hasta la costa de California; zona conocida por su clima cálido, p. 128

surplus/excedente más de lo necesario, p. 372

Swahili/suajili idioma africano que contiene algunas palabras árabes, p. 376

T

taiga/taiga en Rusia, bosque enorme que cubre más de cuatro millones de millas cuadradas, p. 267

tariff/arancel derecho o impuesto que un gobierno cobra por introducir productos en el país, p. 294

technology/tecnología herramientas y destrezas que las personas necesitan usar; uso práctico de las destrezas científicas, especialmente en la industria, p. 48

tectonic plate/placa tectónica porción grande de la corteza terrestre, p. 552

temperature/temperatura grado de calentamiento o enfriamiento de algo, como el agua o el aire; por lo general se mide con un termómetro, p. 34

terrace/terraza plataforma recortada en la ladera de una montaña; se usa para hacer cultivos escalonados en lugares empinados, p. 406

tertiary industry/industria terciaria industias de servicio como bancos, transportes, cuidado de la salud y protección policiaca, pp. 52, 575

textiles/textiles productos de tela, p. 281

totem pole/poste totémico poste alto de madera tallado con símbolos; se encuentra entre los indígenas estadounidenses de la costa noroeste del Pacífico, p. 150

tourism/turismo negocios que dan servicio a los turistas o visitantes de una región, p. 575

traditional economy/economía tradicional economía en que se producen, se compran y se venden bienes de acuerdo con las costumbres, las tradiciones y los hábitos del grupo, pp. 52–53

transportation barrier/barrera de transportación características físicas que impiden viajar o transportar productos de una región o otra, p. 359

transportation corridors/corredores de transportación rutas por las que se puede viajar a pie, en vehículo, en tren, en barco o en avión, pp. 76, 222

treaty/tratado acuerdo por escrito entre dos o más países, p. 187

Treaty of Tordesillas/Tratado de Tordesillas tratado de 1494 que establece la Línea de demarcación, que da a España el derecho de poblar y comerciar al oeste de la línea y a Portugal los mismos derechos al este de la línea, p. 187

682 SPANISH GLOSSARY

tributary/tributario corriente de agua que fluye hacia un gran río o a un depósito de agua mayor, pp. 76, 172, 263, 360

tropics/trópico región de la Tierra entre las líneas de latitud 23° N y 23° S, cuyo clima casi siempre es caluroso, p. 78

tundra/tundra región fría y seca cubierta de nieve más de la mitad del año; gran planicie sin árboles donde el subsuelo siempre está congelado, pp. 79, 267

turbines/turbinas enormes máquinas con hélices por lo general impulsadas por agua y que generan electricidad, p. 270

U

United Empire Loyalists/United Empire Loyalists (Unión de Colonos Leales al Imperio) colonos estadounidenses leales a Gran Bretaña que se trasladaron a Canadá después de la Guerra de Independencia, p. 145

United Nations/Organización de las Naciones Unidas organización de países establecida en 1945, que actúa a favor de la paz y la cooperación entre los países, p. 333

urban/urbano relativo o referente a la ciudad, p. 198

urban area/área urbana zona densamente poblada; una ciudad o un pueblo, p. 46

urbanization/urbanización crecimiento de las ciudades como consecuencia del flujo de personas hacia ellas, pp. 45, 292

vegetation/vegetación

V

vassals/vasallos sirvientes, p. 421

vegetation/vegetación conjunto de plantas de una zona, p. 36

W

weather/tiempo condiciones de la capa inferior de la atmósfera terrestre en un lugar durante un periodo corto, p. 34

weathering/desgaste desintegración de las rocas producida por el viento, la lluvia o el hielo, p. 29

SPANISH GLOSSARY 683

Index

The *italicized* letters preceding page numbers refer to maps *(m)*, charts *(c)*, pictures *(p)*, tables *(t)*, or graphs *(g)*.
Items in blue type refer to the Teacher Edition.

A

D

H

N

O

P

Acknowledgments

Cover Design

Pearson Educational Development Group

Cover Photo

Top right, clockwise: Harald Sund/Image Bank; SuperStock; SuperStock; SuperStock; SuperStock; José Fuste Raga/Corbis StockMarket; David Hiser/Stone; Cartesia/Photodisc; McDaniel Woolf/Photodisc; Travelpix/FPG; **Center image:** Robert Everts/Stone; **Silouette figure with binoculars:** Ken Karp Photography.

Maps

38, 78, 122 T, 126 T, 130 T, 134 T, 146 T, 146 B, 218 T, 242 T, 242 B, 247,266, 269, 276, 312 T, 312 B, 335 T, 335 B, 367 L, 367 R, 417, 420 T, 420 B, 444, 452, 463, 537, 544 T, 544 B, 561, 579, 613 T, 614 T, 616 T, 618 T, 621 T, Ortelius Design, Inc.; all other maps by MapQuest.com, Inc.

Map information sources: Columbia Encyclopedia, Encyclopaedia Britannica, Microsoft® Encarta®, National Geographic Atlas of the world, Rand McNally Commerical Atlas, The Times Atlas of the World.

Staff Credits

Joyce Barisano, Carolyn Casey, Clare Courtney, Stephen Flanagan, Kathryn Fox, **Mary Hanisco, Catherine Holder, Estelle Needleman, Kirsten Richert, Miriam Rodriquez, Peter Sacks,** Betsy Sawyer-Melodia, and the **Pearson Education Development Group.**

Additional Credits

Design, Art, and Production: Pronto Design, Inc.

Text

11, Excerpt from *North American Indian Mythology* by Cottie Burland. Copyright © 1965 by Cottie Burland. Reproduced by permission of The Hamlyn Publishing Group Limited. **87,** Excerpt from *The Crown of Columbus* by Michael Dorris and Louise Erdrich. Copyright © 1991 by Michael Dorris and Louise Erdrich. Reproduced by permission of Harper-Collins Publishers. **94,** Excerpt from *How the Other Half Lives* by Jacob Riis. Copyright © 1971 by Dover Publications, Inc. Reproduced by permission of Dover Publications, Inc. **109,** Excerpt from *Obscure Destinies* by Willa Cather. Copyright © 1930 by Willa Cather. Copyright © renewed 1932 by Willa Cather. Reproduced by permission of Alfred A. Knopf. **120,** Excerpt from *America, the Beautiful* by Katherine Lee Bates. Copyright © 1993 by Neil Waldman. Reproduced by permission of Macmillan Publishing Company. **196,** "Wind and Water and Stone" by Octavio Paz. Copyright © 1979 by The New Yorker Magazine. Reproduced by permission of New Directions Publishing Corporation. **290,** Excerpt from *Pearl in the Egg* by Dorothy Van Woerkom. Copyright © 1980 by Dorothy Van Woerkom. Reproduced by permission of Thomas Y. Crowell. **326,** Excerpt from *Zlata's Diary* by Zlata Filipovic. Copyright © 1994 by Fixot et editions Robert Laffont. Reproduced by permission of Viking. **418,** Excerpt from *Mandela: An Illustrated Autobiography* by Nelson Mandela. Copyright © 1994, 1996 by Nelson Rolihlahla Mandela. Reproduced by permission of Little, Brown and Company. **464,** Excerpt from *Selected Works of Jawaharlal Nehru.* Copyright © 1987. Reproduced by permission of Oxford University Press. **477,** Excerpt from *Voices from Kurdistan,* edited by Rachel Warner. Copyright © 1991 by the Minority Rights Group. Reproduced by permission of the Minority Rights Group. **482,** Excerpt from *Sadako and the Thousand Paper Cranes* by Eleanor Coerr. Copyright © 1977 by Eleanor Coerr. Reproduced by permission of G.P. Putnam's Sons.

Illustration

9, 71, 167, 259, 355 BR, 449, 549 Michael Digiorgio

Photos

Dorling Kindersley 60 C, 60 BL, 61 T, 61 C, 248 BL, 249 TR, 438 TR, 538 BR, 539, 580 C, 581 TL

Table of Contents vi, Sami Sarkis/Photodisc; **vii T,** Larry Chiger/SuperStock; **vii B,** Bettman/Corbis; **viii,** Aubrey Diem/Valan Photos; **ix T,** Thomas Kitchin/Tom Stack & Associates; **ix B,** Art Wolfe/Getty Images; **x,** Alex Irvin/Alex Irvin Photography; **xi,** Wolfgang Kaehler/Liaison Agency, Inc.; **xii,** Stephen Johnson/Getty Images; **xiii,** Wolfgang Kaehler/ Wolfgang Kaehler Photography; **xiv,** M. & E. Bernheim/Woodfin Camp & Associates; **xv,** Frans Lanting/Minden Pictures; **xvi,** Jerry Alexander/Getty Images; **xvii T,** Janette Ostier Gallery, Paris, France/SuperStock; **xvii B,** Matthew Neal McVay/Getty Images; **xviii,** Ahreim Land, Northern Territory, Australia, Explorer SuperStock; **xix T,** Philip & Karen Smith/Getty Images; **xix B,** Wolfgang Kaehler/Wolfgang Kaehler Photography; **Special Features xx,** Christie's Images, London, UK/Bridgeman Art Library; **Unit I xxxviii BL,** Radhinka Chalasani/Getty Image; **xxxviii BC,** Ted Streshinsky/Corbis; **xxxviii BR,** Adam Woolfitt/Corbis; **1 TL,** Andrew Errington/Getty Images; **1 TR,** Andy Sacks/Getty Images; **1 BR,** Andy Sacks/Getty Images; **1 B,** © Victor Englebert/Photo Researchers Inc.; **2 TR,** Philip & Karen Smith/ Getty Images; **2 BL,** Corbis; **2 BR,** Don Smetzer/Getty Images; **3 TR,** Larry Chiger/SuperStock; **3 B,** Bettmann/Corbis; **4 T,** Ken Graham/Getty Images; **4 B,** Robert Frerck/Odyssey/Chicago; **5 TL,** Alan Abramowitz/Getty Images; **5 TR,** Peter Carmichael/Getty Images; **Chapter I 10 T,** Mike Agliolo/Corbis; **10 B,** Jeremy Woodhouse/PhotoDisc, Inc.; **11,** Stocktrek/PhotoDisc, Inc.; **14,**Sami Sarkis/PhotoDisc; **15,** Kevin Kelley/Getty Images; **19,** British Museum; **Chapter 2 26,** ESA/TSADOD/Tom Stack & Associates; **27,** © James A. Sugar/Corbis; **31,** Larry Chiger/ SuperStock; **34,** David Falconer/Getty Images; **36,** Rod Planck/Tom Stack & Associates; **Chapter 3 40,** The Granger Collection; **41,** Paul Chesley/Getty Images; **42,** Ken Fisher/Getty Images; **44,** © Bill Gentile/Corbis; **46,** Donna DeCesare; **47,** Paul Conklin/PhotoEdit; **48,** Don Smetzer/Getty Images; **49,** Donna DeCesare; **51,** Julia Vindasius/Vindasius; **53,** AP/Wide World Photos; **54,** © Bettmann/Corbis; **55,** Adam Woolfitt/Corbis; **56,** Hulton Deutsch Collection/Corbis; **Unit I DK 60 TL,** Jeff Divine/FPG International by Getty Images; **60 C,** Dorling Kindersley; **60 BL,** Dorling Kindersley; **61 T,** Dorling Kindersley; **61 C,** Dorling Kindersley; **61 B,** Mary Evans/Mary Evans Picture Library; **Unit 2 62 T,** Charles Sykes/Visuals Unlimited; **62 BL,** Bruce Forster/Getty Images; **62 BR,** J. Eastcott/Yva Momatiuk/Valan Photos; **63 TL,** Alan Klehr/Getty Images; **63 TR,** Robin Smith/Getty Images; **63 BL,** Corbis-Bettmann; **63 BR,** John Edwards/Getty Images; **64 TR,** Gordon Fisher/Getty Images; **64 BL,** John Trumball/The Granger Collection; **64 BR,** Lawrence Migdale/Getty Images; **65 T,** Thomas Kitchin/Tom Stack & Associates; **65 B,** Celestica, Inc.; **Chapter 4 72,** John Edwards/Getty Images; **73,** Olaf Soot/Getty Images; **75,** Thomas Kitchin/Tom Stack & Associates; **76,** Science VU/Visuals Unlimited; **77,** Donald Nausbaum/Getty Images; **79,** © Lowell Georgia/Corbis; **80,** Harold Sund/Getty Images; **81,** H. Armstrong Roberts; **82,** Vince Streano/Getty Images; **Chapter 5 86 TL,** Corbis Sygma; **86 TR,** Stock Trec/PhotoDisc, Inc; **86 B,** Eric Long/NASA/Smithsonian Inst.; **87,** Steve McCutcheon/Visuals Unlimited; **90,** The Granger Collection; **91,** The Granger Collection; **93,** Corbis; **94,** The Granger Collection; **95,** The Granger Collection; **96,** Library of Congress; **97,** Hutton/Archive

706 ACKNOWLEDGMENTS

Photos; **98,** John D. Cunningham/Visuals Unlimited; **99,** Library of Congress; **Chapter 6 104 T,** Thomas Kitchin/Tom Stack & Associates; **104 B,** Bob Thomason/Getty Images; **105,** Lawrence Migdale/Getty Images; **108,** T. Phillibrown/Library of Congress; **109,** AP/Wide World Photos; **110,** Archive Photos; **111,** J. Eastcott/Yva Momatiuk/Valan Photography; **112,** Corbis/Stock Market; **113,** Dave G. Houser/Houser Stock, Inc.; **115,** Reuters/Corbis-Bettmann; **116,** Hutton/Archive Photos; **Chapter 7 120 T,** Jeremy Woodhouse/PhotoDisc, Inc.; **120 B,** McDaniel Woolf/PhotoDisc, Inc.; **121,** Wayne Eastep/Getty Images; **125,** AFP/Corbis; **127,** Bob Thomason/Getty Images; **129,** Inga Spence/Tom Stack & Associates; **132,** Gurmankin/Morina/Visuals Unlimited; **133,** Rosemary Calvert/Getty Images; **135,** Art Wolfe/Getty Images; **Chapter 8 140 T,** Glen Allison/Getty Images; **140 B,** Aubrey Diem/Valan Photos; **141,** Jean Bruneau/Valan Photos; **143,** Reuters/Corbis-Bettmann; **144,** John Edwards/Getty Images; **145,** ™ and © by Queen's Printer for Ontario 2001, reproduced with permission; **147,** © Cosmo Condina/Getty Images; **148,** © Michael S. Yamashita/Corbis; **149,** Hulton/Getty Images; **150,** Glen Allison/Getty Images; **Unit 2 DK 156 TR,** Corbis; **156 BL,** David G. Houser/Corbis; **156 BR,** Corbis-Bettmann; **157 TL,** Josef Scaylea/Corbis; **157 TR,** Brian Stablyk/Getty Images; **157 BL,** Corbis-Bettmann; **157 BR,** Sandy Felsenthal/Corbis; **Unit 3 158 T,** Ed Simpson/Getty Images; **158 BL,** Ed Simpson/Getty Images; **158 BR,** Robert Frerck/Odyssey/Chicago; **159 TL,** D.E. Cox/Getty Images; **159 TR,** Mark Segal/Getty Images; **159 BL,** © Neil Beer/Corbis; **159 BR,** Corbis-Bettmann; **160 T,** Jaques Jangoux/Getty Images; **160 BR,** D.E. Cox/Getty Images; **160 BL,** Robert Frerck/Odyssey/Chicago; **161 T,** Chip & Rosa María de la Cueva Peterson; **161 B,** Robert Frerck/Odyssey/Chicago; **Chapter 9 168 T,** Chip & Rosa María de la Cueva Peterson; **168 B,** Robert Frerck/Odyssey/Chicago; **169,** Will & Deni McIntyre/Getty Images; **171,** Bryan Parsley/Getty Images; **173,** Robert Frerck/Odyssey/Chicago; **175,** Wolfgang Kaehler/Wolfgang Kaehler Photography; **176,** Erik Svenson/Getty Images; **177,** Robert Frerck/Odyssey/Chicago; **178,** Chip & Rosa María de la Cueva Peterson; **Chapter 10 182,** Ed Simpson/Getty Images; **183,** Chip & Rosa María de la Cueva Peterson; **184,** Chip & Rosa María de la Cueva Peterson; **185,** Chip & Rosa María de la Cueva Peterson; **186,** Daniel Aubry/Odyssey/Chicago; **187,** Stock Montage; **188,** Archivo Iconografico, S.A/Corbis; **189,** North Wind Picture Archives; **190,** Robert Frerck/Odyssey/Chicago; **191,** Robert Frerck/Odyssey/Chicago; **192,** Mark Segal/Getty Images; **Chapter 11 196 T,** Phillipe Columbi/PhotoDisc; **196 B,** Robert Frerck/Odyssey/Chicago; **197,** Demetrio Carrasco/Getty Images; **199,** Chip & Rosa María de la Cueva Peterson; **199 B,** David R. Frazier/Getty Images; **200,** Elizabeth Harris/Getty Images; **201,** Sheryl McNee/Getty Images; **201 BR,** Sheryl McNee/Getty Images; **202,** Robery E. Daemmrich/Getty Images; **203,** Jason Laure'/Laure' Communications; **204,** SuperStock; **205,** Doug Armand/Getty Images; **206,** Alex Irvin/Alex Irvin Photography; **207,** Ed Simpson/Getty Images; **209,** Sheryl McNee/Getty Images; **Chapter 12 212 T,** Jose Diego Maria Rivera, "Sugar Cane," 1931. Fresco. 57 1/8 x 94 1/8 in. (145.1cm x 239.1 cm). Philadelphia Museum of Art. Gift of Mr. and Mrs. Herbert Cameron Morris. 1943–46–2. (C) Banco de Mexico Diego Rivera Museum Trust; **212 B,** James Nelson/Getty Images; **213,** David R. Frazier/Getty Images; **216,** Robert Frerck/Odyssey/Chicago; **217,** Robert Frerck/Odyssey/Chicago; **220,** © Bill Gentile/Corbis; **221,** Chip & Rosa María de la Cueva Peterson; **224,** Robert Freck/Odyssey/Chicago; **Chapter 13 228,** Doug Armand/Getty Images; **229,** © Jeff Greenberg/Omni-Photo Communications, Inc.; **231,** Corbis-Bettmann; **232,** Suzane L. Murphy/D.D. Bryant Photography; **233,** Chip & Rosa María de la Cueva Peterson; **235,** Sylvain Grandadam/Getty Images; **236,** Ary Diesendruck/Getty Images; **237,** Rhonda Klevansky/Getty Images; **238,** Charles Phillip/Photri-Microstock; **241,** Liaison Agency Inc./© Wolfgang Kaehler; **244,** Pan American Airways Corp.; **Unit 3 DK 248 TR,** Chiapas State, Mexico/Index/Bridgeman Art Library; **248 BL, 249 TR,** Dorling Kindersley; **249 BL,** Mary Evans/Mary Evans Picture Library; **249 BR,** Tony Morrison/South American Pictures; **Unit 4 250 T,** SIPA Press; **250 BR,** Michael Rosenfeld/Getty Images; **250 BL,** SuperStock; **251 TL,** Reuters Newsmedia, Inc./Corbis; **251 TR,** SuperStock; **251 BL,** David Barnes/Stock Market; **251 BR,** N. Ray/Art Directors/TRIP; **252 TR,** Julian Calder/Getty Images; **252 BL,** AP/Wide World Photos; **252 BR,** AP/Wide World Photos; **253,** AP/Wide World Photos; **Chapter 14 260,** W. Jacobs/Art Directors/TRIP; **261,** M. Feeney/Art Directors/TRIP; **263,** James Balog/Getty Images; **265,** D. MacDonald/Art Directors/TRIP; **267,** © Len Rue/Photo Researchers, Inc.; **268,** Arnulf Husmo/Getty Images; **Chapter 15 274 TL,** Stock Montage; **274 TR,** Bettmann/Corbis; **274 B,** Erich Lessing/Art Resource; **275,** SuperStock; **277,** Marte Ueda/Getty Images; **278,** The Granger Collection; **279,** Biblioteca Reale, Turin Italy/SuperStock; **281,** North Wind Picture Archives; **283,** AP/Wide World Photos; **284,** Victoria & Albert Museum, London, NY/Bridgeman Art Library/Art Resource; **285,** Historical Museum, Moscow, Russia/SuperStock; **286,** Novosti/Corbis-Bettmann; **Chapter 16 290 T,** Philip Webb, The Red House, Bexley Heath, UK, 1859. Photo by Charlotte Wood; **290 B,** Dewitt Jones/Getty Images; **291,** SuperStock; **292,** Stephen Johnson/Getty Images; **293,** Joseph Okwesa/Art Directors/TRIP; **294,** Michael Rosenfeld/Getty Images; **295,** North Wind Picture Archives; **297,** Ibrahim/Art Directors/TRIP; **298,** AP/Wide World Photos; **299,** SuperStock; **300,** A. Kuznetsov/Art Directors/TRIP; **301,** Alexandra Avakian/Woodfin Camp & Associates; **302,** Wolfgang Kaehler/ Wolfgang Kaehler Photography; **303,** The Forbes Collection, New York; **Chapter 17 306 T,** Erich Lessing/Art Resource; **306 B,** EKA/Eureka Slide; **307,** John Drysdale/Woodfin Camp & Associates; **308,** AP/Wide World Photos; **311,** B. & C. Alexander/Bryan and Cherry Alexander Photography; **313,** © Paul Almasy/Corbis; **314,** Ian Murphy/Getty Images; **315,** AP/Wide World Photos; **317,** AP/Wide World Photos; **318,** Corbis-Bettmann; **319,** Chad Ehlers/Getty Images; **321,** Jean Pragen/Getty Images; **322,** Peter Timmermans/Getty Images; **Chapter 18 326 T,** Jellybean Photographic and Imaging; **326 B,** B & C Alexander/Bryan & Cherry Alexander Photography; **327,** Henryk T. Kaiser/Envision; **330,** SuperStock; **333,** AP/Wide World Photos; **334,** AP/Wide world Photos; **336,** © Richard Oliver/Corbis; **337,** SIPA Press; **339,** Wolfgang Kaehler/Wolfgang Kaehler Photography; **340,** B. Turner/Art Directors/TRIP; **Unit 4 DK 344 T,** National Archaeological Museum, Athens, Greece/Ancient Art & Architecture Collection Ltd/Bridgeman Art Library; **344 L,** Biblioteque Nationale, Paris, France/Bridgeman Art Library; **344 R,** Vatican Museums and Galleries, Vatican City, Italy/Bridgeman Art Library; **344 B,** National Gallery, London; **345 TL,** Wallace Collection, London, UK/Bridgeman Art Library; **345 TR,** Musee d'Orsay, Paris, France/Bridgeman art Library; **345 BL,** Hulton Archive/Getty images; **345 BR,** Los Angeles County Museum of Art,CA, USA/Bridgeman Art Library; **Unit 5 346 T,** Reuters/Corbis-Bettmann; **346 BL,** M. & E. Bernheim/Woodfin Camp & Associates; **346 BR,** Jason Laure'/Laure' Communications; **347 TL,** AP/Wide World Photos; **347 TR,** Jason Laure'/Laure' Communications; **347 BL,** Tim Davis/Getty Images; **347 BR,** Betty Press/Woodfin Camp & Associates; **348,** © John Conrad/Corbis; **348 BL,** Corbis Images Royalty Free; **348 BR,** Miguel Raurich/Getty Images; **349,** Ian Murphy/Getty Images; **349 B,** Paula Bronstein; **Chapter 19 356,** Victor Englebert/Victor Englebert Photography; **357,** Penny Tweedle/Getty Images; **358,** G. Winters/Art Directors/TRIP; **361,** Frans Lanting/Minden Pictures; **364,** Victor Englebert/Victor Englebert Photography; **364 BR,** Cabisco/Visuals Unlimited; **Chapter 20 370,** Jason Laure'/Laure' Communications; **371,** The Granger Collection; **372,** Boltin Picture Library; **373, 374,** SuperStock; **375,** The Granger Collection; **377,** Erich Lessing/Art Resource; **378,** Robert Frerck/Odyssey/Chicago; **379,** AP/Wide World Photos; **380,** Wolfgang Kaehler/Wolfgang Kaehler Photography; **Chapter 21 384 T,** M. & E. Bernheim/ Woodfin Camp & Associates; **384 B,** M. & E. Bernheim/ Woodfin Camp & Associates; **385,** Glen Allison/Getty Images; **386,** Lorne Resnick/Getty Images; **388,** Wolfgang Kaehler/Wolfgang Kaehler Photography; **389,** Wolfgang Kaehler/Wolfgang Kaehler Photography; **390,** M. & E. Bernheim/ Woodfin Camp & Associates;

ACKNOWLEDGMENTS 707

391, Robert Frerck/Odyssey/Chicago; **392,** Boyd Norton/Boyd Norton Photography; **393,** P. Joynson-Hicks/Art Directors/TRIP; **394,** Jason Laure'/Laure' Communications; **395,** Jason Laure'/ Laure' Communications; **Chapter 22 400 T,** Roland & Sabrina Michaud/Woodfin Camp & Associates; **400 B,** Lawrence Manning/Getty Images; **401,** P. Mitchell/Art Directors/TRIP; **403,** Israel Talby/ Woodfin Camp & Associates; **404,** Don Smetzer/Getty Images; **405,** Sylvain Grandadam/Getty Images; **408,** Robert Frerck/Odyssey/Chicago; **411,** AP/Wide World Photos; **413,** Tim Beddow/Getty Images; **414,** AP/Wide World Photos; **415,** David Young-Wolff/PhotoEdit; **Chapter 23 418 T,** Dekeerle/ © Liaison Agency, Inc.; **418 B,** B. Mnguni/Art Directors/TRIP; **419,** © Tom Mchugh/Photo Researchers; **421,** AP/Wide World Photos; **422,** Agence France © AFB/Corbis; **423,** M. & E. Bernheim/Woodfin Camp & Associates; **426,** Victor Englebert/Victor Englebert Photography; **427,** Jason Laure'/Laure' Communications; **429,** M. Jelliffe/Art Directors/TRIP; **430,** AP/Wide World Photos; **431,** Jason Laure'/Laure' Communications; **433,** Paula Bronstein; **Unit 5 DK 438 TR,** Dorling KIndersley; **438 BL,** AP/Wide World Photos; **438 BR,** Mary Evans/Mary Evans Picture Library; **439 TL,** Richard T. Nowitz/Corbis; **439 TR,** Christie's Images, London, UK/Bridgeman Art Library; **439 BL,** Peter Dejong/AP/Wide World Photos; **439 BR,** Liaison Agency; **Unit 6 440 T,** Blaise Musau/AP/Wide World Photos; **440 BL,** Wendy Chan/Getty Images; **440 BR,** Wolfgang Kaehler/Wolfgang Kaehler Photography; **441 TL,** Al Stephenson/Woodfin Camp & Associates; **441 TR,** Karen Kasmauski/Woodfin Camp and Associates; **441 BL,** Kim Newton/Woodfin Camp &Association; **441 BR,** Cary Wolinsky/Getty Images; **442 TR,** Charles Preitner/Visuals Unlimited; **442 BL,** Jerry Alexander/Getty Images; **442 BR,** Andrea Booher/Getty Images; **443,** Natalie Fobes/Getty Images; **443 B,** UPI/Corbis-Bettmann; **Chapter 24 450 T,** Howard Sochurek/Woodfin Camp & Associates; **450 B,** Art Wolfe/Getty Images; **451,** D. Jenkin/Tropix Photographic Library; **454,** Getty Images; **455,** Wayland Publishers Limited/Wayland Publishers Limited; **456,** Reuters/Will Burgess/Getty Images; **458,** Robert Frerck/ Woodfin Camp & Associates; **461,** Janette Ostier Gallery, Paris, France/SuperStock; **Chapter 25 464 T,** © Hulton Getty/Liaison Agency, Inc.; **464 B,** Cameramann International; 465, Vanni/Art Resource; **467,** Scala/Art Resource; **469,** Jerry Alexander/Getty Images; **472,** Dilip Mehta/Woodfin Camp & Associates; **474,** Wolfgang Kaehler/Wolfgang Kaehler Photography; **475,** SuperStock/Culver Pictures, Inc.; **476,** Erich Lessing/Art Resource; **478,** Al Stephenson/ Woodfin Camp & Associates; **Chapter 26 482 T,** Pearson Education; **482 B,** Matthew Neal McVay/Getty Images; **483,** A. Ramey/Woodfin Camp & Associates; **484,** Cary Wolinsky/Getty Images; **486,** Hulton Getty/Liaison Agency; **487,** Wolfgang Kaehler/Wolfgang Kaehler Photography; **488,** Jack Novak/SuperStock; **489,** Robin Smith/Getty Images; 490, Andrea Booher/Getty Images; **491 T,** Cameramann International; **491 B,** M.M.N./Dinodia Picture Library; **492,** Jason Laure'/Laure' Communications; **494,** Zeynep Sumen/Getty Images; **495,** A. Ramey/Woodfin Camp & Associates; **496,** AFP/Corbis-Bettmann; **Chapter 27 500 T,** Yann Layma/ Getty Images; **500 B,** Ettagale Blauer/Laure' Communications; **501,** D.E. Cox/Getty Images; **504,** © Liu Liqun/ Corbis; **505,** Karen Kasmauski/Woodfin Camp & Associates; **507,** AP/Wide World Photos; **508,** Cameramann International; **509,** SuperStock; **511,** Kim Newton/Woodfin Camp & Associates; **512,** Natalie Fobes/Getty Images; **Chapter 28 518 T,** Wolfgang Kaehler/ Wolfgang Kaehler Photography; **518 B,** Barry Iverson/Woodfin Camp & Associates; **519,** SuperStock; **521,** Charles Prietner/Visuals Unlimited; **522,** Photri-Microstock; **523,** Ann & Bury Peerless/Ann & Bury Peerless Picture Library; **525 TL,** Steve Vidler/Getty Images; **525 TR,** Joel Simon/Getty Images; **527,** Nabeel Turner/Getty Images; **529 TR,** Jane Lewis/Getty Images; **529 TL,** Barry Iverson/Woodfin Camp & Associates; **531,** A. Ramsey/Woodfin Camp & Associates; **533 TL,** Cameramann International Limited; **533 TR,** Israel/Talby/Woodfin Camp & Associates; **534,** Richard T. Nowitz/Corbis; **Unit 6 DK 538 TR,** Richard Anthony/Photo Researchers; **538 BL,** Astrid & Hans Frieder Michler/Science Source/Photo Researchers; **538 BR,** Dorling Kindersley; **539,** Dorling Kindersley; **Unit 7 540 T,** AP/Wide World; **540 BL,** Wolfgang Kaehler/Wolfgang Kaehler Photography; **540 BR,** SuperStock; **541 TL,** Wolfgang Kaehler/Wolfgang Kaehler Photography; **541 TR,** Doug Armand/Getty Images; **541 BL,** Kurt Scholtz/SuperStock; **541 BR,** Zigy Kaluzney/Getty Images; **542,** Wolfgang Kaehler/Wolfgang Kaehler Photography; **542 BL,** Wolfgang Kaehler/Wolfgang Kaehler Photography; **542 BR,** Robert Frerck/Getty Images; **543,** Philip & Karen Smith/Getty Images; **543 B,** SuperStock; **Chapter 29 550,** Joseph Green Life File/PhotoDisc, Inc.; **551,** SuperStock; **555,** Patrick Ward/Getty Images; **556,** Philip & Karen Smith/Getty Images; **556 B,** Doug Armand/Getty Images; **558,** B & C Alexander/Bryan & Cherry Alexander Photography; **559,** Roger Ressmeyer/Corbis; **560,** Wolfgang Kaehler/Wolfgang Kaehler Photography; **Chapter 30 564 T,** Ahrem Land, Northern Territory, Australia/Explorer, SuperStock; **564 B,** Robert Frerck/Getty Images; **565,** Wolfgang Kaehler/Wolfgang Kaehler Photography; **566,** Zigy Kaluzney/Getty Images; **567,** Getty Images; **568,** Wolfgang Kaehler/Wolfgang Kaehler Photography; **569,** Randy Wells/Getty Images; **571,** SuperStock; **572,** © James L. Amos/Corbis; **573,** Wolfgang Kaehler/Wolfgang Kaehler Photography; **575,** Dave Hiser/Getty Images; **576,** Oliver Strewe/ Getty Images; **Unit 7 DK 580 TR,** Mary Evans/Mary Evans Picture Library; **580 C,** Dorling Kindersley; **580 BL,** Geoscience Features Picture Library; **580 BR,** Ed Lallo/Index Stock Photography; **581 TL,** Dorling Kindersley; **581 C,** Jeff Sherman/Getty Images; **581 BR,** The Kobal Collection; **Reference 582-583,** Kaz Chiba/PhotoDisc, Inc; **Regional Database 600-601,** Adam Crowley/PhotoDisc, Inc; **Glossary of Basic Geographic Terms 646 TL,** A & L Sinibaldi/Getty Images; **646 BL,** John Beatty/Getty Images; **647 TL,** Hans Strand/ Getty Images; **647 BL,** Spencer Swanger/Tom Stack & Associates; **647 BR,** Paul Chesley/Getty Images; **Gazetteer 649,** Chip & Rosa María de la Cueva Peterson; **650,** D. Jenkin/Tropix Photographic Library; **651,** Nabeel Turner/Getty Images; **652,** Charles Sykes/Visuals Unlimited; **653,** Wolfgang Kaehler/Wolfgang Kaehler Photography; **654,** James Balog/Getty Images; **655,** Jean Pragen/Getty Images; **Glossary 656,** Jacques Jangoux/Getty Images; **658,** Tammy Pelusol/Tom Stack & Associates; **660,** Spencer Swanger/Tom Stack & Associates; **663,** Nabeel Turner/Getty Images; **664,** D. Jenkin/Tropix Photographic Library; **665,** The Granger Collection; **666,** SuperStock; **667,** Nicholas Parfitt/Getty Images; **668,** Don Smetzer/Getty Images; **669,** Rod Planck/Tom Stack & Associates; **Spanish Glossary 680,** AP/Wide World Photos; **681,** Nicholas Parfitt/Getty Images; **683,** Rod Planck/Tom Stack & Associates.

Fabric Borders Unit 1, Japack Company/Corbis; **Unit 2,** Lowe Museum of Art, University of Miami/SuperStock; **Unit 3,** Kevin Schafer/Stone; **Unit 4,** State Hermitage Museum, St. Petersburg, Russia/Corbis; **Unit 5,** PEDG; **Unit 6,** Collection of the Newark Museum, Gift of Jacob E. Henegar, 1986/Art Resource; **Unit 7,** Ralph A. Clevenger/Corbis.

708 ACKNOWLEDGMENTS